BIG DATA

(Covers Hadoop 2, MapReduce, Hive, YARN, Pig, R and Data Visualization)

Black Book™

Authored by:

DT Editorial Services

Published by:

dreamtech PRESS

ISBN: 978-93-5119-931-1

Reprint: 2023

Printed at: Nisha Enterprises

Acknowledgement

DT Editorial Services would like to express its gratitude to Mr. Vikash Kumar Chaudhari for reviewing this book. A Big Data specialist, Mr. Chaudhari has wide experience in providing Big Data solutions in various domains.

Contents at a Glance

Table of Contents

Introduction

Thanks for buying the *Big Data Black Book*. You are going to find as much Big Data crammed into this book as can fit between the covers.

Big data is a popular term that describes the immense growth and availability of data in both structured and unstructured formats. We all know that Big Data is being generated by nearly everything around us at all times. Various sources of Big Data include digital systems, sensors, mobile phones, social media platforms, satellites, online transaction processing systems (OLTPs), Radio Frequency Identification (RFID) chips, etc. Now all these sources generate Big Data at an alarmingly high rate, which need to be processed and analyzed efficiently almost at the same rate at which it is being generated.

Needless to say, the manual handling of such a huge and ever expanding pool of varied data is neither possible nor feasible. To derive any form of meaningful information from Big Data generated from various sources, you need analytical tools and computational techniques. However, first you need to have an extensive knowledge about each of these tools and techniques, their usage, and the specific environments they have been designed to work in. Only then can you select the right tool suitable for your specific needs and utilize the immense benefits offered by the advanced data analytics.

This is what this book provides you—an in-depth knowledge on what the Big Data is all about, its various sources and types, why it has become so important to store, sort, and analyze Big Data, how it can be handled, the various tools and techniques employed to handle Big Data, and much more.

This book introduces you to the big buzzword of today's market—the Big Data, followed by a detailed discussion on the various technologies of Big Data such as MapReduce, Hadoop, HBase, Pig, Hive, Oozie, and NoSQL, and how to implement and work with R, a statistical and graphical programming language that is considered by professionals as one of the most suitable platforms for Big Data Solutions.

The Audience

This book is designed with a perspective to provide an in-depth understanding of all the concepts related to Big Data. This makes it equally beneficial for beginners who want to learn Big Data from scratch as well as professionals who are already into developing applications in R.

This book will cater to the needs of every level of audience, providing an insight into the real-life implementations of Big Data solutions and problem solving in data analytics.

The Black Book Philosophy

Written by experienced professionals, Black Books provide immediate solutions to global programming and administrative challenges, helping you to complete specific tasks, especially critical ones, which are not well documented in other books. They help you understand a concept and then implement it practically by developing codes and applications based on that concept. The unique format of Black Books is structured to help you build your knowledge to solve problems, and quickly master complex technical issues to become an expert. The discussion of complex topics has been split over many subheadings, each dealing with a particular aspect of that topic, facilitating an easy and quick understanding.

Written and edited by the Content and Editorial teams at Dreamtech Press, this book is conceptualized to give you everything you need to know about Big Data.

Journey through the Book

The book contains the following chapters:

1. Getting an Overview of Big Data
2. Exploring the Use of Big Data in Business Context
3. Introducing Technologies for Handling Big Data
4. Understanding Hadoop Ecosystem
5. Understanding MapReduce Fundamentals and HBase
6. Understanding Big Data Technology Foundations
7. Storing Data in Databases and Data Warehouses
8. Processing Your Data with MapReduce
9. Customizing MapReduce Execution and Implementing MapReduce Program
10. Testing and Debugging MapReduce Applications
11. Understanding Hadoop YARN Architecture
12. Exploring Hive
13. Analyzing Data with Pig
14. Using Oozie
15. NoSQL Data Management
16. Data Movement with Flume and Sqoop

17. Introduction to Mahout
18. Understanding Analytics and Big Data
19. Analytical Approaches and Tools to Analyze Data
20. Exploring R
21. Reading Datasets and Exporting Data from R
22. Manipulating and Processing Data in R
23. Working with Functions and Packages in R
24. Performing Graphical Analysis in R
25. Integrating R and Hadoop and Understanding Hive
26. Data Visualization–I
27. Data Visualization with Tableau (Data Visualization–II)
28. Social Media Analytics and Text Mining
29. Mobile Analytics
30. Finding a Job in the Big Data Market

The book covers the concepts and the technical know-how required by two of the most common specialists of Big Data – the Big Data Developer and the Big Data Analyst.

How to Use This Book

In this book, we are using Hadoop 2, version 2.5. If you work on any previous version than this, you might get some errors while running the code given in this book. So pick up Hadoop 2, version 2.5 (or later) from the Internet.

You will also need to install the R software version 3.1 to run R commands and applications given in this book. The R software is available for both 32-bit and 64-bit computers. In this book, some of the chapters are dedicated to R programming.

Learning Elements

Apart from the discussion of the core concepts, this book projects some specific types of content as certain elements for clear presentation and better understanding. For example, all codes are shown as code listings, with a proper caption to explain what is happening in the code. An example of a listing is shown as follows:

Listing 1.1: Using the readline() Function in R

```
msg <- "Hello"
yourname <- readline("What is your name?")   ← Displays a question: "What is your name?"
paste(msg, yourname)
```

The convention of numbering an element goes as *chapter number.element number*. For instance, in the caption of the above-given listing, *1* is the chapter number and *1* is the listing number. Please note that the same convention has been followed while numbering figures and tables.

Additional information is given in the form of notes:

NOTE

By large or huge datasets or Big Data, we mean anything from a petabyte (1 PB = 1000 TB) to an exabyte (1EB = 1000 PB) of data.

Every figure will have a proper lead-in line and caption:

Figure 1.1 shows the features of Big Data:

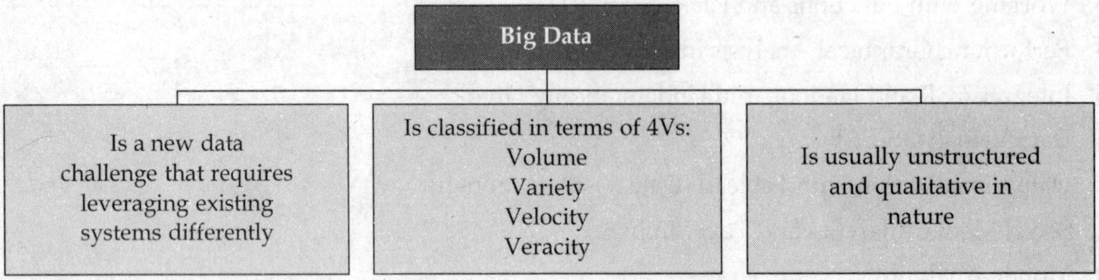

Figure 1.1: Features of Big Data

Tables are placed just below their references:

Table 1.1 lists some common types and sources of data:

Table 1.1: Types and Sources of Data

Type	Description	Source
Social Data	Refers to the information collected from various social networking sites and online portals	Facebook, Twitter, and LinkedIn
Machine Data	Refers to the information generated from Radio Frequency Identification (RFID) chips, bar code scanners and sensors	RFID chip readings, Global Positioning System (GPS) results
Transactional Data	Refers to the information generated from online shopping sites, retailers, and Business-to-Business (B2B) transactions	Retail websites like eBay and Amazon.com

Examples of the real-world implementation of a concept are given as Caselets:

CASELET

Google Inc. applied its expertise of data-collecting, analyzing, and deriving conclusions to raise warnings for the flu plagues in the US approximately two weeks in advance of the existing public health services. To do this, Google monitored millions of users' health-tracking behaviors, and followed a cluster of queries on themes such as symptoms about flu, congestion in chest, and incidences of buying a thermometer. Google analyzed this collected data and generated consolidated results that revealed strong indications of flu levels across America. To determine the accuracy of this data, Google did further research and data comparison before sharing it with the general public.

One of the primary aims of *Big Data Black Book* is to help readers understand how to use various Big Data concepts in real-life business scenarios. This book contains numerous examples presented as Argon Technology Cases, which demonstrate how the data analyst team at Argon Technology (a fictitious organization providing Big Data solutions) handles various client requirements by using concepts discussed in the chapter.

Look out for the **SCENARIO** icon to identify the Argon Technology cases that have been interspersed throughout the chapters:

SCENARIO

Consider the scenario of an organization, Argon Technology, which provides Big Data analytical solutions to customers. Mr. Smith, the data analyst of the Argon Technology, is studying about Big Data and the ways it can be utilized in various sectors. He shares these examples with his team to enhance its knowledge.

Exhibits are excerpts taken from different websites and are included to provide additional information as well as valuable insights on the topic under discussion from a bigger perspective. The URL of the Web page from where an exhibit is taken is mentioned below it:

EXHIBIT 1: Real-World Examples of Big Data

Some real-world examples of Big Data include:

- Consumer product companies and retail organizations are observing data on social media websites such as Facebook and Twitter. These sites help them to analyze customer behavior, preferences, and product perception. Accordingly, the companies can line up their upcoming products to gain profits.
- Manufacturers are monitoring minute vibration data from their equipment, which changes slightly as it wears down, to predict the optimal time to replace or maintain. Replacing it too soon wastes money; replacing it too late triggers an expensive work stoppage
- Manufacturers are also monitoring social networks, but with a different goal than marketers. They are using it to detect aftermarket support issues before a warranty failure becomes publicly detrimental.
- Financial service organizations are using the data mined from customer interactions to slice and dice their users into finely-tuned segments. This enables these financial institutions to create increasingly relevant and sophisticated offers.
- Advertising and marketing agencies are tracking social media to understand responsiveness to campaigns, promotions, and other advertising mediums.
- Insurance companies are using Big Data analysis to see which home insurance applications can be immediately processed, and which ones need a validating in-person visit from an agent.
- By embracing social media, retail organizations are engaging brand advocates, changing the perception of brand antagonists, and even enabling enthusiastic customers to sell their products.
- Hospitals are analyzing medical data and patient records to predict those patients that are likely to seek readmission within a few months of discharge. The hospital can then intervene in hopes of preventing another costly hospital stay.

- Web-based businesses are developing information products that combine data gathered from customers to offer more appealing recommendations and more successful coupon programs.
- The government is making data public at both the national, state, and city level for users to develop new applications that can generate public good.
- Sports teams are using data for tracking ticket sales and even for tracking team strategies.

Source: https://www.acquia.com/examples-big-data-projects

Other Resources

Although this book explains every concept in a very detailed and comprehensive manner, you can refer to the various other sources to explore more about Big Data. To read more about:

- MapReduce, refer to http://hadoop.apache.org/docs/r1.2.1/mapred_tutorial.html
- Apache Hadoop, refer to http://hadoop.apache.org/
- Apache Pig, refer to http://pig.apache.org/
- Apache Hive, refer to https://hive.apache.org/
- Hive, refer to http://www-01.ibm.com/software/data/infosphere/hadoop/hive/
- Insights of Big Data, refer to http://www.sas.com/en_us/insights/big-data/what-is-big-data.html
- Introduction on Big Data, refer to http://www.ibm.com/big-data/us/en/
- Apache HBase, refer to http://hbase.apache.org/
- HBase Cloudera, refer to http://www.cloudera.com/content/cloudera/en/products-and-services/cdh/hbase.html
- R tutorial, refer to http://www.r-tutor.com/
- Introduction on R, refer to http://www.cyclismo.org/tutorial/R/
- Data Visualization, refer to http://www.sas.com/en_us/insights/big-data/data-visualization.html

Book Preview

Chapter 1: Getting an Overview of Big Data

This chapter introduces you to Big Data and discusses the various sources from where it is generated along with the forms in which it is generated such as structured, unstructured, and semi-structured data. You also learn about the evolution of Big Data and the four important Big Data elements, which are Variety, Velocity, Volume, and Veracity. This chapter also explores different professional opportunities available in the career path of Big Data and the technical as well as soft skills required for entering this domain.

Chapter 2: Exploring the Use of Big Data in Business Context

This chapter discusses the role and importance of Big Data in various business contexts, such as social networking and the detection and prevention of fraudulent activities, with a special focus on the insurance and retail sectors.

Chapter 3: Introducing Technologies for Handling Big Data

The chapter begins with a discussion on distributed and parallel computing for Big Data. It explains the importance of virtualization in Big Data. It also introduces Hadoop and cloud computing, covering their features, deployment models, and delivery models in detail.

Chapter 4: Understanding Hadoop Ecosystem

This chapter explains the use of HDFS files and Hadoop-specific file types. It discusses the architecture and features of Hadoop Distributed File System (HDFS). It explains the installation of HDFS and the utility of combining HBase with HDFS. It also introduces the concepts of MapReduce and HBase. You are also familiarized with various technologies used to interact with the Hadoop ecosystem, such as Pig, Sqoop, ZooKeeper, Flume, and Oozie.

Chapter 5: Understanding MapReduce Fundamentals and HBase

This chapter discusses the concepts of MapReduce and HBase in detail. It also describes techniques like network topology, synchronization, and file system, and how they are used to optimize MapReduce jobs. You also learn about the characteristics and the installation process of HBase.

Chapter 6: Understanding Big Data Technology Foundations

This chapter discusses the architecture of the Big Data stack and explores its different layers. It also explains the impact of virtualization on Big Data and the different virtualization approaches used for handling Big Data operations.

Chapter 7: Storing Data in Databases and Data Warehouses

In this chapter, you learn about common storage options that organizations generally use to store Big Data. These include data warehouses and relational and non-relational databases. You also learn how deployment models have changed with the emergence of Big Data.

Chapter 8: Processing Your Data with MapReduce

This chapter explores the basics of the MapReduce framework and describes methods to develop simple applications using the map and reduce functions. It also discusses the points that need to be considered while developing MapReduce applications.

Chapter 9: Customizing MapReduce Execution and Implementing MapReduce Program

This chapter introduces you to the various classes available in the MapReduce framework and how they help you control MapReduce applications. It also discusses the role of Combiner in optimizing MapReduce applications. Finally, you will learn about the use of Partitioners in the MapReduce framework to control the execution of the reducer.

Chapter 10: Testing and Debugging MapReduce Applications

This chapter discusses the testing mechanisms and debugging procedures of MapReduce applications. It also explains the concept of logging and its use in testing Hadoop applications. It describes some defensive approaches used in developing MapReduce applications.

Chapter 11: Understanding Hadoop YARN Architecture

This chapter starts with a background study of YARN. It then describes why YARN is required in the Hadoop ecosystem. You also study about the architecture and working of YARN. This chapter also discusses the use and importance of schedulers and backward compatibility in YARN. It describes how YARN is configured for handling Big Data. Finally, it describes the commands in YARN as well as the management of logs in YARN.

Chapter 12: Exploring Hive

This chapter starts with a discussion of Hive architecture and the metastore. Next, it discusses CLI as well as the variables, commands, and properties in Hive. It also explores the concepts of shell execution, Hadoop dfs commands, comments in Hive, data types used in Hive, built-in Hive functions, Hive DDL, HiveQL queries, and joins in Hive.

Chapter 13: Analyzing Data with Pig

This chapter discusses the architecture, benefits, installation, and properties of Pig. Pig is integral to the analysis of Big Data. Therefore, studying Pig is important for anyone who wants to excel this field. Keeping this in mind, this chapter explains in detail how Pig is run in the Hadoop ecosystem and how Pig Latin is used for programming in Hadoop. This chapter also explores the operators in Pig.

Chapter 14: Using Oozie

This chapter introduces you to Oozie, the Oozie workflow, the Oozie coordinator, and bundle. In addition, you learn about the parameterization of Oozie with EL, the Oozie job execution model, and Oozie SLA. You also learn to install and configure Oozie.

Chapter 15: NoSQL Data Management

This chapter starts with an introduction to NoSQL and further discusses aggregate data models. It also discusses the key-value and document data models and also familiarizes you with the concept of relationships and graph databases. Also discussed are schema-less databases, materialized views, distribution models, the concept of sharding, etc. Toward the end, this chapter explains partitioning and combining operations in MapReduce.

Chapter 16: Data Movement with Flume and Sqoop

This chapter discusses various aspects of Flume and its components in detail. It introduces the Flume architecture designed on the basis of a few concepts, i.e., Flume Event, Flume Agent, Flume Flow, Flume Client, Source, Channel, and Sink. It also explores the concept of Sqoop that has been designed to exchange information between Hadoop and Relational Database. Toward the end, this chapter discusses about importing data into hive and HDFS.

Chapter 17: Introduction to Mahout

This chapter discusses the Apache Mahout, which is the open source library of scalable machine-learning algorithms. It also explains the machine learning techniques followed by 3Cs of machine learning. These 3Cs are collaborative filtering, clustering, and classification. You also learn to install Mahout on the Linux operating system.

Chapter 18: Understanding Analytics and Big Data

The chapter discusses various types of analytical approaches used in Big Data, such as basic analytics, advanced analytics, operationalized analytics, and monetizing analytics. You also learn to design new analytical approaches for Big Data.

Chapter 19: Analytical Approaches and Tools to Analyze Data

This chapter explores the evolution and history of analytical approaches and tools. Here, you learn about different types of analytical tools used in Big Data. It also explains how to install R and RStudio on different operating systems.

Chapter 20: Exploring R

In this chapter, you learn to navigate in the R workspace and use scripts to develop a program, perform mathematical operations, store and calculate values, etc. This chapter also discusses the concept of vectors in R.

Chapter 21: Reading Datasets and Exporting Data from R

In this chapter, you learn about various commands in R and how they are used to perform various types of functions, such as creating and reading datasets, exporting data from datasets, saving your work, etc.

Chapter 22: Manipulating and Processing Data in R

This chapter describes the ways in which data can be manipulated and processed in R. It discusses various concepts, such as selecting the most appropriate data structure to store data, creating data subsets, merging different sets of data, and sorting of data in R. You also learn to use the formula interface in R.

Chapter 23: Working with Functions and Packages in R

This chapter starts with an explanation of the use of R functions in place of scripts. Scripts are a good way to perform various operations, but the increasing complexity of analytics means that scripts will become inadequate in several cases. It also describes the use of parameters with functions and explains the use of packages.

Chapter 24: Performing Graphical Analysis in R

This chapter discusses the use of plots to demonstrate different patterns and trends existing in data. Here, you learn the utility of different types of plots, such as single-variable plots, two-variable plots, multi-variable plots, and special plots. This chapter also explains how to save your R plots in external files.

Chapter 25: Integrating R and Hadoop and Understanding Hive

This chapter starts by discussing the integration of R with Hadoop, creating a new field of data analytics field, i.e., RHadoop. It describes the installation of RHadoop and its use in R. You also learn to implement text mining in RHadoop, and mining data through Hive in the RHadoop configuration.

Chapter 26: Data Visualization–I

This chapter discusses why data visualization is important for presenting data analysis results. You also learn about various applications of data visualization in fields other than Big Data. Data visualization can be carried out by using different tools, which are discussed in detail in the chapter. This chapter also introduces you to an important visualization tool, Tableau.

Chapter 27: Data Visualization with Tableau (Data Visualization–II)

This chapter explores the use of Tableau software products in presenting the outcomes of Big Data analytics. It starts with an introduction to Tableau software and goes on to explain the workspace of a specific Tableau product, known as Tableau Desktop. You will also learn about other Tableau products such as Tableau Server and Tableau Public.

Chapter 28: Social Media Analytics and Text Mining

This chapter discusses the role of social media and the importance of conducting social media analytics by business organizations. In addition, it discusses the role of text mining and sentiment analysis. In the end, it explains how to perform social media analytics and opinion mining on tweets.

Chapter 29: Mobile Analytics

This chapter deals with different aspects of mobile analytics. It draws a comparison between mobile analytics and Web analytics. It also explores the types of results produced in mobile analytics and the applications that are developed for performing mobile analytics. Apart from this, it introduces some mobile analytics tools, which include location-based tracking tools, user-behavior tracking tools, and real-time analytics tools.

Chapter 30: Finding a Job in the Big Data Market

This chapter begins with an overview of the importance and scope of Big Data jobs and moves forward to describe Big Data opportunities. Moreover, it explains how Big Data skills can be assessed in order to land the perfect job in the Big Data market. It also discusses about the roles and responsibilities in Big Data jobs. Next, it describes how you can make a foothold in the Big Data market. You also get an idea of the basic educational and technological requirements for Big Data jobs. In addition, you learn about the tools used in Big Data, the job roles of Big Data professionals, and the tactics used for searching Big Data jobs. In the end, this chapter provides some interview preparation and social media usage tips for getting Big Data jobs.

Big Data Practical

Big Data Practical shows some practical implementation and uses of various Big Data technologies, such as MapReduce, Pig, Hive, and HBase. You perform various tasks on Big Data by using the MapReduce programming paradigm. In addition, you get hands-on experience on how Pig is used to handle Big Data. Further, you perform some Big Data management operations in Hive. In the end, you learn the role of HBase in managing Big Data. Finally, it discusses the updated labs on R and Tableau 9.0 public.

Appendix A: Cassandra

This appendix starts with an introduction to the Cassandra database system. It then explores the main features of Apache Cassandra. It also describes the structure of the Cassandra database system. Moreover, it discusses how read/write operations are performed in Cassandra. In the end, it introduces the basics of Contextual Query Language (CQL).

Appendix B: ZooKeeper

This appendix discusses about the Apache ZooKeeper, providing the open source distributed configuration service, centralized service for naming the large distributed systems and coordination service. It explains the data model, which is used in ZooKeeper. In addition, it describes the Znodes and time in ZooKeeper. Toward the end, you learn about the data storage in ZooKeeper.

1

Getting an Overview of Big Data

"Information is the oil of the 21st century, and analytics is the combustion engine."

–Peter Sondergaard of the Gartner Group.

The 21st century is characterized by the rapid advancement in the field of information technology. IT has become an integral part of daily life as well as various other industries, be it health, education, entertainment, science and technology, genetics, or business operations. In today's competitive and global economy, organizations must possess a number of skills to create their place and sustain in the market. One of the most crucial of these skills is an understanding of and the ability to utilize and harness the immense potential of information technology. According to the Information Technology Association of America, information technology is defined as *"the study, design, development, application, implementation, support or management of computer-based information systems."*

This is truly an information age where data is being generated at an alarming rate. This huge amount of data is often termed as Big Data. Organizations use data generated through various sources to run their businesses. They analyze the data to understand and interpret market trends, study customer behavior, and take financial decisions. The term Big Data is now widely used, particularly in the IT industry, where it has generated various job opportunities.

Big Data consists of large datasets that cannot be managed efficiently by the common database management systems. These datasets range from terabytes to exabytes. Mobile phones, credit cards, Radio Frequency Identification (RFID) devices, and social networking platforms create huge amounts of data that may reside unutilized at unknown servers for many years. However, with the evolution of Big Data, this data can be accessed and analyzed on a regular basis to generate useful information.

The chapter introduces you to Big Data—the big buzzword of the IT industry – and its growing importance in almost every sector of human existence, be it education, health, science, technology, defense, lifestyle, etc.

What is Big Data?

Think of the following:

- Every second, there are around 8,22 tweets on Twitter.
- Every minute, nearly 510 comments are posted, 293,000 statuses are updated, and 136,000 photos are uploaded on Facebook.
- Every hour, Walmart, a global discount departmental store chain, handles more than 1 million customer transactions.
- Every day, consumers make around 11.5 million payments by using PayPal.

We live in a digital world where data is increasing rapidly because of the ever increasing use of the Internet, sensors, and heavy machines at a very high rate. The sheer volume, variety, velocity, and veracity of such data is signified by the term 'Big Data.' Big data is structured, unstructured, semi-structured, or heterogeneous in nature. It becomes difficult for computing systems to manage 'Big Data' because of the immense speed and volume at which it is generated. Traditional data management, warehousing, and analysis systems fizzle to analyze this type of data. Due to its complexity, big data is stored in distributed architecture file system.

Hadoop by Apache is widely used for storing and managing Big Data. Analyzing Big Data is a challenging task as it involves large distributed file systems, which should be fault tolerant, flexible, and scalable.

According to IBM, "Every day, we create 2.5 quintillion bytes of data – so much that 90% of the data in the world today has been created in the last two years alone. This data comes from everywhere: sensors used to gather climate information, posts to social media sites, digital pictures and videos, purchase transaction records, and cell phone GPS signals to name a few. This data is big data."

Data is everywhere, in every industry, in the form of numbers, images, videos, and text. As data continues to grow, so does the need to organize it. Collecting such huge amount of data would just be a waste of time, effort, and storage space if it cannot be put to any logical use. The need to sort, organize, analyze, and offer this critical data in a systematic manner leads to the rise of the much discussed term, Big Data.

The process of capturing or collecting Big Data is known as 'datafication.' Big Data is 'datafied' so that it can be used productively. Big Data cannot be made useful by simply organizing it, rather the data's usefulness lies in determining what we can do with it.

According to IBM, Big data is being generated by nearly everything around us at all times at an alarming velocity, volume, and variety. To extract meaningful value from Big Data, you need optimal processing power, analytical capabilities, and skills.

Figure 1.1 shows the features of Big Data:

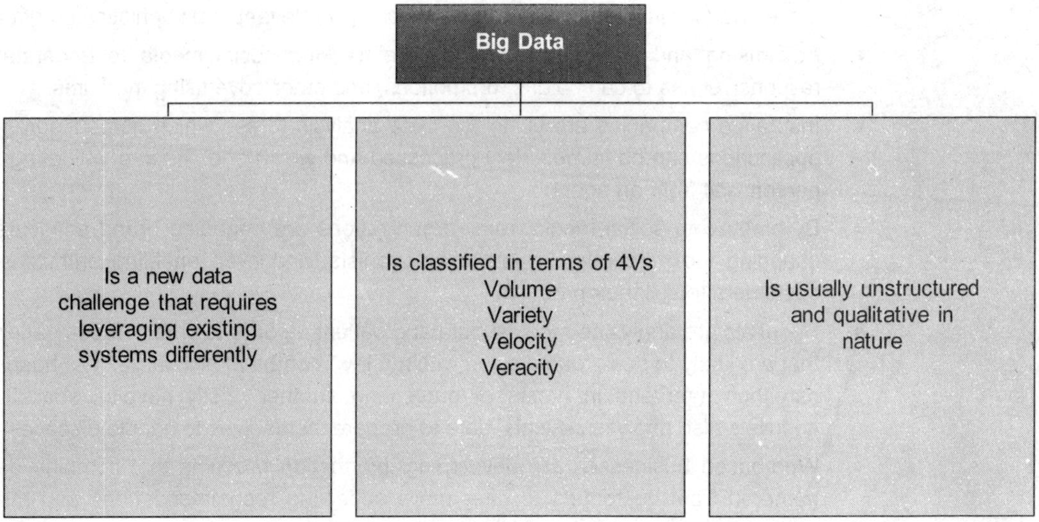

Figure 1.1: Features of Big Data

NOTE

By large or huge datasets or Big Data, we mean anything from a petabyte (1PB = 1000TB) to an exabyte (1EB = 1000PB) of data.

SCENARIO

Consider the scenario of an organization, Argon Technology, which provides Big Data analytical solutions to customers. Mr. Smith, the data analyst of the Argon Technology, is studying about Big Data and the ways in which it can be utilized in various sectors. He shares some examples with his team to enhance their knowledge.

EXHIBIT 1: Real-World Examples of Big Data

Some real-world examples of Big Data include:

- Consumer product companies and retail organizations are observing data on social media websites such as Facebook and Twitter. These sites help them to analyze customer behavior, preferences, and product perception. Accordingly, the companies can line up their upcoming products to gain profits. This phenomenon is also known as social media analytics.
- Manufacturers are monitoring minute vibration data from their equipment, which changes slightly as it wears down, to predict the optimal time to replace or maintain. Replacing it too soon wastes money and replacing it too late triggers an expensive work stoppage.
- Manufacturers are also monitoring social networks but with a different goal than marketers. They are using it to detect aftermarket support issues before a warranty failure becomes publicly detrimental.
- Financial service organizations are using the data mined from customer interactions to slice and dice their users into finely tuned segments. This enables these financial institutions to create increasingly relevant and sophisticated offers.
- Advertising and marketing agencies are tracking social media to understand responsiveness to campaigns, promotions, and other advertising mediums.
- Insurance companies are using Big Data analysis to see which home insurance applications can be immediately processed and which ones need a validating in-person visit from an agent.
- By embracing social media, retail organizations are engaging brand advocates, changing the perception of brand antagonists, and even enabling enthusiastic customers to sell their products.
- Hospitals are analyzing medical data and patient records to predict those patients that are likely to seek readmission within a few months of discharge. The hospital can then intervene in hopes of preventing another costly hospital stay. The hospitals also analyze patients' data to prepare themselves to handle diseases.
- Web-based businesses are developing information products that combine data gathered from customers to offer more appealing recommendations and more successful coupon programs.
- The government is making data public at the national, state, and city level for users to develop new applications that can generate public good. For example, weather data that is helpful for various industries.
- Sports teams are using data for tracking ticket sales and even for tracking team strategies. This is known as sports analytics.

Source: https://www.acquia.com/examples-big-data-projects

As already discussed, Big Data is a pool of huge amounts of data of all types, shapes, and formats collected from varied sources. Table 1.1 lists some common types of data and their sources:

Table 1.1: Types and Sources of Data

Type	Description	Source
Social Data	Refers to the information collected from various social networking sites and online portals	Facebook, Twitter, and LinkedIn
Machine Data	Refers to the information generated from RFID chips, bar code scanners, and sensors	RFID chip readings, Global Positioning System (GPS) results
Transactional Data	Refers to the information generated from online shopping sites, retailers, and Business to Business (B2B) transactions	Retail websites like eBay and Amazon

CASELET

Google Inc. applied its expertise of datacollecting, analyzing, and deriving conclusions to raise warnings for the flu plagues in the US approximately two weeks in advance of the existing public health services. To do this, Google monitored millions of users' health-tracking behaviors and followed a cluster of queries on themes such as symptoms about flu, congestion in chest, and incidences of buying a thermometer. Google analyzed this collected data and generated consolidated results that revealed strong indications of flu levels across America. To determine the accuracy of this data, Google did further research and data comparison before sharing it with the general public.

History of Data Management – Evolution of Big Data

Big Data is the new term of data evolution directed by the enormous velocity, variety, and volume of data. Velocity implies the speed with which the data flows in an organization; variety refers to the varied forms of data, such as structured, semi-structured, or unstructured; and volume defines the amount or quantity of data an organization has to deal with.

Figure 1.2 shows the challenges faced while handling data over the past few decades:

Figure 1.2: Evolution of Big Data

The advent of IT, the Internet, and globalization has facilitated increased volumes of data and information generation at an exponential rate, which has led to 'information explosion.' This, in turn, fueled the evolution of Big Data that started in 1940s and continues till date.

Information explosion is described as a continuous increase in the volume of the published information or data and the effects of this abundant information.

Table 1.2 lists some major milestones in the evolution of Big Data:

Table 1.2: Evolution of Big Data

Year	Milestone
1940s	An American librarian speculated the potential shortfall of shelves and cataloging staff, realizing the rapid increase in information and limited storage.
1960s	Automatic Data Compression was published in the Communications of the ACM. It states that the explosion of information in the past few years makes it necessary that requirements for storing information should be minimized. The paper described 'Automatic Data Compression' as a complete automatic and fast three-part compressor that can be used for any kind of information in order to reduce the slow external storage requirements and increase the rate of transmission from a computer system.
1970s	In Japan, the Ministry of Posts and Telecommunications initiated a project to study information flow in order to track the volume of information circulating in the country.
1980s	A research project was started by the Hungarian Central Statistics Office to account for the country's information industry. It measured the volume of information in bits.
1990s	Digital storage systems became more economical than paper storage. Challenges related to the amount of data and the presence of obsolete data became apparent. Some papers that discussed this concern are as follows: • Michael Lesk published How much information is there in the world? • John R. Masey presented a paper titled Big Data... and the Next Wave of InfraStress. • K.G. Coffman and Andrew Odlyzko published The Size and Growth Rate of the Internet. • Steve Bryson, David Kenwright, Michael Cox, David Ellsworth, and Robert Haimes published Visually Exploring Gigabyte Datasets in Real Time.
2000 onwards	Many researchers and scientists published papers raising similar concerns and discussing ways to solve them. Various methods were introduced to streamline information. Techniques for controlling the Volume, Velocity, and Variety of data emerged, thus introducing 3D data management. A study was carried out in order to estimate the new and original information created and stored worldwide in four types of physical media: paper, film, optical media, and magnetic media.

Table 1.2 is only a synopsis of the evolution. The need for an adequate space and storage of data was always felt, and with time, Big Data grew into a technological phenomenon.

The next chapter will help you in understanding the business applicability of Big Data in various industries. 'Big Data' as a concept has been used for long. When researchers used computers to analyze huge volumes of data, they were actually analyzing the Big Data. The demand for faster access to data and the applications and programs to process this data led to the present concept of Big Data and Big Data analytics in the IT industry.

Suppose a bank plans to establish self-service kiosks in a major metro area. The marketing department wants to determine the busiest spots for establishing the self-service kiosks, on the basis of the traffic patterns of customers across the city. This information is not available in the existing data warehouse of the bank. In this situation, the bank can acquire the GPS location data of the customers through a third party, and thereby, gather the information about the mobility patterns of its customers.

Thus, by using the right set of Big Data with the right technique of data extraction, preparation, and integration, today banks can identify the busiest spots in the city for establishing their self-service kiosks.

NOTE

World Wide Web (WWW) is the biggest source of generating data. More than 60% evolution happening in the field of data is just because of the use of the Internet.

Structuring Big Data

Structuring of data, in simple terms, is arranging the available data in a manner such that it becomes easy to study, analyze, and derive conclusion from it. But, why is structuring required?

In daily life, you may have come across questions like:

- How do I use to my advantage the vast amount of data and information I come across?
- Which news articles should I read of the thousands I come across?
- How do I choose a book of the millions available on my favorite sites or stores?
- How do I keep myself updated about new events, sports, inventions, and discoveries taking place across the globe?

Today, solutions to such questions can be found by information processing systems. These systems can analyze and structure a large amount of data specifically for you on the basis of what you searched, what you looked at, and for how long you remained at a particular page or website, thus scanning and presenting you with the customized information as per your behavior and habits. In other words, structuring data helps in understanding user behaviors, requirements, and preferences to make personalized recommendations for every individual.

When a user regularly visits or purchases from online shopping sites, say eBay, each time he/she logs in, the system can present a recommended list of products that may interest the user on the basis of his/her earlier purchases or searches, thus presenting a specially customized recommendation set for every user. This is the power of Big Data analytics.

Today, various sources generate a variety of data, such as images, text, audios, etc. All such different types of data can be structured only if it is sorted and organized in some logical pattern. Thus, the process of structuring data requires one to first understand the various types of data available today.

Types of Data

Data that comes from multiple sources, such as databases, Enterprise Resource Planning (ERP) systems, weblogs, chat history, and GPS maps, varies in its format. However, different formats of data need to be made consistent and clear to be used for analysis. Data is obtained primarily from the following types of sources:

- Internal sources, such as organizational or enterprise data
- External sources, such as social data

Table 1.3 compares the internal and external sources of data:

Table 1.3: Comparison between the Internal and External Sources of Data

Data Source	Definition	Examples of Sources	Application
Internal	Provides structured or organized data that originates from within the enterprise and helps run business	• Customer Relationship Management (CRM) • Enterprise Resource Planning (ERP), systems • Customers, details • Products and sales data • Generally OLTP and operational data	This data (current data in the operational system) is used to support daily business operations of an organization
External	Provides unstructured or unorganized data that originates from the external environment of an organization	• Business partners • Syndicate data suppliers • Internet • Government • Market research organizations	This data is often analyzed to understand the entities mostly external to the organization, such as customers, competitors, market, and environment

Figure 1.3 shows the various parts of Big Data. It is obvious from Figure 1.3 that in Big Data, we deal with data storage, distributed system, data mining, and many other things.

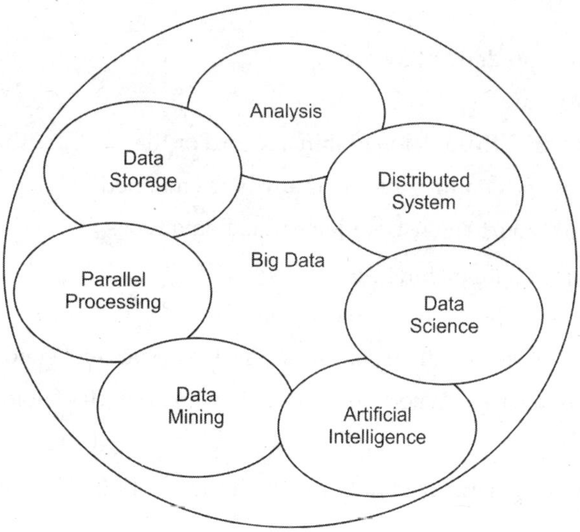

Figure 1.3: Concepts of Big Data.

On the basis of the data received from the sources mentioned in Table 1.3, Big Data comprises:

- Structured data
- Unstructured data
- Semi-structured data

In a real-world scenario, typically, the unstructured data is larger in volume than the structured and semi-structured data, approximately 70% to 80% of data is in unstructured form. Figure 1.4 illustrates the types of data that comprise Big Data:

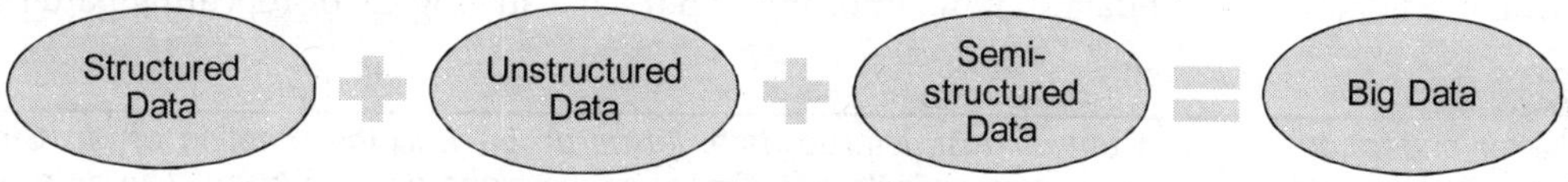

Figure 1.4: Types of Big Data

Let us discuss these types in detail in the following sections.

Structured Data

Structured data can be defined as the data that has a defined repeating pattern. This pattern makes it easier for any program to sort, read, and process the data. Processing structured data is much easier and faster than processing data without any specific repeating patterns.

SCENARIO

Reconsider the scenario of Mr. Smith, the Big Data analyst of Argon Technology, who is sharing his observations on the applications of Big Data with his team. In one such example, he tells that the data in most publishing houses is often captured by suitable software tools and maintained in a relational database, such as Oracle. The data stored in a relational database is in a structured format; therefore, it can directly be put to analysis, and the outcome can be used to take various organizational decisions.

Structured data:

- Is organized data in a predefi ed format
- Is stored in tabular form
- Is the data that resides in fixed fields within a record or file
- Is formatted data that has entities and their attributes mapped
- Is used to query and report against predetermined data types

Some sources of structured data include:

- Relational databases (in the form of tables)
- Flat files in the form of records (like comma separated values (csv) and tab-separated files)
- Multidimensional databases (majorly used in data warehouse technology)
- Legacy databases

Table 1.4 shows a sample of structured data in which the attribute data for every customer is stored in the defined fields:

Table 1.4: Sample of Structured Data

Customer ID	Name	Product ID	City	State
12365	Smith	241	Graz	Styria
23658	Jack	365	Wolfsberg	Carinthia
32456	Kady	421	Enns	Upper Austria

Unstructured Data

Unstructured data is a set of data that might or might not have any logical or repeating patterns.

SCENARIO

To better understand the concept of unstructured data, let us go back to the meeting of Mr. Smith. He explains that the publishing house also collects data from various blogs and websites. The data obtained from Web blogs or social media sites is considered as unstructured data because it does not follow any specific pattern and is inconsistent. The analysis of such data helps the organization to know more about customer preferences, feedback, and demands.

Unstructured data:

- Consists typically of metadata, i.e., the additional information related to data
- Comprises inconsistent data, such as data obtained from files, social media websites, satellites, etc.
- Consists of data in different formats such as e-mails, text, audio, video, or images

Some sources of unstructured data include:

- **Text both internal and external to an organization**—Documents, logs, survey results, feedbacks, and e-mails from both within and across the organization

- **Social media**—Data obtained from social networking platforms, including YouTube, Facebook, Twitter, LinkedIn, and Flickr
- **Mobile data**—Data such as text messages and location information

About 80 percent of enterprise data consists of unstructured content.

CASELET

We all know that nowadays CCTV cameras are installed in almost every supermarket, and its footage is thoroughly analyzed by the management for various purposes. Some focus points of the analysis include the routes customers take to navigate through the store, customer behavior during a bottleneck, such as network traffic; and places where customers typically halt while shopping. This unstructured information from the CCTV footage is combined with structured data, comprising the details obtained from the bill counters, products sold, the amount and nature of payments, etc. to arrive at a complete data-driven picture of customer behavior. The analysis of the obtained information helps the management to provide a pleasant shopping experience to customers as well as improve sales figures.

Challenges Associated with Unstructured Data

Working with unstructured data poses certain challenges, which are as follows:

- Identifying the unstructured data that can be processed
- Sorting, organizing, and arranging unstructured data in different sets and formats
- Combining and linking unstructured data in a more structured format to derive any logical conclusions out of the available information
- Costing in terms of storage space and human resource (data analysts and scientists) needed to deal with the exponential growth of unstructured data

Figure 1.5 shows the result of a survey conducted to ascertain the challenges associated with unstructured datain percentage—from the most to the least-challenging IT areas:

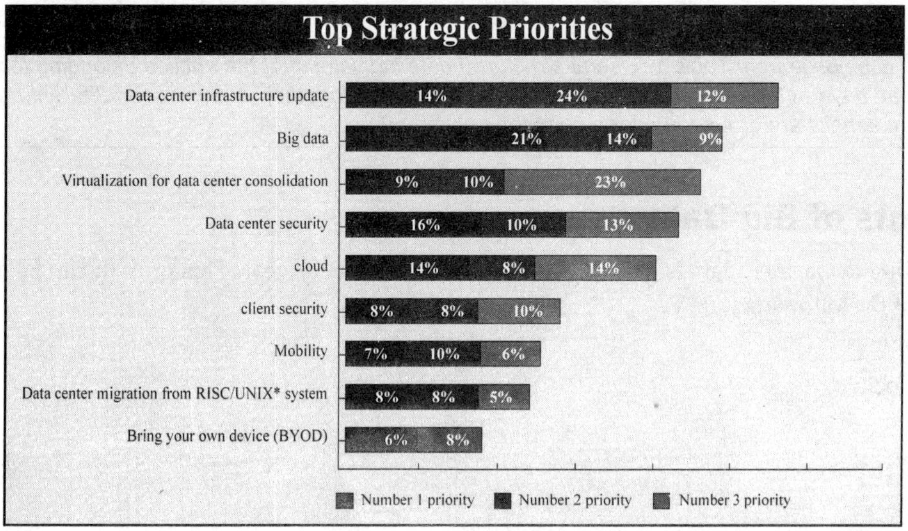

Source: Peer Research Big Data Analytics Intel (August 2013)

Figure 1.5: Challenges in Handling Unstructured Data

The survey reveals that the Big Data is the second biggest challenge followed by virtualization to manage the volume of data. Unstructured data is also generated from files that often have the same name and extension. For example, video files are generally stored with the extension .mp4 or .3gp, whereas audio files have extension .wav or .mp3. As different files of the same category can have the same file name in different sources, merely a name and an extension do not help in data identification, classification, or even basic searches.

Semi-Structured Data

Semi-structured data, also known as having a schema-less or self-describing structure, refers to a form of structured data that contains tags or markup elements in order to separate elements and generate hierarchies of records and fields in the given data. Such type of data does not follow the proper structure of data models as in relational databases. In other words, data is stored inconsistently in rows and columns of a database.

Some sources for semi-structured data include:

- File systems such as Web data in the form of cookies
- Data exchange formats such as JavaScript Object Notation (JSON) data

SCENARIO

Mr. Smith also observes the presence of some semi-structured data saved in the database system of the publishing house. This data contains personal details of the authors working for the publishing house, as shown in Table 1.5:

Table 1.5: Semi-Structured Data

Sl. No	*Name*	*E-Mail*
1.	*Sam Jacobs*	*smj@xyz.com*
2.	*First Name: David* *Last Name: Brown*	*davidb@xyz.com*

As you can notice from Table 1.5, semi-structured data indicates that the entities belonging to the same class can have different attributes even if they are grouped together. In this case, different names and different e-mails are grouped under a common column name.

Elements of Big Data

According to Gartner, data is growing at the rate of 59% every year. This growth can be depicted in terms of the following four Vs:

- Volume
- Velocity
- Variety
- Veracity

Figure 1.6 explains the four Vs of Big Data with examples:

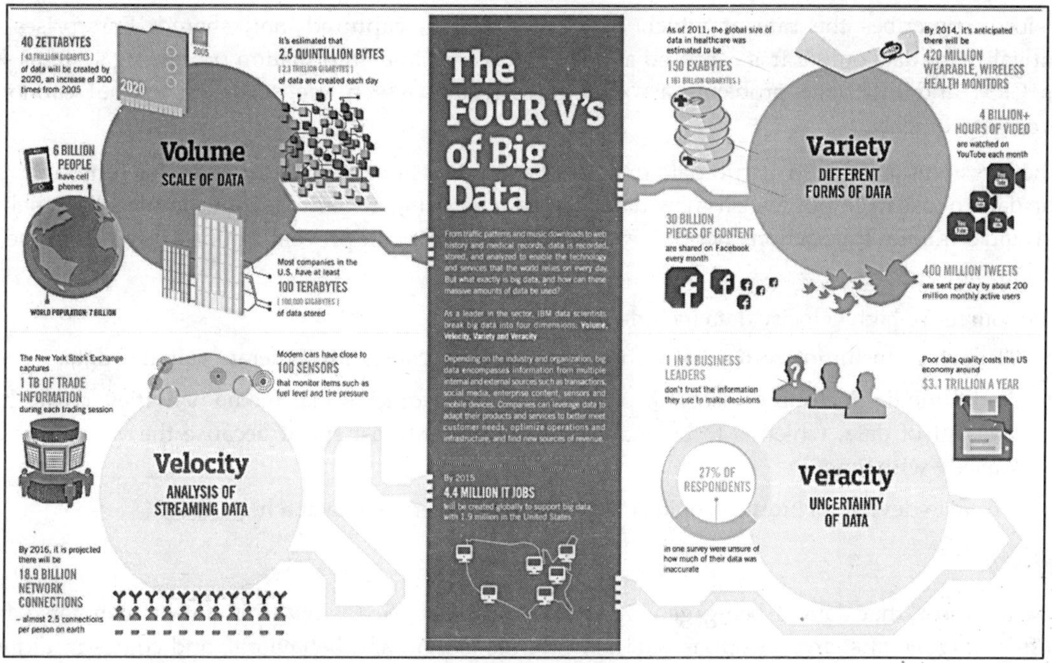

Source: *McKinsey Global Institute, Twitter, Cisco, Gartner, EMC, SAS, IBM, MEPTEC, QAS*

Figure 1.6: Four Vs of Big Data

Volume

Volume is the amount of data generated by organizations or individuals. Today, the volume of data in most organizations is approaching exabytes. Some experts predict the volume of data to reach zettabytes in the coming years. Organizations are doing their best to handle this ever-increasing volume of data. For example, according to IBM, over 2.7 zetabytes of data is present in the digital universe today. Every minute, over 571 new websites are being created. IDC estimates that by 2020, online business transactions will reach up to 450 billion per day.

The Internet alone generates a huge amount of data. The followings figures help us to get an idea of the Internet traffic:

- Internet has around 14.3 trillion live Web pages, and 48 billion Web pages are indexed by Google Inc.; 14 billion Web pages are indexed by Microsoft Bing.
- Internet has around 672 exabytes of accessible data.
- Total world-wide Internet traffic in the year 2013 was 43,639 petabytes.
- Over 9,00,000 servers are owned by Google Inc., which is the largest in the world.
- Total data stored on the Internet is over 1 yottabyte.

Even by underestimation, the total data stored on the Internet, including images, videos, audio, etc., has crossed 1 yottabyte. The exact size of the Internet will never be known!

Source: *Global Internet usages facts and statistics of 2013*

Velocity

Velocity describes the rate at which data is generated, captured, and shared. Enterprises can capitalize on data only if it is captured and shared in real time. Information processing systems such as CRM and ERP face problems associated with data, which keeps adding up but cannot be processed quickly.

These systems are able to attend data in batches every few hours; however, even this time lag causes the data to lose its importance as new data is constantly being generated. For example, eBay analyzes around 5 million transactions per day in real time to detect and prevent frauds arising from the use of PayPal.

The sources of high velocity data include the following:

- IT devices, including routers, switches, firewalls, etc., constantly generate valuable data.
- Social media, including facebook posts, tweets, and other social media activities, create huge amount of data, which is to be analyzed instantly at a fast speed because the value degrades quickly with time.
- Portable device, including mobile, PDA, etc., also generate data at a high speed.

Variety

We all know that data is being generated at a very fast pace. Now, this data is generated from different types of sources, such as internal, external, social, and behavioral, and comes in different formats, such as images, text, videos, etc. Even a single source can generate data in varied formats, for example, GPS and social networking sites, such as Facebook, produce data of all types, including text, images, videos, etc. Figure 1.7 shows the various types of data:

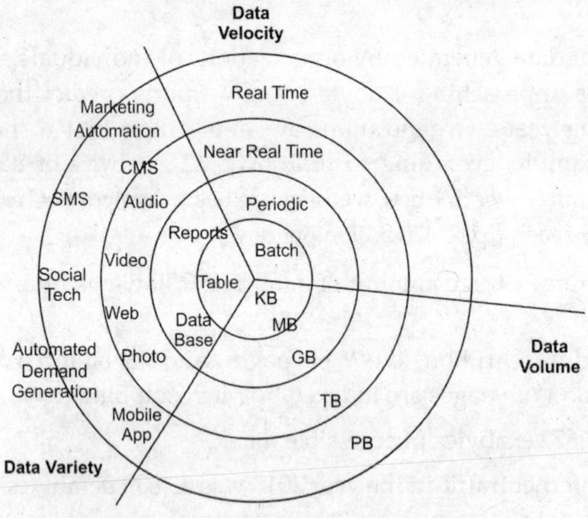

Figure 1.7: Various Types of Data

Veracity

Veracity generally refers to the uncertainty of data, i.e., whether the obtained data is correct or consistent. Out of the huge amount of data that is generated in almost every process, only the data that is correct and consistent can be used for further analysis. Data when processed becomes information; however, a lot of effort goes in processing the data. Big Data, especially in the unstructured and semi-structured forms, is messy in nature, and it takes a good amount of time and expertise to clean that data and make it suitable for analysis.

Big Data Analytics

Big data analytics reformed the ways to conduct business in many ways, such as it improves, decisions making, business process management, etc. Business analytics uses the data and different other techniques like information technology, features of statistics, quantitive methods, and different models to provide results. There are three main types of business analytics: descriptive analytics, predictive analytics, and prescriptive analytics. The conventional database systems are not in a postion to process Big data defined by the four Vs: volume, variety, velocity, and veracity. Big data also affects the analytical process and technologies used for analytics.

There are mainly three types of analytics:

- **Descriptive Analytics**—Descriptive analytics is the most prevalent form of analytics, and it serves as a base for advanced analytics. It answers the question 'What happened in the business?' Descriptive analytics analyses a database to provide information on the trends of past or current business events that can help managers, planners, leaders, etc. to develop a road map for future actions. Descriptive analytics performs an in-depth analysis of data to reveal details such as frequency of events, operation costs, and the underlying reason for failures. It helps in identifying the root cause of the problem.
- **Predictive Analytics**—Predictive analytics is about understanding and predicting the future and answers the question 'What could happen?' by using statistical models and different forecast techniques. It predicts the near future probabilities and trends and helps in what-if analysis. In predictive analytics, we use statistics, data mining techniques, and machine learning to analyze the future. Figure 1.8 shows the steps involved in predictive analytics:

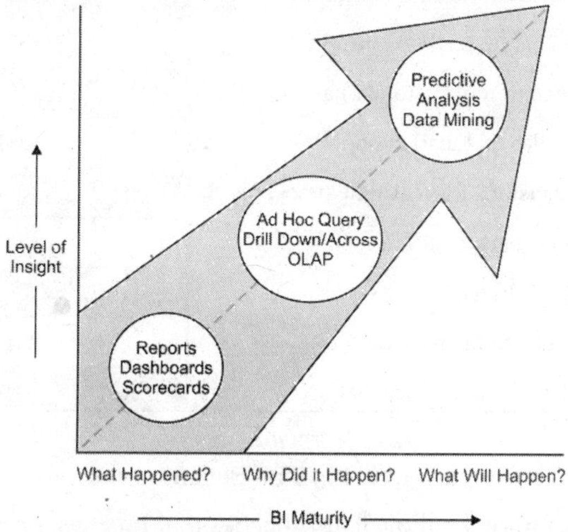

Figure 1.8: Predictive Analytics

- **Prescriptive Analytics**—Prescriptive analysis answers 'What should we do?,' on the basis of complex data obtained from descriptive and predictive analyses. By using the optimization technique, prescriptive analytics determines the finest substitute to minimize or maximize some equitable finance, marketing, and many other areas. For example, if we have to find the best way of shipping goods from a factory to a destination, to minimize costs, we will use the prescriptive analytics. Figure 1.9 shows a diagrammatic representation of the stages involved in the prescriptive analytics:

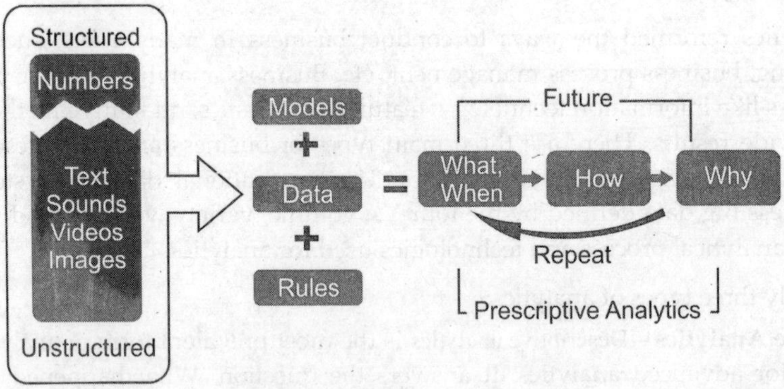

Figure 1.9: Prescriptive Analytics

Data, which is available in abundance, can be streamlined for growth and expansion in technology as well as business. When data is analyzed successfully, it can become the answer to one of the most important questions: how can businesses acquire more customers and gain business insight? The key to this problem lies in being able to source, link, understand, and analyze data.

Figure 1.10 highlights the proportion of business areas that have benefited by using Big Data:

Big Data Analytics Benefit	Proportion of Businesses Reporting Benefit (%)
Better social influences marketing	61%
More accurate business insights	45%
Segmentation of customer base	41%
Identifying sales and market opportunities	38%
Automated decisions for real-time processes	37%
Detection of fraud	33%
Quantification of risks	30%
Better planning and forecasting	29%
Identifying cost drivers	29%

***Source:** TDWI July 2013*

Figure 1.10: Big Data Benefit Areas

Let us understand some common analytical approaches that businesses apply to use Big Data.

Table 1.6 describes various analytical approaches typically associated with Big Data:

Table 1.6: Analytical Approaches

Approach	Possible Evaluations
Predictive Analysis	• How can a business use the available data for predictive and real-time analysis across its different domains? • How can a business avail benefits from the unstructured enterprise data? • How can a business leverage upon new types of data such as sentiment data, social media, clickstream, and multimedia?

Behavioral Analysis	• How will a business leverage complex data in order to create new models for:
	  • Driving business outcomes
	  • Decreasing business costs
	  • Driving innovation in business strategy
	  • Improving overall customer satisfaction
	  • Converting an audience to a customer

Data Interpretation	• What new business analyses can be estimated from the available data? • Which data should be analyzed for new product innovation?

Advantages of Big Data Analytics

According to Atul Butte, Stanford, "Hiding within those mounds of data is knowledge that could change the life of a patient, or change the world." So, the real power of Big Data lies in its analysis. Processing, studying, and implementing the conclusions derived from the analysis of Big Data help you to collect accurate data, take timely and more informed strategic decisions, target the right set of audience and customers, increase benefits, and reduce wastage and costs.

The right analysis of the available data can improve major business processes in various ways. For example, in a manufacturing unit, data analytics can improve the functioning of the following processes:

- **Procurement**—To find out which suppliers are more efficient and cost-effective in delivering products on time
- **Product Development**—To draw insights on innovative product and service formats and designs for enhancing the development process and coming up with demanded products
- **Manufacturing**—To identify machinery and process variations that may be indicators of quality problems
- **Distribution**—To enhance supply chain activities and standardize optimal inventory levels vis-à-vis various external factors such as weather, holidays, economy, etc.
- **Marketing**—To identify which marketing campaigns will be the most effective in driving and engaging customers and understanding customer behaviors and channel behaviors
- **Price Management**—To optimize prices based on the analysis of external factors

- **Merchandising**—To improve merchandise breakdown on the basis of current buying patterns and increase inventory levels and product interest insights on the basis of the analysis of various customer behaviors
- **Sales**—To optimize assignment of sales resources and accounts, product mix, and other operations
- **Store Operations**—To adjust inventory levels on the basis of predicted buying patterns, study of demographics, weather, key events, and other factors
- **Human Resources**—To find out the characteristics and behaviors of successful and effective employees, as well as other employee insights for managing talent better

Every business and industry today is affected by and benefitted from Big Data analytics in multiple ways.

A closer look at some specific industries will help you to understand the application of Big Data in these sectors.

Transportation

Big Data has greatly improved transportation services. The data containing traffic information is analyzed to identify traffic jam areas. Suitable steps can then be taken, on the basis of this analysis, to keep the traffic moving in such areas. Distributed sensors are installed in handheld devices, on the roads and on vehicles to provide real-time traffic information. This information is analyzed and disseminated to commuters and also to the traffic control authority.

Education

Big Data has transformed the modern-day education processes through innovative approaches, such as e-learning for teachers to analyze the students' ability to comprehend and thus impart education effectively in accordance with each student's needs. The analysis is done by studying the responses to questions, recording the time consumed in attempting those questions, and analyzing other behavioral signals of the students. Big Data also assists in analyzing the requirements and finding easy and innovative ways of imparting education, especially distance learning over vast geographical areas.

Travel

The travel industry also uses Big Data to conduct business. It maintains complete details of all the customer records that are then analyzed to determine certain behavioral patterns in customers. For example, in the airline industry, Big Data is analyzed for identifying personal preferences or spotting which passengers like to have window seats for short-haul flights and aisle seats for long-haul flights. This helps airlines to offer the similar seats to customers when they make a fresh booking with the airways.

Big Data also helps airlinesto track customers who regularly fly between specific routes so that they can make the right cross-sell and up-sell offers. Some airlines also apply analytics to pricing, inventory, and advertising for improving customer experiences, leading to more customer satisfaction, and hence, more business. Some airlines even go to the length of evaluating customers who tend to miss their flights. They try to help such customers by delaying the flights or booking them on another flight.

Government

Big Data has come to play an important role in almost all the undertaking and processes of government.

According to the UK free market,"the UK government could save up to £33 billion a year by using public Big Data more effectively." Analysis of Big Data promotes clarity and transparency in various government processes and helps in:

- Taking timely and informed decisions about various issues
- Identifying flaws and loopholes in processes and taking preventive or corrective measures on time
- Assessing the areas of improvement in various sectors, such as education, health, defense, and research
- Using budgets more judiciously and reducing unnecessary wastage and costs
- Preventing fraudulent practices in various sectors

Healthcare

In healthcare, the pharmacy and medical device companies use Big Data to improve their research and development practices, while health insurance companies use it to determine patient-specific treatment therapy modes that promise the best results. Big Data also helps researchers to work towards eliminating healthcare-related challenges before they become real problems. Big Data helps doctors to analyze the requirement and medical history of every patient and provide individualistic services to them, depending on their medical condition.

Telecom

The mobile revolution and the Internet usage on mobile phones have led to a tremendous increase in the amount of data generated in the telecom sector. Managing this huge pool of data has almost become a challenge for the telecom industry. For example, in Europe, there is a compulsion on the telecom companies to keep data of their customers for at least six months and maximum up to two years. Now, all this collection, storage, and maintenance of data would just be a waste of time and resources unless we could derive any significant benefits from this data. Big Data analytics allows telecom industries to utilize this data for extracting meaningful information that could be used to gain crucial business insights that help industries in enhancing their performance, improving customer services, maintaining their hold on the market, and generating more business opportunities.

Consumer Goods Industry

Consumer goods companies generate huge volumes of data in varied formats from different sources, such as transactions, billing details, feedback forms, etc. This data needs to be organized and analyzed in a systemic manner in order to derive any meaningful information from it. For example, the data generated from the Point-of-Sale (POS) systems provides significant real-time information about customers' preferences, current market trends, the increase and decrease in demand of different products at different regions, etc. This information helps organizations to predict any possible fluctuations in prices of goods and make purchases accordingly. It also helps marketing teams in taking suitable actions rapidly if there is a deviation in the expected sales of a product, thus, preventing any further losses to the company. Therefore, we can say that Big Data analytics allows organizations to gain better business insights and take informed and timely decisions.

Aviation Industry

Big Data analytics also plays a significant role in the commercial aviation industry. Like other industries, the aviation industry also maintains a detailed record of all their customers that includes their personal information, flying preferences, and other trends and patterns. The organization analyzes this data to improve their customer services, and thus brand image. In addition, every aircraft generates a significant amount of data during operation. This data is then analyzed for enhancing operational efficiencies, identifying the parts that require repairs, and taking any necessary constructive or preventive measures on time.

Careers in Big Data

Now that you know that Big Data is really BIG in today's world, you can well understand that so are the opportunities associated with it. The market today needs plenty of talented and qualified people who can use their expertise to help organizations deal with Big Data.

Qualified and experienced Big Data professionals must have a blend of technical expertise, creative and analytical thinking, and communication skills to be able to effectively collate, clean, analyze, and present information extracted from Big Data.

Most jobs in Big Data are from companies that can be categorized into the following four broad buckets:

- Big Data technology drivers, e.g., Google, IBM, Salesforce
- Big Data product companies, e.g., Oracle
- Big Data services companies, e.g., EMC
- Big Data analytics companies, e.g., Splunk

Figure 1.11 shows the logos of some companies that hire Big Data professionals:

Source: *Glassdoor Report October 2011*

Figure 1.11: Companies Hiring Big Data Professionals

As shown in Figure 1.11, companies such as Google, Salesforce, and Apple offer various types of opportunities to Big Data professionals. These companies deal in various domains such as retail, manufacturing, information, finance, and consumer electronics. The hiring of Big Data experts in these domains, as per Big Data Analytics 2014 report, is shown in Figure 1.12:

Figure 1.12: Top 20 Industries Hiring Big Data Experts

The most common job titles in Big Data include:

- Big Data analyst
- Data scientist
- Big Data developer
- Big Data administrator
- Big Data engineer

Figure 1.13 illustrates the roles of these profiles:

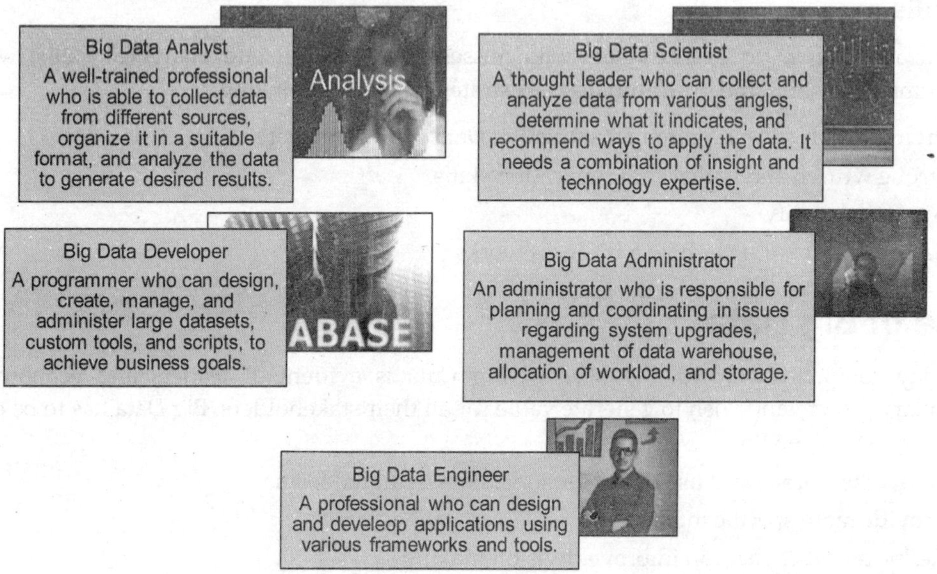

Figure 1.13: Role of Different JobTitles in Data Analytics

In 2011, a report was published by McKinsey & Co. that indicated that by 2018, the United States alone might face a huge shortage (about 140,000 to 190,000) of data analytics professionals.

Skills Required

Big Data professionals can have various educational backgrounds, such as econometrics, physics, biostatistics, computer science, applied mathematics, or engineering. Data scientists mostly possess a master's degree or Ph.D. because it is a senior position and often achieved after considerable experience in dealing with data. Developers generally prefer implementing Big Data by using Hadoop and its components.

Technical Skills

A Big Data analyst should possess the following technical skills:

- Understanding of Hadoop ecosystem components, such as HDFS, MapReduce, Pig, Hive, etc.
- Knowledge of natural language processing
- Knowledge of statistical analysis and analytical tools
- Knowledge of machine learning
- Knowledge of conceptual and predictive modeling

A Big Data developer should possess the following skills:

- Programming skills in Java, Hadoop, Hive, HBase, and HQL
- Understanding of HDFS and MapReduce
- Knowledge of ZooKeeper, Flume, and Sqoop

These skills can be acquired with proper training and practice. This book familiarizes you with the technical skills required by a Big Data analyst and Big Data developer.

Soft Skills

Organizations look for professionals who possess good logical and analytical skills, with good communication skills and an affinity toward strategic business thinking.

The preferred soft skills requirements for a Big Data professional are:

- Strong written and verbal communication skills
- Analytical ability
- Basic understanding of how a business works

Future of Big Data

In today competitive world, the need of Big Data is evident. If leaders and economies want exemplary growth and wish to generate value for all their stakeholders, Big Data has to be embraced and used extensively to:

- Allow the storage and use of transactional data in digital form
- Provide more specific information
- Refine analytics that can improve decision making
- Classify customers for providing customized products and services based on buying patterns

Most organizations today consider data and information to be their most valuable and differentiated asset. By analyzing this data effectively, organizations worldwide are now finding new ways to compete and emerge as leaders in their fields to improve decision making and enhance their productivity and performance. At the same time, the volume and variety of data is also increasing at an immense rate every day. The global phenomena of using Big Data to gain business value and competitive advantage will only continue to grow as will the opportunities associated with it.

Figure 1.14 depicts the tremendous growth in the volume of Big Data over the coming years:

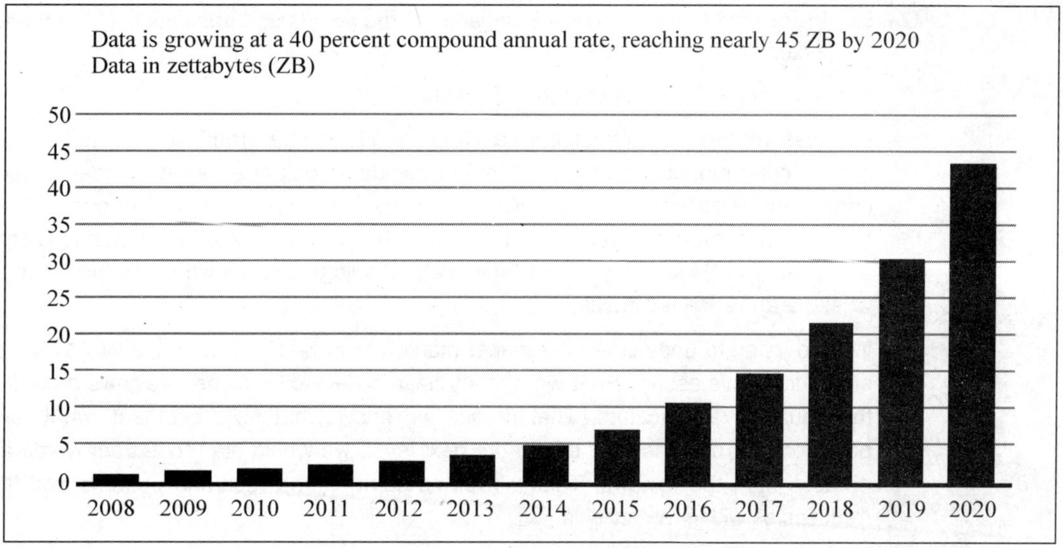

Source: *Oracle, 2012*

Figure 1.14: Growth Pattern of Data

Research conducted by MGI and McKinsey's Business Technology Office suggests that the use of Big Data is most likely to become a key basis of competition for individual firms for success and growth and strengthening consumer surplus, production growth, and innovation.

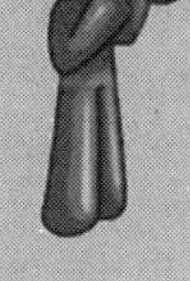

EXHIBIT 2: The Future of Big Data—Moving from Big Data 1.0 to 2.0

The future of Big Data is not about numeric data points but instead about asking the deeper questions and finding out why consumers make the decisions they do.

Today, clients often ask about the future of big data and what the next step is; how can we leverage data on an even deeper level in order to extract meaningful consumer insights that go beyond where we are now? Most of the standard answers are around the ability to get data and insights in real time and from more devices than ever. It's time we move beyond structured data and into the prime time of text analytics.

For us, the easiest way to get started with Big Data 2.0 is to focus on the unstructured data we collect every day. This can be reviews, customer support emails, community forums, or even your own CRM system. The simplest way to look at this data is through a process called text analytics.

Text analytics is a fairly straightforward process that breaks out like this:

1. **Acquisition**—Collecting and aggregating the raw data you want to analyze
2. **Transforming & Preprocessing**—Cleaning and formatting the data to make it easier to read
3. **Enrichment**—Enhancing the data by adding additional data points
4. **Processing**—Performing specific analyses and classifications on the data
5. **Frequencies & Analysis**—Evaluation of the results and translation into numerical indicators
6. **Mining**—Actual extraction of information

Let's assume we are a consumer packaged goods company and we want to introduce a new line of diapers into the market. We decide to look at Amazon in order to better understand which products are category leaders (sales rank and number of sales) and how the consumers like the product itself (reviews). If we analyze these metrics across all diapers, we have a Big Data 1.0 picture that tells us exactly who sells the most and what the audience favorite is.

We are trying to understand the diaper market. In order to not turn this into a step-by-step guide, let's assume that we already have collected all diapers reviews as well as their qualitative indicators. That means we know what sells best and what ranks best/worst. In order to take this to the next level, we would start to extract words and phrases from the reviews. This will tell us some of the recurring patterns and their frequencies within the reviews.

1. **Why Did It Sell So Well**

   When I looked at the reviews of the top-selling product, I found that the most mentioned terms across the majority of the helpful reviews were "price," "special," and "value." This tells us that people did not buy it because of its quality or features but because of its pricing. So, when we are launching our product, we want to look at this one for price/value guidance instead of features.

2. **Why People Did Not Like It**

   This one was very revealing. The brand with the most negative reviews had an extremely high frequency around the terms "tape," "stick," "stay closed," and "open." After a few reads, I discovered that consumers had no issues with the usual key features on a diaper such as "absorbency," "leakage," or "softness" but actually had issues with the tape on the side of the diaper, and the fact that it kept opening. The amount of negative reviews overall that mentioned these issues makes us believe that this is a feature that brands don't talk about but consumers care about. Therefore, we would recommend testing ads that address this issue.

3. **Smart Filtering**

   One interesting issue we came across is the fact that a lot of the negative reviews were not actually about the product but rather focused on shipping, stock level, and packaging concerns. By tagging and removing these from the set, we are able to evaluate product level in order to focus on product-related concerns. If we were to list our diaper on Amazon, we would recommend adding a shipping and stock level guarantee prominently in the copy—a competitive advantage that speaks directly to consumer concerns.

4. **What Do They Want**

From an R&D perspective, this insight is worth gold. By evaluating reviews that have terms like "I wish," "hope," or "they should," we are able to detect common features consumers are looking for when thinking about diapers. These are great insights that address the constantly changing need of the consumers. We can feed these product feature-specific insights to our R&D team as well as our copywriters.

As you can see, when analyzing the diaper category, Big Data 2.0 yielded insights beyond binary performance indicators. We could see the crowd favorites but did not (yet) know the "why" behind purchases or understand the positive or negative reviews until our text analytics exercise. There are countless consumer insights to be mined from textual, unstructured data that give us the voice of the consumer, their motivations, and a deeper understanding of their purchasing behavior.

Source: http://www.clickz.com/clickz/column/2377230/the-future-of-big-data-big-data-20

Summary

This chapter, introduced you to Big Data—the big buzzword of today's IT industry. The chapter discussed some common features and sources of Big Data. Next, you learned about the evolution of Big Data along with its various types, namely, structured, unstructured, and semi-structured. The chapter further discussed the four Vs of Big Data, i.e., Volume, Velocity, Variety, and Veracity. You also learned about the use of Big Data in various domains, such as transportation, education, travel, government, and healthcare. The chapter also familiarized you with professional opportunities available in the career path of Big Data and the technical as well as soft skills required to enter this domain.

Quick Revise

Multiple-Choice Questions

Q1. Which of the following is not a characteristic of Big Data?

a. Volume
b. Variability
c. Variety
d. Velocity

Ans. The correct option is b.

Q2. Who among the following do you think would be able to deal with the growing number of data sources efficiently?

a. Business developer
b. Data scientist
c. Sales executive
d. Web designer

Ans. The correct option is b.

Q3. Which one of the following is not an example of external datasources?

a. Data from CRM
b. Data from Web logs
c. Data from government sources
d. Data from market surveys

Ans. The correct option is a.

Q4. Which of the following does not belong to the traditional database technology?

a. RDBMS
b. DBMS
c. Flat files
d. NoSQL

Ans. The correct option is d.

Q5. If a Big Data analyst were to analyze data from a database of call logs provided by a telecom service provider, which element of Big Data would he be dealing with?

a. Volume
b. Variable
c. Variety
d. Velocity

Ans. The correct option is a.

Q6. Some people call this data as "structured but not relational." Which data are we talking about?

a. Structured data
b. Unstructured data
c. Semi-structured data
d. Mixed data

Ans. The correct option is c.

Q7. The data generated from a GPS satellite and Web logs is classified as ____________.

a. Structured data
b. Unstructured data
c. Both structured and unstructured data
d. Semi-structured data

Ans. The correct option is d.

Q8. The data being captured can be in any form or structure. Which characteristic of Big Data are we talking about?

a. Volume
b. Velocity
c. Variety
d. Value

Ans. The correct option is c.

Subjective Questions

Q1. List and discuss the four elements of Big Data.

Ans. Big Data primarily consists of the following four elements:

- **Volume**—Volume is the amount of data generated by organizations or individuals. Today, the volume of data in most organizations is approaching around exabytes. Some experts predict the volume of data to reach zetabytes in the coming years. Organizations are doing their best to handle this ever-increasing volume of data. For example, Google Inc. processes around 20 petabytes of data, and Twitter feeds generate around 8 terabytes of data every day.

- **Velocity—**Velocity describes the rate at which data is generated, captured, and shared. Enterprises can capitalize on data only if it is captured and shared in real time. Information processing systems such as CRM and Enterprise Resource Planning (ERP) face problems associated with data, which keeps adding up but cannot be processed quickly. These systems are able to attend data in batches every few hours; however, even this time lag causes the data to lose its importance as new data is constantly being generated. For example, eBay analyzes around 5 million transactions per day in real time to detect and prevent frauds arising from the use of PayPal.
- **Variety—**We all know that data is being generated at a very fast pace. Now, this data is generated from different types of sources, such as internal, external, social, and behavioral, and comes in different formats, such as images, text, videos, etc. Even a single source can generate data in varied formats; for example, GPS and social networking sites, such as Facebook, produce data of all types, including text, images, videos, etc.
- **Veracity—**Veracity generally refers to the uncertainty of data, i.e., whether the obtained data is correct or consistent. Out of the huge amount of data that is generated in almost every process, only the data that is correct and consistent can be used for further analysis. Data when processed becomes information; however, a lot of effort goes in processing the data. Big Data, especially in the unstructured and semi-structured forms, is messy in nature, and it takes a good amount of time and expertise to clean that data and make it suitable for analysis.

Q2. As an HR manager of a company providing Big Data solutions to clients, what characteristics would you look for while recruiting a potential candidate for the position of a data analyst?

Ans. A Big Data analyst should be a well-trained professional who is able to collect data from different sources, organize it in a suitable form, and analyze it to generate the desired results. A Big Data analyst should have the following technical and soft skills:

Technical Skills:

- Understanding of Hadoop, Hive, and MapReduce
- Knowledge of natural language processing
- Knowledge of statistical analysis and analytical tools
- Knowledge of conceptual and predictive modeling

Soft Skills:

- Strong written and verbal communication skills
- Analytical ability
- Basic understanding of how a business works

Q3. You are planning the marketing strategy for a new product in your company. Identify and list some limitations of structured data related to this work.

Ans. Structured data has certain limitations associated with it, when it comes to product marketing and advertising.

Some of these limitations are:

- Marketing strategies do not provide space for predefined rules
- There is hardly any definite relation between product sales and marketing strategies
- Structured data cannot find complex correlation patterns
- Behavioral analysis is not possible from structured data

2

Exploring the Use of Big Data in Business Context

Almost all organizations collect and collate relevant data in various forms, such as customers' feedback, inputs from retailers and suppliers, current market trends, etc. The information, thus derived, is used by the management to take major organizational decisions. An organization generally has to spend huge amounts to collect data and information. For example, customer surveys or market research reports require a significant amount of investment by an organization. The cost of collecting information goes on escalating as an organization keeps on collecting more information. The continuously increasing cost decreases the value of the collected information. In other words, collecting and maintaining a pool of data and information is just a waste of resources unless any logical conclusions and business insights can be derived from it. This is where Big Data analytics comes into the picture.

This chapter provides an in-depth look at how Big Data influences businesses in today's world. The key is to understand how Big Data and different methods of data analytics are used in real time and why. How can an organization make optimum use of Big Data? How can large volumes of data be used to get better insights? How can the data obtained be used to form better business strategies, and thereby help in scalability and profitability? The key to implementing a Big Data solution is to manage Big Data for meeting business requirements. Business insights gained from Big Data analytics help organizations to reduce their cycle time, fulfill orders quickly, cut excess inventory, and improve forecast accuracy and customer services by exchanging information, such as inventory levels, forecast data, and sales trends. These insights can be applied to almost all the core domains of an organization and shared with partners, suppliers, customers, and other stakeholders.

In this chapter, you will learn how the data is actually used in the real world to get better business insights and explore future business expansions and also detect and prevent frauds in different industries.

SCENARIO

Mr. Smith, the data analyst of Argon Technology, plans to do some research on the use and effects of Big Data analytics on the business sector. This research requires the extraction and analysis of data from different data sources to derive meaningful insights. He knew that all types of businesses give due importance to their customers' feedback, and customers generally express their opinions on social media platforms. So, Mr. Smith decides to collect data for his research from social networking sites.

Use of Big Data in Social Networking

Human beings are considered social animals and prefer to live in a society. A human being lives in a social environment and gains knowledge and experience through communication. Today, communication is not restricted to meeting in person. The affordable and handy use of mobile phones and the Internet have made communication and sharing data of all kinds possible across the globe. Some popular social networking sites are Twitter, Facebook, and LinkedIn. These social networking sites are also called social media.

In this section, we analyze the effects of Big Data generated from the social media on different industries. Let's first understand the meaning of social network data.

Social network data refers to the data generated from people socializing on social media. On a social networking site, you will find different people constantly adding and updating comments, statuses, preferences, etc. All these activities generate large amounts of data. Analyzing and mining such large volumes of data show business trends with respect to wants and preferences and likes and dislikes of a wide audience.

This data can be segregated on the basis of different age groups, locations, and genders for the purpose of analysis. Based on the information extracted, organizations design products and services specific to people's need.

Figure 2.1 shows the social network data generated daily through various social media:

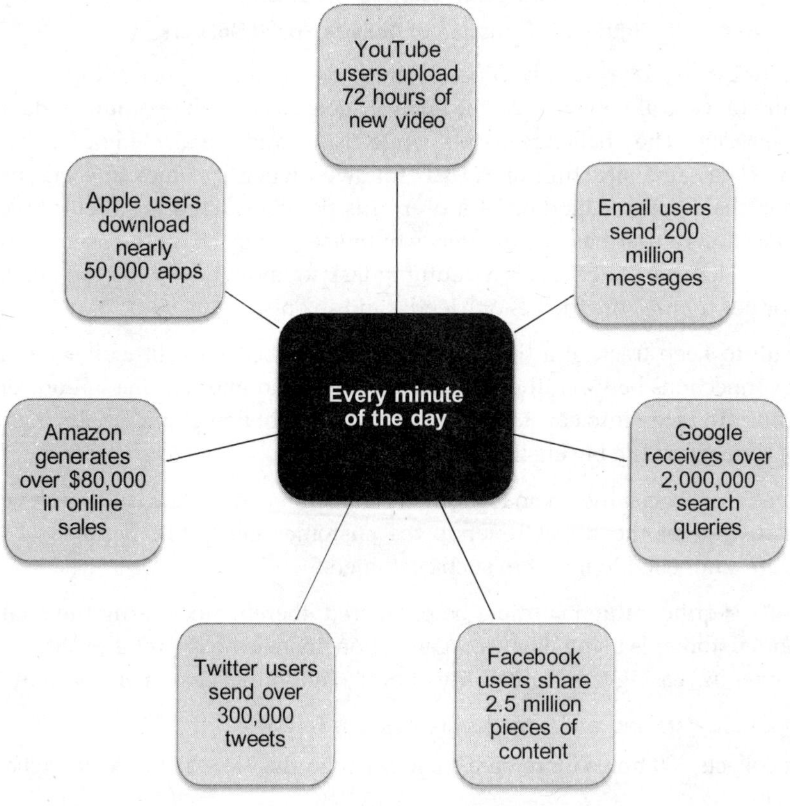

Figure 2.1: Social Network Data Generated Every Minute of the Day

Social Network Analysis (SNA) is the analysis performed on the data obtained from social media. As the data generated is huge in volume, it results in the formation of a Big Data pool.

Let's understand the importance of social network data with the help of an example of a Mobile Network Operator (MNO). The data captured by an MNO in a day, such as the cell phone calls, text messages, and other related details of all its customers is very huge in volume. This type of data is used daily for different purposes.

An MNO does not simply need to record and analyze the calls of a customer but the entire network calls related to that customer. The company must study the data of the people whom the customer called and also of the people in the customer's network who called back the customer. Such a network is called a social network.

Figure 2.2 shows the graphical view of how the caller's social network structure is created:

Figure 2.2: Structure of Caller's Social Network

As seen in Figure 2.2, the data analysis process can go deeper and deeper within the network to get a complete picture of a social network. As the analysis goes deeper, the volume of data to be analyzed also becomes massive. The challenge comes while using traditional methods to analyze the huge volume of data. The same structure of SNA is followed when it comes to social networking sites. While analyzing the social media data of a user, it is not considered a difficult task to identify the number of connections a user has, the frequency of messages posted on the user's timeline, and other standard metrics. However, it becomes a daunting task to know how wide the network of a user is, including his or her friends, the friends of friends, and so on.

It is not difficult to keep track of a thousand users, but it becomes difficult when it comes to one million direct connections between these thousand users, and another one billion connections when friends of friends are taken into consideration. Extracting, obtaining, and analyzing data from every single point of connection is a big challenge faced by SNA.

The data derived from social media enables an organization to calculate the total revenue a customer can influence instead of the direct revenue the customer generates. Because of this advantage, organizations are compelled to invest in such customers.

A customer who is quite influential must be pampered, thereby, increasing the total profitability of the network the customer is using. For an organization, increasing the total profitability of a network takes priority over increasing the profitability of every individual customer's account.

Some facts about big data and social media are listed as follows:

- Facebook collects 500 times more data each day than the New York Stock Exchange. (Source: BI Intelligence)
- Twitter produces 12 times more data each day than the New York Stock Exchange. (Source: BI Intelligence)
- By 2016, there will be 18.9 billion network connections, i.e., 2.5 connections per person. (Source: IBM Big Data Hub)

Social media analytics is nowadays used for online reputation management, crisis management, lead generation, and brand check to measure campaigning reports and much more.

The following are the areas in which decision-making processes are influenced by social network data:

- Business intelligence
- Marketing
- Product design and development

Business Intelligence

Business intelligence is a data analysis process to convert a raw dataset to meaningful information by using different techniques and tools for boosting business performance. This system allows a company to collect, store, access, and analyze data for adding value to decision making.

The data generated from different social media is analyzed to gain important business insights. Social Customer Relationship Management (CRM) data is the latest catch phrase used these days to describe this type of data. Such a data analysis helps in changing the perspective of an organization while valuing its customers. Instead of valuing a single customer, organizations can now calculate the value of the entire network that is influenced by that customer.

Consider an example of a mobile service provider that has a low-value customer. The customer has subscribed for a simple call plan and fails to provide any additional revenue as profit. As per the traditional method of evaluating the profitability of a customer, if the customer is not satisfied with the services and if he or she wants to leave, the company generally has no problems to let the customer go as he/she is providing low revenue.

However, with the help of SNA, the organization can now identify that some connections in the customer's network make a large number calls and text messages and have a large network of friends. With such an analysis, the organization might take an altogether different decision and might start valuing the customer more. This implies that the influence of a customer is very important to the organization.

Studies have shown that when a user of a calling network leaves, others in the network often follow suit. With the help of SNA, the influence a customer can create on the network can be identified instead of the revenue the customer can generate directly. This approach helps to form an entirely different perspective of handling customer requirements. The mobile service provider can now think of investing in the customer to retain him/her.

NOTE

SNA can also help in law enforcement and anti-terrorism efforts as it is possible to identify trouble groups or people who are directly or indirectly connected to each other. Such type of analysis is called link analysis.

From the preceding examples, we can derive the following business insights:

- SNA can help provide new contexts in which decisions are taken on the basis of available data and not on opinions.
- Big Data analysis allows organizations to shift goals from maximizing individual account profitability to maximizing the profitability of the customer's network.
- Big Data helps organizations to identify highly connected customers. It also helps in identifying when, where, and how to align and focus marketing efforts in building a better brand image.
- Big Data enables organizations to lure highly connected customers by offering them free trials of their services and soliciting their feedback for the betterment of their products and services.
- Big Data analysis assists organizations by encouraging internal customers to become more active on corporate social networking sites and provide comments and opinions on various products and services.

Some organizations reward their influential customers with discounts and offers, and these customers in turn keep on spreading a positive brand image of the organization. Social networking sites such as LinkedIn or Facebook can obtain insights on the advertisements that most users prefer. This is achieved by designing advertisements based on interests, likes, and preferences that customers as well as their circle of friends, contacts, and colleagues have personally opted for.

The gaming industry also makes use of social network data to develop business intelligence. Analysis of social network data or link analysis helps in tracking telemetry data about gaming, including the information about who is playing which game, who plays with whom, for how much time they remain online to play the game, changing patterns of playing among people or groups, and much more.

NOTE

The term telemetry is popular in the video gaming industry and refers to the capture of in-game activities. Telemetry is analogous to a weblog analyzer tool and captures the activities performed by players while they navigate through the game.

Telemetry also helps in finding the preferred partner for a player for a particular game. Players are often segmented on the basis of their individual playing style.

For example:

- One player segment can opt for advancing as fast as possible to beat a level with the purpose of only completing that level.
- Another player segment might be focused at collecting the bonus points available prior to the completion of each level.
- Another player segment might target at exploring every aspect of each level during the play.

A game developer might find this information very valuable while designing new games, updating existing ones, and targeting a particular audience for games. This information also enables the game developer to provide options and suggestions to players on the groups available to them when other players/users log in. Such suggestions and options keep the players engaged and interested in the game, which helps in generating revenue.

Marketing

Today, the preferences of consumers have changed due to their busy schedules. They no longer have the time to read newspapers thoroughly, watch all the TV commercials, or go through all the e-mails they receive in their inbox. Consumers can now make their preferences clear and select the marketing messages they wish to receive–when, where, and from whom. In today's competitive scenario, marketers aim to deliver what consumers want by using interactive communication across digital channels such as e-mail, mobile, social, and the Web.

These channels, in turn, generate the social data required to provide insights based upon the brand preferences of a target audience, the tone of its voice, the other brands it discusses, its interests, and other information. Conducting social network analysis of this data can generate very useful and meaningful business insights that may help organizations to take timely and informed decisions. When a comparison is made between the efforts spent on the social media marketing platform and the e-mail marketing platform, it is found that the marketing efforts spent on the former yield more returns as compared to the latter.

Let's now take a case study to understand the importance of social media marketing.

CASELET

Walmart has acquired a social media analytics company, named Kosmix, and created @WalmartLabs, a division that analyzes media communication to understand retail trends. The director of product management at @WalmartLabs, Tracy Chu, said the following in a blog post:

"@WalmartLabs is working on ways to help Walmart interpret social media to predict trends and learn more about what our customers want. We are mining social media sources like Twitter and Facebook, blogs, search activity, as well as transaction data to find useful insights." One of the key responsibilities of this division is to monitor public domain conversations and then position Walmart products accordingly. @WalmartLabs has been tracking social chats for analyzing trends in various categories such as holiday toys, online games, and mobile commerce.

Recently, @WalmartLabs has also launched Shopycat, a Facebook app. This app analyzes data from social networks and accordingly makes gift recommendations as per your friend's likes and dislikes. Then the app matches these recommendations to the products available in Walmart and some other site catalogs. Not only this, the app also suggests gift cards and the location of the closest Walmart store from where the gifts can be purchased.

Brand popularity is very critical in marketing. There are apps in which customers can rate a brand on a scale of 1–10 according to how likely they are to recommend the product or service to a friend. Once a brand's rating crosses 300, the application sends out a report that contains information on what customers feel about the product, along with a detailed analysis of the brand's reputation as compared to the competition.

Affiliate marketing is a reward-based marketing structure, where an affiliated company uses its own market effort to trigger off customers for another company and in turn, is rewarded by the benefited company. Today, one can hardly find any major brand without an affiliate program. According to analysts in this field, affiliate marketing has already become a $3 billion industry. Websites, such as couponmountain.com, earn revenue of multimillion dollars a year by doing affiliate marketing for the brands they promote.

Product Design and Development

With the increasing popularity of social media and growing volume of data every second, organizations competing to make it big in the market must not only identify and extract the information relevant for their company, products, and services but also comprehend and respond to the information on a continuous basis. A system that is able to represent a sentiment as data with a high degree of accuracy provides the client a means to access information on a social platform. To be able to measure sentiments more meticulously is of great value while designing a product or service. Brands must understand the importance of the demographic information they receive to devise better target products and programs.

By listening to what consumers want, by understanding where the gap in the offering is, and so on, organizations can make the right decisions in the direction of their product development and offerings. In this way, social network data can help organizations to improve product development and services, making sure that the consumers ultimately get the products and services they want.

Sentiment analysis refers to a computer programming technique to analyze human emotions, attitudes, and views across popular social networks, including Facebook, Twitter, and blogs. The technique requires analytic skills as well as advanced computing applications.

Businesses, research organizations, and marketing professionals across the globe use sentiment analysis in one form or the other to identify and measure customers' behavior and online trends. However, this technique is still evolving, and the full potential of sentiment analysis is yet to be explored by marketers and other business professionals. Most organizations today simply rely on the number of likes, tweets, and comments, instead of actually studying the quality of the sentiments expressed in the conversations.

CASELET

According to a survey conducted by MSN Money, American Airlines has been ranked as one of the most disliked companies in the US.

Studies reveal that American Airlines has about 346,259 'followers' on Twitter and 273,591 'likes' on Facebook. But this cannot be taken as a true indicator of the company's popularity. Deep studies of the sentiments of customers reveal that the trends of online conversation about the company are negative, which indicate that it is allegedly one of the most disliked airlines. Thus, clearly, the company's efforts to engage social media community have not paid any beneficial returns.

To improve their image and ranking, American Airlines should focus more on the sentiment and emotive data and the 'correct' types of incoming data sources rather than just counting the numbers of 'followers' and 'likes'.

SCENARIO

While going through the feeds collected from social networking data, Smith notices that almost all types of businesses have suffered on account of fraudulent activities and many organizations are now turning to Big Data analytics to solve this problem.

Use of Big Data in Preventing Fraudulent Activities

A fraud can be defined as the false representation of facts, leading to concealment or distortion of the truth. Frauds can be committed by both words and conduct and are intended to deceive the other party, generally to gain an advantage over it in some manner. Frauds that occur frequently in financial institutions, such as banks and insurance and healthcare companies, or involve any type of monetary transactions, such as in the retail industry, are called financial frauds. In such fraudulent cases, online retailers, such as Amazon, eBay, and Groupon, tend to incur huge expenses and losses.

The following are some of the most common types of financial frauds:

- **Credit card fraud**—This type of fraud is quite common these days and is related to the use of credit card facilities. In an online shopping transaction, the online retailer cannot see the authentic user of the card and therefore, the valid owner of the card cannot be verified. It is quite likely that a fake or a stolen card is used in the transaction.

  In an online transaction, in spite of the security checks, such as address verification or card security code, fraudsters manage to manipulate the loopholes in the system.

- **Exchange or return policy fraud**—An online retailer always has a policy allowing the exchange and return of goods and sometimes, people take advantage of this policy. These people buy a product online, use it, and then return it back as they are not satisfied with the product. Sometimes, they even report non-delivery of the product and later attempt to sell it online. What leads to such a fraud is that retailers encourage consumers to order products in bulk and later return the ones that they don't require.

  Such a fraud can be averted by charging a restocking fee on the returned goods, getting customer's signature on the delivery of the product, and staying cautious of such customers who are known to commit such frauds.

- **Personal information fraud**—In this type of fraud, people obtain the login information of a customer and then log-in to the customer's account, purchase a product online, and then change the delivery address to a different location. The actual customer keeps calling the retailer to refund the amount as he or she has not made the transaction. Once the transaction is proved fraudulent, the retailer has to refund the amount to the customer.

All these frauds can be prevented only by studying the customer's ordering patterns and keeping track of out-of-line orders. Other aspects should also be taken into consideration such as any change in the shipping address, rush orders, sudden huge orders, and suspicious billing addresses. By observing such precautions, the frequency of the occurrence of such frauds can be reduced to a certain extent, but cannot be completely eliminated.

Preventing Fraud Using Big Data Analytics

We have seen that one of the ways to prevent financial frauds is to study the customer's ordering pattern and other related data. However, this method works only when the data to be analyzed is small in size. In order to deal with huge amounts of data and gain meaningful business insights, organizations need to apply Big Data analytics. Analyzing Big Data allows organizations to:

- Keep track of and process huge volumes of data
- Differentiate between real and fraudulent entries
- Identify new methods of fraud and add them to the list of fraud-prevention checks
- Verify whether a product has actually been delivered to the valid recipient
- Determine the location of the customer and the time when the product was actually delivered
- Check the listings of popular retail sites, such as e-Bay, to find whether the product is up for sale somewhere else

Fraud Detection in Real time

Big Data also helps to detect frauds in real time. It compares live transactions with different data sources to validate the authenticity of online transactions. For example, in an online transaction, Big Data would compare the incoming IP address with the geo-data received from the customer's smart phone apps. A valid match between the two confirms the authenticity of the transaction.

Big Data also examines the entire historical data to track suspicious patterns of the customer order. These patterns are then used to create checks for avoiding real-time fraud. Big Data analysis is performed in real time by retailers to know the actual time when the products were delivered to customers. Costly products often have sensors attached to them that transmit their location information. When such products are delivered to customers, the streaming data obtained from these sensors provides location information to the retailer, thereby, preventing frauds.

CASELET

Visa uses a powerful fraud management system, and the company has reported the identification and, thus, prevention of potential fraud opportunities that could have cost the company a loss of around $2 billion. The fraud management system was based on a Big Data technology known as Massively Parallel Processing (MPP) database. In order to detect and prevent frauds, the system analyzes each transaction from 500 different aspects and returns with effective results.

Centralization of Big Data takes place through MPP systems. Any organization that aims at improving its analytic scalability needs an MPP system. With the continuous increase in the volume of data, it is not always possible to move data as part of the analysis process except where it is absolutely required. MPP is the most widely used technique of storing and analyzing huge volumes of data.

Let us now understand what an MPP database is and what makes it so special and preferred. An MPP database has several independent pieces of data stored on multiple networks of connected computers. It eliminates the concept of one central server having a single CPU and disk.

The data in an MPP database is divided into different disks managed by different CPUs across different servers, as shown in Figure 2.3:

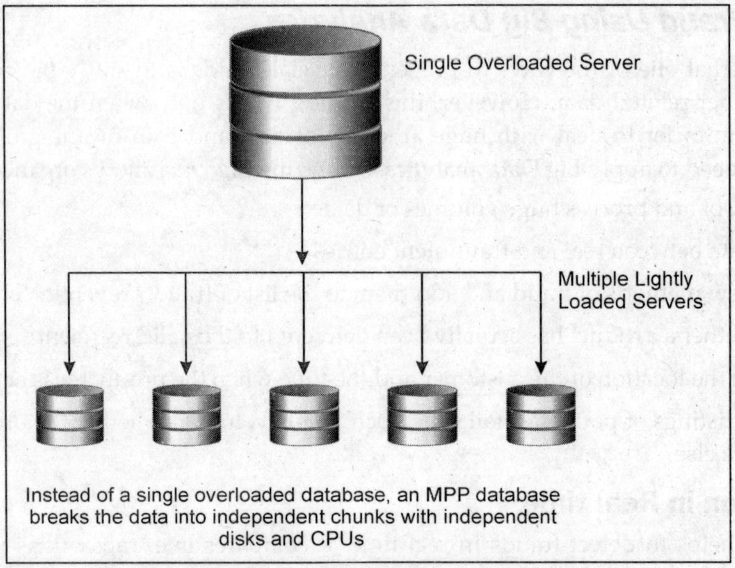

Figure 2.3: MPP System Data Storage

Visually Analyzing Fraud

Image analytics is another emerging field that can help detect frauds. It refers to the process of analyzing image data with the help of digital processing of the image. Examples include the use of bar codes and QR codes. Some other examples include complex solutions such as facial recognition and position-and-movement analysis. Today, images and videos contribute to 80 percent of unstructured data. Analytical systems that deal with Big Data are designed to integrate and understand images, videos, text, and numbers.

Big Data can also help in creating maps and graphs for comparisons that can be used to analyze situations and take decisions. An analysis in the graphical form, for example, can help identify the customers, areas, and products that display a high fraud rate. Big Data can even show comparisons between products and regions, which alert retailers as to where a greater probability of fraud exists. The retailer can then take proper actions to mitigate the risk accordingly.

In the course of his research, Smith finds that most cases of cheatings and fraudulent activities occur in the insurance and retail industries. He concludes that the reason behind such fraudulent activities is that these sectors mainly deal with hardcore financial transactions. He decided to concentrate his study on the role of Big data analytics in these industries.

Use of Big Data in Detecting Fraudulent Activities in Insurance Sector

Let's assume that an insurance company wants to improve its ability to take decisions while processing claims. The company has observed that even a small mistake on its part can make it vulnerable to fraudulent claims, causing huge economic losses. The company has policies and procedures to help underwriters evaluate fraudulent claims; however, the underwriters do not have the required data at the right time to take necessary decisions, thus delaying the processing time and increasing the chances of frauds.

As a solution to this problem, the company decides to implement a Big Data analytical platform, which will use data from social media to provide a real-time view of the case in hand. The information obtained from this platform will enable the insurance agent to diagnose the patterns of customer's claims, behavior, and other related issues. In some cases, social media could also provide great triggers to identify fraud; for example, a customer might indicate that his or her car was destroyed in a flood, but the documentation from the social media feed may show that the car was actually in another city on the day the flood occurred. These discrepancies reflect fraud.

Insurance frauds affect the economics as well as the reputation of an organization tremendously. That is why companies prefer using Big Data analytics and other advanced technologies to handle this issue. Big Data can detect patterns of fraudulent behavior from large amounts of structured and unstructured data and help in detecting frauds in real time, thereby, reducing the number of days to process a claim and ensuring a better return.

Fraud Detection Methods

Traditionally, fraudulent claims were identified by insurance companies by using statistical models. These models have many limitations and can prevent fraud only to a limited extent. This section examines these limitations and how Big Data can overcome them.

Insurance companies used to analyze small samples of data to detect frauds. This was not a fool proof method as it left much room for frauds to go undetected in the data that was not analyzed. Moreover, traditional methods of fraud detection are not capable of handling various sources of information from different channels in an integrated way. Big Data analytics, on the other hand, can handle this kind of challenge.

Public data is an important source to conduct predictive analysis in order to avoid frauds. Bank statements, legal judgments, criminal records, and medical bills are a few examples of public data that can be used to identify suspicious behavior of people. To get the most effective predictive value from public data, business organizations integrate their internal data with third-party data. This integration helps in investigating and restricting fraudulent activities.

Social Network Analysis

Earlier, we learned about SNA and how Big Data can help in getting more clear and concise business insights. SNA is an innovative and effective way to identify and detect frauds. The SNA tool uses a mix of analytical methods. This mixed approach includes statistical methods, pattern analysis, and link analysis to identify any kind of relationships or patterns within large amounts of data collected from different sources. When link analysis is used in fraud detection, one looks for clusters of data and how these data clusters are linked to other data clusters. As already mentioned, public records, such as criminal records, judgments, address change frequency, foreclosures, and declarations of bankruptcy are various data sources that can be assimilated into the model.

Using this approach of incorporating the information obtained from various data sources into a model, the insurer can rate claims. A high rating indicates that the claim is a fraudulent one. Organizations should keep the following points in mind while implementing SNA:

- The speed at which data is arriving
- The quantity of data that is potentially useless for deriving any logical conclusions
- The depth of analysis needed to determine the accurate results
- The type of user interface components that need to be included on the SNA dashboard

The following are the steps followed in the SNA method to detect fraud:

1. Both structured and unstructured data gathered from different sources are loaded into the Extract, Transform, and Load (ETL) tool. This data is then processed and loaded into a data warehouse.

NOTE

ETL refers to a process used to extract data from external sources, transform that data to fit operational requirements, and load the data into a database.

2. The analytics team uses data from different sources, marks the risk of fraud, and ranks the likelihood of fraud. The information used can come from varied sources, such as a prior belief, a relationship of any kind with another individual of an earlier case, the number of rejected claims, doubtful combination of data, or dubious alterations in personal information.
3. Several Big Data technologies, including text mining and content categorization can be included into the fraud detection and predictive modeling mechanism.
4. On the basis of the score of a specific network, an alert is made.
5. The investigators start working on the fraudulent claim.
6. Finally, frauds that are detected are added into the use case system.

CASELET

In GE Consumer & Industrial Home Services Division, technicians who perform repair operations on consumer products, which are still under the warranty period, usually also process their claims. The biggest challenge in this traditional process was that the technicians could not identify any patterns with the data that was available to them. After some time, the company noticed that it is incurring losses as a result of the settlement of lots of claims. To check the credibility of claims, GE Consumer & Industrial Home Services Division decided to implement the SNA solution from Statistical Analysis System (SAS)—a *developer of business analytics software. Within a year of implementing the SNA solution, the company had saved around $5.1 million by detecting fraudulent claims.*

Consider a case where a customer files a case to get the insurance money of a car claiming that it is destroyed in a fire. However, the customer's statements on file indicate that most of the valuable items were removed from the car prior to the fire. This might indicate that the car was torched on purpose. This is an example of predictive analysis, which is used to detect frauds by using text and sentiment analytics.

Generally, claim reports are of multiple pages, making it difficult for the text analytics team to detect the fraud easily. Big Data analytics helps to solve this problem as it can examine huge volume of unstructured data quickly and efficiently.

EXHIBIT 1: Implementing Social Network Analysis for Fraud Prevention

Social network analysis: The use of social network analysis for combating fraud is slowly gaining acceptance within a range of sectors, primarily in financial services, telecommunications, and public organizations. Anti-money laundering, identity fraud, network fraud, denial of service attacks, and terrorist financing are some of the areas of fraud where SNA could be used to significantly improve fraud detection. SNA techniques and tools have been deployed in landmark cases like tracing terrorist funding after 9/11 attacks by FinCEN and insider trading cases identified by the Australian Securities and Investment Commission. For most business though, profit loss continues to be a key reason to invest in fraud detection. More than 15% of income loss for medium-sized businesses in Germany is due to fraud, corruption, and defalcation. This is the second largest area of loss after theft, burglary, and assault [Corporate Trust 2009]. Financial crimes are continuously evolving into more complex systems of attack on businesses and, therefore, the technologies that financial institutions use to detect and stop these crimes from occurring need to evolve. In Germany, there were more than 4,100 reported cases of check fraud in 2002. By 2009, this dropped to only a little more than 600 cases [BKA, 2002&2009]. In contrast, reported fraud cases related to card payments have risen 345% just from 2007 to 2009 [BKA, 2008&2009]. With the recent economic crisis and obvious changes in technology, it is important to be more vigilant regarding fraud detection. Increasingly sophisticated fraudsters are able to easily slip behind risk-score based analysis to avoid detection, and to overcome this issue, organizations need to better understand the dynamics and patterns of fraud and fraud networks. This is where the visual and analytical capabilities of SNA can help the fraud prevention function to effectively detect and prevent fraud originating from web-based and other more traditional business channels. In general, SNA is a "data mining technique that reveals the structure and content of a body of information by representing it as a set of interconnected, linked objects or entities." [Mena, 2003]. The perfect combination of advances in knowledge management, visualization techniques, data availability, and increased computing power enabled the steady rise of SNA as an interdisciplinary investigative technique in a wide array of sectors. Unlike other analytical techniques like statistics that are based on the notion of independence of subjects, SNA can provide useful insight into large datasets along network, spatial, and time dimensions based on the interconnectedness of the subjects being analyzed.

Source: http://www.cgi.com/sites/default/files/white-papers/Implementing-social-network-analysis-for-fraud-prevention.pdf

Social Customer Relationship Management

Social CRM enables effective fraud detection in the insurance sector. Social CRM is not a platform or technology, but a process. It makes it critical for insurance companies to link social media sites, such as Facebook and Twitter, to their CRM systems. When social media is integrated within an organization, it provides high transparency in various issues related to customers.

This amalgamation also promotes mutually beneficial transparency, which means that the organization trusts its consumers and vice versa. This consumer-centric ecosystem helps businesses to retain and expand their customer base.

The following points briefly describe how a Social CRM process works:

- It collects data from an organization's existing CRM and different social media platforms.
- The reference data obtained from the social media platform and the data stored in the CRM are then loaded into a claim management system, which compares and analyzes the data for any discrepancies and provides results.
- The response received from the claim management system is then investigated by investigators. This is because the result of social analytics is just an indicator and should not be considered as the final reason to reject a claim.

CASELET

A Turkish insurance company called AXA OYAK uses the SAS Social CRM solution to deal with risks and avoid frauds. With the help of the social CRM, AXA cleans its customer portfolio data at regular intervals. This helps AXA OYAK to detect and rectify inconsistencies in customer data that enables it to relate even two slightly different records of the same customer. Thus, AXA OYAK is able to make more accurate analysis of customer data and examine fraudulent claims more efficiently. SAS enables the insurance company to detect the relationships between customer behavior and fraudulent claims quickly and efficiently. Using a SAS data warehouse, AXA could check its customer data on the basis of the flags generated while analyzing certain relationships between datasets.

EXHIBIT 2: Analytics: Real-World Use of Big Data in Insurance

"Big Data" – which admittedly means many things to many people – is no longer confined to the realm of technology. Today, it is a business imperative. In addition to providing solutions to insurance companies' long-standing business challenges, Big Data solutions offer the power to transform processes, organizations, and entire industries.

Big Data is especially promising for insurance companies. With no physical products to manufacture, data is arguably one of their most important assets. Financial, actuarial, claims, risk, consumer, producer/wholesaler, and many other types of data form the basis for virtually every decision an insurer makes. And while the industry has made progress in capturing and analyzing much of the structured information associated with their products and policyholders, there is value in unstructured and semi-structured information that remains untapped.

At the same time, the industry is undergoing a significant transformation as insurers work to sell to continually more demanding and empowered consumers who have real-time access to more diverse and instant insurance services than ever before. To compete and win in this dynamic environment, insurers must leverage and optimize the value of Big Data.

The latest Big Data study found that 74 percent of insurance companies surveyed report that the use of information (including Big Data) and analytics is creating a competitive advantage for their organizations, compared with 63 percent of cross-industry respondents. Compared to 35 percent of insurance companies that reported an advantage in IBM's 2010 New Intelligent Enterprise Global Executive Study and Research Collaboration, this represents a staggering 111 percent increase in just two years.

It is increasingly clear that insurance companies must leverage their information assets to gain a comprehensive understanding of markets, customers, products, distribution channels, regulations, competitors, employees and more. Insurance companies will realize value by effectively managing and analyzing the rapidly increasing volume, velocity, and variety of new and existing data. By putting the right skills and tools in place to better understand their operations, customers and new markets, insurance organizations will be on the right track to compete and thrive in this global, dynamic marketplace.

Source: *http://www-935.ibm.com/services/us/gbs/thoughtleadership/big-data-insurance/*

Use of Big Data in Retail Industry

Big Data has huge potential for the retail industry as well. Considering the immense number of transactions and their correlation, the retail industry offers a promising space for Big Data to operate.

Seemingly simple questions, such as the following, are easy to answer when there is a single retail location and a small customer base:

- How many basic tees did we sell today?
- What time of the year do we sell most leggings?
- What else has customer X bought, and what kind of coupons can we send to customer X?

However, with millions of transactions spread across multiple disconnected legacy systems and IT teams, it is impossible to find answers to such questions. Business insights in customer behavior and company health can be obtained by finding a relation between the organization's sales between in-store and online sales. It could be very difficult for a marketing analyst to understand the health and strength of different types of products and campaigns and reconcile the data obtained from these systems. While omni-channel retailing solutions do exist, they require both store managers and Web developers to learn entirely new systems. The company-wide training and deployment of these systems would incur huge costs in terms of time and money.

NOTE

The omni-channel retailing process is similar to multi-channel retailing in its early stages. The process focuses on the consumer experiences by using all available channels, including mobile, Internet, actual stores, television, radio, mails, and more. To meet demands of new customers, retailers implement specialized software applications.

Many times, extracting data in real time is not feasible as systems are affected because of scaling issues. Suppose you want to know if a particular item is in stock in another nearby store. This data cannot be found immediately and needs some phone calls or other ways of accessing information and therefore, prevents the immediate sale of the item.

If access to the data is possible, there may not be anything particularly rich or useful about it. Raw transactional data can only help a company understand its sales but does not provide any relationships, patterns, or other clues for deeper analysis.

Also, the fact remains that most of the Big Data is just not required and not useful either. Some information in a Big Data feed can have a long-term strategic value while some information will be used immediately and some information will not be used at all. The main part of taming Big Data is to identify which portions fall into which category.

CASELET

Walmart uses about 10 different websites for collecting and providing shopping and transaction data into an analytical data processing system. Other companies such as Sears and Kmart are focused on personalizing marketing strategy according to the likes and dislikes of their particular customers, with Big Data technology. Amazon also uses Big Data technology for building an affiliate network support, providing risk management, and updating their website.

Use of RFID Data in Retail

The introduction of Radio Frequency Identification (RFID) technology automated the process of labeling and tracking of products, thereby, saving significant time, cost, and effort. Walmart was one of the first retailers to implement RFID in its merchandise.

The RFID technology helps better item tracking by differentiating the items that are out of stock and that are available on shelves. For instance, if an item is not available on the shelves, it does not imply that the item is not available throughout. With the help of an RFID reader and a mobile computer, the inventory can be immediately verified and stocks replenished, if required.

Various types of RFID tags are available for various environments such as cardboard boxes, wooden, glass, or metal containers. Tags also come in various sizes and are of varied capabilities, including read and write capability, memory, and power requirements. They also have a wide range of durability. Some varieties are paper-thin and are typically for one-time use and are called 'smart labels.' RFID tags can also be customized and withstand heat, moisture, acids, and other extreme conditions. Some RFID tags are also reusable, thus offering a Total Cost of Ownership (TCO) benefit over bar code labels.

The use of RFIDs saves time, reduces labor, enhances the visibility of products throughout the production-delivery cycle, and saves costs.

Some common benefits of using RFID are shown in Figure 2.4:

Figure 2.4: Advantages of Using RFID

Asset Management

Organizations can tag all their capital assets, such as pallets, vehicles, and tools, in order to trace them anytime and from any location. Readers fixed at specific locations can observe and record all movements of the tagged assets with great accuracy. This mechanism also works as a security check and alerts supervisors and raises an alarm in case anyone tries to take the asset outside the authorized area.

When containers are loaded for shipment, tracking pallets with RFIDs are included in them. These RFIDs contain records of what is stored in the container. This helps production managers to have a complete view of the inventory level and location of containers. This information can be used to locate items and fulfil rush orders without any waste of time.

Shipping containers, pallets, cylinders, and reusable plastic bottles having RFID tags can be easily identified at the dock entry as they leave with an outbound consignment. After the database is matched with the shipping information, the manufacturers of the products create a log of each shipping container with its details and develop a procedure for tracking their goods. This information can be utilized to reduce the time required for documentation and can be of great value in resolving disputes of lost and damaged goods.

Inventory Control

One of the primary benefits of using RFID is inventory tracking, especially in areas where tracking has not been done or was not possible before. RFID tags can be read even if the contents are packed and are not in the direct line of sight. This means that an entire pallet with an assortment of goods can be read without disturbing the arrangement of goods in the pallet. RFID tags are resistant to temperature and environmental variances such as dirt, moisture, heat, and contaminants. On the other hand, bar codes cannot handle such conditions and are prone to damage or errors.

Using an RFID tracking system can result in an optimized inventory level, and thus reduce the overall cost of stocking and labor. RFID allows manufacturers to track inventory for raw materials, work in progress, or finished goods. Readers installed on shelves can update inventory automatically and raise alarms in case the requirement for restocking arises.

RFIDs are used to create secure storage areas wherein readers can be programed to raise an alarm in case the items are removed or placed elsewhere. A study has indicated that a consumer goods manufacturer can reduce the chance of shrinkage and loss of inventory by approximately 10% by using RFID tags.

Shipping and Receiving

RFID tags can also be used to trigger automated shipment tracking applications. Manufacturers use the readings obtained from these tags for generating a shipment manifest, which is used for many tasks including:

- Printing a shipping document
- Recording the shipment automatically in the shipping system
- Printing a 2D bar code for a shipping label

Nowadays, Serial Shipping Container Code (SSCC) is widely used in shipping labels. SSCC can be easily converted into RFID tags in order to provide automatic handling of shipment.

The data contained in the RFID tag can be considered with the shipment information, which can easily be read by the receiving organization to simplify the receiving process and eliminate processing delays.

Regulatory Compliance

The entire custody trail can be produced before regulatory bodies such as the Food and Drug Administration (FDA), Department of Transportation (DOT), and Occupational Safety and Health Administration (OSHA) along with other regulatory requirements, provided the RFID tag that travels with the material has been updated with all the handling data. This could be of great use for companies that work with hazardous items, food, pharmaceuticals, and other regulated materials.

A logistic company brings various packages from different locations to a hub. Thereafter, it sorts out the urgent ones for a morning delivery from the regular delivery ones. This is where RFID can help in locating these packages or pallets and loading them for a faster and quicker delivery.

Service and Warranty Authorizations

A warranty card or document to request for a service warranty would no longer be necessary because an RFID tag can hold all this information. Once the repair or service has been completed, the information can be fed into the RFID tag as the maintenance history. This is something that will always remain on the product. If future repairs are required, the technician can access this information without accessing any external database, which helps in reducing calls and time-expensive enquiries into documents.

Summary

This chapter explored the need and importance of conducting Big Data analytics in the business context. You first learned how businesses process and use the data collected from various social network platforms. Next, the chapter discussed how Big Data analytics helps in detecting and preventing fraudulent activities in businesses, especially in the insurance and retail sectors. Toward the end, you learned the use of RFID tags in the retail industry.

Quick Revise

Multiple-Choice Questions

Q1. Which application of social network data analysis is used by a customer retention manager?

a. Business intelligence
b. Marketing
c. Product design and development
d. Insurance fraud

Ans. The correct option is a.

Q2. Identify the types of frauds that typically impact online retailers.

a. Credit card fraud
b. Forward fraud
c. Corporate fraud
d. Insurance fraud

Ans. The correct option is a.

Q3. How can Big Data analytics help prevent fraud?

a. Analyze all the data
b. Detect fraud in real time
c. Use predictive analytics
d. All of the above

Ans. The correct option is d.

Q4. From the following, select the analytical method that SNA uses to show relationships via links:

a. Organizational business rules
b. Pattern framework
c. Link analysis
d. Statistical methods

Ans. The correct option is c.

Q5. Identify the technologies that enable fraud identification and the predictive modeling process:

a. Text mining
b. Social media data analysis
c. Regression analysis
d. All of the above

Ans. The correct option is a.

Q6. Predictive models based on both historical and real-time data can help _______________ to identify suspected cases of fraud in the early stages.

a. Marketing companies
b. Medical claims companies
c. Construction companies
d. CRM-based manufacturing companies

Ans. The correct option is b.

Q7. Before implementing SNA, insurers should consider _______________.

a. The speed of the data
b. The format of the data
c. The type of analysis to be performed on the data
d. The potential output of SNA

Ans. The correct option is a.

Q8. In which of the following cases can RFIDs reduce manual labor cost and time and improve the visibility of assets through product delivery?

a. Asset management
b. Identify fraud detection
c. SNA
d. Corporate fraud detection

Ans. The correct option is a.

Q9. Which of the following can be tracked by using the RFID tags?

a. Raw materials
b. Scrap materials
c. Finished goods inventory
d. Insurance frauds

Ans. The correct option is c.

Q10. Which of the following is an RFID reader action?

a. Text mining
b. Credit notes management
c. Insurance fraud detection
d. Inventory management

Ans. The correct option is d.

Subjective Questions

Q1. Discuss some areas in which decision-making processes are influenced by social network data.

Ans. The following are the areas in which decision-making processes are influenced by social network data:

- **Business intelligence**—The data generated from different social media is analyzed to gain important business insights. Social Customer Relationship Management (CRM) data is the latest catchphrase used these days to describe this type of data. Such a data analysis helps in changing the perspective of an organization while valuing its customers. Instead of valuing a single customer, organizations can now calculate the value of the entire network that is influenced by that customer.

  The business intelligence gained from social network analysis on Big Data can:

  - Provide new contexts in which decisions are taken on the basis of the available data and not on opinions
  - Allow organizations to shift goals from maximizing individual account profitability to maximizing the profitability of the customer's network
  - Help organizations to identify highly connected customers. It also helps in identifying when, where, and how to align and focus marketing efforts in building a better brand image.
  - Enable organizations to lure highly connected customers by offering them free trials of their services and soliciting their feedback for the betterment of their products and services.
  - Assist organizations to encourage internal customers to become more active on corporate social networking sites and provide comments and opinions on various products and services.

- **Marketing**—Nowadays, marketers aim to deliver what consumers want by using interactive communication across digital channels such as e-mail, mobile, social, and the Web. These channels, in turn, generate the social data required to provide insights based upon the brand preferences of a target audience, the tone of its voice, the other brands it discusses, its interests, and other information. Conducting social network analysis of this data can generate very useful and meaningful business insights that may help organizations to take timely and informed decisions. When a comparison is made between the efforts spent on the social media marketing platform and the e-mail marketing platform, it is found that the marketing efforts spent on the former yields more returns as compared to the latter.

- **Product design and development**—With the increasing popularity of social media and growing volume of data every second, organizations competing to make it big in the market must not only identify and extract the information relevant for them, and their products, and services but also comprehend and respond to the information on a continuous basis. A system that is able to represent a sentiment as data with a high degree of accuracy provides the client a means to access information on a social platform. To be able to measure sentiments more meticulously is of great value while designing a product or service. Brands must understand the importance of the demographic information they receive to devise better target products and programs. By listening to what consumers want, by understanding where the gap in the offering is, and so on, organizations can make the right decisions in the direction of their product development and offerings. In this way, social network data can help organizations to improve product development and services, making sure that the consumers ultimately get the products and services they want.

Q2. List some common types of financial frauds prevalent in the current business scenario.

Ans. The following are some of the most common types of financial frauds:

- **Credit card fraud**—This type of fraud is quite common these days and is related to the use of credit card facilities. In an online shopping transaction, the online retailer cannot see the authentic user of the card and therefore, the valid owner of the card cannot be verified. It is quite likely that a fake or a stolen card is used in the transaction.

  In an online transaction, in spite of the security checks, such as address verification or card security code, fraudsters manage to manipulate loopholes in the system.

- **Exchange or return policy fraud**—An online retailer always has a policy allowing the exchange and return of goods, and sometimes, people take advantage of this policy. These people buy a product online, use it, and then return it back as they are not satisfied with the product. Sometimes, they even report non-delivery of the product and later attempt to sell it online. What leads to such a fraud is that retailers encourage consumers to order products in bulk and later return the ones that they don't require. Such a fraud can be averted by charging a restocking fee on the returned goods, getting customer's signature on the delivery of the product, and staying cautious of such customers who are known to commit such frauds.

- **Personal information fraud**—In this type of fraud, people obtain the login information of a customer and then log-in to the customer's account, purchase a product online, and then change the delivery address to a different location. The actual customer keeps calling the retailer to refund the amount as he or she has not made the transaction. Once the transaction is proved as a fraudulent one, the retailer has to refund the amount to the customer.

Q3. In what ways does analyzing Big Data help organizations prevent fraud?

Ans. Analyzing Big Data allows organizations to:

- Keep track of and process huge volumes of data
- Differentiate between real and fraudulent entries
- Identify new methods of fraud and add them to the list of fraud-prevention checks
- Verify whether a product has actually been delivered to the valid recipient
- Determine the location of the customer and the time when the product was actually delivered
- Check the listings of popular retail sites, such as e-Bay, to find whether the product is up for sale somewhere else

Q4. List some methods used for the verification of credit cards.

Ans. There are several methods for the verification of credit cards. Some prominently used ones are:

- Address Verification
- Online Personal Identification Number (PIN) Generation
- Offline PIN Verification
- Payer Authentication

Q5. List the steps that SNA follows to detect fraud.

Ans. The step-by-step approach followed by SNA to detect fraud is:

1. The data, both structured and unstructured, from various sources is fed into the (Extract, Transform, and Load (ETL) tool. This data is then transformed and loaded into a data warehouse.
2. The analytics team uses data from different sources, marks the risk of fraud and ranks the likelihood of fraud. The information used can come from varied sources, such as a prior belief, a relationship of any kind with another individual of an earlier case, the number of rejected claims, doubtful combination of data, or dubious alterations in personal information.
3. Several Big Data technologies, including text mining and content categorization can be included into the fraud detection and predictive modeling mechanism.
4. On the basis of the score of a specific network, an alert is made.
5. The investigators start working on the fraudulent claim.
6. Finally, frauds that are detected are added into the use case system.

Q6. Write a note on Social Customer Relationship Management.

Ans. Social CRM enables effective fraud detection in the insurance sector. Social CRM is not a platform or technology, but a process. It is critical for insurance companies to link social media sites, such as Facebook and Twitter, to their CRM systems.

When social media is integrated within an organization, it provides high transparency in various issues related to the customers. This amalgamation also promotes mutually beneficial transparency, which means that the organization trusts its consumers and vice versa. This consumer-centric ecosystem helps businesses to retain and expand its customer base.

The following points briefly describe how a Social CRM process works:

- It collects data from an organization's existing CRM and different social media platforms.
- The reference data obtained from the social media platforms and the data stored in the CRM are then loaded into a claim management system, which compares and analyzes data for any discrepancies and provides results.
- The response received from the claim management system is then investigated by investigators. This is because the result of social analytics is just an indicator and should not be considered as the final reason to reject a claim.

Q7. What kind of analysis does the following figure represent?

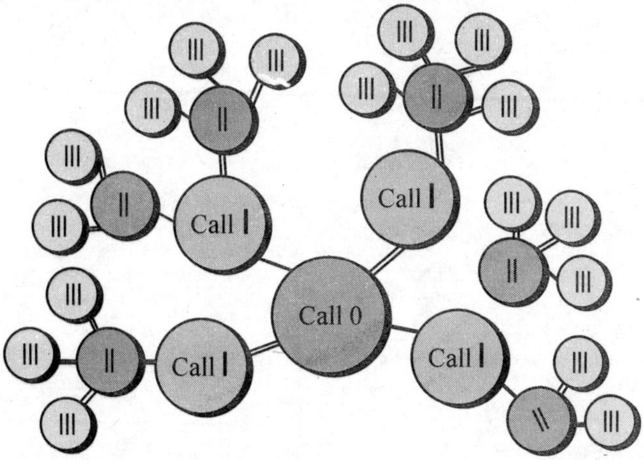

Ans. Social Network Analysis

Q8. How does the use of RFID tags help in inventory control? Explain.

Ans. One of the primary benefits of using RFID is inventory tracking, especially in areas where tracking has not been done or was not possible before. RFID tags can be read even if the contents are packed and are not in the direct line of sight. This means that an entire pallet with an assortment of goods can be read without disturbing the arrangement of goods in the pallet. RFID tags are resistant to temperature and environmental variances such as dirt, moisture, heat and contaminants. On the other hand, bar codes cannot handle such conditions and are prone to damage or errors.

Using an RFID tracking system can result in an optimized inventory level, and thus reduce the overall cost of stocking and labor. RFID allows manufacturers to track inventory for raw materials, work in progress, or finished goods. Readers installed on shelves can update inventory automatically and raise alarms in case the requirement for restocking arises.

RFIDs are used to create secure storage areas wherein readers can be programmed to raise an alarm in case the items are removed or placed elsewhere. A study has indicated that a consumer goods manufacturer can reduce the chance of shrinkage and loss of inventory by approximately 10% by using RFID tags.

3

Introducing Technologies for Handling Big Data

In the previous chapters, we have already learned that the huge amounts of data generated by different sources need to be managed properly, if it is to be utilized in any productive manner. Now, such voluminous, varied, and scattered data cannot be handled by traditional data storage and processing systems. This requirement prompted the development of various technologies used for processing Big Data. Among the technologies that are used to handle, process, and analyze Big Data, the most effective and popular innovations have been in the fields of distributed and parallel processing, Hadoop, In-Memory Computing (IMC), Big Data cloud, etc. Hadoop, which is an open-source platform, has been by far the most popular technology associated with Big Data storage and processing different types of data. Hadoop is commonly used by data-driven organizations to extract maximum output from their normal data-usage practices at a rapid pace. Besides Hadoop, the other techniques used for Big Data processing are cloud computing and IMC.

These technologies help organizations to analyze data in different ways under varying circumstances. Cloud computing helps businesses to save cost and better manage their resources by allowing them to use resources as a service on the basis of specific requirements and paying for only those services that have actually been used. IMC helps you to organize and complete your tasks faster by carrying out all the computational activities from the main memory itself. You can use all these techniques, as per specific requirements, for analyzing Big Data.

This chapter mainly focuses on explaining the basics and exploring the relevance and role of various technologies that are used for storing, processing, and analyzing Big Data. Here, you will first learn about the concept of distributed and parallel computing followed by a discussion on various technologies, such as Hadoop, cloud computing, and IMC, used to handle Big Data.

SCENARIO

Mr. Richard Stephens is the global business head of Argon Technology and wants to use some latest technologies while analyzing Big Data. He carried out some research and found that as compared to traditional methods of computing, distributed and parallel computing technologies are more suitable to handle Big Data. The following section discusses distributed and parallel computing technologies, especially for Big Data analytics.

Distributed and Parallel Computing for Big Data

In distributed computing, multiple computing resources are connected in a network and computing tasks are distributed across these resources. This sharing of tasks increases the speed as well as the efficiency of the system. Because of reason, the distributed computing is considered faster and much more efficient than traditional methods of computing. It is also more suitable to process huge amounts of data in a limited time.

Another way to improve the processing capability of a computer system is to add additional computational resources to it. This will help in dividing complex computations into subtasks, which can be handled individually by processing units that are running in parallel. We call such systems as parallel systems in which multiple parallel computing resources are involved to carry out calculations simultaneously. The concept behind involving multiple parallel resources is that the processing capability will increase with the increase in the level of parallelism.

Figure 3.1 shows a comparison between distributed and parallel processing techniques:

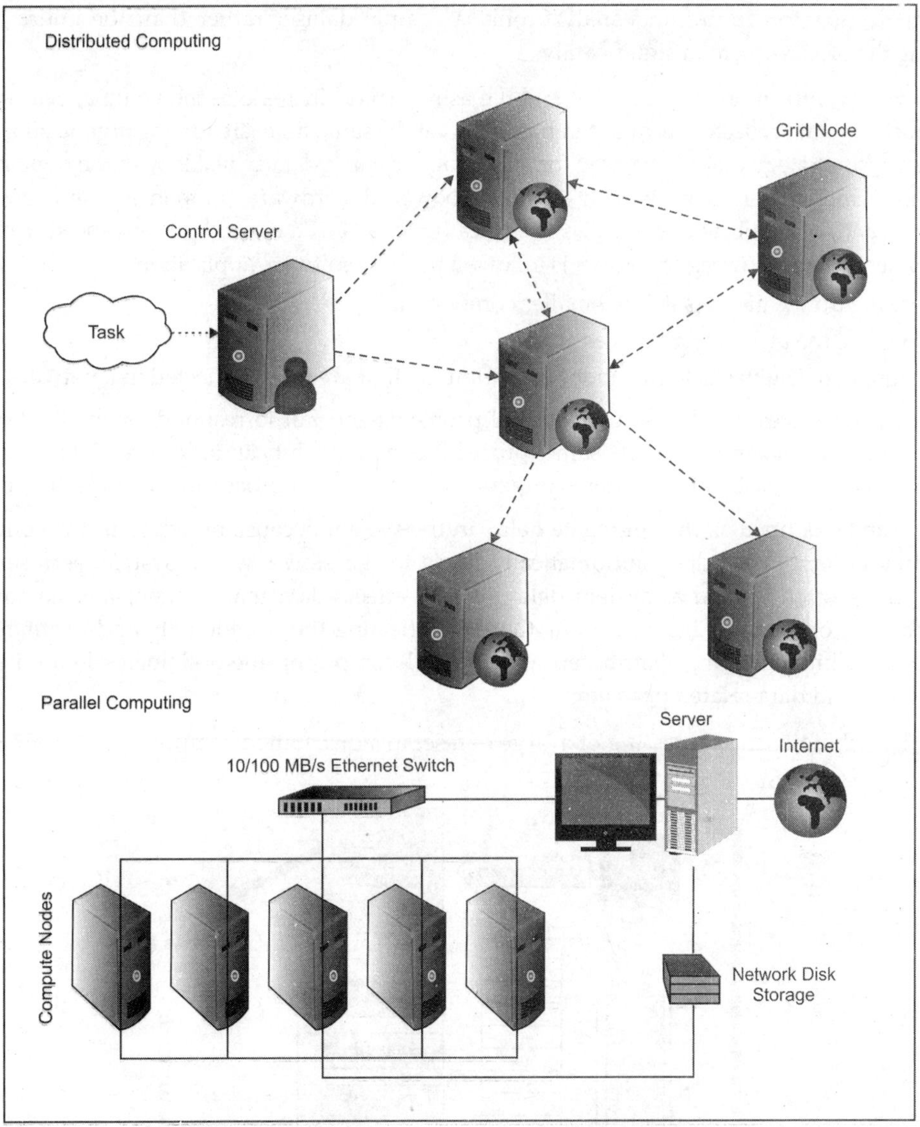

Figure 3.1: Distributed Computing and Parallel Computing

Organizations use both parallel and distributed computing techniques to process Big Data. The most important constraint for businesses today is time. In case there was no restriction on time, every organization would hire outside (or third-party) sources to perform the analysis of its complex data. The direct benefit of adopting this method is that the organization would not require any resources and data sources to process and analyze complex data. These third parties are usually specialized agencies in the field of data manipulation, processing, and analysis. Apart from being effective, hiring third party agencies also reduces the storage and processing costs of handling large amounts of data.

Moreover, data processing and analysis activities carried out within an organization would require the organization to capture and analyze only a sample dataset rather than the entire data thus, reducing the processing load significantly.

The growing competition in the market and the astronomical increase in the volume, velocity, variety, and veracity of data collected from different sources, at the same time, are forcing organizations to adopt a data analysis strategy that can be used for analysing the entire data available with the organization in a very short time. This is done with the help of powerful hardware components and new software programs and/or applications written specifically to fulfill the need of advanced technological developments. The following procedure is followed by these software applications:

1. Breaking up the given task into smaller components
2. Surveying the available resources at hand
3. Assigning the subtasks to the nodes or computers that are interconnected in a network

Sometimes, resources develop some technical problems and fail to respond. Such situations can be handled by virtualization, where some processing and analytical tasks are delegated to other resources. Another problem that often hampers data storage and processing activities is latency.

Latency can be defined as the aggregate delay in the system because of delays in the completion of individual tasks. Such a delay automatically leads to the slowdown in system performance as a whole and is often termed as system delay. It also affects data management and communication within and across various business units there by, affecting the productivity and profitability of an organization. Implementing distributed and parallel computing methodologies helps in handling both latency and data-related problems.

Figure 3.2 elaborates the processing of a large dataset in a distributed computing environment:

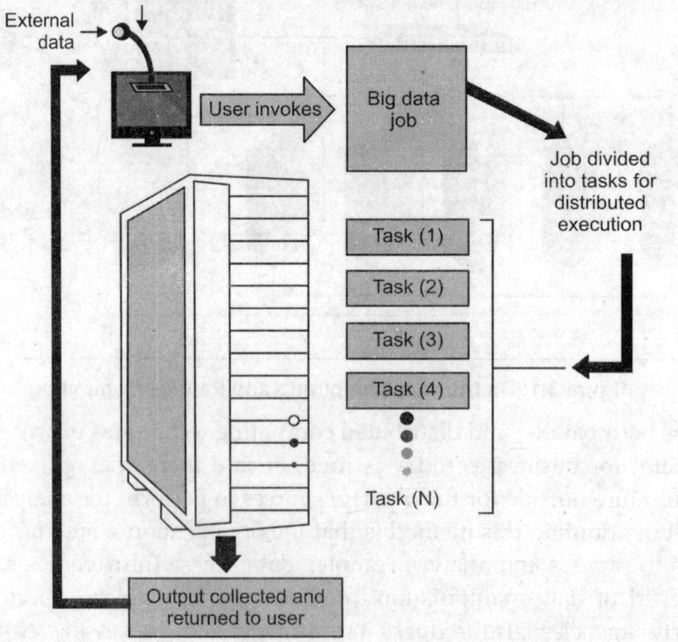

Figure 3.2: Distributed Computing Technique for Processing Large Data

As you can notice in Figure 3.2, the nodes are arranged within a system along with the elements that form the core of computing resources. These resources include CPU, memory, disks, etc. Big Data systems, usually, have higher scaling requirements. Therefore, these nodes are more beneficial for adding scalability to the Big Data environment, as and when required. The system, with added scalability, can accommodate the growing amounts of data more efficiently and flexibly. Distributed computing technique also makes use of virtualization and load balancing features. The sharing of workload across various systems throughout the network to manage the load is known as load balancing. The virtualization feature creates a virtual environment in which hardware platform, storage device, and Operating System (OS) are included.

NOTE

Distributed computing has been around for almost 50 years. Initially, the technology was used in computer science research as a way to scale computing tasks and solve complex problems without incurring the expenses of using massive computing systems.

Parallel computing technology uses a number of techniques to process and manage huge amounts of data produced at a high velocity. Some of these techniques are shown in Table 3.1:

Table 3.1: Techniques of Parallel Computing

Parallel Computing Method	Description	Uses
Cluster or Grid Computing (Primarily used in Hadoop)	Cluster or grid computing is based on a connection of multiple servers in a network. This network is known as a cluster in which the servers share the workload among them. A cluster can be either homogeneous (comprising the same type of commodity hardware) or heterogeneous (consisting of different types of hardware).	A cluster can be created even by using hardware components that were acquired a long time back to provide cost-effective storage options. The overall cost may be very high in cluster computing.
Massively Parallel Processing (MPP) (Used in data warehouses)	A single machine working as a grid is used in the MPP platform, which is capable of handling the activities of storage, memory, and computing. Software written specifically for MPP platform is used for the optimization of MPP capabilities.	MPP platforms, such as EMC Greenplum, and ParAccel are most suited for high-value use cases.
High-Performance Computing (HPC)	HPC environments are known to offer high performance and scalability by using IMC. This technology is especially suitable for processing floating-point data at high speeds.	HPC environments can be used to develop specialty and custom applications for research and business organizations where the result is more valuable, than the cost or where strategic importance of the project is of high priority.

After learning about both distributed and parallel computing techniques, we can compare these in certain aspects. Table 3.2 shows how parallel systems are different from distributed systems:

Table 3.2: Difference Between Parallel Systems and Distributed Systems

Distributed System	Parallel System
An independent, autonomous system connected in a network for accomplishing specific tasks	A computer system with several processing units attached to it
Coordination is possible between connected computers that have their own memory and CPU	A common shared memory can be directly accessed by every processing unit in a network
Loose coupling of computers connected in a network, providing access to data and remotely located resources	Tight coupling of processing resources that are used for solving a single, complex problem

SCENARIO

During the discussion about distributed and parallel computing for Big Data analytics, Mr. Stephens learned that Hadoop is a technology that works on the distributed computing technique and is vastly used by large organizations to manage their Big Data requirements. He concludes that implementing Hadoop in the company would help them handle their business problems in a better way.

How Data models and Computing models are different?

As we know Hadoop is a distributed system like distributed databases; however, there are several key differences between the two infrastructures with respect to computing model and data model in a distributed architecture. Figure 3.3 shows the distributed databases and Figure 3.4 shows Hadoop:

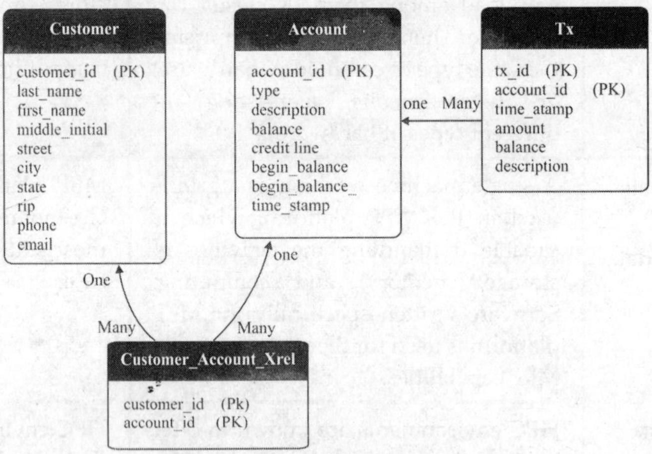

Figure 3.3: Distributed Databases

- Distributed Databases:
  - Deal with tables and relations
  - Must have a schema for data
  - Implements data fragmentation and partitioning

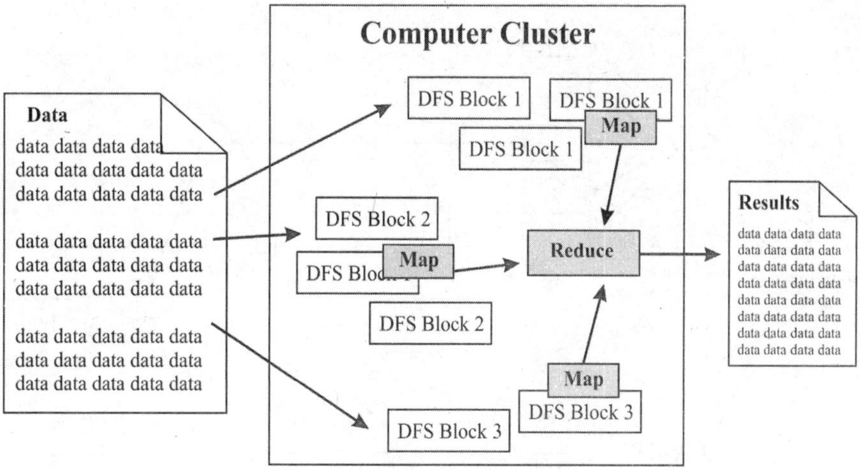

Figure 3.4: Hadoop

- Hadoop:
  - Deals with flat files in any format
  - Operates on no schema for data
  - Divides files automatically into blocks

The computing models of a distributed database and Hadoop are shown in figure 3.5 and figure 3.6, respectively:

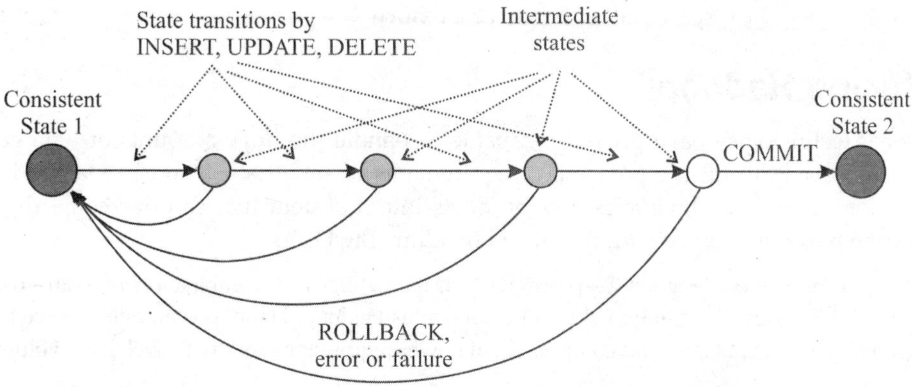

Figure 3.5: Computing Model of Distributed Database

Distributer Databases:

- Generate notations of a transaction
- Implement ACID transaction properties
- Allow distributed transactions

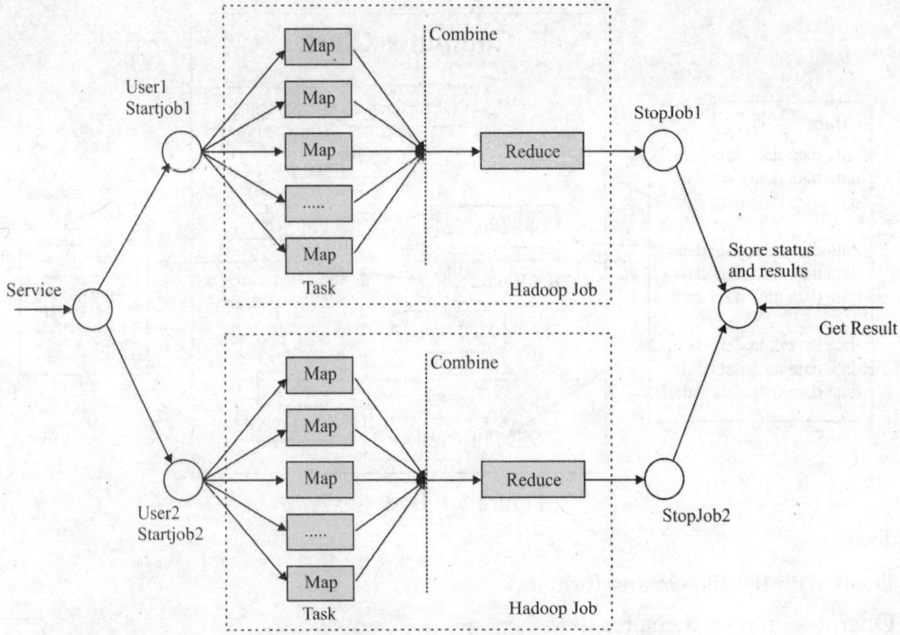

Figure 3.6: Computing Model of Hadoop

- Generates notations of a job divided into tasks
- Implements MapReduce computing model
- Considers every task as either a map or a reduce

Introducing Hadoop

Traditional technologies have proved incapable to handle the huge amounts of data generated in organizations or to fulfill the processing requirements of such data. Therefore, a need was felt to combine a number of technologies and products into a system that can overcome the challenges faced by the traditional processing systems in handling Big Data.

One of the technologies designed to process Big Data (which is a combination of both structured and unstructured data available in huge volumes) is known as Hadoop. Hadoop is an open-source platform that provides analytical technologies and computational power required to work with such large volumes of data.

Earlier, distributed environments were used to process high volumes of data. However, multiple nodes in such an environment may not always cooperate with each other through a communication system, leaving a lot of scope for errors. Hadoop platform provides an improved programming model, which is used to create and run distributed systems quickly and efficiently.

A Hadoop cluster consists of single MasterNode and multiple worker nodes. The master node contains a NameNode and JobTracker and a slave or worker node acts as both a DataNode and TaskTracker. Hadoop requires Java Runtime Environment (JRE) 1.6 or a higher version of JRE. The standard start-up and shutdown scripts require Secure Shell to be set up between nodes in the cluster. In a larger cluster, the HDFS is managed through a NameNode server to host the file system index and a secondary NameNode that keeps snapshots of the NameNodes and at the time of failure of NameNode the secondary NameNode replaces the primary NameNode, thus preventing file-system from getting corrupt and reducing data loss. Figure 3.7 shows Hadoop multinode cluster architecture:

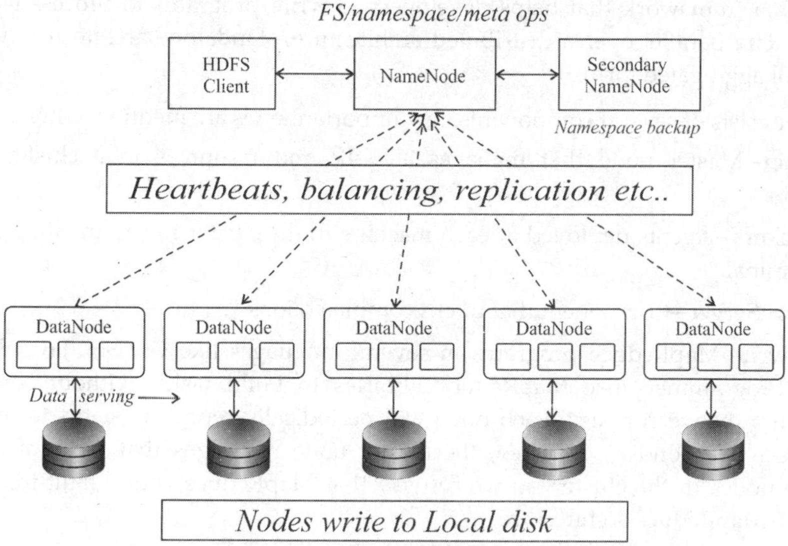

Figure 3.7: Hadoop multinode cluster architecture

The secondary NameNode takes snapshots of primary NameNode directory information after a regular interval of time, which is saved in local or remote directories. These checkpoint images can be used in the place of the primary NameNode to restart a failed primary NameNode without replaying the entire journal of file-system actions and without editing the log to create an up-to-date directory structure. NameNode is the single point for storage and management of metadata. To process the data, Job Tracker assigns tasks to the Task Tracker. Let us assume that a DataNode cluster goes down while the processing is going on, then the NameNode should know that the some DataNode is down in the cluster, otherwise it cannot continue processing. Each DataNode sends a "Heart Beat Signal" to NameNode after every few minutes (as per Default time set) to make NameNode aware of the active / inactive status of DataNodes. This system is called as Heartbeat mechanism.

HDFS and MapReduce

There are two main components of Apache Hadoop–the Hadoop Distributed File System (HDFS) and the MapReduce parallel processing framework. Both of these open source projects, HDFS is used for storage and MapReduce is used of processing.

Hadoop includes a fault-tolerant storage system called Hadoop distributed file system (HDFS). It stores large size files from terabytes to petabytes across different terminals. HDFS attains reliability by replicating the data over multiple hosts. The default replication value is 3. Data is replicated on three nodes: two on the same rack and one on a different rack. The file in HDFS is split into large blocks size of 64 MB by default (typically 64 to 128 megabytes) and each block of the file is independently replicated at multiple data nodes. The NameNode actively monitors the number of replicas of a block (by default 3 times). When a replica of a block is lost due to a DataNode failure or disk failure, the NameNode creates another replica of the block.

MapReduce is a framework that helps developers to write programs to process large volumes of unstructured data parallel over a distributed architecture/standalone architecture which produces result in useful aggregated form.

MapReduce consists of several components, few important ones are mentioned here:

- **JobTracker**—Master node that manages all jobs and resources in a cluster of commodity computers
- **TaskTrackers**—Agents deployed at each machine in the cluster to run the map and reduce task at the terminal
- **JobHistoryServer**—Component that tracks completed jobs

  We can write MapReduce programs in several languages like C, C++, Java, Ruby, Perl, and Python. Programmers use MapReduce libraries to build tasks, without communication or coordination between nodes. Each node will periodically report its status to master node, if a node doesn't respond as expected, the master node re-assigns that piece of the job to other available nodes in the cluster, so we can say that MapReduce is also fault-tolerant. Figure 3.8 shows the MapReduce architecture.

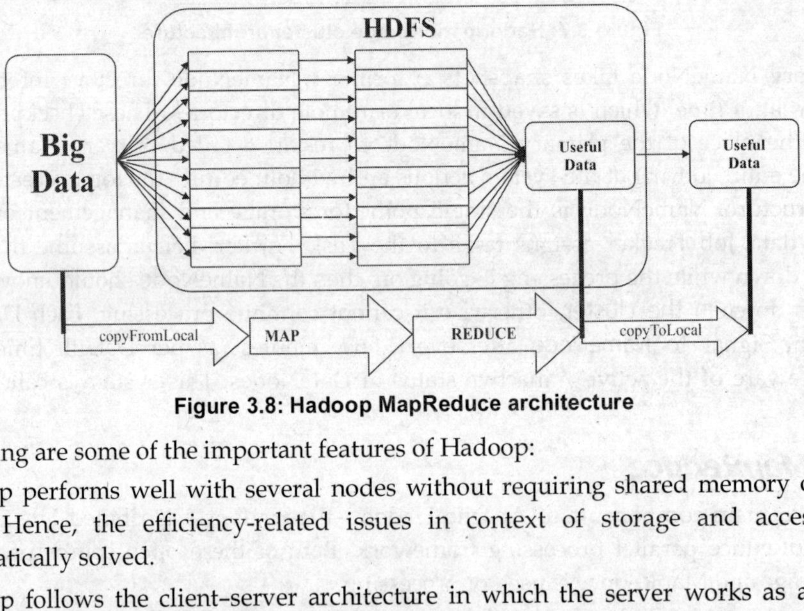

Figure 3.8: Hadoop MapReduce architecture

The following are some of the important features of Hadoop:

- Hadoop performs well with several nodes without requiring shared memory or disks among them. Hence, the efficiency-related issues in context of storage and access to data get automatically solved.
- Hadoop follows the client-server architecture in which the server works as a master and is responsible for data distribution among clients that are commodity machines and work as slaves to carry out all the computational tasks. The master node also performs the tasks of job controlling, disk management, and work allocation.
- The data stored across various nodes can be tracked in Hadoop NameNode. It helps in accessing and retrieving data, as and when required.

- Hadoop improves data processing by running computing tasks on all available processors that are working in parallel. The performance of Hadoop remains up to the mark both in the case of complex computational questions and of large and varied data.
- Hadoop keeps multiple copies of data (data replicas) to improve resilience that helps in maintaining consistency, especially in case of server failure. Usually, three copies of data are maintained, so the usual fault-replication factor in Hadoop is 3.

How does Hadoop Function?

The first thing to know about the functioning of Hadoop is the way it utilizes multiple computing resources for executing a particular task. The core components of Hadoop include the following:

- **Hadoop Distributed File System (HDFS)**—It is a cluster of storage solutions that is highly reliable, more efficient, and economical and provides facilities to manage files containing related data across machines.
- **Hadoop MapReduce**—It is a computational framework used in Hadoop to perform all the mathematical computations. It is based on a parallel and distributed implementation of MapReduce algorithm that provides high performance.

Hadoop facilitates the processing of large amounts of data present in both structured and unstructured forms. Hadoop clusters are created from the racks of commodity machines. Tasks are distributed across these machines (also known as nodes), which are allowed to work independently and provide their responses to the starting node. Moreover, it is possible to add or remove nodes dynamically in a Hadoop cluster on the basis of varying workloads. Hadoop has an ability to detect changes (which also include server failure) in the cluster and adjust to them, without causing any interruption in the system.

Hadoop accomplishes its operations (of dividing the computing tasks into subtasks that are handled by individual nodes) with the help of the MapReduce model, which comprises two functions, namely, a mapper and a reducer. The mapper function is responsible for mapping the computational subtasks to different nodes, and the reducer function takes the responsibility of reducing the responses from compute nodes, to a single result. The MapReduce model implements the MapReduce algorithm, as discussed earlier, to incorporate the capability of breaking data into manageable subtasks, processing the data on the distributed cluster simultaneously, and making the data available for additional processing or user consumption.

In the MapReduce algorithm, the operations of distributing task across various systems, handling the task placement for load balancing, and managing the failure recovery are accomplished by the map component (or the mapper function). The reduce component (or the reducer function), on the other hand, has the responsibility to aggregate all the elements together after the completion of the distributed computation.

When an indexing job is provided to Hadoop, it requires the organizational data to be loaded first. Next, the data is divided into various pieces, and each piece is forwarded to different individual servers. Each server has a job code with the piece of data it is required to process. The job code helps Hadoop to track the current state of data processing. Once the server completes operations on the data provided to it, the response is forwarded with the job code being appended to the result.

In the end, results from all the nodes are integrated by the Hadoop software and provided to the user, as shown in Figure 3.9:

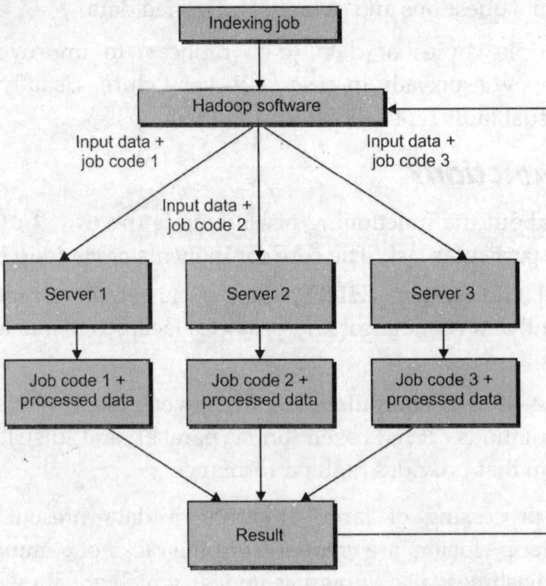

Figure 3.9: Job Tracking Process in MapReduce

We can understand the working of Hadoop by referring to the following example:

The call records of all the telephones in a city are being examined by a researcher who wants to know about those calls that are made by college students on the occasion of an event. The fields required as a result of the analysis carried out by the researcher include the timing of the event and the relevant information of the user. The query is fired on every machine to search the results from the call records stored with the machine, which will return the relevant results. Finally, a single result will be generated by aggregating individual results obtained from all the machines. We are considering that the records are collected in a Comma Separated Value (CSV) file.

- The processing starts by first loading the data into Hadoop and then applying the MapReduce programming model. Let us consider the following five columns to be contained in the CSV file:
  - `u_id`
  - `u_name`
  - `c_name`
  - `sp_name`
  - `call_time`

  To identify individual users who made phone calls at a specific time, the `u_id` field is used. It helps us to determine the number of users who have called at the time. We can, thus, get the final output in terms of the number of users by whom calls were made during the specified time.
- To obtain the final output, each mapper receives data line by line. Once the mapper completes its job, the results are shuffled or sorted by the Hadoop framework, which then combines the data in groups that are forwarded to the reducer. Ultimately, the final output is obtained from the reducer.

- Data in Hadoop can be stored across multiple machines. Businesses can take the advantage of this storage facility to use multiple commodity machines. These machines are capable of hosting the Hadoop software. In this case, businesses will not need to create integrated systems.

  Today, Hadoop is the most popular and used platform in businesses for Big Data processing. It helps in Big Data analytics by overcoming the obstacles that are usually faced in handling Big Data. In Hadoop, we can break down large computational problems into smaller tasks as smaller elements can be analyzed economically and quickly. All these parts are analyzed in parallel, and the results of the analysis are regrouped to produce the final output.

SCENARIO

Big Data is a vast field that needs involvement of various technologies and equipment. The hardware and infrastructure required for storing and handling Big Data is usually much higher than the existing infrastructure or hardware. To deal with this issue, Mr. Richard Stephens decides to utilize the services of cloud computing. He tells his team that cloud computing is a technique that helps organizations to hire infrastructure and other resources on rent, thereby saving a lot of initial investment.

Cloud Computing and Big Data

One of the vital issues that organizations face with the storage and management of Big Data is the huge amount of investment to get the required hardware setup and software packages. Some of these resources may be over utilized or underutilized with the varying requirements overtime. We can overcome these challenges by providing a set of computing resources that can be shared through cloud computing. These shared resources comprise applications, storage solutions, computational units, networking solutions, development and deployment platforms, business processes, etc. The cloud computing environment saves costs related to infrastructure in an organization by providing a framework that can be optimized and expanded horizontally. In order to operate in the real world, cloud implementation requires common standardized processes and their automation.

Figure 3.10 shows the cloud computing model:

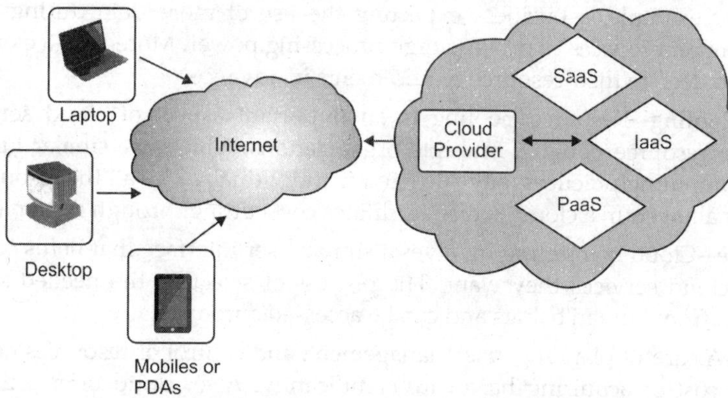

Figure 3.10: Cloud Computing Model

In cloud-based platforms, applications can easily obtain the resources to perform computing tasks. The costs of acquiring these resources need to be paid as per the acquired resources and their use. In cloud computing, this feature of resource acquisition is in accordance with the requirements and payment of cost and is known as elasticity. Cloud computing makes it possible for organizations to dynamically regulate the use of computing resources and access them as per the need while paying only for those resources that are used. This facility of dynamic use of resources provides flexibility; however, an organization needs to plan, monitor, and control its resource utilization carefully. Careless resource monitoring and control can result in unexpectedly high costs.

The cloud computing technique uses data centers to collect data and ensures that data backup and recovery are automatically performed to cater to the requirements of the business community. Both cloud computing and Big Data analytics use the distributed computing model in a similar manner and hence, are complementary to each other.

CASELET

Companies, such as Google and Amazon, require systems that could provide massive capabilities for managing large amounts of data in order to take their business forward. This requires strong infrastructure and advanced technologies to assist their applications at a large scale. For example, Google processes millions of Gmail messages every minute through an optimized Linux OS and its software environment, and Amazon handles massive workloads through its Infrastructure as a Service (IaaS) data centers. These companies also offer cloud-based services to contribute in the field of Big Data processing.

Features of Cloud Computing

The following are some features of cloud computing that can be used to handle Big Data:

- **Scalability**—Scalability means addition of new resources to an existing infrastructure. The increase in the amount of data being collected and analyzed requires organizations to improve their hardware components' processing ability. These organizations may, at times, need to replace the existing hardware with a new set of hardware components in order to improve data management and processing activities. The new hardware may not provide complete support to the software that used to run properly on the earlier set of hardware. We can solve such issues by using cloud services that employ the distributed computing technique to provide scalability to the architecture.
- **Elasticity**—Elasticity in cloud means hiring certain resources, as and when required, and paying for the resources that have been used. No extra payment is required for acquiring specific cloud services. For example, a business expecting the use of more data during in-store promotion could hire more resources to provide high processing power. Moreover, a cloud does not require customers to declare their resource requirements in advance.
- **Resource Pooling**—Resource pooling is an important aspect of cloud services for Big Data analytics. In resource pooling, multiple organizations, which use similar kinds of resources to carry out computing practices, have no need to individually hire all the resources. The sharing of resources is allowed in a cloud, which facilitates cost cutting through resource pooling.
- **Self Service**—Cloud computing involves a simple user interface that helps customers to directly access the cloud services they want. The process of selecting the needed services requires no intervention from human beings and can be accessed automatically.
- **Low Cost**—A careful planning, use, management, and control of resources help organizations to reduce the cost of acquiring hardware significantly. Also, cloud offers customized solutions, especially to organizations that cannot afford too much initial investment in purchasing the resources that are used for computation in Big Data analytics. The cloud provides them the pay-as-you-use option in which organizations need to sign for those resources only that are essential. This also helps the cloud provider in harnessing benefits of economies of scale and providing benefit to their customers in terms of cost reduction.

- **Fault Tolerance**—Cloud computing provides fault tolerance by offering uninterrupted services to customers, especially in cases of component failure. The responsibility of handling the workload is shifted to other components of the cloud.

Cloud Deployment Models

Depending upon the architecture used in forming the network, services and applications used, and the target consumers, cloud services are offered in the form of various deployment models. The following are the most-commonly used cloud deployment models:

- Public Cloud
- Private Cloud
- Community Cloud
- Hybrid Cloud

Public Cloud (End-User Level Cloud)

A cloud that is owned and managed by a company than the one (which can be either an individual user or a company) using it is known as a public cloud. In this cloud, there is no need for the organizations (customers) to control or manage the resources; instead, they are being administered by a third party. Some examples of public cloud providers are Savvis, Verizon, Amazon Web Services, and Rackspace. You should understand that in case of a public cloud, the resources are owned or hosted by the cloud service providers (a company), and the services are sold to other companies. Companies or individuals can obtain various services in a public cloud. The workload is categorized on the basis of service category, and therefore, in this cloud, the hardware customization is possible to provide optimized performance. The process of computing becomes very flexible and scalable through customized hardware resources. For example, a cloud can be used specifically for video storage that can be streamed live on YouTube or Vimeo. You can also optimize this cloud for handling large traffic volumes.

Businesses can obtain economical cloud storage solutions in a public cloud, which provides efficient mechanisms for complex data handling. The primary concerns with a public cloud include security and latency, which can be overlooked citing the benefits of this cloud.

Figure 3.11 demonstrates the use of a public cloud:

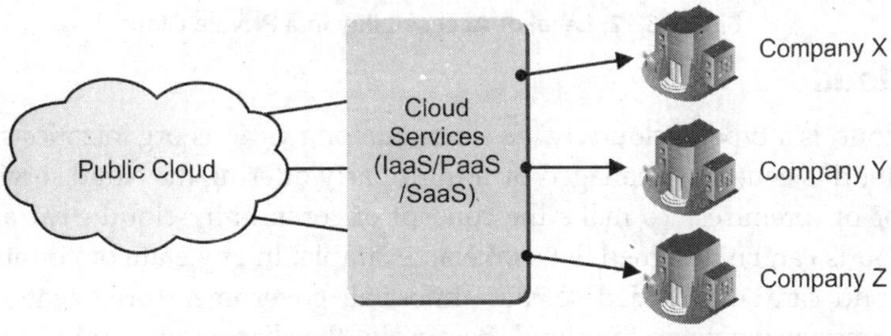

Figure 3.11: Level of Accessibility in a Public Cloud

Private Cloud (Enterprise Level Cloud)

The cloud that remains entirely in the ownership of the organization using it is known as a private cloud. In other words, in this cloud, the cloud computing infrastructure is solely designed for a single organization and cannot be accessed by other organizations. However, the organization may allow this cloud to be used by its employees, partners, and customers. The primary feature of a private cloud is that an organization installs the cloud for its own requirements. These requirements are customary to the organization that plans and manages the resources and their use. A private cloud integrates all the processes, systems, rules, policies, compliance checks, etc. of the organization at a place. In a private cloud, you can automate several processes and operations that require manual handling in a public cloud. Moreover, you can also provide firewall protection to the cloud; thereby, solving many latency and security concerns. A private cloud can be either on-premises or hosted externally. In case of on-premises private clouds, the service is exclusively used and hosted by a single organization. However, the private clouds that are hosted externally are used by a single organization and are not shared with other organizations. Moreover, the cloud services are hosted by a third party that specializes in cloud infrastructure. Note that on-premises private clouds are costlier as compared to the externally hosted private clouds. In case of a private cloud, security is kept in mind at every level of design. The general objective of a private cloud is not to sell the cloud services (IaaS/PaaS/SaaS) to the external organizations but to get the advantages of cloud architecture by not providing the privilege to manage your own data center.

Figure 3.12 demonstrates the use of a private cloud:

Figure 3.12: Level of Accessibility in a Private Cloud

Community Cloud

Community cloud is a type of cloud that is shared among various organizations with a common tie. This type of cloud is generally managed by a third party offering the cloud service and can be made available on or off premises. To make the concept of community cloud clear and to explain when community clouds can be designed, let's take an example. In any state or country, say England, the community cloud can be provided so that almost all government organizations of that state can share the resources available on the cloud. Because of the sharing of cloud resources on community cloud, the data of all citizens of that state can be easily managed by the government organizations.

Figure 3.13 shows the use of community clouds:

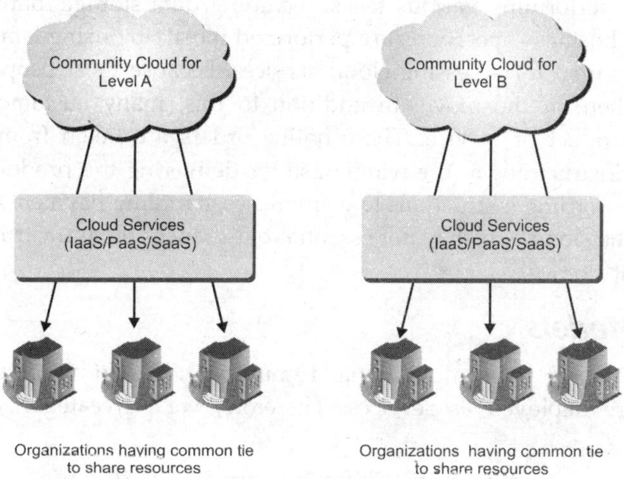

Figure 3.13: Level of Accessibility in Community Clouds

Hybrid Cloud

The cloud environment in which various internal or external service providers offer services to many organizations is known as a hybrid cloud. Generally, it is observed that an organization hosts applications, which require high level of security and are critical, on the private cloud. It is also possible that the applications that are not so important or confidential can be hosted on the public cloud. In hybrid clouds, an organization can use both types of cloud, i.e. public and private together. Such type of cloud is generally used in situations such as cloud bursting. In case of cloud bursting, an organization generally uses its own computing infrastructure; however, in high load requirements, the organization can access clouds. In other words, the organization using the hybrid cloud can manage an internal private cloud for general use and migrate the entire or a part of an application to the public cloud during the peak periods.

Figure 3.14 shows a hybrid cloud:

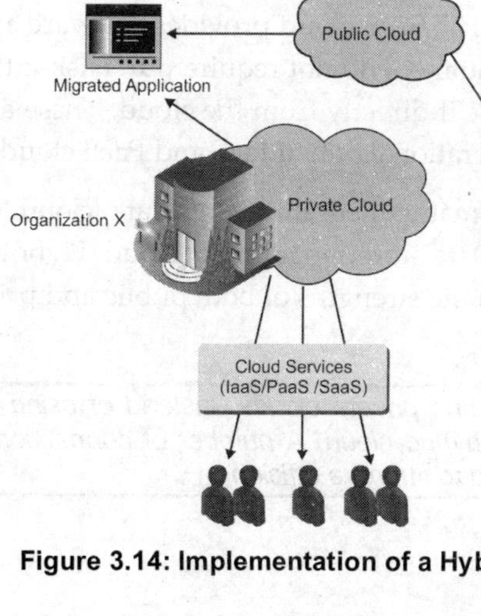

Figure 3.14: Implementation of a Hybrid Cloud

Cloud is a multipurpose platform that helps in, not only helps in handling Big Data analytics operations but also performing various tasks, including data storage, data backup, and customer service. Nowadays, business operations are performed mostly by using laptops, tablets, and mobile devices, which are suited for accessing cloud services, because most people today want to access computers even when on the move. In addition to this, many customers use the Internet for purchasing some product or service. These online orders are taken from customers by product stores, which send instructions to the warehouse for delivering the product. The entire process of receiving orders, forwarding instructions to warehouses, handling payments, and tracking deliveries can be assisted by the cloud, which is not essential but reduces the infrastructure cost and improves scalability in content storage.

Cloud Delivery Models

Cloud environment provides computational resources in the form of hardware, software, and platform, which are deployed as services. Therefore, we can categorize these services in the following manner:

- **Infrastructure as a Service (IaaS)**—Infrastructure in cloud computing can be defined as a combination of various elements. These elements include network, storage, and hardware components. A public IaaS is used when a user selects cloud for storing one's data, which may include photographs captured at an event or the favorite videos of the user. On the other hand, the server backups used by the employees of an organization for saving the daily status report of the work come under private IaaS. Virtual machines, load balancers, and network-attached storage are some examples of IaaS that include network, hardware, and storage as services. In a public cloud, IaaS may help businesses to save their investments required for purchasing physical infrastructure. A business can select the OS of its choice to create a virtual machine that includes scalable storage and processing abilities.
- **Platform as a Service (PaaS)**—User applications are provided a platform for writing code and executing it through the PaaS cloud. In terms of cloud, platform means the OS that combines software development and deployment tools along with middleware services. Windows Azure and Google App Engine (GAE) are examples of PaaS cloud. In organizations having a private PaaS, it is possible for programmers to create and deploy applications for their requirements.
- **Software as a Service (SaaS)**—The SaaS cloud provides software applications that are accessible from wherever the user is. Customers do not require purchasing the software or installing it on their own devices. They can use it directly from the cloud. These applications are hired through annual contracts, which are operational only if IaaS and PaaS clouds are already being used.

Customized applications can be maintained in the private cloud of organizations, which can interlink the applications and Big Data stored in a public cloud. Hybrid clouds allow applications to analyze the data efficiently through the strengths of both public and private clouds.

NOTE

Many organizations use both public and private clouds. Instead of using them separately, organizations combine the two cloud models in a hybrid cloud. A number of connections are formed between the two clouds, and operations are automated to improve efficiency.

EXHIBIT 1: Difference between SaaS, PaaS, IaaS

When your business has made the decision to consider cloud services for your application or infrastructure deployment, it's important that you grasp the fundamental differences between the core categories of cloud services available.

The cloud is a very broad concept, and it covers just about every possible sort of online service, but when businesses refer to cloud procurement, there are usually three models of cloud service under consideration: Software as a Service (SaaS), Platform as a Service (PaaS), and Infrastructure as a Service (IaaS). Each has its own intricacies and hybrid cloud models, but today we're going to help you develop an understanding of the high-level differences between SaaS, PaaS, and IaaS.

Software as a Service

In some ways, SaaS is very similar to the old thin-client model of software provision, where clients, in this case usually Web browsers, provide the point of access to software running on servers. SaaS is the most familiar form of cloud service for consumers. SaaS moves the task of managing software and its deployment to third-party services. Among the most familiar SaaS applications for business are customer relationship management applications like Sales force, productivity software suites like Google Apps, and storage solutions brothers like Box and Drop box.

Use of SaaS applications tends to reduce the cost of software ownership by removing the need for technical staff to install, manage, and upgrade software, as well as reduce the cost of licensing software. SaaS applications are usually provided on a subscription model.

Platform as a Service

PaaS functions at a lower level than SaaS, typically providing a platform on which software can be developed and deployed. PaaS providers abstract much of the work of dealing with servers and give clients an environment in which the operating system and server software, as well as the underlying server hardware and network infrastructure are taken care of, leaving users free to focus on the business side of scalability and the application development of their product or service. Businesses can requisition resources as they need them, scaling as demand grows, rather than investing in hardware with redundant resources. Examples of PaaS providers include Heroku, Google App Engine, and Red Hat's OpenShift.

Infrastructure as a Service

Moving down the stack, we get to the fundamental building blocks for cloud services. IaaS is comprised of highly automated and scalable compute resources, complemented by cloud storage and network capability, which can be self-provisioned, metered, and available on-demand.

IaaS providers offer these cloud servers and their associated resources via dashboard and/or API. IaaS clients have direct access to their servers and storage, just as they would with traditional servers but gain access to a much higher order of scalability. Users of IaaS can outsource and build a "virtual data center" in the cloud and have access to many of the same technologies and resource capabilities of a traditional data center without having to invest in capacity planning or the physical maintenance and management of it.

IaaS is the most flexible cloud computing model and allows for automated deployment of servers, processing power, storage, and networking. IaaS clients have true control over their infrastructure than users of PaaS or SaaS services. The main uses of IaaS include the actual development and deployment of PaaS, SaaS, and web-scale applications.

Source: *https://www.computenext.com/blog/when-to-use-saas-paas-and-iaas/*

Cloud Services for Big Data

Cloud services are associated with various models that are used for delivery and deployment. Cloud follows the same architecture as Big Data, both requiring distributed clusters of computing devices. Big Data systems include different specifications of cloud as an integral part; therefore, a cloud is termed as an ideal computing environment for handling Big Data.

In Big Data, the IaaS, PaaS, and SaaS clouds are used in the following manner:

- **IaaS**—The huge storage and computational power requirements for Big Data are fulfilled by the limitless storage space and computing ability obtained by the IaaS cloud.
- **PaaS**—PaaS offerings of various vendors have started adding various popular Big Data platforms that include MapReduce and Hadoop. These offerings save organizations from a lot of hassle, which may occur in managing individual hardware components and software applications.
- **SaaS**—Various organizations require identifying and analyzing the voice of customers, particularly on social media platforms. The social media data and the platform for analyzing the data are provided by SaaS vendors. In addition, private cloud facilitates the access to enterprise CRM data, which enables these analyses.

Cloud Providers in Big Data Market

Big Data cloud providers have been gearing up to bring the most advanced technologies at competitive prices in the market. Some providers are established, whereas some of them are relatively new to the field of cloud services. Some of these providers are rendering services that are relevant to Big Data analytics only. Some such providers are discussed as follows:

- **Amazon**—Amazon is one of the largest cloud service provider, and it offers its cloud services as Amazon Web Services (AWS).AWS includes some of the most popular cloud services, such as Elastic Compute Cloud (EC2), Elastic MapReduce, Simple Storage Service (S3), etc. Some of these services are discussed as follows:
  - **EC2**—Refers to a Web service that employs a large set of computing resources to perform its business operations. These resources are not properly utilized by Amazon, and therefore, they are pooled in the form of an IaaS cloud so that other organizations can take the benefit of these resources, ultimately benefitting Amazon through the rental cost. Organizations can use these resources elastically in a way that the hiring of resources is possible on an hourly basis.
  - **Elastic MapReduce**—It is a Web service that uses Amazon EC2 computation and Amazon S3 storage for storing and processing large amounts of data so that the cost of processing and storage is reduced significantly.
  - **DynamoDB**—Refers to a NoSQL database system in which data storage is done on Solid State Devices (SSDs). DynamoDB allows data replication for high availability and durability.
  - **Amazon S3**—Amazon Simple Storage Service (Amazon S3)is a Web interface that allows data storage over the Internet and makesweb-scale computing possible.
  - **High Performance Computing (HPC)**—Refers to a network that is replete with high bandwidth, low latency, and high computational abilities, which are required for processing Big Data, especially for solving issues related to education and business domains.
  - **RedShift**—Refers to a data warehouse service that is used to analyze data with the help of existing tools of business intelligence in an economical manner. You can scale Amazon RedShift for handling data up to a petabyte.
- **Google**—The cloud services that are provided by Google for handling Big Data include the following:
  - Google Compute Engine is a computing environment, which is secure, flexible, and based on virtual machine.
  - Google BigQuery is a Desktop as a Service (DaaS), which is used for searching huge amounts of data at a faster pace on the basis of SQL-format queries.
  - Google Prediction API, which is used for the identifying patterns in data, storingof patterns, and improving the patterns with successive utilizations.
- **Windows Azure**—Microsoft offers a PaaS cloud that is based on Windows and SQL abstractions and consists of a set of development tools, virtual machine support, management and media services, and mobile device services. Windows Azure PaaS is easy-to-adopt for people who are well equipped with the operations of .NET, SQL Server, and Windows. In addition, the Windows Azure HD Insight option added to the PaaS cloud makes it possible for the cloud users to address the emerging requirements to for integrating Big Data into Windows Azure

solutions. The platform used for building the Windows Azure PaaS is Horton works Data Platform (HDP) that, as stated by Microsoft, is fully compatible with Apache Hadoop. Moreover, Microsoft Excel and various other Business Intelligence (BI) tools can be connected to Windows Azure with support from HDInsight, which can be developed on the Windows Server also.

Hadoop is used as a cloud service in Windows Azure PaaS with the help of HDInsight. HDFS and MapReduce related frameworks are thus, offered economically, and in a simpler way, by the integration of Hadoop in this PaaS. The efficient management and storage of data are important features of HDInsight, which also uses Sqoop connector for importing the Windows Azure SQL data into HDFS or for exporting the data to a Windows Azure SQL database from HDFS.

SCENARIO

While discussing various Big Data handling technologies, Mr. Richard Stephens finds that a technology known as In-Memory Computing (IMC) can be used for carrying out calculations within the main memory. You will learn about IMC in the following section.

In-Memory Computing Technology for Big Data

We learned that distributed computing can help us meet requirements of storage and processing power for Big Data analytics. Another way to improve the computational speed and power of processing data is to use IMC. The representation of data in the form of rows and columns makes data processing easier and faster. Data stored in this manner is known as structured data in which a set of variables, each of which is associated with certain values, is used. Today, however, the data being generated is largely unstructured. The volume of data being generated today must be processed at a very high speed because the data is growing at a very fast rate. IMC is used to facilitate high-speed data processing. For example, IMC can help in tracking and monitoring consumers' activities and behaviors, which allow organizations to take timely actions for improving customer services and, thus, customer satisfaction.

We all know that data is stored on external devices known as secondary storage space. This data had to be accessed from the external source whenever an operation or any kind of modification on the data was required. External sources are accessed through Input/Output (I/O) channels that transfer data temporarily from secondary storage space to primary storage for processing purposes. The process of accessing external devices used to consume too much time during which the CPU could not be used for any other operation. The advantage of using external devices for data storage is that secondary storage is economical as compared to primary storage.

In the IMC technology, the RAM (or the primary storage space) is used for analyzing data. RAM helps us to increase the computing speed. Simultaneously, the reduction of primary storage cost has also made it possible to store data in the primary memory. The application finds data in the same location where it (the application) resides. Therefore, the analysis of data can be carried out in a more quick and efficient manner. Figure 3.15 shows the working of IMC:

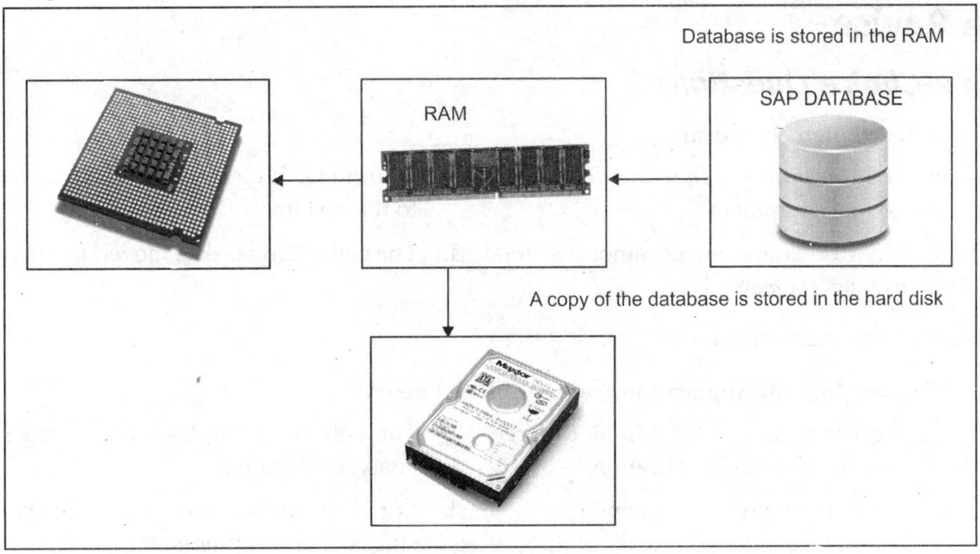

Figure 3.15: IMC Process

Relational Databases (RDBs) are used to store relational data. RDBs are the sources of information that are obtained by using SQL queries. The data stored in the RDBs is mostly structured, for example, accessing your marksheet from the college's website by filling in your roll number. Unstructured data, which comprises a wide range of text, images, videos, Web pages, blogs, business reports, press releases, emails, and text messages, provides information in the form of search results that are obtained by searching for specific keywords. Unstructured data is stored in a special kind of databases known as NoSQL databases. Entering a name in the Google search space to find the Web page, blog, or birthday video of a person is an example of accessing unstructured data.

The volume-related issues of Big Data are addressed by using IMC, and the diversity of Big Data is taken care of by NoSQL databases. Large organizations have centralized data warehouses for keeping the data safe. Users can access these warehouses only with the help of the IT department. The IMC technology helps different departments or business units of an organization to access and process the data that is relevant to them. This reduces the load on the central warehouse as every department takes care of processing its own data.

Summary

This chapter discussed the concept of distributed and parallel computing technologies and the role they play in handling Big Data. You also learned about various techniques used in parallel computing. Next, you learned about Hadoop and its functioning. The chapter further discussed cloud computing in detail, including its features, cloud deployment models, cloud delivery models, cloud services for Big Data, and cloud providers in the Big Data market. Finally, you learned about IMC and its importance in the context of Big Data.

Quick Revise

Multiple-Choice Questions

Q1. In distributed computing, _______________.

a. The computing task is divided among several computers

b. Additional high-capacity disks are added to the system

c. The results are shared among several users of the network

d. The computing task is moved to the cloud

Ans. The correct option is a.

Q2. Why are Big Data applications susceptible to latency?

a. Big Data may reside in a different location from the application.

b. The volume of Big Data is too large to be analyzed rapidly.

c. Big Data cannot use in-memory computing.

d. Big Data applications are still in the early stages of development.

Ans. The correct option is b.

Q3. The three major parallel computing platforms are _________.

a. IaaS, PaaS, and SaaS

b. Clusters or grids, MPP, and HPC

c. Database, SQL, and network

d. Network, cloud, and DaaS

Ans. The correct option is b.

Q4. How does the Hadoop architecture use computing resources?

a. By distributing software to computing resources.

b. By distributing data and computing tasks to computing resources.

c. By creating shared memory for computing resources.

d. By distributing data to computing resources.

Ans. The correct option is d.

Q5. Hadoop makes the system more resilient by __________.

a. Using an effective firewall and anti-virus.

b. Keeping multiple copies of data.

c. Keeping each computing resource isolated.

d. Uploading data to a cloud for backup.

Ans. The correct option is c.

Q6. Which of the following are the disadvantages of using a public cloud?

a. Latency and risk to data security

b. Latency and software incompatibility

c. Higher cost and risk to data security

d. Higher cost and legal issues of location

Ans. The correct option is c.

Q7. Which of the following is an appropriate combination of resources in a hybrid cloud?

a. Backup in the private cloud and HR policies in the public cloud

b. Internal processes in the private cloud and Big Data in the public cloud

c. Customer communication in the private cloud and financial compliance in the public cloud

d. Big Data in the private cloud and backup in the public cloud

Ans. The correct option is b.

Q8. To be able to use accounting software on a cloud, you should have an appropriate __________ and __________.

a. Infrastructure and data

b. Platform and network

c. Infrastructure and platform

d. Platform and data

Ans. The correct option is c.

Q9. Cloud computing offers cost-effective solutions for computing resources because______.

a. Cloud vendors negotiate for lower prices of resources.

b. Each resource has multiple users, which divides the cost.

c. All computing resources are located in low-cost regions.

d. Distributed computing lowers the cost of each resource.

Ans. The correct option is c.

Q10. A business that has customers' confidential information wants to use a public cloud for backup. Which of the following must the business ensure?

a. The cloud resources are compatible with the business' hardware and software.

b. The expected performance of the cloud is specified in detail in the service agreement.

c. The cloud allows access to government regulators and authorized third parties.

d. The cloud provides access to data only to designated persons of the business.

Ans. The correct option is a.

Subjective Questions

Q1. What is distributed computing? Explain the working of a distributed computing environment.

Ans. In distributed computing, multiple computing resources are connected in a network and computing tasks are distributed across these resources. This sharing of tasks increases the speed as well as the efficiency of the system. Because of this reason, distributed computing is considered faster and much more efficient than traditional methods of computing. It is also more suitable to process huge amounts of data in a limited time.

The following figure elaborates the processing of a large dataset in a distributed computing environment:

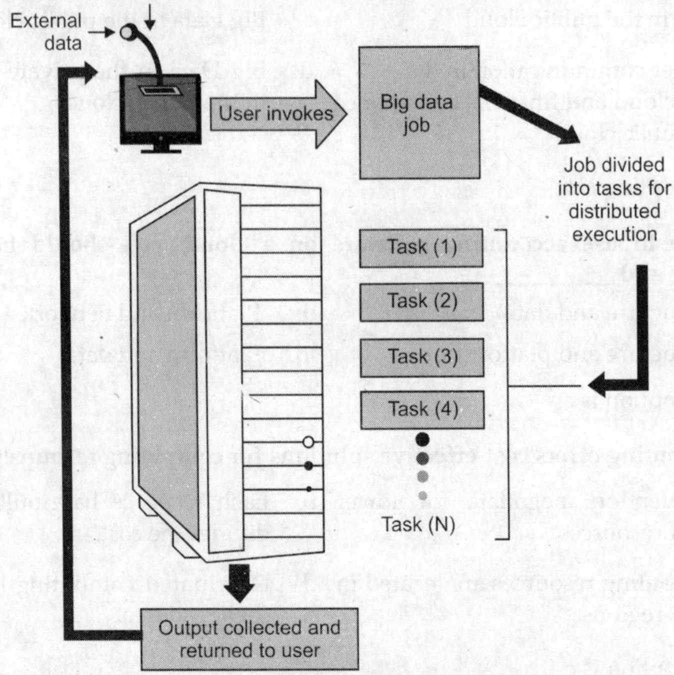

Distributed Computing Technique for Processing Large Data

As you can notice, the nodes are arranged within a system and are the elements that form the core of computing resources. These resources include CPU, memory, disks, etc. Big Data systems, usually, have higher scaling requirements. Therefore, these nodes are more beneficial for adding scalability to the Big Data environment, as and when required. The system, with added scalability, can accommodate the growing amounts of data more efficiently and flexibly. Distributed computing technique also makes use of virtualization and load balancing features.

The sharing of workload across various systems throughout the network to manage the load is known as load balancing. The virtualization feature creates a virtual environment in which hardware platform, storage device, and OS are included.

Q2. List the differences between parallel and distributed systems.

Ans. The following table lists the differences between parallel and distributed systems:

Distributed System	Parallel System
An independent, autonomous system connected in a network for accomplishing specific tasks	A computer system with several processing units attached to it

Distributed System	Parallel System
Coordination is possible between connected computers that have their own memory and CPU	A common shared memory can be directly accessed by every processing unit in a network
Loose coupling of computers connected in a network, providing access to data and remotelylocated resources	Tight coupling of processing resources that are used for solving a single, complex problem

Q3. Discuss the techniques of parallel computing.

Ans. Some of the techniques of parallel computing are given in the table followings:

Parallel Computing Method	Description	Uses
Cluster or Grid Computing (Primarily used in Hadoop)	Cluster or grid computing is based on a connection of multiple servers in a network. This network is known as a cluster in which the servers share the workload among them. A cluster can be either homogeneous (comprising the same type of commodity hardware) or heterogeneous (consisting of different types of hardware).	A cluster can be created even by using hardware components that were acquired a long time back to provide cost-effective storage options. The overall cost may be very high in cluster computing.
Massively Parallel Processing (MPP) (Used in data warehouses)	A single machine working as a grid is used in the MPP platform, which is capable of handling the activities of storage, memory, and computing. Software written specifically for MPP platform is used for the optimization of MPP capabilities.	MPP platforms, such as EMC Greenplum, and ParAccel, are most suited for high-value use cases.
High-Performance Computing (HPC)	HPC environments are known to offer high performance and scalability by using IMC. This technology is especially suitable for processing floating-point data at high speeds.	HPC environments can be used to develop specialty and custom applications for research and business organizations where the result is more valuable, than the cost or where strategic importance of the project is of high priority.

Q4. List the important features of Hadoop.

Ans. The following are some of the important features of Hadoop:

- Hadoop performs well with several machines without requiring shared memory or disks among them. Hence, the efficiency-related issues related to storage and access to data get automatically solved.
- Hadoop uses various servers for data distribution, thus improving data loading and data storage operations.
- The data stored across various servers can be tracked by Hadoop. It helps in accessing and retrieving data, as and when required.
- Hadoop improves data processing by running computing tasks on all available processors that are working in parallel. The performance of Hadoop remains up to the mark both in the case of complex computational questions and of large and varied data.
- Hadoop keeps multiple copies of data to improve resilience that helps in maintaining consistency, especially in case of server failure.

Q5. Discuss the features of cloud computing that can be used to handle Big Data.

Ans. The following are some features of cloud computing that can be used to handle Big Data:

- **Scalability**—Scalability means addition of new resources to an existing infrastructure. The increase in the amount of data being collected and analyzed requires organizations to improve their hardware components' processing ability. These organizations may, at times, need to replace the existing hardware with a new set of hardware components in order to improve data management and processing activities. The new hardware may not provide complete support to the software that used to run properly on the earlier set of hardware. We can solve such issues by using cloud services that employ the distributed computing technique to provide scalability to the architecture.
- **Elasticity**—Elasticity in cloud means hiring certain resources, as and when required, and paying for the resources that have been used. No extra payment is required for acquiring specific cloud services. For example, a business expecting the use of more data during in-store promotion could hire more resources to provide high processing power. Moreover, a cloud does not require customers to declare their resource requirements in advance.
- **Resource Pooling**—Resource pooling is an important aspect of cloud services for Big Data analytics. In resource pooling, multiple organizations, which use similar kinds of resources to carry out computing practices, have no need to individually hire all the resources. The sharing of resources is allowed in a cloud, which facilitates cost cutting through resource pooling.
- **Self Service**—Cloud computing involves a simple user interface that helps customers to directly access the cloud services they want. The process of selecting the needed services requires no intervention from human beings and can be accessed automatically.

- **Low Cost—**A careful planning, use, management, and control of resources help organizations to reduce the cost of acquiring hardware significantly. Also, cloud offers customized solutions especially to organizations that cannot afford too much initial investment in purchasing the resources that are used for computation in Big Data analytics. The cloud provides them the pay-as-you-use option in which organizations need to sign for those resources only that are essential. This also helps the cloud provider in harnessing benefits of economies of scale and providing benefit to their customers in terms of cost reduction.
- **Fault Tolerance—**Cloud computing provides fault tolerance by offering uninterrupted services to customers, especially in cases of component failure. The responsibility of handling the workload is shifted to other components of the cloud.

Q6. Discuss the role cloud services play in handling Big Data.

Ans. Cloud services are associated with various models that are used for delivery and deployment. Cloud follows the same architecture as Big Data, both requiring distributed clusters of computing devices. Big Data systems include different specifications of cloud as an integral part; therefore, a cloud is termed as an ideal computing environment for handling Big Data.

In Big Data, the IaaS, PaaS, and SaaS clouds are used in the following manner:

- **IaaS—**The huge storage and computational power requirements for Big Data are fulfilled by the limitless storage space and computing ability obtained by the IaaS cloud.
- **PaaS—**PaaS offerings of various vendors have started adding various popular Big Data platforms that include MapReduce and Hadoop. These offerings save organizations from a lot of hassles, which may occur in managing individual hardware components and software applications.
- **SaaS—**Various organizations require identifying and analyzing the voice of customers, particularly on social media platforms. The social media data and the platform for analyzing the data are provided by SaaS vendors. In addition, private cloud facilitates the access to enterprise CRM data, which enables these analyses.

Q7. Write a short note on In-Memory Computing technology.

Ans. IMC is used to facilitate high-speed data processing. For example, IMC can help in tracking and monitoring consumers' activities and behaviors, which allow organizations to take timely actions for improving customer services and, thus, customer satisfaction.

We all know that data is stored on external devices known as secondary storage space. This data had to be accessed from the external source whenever an operation or any kind of modification on the data was required. External sources are accessed through Input/Output (I/O) channels that transfer data temporarily from secondary storage space to primary storage for processing purposes. The process of accessing external devices used to consume too much time during which the CPU could not be used for any other operation. The advantage of using external devices for data storage is that secondary storage is economical as compared to primary storage.

In the IMC technology, the RAM (or the primary storage space) is used for analyzing data. RAM helps us to increase the computing speed. Simultaneously, the reduction of primary storage cost has also made it possible to store data in the primary memory. The application finds data in the same location where it (the application) resides. Therefore, the analysis of data can be carried out in a more quick and efficient manner.

4

Understanding Hadoop Ecosystem

Handling huge volumes of data generating from billions of online activities and transactions requires continuous upgradation and evolution of Big Data. One such upcoming technology is Hadoop. People often confuse Hadoop with Big Data. Hadoop is not Big Data; however, it is also true that Hadoop plays an integral part in almost all Big Data processes. In fact, it is almost impossible to use Big Data without the tools and techniques of Hadoop. So what exactly is Hadoop?

According to Apache, "Hadoop is a framework that allows for the distributed processing of large data sets across clusters of computers using simple programming models. It is designed to scale up from single servers to thousands of machines, each offering local computation and storage. Rather than rely on hardware to deliver high-availability, the library itself is designed to detect and handle failures at the application layer, so delivering a highly-available service on top of a cluster of computers, each of which may be prone to failures." In simple words, Hadoop is a 'software library' that allows its users to process large datasets across distributed clusters of computers, thereby enabling them to gather, store and analyze huge sets of data. Hadoop provides various tools and technologies, collectively termed as the Hadoop ecosystem, to enable development and deployment of Big Data solutions.

Hadoop Distributed File System (HDFS) is a resilient, flexible, grouped method of file management in a Big Data setup. HDFS is a data service offering unique abilities required when data variety, volumes, and velocity are beyond the controllable levels of traditional data management systems. In case of traditional data management systems, data is read many times after it is inserted into a system but written only once in its lifetime. However, in the case of systems performing continuous read-write cycles, HDFS offers excellent Big Data analysis and support. HDFS consists of a central DataNode and multiple DataNodes running on the appliance model cluster and offers the highest performance levels when the same physical rack is used for the entire cluster. HDFS is capable of managing the inbuilt environment redundancy and its design can detect failures and resolve them by running particular programs automatically on multiple servers present in the cluster. HDFS allows simultaneous application execution across multiple servers consisting of economical internal disk drives.

This session introduces you to the various elements of the Hadoop ecosystem, such as HDFS and its architecture, MapReduce, YARN, HBase, and Hive. You will also learn about various tools used to interact with Hadoop ecosystem including Pig and Pig Latin, Sqoop, ZooKeeper, Flume, and Oozie in later chapters. In the end, the chapter discusses the need for selecting a suitable Hadoop data organization for applications.

Hadoop Ecosystem

Hadoop ecosystem is a framework of various types of complex and evolving tools and components. Some of these elements may be very different from each other in terms of their architecture; however, what keeps them all together under a single roof is that they all derive their functionalities from the scalability and power of Hadoop. In simple words, the Hadoop ecosystem can be defined as a comprehensive collection of tools and technologies that can be effectively implemented and deployed to provide Big Data solutions in a cost-effective manner. **MapReduce** and **Hadoop Distributed File System (HDFS)** are two core components of the Hadoop ecosystem that provide a great starting point to manage Big Data; however, they are not sufficient to deal with the Big Data challenges. Along with these two, the Hadoop ecosystem provides a collection of various elements to support the complete development and deployment of Big Data solutions.

Figure 4.1 depicts the elements of the Hadoop ecosystem:

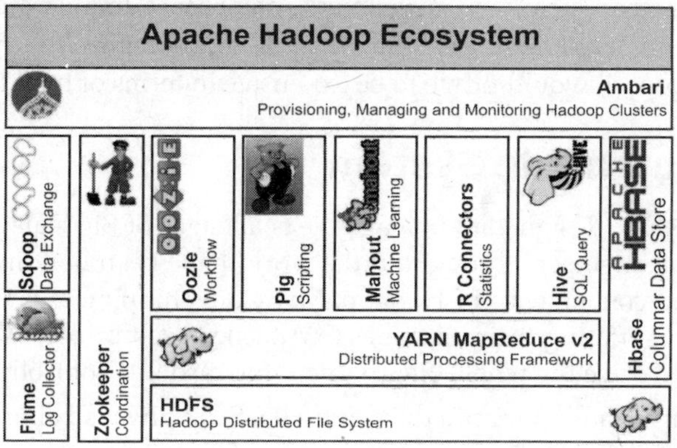

Source: *http://blog.agro-know.com/?p=3810*

Figure 4.1: Hadoop Ecosystem

All these elements enable users to process large datasets in real time and provide tools to support various types of Hadoop projects, schedule jobs, and manage cluster resources.

Figure 4.2 depicts how the various elements of Hadoop involve at various stages of processing data:

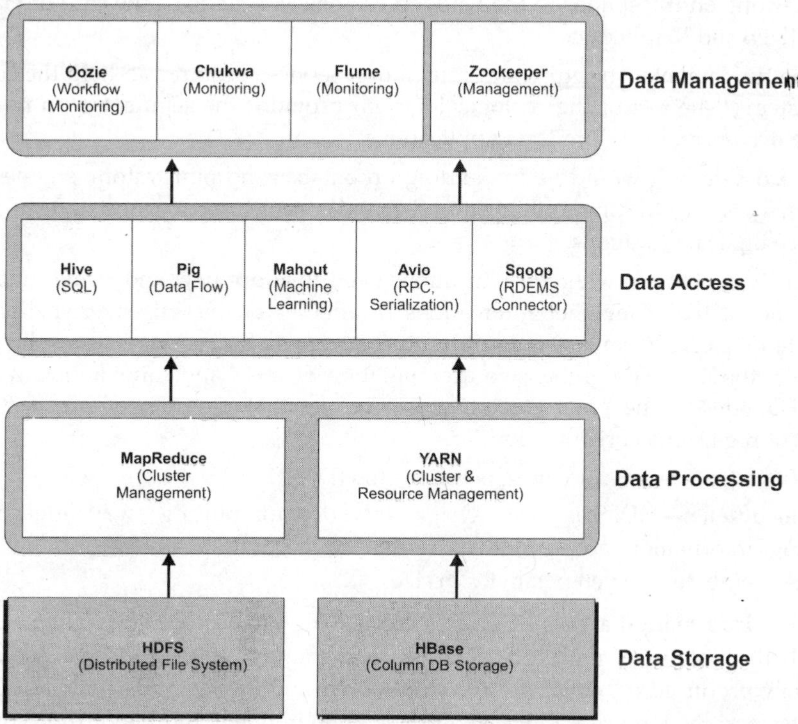

Figure 4.2: Hadoop Ecosystem Elements at Various Stages of Data Processing

MapReduce and HDFS provide the necessary services and basic structure to deal with the core requirements of Big Data solutions. Other services and tools of the ecosystem provide the environment and components required to build and manage purpose-driven Big Data applications. In the absence of an ecosystem, the developers, database administrators, system and network managers will have to implement separate sets of technologies to create Big Data solutions. However, such an approach would prove to be expensive in terms of both time and money.

Hadoop Distributed File System

File systems like HDFS are designed to manage the challenges of Big Data. For some time now, open source and commercial engineers throughout the world have been building and testing instruments to expand the role and convenience of Hadoop. Many are chipping away at the components of the Hadoop ecosystem and offering their upgrades to Apache-based projects. This steady stream of fixes and upgrades serves to drive the whole environment forward in a controlled and secure way.

Being core components, Hadoop MapReduce and HDFS are always being enhanced and hence they provide greater stability. The Hadoop ecosystem provides a constantly increasing collection of tools and technology particularly made to abridge the deployment, development and support of Big Data setups. Attempting to handle enormous information challenges without a toolkit loaded with innovation and credibility is similar to attempting to drain the sea with a spoon.

No building is steady without a solid base. Each part of the building must justify its existence. The walls, stairs, floors, electrical equipment, pipes—all need to support one another for the building to exist as one strong entity, similar to the Hadoop ecological system. In the case of Hadoop, the base consists of HDFS and MapReduce.

Both give the fundamental structure and integration services required to help the core condition of Big Data systems. The rest of the ecological system provides the segments you need to build and oversee goal-driven, real-time Big Data applications.

Without an ecosystem, it would be impending on database administrators, engineers, system and network managers, etc., to commonly distinguish and concur upon a group of technologies to create and introduce Big Data solutions.

This is routinely a situation where organizations need to adopt new and rising innovation patterns and the errand of fixing together innovations in another business is overwhelming. That is the reason the Hadoop ecosystem is very important: it acknowledges and unleashes the net capability of Big Data. It is the most comprehensive accumulation of tools and innovations available today to target Big Data tests. The environment assists in the making of new prospects for extensive deployment of Big Data by organizations.

Let's now discuss some terms or concepts related to HDFS:

- **Huge documents**—HDFS is a file system intended for putting away huge documents with streaming information access. Huge in this connection means records in the vicinity of gigabytes, terabytes or even petabytes in size.
- **Streaming information access**—HDFS is created for batch processing. The priority is given to the high throughput of data access rather than the low latency of data access. A dataset is commonly produced or replicated from the source, and then various analyses are performed on that dataset in the long run. Every analysis is done in detail and hence time consuming, so the time required for examining the entire dataset is quite high.

- **Appliance hardware**—Hadoop does not require large, exceptionally dependable hardware to run.
- **Low-latency information access**—Applications that permit access to information in milliseconds do not function well with HDFS. Therefore, HDFS is upgraded for conveying a high transaction volume of information, and this may be at the expense of idleness. HBase is at present a superior choice for small latency access.
- **Loads of small documents**—Since the NameNode holds file system data information in memory, the quantity of documents in a file system is administered in terms of the memory on the server. As a dependable guideline, each document and registry takes around 150 bytes. Thus, for instance, if you have one million documents, you would require no less than 300 MB of memory. While putting away a huge number of records is achievable, billions is past the capacity of the current equipment.

HDFS Architecture

HDFS has a master-slave architecture. It comprises a NameNode and a number of DataNodes. The NameNode is the master that manages the various DataNodes, as shown in Figure 4.3:

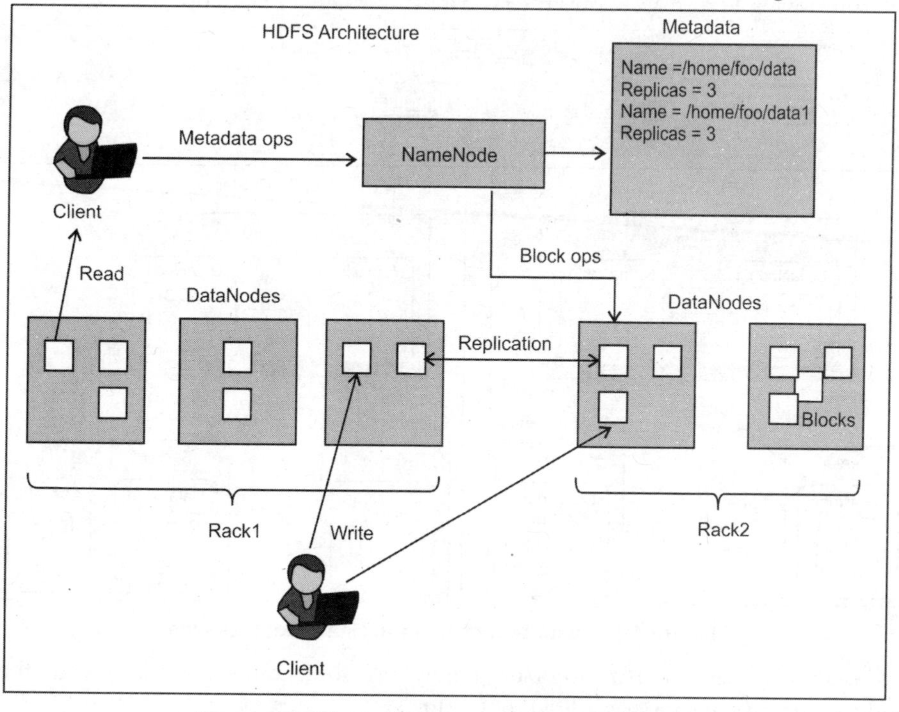

Figure 4.3: Displaying the Architecture of HDFS

The NameNode manages HDFS cluster metadata, whereas DataNodes store the data. Records and directories are presented by clients to the NameNode. These records and directories are managed on the NameNode. Operations on them, such as their modification or opening and closing them are performed by the NameNode. On the other hand, internally, a file is divided into one or more blocks, which are stored in a group of DataNodes. DataNodes read and write requests from the clients. Data...odes can also execute operations like the creation, deletion, and replication of blocks, depending on the instructions from the NameNode.

Concept of Blocks in HDFS Architecture

A disk has a certain block size, which is the basic measure of information that it can read or compose. File systems expand by managing information in pieces, which are an indispensable part of the disk block size. File system blocks are commonly a couple of kilobytes in size, while disk blocks are regularly 512 bytes. This is by and large straightforward for the file system client that is essentially perusing or composing a record of whatever length.

HDFS blocks are huge in contrast to disk blocks because they have to minimize the expense of the seek operation. Consequently, the time to transfer a huge record made of multiple blocks operates at the disk exchange rate. A quick computation demonstrates that if the seek time is around 10ms, and the exchange rate is 100 MB/s, then to assign the seek time that is 1% of the exchange time, we have to create a block size of around 100 MB. The default size is 64 MB, although numerous HDFS installations utilize 128 MB blocks. Map tasks of MapReduce (component of HDFS) typically work on one block at once, so if you have fewer assignments (fewer than the nodes in the group), your tasks will run slower. Figure 4.4 shows the Heartbeat message of Hadoop:

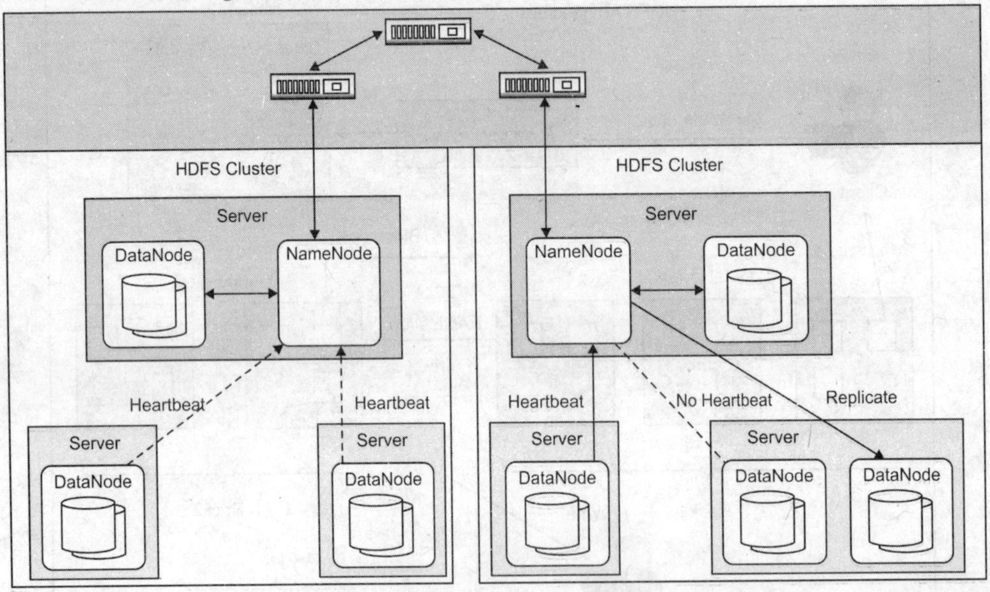

Figure 4.4: Illustration of Hadoop Heartbeat Message

When a heartbeat message reappears or a new heartbeat message is received, the respective DataNode sending the message is added to the cluster.

HDFS performance is calculated through distribution of data and fault tolerance by detecting faults and quickly recurring the data. This recovery is completed through replication and resents in a reliable file system. It results in a reliable huge file storage.

To enable this task of reliability, one should facilitate number of tasks for failure management, some of which are utilized within HDFS and others are still in a process to be implemented:

- **Monitoring**—DataNode and NameNode communicate through continuous signals ("Heartbeat"). If signal is not heard by either of the two, the node is considered to have failed and would be no longer available. The failed node is replaced by the replica and replication scheme is also changed.
- **Rebalancing**—According to this process, the blocks are shifted from one to another location where ever the free space is available. Better performance can be judged by the increase in demand of data as well as the increase in demand for replication towards frequent node failures.
- **Metadata replication**—These files are prove to failures; however, they maintain the replica of the corresponding file on the same HDFS.

There are a few advantages of abstracting a block for a distributed file system. The principal advantage is most evident: a record can be bigger than any single disk in a system. There is nothing that requires the blocks from a record to be put away on the same disk; so, they can exploit any of the disks in the cluster. It would still be possible to store a single document on a HDFS cluster with the entire cluster disks filled by its blocks.

Second, making the abstraction unit a block instead of a file improves the storage subsystem. The storage subsystem manages blocks, improving storage management (since blocks are of a fixed size, it is not difficult to compute the number of blocks that can be stored on a disk), and dispensing with metadata concerns.

To protect against corrupt blocks and disks and machine failure, each block is recreated on a few separate machines (usually three). In the event that a block gets occupied, a copy or duplicate block can be read from an alternate location in a straightforward manner to the client. A block that is no more accessible because of such issues can be replicated from its alternative location to other live machines.

Just like a disk file system, HDFS's fsck command can issue directives to blocks. For example, running the *% hadoop fsck -files –blocks* command lists the blocks that create each file in a file system.

NameNodes and DataNodes

An HDFS cluster has two node types working in a slave master design: a NameNode (the master) and various DataNodes (slaves). The NameNode deals with the file system. It stores the metadata for all the documents and indexes in the file system. This metadata is stored on the local disk as two files: the file system image and the edit log. The NameNode is aware of the DataNodes on which all the pieces of a given document are found; however, it doesn't store block locations necessarily, since this data is recreated from DataNodes.

A client accesses the file system on behalf of the user by communicating with the DataNodes and NameNode. The client provides a file system, like the POSIX interface, so the user code does not require the NameNode and DataNodes in order to execute.

DataNodes are the workhorses of a file system. They store and recover blocks when they are asked to (by clients or the NameNode), and they report back to the NameNode occasionally with a list of blocks that they store externally.

Without the NameNode, the file system cannot be used. In fact, if the machine using the NameNode crashes, all files on the file system would be lost since there would be no way of knowing how to reconstruct the files from the blocks on DataNodes. This is why it is important to make the NameNode robust to cope with failures, and Hadoop provides two ways of doing this.

The first way is to take the back up of file documents. Hadoop can be set in a way that NameNode creates its state for various file systems. The normal setup choice is to write to the local disk and to a remote NFS mount.

Another way is to run a secondary NameNode, which does not operate like a normal NameNode.

Secondary NameNode periodically reads the filesystem, changes the log, and apply them into the fsimage file. When the NameNode is down, secondary NameNode will be online but this node will only have read permissions to fsimage and editlog file.

DataNodes ensure connectivity with the NameNode by sending heartbeat messages. Whenever the NameNode ceases to receive a heartbeat message from a DataNode, it unmaps the DataNode from the cluster and proceeds with further operations.

The Command-Line Interface

We are going to view HDFS by interfacing with it from the command line. There are numerous different interfaces for HDFS; however, the command line is one of the easiest and most popular among developers. We are going to execute HDFS on a machine. For this, we need to first set up Hadoop in a distributed mode prototype.

There are two properties that we set in the distributed mode prototype setup that calls for further clarification. The principal is fs.default.name, set to `hdfs://localhost/`, which is used to set a default Hadoop file system. File systems are tagged by a URI, and here we have utilized an HDFS URI to design Hadoop. The HDFS daemons will utilize this property to focus the host and port for the HDFS NameNode. We'll be running it on localhost, on the default HDFS port, 8020. Furthermore, HDFS clients will utilize this property to figure out where the NameNode is running so they can connect with it.

Using HDFS Files

The HDFS file system is accessed by user applications with the help of the HDFS client. It is a library that reveals the interface of the HDFS file system and hides almost all the complexities that appear during the implementation of HDFS.

The user application is not required to know whether the metadata of the file system and its storage are on the same servers or have multiple replicas.

The object of a Filesystem class is created for accessing HDFS. The Filesystem class is an abstract base class for a generic file system. The code created by a user referring to HDFS must be written in order to use an object of the Filesystem class. An instance of the FileSystem class can be created by passing a new Configuration object into a constructor. Assume that Hadoop configuration files, such as hadoop-default.xml and hadoopsite.xml are present on the class path.

The code to create an instance of the FileSystem class is shown in Listing 4.1:

Listing 4.1: Creating a FileSystem Object

```
Configuration config = new Configuration();   ← Creates a configuration object config

FileSystem fsys = FileSystem.get(config);   ← Creates a FileSystem object fs
```

Path is another important HDFS object, which specifies the names of the files or directories in a file system. You can create a Path object from a string specifying the location of the file/directory on HDFS. Both the FileSystem and Path objects allow you to perform programmatic operations on HDFS files and directories.

Listing 4.2 shows the manipulation of HDFS objects:

Listing 4.2: Manipulating HDFS Objects

```
Path fp=new Path(file name);   ← Creating an object for the Path class

if (fsys.exists(fp))   ← Checking the file path
//statement 1
If(fsys.isFile(fp))
//statement 1
Boolean result=fsys.createNewFile(fp);
Boolean result=fsys.delete(fp);

FSDataInputStream fin=fsys.open(fp);   ← Reading from the file

FSDataOutputStream fout=fsys.create(fp);   ← Writing to the file
```

You must note that whenever a file is opened to perform the writing operation, the client opening this file grants an exclusive writing lease for it. Due to this, no other client can perform write operations on this file until the operation of this client gets completed. In order to ensure that a lease is held by no "runaway" clients, it gets expired periodically. The effective use of a lease ensures that no two applications can perform the write operation to a given file simultaneously.

The lease duration is bounded by a soft limit and a hard limit. In the case of the soft limit, a writer gets access to a file exclusively. In case the soft limit expires and the client fails to close the file or renew the lease, another client can preempt the lease. On the other hand, if the hard limit expires and the client fails to renew the lease, HDFS assumes that the client has quitted and closes the file automatically.

Hadoop-Specific File System Types

In addition to ordinary files, HDFS also provides several specific file system types that provide richer functionality and simplify the processing of data. The local file system of Hadoop performs the client-side checksum operation. When you write a record to a file, the client of the file system directly creates a hidden document, `.filename.crc`, in the same index containing checksums for each chunk of the document. The size of the chunk is managed by the `io.bytes.per.checksum` property, which is 512 bytes by default. The chunk size is stocked up as metadata in the .crc document, so the file can be read correctly regardless of the changed setting for the chunk size. Checksums are checked when a record is analyzed, and if an error is found, the local file system throws a checksumexception exception.

NOTE

A checksum refers to the number of bits in a transmission unit included with the unit to enable the receiver to see whether the same number of bits has arrived.

Checksums are economical to calculate (in Java, they are executed in local code), normally adding a marginal overhead to the time to analyze or write a record. For most systems, the cost is worth the value additions it brings to the application. The disabling of checksums is possible. This is achieved by using the `Rawlocalfilesystem` class instead of the `Localfilesystem` class. Table 4.1 lists some Hadoop-specific file systems types:

Table 4.1: Hadoop-Specific File System Types

File System	URI Scheme	Java Implementation (org.apache.hadoop)	Definition
Local	file	fs.LocalFileSystem	A file system for a locally connected disk with client-side check-sums. Use `RawLocalFileSystem` for a local file system with no checksums.
HDFS	hdfs	hdfs.DistributedFile System	Hadoop's distributed file system. HDFS is designed to work efficiently with MapReduce.
HFTP	hftp	hdfs.HftpFileSystem	A file system providing read-only access to HDFS. (Despite its name, HFTP has no link with FTP.) Often used with distcp to copy data between HDFS clusters running different versions.
HSFTP	hsftp	hdfs.HsftpFileSystem	A file system providing read-only access to HDFS over HTTPS. (Again, this has no connection with FTP.)
HAR	har	fs.HarFileSystem	A file system layered on another file system for archiving files. Hadoop archives are typically used for archiving files in HDFS to reduce the NameNode's memory usage.
KFS (CloudStore)	kfs	fs.kfs.KosmosFile System	CloudStore (formerly the Kosmos file system) is a distributed file system like HDFS or Google's GFS, written in C++.
FTP	ftp	fs.ftp.FTPFileSystem	A file system backed by an FTP server.
S3 (native)	s3n	fs.s3native.NativeS3 FileSystem	A file system backed by Amazon S3.

Table 4.1: Hadoop-Specific File System Types			
File System	**URI Scheme**	**Java Implementation (org.apache.hadoop)**	**Definition**
S3 (blockbased)	s3	fs.s3.S3FileSystem	A file system backed by Amazon S3, which stores files in blocks (much like HDFS) to overcome S3's 5 GB file size limit.

HDFS Commands

Various shell like commands interact with HDFS directly as well as with other file systems supported by Hadoop such as Local FS, HFTP FS, S3 FS, and others. These commands are provided by the File System (FS) shell. The FS shell can be invoked by the following command:

```
bin/hadoop fs <args>
```

Most commands in the FS shell are similar to the Unix commands and perform almost similar functions. Some commonly used HDFS commands are shown in Table 4.2:

Table 4.2: HDFS Commands and their Description		
Commands	**Description**	**Syntax**
appendToFile	Used for appending a single src or multiple srcs from the local file system to the destination file system. This command also reads input from stdin and appends to the destination file system.	hdfs dfs -appendToFile <localsrc> ... <dst>
cat	Used for copying source paths to stdout. This command returns 0 on success and -1 in case of error.	Usage: hdfs dfs -cat URI [URI ...]
chmod	Used for changing the permissions of files.	hdfs dfs -chmod [-R] <MODE[,MODE]... | OCTALMODE> URI [URI ...]
chown	Used for changing the owner of files.	hdfs dfs -chown [-R] [OWNER][:[GROUP]] URI [URI]
count	Used for counting the number of directories, files, and bytes under the paths that match the mentioned file pattern.	hdfs dfs -count [-q] [-h] <paths>
cp	Used for copying files from the source to the destination. This command enables multiple sources as well in which case the destination must be a directory.	hdfs dfs -cp [-f] [-p | -p[topax]] URI [URI ...] <dest>

Table 4.2: HDFS Commands and their Description

Commands	Description	Syntax
get	Used for copying files to the local file system.	hdfs dfs -get [-ignorecrc] [-crc] <src> <localdst>
mkdir	Used for creating directories by taking the path URI as an argument.	hdfs dfs -mkdir [-p] <paths>
mv	Used for moving files from the source to the destination.	hdfs dfs -mv URI [URI ...] <dest>
rm	Used for deleting files specified as args.	hdfs dfs -rm [-f] [-r|-R] [-skipTrash] URI [URI ...]

The org.apache.hadoop.io package

This `org.apache.hadoop.io` package provides generic I/O code to be used while reading and writing data to the network, to databases, and to files. This package provides various interfaces, classes, and exceptions. The interfaces provided by this package are listed in Table 4.3:

Table 4.3: Interfaces of the org.apache.hadoop.io Package and their Description

Interface	Description
RawComparator<T>	Refers to a comparator that operates directly on byte representations of objects.
Stringifier<T>	Provides two methods for converting an object to a string representation and restore the object given in its string representation.
Writable	Refers to a serializable object that implements a simple, efficient, serialization protocol based on DataInput and DataOutput.
WritableComparable<T>	Refers to a Writable object which is also a Comparable object.
WritableFactory	Refers to a factory for a class of Writable.

Table 4.4 lists the classes of the `org.apache.hadoop.io` package:

Table 4.4: Classes of the org.apache.hadoop.io Package and their Description

Class	Description
AbstractMapWritable	Refers to an abstract base class for MapWritable and SortedMapWritable. Unlike org.apache.nutch.crawl.MapWritable, this class enables the creation of MapWritable<Writable, MapWritable>.
ArrayFile	Performs a dense file-based mapping from integers to values.
ArrayPrimitiveWritable	Refers to a wrapper class.

Table 4.4: Classes of the org.apache.hadoop.io Package and their Description	
Class	**Description**
ArrayWritable	Acts as a Writable object for arrays containing instances of a class.
BinaryComparable	Refers to the interface supported by WritableComparable types that support ordering/permutation by a representative set of bytes.
BloomMapFile	Extends MapFile and provides almost the same functionality.
BooleanWritable	Refers to a WritableComparable object for booleans.
BytesWritable	Refers to a byte sequence that is usable as a key or value.
ByteWritable	Refers to a WritableComparable object for a single byte.
CompressedWritable	Refers to a base class for Writables that store themselves in a compressed form.
DataOutputOutputStream	Refers to an OutputStream implementation that wraps a DataOutput.
DefaultStringifier<T>	Refers to the default implementation of the Stringifier interface, which stringifies the objects using base64 encoding of the serialized version of the objects.
DoubleWritable	Refers to a Writable object for double values.
ElasticByteBufferPool	Refers to a simple ByteBufferPool that creates ByteBuffers as required.
EnumSetWritable<E extends Enum<E>>	Refers to a Writable wrapper for EnumSet.
FloatWritable	Refers to a WritableComparable object for floats.
GenericWritable	Refers to a wrapper for Writable instances.
IntWritable	Refers to a WritableComparable object for ints.
IOUtils	Refers to a utility class for I/O related functionality.
LongWritable	Refers to a WritableComparable object for longs.
MapFile	Performs a file-based mapping from keys to values.
MapWritable	Refers to a Writable Map.
MD5Hash	Refers to a Writable object for MD5 hash values.
NullWritable	Refers to a singleton Writable with no data.
ObjectWritable	Refers to a polymorphic Writable that writes an instance with its class name.
SequenceFile	Refers to flat files comprising binary key/value pairs.

Table 4.4: Classes of the org.apache.hadoop.io Package and their Description	
Class	**Description**
SetFile	Refers to a file-based set of keys.
ShortWritable	Refers to a WritableComparable object for shorts.
SortedMapWritable	Refers to a Writable SortedMap.
Text	Uses standard UTF8 encoding for storing text.
TwoDArrayWritable	Contains a matrix of instances of a class and is a writable for 2D arrays.
VersionedWritable	Refers to a base class for Writables that provides version checking.
VIntWritable	Refers to a WritableComparable object for integer values stored in the variable-length format.
VLongWritable	Refers to a WritableComparable for longs in a variable-length format.
WritableComparator	Refers to a comparator for WritableComparables.
WritableFactories	Refers to the factories for non-public writables.

Table 4.5 lists exceptions of the `org.apache.hadoop.io` package:

Table 4.5: Exceptions of the `org.apache.hadoop.io` Package and their Description	
Exceptions	**Description**
MultipleIOException	Encapsulates a list of IOException into an IOException
VersionMismatchException	Occurs when the version of the object being read does not match with the current implementation version as returned by VersionedWritable.getVersion(), which throws this VersionedWritable.readFields(DataInput) exception.

HDFS High Availability

In an HDFS cluster, the NameNode was a Single Point Of Failure (SPOF) prior to Hadoop 2.0. Each Hadoop cluster contains a NameNode. The availability of an HDFS cluster depends upon the availability of the NameNode. In other words, the HDFS cluster would not be available if its NameNode cluster is not active.

This kind of situation affects the total availability of the HDFS cluster in mainly two ways:

- If an unplanned event such as a machine crash occurs, then the cluster would remain unavailable till an operator restarts the NameNode.
- Planned maintenance such as upgradation of software or hardware on the NameNode machine would result in cluster downtime.

The preceding problems are addressed by the HDFS High Availability feature which provides the facility of running two redundant NameNodes in the same cluster. These NameNodes can run in an

Active/Passive configuration which enables a fast failover to a new NameNode in case a machine crashes.

A typical HA cluster comprises two separate machines that are configured as NameNodes. At any instant, only one NameNode is in an Active state, and the other will be in the Standby state. The Active NameNode performs all the client operations in the cluster, and the Standby NameNode acts as a slave, which maintains enough state for providing a fast failover, if required.

You can deploy an HA cluster by preparing the following:

- **NameNode machines**—These are the machines on which you can run the Active and Standby NameNodes. These NameNode machines must have similar hardware configurations.
- **Shared storage**—Both NameNode machines must have read/write accessibility on a shared directory.

EXHIBIT 1: Streamlining Healthcare Connectivity with Hadoop and Big Data

Company Overview

The connectivity and information technology subsidiary of a major pharmaceutical company were created to simplify how the business of healthcare is managed while making the delivery of care safer and more efficient. As more and more of healthcare systems in the US go electronic, the company meets challenges and opportunities through an open network that supports future growth via interoperability among organizations, systems and solutions.

Business Challenges Before Cloudera

With regulations such as the Health Insurance Portability and Accountability Act of 1996 (HIPAA), healthcare organizations are required to store healthcare data for extended periods of time. This company instituted a policy of saving seven years' historical claims and remit data, but its in-house database systems had trouble meeting the data retention requirement while processing millions of claims every day.

A software engineer at the company explained, "All of our systems were maxed out. We were constantly having database issues. It was just too much data for what they were meant to handle. They were overworked and overloaded, and it started to cause problems with all of our real-time production processing."

Further, the company sought a solution that would allow users to do more than just store data. The manager of software development at the company explained, "In today's data driven world, data really is this huge asset. We wondered, 'What framework, what platform will allow us to optimize the data that we have?'"

The team set out to find a new solution. "We could have gone the SAN route, but it's expensive and cumbersome," said the software engineer. They did some searching online and came across Hadoop, MongoDB, and Cassandra. "We analyzed them and came up with a prototype for each one. In the end, we decided Hadoop was what we wanted."

Initially the company downloaded Hadoop from Apache and configured it to run on 10 Dell workstations that were already in house. Once the small Hadoop cluster showed its functionality and demonstrated value, the team decided to make a commitment to the platform, but needed support to do so. When evaluating various Hadoop distributions and management vendors, they recognized that Cloudera was different: its Hadoop distribution — CDH — is a 100% Apache open source. This allows Cloudera customers to benefit from rapid innovations in the open source community while also taking advantage of enterprise-grade support and management tools offered with the Cloudera Enterprise subscription.

When deciding to deploy CDH, the team set out to identify applications that were already seeing performance issues in production. "One of the big advantages of Hadoop has been to be able to segregate Big Data from transactional processing data and allow smoother processing of information. Basically, it allows us to offload a lot of stress from the database," said the company's manager of software development.

They quickly identified two areas that were a strong fit for Hadoop:

- Archiving seven years' claims and remit data, which requires complex processing to get into a normalized format
- Logging terabytes of data generated from transactional systems daily, and storing them in CDH for analytical purposes

Today, the company uses Flume to move data from its source systems into the CDH cluster on a 24x7 basis. The company loads data from CDH to an Oracle Online Transaction Processing (OLTP) database for billing purposes. This load runs once or twice each day via Sqoop.

Impact: Helping Providers Collect Payment Faster through Operational Efficiencies

"If you look at the margin that the average hospital has, it's between 2-3%," stated the manager of software development. "So their cash flow is very tight. Anything you can do to reduce the time to get paid is very valuable to a healthcare provider."

Since deploying Cloudera Enterprise, the company has reduced the time it takes for healthcare providers to get paid by streamlining their transfer of messages to payers. The ability to expedite this process is especially valuable when regulatory changes come into play, such as the recent conversion from HIPAA 4010 to HIPAA 5010.

"We assist with the conversion and processing of these messages," said the company's manager of software development. "For example, 4010 messages came in and we'd convert them to 5010 to allow seamless processing. The providers didn't have to upgrade any of their systems when the regulations went into effect. We gave them a bit of a buffer to implement changes. And since we do a lot of electronic processing, we can do basic sanity checks on the messages as they come in and let providers know what adjustments need to be made in order to get paid faster."

Impact: Low Cost + Greater Analytic Flexibility

Because Hadoop uses industry standard hardware, the cost per terabyte of storage is, on average, 10 times cheaper than a traditional relational data warehouse system. "One of my pet peeves is: you buy a machine, you buy SAN storage, and then you have to buy licensing for the storage in addition to the storage itself," explained the manager of software development. "You have to buy licensing for the blades, and it just becomes an untenable situation. With Hadoop you buy commodity hardware and you're good to go. In addition to the storage, you get a bigger bang for your buck because it gives you the ability to run analytics on the combined compute and storage. The solutions that we had in place previously really didn't allow for that. Even if the costs were equivalent, the benefit you get from storing data on a Hadoop type solution is far greater than what you'd get from storing it in a database."

Impact: Simple Deployment & Administration

After deciding on the Cloudera solution, "the deployment process into production with Hadoop was actually quite easy," said a software engineer at the company. "Cloudera Manager really helped us a lot. It's as easy as just clicking a few buttons, and you're up and running. It's really simple. And the support staff at Cloudera have been great. They really helped us out with a couple of issues we had along the way." Further, this company appreciates the proactive customer support offered by Cloudera Enterprise.

Source: http://hadoopilluminated.com/hadoop_illuminated/cached_reports/Cloudera_Case_Study_Healthcare.pdf

Features of HDFS

Data replication, data resilience, and data integrity are the three key features of HDFS. You have already learned that HDFS allows replication of data; thus automatically providing resiliency to data in case of an unexpected loss or damage of the contents of any data or location. Additionally, data pipelines are also supported by HDFS. A block is written by a client application on the first DataNode in the pipeline. The DataNode then forwards the data block to the next connecting node in the pipeline, which further forwards the data block to the next node and so on. Once all the data replicas are written to the disk, the client writes the next block, which undergoes the same process. This feature is supported by Hadoop MapReduce.

When a file is divided into blocks and the replicated blocks are distributed throughout the different DataNodes of a cluster, the process requires careful execution as even a minute variation may result in corrupt data.

HDFS ensures data integrity throughout the cluster with the help of the following features:

- **Maintaining Transaction Logs**—HDFS maintains transaction logs in order to monitor every operation and carry out effective auditing and recovery of data in case something goes wrong.
- **Validating Checksum**—Checksum is an effective error-detection technique wherein a numerical value is assigned to a transmitted message on the basis of the number of bits contained in the message. HDFS uses checksum validations for verification of the content of a file. The validations are carried out as follows:

1. When a file is requested by a client, the contents are verified using checksum.
2. If the checksums of the received and sent messages match, the file operations proceed further; otherwise, an error is reported.
3. The message receiver verifies the checksum of the message to ensure that it is the same as in the sent message. If a difference is identified in the two values, the message is discarded assuming that it has been tempered with in transition. Checksum files are hidden to avoid tempering.

- **Creating Data Blocks—**HDFS maintains replicated copies of data blocks to avoid corruption of a file due to failure of a server. The degree of replication, the number of DataNodes in the cluster, and the specifications of the HDFS namespace are identified and implemented during the initial implementation of the cluster. However, these parameters can be adjusted any time during the operation of the cluster.

Data blocks are sometimes, also called **block servers.** A block server primarily stores data in a file system and maintains the metadata of a block. A block server carries out the following functions:

- Storage (and retrieval) of data on a local file system. HDFS supports different operating systems and provides similar performance on all of them.
- Storage of metadata of a block on the local file system on the basis of a similar template on the NameNode.
- Conduct of periodic validations for file checksums.
- Intimation about the availability of blocks to the NameNode by sending reports regularly.
- On-demand supply of metadata and data to the clients where client application programs can directly access DataNodes.
- Movement of data to connected nodes on the basis of the pipelining model.

NOTE

A connection between multiple DataNodes that supports movement of data across servers is termed as a pipeline.

The manner in which the blocks are placed on the DataNodes critically affect data replication and support for pipelining. HDFS primarily maintains one replica of each block locally. A second replica of the block is then placed on a different rack to guard against rack failure. A third replica is maintained on a different server of a remote rack. Finally additional replicas are sent to random locations in local and remote clusters.

However, without proper supervision, one DataNode may get overloaded with data while another is empty. To address and avoid these possibilities, HDFS has a rebalancer service that balances the load of data on the DataNodes. The rebalancer is executed when a cluster is running and can be halted to avoid congestion due to network traffic. The rebalancer provides an effective mechanism; however, it has not been designed to intelligently deal with every scenario. For instance, the rebalancer cannot optimize for access or load patterns. These features can be anticipated from further releases of HDFS.

The HDFS balancer rebalances data over the DataNodes, moving blocks from over-loaded to under-loaded nodes. System administrator can run the balancer from the command-line when new DataNodes are added to the cluster.

NOTE

- *Superuser of HDFS has the capabilities to run balancer.*
- *Balancer will not balance between individual volumes on single DataNode.*

The command to run the balancer is as follows:

```
sudo -u hdfs hdfs balancer
```

MapReduce

The algorithms developed and maintained by the Apache Hadoop project are implemented in the form of Hadoop MapReduce, which can be assumed analogous to an engine that takes data input, processes it, generates the output, and returns the required answers.

MapReduce is based on the parallel programming framework to process large amounts of data dispersed across different systems. The process is initiated when a user request is received to execute the MapReduce program and terminated once the results are written back to the HDFS.

Nowadays, organizations need to quickly analyze the huge amount of gathered data and information to make effective and smart decisions. MapReduce facilitates the processing and analyzing of both unstructured and semi-structured data collected from different sources, which may not be analyzed effectively by other traditional tools.

MapReduce enables computational processing of data stored in a file system without the requirement of loading the data initially into a database. It primarily supports two operations: map and reduce. These operations execute in parallel on a set of worker nodes. MapReduce works on a master/worker approach in which the master process controls and directs the entire activity, such as collecting, segregating, and delegating the data among different workers.

Figure 4.5 depicts the working of MapReduce:

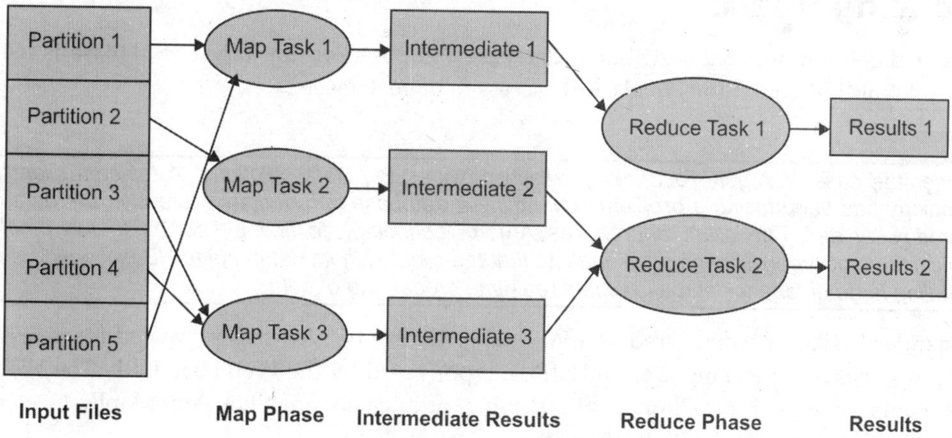

Figure 4.5: Working of MapReduce

The working of MapReduce can be summed up in the following steps:

1. A MapReduce worker receives data from the master, processes it, and sends back the generated result to the master.

2. MapReduce workers run the same code on the received data; however, they are not aware of other co-workers and do not communicate or interact with each other.
3. The master receives the results from each worker process, integrates and processes them, and generates the final output.

CASELET

Consider a case where Web logs are received as a steady stream, and then passed to various worker nodes for processing. A simple method to distribute and process incoming data blocks, in this case, is the round-robin procedure where every node receives the data packets sequentially. It can be further supported with some sort of hashing wherein data blocks are forwarded to workers on the basis of a formula so that the same worker receives similar data blocks. For example, implementing hashing on customer ID will direct all records of a particular customer to the same worker process.

Hadoop YARN

Job scheduling and tracking are primarily encoded in the functioning of Hadoop MapReduce. The early versions of Hadoop were accompanied with a rudimentary job and task-scheduling system. However, as the mix of work processed by Hadoop changed with time, the scheduler became obsolete.

The old scheduler was no more able to manage non-MapReduce jobs, and could not optimize cluster utilization. In order to address these shortcomings and provide more flexibility, efficiency, and performance boost, a new functionality was developed.

Yet Another Resource Negotiator (YARN) is a core Hadoop service that supports two major services Global resource management (ResourceManager) and Per-application management (ApplicationMaster). Global resource management (ResourceManager) and Per-application management (ApplicationMaster) have been discussed in detail in later chapters.

Introducing HBase

HBase is a column-oriented distributed database composed on top of HDFS. HBase is used when you need real-time continuous read/write access to huge datasets.

SCENARIO

Consider the case of Argon Technology, which provides Big Data solutions. A telecom client of Argon Technology has been facing a problem in handling a database in real time. Moreover, the data is getting bigger day by day. The client approaches Argon Technology to find a solution to the problem. The technical team at Argon Technology suggests that the client shift its database to HBase, which is proficient in handling large databases and allows fast real-time processing of data.

The standard HBase is considered as a Web table, a table of Web pages crawled (or accessed), and their properties (such as language and MIME type) keyed by the Web page URL. The Web table is large, containing over a billion rows. Parsing and batch analytics are MapReduce jobs that continuously run against the Web table.

These jobs derive statistics and add new columns of MIME type and parsed text content for later indexing by a search engine. Simultaneously, the Web table is accessed randomly by crawlers (search engines) running at various rates and updating random rows. The random pages in the Web table are served in real-time as users click on a website's cached-page feature.

Though there are innumerable techniques and implementations for database storage and recovery, most settings - particularly those with relational variety - are not constructed on a huge scale and allocation in mind. Most vendors offer replication and partition solutions to increase the database beyond the restrictions of a single node; yet these additional solutions are by and large an idea in retrospect and are complicated to install and maintain. Joins, triggers, complex queries, outside key requirements, and perspectives get to be incredibly expensive to run on a scaled RDBMS or do not work at all.

HBase takes the scaling issue head on and is constructed from the ground up scale just by adding nodes. HBase is not relational and thus does not support SQL, but it still has the capacity to do what an RDBMS cannot: host large, inadequately populated tables on clusters produced using appliance hardware.

HBase is one of the projects of Apache Software Foundation that is distributed under Apache Software License v2.0. It is a non-relational (columnar) database suitable for distributed environments and uses HDFS as its persistence storage. Modeled after **Google Big Table** (a way of storing non-relational data efficiently), HBase can host very large tables (billions of columns/rows). HBase facilitates reading/writing of Big Data randomly and efficiently in real time. It is highly configurable, allows efficient management of huge amount of data, and helps in dealing with Big Data challenges in many ways. It stores data into tables with rows and columns as in RDBMSs. The intersection of a row and column is called a cell. However, HBase tables have one key feature called versioning, which differentiates them from RDBMS tables. Each cell in an HBase table has an associated attribute termed as "version", which provides a timestamp to uniquely identify the cell. Versioning helps in keeping a track of the changes made in a cell and allows the retrieval of the previous version of the cell contents, if required.

HBase also provides various useful data processing features, such as scalability, persistence, sparseness, and support for distributed environments and multidimensional maps. HBase indexes are mapped with a row/column key pair and a timestamp. Each map value is represented by a continuous array of bytes. HBase also allows storage of results for later analytical processing.

HBase Architecture

Applications store information in labeled tables, and the values stored in table cells get updated from time to time. A cell's value is an unread array of bytes.

Keys in table rows are also byte arrays, so hypothetically anything can act as a row key. Table rows are categorized by the row key, which is the table's primary key. By default, the data type of the primary key is byte-ordered. All table access is via the table primary key.

Row/columns are clustered into column families. All family members of a column share a common prefix, e.g., the columns *java:android* and *java:servlets* are both members of the *java* family. The column family should consist of printable characters. The suffix can be made of any random bytes.

A table's column family members must be specified beforehand as an aspect of the table schema meaning, but new column family members can be added on a need basis. For example, a new column address:pincode can be provided by a client as part of an upgrade, and its value continued, as long as the column family exists in place on the targeted table.

Physically, all family members of a column are saved together on the file system. So, previously we described HBase as a column-oriented entity, but it would be more precise if it is described as a *column-family* oriented entity. Because storage requirements are fulfilled at the column family level, all column family members are recommended to have the same general access design and size features. In short, HBase tables are like the ones in RDBMS, with cells being versioned, sorted rows, and on-the-fly addition of columns as per the client's requirements.

Regions

Tables are automatically partitioned horizontally into regions by HBase. Each region consists of a subset of rows of a table. Initially, a table comprises a single region but as the size of the region grows, after it crosses a configurable size limit, it splits at the boundary of a row into two new regions of almost equal size, as shown in Figure 4.6:

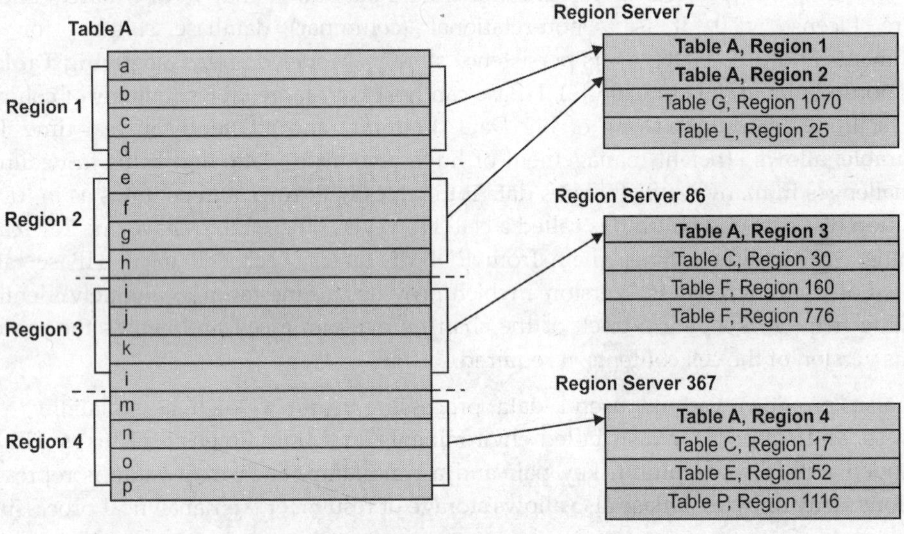

Figure 4.6: Displaying Regions in HBase

Regions are units that get spread over a cluster in HBase. Hence, a table too big for any single server can be carried by a cluster of servers with each node hosting a subset of all the regions of a table. This is also the medium by which the loading on a table gets spread. At a given time, the online group of sorted regions comprises the table's total content.

HBase persists data via the Hadoop file system API. There are multiple implementations of the file system interface—one each for the local file system, the KFS file system, Amazon's S3, and HDFS. HBase can persist to any of these implementations. By default, unless set otherwise, HBase writes into the local file system. The local file system is fine for experimenting with your initial HBase install, but thereafter, usually the first configuration made in an HBase cluster involves pointing HBase at the HDFS cluster to use.

Storing Big Data with HBase

HBase is a dispersed, non-relational (columnar) database that uses HDFS. It is designed according to Google Bigtable (a compressed, high performance proprietary data storage system built on the Google file system) and is equipped for facilitating extensive tables (billions of sections/columns) on the grounds that it is layered on Hadoop clusters of appliance hardware. HBase gives arbitrary, continuous read/write access to enormous information. It is exceptionally configurable, giving a lot of flexibility to address immense measures of information proficiently.

In HBase, all information is put away into tables with columns and sections like relational frameworks (RDBMS). The cell is known as an intersection of a row and column. One essential distinction between HBase tables and RDBMS tables is versioning. Each cell value consists of a version property, which is just a timestamp uniquely distinguishing the cell. Versioning tracks changes in the cell and makes it possible to retrieve any version of the contents, if required. HBase stores the information in cells in descending order (utilizing the timestamp), so a read will obviously find the newer values first.

Interacting with the Hadoop Ecosystem

Writing programs or using specialty query languages is not the only way you interact with the Hadoop ecosystem. IT teams that manage infrastructures need to control Hadoop and the Big Data applications created for it. As Big Data becomes mainstream, non-technical professionals will want to try to solve business problems with it.

Hadoop-supported business distributions are always showing signs of change. New tools and technologies are presented, existing technologies are enhanced, and a few innovations are replaced by better substitutions. This is one of the key advantages of open source. An alternate is the selection of open-source innovations or applications by business organizations. These organizations upgrade the applications, making them better for everybody at an economical cost. This is how the Hadoop ecosystem has developed and why it is a good decision for serving to tackle your enormous information challenges.

HBase in Operation – Programming with HBase

HBase keeps individual catalog tables internally, called `-ROOT-` and `.META.`, within which it maintains the current list, state, recent history, and location of all regions at the top of the cluster. The `-ROOT-` table has the list of `.META.` table regions. The `.META.` table has a list of all the regions in it. Entries in these tables are keyed utilizing the region's starting row. Column keys, as noted earlier, are sorted so discovering the region that has a specific row is a matter of a lookup to discover the first entry whose key is more noteworthy than or equivalent to that of the asked for row key. Figure 4.7 displays an HBase cluster:

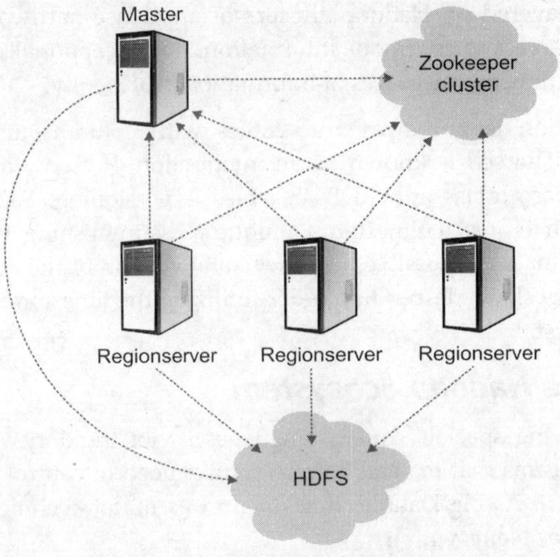

Source: *http://www.programering.com/a/MzNwgjNwATY.html*

Figure 4.7: Displaying an HBase Cluster

Fresh clients that connect to the ZooKeeper cluster need to first learn the location of the `-ROOT-` table. Clients consult `-ROOT-` to elicit the location of the `.META.` region, the scope of which covers the requested row. The client searches for the located `.META.` region to know the hosting region and its location. Thereafter, the client interacts directly with the hosting region-server.

To avoid making three round-trips per row operation, clients store all they learn while traversing `-ROOT-` and `.META.` caching locations as well as user-space region rows, so they can find hosting regions themselves without looking at the `.META.` table. As the clients work, they carry on using the cached entry, until there is a fault. When this happens, it means that the region has moved, and the client consults the `.META.` again to learn the new location. Therefore, if the contacted `.META.` region has moved, then `-ROOT-` is reconsulted.

Writes incoming at a region-server are first connected to a commit log file and then added to a cache. When the cache fills up, its content is moved to the file system. The log is stored on HDFS, so it stays available.

Combining HBase and HDFS

HBase's utilization of HDFS is different from how it is utilized by MapReduce. In MapReduce, by and large, HDFS documents are opened, their content streamed through a map task(which takes a set of data and converts it into another set of data), and are closed. In HBase, data files are opened on group startup and kept open so that the user does not have to pay the file open expenses on each access. Hence, HBase has a tendency to handle issues not commonly experienced by MapReduce clients, which are as follows:

- **File descriptors shortage**—Since we keep documents open on a loaded cluster, it doesn't take too long to run the documents on a framework. For example, we have a cluster having three hubs, each running an instance of a DataNode and region server, and we are performing an upload on a table that presently has 100 regions and 10 column families. Suppose every column family has two file records. In that case, we will have 100 × 10 × 2 = 2000 records open at any given time. Add to this the collective random descriptors consumed by good scanners, and Java libraries. Each open record devours no less than one descriptor on the remote DataNode. The default quantity of record descriptors is 1024.

- **Not many DataNode threads**—Essentially, the Hadoop DataNode has a higher limit of 256 threads it can run at any given time. Suppose we use the same table measurements cited earlier. It is not difficult to perceive how we can surpass this figure given in the DataNode since each open connection with a record piece consumes a thread. If you look in the DataNode log, you will see an error like xceivercount 258 limit exceeds point of simultaneous xcievers 256; therefore, you need to be careful in using the threads.

  Bad blocks—The Dfsclient class in the region server will have a tendency to mark document blocks as bad if the server is heavily loaded. Blocks can be recreated only three times. Therefore, the region server will proceed onward for the recreation of the blocks. But if this recreation is performed during a period of heavy loading, we will have two of the three blocks marked as bad. In the event that the third block is discovered to be bad, we will see an error, stating, No live hubs contain current block in region server logs. During startup, you may face many issues as regions are opened and deployed. At the worst case, set the dfs.datanode.socket.write.timeout property to zero. Do note that this configuration needs to be set in a location accessible to HBase Dfsclient; set it in the hbase-site.xml file or by linking the hadoop-site.xml (or hdfssite.xml) file to your HBase conf directory.
- **UI**—HBase runs a Web server on the master to present a perspective on the condition of your running cluster. It listens on port 60010 by default. The master UI shows a list of basic functions, e.g., software renditions, cluster load, request rates, list of group tables, and participant region servers. In the master UI, click a region server and you will be directed to the Web server running the individual region server. A list of regions carried by this server and metrics like consumed resources and request rate would be displayed.
- **Schema design**—HBase tables are similar to RDBMS tables, except that HBase tables have versioned cells, sorted rows, and columns. The other thing to keep in mind is that an important attribute of the column `(-family)`-oriented database, like HBase, is that it can host extensive and lightly populated tables at no extra incurred cost.
- **Row keys**—Spend a good time in defining your row key. It can be utilized for grouping information as a part of routes. If your keys are integers, utilize a binary representation instead of a persistent string form of a number as it requires lesser space.

Now, let's create a table in Hbase, insert data in it, and then perform a cleanup.

To create a table, you must define its schema. The schema has table attributes and a table column family list. Column families have properties that you set at the time of schema definition. The schemas can be revised later by putting the table off line using the disable command (shell), making the changes using the alter command, and then restoring the table with the enable command.

You can create a table with the name `test` having a single column family `-data-` by using the following command:

```
hbase(main):007:0> create 'test', 'data' 0  row(s) in 4.3066 seconds
```

To view if the creation of the new table was successful, run the list command. This displays all the existing tables, as follows:

```
hbase(main):019:0> list
test        1  row(s) in 0.1112 seconds
```

Insert data into different rows, and columns at the `data` column family, and then list the content, by using the following commands:

```
hbase(main):021:0> put 'test', 'row1', 'data:1', 'value1'
0  row(s) in 0.0454 seconds
hbase(main):022:0> put 'test', 'row2', 'data:2', 'value2'
0  row(s) in 0.0035 seconds
hbase(main):023:0> put 'test', 'row3', 'data:3', 'value3'
0  row(s) in 0.0090 seconds hbase(main):024:0> scan 'test'
ROW            COLUMN+CELL
row1           column=data:1, timestamp=1240148026198, value=value1
row2           column=data:2, timestamp=1240148040035, value=value2
row3           column=data:3, timestamp=1240148047497, value=value3
              3  row(s) in 0.0825 seconds
```

To remove a table, you must first disable it, as follows:

```
hbase(main):025:0> disable 'test'
15/02/15 06:40:13 INFO client.HBaseAdmin: Disabled test
0  row(s) in 6.0426 seconds hbase(main):026:0> drop 'test'
15 /02/10 06:40:17 INFO client.HBaseAdmin: Deleted test
0  row(s) in 0.0210 seconds
hbase(main):027:0> list 0  row(s) in 2.0645 seconds
```

Shut down your HBase instance by running the following command:

```
% stop-hbase.sh
```

HBase is written in Java. Its classes and utilities are included in the `org.apache.hadoop.hbase.mapred` package, aided by using HBase in MapReduce jobs as a source. The `TableInputFormat` class splits the region borders, so maps are assigned a single region to work. The `TableOutputFormat` class writes the reduce result in HBase. The `RowCounter` class runs a map task using `TableInputFormat`, for counting rows. This class implements the Tool and HBase TableMap interfaces, as well as the `org.apache.hadoop.mapred.Mapper` interface, which sets the map inputs types passed by using the table input format. The `createSubmittableJob()` method analyses the added arguments command line configuration and estimates the table and columns we are to run using the `RowCounter` class. It also invokes the `TableMapReduceUtil.initTableMap Job()` utility method and sets the input format to `TableInputFormat`. MapReduce checks all the columns. In case some are found to be empty, it does not count the related rows; otherwise, it increments the `Counters.ROWS` property by one.

REST and Thrift

HBase contains the REST and Thrift interfaces, which are used when the interacting application is written in a language other than Java. In both cases, a Java server hosts the HBase instance, and the REST and thrift interfaces request for HBase storage. This extra work makes these interfaces slower than the Java client.

You can start REST by using the following command:

```
% hbase-daemon.sh start rest
```

This command starts a server instance, on the default port 60050, in the background, and catches any output by the server into a log file in the HBase *logs* directory.

Clients can ask for a response to be formatted as JSON or as XML, depending on how the client *HTTP Accept* header is set. You can stop the REST server by using the following command:

```
% hbase-daemon.sh stop rest
```

Similarly, you can start Thrift by running the following command:

```
% hbase-daemon.sh start thrift
```

This will start the Thrift instance on the default port 9090, in the background, and catch any output by Thrift in a log file in the HBase logs directory.

You can stop Thrift by using the following command:

```
% hbase-daemon.sh stop thrift
```

Figure 4.8 shows the mechanism of writing data to HDFS:

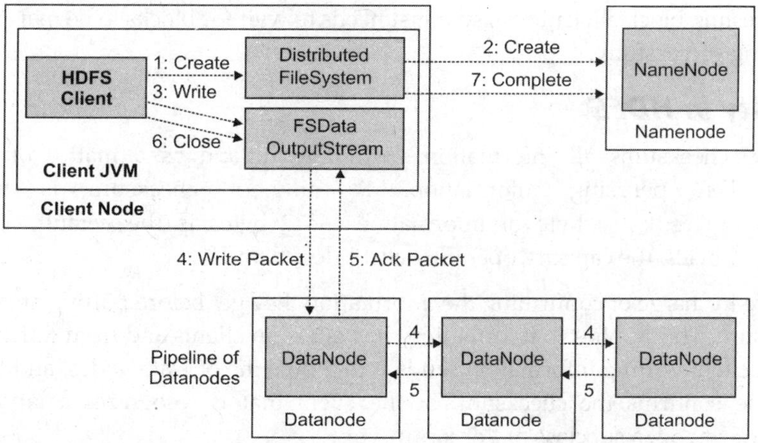

Source: *http://hadoopguide.blogspot.in/2013/05/hadoop-hdfs-data-flow-io-classes.html*

Figure 4.8: Displaying the Process of Writing Data to HDFS

As shown in Figure 4.8, the client creates a record by calling the `make()` function on a distributed file system (step 1). The distributed file system makes a RPC call to the NameNode to make another record in the file system's namespace, with no pieces connected with it (step 2). The NameNode performs different checks to verify that the document doesn't currently exist, and that the client has the right contents to create the record. After passing these checks, the NameNode creates a record of the new document. Generally, the `Fsdataoutputstream` class encapsulates the `Dfsoutput` stream like in the read case, which manages the correspondence with the data as well as the NameNodes.

As the client composes information (step 3), `Dfsoutputstream` splits it into fragments, called the data queue. The information line is consumed by the `DataStreamer` class, whose obligation is to ask the NameNode to dispense new blocks by picking suitable DataNodes to store the copy. The DataNodes are structured in a pipeline, so there are three hubs in the pipeline. The `DataStreamer` class streams the packages in the first DataNode of the pipeline, where the packet is stored, and advances it to the second DataNode in the pipeline. Also, the second DataNode stores the packet and advances it to the third (and last) DataNode in the pipeline (step 4). The `Dfsoutputstream` class additionally keeps an internal queue of packets that are waiting to be recognized by DataNodes, called the ack queue. A packet is expelled from the ack line just when it has been recognized by all the DataNodes in the pipeline (step 5).

In the event that a DataNode fails while information is being written to it, the pipeline is shut, and any packets in the ack line (step 5) are added to the front of the data line so that DataNodes that are downstream from the failure hub will not miss any packets. The present block of the good DataNodes is given a new identity, which is conveyed to the NameNode, so that the partial block on the failed DataNode is erased. The failed DataNode is expelled from the pipeline, and the rest of the block's information is written to the two good DataNodes in the pipeline.

At the point when the client has completed the process of writing information, on stream, it calls the `close ()` function (step 6). This activity pushes all the remaining packets to the DataNode pipeline and waits for affirmations before reaching the NameNode to signify that the work on the records is completed (step 7). The NameNode knows which blocks the document is made up of (through Data Streamer requesting block allocations), so it just needs to wait for blocks to be marginally reproduced before returning successfully.

Data Integrity in HDFS

HDFS directly checksums all information written to it, and as a matter of course, confirms checksums when perusing information. A different checksum is made for each `io.bytes.per.checksum` byte of information - 512 bytes is the default, and since CRC-32 checksum is of 4 bytes, the capacity operating cost is less than 1%.

DataNodes are in charge of confirming the information they get before putting away the information and its checksum. This applies to information they get from clients and from different DataNodes in replication. A client writing information sends it to a pipeline of DataNodes, and the last DataNode in the pipeline confirms the checksum. In the event that it recognizes a lapse, the client gets `Checksumexception`, a subclass of `Ioexception`.

When clients read information from DataNodes, they check checksums also, looking at them with the ones put away at the DataNode. Every DataNode keeps a determined log of checksum confirmations, so it knows when each of its blocks was last confirmed. At the point when a client effectively confirms a block, it tells the DataNode, which overhauls its log. This action is profitable in detecting bad disks.

Every DataNode runs a Datablockscanner in a background thread that occasionally checks all the blocks put away on the DataNode. This is to prepare for debasement because of "bit decay" in the physical storage media.

Since HDFS stores imitations of pieces, it can "repair" corrupted blocks by replicating one of the good copies to deliver another, uncorrupted copy. The way this works is that if a client identifies an error when examining a piece, the client reports the bad block in the related file system before throwing the `Checksumexception` exception. The NameNode marks the block copy as corrupt, so it doesn't forward clients to it. It then schedules the block to be duplicated on an alternate DataNode.

It is possible to disable checksum verifications by passing false to the setverify `Checksum()` method on the related file system, before utilizing the `open()` system to peruse a record. The same impact is possible from the shell by utilizing the `-ignorecrc` choice with the -get or equal `-copytolocal` charge. This feature is useful when you have a corrupt document that you need to assess so you can choose what to do with it.

NOTE

HBase stores data in column-oriented fashion instead of the record storage pattern as done in RDBMS.

Features of HBase

Some of the main features of HBase are:

- **Consistency**—In spite of not being an ACID implementation, HBase supports consistent read and write operations. This makes HBase suitable for high-speed requirements where RDBMS-supported extra features, such as full transaction support or typed columns, are not required.
- **Sharding**—HBase allows distribution of data using an underlying file system and supports transparent, and automatic splitting and redistribution of content.
- **High availability**—HBase implements region servers to ensure the recovery of LAN and WAN operations in case of a failure. The master server at the core monitors the regional servers and manages all the metadata for the cluster.
- **Client API**—HBase supports programmatic access using Java APIs.
- **Support for IT operations**—HBase provides a set of built-in Web pages to view detailed operational insights about the system.

NOTE

ACID stands for Atomicity, Consistency, Isolation, and Durability. It is a set of properties that ensures reliable processing of database transactions.

HBase implementations are most suitable in situations where:

- Gathering and processing of high volume, incremental data is required
- Real-time information processing and exchange take place
- Content changes at frequent intervals

EXHIBIT 2: Nokia: Using Big Data to Bridge the Virtual & Physical Worlds

Company Overview

Nokia has been in business for more than 150 years, starting with the production of paper in the 1800s and evolving into a leader in mobile and location services that connects more than 1.3 billion people today. Nokia has always transformed resources into useful products — from rubber and paper, to electronics and mobile devices — and today's resource, which is data.

Nokia's goal is to bring the world to the third phase of mobility: leveraging digital data to make it easier to navigate the physical world. To achieve this goal, Nokia needed to find a technology solution that would support the collection, storage, and analysis of virtually unlimited data types and volumes.

Use Case

Effective collection and use of data have become central to Nokia's ability to understand and improve users' experiences with their phones and other location products. "Nokia differentiates itself based on the data we have," stated Amy O'Connor, Senior Director of Analytics at Nokia. The company leverages data processing and complex analyses in order to build maps with predictive traffic and layered elevation models, to source information about points of interest around the world, to understand the quality of phones, and more.

To grow and support its extensive use of Big Data, Nokia relies on a technology ecosystem that includes a Teradata Enterprise Data Warehouse (EDW), numerous Oracle and MySQL data marts, visualization technologies, and at its core: Hadoop. Nokia has over 100 terabytes (TB) of structured data on Teradata and petabytes (PB) of multi-structured data on the Hadoop Distributed File System (HDFS), running on Dell PowerEdge servers. The centralized Hadoop cluster that lies at the heart of Nokia's infrastructure contains .5 PB of data. Nokia's data warehouses and marts continuously stream multi-structured data into a multi-tenant Hadoop environment, allowing the company's 60,000+ employees to access the data. Nokia runs hundreds of thousands of Scribe processes each day to efficiently move data from, for example, servers in Singapore to a Hadoop cluster in the UK data center. The company uses Sqoop to move data from HDFS to Oracle and/or Teradata. And Nokia serves data out of Hadoop through HBase.

Business Challenges before Hadoop

Prior to deploying Hadoop, numerous groups within Nokia were building application silos to accommodate their individual needs. It didn't take long before the company realized it could derive greater value from its collective data sets if these application silos could be integrated, enabling all globally captured data to be cross-referenced for a single, comprehensive version of truth.

"We were inventorying all of our applications and data sets," O'Connor noted. *"Our goal was to end up with a single data asset."*

Nokia wanted to understand at a holistic level how people interact with different applications around the world, which required them to implement an infrastructure that could support daily, terabyte-scale streams of unstructured data from phones in use, services, log files, and other sources. Leveraging this data also requires complex processing and computation to be consumable and useful for a variety of uses, like gleaning market insights, or understanding collective behaviors of groups; some aggregations of that data also need to be easily migrated to more structured environments in order to leverage specific analytic tools.

However, capturing petabyte-scale data using a relational database was cost prohibitive and would limit the types of data that could be ingested.

"We knew we'd break the bank trying to capture all this unstructured data in a structured environment," O'Connor said.

Because Hadoop uses industry standard hardware, the cost per terabyte of storage is, on average, 10 times cheaper than a traditional relational data warehouse system. Additionally, unstructured data must be reformatted to fit into a relational schema before it can be loaded into the system. This requires an extra data processing step that slows ingestion, creates latency and eliminates elements of the data that could become important down the road.

Various groups of engineers at Nokia had already begun experimenting with Apache Hadoop, and a few were using Cloudera's Distribution Including Apache Hadoop (CDH). The benefits of Hadoop were clear — it offers reliable, cost-effective data storage and high performance parallel processing of multi-structured data at petabyte scale — however, the rapidly evolving platform and tools designed to support and enable it are complex and can be difficult to deploy in production. CDH simplifies this process, bundling the most popular open source projects in the Apache Hadoop stack into a single, integrated package with steady and reliable releases.

After experimenting with CDH for several months, the company decided to standardize the use of the Hadoop platform to be the cornerstone of its technology ecosystem. With limited Hadoop expertise in-house, Nokia turned to Cloudera to augment their internal engineering team with strategic technical support and global training services, giving them the confidence with expertise necessary to deploy a very large production Hadoop environment in a short timeframe.

Impact

In 2011, Nokia put its central CDH cluster into production to serve as the company's enterprise-wide information core. Cloudera supported the deployment from start to finish, ensuring the cluster was successfully integrated with other Hadoop clusters and relational technologies for maximum reliability and performance.

Nokia is now using Hadoop to push the analytics, creating 3D digital maps that incorporate traffic models that understand speed categories, recent speeds on roads, historical traffic models, elevation, ongoing events, video streams of the world, and more.

"Hadoop is absolutely mission critical for Nokia. It would have been extremely difficult for us to build traffic models or any of our mapping content without the scalability and flexibility that Hadoop offers," O'Connor explained. "We can now understand how people interact with the apps on their phones to view usage patterns across applications. We can ask things like, 'Which feature did they go to after this one?' and 'Where did they seem to get lost?' This has all been enabled by Hadoop, and we wouldn't have gotten our Big Data platform to where it is today without Cloudera's platform, expertise and support."

Source: *http://hadoopilluminated.com/hadoop_illuminated/cached_reports/Cloudera_Nokia_Case_Study_Hadoop.pdf*

Hive

Hive is a data-warehousing layer created with the core elements of Hadoop (HDFS and MapReduce) to support batch-oriented processes. It exposes a simple SQL-like implementation called HiveQL for easy interaction along with access via mappers and reducers. In this manner, Hive provides the best of both worlds with an SQL-like access to structured data and sophisticated analysis of Big Data using MapReduce. Hive looks somewhat similar to traditional database. Hive uses map-reduce operations over Hadoop ecosystem, and there are many differences between Hive and traditional SQL. Hive has not been designed for quickly addressing queries, like other data warehouses. In fact, query processing and execution in Hive may take several hours depending on the complexity involved. On the other hand, Hive is used effectively for data mining and intense analysis, which does not involve real-time processing. Since Hive works on underlying Hadoop functions, it is scalable, resilient, and extensible.

Pig and Pig Latin

The official website of Hadoop, *http://hadoop.apache.org/*, defines Pig as "a platform for analyzing large data sets that consists of a high-level language for expressing data analysis programs, coupled with infrastructure for evaluating these programs. The salient property of Pig programs is that their structure is amenable to substantial parallelization, which in turns enables them to handle very large data sets."

Pig is used as an ELT tool for Hadoop. It makes Hadoop more approachable and usable for non-technical persons. It opens an interactive and script-based execution environment for non-developers with its language, Pig Latin. Pig Latin loads and processes input data using a series of operations and transforms that data to produce the desired output.

Sqoop

Sqoop (SQL-to-Hadoop) is a tool used for data transfer between Hadoop and relational databases. Critical processes are employed by MapReduce to move data into Hadoop and back to other data sources.

Similar to Pig, Sqoop is also a command-line interpreter, which sequentially executes Sqoop commands. Sqoop can be effectively used by non-programmers as well and relies on underlying technologies like HDFS and MapReduce.

ZooKeeper

Hadoop works by the divide-and-conquer approach. Once a problem is divided, it is approached and processed by using distributed and parallel processing techniques across Hadoop clusters. In case of Big Data problems, traditional interactive tools do not provide enough insight or timelines required to take business decisions. In that case, Big Data problems are approached with distributed applications. ZooKeeper helps in coordinating all the elements of the distributed applications.

Flume

Apache Flume aids in transferring large amounts of data from distributed resources to a single centralized repository. It is robust and fault tolerant, and efficiently collects, assembles, and transfers data. Flume is used for real-time data capturing in Hadoop. It can be applied to assemble a wide variety of data such as network traffic, data generated via social networking, business transaction data, and emails. The simple and extensible data model of Flume facilitates fast online data analytics.

As an implied tool, Flume covers a wide range of common requirements for transferring data into HDFS. It is a very popular system for moving large amounts of streaming data into HDFS. A common case where Flume can be applied is of collecting the log data from different systems, and collecting the aggregated data into HDFS for later analysis. Flume is also used for collecting data from various social media websites such as Twitter and Facebook.

Oozie

Oozie is an open-source Apache Hadoop service used to manage and process submitted jobs. It supports the workflow/coordination model and is highly extensible and scalable. Oozie is a dataware service that coordinates dependencies among different jobs executing on different platforms of Hadoop, such as HDFS, Pig, and MapReduce.

Hive, Pig and Pig Latin, Sqoop, ZooKeeper, Flume, and Oozie have been discussed in detail in further chapters.

Summary

In this chapter, you have learned about the Hadoop ecosystem and explored its major components. We have discussed various aspects of data storage in Hadoop. In the beginning, it has introduced HDFS and its architecture. After that, it has described HDFS files and Hadoop-specific file types. Next, the chapter has explained HBase and its architecture. The chapter has also shown the procedure of installing HDFS in a system. In addition, you have learned how to combine HBase with HDFS. We have learned the other components like MapReduce, YARN, HBase, and Hive. The chapter has also discussed various tools used to interact with the Hadoop ecosystem including, Pig and Pig Latin, Sqoop, ZooKeeper, Flume, and Oozie.

Quick Revise

Multiple-Choice Questions

Q1. Which of the following terms is used to denote the small subsets of a large file created by HDFS?

a. NameNode

b. DataNode

c. Blocks

d. Namespace

Ans. The correct option is c.

Q2. What message is generated by a DataNode to indicate its connectivity with NameNode?

a. Beep
b. Heartbeat
c. Analog pulse
d. Map

Ans. The correct option is b.

Q3. Which of the following defines metadata?

a. Data about data
b. Data from Web logs
c. Data from government sources
d. Data from market surveys

Ans. The correct option is a.

Q4. Which of the following is managed by the MapReduce environment?

a. Web logs
b. Images
c. Structured data
d. Unstructured data

Ans. The correct option is d.

Q5. Which of the following services is provided by YARN?

a. Global resource management
b. Record reader
c. MapReduce engine
d. Data mining

Ans. The correct option is a.

Q6. In an HDFS cluster, _______ manages cluster metadata.

a. NameNode
b. DataNode
c. Inode
d. Namespace

Ans. The correct option is a.

Q7. Which of the following commands of HDFS can issue directives to blocks?

a. fcsk
b. fkcs
c. fsck
d. fkcs

Ans. The correct option is c.

Q8. Which of the following file systems provides read-only access to HDFS over HTTPS?

a. HAR
b. HDFS
c. HFTP
d. HSFTP

Ans. The correct option is d.

Subjective Questions

Q1. Write a short note on the Hadoop ecosystem.

Ans. The Hadoop ecosystem is a framework of various types of complex and evolving tools and components. Some of these elements may be very different from each other in terms of their architecture; however, what keeps them all together under a single roof is that they all derive their functionalities from the scalability and power of Hadoop. In simple words, the Hadoop ecosystem can be defined as a comprehensive collection of tools and technologies that can be effectively implemented and deployed to provide Big Data solutions in a cost-effective manner.

MapReduce and **Hadoop distributed File System (HDFS)** are two core components of the Hadoop ecosystem that provide a great starting point to manage Big Data; however, they are not sufficient to deal with the Big Data challenges. Along with these two, the Hadoop ecosystem provides a collection of various elements to support the complete development and deployment of Big Data solutions.

Q2. What is metadata? What information does it provide?

Ans. Metadata refers to data about data. It acts as a template that provides the following information:

- The time of creation, last access, modification, and deletion of a file
- The storage location of the blocks of files on a cluster
- The access permissions to view and modify a file
- The number of files stored on a cluster
- The number of DataNodes connected to form a cluster
- The location of the transaction log on a cluster

Q3. How does HDFS ensure data integrity in a Hadoop cluster?

Ans. HDFS ensures data integrity throughout the cluster with the help of the following features:

- **Maintaining Transaction Logs**—HDFS maintains transaction logs in order to monitor every operation and carry out effective auditing and recovery of data in case something goes wrong.

- **Validating Checksum**—Checksum is an effective error-detection technique wherein a numerical value is assigned to a transmitted message on the basis of the number of bits contained in the message. HDFS uses checksum validations for verification of the content of a file. The validations are carried out as follows:

  1. When a file is requested by a client, the contents are verified using checksum.
  2. If the checksums of the received and sent messages match, the file operations proceed further; otherwise, an error is reported.
  3. The message receiver verifies the checksum of the message to ensure that it is the same as in the sent message. If a difference is identified in the two values, the message is discarded assuming that it has been tempered in transition. Checksum files are hidden to avoid tempering.

- **Creating Data Blocks**—HDFS maintains replicated copies of data blocks to avoid corruption of a file due to failure of a server. The degree of replication, the number of DataNodes in the cluster, and the specifications of the HDFS namespace are identified and implemented during the initial implementation of the cluster. However, these parameters can be adjusted any time during the operation of the cluster.

Data blocks are sometimes, also called block servers. A block server primarily stores data in a file system and maintains metadata of a block. A block server carries out the following functions:

- Storage (and retrieval) of data on a local file system. HDFS supports different operating systems and provides similar performance on all of them.
- Storage of metadata of a block on the local file system on the basis of similar template on the NameNode.
- Conduction of periodic validations for file checksums.
- Intimation about the availability of blocks to the NameNode by sending reports regularly.
- On-demand supply of metadata and data to the clients where client application programs can directly access DataNodes.
- Movement of data to connected nodes on the basis of the pipelining model.

Q4. Discuss the working of MapReduce.

Ans. MapReduce enables computational processing of data stored in a file system without the requirement of loading the data initially into a database. It primarily supports two operations: map and reduce. These operations execute in parallel on a set of worker nodes. MapReduce works on a master/worker approach in which the master process controls and directs the entire activity, such as collecting, segregating, and delegating the data among different workers.

The following figure depicts the working of MapReduce:

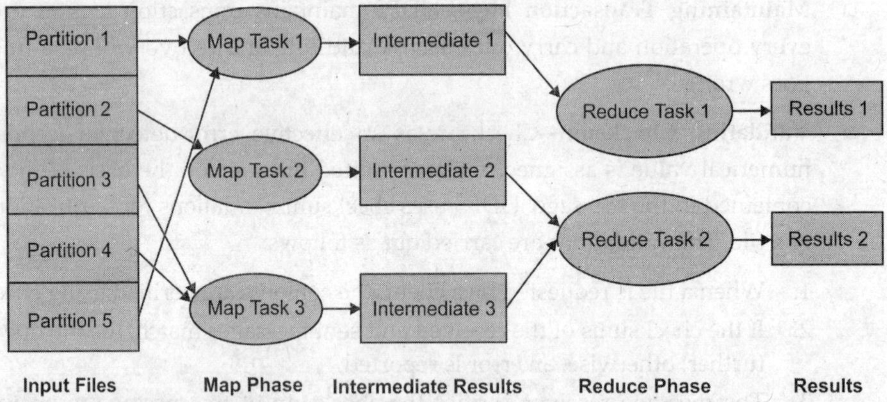

The working of MapReduce can be summed up in the following steps:

1. A MapReduce worker receives data from the master, processes it, and sends back the generated result to the master.
2. MapReduce workers run the same code on the received data; however, they are not aware about other co-workers and do not communicate or interact with each other.
3. The master receives the results from each worker process, integrates the results received, processes the integrated result, and generates the final output.

Q5. Discuss the following terms:

- **Streaming information access**
- **Low-latency information access**

Ans. **Streaming information access**—HDFS is created for batch processing. The priority is given to high throughput to data access rather than the low latency of data access. A dataset is commonly produced or replicated from the source, and then various analyses are performed on that dataset in the long run. Every analysis is done in detail and hence time consuming, so the time required for examining the entire dataset is quite high.

Low-latency information access—Applications that permit access to information in milliseconds do not function well with HDFS. Therefore, HDFS is upgraded for conveying a high transaction volume of information, and this may be at the expense of idleness. HBase is at present a superior choice for low latency access.

Q6. What is the role of NameNode in an HDFS cluster?

Ans. HDFS cluster has two node types working in a slave master design: a NameNode (the master) and various DataNodes (slaves). The NameNode deals with the file system. It stores the metadata for all the documents and indexes in the file system. This metadata is stored on the local disk as two files: the file system image and the edit log. The NameNode is aware of the DataNodes on which all the pieces of a given document are found; however, it doesn't store block locations necessarily, since this data is recreated from DataNodes.

A client accesses the file system on behalf of the user by communicating with the DataNodes and the NameNode. The client provides a file system, like the POSIX interface, so the user code does not require the NameNode and DataNodes in order to execute.

Q7. What is HBase?

Ans. HBase is a column-oriented distributed database composed on top of HDFS. HBase is the Hadoop application used when you need real-time continuous read/write access to huge datasets. Consider a case of Argon Technology, which provides Big Data solutions. A telecom client of Argon Technology has been facing a problem in handling a database in real time. Moreover, the data is getting bigger day by day. The client approaches Argon Technology to find a solution to the problem. The technical team at Argon Technology suggests that the client shift its database to HBase, which is proficient in handling large databases and allows fast real-time processing of data.

The standard HBase is considered as a Web table, a table of Web pages crawled (or accessed) and their properties (such as language and MIME type) keyed by the Web page URL. The Web table is large, containing over a billion rows. Parsing and batch analytics are MapReduce jobs that continuously run against the Web table. These jobs derive statistics and add new columns of the MIME type and parsed text content for later indexing by a search engine. Simultaneously, the Web table is accessed randomly by crawlers (search engines) running at various rates and updating random rows. The random pages in the Web table are served in real-time as users click on a website's cached-page feature.

Q8. Discuss the concept of regions in HBase.

Ans. Tables are automatically partitioned horizontally into regions by HBase. Each region consists of a subset of rows of a table. Initially, a table comprises a single region but as the size of the region grows, after it crosses a configurable size limit, it splits at the boundary of a row into two new regions of almost equal size, as shown in the following figure:

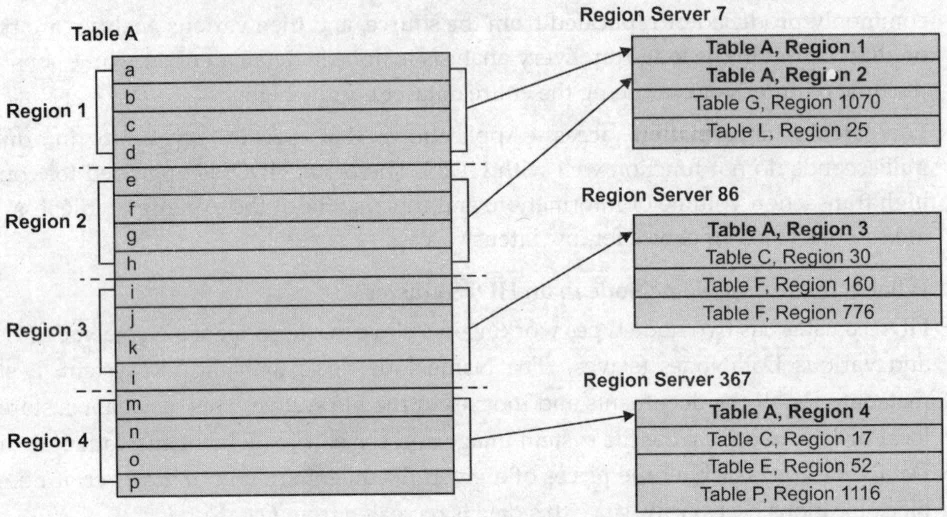

Regions are units that get spread over a cluster in HBase. Hence, a table too big for any single server can be carried by a cluster of servers with each node hosting a subset of the total regions of a table. This is also the medium by which the loading on a table gets spread. At a given time, the online group of sorted regions comprises the table's total content.

5

Understanding MapReduce Fundamentals and HBase

Over the last few years, Big Data has been a headline-grabbing advancement in the fastest growing field of Information Technology (IT). Big Data analysis involves processing huge amounts of data, which is not a very new thing in the field of computers and IT. Computers have evolved overtime in terms of their speed of processing, their capability to handle more and more data, and advanced technologies. However, thc requirements of effective and faster processing have also grown with each evolution. The advent of Local Area Networks (LANs) and other networking technologies shifted the focus of IT industry toward solving bigger and bigger problems by combining computing and storing capacities of systems on the network. Nowadays, applications involving intense calculations on large amounts of data are distributed across the connected systems. To handle these computations, various new approaches have been developed, and one of these approaches is MapReduce, which assists in processing data in a parallel manner by integrating different functions as a single software framework. Developers can utilize this platform to write programs that can process large amounts of data (structured, semi-structured or unstructured data) by using a number of distributed processors simultaneously.

This chapter focuses on explaining the basics and exploring the relevance and role of various functions that are used in the MapReduce framework. Here, you learn about the working of the map and reduce functions, which form the core of the MapReduce algorithm. The chapter next discusses various techniques used to draw maximum benefits from the MapReduce approach. Finally, the chapter introduces you to HBase, discusses its use in connection with the MapReduce programming model, and explains the process of its installation.

SCENARIO

Mr. Richard Paul, the Vice President (Operations) of Argon Technology, wants to view customer feedbacks about the company's services. The feedbacks are recorded in log files, which need to be parsed on the basis of different words appearing in the file so that the sentiments can be analyzed. The VP finds that the MapReduce programming can help in parsing the text and providing the output in a structured format. He tells the members of his team about MapReduce, its different features, and the way it works.

The MapReduce Framework

At the start of the 21st century, the team of engineers working with Google concluded that because of the increasing number of Internet users, the resources and solutions available would be inadequate to fulfill the future requirements. As a preparation to the upcoming issue, Google engineers established that the concept of task distribution across economical resources, and their interconnectivity as a cluster over the network, can be presented as a solution. The concept of task distribution, though, could not be a complete answer to the issue, which requires the tasks to be distributed in parallel. A parallel distribution of tasks:

- Helps in automatic expansion and contraction of processes
- Enables continuation of processes without being affected by network failures or individual system failures
- Empowers developers with rights to access the services that other developers have created in context of multiple usage scenarios

In addition to the task distribution concept, location independence in terms of data and applications working on the data was also a necessity. A generic implementation to the entire concept was, therefore, provided with the development of the MapReduce programming model. The name, MapReduce, is effectively and practically a combination of the two capabilities of the existing computer languages. These capabilities are map and reduce. The MapReduce implementations have evolved over the years to be available both as commercial products and open-source models.

NOTE

The map and reduce functions are operators that do not modify the original data. Instead, create new data structures to display their output. Thus, these functions do not affect the stored data.

Exploring the Features of MapReduce

MapReduce keeps all the processing operations separate for parallel execution. Problems that are extremely large in size are divided into subtasks, which are chunks of data separated in manageable blocks. The subtasks are executed independently from each other and then, the results from all independent executions are combined to provide the complete output.

The principal features of MapReduce include the following:

- **Scheduling**—MapReduce involves two operations: map and reduce, which are executed by dividing large problems into smaller chunks. These chunks are run in parallel by different computing resources. The operation of breaking tasks into subtasks and running these subtasks independently in parallel is called mapping, which is performed ahead of the reduce operation. The mapping operation requires task prioritization based on the number of nodes in the cluster. In case nodes are fewer than tasks, then tasks are executed on a priority basis. The reduction operation cannot be performed until the entire mapping operation is completed. The reduction operation then merges independent results on the basis of priority. Hence, the MapReduce programming model requires scheduling of tasks.
- **Synchronization**—Execution of several concurrent processes requires synchronization. The MapReduce program execution framework is aware of the mapping and reducing operations that are taking place in the program. The framework tracks all the tasks along with their timings and starts the reduction process after the completion of mapping. A method known as shuffle and sort produces the intermediate data, which is transmitted across the network. The shuffle and sort mechanism is used for collecting the mapped data and preparing it for reduction.
- **Co-location of Code/Data (Data Locality)**—The effectiveness of a data processing mechanism depends largely on the location of the code and the data required for the code to execute. The best result is obtained when both code and data reside on the same machine. This means that the co-location of the code and data produces the most effective processing outcome.
- **Handling of Errors/Faults**—MapReduce engines usually provide a high level of fault tolerance and robustness in handling errors. The reason for providing robustness to these engines is their high propensity to make errors or faults. There are high chances of failure in clustered nodes on which different parts of a program are running. Therefore, the MapReduce engine must have the capability of recognizing the fault and rectify it. Moreover, the MapReduce engine design involves the ability to find out the tasks that are incomplete and eventually assign them to different nodes.

- **Scale-Out Architecture**—MapReduce engines are built in such a way that they can accommodate more machines, as and when required. This possibility of introducing more computing resources to the architecture makes the MapReduce programming model more suited to the higher computational demands of Big Data.

Working of MapReduce

We all know that different types of operations are performed on the input data to generate outputs. The original dataset, however, must remain the same while performing these operations. The data analysis operations must not destroy the data in any case, because the input data is not accessible to the user all the time. Any changes in the input data might disable the user from using the same dataset for other computations or purposes.

Applications to handle data are designed by software professionals on the basis of algorithms, which are stepwise processes to solve a problem or achieve a goal. The MapReduce programming model also works on an algorithm to execute the map and reduce operations. This algorithm can be depicted as follows:

1. Take a large dataset or set of records.
2. Perform iteration over the data.
3. Extract some interesting patterns to prepare an output list by using the map function.
4. Arrange the output list properly to enable optimization for further processing.
5. Compute a set of results by using the reduce function.
6. Provide the final output.

The MapReduce approach of analyzing data can be used by programmers for implementing various kinds of applications. This algorithm can also work with extremely large datasets, ranging from hundreds of gigabytes to few terabytes, or even beyond.

To sum up the things we have learned till now, the MapReduce model executes a given task by dividing it into two functions, map and reduce. The map function is executed first in parallel on different machines. The reduce function takes the output of the map function to present the final output in an aggregate form. The working of the MapReduce approach is shown in Figure 5.1:

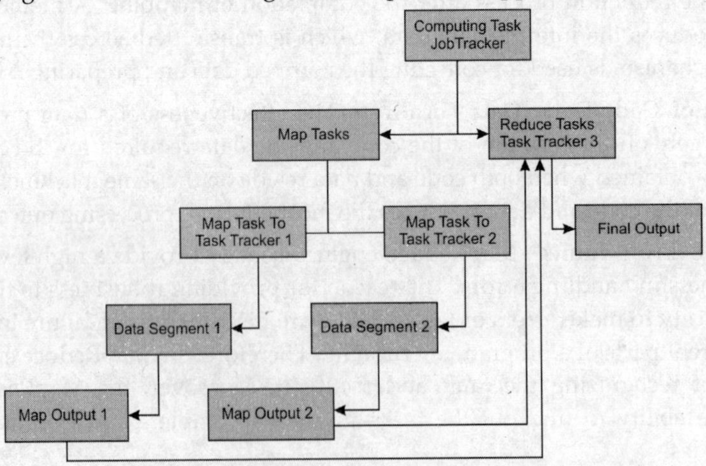

Figure 5.1: Working of the MapReduce Approach

The MapReduce framework, shown in Figure 5.1, is a combination of a master and three slaves. The master monitors the entire job assigned to the MapReduce algorithm and is given the name of JobTracker. Slaves, on the other hand, are responsible for keeping track of individual tasks and are called TaskTrackers. First, the given job is divided into a number of tasks by the master, i.e., the JobTracker, which then distributes these tasks into slaves. It is the responsibility of the JobTracker to further keep an eye on the processing activities and the re-execution of the failed tasks. Slaves coordinate with the master by executing the tasks they are given by the master.

The JobTracker receives jobs from client applications to process large information. These jobs are assigned in the forms of individual tasks (after a job is divided into smaller parts) to various TaskTrackers. The task distribution operation is completed by the JobTracker. The data after being processed by TaskTrackers is transmitted to the reduce function so that the final, integrated output, which is an aggregate of the data processed by the map function, can be provided.

A cluster uses commodity servers to store nodes. The data processing job is accomplished through MapReduce and Hadoop Distributed File System (HDFS), which are based on these nodes.

The logical flow of data in the MapReduce programming framework is shown in Figure 5.2:

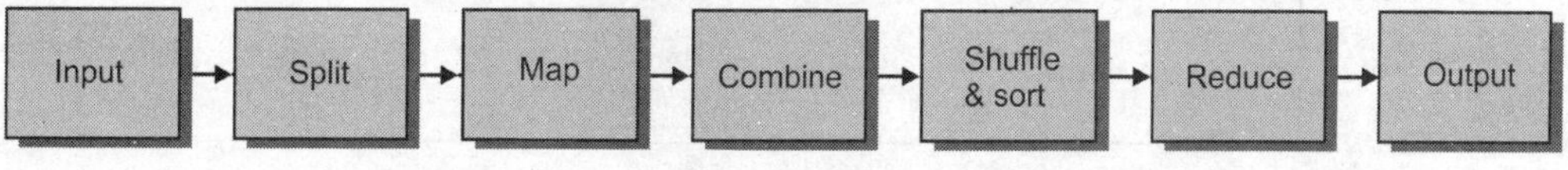

Figure 5.2: Logical Flow of Data in MapReduce

Operations performed in the MapReduce model, according to the data flow (as shown in Figure 5.2) are as follows:

- The input is provided from large data files in the form of key-value pair (KVP), which is the standard input format in a Hadoop MapReduce programming model.
- The input data is divided into small pieces, and master and slave nodes are created. The master node usually executes on the machine where the data is present, and slaves are made to work remotely on the data.
- The map operation is performed simultaneously on all the data pieces, which are read by the map function. The map function extracts the relevant data and generates the KVP for it.

The input/output operations of the map function are shown in Figure 5.3:

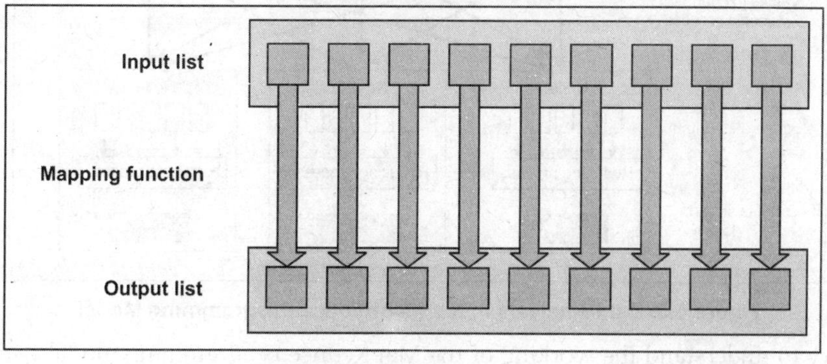

Figure 5.3: Working of the Map Function in the MapReduce Model

The output list is generated from the map operation, and the master instructs the reduce function about further actions that it needs to take. The list of KVPs obtained from the map function is passed on to the reduce function.

The reduce function sorts the data on the basis of the KVP list. The process of collecting the map output list from the map function and then sorting it as per the keys is known as shuffling.

Every unique key is then taken by the reduce function. These keys are called, as required, for producing the final output to be sent to the file. The input/output operations of the reduce function are shown in Figure 5.4:

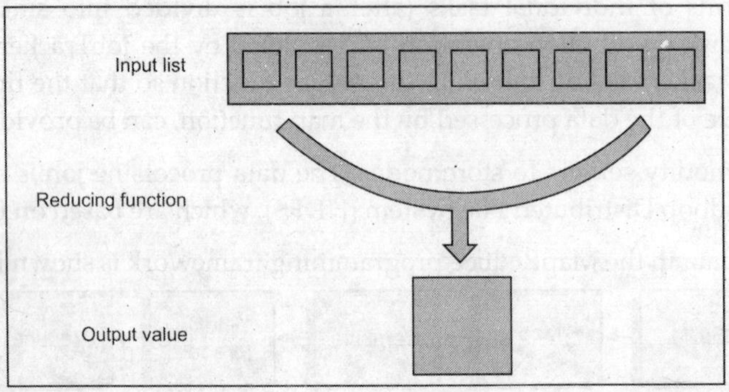

Figure 5.4: Working of the Reduce Function in the MapReduce Model

The output is finally generated by the reduce function, and the control is handed over to the user program by the master.

Figure 5.5 shows the entire process of data analysis conducted in the MapReduce programming model:

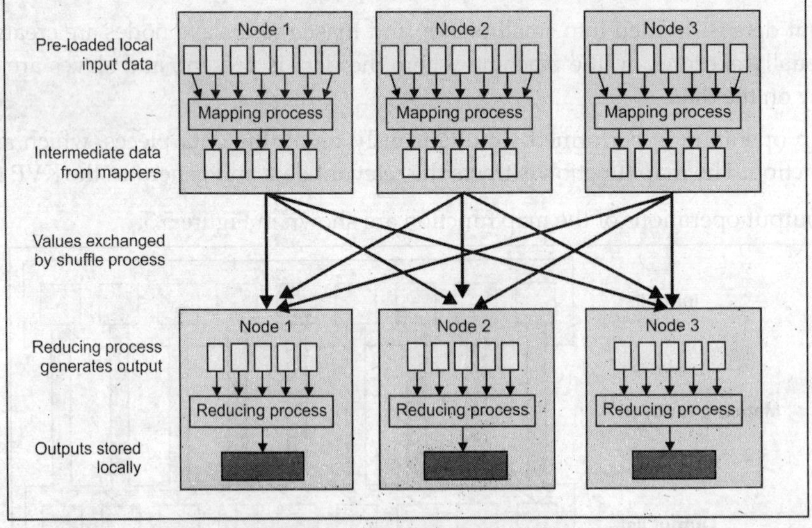

Figure 5.5: Data Analysis in the MapReduce Programming Model

Let's now try to understand the working of the MapReduce programming model with the help of a few examples.

Example 1: Consider that there is a data analysis project in which 20 terabytes of data needs to be analyzed on 20 different MapReduce server nodes. At first, the data distribution process simply copies data to all the nodes before starting the MapReduce process. You need to keep in mind that the determination of the format of the file rests with the user and no standard file format is specified in MapReduce as in relational databases.

Next, the scheduler comes into the picture as it receives two programs from the programmer. These two programs are the map and reduce programs. The data is made available from the disk to the map function, which runs the logic on the data. In our example, all the 20 nodes independently perform the operation. The map function passes the results to the reduce function for summarizing and providing the final output in an aggregate form.

The ancient Rome census can help to understand the mapping process of the map and reduce functions. In the Rome census, volunteers were sent to cover various places that are situated near the kingdom of Rome. Volunteers had to count the number of people living in the area assigned to them and send the report of the population to the organization. The census chief added the count of people recorded from all the areas to reach an aggregate whole. The map function performs the processing operation in parallel to counting the number of people living in an area, and the reduce function combines the entire result.

Example 2: A data analytic professional parses out every term available in the chat text by creating a map step. He creates a map function to find out every word of the chat. The count is incremented by one after the word is parsed from the paragraph. The map function provides the output in the form of a list that involves a number of KVPs, for example, "<my, 1>," "<product, 1>," "<broke, 1>." Once the operations of all map functions are complete, the information is provided to the scheduler by the map function itself.

After completing the map operation, the reduce function starts performing the reduce operation. Keeping the current target of finding the count of the number of times a word appears in the text, shuffling is performed next. This process involves distribution of the map output through hashing in order to map the same keywords to the respective node of the reduce function. Assuming a simple situation of processing an English text, for example, we require 26 nodes that can handle words starting with individual letters of the alphabet. In this case, words starting with A will be handled by one node, words that start with B will be handled by another node, and so on. Thus, the number of words can easily be counted by the reduce step.

Figure 5.6 depicts the detailed MapReduce process used in this example:

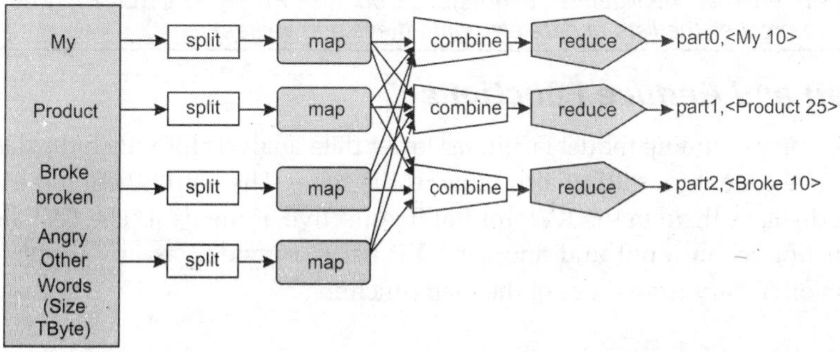

Figure 5.6: Description of MapReduce Process for a Specific Case

The final output of the process will include "<my, 10>," "<product, 25>," "<broke, 20>," where the first value of each angular bracket (<>) is the analyzed word, and the second value is the count of the word, i.e., the number of times the word appears within the entire text. The result set will include 26 files. Each of these files is produced from an individual node and contains the count of words in a sorted order. You need to keep in mind that the combining operation will also require a process to handle all the 26 files obtained as a result of the MapReduce operations.

After we obtain the count of words, we can feed the results for any kind of analysis. For example, we can identify the frequency of some product names that are doing rounds in online chats or assess whether customers are satisfied with the services of a particular company or not. Thus, the unstructured stream of textual data has been converted in a structured list of KVPs, and we can use the result for various purposes such as data analysis, pattern prediction, etc.

NOTE

MapReduce usually indicates the initiation of a data analysis process in which the input data is the outcome of the MapReduce operation.

The strength of MapReduce can be assessed by the fact that it involves several thousands of machines that work on thousands of map and reduce functions to find out the desired result. We can break a huge data stream into smaller parts, which means no single machine will have to bear too much of workload in MapReduce. Moreover, MapReduce facilitates complete parallel processing by allowing different slaves to perform the tasks independently, without requiring other slaves to worry about the task being performed and the manner in which it is performed. Our example processes words in such a way that each word is parsed individually, and the map worker (or slave) remains unaware of the contents of other words.

In parallel processing, two different slaves have no knowledge of each other's tasks. This enables us to determine the use cases for MapReduce. We studied about the Rome census, wherein each volunteer collected data from his/her own area and provided the record directly to the organization; this means that no volunteer was aware about that data collected by any other volunteer. In the same way, MapReduce cannot be used in a scenario where data sharing is required. The MapReduce programming model can also be used for data analysis. For example, we can parse a weblog or an RFID record by dividing the data into pieces that are independent of each other.

TIP

The map function has been a part of many functional programming languages for years. It gained popularity with an artificial intelligence language called List Processing (LISP). The map function is commonly used to process the lists of data elements (keys and values).

Exploring Map and Reduce Functions

The MapReduce programming model facilitates faster data analysis for which the data is taken in the form of KVPs. The format for output also remains the same. The map function retrieves its features of interest and displays them in the KVP format irrespective of the data. The KVP list is received by the reduce function as an input and another KVP list is provided as an output. The keys of the reduce function often vary from those of the map function.

Both MapReduce functions and Hadoop can be created in many languages; however, programmers generally prefer to create them in Java. The Pipes library allows C++ source code to be utilized for map and reduce code. The generic Application Programming Interface (API) called streaming allows programs created in most languages to be utilized as map and reduce functions in Hadoop.

NOTE

Today, it is possible for programmers to write MapReduce programs by using various popular, high-level programming languages, which include R, Python, Perl, etc.

Streaming is used for expressing input and output in the text format. The input and output are KVPs, in which the key and value are separated by tab.

The `stdin()` function includes the input KVP, which is the standard input for reading data from a file. On the other hand, the `stdout()` function includes the output KVPs, which is the standard output for writing data into a file. While converting the map output to the reduce input, a list is structured to bring together all the values for each key.

Consider an example of a program that counts the number of Indian cities having a population of above one lakh. You must note that the following is not a programming code instead a plain English representation of the solution to the problem.

One way to achieve the following task is to determine the input data and generate a list in the following manner:

```
    mylist = ("all counties in the India that participated in the most recent general
election")
```

Use the map function to create a function, `howManyPeople`, which selects the cities having a population of more than one lakh:

```
    map howManyPeople (mylist) = [howManyPeople "city 1";howManyPeople"city 2";
howManyPeople "city 3"; howManyPeople "city 4"; . . . ]
```

Now, generate a new output list of all the cities having a population of more than one lakh:

```
      (no, city 1; yes, city 2; no, city 3; yes, city 4; ?, city nnn)
```

The preceding function gets executed without making any modifications to the original list. Moreover, you can notice that each element of the output list gets mapped to a corresponding element of the input list, having a "yes" or "no" attached.

If a city fulfils the requirement of having more than one lakh people, the map function determines it with a yes; otherwise, a no is specified.

The new list provided by the `howManyPeople` map function is utilized as an input for the reduce function. This function processes each element of the list and returns a list of all the cities with a population greater than one lakh.

EXHIBIT 1: What is MapReduce?

MapReduce is the heart of Hadoop. It is this programming paradigm that allows for massive scalability across hundreds or thousands of servers in a Hadoop cluster. The MapReduce concept is fairly simple to understand for those who are familiar with clustered scale-out data processing solutions.

The term MapReduce actually refers to two separate and distinct tasks that Hadoop programs perform. The first is the map job, which takes a set of data and converts it into another set of data, where individual elements are broken down into tuples (key/value pairs). The reduce job takes the output from a map as input and combines those data tuples into a smaller set of tuples. As the sequence of the name MapReduce implies, the reduce job is always performed after the map job.

An example of MapReduce

Let's look at a simple example. Assume you have five files, and each file contains two columns (a key and a value in Hadoop terms) that represent a city and the corresponding temperature recorded in that city for the various measurement days. Of course we've made this example very simple, so it's easy to follow. You can imagine that a real application won't be quite so simple, as it's likely to contain millions or even billions of rows, and they might not be neatly formatted rows at all; in fact, no matter how big or small the amount of data you need to analyze, the key principles we're covering here remain the same. Either way, in this example, city is the key and temperature is the value.

Toronto, 20
Whitby, 25
New York, 22
Rome, 32
Toronto, 4
Rome, 33
New York, 18

Out of all the data we have collected, we want to find the maximum temperature for each city across all of the data files (note that each file might have the same city represented multiple times). Using the MapReduce framework, we can break this down into five map tasks, where each mapper works on one of the five files, and the mapper task goes through the data and returns the maximum temperature for each city. For example, the results produced from one mapper task for the data above would look like this:

- (Toronto, 20) (Whitby, 25) (New York, 22) (Rome, 33)

Let's assume the other four mapper tasks (working on the other four files not shown here) produced the following intermediate results:

(Toronto, 18) (Whitby, 27) (New York, 32) (Rome, 37)(Toronto, 32) (Whitby, 20) (New York, 33) (Rome, 38)(Toronto, 22) (Whitby, 19) (New York, 20) (Rome, 31)(Toronto, 31) (Whitby, 22) (New York, 19) (Rome, 30)

All five of these output streams would be fed into the reduce tasks, which combine the input results and output a single value for each city, producing the final result set as follows:

- (Toronto, 32) (Whitby, 27) (New York, 33) (Rome, 38)

As an analogy, you can think of map and reduce tasks as the way a census was conducted in Roman times, where the census bureau would dispatch its people to each city in the empire. Each census taker in each city would be tasked to count the number of people in that city and then, return their results to the capital city. There, the results from each city would be reduced to a single count (sum of all cities) to determine the overall population of the empire. This mapping of people to cities, in parallel, and then, combining the results (reducing) is much more efficient than sending a single person to count every person in the empire in a serial fashion.

Source: *http://www-01.ibm.com/software/data/infosphere/hadoop/mapreduce/*

SCENARIO

After learning about the working of MapReduce programming model, some of the team members working with Mr. Richard Paul asked about the different ways in which MapReduce jobs can be optimized. Mr. Paul answered by describing the different approaches that can be used for MapReduce job optimization.

Techniques to Optimize MapReduce Jobs

An analysis of the MapReduce program execution shows that it involves a series of steps in which every step has its own set of resource requirements. In addition, you must avoid any bottlenecks of resources in order to draw the maximum benefits from the MapReduce resources. These resources, if utilized to the fullest, can help you to reduce the response time of your MapReduce job to a minimum level.

In case of short jobs, especially the ones where the user requires a quick response to his/her query, the response time becomes more important. Hence, we need the MapReduce job to be optimized. Encountering a deadlock for even a single resource, during the execution of the program, slows down the execution process.

The performance of MapReduce jobs and their reliability, in addition to the code written for the main application, can be optimized by using some techniques. We can organize the MapReduce optimization techniques in the following categories:

- Hardware or network topology
- Synchronization
- File system

Hardware/Network Topology

MapReduce makes it possible for hardware to run the MapReduce tasks on inexpensive clusters of commodity computers. These computers can be connected through standard networks. The performance and fault tolerance required for Big Data operations are also influenced by the physical location of servers. Usually, the data center arranges the hardware in racks. The performance offered by hardware systems that are located in the same rack where the data is stored will be higher than the performance of hardware systems that are located in a different rack than the one containing the data. The reason for the low performance of the hardware that is located away from the data is the requirement to move the data and/or application code.

When the program is being executed, we can configure the MapReduce engine to exploit the advantages of its closeness to the data. The best way to optimize the performance of your MapReduce engine is to keep the application code and data together. You can, thus, minimize the latency in MapReduce processing by keeping the hardware elements close to each other.

Synchronization

The completion of map processing enables the reduce function to combine the various outputs for providing the final result. However, the performance will degrade if the results of mapping are contained within the same nodes where the data processing began. In order to improve the performance, we should copy the results from mapping nodes to the reducing nodes, which will start their processing tasks immediately. In addition, the hashing function sends all the values marked with the same key to the same reducer node. Thus, the overall performance of the system enhances with an increased efficiency. You can extract the best possible outcomes by writing the outputs of reduction operations directly to the file system. This entire process is synchronized to provide efficiency to the MapReduce programming model.

File System

A distributed file system is used to support the implementation of the MapReduce operation. Distributed file systems are different from local file systems in a manner that local file systems have less capability of storing and arranging data. The Big Data world has immense information to be processed and requires data to be distributed among a number of systems or nodes in a cluster so that the data can be handled efficiently. The distribution model followed in implementing the MapReduce programming approach is to use the master and slaves model. All the metadata and access rights, apart from the mapping, block, and file locations are stored with the master. On the other hand, the data on which the application code will run is kept with the slaves. The master node receives all the requests, which are forwarded to appropriate slaves for performing the required actions.

You need to keep the following points in mind while designing a file that supports MapReduce implementation:

- **Keep it Warm**—The master handles various operations, which may lead to a stage of overworking for it. In case of the failure of the master node, you will be unable to access the entire file system unless the master becomes active again. In order to optimize the file system, you can develop a standby master node that can remain warm and, whenever the primary master fails to deliver, can take the responsibility.
- **The Bigger the Better**—In Big Data environment, files with a size less than 100 MB are not preferred, so you need to avoid using them. The best results are obtained when the distributed file systems that are used with MapReduce are loaded with a small number of large-sized files.
- **The Long View**—MapReduce handles the workload by keeping large jobs in small data batches. Hence, MapReduce needs a network bandwidth that remains available for a long time instead of having quick execution times of mappers and reducers. To use the network optimally, a long stream of data should be sent by the application code when it is reading from or writing to the file system.
- **Right Degree of Security**—The increasing number of security layers hampers the performance of distributed file systems. The permissions associated with file systems are meant to protect files from any unauthorized access and damage. It is always advisable to allow only authorized users to access the data center environment and protect the distributed file system.

SCENARIO

To fully exploit the potential of MapReduce, it is important to learn about the areas in which MapReduce has particular relevance. With this perspective in mind, Mr. Paul decided to brief his team about the uses and applications of MapReduce.

Uses of MapReduce

MapReduce is used to process various types of data obtained from various sectors. Some of the fields benefitted by the use of MapReduce are:

- **Web Page Visits**—Suppose a researcher wants to know the number of times the website of a particular newspaper was accessed. The map task would be to read the logs of the Web page requests and make a complete list. The map outputs may look similar to the following:

```
<emailURL, 1>
<newspaperURL, 1>
<socialmediaURL, 1>
<sportsnewsURL, 1>
<newspaperURL, 1>
<emailURL, 1>
<newspaperURL, 1>
```

The reduce function would find the results for the newspaper URL and add them. The output of the preceding code is:

```
<newspaperURL, 3>
```

- **Web Page Visitor Paths**—Consider a situation in which an advocacy group wishes to know how visitors get to know about its website. To determine this, they designed a link known as "source," and the Web page to which the link transfers the information is known as "target." The map function scans the Web links for returning the results of the type <target, source>. The reduce function scans this list for determining the results where the "target" is the Web page. The reduce function output, which is the final output, will be of the form <advocacy group page, list (source)>.
- **Word Frequency**—A researcher wishes to read articles about flood but, he does not want those articles in which the flood is discussed as a minor topic. Therefore, he decided that an article basically dealing with earthquakes and floods should have the word "tectonic plate" in it more than 10 times. The map function will count the number of times the specified word occurred in each document and provide the result as <document, frequency>. The reduce function will count and select only the results that have a frequency of more than 10 words.
- **Word Count**—Suppose a researcher wishes to determine the number of times celebrities talk about the present bestseller. The data to be analyzed comprises written blogs, posts, and tweets of the celebrities. The map function will make a list of all the words. This list will be in the KVP format, in which the key is each word, and the value is 1 for every appearance of that word.

The output from the map function would be obtained somewhat as follows:

```
<global warning, 1>
<food, 1>
<global warning, 1>
<bestseller, 1>
<Afghanistan, 1>
<bestseller, 1>
```

The preceding output will be converted in the following form by the reduce function:

```
<global warning, 2>
<food, 1>
<bestseller, 2>
<Afghanistan, 1>
```

The MapReduce programming model can utilize other components of the Hadoop ecosystem to perform its operations better. One such components is HBase.

SCENARIO

The team members working with Mr. Richard Paul now wanted to know whether MapReduce is enough to process all the data by itself or it gets any assistance from other technologies that are used in the field of Big Data processing. They were told about some of the technologies such as HBase and Hive, which are used mainly for data storage and management. The team members were particularly interested to know about HBase.

Let us examine the ways in which HBase can help perform MapReduce operations better.

Role of HBase in Big Data Processing

HBase is an open source, non-relational, distributed, column-oriented database developed as a part of Apache Software Foundation's Hadoop project. It is beneficial when large amounts of information is required to be stored, updated, and processed at a fast speed.

Because of the vast size of Big Data, its storage and processing are challenging tasks. While MapReduce enhances Big Data processing, HBase takes care of its storage and access requirements.

Characteristics of HBase

HBase helps programmers to store large quantities of data in such a way that it can be accessed easily and quickly, as and when required. It stores data in a compressed format and thus, occupies less memory space. HBase has low latency time and is, therefore, beneficial for lookups and scanning of large amounts of data. HBase saves data in cells in the descending order (with the help of timestamp); therefore, a read will always first determine the most recent values. Columns in HBase relate to a column family. The column family name is utilized as a prefix for determining members of its family; for instance, Cars: Wagon R and Cars: i10 are the members of the Cars column family.

A key is associated with rows in HBase tables. The structure of the key is very flexible. It can be a calculated value, a string, or any other data structure. The key is used for controlling the retrieval of data to the cells in the row. All these characteristics help build the schema of the HBase data structure before the storage of any data. Moreover, tables can be modified and new column families can be added once the database is up and running.

This extensibility is beneficial while dealing with Big Data, because every time you do not always know the diversity of your data streams. Relational databases are row-oriented, because the data in each row of a table is saved together. In a columnar or column-oriented database, the data is saved across rows. The columns can be added very easily and are added row-by-row, providing great flexibility, performance, and scalability.

In case you have large volume and variety of data, you can use a columnar database. HBase is suitable in conditions where the data changes gradually and rapidly. In addition, HBase can save the data that has a slow-changing rate and ensure its availability for Hadoop tasks. Examples of data that changes at a very slow pace include demographic data, IP addresses, geolocation lookup tables, and product dimensional data.

Application logs, clickstream data, and in-game usage data are developed rapidly and are used in real-time log ingestion and batch log analytics. HBase can obtain this data and quickly update the database to enable instant processing of the updated data.

Installation of HBase

HBase is a framework written in Java for supporting applications that are used to process Big Data. HBase is a non-relational Hadoop database that provides fault tolerance for huge amounts of data. Before starting the installation of HBase, you need to install the Java Software Development Kit (SDK). The installation of HBase requires the following operations to be performed in a stepwise manner:

In the Windows terminal, install the dependency `$sudo apt-get installntp libopts25`. Figure 5.7 shows the installation of dependency for HBase:

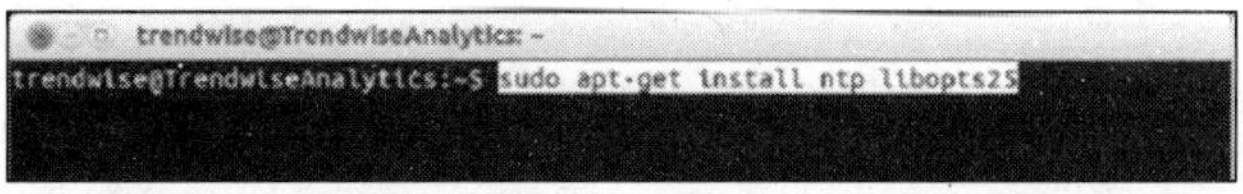

Figure 5.7: Dependency Installation for HBase

The HBase file can be customized as per the user needs by exporting `JAVA_HOME` and `HBase Opts (hbase-env.sh)`. To customize an HBase file, type the following code:

```
export JAVA_HOME/home/WCBDD/apache/jdk1.6.0_25
export PATH=$PATH:$JAVA_HOME/bin
export HBASE_OPTS='$HBASE_OPTS -XX:UseConMarkSweepGC'
```

Figure 5.8 shows how to export `JAVA_HOME` and `HBase Opts (hbase-env.sh)`:

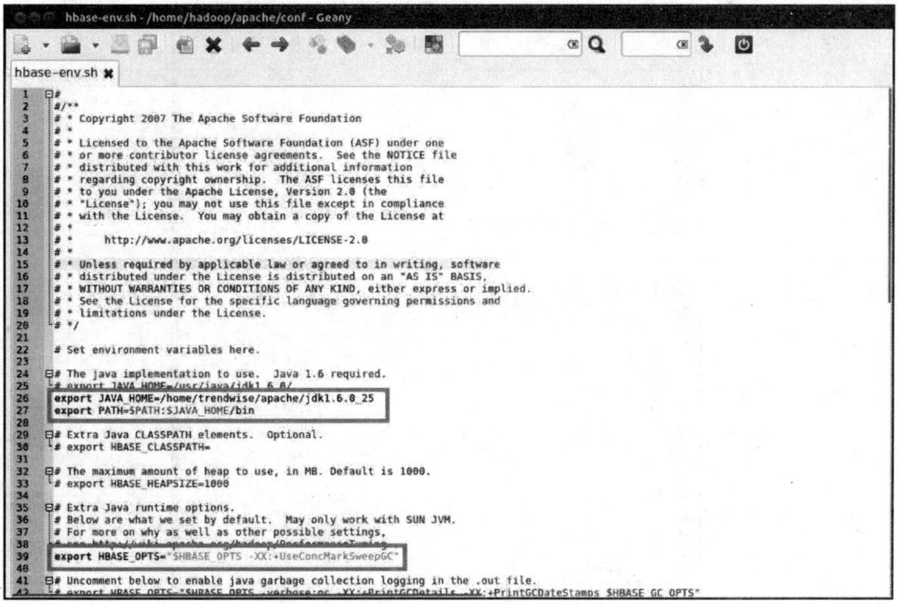

Figure 5.8: Exporting JAVA_HOME and HBase Options

Zookeeper, the file management engine of the Hadoop ecosystem, manages the files thatHBase plans to use currently and in the future. Therefore, to manage zookeeper in HBase and ensure that it is enabled, use the following command:

```
export HBASE_MANAGES_ZK=true
```

Figure 5.9 shows zookeeper enabled in HBase:

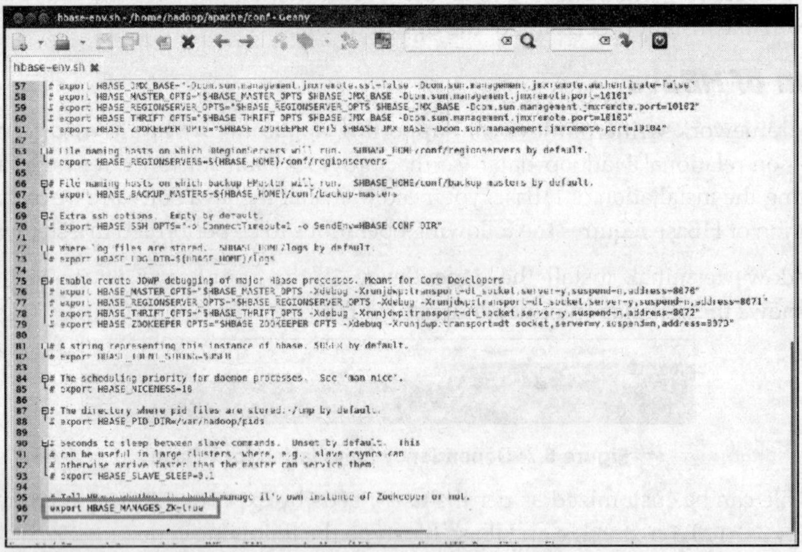

Figure 5.9: Zookeeper Enabled in HBase

Site-specific customizations are done in `hbase-site.xml (HBASE_HOME/conf)`. Figure 5.10 shows customized `hbase-site.xml (HBASE_HOME/conf)`:

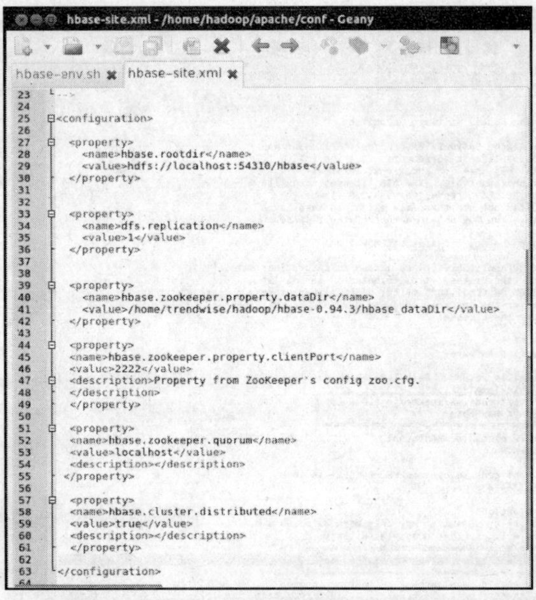

Figure 5.10: Customized hbase-site.xml

To enable connection with remote HBase server, edit `/etc/hosts`. Figure 5.11 shows the edited `/etc/hosts`:

Figure 5.11: Edited etc/hosts

Start HBase by using the following command:

```
$bin/start-hbase.sh
```

Figure 5.12 shows the initiation process of HBase daemons:

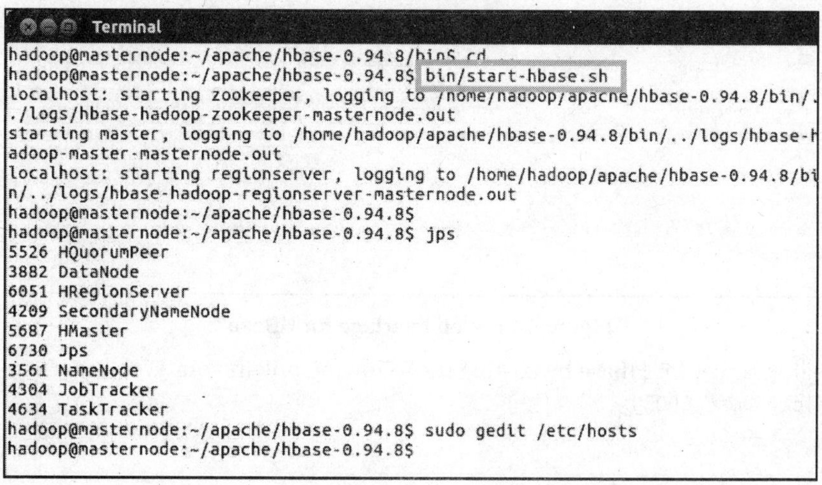

Figure 5.12: Initiating HBase Daemons

Check all HBase daemons by using the following command:

```
$jps
```

Figure 5.13 shows the implementation of the `$jps` command:

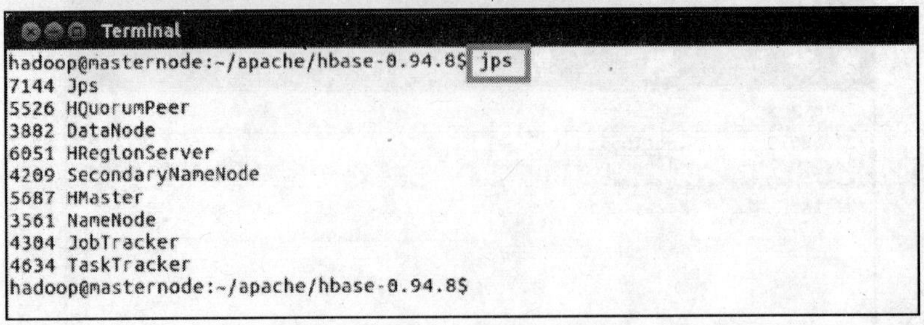

Figure 5.13: Checking HBase Daemons

Paste the following link to access the Web interface, which has the list of tables created, along with their definition:

```
http://localhost:60010
```

Figure 5.14 shows the Web interface for HBase:

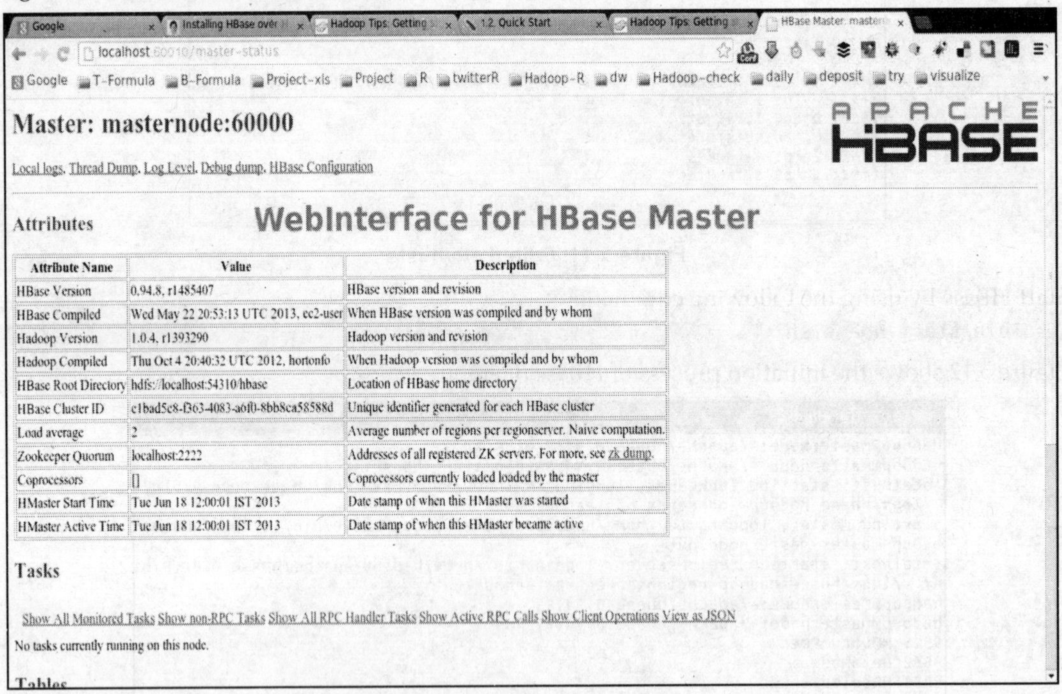

Figure 5.14: Web Interface for HBase

Check the region server for HBase by pasting the following link in your Web browser:

```
http://localhost:60030
```

Figure 5.15 shows a sample of regional HBase servers:

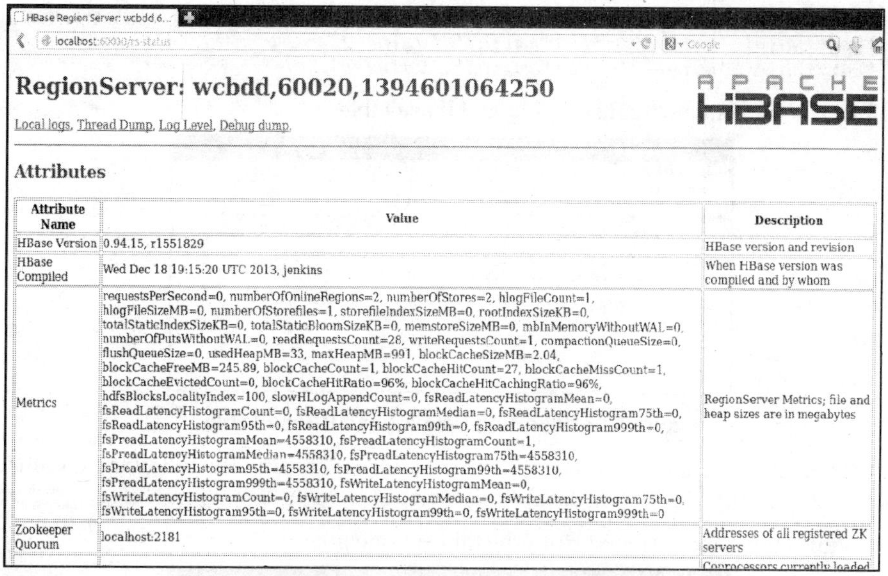

Figure 5.15: Regional HBase Servers

Start the HBase shell by using the following command:

```
$bin/hbase shell
```

Figure 5.16 shows the `$bin/hbase` shell running in a terminal:

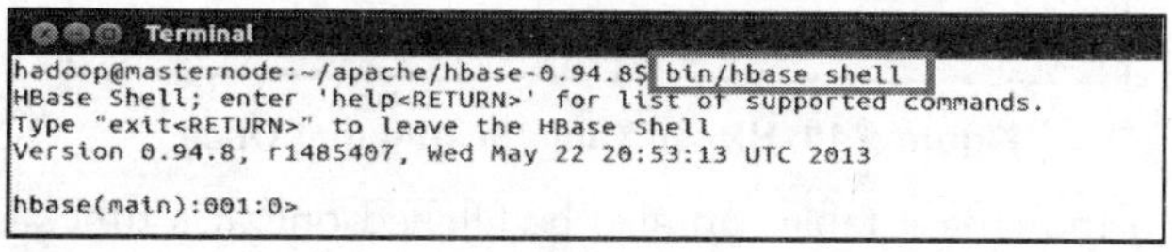

Figure 5.16: HBase Shell in Execution

Create an HBase table by typing the following commands:

```
>list
> create 'testtable','colfam1',{SPLITS => ['row-300','row-
700','row-900']}
>list
```

Figure 5.17 shows the creation of an HBase table in a terminal:

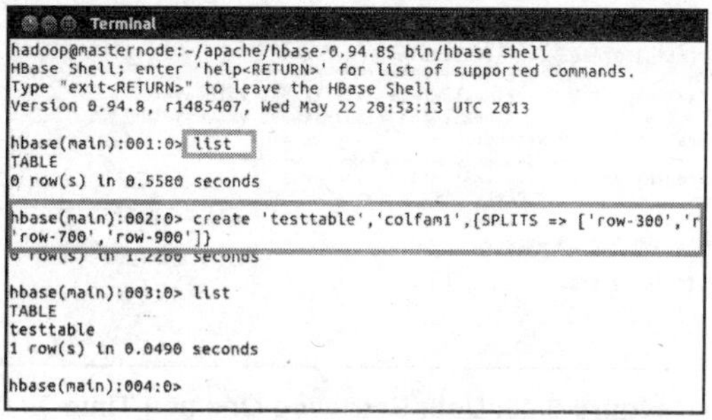

Figure 5.17: Creating an HBase Table

Insert sample data into the table by typing the following commands:

```
>put 'testtable','myrow-1','colfam1:q1','value-1'
>put 'testtable','myrow-2','colfam1:q2','value-2'
>put 'testtable','myrow-3','colfam1:q3','value-3'
```

Figure 5.18 shows the data being inserted to an HBase table:

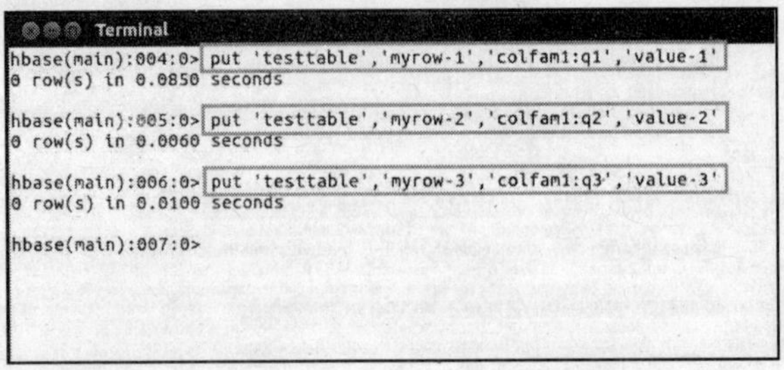

Figure 5.18: Inserting Data into an HBase Table

All the data from the HBase table can be retrieved at once by typing the following command:

```
> scan 'testtable'
```

Figure 5.19 shows the data retrieved from the table at one go:

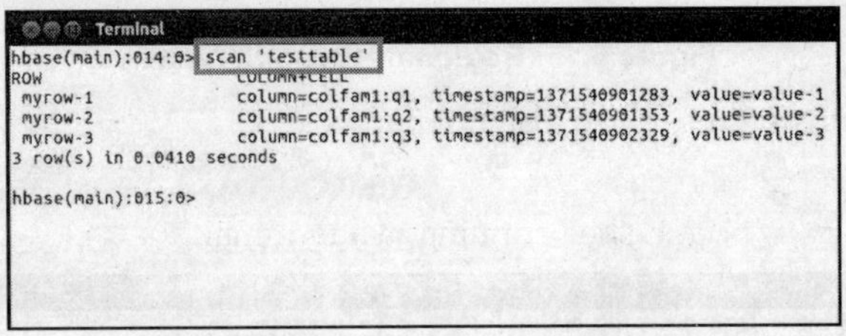

Figure 5.19: HBase Table Scanned at Once

The data records from the HBase table can also be fetched one at a time, as per requirement. The following commands return the records from individual rows:

```
>get 'testtable','myrow-1'
>get 'testtable','myrow-2'
>get 'testtable','myrow-3'
```

Figure 5.20 shows the data being retrieved as per requirement:

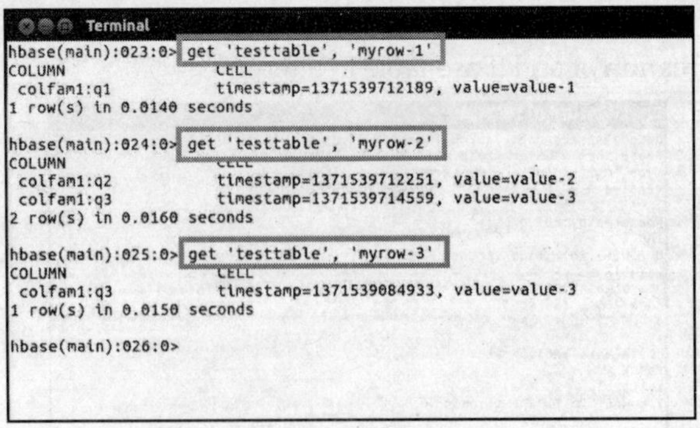

Figure 5.20: Data Retrieved One at a Time

Data can be inserted randomly into an HBase table as easily as it can be retrieved from it. Insert 10 records into the `testtable` table by typing the following command:

```
>for i in '0'..'9' do for j in '0'..'9' do for k in '0'..'9' do put
'testtable','row-#(i)#(j)#(k)','colfam1:#(j)#(k)','#(j)#(k)' end end end
```

Figure 5.21 shows a query to insert 1000 rows randomly into an HBase table:

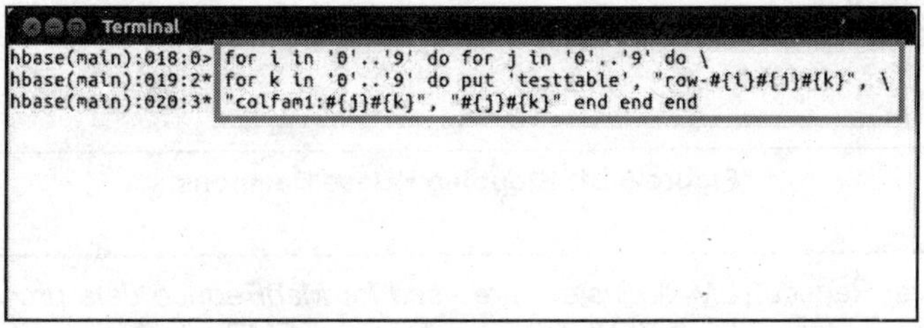

Figure 5.21: Insertion of Rows in an HBase Table

To delete data from an HBase table, type the following command:

```
>delete 'testtable','myrow2','colfam1:q2'
```

Figure 5.22 shows the deletion of data from a particular cell in an HBase table:

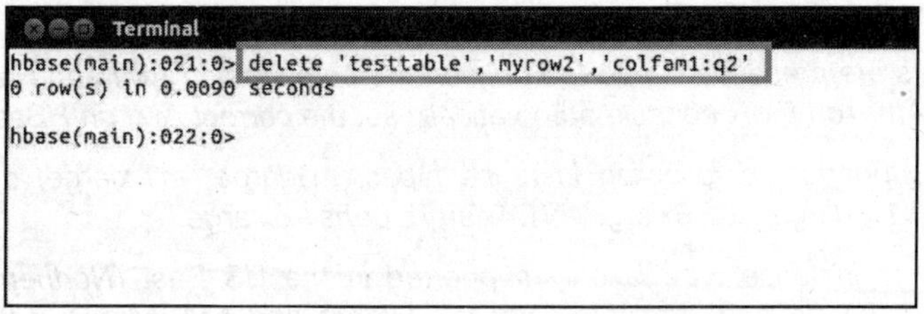

Figure 5.22: Deletion of Records from a Cell

Deletion of complete tables is also possible in HBase. You can delete the test table by typing the following commands:

```
>disable 'testtable'
>drop 'testtable'
>exit
```

Figure 5.23 shows the deletion of an HBase table:

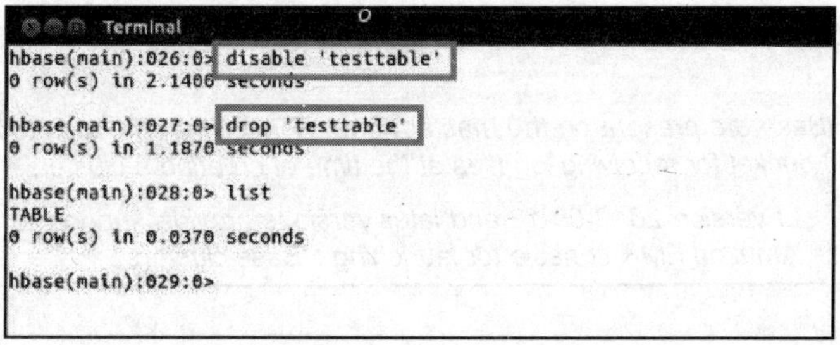

Figure 5.23: Deletion of an HBase Table

HBase daemons can be stopped once their functionality is no longer required. You can stop the HBase daemons by typing the following commands:

```
$bin/stop-hbase.sh
$jps
```

Figure 5.24 shows the stopping of HBase daemons:

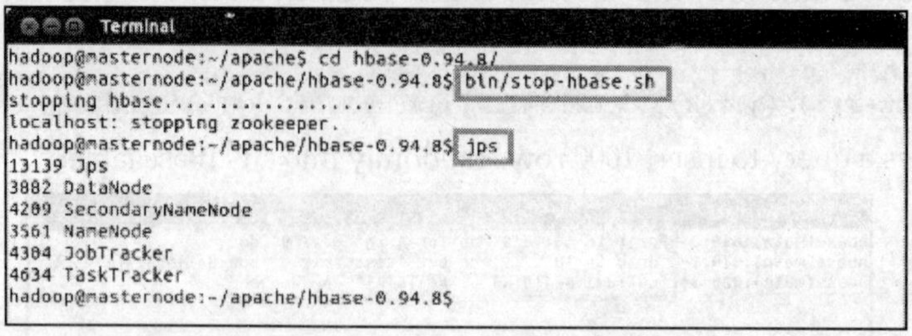

Figure 5.24: Stopping HBase Daemons

NOTE

Amazon Elastic MapReduce (EMR) clusters are used for MapReduce data processing, which can be improved by using HBase. To run HBase, an Amazon EMR cluster should meet the following requirements:

- *HBase can run only on persistent clusters, which are built automatically by the Amazon EMR Command Line Interface (CLI) and Amazon EMR console.*
- *While creating the HBase cluster, an Amazon EC2 key pair must be set. An HBase shell requires the Secure Shell (SSH) network protocol to connect to the master node.*
- *HBase clusters are presently supported only on the beta version AMI and Hadoop 20.205 or later. The CLI and Amazon EMR console automatically set the correct AMI on HBase clusters.*
- *HBase only supports the following instance types: m1.large, m1.xlarge, c1.xlarge, m2.2xlarge, m2.4xlarge, cc1.4xlarge, cc2.8xlarge, hi1.4xlarge, or hs1.8xlarge.*
- *The cc2.8xlarge instance type is only supported in the US East (Northern Virginia), US West (Oregon), and EU (Ireland) regions. The cc1.4xlarge and hs1.8xlarge instance types are only supported in the US East (Northern Virginia) region. The hi1.4xlarge instance type is only supported in the US East (Northern Virginia) and EU (Ireland) regions.*

There are some other considerations that do not necessarily enhance performance. Therefore, these are considered as optional requirements:

- *The cluster's master node runs the HBase master server and Zookeeper, and slave nodes run the HBase region servers. For getting the best performance, HBase clusters must run on at least two EC2 instances, though HBase can be executed on a single node.*
- *To monitor HBase performance metrics, use a bootstrap action for installing Ganglia while creating the cluster.*
- *The logs for HBase are present on the master node. For copying the logs to Amazon S3, mention an Amazon S3 bucket for receiving log files at the time of creating a cluster.*
- *Amazon EMR CLI version 2012-06-12 and later versions provide support to HBase. Alternatively, you can use the Amazon EMR console for launching HBase clusters.*

Summary

In this chapter, you learned about the MapReduce framework, which is an integration of different functions to sort, process, and analyze Big Data. The chapter discussed the features and benefits of using MapReduce with the help of examples. Next, you learned about the working of the map and reduce functions as well as the algorithm on which the MapReduce model works. The chapter further explored various techniques to draw the maximum benefits from the MapReduce approach. Toward the end, the chapter discussed HBase, its installation process, and how integrating HBase with MapReduce helps in better and faster processing of Big Data.

Quick Revise

Multiple-Choice Questions

Q1. Which of the following options most aptly explains the reason behind the creation of MapReduce? Select all that apply.

a. Need to increase the processing power of new hardware

b. Need to perform complex analysis of structured data

c. Need to increase the number of Web users

d. Need to spread distributed computing

Ans. The correct option is a.

Q2. In designing the MapReduce framework, which of the following needs did the engineers consider? Select all that apply.

a. It should be cheap and distributed free of cost.

b. Processing should expand and contract automatically.

c. Processing should be stopped in the case of network failure.

d. Developers should be able to create new languages.

Ans. The correct option is b.

Q3. Which of the following describes the map function? Select all that apply.

a. It processes data to create a list of key-value pairs.

b. It indexes the data to list all the words occurring in it.

c. It converts a relational database to key-value pairs.

d It tracks data across multiple tables and clusters in Hadoop.

Ans. The correct option is a.

Q4. Which of the following describes the reduce function? Select all that apply.

a. It analyzes the map function results to show the most frequently occurring values.

b. It combines the map function results to return a list of the best matches for the query.

c. It adds the results of the map function to convert the key-value pair lists to columnar databases.

d. It processes map function results and creates a new key-value pair list to answer the query.

Ans. The correct option is d.

Q5. In the MapReduce framework, map and reduce functions can be run in any order. Do you agree and why?

a. Yes, because in functional programming, the order of execution is not important.

b. Yes, because the functions use KVP as input and output; order is not important.

c. No, because the output of the map function is the input for the reduce function.

d. No, because the output of the reduce function is the input for the map function.

Ans. The correct option is c.

Q6. How does MapReduce achieve co-location? Select all that apply.

a. The scheduler sends the code to the machine where the relevant data resides.

b. The process scheduler distributes data of the same type to machines in the same cluster.

c. The master JobTracker sends map and reduce functions to the same machines or nodes in a cluster.

d. The slave TaskTrackers copy related data and code to adjacent clusters in case of processing failure.

Ans. The correct option is a.

Q7. How does HBase help real-time analytics? Select all that apply.

a. It uses column-based storage and compression suitable for unstructured data.

b. It updates data fast enough to allow processing of the latest data.

c. As a non-relational database, it is flexible and allows SQL-like queries with Hive.

d. It enables sequential and batch processing of write and update requests.

Ans. The correct option is b.

Q8. What role does the map function play in a word count query? Select all that apply.

a. It sorts the words alphabetically and returns a list of the most frequently used words.

b. It creates a list with each word as a key and the number of occurrences as the value.

c. It creates a list with each word as a key and every occurrence as value 1.

d. It returns a list with each document as a key and the number of words in it as the value.

Ans. The correct option is c.

Subjective Questions

Q1. List the main features of MapReduce.

Ans. The principal features of MapReduce include the following:

- **Scheduling**—MapReduce involves two operations:map and reduce, which are executed by dividing large problems into smaller chunks. These chunks are run in parallel by different computing resources. The operation of breaking tasks into subtasks and running these subtasks independently in parallel is called mapping, which is performed ahead of the reduce operation. The mapping operation requires task prioritization based on the number of nodes in the cluster.

  In case nodes are fewer than tasks, then tasks are executed on a priority basis. The reduction operation cannot be performed until the entire mapping operation is completed. The reduction operation then merges independent results on the basis of priority. Hence, the MapReduce programming model requires scheduling of tasks.

- **Synchronization**—Execution of several concurrent processes requires synchronization. The MapReduce program execution framework is aware of the mapping and reducing operations that are taking place in the program. The framework tracks all the tasks along with their timings and starts the reduction process after the completion of mapping. A method known as shuffle and sort produces the intermediate data, which is transmitted across the network. The shuffle and sort mechanism is used for collecting the mapped data and preparing it for reduction.

- **Co-location of Code/Data**—The effectiveness of a data processing mechanism depends largely on the location of the code and the data required for the code to execute. The best result is obtained when both the code and data reside on the same machine. This means that the co-location of the code and data produces the most effective processing.

- **Handling of Errors/Faults**—MapReduce engines usually provide a high level of fault tolerance and robustness in handling errors. The reason for providing robustness to these engines is their high propensity to incur errors or faults. There are high chances of failure in clustered nodes on which different parts of a program are running.

  Therefore, the MapReduce engine must have the capability of recognizing the fault and taking the required action to rectify it. Moreover, the MapReduce engine design involves the ability to find out the tasks that are incomplete and eventually assign them to different nodes.

- **Scale-out Architecture**—MapReduce engines are built in such a way that they can accommodate more machines, as and when required. This possibility of introducing more computing resources to the architecture makes the MapReduce programming model more suited to the higher computational demands of Big Data.

Q2. Describe the working of the MapReduce algorithm.

Ans. The working of the theMapReduce algorithm can be explained in the following steps:

1. Take a large dataset or set of records.
2. Perform iteration over the data.
3. Extract some interesting patterns to prepare an output list by using the map function.
4. Arrange the output list properly to enable optimization for further processing.
5. Compute a set of results by using the reduce function.
6. Provide the final output.

Q3. Discuss some techniques to optimize MapReduce jobs.

Ans. The performance of MapReduce jobs and their reliability, in addition to the code written for the main application, can be optimized by using some techniques. We can organize the MapReduce optimization techniques in the following categories:

- **Hardware/Network Topology**—MapReduce makes it possible for hardware to run the MapReduce tasks on inexpensive clusters of computers. These computers can be connected through standard networks. The performance and fault tolerance required for Big Data operations are also influenced by the physical location of servers. Usually, the data center arranges the hardware in racks. The performance offered by hardware systems that are located in the same rack where the data is stored will be higher than the performance of hardware systems that are located in a different rack than the one containing the data. The reason for the low performance of the hardware that is located away from the data is the requirement to move the data and/or application code. When the program is being executed, we can configure the MapReduce engine to exploit the advantages of its closeness to the data. The best way to optimize the performance of your MapReduce engine is to keep the application code and data together. You can, thus, minimize the latency in MapReduce processing by keeping the hardware elements close to each other.

- **Synchronization**—The completion of map processing enables the reduce function to combine the various outputs for providing the final result. However, the performance will degrade if the results of mapping are contained within the same nodes where the data processing began. In order to improve the performance, we should copy the results from mapping nodes to the reducing nodes, which will start their processing tasks immediately. In addition, the hashing function sends all the values marked with the same key to the same reducer node. Thus, the overall performance of the system enhances with an increased efficiency. You can extract the best possible outcomes by writing the outputs of reduction operations directly to the file system. This entire process is synchronized to provide efficiency to the MapReduce programming model.

- **File System**—A distributed file system is used to support the implementation of the MapReduce operation. Distributed file systems are different from local file systems in a manner that local file systems have less capability of storing and arranging data. The Big Data world has immense information to be processed and requires data to be distributed among a number of systems or nodes in a cluster so that the data can be handled efficiently. The distribution model followed in implementing the MapReduce programming approach is to use the master and slaves model.

All the metadata and access rights, apart from the mapping, block, and file locations are stored with the master. On the other hand, the data on which the application code will run is kept with the slaves. The master node receives all the requests, which are forwarded to appropriate slaves for performing the required actions.

Q4. Discuss the points you need to consider while designing a file system in MapReduce.

Ans. You need to keep the following points in mind while designing a file that supports MapReduce implementation:

- **Keep it Warm**—The master handles various operations, which may lead to a stage of overworking for it. In case of the failure of the master node, you will be unable to access the entire file system unless the master becomes active again. In order to optimize the file system, you can develop a standby master node that can remain warm and, whenever the primary master fails to deliver, can take the responsibility.
- **The Bigger the Better**—In Big Data environment, files with a size less than 100 MB are not preferred, so you need to avoid using them. The best results are obtained when the distributed file systems that are used with MapReduce are loaded with a small number of large-sized files.
- **The Long View**—MapReduce handles the workload by keeping large jobs in small data batches. Hence, MapReduce needs a network bandwidth that remains available for a long time instead of having quick execution times of mappers and reducers. To use the network optimally, a long stream of data should be sent by the application code when it is reading from or writing to the file system.
- **Right Degree of Security**—The increasing number of security layers hampers the performance of distributed file systems. The permissions associated with file systems are meant to protect files from any unauthorized access and damage. It is always advisable to allow only authorized users to access the data center environment and protect the distributed file system.

Q5. Write a short note on HBase.

Ans. HBase is an open source, non-relational, distributed database developed as a part of Apache Software Foundation's Hadoop project. It is beneficial when large amounts of information is required to be stored, updated, and processed at a fast speed.

Because of the vast size of Big Data, its storage and processing are challenging tasks. While MapReduce enhances Big Data processing, HBase takes care of its storage and access requirements.

HBase helps programmers to store large quantities of data in such a way that it can be accessed easily and quickly, as and when required. It stores data in a compressed format and thus, occupies less memory space.

HBase has low latency time and is, therefore, beneficial for lookups and scanning of large amounts of data. HBase saves data in cells in the descending order (with the help of timestamp); therefore, a read will always first determine the most recent values. Columns in HBase relate to a column family. The column family name is utilized as a prefix for determining members of its family; for instance, Cars: Wagon R and Cars: i10 are the members of the Cars column family.

6

Understanding Big Data Technology Foundations

In the previous chapter, you learned about various technologies such as Hadoop and MapReduce that help in improving the processing power of the system analyzing Big Data. As it deals with huge volumes of varied data, Big Data analysis requires the use of best technologies at every stage, be it collecting data, cleaning it, sorting and organizing it, integrating it, analyzing it, or deriving final conclusions. Each of these steps needs the implementation of the most advanced architectures that are not just efficient and fast but also economical. One of the ways to achieve this combination of efficiency and economy is virtualization.

Virtualization means creating a virtual projection of data, such as an operating system, network resource, a server, etc. It keeps the virtual version of resources and services separate from the underlying physical implementation. Applying virtualization across the Big Data environment helps in fulfilling its resource-related requirements to a great extent.

In this chapter, you learn about the design and configuration of the architecture used to analyze Big Data. Next, you learn about the different layers of this model in detail. Finally, the chapter discusses the technique of virtualization, its features, and the role it plays in the Big Data environment.

SCENARIO

In one of Mr. Smith's meetings with his team, the team members expressed their desire to know more about the Big Data architecture. They have heard that this architecture is also open to variations as per the workload and processing requirements. Smith explained that the Big Data stack architecture consists of different layers and components and is not a fixed, one-size-fits-all approach. He further tells them that this architecture is very flexible and can be customized and used according to different analysis requirements.

Exploring the Big Data Stack

The first step in the process of designing any data architecture is to create a model that should give a complete view of all the required elements. Although, initially, creating a model may seem to be a time-consuming task; however, it can save a significant amount of time, effort, and rework during the subsequent implementations.

Big Data analysis also needs the creation of a model or architecture, commonly known as the Big Data architecture. Here, you must note that the configuration of the model may vary depending upon the specific needs of the organization; however, the basic layers and components, more or less, remain the same. To create a Big Data architecture model, you need to think of Big Data as a strategy and not a project. This strategy also includes certain design principles related to the creation of an environment to support Big Data. Basically, these principles deal with the storage of data, analytics, reporting, or applications. However, while creating Big Data environment, we must also take hardware, infrastructure software, operational software, management software, Application Programming Interfaces (APIs), and software developer tools into consideration. In short, we can say that the architecture of the Big Data environment must fulfill all the foundational requirements and must be able to perform the following functions:

- Capturing data from different sources
- Cleaning and integrating data of different types of formats
- Sorting and organizing data
- Analyzing data

- Identifying relationships and patterns
- Deriving conclusions based on the data analysis results

Figure 6.1 shows the arrangement of various layers in the Big Data architecture:

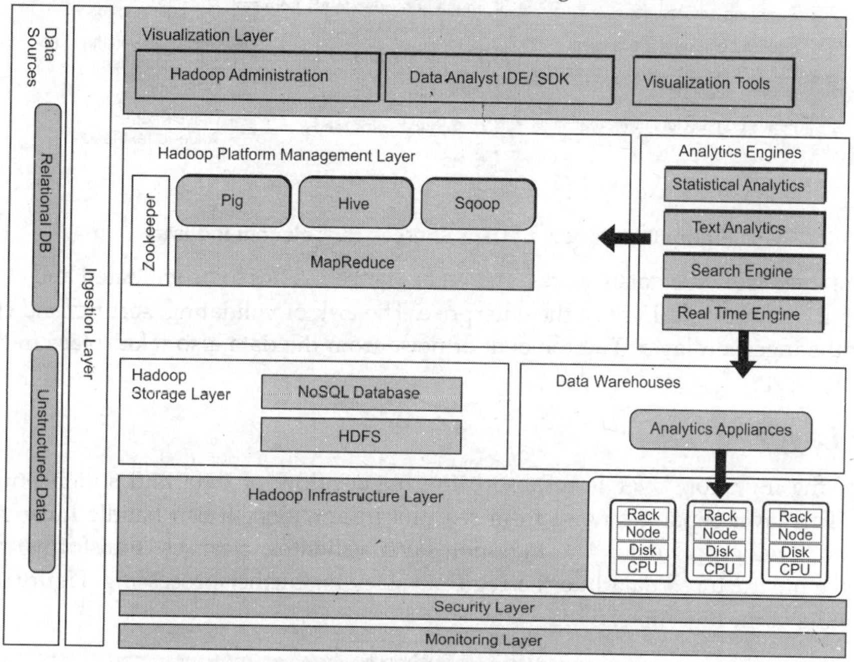

Figure 6.1: Stack of Layers in Big Data Architecture

Figure 6.1 shows a sample diagram of the Big Data architecture, comprising the following basic layers and components:

- Data Sources layer
- Ingestion layer
- Storage layer
- Physical Infrastructure layer
- Platform Management layer
- Security layer
- Monitoring layer
- Analytics engine
- Visualization layer
- Big Data applications

Let's learn about these layers and components in detail in the following sections.

Data Sources Layer

Organizations generate a huge amount of data on a daily basis. The basic function of the data sources layer is to absorb and integrate the data coming from various sources, at varying velocity and in different formats. Before this data is considered for big datastack, we have to differentiate between the noise and relevant information.

Figure 6.2 shows different data sources from where the telecom industry obtains its data:

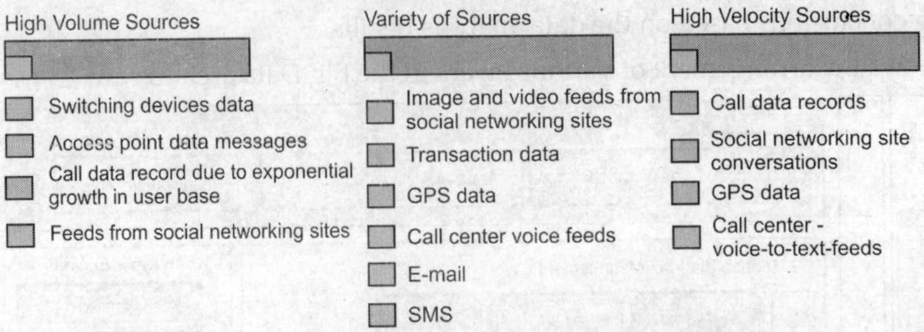

Figure 6.2: Variety of Data Sources for Telecom Industry

The data obtained from the data sources, shown in Figure 6.2, has to be validated and cleaned before introducing it for any logical use in the enterprise. The task of validating, sorting, and cleaning data is done by the ingestion layer. The removal of noise from the data also takes place in the ingestion layer.

Ingestion Layer

The role of the ingestion layer is to absorb the huge inflow of data and sort it out in different categories. This layer separates noise from relevant information. It can handle huge volume, high velocity, and a variety of data. The ingestion layer validates, cleanses, transforms, reduces, and integrates the unstructured data into the Big Data stack for further processing. Figure 6.3 illustrates the functioning of the ingestion layer:

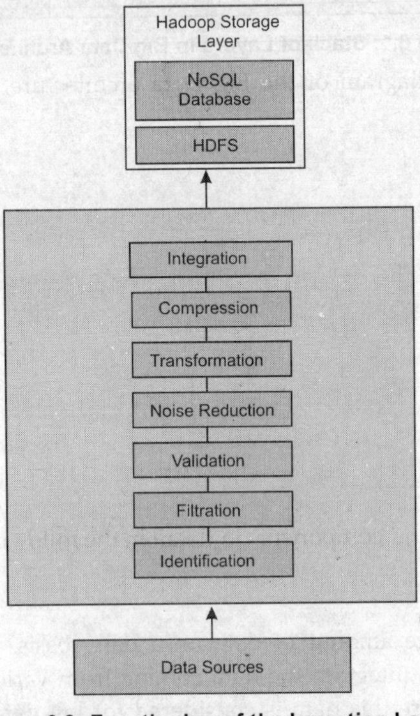

Figure 6.3: Functioning of the Ingestion Layer

In the ingestion layer, the data passes through the following stages:

- **Identification**—At this stage, data is categorized into various known data formats, or we can say that unstructured data is assigned with default formats.
- **Filtration**—At this stage, the information relevant for the enterprise is filtered on the basis of the Enterprise Master Data Management (MDM) repository.
- **Validation**—At this stage, the filtered data is analyzed against MDM metadata.
- **Noise reduction**—At this stage, data is cleaned by removing the noise and minimizing the related disturbances.
- **Transformation**—At this stage, data is split or combined on the basis of its type, contents, and the requirements of the organization.
- **Compression**—At this stage, the size of the data is reduced without affecting its relevance for the required process. It should be noted that compression does not affect the analysis results.
- **Integration**—At this stage, the refined dataset is integrated with the Hadoop storage layer, which consists of Hadoop Distributed File System (HDFS) and NoSQL databases.

Storage Layer

Hadoop is an open source framework used to store large volumes of data in a distributed manner across multiple machines. The Hadoop storage layer supports fault-tolerance and parallelization, which enable high-speed distributed processing algorithms to execute over large-scale data. There are two major components of Hadoop: a scalable Hadoop Distributed File System (HDFS) that can support petabytes of data and a MapReduce engine that computes results in batches.

HDFS is a file system that is used to store huge volumes of data across a large number of commodity machines in a cluster. The data can be in terabytes or petabytes. HDFS stores data in the form of blocks of files and follows the write-once-read-many model to access data from these blocks of files. The files stored in the HDFS are operated upon by many complex programs, as per the requirement.

Consider an example of a hospital that used to perform a periodic review of the data obtained from the sensors and machines attached to the patients. This review helped doctors to keep a check on the condition of terminal patients as well as analyze the effects of various medicines on them. With time, the growing volume of data made it difficult for the hospital staff to store and handle it. To find a solution, the hospital consulted a data analyst who suggested the implementation of HDFS as an answer to this problem. HDFS can be implemented in an organization at comparatively low costs than other advanced technologies and can easily handle the continuous streaming of data.

Earlier, we needed to have different types of databases, such as relational and non-relational, for storing different types of data. However, now, all these types of data storage requirements can be addressed by a single concept known as Not Only SQL (NoSQL) databases. Some examples of NoSQL databases include HBASE, MongoDB, AllegroGraph, and InfiniteGraph.

Different NoSQL databases used for different types of business applications are shown in Figure 6.4:

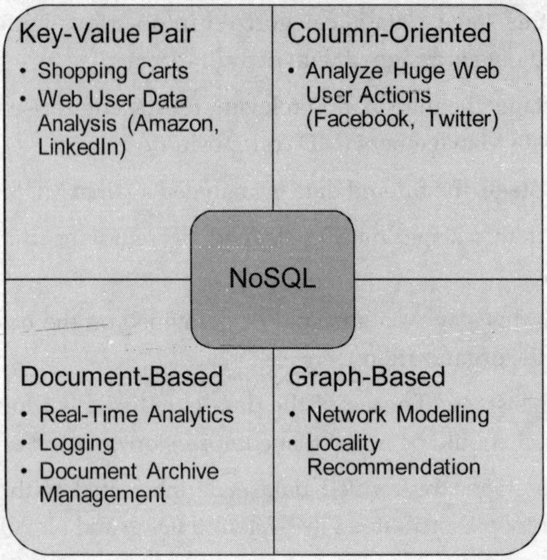

Figure 6.4: Different NoSQL Databases for Different Business Applications

Figure 6.4 shows that different types of NoSQL databases, such as graph-based, document-based, key-value pair, and column-oriented, can be used to store different types of data.

Physical Infrastructure Layer

Before learning about the physical infrastructure layer, you need to know about the principles on which Big Data implementation is based. Some of these principles are:

- **Performance**—High-end infrastructure is required to deliver high performance with low latency. Performance is measured end to end, on the basis of a single transaction or query request. It would be rated high if the total time taken in traversing a query request is low. The total time taken by a data packet to travel from one node to another is described as latency. Generally, the setups that provide high performance and low latency are quite expensive than normal infrastructure setups.
- **Availability**—The infrastructure setup must be available at all times to ensure nearly a 100 percent uptime guarantee of service. It is obvious that businesses cannot wait in case of a service interruption or failure; therefore, an alternative of the main system must also be maintained.
- **Scalability**—The Big Data infrastructure should be scalable enough to accommodate varying storage and computing requirements. They must also be capable to deal with any unexpected challenges.
- **Flexibility**—Flexible infrastructures facilitate adding more resources to the setup and promote failure recovery. It should be noted that flexible infrastructure is also costly; however, costs can be controlled with the use of cloud services, where you need to pay for what you actually use.
- **Cost**—You must select the infrastructure that you can afford. This includes all the hardware, networking, and storage requirements. You must consider all the above parameters in the context of your overall budget and then make trade-offs, where necessary.

From the above points, it can be concluded that a robust and inexpensive physical infrastructure can be implemented to handle Big Data. This requirement is addressed by the Hadoop physical infrastructure layer. This layer is based on a distributed computing model, which allows the physical storage of data in many different locations by linking them through networks and the distributed file system. The Hadoop physical infrastructure layer also supports redundancy of data, because data is collected from so many different sources.

Figure 6.5 shows the hardware topology used for Big Data implementation:

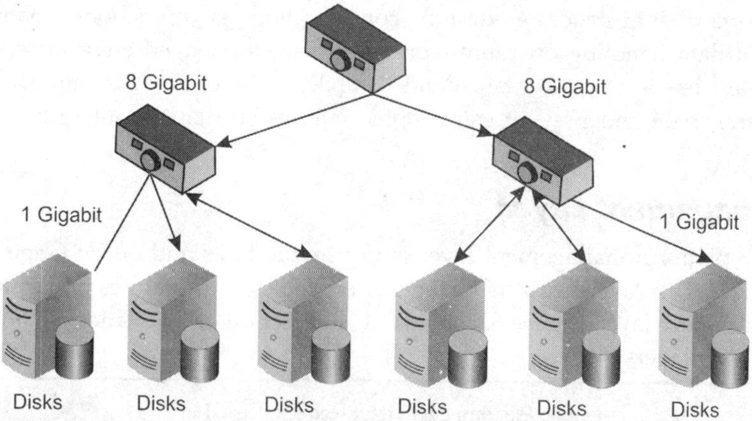

Figure 6.5: Hardware Topology Used for Big Data Implementation

Hadoop infrastructure layer takes care of the hardware and network requirements. It can provide a virtualized cloud environment or a distributed grid of commodity servers over a fast gigabit network. Following are the main components of a Hadoop infrastructure:

- N commodity servers (8-core, 24 GBs RAM, 4 to 12 TBs, gig-E)
- 2-level network (20 to 40 nodes per rack)

NOTE

Big Data implementations need to be highly available, for which the networks, servers, and physical storage hardware should be both resilient and redundant.

The term 'resilience' means flexible, and the term 'redundant' means jobless. In case of Big Data implementation, both these terms are related to each other. The physical infrastructure, or a system, should be resilient so that in case of any type of change or failure, it can accommodate with redundant resources and get ready to jump into action again.

Physical Redundant Networks

In the Big Data environment, networks should be redundant and capable of accommodating the anticipated volume and velocity of the inbound and outbound data in case of heavy network traffic. Organizations that plan to make Big Data an integral part of their computing strategy must be prepared for improving their network performance to handle the increase in the volume, velocity, and variety of data. It is necessary for infrastructure designers to plan for these increases and try to create a flexible physical infrastructure.

Managing Hardware: Storage and Servers

Similar to the redundant networks, hardware resources for storage and servers must also have sufficient speed and capacity to handle all expected types of Big Data. If slow servers are connected to high-speed networks, the slow performance of the servers will be of little use and can, at times, also become a bottleneck.

Infrastructure Operations

Another important infrastructure design consideration is operations management. Proper management of data handling operations provides a well-managed environment, which, in turn, gives the greatest levels of performance and flexibility. Therefore, it is important for data center managers to anticipate and prevent catastrophic failures so that the integrity of the data can be maintained.

Platform Management Layer

The role of the platform management layer is to provide tools and query languages for accessing NoSQL databases. This layer uses the HDFS storage file system that lies on the top of the Hadoop physical infrastructure layer. Figure 6.6 shows the interaction of the Hadoop platform management layer with its lower layers:

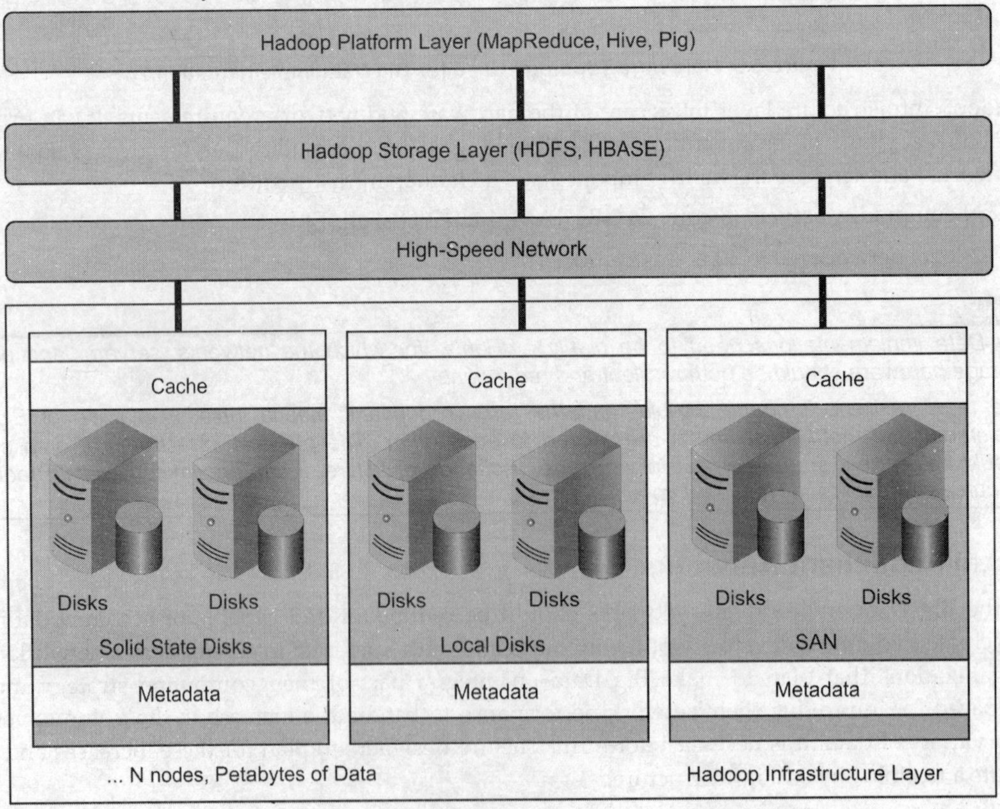

Figure 6.6: Hadoop Platform Management Layer with Other Layers

There is a new technology called Hadoop; it consists of two core components: HDFS and Map-Reduce, and different types of tools that work on Hadoop framework to store, access, and analyze large amounts of data by using real-time analysis. These technologies handle the most fundamental problem of processing huge amounts of data timely, efficiently, and cost-effectively.

The following are the key building blocks of the Hadoop platform management layer:

- **MapReduce**—Refers to a technology that simplifies the creation of processes for analyzing huge amounts of unstructured and structured data. It is a combination of map and reduce features. Map is a component that distributes a problem (of multiple tasks) across a large number of systems and also handles the task of distributing the load for recovery management against failure. When the task of distributed computation is completed, the reduce function combines all the elements back together to provide an aggregate result.
- **Hive**—Refers to a data warehousing package built over Hadoop architecture. Hive provides SQL type query language, called Hive Query Language (HQL) for querying data stored in a Hadoop cluster.
- **Pig**—Refers to a scripting language that is used for batch processing huge amounts of data and allows us to process the data in HDFS in parallel. Pig is not suitable to perform queries on a small portion of a dataset because it scans the entire dataset in one go.
- **HBase**—Refers to a column-oriented database that provides fast access for handling Big Data. It is Hadoop compliant and suitable for batch processing.
- **Sqoop**—Refers to a command-line tool that can import individual tables, specific columns, or entire database files directly in the distributed file system or data warehouse.
- **ZooKeeper**—Refers to a coordinator that keeps multiple Hadoop instances and nodes in synchronization and provides protection to every node from failing because of the overload of data.

Security Layer

The security layer handles the basic security principles that Big Data architecture should follow. Big Data projects are full of security issues because of using the distributed architecture, a simple programming model, and the open framework of services. Therefore, the following security checks must be considered while designing a Big Data stack:

- It must authenticate nodes by using protocols, such as Kerberos.
- It must enable file-layer encryption.
- It must subscribe a key management service for trusted keys and certificates.
- It must use tools such as Chef or Puppet for validating data during the deployment of datasets or while applying service patches on virtual nodes.
- It must maintain logs of the communication that occurs between nodes and trace any anomalies across layers by using distributed logging mechanisms.
- It must ensure a secure communication between nodes by using the Secure Sockets Layer (SSL).

Monitoring Layer

The monitoring layer consists of a number of monitoring systems. These systems remain automatically aware of all the configurations and functions of different operating systems and hardware. They also provide the facility of machine communication with the help of a monitoring tool through high-level protocols, such as Extensible Markup Language (XML). Monitoring systems also provide tools for data storage and visualization. Some examples of open source tools for monitoring Big Data stacks are Ganglia and Nagios.

Analytics Engine

The role of an analytics engine is to analyze huge amounts of unstructured data. This type of analysis is related to text analytics and statistical analytics. Some examples of different types of unstructured data that are available as large datasets include the following:

- Documents containing textual patterns
- Text and symbols generated by customers or users using social media forums, such as Yammer, Twitter, and Facebook
- Machine generated data, such as Radio Frequency Identification (RFID) feeds and weather data
- Data generated from application logs about upcoming or down time details or about maintenance and upgrade details

Figure 6.7 shows some statistical and numerical methods used for analyzing various unstructured data sources:

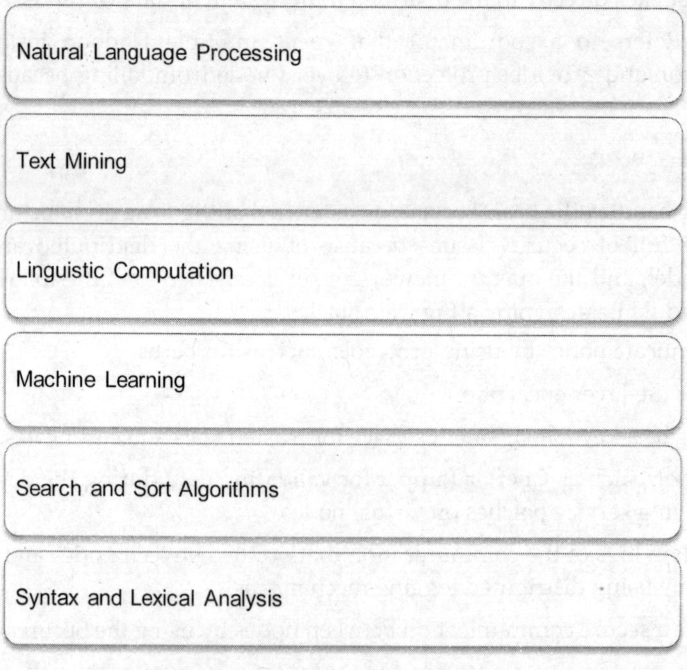

Figure 6.7: Different Statistical and Numerical Methods for Analyzing Big Data

The following types of engines are used for analyzing Big Data:

- **Search engines**—Big Data analysis requires extremely fast search engines with iterative and cognitive data discovery mechanisms for analyzing huge volumes of data. This is required because the data loaded from various sources has to be indexed and searched for Big Data analytics processing.
- **Real-time engines**—These days, real-time applications generate data at a very high speed and even a few-hour old data becomes obsolete and useless as new data continues to flow in. Real-time analysis is required in the Big Data environment to analyze this type of data. For this purpose, real-type engines and NoSQL data stores are used.

Visualization Layer

The visualization layer handles the task of interpreting and visualizing Big Data. Visualization of data is done by data analysts and scientists to have a look at the different aspects of the data in various visual modes. It can be described as viewing a piece of information from different perspectives, interpreting it in different manners, trying to fit it in different types of situations, and deriving different types of conclusions from it.

Figure 6.8 shows the role of the visualization layer:

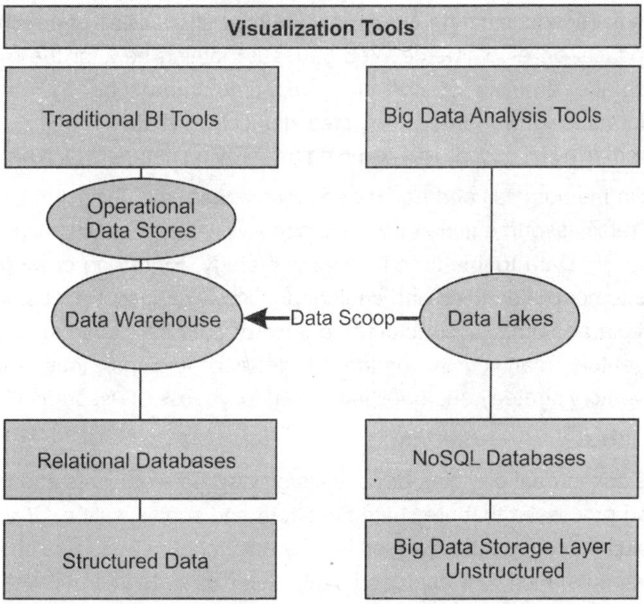

Figure 6.8: Role of the Visualization Layer

The visualization layer works on top of the aggregated data stored in traditional Operational Data Stores (ODS), data warehouse, and data marts. These ODSs get the aggregated data through the data scoop, as shown in Figure 6.8. Some examples of visualization tools are Tableau, Clickview, Spotfire, MapR, and revolution R. These tools work on top of the traditional components such as reports, dashboards, and queries.

NOTE

The aggregated output of Big Data Hadoop processing is scooped into the traditional ODS, data warehouse, and data marts for a further analysis along with the transaction data.

Big Data Applications

Different types of tools and applications are used to implement Big Data stack architecture. These applications can be either horizontal or vertical. Horizontal applications are used to address the problems that are common across industries, whereas vertical applications are used to solve an industry-specific problem.

EXHIBIT 1: World Wide Technology Big Data Use Case for Retail

Improving the Role of Assortment Planning as Part of a Successful Retail Inventory Strategy

Introduction

This year, retailers aren't just pitching the latest fashion trends to students. Retail inventory strategists and assortment planners are also going "back to school" as they seek to learn about customer preferences by turning data into information. Striving to predict how customers will behave as they stroll aisles of merchandise and browse for products on e-commerce Web pages is nothing new for the retail industry. However, with the promise of delivering real-time knowledge by gathering key pieces of information from large, integrated datasets, initiatives focused on using Big Data to improve retail assortment planning are proving compelling, if not imperative.

With the busy fall and holiday seasons ahead, the distinct innovation stirring the world of retail assortment planning, and sending retailers back to school, is the opportunity to use Big Data to fine-tune inventory strategy. By drilling down in new ways to explore customer preferences and capturing a timely snapshot of customer trends using social media and other unstructured sources of data, retailers can study shoppers and treat inventory planning according to detailed findings, thus sharpening their overall inventory strategy and boosting the effectiveness of assortment planning.

Context

As assortment planning often relies on disparate datasets and leans on analytical tools and processes that are limited in depth and sophistication, WWT approaches Big Data solutions for assortment planning by developing strong use cases based on three key elements. First, our approach integrates disparate internal datasets and evaluates the incorporation of third-party datasets, when applicable. Second, our approach develops predictive analytical models that provide superior guidance and better forecasting by essentially turning business problems into math problems. Finally, our approach uses best-in-breed technology, including world-class analytics, to augment legacy IT and produce useful business information that drives successful outcomes.

Use case definition in the area of assortment planning begins with an understanding that success depends on improving the ability to project inventory level requirements in terms of variety and volume, and accurately measure performance at the SKU level.

Additionally, use cases must recognize that improvements in the key areas of assortment planning likely depend on the ability to provide for regional and local preferences. Indeed, use cases focused on inventory strategy and assortment planning need to assume that the range of factors involved in decision model analysis is likely undefined and that the process of defining what data to integrate will carry a significant level of effort.

Description of Solution

WWT's approach to determining what datasets should be integrated and prepared for analysis begins with an evaluation of a retailer's data across business and supplier silos. Our approach then coordinates data from the organization's brands with sales activity at the regional layer that includes discrete variables such as seasonal purchases and online browsing history. If the retailer has yet to undertake data virtualization, efforts will be made to initiate such a program to assess all sources of data across silos, including all available unstructured data. This linkage of data is conducted via abstraction of datasets; no data is moved and no data warehouses are re-architected.

In parallel to data virtualization, or engagement with current data virtualization efforts, WWT will scope the specific business forecasting outcomes required to refine and enhance inventory strategy decision making and subsequent assortment planning processes. The result of this effort will be a roadmap for developing effective predictive analytical models using technology that either augments the existing infrastructure or establishes a scalable platform for supporting inventory strategy and assortment planning, as well as other areas of business decision making that are likely to benefit from Big Data engagements.

Implementation

The objective of WWT's implementation effort is twofold. First, our team will deploy a solution that captures the benefits of data virtualization and provides rapid visibility into possible insights revealed by the correlations across previously isolated datasets. Second, WWT will implement a Big Data stack in conjunction with the customer's IT strategy so that, depending on the available technology and data integrity, an experienced analyst or data scientist with retail expertise can begin to align the assortment of items to reflect marketplace trends for regions, seasons, styles, and demand for specific brands.

In small steps, the choices recommended by WWT's predictive models will then be compared to actual store performance, leading to a refinement of the models, where needed. Data-driven insights are then used to augment human judgment for scenario planning, and visualization layers are introduced to enable a common platform for assortment planning collaboration, budgeting, marketing promotional campaigns, and inventory rotation.

Conclusion and Benefits

The goal of quickly providing the decision-making tools necessary to improve inventory strategy and associated assortment planning programs is primary to WWT's approach of employing data virtualization versus data aggregation. The key advantage is that the costly and time-consuming process of moving and normalizing data across multiple data warehouses and sources is eliminated. WWT's model allows data to be viewed by business analysts using a variety of business intelligence reports that can be generated to improve performance across all retail platforms — in-store, online, outlets, brands, suppliers, regions, departments, and styles – leading to a more holistic view of customer interests and future demand. The resulting enhanced view of customer demand enables wiser inventory investment strategies that can provide meaningful improvement across all areas of the retailer's operations.

About World Wide Technology's Big Data Practice

World Wide Technology's Big Data Practice focuses on business outcomes and end-to-end Big Data planning and design to help customers create valuable pilot use cases that can integrate the platform, analytics tools, and workflows needed to operationalize and sustain long-term solutions. WWT helps customers move from successful proof-of-concept design to implementation using a phased rollout with live data that is processed and analyzed to provide meaningful value for an organization. WWT provides sustainment training to ensure that customer business units enjoy coordination across the enterprise to scale Big Data solutions.

WWT's core consultants, data scientists, technology practice resources, and OEM partners support each stage of a Big Data engagement from developing an analytical model to building out technology. Our objective is to enable customers to achieve long-term success with Big Data by arming them with analytical intelligence customized for their business needs and the Big Data technology to operationalize and scale these valuable solutions.

Source: *https://www2.wwt.com/using-big-data-to-improve-retail-assortment-planning/*

Virtualization and Big Data

To meet everyday challenges of Big Data, regarding the management of huge volumes of distributed data stores and use of computing applications, you need a highly efficient IT environment. One of the answers to this need is virtualization.

Virtualization is a process that allows you to run the images of multiple operating systems on a physical computer. These images of operating systems are called virtual machines. A virtual machine is basically a software representation of a physical machine that can execute or perform the same functions as the physical machine. Each virtual machine contains a separate copy of the operating system with its own virtual hardware resources, device drivers, services, and applications. Although virtualization is not a requirement for Big Data analysis, the required software frameworks such as MapReduce works very efficiently in a virtualized environment.

Figure 6.9 shows the virtualization environment:

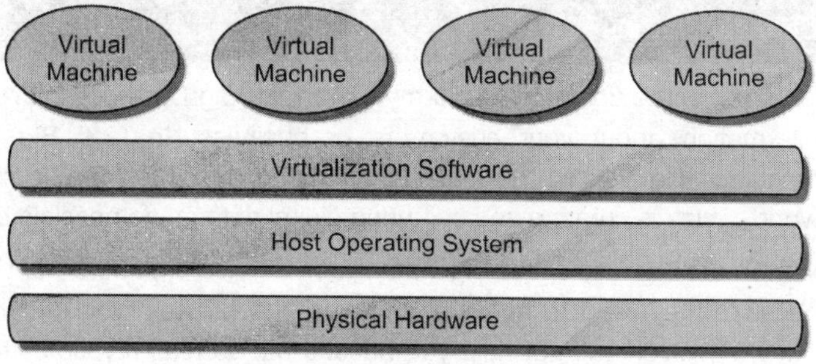

Figure 6.9: Virtualization Environment

The operating system that runs as a virtual machine is known as the guest, while the operating system that runs a virtual machine is known as the host. A guest operating system runs on a hardware virtualization layer, which is at the top of the hardware of a physical machine.

The following are the basic features of virtualization:

- **Partitioning**—Multiple applications and operating systems are supported by a single physical system by partitioning (separating) the available resources.
- **Isolation**—Each virtual machine runs in an isolated manner from its host physical system and other virtual machines. The benefit of such isolation is that if one virtual instance crashes, the other virtual machines and the host system are not affected. In addition, data is not shared between virtual machines.
- **Encapsulation**—Each virtual machine encapsulates its state as a file system. Like a simple file on a computer system, a virtual machine can also be moved or copied. It works like an independent guest software configuration.
- **Interposition**—Generally, in a virtual machine, all the new guest actions are performed through the monitor. A monitor can inspect, modify, or deny operations, such as compression, encryption, profiling, and translation. For instance, a monitor encrypts the data written to a disk. The benefit of this feature is that such types of actions are done without the knowledge of the operating system.

Virtualization is implemented to increase the performance and efficiency of processing a variety of workloads. Instead of assigning a new set of physical system to perform a set of tasks, a set of virtual resources are quickly allocated for meeting all work requirements. Using virtual resources provides the following benefits:

- Enhance service delivery speed by decreasing latency
- Enable better utilization of resources and services
- Provide a foundation for implementing cloud computing
- Improve productivity, implement scalability, and save costs
- Provide a level of automation and standardization for optimizing the computing environment

EXHIBIT 2: Data Visualizations: Converting Big Data into Big Ideas in Madras Cement Company

Let's put some commonly held myths to rest. Big Data doesn't reveal earth-shattering information about your customers or business. In fact, Big Data doesn't reveal anything. If anything, Big Data is a term to describe the current state of the digital world, which is creating and capturing digital data made possible by technology.

What's the big fuss about Big Data then? Service providers want you to think it's huge because they want to sell you solutions that will help you to capture and store data. They, however, will not help you decode the various cryptic patterns and lead you to discover what your customers want or the market is demanding. Even Dan Brown can't help you with that.

The fundamental problem is that traditional forms of data interpretation have stuck to text- or table-based reports like Excel sheets. But humans are visual creatures. Our ability to quickly interpret visual information is far greater than with written words. The data deluge we are witnessing further compounds the problem. Our attention spans are shrinking; there's a constant overload of information and our ability to retain what we read is abysmal.

Data visualization or the art of interpreting data through info graphics, color-codes, geo-mapping, and 3D modeling among others is paving the way to make complex data into simple, consumable information sets. N. Varadarajan, the AVP-IT of Madras Cements, is one of the few Indian CIOs who has successfully embraced it to spectacular business results.

Madras Cements is the fifth largest cement manufacturer in the country and second biggest in Tamil Nadu. It had all the traditional IT instruments that it needed to function efficiently. An ERP, business intelligence software, a great supply chain, and an efficient workforce, and yet the top-line didn't grow as much as expected. It's true in cement industry; supply has always been higher than demand and competition is tight. But the demand too was growing, so how could Madras Cements leverage Information Technology to tap the potential for top-line and bottom-line growth?

This was the challenge faced by the company. The IT team of Madras Cements knew there was lot of scope and untapped potential in managing information. Their ERP was generating rich data, but the lack of visualizations was hindering the company's ability to leverage it and get better insight. It led to the conclusion that the only way to avoid it was to radically change the way the end users saw, read, and interpreted data on any device, whether it was desktops, laptops, mobiles, or tablets.

Information can be presented in many ways. But complex information such as a salesperson performance or cement outlet performance benchmarking or location mapping of the company's wagon movements are best understood not through numbers but through color coding and representation on a map.

Hence, Madras Cements decided to integrate its entire business intelligence system with the enterprise version of Google Maps, while its Ramco ERP application provided the underlying data. Super-imposing its data onto Google Map layer led to some stunning results.

All across India, over 300 field salespersons access reports and transactions on a daily basis from the company's ERP system and integrated Google Maps based BI. Management at Madras Cements started using Google Maps for visual analysis – for monitoring benchmarks and identifying discrepancies and deviation.

The technique followed is called *Geocoded Color Banding*. They assigned color codes to denote a range of performance. For example, performance beyond expectation was assigned a dark green, expected performance green, average orange, below average red, and very bad performance is given dark red. Such color-coded icons are depicted on Google Map using longitude and latitude data captured. For example, the delivery time from factory to each customer outlet can be shown as color coded dots with the dots placed on their longitude and latitude values.

Gap Analysis

Now using the tool, the dark red dots among predominantly green dots quickly pointed them to the areas of weakness and anomalies. More than 60 such KPIs/parameters can be visualized as color-coded icons or regions on the map. This brings out additional insights than what is normally available through a table or a chart. For example, it is very useful to compare and benchmark information such as dealer outlets, delivery points, marketing region, or sales person performance. The tool allows choosing a particular geographical entity (like Kerala) and analyzing the chosen KPI based on a slice (say district, customer point, etc). It helps to analyze patterns of distribution of these color dots on the selected area.

For example, the company monitored one KPI called "Ontime Delivery Index" of its shipments to customers to measure if shipments were reaching on time. Understandably, all areas around the factory performed well as the time taken to reach was much shorter. But amidst all the green or light green dots emerged a single orange spot. The business started to ask, Why was the delivery to this particular dealer so late despite its proximity to the factory?

A little investigation revealed that a particular customer was located on a hilly terrain, because of which it was taking more time for delivery when a truck used was less powerful or old. When the problem was identified, logistics took up the matter with transporters and advised them to use better trucks for that particular location. From the next dispatch, the deliveries were on time.

Insights like these would be impossible without such a visualization tool based on maps. Such data, known as "geographically significant information" forms bulk of Marketing Performance BI, explains **Varadarajan**.

The tool has an Exception Module, which alerts management immediately when any performance parameter downgrades in color (say a green moves to an orange, indicating that performance is dipping) and prompts them to take corrective action before it's too late. This module also helps to analyze and focus on only exceptional items for a particular KPI, say **Dark Reds**, instead of viewing all data. Another aspect of this tool is that no data is entered for this purpose. The data is captured as physical process is done (like invoicing, accounts receivable, etc.), and KPI is built on this vast volume of data. This ensures transparency and objectivity. There is an inbuilt Issue Tracker, which can be used to raise queries to the concerned salesperson (by mail/sms) based on the depicted data and to track responses/actions taken.

Madras Cements' sales and marketing divisions also benefited from this system of BI based on Google Maps. The field sales team now has the capability to easily view information on their mobile devices – information ranging from competitor distribution networks in their area to the best and worst performing dealers and salespersons. This not only enabled them to make better sales strategies on-the-go but also helped management improve their market penetration strategy based on competitiveness in a particular market. They can now locate their cement warehouses and outlets and key customers on Google Maps vis-à-vis critical operation information, empowering them to devise effective supply chain strategies and enhance customer service. Google Maps based BI helped to visualize data at various levels of detail; for example, which regions were experiencing strong growth, which dealers were performing best or had the most potential for growth. Google Maps also made it easier to identify and analyze performing markets with the potential for growth.

IT Departments Battle for Data Analytics Talent

The results have been stupendous. Madras Cements reduced penalties, losses, and damages arising during the wagon clearance process by up to 70 percent, and improved consignment clearance time by up to 40 percent. By implementing Google Maps, the company has successfully captured 20–30 percent market share in these specific markets. *We've also noticed a 10–12 percent increase in sales. But that's just quantitative data. The customer satisfaction that has improved is immeasurable!*, says **Varadarajan**.

Big data can only lead you to big ideas if you ask the right questions. But technology can take you a little further, if you have the right tools.

Source: http://www.cio.in/article/data-visualizations-converting-big-data-big-ideas

Virtualization Approaches

In the Big Data environment, you can virtualize almost every element, such as servers, storage, applications, data, networks, processors, memory, and services. Let's now learn about the virtualization processes of these elements.

Server Virtualization

In case of server virtualization, a single physical server is partitioned into multiple virtual servers. Each virtual server has its own hardware and related resources, such as Random Access Memory (RAM), CPU, hard drive, and network controller. A thin layer of software is also inserted with the hardware, which consists of a virtual machine monitor, also called hypervisor. Hypervisor is a technology that manages the traffic between the virtual machines and the physical machine.

In Big Data analysis, server virtualization can ensure the scalability of the platform as per the volume of the data. Server virtualization also provides the foundation of using cloud services as data sources.

Application Virtualization

Application virtualization means encapsulating applications in a way that they would not be dependent on the underlying physical computer system. Application virtualization improves the manageability and portability of applications. It can be used along with server virtualization to meet business SLAs (Service Level Agreements).

Application virtualization ensures that Big Data applications can access resources on the basis of their relative priority with each other. Big Data applications have significant IT resource requirements, and application virtualization can help them in accessing resources at low costs.

NOTE

Server virtualization helps in monitoring the CPU and memory usage but does not provide information regarding the variations in business priority while allocating resources. However, by implementing application virtualization along with server virtualization, you can ensure that the most high-priority applications will always have the top priority while accessing resources.

Network Virtualization

Network virtualization means using virtual networking as a pool of connection resources. While implementing network virtualization, you do not need to rely on the physical network for managing traffic between connections. You can create as many virtual networks as you need from a single physical implementation. In the Big Data environment, network virtualization helps in defining different networks with different sets of performance and capacities to manage the large distributed data required for Big Data analysis.

Processor and Memory Virtualization

Processor virtualization optimizes the power of the processor and maximizes its performance. Memory virtualization decouples memory from the servers. Big Data analysis needs systems to have high processing power (CPU) and memory (RAM) for performing complex computations. These computations can take a lot of time in case CPU and memory resources are not sufficient. Processor and memory virtualization, thus, can increase the speed of processing and get your analysis results sooner.

Data and Storage Virtualization

Data virtualization provides an abstract service that delivers data continuously in a consistent form without the knowledge of the underlying physical database. It is used to create a platform that can provide dynamic linked data services. On the other hand, storage virtualization combines physical storage resources so that they can be shared in a more effective way.

In the Big Data environment, sometimes, you need to access only a certain type of data, say only a columnar database. Data virtualization proves to be useful in these cases, as the virtual images of the database can be stored and invoked, whenever required, without consuming valuable data center resources or capacity. In addition, storage virtualization is used to store large volumes of unstructured and structured data.

Managing Virtualization with Hypervisor

Hypervisor is a program that allows multiple operating systems to share a single hardware. Hypervisor is also known as virtual machine manager. It controls the host processor and resources. It allocates what the other operating system needed and takes care that the guest operating systems (virtual machines) do not disrupt each other. There are two types of hypervisor:

- **Type 1**—It runs directly on the system hardware with VM resources provided by the hypervisor. They are often called "native" or "embedded" hypervisors. Examples of type 1 hypervisor are VMwareESXi and Citrix XenServer.
- **Type 2**—It runs on a host operating system to provide virtualization services. Administrators could buy the software and install it on a server. It is also known as hosted hypervisor. Examples of type 2 hypervisor are Sun VirtualBox, VMware Server, and Microsoft Virtual PC. Figure 6.10 shows the two types of hypervisor:

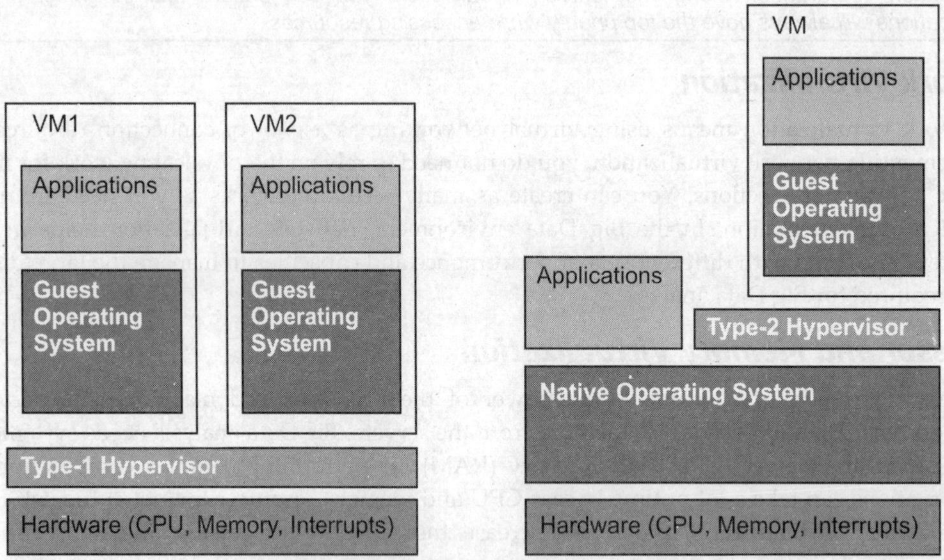

Figure 6.10: Type 1 and Type 2 Hypervisors

Hyper-V is a hypervision technology that provides the hypervisor a thin software layer that runs on top of the hardware and under the host operating system. It grants both parent (host) and child (guest) operating systems an equal access to the hardware. Actually, a hypervisor turns all locally installed operating systems into virtual machines. In Hyper-V, guest operating systems are installed in separate partitions and have equal access to the hardware.

Figure 6.11 shows the architecture of the hypervision technology:

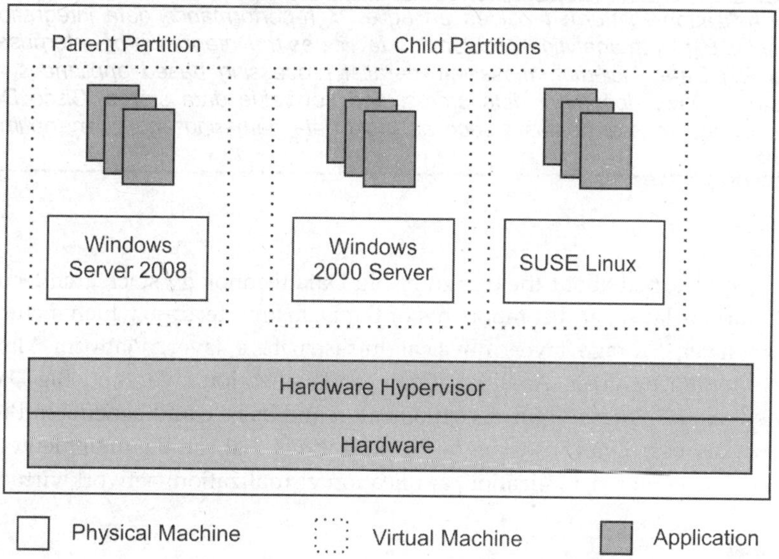

Figure 6.11: Architecture of the Hypervision Technology

Hyper-V has some strict hardware requirements that are related to the processor. It requires an x64-based processor that includes AMD-V and IntelVT hardware-assisted virtualization and hardware data execution protection. In Advanced Micro Dynamics (AMD) systems, the data execution protection feature is known as No Execute or NX bit, and in Intel systems, this feature is called Execute Disable or XD bit. Note that these features are disabled by default, so you have to enable them.

In the Big Data environment, hypervisor can provide a practical way of getting things virtualized quickly and efficiently. Hypervisor can provide different operating system environments for different applications running on a physical computer system.

Implementing Virtualization to Work with Big Data

To handle Big Data, you need to access, manage, and analyze structured and unstructured data in a distributed environment. Virtualization helps in Big Data analysis by optimizing various elements related to the computer system, including hardware, software, and storage, for processing and managing large volumes of structured and unstructured data.

In practice, any kind of MapReduce engine can work much better in a virtualized environment. Configuring multiple MapReduce engines in parallel in a virtual environment reduces the management overhead and related task workload.

Moreover, implementing virtualization increases the utilization of the assets for which organizations have already paid and, in fact, turns these assets into generic pools of resources.

CASELET

Cisco Data Virtualization Platform provides an agile, high-performance data integration approach that addresses complex Big Data analytical problems. It facilitates the integration of enterprise data with all the major types of Big Data, including massively parallel processing based appliances, columnar/tabular NoSQL data stores, XML document data stores, and key/value data stores. Cisco Data Virtualization Platform also provides several benefits, such as rapid data gathering and query optimization for timely business insight.

Summary

In this chapter, you learned about the design of Big Data technology stack architecture. The chapter also discussed various layers and components of Big Data architecture, which includes Data Sources layer, Ingestion layer, Storage layer, Physical Infrastructure layer, Platform Management layer, Security layer, Monitoring layer, Analytics Engine, Visualization layer, and Big Data Applications. You also learned about the technique of virtualization and its role and benefits in Big Data analytics. The chapter then discussed various types of virtualizations that can be implemented in the Big Data environment, such as server virtualization, application virtualization, network virtualization, etc.

Quick Revise

Multiple-Choice Questions

Q1. The role of the ____ layer is to absorb the huge inflow of data and sort it out in different categories.

a. Data sources
b. Ingestion
c. Security
d. Visualization

Ans. The correct option is b.

Q2. Which of the following stages in the Ingestion layer reduces the size of data without affecting its relevance for the required process?

a. Identification
b. Filtration
c. Compression
d. Noise reduction

Ans. The correct option is c.

Q3. _________ is an open source framework that enables you to store large volumes of data in a distributed manner across multiple machines.

a. Hadoop
b. Hive
c. Pig
d. ZooKeeper

Ans. The correct option is a.

Q4. Which of the following is not an example of NoSQL databases?

a. Hbase
b. MongoDB
c. AllegroGraph
d. Oracle

Ans. The correct option is d.

Q5. The role of the ___ layer is to provide tools and query languages for accessing NoSQL databases by using the HDFS storage file system.

a. Platform management
b. Physical infrastructure
c. Storage
d. Analytics engine

Ans. The correct option is a.

Q6. ____ is a command-line tool that can import individual tables, specific columns, or entire database files directly in the distributed file system or data warehouse.

a. Sqoop
b. ZooKeeper
c. Pig
d. HBase

Ans. The correct option is a.

Q7. Technology that manages traffic between virtual and physical machines is known as:

a. MapReduce
b. Hadoop
c. Hypervisors
d. Virtualization

Ans. The correct option is c.

Q8. Which of the following features of virtualization means that a virtual machine can be represented by using a single file?

a. Partitioning
b. Isolation
c. Encapsulation
d. Application virtualization

Ans. The correct option is c.

Q9. Which of the following can improve the speed of processing of data and get your analysis results sooner?

a. Network virtualization
b. Processor and memory virtualization
c. Data and storage virtualization
d. Application virtualization

Ans. The correct option is b.

Q10. Which of the following statements is not true?

a. Hypervisor is a thin software layer that runs on top of the hardware and under the host operating system
b. A MapReduce engine can work much better in a virtualized environment
c. Application virtualization improves the processing speed of applications
d. The operating system that runs as a virtual machine is known as the guest

Ans. The correct option is c.

Subjective Questions

Q1. List some major functions of the Big Data architecture model.

Ans. The Big Data architecture model must be able to perform the following functions:

- Capturing data from different sources
- Cleaning and integrating data of different types of formats
- Sorting and organizing data
- Analyzing data
- Identifying relationships and patterns
- Deriving logical conclusions based on the data analysis results

Q2. List the components of the Big Data architecture.

Ans. The Big Data architecture comprises the following layers and components:

- Data Sources layer
- Ingestion layer
- Storage layer
- Physical Infrastructure layer
- Platform Management layer
- Security layer
- Monitoring layer
- Analytics engine
- Visualization layer
- Big Data applications

Q3. Explain the functioning of the ingestion layer in the Big Data architecture.

Ans. The role of the ingestion layer is to absorb the huge inflow of data and sort it out in different categories. This layer separates the noise from the relevant information. It can handle huge volume, high velocity, and a variety of data. The ingestion layer validates, cleanses, transforms, reduces, and integrates the unstructured data into the Big Data stack for further processing.

The following figure illustrates the functioning of the ingestion layer:

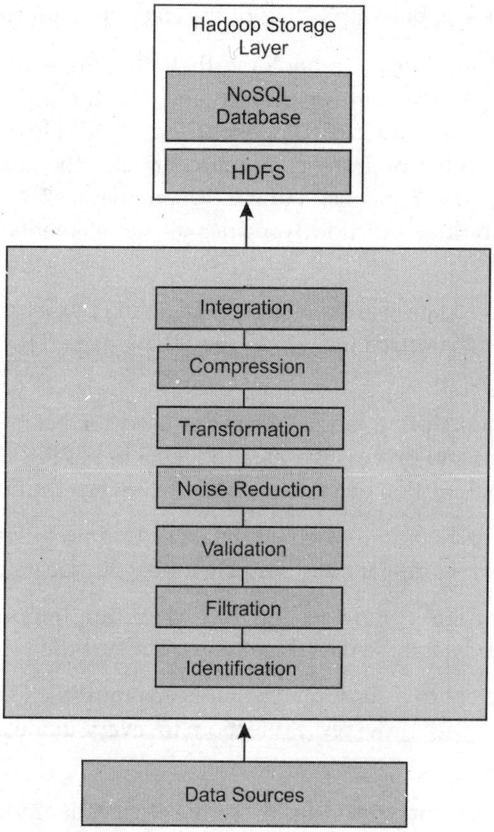

In the ingestion layer, the data passes through the following stages:

- **Identification**—At this stage, data is categorized into various known data formats, or we can say that unstructured data is assigned with default formats.
- **Filtration**—At this stage, the information relevant for the enterprise is filtered on the basis of the enterprise MDM repository.
- **Validation**—At this stage, the filtered data is analyzed against MDM metadata.
- **Noise Reduction**—At this stage, data is cleaned by removing the noise and minimizing the related disturbances.
- **Transformation**—At this stage, data is split or combined on the basis of its type, contents, and the requirements of the organization.
- **Compression**—At this stage, the size of the data is reduced without affecting its relevance for the required process. It should be noted that compression does not affect the analysis results.
- **Integration**—At this stage, the refined dataset is integrated with the Hadoop storage layer, which consists of Hadoop Distributed File System (HDFS) and NoSQL databases.

Q4. Discuss the key building blocks of the Hadoop platform management layer.

Ans. The following are the key building blocks of the Hadoop platform management layer:

- **MapReduce**—Refers to a technology that simplifies the creation of processes for analyzing huge amounts of unstructured and structured data. It is a combination of map and reduce features. Map is a component that distributes a problem (of multiple tasks) across a large number of systems and also handles the task of distributing the load for recovery management against failure. When the task of distributed computation is completed, the reduce function combines all the elements back together to provide an aggregate result.
- **Hive**—Refers to a data warehousing package/infrastructure built on top of Hadoop. It provides an SQL dialect, called Hive Query Language (HQL) for querying data stored in a Hadoop cluster.
- **Pig**—Refers to a scripting language that is used for batch processing huge amounts of data and allows us to process the data in HDFS in parallel. Pig is not suitable to perform queries on a small portion of a dataset because it scans the entire dataset in one go.
- **HBase**—Refers to a column-oriented database that provides fast access for handling Big Data. It is Hadoop-compliant and suitable for batch processing.
- **Sqoop**—Refers to a command-line tool that can import individual tables, specific columns, or entire database files directly in the distributed file system or data warehouse.
- **ZooKeeper**—Refers to a coordinator that keeps multiple Hadoop instances and nodes in synchronization and provides protection to every node from failing because of the overload of data.

Q5. What is the role of an analytical engine in the Big Data environment? Describe different types of engines used to analyze Big Data.

Ans. The role of an analytics engine is to analyze huge amounts of unstructured data. This type of analysis is related to text analytics and statistical analytics. The following types of engines are used for analyzing Big Data:

- **Search engines**—Big Data analysis requires extremely fast search engines with iterative and cognitive data discovery mechanisms for analyzing huge volumes of data. This is required because the data loaded from various sources has to be indexed and searched for Big Data analytics processing.
- **Real-time engines**—These days, real-time applications generate data at a very high speed, and even a few-hour old data becomes obsolete and useless as new data continues to flow in. Real-time analysis is required in the Big Data environment to analyze this type of data. For this purpose, real-type engines and NoSQL data stores are used.

Q6. What is virtualization? Explain its features.

Ans. Virtualization is a process that allows you to run the images of multiple operating systems on a physical computer. These images of operating systems are called virtual machines. A virtual machine is basically a software representation of a physical machine that can execute or perform the same functions as the physical machine. Each virtual machine contains a separate copy of the operating system with its own virtual hardware resources, device drivers, services, and applications.

Although virtualization is not a requirement for Big Data analysis, the required software framework such as MapReduce works very efficiently in a virtualized environment.

The following are the basic features of virtualization:

- **Partitioning**—Multiple applications and operating systems are supported by a single physical system by partitioning (separating) the available resources.
- **Isolation**—Each virtual machine runs in an isolated manner from its host physical system and other virtual machines. The benefit of such isolation is that if one virtual instance crashes, the other virtual machines and the host system are not affected. In addition, data is not shared between virtual machines.
- **Encapsulation**—Each virtual machine encapsulates its state as a file system. Like a simple file on a computer system, a virtual machine can also be moved or copied. It works like an independent guest software configuration.
- **Interposition**—Generally, in a virtual machine, all the new guest actions are performed through the monitor. A monitor can inspect, modify, or deny operations, such as compression, encryption, profiling, and translation. For instance, a monitor encrypts the data written to a disk. The benefit of this feature is that such types of actions are done without the knowledge of the operating system.

Q7. Write short notes on the following:

a. Server virtualization

b. Processor and memory virtualization

c. Hyper-V

Ans. a. **Server virtualization**—In case of server virtualization, a single physical server is partitioned into multiple virtual servers. Each virtual server has its own hardware and related resources, such as Random Access Memory (RAM), CPU, hard drive, and network controller. A thin layer of software is also inserted with the hardware, which consists of a virtual machine monitor, also called hypervisor. Hypervisor is a technology that manages the traffic between the virtual machine and the physical machine.

In Big Data analysis, server virtualization can ensure the scalability of the platform as per the volume of the data. Server virtualization also provides the foundation of using cloud services as data sources.

b. **Processor and memory virtualization**—Processor virtualization optimizes the power of the processor and maximizes its performance. Memory virtualization decouples memory from the servers. Big Data analysis needs systems to have high processing power (CPU) and memory (RAM) for performing complex computations. These computations can take a lot of time in case CPU and memory resources are not sufficient. Processor and memory virtualization, thus, can increase the speed of processing and get your analysis results sooner.

c. **Hyper-V**—Hyper-V is a hypervision technology that provides the hypervisor a thin software layer that runs on top of the hardware and under the host operating system. It grants both parent (host) and child (guest) operating systems an equal access to the hardware. Actually, a hypervisor turns all locally installed operating systems into virtual machines. In Hyper-V, guest operating systems are installed in separate partitions and have equal access to the hardware.

7

Storing Data in Databases and Data Warehouses

A simple Database Management System (DBMS) stores data in the form of schemas or tables, comprising rows and columns. The main goal of a DBMS is to provide a solution for storing and retrieving information in a convenient and efficient manner. The most common way of fetching data from these tables is by using Structured Query Language (SQL). A Relational Database Management System (RDBMS) stores the relationships between these tables in columns that serve as a reference for another table. These columns are known as primary keys and foreign keys, both of which can be used to reference other tables so that data can be related between the tables and retrieved as and when it is required.

Such a database system usually consists of several tables and relationships between those tables, which help in classifying the information contained in them. These tables are also stored in Boyce-Codd Normal Form (BCNF), and a relationship is sustained within these tables using primary/foreign keys.

As you know, data in tables is stored in the form of rows and columns. The size of a file increases as new data and records are added, resulting in an increase in the size of the database. All these files are commonly shared by several users through a database server. In systems requiring consistent availability, these data files are shared across nodes so that each node has access to the same data file.

In addition to data files, a Data Warehouse (DWH) is also used for handling large amounts of data or Big Data. A DWH can be defined as the association of data from various sources that are created for supporting planned decision making. According to William (Bill) H. Inmon, the Father of Data Warehousing, "A data warehouse is a subject-oriented, integrated, time-variant and non-volatile collection of data in support of management's decision-making process."

The primary goal of a data warehouse is to provide a consistent picture of the business at a given point of time. Using various data warehousing toolsets, employees in an organization can efficiently execute online queries and mine data according to their requirement.

This chapter begins by describing RDBMS and its use in managing Big Data. It also introduces you to non-relational databases. Further, you learn about polyglot persistence, which is defined as a set of applications that use several core database technologies. The chapter also discusses the integration of Big Data with traditional data warehouses. In addition, it explains the role and importance of Big Data analysis and data warehouses. In the end, the chapter discusses the change in deployment models in the era of Big Data.

RDBMS and Big Data

An RDBMS uses a relational model where all the data is stored using preset schemas. These schemas are linked using the values in specific columns of each table. The data is hierarchical, which means for data to be stored or transacted it needs to adhere to ACID standards, namely:

- **Atomicity**—Ensures full completion of a database operation.
- **Consistency**—Ensures that data abides by the schema (table) standards, such as correct data type entry, constraints, and keys.
- **Isolation**—Refers to the encapsulation of information. Makes only necessary information visible.
- **Durability**—Ensures that transactions stay valid even after a power failure or errors.

In traditional database systems, every time data is accessed or modified, it requires to be moved (indexed) to a central location for processing. Therein lies a major limitation of hardware upgradation. You can upgrade your hardware to improve performance; however, depending on the hardware platform, there is a limitation on the number of processors and system memory that can be used to concurrently perform database operations. Besides the processing power restraint, network latency can also occur during data transfer to the central node.

NOTE

The data in a database is stored in primary data files with the extension .mdf and secondary data files are identified with the .ndf extension. Log files are identified with the .ldf extension.

Let's assume that you can buy a server with 2 terabytes of RAM. It is a bit expensive, but not unworkable for a large organization. Also, currently there are very few databases that will lag with 2 terabytes of RAM. The problem lies in its design.

RDBMS presumes your data to be essentially correct beforehand. Mapping real-world problems to a relational database model comprises many improvised strategies, but the textbook approach recommends following a three-step process: conceptual, logical, and physical modeling. But simply mapping the problem in such a way doesn't work. It makes some incorrect assumptions, such as your information system staying consistent and static all the time. However in the real world, data is only partially legible.

For example, a bank cannot maintain its Web server access logs using the same database that it uses for financial transactions. This is because it is more important for financial transactions to be highly consistent than the other requirement of maintaining logs. But since one of the operations (transactions) happens to be absolute and the other not, we clearly defy the presumption of information staying consistent all the time, which we had about our information systems.

The Internet has grown by leaps and bounds in the past two decades. Numerous domains have been registered, more than a billion gigabytes of Web-space has been reserved. With the digital revolution of the early 1990s aiding the personal computer segment, Web transactions have grown rapidly. With the advent of various search engines, lure of easily available information, and freely distributable information, the social media platform has recorded a threefold increase in the volume of transactions. Although solutions for such situations occurring in corporate scenarios have been there, coping with Web-based transactions has turned out to be a compelling factor while addressing database-related issues with Big Data solutions.

Big Data mainly takes three Vs into account: Volume, Variety, and Velocity. These three terms can be briefly explained as follows:

- **Volume of Data**—Big Data is designed to store and process a few hundred terabytes, or even petabytes or zettabytes of data.
- **Variety of Data**—Collection of data, different from a format suiting relational database systems, is stored in a semi-structured or an unstructured format.
- **Velocity of Data**—The rate of data arrival might make an enterprise data warehouse problematic, particularly where formal data preparation processes like conforming, examining, transforming, and cleansing of the data needs to be accomplished before it is stored in data warehouse tables.

Big Data solutions are designed for storing and managing enormous amounts of data using a simple file structure, formats, and highly distributed storage mechanisms with the initial handling of the data occurring at each storage node, unlike RDBMS. This obviates the need for data to be moved every time over the network for even a simple processing.

One of the biggest difficulties with RDBMS is that it is not yet near the demand levels of Big Data. The volume of data handling today is rising at a fast rate.

Facebook stores 1.5 petabytes (PB) of photos. Google processes around 20 PB of data each day. Every minute, over 204 million emails are sent and received, 3,500 photos are shared on Instagram, and over two million search queries are processed by Google. An RDBMS fails to live up to the required expectation of processing data volumes of such massive scales, and RDBMS solutions turn out to be ridiculously expensive.

Big Data primarily comprises semi-structured data, such as social media sentiment analysis and text mining data, while RDBMSs are more suitable for structured data, such as weblog, sensor, and financial data.

Table 7.1 shows a comparative study of the features of relational database solutions and Big Data solutions:

Table 7.1: Feature of Relational Databases and Big Data Solutions

Feature	Relational Database Systems	Big Data Solutions
Data types and formats	Structured	Structured, semi-structured and unstructured
Data integrity	High transactional updates	Depends on the technology used—often follows consistent models
Schema	Static	Dynamic
Read and write pattern	Fully repeatable read/write	Write once, repeatable read
Storage volume	Gigabytes to terabytes	Terabytes, petabytes, and beyond
Scalability	Scale up with more powerful hardware	Scale out with additional servers
Data processing distribution	Limited or none	Distributed across clusters
Economics	Expensive hardware and software	Commodity hardware and open-source software

It is a misconception that Big Data deals only with volume, as Big Data talks about 4Vs. A report of a survey done by Forrester on 60 clients brings out some interesting facts. Three-quarters of the respondents indicate volume as the main reason for contemplating Big Data solutions, while others state velocity, variety as well as variability as the major cause toward shifting to Big Data technologies.

Figure 7.1 shows the fourth V, that is, variability:

Volume - exceeds physical limits of vertical scalability	**Velocity** - decision window small compared to data change rate
Variety - many different formats makes integration expensive	**Variability** - many options or variable interpretations confound analysis

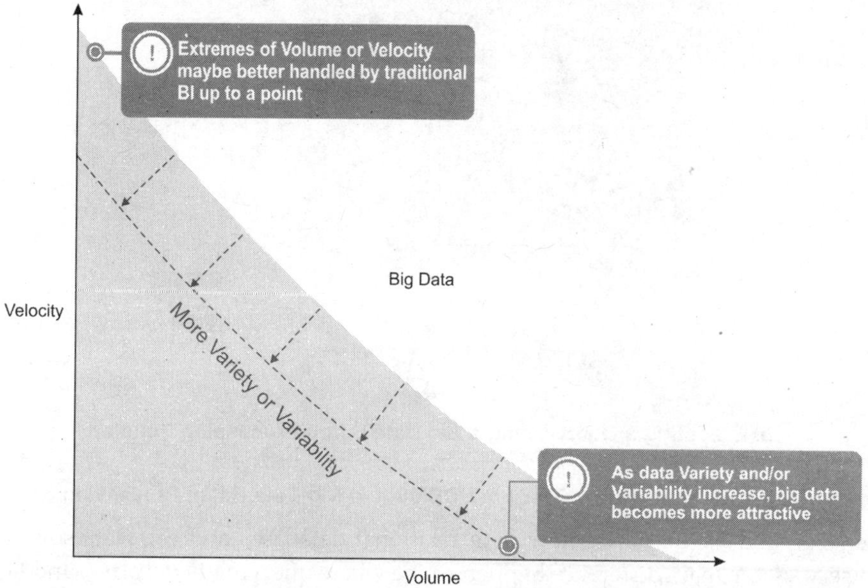

Source: *Expand your Digital Horizon with Big Data by Brain Hopkins & Boris Evelson, Sep 30-2011*

Figure 7.1: The Four Vs of Big Data

Big Data does not force a relational model on the stored data. Rather, the data can be of any type—structured, semi-structured, or unstructured. A suitable schema can be applied later on, when you query this data. Big Data stores data in its raw format and applies a schema only when the data is read, which preserves all of the information within the data.

Figure 7.2 (a) and 7.2 (b) show some basic differences between an RDBMS and a Big Data system in terms of storage and querying of data:

a. Executing a Query Using a Relational Database System

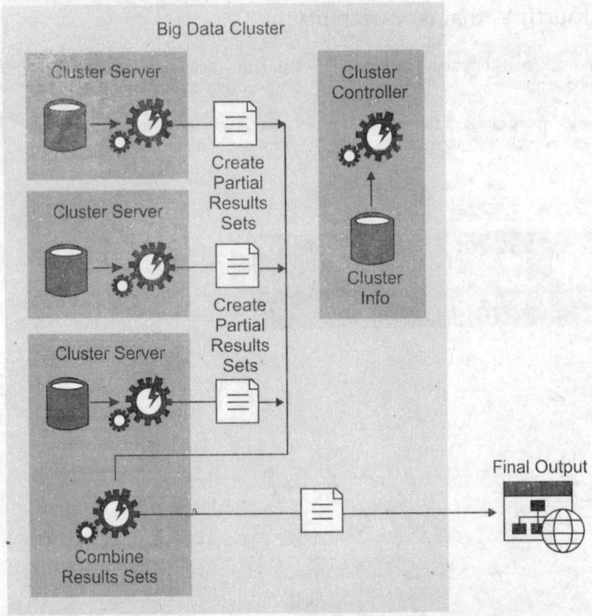

b. Executing a Query Using a Big Data Batch Processing Solution

Source: *https://msdn.microsoft.com/en-us/library/dn749785.aspx*

Figure 7.2 (a & b): Executing a Query in RDBMS and Big Data Batch Processing Solution

In Figure 7.2(a) and 7.2(b), notice how both relational databases and Big Data solutions employ a cluster of servers; the main difference happens to be where querying takes place, and how the data is moved across.

Big Data solutions are adjusted for loading huge amounts of data using simple file formats and highly distributed storage mechanisms, with initial processing of the data occurring at every storage node. This means that once the data is loaded on to the cluster storage, the data bulk need not be moved over the network for processing.

If Big Data uses unstructured, non-relational jumbled raw data, how can it act in demanding environments, where need for data retrieval, archival, and other operations at steady and faster speed are important?

Big Data solutions provide a way to avoid storage limitations and reduce the cost of processing and storage, for immense volumes of data. Even in the case of RDBMS, with the advancement of technology and development in hardware and software for such an essential business function, capabilities for storing huge amounts of data are available. For example, Analytics Platform System (APS) from Microsoft can easily store a few hundred terabytes of data.

In fact, relational database systems and Big Data batch processing solutions are seen as complementary mechanisms instead of being competitive. Batch processing solutions of Big Data are very unlikely to ever replace relational database solutions and in most cases, they balance and enhance the capabilities for managing data and generating BI cases.

Big Data is an important tool when you need to manage data that is arriving very quickly in random formats, which you can process later. You can store the data in clusters in its original format, and then process it when required using a query that extracts the required result set and stores it in a relational database, or makes it available for reporting. Figure 7.3 shows this approach in schematic form:

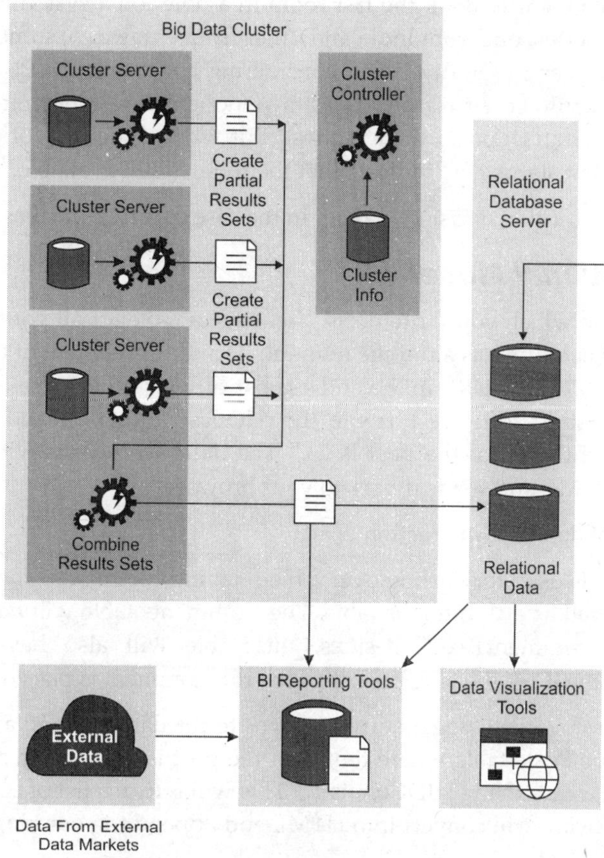

Source: *https://msdn.microsoft.com/en-us/library/dn749785.aspx*

Figure 7.3: Combining Big Data Batch Processing with a Relational Database

In the 'data-tsunami' kind of environment, where data inflow is beyond usual conventions and rationales, Big Data acts as the dam to contain the water (data), and then utilizes RDBMS cleverly to make channels in order to distribute data specifically to the hydro-electric stations, irrigation canals, and other places where the water is required most.

Hence, Big Data happens to be non-relational when it comes to storing and handling incoming data, and then it abides by a conventional RDBMS system to actually disintegrate the raw, typically structure-less data into fragments of meaningful information.

CAP Theorem

CAP Theorem is also known as Brewer's theorem. It states that it is not possible for a distributed system to provide all the following three conditions at the same point of time:

- **Consistency**—Same data is visible by all the nodes.

- **Availability**—Every request is answered, whether it succeeds or fails.
- **Partition-tolerance**—Despite network failures, the system continues to operate.

For example, Alice and Bob want to book the last room in a hotel on a system which is in peer-to-peer topology having two nodes, one from India and other from Ottawa. Assume that the two nodes reside on the same data center in Ottawa. Now considering consistency (CP) when Alice tries to book the room, the node should confirm from the Ottawa node before confirming the room. Ideally both nodes are based on serialization of their request. But what if the network connection breaks between the two? The current status may indicate that the room is still available.

The CAP theorem is very helpful in decision making in the case of future databases.

Issues with the Relational Model

Imagine you have a blog on which you write posts. You have a table for all your posts in which, for each post, there is a row. Each row has a unique numeric ID and text content of that post. When you want to view/read a blog post, the URL in the address bar of your browser says "give me post #23 for example." The blog hosting software turns to the database and commands "select everything from the posts table where the ID of the post is 23." The database reverts with the post, and the software converts it into HTML and sends it back to your browser.

This is the simplest form of database interaction.

Now, the relational model is used for surfing over a blog having comments. The relational database includes a Posts table as well as a Comments table. The Comments table will have a unique ID and another column called "commentText." Besides, this table will also have a column called "postIDCom," to identify the ID of the blog post at which this comment is placed.

So now when visitor comes by, the blogger software turns to the database and asks for two things—"select everything from the Posts table where the ID of the post is 23," and then "select everything from the Comments table where the postIDCom is 1." This will return a list of comments in the form of an array, which the software will convert into HTML and append to your blog post in the form of the comments section.

For explanative purposes, this is a straightforward real-time equation. But, does it really make sense to store blog posts and comments at different places? They're clearly related. Will you evaluate a post's comments without knowing what that post is all about?

Because of these issues, a non-relational (NoSQL, MongoDB, etc.) database can appear to be a lot more rational approach.

Non-Relational Database

The database that does not integrate in the table/key model is known as a non-relational database.

In other words, a database that does not use the table/key model of RDBMS is a non-relational database. Such a kind of database requires effective data operation techniques and processes, often custom-designed, to provide solutions to Big Data problems. NoSQL (Not Only SQL) is one such example of a popular emerging non-relational database. It is a BASE system (Basically Available, Soft state, and Eventual Consistency).

Most non-relational databases are associated with websites such as Google, Amazon, Yahoo!, and Facebook. These websites introduce new applications almost every day with millions of users. So they require non-relational databases to handle unexpected traffic spikes, since the existing RDBMS cannot withstand the fluctuation. An appealing feature of a non-relational database is scalability. Non-relational databases do scaling without the table, which comprises rows and columns, and relational databases use specialized frameworks to store data, accessible by special query APIs.

Another important class of non-relational databases is the one that does not support the relational model, but uses and relies on SQL as the primary means of manipulating existing data. Despite relational and non-relational databases having similar fundamentals, the difference lies in how they individually achieve the fundamentals.

Non-relational database technologies have the following characteristics in common:

- **Scalability**—It refers to the capability to write data across multiple data clusters simultaneously, irrespective of physical hardware or infrastructure limitations.
- **Seamlessness**—Another important aspect that ensures the resiliency of non-relational databases, is their capability to expand/contract to accommodate varying degrees of increasing or decreasing data flows, without affecting the end-user experience.
- **Data and Query Model**—Instead of the traditional row/column, key-value structure, non-relational databases use frameworks to store data with a required set of queries or APIs to access the data.
- **Persistence Design**—Persistence is an important element in non-relational databases, ensuring faster throughput of huge amounts of data by making use of dynamic memory rather than conventional reading and writing from disks. This is a vital element in non-relational databases. Due to the high variety, velocity, and volume of data, these databases utilize different mechanisms, maintain persistency in data. The highest performance option is "in-memory," where the entire database is stored in a huge cache, so as to avoid time-consuming read-write cycles.
- **Eventual Consistency**—While RDBMS use ACID (Atomicity, Consistency, Isolation, Durability) for ensuring data consistency, non-relational DBMS use BASE Basically available soft state, eventual consistency to ensure that inconsistencies are resolved when data is midway between the nodes in a distributed system.

However, there are issues with the non-relational database model. Let's discuss them in detail.

Issues with the Non-Relational Model

The non-relational data model looks more like a concept of one entity, and all the data that relates to that one entity is called a document.

The way your blogging software interacts with the blog post is theoretically a lot simpler in a non-relational database. The request comes in, and the blogging software queries the database and says "Return a specific post and everything related to it." But, since we are not concerned about data structure right now, what if we want to tag that post with different categories? You need to join them with some document and when the blog software asks "Give me everything on Post #1," the tags, the comments, and any other randomly associated data are returned as a query result. The bottom line is that you should be well aware of what you are doing at the software level.

Imagine a grocery list. You can make a grocery list in a simple way—you write down the items you want on a piece of paper. But say, after few months, you want to know how many bread loaves you bought last year. In such a case, with the non-relational database model you have to go through each list and count every loaf separately, whereas in a relational database modeling, you can get that count instantly. Yes, it means a bit of extra work on the front end, but modeled correctly, it is indeed an efficient way. In situations where you want to be careful about your data and its structure—bank accounts, for example—a relational database is an absolute must, theoretically better, and a tried and proven technology.

To sum up, individual limitations of the relational and non-relational data models may appear as trivial at a lower level but going up in the Big Data ecosystem, things become too evident to be overlooked. Some popular non-relational databases are CouchDB, MongoDB, Cassandra, Bigtable (Google) and Neo4j.

Polyglot Persistence

The term polyglot in Big Data is applied to a set of applications that use several core database technologies. A polyglot database is often used to solve a complex problem by breaking it into fragments and applying different database models. Then, the results of different sets are aggregated into a data storage and analysis solution. We can attain the results by using multiple data storage technologies for a particular application, which is chosen based upon the best way data can be stored and retrieved for an application. In Big Data, it means picking the right NoSQL DB for the right application.

For examples, Disney in addition to RDBMS also uses Cassandra and MongoDB. Netflix uses Cassandra, Hbase, and SimpleDB. Twitter uses Cassandra, FlockDB, Hbase, and MYSQL. Mendeley uses Hbase, MongoDB, Solr, and Voldemort.

A lot of corporations still use relational databases for some data, but the increasing persistence requirements of dynamic applications are growing from predominantly relational to a mixture of data sources.

Imagine you're working on an e-commerce website and have a central database for all your transactional requirements, say storing user sessions, cookies, caching user history, etc. If the database fails for some reason, it may lead to serious consequences.

However, like distributed or parallel computing, if the data is scattered over different database nodes, you can at least be sure that not all functionalities would be hampered in an unlikely event.

NOTE

Data warehouses, multiple RDBMSs, flat files, data marts, content management servers, etc., are examples of behind-the-scene polyglot persistence you often find at a typical corporate workplace.

Polyglot persistence is quite a common and popular paradigm among database professionals, but an important reason is that users, like applications, come studded with rich experiences—where they can easily search for what they are looking, without caring about rest of the frills— such as finding friends, nearby restaurants, accurate information, etc.

Figure 7.4 shows an example of a Web application using different types of databases for handling complex user queries:

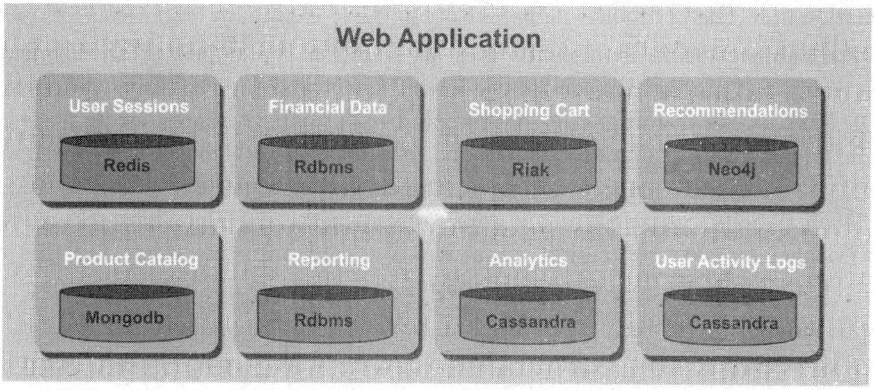

Source: *http://martinfowler.com/bliki/PolyglotPersistence.html*

Figure 7.4: Displaying a Web Application with Multiple Databases

To build a useful app for a user, developers are required to make clever improvisations with the existing ways of storing and querying data. They need tools to provide the required context-based content to the users.

Integrating Big Data with Traditional Data Warehouses

After a feasibility study of Big Data requirement, the identification and transition phase commences. Planning a heterogeneous data environment is a task that involves multiple phases of undo-redo, quality checks, and integrity assurances, whereas implementing a Big Data solution to a previously non-existent environment includes key challenges to be taken care of, before any further commitments ensue. While Big Data and the traditional data warehouse confront each other often, they are more likely to stay homogenous than to come up with a new version of Big Data. Data warehouses are highly structured and adjusted for custom purposes. Besides, these structures of records happen to be highly centralized as well.

The relational data model is here to stay for a long time, since organizations will continue to use data warehouses to manage organized and operational type of data that characterize record systems. For business analysts, these data warehouses will have the ability to analyze trends in Big Data. A relationship between Big Data and a data warehouse can be best described as a hybrid structure in which the well-structured, optimized, and operational data remains in the heavily guarded data warehouse, while the highly distributed data subject to variations in real time is managed by a Hadoop- or NoSQL-based infrastructure.

Gradually, organizations are beginning to realize that they have an inevitable business requirement of combining traditional data warehouses with their archived business data sources to less structured and scrutinized Big Data sources. A hybrid approach helps in accomplishing these business goals, which supports a cross between traditional and Big Data sources.

The main challenges confronting the physical architecture of the next-gen data warehouse platform include data availability, loading, storage performance, data volume, scalability, assorted and varying query demands against the data, and operational costs of maintaining the environment. To cope with any issues that might hamper the overall implementation and integration process, a number of challenges are pre-studied and dealt with before actually assigning bandwidth to the data implementation unit. The key methods that we are going to explain in brief are as follows:

- **Data Availability**—Data availability is a well-known challenge for any system related to transforming and processing data for use by end-users, and Big Data is no different. Hadoop or NoSQL is beneficial in mitigating this risk and make data available for analysis immediately upon acquisition. The challenge is to sort and load the data, which is unstructured and in varied formats. Also, context-sensitive data involving several different domains may require another level of availability check. Since the data present in the Big Data hierarchy is not updated, reprocessing new data containing updates will create duplicate data, and this needs to be handled to minimize the impact on availability.
- **Pattern Study**—Pattern study is nothing but the centralization and localization of data according to the demands. A global e-commerce website can centralize requests and fetch directives and results on the basis of end user locations, so as to return only meaningful contextual knowledge than to impart the entire data to the user. Trending topics are one of the pattern-based data study models that are a popular mode of knowledge gathering for all platforms. The trending pattern to be found for a given regional location is matched for occurrence in the massive data stream, in terms of keywords or popularity of links as per the hits they receive, and based on the geographical diversifications and stream filtering methods, data with similar characteristics is conjoined to form a pattern.
- **Data Incorporation and Integration**—Since no guidebook format or schema metadata exists, the data incorporation process for Big Data is about just acquiring the data and storing as files. However, continuous data processing on a platform can create a conflict for resources over a given period of time, often leading to deadlocks. Especially in case of big documents, images or videos, if such requirements happen to be the sole architecture driver, a dedicated machine can be allocated for this task, bypassing the guesswork involved in the configuration and setup process.
- **Data Volumes and Exploration**—Traffic spikes and volatile surge in data volumes can easily dislocate the functional architecture of corporate infrastructure due to the fundamental nature of the data streams. On each cycle of data acquisition completion, retention requirements for data can vary depending on the nature and the freshness of the data and its core relevance to the business. Data exploration and mining is an activity responsible for Big Data procurements across organizations and also yields large data sets as processing output. These data sets are required to be preserved in the system by occasional optimization of intermediary data sets. This is an important area normally ignored by organizations, which can be a potential performance drain over a given period of time.
- **Compliance and Localized Legal Requirements**—Various compliance standards such as Safe Harbor, GLBA, and PCI regulations can have some impact on data security and storage. Therefore, these standards should be judiciously planned and executed. Moreover, there are several cases of transactional data sets not being stored online required by the courts of law. Big Data infrastructure can be used as a storage engine for such data types, but the data needs to comply with certain standards and additional security. Large volumes of data can affect overall performance, and if such data sets are processed on the Big Data platform, the appliance configurator can provide administrators with tools/tips to mark the data in its own area of infrastructure zoning, minimizing both risk and performance impact.

- **Storage Performance**—In all these years, storage-based solutions didn't advance as rapidly as their counterparts, processors, memories, or cores did. Disk performance is a vital point to be taken care of while developing Big Data systems, and appliance architecture can throw better light on the storage class and layered architecture. If a combination of Solid State Drive (SSD), in-memory, and traditional storage architecture is intended for Big Data processing, the exchange and persistence of data across the different layers can be time-consuming and vapid.

An often misunderstood conviction among corporations is that once a Big Data solution is implemented, the existing relational data warehousing becomes redundant and are not required anymore, since they already have the best technology of recent times.

A few parallels can be drawn between a data warehouse and Big Data solution. Both store a lot of data. Both can be used for reporting and are managed by electronic storage devices.

EXHIBIT 1: HP Vertica Enables Fast, Scalable Customer Analytics

Founded in 2000, Conclusive Analytics offers Conclusive Sales Analyst (CSA), a sales and marketing analytics solution, to its customers across industries—from financial services to healthcare and technology. When Conclusive Analytics reached performance limits with its existing reporting tools, it evaluated alternatives, including EMC Greenplum, open-source Infobright, and HP Vertica. During the evaluation process, Conclusive Analytics put the three solutions through a standard set of operations, and selected HP Vertica for its superior performance.

Challenges

Conclusive Analytics faced the following challenges:

- Customers needed immediate access to data; Conclusive Analytics' flagship product, CSA, requires fast analytics and reporting
- Platform required the capacity to accommodate a large volume of data records—up to three-to-four billion records for some clients
- Scalability to accommodate expanding customer needs
- Versatile solution capable of meeting a range of analytics requirements

Benefits

By analyzing clients' customer data on a daily basis, CSA gains insights into customer behavior and identifies opportunities for improving customer loyalty, reducing churn, and increasing sales. With HP Vertica, the company has a Big Data tool for rapid analysis of large volumes of data.

Today, Conclusive Analytics has a powerful analytics engine that enables it to:

- Generate a range of reports including complex nightly batch reports that generate actionable alerts
- Actionable alerts enable the salesforce to improve customer relationships, reduce churn and increase sales

- Provide sales reps at customer sites with access to data in seconds instead of hours
- Scale up to meet customer demand

Here's what Conclusive Analytics has to say about the HP Vertica data analytics platform:

"We help our clients' customers look at leading indicators to prevent customer churn. Without our columnar database platform, HP Vertica, we would not be able to analyze the volume of data that we do, and the speed has been phenomenal."

—Wade MacNeil, chief architect, Conclusive Analytics

"Our developers seamlessly and almost immediately begin working in HP Vertica because of its standard SQL interface."

—Wade MacNeil, chief architect, Conclusive Analytics

"From a systems administration standpoint, redundancy, K-safety and clustering make it a breeze to support multiple 3-node clusters."

—Brian Allen, manager, IT and Infrastructure, Conclusive Analytics

The HP Vertica Analytics platform enables organizations to manage and analyze massive volumes of data quickly and reliably without the compromises that accompany traditional enterprise data warehouses. You can also accelerate business value from a vastly expanded variety of data by exploring and analyzing of all forms of data, including "dark data." And with expanded deployment options, you get the flexibility to deploy analytics where it's needed – on industry-standard hardware, virtual machines, or in the cloud.

Source: http://h20195.www2.hp.com/V2/GetDocument.aspx?docname=4AA5-3410ENW&cc=us&lc=en

Big Data Analysis and Data Warehouse

Big Data is analyzed to know the present behavior or trends and make future predictions. Various Big Data solutions are used for extracting useful information from Big Data. A simple working definition of a Big Data solution is that it is a technology that:

- Enables the storage of very large amounts of heterogeneous data
- Holds data in low-cost storage devices
- Keeps data in a raw or unstructured format

Big Data analytics performed by a Big Data solution helps organizations in the following ways:

- Brings improvement in the tourism industry by analyzing the behavior of tourists and their trends
- Enables improvement in technological research
- Enables improvement in the medical field for diagnosing diseases quickly

- Helps the defense sector by enabling better monitoring
- Helps the insurance industry by better customer relationship management

Data warehousing, on the other hand, is a group of methods and software to enable data collection from functional systems, integration, and synchronization of that data into a centralized database, and then the analytical visualization and report-tracking of key performance indicators in a dashboard-driven environment. There are different interpretations of the meaning of data warehousing. However, it is generally agreed that data warehouse means something that is achieved by incorporating data from multiple heterogeneous sources that support logical reporting, structured decision making, and random queries. The data warehousing process comprises cleaning, integration, and consolidation of data. A data warehouse acts as a single point of reference for a granular and integrated data of the company.

Consider the case of Argon Technology, which provides Big Data solutions worldwide. A big client of Argon Technology wants a solution for analyzing the data of 100,000 employees across the world. Assessing the performance manually of each employee is a huge task for the administrative department before rewarding bonuses or increasing salaries. Argon Technology experts set up a data warehouse in which information related to each employee is stored. The administrative department extracts that information with the help of Argon's Big Data solution easily and analyzes it before providing benefits to an employee.

Complexity of the data warehouse environment has risen dramatically in recent years with the influx of data warehouse appliances architecture, NoSQL/Hadoop, databases, and several API-based tools for many forms of cutting-edge analytics or real-time tasks. New vendor and open-source platforms have appeared as a response to users' growing demands for optimized platforms for various Big Data analytics, real-time operations, and workloads involving them.

A Big Data solution is preferred because there is a lot of data that has to be manually and relationally handled. In organizations handling Big Data, if the data is potentially used, it can provide much valuable information leading to superior decision making which, in turn, can lead to more profitability, revenue, and happier customers. Isn't this what most organizations want?

Such organizations require a data warehouse in order to make rational decisions. In order to have a good knowledge of what actually is going on in your company, you need your data to be reliable, credible, and available to everyone.

On comparing a data warehouse to a Big Data solution, we find that a Big Data solution is a technology and data warehousing is an architecture. They are two distinct things.

Technology is just a medium to store and operate huge amounts of data. A data warehouse is a way of organizing data so that when someone queries or fetches data from it, that person knows about other people having the same data for different purposes. There is a scope of data reconcilability in the case of a data warehouse.

For example, can an organization:

- Have a Big Data solution and no data warehouse or vice versa? Yes.
- Have a Big Data solution and data warehouse or vice versa? Yes.

There is hardly a correlation between a Big Data analysis and a data warehouse. They are not the same thing.

In a typical data warehouse, you will find a combination of flat files, relational database tables, and non-relational sources. A well-constructed data warehouse will be architected so that the data is converted into a common format, allowing queries to be correctly and consistently processed.

So if you have Big Data, will you ever need a data warehouse?

If your corporation has a need for credible, reliable, and accessible data that everyone can rely on, then a data warehouse is recommended.

Big Data is not a substitute for a data warehouse.

Data warehouses work with abstracted data that has been operated, filtered, and transformed into a separate database, using analytics such as sales trend analysis or compliance reporting. That database is updated gradually with the same filtered data, either at a weekly or monthly basis. But Big Data systems have raw data whether from operations, for example, reporting, user activity such as session tracking, or other real-world norms. That data is left untouched since the actual usage pattern or requirement is not known or predetermined.

Actually, organizations that use data warehousing technology will continue to do so and those that use both Big Data and data warehousing are future-proof from any further technological advancements only up till the point where the thin line of separation starts depleting. Big Data systems are normally used to understand strategic issues, for example, for inventory maintenance or target-based individual performance reports.

Enterprises still use data warehousing for reports and visualizations for management purposes to report a clearer and more lucid picture about company finances. Conventional data warehouse systems are proven systems and with investments to the tune of millions of dollars for their development, those systems, are not going anywhere, soon. Regardless of how good and profitable Big Data analytics is or turns out, data warehousing will still continue to provide crucial database support to many enterprises, and in all circumstances, will complete the lifecycle of current systems.

EXHIBIT 2: Big Data Analysis in GE

General Electric Co. (GE) is known for making what it refers to as 'big swings' – large bets to grab the lead in emerging markets with enormous potential. The $145 billion manufacturer of jet engines, power plants, and locomotives believes Big Data and analytics is one of these markets. How big an opportunity does GE see with Big Data, and how much and where it is investing?

In 2011, Fairfield, a Connecticut-based industrial giant announced the launch of a global software center and a $1 billion investment to build software and expertise for GE's version of Big Data analytics. "What we've done is centralized what I would call the real rocket science of Big Data," says William Ruh, vice president and corporate officer of the center. "These are people with deep expertise and experience. We use them to develop the most complex capabilities and reusable components."

GE brought in Ruh from Cisco Systems in 2011 to lead the center, located in San Ramon, California. That's a short drive from Silicon Valley, an emerging epicenter of Big Data startups and established technology companies. Ruh's charter is to build a center that powers up software development and data science capabilities in GE's Big Data domain of interest – a niche it refers to as 'the industrial Internet'. In 2012, GE CEO Jeffrey Immelt announced that the company would commit $1 billion to its analytics and software center over four years. According to a survey conducted at that time, such an amount would put the company among the top in the world in terms of Big Data and analytics investments.

While a sizable amount, it's a small down payment on what GE envisions as a $30 trillion opportunity by 2030. Using what it believes to be a conservative 1% savings in five sectors that buy its machinery (aviation, power, healthcare, rail, and oil and gas), a GE report estimates the savings from an industrial Internet for these sectors alone could be nearly $300 billion in the next 15 years.

Take the aviation industry. A 1% boost in fuel efficiency would put $2 billion a year into airlines' coffers.

A growing percentage of GE's business is services that support its industrial products – services that help customers use GE's machines more effectively and efficiently. Providing insights based on Big Data will be one more service offering. "We believe this is a foundational change, in the same way that the consumer Internet has remade consumer industries in the past decade," Ruh said. "Who does Walmart view as its competitor? Amazon? Who does American Express see as its competitor? PayPal. In the next 10 years, the changes that we saw in the consumer Internet will happen in the industrial world", he added.

Today, the center has a staff of about 300, up from just two people (Ruh and his executive assistant) in late 2011. Not all of them are in San Ramon, however. Ruh has employees located around the globe – Bangalore, New York and Cambridge – who report to the center. The company plans to staff up to about 1,000 people at the San Ramon facility, which is between San Francisco and Silicon Valley. Their work will support the efforts of another 9,000 GE software engineers who operate in its various product businesses globally.

Of the 300 currently in San Ramon, there are a number of 'hardcore data scientists' as Ruh refers to them. Why centralize these people? Ruh said it came down to three factors:

- **An acute shortage of talent**—"The first reason for centralization is that there is only a limited amount of talent – and I actually mean extraordinarily limited," said Ruh, who added that his center hires less than 5% of job applicants. "You can find a lot of people who are subject matter experts, basically analysts. You can find a lot of people who do business intelligence. You can find programmers. But the fact is that you're still probably not getting a whole lot out of your data other than reporting. The in-depth data science and deep analytics capabilities are held by such a small number of people."
- **Employee retention**—Data scientists at GE will need a career path if they're to stay for long. "They need to feel coupled and placed into a leadership program where they can get promoted based on their capabilities. When you put them in the businesses, their ability to grow, get promoted, and take on increasingly

bigger roles is limited in many ways by the hierarchal structure of those businesses."

- **Reusability in technology**—"We need to build high-end capabilities [in solving deep technical problems]," Ruh said. "That cannot be built by each group over and over again. The reason is you can't find the talent, you can't maintain it, and so on. We believe this idea of reuse is going to differentiate the winners from the losers."

The center has begun to organize employees into disciplines such as machine learning, statistics, and operations research. "They are very different approaches, and there isn't one approach that solves every problem," Ruh said. The keys to success for GE software and analytics? Ruh boils it down to this: continually bringing a new portfolio of compelling service offerings. To be attractive to the market, those services must help airlines, electric utilities, hospitals and other customers tap GE's Big Data expertise and generate big savings and other improvements.

"In the end, our service offerings must foundationally improve how our customers manage, operate and maintain these big machines," Ruh concluded. "If we do that, we will be a leader in helping bring about this industrial Internet."

Source: http://sites.tcs.com/big-data-study/ge-big-data-case-study/

Changing Deployment Models in Big Data Era

Data managing deployment models are shifting to altogether different levels ever since the inception of Big Data. From implementation of traditional data on a large and an individual system in the data center to distributed database nodes located in several computers within the same data center, the costs-price ratio of such a model has led companies to optimize these warehouses and limit the scope and size of the data being managed.

The inevitable trend is toward hybrid environments that address the following enterprise Big Data necessities:

- **Scalability and Speed**—The developing hybrid Big Data platform supports parallel processing, optimized appliances and storage, workload management, and dynamic query optimization.
- **Agility and Elasticity**—The hybrid model is agile, which means it is flexible and responds rapidly in case of changing trends. It also provides elasticity, which means this model can be increased or decreased as per the demands of the user.
- **Affordability and Manageability**—The hybrid environment will integrate flexible pricing, including licensed software, custom designed appliances, and cloud-based approaches for future proofing.

  However, when organizations want to utilize the huge information generated by Big Data sources, the curbs on the traditional models are more evident and apparent in real-time functioning. Hence, appliance data warehouse has become a real-world method of producing an enhanced environment to support the transition to new information management.

When companies need to merge their existing data warehouse structure with a relatively new Big Data solution, the appliance model is a scalable and noteworthy first step in terms of upgrade.

- **Appliance Model (also known as Commodity Hardware)** – Appliance is a system used in data centers to optimize data storage and management. Since appliance is autonomous, it can be easy and quick to implement, and offers low cost in terms of operation and maintenance. The Appliance model is pre-loaded with a relational DB model, MapReduce, the Hadoop framework, and many other tools to use and organize data from different sources. It also integrates logical engines and tools to shorten the process of examining data from several sources. The appliance is thus a single-purpose machine that usually includes different interfaces to easily connect to an existing data warehouse.

  But then, like any other appliance, it is bound to be subjected to extremes of massive data onslaught and storage clusters, and since it is built principally around a mechanical disk using it as primary storage, there are not-so-rare chances of a central node or distributed node failure, leading to a complete warehouse blackout. Though various backups systems and central node transfer techniques have made it a real easy deal for the present-day appliance model to be fairly reliant, oddities still remain.

- **Cloud Deployment** – Big Data business applications with cloud-based approaches have an advantage that other methods (such as software on commodity hardware or pre-integrated appliances) lack. Let's have a look at the advantages of cloud deployment:
  - **On-demand self-service** – Enables the customer to use a self-propelled cloud service with minimal interaction involving the cloud service provider
  - **Broad network access** – Allows Big Data cloud resources to be available over the network and accessible across different client platforms
  - **Multi-user** – Allows cloud resources to be allocated so that isolation can be guaranteed to multiple users, their computations, and data from one another
  - **Elasticity and scalability** – Allows cloud resources to be elastically, rapidly, and automatically scaled out, up, and down as the need be
  - **Measured service** – Enables remote monitoring and billing of Big Data cloud resources

However, cloud-based deployment actually requires a few concerns to be addressed. Some of the challenges for a Big Data architecture and cloud computing are as follows:

- The data involved, and its magnitude and location. Big Data may end up unrelated and start out in different locations. These sites may or may not be serviceable by a cloud service.
- The type of processing required on the data. Continuous or burst mode? Can the data be parallelized?
- Does data need to be moved to the processing environment or does the processing environment need to be moved to where data is, depending on the data volumes involved?
- Technical and supportability requirements of cloud-based Big Data
- Service models and deployment of Big Data in the cloud

Summary

The chapter has discussed databases and data warehouses in terms of their utility in data storage. It begins by describing RDBMS and its role in managing Big Data. The chapter has also introduced non-relational databases and explained the concept of polyglot persistence. Apart from this, it has described the integration of Big Data with traditional data warehouses. Big Data analysis and data warehousing have also been discussed in detail. In the end, the chapter has elaborated on the change in the deployment models in the era of Big Data.

Quick Revise

Multiple-Choice Questions

Q1. BCNF stands for:

a. Boyce-Codd Normal Form
b. Boy-Codd Normal Form
c. Boyce-Cord Normal Form
d. Boyce-Codd Normalization Form

Ans. The correct option is a.

Q2. Which ACID property is related to the encapsulation of information?

a. Atomicity
b. Consistency
c. Isolation
d. Durability

Ans. The correct option is c.

Q3. APS stands for:

a. Analytical Platform System
b. Analytics Performance System
c. Analytics Platform Server
d. Analytics Platform System

Ans. The correct option is d.

Q4. Which of the following is an example of a non-relational database?

a. SQL
b. ORACLE
c. Mongo DB
d. SQL SERVER 2012

Ans. The correct option is c.

Q5. Which of the following models is also known as commodity hardware?

a. Appliance model
b. Cloud model
c. Hybrid model
d. Private model

Ans. The correct option is a.

Subjective Questions

Q1. What do you understand by the Appliance model?

Ans. Appliance is a system used in data centers to optimize data storage and management. Since appliance is autonomous, it can be easy and quick to implement, and offers low cost in terms of operation and maintenance. Appliance model is pre-loaded with a relational DB model,

MapReduce, the Hadoop framework, and many other tools to use and organize data from different sources. It also integrates logical engines and tools to shorten the process of examining data from several sources. The appliance is thus a single-purpose machine that usually includes different interfaces to easily connect to an existing data warehouse.

Q2. What are the advantages of cloud deployment?

Ans. The advantages of cloud deployment are as follows:

- **On-demand self-service**—Enables the customer to use a self-propelled cloud service with minimal interaction involving the cloud service provider
- **Broad network access**—Allows Big Data cloud resources available over the network and accessible across different client platforms
- **Multi-user**—Allows cloud resources to be allocated so that isolation can be guaranteed to multiple users, their computations, and data from one another
- **Elasticity and scalability**—Allows cloud resources to be elastically, rapidly, and automatically scaled out, up, and down as the need be
- **Measured service**—Enables remote monitoring and billing of Big Data cloud resources.

Q3. What is RDBMS? Discuss its ACID standards.

Ans. RDBMS stands for Relational Database Management System. It uses a relational model where all the data is stored using preset schemas. These schemas are linked using the values in specific columns of each table. The data is hierarchical, which means the data to be stored or transacted needs to adhere to ACID standards, namely:

- **Atomicity**—Ensures full completion of a database operation
- **Consistency**—Ensures that data abides by the schema (table) standards, such as correct data type entry, constraints, and keys.
- **Isolation**—Refers to the encapsulation of information. Makes only necessary information visible.
- **Durability**—Ensures that transactions stay valid even after a power failure or errors.

Q4. What are the three Vs of Big Data?

Ans. The three Vs of Big Data are as follows:

- **Volume of Data**—Big Data is designed to store and process hundreds of terabytes, or even petabytes or zettabytes of data
- **Variety of Data**—Collection of data, different from a format suiting relational database systems, is stored in a semi-structured or unstructured format.
- **Velocity of Data**—The rate of data arrival might make an enterprise data warehouse problematic, particularly where formal data preparation processes like conforming, examining, transforming, and cleansing of the data needs to be accomplished before it is stored into the data warehouse tables.

Q5. What is a non-relational database?

Ans. A database that is not relational or non-RDBMS styled is known as a non-relational database. In other words, a database that does not use the table/key model of RDBMS is a non-relational database. Such a kind of database requires effective data operation techniques and processes, often custom-designed, to provide solutions to Big Data problems. NoSQL (Not Only SQL) is one such example of a popular emerging non-relational database.

8

Processing Your Data with MapReduce

At the beginning of the 21st century, Google faced a major challenge of analyzing large volumes of data measuring in petabytes. It had to process huge data present in Web access logs in order to rank websites in its Web search engine result. A Web log contained a complete list of the requests made by several Web users to access any website. The algorithm used to process such a huge volume of data was quite simple. The challenge, however, was to complete the data-processing task within a reasonable amount of time. For this, the data-processing task had to be distributed on thousands of machines simultaneously. To do so, developers had to develop software that split and forwarded the data across multiple machines, processed the data, and retrieved and organized the data to arrive at a final result. The entire process was very tedious, error-prone, and time consuming. In addition, the process had to be repeated for each split.

Given the huge volumes of data that Google developers were working on and the amount of time the tasks took, developers knew they needed a programming model that could work in parallel, was fault tolerant, and could share the workload across distributed computers. To fulfill these requirements, Google invented Google MapReduce, which uses Google File System (GFS) to work with distributed file systems. Inspired by the Google MapReduce concepts presented in the Google paper, Hadoop developers thought of creating an open-source variant of the proprietary technology Google MapReduce. Later in 2006, Apache Software Foundation (ASF) released Apache Hadoop, which is an open-source project with two main functions, Hadoop MapReduce for processing data, and Hadoop Distributed File System (HDFS) for storing data.

One of the main advantages of using Hadoop is that it provides data processing and storage capabilities. The biggest benefit of using the processing engine, MapReduce, in Hadoop is that you can actually query live data (data that is delivered instantly). MapReduce helps in solving problems related to data sorting, graph processing, Web log analysis, text processing, and much more. In the case of Big Data, MapReduce can prove to be the key tool in data processing.

You have already learned the basic concepts of MapReduce in Chapter 5. In this chapter, we recall the concepts related to MapReduce as well as execution of MapReduce applications. The chapter also familiarizes you with the basics of designing MapReduce applications.

Recollecting the Concept of MapReduce Framework

MapReduce refers to integrated software clubbed in Hadoop framework that enables distributed processing of huge amounts of data on different clusters of computers or nodes. The MapReduce programming model is a combination of map() and reduce() functions as used in the Lisp programming language. In Lisp, a map takes a function and a set of values as input. It then applies the function to individual values in the set. Finally, the reduce function combines all the values using a binary operation.

The main task of MapReduce is to solve large computational problems using the principle of divide-and-conquer. A large dataset is divided into independent pieces that are later processed together by various mappers (machines that perform the map function). The results obtained from the mappers are then provided to the reducers as input.

To use the MapReduce, developers must implement mappers and reducers by creating classes that extend the base classes of Hadoop to solve a particular problem.

MapReduce helps in coordinating the entire execution process, including:

- Selection of suitable machines for running mappers
- Starting and monitoring of the execution of a mapper
- Selection of locations for executing reducers
- Starting and monitoring of the execution of a reducer
- Sorting and shuffling of a mapper's output and forwarding it to reducer machines

Shuffle and sort is the process between the mapper and reducer. Mapper gives the key and value pair, which need to be rearranged. This rearrangement happens in shuffle and then the sorting takes place. Combiner (combiners do the rearrangement of the key and values) and partitioner (partitions the values on the basis of keys) are the middle steps in shuffle sort.

1. Input Reader()
2. Mapper()
3. Shuffle and sort
   i. Combiner
   ii. Partitioner
4. Reducer()

Developing Simple MapReduce Application

You are already familiar with MapReduce and its different components. Now, you will understand how these components interact with each other in a MapReduce application. In this section, we will use a simple word count example to illustrate the role of the Mapper and Reducer classes.

SCENARIO

To perform text analysis, Argon Technology requires an application that will analyze text after the number of lines, characters, and words appearing in it are known. The company has already created separate applications to find the total number of lines and characters. Now, it needs a separate application to know the total word count in a given text. John, a data analyst at Argon Technology, is assigned the task to create the word count application.

In this section, you learn to write MapReduce programs to obtain the total count of words in a text with the help of Eclipse Integrated Development Environment (IDE).

NOTE

Before creating an application, you need to ensure that you have Eclipse, Hadoop, and Java Development Kit (JDK) installed on your Linux Ubuntu computer.

The following are the broad-level steps to create a word count application:

1. **Defining the objective**—The text given as input is processed to count the frequency of words appearing in it.
2. **Deciding the action**—Hadoop MapReduce programs are implemented for word count.
3. **Breaking the program modules**—The program module is divided into the following main classes:
   - The `WCount` class, which reads text files and counts words. The input and output files are text files.

- The `WCMapper` class, which takes the input file and breaks it into words.
- The `WCReducer` class, which counts all the words and generates the output in the form of word count.

Now, perform the following steps to create the `WCountExample` application:

1. Start Eclipse by clicking the Eclipse icon, as shown in Figure 8.1:

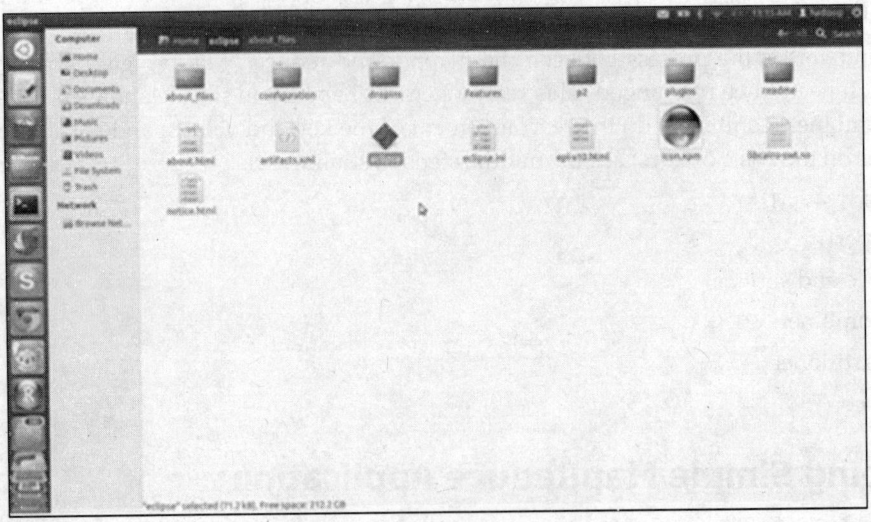

Figure 8.1: Starting Eclipse

The Select a workspace dialog box opens, as shown in Figure 8.2:

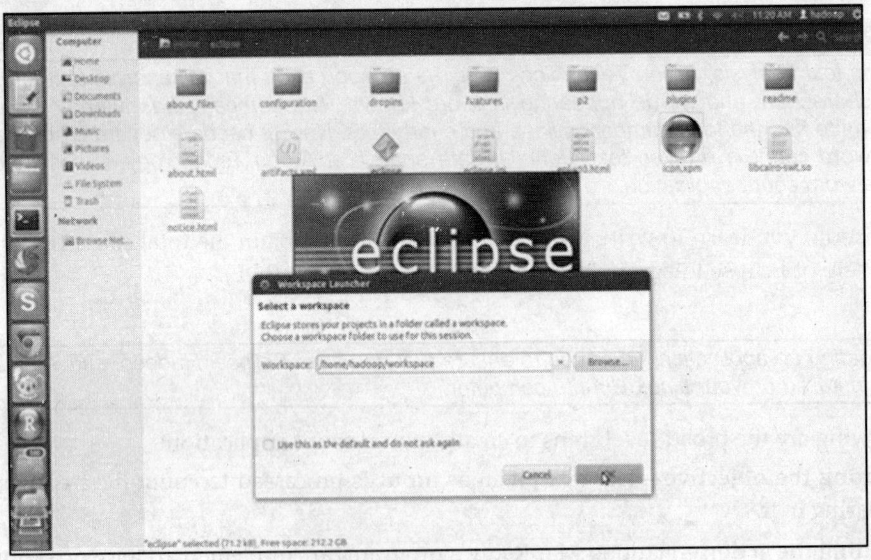

Figure 8.2: Selecting the Workspace

2. Select (or assign) a workspace location from the Workspace drop-down list in the dialog box. In our case, we have selected the location `/home/Hadoop/workspace` (Figure 8.2).

3. Click the OK button (Figure 8.2). The Eclipse IDE appears, as shown in Figure 8.3:

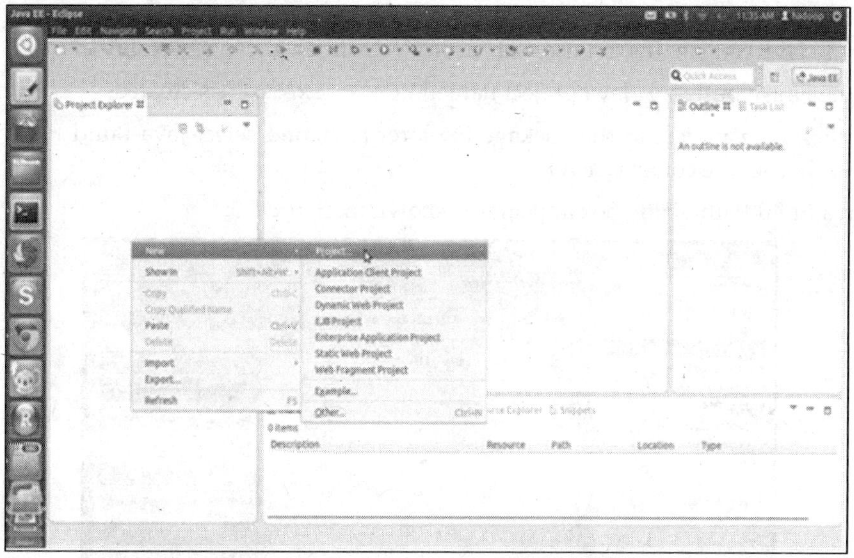

Figure 8.3: Displaying the Eclipse IDE

4. Right-click the Project Explorer area and select New → Project from the context menu to create a new project (Figure 8.3).

   The New Project wizard appears, as shown in Figure 8.4:

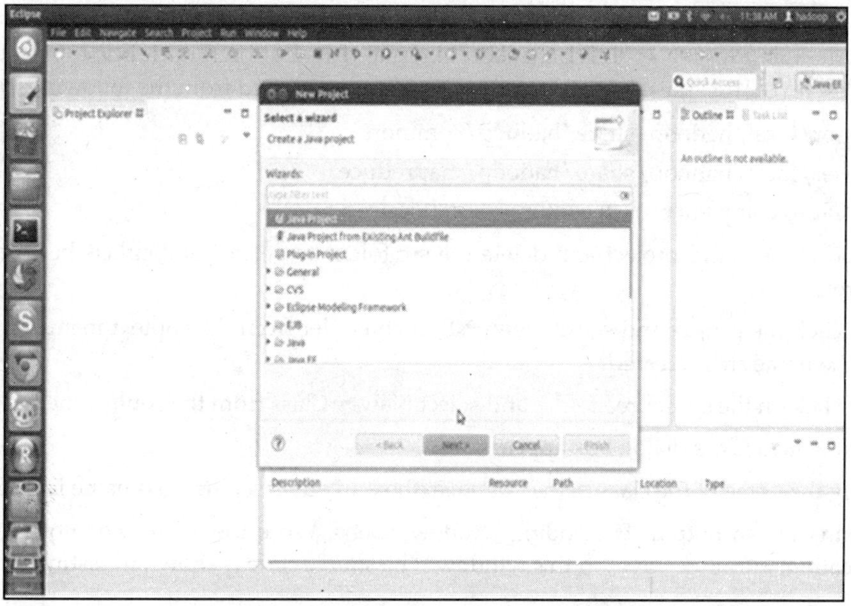

Figure 8.4: Showing the New Project Wizard

5. Select Java Project as the type of project and click the Next button (Figure 8.4).

   The Create a Java Project page appears.

6. Enter the name of the project in the Project name field. In our case, we have entered the project name as `WCountExample`.
7. Select the Java version. In our case, we have selected the version as JavaSE-1.7.
8. Click the Finish button. A Java project named `WCountExample` is created.
9. Right-click your project in the Package Explorer area, and select Java Build Path → Configure Build Path from the context menu.

   The Java Build Path dialog box appears, as shown in Figure 8.5:

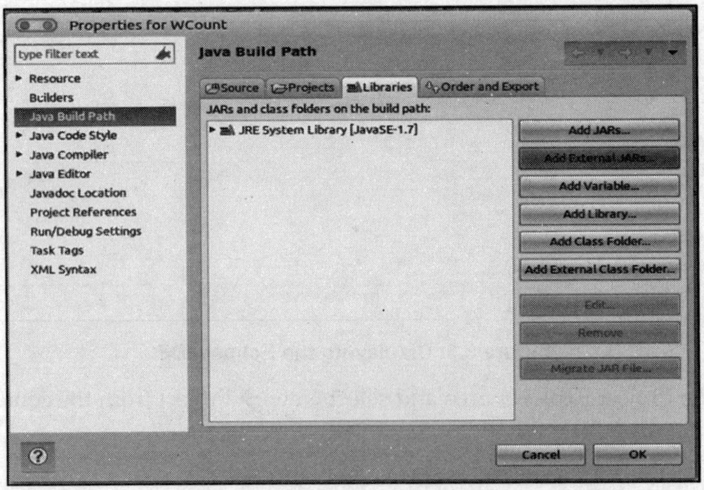

Figure 8.5: Showing the Java Build Path Dialog Box

10. Select the Libraries tab and click the Add External JARs button (Figure 8.5) to select the required Java ARchive (JAR) files. In our case, the JAR files are selected from the following locations:
    - /user/local/hadoop/share/hadoop/common
    - /user/local/hadoop/share/hadoop/mapreduce
11. Click OK to complete project configuration (Figure 8.5).
12. Expand the `WCount` project and delete the src folder to get rid of conflicts between the files in the project.
13. Right-click the project and select New → Source Folder from the context menu. A source folder with the name src is created.
14. Right-click on the src source folder and select New →Class from the context menu.

    The New Java Class dialog box appears.
15. Specify the name of the class in the Name textbox. In our case, the class name is `WCount`.
16. Click the Finish button. The coding window opens. Write the source code of the MapReduce application, `WCount.java`, in this window. The source code is shown in Listing 8.1:

Listing 8.1: Code of `WCount.java`

```
import org.apache.hadoop.fs.Path;
import org.apache.hadoop.conf.*;
import org.apache.hadoop.io.*;
```

```
import org.apache.hadoop.mapred.*;
import org.apache.hadoop.util.*;

public class WCount extends Configured implements Tool{
      public int run(String[] args) throws Exception
      {
//creating a JobConf object and assigning a job name for identification purposes
            JobConf conf = new JobConf(getConf(), WCount.class);
            conf.setJobName("WCount");
//Setting configuration object with the Data Type of output Key and Value
            conf.setOutputKeyClass(Text.class);
            conf.setOutputValueClass(IntWritable.class);
            //Providing the mapper and reducer class names
            conf.setMapperClass(WCMapper.class);
            conf.setReducerClass(WCReducer.class);
//We wil give 2 arguments at the run time, which are input path and output path
            Path inp = new Path(args[0]);
            Path out = new Path(args[1]);
//the hdfs input and output directories to be fetched from the command line
            FileInputFormat.addInputPath(conf, inp);
            FileOutputFormat.setOutputPath(conf, out);
            JobClient.runJob(conf);
            return 0;
      }
      public static void main(String[] args) throws Exception
      {
            // this main function will call run method defined above.
            int res = ToolRunner.run(new Configuration(), new WCount(),args);
            System.exit(res);
      }
}
```

In Listing 8.1, a `WCount` class is created, which reads text files and counts words. In this class, an object `conf` of the `JobConf` class is created, and a job name is assigned to it to identify the job. The data type of the output key/value pair is then set to the configuration object `conf`. After this, the names of the mapper and reducer classes are specified on the configuration object. The objects to store the input path and output path that we specify during the execution of the application are created in the `WCount` class. Finally, the HDFS input and output directories to be retrieved from the command line are defined in this class.

TIP

If the output directory specified in the output format already exists, MapReduce execution throws an error. In such cases, you need to remove this directory prior to job execution.

17. Add the code given in Listing 8.2 for the `WCMapper.java` file:

Listing 8.2: Code of the `WCMapper.java` File

```
import java.io.IOException;
import java.util.StringTokenizer;
import org.apache.hadoop.io.*;
import org.apache.hadoop.mapred.*;
public class WCMapper extends MapReduceBase implements Mapper<LongWritable, Text,
  Text, IntWritable>
{
      //hadoop supported data types
      private final static IntWritable one = new IntWritable(1);
      private Text word = new Text();

//map method that performs the tokenizer job and framing the initial key value pairs
```

```
// after all lines are converted into key-value pairs, reducer is called.

    public void map(LongWritable key, Text value, OutputCollector<Text,
  IntWritable> output, Reporter reporter) throws IOException
    {
           //taking one line at a time from input file and tokenizing the same

           String line = value.toString();
           StringTokenizer tokenizer = new StringTokenizer(line);

//iterating through all the words present in that line and forming key value pair
           while (tokenizer.hasMoreTokens())
           {
              word.set(tokenizer.nextToken());
//sending to output collector which in turn passes the same to reducer
                 output.collect(word, one);
           }
    }
}
```

In Listing 8.2, the `WCMapper` class is created where the MapReduce algorithm to take the input file and split it into words is defined. In the class, a `map()` method is defined, which creates key/value pairs and then calls a reducer. In the `map()` method, a `StringTokenizer` object is defined, which takes one line from the input file and tokenizes it. A `while` loop is used to iterate through all the words in each line and convert them into key/value pairs.

18. Add the code given in Listing 8.3 for the `WCReducer.java` file:

Listing 8.3: Code of the `WCReducer.java` File

```
import java.io.IOException;
import java.util.Iterator;
import org.apache.hadoop.io.*;
import org.apache.hadoop.mapred.*;
public class WCReducer extends MapReduceBase implements Reducer<Text, IntWritable,
  Text, IntWritable>
{
     public void reduce(Text key, Iterator<IntWritable> values,
  OutputCollector<Text, IntWritable> output, Reporter reporter) throws IOException
     {
          int sum = 0;
          /*traverse through all the values of a key and add them together and
  give the final result as the key and sum of its values*/
        while (values.hasNext())
        {
             sum += values.next().get();
        }
        output.collect(key, new IntWritable(sum));
     }
}
```

In Listing 8.3, the `WCReducer` class is created where the MapReduce algorithm to count all the words and generate the output in the form of word count is defined. In the class, the `reduce()` method is defined, which uses a `while` loop to traverse through all the values of a key/value pair, adds them, and provides the final output in the form of a key and the total of its values.

Building the Application

Hadoop uses Java as the programming language and therefore you must use a Java IDE. In this chapter, we have used Eclipse as the Java IDE.

Consider that the Eclipse IDE you are using is configured with Maven. In that case, you need to first create a Maven project. Maven refers to a built-in automation tool that is mainly used for Java projects. There is no Hadoop Maven archetype (a Maven project templating tool that consists of the project prototype you want to create). Therefore, begin with the building process by using a simple Maven project, and then add the `pom.xml` file manually. You need to add the code shown in Listing 8.4 in this file:

Listing 8.4: The `pom.xml` File for Hadoop 2.0

```
<project xmlns="http://maven.apache.org/POM/4.0.0"
xmlns:xsi="http://www.w3.org/2001/XMLSchema-instance"
xsi:schemaLocation="http://maven.apache.org/POM/4.0.0
http://maven.apache.org/xsd/maven-4.0.0.xsd">
<modelVersion>4.0.0</modelVersion>

<groupId>com.nokia.lib</groupId>
<artifactId>nokia-cgnr-sparse</artifactId>
<version>0.0.1-SNAPSHOT</version>
<name>cgnr-sparse</name>

<properties>
<hadoop.version>2.0.0-mr1-cdh4.1.0</hadoop.version>
<hadoop.common.version>2.0.0-cdh4.1.0</hadoop.common.version>
<hbase.version>0.92.1-cdh4.1.0</hbase.version>
</properties>
<repositories>

<repository>
<id>CDH Releases and RCs Repositories</id>
<url>https://repository.cloudera.com/content/groups/cdh- releasesrcs</
url>
</repository>
</repositories>

<build>
<plugins>
<plugin>
<groupId>org.apache.maven.plugins</groupId>
<artifactId>maven-compiler-plugin</artifactId>
<version>2.3.2</version>

<configuration>
<source>1.6</source>
<target>1.6</target>
</configuration>
</plugin>

</plugins>
</build>
<dependencies>
<dependency>

<groupId>org.apache.hadoop</groupId>
<artifactId>hadoop-core</artifactId>
<version>${hadoop.version}</version>
<scope>provided</scope>
</dependency>
<dependency>
<groupId>org.apache.hbase</groupId>
<artifactId>hbase</artifactId>
```

```
<version>${hbase.version}</version>
<scope>provided</scope>
</dependency>
<dependency>

<groupId>org.apache.hadoop</groupId>
<artifactId>hadoop-common</artifactId>
<version>${hadoop.common.version}</version>
<scope>provided</scope>
</dependency>

<dependency>
<groupId>junit</groupId>
<artifactId>junit</artifactId>
<version>4.10</version>

</dependency>
</dependencies>
</project>
```

Project Object Model (POM) refers to the basic unit of work done in Maven. POM is an XML file that consists of configuration details used by Maven for building a project. The POM file displayed in Listing 8.4 is for Cloudera CDH4.1. Note that the POM file includes the Cloudera repository. It also specifies the minimal dependencies, `Hadoop-core` and `Hadoop-common`, required for developing a Hadoop MapReduce job. Further, if you intend to use HBase in your MapReduce application, you must also include an hbase dependency. You can also enable support for basic unit tests by including junit. Further, all the dependencies related to Hadoop have been provided. This implies that these dependencies will not be provided in the final JAR file generated by Maven.

After creating the Eclipse Maven project, all the code for MapReduce is added to the project. Eclipse then loads the required libraries, compiles the Java code, and takes further action as required.

Executing the Application

Once you write a MapReduce job, you need to execute it. For this, you can generate a JAR file containing all the required code by using the Maven install command. After creating a JAR file, you can send it to the cluster's edge node over FTP and then use the following command to execute the file:

```
hadoop jar your.jar mainClass inputpath outputpath
```

The preceding command is the Hadoop execution command. You need to use it only if you are using the Maven build tool. Now let's look at the steps to execute the MapReduce application if Maven is not used.

After writing the code in Eclipse, create a `JAR` file of the project using the following steps:

1. Select Run→Run Configurations. The Run Configurations dialog box appears, as shown in Figure 8.6:

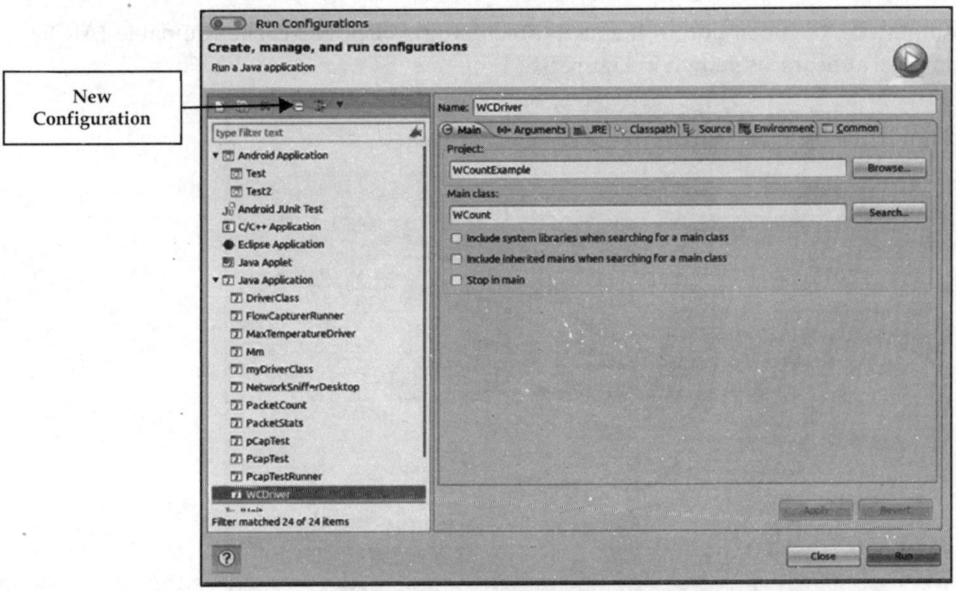

Figure 8.6: Displaying the Run Configurations Dialog Box

2. Click the New Configuration button at the top left side of the dialog box.
3. Enter the name `WCountDriver` in the Name textbox.
4. Select your project by clicking the Browse button.
5. Enter `WCount` in the Main class textbox and click the Apply button and then the Close button.
6. Right-click the project name (`WCountExample`) and select the Export option.

   The Export wizard appears, as shown in Figure 8.7:

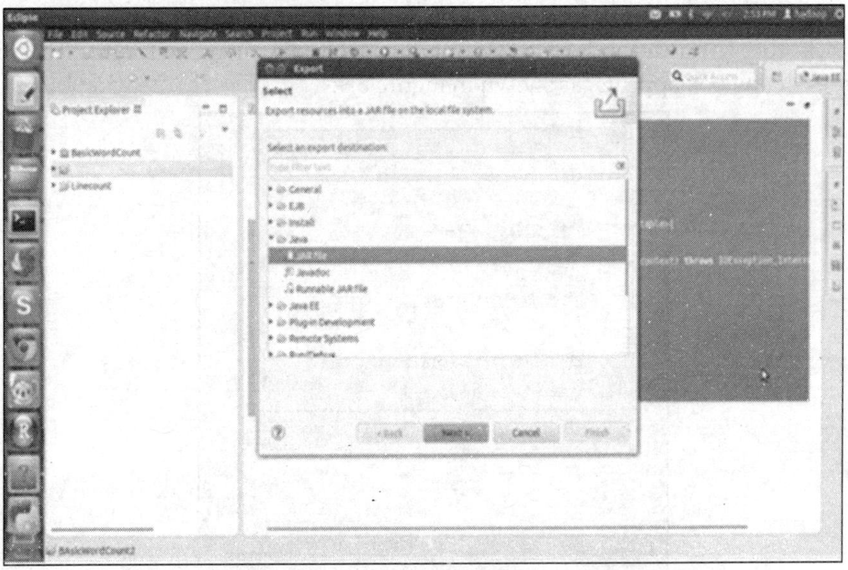

Figure 8.7: Displaying the Export Wizard

7. Select the Runnable JAR file option in the Java directory and click Next. The Runnable JAR File Specification page appears, as shown in Figure 8.8:

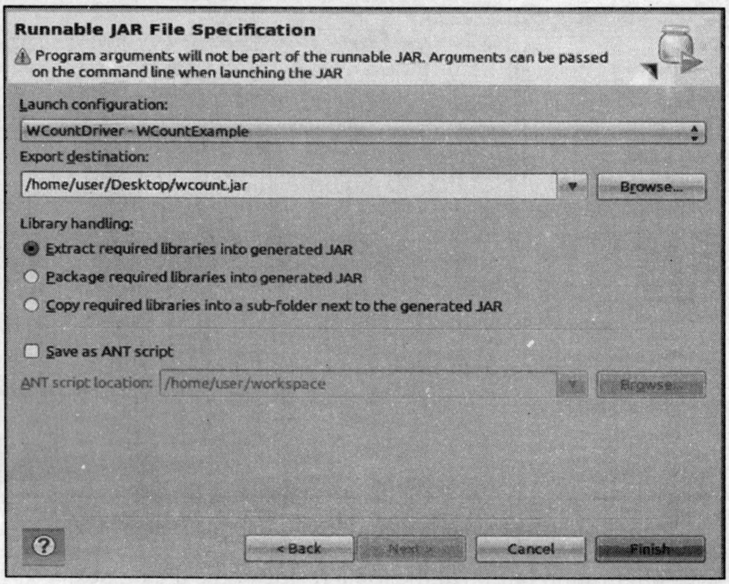

Figure 8.8: Selecting the Location to Export the Project JAR File

8. Select the `WCountDriver` config file from the Launch Configuration drop-down list.
9. Specify the location where you want to export the project JAR file. You can store it in the folder for your home folder with your user name. Name the JAR file as `wcount`.
10. Select the Extract required libraries into generated JAR radio button and click Finish.

    The `wcount.jar` file gets created.
11. Right-click the JAR file and select Properties from the context menu. The `wcount.jar` Properties dialog box appears, as shown in Figure 8.9:

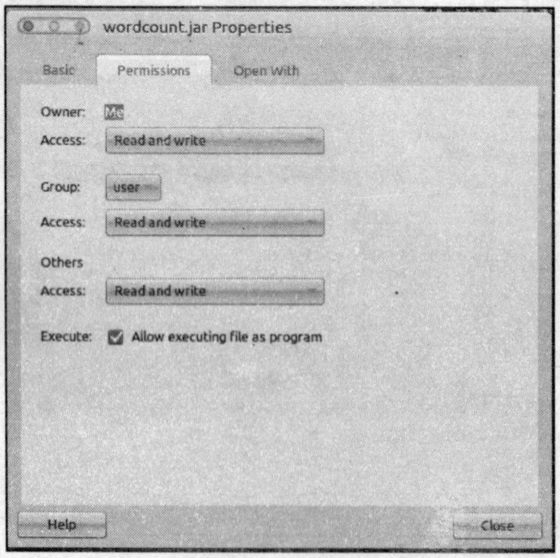

Figure 8.9: Displaying the wordcount.jar Properties

12. Select the Permissions tab and provide read and write access to all the users. Also, select the Allow executing file as a program checkbox (Figure 8.9).
13. Start Hadoop and ensure it is running by typing `jps` on the terminal. The terminal returns the running processes, as follows:

```
DataNode,
NameNode,
JobTracker,
TaskTracker,
SecondaryNameNode
Jps

Also in the new Version of Hadoop 2.x another deamon runs, which is YARN
So when we use Jps command on terminal it will give

Namenode
Datanode
Secoundary Namenode
Application manager
Resource manager
Yarn
jps
```

14. Switch to `hduser` by using the following command:

```
sudo su hduser
```

15. Change the directory to suit the Hadoop configuration with the help of the following command:

```
cd /user/local/hadoop/etc/hadoop
```

16. Delete all temporary folders by using the following command:

```
sudo rm -R /app/*
sudo rm -R /tmp/*
```

17. Format the `namenode` directory by using the following command:

```
hadoop namenode -format
```

18. Start all daemons by using the following command:

```
    start-dfs.sh && start-yarn.sh or instead of starting each demons separately we can
start all demons in one go by the command:

    Start-all.sh
```

19. Check if DataNode and NameNode are running by using the following command:

```
jps
```

20. In case DataNode or Namenode fails to start, check if other programs are running in the ports reserved for Hadoop by using the following command:

```
sudo netstat -tulpn | grep :8040
sudo netstat -tulpn | grep :8042
sudo netstat -tulpn | grep :50070
sudo netstat -tulpn | grep :50075
```

21. Enter the following command to kill a running program if PID is detected as the last number (in our case, it is 10234. You can get a process ID with the help of the `sudo netstat -tulpn | grep :port` command):

```
sudo kill -9 10234
```

Once you find that the DataNode and Namenode are running, you can proceed to the next step.

22. Make an HDFS directory by using the following command:

```
hadoop dfs -mkdir -p /user/local/hadoop/input
```

NOTE

An HDFS directory cannot be viewed in the terminal if it is being used. Also, it will not be visible in File Explorer.

23. Copy the input text file into the HDFS directory by using the following command:

```
hadoop dfs -copyFromLocal /home/user/Desktop/sample.txt /user/local/hadoop/input
```

Also, you can directly put the text file or the data file on Hadoop by the following command:

```
    hadoop fs -put /home/user/desktop/sample.txt  /hadoopfs ( instead of hadoopfs you
can give the full path like /opt/Hadoop/ This command is for Hadoop 2.x as it use
"fs"instead of "dfs" and can also be used with the "hadoop dfs".
```

As we know that Hadoop's stable version 2.x is also released and there is only one change in the command ,i.e., instead of using "dfs" with Hadoop, we can use the "fs." It doesn't mean we can't use "dfs" in commands, but few commands will not work in hadoop 2.x with "dfs."

Note that for our MapReduce application, we are using `sample.txt` as the input file. The file contains the following text:

```
user01|1|2|3|4|5
user02|1|2|3|4|5
user03|1|2|3|4|5

user01|1|2|3|4|5
user02|1|2|3|4|5
user01|1|2|3|4|5

user03|1|2|3|4|5
user01|1|2|3|4|5
user04|1|2|3|4|5

user01|1|2|3|4|5
```

24. Now, change the directory to run our Word count application through a JAR file:

```
cd /home/user/Desktop
hadoop jar wcount.jar /user/local/hadoop/input /user/local/hadoop/output
```

NOTE

You need not create the output folder as it is created by default. However, provide a new directory path every time you execute the code.

25. Type the following command to see the results:

```
hadoop dfs -cat /user/local/hadoop/output/part-r-00000   or
hadoop dfs -cat /user/local/hadoop/output/part-00000
```

The output file part-r-00000 will show the following output:

```
user01    5
user02    2
user03    2
user04    1
```

26. Remove the folders created by using HDFS with the help of the following command:

```
    hadoop dfs -rm -R /user/local/hadoop/output
    use the -rm commond carefully as if you apply -rm on any of the other folder on HDFS
it will damage the hadoop distributed file system in other words the hadoop Hdfs cluster
went down. Simple instead of -rm (remove command) you can use the -mv (move command) for
better and safe work.
```

27. View the folders in HDFS by using the following command:

```
hdfs dfs -ls /user/local/hadoop/
```

28. Change the Hadoop directory by using the following command:

```
cd /user/local/hadoop/etc/hadoop
```

29. Now, stop all the Hadoop daemons by using the following command:

```
stop-all.sh Thus, in the way, we can implement Hadoop MapReduce applications to perform different operations.
```

Points to Consider while Designing MapReduce

You need to consider the following guidelines while implementing MapReduce applications:

- When dividing information among map tasks, make sure that you do not create too many mappers. Usually, the number of mappers should be in hundreds and not thousands.

  Having the right number of mappers has the following benefits for applications:

  - Excessive mappers might create scheduling and infrastructure overhead. In some cases, this can even terminate a JobTracker. However, excessive mappers improve resource utilization (due to the creation of excessive JVMs) and execution time (in light of the limited number of execution slots).
  - Having fewer mappers can lead to underutilization of some part of the storage and excessive burden on other parts of the storage. Furthermore, because of huge map tasks, retries and theoretical execution become exceptionally costly and take a longer time to complete.
  - A vast number of small mappers perform a large number of seek operations during map shuffle output to the reducers. Mappers also establish excessive connections to deliver map outputs to the reducer.
- Another important factor is the number of reducers configured for the application. Creating too many or too few reducers can have a negative impact on productivity. Remember the following:
  - The number of reducers designed for an application is an essential variable for the application.
  - Besides planning and framework overhead, having too many reducers generates a corresponding number of output documents (since every reducer makes its own output records), which has a negative effect on a NameNode. In addition, it makes it difficult for different jobs to leverage results from the MapReduce work.
  - Having very few reducers has the same negative impact as having very few mappers, which is underutilization of resources and expensive retries.
- Use job counters properly as described below:
  - Counters are suitable for keeping track of global data bits of information. They are not meant to calculate aggregate statistics of applications.
  - Counters are costly, because the JobTracker must keep track of every counter of each map/reduce task for the whole duration of the application.
- You must compress the output of an application with an appropriate compressor to enhance the write operation.
- Use a suitable file format for storing the output of MapReduce jobs. Using SequenceFiles is the best option as these files can be partitioned and are compressible.
- You must use a large output block size for individual input/output documents with size measuring in gigabytes.

- Try not to create any new object instances within the `map()` and `reduce()` methods. These methods get executed within a loop, which means that object creation and transfer will increase execution time and create additional work for the garbage collector. It is best to make the most of your intermediate classes in a setup method, and after that, rearrange these classes within `map()/reduce()` methods.
- Do not use a distributed cache to move an extensive number of objects and/or large objects of hundreds of megabytes each. The distributed cache is generally meant for distributing a small number of medium-sized objects, ranging from a few to several hundred megabytes.
- Do not create workflows containing hundreds of small jobs handling small datasets.
- Do not try to re-implement existing Hadoop classes—extend them and explicitly specify your implementation in the configuration. Unlike application servers, a Hadoop command specifies user classes last, which means that existing Hadoop classes always have precedence.

Summary

This chapter helped you to recall the concepts related to the MapReduce framework. It mainly discussed data procession in MapReduce applications and how different components interact with each other in the application to display the required result. Toward the end, the chapter provided guidelines that one needs to consider while designing a MapReduce application.

Quick Revise

Multiple-Choice Questions

Q1. In a MapReduce model, the language Lisp uses 'reduce' to:

a. Reduce elements
b. Combine all elements using tertiary operations
c. Combine all elements using binary operations
d. Eliminate errors

Ans. The correct option is c.

Q2. Which of the following is/are performed by MapReduce?

a. Selection of suitable machines for running mappers
b. Starting and monitoring of the execution of a mapper
c. Selection of locations for executing reducers
d. All of the above

Ans. The correct option is d.

Q3. If the output directory specified in the output format already exists, MapReduce execution:

a. Throws an error
b. Shuts down completely
c. Seeks further instructions
d. Continues execution

Ans. The correct option is a.

Q4. In a MapReduce job, you want each of the input files processed by a single map task. How do you configure a MapReduce job so that a single map task processes each input file regardless of how many blocks the input file occupies?

a. By increasing the parameter that controls the minimum split size in the job configuration

b. By writing a custom MapRunner that iterates over all key/value pairs in the entire file

c. By setting the number of mappers equal to the number of input files you want to process

d. By writing a custom FileInputFormat and overriding the isSplittable() method to always return false

Ans. The correct option is c.

Q5. What happens if the mapper output does not match the reducer input?

a. The Hadoop API will convert the data to the type needed by the reducer

b. Data input/output inconsistency is not permitted. Therefore, a preliminary validation check is executed prior to the full execution of the job to ensure consistency

c. The Java compiler will report an error during compilation, but the job will complete with exceptions

d. A real-time exception will be thrown, and the MapReduce job will fail

Ans. The correct option is d.

Subjective Questions

Q1. What are the functions of Eclipse with respect to MapReduce?

Ans. Using Eclipse for developing Hadoop code is really straightforward. Eclipse helps in creating and implementing projects in Maven. Once an Eclipse Maven project is created, all the code for MapReduce is added to the project. Eclipse then loads the required libraries, compiles the Java code, and takes further action as required.

An easier way to manipulate files in HDFS is by using the Eclipse plugin. Eclipse copies the files directly into HDFS, bypassing the local drive of the virtual machine. You may have to refresh the directory view to see your changes.

Q2. What conditions must be met to implement MapReduce applications?

Ans. Implementation of a MapReduce application requires the following conditions to be satisfied:

- The dataset size should be large enough or the calculations long enough so that the infrastructure overhead of splitting it up for independent computations and merging results does not affect the overall performance.
- The computation depends mostly on the dataset being processed. Therefore, additional small datasets can be added using HBase, distributed caches, or some other techniques.

Q3. Can MapReduce be used to solve any kind of computational problem? If not, explain the cases where MapReduce is not applicable.

Ans. MapReduce is not applicable in scenarios where the dataset must be accessed randomly to perform the operation (for example, if a given dataset record must be combined with additional records to perform the operation). However, in this case, it is sometimes possible to run additional MapReduce jobs to 'prepare' data for calculations.

MapReduce is also not applicable while dealing with recursive problems (for example, a Fibonacci problem). MapReduce is not applicable in this case because computation of the current value requires knowledge of the previous one. This means that you cannot break it apart into sub-computations that can be run independently.

If a data size is small enough to fit in a single machine's memory, it is probably going to be faster to process it as a standalone application. Usage of MapReduce, in this case, makes implementation unnecessarily complex and typically slower.

9

Customizing MapReduce Execution and Implementing MapReduce Program

In the previous chapter, you studied about MapReduce and identified the roles of its components. All these components are implemented as a Java class with a specific interface defined within a MapReduce framework. In this chapter, you will study how to customize MapReduce execution to get better performance of the cluster network. The chapter starts with the concept of controlling MapReduce execution with the `InputFormat` class. Here, you will learn how to implement `InputFormat` for compute-intensive applications and multiple HBase tables. The performance of a cluster network greatly depends on the number of maps it has; therefore, you will also learn how to manage the number of maps using the `InputFormat` class for efficient pertormance. Moreover, you will study how to input or generate output using the `RecordReader` and `OutputFormats` classes. Apart from this, you will learn the role of the combiner and reducer in optimizing MapReduce execution.

Controlling MapReduce Execution with InputFormat

Let us start with a discussion on the utility of the `InputFormat` class for controlling the number of maps and the location of a map's execution. In the previous chapter, you have studied about the `InputFormat` class. This is the most important class of the MapReduce framework and is responsible for defining input splits and record readers.

InputSplit

A MapReduce program is designed to do some work on the given dataset. This work is known as a job. Furthermore, a job can have several tasks. Now the question arises, Who divides the job into several tasks? The class `InputSplit` does this for the MapReduce program.

An input split is a unit of work in a MapReduce program that can be processed by an individual map. In other words, input split represents the data to be processed by an individual map. Each split can be divided into small segments known as records. All records of a split can be processed by a map.

NOTE

InputSplit contains only a reference to its data.

You can measure the size of `InputSplit` in bytes. Each `InputSplit` is associated with some storage locations, which are used to store a map close to the data of a split. An important point to note here is that the splits can be of different sizes. Each split executes according to its size, with the largest split executing first. As a programmer, you cannot use `InputSplits` directly. The `InputFormat` class does this job for you.

Figure 9.1 shows the functionality of the `InputFormat` clas.

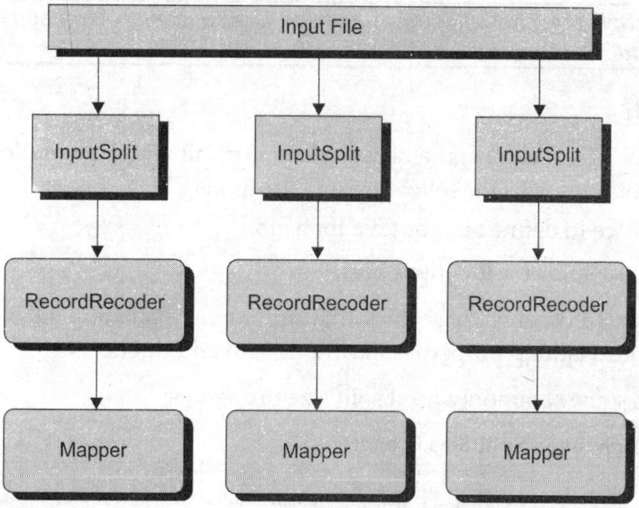

Figure 9.1: Functionality of InputFormat

In Figure 9.1, you can see that the `InputFormat` class provides the following functionality:

- It selects the required input file.
- It divides the input file into tasks and defines the `InputSplits` class.
- It provides a `RecordReader` class that reads the input file for the mapper.

The split implementation extends the `InputSplit` class, which is a base abstract class of Hadoop. It is able to define split lengths and split locations.

`InputSplit` can be defined as:

```
public abstract class InputSplit
{
   public abstract long getLength() throws IOException, InterruptedException;
   public abstract String[] getLocations() throws IOException,InterruptedException;
}
```

What do we mean by split size and split locations? Split size and split locations can have different meaning, depending on the storage mechanisms and execution strategy used. For example, in the case of HDFS (Hadoop Distributed File System), an input split corresponds to a physical data block, and the location is a set of machines where that block is physically located.

RecordReader

As we know, the input split (or just split) defines the unit of work in a MapReduce program. But, the input split does not describe the way to access the unit of work. The `RecordReader` class loads all required data from its source and converts it into a key/value pair, i.e., pairs that can be read by the mapper. An input file is a plain text file that is broken into lines through either linefeed or carriage-return. In a key/value pair, the key refers to the position of a value in a file, while a value refers to a line of text. To read the input, the `RecordReader` class is invoked continually until the entire input splits are consumed. Each invocation of `RecordReader` calls the `map()` method of the mapper.

NOTE

Input split and InputSplit are different terms. Input split is a conceptual term and InputSplit is a class name to implement the input split.

FileInputFormat

The `FileInputFormat` class is a base class for all implementations of `InputFormat`. `FileInputFormat` performs the following two functions:

- It provides a place to define an input file for a job.
- It generates input splits for the input files.

`FileInputFormat` splits only those files that are larger than the HDFS block. Split size can be controlled by various Hadoop properties like input path and filters.

Table 9.1 describes some commonly used split size properties:

Table 9.1: Commonly Used Split Size Properties

Property Name	Data Type	Value	Description
`mapred.min.split.size`	int	1 byte	This is the smallest valid size for a split.
`mapred.max.split.size`	long	Long.MAX_VALUE, that is 9223372036854775807 bytes	This is the largest valid size for a split.
`dfs.block.size`	Long	64MB	This is an HDFS block size.

As you can see in Table 9.1, the minimum split size is usually 1 byte, although some formats have a lower bound on the split size. We may impose a minimum split size. By setting this to a value larger than the block size, you can force splits to be larger than a block. However, this is not good while using HDFS, because doing so will increase the number of blocks that are not local to a map task. The maximum split size defaults to the maximum value that can be represented by a Java long type. It has an effect only when it is less than the block size, forcing splits to be smaller than a block.

The `computeSplitSize()` method in the `FileInputFormat` class can compute the split size by using the `max(minimumSize, min(maximumSize, blockSize))` and by default `minimumSize < blockSize < maximumSize`. Thus, the split size will be equal to `blockSize`.

The steps used by the `FileInputFormat` class to calculate the splits for the given input file are as follows:

1. Extend the `InputSplit` class to get information about the location of the input file and the block length.
2. Get a list of blocks for the input file.

3. For every block, do the following:
   - Create a split equal to the block size.
   - Set the split locations as the locations of a given block.
   - Save the block offset, length, and file location in the split.

Implementing InputFormat for Compute-Intensive Applications

The term 'compute-intensive' is used for any computer application that requires a lot of computation. A compute-intensive application is a special class of MapReduce applications. For example, face recognition applications require complex calculations and make use of MapReduce to achieve parallelization.

The fundamental characteristic of compute-intensive applications is that the execution of the `Mapper.map()` function in the application is considerably longer than the application's data access time.

Technically, compute-intensive applications can use standard input format implementation. However, this implementation can cause a problem by creating a large number of data nodes and leaving other nodes within the cluster underutilized.

Figure 9.2 shows the utilization of the nodes of the cluster in compute-intensive applications:

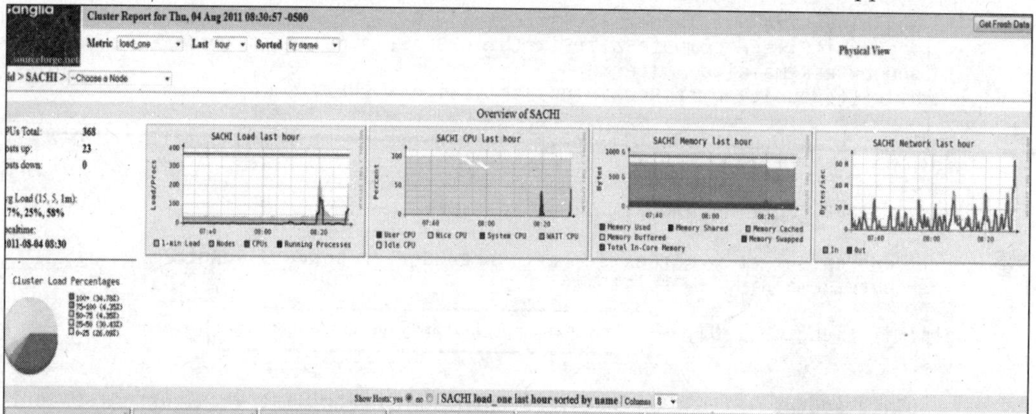

Source: *http://cdn.infoq.com/statics_s2_20150807-0037u2/resource/articles/HadoopInputFormat/en/resources/figure1large.jpg*

Figure 9.2: Utilization of Nodes of the Cluster in Compute-Intensive Applications

In Figure 9.2, you will notice large variations in the utilization of nodes. Overutilization is shown by the dark gray color, while underutilization is shown by the light gray color.

On the basis of the above figure, we have reviewed the notion of locality for the compute-intensive applications. Here, locality means balanced delivery of maps for execution among all available nodes. Balanced delivery of maps for execution can maximize the utilization of cluster's machines.

Calculating Split Using Custom InputFormat

In this section, we are going to calculate a split by using the custom `InputFormat` class. Here, we have input in a sequential text file. Listing 9.1 shows this implementation:

Listing 9.1: Implementation of the `ComputeIntensiveSequenceFile` Class to Calculate a Split

```
public class ComputeIntensiveSequenceFile <K, V> extends SequenceFileInputFormat
   <K,V>
{
@Override
public List<InputSplit> getSplits(JobContext job) throws IOException
{
   String[] servers = getActiveServersList(job);
   if(servers == null) return null;
   List<InputSplit> splits = new ArrayList<InputSplit>();
   List<FileStatus>files = listStatus(job);
   int currentServer = 0;
   for (FileStatus file: files) { Path path = file.getPath();
   long length = file.getLen();
   if ((length != 0) && isSplitable(job, path))
   {
     long blockSize = file.getBlockSize();
     long splitSize = computeSplitSize(blockSize, minSize, maxSize);
     long bytesRemaining = length;
     while (((double) bytesRemaining)/splitSize > SPLIT_SLOP)
     {
       splits. add(new FileSplit(path, length-bytesRemaining, splitSize, new
  String[]
        {
         servers[currentServer]
        }));
         currentServer = getNextServer(currentServer,servers.length);
         bytesRemaining -= splitSize;
     }
    else if (length != 0)   <-- Creates an empty host array for zero-length files
    {

      splits.add(new FileSplit(path,0,length,new String[]{servers[currentServer]}));
      currentServer = getNextServer(currentServer, servers.length);
    }
    }
     // Save the number of input files in the job-conf job.
  getConfiguration().setLong(NUM_INPUT_FILES, files.size());
   return splits;
}
                 A method that calculates an array of
                 servers (names) currently active in
                 the cluster
                              |
                              v
 private String[] getActiveServersList(JobContext context)
 {
  String [] servers = null;
  try {
        JobClient jc = new JobClient((JobConf)context.getConfiguration());
        ClusterStatus   status = jc.getClusterStatus(true); Collection<String> atc =
        status.getActiveTrackerNames();
         servers = new String[atc.size()]; int s = 0;
```

```
        for(String serverInfo : atc)
        {
            StringTokenizer st = new StringTokenizer(serverInfo, ":");
            String trackerName =        st.nextToken();
            StringTokenizer st1 = new StringTokenizer(trackerName, "_");
            st1.nextToken();
            servers[s++] = st1.nextToken();
        }
    } catch (IOException e) { e.printStackTrace();}
  return servers;
}

private static int getNextServer(int current, int max)
{
  current++; if(current >= max)
  current = 0; return current;
} }
```

Calculates the next server in the server array when the array of servers is exhausted

In the code given in Listing 9.1, we have implemented the `ComputeIntensiveSequenceFile` class to extend the `SequenceFileInputFormat` class. The `ComputeIntensiveSequenceFile` class calculates splits and distributes them among all available servers of the cluster.

The `ComputeIntensiveSequenceFile` class overrides the `getSplits()` method and calculates splits and assigns them to all available servers in the cluster uniformly. All these assignments are done by following two methods:

- The `getActiveServersList()` method, which creates a list of all active servers in the cluster.
- The `getNextServer()` method, which finds the nearest server around an exhausted server in the cluster.

You can see in Figure 9.3 that dark gray nodes (exhausted servers) are not present as they are in Figure 9.3:

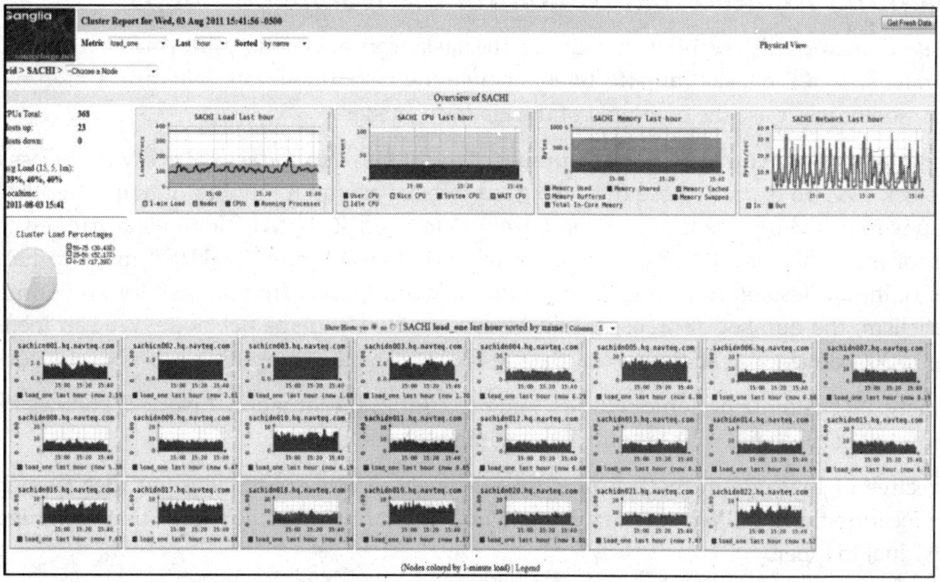

Source: *http://www.infoq.com/articles/HadoopInputFormat*

Figure 9.3: Node Utilization with the Execution Locality InputFormat() Method

Thus, we can say that calculating splits using custom `InputFormat` produces better results.

Calculating Split Using Hadoop Fair Scheduler

You can also use another solution, known as Hadoop Fair Scheduler, to calculate splits. Hadoop Fair Scheduler is used for organizing, scheduling, and preempting MapReduce jobs in the clusters. The main characteristics of Fair Scheduler are as follows:

- It can run small jobs first without starving the big job.
- It provides guaranteed service levels to jobs in a shared cluster.
- It is simple to configure.
- Fair Scheduler at runtime is possible, without restarting the cluster.

In our case, we are assuming that Hadoop Fair Scheduler is available on our system. Add the following block of code to the `mapred-site.xml` file in order to enable the scheduler:

```
<property>
        <name>mapred.fairscheduler.locality.delay</name>
        <value>360000000</value>
<property>
```

The execution time of Hadoop Fair Scheduler is about 30% less than when the custom `InputFormat` approach is used.

NOTE

MapReduce is an application that can run on the Hadoop 2.x framework. All the configuration options of MapReduce are stored in the /opt/mapr/hadoop/hadoop-2.x.x/etc/hadoop/mapred-site.xml file. The mapred-site.xml file is editable by the root user. This file contains configuration information that overrides the default values for MapReduce parameters.

Implementing InputFormat to Control the Number of Maps

In this section, we will see how the size of the tasks can affect the performance of Hadoop. An appropriate size of the tasks can effectively change the performance of Hadoop. A high number of tasks can sometimes raise the overhead of the Hadoop cluster.

For example, suppose you have a large number of input files and the size of every file is less than the HDFS block size. To execute these files, we need to have an equal number of maps. In other words, one map is required for one input file because nothing is distributed. Now, what happen when the number of input files is 1,000,000? Unfortunately, Hadoop requires 1,000,000 maps to handle this number of input files and can run out of resources. It is important to note that for an optimum level of parallelism, the number of maps should be around 10–100 maps per node. We can increase this number to 300, depending on how small the file is as well as the computing power of the node.

Fortunately, by customizing some settings, you can control the situation. Listing 9.2 shows the utility of the concept of multi file split to control the number of maps.

The objective of the code in the listing is to copy a set of non-splittable input files from HDFS to another location through Web services. Here, a non-splittable input file means that each file requires an individual mapper.

NOTE

The code given in Listing 9.2 shows only the implementation of relevant methods, not the complete program.

Listing 9.2 implements the solution by using the `MultiFileSplit` class, which is extended by the `InputSplit` class. The `MultiFileSplit` class contains both, a list of files and information of the locality. Listing 9.2 shows the implementation of the `MultiFileSplit` class for creating multiple input splits:

Listing 9.2: Creation of Multiple InputSplits by Using the `MultiFileSplit` Class

```
public class MultiFileSplit extends InputSplit implements
Writable{
private long length;
private String[] hosts;
private List<String> files = null;
public MultiFileSplit(){
}
```

MultiFileSplit is a constructor with two arguments

```
public MultiFileSplit(long l, String[] locations){
}
@Override
```

Returns an array containing the length of the files

```
public long getLength() throws IOException, InterruptedException {
  return files.size();
}
@Override
```

Gets the location of the host

```
public String[] getLocations() throws IOException,InterruptedException {
 return hosts;
}
@Override
public void write(DataOutput out) throws IOException {
}
@Override
public void readFields(DataInput in) throws IOException {
}
}
```

Implementing InputFormat for Multiple HBase Tables

HBase is an open-source, non-relational, and distributed database model. It is a column-oriented DBMS that can run on top of HDFS. HBase is written in Java and does not support any structured query language like SQL.

There are two types of MapReduce applications:

- **HBase data source**—This type of MapReduce application stores a set of data that can be used in analysis.
- **HBase sink**—This type of MapReduce application stores the output.

HBase provides a `TableInputFormat` class for scanning an HBase table; this scanning process is known as a table scan. It can split rows resulting from the table scan into regions in which these rows reside.

Listing 9.3 helps you understand how to define a class that can hold the definition of a table:

Listing 9.3: The `TableDefinition` Class

```
public class TableDefinition implements Writable
{
 private Scan _scan = null;
 private HTable _table = null;
 private String _tableName = null;
}
```

The `MultiTableSplit` class helps to identify the table during the processing of MapReduce jobs. The process of defining a rowspan (or columns) of the table relevant to the requirement of the user is known as a row scan (or column scan).

In Listing 9.3, the `TableDefinition` class defines a table that initializes three variables — `_scan`, `_table`, and `_tableName`, with null values.

We know `TableInputFormat` supports a single table per scan; thus, we need not define the table in the `InputSplit` class. Because of this concept, different splits can refer to different tables in every scan.

Listing 9.4 shows the `MultiTableSplit` class (code file:class `MultiTableSplit`) that extends the `TableSplit` class to store table-related information as well as scan a given table:

Listing 9.4: The `MultiTableSplit` Class

```
public class MultiTableSplit extends TableSplit {
private Scan scan;
public MultiTableSplit() {
.......................................................
}
public MultiTableSplit(byte [] tableName, byte [] startRow, byte [] endRow,
final String location, Scan scan) {
.......................................................
}
..........................................................
}
```

In Listing 9.4, you can see that the `MultiTableSplit` class contains two constructors: a default constructor and a parameterized constructor. These two constructors contain table-related information like name, start and end rows, etc., as well as scan the given table.

With these two supporting classes in place, the `MultiTableInputFormat` class can be implemented by using the code shown in Listing 9.5:

Listing 9.5: The `MultiTableInputFormat` Class

```
public class MultiTableInputFormat extends InputFormat<ImmutableBy
tesWritable, Result> implements Configurable{
..........................................................................
protected void setTableRecordReader(TableRecordReader
tableRecordReader) {
   this.tableRecordReader = tableRecordReader;
}
@Override
```

Get a split based on region and store it in a list

```
public List<InputSplit> getSplits(JobContext context) throws
IOException, InterruptedException {
```

```
List<InputSplit> splits = new LinkedList<InputSplit>();
int count = 0;
for(TableDefinition t : tables){ HTable table = t.getTable(); if
(table == null) {
  continue;
}
Pair<byte[][], byte[][]> keys = table.getStartEndKeys();
if (keys == null || keys.getFirst() == null || keys.getFirst().
length == 0) {
  continue;
}
Scan scan = t.getScan();
for (int i = 0; i < keys.getFirst().length; i++) {

  String regionLocation =

table.getRegionLocation(keys.getFirst()[i]). getServerAddress().getHostname();
byte[] startRow = scan.getStartRow();
byte[] stopRow = scan.getStopRow();
if ((startRow.length == 0 || keys.getSecond()[i].length == 0 ||
  Bytes.compareTo(startRow, keys.getSecond()[i]) <
0) && (stopRow.length == 0 || Bytes.compareTo(stopRow, keys.getFirst()[i]) > 0))
{
    byte[] splitStart = startRow.length == 0 || Bytes.compareTo(keys.
    getFirst()[i], startRow) >= 0 ?
    keys.getFirst()[i] : startRow;
    byte[] splitStop = (stopRow.length == 0 || Bytes.compareTo(keys.getSecond()[i],
  stopRow) <= 0) &&
keys.getSecond()[i].length > 0 ? keys.getSecond()[i] : stopRow;
InputSplit split = new

MultiTableSplit(table.getTableName(), splitStart, splitStop, regionLocation, scan);
splits.add(split);
}
}
 if(splits.size() == 0){
   Throw new IOException ("Expecting at least one region.");
}
Return splits;
}
@Override
public RecordReader<ImmutableBytesWritable, Result>
createRecordReader( InputSplit split, TaskAttemptContext context)
throws IOException,
InterruptedException {

MultiTableSplit tSplit = (MultiTableSplit) split;
TableRecordReader trr = this.tableRecordReader; if (trr == null) {
trr = new TableRecordReader();
}
 Scan sc = tSplit.getScan(); sc.setStartRow(tSplit.getStartRow());
 sc.setStopRow(tSplit.getEndRow()); trr.setScan(sc);
 byte[] tName = tSplit.getTableName();
 trr.setHTable(new HTable(HBaseConfiguration.create(conf), tName));
 trr.init();
 return trr;
}
```

To iteratively get information about the RegionLocation.hostsname host and the startrow and stoprow locations

Creating a MultiTableSplit based on the values obtained for splitStart, splitStop, and RegionLocation

Creating and setting values for the RecordReader class

```
public static void initTableMapperJob(List<TableDefinition> tables,
Class<? extends TableMapper> mapper,
Class<? extends WritableComparable> outputKeyClass,
```

The initTableMapperJob method used to set the MapReduce job

```
Class<? extends Writable> outputValueClass, Job job) throws
IOException {
job.setInputFormatClass(MultiTableInputFormat.class);
if (outputValueClass != null)
job.setMapOutputValueClass(outputValueClass);
if (outputKeyClass != null) job.setMapOutputKeyClass(outputKeyCla
ss); job.setMapperClass(mapper); job.getConfiguration().set(INPUT_
TABLES,convertTablesToString(tables));
}
}
```

The `MultiTableInputFormat` class contains the following key methods:

- The `getSplits()` method, which iterates through the list of tables, and for every table, calculates a list of regions with a set of keys inside scan boundaries. For every region, the implementation creates a new split and populates the `MultitableSplit` class with the appropriate information.
- The `createRecordReader()` method creates a new record reader based on the table and scans information. By default, the `InputFormat` class uses the default implementation provided by Hadoop. Additionally, the `setTableRecordReader()` method allows subclasses of the `InputFormat` class to overwrite `RecordReader` implementation.
- Finally, `initTableMapperJob()` method, which simplifies the setting up of a MapReduce job. It takes a list of table definitions, a mapper class, output keys and values, and a job, and sets job parameters correctly. It also 'stringifies' a list of table definitions and sets the resulting string to the context object, which makes it available to the `InputFormat` implementation.

Now, you know how to write custom `InputFormats` to control a mapper's execution. The next section looks at how to implement a custom `RecordReader` that enables you to control how input data is read, processed, and delivered to the mappers.

Reading Data with Custom RecordReader

The `RecordReader` class generates key/value pairs from data within the boundaries created by the input split. In the input file, we have a start and a corresponding end. The start is a byte and tells the `RecordReader` to start generating key/value pairs. Similarly, the end tells the `RecordReader` to stop reading records.

To understand more about the reading process, let's take an example. Suppose your dataset is composed in an input file of size 300MB. The file has three blocks, each of a size of 128MB. Suppose you have an `InputSplit` class for each block.

Now, let's consider three different scenarios or cases to read the lines by record readers. These cases are given as follows:

Case 1 – If the input file has six lines of 50MB each, as shown in Figure 9.4:

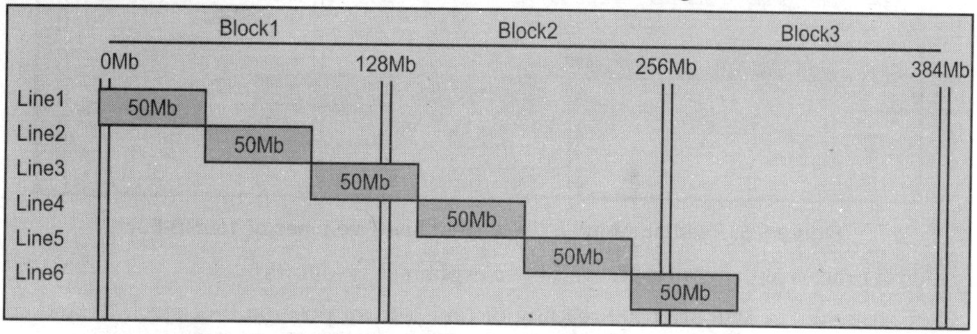

Figure 9.4: Reading of Input File with Six Lines of 50MB Each

The reading process shown in Figure 9.4 can be explained as follows:

- `RecordReader 1` will start reading bytes from position 0 of Block B1. The first EOL (End of Line) will be met after the first 50MB, and Line 1 will be read and sent as a key/value pair to `Mapper 1`. Moreover, the second EOL will be met after the second 50MB, and Line 2 will be read and sent as a key/value pair to `Mapper 1`.
- Now, `RecordReader 1` starts reading Line 3 starts from byte 100MB, and its EOL is outside Block 1 (i.e., at 128Mb). The complete reading of the line will end on bytes 150MB in Block B2. The entire reading process will be done in two phases. In the first phase, the first part of Line L3 will be read locally from Block B1, while the next part will be read from Block B2 remotely. After reading a complete line, it will send as a key/value pair to `Mapper 1`.
- Now, `RecordReader 2` starts on Block B2. The start of Block 2 is at position 128MB, but this is not the start of any line actually. In this case, Reader 2 needs to jump on the first EOL of Block 2, which can be found at position 150MB. Now, the actual start of `RecordReader 2` will be at 150MB instead of 128MB.
- What happens when a `RecordReader` reads a block that starts exactly on an EOL? In this case, the `RecordReader` might miss one record. To prevent this situation, before moving to the next EOL, the `RecordReader` needs to move back until a start is met and decrement the initial start value to start - 1. This will ensure that no record is skipped.
- The remaining process follows the same logic.

The points discussed above are summarized in Table 9.2:

Table 9.2: Reading of Line by Three RecordReaders

	Start	Actual Start	End	Line(s)
Mapper1	B1:0	B1:0	B2:150	L1,L2,L3
Mapper2	B2:128	B2:150	B3:300	L4,L2,L6
Mapper3	B3:256	B3:300	B3:300	N/A

Case 2—If the input file has only two lines of 150MB each, as shown in Figure 9.5:

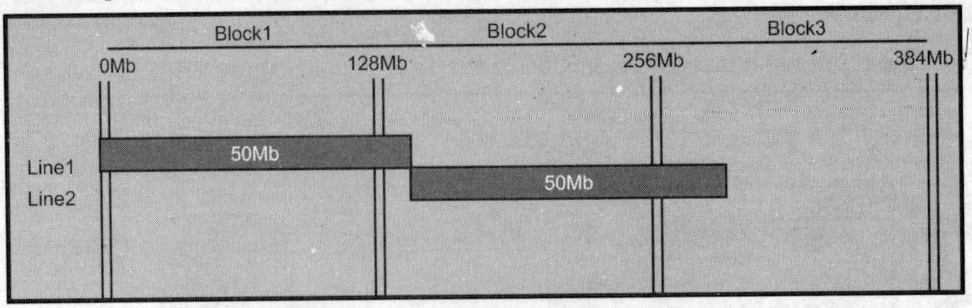

Figure 9.5: Reading of Input file when it has Two Lines of 150MB Each

The reading process shown in Figure 9.5 can be explained as follows:

- `RecordReader 1` will start the reading of Line 1 from position 0 of block B1 and continually read this line locally until the end of Block 1 (128MB). Till now, the EOL is not met, so it will continually read Line 1 remotely on Block 2 until EOL (150MB).
- Similarly, `RecordReader 2` will start reading from 128MB, but Line 2 starts on 150MB. So, `RecordReader 2` actually starts reading from 150MB to 256MB locally and from 256MB to 300MB remotely.

The points discussed above are summarized in Table 9.3:

Table 9.3: Summary of Reading by Two RecordReaders

	Start	Actual Start	End	Line(s)
Mapper1	B1:0	B1:0	B2:150	L1
Mapper2	B2:128	B2:150	B3:300	L2
Mapper3	B3:256	B3:300	B3:300	N/A

Case 3—If the input file has only two lines of 300MB each, as shown in Figure 9.6:

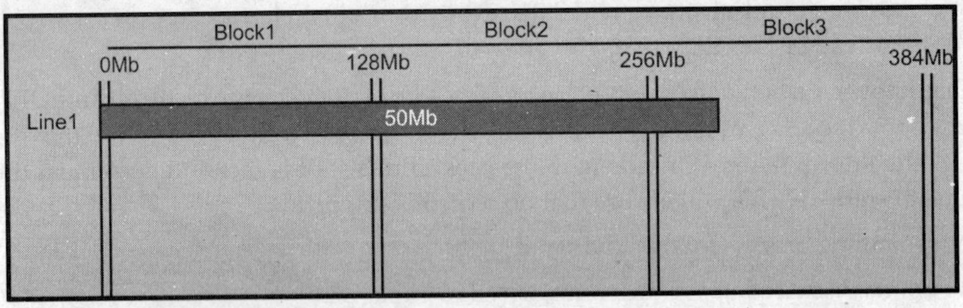

Figure 9.6: Reading of Input File when it has One Line of 300MB

The reading process shown in Figure 9.6 can be explained as follows:

- `RecordReader 1` will start reading locally from position 0 of Block 1 to the end of Block 1, while it will continually read Line 1 from 128MB to 256 of Block 2, and from 256MB to EOL (300MB) of Block 3 remotely. This creates some overhead because `RecordReaders` are trying to read a lot of data remotely.

- The points discussed above are summarized in Table 9.4:

Table 9.4: Summary of Reading by a RecordReader

	Start	Actual Start	End	Line(s)
Mapper1	B1:0	B1:0	B3:300	L1

Organizing Output Data with OutputFormats

The `OutputFormat` and `RecordWriter` interfaces are used to write the results of execution of a MapReduce's job back to the permanent storage of the various nodes of a cluster.

`TextOutputFormat` is a default format that can write key/value pairs in the form of a string into the specific lines of an output file. The `TextOutputFormat` format writes output data using the `toString()` method, while the `SequenceFileOutputFormat` format keeps the data in binary format so that it can be read quickly later if required.

By defining your own `OutputFormat` implementation, you can write data into the output file in the format you want. To write output files on your local system or in HDFS (Hadoop Distributed File System), you must extend the `FileOutputFormat` class. Moreover, to write the output in a different format, you must use the `JobConf.setOutputFormat()` method.

Figure 9.7 shows the complete output process using the `FileOutputFormat` class:

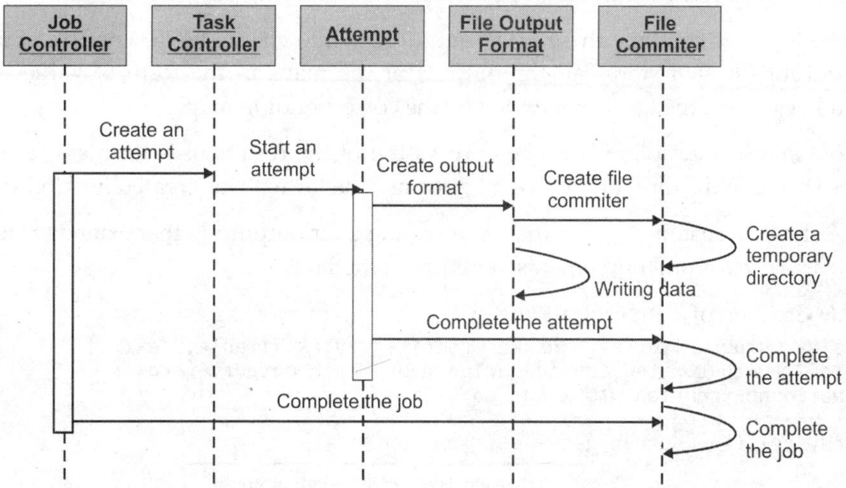

Figure 9.7: Output Process of the FileOutputFormat Class

As the job splits into multiple input splits, a task controller attempts to perform task execution. Execution of a job creates a subclass of the `FileOutputFormat` class which, in turn, creates a `FileCommitter` class to complete the task. Now, a temporary directory is created in the output directory as specified by `FileOutputFormat`. Once an attempt is completed, the `FileOutputCommitter` is invoked, and the entire process is repeated. The temporary directory allows each task to write its output independently during multiple attempts of each task.

An execution also creates one of the subclasses of `FileOutputFormat`, which, in turn, creates a `FileCommitter` class. If any attempt fails, the corresponding temporary directory will be removed automatically. When the attempt completes successfully, the output will be copied into the main directory from the temporary directory, and the temporary directory can be removed. As the execution of the job is completed, the `FileCommitter` class is invoked and finalizes the output data.

Customizing Data with RecordWriter

As we have studied in the previous section, the `OutputFormat` and `RecordWriter` interfaces are responsible for writing the results in the desired format. In other words, these interfaces can determine where the result is stored and how the result is written in the storage of the nodes of the cluster.

Why would we require customizing the behavior of `RecordWriter`? One reason for doing this is to keep the output of a MapReduce job in various directories separately. Another reason is to create the output in the required form.

Hadoop provides the facility to customize `RecordWriter`, allowing you to write data (or the result) into HBase, HDFS, and other external systems. Let's see how to implement a custom `RecordWriter`.

Suppose you have a mapper, and it generates a complete output file after every function invocation. When the mapper writes these output files into HDFS directly, it creates a large number of small output files. As you can see, this is not a practical way of storing output files.

It will be better if we combine these small output files into a large file. Using this approach, we will have an output file that stores all the outputs of the maps in the form of values by using their associated keys. Here, the key is generated by the corresponding map.

There is one more assumption here, i.e., processing of the results uses tar files. Tar is a file format that stores values in the form of archive bit streams. The format was created for UNIX.

Listing 9.6 shows a custom `RecordWriter` creating a tar output file that extends Hadoop's abstract `RecordWriter` class and implements all required methods:

Listing 9.6: Creation of a Tar Output File by the `TarOutputWriter` Class

```
class TarOutputWriter extends RecordWriter<BytesWritable, Text> {
public TarOutputWriter(Configuration conf, Path output) throws
FileNotFoundException, IOException
{
 FileSystem fs = output.getFileSystem(conf);
```

Each reader is added to the output stream

```
 FSDataOutputStream fsOutStream = fs.create(output, REWRITE_FILES, BUFFER_SIZE);
 tarOutStream = new TarArchiveOutputStream(fsOutStream);
}
@Override
```

This creates the tar entry from keys and values

```
public void write(BytesWritable key, Text value) throws
IOException {
if (key == null || value == null ) {
 return;
}
```

```
    TarArchiveEntry mtd = new TarArchiveEntry(key.toString());
    mtd.setSize(value.getLength());
    tarOutStream.putArchiveEntry(mtd);
    IOUtils.copy(new ByteArrayInputStream(value.getBytes()),
    tarOutStream);
  }
  @Override
  public void close(TaskAttemptContext context) throws IOException {
   if (tarOutStream != null) { tarOutStream.flush();
    tarOutStream.close();
  }}}
```

In the above code, the main function is performed by the `write()` method. The `write()` method first creates an entry from key/value pairs and then adds it to the `OutputStream` class. The `close()` method finally clears `OutputStream`.

Optimizing MapReduce Execution with Combiner

The combiner is an important Hadoop's feature. It takes a list of key/value pairs from various maps and optimizes (or combines) them. After optimization, the combiner passes the optimized key/value pairs to the partitioner for further processing. By reducing the number of key/value pairs, the combiner saves a lot of bandwidth.

Figure 9.8 shows the role of the combiner in MapReduce processing:

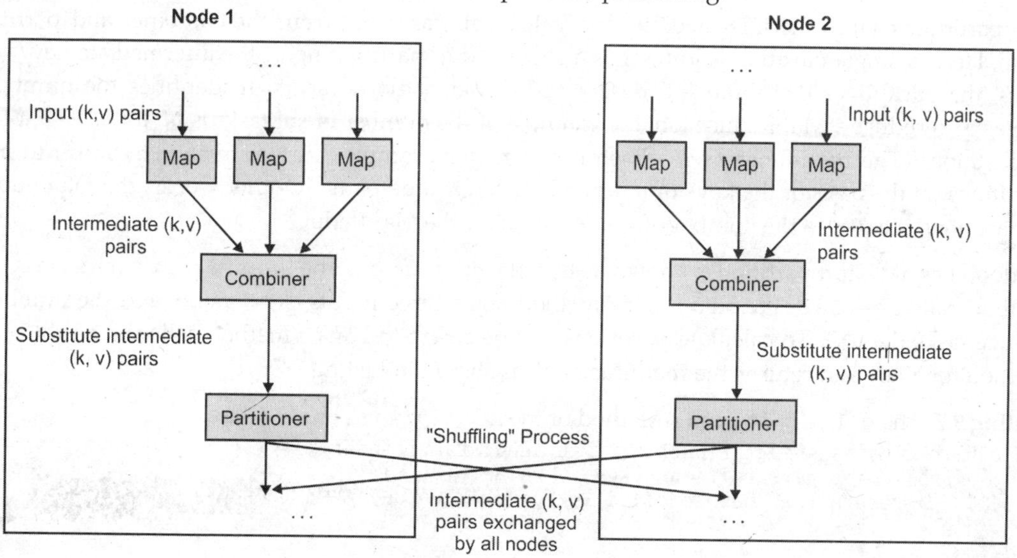

Figure 9.8: Role of Combiner in Hadoop's Processing Pipeline

Let's see how the combiner helps to reduce the amount of data. Take word count as an example. Suppose there are several occurrences of the word 'the' in a piece of text, and we want to know the exact number. Without the help of the combiner, the mapper will send many key/value pairs in the 'the/1' format. However, if we use combiners, they will send a single key/value pair as 'the/N', where N is bigger than 1.

Informally, we can say that the combiner is a mini reducer that reduces a list of key/value pairs and sends these reduced pairs to the reducer.

The combiner does not have its own interface; however, you can implement it by using the `Reducer` interface, and the `reduce()` method of the `Combiner` class will be called on each map output key.

Using the `Combiner` class seems simple, but be careful as it does not always produce the desired result. Let's look at the counter example to understand this. Suppose we have a mean reducer that computes the mean value from the given key/value pairs. Let's suppose we have five such key/value pairs: (k, 40), (k, 30), (k, 20), (k, 2), and (k, 8) generated from the mapper for a given key k. As the mean reducer receives this list as (k, <40, 30, 20, 2, 8>), it gives 20 as the output, which is true. However, when two mean combiners are applied on two lists {(k, 40), (k, 30), (k, 20)} and {(k, 2), (k, 8)} separately, the reducer would receive the list as (k, <30, 5>) and give the output as 17.5, which is wrong.

Generally, we can say that the use of the `Combiner` class is appropriate only when its function is both associative and commutative. For example, an addition function is both associative and commutative. Thus, we can use the additive combiner.

Controlling Reducer Execution with Partitioners

Every map takes some key/value pairs and produces a key/value pair as a result. This resultant key/value pair is known as intermediate key/value pair. Partitioning is the process of making partitions of the received intermediate (key, value) pairs and of deciding which reducer will receive which partition. The process of partitioning is done by the partitioner.

The partitioner takes the intermediate key/value pairs as input from the combiner and partitions them. Here, a single partition is known as a single. After partitioning of the intermediate key/value pairs, the partitioner distributes all reduce tasks among the reducers. It identifies the number of subtasks to reduce a MapReduce job. For example, if the number of subtasks is N, it makes a total of N partitions. The partitioner uses a hash function (for example, the `HashPartitioner`) to make partitions on the basis of the keys of intermediate key/value pairs. In other words, the total number of partitions is equal to the number of reduce tasks for the MapReduce.

Hadoop has a default partitioner known as `HashPartitioner`. The `HashPartitioner` class has a method called `getPartition()`. This method takes three inputs—key, value, and the number of reduce tasks (i.e., N). To calculate partitions, the `getPartition()` method calls the `hashCode()` method for a key and returns the modulus of N, as shown in Listing 9.7:

Listing 9.7: The `getPartition()` Method of the `HashPartitioner` Class

```
public class HashPartitioner<K, V> extends Partitioner<K, V> {
    public int getPartition(K key, V value, int N) {
        return (key.hashCode() & Integer.MAX_VALUE) % N;
    }
}
```

Suppose the total number of reduce tasks is five. In that case, the `getPartition()` method will return any of the values from 0 to 4 for all keys.

Customizing the MapReduce Execution in Terms of YARN

As we know, YARN is the MapReduce of the second-generation Hadoop. In case of YARN, there is an application manager and the resource manager. In YARN, there is another daemon that manages every task and coordinates with the application manager and the resource manager to take the live status of the job. This daemon is known as the node manager. Let us now talk about the job execution in YARN, which is shown in Figure 9.9:

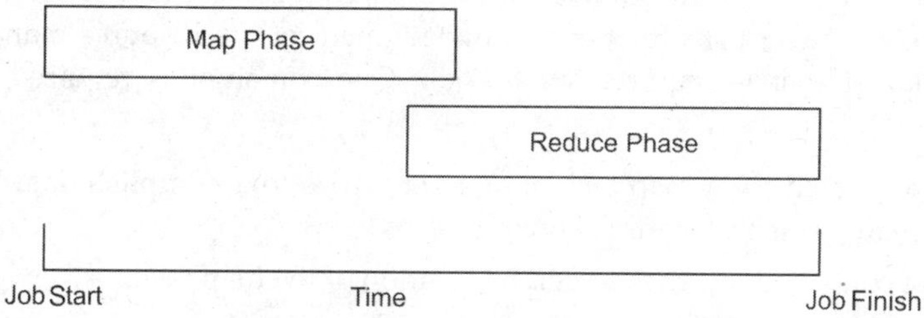

Figure 9.9: Layout of the Job Timeline

The MapReduce job execution timeline is as follows:

- **Map phase**—Several map tasks are executed in this phase.
- **Reduce phase**—In this phase, several reducer tasks will run.

Note that the reduce phase always starts before the end of the map phase. That is why an interleaving is possible between them.

Let us now discuss these two phases in detail in the following sections.

Map Phase

Question arises that how many map tasks/mappers are invoked by the application manager (or we can say application master) so that it can start the current job, which is provided by the user. As we know that when a user submits an application (job), much information is provided to the YARN. This information is as follows:

- **Configuration**—Configurations are the settings that are necessary for the execution of the job. Also, job can be executed with the default configuration that YARN already holds.
- **JAR**—A jar of the job is needed for the processing. It should contain the following information:
  - Map () implementation
  - Combiner implementation
  - Reducer() implementation
  - Driver () implementation, which is nothing but the repository of the data flow connection that joins the map, combiner, and reducer functions
- **Input and output information**—Input and output information is basically the path of the file on which the operations need to be done. If the input path is wrong or the file is not available, the job will fail. Similarly, the output information is the information about the storage, where the output gets stored after processing.

Now the question is, How many map tasks run?

After the submission of the job, application manager/master launches the map tasks for each input split. If the input file is bigger than the HDFS block size, two or more splits are associated with the same input file. The default HDFS block size is 128MB in second generation Hadoop. So, the application master divides the file in input split, and due to this, the application master launches the mapper.

Map Task Launching

Now this is the part that somehow controls or customizes the execution of the MapReduce task in YARN. Application manager asks for the acknowledgment of the resource manager regarding the status of the container that is required by the job. One container is required for one map task (map splits).

Container that is requested for a map task (job) always tries to accomplish data locality of the map split. Application manager asks for the following:

- Location of the container and tries to get the location of the map task.
- Else, it can identify whether they are both in the same node or in the same rack.
- Otherwise, it will query for the container on the other node manager on the cluster.

The above information is just a hint for the resource scheduler. It can ignore the data locality if the suggested job is conflicting with the resource scheduler's aim. After this entire job execution, if a container is assigned to the application manager, the map task is launched.

Map Phase: Execution

As we know that in the first generation of Hadoop, everything is controlled by the NameNode, which is responsible for the execution and allotment of the nodes for the MR. Similarly, in YARN, the node manager takes care of the job execution. It timely takes the status of the Map task and simultaneously coordinates with the containers and the resource scheduler. Following are some steps that take place in execution:

1. **INIT**—This is the step in which we set up the map task.
2. **Execution**—This is the process in which the map task gives the key, value tuple when we run the map () function.
3. **Spilling phase**—This is the phase in which each output generated from the map task is stored in memory buffer. When the buffer is about to fill, it simultaneously starts removing the data from the buffer stack.
4. **Shuffle**—After the spilling phase, we merge all the outputs received from the mapper and then pack them for the reduce phase.

Reduce Phase

In this phase, the mappers output is already processed as it has undergone execution, spilling, and shuffling. Finally, it reaches the reducer. Now, it goes for final processing under the reducer in which the values are associated and processed to give a (key $_{final}$, Value $_{final}$) pair.

Concept of Containers

- Container is the basic resource for completing the MapReduce job in YARN.
- Containers are under the supervision of the node manager.
- Status of the container is directly taken by the node manager.
- Job is allocated by the application manager, and the resource is allocated by the resource manager, which undergoes processing in a container that is reported to node manager.

- Now, in terms of customizing the MR process in YARN, resource scheduler and the container play an important role.

For example, if the job needs 70% of the resources and resource manager is having only 30% of the resources, the resource scheduler processes the 30% resources with the acknowledgment of the node manager and transfers the 30% resources to the container where the job gets processed. After processing, the resource gets available for the job, and it gives the rest of the resources to the job for further processing.

Implementing a MapReduce Program for Sorting Text Data

Many times, we need to arrange large amounts of data either in ascending or in descending order. Sorting of data is important for many types of applications like in employee management, online trading and store management, etc. In this section, we will implement a MapReduce program to sort text data in ascending or descending order.

SCENARIO

Argon Technologies, a marketing company, has a file named sorting.txt that contains some important information in text format. The HR manager of the company wants to sort the content of the file for extracting important information.

Now, you are required to write a MapReduce program that takes an input text file and sorts the content of the file in ascending or descending order. Note that sorted data must be separated from each other by a tab space.

Before writing the code for the required program, you need to ensure that you have Eclipse 4.3 installed on your system. Now, perform the following steps to implement a MapReduce program for sorting text data:

1. Start Eclipse by clicking the Eclipse icon, as shown in Figure 9.10:

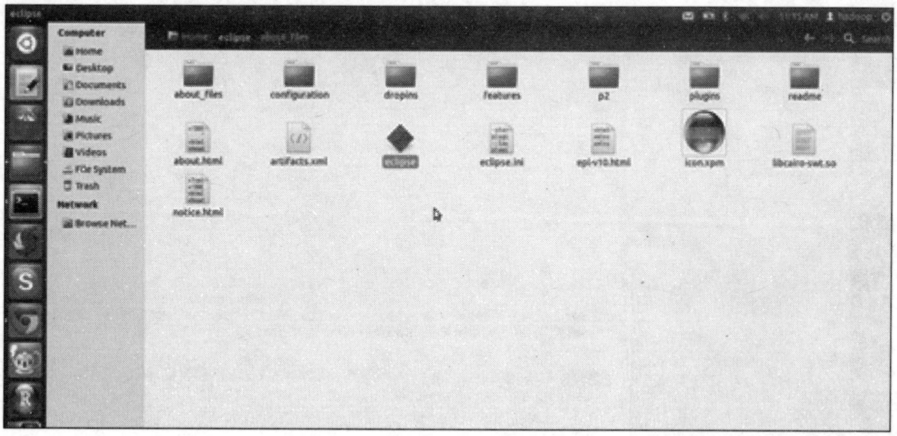

Figure 9.10: Starting Eclipse

A dialog box opens, prompting you to select (or assign) a workspace, as shown in Figure 9.11:

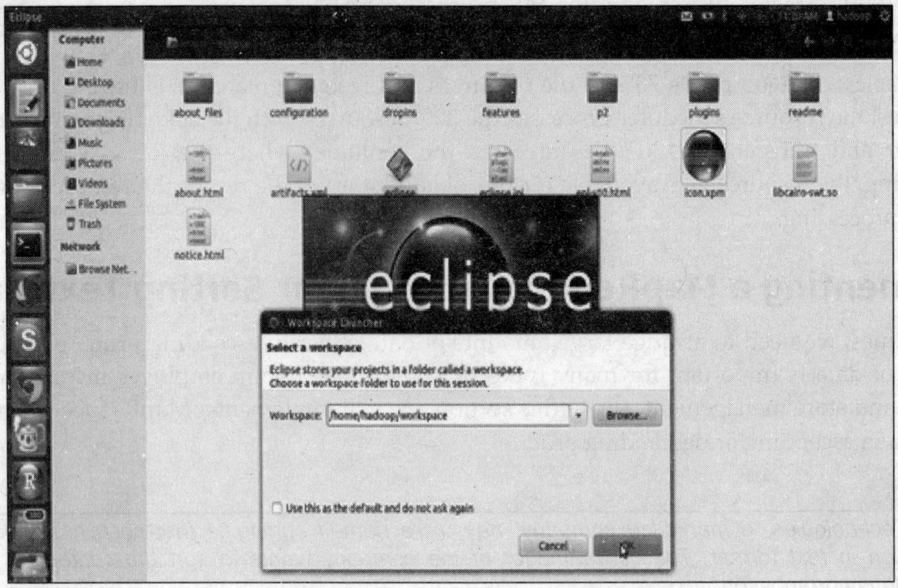

Figure 9.11: Selecting the Workspace

2. Assign a location for your workspace. You can use the drop-down menu or the Browse feature, for this. Once you are done, click the OK button (Figure 9.11).

The Eclipse startup screen appears, as shown in Figure 9.12:

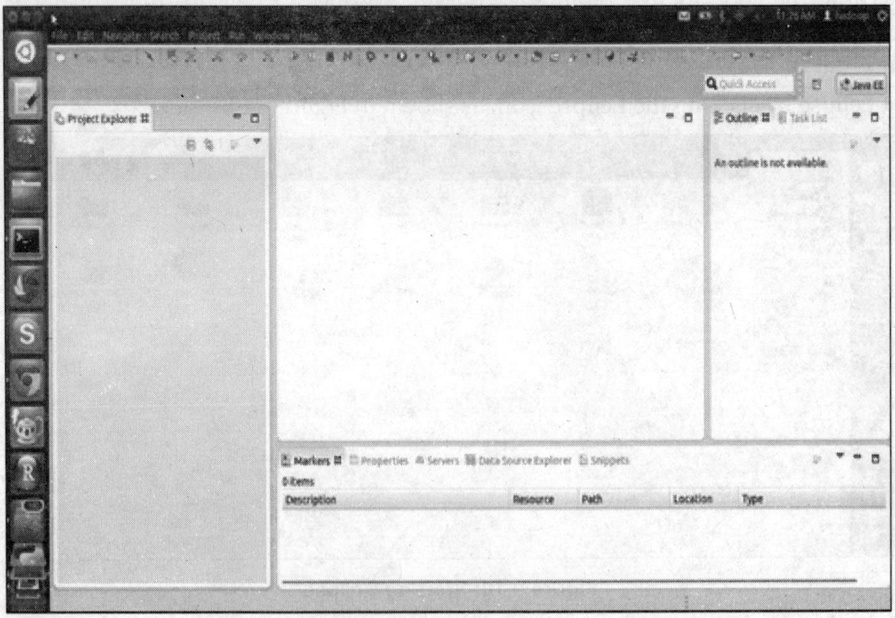

Figure 9.12: Showing the Eclipse Startup Screen

3. Right-click the Project Explorer area to open a context menu, as shown in Figure 9.13:

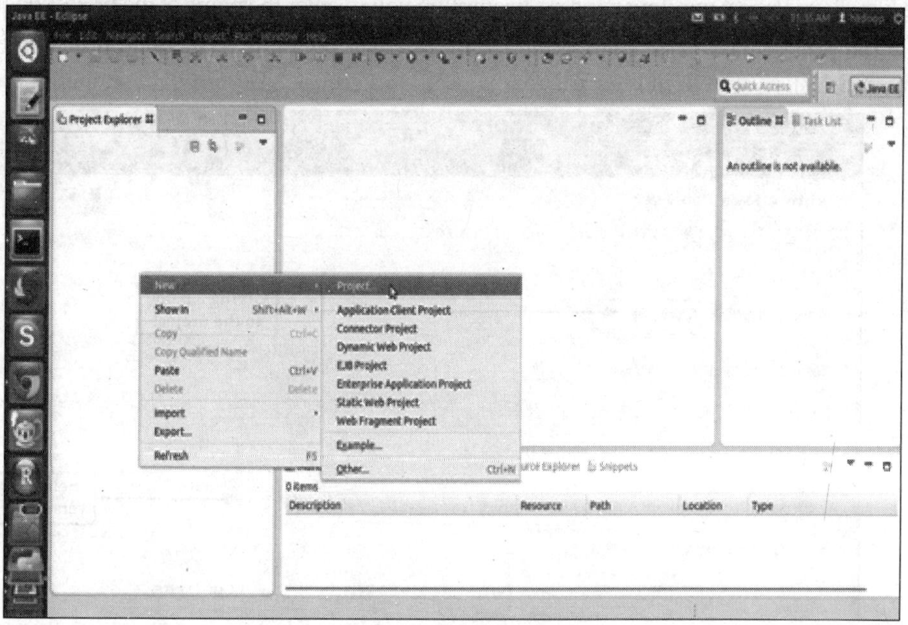

Figure 9.13: Creating a New Project in Eclipse

4. Select New→ Project from the context menu (Figure 9.13).

   The New Project window appears, prompting you to select the type of project, as shown in Figure 9.14:

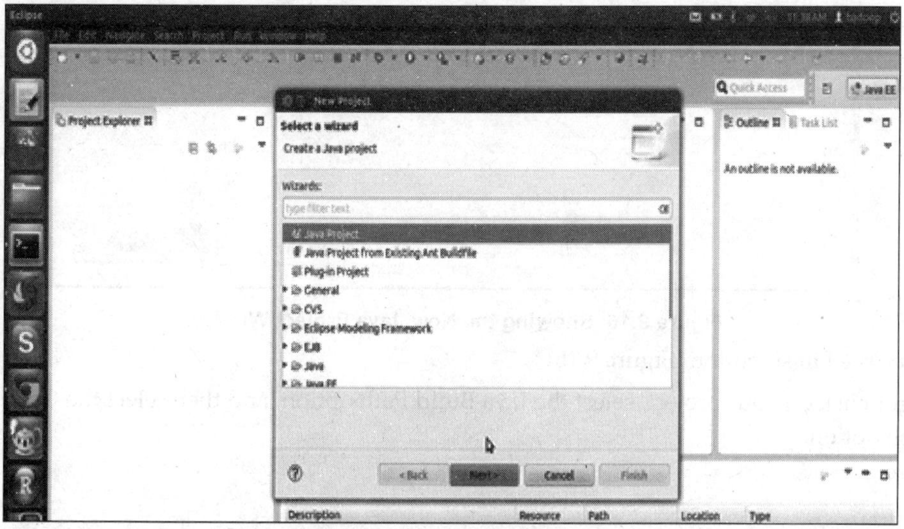

Figure 9.14: Showing the New Project Window

5. Select Java Project and click the Next button (Figure 9.14).

   The New Java Project window appears, prompting you to enter the name of the project (Figure 9.15).

6. Type the project name and change the Java version to JavaSE-1.6 (by default, it will be selected as JavaSE-1.7), as shown in Figure 9.15:

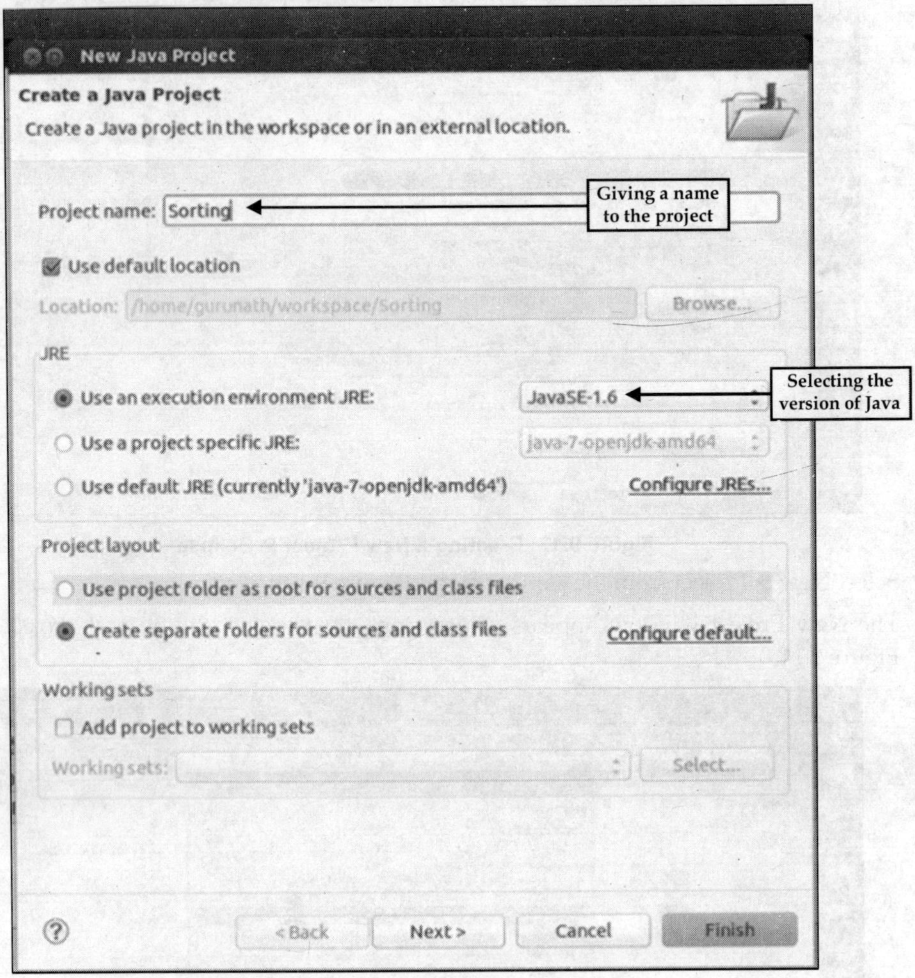

Figure 9.15: Showing the New Java Project Window

7. Click the Finish button (Figure 9.15).

8. Right-click on your project, select the Java Build Path option, and then select the Configure Build Path option.

The Java Build Path window appears, as shown in Figure 9.16:

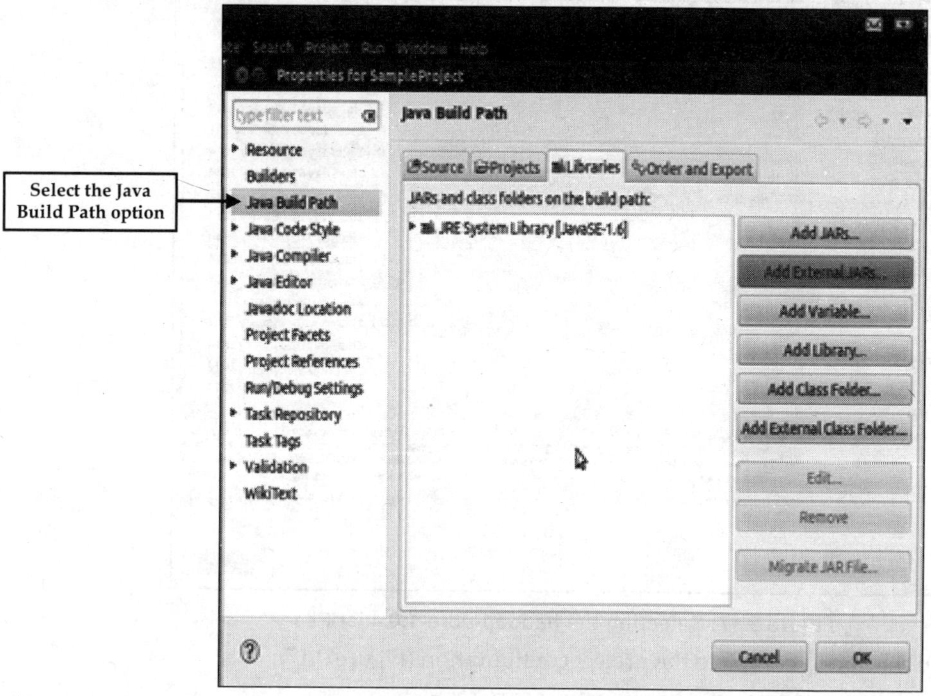

Figure 9.16: Setting Properties for the Java Project

9. Select the Library tab and click the Add External JARs button (Figure 9.16).
10. Select the folder with your user name (The Apache/Hadoop 1.0.4 folder, in our case). Select the lib folder inside this folder. Then, select the following Java ARchive (JAR) files inside the lib folder:

```
commons-collections-3.2.1.jar
commons-configuration-1.6.jar
commons-httpclient-3.0.1.jar
commons-lang-2.4.jar
commons-logging-1.1.1.jar
commons-logging-api-1.0.4.jar
jackson-core-asl-1.8.8.jar
jackson-mapper-asl-1.8.8.jar
log4j-1.2.15.jar
```

11. Add the `hadoop-core-1.0.4.jar` file from the Hadoop 1.0.4 folder, as shown in Figure 9.17:

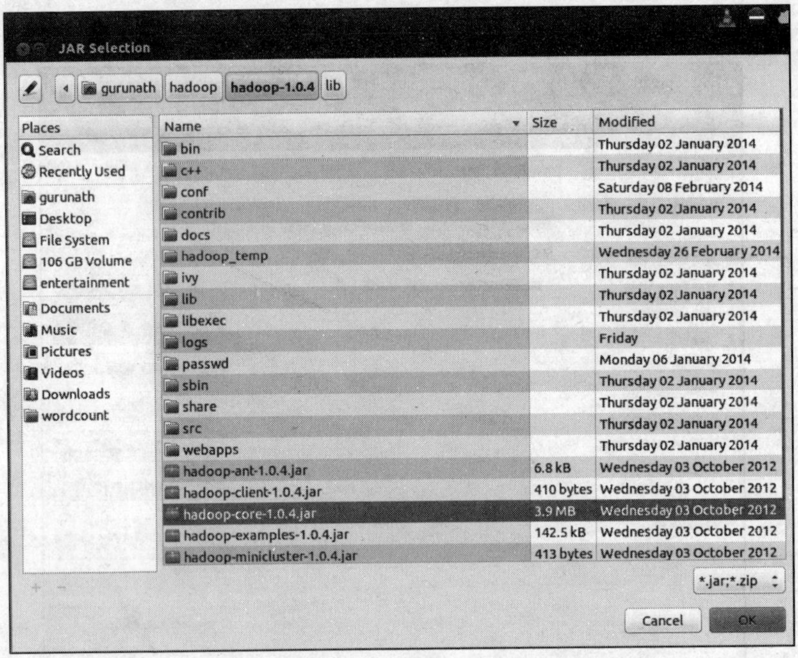

Figure 9.17: Selecting the hadoop-core-1.0.4.jar File

12. Click the OK button to complete the project configuration (Figure 9.17).
13. Right-click the project and select New→Source Folder to create a source folder, as shown in Figure 9.18:

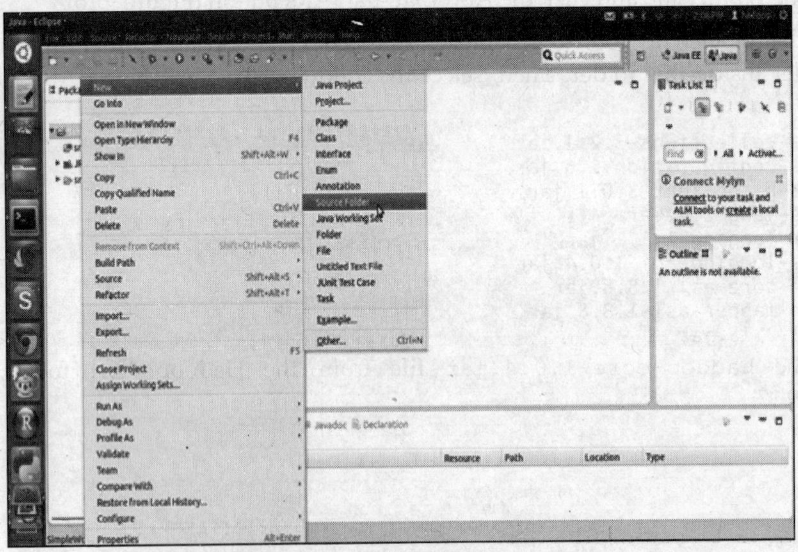

Figure 9.18: Creating a New Source Folder

14. After creating a new source folder, right-click the folder and select the New option. The New Java Class window opens (Figure 9.19).

15. Enter the class name as `IdentifyMapper` in the Name textbox and then click the Finish button, as shown in Figure 9.19:

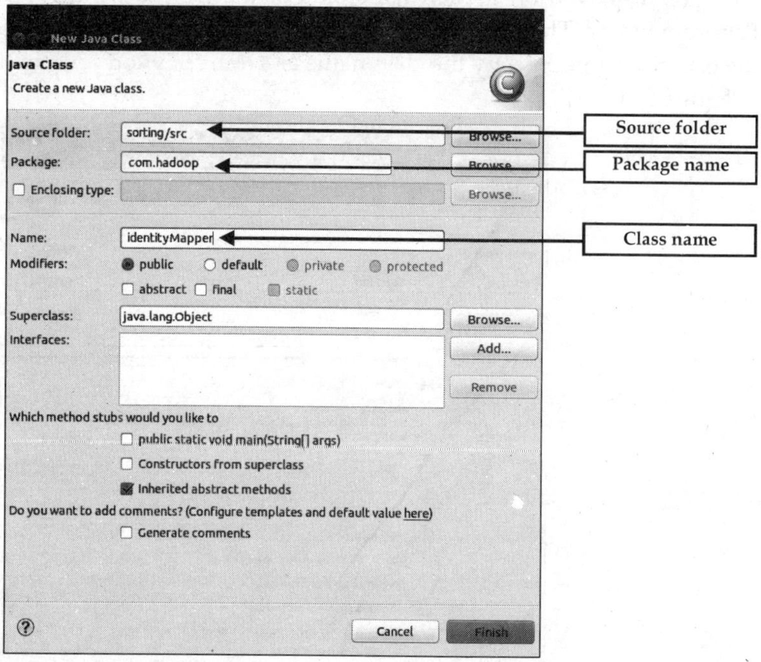

Figure 9.19: Creating the New Class with Package Name

Let us now write the source code for the MapReduce program for sorting text data. In this program, four mapper classes are used. Let's create the first mapper class.

16. Create the first mapper class (`IdentityMapper`, in our case). This class implements the identity function that can map inputs to outputs. The `IdentityMapper` class can be created by adding the following code in the coding window:

```
//This is a Mapper module IdentityMapper.java created in com.hadoop package.
package com.hadoop;
import java.io.IOException;
import org.apache.hadoop.mapred.Mapper;
import org.apache.hadoop.mapred.OutputCollector;
import org.apache.hadoop.mapred.Reporter;
import org.apache.hadoop.mapred.MapReduceBase;
/** Implements the identity function, mapping inputs directly to outputs. */
public class IdentityMapper<K, V> extends MapReduceBase implements Mapper<K,V,K,
  V>
{
/** The identify function. Input (key, value) pair is written directly to *
  output.*/
 public void map(K key, V val, OutputCollector<K, V> output, Reporter reporter)
 throws IOException
 {
    output.collect(key, val);
 }
}
```

17. Let's create the second class, which is the reducer class. For this, right-click the `com.hadoop` package, displayed on the left hand side of the Eclipse window. Select New→Class from the Eclipse window. The New Java Class dialog box appears (Figure 9.19). In this dialog box, retain the package name. Specify the class name as `IdentityReducer` in the Name textbox, as shown in Figure 9.20:

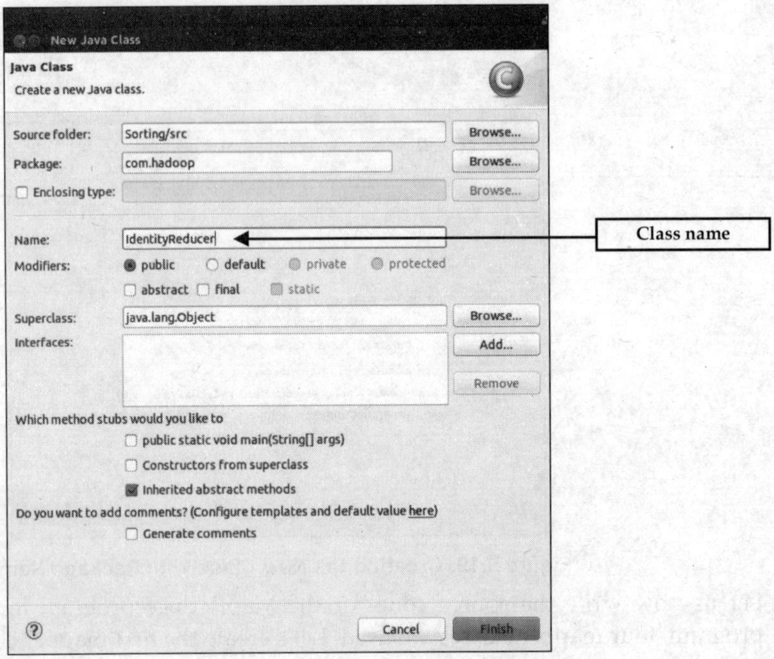

Figure 9.20: Creating the New IdentityReducer Class

18. Click the Finish button (Figure 9.20) to open the coding window and add the following code in the window:

```
//This is a Reducer module IdentityReducer.java created in the com.hadoop package.
package com.hadoop;
import java.io.IOException;
import java.util.Iterator;
import org.apache.hadoop.mapred.Reducer;
import org.apache.hadoop.mapred.OutputCollector;
import org.apache.hadoop.mapred.Reporter;
import org.apache.hadoop.mapred.MapReduceBase;
/** Performs no reduction, writing all input values directly to the output. */
public class IdentityReducer<K, V> extends MapReduceBase implements Reducer<K, V, K, V>
{
 /** Writes all keys and values directly to output. */
 public void reduce(K key, Iterator<V> values, OutputCollector<K, V> output,
  Reporter reporter) throws IOException
{
 while (values.hasNext())
 {
   output.collect(key, values.next());
 }
}
}
```

19. To create the third class, right-click the `com.hadoop` package, which is displayed on the left hand side of the Eclipse window. Select New→Class from the Eclipse window. The New Java Class dialog box appears (Figure 9.21). In this dialog box, retain the package name. Specify the class name as `MapReduceIntro` in the Name textbox, as shown in Figure 9.21:

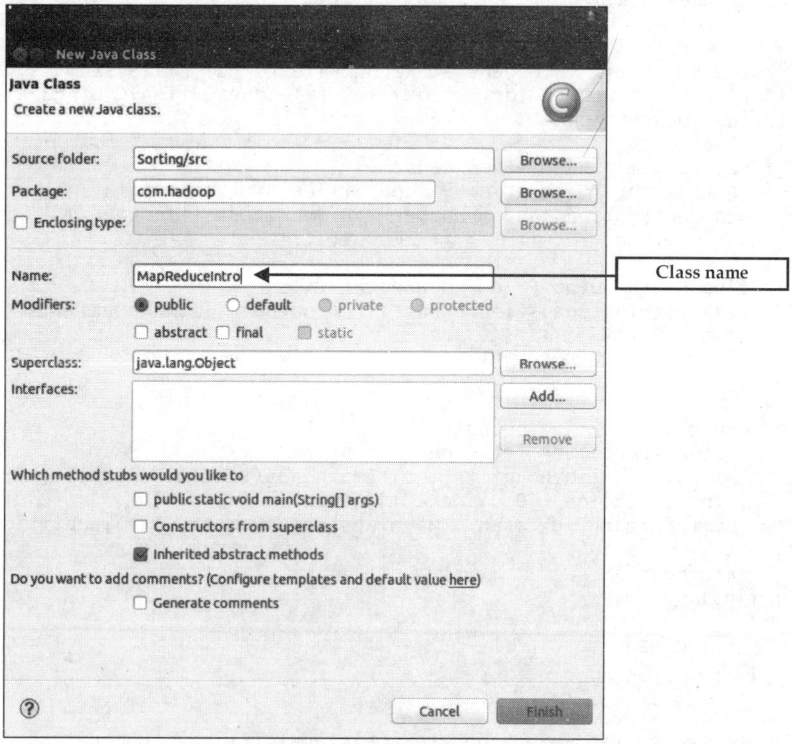

Figure 9.21: Creating the New MapReduceIntro Class

20. Click the Finish button to open the coding window and add the following code in this window:

```
package com.hadoop;
import java.io.IOException;
import java.util.Formatter;
import java.util.Random;
import org.apache.hadoop.fs.FSDataOutputStream;
import org.apache.hadoop.fs.FileStatus;
import org.apache.hadoop.fs.FileSystem;
import org.apache.hadoop.fs.Path;
import org.apache.hadoop.mapred.JobConf;
import org.apache.log4j.Logger;
public class MapReduceIntroConfig {
protected static Logger logger =
Logger.getLogger(MapReduceIntroConfig.class);
protected static Path inputDirectory =
new Path("file:///home/gurunath/sorting1");
protected static Path outputDirectory =
new Path("file:///home/gurunath/out250");
protected static void exampleHouseKeeping(final JobConf conf,
final Path inputDirectory, final Path outputDirectory)
throws IOException {
conf.set("mapred.job.tracker", "local");
```

```
conf.set("fs.default.name", "file:///");
conf.setInt("io.sort.mb", 1);
generateSampleInputIf(conf, inputDirectory);
if (!removeIf(conf, outputDirectory))
{
 logger.error("Unable to remove " + outputDirectory + "job aborted");
 System.exit(1);
}
}
protected static void generateRandomFiles(final FileSystem fs,
final Path inputDirectory, final int fileCount, final int maxLines)
throws IOException
{
 final Random random = new Random();
 logger .info( "Generating 3 input files of random data," +
 "each record is a random number TAB the input file name");
 for (int file = 0; file < fileCount; file++)
 {
   final Path outputFile = new Path("file-");
   final String qualifiedOutputFile = outputFile.makeQualified(fs).
  toUri().toASCIIString();
   FSDataOutputStream out = null;
 try
 {
     out = fs.create(outputFile);
     final Formatter fmt = new Formatter(out);
     final int lineCount = (int) (Math.abs(random.nextFloat())* maxLines + 1);
     for (int line = 0; line < lineCount; line++) {
     fmt.format("%d\t%s%n", Math.abs(random.nextInt()),qualifiedOutputFi le);
}
   fmt.flush();
} finally
  {
    out.close();
  }
}
}
protected static void generateSampleInputIf(final JobConf conf, final Path
  inputDirectory) throws IOException
{
 boolean inputDirectoryExists;
 final FileSystem fs = inputDirectory.getFileSystem(conf);
if ((inputDirectoryExists = fs.exists(inputDirectory)) && !isEmptyDirectory(fs,
  inputDirectory))
 {
  if (logger.isDebugEnabled()) {
   logger.debug("The inputDirectory " +       inputDirectory +       " exists and is
  either a" +   " file or a non-empty directory");
 }
  return;
}
if (!inputDirectoryExists) {
if (!fs.mkdirs(inputDirectory)) { logger.error("Unable to make the inputDirectory "
+ inputDirectory.makeQualified(fs) + " aborting job"); System.exit(1);
}
}final int fileCount = 3; final int maxLines = 100;
 generateRandomFiles(fs, inputDirectory, fileCount, maxLines);
}
public static Path getInputDirectory() { return inputDirectory;
}
public static Path getOutputDirectory() { return outputDirectory;
}
```

```
private static boolean isEmptyDirectory(final FileSystem fs, final Path
   inputDirectory) throws IOException {
final FileStatus[] statai = fs.listStatus(inputDirectory); if ((statai == null) ||
   (statai.length == 0)) {
if (logger.isDebugEnabled()) { logger.debug(inputDirectory.makeQualified(fs).toUri()
+ " is empty or missing");
}
 return true;
}
if (logger.isDebugEnabled()) {logger.debug(inputDirectory.makeQualified(fs).toUri()
+ " is not empty");
}
for (final FileStatus status : statai) {
if (!status.isDir() && (status.getLen() != 0)) { if (logger.isDebugEnabled()) {
logger.debug("A non-empty file "
+ status.getPath().makeQualified(fs).toUri() + " was found");
return false;
}
}
}
for (final FileStatus status : statai) {
if (status.isDir() && isEmptyDirectory(fs, status.getPath())) {
 continue;
}
if (status.isDir()) {
 return false;
}
}
 return true;
}protected static boolean removeIf(final JobConf conf, final Path outputDirectory)
   throws IOException {
final FileSystem fs = outputDirectory.getFileSystem(conf);
if (!fs.exists(outputDirectory)) {
if (logger.isDebugEnabled()) {
logger.debug("The output directory does not exist,"
+ " no removal needed.");
}
  return true;
}
final FileStatus status = fs.getFileStatus(outputDirectory); logger.info("The job
  output directory " + outputDirectory.makeQualified(fs) + " exists"
+ (status.isDir() ? " and is not a directory" : "")
+ " and will be removed");
if (!fs.delete(outputDirectory, true)) {
logger.error("Unable to delete the configured output directory "
+ outputDirectory);
return false;
}
return true;
}
public static void setInputDirectory(final Path inputDirectory) {
 MapReduceIntroConfig.inputDirectory = inputDirectory;
}
public static void setOutputDirectory(final Path outputDirectory) {
 MapReduceIntroConfig.outputDirectory = outputDirectory;
}
}
```

21. Now, to create the fourth class, right-click the `com.hadoop` package displayed on the left hand side of the Eclipse window. Select New→Class from the Eclipse window. The New Java Class dialog box appears (Figure 9.22). In this dialog box, retain the package name. Specify the class name as `MapReduceIntroConfig` in the Name textbox, as shown in Figure 9.22:

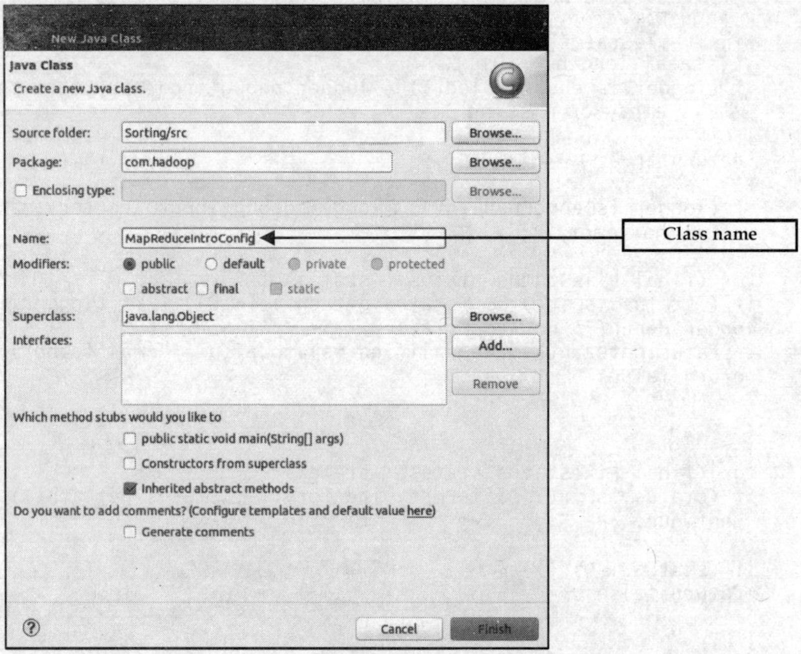

Figure 9.22: Creating the New Class MapReduceIntroConfig

22. Click the Finish button to open the coding window and add the following code in this window:

```
package com.hadoop;
import java.io.IOException;

import java.util.Formatter;
import java.util.Random;

import org.apache.hadoop.fs.FSDataOutputStream;
import org.apache.hadoop.fs.FileStatus;
import org.apache.hadoop.fs.FileSystem;

import org.apache.hadoop.fs.Path;
import org.apache.hadoop.mapred.JobConf;

import org.apache.log4j.Logger;
public class MapReduceIntroConfig {

protected static Logger logger = Logger. getLogger(MapReduceIntroConfig.class);
protected static Path inputDirectory=new Path("file:///home/wcbdd/ sort4"); //INPUT
protected static Path outputDirectory=new Path("file:///home/wcbdd/ out2"); //OUTPUT
protected static void exampleHouseKeeping(final JobConf conf, final Path
  inputDirectory, final Path outputDirectory) throws IOException
{

 conf.set("mapred.job.tracker", "local");
 conf.set("fs.default.name", "file:///");
 conf.setInt("io.sort.mb", 1);

 generateSampleInputIf(conf, inputDirectory);
 if (!removeIf(conf, outputDirectory)) {
 logger.error("Unable to remove " + outputDirectory + "job aborted");
 System.exit(1);
```

```
    }
  }

  protected static void generateRandomFiles(final FileSystem fs,final Path
     inputDirectory, final int fileCount, final int maxLines) throws IOException {
  final Random random = new Random();

  logger .info( "Generating 3 input files of random data," + "each record is a random
     number TAB the input file name");
  for (int file = 0; file < fileCount; file++) {

   final Path outputFile = new Path(inputDirectory, "file-" + file);
   final String qualifiedOutputFile = outputFile.makeQualified(fs).
    toUri().toASCIIString();
  FSDataOutputStream out = null;
  try {
   out = fs.create(outputFile);
   final Formatter fmt = new Formatter(out);

   final int lineCount = (int) (Math.abs(random.nextFloat())* maxLines + 1);
   for (int line = 0; line < lineCount; line++) {
   fmt.format("%d\t%s%n", Math.abs(random.nextInt()),
   qualifiedOutputFile);
  }
   fmt.flush();
  } finally {
   out.close();
  }
  }
  }

  protected static void generateSampleInputIf(final JobConf conf, final Path
     inputDirectory) throws IOException {
  boolean inputDirectoryExists;
  final FileSystem fs = inputDirectory.getFileSystem(conf);

  if ((inputDirectoryExists = fs.exists(inputDirectory))
  && !isEmptyDirectory(fs, inputDirectory)) {
  if (logger.isDebugEnabled()) {
  logger.debug("The inputDirectory "+ inputDirectory+ " exists and is either a"

  + " file or a non-empty directory");
  }
   return;
  }
  if (!inputDirectoryExists) {
   if (!fs.mkdirs(inputDirectory)) {
    logger.error("Unable to make the inputDirectory " + inputDirectory.
    makeQualified(fs) + " aborting job");
   System.exit(1);
  }
  }

  final int fileCount = 3;
  final int maxLines = 100;
  generateRandomFiles(fs, inputDirectory, fileCount, maxLines);
  }
  public static Path getInputDirectory() {
   return inputDirectory;
  }
  public static Path getOutputDirectory() {
   return outputDirectory;

  }
  private static boolean isEmptyDirectory(final FileSystem fs,
```

```
final Path inputDirectory) throws IOException {

final FileStatus[] statai = fs.listStatus(inputDirectory);
if ((statai == null) || (statai.length == 0)) {

if (logger.isDebugEnabled()) {
 logger.debug(inputDirectory.makeQualified(fs).toUri() + " is empty or missing");
}
return true;
}

if (logger.isDebugEnabled()) {
 logger.debug(inputDirectory.makeQualified(fs).toUri() + " is not empty");
}
for (final FileStatus status : statai) {
 if (!status.isDir() && (status.getLen() != 0)) {
 if (logger.isDebugEnabled()) {

 logger.debug("A non-empty file " + status.getPath(). makeQualified(fs).toUri() + "
   was found");
 return false;
}
}
}

for (final FileStatus status : statai) {
 if (status.isDir() && isEmptyDirectory(fs, status.getPath())) {
 continue;
}
if (status.isDir()) {
 return false;
}
}
 return true;

}protected static boolean removeIf(final JobConf conf, final Path outputDirectory)
   throws IOException {
    final FileSystem fs = outputDirectory.getFileSystem(conf);

if (!fs.exists(outputDirectory)) {
if (logger.isDebugEnabled()) {
   logger .debug("The output directory does not exist," + " no removal needed.");

}
 return true;
}
final FileStatus status = fs.getFileStatus(outputDirectory);
logger.info("The job output directory " + outputDirectory. makeQualified(fs) + "
   exists"

+ (status.isDir() ? " and is not a directory" : "") + "and will be removed");
if (!fs.delete(outputDirectory, true)) {
 logger.error("Unable to delete the configured output directory " +
   outputDirectory);
 return false;

}
 return true;
}

public static void setInputDirectory(final Path inputDirectory) {
 MapReduceIntroConfig.inputDirectory = inputDirectory;
}

public static void setOutputDirectory(final Path outputDirectory) {
```

```
    MapReduceIntroConfig.outputDirectory = outputDirectory;
  }
}
```

23. Right-click the Project menu and go to the Export option in the Eclipse window. The Export window opens, as shown in Figure 9.23:

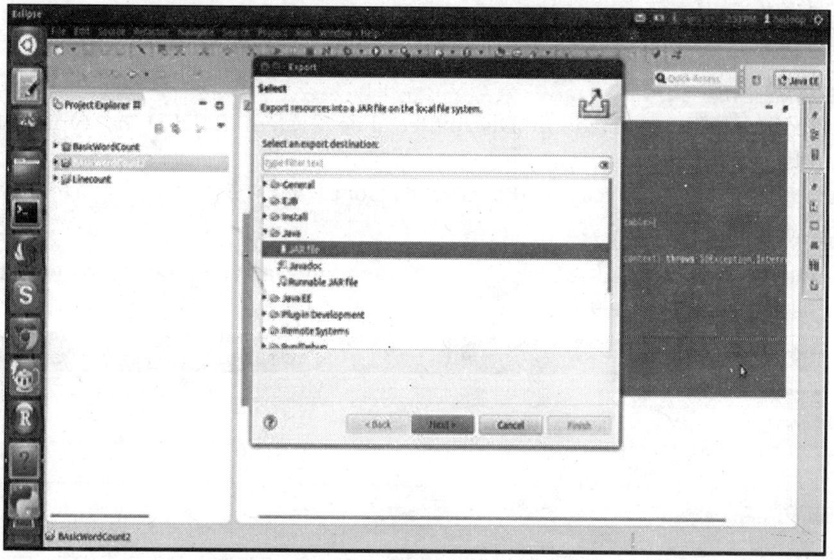

Figure 9.23: Exporting the Project JAR File

24. Select the JAR file option in the Java directory and click the Next button (Figure 9.23). The JAR Export window appears, as shown in Figure 9.24:

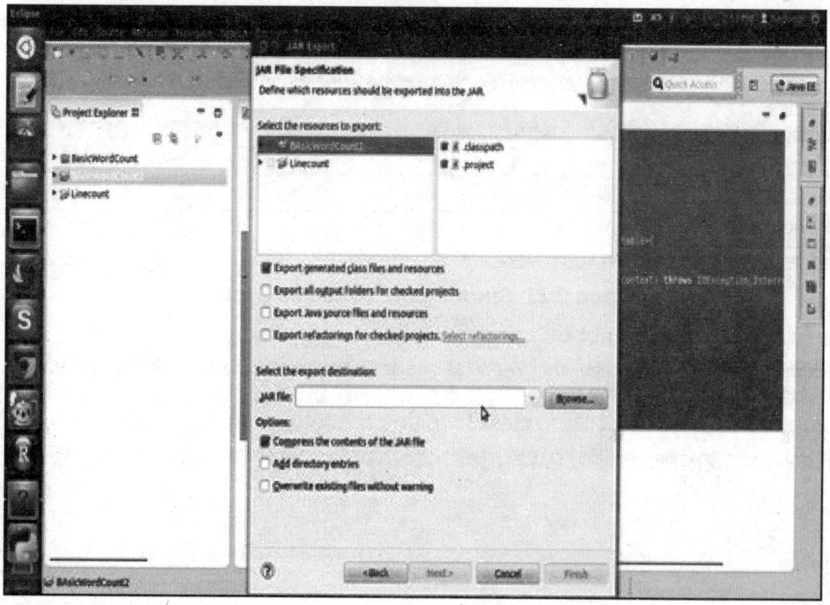

Figure 9.24: Showing the JAR Export Window

25. Click the Browse button (Figure 9.24) to open the Browse window. In this window, specify the location where you want to export the project JAR file. After doing this, click the Finish button to complete the process.
26. Start Hadoop and ensure it is running by typing `jps` on the terminal. The terminal returns the running processes, as follows:

```
DataNode,
NameNode,
JobTracker,
TaskTracker,
SecondaryNameNode
```

27. Copy the input file to Hadoop Distributed File System (HDFS) by typing the following commands:

```
bin/hadoop dfs -copyFromLocal /home/wcbdd/sort3 hdfs:/
bin/hadoop dfs -ls hdfs:/
Web Link: localhost: 50070
```

As the line `Web Link: localhost: 50070` executes, a Web page opens with the `sort3` file system, as shown in Figure 9.25:

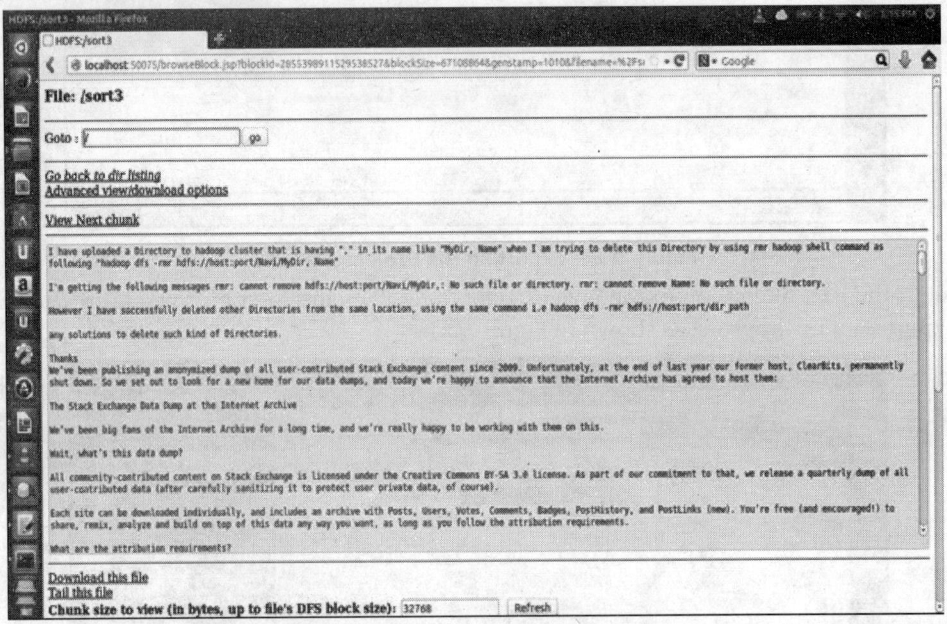

Figure 9.25: Showing the sort3 File System

28. Run the MapReduce program by using the following syntax:

```
bin/hadoop jar jarfilename DriverClassname(path-to-driver class or package path)
inputfilename outputfilename
```

29. Now, run the `MapReduceIntro` class by using the following commands:

```
bin/hadoop jar /home/wcbdd/sort2.jar com.hadoop.MapReduceIntro
```

The progress of the execution is shown in Figure 9.26:

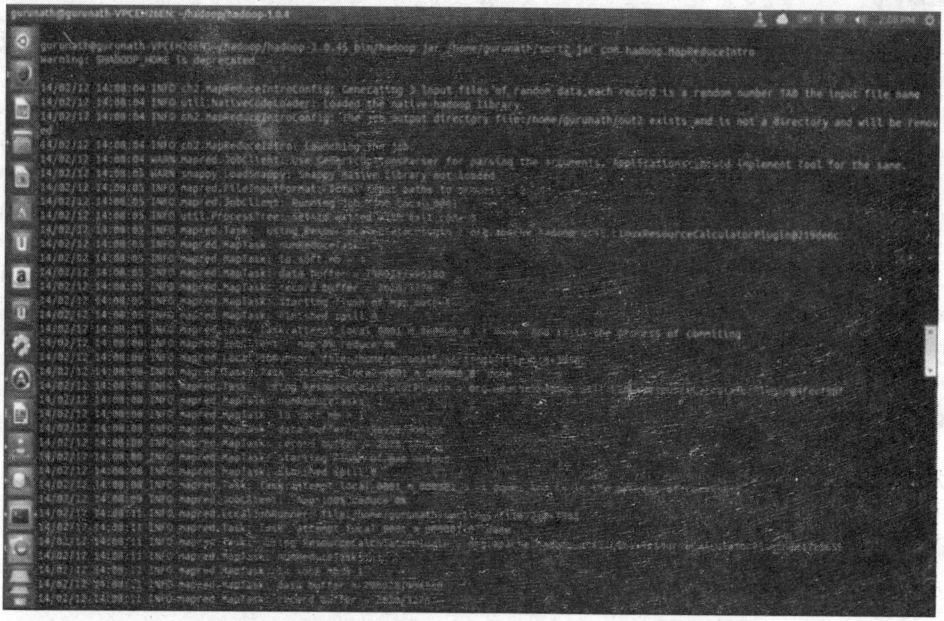

Figure 9.26: Running the Hadoop MapReduce Program

30. In order to view the `output.txt` file on your local system, open a new terminal and enter the following commands:

```
$ cd /home/wcbdd/
$ gedit output.txt
```

The output of the program is shown in Figure 9.27:

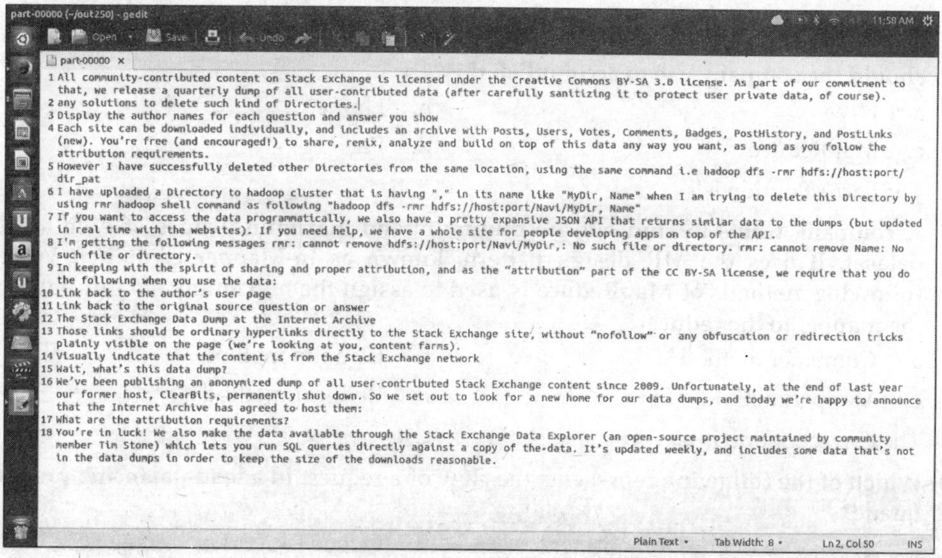

Figure 9.27: Output of the MapReduce Program for Sorting Text Data

Summary

The chapter covered different aspects of customization of a MapReduce program. In the beginning, it introduced the `InputFormat` class and its three important subclasses—`InputSplit`, `RecordReader`, and `FileInputFormat`. You also learned how to control MapReduce execution with `InputFormat` and calculate splits using the custom `InputFormat` and Hadoop Fair Scheduler. After this, the chapter discussed how to control the number of maps that can be created during execution by the `InputFormat` class. Additionally, you learned how to read data with the custom `RecordReader`. Also, you learned how to obtain output from the different nodes of a network. Apart from this, the chapter explained the optimization of MapReduce execution with combiners and partitioners. Toward the end, the chapter took you through the steps of implementing a MapReduce program for sorting textual data.

Quick Revise

Multiple-Choice Questions

Q1. The size of an HDFS block is:

a. 1 byte
b. 16MB
c. 32MB
d. 64MB

Ans. The correct option is d.

Q2. In HDFS, an input split corresponds to:

a. Physical data block
b. Logical data block
c. File controlling system
d. None of these

Ans. The correct option is a.

Q3. A company needs to import a portion of a relational database every day as files to HDFS and generate Java classes to interact with the imported data. Which of the following tools should the company use to accomplish this?

a. Hive
b. Flume
c. MapReduce
d. Pig

Ans. The correct option is a.

Q4. A company wants to find out the minimum and maximum values of each attribute in a dataset. It uses the MR design pattern, known as in-Mapper combiner. Which of the following methods of MapReduce is used to assign the maximum and minimum values of the mapper to the reducer?

a. Combiner method
b. Cleanup method
c. Mapper method
d. Reducer method

Ans. The correct option is b.

Q5. Which of the following represents the flow of a request in a load-balancing process using a queue?

a. Worker → queue → requester
b. Queue → worker → requester
c. Requester → worker → queue
d. Requester → queue → worker

Ans. The correct option is d.

Q6. Which of the following static method implementations provides an API to set the value of maps in a job driver and leverage a standard Hadoop approach to pass parameters between the Hadoop components?

a. setMapCount()
b. getShifts()
c. fileListInputFormat()
d. cleanup()

Ans. The correct option is a.

Q7. Which of the following frameworks is used to run multiple instances of slow tasks and where the output is determined from the instance that first finishes the task?

a. Compression
b. Speculative execution
c. Scalding
d. Scroobi

Ans. The correct option is b.

Q8. Which of the following is not a property of an input split?

a. mapred.min.split.size
b. mapred.max.split.size
c. mapred.max.block.size
d. dfs.block.size

Ans. The correct option is c.

Q9. Which of the following represents the block size of HDFS?

a. mapred.min.split.size
b. mapred.max.split.size
c. mapred.max.block.size
d. dfs.block.size

Ans. The correct option is d.

Q10. Which of the following formulas is used to compute a block size by the `computeSplitSize()` method?

a. min(minimumSize, max (maximumSize, blockSize))
b. max(minimumSize, min(maximumSize, blockSize))
c. min(minimumSize, min (maximumSize, blockSize))
d. max(minimumSize, max(maximumSize, blockSize))

Ans. The correct option is b.

Subjective Questions

Q1. Reducers do not start before all the mappers have finished the mapping process, but the progress on a MapReduce job shows something like Map(50%) Reduce(10%). Why is the percentage of a reducer displayed with the mapper percentage, given that the reducers have not yet started?

Ans. Reducers start copying intermediate key/value pairs from the mappers as soon as they are available. The progress calculation also takes into account the process of data transfer, which is done by the reduce process; therefore, the reduce progress starts showing up as soon as any intermediate key/value pair for a mapper is available to be transferred to the reducer.

Q2. A company needs to input a large file to a MapReduce program; however, the input file should not be split and passed as a whole to the map function. Explain how the company can achieve this.

Ans. This can be done by passing the minimum input split size as a parameter, as follows:

```
-D mapred.min.split.size=9223372036854775807L
```

Here, you need to set the minimum input split size to the largest possible value or at least a size larger than any of your input file:

`9223372036854775807L == Long.MAX_VALUE, and 2^31-1 (2147483647) = Integer.MAX_VALUE`

Q3. Write a short note on InputSplit.

Ans. A MapReduce program is designed to do some work on the given dataset. This work is known as a job. Furthermore, a job can have several tasks. Now the question arises, Who divides the job into several tasks? The class `InputSplit` does this for the MapReduce program.

An input split is a unit of work in a MapReduce program that can be processed by an individual map. In other words, input split represents the data to be processed by an individual map. Each split can be divided into small segments known as records. All records of a split can be processed by a map.

You can measure the size of `InputSplit` in bytes. Each `InputSplit` is associated with some storage locations, which are used to store a map close to the data of a split. An important point to note here is that the splits can be of different sizes. Each split executes according to its size, with the largest split executing first.

Q4. Explain the types of MapReduce applications.

Ans. There are two types of MapReduce applications:

- **HBase data source**—This type of MapReduce application stores a set of data that can be used in analysis.
- **HBase sink**—This type of MapReduce application stores the output.

Q5. Write a short note on the FileInputFormat class.

Ans. The `FileInputFormat` class is a base class for all implementations of `InputFormat`. `FileInputFormat` performs the following two functions:

- It provides a place to define an input file for a job.
- It generates input splits for the input files.

`FileInputFormat` splits only those files that are larger than the HDFS block. The split size can be controlled by various Hadoop properties like input path and filters.

10

Testing and Debugging MapReduce Applications

You have already learned that MapReduce programs, which are used for analyzing Big Data, are based on the Java programming language. With most of the modern day programming being focused on Test-Driven Development (TDD), programmers prefer to develop applications that are simultaneously tested and corrected for any errors and bugs. Now, it is really difficult to create an entirely bug-free application. Such an effort requires careful inspection and repeated test trials of the application on different platforms and environments, which is sometimes not feasible in terms of time and cost. Application testing becomes all the more important in case of Big Data analytics, where even a small mistake can lead to huge differences in the outcome. Testing and debugging of MapReduce applications involve unit testing in which each module is developed and tested individually. The tested modules are then integrated together to make up a complete system. The completed system requires integration testing to ensure that all the components are working well together. However, even after having gone through an intense testing process, some bugs might still creep in the system. You can debug a MapReduce program by using system logs, which collect the entire information about system performance and errors that may occur. Logging is also an important element of MapReduce application programming and testing. These techniques are not the only measures used in MapReduce application testing and debugging; you can also adopt some defensive programming strategies to reduce the testing work in MapReduce application programming.

In this chapter, you learn how to test and debug MapReduce programs. Here, you learn about the techniques of unit testing, integration testing, and logging, which are used to test and debug MapReduce applications. Toward the end, the chapter discusses the need and importance of adopting the approach of defensive programming while developing MapReduce applications.

Debugging Hadoop MapReduce Locally

Before discussing testing and debugging, we need to know the system architecture of Hadoop as Hadoop itself has three modes, which we will discuss in this section. Eclipse is a java developing tool, which can be used for both testing and debugging. These days most of the coders code their codes in the eclipse, and they prefer to test their code locally before making it a jar file and shooting it to any machine or on any cluster. As we all know, running a Hadoop in local mode is easy, but debugging the code on the local is very difficult.

Hadoop runs mainly in three modes, which are as follows:

- **Standalone (or local) mode (#1)**—In this mode, no daemons are present in the node. If you type JPS on the terminal, it will show nothing because Hadoop just uses its local filesystem as backend for the HDFS file system.
- **Pseudo-distributed mode (#2)**—This is the single node cluster in which all the daemons run on the same machine and act as a cluster. All the daemons run in the same machine locally by using the HDFS protocols.
- **Fully distributed mode (#3)**—This is the cluster of more than 100 of machines setup in a proper manner. This is a very high cost setup, and this cluster is called the Hadoop distributed cluster, which shows the real power of Hadoop where the data really get on HDFS and remain there for analysis.

As it is shown and mentioned earlier that most of the coders code and test on locally setup eclipse before doing the final job. For doing that, Hadoop gives you two options: #1(local mode) and #2(Pseudo mode).

To debug Hadoop jobs, you need to make the following configuration:

a. While opening the `conf` folder of your HADOOP_HOME, just add the following line in hadoop-env.sh.

```
export HADOOP_OPTS="-
agentlib:jdwp=transport=dt_socket,server=y,suspend=y,address=5002"
```

b. By changing the configuration, it will send the code in a remote java application's mode; whereas to run in the remote mode, you need to follow these steps:
   i. Click on Debug Configurations in eclipse.
   ii. Select Remote Java Application on the menu on left.
   iii. In the host file, provide the local host name and port number. This should be the one as provided in the address variable.

What makes you opt the mode #1 over #2?

Modes #1 and #2 are alike as all the code is running locally in the system. However, it is very difficult to debug your mappers and reducer using mode #2. The reason here is that in pseudo mode, every mapper and reducer runs in its own JVM and it's quite impossible to debug the MapReduce application code in one instance of eclipse. The only best way to debug the Hadoop's MapReduce application code, in the full potential, is by using the local mode (#1) because all mappers and reducers run in a single JVM of the system and it is easy to debug variables.

SCENARIO

Ms. Caroline is an application testing and debugging professional working with Argon Technology. She has been asked by the organization's Chief Technical Officer (CTO), Mr. Daniel Clark, to test some MapReduce applications by employing various techniques, including unit testing, integration testing, logging, etc. Ms. Caroline takes a WordCount MapReduce application and tests it by applying various methods. All the steps taken by her during the testing and debugging operation are discussed in this chapter.

Performing Unit Testing for MapReduce Applications

Testing applications is increasingly becoming an integral part of the software development process. This is also one of the reasons why the TDD approach is being implemented by more and more programmers. TDD is a programming technique that requires you to simultaneously write the actual application code as well as the automated tests for the code. As the process is automated, the simultaneous writing of application code and test procedures enables you to test and retest your code quickly and easily.

TDD is based on unit testing, which involves an alternative mechanism for the JUnit framework that is customarily used for testing MapReduce implementations. The JUnit framework is used to create a set of mock classes for testing MapReduce programs. In Hadoop, unit testing is usually performed through MRUnit framework, which first started in the form of an open-source service in the Hadoop Cloudera distribution. Now, the framework has been brought under the Apache Incubator project. You can perform unit and integration testing on mappers and reducers. These tests are performed through the MRUnit framework for which the JUnit framework works as a foundation. The integration testing involves testing the mapper-reducer interaction, the combiner, custom counters, partitioners, etc.

You are already aware that Eclipse Integrated Development Environment (IDE) is a suitable platform for MapReduce application development. Moreover, all the dependencies required in MapReduce applications can be contained within a single Extensible Markup Language (XML) file, which can be created in Eclipse. Eclipse not only provides a good development platform for MapReduce applications but also a great testing environment based on the MRUnit framework.

Performing unit testing on the basis of the MRUnit framework requires some changes to be made in the XML file that contains dependencies related to MapReduce applications. You need to include the MRUnit dependencies in the standard MapReduce Maven pom.xml file, as shown in Listing 10.1:

Listing 10.1: Including MRUnit Dependencies for `Maven pom.xml` File

```
<artifactId>nokia-cgnr-sparse</artifactId>
<version>0.0.1-SNAPSHOT</version>
<name>cgnr-sparse</name>
<properties>
<hadoop.version>2.0.0-mr1-cdh4.1.0</hadoop.version>
<hadoop.common.version>2.0.0-cdh4.1.0</hadoop.common.version>
<hbase.version>0.92.1-cdh4.1.0</hbase.version>
</properties>
<repositories>
<repository>
<id>CDH Releases and RCs Repositories</id>
<url>https://repository.cloudera.com/content/groups/cdh-releasesrcs</url>
</repository>
</repositories>
<build>
<plugins>
<plugin>
<groupId>org.apache.maven.plugins</groupId>
<artifactId>maven-compiler-plugin</artifactId>
<version>2.3.2</version>
<configuration>
<source>1.6</source>
<target>1.6</target>
</configuration>
</plugin>
</plugins>
</build>
<dependencies>
<dependency>
<groupId>org.apache.hadoop</groupId>
<artifactId>hadoop-core</artifactId>
<version>${hadoop.version}</version>
<scope>provided</scope>
</dependency>
<dependency>
<groupId>org.apache.hbase</groupId>
<artifactId>hbase</artifactId>
<version>${hbase.version}</version>
<scope>provided</scope>
</dependency>
<dependency>
<groupId>org.apache.hadoop</groupId>
<artifactId>hadoop-common</artifactId>
```

Configures the source and target elements of maven compiler plugin

```
<version>${hadoop.common.version}</version>
<scope>provided</scope>
</dependency>
<dependency>
<groupId>junit</groupId>
<artifactId>junit</artifactId>
<version>4.10</version>
</dependency>
<dependency>
<groupId>org.apache.mrunit</groupId>
<artifactId>mrunit</artifactId>
<version>0.9.0-incubating</version>
<classifier>hadoop2</classifier>
</dependency>
</dependencies>
</project>
```

Configures the JUnit framework in Hadoop

Configures the JUnit framework in Hadoop

In Listing 10.1, the highlighted portion can be changed on the basis of the version being used by the user. The MRUnit jar file and the Maven dependency come in two versions: `mrunit-0.9.0-incubatinghadoop1.jar` is for MapReduce version 1 of Hadoop, and `mrunit-0.9.0-incubatinghadoop2.jar` is for working with the new version of Hadoop's MapReduce. The newer version is the Hadoop-2.0 version from Cloudera's CDH 4.

Now, the XML file has been changed and the dependencies have been listed. We can use this XML file to perform unit testing on the primary MapReduce application components. In this chapter, we are going to test a WordCount MapReduce application for counting the number of words in a text file. This example takes the mapper and reducer components of the WordCount application as parameters to perform unit testing.

Unit Testing the Mapper Component

Performing a unit test on the mapper component of a MapReduce application by using the MRUnit framework is simple. We can explain the use of MRUnit for unit testing of the mapper component of the WordCount application by taking a look at the code shown in Listing 10.2:

Listing 10.2: Unit Testing a Mapper

```
@Test
public void testMapper() throws Exception {
new MapDriver<LongWritable, Text, Text, IntWritable>()
        .withMapper(new WordCount.Map())
        .withConfiguration(new Configuration())

        .withInput(new LongWritable(1), new Text("cat cat dog"))

        .withOutput(new Text("cat"), new IntWritable(1))
        .withOutput(new Text("cat"), new IntWritable(1))
        .withOutput(new Text("dog"), new IntWritable(1))

       .runTest();
}
```

Enables you to supply the desired key/value pair to the mapper

Specifies the expected output

Feeds the specified input values into the mapper

The first line in the `testMapper()` method instantiates the `MapDriver` class that is parameterized exactly as the mapper under test. In the next line, an instance of the mapper you are testing is added by using the with Mapper call. You can use an optional with Configuration method to pass in a desired configuration to the mapper. Moving forward, the `withInput` call enables you to supply a desired key/value pair to the mapper under test. We, in our case, are passing the `LongWritable` object with an arbitrary value and a Text object containing the line "cat cat dog" to the `withInput()` method.

The expected output is specified using the `withOutput` call. The output expected in our example is three text objects with values of "cat," "cat," and "dog" with the corresponding `intWritable` values of occurrences—all equal to 1.

If the mapper is incrementing a counter, an optional `.withCounter(group,name, expectedValue)` method, which is not shown in Listing 10.2, enables you to specify the expected value of the counter.

The last call, `runTest,` feeds the specified input values into the mapper and compares the actual output against the expected output set in the `withOutput()` method.

The unit test written for testing the mapper using the MRUnit framework is very simple. We can enhance the simplicity of the test further by using the approach of Application Programming Interfaces (APIs).

The `MapDriver` class in the WordCount application has a limitation of responding to only a single input/output pair for every test. You can use the `withInput()` and `withOutput()` methods as many times as you want, but the preceding values of the input/output pair shall be overwritten by the next value that is obtained from the `MapDriver` class. Therefore, the testing continues to be performed with a single pair of input/output values at a given point of time. You can use multiple values as input by using an object of `MapReduceDriver`.

Unit Testing the Reducer Component

The process of performing a unit test on the reducer component of a MapReduce application by using the MRUnit framework is similar to the unit testing of the mapper. We can explain the use of MRUnit for unit testing of the reducer component of the WordCount application by taking a look at the code shown in Listing 10.3:

Listing 10.3: Unit Testing a Reducer

```
@Test
public void testReducer() throws Exception {List<IntWritable>
   values = new ArrayList<IntWritable>();
   values.add(new IntWritable(1));
   values.add(new IntWritable(1));
   new ReduceDriver<Text, IntWritable, Text, IntWritable>()

  .withReducer(new WordCount.Reduce())
  .withConfiguration(new Configuration())

  .withInput(new Text("cat"), values)


  .withOutput(new Text("cat"), new IntWritable(2))

  .runTest();
}
```

- Creates a list of IntWritable objects
- Instantiates a ReducerDriver
- Supplies an instance of the reducer to be tested
- Enables you to supply the input key/value pair to the reducer
- Specifies the expected output
- Feeds the specified input values into the reducer

In Listing 10.3, a list of `IntWritable` objects is created to be used as input to the reducer, and a `ReducerDriver` is instantiated. Similar to the `MapperDriver` class, the `ReducerDriver` class is parameterized exactly as the reducer under test. An instance of the reducer that you want to test is passed by using the `withReducer` call. An optional `withConfiguration()` method enables you to pass a desired configuration to the reducer. The `withInput` call enables you to pass input values for the reducer. Here, you pass the key of "cat" and the list created by the `IntWritable` object at the start of the test. You can specify the expected reducer output by using the `withOutput` call. Here, you also mention the same key of "cat" and an `IntWritable` object representing the number of "cat" words (2) you expect. If the reducer is incrementing a counter, an optional `withCounter(group, name, expectedValue)` method, not shown in Listing 10.3, enables you to specify the expected value of the counter. Finally, you call runTest, which feeds the reducer with the specified inputs and compares the output from the reducer against the expected output.

The limitation of the `ReducerDriver` class in the WordCount application is the same as the `MapperDriver` class. The `ReducerDriver` class responds to a single input/output pair only for every individual test.

Till now, you learned to test individual components of a MapReduce application. Sometimes, we may need to test these components together in an integrated environment. This can be done with the help of the `MapReduceDriver` class that is also used for testing combiners.

Integration Testing of the Mapper-Reducer Combination

The `MapReduceDriver` class is provided by the MRUnit framework to enable the user to carry out tests on how the mapper and reducer work with each other. Parameters in the `MapReduceDriver` class are passed in a different manner than the way they are passed in the `MapperDriver` and `ReducerDriver` classes.

While configuring `MapReduceDriver` parameters, the input types and output types of respective mappers and reducers are parameterized individually. You will obtain three types of input/output parameters (one is the input type to the mapper, second is the output type obtained from the mapper, which is the same as the input type to the reducer, and third is the output type from the reducer) in the integration testing of mapper-reducer combination. Since the mapper output type is the same as the reducer input type, we obtain three types of input/output key/value pairs. You can provide multiple inputs and specify multiple expected outputs in the integration testing procedure.

A sample code for integration testing of a mapper-reducer combination is shown in Listing 10.4:

Listing 10.4: Testing a Combination of Mapper and Reducer

```
@Test
public void testMapReduce() throws Exception {                Takes a list of objects in parameters

    new MapReduceDriver<LongWritable, Text, Text, IntWritable, Text, IntWritable>()

    .withMapper(new WordCount.Map()) ← Connects to the mapper

    .withReducer(new WordCount.Reduce()) ← Connects to the reducer
    .withConfiguration(new Configuration())
    .withInput(new LongWritable(1), new Text("dog cat dog"))
    .withInput(new LongWritable(2), new Text("cat mouse"))
    .withOutput(new Text("cat"), new IntWritable(2))
    .withOutput(new Text("dog"), new IntWritable(2))
    .withOutput(new Text("mouse"), new IntWritable(1))
    .runTest();
}
```

In Listing 10.4, the `MapReduceDriver` class first takes a list of objects in parameters. Examples of these objects include `LongWritable, text,` and `IntWritable`. Next, the driver connects the mapper and the reducer by calling `Map()` and `Reduce()` functions. The driver also completes the configuration of the mapper and reducer classes. The `withInput` call enables you to pass the input values for a reducer. Here, you pass the key of "cat" and the list created by `IntWritable` at the start of the test. You can specify the expected reducer output by using the `withOutput` call. You can also specify the same key of "cat" and an `IntWritable` object representing the number of "cat" words (2) you expect.

The preceding code shows that the setup of mapper-reducer combination is similar to the one used by the individual `MapperDriver/ReducerDriver` classes. The instances of mapper and reducer are passed to the original class. An alternate option available for this is to use `withConfiguration()` and `withCombiner()` methods to test the configuration and combiner, if required.

The `MapReduceDriver` class accepts multiple inputs being provided with different keys. In our MapReduce application, we are supplying two records to the `MapReduceDriver` class. The first record is passed with a `LongWritable` type arbitrary value and a `Text` object containing a line "dog cat dog". The second record is supplied with a `LongWritable` type arbitrary value and a `Text` object containing the line "cat mouse."

Additionally, specifications on the expected reducer output are provided by using the `withOutput` method. In our case, we are specifying three keys, "cat," "dog," and "mouse", along with respective counters of 2, 2, and 1. In the end, you can alternatively add an additional `.withCounter(group, name, expectedValue)` method that would enable mapper/reducer to increment the counter as an optional mechanism (which has not been discussed in Listing 10.4).

In case of test failure, the MRUnit provides a similar output as shown in Listing 10.5 to explicitly reveal the error information:

Listing 10.5: Result of the Unsuccessful MRUnit Execution

```
13/01/05 09:56:30 ERROR mrunit.TestDriver: Missing expected output (mouse, 2) at
  position 2.
13/01/05 09:56:30 ERROR mrunit.TestDriver: Received unexpected output (mouse, at
  position 2.
```

The success of the test indicates that mappers and reducers are working together properly. The MRUnit framework performs well, making the unit tests of mappers and reducers easy, especially for simple MapReduce applications. To handle the increasing level of complexity in the map and/or reduce programs, you need to improve your test designs. This can be done by decoupling application-specific business processing from the Hadoop framework support. The best way to improve the testing mechanism is to test the business logic on its own and use the Hadoop framework only for the purpose of application development. Testing MapReduce applications in an integrated manner provides a good assessment of how all the components of the application work together. However, after continuing to test for some time, we reach a point where the test can no more be performed for the business logic. However, the Hadoop framework continues to be tested over and over again, thus increasing the workload. Hence, in such cases, separating the business logic from the Hadoop MapReduce framework becomes important.

The next section discusses the local application testing of MapReduce applications through a local job runner.

Performing Local Application Testing with Eclipse

Eclipse is an IDE that is extensively used for developing applications in different languages. A complete MapReduce code can be executed as a single instance in Eclipse. To run Hadoop jobs on local machines, we require a local job runner. Hadoop distribution (Hadoop-core) already involves a local job runner, which can be used to run Hadoop on a local machine in a single JVM. In our application, the Eclipse debugger can be used to set breakpoints within the mapper and the reducer modules. These breakpoints enable you to find out errors in the program code.

The Eclipse IDE does not require any specific configuration or setup to run MapReduce applications locally. You can run a MapReduce application in a local mode by performing the following steps:

1. Right-click the main class to open a list of selection options.
2. Select the Run As option to open a dialog box asking you to select the specific type of application.
3. Select the Java Application option to start running your application.

NOTE

Eclipse IDE supports local MapReduce execution on both Windows and Linux systems. However, you need to install Cygwin to execute MapReduce programs on Windows.

The default configuration of the local job runner performs the data read/write operation by using the local file system. You must remember that the default configuration of Hadoop execution also uses the local file system. Usually, the Hadoop framework stores data files in Hadoop Distributed File System (HDFS), and the HDFS implementation assists the local data system, which requires copying all testing data to the local system where the outcomes of execution are produced.

In case, you are unable to copy the data required for testing on the local system for some reasons, you have an alternate mechanism to run MapReduce applications locally. In this method, configuration of the local job runner to operate on a cluster's data (including HBase) is required.

Hadoop cluster provides access to data during local program execution through a configuration file, as shown in Listing 10.6:

Listing 10.6: Hadoop Configuration for Accessing Cluster Data

```
<?xml version="1.0" encoding="UTF-8"?>
<configuration>
<!-- hbase access -->
<property>
<name>hbase.zookeeper.quorum</name>
<value>Comma separated list of zookeeper nodes</value>
</property>
<property>
<name>hbase.zookeeper.property.clientPort</name>
<value>zookeeper port</value>
</property>
<!-- hdfs -->
<property>
<name>fs.default.name</name>
<value>hdfs://<url>/</value>
</property>
<!-- impersonation -->
<property>
<name>hadoop.job.ugi</name>
<value>hadoop, hadoop</value>
```

```
</property>
</configuration>
```

In Listing 10.6, three primary constituents have been defined:

- HBase access (the ZooKeeper quorum reference is used to define HBase access)
- HDFS access (an HDFS URL is used to define it)
- Security impersonation (needed to avoid the identity constraint in case your development machine is a part of a different security domain than that of your Hadoop cluster, or in case your login name is different on your local machine than what it is on the Hadoop cluster)

You need to follow a simple and straightforward mechanism to add the configuration to the execution, as shown in Listing 10.7:

Listing 10.7: Adding Cluster Information to Configuration

```
Configuration.addDefaultResource("Hadoop properties");
Configuration conf = new Configuration();
```

In Listing 10.7, the default resource is added by using the `addDefaultResource()` method of the `Configuration` class. Then, an object of the `Configuration` class is created to access the default resources.

The local execution of the MapReduce testing procedure by using the local job runner is much more thorough as compared to unit testing, but there can be an issue of size when we are performing MapReduce testing by using local job runners.

In Hadoop MapReduce job execution, the size of application plays an important role. Testing a MapReduce job multiple times on a local system does not guarantee correct working of the code unless the tests are performed on realistic samples of data. Hence, we cannot verify various points in local application testing without performing the full scale tests with real-time data. Some points that cannot be verified include the following:

- How many mappers are going to be created during an application run, and how well is the data going to be split between them?
- What is a realistic timing for the shuffle and sort operation in MapReduce? Is it necessary to implement a combiner? Will an in-memory combiner be a better option?
- What kind of hardware/software/network load does an application create? Is it necessary to do additional application/cluster parameter tuning?

Thus, we can verify proper working of our MapReduce application only by testing the application on a real Hadoop cluster, after we are done with testing it on a local machine by using a local job runner.

MapReduce programs are highly distributed in nature, and their execution vastly depends on the amount of data being used. Therefore, testing professionals find debugging of MapReduce applications a challenging task.

Logging for Hadoop Testing

Logging is a mechanism to collect data about a system and the various tasks performed by it. In this mechanism, a log file is generated containing all the information about the system. Logging is widely used by various software projects to serve a number of purposes. For example, you can use logging to:

- Create an execution audit trail that can be used to perform execution analyses or identify potential improvements
- Collect execution metrics that can be used to perform both real-time and post-mortem analyses, automate test procedures, identify errors, etc.

All the important events occurring during the MapReduce program execution are saved in the form of logs by the MapReduce framework itself. The default location of storing the configuration files in Hadoop is the logs subdirectory of the Hadoop version directory. TaskTracker logs that are used to store the exceptions thrown by a MapReduce job are the most crucial logs for debugging individual MapReduce applications.

Each task that runs in the Hadoop MapReduce framework generates its individual log directory. All these individual directories are contained in the userlogs directory, which is a subdirectory under the log directory. The stdout and stderr information recorded by every task is stored as two separate files in the individual log record directory. The logging information that is particularly related to the application being executed is also contained within these files. A multi-node Hadoop cluster does not aggregate these logs on central servers, so you must check the individual log directory of jobs on the respective compute nodes for their content.

You can also use the Web page of a JobTracker to conveniently view the content of the logs. Accessing the Web page of a JobTracker is a mechanism through which the logs for all mappers and reducers that are produced by the Job are displayed.

You can access the logging information about all the jobs from the job page of a TaskTracker. This job page contains information on job setup and cleanup logs, as well as mappers and reducers pages, which are linked to the corresponding log pages.

You can navigate to the job configuration section from the job page. The content of a configuration object is given on the job configuration page. This page is more important for us to access when large amounts of custom configurations are used. For example, a job configuration page is especially helpful in confirming whether the desired values are supplied with the parameters when parameters are passed from the driver to mappers and reducers.

Moreover, log pages have direct linking with the corresponding job setup and cleanup logs, as well as mappers and reducers pages. These log pages contain stdout, stderr, and syslog logs that contain logging information specifically related to applications. You can refresh this page in the real time and, hence, can effectively use to check the progress of individual executions with an assumption that your application is providing the appropriate logging information.

You can make log processing more powerful and effective by using a facility of the MapReduce framework to run scripts provided by the user for debugging. Any problem-at-hand can be effectively understood by using the most important information distilled from the output logs of these user-defined scripts. These scripts have permission for data mining from the output of a task (stdout and stderr), syslog, and jobconf. The outputs from the debug script's stdout and stderr are available through the job user interface.

The failure of MapReduce tasks can be scripted separately for mappers and reducers. You need to set up values for the properties `mapred.map.task.debug.script` (used to debug map tasks) and `mapred.reduce.task.debug.script` (used to debug reduce tasks). You also have APIs for setting up these properties. The script uses the task's `stdout`, `stderr`, `syslog`, and `jobconf` files as its arguments.

You need to objectively decide what information needs to be saved in the form of logs and what exactly to log in a MapReduce job. Some recommendations for designing logs are as follows:

- Exception/error handling code should always log exception information.
- Any unexpected variable's values (e.g., nulls) should be logged during execution.
- Detection of unexpected execution paths should be logged.
- If execution performance becomes a concern, the execution timing of the main code blocks should be logged.
- Too much logging is useless. It makes it impossible to find relevant information within a log.

In some applications, log files can be viewed conveniently by using the JobTracker, but in automatic mining and processing logs, using JobTracker is not effective. Some approaches for automated processing of logs are discussed in the following section.

Application Log Processing

You can use a wide range of solutions for logging, starting from specialized software (e.g., the Splunk App for HadoopOps) to a custom log-processing application. To implement custom log processing, all the log data from all mappers and reducers must be brought together in a single file. You can bring all the logs related to a specific application together by using screen scraper. In addition, you can store the logs in a single file for subsequent processing.

The use of screen scraper is shown in Listing 10.8 (code file:class `HadoopJobLogScraper`):

Listing 10.8: Simple Log Screen Scraper

```
public class HadoopJobLogScraper
{
  private String _trackerURL = null;  ◄── Contains the scraper method that helps you to bring
                                          together all the log data of mapper and reducer

  public static void main(String[] args) throws IOException
  {
   if (args.length != 2) {
     System.err.println("usage: <JobTracker URL>, <job id>");
     }
   String jobId = args[1]; String trackerURL = args[0];
   HadoopJobLogScraper scraper = new HadoopJobLogScraper(trackerURL);

   scraper.scrape(jobId, JobType.MAP);  ◄── Specifies the type of job with a job ID

   scraper.scrape(jobId, JobType.REDUCE); System.out.println("done");
 }
 public enum JobType
 {
  MAP("map"), REDUCE("reduce");
  private String urlName;
```

```
    private JobType(String urlName){this.urlName = urlName;
   }
    public String getUrlName(){return urlName;}
   }
    private Pattern taskDetailsUrlPattern = Pattern.compile("<a 
    href=\"(taskdetails\\.jsp.*?)\">(.*?)</a>");
    private Pattern logUrlPattern = Pattern.compile("<a href=\"([^\"]*)\">All</a>");
    public HadoopJobLogScraper (String trackerURL){_trackerURL = trackerURL;}
    public void scrape(String jobId, JobType type) throws IOException
    {
     System.out.println("scraping " + jobId + " - " + type);
     String jobTasksUrl = _trackerURL + "/jobtasks.jsp?jobid=" + jobId + "&type=" + 
     type.getUrlName() + "&pagenum=1";
     String jobTasksHtml = IOUtils.toString(new URL(jobTasksUrl).openStream());
     Matcher taskDetailsUrlMatcher = taskDetailsUrlPattern.matcher(jobTasksHtml);
     File dir = new File(jobId);
     if (!dir.exists()){dir.mkdir();
     }
     File outFile = new File(dir, type.getUrlName());
     BufferedWriter out = new BufferedWriter(new FileWriter(outFile));
     while (taskDetailsUrlMatcher.find())
     {
       out.write(taskDetailsUrlMatcher.group(2) + ":\n");
       String taskDetailsUrl = new String(_trackerURL + "/" + 
     taskDetailsUrlMatcher.group(1));
       String taskDetailsHtml = IOUtils.toString(new URL(taskDetailsUrl).openStream());
       Matcher logUrlMatcher = logUrlPattern.matcher(taskDetailsHtml);
       while (logUrlMatcher.find())
       {
         String logUrl = logUrlMatcher.group(1) + "&plaintext=true&filter=stdout";
         out.write(IOUtils.toString(new URL(logUrl).openStream()));
       }
      }
      out.flush();
      out.close();
    }
   }
```

In Listing 10.8, a class named `HadoopJobLogScraper` contains a scraper method that helps you to bring together all the log data of mapper and reducer. The scraper method specifies the type of job with a job ID.

The `main()` method creates a screen scraper for recording and logging information by using the JobTracker URL and Job ID. The `main()` method then scrapes all the logging information about both mappers and reducers through this screen scraper. All the mapper/reducer pages are located by the scraper method by using regular expressions. The scraper mainly performs the following tasks:

- Locate mapper/reducer pages by using regular expressions
- Read the pages
- Print out the content of the pages

MapReduce executions are quite complex, and accessing the logging information may not always be the best way to check for programming or other kinds of errors. At times, testing errors may even reduce the productivity. Therefore, you can apply some strategies for defensive programming of applications in the MapReduce framework.

Defensive Programming in MapReduce

Hadoop records are based on large volumes of data supplied as the mapper input. Therefore, the productivity of Hadoop MapReduce programming framework usually decreases when we start killing jobs every time a mapper is unable to process the given input data. The mapper may not complete the processing task because of the following two reasons:

- A record itself is corrupt and cannot be accessed.
- The map function has bugs and is unable to access all or specific records. For instance, the source code that may have caused the error in some third-party libraries may not be available.

In Big Data solutions, skipping a few input values does not affect the end results by a huge margin. Hence, if we can develop a MapReduce application that can handle skipping some of the input values in order to save the mapper from failing, we can correctly process the aforementioned error situations. This can help you to develop an application that is overall more reliable and easy to maintain. However, existence of such applications is mostly hypothetical, as either the reader responsible for data reading operation will throw an exception or the mapper responsible for processing the data will cause an exception. You can correctly process such situations in applications by implementing the following:

- Careful error handling in the reader so that all read errors are correctly processed and the file pointer is moved to the next record
- A mechanism for communicating with the mapper to report reader errors so that the mapper can correctly output information about them
- Careful error handling in the mapper so that all the errors are correctly processed
- A custom OutputFormat object that writes error data in a dedicated error output directory

Hadoop provides a skipping mechanism to handle difficult implementations. This feature enables your MapReduce applications to skip the records that may possibly cause a task failure. When you turn on the skipping feature of Hadoop, the task enters the skipping mode after the efforts to read a particular record have failed multiple times in succession. When a task enters the skipping mode, the range of records that is causing failure is determined by the TaskTracker, which will then restart the task. When the task is restarted, it skips the range of corrupt input records.

The `SkipBadRecords` class, which includes numerous static methods, provides control of the skipping feature to the applications. In order to turn on the record skipping feature for map and reduce tasks, the job driver must call one or both of the following methods:

- `setMapperMaxSkipRecords(Configuration conf,long maxSkipRecs)`
- `setReducerMaxSkipGroups(Configuration conf,long maxSkipGrps)`

No records are skipped when the maximum range of records to be skipped is set to 0, which means that the record skipping is disabled. The application increments the record pointer with a certain frequency that determines the number of records to be skipped during the skipping mode. Normally, the counter should be increased every time a record is processed. In certain cases, this is not possible (e.g., in applications where batching of jobs is possible). In this case, some additional records that are adjacent to the bad ones can be skipped. In Hadoop, the divide-and-conquer mechanism is used to determine the range of records to be skipped.

In this approach, the skip range is divided by two every time to obtain two halves that contain bad records. The process is executed repeatedly to determine an acceptable size of the skip range. The determination of the skip range is an expensive operation, even more when the range of maximum skip is small. Therefore, at times, you may need to increase the maximum number of task attempts for normal recovery methods in Hadoop. In that case, extra recovery attempts can be added to the application.

When a task is in the skipping mode, it reports to the TaskTracker about the records being processed. In case of a task failure, the TaskTracker retries and the record that resulted in failure is skipped. The skipping mode is enabled only after the task fails twice to access a given input record.

Sometimes, a task keeps failing over a corrupt record, even after the repeated attempts of the TaskTracker. In such cases, the following results are possible:

- Failed attempt with no special actions (twice)
- Failed attempt with a failed record being stored by the TaskTracker
- New attempt skipping the bad record that has failed in the previous attempt

You can modify the number of task failures needed to trigger the skipping mode by using the `setAttemptsToStartSkipping(int attempts)` method on the `SkipBadRecords` class. Hadoop saves the log of skipped records to HDFS for later analysis. These records are written as sequence files in the `_log/skip` directory.

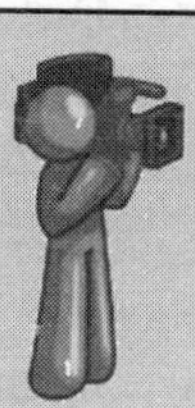

EXHIBIT 1: Obtaining Debugging Information from Log Files

The core Hadoop engine in HDInsight generates a range of information in log files, counters, and status messages, which is useful for debugging and testing the performance of your solutions. Much of this information is accessible through the Hadoop YARN Status portal.

The following list contains some suggestions to help you obtain debugging information from HDInsight:

- Use the Applications section of the Hadoop YARN Status portal to view the status of jobs. Select FAILED in the menu to see failed jobs. Select the History link for a job to see more details. In the details page are menu links to show the job counters, and details of each map and reduce task. The Task Details page shows the errors and provides links to the log files and the values of custom and built-in counters.
- View the history, job configuration, syslog, and other log files. The Tools section of the Hadoop YARN Status portal contains a link that opens the log files folder where you can view the logs, and also a link to view the current configuration of the cluster. In addition, see **Monitoring and logging** in the section **Building end-to-end solutions using HDInsight**.
- Run a debug information script automatically to analyze the contents of the standard error, standard output, job configuration, and syslog files. For more information about running debug scripts, see **How to Debug Map/Reduce Programs** and **Debugging** in the MapReduce Tutorial on the Apace website.

Using a single-node local cluster for testing and debugging

Performing runtime debugging and single-stepping through the code in map and reduce components is not possible within the Hadoop environment. If you want to perform this type of debugging, or run unit tests on components, you can create an application that executes the components locally, outside of Hadoop, in a development environment that supports debugging. You can then use a mocking framework and test runner to perform unit tests.

Sometimes, errors can occur due to the parallel execution of multiple map and reduce components on a multinode cluster. Consider emulating distributed testing by running multiple jobs on a single node cluster at the same time to detect errors, then expand this approach to run multiple jobs concurrently on clusters containing more than one node in order to help isolate the issue.

You can create a single-node HDInsight cluster in Azure by specifying the advanced option when creating the cluster. Alternatively, you can install a single-node development environment on your local computer and execute the solution there. A single-node local development environment for Hadoop-based solutions, which is useful for initial development, proof of concept, and testing, is available from Hortonworks. For more details, see **Hortonworks Sandbox**.

By using a single-node local cluster, you can rerun failed jobs and adjust the input data, or use smaller datasets, to help you isolate the problem. To rerun the job, go to the \taskTracker\task-id\work folder and execute the command %hadoop.org.apache.hadoop.mapred.IsolationRunner ../job.xml.

This runs the failed task in a single Java virtual machine over the same input data.

Source: https://msdn.microsoft.com/en-us/library/dn749854.aspx

Summary

This chapter discussed the techniques to test and debug MapReduce programs. The chapter started with an overview of unit testing in the TDD environment. Next, the concepts of integration testing and logging were explained in detail. Finally, you learned about defensive programming and the importance of its implementation while developing MapReduce applications.

Quick Revise

Multiple-Choice Questions

Q1. For a task that consistently fails on a bad record, the TaskTracker gives the following outcomes:

a. Runs an error message

b. Failed attempt with no special actions (once)

c. Failed attempt with special actions (twice)

d. Failed attempt with no special actions (twice)

Ans. The correct option is d.

Q2. The MRUnit jar file and Maven dependency version mrunit-0.9.0-incubating hadoop2.jar are from:

a. MapReduce version 1 of Hadoop
b. COBRA's CDH4
c. Cloudera's CDH4
d. New version of Hadoop's MapReduce

Ans. The correct option is c.

Q3. Local application testing with Eclipse helps MapReduce:

a. To make debugging easier
b. To create maps
c. To reduce the fragments
d. To run Hadoop in 10 JVMs

Ans. The correct option is d.

Q4. To run MapReduce on Windows, you must install:

a. LISP
b. Cloudera's CDH4
c. Cygwin
d. Windows 14

Ans. The correct option is c.

Q5. TDD:

a. Is a testing technique that requires you to write actual code and automated code tests simultaneously
b. Is a programming technique that requires you to write existing code and automated code tests simultaneously
c. Is a testing technique that requires you to simultaneously write actual code and manual code tests
d. Is a programming technique that requires you to write actual code and automated code tests simultaneously

Ans. The correct option is a.

Q6. The location of files in MapReduce is controlled by:

a. Hadoop file manager
b. MapReduce files list
c. Hadoop configuration files
d. Hadoop cluster

Ans. The correct option is c.

Q7. The log directory also has a subdirectory called:

a. Log users
b. Directory users
c. Userlogs
d. Useful logs

Ans. The correct option is c.

Q8. One recommendation for designing useful logging is:

a. Unexpected variable's value should be logged after execution
b. Detection of unexpected execution paths should not be logged
c. Error handling code should always log acceptance information
d. Too much logging should be avoided

Ans. The correct option is a.

Q9. If a job tries to create millions of counters, the JobTracker will generate:

a. A "loss of memory" error
b. An "out of memory" error
c. An "out of date" error
d. An error message

Ans. The correct option is b.

Subjective Questions

Q1. What do you understand by TDD? Explain its importance in the context of Hadoop MapReduce implementations.

Ans. Test-Driven Development (TDD) is a programming technique that requires you to simultaneously write the actual application code and the automated tests for the code. As the process is automated, the simultaneous writing of application code and test procedures enables you to test and retest your code quickly and easily.

TDD is based on unit testing, which involves an alternative mechanism for the JUnit framework that is customarily used for testing MapReduce implementations. The JUnit framework is used to create a set of mock classes for testing MapReduce programs. In Hadoop, unit testing is usually performed through MRUnit framework, which first started in the form of an open-source service in the Hadoop Cloudera distribution. Now, the framework has been brought under the Apache Incubator project. You can perform unit and integration testing on mappers and reducers. These tests are performed through the MRUnit framework for which the JUnit framework works as a foundation. The integration testing involves testing the mapper-reducer interaction, combiner, custom counters, partitioners, etc.

Q2. How will you perform local application testing on MapReduce applications with Eclipse?

Ans. Eclipse is an IDE that is extensively used for developing applications in different languages. A complete MapReduce code can be executed as a single instance in Eclipse. To run Hadoop jobs on local machines, we require a local job runner. Hadoop distribution (Hadoop-core) already involves a local job runner, which can be used to run Hadoop on a local machine in a single JVM. In our application, the Eclipse debugger can be used to set breakpoints within the mapper and the reducer modules. These breakpoints enable you to find out errors in the program code.

The Eclipse IDE does not require any specific configuration or setup to run MapReduce applications locally. You can run a MapReduce application in a local mode by performing the following steps:

1. Right-click the main class to open a list of selection options.
2. Select the Run As option to open a dialog box asking you to select the specific type of application.
3. Select the Java Application option to start running your application

Q3. What is logging? Explain the role it performs in testing Hadoop applications.

Ans. Logging is a mechanism to collect data about a system and the various tasks performed by it. In this mechanism, a log file is generated containing all the information about the system. Logging is widely used by various software projects to serve a number of purposes. For example, you can use logging to:

- Create an execution audit trail that can be used to perform execution analyses or identify potential improvements
- Collect execution metrics that can be used to perform both real-time and post-mortem analyses, automating test procedures, identifying errors, etc.

All the important events occurring during the MapReduce program execution are saved in the form of logs by the MapReduce framework itself. The default location of storing the configuration files in Hadoop is the logs subdirectory of the Hadoop version directory. TaskTracker logs that are used to store the exceptions thrown by a MapReduce job are the most crucial logs for debugging individual MapReduce applications.

Each task that runs in the Hadoop MapReduce framework generates its individual log directory. All these individual directories are contained in the userlogs directory, which is a subdirectory under the log directory. The stdout and stderr information recorded by every task is stored as two separate files in the individual log record directory. The logging information that is particularly related to the application being executed is also contained within these files. A multi-node Hadoop cluster does not aggregate these logs on central servers, so you must check the individual log directory of jobs on the respective compute nodes for their content.

You can also use the Web page of a JobTracker to conveniently view the content of the logs. Accessing the Web page of a JobTracker is a mechanism through which the logs for all mappers and reducers that are produced by the job are displayed. You can access the logging information about all the jobs from the job page of a TaskTracker. This job page contains information on job setup and cleanup logs, as well as mappers and reducers pages, which are linked to the corresponding log pages.

You can navigate to the job configuration section from the job page. The content of a configuration object is given on the job configuration page. This page is more important for us to access when large amounts of custom configurations are used. For example, a job configuration page is especially helpful in confirming whether the desired values are supplied with the parameters when parameters are passed from the driver to mappers and reducers.

Moreover, log pages have direct linking with the corresponding job setup and cleanup logs, as well as mappers and reducers pages. These log pages contain stdout, stderr, and syslog logs that contain logging information specifically related to applications. You can refresh this page in the real time and, hence, can effectively use to check the progress of individual executions with one assumption that your application is providing the appropriate logging information.

Q4. Write a note on defensive programming in MapReduce.

Ans. Hadoop records are based on large volumes of data supplied as the mapper input. Therefore, the productivity of Hadoop MapReduce programming framework usually decreases when we start killing jobs every time a mapper is unable to process the given input data. The mapper may not complete the processing task because of the following two reasons:

- A record itself is corrupt and cannot be accessed.
- The map function has bugs and is unable to access all or specific records. For instance, the source code, which may have caused the error, in some third-party libraries may not be available.

In Big Data solutions, skipping a few input values does not affect the end results by a huge margin. Hence, if we can develop a MapReduce application that can handle skipping some of the input values in order to save the mapper from failing, we can correctly process the aforementioned error situations. This can help you to develop an application that is overall more reliable and easy to maintain. However, existence of such applications is mostly hypothetical, as either the reader responsible for data reading operation will throw an exception or the mapper responsible for processing the data will cause an exception. You can correctly process such situations in applications by implementing the following:

- Careful error handling in the reader so that all read errors are correctly processed and the file pointer is moved to the next record
- A mechanism for communicating with the mapper to report reader errors so that the mapper can correctly output information about them
- Careful error handling in the mapper so that all the map errors are correctly processed
- A custom `OutputFormat` object that writes error data in a dedicated error output directory

11

Understanding Hadoop YARN Architecture

Most Big Data architectures are based on Hadoop ecosystem, which has evolved rapidly over the years. The first version of Hadoop ecosystem (Hadoop 1) included MapReduce data processing model, which provides limited scalability and performance because of the batch-oriented nature of processing data. However, the MapReduce model improved over time to become more interactive and specialized in Hadoop 2. Among the various improvements of the second-generation Hadoop ecosystem (Hadoop 2.0), Yet Another Resource Negotiator (YARN) is one of the most important improvements. YARN is also, sometimes, called MapReduce version 2, which is a part of the core Hadoop project in Apache Software Foundation's distributed processing framework.

YARN is a key element of the Hadoop data processing architecture that provides different data handling mechanisms, including interactive Structured Query Language (SQL) and batch processing. It improves the performance of data processing in Hadoop by separating the resource management and scheduling capabilities of MapReduce from its data processing component. YARN has more flexible data processing engine and supports additional processing models such as Bulk Synchronous and Parallel (BSP) model. Thus, YARN can be considered as the operating system of Hadoop ecosystem, because it is responsible for managing, monitoring, and maintaining a multi-tenant environment.

In this chapter, you will learn about the YARN architecture in detail. The chapter starts with a discussion on the history of YARN with a revision of the MapReduce model. The chapter next explains the YARN architecture and its various components in detail. You also learn about different types of schedulers that are used by YARN for managing processing tasks. Towards the end, the chapter describes the backward compatibility feature of YARN architecture and introduces different commands used in YARN for various purposes. Finally, the chapter introduces the log management feature of YARN.

SCENARIO

Mr. Benson Rodriguez is the Chief Technology Officer (CTO) of Argon Technology, which is a Big Data management company. Mr. Rodriguez had already introduced the Hadoop ecosystem in his team, which has some experience working with the MapReduce model. While working with the MapReduce model, the IT team of Argon Technology encountered certain issues in dealing with some real-world problems related to Big Data. Mr. Rodriguez concluded that the issues can be overcome by introducing YARN to the core Hadoop ecosystem. He immediately decided to familiarize his team with the need, architecture, and working of YARN. In this chapter, we will learn everything that Mr. Rodriguez told his team about YARN.

Background of YARN

Apache Hadoop is an ecosystem used for processing large amounts of data through the MapReduce data processing model. This ecosystem was originally developed by Google Inc. and was handed over to the Apache Software Foundation in 2005. Hadoop supports distributed processing of large amounts of data through the core MapReduce processing mechanism. In 2012, the Hadoop project was upgraded to introduce a new architecture, known as YARN, which provides a more general-purpose data processing framework. This framework supports the MapReduce model as well as some other data processing models based on the distributed processing of data.

In YARN, the data processing component is separated from the resource management and scheduling components of MapReduce. This helps Hadoop ecosystem to run interactive queries and streaming data applications simultaneously through MapReduce batch jobs. It also helps Hadoop to support a broader range of applications and different types of processing approaches. In Hadoop ecosystem, YARN works as an operating system that manages, monitors, and maintains multi-tenant environment. In this environment, you can run various user applications of different types on multiple platforms simultaneously.

Hadoop 1, with the core MapReduce processing model, provides a way in which MapReduce programs can be written in various languages, such as Java, Python, Ruby-on-Rails, Pig, etc. However, the issue with Hadoop 1 is that the programs are run on the basis of the MapReduce processing model that cannot deal with all Big Data processing problems alone. The MapReduce processing model is a program-based model, which includes tools such as Pig and Hive to provide simplicity to data processing tasks. However, it does not solve all kinds of Big Data problems. Therefore, YARN was introduced to fill the gap resulted due to the incapability of the MapReduce model to fulfill all kinds of data processing requirements.

Before we proceed, we need to understand how Hadoop 1 manages resources in a cluster and what kinds of general issues are there with this approach. Let's start with a revision of the MapReduce model.

Revisiting MapReduce

We have learned earlier that MapReduce is a programming model used for processing large amounts of data. It is a part of Apache Hadoop project that has been widely used for handling Big Data. The MapReduce model is based on the MapReduce programming paradigm that divides large datasets into multiple small datasets distributed over a number of mapper and reducer nodes used for processing data. The MapReduce system consists of a JobTracker node that is also called the master and multiple TaskTracker nodes that are known as slaves.

Figure 11.1 shows the architecture of the MapReduce model:

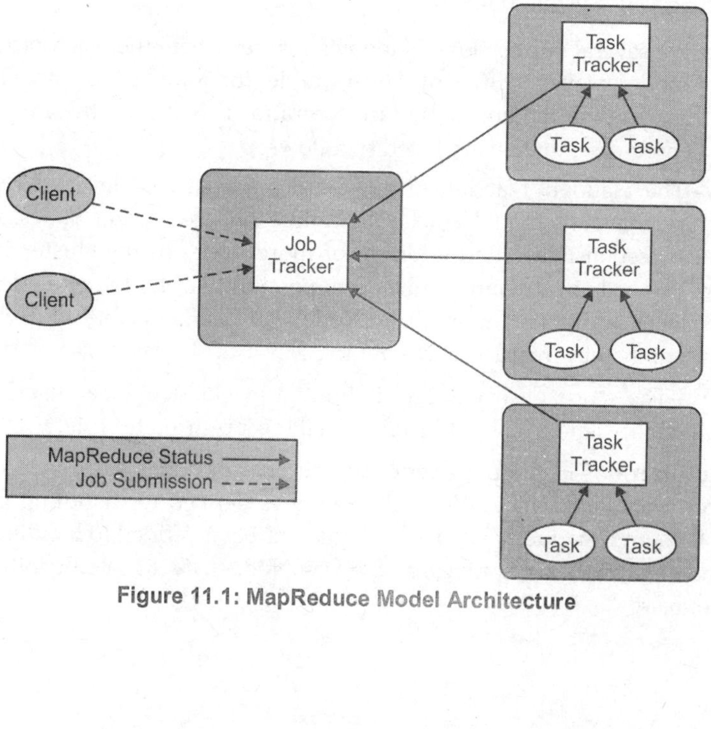

Figure 11.1: MapReduce Model Architecture

In Figure 11.1, the JobTracker performs the resource management tasks, which include managing slaves (or TaskTracker nodes), tracking the availability and consumption of resources, and managing the job lifecycle. The management of a job lifecycle involves individual task scheduling, progress tracking, providing fault tolerance, etc. TaskTracker nodes, on the other hand, perform fundamental operations that include breaking down of tasks on the orders of the JobTracker and providing periodic status information to the JobTracker.

Limitations of MapReduce

The MapReduce model is used as the standard processing model in Hadoop 1. However, this model involves certain limitations, which become more pronounced in dealing with large clusters. For example, clusters with 4,000 nodes or more (wherein every node may involve multiple cores) are likely to face issues such as node failure, system downtime, etc. The failure of nodes is one of the most concerning issues because the failure of even a single node may cause the entire cluster to fail. This case arises because the JobTracker tries to replicate the data on live nodes that are overloaded due to network flooding.

Apart from cluster failure, large clusters can face the issue of multi-tenancy, which is required to provide effective resource utilization. Some of the nodes in large clusters may be sitting idle and should be used for other tasks. The increasing size of clusters implies that the user can use the cluster for various purposes with different processing models to provide improved efficiency and performance. However, this is hardly achievable in the MapReduce model.

MapReduce does not fulfill all kinds of requirements, and in many cases, we may need to use other data processing models for more efficient output. For example, Apache Giraph can be used in place of the MapReduce model in graph processing and iterative modeling. Similarly, we need to have multiple paths for processing the data when all the data in an enterprise is already available in the Hadoop Distributed File System (HDFS).

Moreover, there are several applications in today's market where the batch processing framework of the MapReduce model proves inefficient. For example, the MapReduce model is unable to process the streaming data and in-memory interface operations. Some of the limitations of Hadoop 1 MapReduce data processing model are listed as follows:

- **Scalability—**The Hadoop 1 architecture provides a restricted level of scaling because of the single machine that runs the JobTracker to handle all TaskTracker nodes. A JobTracker already has too much responsibility and addition of more nodes to the cluster increases the work of JobTracker. This reduces resource utilization, possibility of more node addition, and chances of scalability. Some additional nodes (DataNode) are also available in a cluster but they often remain unused; thereby, restricting scalability.
- **Availability—**The scope of availability is limited in Hadoop 1 because JobTracker is the only point of availability, and in case of its failure, all the jobs need to restart.
- **Resource utilization—**Hadoop 1 defines the number of nodes separately to handle the mapper and reducer tasks in advance. When all the nodes defined for handling mapper tasks are full, you cannot assign a mapper task to a node that has been defined to handle the reducer task. This restricts the utilization of resources, as the DataNodes will sit idle in spite of the availability of empty resources.

- **Non-MapReduce applications**—Hadoop 1 is designed to do only MapReduce programming jobs, which means that you cannot handle non-MapReduce applications with it.

These are some of the limitations of the MapReduce model to overcome which YARN has been introduced in the Hadoop ecosystem.

EXHIBIT 1: WGBH deploys the RedPoint Convergent Marketing Platform™ to engage its next generation of donors and transform public media marketing nationwide.

Overview

WGBH Boston isn't just a world-renowned public media organization: it's also PBS's #1 content producer, the source of programs ranging from Masterpiece: Downton Abbey to Frontline. But, like many public media stations, WGBH faces an existential threat. Its donors are aging and recruiting younger donors is difficult. Its system for communicating appropriately with these donors was not working.

In 2011, WGBH upgraded its 17-year-old donor management system to a robust, cloud based solution, but it had a few limitations that made it difficult to fully leverage all of the necessary communications channels.

So WGBH turned to RedPoint's Convergent Marketing Platform™, a data-driven marketing solution designed to improve customer engagement. The RedPoint Convergent Marketing Platform extracts customer data from wherever it's located; delivers insights from customer behaviors, sentiments and preferences; and creates precisely the right interactions – whenever and through whatever channel is required – all from a single platform. Using RedPoint, WGBH created an authoritative "record of engagement" for every donor, establishing a strong foundation for its donor relationships. The RedPoint platform also allows WGBH to quickly create, automate, test, execute, modify, and reuse marketing campaigns of all kinds, across all channels. RedPoint's Big Data for Hadoop 2.0 application will help WGBH capture streaming information from social networks and fully integrate social media channels into its marketing mix.

WGBH now is making its immensely valuable donor engagement platform available to other public media outlets – helping local stations strengthen their donor bases and finances, so they can offer great programming locally for years to come.

About WGBH

Public media powerhouse WGBH Boston serves New England, the nation, and the world with educationally rich content that informs, inspires, and entertains. WGBH is the single largest producer of TV and Web content for PBS, and a major supplier of programming for public radio nationwide.

WGBH has been recognized with hundreds of honors: Emmys, Peabodys, duPontColumbia Awards, and even two Academy Awards. It has earned honors for Nova, Masterpiece (including Downton Abbey), American Experience, Frontline, Arthur, Curious George, The World, and many other outstanding programs.

Today, WGBH delivers content wherever its audiences choose, through broadcast media, podcasts/vodcasts, streaming media, iPhone/iPad apps, educational multimedia, and beyond. As a local public broadcaster, WGBH serves southern New England with 11 public TV services, three public radio services, and local productions reflecting its region's concerns and cultural riches. The challenges like most public media organizations, WGBH has an aging donor base. Engaging younger donors is challenging even in the best circumstances. However, WGBH's engagement efforts were complicated by its 17-year-old system that required deep, specialized expertise and made it difficult to take advantage of new marketing channels. The older system limited WGBH to traditional campaigns and channels that were increasingly out-of-step with younger audiences, who live on social, mobile, and Web platforms.

In response, WGBH committed to building a world-class CRM system for public media. Its first step was to upgrade to a Salesforce.com cloud environment enhanced by roundCause from roundCorner.

This step immediately reduced total cost of ownership and made the data much more accessible to WGBH's marketers regardless of their technical acumen. However, over time they kept finding that they couldn't regularly extract specific data in order to meet their B2C marketing needs. Also, their active donor engagement programs rely extensively on heuristic matching rules and, without them in their new platform, they ended up inadvertently creating thousands of duplicate account and contact records. Not only was WGBH wasting money through duplicate records, it also was alienating donors by over-communicating or miscommunicating to them.

Custom solutions to these problems would have required costly development and ongoing maintenance at a time when WGBH wanted to refocus its limited resources on "boots-on-the-ground" fundraising.

The Solution

To overcome these problems, WGBH enhanced its technical ecosystem by implementing and integrating RedPoint's Convergent Marketing Platform. A leading customer engagement solution, the RedPoint platform proved uniquely capable of addressing WGBH's challenges by bringing together all the customer data WGBH needed to create precise, one-to-one interactions with donors across all of its marketing channels. And it allowed WGBH to continue driving value from the other technology investments it had already made.

RedPoint also is the only customer engagement platform vendor with a YARN-certified data management application for Hadoop 2.0, which will allow WGBH to drive even more value from its large streams of structured and unstructured audience and donor data.

The Results

WGBH now has a comprehensive, next-generation donor engagement ecosystem that supports constant marketing innovation and experimentation. With RedPoint, WGBH has the ability to individually engage donors, wherever and whenever they prefer.

RedPoint's technology allows WGBH to leverage its existing investments and to better utilize everything the organization knows about its constituents to more accurately communicate with them.

Everything starts with accurate and consistent data: without that, no organization can build a reliable 360° view of its donors. This is especially challenging for WGBH, given its many donor touchpoints – from lockbox processed direct mail, to pledge drive 800 numbers and online donations to social and mobile media.

"Identity resolution is a huge issue for us," says Cate Twohill, WGBH's Director, Technical Product Development. "Without solid heuristic matching rules in place, we were regularly creating duplicate accounts. This would lead to miscommunications with donors. For example, sometimes we'd communicate with long-time donors as if they had just made their first contribution."

"RedPoint solved this problem right out of the box. It has amazing identity resolution tools. It allows us to match at both the individual and household levels. We're on the path to cleaning up all the duplicate records, and since we've been live on RedPoint, the duplicate record problem is under control."

"At last, we can keep identities clean and perfect for all our ongoing donor communications. Not having to manage duplicate accounts has, by itself, nearly paid for the cost of the solution."

WGBH relies heavily on their direct mail channel for benefit delivery and donor communications. RedPoint's data management capabilities provide NCOA, CASS, and other certifications to optimize direct mail programs. For the new, younger donors who are WGBH's future, the solution offers social media integration and geo-data – information that will be indispensable in new mobile and in-person canvassing programs.

And, since RedPoint is API-based and applications-agnostic, says Twohill, "We have access to any data source or any analytics tools we want."

Building on this strong and flexible data management foundation, RedPoint's Convergent Marketing Platform gives WGBH's marketers easy and powerful tools for executing on their omni-channel marketing vision.

"Our marketers are thrilled," says Twohill. "RedPoint's campaign management tools put all the power in their hands – not just the hands of a few people with deep technical skills. The tools offer a graphical, drag-and-drop user interface. We love them."

Thanks to RedPoint's simplicity, more than 30 marketing professionals were able to quickly get up to speed to build, modify, run, and reuse even the most complex campaigns. From one visual tool, marketers can define segments, create splits, control data delivery to external vendors, and much more. They can develop automated campaigns encompassing everything from email and direct mail to SMS communications.

"RedPoint's tools have made us smarter segmenters," Twohill notes. "Previously, we couldn't select data from more than a few of our connected data tables at a time. This made it very difficult for us to perform complex segmentations for omni-channel marketing.

We couldn't create and reach out to that segment before. But with RedPoint, we can." Whatever task they are engaged in, marketers get the information and control they need – and when they need more, says Twohill, it's easy to drill down and get that, too.

Even before implementing RedPoint, WGBH's marketers focused heavily on testing. "With RedPoint," says Twohill, "we feel even stronger about our ability to test and track, and know that we're getting reliable results across platforms."

In the end, RedPoint not only helps improve productivity, it supports WGBH's strategic goal of reallocating resources to projects that engage younger donors.

Transitioning Campaigns to Engagement

Building donor engagement isn't always about traditional "campaigns" anymore. Now, it's also about promoting conversations with individuals. That's especially true at WGBH, which produces much of PBS's highest-profile programming, from provocative Frontline documentaries to the cultural phenomenon Downton Abbey on Masterpiece.

"Lots of people talk about WGBH in social media," says Twohill. "We want to know what's being said, both positive and negative, so we can address it immediately. RedPoint will make it possible for us to listen to what people are saying about us, connect with anyone who chooses to talk about us, and leverage all the information that's out there."

Unstructured social data streams have been notoriously difficult to integrate into marketing programs. At WGBH, RedPoint Data Management for Hadoop will change all that. With its pioneering support for Hadoop 2.0/YARN, RedPoint will make Big Data accessible to WGBH analysts without requiring highly specialized programming skills.

"I'm not a Hadoop expert," says Twohill, "but I can already see how this Big Data tool will help us run analytics against data from lots of different sources – work we couldn't even have considered before."

By linking social listening with a growing understanding of donor behavior and preferences, WGBH can more consistently take the right next action with each donor in real time.

"We want to track how people are engaging with us from any device, at any time," Twohill says. "If we know how people are consuming our content, and what they're - engaging with, we can integrate that with our CRM data. We can personalize their experience in the specific channels where they want to engage. Through platforms like Facebook and Twitter, we can encourage them to let their friends know what they like. We can build a virtuous marketing cycle that grows and grows."

Strengthening Public Broadcasting Everywhere

Taken together, these innovations transform the way public media organizations engage their donors. They could help hundreds of financially challenged public broadcasters – and WGBH is making sure they do. The Boston-based organization is offering other public broadcast organizations the opportunity to benefit from what it's learned and implemented.

"Because we produce so much content," says Twohill, "it's in our interest to keep all public broadcasters viable so they may offer great content to their local markets.

Everything we are doing – including the development of our new MyWGBH online member portal – is being done in a way that will enable any public media outlet to adopt the same solution without needing to build it themselves. With these sophisticated tools, any station will be able to improve their own engagement and strengthen their donor bases."

Finally, many of these innovations wouldn't be practical for WGBH if they required extensive internal IT investments for custom development and integration. But, with RedPoint's technology and support, this is no longer an issue.

Says Twohill, "I tell people I feel like we've added ten people to our staff: RedPoint Global professionals who help us set up, answer our questions, provide new versions, and support us day and night. We hope to offer the same kind of support to other public media outlets so they can leverage RedPoint and find success, too.

Source: http://www.redpoint.net/wp-content/uploads/2014/09/RedPoint-WGBH-Case-Study-8.5x11-0814-PRINT.pdf.

Advantages of YARN

In Hadoop 2, the task of cluster management is handled by YARN and the tasks of data processing are performed by using the MapReduce programming paradigm. YARN manages the cluster through a component called central resource manager, which manages the resources and allocates them to applications.

YARN provides a way for Hadoop to run a number of applications simultaneously wherein applications can share common resource management. The inclusion of YARN in Hadoop 2 also means that the terms JobTracker and TaskTracker are not required any more. The isolation and scalability provided to the data processing applications are more in this model than in the previous MapReduce model. In Hadoop 2, the processing of data is done by the MapReduce framework via YARN.

The following are some advantages of using YARN with MapReduce in Hadoop 2:

- YARN provides efficient resource utilization. The available resources are scheduled to perform map and reduce tasks as per the requirement instead of the prior allocation of resources for map and reduce job execution.
- YARN provides a mechanism to Hadoop 2 through which multiple applications, sharing common resources, can be run simultaneously. In Hadoop 1, this is achieved only by running applications on different clusters.
- YARN allows Hadoop ecosystem to even run those applications in which the MapReduce model is not followed. The resource management and scheduling tasks of the MapReduce model are

separated from the data processing component by YARN. Hence, a large variety of data processing tasks and a wide range of applications, such as streaming applications, are supported by Hadoop 2.

- YARN provides backward compatibility that means applications developed on Hadoop 1 can run on Hadoop 2 directly.
- YARN does not have JobTracker and TaskTracker nodes. Instead, the two main functionalities of JobTracker (managing resources and monitoring/scheduling of jobs) are assigned to different components.

Let's now learn about the YARN architecture.

YARN Architecture

We have already studied that the Hadoop 1 architecture relies on MapReduce programming model's two main components, JobTracker and TaskTracker. In Hadoop 2, the JobTracker and TaskTracker nodes are replaced with a new set of components that are not prone to node failures. The fundamental idea of YARN is to split the tasks of the JobTracker, i.e. managing resources and scheduling/monitoring jobs to separate components. These components are known as ResourceManager and ApplicationMaster (also called ApplicationManager).

In Hadoop 2, ResourceManager shares the overall responsibility of controlling and managing resources and the ApplicationManager component allows a cluster to handle multiple applications at a time. Each application in the cluster will have its own ApplicationManager instance. ResourceManager and per-node slave (also called NodeManager) together manage applications in a distributed manner by forming data-computation framework.

Let's now learn about the two primary components of YARN: ResourceManager and ApplicationManager.

ResourceManager

ResourceManager, in YARN architecture, is the supreme authority that controls all the decisions related to resource management and allocation. It has a Scheduler Application Programming Interface (API) that negotiates and schedules resources. However, the Scheduler API does not monitor or track the status of applications. Hence, no guarantee is offered by the Scheduler to restart the tasks that have failed due to application or hardware failure. This API schedules resources, such as CPU, memory, disk, and network, on the basis of the resource requirements of applications.

The main purpose of introducing ResourceManager in YARN is to optimize the utilization of resources all the time by managing all the restrictions, which involve capacity guarantees, fairness in allocation of resources, etc. Thus, we can say that the YARN ResourceManager is responsible for almost all the tasks performed by the JobTracker in the MapReduce model.

ResourceManager performs all its tasks in integration with NodeManager and ApplicationManager components. Resources on each node are allocated and managed by its respective NodeManager. The ResourceManager gives instructions to the NodeManager, which is responsible for managing resources available on the node it manages. Similarly for each application, there is an

ApplicationManager instance that negotiates resources with the ResourceManager and, in association with NodeManager instances, starts the containers.

NOTE

Containers are physical resources, i.e., memory, CPU cores, and disks, available on every node.

In a cluster, applications can request resources at various levels, such as nodes, racks, etc. However, the resource allocation is done by the Scheduler on the basis of the availability of resources and the configured resource sharing policy in YARN. In short, we can say that the Scheduler uses the abstract notion of a resource container to perform its scheduling function on the basis of the amount of resources required for an application. The resource container incorporates various resource dimensions, including memory, CPU, disk, network, etc.

All the tasks related to resource management, allocation, and status tracking are performed by the JobTracker in Hadoop 1. There are several functions that the ResourceManager in Hadoop 2 is not responsible for. For example, the ResourceManager is not responsible for providing access to the application status servlet. Moreover, it is not concerned with monitoring of previously executed jobs, as this responsibility has been provided to the Job History Service (a component running on a separate node). Hence, the ResouceManager in YARN architecture is only responsible for resource scheduling and providing more scalability and flexibility.

ApplicationManager

Every instance of an application running within YARN is managed by an ApplicationManager, which is responsible for the negotiation of resources with the ResourceManager. ApplicationManager also keeps track of the availability and consumption of container resources, i.e. CPU, memory, etc., and provides fault tolerance for resources. Thus, we can say that ApplicationManager is responsible for negotiating for appropriate resource containers from the Scheduler, monitoring of their status, and checking the progress.

Integration of ResourceManager and ApplicationManager

With multiple applications residing within a cluster, ResourceManager needs to have information about the resources needed for each application. This information helps ResourceManager to negotiate for resources with ApplicationManager and provide optimum resource utilization. This concept of requesting for the appropriate resource is known as ResourceRequest. ApplicationManager sends ResourceRequest to ResourceManager for allocating the required resources. When ResourceManager approves a ResourceRequest of ApplicationManager, a container is created. Each successful request of ApplicationManager means that a container has been allocated by ResourceManager.

Containers

A container is nothing but a set of physical resources on a single node. A container consists of memory (RAM), CPU cores, and disks. Depending upon the resources in a node, a node can have multiple containers that are assigned to a specific ApplicationManager. A container thus represents a resource (memory, CPU, etc.) on a single node in a given cluster. A container is supervised by the NodeManager and scheduled by the ResourceManager. ApplicationManager itself is launched in a container, which is referred as container 0.

NodeManager

NodeManager is the per-machine slave, which is responsible for launching the applications' containers (containers that result from a successful ResourceRequest), monitoring their resource usage (CPU, memory, disk, network, etc.), and reporting the status of the resource usage to the ResourceManager. NodeManager manages each node within a YARN cluster. It provides per-node services within the cluster. These services range from managing a container to monitoring resources and tracking the health of its node.

Unlike MapReduce, which manages the execution of map and reduce tasks via slots, the NodeManager manages containers that represent per-node resources available for a particular application.

Job History Service

In Hadoop version 1, JobTracker is the master scheduler and tracker of all MapReduce jobs on the cluster. On the other hand, the new YARN-based Hadoop architecture has ResourceManager acting as a scheduler and does not track the job status. The task of tracking the job status is now the responsibility of the JobHistoryService component, which is usually run on a separate node. The architectural view of YARN is shown in Figure 11.2:

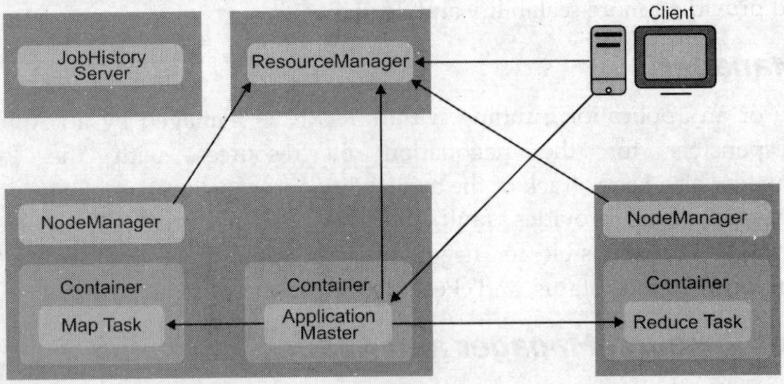

Figure 11.2: Architectural View of YARN

As we understood the role of each component in YARN, let's now get into its detailed processing.

Working of YARN

The overall process flow within YARN begins with a request from a client that consists of an application. ResourceManager negotiates necessary resources for a container and launches an ApplicationManager. ApplicationManager negotiates resource containers for the application at each node by sending the ResourceRequest. Upon execution of the application, ApplicationManager monitors the container until the application completes. When the application is complete, the ApplicationManager unregisters its container with the ResourceManager and the cycle is complete.

The following steps explain the working of YARN:

1. A client program submits the application to ResourceManager, which contains all the necessary information required to launch the application-specific ApplicationManager.

2. Now, we need a container where we can launch the ApplicationManager, which is specific to the application submitted by the client. Here, the ResourceManager negotiates for a specified container in which the ApplicationManager is to be started and then launches the ApplicationManager.
3. The ApplicationManager then registers itself with ResourceManager. This registration allows the client to directly communicate with its own ApplicationManager.
4. As ApplicationManager needs resources to complete its work, it will send a ResourceRequest to the ResourceManager, which has the detailed information about the application.
5. The ResourceManager allocates the appropriate container that is specific to the application. This container can reside in any node irrespective of the node on which ApplicationManager resides.
6. Now that the container is allocated, ApplicationManager launches the container by providing the container launch specification to the NodeManager. This will allow the container to directly communicate with the ApplicationManager.
7. The application code executing within the container provides necessary information that includes progress, status, resource availability, etc. to its ApplicationManager. During the entire process, the client directly communicates with ApplicationManager to get the status and other details on the application.
8. On completion of the submitted application, ApplicationManager deregisters the container with the ResourceManager. This is necessary because deregistration of the allocated container to ApplicationManager makes the container free for another ApplicationManager.

YARN permits the simultaneous execution of a variety of programming models including iterative processing, graph processing, machine learning, and general cluster computing with the help of application-specific ApplicationManager. Figure 11.3 shows the working of YARN:

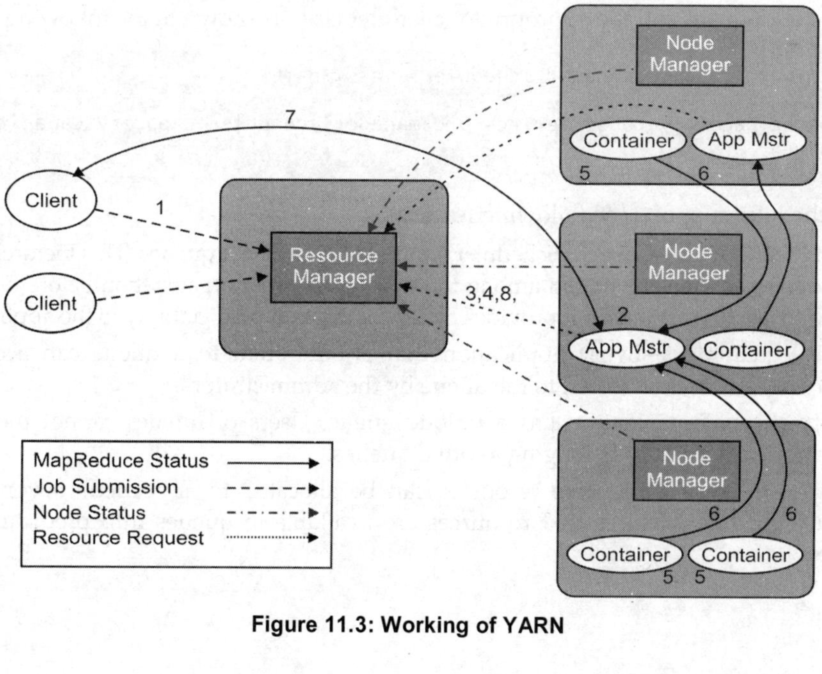

Figure 11.3: Working of YARN

In Figure 11.3, you can see that the two clients are submitting their application to the ResourceManager. This launches two ApplicationManager instances, each of which further launches their respective containers.

After discussing the working of YARN, let's learn about YARN schedulers.

YARN Schedulers

As discussed in the previous section, the sole purpose of ResourceManager is scheduling. There are two types of schedulers commonly available with YARN for negotiating resources with ApplicationManager via ResourceManager. These schedulers are known as CapacityScheduler and FairScheduler.

CapacityScheduler

CapacityScheduler is the default scheduler used in Hadoop 2. Its purpose is to allow multi-tenancy and share resources between multiple organizations and applications on the same cluster. The job of CapacityScheduler is to make sure that any user, application, or queue should not consume a lot of resources available in the cluster. By applying limitation on the initialized or pending applications from a single user and queue, CapacityScheduler ensures stability and fairness among the clusters.

CapacityScheduler works on the concept of queues that are setup by administrators to provide control and predictability on sharing of resources. CapacityScheduler uses hierarchy of queues to ensure that resources are shared among the subqueues of an organization before other queues are allowed to use free resources. Thus, it provides affinity for sharing free resources among applications of a given organization.

To use the scheduler, assign the appropriate scheduler class as shown in the following example:

```
<property>
  <name>yarn.resourcemanager.scheduler.class</name>
  <value>
org.apache.hadoop.yarn.server.resourcemanager.scheduler.capacity.CapacityScheduler
  </value>
</property>
```

CapacityScheduler supports the following features:

- **Hierarchical queues**—CapacityScheduler supports hierarchy of queues. This hierarchy ensures that the resources are equally shared among the subqueues of an organization before other queues are allowed to use free resources. It provides better control and predictability to the application.
- **Capacity guarantees**—Every application that is submitted to a queue can access the entire capacity of resources allocated to the queue by the administrators.
- **Security**—Every organization has a unique queue. Users of queues cannot modify or delete application or properties belonging to other queues.
- **Elasticity**—In some cases, free resources can be allocated to any queue beyond its capacity. CapacityScheduler ensures that resources are available to queues in a predictable and elastic manner.

- **Multi-tenancy—**CapacityScheduler does not provide a comprehensive set of limits to a single application, user, and queue. This prevents overutilization of resources.
- **Resource-based scheduling—**CapacityScheduler supports resource-intensive applications. These applications specify higher resource requirements than the default.

Some of the major properties that can be configured in CapacitySchedulers are allocation-related properties, running and pending application-related properties, and queue administration and permission-related properties. Let's now learn about these properties.

Allocation-related Properties

Table 11.1 lists the allocation-related properties of YARN with their descriptions:

Table 11.1: Allocation-related Properties

Property	Description
`yarn.scheduler.capacity.<queue-path>.capacity`	This property measures the queue capacity in percentage (%). Total capacities of all available queues (available at any level) must be 100%. Applications in the queue may consume more resources than the queue's capacity.
`yarn.scheduler.capacity.<queue-path>.maximum-capacity`	This property limits the maximum capacity or elasticity of applications in the queue. Its default value is -1 which denotes that the queue is disabled.
`yarn.scheduler.capacity.<queue-path>.minimum-user-limit-percent`	This property defines the limit (in %), which is applied on each queue. This limit is known as the user-limit and it can vary between a minimum and maximum value. The minimum value is always set; while the maximum value depends on the number of users who submit applications.
`yarn.scheduler.capacity.<queue-path>.user-limit-factor`	This property defines the limit up to which a user can take the queue's configured capacity. This value is specified as a float. The default value of this property is 1.

Running and Pending Application-related Properties

Table 11.2 lists the running and pending application-related properties of YARN with their descriptions:

Table 11.2: Running and Pending Application-related Properties

Property	Description
`yarn.scheduler.capacity.maximum-applications /yarn.scheduler.capacity.<queue-path>.maximum-`	This property shows the maximum number of applications in the system that can be concurrently active. This includes both running

Table 11.2: Running and Pending Application-related Properties	
Property	**Description**
applications	and pending applications. The maximum-applications limit of each queue is directly proportional to its queue capacity and user limits. When this limit is reached, the application will be rejected. The default value of this property is 10000 (only integer).
yarn.scheduler.capacity.maximum-am-resource-percent /yarn.scheduler.capacity.<queue-path>.maximum-am-resource-percent	This property shows the maximum percentage of resources in the cluster which can be used to run application masters. The maximum-am-resource-percent limit is directly proportional to its queue capacities and user limits. It can be specified as a float, i.e. 0.5 = 50%. Its default value is 10%.

Queue Administration and Permissions-related Properties

Table 11.3 lists the queue administration and permissions related properties of YARN and their descriptions:

Table 11.3: Queue Administration and Permissions Related Properties	
Property	**Description**
yarn.scheduler.capacity.<queue-path>.state	This property describes the state of the queue: RUNNING or STOPPED. If a queue is in the STOPPED state, then any new application cannot be submitted to itself or to any of its child queues. On the other hand, if the root queue is RUNNING, then no application can be submitted to the entire cluster. Only existing applications can continue and get completed. Its value is specified as Enumeration.
yarn.scheduler.capacity.root.<queue-path>.acl_submit_applications	This property decides who can submit applications to the given queue. Only the user or group that contains necessary Access Control List (ACL) on the given queue or one of the parent queues in the hierarchy can submit applications.
yarn.scheduler.capacity.root.<queue-path>.acl_administer_queue	This property decides who can administer applications on the given queue. Only the given user/group has necessary ACLs on the given queue or one of the parent queues in the hierarchy they can administer applications.

Fair Scheduler

Fair scheduling is a method of assigning resources to applications via Application Manager such that all applications get an equal share of resources during their course of running.

YARN is capable of scheduling various types of multiple resources. By default, FairScheduler schedules memory; however, it can be configured to schedule memory and CPU both. When there is a single application running in a cluster, the ApplicationManager uses the entire cluster; but when more than one application is running, then resources that are free can be assigned to the new application. Fair scheduling can also be done on the basis of the priorities, which decide the fractions of the total resources that are needed to assign to the application. The scheduler organizes application into queues and shares resources fairly among these queues. By default, all users share a single queue known as the 'default'; however, it is also possible that multiple queues are shared by a single user.

To use FairScheduler, assign the appropriate scheduler class in the yarn-site.xml file as shown in the following example:

```
<property>
<name>yarn.resourcemanager.scheduler.class</name>
<value>
org.apache.hadoop.yarn.server.resourcemanager.scheduler.fair.FairScheduler
</value>
</property>
```

You can also specify your own allocation file in yarn-site.xml :

```
<property>
  <name>yarn.scheduler.fair.allocation.file</name>
  <value>/etc/gphd/hadoop/conf/fair-scheduler.xml</value>
</property>
```

Common Properties of the yarn-site.xml File

The yarn-site.xml file is used to define the configuration of YARN in Hadoop 2. Table 11.4 lists the common properties of the `yarn-site.xml` file:

Table 11.4: Common Properties of the yarn-site.xml File

Property	Description
`yarn.scheduler.fair.allocation.file`	This property describes the path to allocate a file. An allocation file is an XML manifest describing queues and their properties, in addition to certain policy defaults. This file must be in the XML format. If a relative path is given, the file is searched on the classpath. Its default value is fair-scheduler.xml.
`yarn.scheduler.fair.user-as-default-queue`	This property decides whether or not the username associated with the allocation can be used as a default queue name, in case the queue name is not specified. If this property is set to FALSE/UNSET, then all the jobs can share the default queue. The default value of this property is TRUE.

Table 11.4: Common Properties of the yarn-site.xml File

Property	Description
`yarn.scheduler.fair.preemption`	This property decides whether or not the scheduler can use preemption. The default value of this property is FALSE.
`yarn.scheduler.fair.sizebasedweight`	This property decides whether or not to assign shares to individual apps based on their size, rather than providing an equal share to all apps regardless of size. If the value is set is TRUE, it means that the apps are weighted by the natural logarithm of one plus the app's total requested memory, divided by the natural logarithm of 2. The default value of this property is FALSE.
`yarn.scheduler.fair.assignmultiple`	This property decides whether or not to allow multiple container assignments in one heartbeat. The default value of this property is FALSE.
`yarn.scheduler.fair.max.assign`	This property defines the limit of the maximum containers that can be assigned in a single heartbeat. The default value of this property is -1, which means no limit.
`yarn.scheduler.fair.locality.threshold.node`	This property explains the number of scheduling opportunities for which a node needs to wait when an application requests container on this node before the container is assigned to it. It is expressed as a float between 0 and 1, which as a fraction of the cluster size is the number of scheduling opportunities to pass up.
`yarn.scheduler.fair.locality.threshold.rack`	This property explains the number of scheduling opportunities for which a rack needs to wait when an application requests container on this rack before the container is assigned to it. It can be expressed as a float between 0 and 1.

Allocation File Format Elements

There are various formatting elements defined in the resource allocation file of FairScheduler. Some of the elements of this file are enlisted as follows:

- **Queue element–**It has the following properties:
  - **minResources–**Sets the minimum resources of a queue.
  - **maxResources–**Sets the maximum resources of a queue.
  - **maxRunningApps–**Sets the maximum number of apps from a queue to run at once.

- **weight**—Specifies that the sharing of the cluster is non-proportional with other queues. Its default value is 1.
- **schedulingPolicy**—Specifies the values like "fifo", "fair", "drf" or any class that extends org.apache.hadoop.yarn.server.resourcemanager.scheduler.fair.SchedulingPolicy.
- **aclSubmitApps**—Lists the users who can submit apps to the queue.
- **minSharePreemptionTimeout**—Specifies the number of seconds the queue is under its minimum share before it tries to preempt containers to take resources from other queues.

- **User elements**—Sets the maximum number of applications for a particular user.
- **UserMaxAppsDefault**—Specifies the default running applications limit for users.
- **FairSharePreemptionTimeout**—Sets the number of seconds a queue is under its fair share before it tries to preempt containers to take resources from other queues.
- **defaultQueueSchedulingPolicy**—Specifies the default scheduling policy for queues that is overridden by the schedulingPolicy element in each queue if specified.

Now, let's create a sample XML configuration file by using the above-mentioned elements. The code for the sample XML configuration file for fair scheduling is given as follows:

```
   <?xml version="1.0"?>
<allocations>
  <queue name="test">
    <minResources>2000 mb, 1 vcores</minResources>
    <maxResources>10000 mb, 1 vcores</maxResources>
    <maxRunningApps>20</maxRunningApps>
    <aclSubmitApps>hdfs,gpadmin</aclSubmitApps>
    <weight>2.0</weight>
    <schedulingPolicy>fair</schedulingPolicy>
    <queue name="test-sub">
        <aclSubmitApps>root</aclSubmitApps>
        <minResources>1000 mb, 1 vcores</minResources>
    </queue>
  </queue>
  <user name="root">
    <maxRunningApps>20</maxRunningApps>
  </user>
 <user name="hdfs">
    <maxRunningApps>10</maxRunningApps>
  </user>
  <user name="gpadmin">
    <maxRunningApps>10</maxRunningApps>
  </user>
  <userMaxAppsDefault>10</userMaxAppsDefault>
 <fairSharePreemptionTimeout>20</fairSharePreemptionTimeout>
</allocations>
```

The preceding code configures a FairScheduler by using different scheduling properties.

Let's now understand how backward compatibility is provided by YARN to the MapReduce processing.

Backward Compatibility with YARN

YARN is backward compatible, which means that the code developed using MapReduce can run on YARN Hadoop 2 without any or some minor changes. This is a very important feature as applications that are developed using MapReduce usually cater to a large user base and run on widespread distributed systems. YARN provides different types of backward compatibilities that are discussed in this section.

Script Compatibility

Most of the command line scripts of Hadoop 1 can run on Hadoop 2. This means that you can continue to use Hadoop JAR files to launch jobs of Hadoop 1. The only exception is MRAdmin whose functionality is removed from MapReduce as JobTracker and TaskTracker are now replaced with ResourceManager. The MRAdmin functionality is also replaced with ResourceManager Admin. In YARN, when rmadmin commands are executed, warning messages will appear and remind users of using new YARN commands.

NOTE

Pig and Hive are two major data process applications in the Hadoop ecosystem and, fortunately, for both of them, you do not need any change.

Binary Compatibility

The MapReduce bytecode remained unchanged in YARN. This means that the application developed on Mapreduce can run on YARN directly without recompilation. You just need to provide the location of the application files to the YARN installation suite and the location of the configuration directory to HADOOP_CONF_DIR path.

Source Compatibility

MapReduce API, `org.apache.hadoop.mapreduce`, has gone through several changes over the years from Hadoop 1 to Hadoop 2. If MapReduce-based applications fail to run on YARN, you need to investigate their source code and check whether or not the MapReduce API is referred to. If it is referred to, then you have to recompile the MapReduce application against the new YARN JAR files.

After understanding how backward compatibility is provided with YARN, let's now learn about YARN configurations.

YARN Configurations

YARN configuration involves a number of properties defined to serve specific purposes in Hadoop 2. While most of the properties have been retained from Hadoop 1, several new properties are also added in Hadoop 2 with the inclusion of YARN. Some of the frequently used properties of YARN are listed in Table 11.5:

Table 11.5: New Properties of YARN

Name	Value	Description
`mapreduce.framework.name`	Local	This property denotes the runtime framework for running the MapReduce jobs. Its value can be classic, local, or yarn.
`mapreduce.job.ubertask.enable`	False	This property enables the small-jobs "ubertask" optimization, which runs "sufficiently small" jobs sequentially within a single JVM. By the maxmaps, maxbytes, and maxreduces settings, we can define the meaning of "small" and users can override the value.

Table 11.5: New Properties of YARN

Name	Value	Description
mapreduce.shuffle.max.connections	0	This property denotes the maximum allowable connections for the shuffle. Here, 0 (zero) means that unlimited connections can be made.
yarn.resourcemanager.am.max-attempts	2	This property denotes the maximum number of application attempts. It is a global setting for all application masters. Each application master can specify its individual maximum number of application attempts via the API, but the individual number cannot be more than the global upper bound. If it is, the ResourceManager will override it. The default number is set to 2 to allow at least one retry for ApplicationManager.
yarn.resourcemanager.recovery.enabled	False	This property enables ResourceManager to recover its state after starting. If it is true, then `yarn.resourcemanager.store.class` must be specified.
yarn.resourcemanager.store.class	org.apache.hadoop.yarn.server.resourcemanager.recovery.FileSystemRMStateStore	This is the class to be used as the persistent store. If `org.apache.hadoop.yarn.server.resourcemanager.recovery.ZKRMStateStore` is used and the store is implicitly fenced, then a single ResourceManager is able to use the store at any point in time.

Many MapReduce property names are no longer in effect in YARN. Table 11.6 lists the old MapReduce properties that are no longer in use:

Table 11.6: Old MapReduce Properties Not Used in YARN

Name	Value	Description
mapred.job.tracker	Local	This property specifies the host and port that the MapReduce job tracker runs at. If its value is local, it means that the jobs are running as a single map-reduce task.
mapred.job.tracker.http.address	0.0.0.0:50030	This property specifies the address of the job tracker http server and the port where the server will listen on. If the value of the port is 0, then the server starts on a free port.

Table 11.6: Old MapReduce Properties Not Used in YARN

Name	Value	Description
mapred.task.tracker.report.address	127.0.0.1:0	This property specifies the interface: port where the task tracker server listens on. Since it is only connected by the tasks, it uses the local interface.
mapred.local.dir	${hadoop.tmp.dir}/mapred/local	This property specifies the local directory where intermediate data files are stored by MapReduce. There may be a comma-separated list of directories on the different devices in order to distribute I/O. When any directory does not exist, then it is simply ignored.
mapred.system.dir	${hadoop.tmp.dir}/mapred/system	This property specifies the directory where MapReduce stores the control files.
mapred.tasktracker.map.tasks.maximum	2	This property specifies the maximum number of map tasks that can execute simultaneously by any task tracker.
mapred.tasktracker.reduce.tasks.maximum	2	This property specifies the maximum number of reduce tasks that can execute simultaneously by any task tracker.
mapred.job.reuse.jvm.num.tasks	1	This property specifies the number of tasks to run on a jvm. If its value is -1, then any number of tasks can be run on a jvm.
tasktracker.http.threads	40	This property specifies the number of the worker threads for any http server.
io.sort.record.percent	0.05	This property specifies the percentage of io.sort.mb dedicated to tracking record boundaries. Let this value be r and io.sort.mb is x then the maximum number of records collected before the collection thread can be calculated by the equation (r * x) / 4.

Resource scheduling requests are served by YARN through containers that have various properties in Hadoop 2.

Table 11.7 lists some frequently-used container properties:

Table 11.7: Container Properties

Name	Value	Description
`mapreduce.map.memory.mb`	1024	The amount of memory to request from the scheduler for each map task.
`mapreduce.map.cpu.vcores`	1	The number of virtual cores to request from the scheduler for each map task.
`mapreduce.reduce.memory.mb`	1024	The amount of memory to request from the scheduler for each reduce task.
`mapreduce.map.cpu.vcores`	1	The number of virtual cores to request from the scheduler for each map task.
`mapred.child.java.opts`	-Xmx200m	Java opts for the task processes. If the symbol @taskid@ is present, then it will be replaced by current TaskID. But, any other occurrences of @ will not be changed. For example, to enable verbose gc logging to a file named for the taskid in /tmp and to set the heap maximum to be a gigabyte, pass a 'value' of: -Xmx1024m -verbose:gc Xloggc:/tmp/@taskid@.gc
`mapreduce.reduce.java.opts`	None	Old PropertyName mapred.reduce.child.java.opts has been deprecated
`mapred.map.child.java.opts`	None	Old PropertyName mapred.map.child.java.opts has been deprecated

Let's now learn some commands used in the YARN architecture to perform certain operations.

YARN Commands

YARN provides various commands to manage the YARN environment. There are following two categories of the YARN commands:

- **Administration commands**—These types of commands are used by the cluster administrator.
- **User commands**—These types of commands are used by the cluster user.

Both the administration and user commands are invoked by `/bin/yarn` script. The general syntax of the YARN script is as follows:

```
Syntax: yarn [--config <config_dir>] command [other_options]
```

Where:

- **--config <config_dir>**—It is used to override the default configuration. The default directory is `$HADOOP_PREFIX/conf`.
- **Command**—It denotes the YARN commands.
- **other_options**—It denotes the options associated with the YARN commands.

Let's first look at some of the Administration Commands.

Administration Commands

The commands used for performing administrative activities, such as managing, scheduling, and allocating resources are known as administration commands. These commands can only be used by the users having administrative rights. Some of the most commonly used administration commands are given as follows:

- To Start a ResourceManager

```
Syntax: yarn resourcemanager
```

- To Start a NodeManager

```
Syntax: yarn nodemanager
```

- To Start a WebProxy Server

```
Syntax: yarn proxyserver
```

- To Run a ResourceManager Admin

```
Syntax: yarn rmadmin   [-refreshQueues] [-refreshNodes]
[-refreshUserToGroupsMapping]
[-refreshSuperUserGroupsConfiguration]
[-refreshAdminAcls][-refreshServiceAcl]
[-help [cmd]]
```

Where:

- **-refreshQueues**—It is used to reload the states and scheduler specific properties of queue.
- **-refreshNodes**—It is used to reload the host information at the ResourceManager.
- **-refreshUserToGroupsMappings**—It is used to reload user-to-groups mappings.
- **-refreshSuperUserGroupsConfiguration**—It is used to reload the super-user proxy group mappings.
- **-refreshAdminAcls**—It is used to reload AdminAcls.
- **-refreshServiceAcl**—It is used to reload the service-level authorization policy file.
- **-help [cmd]**—It is used to display help for the given command. If the command is not specified by the user, then it displays help for all commands.
- To get the log level for each daemon

```
Syntax: yarn daemonlog -getlevel <host_and_port> <log_name>
```

This command prints the log-level of the daemon running at the given port of the host. This command connects to the http://host:port/logLevel?log=name link internally.

- To set the log level for each daemon

```
Syntax: yarn daemonlog -setlevel <host_and_port> <log_name> <log_level>
```

This command sets the given log level <log_level> of the daemon running at the given port of the host. This command connects to the http://host:port/logLevel?log=name link internally.

User Commands

The commands that can be used by all the system users (both administrators and guests) to perform a variety of tasks are known as the user commands. Some of these commands are given as follows:

- To Run a JAR file

```
Syntax: yarn jar <jar> [mainClass] args...
```

- To View the Status of the Application

```
Syntax: yarn application -status ApplicationId
```

  This command displays the status of the specified ApplicationId.

- To List the Number of Applications

```
Syntax: yarn application -list
```

  This command lists all the applications registered with ResourceManager.

- To Kill an Application

```
Syntax: yarn application - kill ApplicationId
```

  This command is used to kill an application.

- To Print Node Details

```
Syntax: yarn node <options>
```

  Where options are:

  - **-status NodeId**—It specifies the status of the specified NodeId.
  - **-list**—it is used to list all the nodes.

- To Dump Container Logs

```
Syntax: yarn logs <options>
```

  Where options are:

  - **-applicationId**—It is used to specify the application id.
  - **-appOwner AppOwner**—It is used to specify the owner of the application.
  - **-containerId ContainerId**—It is used to specify the container id.
  - **-nodeAddress NodeAddress**—It is used to specify the node address.

- To Print ClassPath

```
Syntax: yarn classpath
```

- To Print the Version of YARN

```
Syntax: yarn version
```

Let's learn about YARN Containers.

YARN Containers

Yarn containers are a process space where a given task is executed in isolation using resources from resource pool. It is the authority of the ResourceManager to assign any container to applications. The assigned container has a unique CustomerId and is always on a single node.

One of the most important things about secure container is that they will only work in the context of secured YARN clusters.

- **Container isolation requirements**—The local files (jars, log files, configuration files, shared objects, etc.) and directories should be accessed by container executor. The containers will not have access to the private files and confirmation files of Node managers, even if it is being launched by Node manager. The user should submit their executing application in isolation. Also, the different users should not have access to each other files and directories.

  The executing applications submitted by different users should be isolated and should not be able to access each other's files and directories. Similarly, the same requirement will apply to other systems like LPC queues, critical sections, etc., which are non-file securable objects.

- **Linux Secure Container Executor**—To launch the container, secure container executor `LinuxContainerExecutor` uses an external program (also called container executor) in linux environment.

  This program has the `setuid` access right flag set which helps to launch the container with the restricted permissions of the YARN application user.

- **Configuration**—The configured NodeManger user(yarn) and group(hadoop) must hold the configured directories `yarn.nodemanager.local-dirs` and`yarn.nodemanager.log-dirs`.

```
drwxr-xr-x are the permissions set on these directories.
---sr-s--- are the permsiion set of the container-executor which is owned by owned
  root.
```

  Set the following in the conf/yarn-site.xml to configure the `NodeManager` to use the `LinuxContainerExecutor`.

```
<property>
  <name>yarn.nodemanager.container-executor.class</name>
  <value>org.apache.hadoop.yarn.server.nodemanager.LinuxContainerExecutor</value>
</property>

<property>
  <name>yarn.nodemanager.linux-container-executor.group</name>
  <value>hadoop</value>
</property>
The container-executor program reads the LCE file named container-executor.cfg
yarn.nodemanager.linux-container-executor.group=#configured value of
yarn.nodemanager.linux-container-executor.group
banned.users=#comma separated list of users who can not run applications
allowed.system.users=#comma separated list of allowed system users
min.user.id=1000#Prevent other super-users
```

- **Windows Secure Container Executor (WSCE)**—To launch the container, secure container executor the `WindowsSecureContainerExecutor` uses the Windows S4U infrastructure in Windows environment. `hadoopwinutilsvc` service is required by WSCE. This service started with `service` command line arugment and is hosted by `%HADOOP_HOME%\bin\winutils.exe`.

  This service has some special operations that require LocalSystem authority. This is being done so that NameNode is not required to run the complete JVM.

  The communication is done with `hadoopwintulsvc` service by means of RPC(LRPC) via calls JNI to the RCP client which is hosted in `hadoop.dll`.

- **Configuration—**Set the following in the **conf/yarn-site.xml** to configure the `NodeManager` to use the `WindowsSecureContainerExecutor`:

```
<property>
  <name>yarn.nodemanager.container-executor.class</name>
<value>org.apache.hadoop.yarn.server.nodemanager.WindowsSecureContainerExecutor</val
  ue>
</property>
<property>
  <name>yarn.nodemanager.windows-secure-container-executor.group</name>
  <value>yarn</value>
</property>
```

- **wsce-site.xml—**To access the privileged operations, the `hadoopwinutilsvc` uses `%HADOOP_HOME%\etc\hadoop\wsce_site.xml`.

```
    <property>
      <name>yarn.nodemanager.windows-secure-container-
executor.impersonate.allowed</name>
      <value>HadoopUsers</value>
    </property>
```

The details of service running by the nodemanager can be taken from `yarn.nodemanager.windows-secure-container-executor.allowed`. The user has the privileged to access the hadoopwintuilsvc functions. This code contains the users who are allowed to create containers in clusters. Also, these users are allowed to be impersonated by hadoopwinutilsvc.

Now, let's learn about registry.

Registry

A user of the registry can be both:

1. publisher of entries, i.e., service records
2. consumer of other services which are located by their service records.

   Distributed applications use different processes for different tasks. For example, the binding of the worker container of YARN is published by its application manager. If a container has a code running inside it and it gets restarted on different nodes of the cluster, it will be able to search the application manager tc communicate and look for bindings. Application on client side can have a look to the external service extreme point to communicate with application manager through an API.

YARN registry can be used in the following manner:

1. When we have to register dynamic YARN-deployed applications where entries match the lifespan of YARN application, few service records can be altered, for example, these records can be deleted on the completion of the YARN application, the application attempt, or an individual container.
2. To clarify that a service binding is published by a particular user or by a system account on a secure cluster. This can be verified by checking the path under which the entry has been executed.
3. Registering static applications. These files will remain in the registry unless deleted and they can be updated if required.

YARN registry is not used for the following:

1. It directly shares the requested data from the server on the customer request. This data should be published by some means where the entry of registry can be seen.
2. We cannot share secret between processes as registry can be read by anyone.

Log Management in Hadoop 1

In MapReduce, logs are used to debug applications, record the status of running applications, identify race conditions, and track job failures due to hardware or platform bugs. In Hadoop 1, user-logs are left on the individual nodes by the TaskTracker. Due to this, the management of the log files on local nodes is both insufficient as well as non-deterministic for user access.

In order to view log files in Hadoop 1, users were required to login to individual nodes. The map reduce tasks write the log files directly into the local disk. Logging into individual nodes and inspecting logs was a tiring job and sometimes access restriction on node levels made it impossible to view log files.

There were also issues related to the space within the individual nodes and log retention time period. Another problem associated with the logs is that it can run on HTTP that exists only on the local node. This implies that if users want to perform any post analyses of the application, then they have to employ some log-collection methods to collect data. In addition, all the logs were written in a single log-directory. Thus, there is no load balancing across disks and if one disk is down, then all jobs lose all the logs.

With the introduction of YARN, many issues faced with the log management in Hadoop 1 were addressed.

Log Management in YARN

One of the major problems with Hadoop1 was that the user-logs are individual nodes that are left idle for a certain time period by the TaskTracker. In YARN, the NodeManager is employed to move these nodes securely to a file-system, for example, HDFS, after the application completes. This way logs are not retained on the node and the problem of running out of space for individual nodes no longer exists.

Logs belonging to a single application running on a given NodeManager are aggregated and written to a single log file at a configured location in the file system. After completion of an application, two logs known as application-level log directory and per-node log file are created.

Users can easily access both of these logs by using YARN commands, the Web UI, or directly from the file system.

- **Using YARN commands—**
  - To print all the logs for a given application:

```
Syntax: yarn logs -applicationId <application ID>
```

  - To print the logs of only one container:

```
Syntax: yarn logs -applicationId <application ID> -containerId <Container ID> -
nodeAddress <Node Address>
```

- **Using the Web UI—**

  YARN provides access to ApplicationManager via ResourceManager UI. While a MapReduce application is running, users can see the logs from the ApplicationManager UI, which can redirect to the NodeManager UI. Once an application finishes, the completed information is owned by the MapReduce JobHistoryServer that again provides transparent user logs.

Moreover, in YARN, logs can be retained for a much longer time period, and the log viewing is not restricted to UI-based applications. Unlike Hadoop 1, there is no need to truncate logs into small parts as YARN provides enough space to store all the logs. In addition, YARN logs are written to multiple directories, thus resulting in effective load balancing and improved fault tolerance.

Table 11.8 lists the common log-related configuration properties of YARN:

Table 11.8: Common Log-related Configuration Properties

Property	Description
`yarn.nodemanager.log-dirs`	This property determines where the container logs are stored on the node and also when the containers will run. Its default value is ${yarn.log.dir}/userlogs.
`yarn.log-aggregation-enable`	This property determines whether to enable log aggregation or not. If it is disabled, NodeManagers will keep the logs locally.
`yarn.nodemanager.remote-app-log-dir`	This property represents the default file-system (usually HDFS) and indicates where the NodeManager aggregates logs. The directory should not be in the local file system; otherwise, serving daemons will not able to serve the aggregated logs. Its default value is /tmp/logs.
`yarn.nodemanager.remote-app-log-dir-suffix`	The remote log dir will be created at {yarn.nodemanager.remote-app-log-dir}/${user}/{thisParam}. Its default value is 'logs'.
`yarn.log-aggregation.retain-seconds:`	This property specifies how long to wait before deleting aggregated-logs. The -1 or any negative number prevents the deletion of the aggregated-logs.
`yarn.log-aggregation.retain-check-interval-seconds:`	This property specifies how long to wait between aggregated-log retention-checks. If its value is zero or in negative, then the value is computed as one-tenth of the aggregated-log retention-time. Its default value is -1.

Table 11.8: Common Log-related Configuration Properties

Property	Description
`yarn.log.server.url`	This property specifies the URL where NodeManagers redirect the application after its completion.
`yarn.nodemanager.log.retain-.seconds`	This property specifies the time in seconds to retain user logs on the individual nodes if log aggregation is disabled. Its default value is 10800.
`yarn.nodemanager.log.deletion-threads-count`	This property determines the number of threads used by NodeManagers to clean-up logs.

Summary

Hadoop version 2 has completely transformed the way Hadoop version 1 works. In Hadoop 2, you are no longer restricted only to the processing of MapReduce jobs in your cluster. This chapter first provided you with an overview of YARN and its major functionalities. In this chapter, you learned why there is a need for another approach for processing data when MapReduce is already there. Also, you studied the high-level architecture of YARN. In addition, you learned how the responsibilities of the JobTracker have been distributed and how multiple applications can be run on a single cluster. Further, you learned how YARN maximizes the resource utilization and how Hadoop 2 supports the MapReduce application developed in Hadoop 1. Moreover, you came to know about the type of schedulers available in YARN to ensure maximum resource utilization. Next, the chapter discussed the properties that can be configured while using any type of scheduler and described some of the common commands available to users and administrators in YARN. Towards the end, the chapter described the improvement in the log management in YARN as compared to Hadoop 1.

Quick Revise

Multiple-Choice Questions

Q1. YARN stands for:

a. Yet Another Resource Name
b. Yet Another Resource Negotiator
c. Yet Another Recovery Negotiator
d. Yet Another Resource Navigation

Ans. The correct option is b.

Q2. In the YARN cluster, _______ manages resource allocation.

a. ResourceManager
b. Container
c. NodeManager
d. ApplicationManager

Ans. The correct option is a.

Q3. A container consists of:

a. CPU
b. Disk
c. RAM
d. All of these

Ans. The correct option is d.

Q4. Which type of the following jobs MapReduce is suitable for?

a. Graph Processing
b. Batch Processing
c. Real Time Processing
d. Stream Processing

Ans. The correct option is b.

Q5. Which of the following are YARN schedulers?

a. Fair Scheduler
b. Quartz Scheduler
c. CapacityScheduler
d. Huge Database Scheduler

Ans. The correct options are a and c.

Subjective Questions

Q1. What do you understand by ResourceManager?

Ans. ResourceManager, in YARN architecture, is the supreme authority that controls all the decisions related to resource management and allocation. It has a Scheduler Application Programming Interface (API) that negotiates and schedules resources. However, the Scheduler API does not monitor or track the status of applications. Hence, no guarantee is offered by the Scheduler to restart the tasks that have failed due to application or hardware failure. This API schedules resources, such as CPU, memory, disk, and network, on the basis of the resource requirements of applications.

The main purpose of introducing ResourceManager in YARN is to optimize the utilization of resources all the time by managing all the restrictions, which involve capacity guarantees, fairness in allocation of resources, etc. Thus, we can say that the YARN ResourceManager is responsible for almost all the tasks performed by the JobTracker in the MapReduce model.

Q2. Discuss the following terms:

- **NodeManager**
- **Job History Service**

Ans. **NodeManager**—NodeManager is the per-machine slave, which is responsible for launching the applications' containers (containers that result from a successful ResourceRequest), monitoring their resource usage (CPU, memory, disk, network, etc.), and reporting the status of the resource usage to the ResourceManager. NodeManager manages each node within a YARN cluster. It provides per-node services within the cluster. These services range from managing a container to monitoring resources and tracking the health of its node.

Job History Service—The task of tracking the job status in Hadoop 2 is the responsibility of the JobHistoryService component, which is usually run on a separate node.

Q3. Explain the YARN architecture.

Ans. YARN architecture involves two main components, named ResourceManager and ApplicationManager, which form the core of Hadoop 2. In Hadoop 2, the JobTracker and TaskTracker nodes of MapReduce architecture used in Hadoop 1 are replaced with a new set of components that are not prone to node failures. The fundamental idea of YARN is to split the tasks of the JobTracker, i.e. managing resources and scheduling/monitoring jobs to separate components. These components are known as ResourceManager and ApplicationMaster (also called ApplicationManager).

In Hadoop 2, ResourceManager shares the overall responsibility of controlling and managing resources and the ApplicationManager component allows a cluster to handle multiple applications at a time. Each application in the cluster will have its own ApplicationManager instance. ResourceManager and per-node slave (also called NodeManager) together manage applications in a distributed manner by forming data-computation framework.

The architectural view of YARN is shown in the following figure:

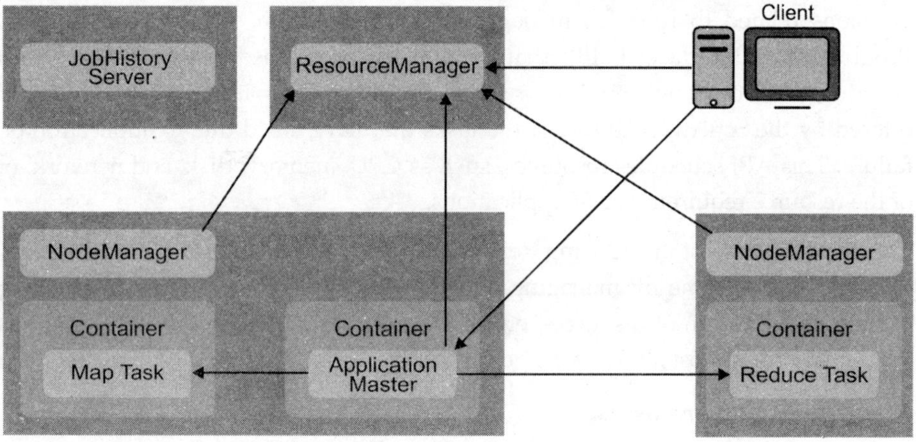

Q4. What is the role of ApplicationManager in Hadoop 2?

Ans. Every instance of an application running within YARN is managed by an ApplicationManager, which is responsible for the negotiation of resources with the ResourceManager. ApplicationManager also keeps track of the availability and consumption of container resources, i.e. CPU, memory, etc., and provides fault tolerance for resources. Thus, we can say that ApplicationManager is responsible for negotiating for appropriate resource containers from the Scheduler, monitoring of their status, and checking the progress.

Q5. Discuss the advantages of YARN over MapReduce.

Ans. The following are some advantages of using YARN with MapReduce in Hadoop 2:

- YARN provides efficient resource utilization. The available resources are scheduled to perform map and reduce tasks as per the requirement instead of the prior allocation of resources for map and reduce job execution.
- YARN provides a mechanism to Hadoop 2 through which multiple applications, sharing common resources, can be run simultaneously. In Hadoop 1, this is achieved only by running applications on different clusters.
- YARN allows Hadoop ecosystem to even run those applications in which the MapReduce model is not followed. The resource management and scheduling tasks of the MapReduce model are separated from the data processing component by YARN. Hence, a large variety of data processing tasks and a wide range of applications, such as streaming applications, are supported by Hadoop 2.
- YARN provides backward compatibility that means applications developed on Hadoop 1 can run on Hadoop 2 directly.
- YARN does not have JobTracker and TaskTracker nodes. Instead, the two main functionalities of JobTracker (managing resources and monitoring/scheduling of jobs) are assigned to different components.

Q6. Discuss fair scheduling in YARN.

Ans. Fair scheduling is a method of assigning resources to applications via ApplicationManager such that all applications get an equal share of resources during their course of running.

YARN is capable of scheduling various types of multiple resources. By default, FairScheduler schedules memory; however, it can be configured to schedule memory and CPU both. When there is a single application running in a cluster, the ApplicationManager uses the entire cluster but when more than one application is running then resources that are free can be assigned to the new application. Fair scheduling can also be done on the basis of the priorities, which decide the fractions of the total resources that are needed to assign to the application. The scheduler organizes application into queues and shares resources fairly among these queues. By default, all users share a single queue known as the 'default'; however, it is also possible that multiple queues are shared by a single user.

Q7. Explain backward compatibility with YARN.

Ans. YARN is backward compatible, which means that the code developed using MapReduce can run on YARN Hadoop 2 without any or some minor changes. This is a very important feature as applications that are developed using MapReduce usually cater to a large user base and run on widespread distributed systems. YARN provides the following types of backward compatibilities:

- Script Compatibility
- Binary Compatibility
- Source Compatibility

Q8. How can you access logs in Hadoop 2 using YARN commands?

Ans. You can access logs in Hadoop 2 by using the following YARN commands:

- To print all the logs for a given application:

```
Syntax: yarn logs -applicationId <application ID>
```

- To print the logs of only one container:

```
Syntax: yarn logs -applicationId <application ID> -containerId <Container ID>
-nodeAddress <Node Address>
```

12

Exploring Hive

You have already learned that Hadoop is a framework that handles huge volumes of datasets in a distributed computing environment. In fact, these datasets can be in any form, unstructured or structured. To carry out operations like querying and analyzing on such huge amounts of data, Hadoop offers an open-source data warehouse system called Hive or Apache Hive. Hive is a mechanism through which we can access the data stored in Hadoop Distributed File System (HDFS). It provides an interface, similar to SQL, which enables you to create databases and tables for storing data. In this way, you can achieve the MapReduce concept without explicitly writing the source code for it.

Hive also supports a language called HiveQL, which is considered as the primary data processing method for Treasure Data. Treasure Data is a cloud data platform that allows you to collect, store, and analyze data on the cloud. It manages its own Hadoop cluster, which accepts your queries and executes them using the Hadoop MapReduce framework. HiveQL automatically translates SQL-like queries into MapReduce jobs executed on Hadoop.

In this chapter, you learn about Hive, Hive architecture, and Hive metastore. Next, you learn about the variables, properties, and commands used in Hive. You also learn to execute Hive queries from files. The chapter next discusses Data Definition Language (DDL) and data manipulation in Hive. Toward the end, you learn how to execute HiveQL queries and use joins in Hive.

Introducing Hive

Hive provides a Structured Query Language (SQL) interface, HiveQL, or the Hive Query Language. This interface translates the given query into a MapReduce code. Hive can be seen as a mechanism through which one can access the data stored in the HDFS. HiveQL enables users to perform tasks using the MapReduce concept but without explicitly writing the code in terms of the map and reduce functions. The data stored in HDFS can be accessed through HiveQL, which contains the features of SQL but runs on the MapReduce framework.

It should be noted that Hive is not a complete database and is not meant to be used in Online Transactional Processing Systems, such as online ticketing, bank transactions, etc. It is mostly used in data warehousing kind of applications, where you need to perform batch processing on a huge amount of data. Typical examples of this kind of data include Web logs, call data records, weather data, etc.

As Hive queries are converted into MapReduce jobs, their latency period is also increased because of the overhead involved in the startup. This means that queries that usually take around a few milliseconds to execute in traditional database systems now take more time on Hive.

Figure 12.1 shows the architecture of Hive:

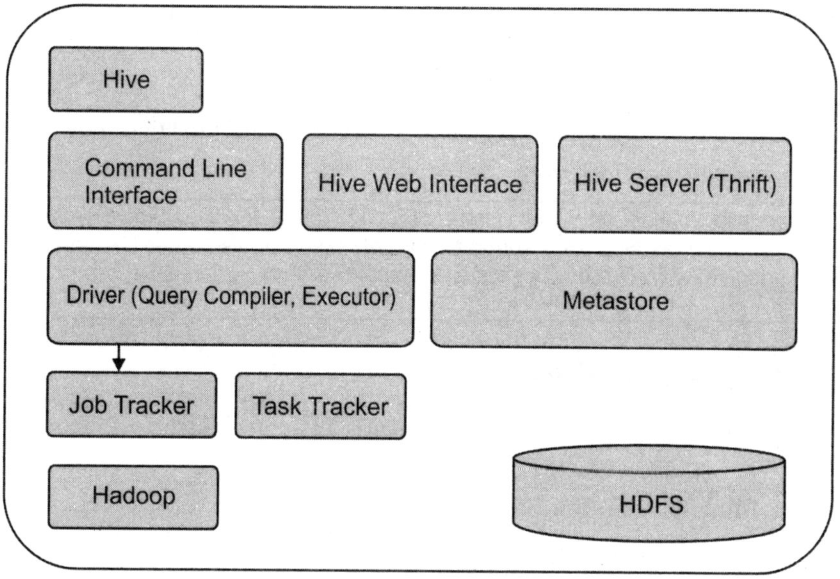

Figure 12.1: Displaying the Architecture of Hive

The architecture of Hive consists of various components. These components are described as follows:

- **User Interface (UI)**—Allows you to submit queries to the Hive system for execution.
- **Driver**—Receives the submitted queries. This driver component creates a session handle for the submitted query and then sends the query to the compiler to generate an execution plan.
- **Compiler**—Parses the query, performs semantic analysis on different query blocks and query expressions, and generates an execution plan.
- **Metastore**—Stores all the information related to the structure of the various tables and partitions in the data warehouse. It also includes column and column type information and the serializers and deserializers necessary to read and write data. It also contains information about the corresponding HDFS files where your data is stored.
- **Execution Engine**—Executes the execution plan created by the compiler. The plan is in the form of a Directed Acyclic Graph (DAG) to be executed in various stages. This engine manages the dependencies between the different stages of a plan and is also responsible to execute these stages on the appropriate system components.

NOTE

DAG is a model for scheduling work. In this model, jobs are represented as vertices in a graph, and the order of the execution of jobs is specified by the directions of the edges in the graph. The term "acyclic" means there are no loops (or cycles) in the graph.

The following are the different ways to access Hive:

- **Hive Command Line Interface**—This is the most commonly used interface of Hive. It is mostly referred to as Hive CLI.

- **Hive Web Interface**—This is a simple Graphical User Interface (GUI) used to connect to Hive. To use this interface, you need to configure it during the Hive installation.
- **Hive Server**—This is an optional server. By using this server, users can submit their Hive jobs from a remote client.
- **JDBC/ODBC**—This is a JDBC client that allows users to connect to Hive and submit their jobs.

NOTE

Most Hadoop users wish to work on a GUI instead of a CLI. The GUI of Apache Hive is provided by a Web browser technology known as Hue. Hue supports not only Hive but also other Hadoop technologies, such as HDFS, MapReduce/YARN, Oozie, Zookeeper, HBase, Pig, and Sqoop. Hue is an open-source project and its Apache Hive GUI is called BeesWax.

Getting Started with Hive

As we know that before using Hive, we need to first install and set the home variable to use Hive on Hadoop.

The steps for installing Hive on Hadoop are as follows:

Installing Hive with embedded metastore:

1. Download the latest version of Hive.
2. Untar the package:

```
$  tar -xzvf  apache-hive-0.13.1-bin.tar.gz
```

3. Add following to ~/.bash_profile:

```
$ sudo nano ~/.bash_profile
export HIVE_HOME=/home/hduser/hive-0.13.1
export PATH=$PATH:$HIVE_HOME/bin
```

   Where hduser is the user name and Hive-0.13.1 is the Hive directory extracted from tar.

4. Run Hive from terminal:

```
$    hive
```

5. Make sure that the Hive node is connected to the hadoop cluster.

   This installation uses embedded Derby database and stores the data on local filesystem. Only one Hive session could be open on the node. If different users try to run the Hive shell, the second would get: "**Failed to start database 'metastore_db'**" error.

6. Run Hive queries for datastore to test for the installation:

```
hive>  SHOW TABLES;
hive> CREATE TABLE sales(id INT, product String) ROW FORMAT DELIMITED FIELDS
TERMINATED BY '\t';
```

7. Logs are generated per user bases in /tmp/<usrename> folder.

Installing Hive with local metastore:

1. Download the latest version of Hive.
2. Untar the package:

```
$  tar -xzvf  apache-hive-0.13.1-bin.tar.gz
```

3. Add following to ~/.bash_profile:

```
$ sudo nano ~/.bash_profile
  export HIVE_HOME=/home/hduser/hive-0.13.1
  export PATH=$PATH:$HIVE_HOME/bin
```

Where hduser is the user name and Hive-0.13.1 is the Hive directory extracted from tar.

4. Install a sql database like MySql on the same machine where you want to run Hive.
5. Add following entries to Hive-site.xml:

```
<configuration>
   <property>
<name>javax.jdo.option.ConnectionURL</name>
<value>jdbc:mysql://localhost:3306/metastore_db?createDatabaseIfNotExist=true</value>
  <description>metadata is stored in a MySQL server</description>
   </property>
   <property>
 <name>javax.jdo.option.ConnectionDriverName</name>
  <value>com.mysql.jdbc.Driver</value>
  <description>MySQL JDBC driver class</description>
   </property>
   <property>
            <name>javax.jdo.option.ConnectionUserName</name>
            <value>hduser</value>
            <description>user name for connecting to mysql server
            </description>
      </property>
      <property>
   <name>javax.jdo.option.ConnectionPassword</name>
              <value>passwd</value>
        <description>password for connecting to mysql server</description>
</property>
</configuration>
```

6. Run Hive from terminal:

```
$ hive
```

Installing Hive with remote metastore:

1. Download the latest version of Hive.
2. Untar the package:

```
$  tar -xzvf  apache-hive-0.13.1-bin.tar.gz
```

3. Add following to ~/.bash_profile:

```
$ sudo nano ~/.bash_profile
export HIVE_HOME=/home/hduser/hive-0.13.1
export PATH=$PATH:$HIVE_HOME/bin
```

Where hduser is the user name and Hive-0.13.1 is the Hive directory extracted from tar.

4. Install a sql database like MySql on a remote machine to be used for metastore.
5. Add following entries to Hive-site.xml:

```
<configuration>
      <property>
   <name>javax.jdo.option.ConnectionURL</name>
<value>jdbc:mysql://<ip_of_remote_host:3306/metastore_db?createDatabaseIfNotExist=tr
ue</value>
      <description>metadata is stored in a MySQL server</description>
      </property>
       <property>
   <name>javax.jdo.option.ConnectionDriverName</name>
    <value>com.mysql.jdbc.Driver</value>
```

```
        <description>MySQL JDBC driver class</description>
          </property>
         <property>
                    <name>javax.jdo.option.ConnectionUserName</name>
                    <value>hduser</value>
                    <description>user name for connecting to mysql server
                    </description>
            </property>
            <property>
         <name>javax.jdo.option.ConnectionPassword</name>
                      <value>passwd</value>
                      <description>password for connecting to mysql
server</description>
</property>
</configuration>
```

6. Run Hive from terminal:

```
$ hive
```

You have already learned that Apache Hive is a data warehouse system for Hadoop that facilitates the analysis of large datasets and ad-hoc queries. In addition, HiveQL the SQL-like language enables programmers, who are familiar with the MapReduce framework, to plug in their custom mappers and reducers to perform complex analysis, which might not be supported by the built-in capabilities of the language. Let's learn some basic language capabilities of Hive in the following subsections.

Hive operates in a shell interactive mode; therefore, to work with Hive, you first need to enter this mode. The shell interactive mode is also known as command-line interface (CLI). You can enter the shell interactive mode of Hive by running the `$HIVE_HOME/bin/Hive` command.

Table 12.1 lists some commonly used Hive commands to be used in the shell interactive mode:

Table 12.1: Hive Commands Used in the Shell Interactive Mode

Command	Description
! <command>	Executes a shell command from the Hive shell
<query string>	Executes a Hive query and prints results to standard output
add FILE[S] <filepath> <filepath>* add JAR[S] <filepath> <filepath>* add ARCHIVE[S] <filepath> <filepath>*	Adds one or more files, jars, or archives to the list of resources in the distributed cache
delete FILE[S] <filepath>* delete JAR[S] <filepath>* delete ARCHIVE[S] <filepath>*	Removes the resource(s) from the distributed cache
dfs <dfs command>	Executes a `dfs` command from the Hive shell
list FILE[S] <filepath>* list JAR[S] <filepath>* list ARCHIVE[S] <filepath>*	Checks whether the given resources are already added to the distributed cache or not

Table 12.1: Hive Commands Used in the Shell Interactive Mode	
Command	**Description**
list FILE[S] list JAR[S] list ARCHIVE[S]	Lists the resources already added to the distributed cache
quit exit	Quits or exits from the interactive shell
Reset	Resets the configuration to the default values
Set	Prints a list of configuration variables that are overridden by the user or Hive
set –v	Prints all Hadoop and Hive configuration variables
set <key>=<value>	Sets the value of a particular configuration variable (key)
source FILE <filepath>	Executes a script file inside the CLI

The following are some examples of using commands in the shell interactive mode of Hive:

```
hive> set;  ← Prints a list of configuration variables
hive> select my.* from mytable;  ← Executes a query
hive> dfs -ls;  ← Lists the directory content
```

In the preceding examples, the `set` command prints a list of configuration variables the `select` query displays the columns beginning with `my.` from the `mytable` table, and `dfs -ls` executes the `dfs` command to list the directory content. The semicolon `(;)` symbol is used to terminate a command, and – is used to insert comments.

You can use the `$HIVE_HOME/bin/hive` utility to run Hive queries in either shell interactive or batch mode.

Table 12.2 lists all the options provided by Hive CLI:

Table 12.2: Options Provided by Hive CLI	
Option	**Description**
-d,--define <key=value>	Applies variable substitution to Hive commands, e.g. `-d A=B or --define A=B`
-e <quoted-query-string>	Executes SQL commands from command line
-f <filename>	Executes SQL commands from one or more files
-H,--help	Prints help information
-h <hostname> --hiveconf <property=value>	Connects to Hive Server on remote host Uses value for the given property

Table 12.2: Options Provided by Hive CLI

Option	Description
--hivevar <key=value>	Variable substitution to apply to Hive commands. e.g. --hivevar A=B
-i <filename>	Initializes SQL file
-p <port>	Connects to Hive Server on port number
-S,--silent	Connects to the silent mode in interactive shell
-v,--verbose	Connects to the verbose mode (echo executed SQL to the console)

Some examples of using Hive CLI are as follows:

```
1.  $HIVE_HOME/bin/hive -e 'select x.col from table x'
2.  $HIVE_HOME/bin/hive -f /home/my/hive-script.sql
```

Executes the select query from the command line

Executes a script non-interactively from the local disk

The Hive command in the first example executes the select query from the command line, while the second command executes a script non-interactively from the local disk.

Hive Services

You can get all the Hive services you want by typing Hive service help. Some Hive services are as follows:

- **CLI**—It is the black window or the panel that we get after the installation of Hive. This is nothing but a command line interface of Hive. This is an inbuilt default service present in Hive.
- **Hive server**—Runs Hive as an integrated server to expose a thrift service, which integrates the access to the number of clients that are written in different types of languages. There are many applications like JDBC, ODBC connectors that need to execute a Hive server to get in communication loop with Hive.
- **Hive Web Interface (HWI)**—The Hive Web Interface is the GUI of Hive on which we can execute the queries. It is an alternative to the shell. HWI uses the following command:

```
% export ANT_LIB=/path/to/ant/lib
% hive --service hwi
```

- **JAR**—Hive is somewhat equal to Hadoop JAR, as it is convenient to run Java applications including the java applications, Hadoop, and Hive classes on the classpath. It is not required to make a special jar to do factual analysis. Hive itself does it just by a simple query.
- **Metastore**—It is the service that runs with the Hive services whenever Hive starts. This is a default process. Using the metastore service, it is possible to run it on a standalone (remote) process. For this, you just need to set the property of the Hive "METASTORE_PORT" environment variable so that the specified port gets listened by the server.
- **Hive client**—There are many different mechanisms to get in contact with the applications when you run Hive as a server that is hiveserver. Following is one of the clients of Hive:

- **Thrift Client**—It is very easy to run Hive commands from the extensive variety of programming dialects through the Hive thrift client. There are numerous programming dialects such as C++, Java, php, python, and ruby for which Hives has the thrift client, to make these dialects accessible.

Similarly, there are JDBC and ODBC drivers that are compatible with Hive. These drivers connect Hive with the metastores and help run applications.

Hive Variables

Hive allows you to set variables that can be referred in the Hive script. For this purpose, you need to use the `-d` or `-define` option, as shown in the following commands:

```
$hive -define db_name = sampledatabase;   ← Defines the db_name variable

hive> CREATE TABLE ${db_name}.sampletable ( x INT);   ← Creates a table by referring to the db_name variable
```

In the preceding commands, a table named `sampletable` is created in the database `sampledatabase`.

By default, the variable substitution option is enabled. However, you can disable this option by using the following command:

```
set hive.variable.substitute=false;
```

In general, there are three namespaces for defining variables `hiveconf`, `system`, and `env`. You can also define custom variables in separate namespaces using the define or hivevar options.

Hive Properties

The `hive-site.xml` file stores the configuration properties of Hive. These properties can be overwritten by the developers. To overwrite the properties of the `hive-site.xml` file, the set command is used. For example, the following command sets the path of the current directory to `/tmp/mydir` for all subsequent commands:

```
set hive.exec.scratchdir=/tmp/mydir;
```

In the `hive-site.xml` file, you can also enable the automatic optimization of joins. This can be done by using the following command:

```
hive> SET hive.auto.convert.join.noconditionaltask = true;   ← Turns on the automatic optimization of joins
```

It should be noted that these properties are valid only until the Hive CLI session is alive.

Hive Queries

Hive allows you to simultaneously execute one or more queries. These queries can be stored in and executed from files. The extension of a query file in Hive is `.hql` or `.q`. Let's take an example of a Hive query file, named `ourquery.hql`, stored in the .../`home/weusers/ queries/`folder.

Now, type the following commands to execute the query stored in the `ourquery.hql` file:

```
$cat /home/weusers/queries/ourquery.hql   ← Writes content in a file
```

```
SELECT roll_no, name FROM students;

$hive -f /home/weusers/queries/ourquery.hql
```

Executes a query from a file

You can also execute a Hive query in the background, as shown in the following command:

```
$nohup hive - /home/weusers/queries/ourquery.hql &
```

Executes a query as a background process

To list the directory content in the Hadoop dfs, type the following command:

```
hive> dfs -ls /user/hduser/input;
```

Lists the directory content

The preceding command gives the following output:

```
Found 2 items
rwxr-xr-x - hduser supergroup 0 2015-02-06 17:02
/user/hduser/input/ hellog.txt
rwxr-xr-x - hduser supergroup 0 2015-02-04 14:30
/user/hduser/input/ hiyou.txt
```

Data Types in Hive

Hive supports two kinds of data types: primitive type and complex type. Primitive data types are built-in data types, which also act as basic structures for building more sophisticated data types. Primitive data types are associated with columns of a table. Figure 12.2 shows a list of primitive data types available in Hive:

Integers
- TINYINT - 1 byte integer
- SMALLINT - 2 byte integer
- INT - 4 byte integer
- BIGINT - 8 byte integer

Boolean type
- BOOLEAN - TRUE/FALSE

Floating point numbers
- FLOAT - single precision
- DOUBLE - double precision

String type
- STRING - sequence of characters in a specified character set

Figure 12.2: Primitive Data Types Available in Hive

Complex data types are customized data types that can be created by using primitive data types. The following types of complex data types are available in Hive:

- **Structs**—The elements within this type can be accessed by using the Dot (.) operator.
- **Maps**—The elements in a map are accessed by using the `['element name']` notation.
- **Arrays**—The elements in an array have to be of the same data type. Elements can be accessed by using the `[n]` notation where `n` represents the index of the array.

Built-In Functions in Hive

You must already be aware of the concept of functions and the role they play in the development of an application. A function is a group of commands used to perform a particular task in a program and return an outcome. Like every programming language, Hive also has its set of built-in functions (also known as pre-defined functions). Table 12.3 lists the built-in functions available in Hive:

Table 12.3: Built-in Functions Available in Hive

Function	Function Return Type	Description
round(double a)	BIGINT	Returns the rounded BIGINT value of a double variable.
floor(double a)	BIGINT	Returns the maximum BIGINT value that is equal or less than a double variable.
ceil(double a)	BIGINT	Returns the minimum BIGINT value that is equal or greater than a double variable.
rand(), rand(int seed)	double	Returns a random number. The sequence of the generated numbers is fixed according to the seed number, if specified.
concat(string A, string B,...)	string	Returns the string resulting from concatenating B after A. This function accepts an arbitrary number of arguments, concatenates them, and returns the result.
substr(string A, int start)	string	Returns the substring of A starting from the start position till the end of string A.
substr(string A, int start, int length)	string	Returns the substring of A starting from the start position with the given length.
upper(string A) or ucase(string A)	string	Returns the resulting string by converting all characters of A to upper case.
lower(string A) or lcase(string A)	string	Returns the resulting string by converting all characters of A to lower case.
trim(string A)	string	Returns the resulting string by trimming spaces from both ends of A.
ltrim(string A)	string	Returns the resulting string by trimming spaces from the beginning (left hand side) of A.
rtrim(string A)	string	Returns the resulting string by trimming spaces from the end (right hand side) of A.
regexp_replace(string A, string B, string C)	string	Returns the resulting string by replacing all substrings in B that match with the Java regular expression syntax with C.

Table 12.3: Built-in Functions Available in Hive		
Function	**Function Return Type**	**Description**
size(Map<K.V>)	int	Returns the number of elements in the 'map' type.
size(Array<T>)	int	Returns the number of elements in the 'array' type.
cast(<expr> as <type>)	value of <type>	Converts the results of the expression expr to <type>. A null is returned if the conversion fails.
from_unixtime(int unixtime)	string	Converts the number of seconds from unix epoch (1970-01-01 00:00:00 UTC) to a string representing the timestamp of that moment in the current system time zone in the format of "1970-01-01 00:00:00".
to_date(string timestamp)	string	Returns the date part of a timestamp string: to_date("1970-01-01 00:00:00") = "1970-01-01".
year(string date)	int	Returns the year part of a timestamp string: year("1970-01-01 00:00:00") = 1970, year("1970-01-01") = 1970.
month(string date)	int	Returns the month part of a timestamp string: month("1970-11-01 00:00:00") = 11, month("1970-11-01") = 11.
day(string date)	int	Returns the day part of a timestamp string: day("1970-11-01 00:00:00") = 1, day("1970-11-01") = 1.
get_json_object(string json_string, string path)	string	Extracts a json object from a json string based on the json path specified and returns a json string of the extracted json object. If the input json string is invalid, it will return null.

To perform various types of computations, Hive provides aggregate functions. Table 12.4 lists the aggregate functions available in Hive:

Table 12.4: Aggregate Functions Available in Hive		
Aggregation Function	**Return Type**	**Description**
`count(*)`	BIGINT	Returns the total number of retrieved rows, including the rows having NULL values
`count(expr)`	BIGINT	Returns the number of rows for which the supplied expression is non-NULL
`count(DISTINCT expr[, expr_.])`	BIGINT	Returns the number of rows for which the supplied expression(s) are unique and non-NULL
`sum(col)`	DOUBLE	Returns the sum of elements in a group

Table 12.4: Aggregate Functions Available in Hive		
Aggregation Function	**Return Type**	**Description**
`sum(DISTINCT col)`	DOUBLE	Returns the sum of distinct values of a column in a group
`avg(col)`	DOUBLE	Returns the average of elements in a group
`avg(DISTINCT col)`	DOUBLE	Returns the average of distinct values of a column in a group
`min(col)`	DOUBLE	Returns the minimum value of a column in a group
`max(col)`	DOUBLE	Returns the maximum value of a column in a group

Hive DDL

Data Definition Language (DDL) is used to describe data and data structures of a database. Hive has its own DDL, such as SQL DDL, which is used for managing, creating, altering, and dropping databases, tables, and other objects in a database. Similar to other SQL databases, Hive databases also contain namespaces for tables. If the name of the database is not specified, the table is created in the default database. Some of the main commands used in DDL are as follows:

```
Create
Alter
Drop
Show
Truncate
Describe
```

Let's learn more about these commands and the operations that can be performed by using them.

Creating Databases

In order to create a database, we can use the following command:

```
hive> CREATE DATABASE temp_database;   ← Creates temp_database
```

The preceding command creates a database with the name `temp_database`. In case a database already exists with the same name, an error is thrown. You can avoid the error by creating the database by using the following command:

```
hive> CREATE DATABASE IF NOT EXISTS temp_database;
```

NOTE

When a database is created in Hive, a folder with the same name is created under Hive's directory on HDFS.

You can also add a table in a particular database by using the following command:

```
hive> CREATE TABLE temp_database.temp _table (z int);   ← Creates temp_table in temp_database
```

In the preceding command, the name of the database is added before the name of the table. Therefore, `temp_table` gets added in the `temp_database`. In addition, you can also create a table in the database by using the following commands:

```
hive> USE temp_database;
hive> CREATE TABLE temp_table (z int);
```

In the preceding commands, the `USE` statement is used for setting the current database to execute all the subsequent HiveQL statements. In this way, you do not need to add the name of the database before the table name. The table `temp_table` is created in the database `temp_database`. Furthermore, you can specify `DBPROPERTIES` in the form of key-value pairs in the following manner:

```
hive> CREATE DATABASE temp_database
> WITH DBPROPERTIES ('owner' ='Joseph ', 'company' = 'Argon Technologies');
```

Assigns properties to a database

Viewing a Database

You can view all the databases present in a particular path by using the following command:

```
hive> SHOW DATABASES;
```

Shows all databases

The preceding command shows all the databases present at a particular location.

Dropping a Database

Dropping a database means deleting it from its storage location. The database can be deleted by using the following command:

```
hive> DROP DATABASE IF EXISTS temp_database;
```

You must note that if the database to be deleted contains any tables, you first need to delete tables from the database by using the `DROP` command. Deleting each table individually from a database is a tedious task. Hive allows you to delete tables along with the database by using the following command:

```
hive> DROP DATABASE temp_database CASCADE;
```

In the preceding command, the cascade functionality allows you to drop all the tables in the database as well as the actual database itself.

Altering Databases

Altering a database means making changes in the existing database. You can alter a database by using the following command:

```
hive> ALTER DATABASE temp_database;
> SET DBPROPERTIES ('owner' ='Joseph ');
```

Alters temp_database

In the preceding command, we are altering `'DBPROPERTIES'` of the `temp_database`. It should be noted that, in any case, Hive does not allow you to alter the name of the database.

Creating Tables

You can create a table in a database by using the CREATE command, as discussed earlier. Now, let's learn how to provide the complete definition of a table in a database by using the following commands:

```
Use temp_database
CREATE TABLE IF NOT EXISTS employee (ename STRING, salary FLOAT, designation STRING)
TBLPROPERTIES ('owner' = 'Joseph', 'created at' = '05/02/2015') ROW FORMAT DELIMITED
FIELDS TERMINATED BY '\t'
LINES TERMINATED BY '\n'
LOCATION '/user/hive/warehouse/temp_database.db/employee' STORED AS TEXTFILE;
```

In the preceding commands, `temp_database` is first set and then the table is created with the name employee. In the employee table, the columns (ename, salary, and designation) are specified with their respective data types. The `TBLPROPERTIES` is a set of key-value properties. C comments are also added in the table to provide more details.

External Table

External tables are created by accessing the query written in files stored on some other computer system. You can specify the location of a data file by using the `LOCATION` keyword while creating the external table. Execute the following commands for creating an external table:

```
CREATE EXTERNAL TABLE IF NOT EXISTS employee external (name STRING, percentage
FLOAT, grade STRING)
TBLPROPERTIES ('owner' = 'Joseph', 'created at' = '05/02/2015') ROW FORMAT DELIMITED
FIELDS TERMINATED BY '\t'
LINES TERMINATED BY '\n'
LOCATION '/user/hive/warehouse/details.db/student' STORED AS TEXTFILE;
```

The concept of external table proves to be very useful when HDFS has huge data files, making copies of which is not feasible due to space constraints.

Creating a Table Using the Existing Schema

You can also create a table having the same schema as another table by using the following command:

```
CREATE TABLE details.employee LIKE details.student;
```

In the preceding command, the schema of the student table present in the details database gets copied in the employee table present in the same database. The name of the table to which the schema gets copied is specified before the `LIKE` keyword, and the name of the table from which the schema gets copied is specified after the `LIKE` keyword.

You can know the structure of the existing table by using the following command:

```
hive> DESCRIBE details.student;  ← Describes the details of the student table
```

The `DESCRIBE` command shows the structure of the student table present in the details database.

NOTE

You can also use the short notation of DESCRIBE as DESC for knowing the structure of the table.

You can also find the details about any column present in a table by using the following command:

```
hive> DESCRIBE details.student.name;
```

In the preceding command, the name of the column is specified with the table name using a dot between them. This will return the data type of the name column of the student table.

Partitioning Tables

Partitioning of a table means dividing a table into different sections (also called partitions) in order to view the required data. It helps you to create and view only a particular set of data of a table. You can create partitions in a table by using the PARTITIONED BY keyword. Consider the following command:

```
CREATE TABLE employee(
ename STRING,
sal FLOAT )
PARTITIONED BY (designation STRING);
```

Creates partition in the employee table

Here, we are creating a table named employee with the ename and sal columns. The table is partitioned from the column designation.

Dropping Tables

You can delete or drop a table by using the following command:

```
hive> DROP TABLE IF EXISTS students;
```

Deletes students table

On execution, the preceding command deletes the students table.

Altering Tables

Altering a table means modifying or changing an existing table. By altering a table, you can modify the metadata associated with the table. The table can be modified by using the ALTER TABLE statement. The altering of a table allows you to:

- Rename tables
- Modify columns
- Add new columns
- Delete some columns
- Change table properties
- Alter tables for adding partitions

Let's now learn how to perform the preceding operations by using the ALTER TABLE statement.

Rename Tables

You can rename a table by using the following command:

```
hive>ALTER TABLE employees RENAME TO employees_new;
```

Renames a table from employees to employees_new

In the preceding command, the employees table gets renamed to employees_new.

Modify Columns

You can modify the name of a column in Hive by using the following command:

```
ALTER TABLE employees_new
CHANGE COLUMN ename emp_name STRING;
```

In the preceding command, the column, ename, gets renamed to emp_name.

Add Columns

In Hive, you can also add an extra column to a given table by using the `ADD COLUMN` statement:

```
ALTER TABLE employees_new ADD COLUMNS (sales_month);
```
← Adds the sales_month column

The preceding command adds an extra column with the name `sales_month` in the `employees` table. By default, the new column is added at the last position before the partitioned columns.

Replace Columns

You can replace all the existing columns with new columns in a table by using the following command:

```
ALTER TABLE employees_new REPLACE COLUMNS (ename STRING, projectname STRING,
plocation INT);
```

The `REPLACE COLUMNS` statement is used to delete all the existing columns and add new columns in their place.

Let's now learn how to use Hive DDL statements.

Using Hive DDL Statements

SCENARIO

Mark works as a team leader of the research department in Argon Technology. His department deals with data on stocks and shares and requires running a set of standard queries on Big Data in order to prepare some ad-hoc reports. Instead of writing the MapReduce source code for the desired results, Mark decides to use Hive for writing queries similar to SQL on Big Data. His team compiles the data available in the CSV file format and saves it in a sequence format.

Let's learn how to write HQL queries for importing data given in a text file named `Sample1.txt` into HDFS first as a CSV table named `stock_data`, and then copy it in a sequence table named `stock_data2`.

Log into Hive and type the following command on the terminal to go to the `bin` folder of the Hive directory:

```
cd ~/$HIVE_HOME/bin/
./hive
```

Now, let us practice some generic commands on Hive.

1. To view a list of all the databases in Hive, type the following command on the terminal:

```
show databases;
```

The preceding command, along with its output, is shown in Figure 12.3:

Figure 12.3: Showing the List of Databases

2. To get a list of tables in a database, type the following command:

```
Show tables [IN database_name]
```

3. To create a database in Hive, type the following command on the terminal:

```
create database IF NOT EXISTS demo;
```

The preceding command, along with its output, is shown in Figure 12.4:

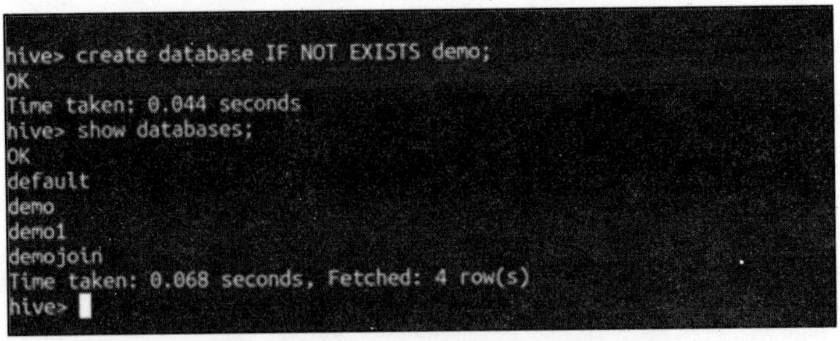

Figure 12.4: Creating a Database in Hive

4. To use the demo database in Hive, type the following command:

```
USE demo
```

5. To create a table named `stock_data`, type the following command on the terminal:

```
create table stock_data(Date1 string,Open float,High float,Low
float,Close float,Volume int,AdjClose float)row format delimited fields
terminated by ',' stored as textfile;
```

6. To create a table in Hive for sequence file, type the following command on the terminal:

```
create table stock_data2(Date1 string, Open float, High float, Low
float, Close float, Volume int, AdjClose float) stored as sequencefile;
```

7. To view the structure of the `stock_data` table and the records stored in it, type the following command:

```
describe stock_data;
```

The operations of creating the `stock_data` table and viewing its structure are shown in Figure 12.5:

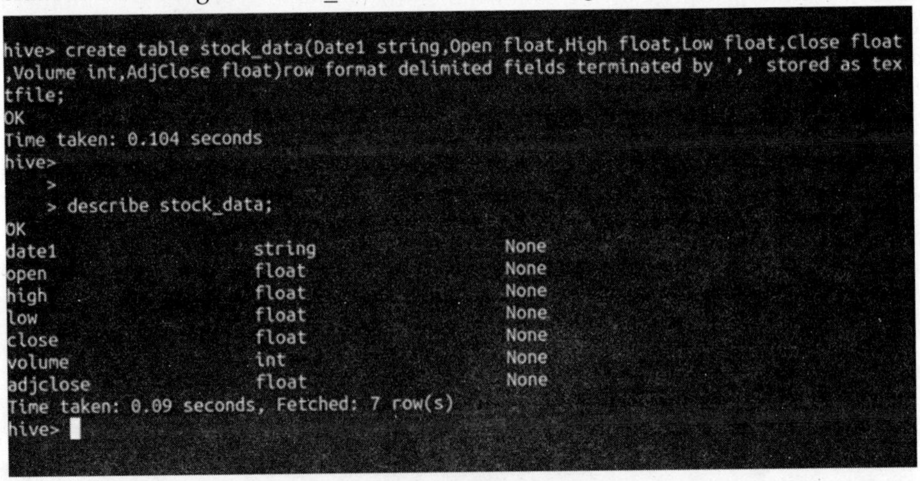

Figure 12.5: Creating and Describing a Table in Hive

Data Manipulation in Hive

After specifying the database schema and creating a database, the data can be modified by using a set of procedures/mechanisms defined by a special language known as Data Manipulation Language (DML). Data can be manipulated in the following ways:

- Loading files into tables
- Inserting data into Hive table from queries
- Updating existing tables
- Deleting records in tables

Let's learn about each of these mechanisms in detail.

Loading Files into Tables

While loading data into tables, Hive does not perform any type of transformations. The data load operations in Hive are, at present, pure copy/move operations, which move data files from one location to another. You can upload data into Hive tables from the local file system as well as from HDFS. The syntax of loading data from files into tables is as follows:

```
LOAD DATA [LOCAL] INPATH 'filepath' [OVERWRITE] INTO TABLE tablename [PARTITION
(partcol1=val1, partcol2=val2 ...)]
```

When the `LOCAL` keyword is specified in the `LOAD DATA` command, Hive searches for the local directory. If the `LOCAL` keyword is not used, Hive checks the directory on HDFS. On the other hand, when the `OVERWRITE` keyword is specified, it deletes all the files under Hive's warehouse directory for the given table. After that, the latest files get uploaded. If you do not specify the `OVERWRITE` keyword, the latest files are added in the already existing folder.

Inserting Data into Tables

You can also insert data into tables through queries by using the `INSERT` command. The syntax of using the `INSERT` command is as follows:

```
INSERT OVERWRITE TABLE tablename1 [PARTITION (partcol1=val1, partcol2=val2 ...) [IF
NOT EXISTS]] select_statement1 FROM from_statement;
INSERT INTO TABLE tablename1 [PARTITION (partcol1=val1, partcol2=val2 ...)]
select_statement1 FROM from_statement;
Hive extension (multiple inserts):
FROM from_statement
INSERT OVERWRITE TABLE tablename1 [PARTITION (partcol1=val1, partcol2=val2 ...) [IF
NOT EXISTS]] select_statement1
[INSERT OVERWRITE TABLE tablename2 [PARTITION ... [IF NOT EXISTS]]
select_statement2]
[INSERT INTO TABLE tablename2 [PARTITION ...] select_statement2] ...;
FROM from_statement
INSERT INTO TABLE tablename1 [PARTITION (partcol1=val1, partcol2=val2 ...)]
select_statement1
[INSERT INTO TABLE tablename2 [PARTITION ...] select_statement2]
[INSERT OVERWRITE TABLE tablename2 [PARTITION ... [IF NOT EXISTS]]
select_statement2] ...;

Hive extension (dynamic partition inserts):
INSERT OVERWRITE TABLE tablename PARTITION (partcol1[=val1], partcol2[=val2] ...)
select_statement FROM from_statement;
INSERT INTO TABLE tablename PARTITION (partcol1[=val1], partcol2[=val2] ...)
select_statement FROM from_statement;
```

In the preceding syntax, the `INSERT OVERWRITE` statement overwrites the current data in the table or partition. The `IF NOT EXISTS` statement is given for a partition. On the other hand, the `INSERT INTO` statement either appends the table or creates a partition without modifying the existing data. The insert operation can be performed on a table or a partition. You can also specify multiple insert clauses in the same qucry.

Consider two tables, `T1` and `T2`. We want to copy the `sal` column from `T2` to `T1` by using the `INSERT` command. It can be done as follows:

```
CREATE TABLE T1 (sal STRING);
INSERT OVERWRITE TABLE T1 SELECT sal FROM T2;
```

Here, we use the keyword `OVERWRITE`. It means that any previous data in table `T1` will be deleted, and new data from table `T2` will be inserted. If we want to retain the previous data in table `T1`, we can use the following command:

```
INSERT INTO TABLE T1 SELECT sal FROM T2;
```

Static Partition Insertion

Static partition insertion refers to the task of inserting data into a table by specifying a partition column value. Consider the following example:

```
INSERT OVERWRITE TABLE T1 PARTITION (month = "JANUARY") SELECT sal FROM T2;
```

In the preceding command, we are inserting data into the `JANUARY` partition of the `T1` table.

Dynamic Partition Insertion

In dynamic partition insertion, you need to specify a list of partition column names in the `PARTITION()` clause along with the optional column values. A dynamic partition column always has a corresponding input column in the `SELECT` statement. If the `SELECT` statement has multiple column names, the dynamic partition columns must be specified at the end of the columns and in the same order in which they appear in the `PARTITION()` clause. By default, the feature of dynamic partition is disabled.

The following command shows an example of dynamic partition insertion:

```
INSERT OVERWRITE TABLE myt PARTITION (ds, hr) SELECT key, value, ds, hr FROM mysrc
WHERE ds is not null and hr>15;
```

In the preceding command, dynamic partition insertion takes place by including all ds and hr columns. In the `SELECT` statement, these columns are listed at the end, in the same order in which they appear in the `PARTITION` clause.

Table 12.5 shows the relevant configuration properties for dynamic partition inserts:

Table 12.5: Various Properties of Dynamic Partition Inserts

Property	Description
hive.exec.max.dynamic.partitions.pernode	This value gives the maximum number of dynamic partitions created by each mapper or reducer (the default value is 100).
hive.exec.max.dynamic.partitions	This value gives the maximum number of dynamic partitions that can be created by a single DML operation (the default value is 1000).

Table 12.5: Various Properties of Dynamic Partition Inserts

Property	Description
hive.exec.max.created.files	This value gives the maximum number of files that can be generated by all mappers or reducers (the default value is 100000).
hive.exec.dynamic.partition	This parameter needs to be set to TRUE to enable dynamic data partitions. The default value is FALSE.
hive.exec.dynamic.partition.mode	This parameter needs to be set to nonstrict so that all partitions can be determined dynamically. The default value is STRICT.

You can set the various parameters in the following manner:

```
hive> SET hive.exec.dynamic.partition = true;
hive> SET hive.exec.dynamic.partition.mode = nonstrict;
hive> INSERT OVERWRITE TABLE log1
        PARTITION (day)
        SELECT * FROM log2;
```

Inserting Data into Local Files

Sometimes, you might require to save the result of the `SELECT` query in flat files so that you do not have to execute the queries again and again. Consider the following example:

Overwrites data from the employee table to myfile

```
INSERT OVERWRITE LOCAL DIRECTORY '/usr/local/myfile' SELECT * FROM employee;
```

The preceding command inserts the `SELECT` query result of the employee table in the `myfile` file of the local directory.

Creating and Inserting Data into a Table Using a Single Query

In Hive, you can create and load data into a table using a single query as follows:

```
CREATE TABLE T1
AS SELECT name, sal, month FROM T2;
```

Here, a new table called `T1` would be created, and the schema for the table would be three columns named `name, sal,` and `month`, with the same data types as mentioned in the `T2` table.

Update in Hive

The update operation in Hive is available from Hive 0.14 version. The `update` operation can only be performed on tables that support the ACID property. The syntax for performing the update operation in Hive is as follows:

```
UPDATE tablename SET column = value [, column = value ...] [WHERE expression]
```

In the preceding syntax, the name of the table will be followed by the `UPDATE` statement. Only those rows that match with the `WHERE` clause will be updated. You must note that the partitioning and bucketing columns cannot be updated.

Consider the following update operation performed on the `sal` column:

Updates sal = 20000, where empid is 10001 in the employee table

```
Update employee set sal=20,000 where empid='10001'
```

In the preceding command, the salary of the employee whose `empid` is 10001 is updated.

Delete in Hive

The delete operation is available in Hive from the Hive 0.14 version. The delete operation can only be performed on those tables that support the ACID property. The syntax for performing the delete operation is as follows:

```
DELETE FROM tablename [WHERE expression]
```

In the preceding syntax, only those rows that match the `WHERE` clause will be deleted. The table name from which the records are deleted are specified after the `DELETE FROM` statement. To delete the records of an employee whose `empid` is 10001, type the following command:

```
DELETE FROM employee where empid=10001
```

Deletes the record from the employee table where empid is 10001

When the preceding command is executed, the records of the employee whose employee id is 10001 get deleted.

Using Hive DML Statements

SCENARIO

Mark now wants to load the data of the `sample1.txt` file into the `stock_data` table. He also needs to overwrite the data stored in the `stock_data2` table with the data stored in the `stock_data` table.

The data stored in a table can be modified either by using the `LOAD` command or by using the `INSERT` command. The general syntax of the `LOAD` command is as follows:

```
LOAD DATA [LOCAL] INPATH 'filepath' [OVERWRITE] INTO TABLE tablename
[PARTITION (partcol1=val1, partcol2=val2 ...)]
```

Mark needs to type the following command on the terminal to access the data stored in the `stock_data` table:

```
load data local inpath '~/DataSet/Hive/sample1.txt' into table
stock_data;
```

The preceding command, along with its output, is shown in Figure 12.6:

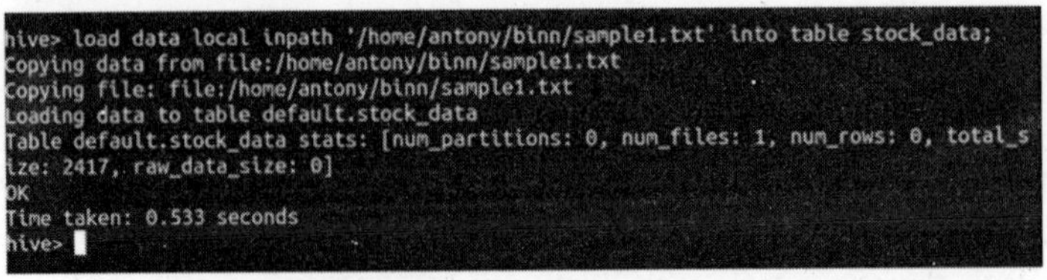

Figure 12.6: Accessing Table Data in Hive

To overwrite the content of the table, Mark uses the `INSERT` command as follows:

```
INSERT OVERWRITE TABLE tablename1 [PARTITION (partcol1=val1,
partcol2=val2 ...) [IF NOT EXISTS]] select_statement1 FROM from_
statement;
INSERT INTO TABLE tablename1 [PARTITION (partcol1=val1,
partcol2=val2 ...)] select_statement1 FROM from_statement;
```

Mark types the following command on the terminal to overwrite the data stored in the `stock_data2` table with the data stored in the `stock_data` table:

```
insert overwrite table stock_data2 select * from stock_data;
```

The preceding command, along with its output, is shown in Figure 12.7:

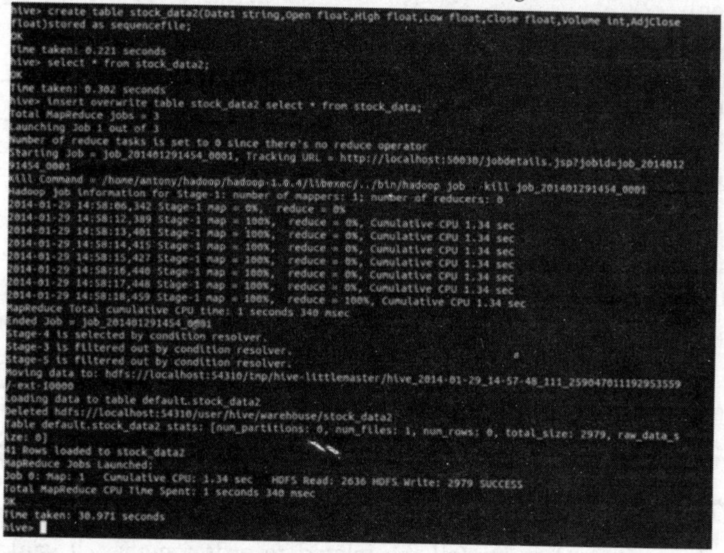

Figure 12.7: Copying the Data in Hive from One Table into Another

You have successfully created two tables, `stock_data` and `stock_data2`, and loaded data in the CSV format in the first file and as a sequence file in the second file.

Data Retrieval Queries

Hive allows you to perform data retrieval queries by using the `SELECT` command along with various types of operators and clauses.

In this section, you learn about the following:

- Using the SELECT command
- Using the WHERE clause
- Using the GROUP BY clause
- Using the HAVING clause
- Using the LIMIT clause
- Executing HiveQL queries

Using the SELECT Command

The `SELECT` statement is the most common operation in SQL. You can filter the required columns, rows, or both. The syntax for using the `SELECT` command is as follows:

```
[WITH CommonTableExpression (, CommonTableExpression)*]
SELECT [ALL | DISTINCT] select_expr, select_expr, ...
FROM table_reference
[WHERE where_condition]
[GROUP BY col_list]
[CLUSTER BY col_list  |
[DISTRIBUTE BY col_list]
[SORT BY col_list]]
[LIMIT number]
```

The following query retrieves all the columns and rows from table, `mydemotable`:

```
SELECT * FROM mydemotable
```

Retrieves all columns and all rows from mydemotable

Using the WHERE Clause

The `WHERE` clause is used to search records of a table on the basis of a given condition. This clause returns a boolean result. For example, a query can return only those sales records that have an amount greater than 15000 from the US region. Hive also supports a number of operators (such as > and <) in the `WHERE` clause. The following query shows an example of using the `WHERE` clause:

```
SELECT * FROM sales WHERE amount > 15000 AND region = "US"
```

Retrieves sales records where amount is greater than 15000 and region is equal to US

Using the GROUP BY Clause

The `GROUP BY` clause is used to put all the related records together. It can also be used with aggregate functions. Often, it is required to group the resultsets in complex queries. In such scenarios, the '`GROUP BY`' clause can be used.

For example, if you wish to calculate the average `marks` obtained by the students from all semesters, you may use the `GROUP BY` clause as shown in the following example:

```
SELECT sem, avg(marks) FROM student
GROUP BY sem;
```

The following example helps you to count the number of distinct users by gender:

```
INSERT OVERWRITE TABLE pv_gender_sum
SELECT pv_users.gender, count (DISTINCT pv_users.userid)FROM pv_users
GROUP BY pv_users.gender;
```

You can also use aggregate functions at the same time, but no two aggregations can have different `DISTINCT` columns.

It should be noted that when the `GROUP BY` clause is used with the `SELECT` query, the `SELECT` statement can only include columns included in the `GROUP BY` clause.

The following queries create a table and use the `GROUP BY` clause on it:

```
CREATE TABLE mydemotable(x INTEGER, y INTGER);
SELECT   x,   sum(y) FROM   mydemotable
GROUP BY   a;
```

Using the HAVING Clause

The `HAVING` clause is used to specify a condition on the use of the `GROUP BY` clause. The use of the `HAVING` clause is added in the version 0.7.0 of Hive. The following query shows an example of using the `HAVING` clause:

```
SELECT clmn 1 FROM mydemotable GROUP BY clmn1 HAVING SUM(clmn2) > 15
```

The preceding command displays the `clmn1` column of the `mydemotable` table grouped by `clmn1` where the sum of `clmn2` is greater than `15`.

Using the LIMIT Clause

The `LIMIT` clause is used to restrict the number of rows to be returned. The rows that are to be returned are chosen at random. The following query returns 8 rows from `mydemotable` at random:

```
SELECT * FROM mydemotable LIMIT 8
```

Restricts the number of rows to 8

Executing HiveQL Queries

SCENARIO

The research department of Argon Technology is asked to query the `stock_data` file in HDFS. Mark decides to use HiveQL queries for accessing and manipulating HDFS data.

Let's perform the following steps to query the `stock_data` file:

1. Type the following command on the terminal to go to the `bin` folder of the Hive directory:

```
cd $HIVE_HOME/bin/
./hive
```

The preceding command performs the logging procedure in Hive, as shown in Figure 12.8:

Figure 12.8: Logging into Hive

2. To retrieve the data stored in the `stock_data` table on a particular date, you can type the following HiveQL command on the terminal:

```
select * from stock_data where date1="2013-12-12";
```

The preceding command, along with its output, is shown in Figure 12.9:

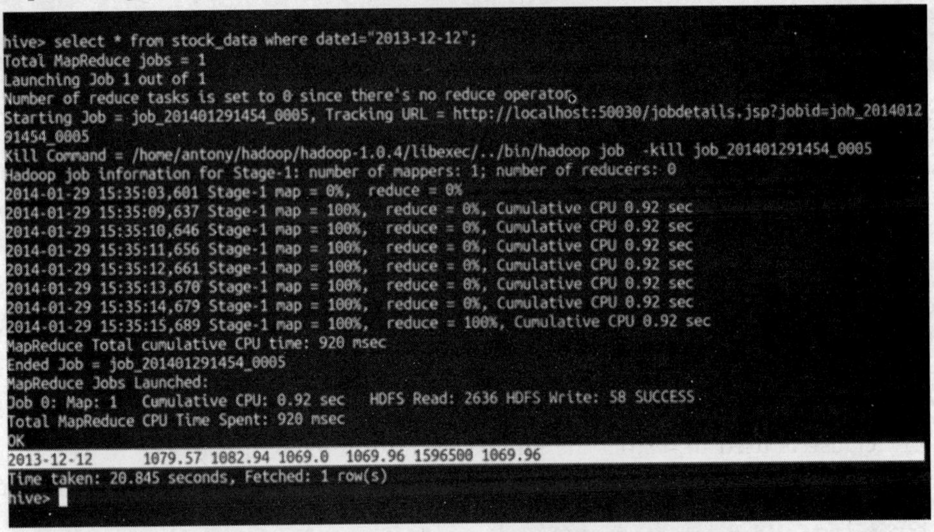

Figure 12.9: Retrieving Records from an HDFS Table

3. In order to retrieve a fixed number of records from a table, you need to specify its limit. Type the following command on the terminal to retrieve three records from the `stock_data` table, having volume less than 1,500,000:

```
select * from stock_data where volume<1500000 limit 3;
```

The preceding command, along with its output, is shown in Figure 12.10:

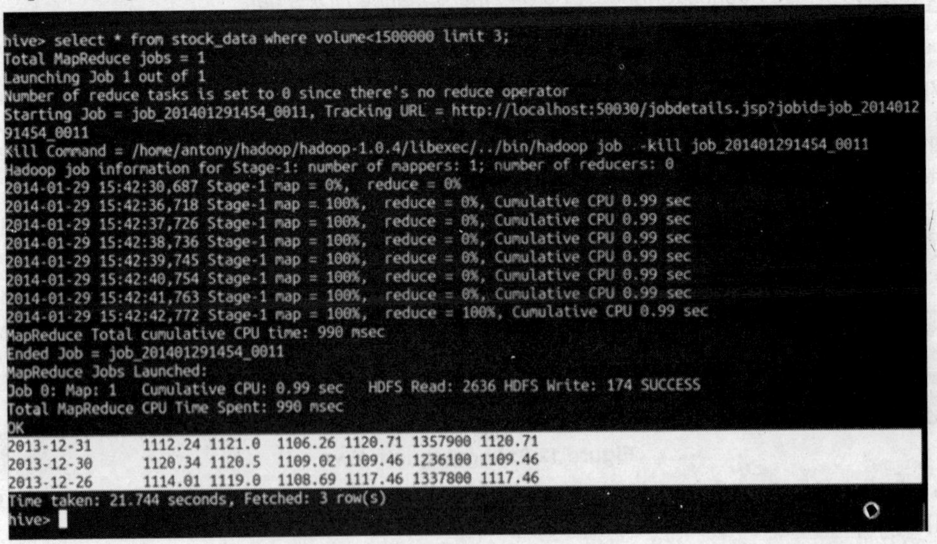

Figure 12.10: Retrieving Specific Number of Records from an HDFS Table

Using JOINS in Hive

Hive supports joining of one or more tables to aggregate information. The various joins supported by Hive are:

- Inner joins
- Outer joins

Inner Joins

In case of inner joins, only the records satisfying the given condition get selected. All the other records get discarded. Figure 12.11 illustrates the concept of inner joins:

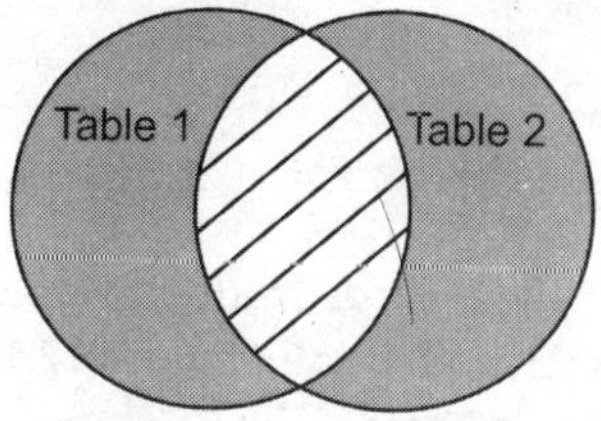

Figure 12.11: Inner Joins

Let's take an example to describe the concept of inner joins. Consider two tables, order and customer. Table 12.6 lists the data of the order table:

Table 12.6: Data of the order Table

order_id	cust_id
1	12
2	15
3	16
4	20
5	25

The above table contains the order id (`order_id`) and the corresponding customer id (`cust_id`).

Table 12.7 lists the data of the customer table:

Table 12.7: Data of the customer Table

cust_id	cust_name
12	Bob
15	Joseph
20	Lisa
23	Monty

The above table contains the customer id (`cust_id`) and the corresponding customer name (`cust_name`).

To know the names of the customers who have placed orders, we need to take the inner join of the two tables, as follows:

```
SELECT order.order_id, customer.cust_name
FROM  order o
JOIN
customer c
ON ( o.cust_id = c.cust_id);
```

The output of the previous command is as follows:

```
order_id                                    cust_name
1                                           Bob
2                                           Joseph
4                                           Lisa
```

Outer Joins

Sometimes, you need to retrieve all the records from one table and only some records from the other table. In such cases, you have to use the outer join. Figure 12.12 illustrates the concept of outer joins:

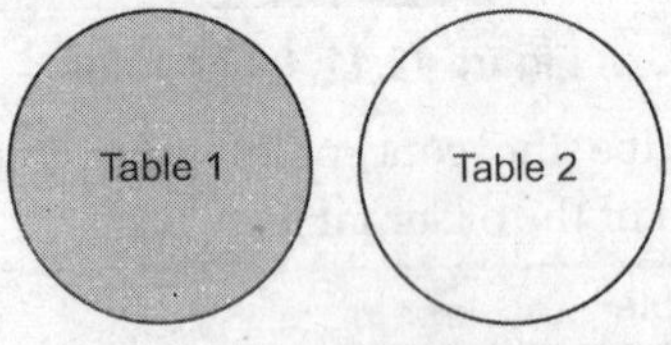

Figure 12.12: Outer Joins

Outer joins are of three types:

- Right Outer Join
- Left Outer Join
- Full Outer Join

Right Outer Join

In this type of join, all the records from the table on the right side of the join are retained. Figure 12.13 illustrates the concept of right outer join:

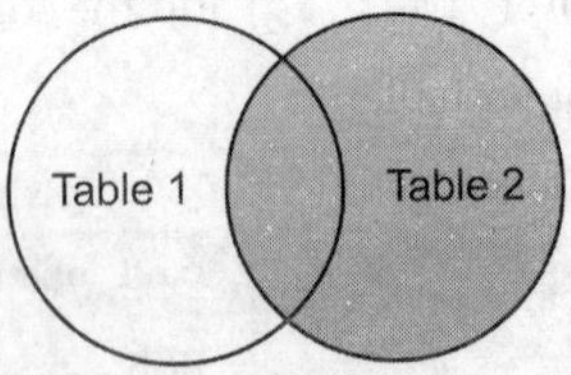

Figure 12.13: Right Outer Join

The query involving right outer join can be written as follows:

```
SELECT  order.order_id, customer.cust_name
        FROM    order o
RIGHT OUTER JOIN
customer  c
ON ( o.cust_id = c.cust_id);
```

The output of the preceding query is as follows:

```
order_id                    cust_name
1                           Bob
2                           Joseph
4                           Lisa
NULL                        Monty
```

You can see that the `order_id` field for the customer 'Monty' is marked as `NULL`. It is because there is no related record matching the given customer id in the `order` table.

Left Outer Join

In this type of join, all the records from the table on the left side of the join are retained. Figure 12.14 illustrates the concept of left outer joins:

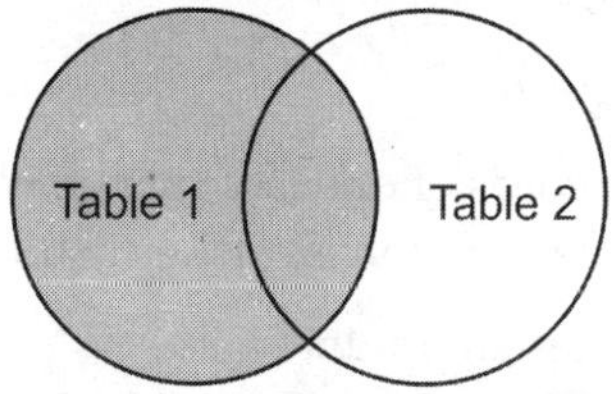

Figure 12.14: Left Outer Join

The query involving left outer joins can be written as follows:

```
SELECT order.order_id, customer.cust_name
FROM order o
LEFT OUTER JOIN
customer c
ON ( o.cust_id = c.cust_id);
```

Here, all the entries from the `order` table are present in the output. A field is kept blank as there is no corresponding value for the key in the `customer` table. The preceding query gives the following output:

```
order_id               cust_id
1                      Bob
2                      Joseph
3                      NULL
4                      Lisa
5                      NULL
```

Full Outer Join

In this case, all the fields from both tables are included. For the entries that do not have any match, a `NULL` value would be displayed.

Figure 12.15 illustrates the concept of full outer join:

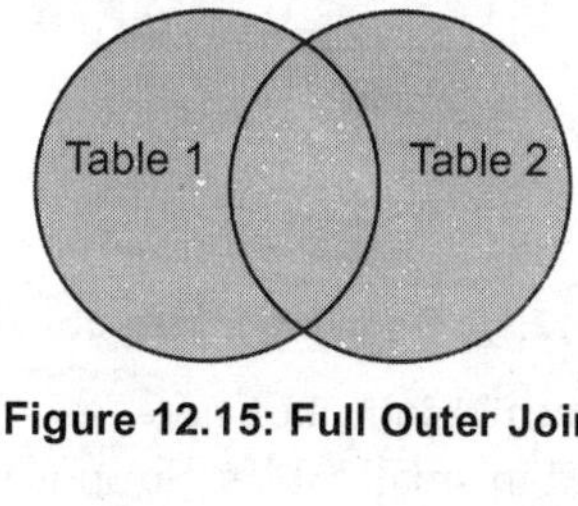

Figure 12.15: Full Outer Join

The query involving a full outer join can be written as follows:

```
SELECT order.order_id, customer.cust_name
FROM order o
FULL OUTER JOIN
customer c
ON ( o.cust_id = c.cust_id);
```

The preceding query gives the following output:

```
order_ id          cust_id
1                  Bob
2                  Joseph
3                  NULL
4                  Lisa
5                  NULL
NULL               Monty
```

Cartesian Product Joins

In cartesian product joins, all the records of one table are combined with another table in all possible combinations. This type of join does not involve any key column to join the tables.

The following is a query with a Cartesian product joint:

```
SELECT * FROM order JOIN customer;
```

Joins the order table with the customer table in all combinations

Map-Side Joins

In a map-side join operation in Hive, the job is assigned to a Map Reduce task that consists of two stages: Map and Reduce. At the Map stage, the data is read from join tables and the 'join key' and 'join value' pair are returned to an intermediate file. This intermediate file is then sorted and merged in the shuffle stage. At the Reduce stage, the sorted result is taken as input, and the joining task is completed.

Figure 12.16 shows the map join procedure in Hive:

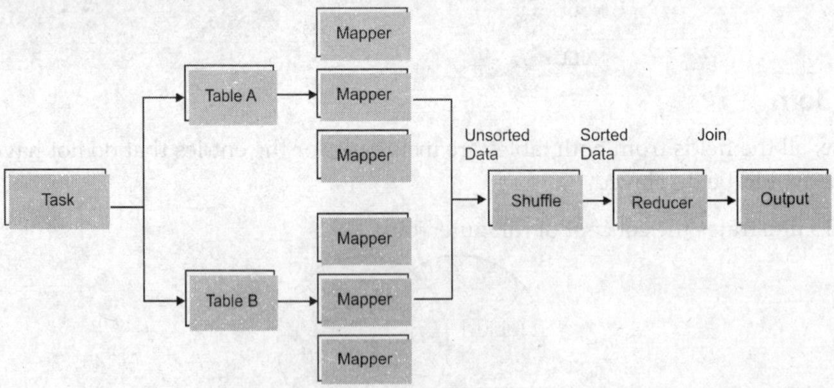

Figure 12.16: Showing a Map Join in Hive

A map-side join is similar to the normal join, but here, all the tasks are performed by the mapper alone. The map-side join is preferred in small tables. Suppose you have two tables, out of which one is a small table. Now, when a map reduce task is submitted, a Map Reduce local task will be created to read the data of the small table from HDFS and store it into an in-memory hash table. After reading the data, the Map Reduce local task serializes the in-memory hash table into a hash table file.

In the next stage, the main join Map Reduce task runs and moves the data from the hash table file to the Hadoop distributed cache, which supplies these files to each mapper's local disk. It means that all the mappers can load this hash table file back into the memory and continue with the join work.

Figure 12.17 shows the map-side join in Hive:

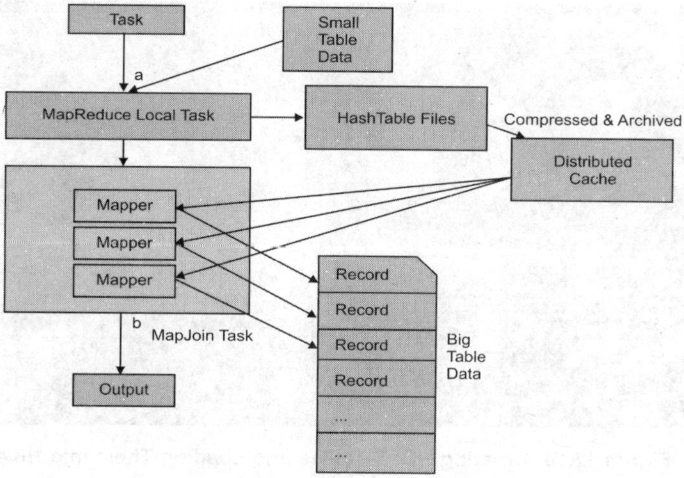

Figure 12.17: Map-Side Join in Hive

In a map-side join, the small table is read only once, and if multiple mappers are running on the same machine, the distributed cache needs to push only one copy of the hash table file to this machine. Map-side joins help in improving the performance of a task by decreasing the time to finish the task. Moreover, it helps in minimizing the cost involved in sorting and merging in the shuffle and reduce stages.

NOTE

Map-side joins are not suitable for tables that store huge data.

Joining Tables

You can combine the data of two or more tables in Hive by using HiveQL queries. For this, we need to create tables and load them into Hive from HDFS.

Let us create two tables, `Post_data_uk` and `Post_data_us`, in HDFS through HQL.

1. To create the table `Post_data_uk`, type the following command on the terminal:

```
create table Post_data_uk(first_name string,last_name
string,company_name string,address string,city string,county
string,postal string,phone1 string,phone2 string,email string,web
string)row format delimited fields terminated by ',' stored as
textfile;
```

2. Type the following command on the terminal to create the table `Post_data_us`:

```
create table Post_data_us(first_name string,last_name
string,company_name string,address string,city string,county
```

```
string,postal string,phone1 string,phone2 string,email string,web
string)row format delimited fields terminated by ',' stored as
textfile;
```

3. To load the two tables, `Post_data_uk` and `Post_data_us`, type the following commands:

```
load data local inpath '~/DataSet/Hive /uk_data.txt' into table
Post_data_uk;
load data local inpath '~/DataSet/Hive /us_data.txt' into table
Post_data_us;
```

The preceding commands, along with their outputs, are shown in Figure 12.18:

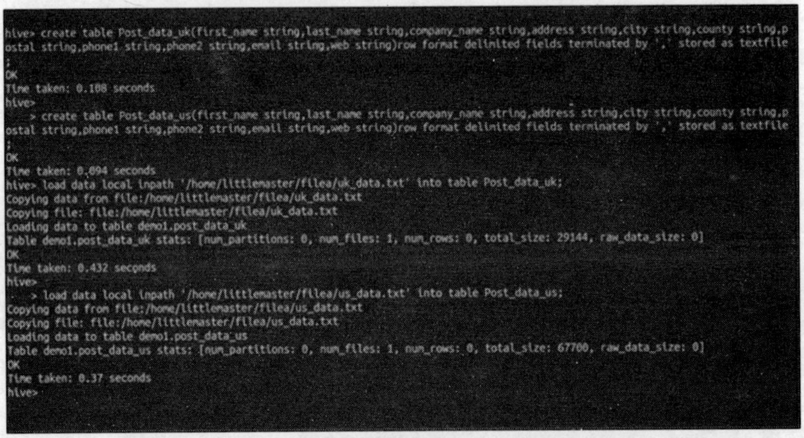

Figure 12.18: Creating HDFS Tables and Loading Them into Hive

4. To perform join operations on tables, we have specific HQL queries. To join the `Post_data_uk` table with the `Post_data_us` table on the basis of the `first_name` column, type the following command:

```
select us.first_name from Post_data_uk uk join Post_data_us us on
(us.first_name=uk.first_name);
```

The preceding command, along with its output, is shown in Figure 12.19:

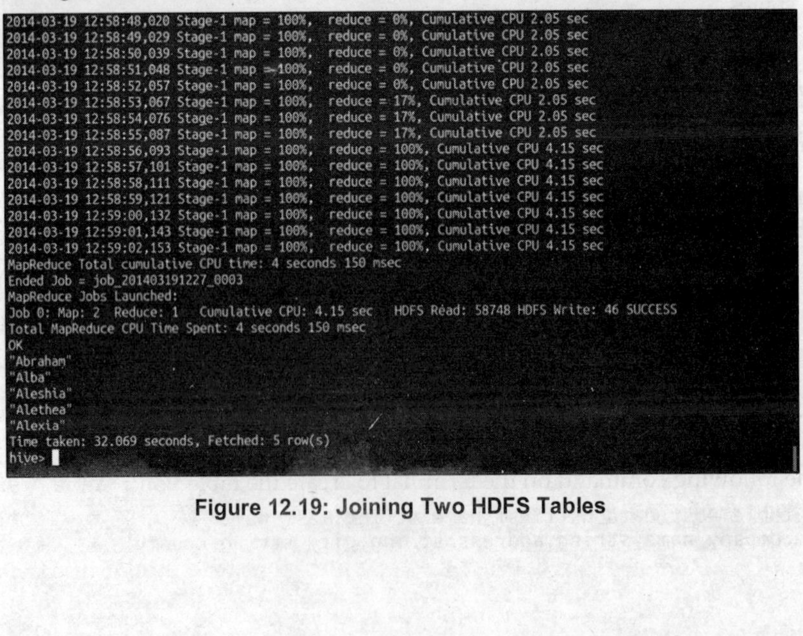

Figure 12.19: Joining Two HDFS Tables

5. Type the following command to select five records after performing the left outer join operation on the two tables, namely, `Post_data_uk` and `Post_data_us`:

```
select uk.company_name from Post_data_uk uk left outer join Post_data_us us on
(us.first_name=uk.first_name) limit 5;
```

Note that here we have limited the results to five entries. The preceding command, along with its output, is shown in Figure 12.20:

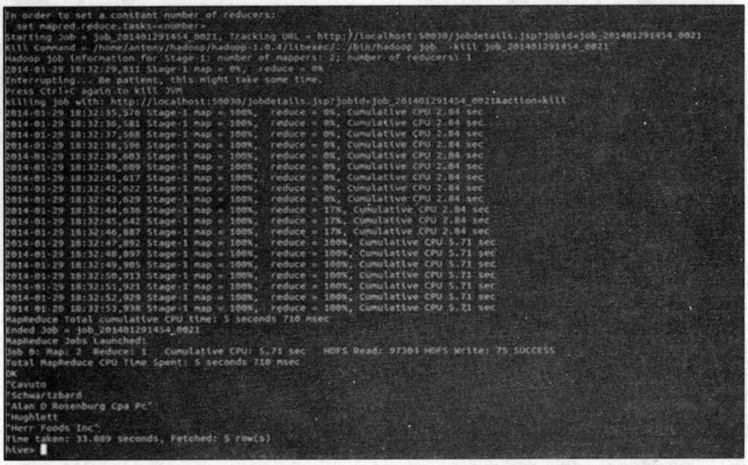

Figure 12.20: Performing the Left Outer Join Operation on Two HDFS Tables

6. To perform the right outer join on the tables, type the following command on the terminal:

```
select us.company_name from Post_data_uk uk right outer join Post_data_us us on
(us.first_name=uk.first_name) limit 5;
```

The preceding command, along with its output, is shown in Figure 12.21:

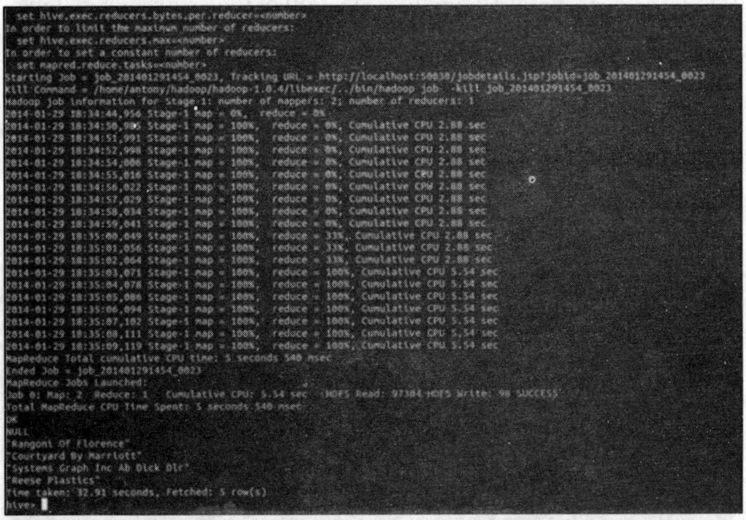

Figure 12.21: Performing the Right Outer Join Operation on Two HDFS Tables

7. To perform a full outer join operation, type the following command on the terminal:

```
select us.company_name,uk.company_name from Post_data_uk uk full
outer join Post_data_us us on (us.first_name=uk.first_name) limit 5;
```

The preceding command, along with its output, is shown in Figure 12.22:

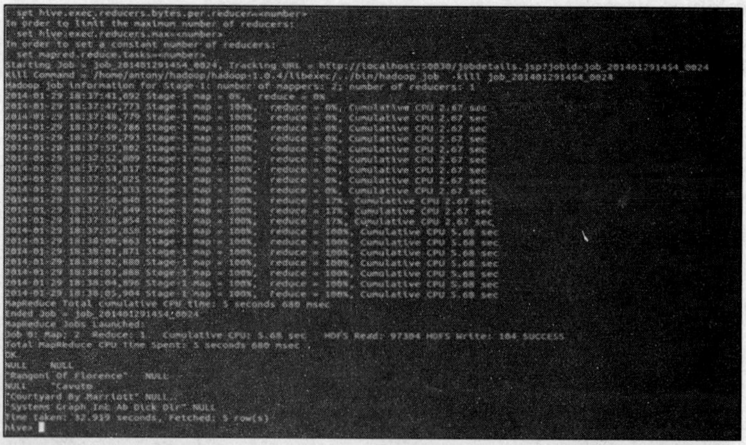

Figure 12.22: Performing the Full Outer Join Operation on Two HDFS Tables

You can also create partitions on the records stored in HDFS tables through HQL queries. For this, let's create a table named `Post_data` with partitions.

8. Type the following command to create the `Post_data` table with partitions:

```
create table Post_data(first_name string,last_name
string,company_name string,address string,city string, state
string,postal string,phone1 string,phone2 string,email string,web
string) partitioned by(country string) row format delimited
fields terminated by ',' stored as textfile;
```

The preceding command creates a table that would be partitioned on the basis of a string, `country`. To load data from the `post_uk` file in the first partition of the `Post_data` table, type:

```
load data local inpath '~/DataSet/Hive /uk_data.txt' overwrite into table Post_data
partition(country='uk');
```

To load data from the `post_us` file in the second partition of the `Post_data` table, type:

```
load data local inpath '~/DataSet/Hive /us_data.txt' overwrite into table Post_data
partition(country='us');
```

The preceding commands, along with their outputs, are shown in Figure 12.23:

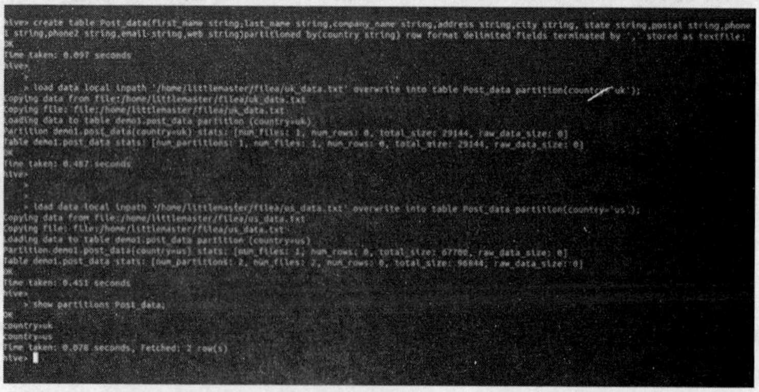

Figure 12.23: Creating Partitions on Tables and Loading Data into the Partitions

The `post_data` file now contains the data given in both the `post_uk` and `post_us` datasets.

Bucketing

Bucketing is the other method for partitioning, but there is a difference between both the methods i.e. partitioning and bucketing. In partitioning, we always create a partitioning table that holds each unique value of column. But, sometimes, there is a problem in creating the partitions as there are so many values that are unique in nature due to which we need to make a lot of small partitions. But, when we use bucketing, we can limit it to an extent of number of your choice and extract your data to that bucket. In Hive, partitions are basically the directories, whereas bucket is a file.

In Hive, bucketing is not automatically defined; **bucketing property** need to be set before using it. `set.hive.enforce.bucketing=true` is the property that should be "true" to use bucketing.

Let's perform the following steps to insert tables in bucket:

1. Create a table, say, abhitbl to store your data:

```
create external table abhitbl (EmployeeID Int,FirstName String,Designation
String,Salary Int,Department String) row format delimited fields terminated by ","
location '/user/admin/Hive';
```

2. Now, create a bucketed table:

```
create table emp_bucket (EmployeeID Int,FirstName String,Designation String,Salary
Int,Department String) clustered by (department) into 3 buckets row format delimited
fields terminated by ",";
```

3. Load the data from abhitbl to the bucketed table:

```
from abhitbl insert into table emp_bucket
select employeeid,firstname,designation,salary,department;
```

4. Check how many data files have been created in Hive metastore:

```
abhiadmin@hadoopnode1:~$ hadoop fs -ls /user/hive/warehouse/emp_bucket
found 3 items
-rw-r- - r--   3 admin hadoop   218 2015-08-18 10:08 /user/hive/warehouse/emp_bucket/000000_0
-rw-r- - r--   3 admin hadoop   218 2015-08-18 10:08 /user/hive/warehouse/emp_bucket/000001_0
-rw-r- - r--   3 admin hadoop   218 2015-08-18 10:08 /user/hive/warehouse/emp_bucket/000002_0
abhiadmin@hadoopnode1:~$
```

Let's have a look on the table content in Hive warehouse.

```
abhiadmin@hadoopnode1:~$ hadoop fs -cat /user/hive/warehouse/emp_bucket/000000_0
15,Abhishek Rai,CEO,100000,B
8,Aastha,engineer,45000,B
7,Pankaj,Tech,12000,B
18,Arun,Admin,60000,B
12,Dev Raj,TL,55000,B
2,Banarjee,STL,75000,B
abhiadmin@hadoopnode1:~$
```

There are three files in the warehouse directory for department A, B, and C. Each bucket contains unique values.

Summary

This chapter discussed the concept of Hive. You learned about Hive architecture and Hive metastore. Next, you learned about Hive Command Line Interface (CLI), and the variables, properties, and commands used in Hive.

You also learned how to execute Hive queries from files. Next, the chapter discussed shell execution, data types, and built-in functions in Hive. You also learned about Hive DDL and data manipulation. Finally, you learned how to execute HiveQL queries and use joins in Hive. Finally, you learned about the bucketing concept and how to use it.

Quick Revise

Multiple-Choice Questions

Q1. The syntax ALTER TABLE old_table_name RENAME TO new_table_name is used for:

a. Renaming an existing database
b. Renaming an existing field name
c. Renaming an existing table name with a new name
d. None of the above

Ans. The correct option is c.

Q2. In Hive, the term 'aggregation' is used to:

a. Count the number of distinct users by gender.
b. Get the best performance of a table
c. Use to merge the data in a table to another table.
d. There is no term like 'aggregation'

Ans. The correct option is c.

Q3. Hive uses ________ to store metadata:

a. Derby database
b. HiveQl
c. NoSQL
d. SQL

Ans. The correct option is a.

Q4. The command `SET` in Hive is useful when:

a. You want to set an explicit property in 'hive-site.xml'.
b. You want to set an internal property in 'hive-site.xml'.
c. You are not permitted to use any other command.
d. You cannot add external properties like SET.

Ans. The correct option is a.

Q5. You want to write a query in a file called `firstquery.hql`, which is stored under the folder .../`home/guru/queries/`. Which of the following commands will you use?

a. hive -f/home/guru/queries/firstquery.hql
b. cat/home/myuser/queries/myquery.hql
c. SELECT * FROM student;
d. All the three commands

Ans. The correct option is a.

Q6. What is the syntax to declare the struct data type?

a. STRUCT<col_name : data_type [COMMENT col_comment], ...>
b. STRUCTS<col_name : data_type [COMMENT col_comment], ...>

c. STRUCT<[COMMENT col_comment], ...>

d. None of the above

Ans. The correct option is a.

Q7. The Hive built-in function size (Map<K.V>) is used to:

a. Return the number of elements in the map type

b. Convert the results in the Map type

c. Return null if the conversion does not succeed

d. Only options (i) and (iii)

Ans. The correct option is a.

Q8. The CREATE statement in Hive is related to:

a. DDL statements

b. DML statements

c. Session control statements

d. Embedded SQL statements

Ans. The correct option is a.

Subjective Questions

Q1. Write the Hive command to create a table with four columns: First name, last name, age, and income.

Ans. The command is as follows:

```
CREATE TABLE sample(First_name string, Last_name string, age int, income int);
```

Q2. Write a script to copy the same table structure into a new table.

Ans. The command is as follows:

```
CREATE TABLE sample_empty_table LIKE sample_table;
```

Q3. A start-up company wants to use Hive for storing its data. List the collection types provided by Hive for this purpose.

Ans. Hive offers several collection data types: struct, map, and array. Struct, like in most programming languages, allows you to define a structure with established columns and data types.

```
For example, a column; named address, can be declared as follows:
address struct<street:string, city:string, state:string, zipcode:int>
```

Map is a little less structured than the struct data type. Instead of predefining the sub-attributes of this column, you need to define a key-value pair and declare the data type for each. For example, an acceptable map could be:

```
preferences map<pref_code string, pref_value string>
```

Finally, an array allows you to store n number of values of the same data type. In other words, you wouldn't use an array unless the objects are representing the same type of information and using the same data type. An example where an array could be used:

```
household_ages array[smallint]
```

Q4. Write a shell command in Hive to list all the files in the current directory.

Ans. The command is as follows:

```
!ls;
```

Q5. Write Hive commands for:

- Creating a database named Super_store
- Creating two tables with the given properties:
  - Customers
  - Custname –char
  - Cust avg expenses –num
  - Items
  - Item name-char
  - Item value –num

Ans. a. The command is as follows:

```
create database Super_store;
```

b. The commands are as follows:

```
create table Customers (Custname string, Cust_avg_expenses int);
create table Items (Item_name string, Item value int);
```

Q6. Write the command to print a list of default Hive tables.

Ans. The command is as follows:

```
show tables;
```

Q7. Write the command to print the content of the first two tables.

Ans. The command is as follows:

```
select * from table_one;
select * from table_two;
```

13

Analyzing Data with Pig

While programming with Hadoop, we use the MapReduce model. It consists of the map phase and the reduce phase. In the map phase, a significant portion of the dataset is processed, and the output is represented into an intermediate representation. On the other hand, in case of the reduce phase, the results from the map phase are combined, and the final output is produced.

The MapReduce model is not always convenient and efficient, but it can be extended to many real-world problems. However, when there is a large amount of data that needs to be processed using Hadoop, the processing involves more overhead and becomes complex. A better solution to such kind of problems is Pig, which is a Hadoop extension. Pig is recommended if you need to handle gigabytes or terabytes of data. However, it is not recommended in case you are required to write a single or a small group of records or search various records randomly. Yahoo uses Hadoop heavily and executes 40 percent of all its Hadoop jobs with Pig. The well-known company Twitter is also another user of Pig. The main philosophy behind the development of Pig is its ease of use, high performance, and massive scalability.

This chapter begins by introducing Pig. It then discusses the architecture and benefits of Pig. After that, you learn how to install and run Pig. Next, the chapter explains the Pig language, called Pig Latin, along with its structure. In the end, the chapter explores the operators and functions used in Pig.

Introducing Pig

Pig was designed and developed for performing a long series of data operations. The Pig platform is specially designed for handling many kinds of data, be it structured, semi-structured, or unstructured. Pig enables users to focus more on what to do than on how to do it. Pig was developed in 2006 at Yahoo. It was a part of a research project, the aim of which was to provide an easy option to simplify the process of using Hadoop and concentrate on examining large datasets instead of wasting time on MapReduce. Pig became an Apache project in 2007. In 2009, Pig started being used by other companies and emerged as a top-level Apache project in 2010. Pig can be divided into three categories: ETL (Extract, Transform, and Load), research, and interactive data processing.

Pig consists of a scripting language, known as Pig Latin, and a Pig Latin compiler. The scripting language is used to write the code for analysing the data, and the compiler converts the code into the equivalent MapReduce code. So, we can say that Pig automates the process of designing and implementing MapReduce applications. It becomes easier to write code in Pig compared to programming in MapReduce. Pig has an optimizer that decides how to get the data quickly. This essentially means that Pig is smart and intelligent in terms of data processing.

The Pig Architecture

Pig is simple and easy to use. As stated earlier, Pig is made up of two components: a scripting language called Pig Latin and the Pig Latin compiler.

In other words, Pig Latin is the programming language for the Pig platform. It is a high-level language that is used to write programs for data processing and analysis.

The Pig Latin compiler, on the other hand, is used to convert the Pig Latin code into executable code. The executable code can be in the form of MapReduce jobs.

Figure 13.1 shows how Pig relates to the Hadoop ecosystem:

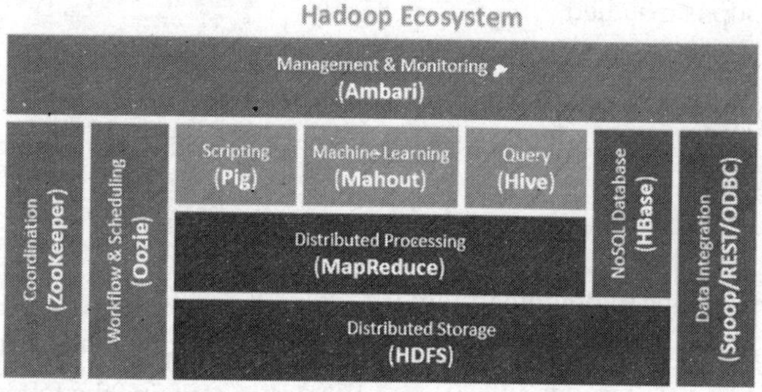

Figure 13.1: Pig Architecture in Relation to Hadoop Ecosystem

NOTE

A good strategy to test Pig scripts is to run the Pig job in the virtual Hadoop instance. No change in the code is required to execute Pig programs on MapReduce v1 or MapReduce v2.

Pig scripts can also be run on Apache Tez, which provides a more efficient execution framework than MapReduce. YARN (Yet Another Resource Negotiator) is a cluster management technology that enables application frameworks other than MapReduce (such as Tez) to run on Hadoop. Pig is a good choice when you are dealing with gigabytes or terabytes of data. It is, however, not recommended if you need to write for a small group of records or for random look up of records.

Benefits of Pig

The Pig programming language offers the following benefits:

- **Ease of coding**—Pig Latin lets you write complex programs. The code is simple and easy to understand and maintain. It explicitly encodes the complex tasks, involving interrelated data transformations, as data flow sequences.
- **Optimization**—Pig Latin encodes tasks in such a way that they can be easily optimized for execution. This allows users to concentrate on the data processing aspects without bothering about efficiency.
- **Extensibility**—Pig Latin is designed in such a way that it allows you to create your own custom functions. These can be used for performing special tasks. Custom functions are also called user-defined functions.

Installing Pig

You can run Pig from your laptop/desktop computers. It can also operate on the machine from which Hadoop jobs are launched. Pig can be installed on a UNIX or Windows system.

NOTE

Windows users also need to install the Cygwin and Perl packages. The packages can be installed from http://www.cygwin.com/.

Before installing Pig, you need to make sure that your system has the following applications:

- **Hadoop** (version 0.20.2 onwards)
  - It can be downloaded from *http://hadoop.apache.org/common/releases.html*.

- The HADOOP_HOME environment variable can be set accordingly to indicate the directory where Hadoop is installed.

❑ **Java** (version 1.6 onwards)

- It can be downloaded from *//java.sun.com/javase/downloads/index.jsp*.
- The JAVA_HOME environment variable can be set accordingly to indicate the directory where Java is installed.

Downloading Pig

Perform the following steps to download Pig:

1. Download a recent stable release from one of the Apache Download Mirrors.
2. Unpack the downloaded Pig distribution and ensure it contains the following files:
   - The Pig script file, Pig, which is located in the bin directory.
   - The Pig properties file, `pig.properties`, which is located in the `conf` directory.
3. Add `/pig-n.n.n/bin` to your path. Then, use either the export (`bash.sh.ksh`) or the `setenv (tcsh.csh)` command, as shown here:

```
$ export PATH=/<my-path-to-pig>/pig-n.n.n/bin:$PATH
```

   This completes the process of downloading and installing Pig on your local machine.

4. Now, the Pig installation can be tested with the following command:

```
$ pig-help
```

Building a Pig Repository

Perform the following steps to build a Pig repository:

1. Download the Pig code from Apache Subversion (SVN), which is available at the following URL: *http://svn.apache.org/repis/asf/pig/trunk*.
2. You can build the code in the working directory. A successfully completed build would result in the creation of the `pig.jar` file in the working directory.
3. You can validate the `pig.jar` file by running a unit test, such as the ant test.

When you start Pig, the Hadoop properties can be specified with the `-D` option and the Pig properties with the `-P` option in the Pig interface. You can also use the `set` command to change individual properties in the Grunt mode of Pig.

The following precedence order is supported by the Pig Latin properties:

```
-D Pig property < -P properties file < set command
```

Pig does not interpret Hadoop properties. These are directly passed to Hadoop.

The Hadoop properties that you specify support the following precedence order:

```
Hadoop configuration files < -D Hadoop property < -P properties_file < set command
```

Properties of Pig

Pig programming language is written in Java; therefore, it supports the properties of Java and uses the Java notation.

Table 13.1 shows some important properties of Pig:

Table 13.1: Important Properties of Pig

Property	Description	Values	Default
stop.on.failure	Decides whether to exit at the first error.	True/False	False
udf.import.list	Refers to a comma-separated list of imports for Universal Disk Format (UDF).		
pig.additional.jars	Refers to a command-separated list of JavaArchive (JAR) files.	JAR files	
Exectype	Describes the execution model.	local/MapReduce	MapReduce
pig.exec. filterLogicExpressionSimplifier	Allows optimization to simplify filter expressions.	True/False	False
pig.noSplitCombination	Checks whether small files are joined to a single map.	True/False	True
pig.tmpfilecompress.codec	Specifies the compression codec.	lzo/gzip	Gzip
pig.tmpfilecompression	Determines whether temporary files should be compressed or not.	True/False	False
opt.multiquery	Disables multi-query (workaround).	True/False	False
pig.exec.nocombiner	Disables the combiner optimizer.	True/False	False

Table 13.1: Important Properties of Pig

Property	Description	Values	Default
aggregate.warning	Generates a set of warnings.	True/False	True
Brief	Omits timestamps on log messages.	True/False	False
Verbose	Prints all log messages on the screen.	True/False	False

Running Pig

Pig scripts can be run in the following two modes:

- **Local mode**—In this mode, several scripts can run on a single machine without requiring Hadoop MapReduce and Hadoop Distributed File System (HDFS). This mode is useful for developing and testing Pig logic. The local mode is faster when you are using a small set of data to develop or test your code than the MapReduce infrastructure. This mode does not require Hadoop. The Pig program runs in the context of a local Java Virtual Machine (JVM). The data is accessed through the local file system on a single machine. This process is a separate one, outside of the Pig Latin compiler.
- **MapReduce mode**—It is also known as the Hadoop mode. In this case, the Pig script gets converted into a series of MapReduce jobs, which are then run on the Hadoop cluster.

Figure 13.2 shows the modes available for running Pig scripts:

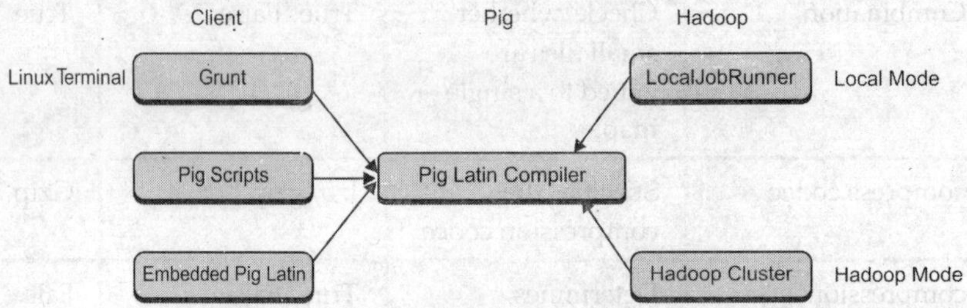

Figure 13.2: Pig Models

The decision whether to use the local mode or the Hadoop mode is made on the basis of the amount of the data available. Suppose you want to perform operations on several terabytes of data and create a program. You may notice that the operations slow down significantly after some time. The local mode enables you to perform tasks with subsets of your data in a highly interactive manner. You can determine the logic and rectify bugs in your Pig program. After performing these tasks, and when your operations are running smoothly, you can use the MapReduce mode.

Running Pig Programs

Before running the Pig program, it is necessary to know about the pig shell. As we all know, without a shell, no one can access the pig's in-built characteristics. Pig shell is known as "Grunt." Grunt is a command shell, which is graphical in nature and used for scripting of pig. Grunt saves the previously used command in "pig_history" file in Home directory. There is one handier feature of Grunt: if you are writing a script on grunt, it will automatically complete the keywords that you are typing. For example, if you are writing a script and you need to just type "for" and press Tab button, it will automatically type "foreach" keyword.

```
grunt> a=for(press Tab it will automatically give "foreach") b ge(press Tab it will automatically give "generate") names;
```

The above code after competition looks like this:

```
grunt> a= foreach b generate name;
```

Schema

After getting the knowledge of grunt, we need to know the schema for writing the script. For every scripting language, there is a schema definition that tells everything about the script. Let us have an example,

```
grunt> a = LOAD 'input/sample.txt' AS (year: int, temp: int, name: chararray);
grunt> DESCRIBE a;
a:{ year: int, temp: int, name: chararray)
```

Here, we declared the columns in the script, and year is given a datatype of integer, temp as an integer, and name as a char array. This is nothing but a schema declaration of the script for "a".

SCENARIO

Consider the case of Argon Technology, which provides Big Data solutions. An input file containing weather data is provided to the project manager of this company. This is a simple CSV file and has three columns. The first column indicates the serial number, the second column indicates the year, and the third column indicates the temperatures recorded over various years.

The manager is interested in finding the maximum temperature from the given dataset. To do this, a Pig program is required, which can be implemented on Pig Grunt. He will have to write a Pig program and execute the commands for running it. This scenario involves implementation of a Pig program to find out the maximum temperature year-wise from the given dataset.

The manager has to first ensure that Hadoop, Java, and Pig are installed and running smoothly on his system. He can set the environment variables, if required, by using the following commands:

```
export JAVA HOME=/home/apache/jdk1.8.0 25
export HADOOP HOME=/home/apache/hadoop-2.6.0
export PIG HOME=/home/apache/pig-0.14.0
export PIG CLASSPATH=$HADOOP HOME/conf
export PATH=$PATH:$JAVA HOME/bin:$HADOOP HOME/bin:PIG_HOME/bin
```

Next, he starts Pig Grunt with the following command:

```
$bin/pig -x local
```

Then, he writes the Pig program to find the maximum temperature from the given set of data. The program is shown in Listing 13.1:

Listing 13.1: Displaying the Program to Find the Maximum Temperature

```
records = LOAD '/home/your-dir/apache/pig-n.n.n/temperature ' AS (year:chararray,
temperature:int, quality:int);
```

```
filtered_records = FILTER records BY temperature != 9999 AND (quality == 0 OR
quality == 1 );
grouped_records = GROUP filtered_records BY year;
max_temp = FOREACH grouped_records GENERATE group, MAX(filtered_
records.temperature);
DUMP max_temp;
```

Finally, he runs this 'Dump' command, shown in Listing 13.1, on a terminal to generate the output.

Getting Started with Pig Latin

Pig is a high-level programming platform that uses Pig Latin language for developing Hadoop MapReduce programs. Pig Latin abstracts its programming from the Java MapReduce idiom and extends itself by allowing direct calling of user-defined functions written in Java, Python, JavaScript, Ruby, or Groovy. Pig Latin is compliant with parallelism, which enables it to handle very large datasets. Pig translates the Pig Latin script into MapReduce jobs. The main reasons for developing Pig Latin are as follows:

- **Simple**—A streamlined method is provided in Pig Latin for interacting with MapReduce. This makes the creation of parallel programs simpler for analysis and processing on the Hadoop cluster. Complex tasks may need many interrelated transformations of data. These transformations can be easily encoded as data flow sequences in Pig Latin.
- **Smart**—The Pig Latin compiler transforms a Pig Latin program into a series of Java MapReduce jobs. The logic here is to ensure that the compiler can optimize the execution of these Java MapReduce jobs automatically. This allows the user to concentrate on semantics and not on how to optimize and access the data.
- **Extensible**—Pig Latin is extensible, which allows developers to add functions for addressing their business problems specifically.

Compared to Java MapReduce programs, Pig Latin scripts make writing, understanding, and maintaining programs easier. All this is made possible because:

- You are not required to write the jobs in Java.
- You are not required to think in terms of MapReduce.
- You do not need to develop custom code for dealing with rich data types.

Pig Latin provides an easy and simple language to effectively use Hadoop. It thus makes it easier for more and more users to leverage the power of Hadoop, reduce time, and enhance productivity.

NOTE

RDBMS data warehouses traditionally make use of a specific data processing pattern, which includes Extract, Transform, and Load (usually called ETL). Data is extracted from outside sources, transformed to make it suitable for the user's operational needs, and loaded into the operational data store or another database or data warehouse.

With Big Data, however, you do not want the large amount of data to be moving around. So, the processing is brought to the data itself. The Pig Latin language goes with ELT instead of the old ETL approach: Extract the data from various sources, load it into HDFS, and then transform it as needed in order to make it ready for further analysis.

Pig Latin Application Flow

Pig Latin is regarded as a data flow language. This simply means that we can use Pig Latin to define a data stream and a sequence of transformations, which can be applied to the data as it moves throughout your application. In the case of a control flow language, on the other hand, we write a sequence of instructions. We also use concepts such as conditional logic and loops. In Pig Latin, we won't find loops and if statements.

The Pig syntax used for data processing flow is as follows:

```
X = LOAD 'file_name.txt';
...
Y = GROUP ... ;
...
Z= FILTER ... ;
...
DUMP Y;
..
STORE Z into 'temp';
```

As you can see from the preceding syntax, Pig Latin makes use of the following statements:

- The LOAD statement is used for reading data from the file system. The data that requires to be manipulated is first loaded. It is typically stored in HDFS. For a Pig program to access the data, you first need to specify the file to use. For this, you use the LOAD statement. The specified file can be either an HDFS file or a directory. If a directory is specified, all files in that directory are loaded into the program.
- The FILTER statement is used for filtering the records.
- The GROUP statement is used for grouping the data.
- The DUMP statement is used for viewing the results on the screen. Typically, you use the DUMP command to show the output on to the screen when the program needs to be debugged. When working in a production environment, you can use the STORE command to save the results in a file. These results can be used for further processing or analysis.
- The STORE statement is used for saving the results.

Pig Latin Structure

To explain the Pig Latin structure, let us consider an example of a dataset named Aircraft. We want to calculate the total distance covered by aircraft flown by different companies.

The Pig Latin script to calculate the total distance covered by aircraft is shown in Listing 13.2:

Listing 13.2: Displaying the Pig Latin Script to Calculate Total Distance Covered by Aircraft

```
input_records = LOAD '2014 Aircraft.csv' USING PigStorage(',') AS (YearNum, No_Mo
nth, Month_Day,Week_Day,Departure_Time,CRSDeparture_Time,Arrival_Time,
CRSArrival_Time, U_Carrier, Flight_Number, Tail_Number, Real_ElpsdTime,
CRS_Elpsd_Time,
AirTime,Arrival_Delay,Departure_Delay,Source,Destination,Distance:int,CabIn,CabOut
,Canclled,CodeCancellation,Diverted,Delay_Carrier,Delay_Weather,Delay_NAS,
Delay_Security, LateFlight_Delay);
average = GROUP input_records ALL;
totalmilesCovered = FOREACH average GENERATE SUM(input_records.Distance);
DUMP totalmilesCovered;
```

An explanation for the script in Listing 13.2 is as follows:

- The `LOAD` operator is used for reading data from HDFS.
- The `GROUP` operator is used for aggregating `input_records`.
- The `ALL` statement is used for aggregating all the tuples into a single group.
- The `FOREACH` operator is used for iteration.
- The `DUMP` statement is used for executing the operators and displaying the results on the screen.

Please note the following points about the preceding script:

- The Pig script is much shorter than the MapReduce script for performing a given task.
- In Pig, you are not required to be aware of the logic of performing a given task.
- The Pig Latin script generally starts with the `LOAD` operator for reading data from HDFS.
- Pig has a data model for itself. You need to map the data model of files to Pig's data model. This is done with the help of the `USING` operator. The code says that it is a comma-delimited file with the `PigStorage(',')` statement, followed by the `AS` statement that defines the name of columns.
- Generally, we use aggregations in Pig for summarizing datasets. The `GROUP` operator is used for aggregating records into a single record. The `ALL` statement is used for aggregating all tuples into a single group.
- The `FOREACH GENERATE` statements are used for transforming columnar data. Here, we want to calculate the total distance travelled by all aircraft. The `SUM` statement calculates the sum of the `input_records`. Distance column is combined into a single column collection named `totalmilesCovered`.
- The `DUMP` operator is used to execute Pig Latin statements and display the output on to the screen. The operator is used in the interactive mode. Therefore, the statements are immediately executed, and the results are not saved.

Working with Operators in Pig

In Pig Latin, relational operators are used for transforming data. Different types of transformations include grouping, filtering, sorting, and joining. The following are some basic relational operators used in Pig:

- FOREACH
- ASSERT
- FILTER
- GROUP
- ORDER BY
- DISTINCT
- JOIN
- LIMIT
- SAMPLE
- SPLIT

Let's learn about each operator in detail in the following sections.

FOREACH

The FOREACH operator performs iterations over every record to perform a transformation. When the given expressions are applied, the FOREACH operator generates a new collection of records. The syntax for using the FOREACH operator is as follows:

```
alias = FOREACH { block | nested_block };
```

In the preceding syntax,

- **alias**—Refers to name of the relation, which is also known as a variable
- **block**—Refers to the outer block
- **nested_block**—Refers to the name of the inner block

Suppose we have a student's data and we load it from the HDFS and want to extract the data from it. The following script illustrates the use of the FOREACH operator on the student data:

```
student = load '/home/Your Dir/hadoop/pig/pig-0.14.0/data' using PigStorage('');
output = FOREACH student GENERATE *;
DUMP output;
```

The result of the preceding script is as follows:

```
(John,3,M)
(Robinson,2,M)
(Jilly,6,F)
(Peter,7,M)
```

The preceding example uses the relations 'student', 'rollno', and gender. The asterisk (*) symbol is used for projecting all the fields. You can also use the FOREACH operator for projecting only two fields of the student table by using the following script:

```
student = load '/home/Your Dir/hadoop/pig/pig-0.14:0/data' using PigStorag ('');
output = FOREACH student GENERATE sname, rollno;
DUMP output;
```

The output of the preceding script is as follows:

```
(John,3,M)
(Robinson,2,M)
(Jilly,6,F)
(Peter,7,M)
```

ASSERT

The ASSERT operator asserts a condition on the data. Assertions are used for ensuring that a condition is true on the data. The processing fails if any of the records violate the condition. The syntax for using the ASSERT operator is as follows:

```
ASSERT alias BY expression [, message];
```

In the preceding syntax,

- **alias**—Refers to the name of the relation
- **BY**—Refers to a keyword
- **expression**—Refers to a boolean expression
- **message**—Refers to an error message when assertion fails

The following script shows the use of the ASSERT operator:

```
temp = LOAD 'data' AS (first:int, second:int, third:int);
DUMP temp;
```

The output of the preceding script is as follows:

```
(2,3,4)
(4,1,2)
(3,4,7)
(5,8,2)
```

Suppose you want to ensure that the size of the first column in your data is >0. In that case, you can use the following script:

```
ASSERT temp BY first > 0, 'first should be greater than 0';
```

FILTER

The FILTER operator enables you to use a predicate for selecting the records that need to be retained in the pipeline. Only those records will be passed down the pipeline successfully for which the predicate defined in the FILTER statement remains true. The syntax for using the FILTER operator is as follows:

```
alias = FILTER alias BY expression;
```

In the preceding syntax:

- **alias**—Refers to the name of a table
- **BY**—Refers to a keyword
- **expression**—Refers to a boolean expression

The use of the FILTER operator is illustrated by the following script:

```
table = load '/home/Your Dir/hadoop/pig/pig-0.14.0/numbers' AS
   (first:int,second:int,third:int);
Dump table;
(1,2,3)
(1,2,4)
(6,1,3)
(6,1,2)
result = FILTER table by third == 3;
DUMP result;
```

The result of the preceding script is as follows:

```
(1,2,3)
(6,1,3)
temp = FILTER table BY (first == 6) OR (NOT (second+third > a1));
DUMP temp;
(6,1,3)
(6,1,2)
```

GROUP

Various operators are provided by Pig Latin for group and aggregate functions. The syntax of the GROUP operator in Pig Latin is similar to SQL, but it is different in functionality when compared to the GROUP BY clause in SQL. In Pig Latin, the GROUP operator is used for grouping data in single or multiple relations. The GROUP BY clause in SQL is used to create a group that can be input directly into single or multiple aggregate functions. You cannot include a star expression in a GROUP BY column in Pig Latin.

The syntax for using the GROUP operator is as follows:

```
alias = GROUP alias { ALL | BY expression } [, alias ALL | BY expression…]
[ USING 'collected' | 'merge' ] [ PARTITION BY partitioner ] [ PARALLEL n ];
```

In the preceding syntax:

- **alias**—Refers to the name of a table
- **ALL**—Refers to the keyword used for inputting all the tuples into a group; for example, Z = GROUP A ALL;
- **BY**—Refers to a keyword used for grouping relations by field, tuple, or expression; for example, X = GROUP A BY f1;
- **PARTITION BY partitioner**—Describes the Hadoop Partitioner, used for controlling the keys that partition intermediate map-outputs.

The following script shows the use of the GROUP operator:

```
X = LOAD 'student' AS (name:chararray, age:int);
DESCRIBE X;
X: {name: chararray, age: int}
DUMP X;
```

The output of the preceding script is as follows:

```
(George,20)
(Lisa,21)
(Paul,22)
(Joseph,20)
```

Now, let's suppose that you want to group relation X on the field age to form relation Z, as shown in the following script:

```
Z = GROUP X BY age;
DESCRIBE Z;
Z: {group: int, X: {name: chararray, age: int}}
DUMP Z;
```

The output of the preceding script is as follows:

```
(20,{(George,18),(Joseph,18)})
(21,{(Lisa,19)})
(22,{(Paul,20)})
```

In the output, you can see a group of teenagers of age 18 is created.

NOTE

The GROUP and COGROUP operators are similar in several respects. Both these operators can perform their functions with one or multiple relations. The GROUP operator can be used when the statements deal with a single relation, while the COGROUP operator is used when two or more relations are involved in statements. COGROUP can handle a maximum of 127 relations at a time.

ORDER BY

The ORDER BY operator in Pig Latin is used for sorting a given relation, depending on one or more fields. The syntax of the ORDER BY operator is as follows:

```
alias = ORDER alias BY {* [ASC|DESC] | field_alias [ASC | DESC] [, field_alias
[ASC|DESC]…] }
[PARALLEL n];
```

In the preceding syntax:

- **alias**—Refers to the name of a relation
- *—Signifies a tuple designator
- **field_alias**—Refers to a field in the relation
- **ASC**—Sorts data in ascending order
- **DESC**—Sorts data in descending order
- **PARALLEL n**—Enhances the parallelism of a task by mentioning the number of reduce tasks, n

Pig supports the ordering on fields with simple data types or by using the tuple designator (*). You cannot impose order fields with complex types or by expressions.

The following commands describe the syntax used for ordering fields in Pig:

```
data = LOAD 'mydata' AS (x: int, y: map[]);
order1 = ORDER data BY x;
order2 = ORDER data BY y;
order3 = ORDER data BY y#'id';
```

The following script depicts some examples of the ORDER BY operator in Pig:

```
temp = load '/home/Your Dir/hadoop/pig/pig-0.14.0/employees' AS
(first:int,second:int,third:int);
DUMP temp;
```

The output of the preceding script is as follows:

```
(1,2,4)
(2,4,1)
(4,2,5)
(3,5,7)
```

Now, consider the following script that arranges the data in decreasing order in terms of the third element:

```
Z = ORDER data BY third DESC;
DUMP Z;
```

The output of the preceding script is as follows:

```
(3,5,7)
(4,2,5)
(1,2,4)
(2,4,1)
```

DISTINCT

In Pig Latin, the DISTINCT operator works on the entire records and not on individual fields. This operator is used for removing duplicate fields from a given set of records. The syntax of the DISTINCT operator is as follows:

```
alias = DISTINCT alias [ PARTITION BY partitioner ] [ PARALLEL n ];
```

In the preceding syntax:

- **alias**—Refers to the name of the relation
- **PARTITION BY partitioner**— Refers to the Hadoop partitioner
- **PARALLEL n**—Enhances the parallelism of a task by mentioning the number of reduce tasks, n

Consider the following script that illustrates the use of the `DISTINCT` operator:

```
my_student  =  load '/home /Your Dir/hadoop/pig/pig-0.14.0/students' AS ( first :
chararray,     second : int, third : int ) ;
DUMP my_student;
```

The output of the preceding script is as follows:

```
(Sam, 2,4)
(Sam, 2,4)
(Paul, 3,2)
(Peter, 3,6)
(John, 3,6)
```

Consider the following example in which all the redundant tuples are removed:

```
original = DISTINCT my_student;
DUMP original;
```

The output of the preceding script is as follows:

```
(sam,2,4)
(Paul, 3,2)
(Peter,3,6)
```

JOIN

The `JOIN` operator in Pig Latin is used for joining two or more relations. The joining of two rows is possible in case they have identical keys. If some records in the two rows do not match, these records can be deleted or dropped. The following two types of joins can be performed in Pig Latin:

- Inner join
- Outer join

We will learn about these joins shortly in the chapter.

The syntax of the `JOIN` operator is as follows:

```
alias = JOIN alias BY {expression|'('expression [, expression…]')'}
(, alias BY {expression|'('expre
ssion [, expression…]')'}…) [USING 'replicated' |
'skewed' | 'merge' | 'merge-sparse']
```

In the preceding syntax:

- **alias**—Refers to the name of a relation
- **BY**—Refers to a keyword
- **expression**—Refers to a field expression
- **USING**—Refers to a keyword
- **replicated**—Performs replicated joins
- **skewed**—Performs skewed joins
- **merge**—Performs merge joins
- **merge-sparse**—Performs merge-sparse joins

Inner Join

In an inner join, the same dataset is used with different aliases. As we know, the Pig script works upon the nomenclature and that is why different aliases are used to avoid naming conflicts. Let's take an example to show the inner join on a data file "mydata" with different aliases:

```
grunt> data1 = load  'mydata' ;
grunt> data2 = load  'mydata' ;
grunt> result = join data1 by $0, data2 by $0 ;
```

In the preceding code, the two different aliases, data1 and data2, of the mydata table are created. Then, the join operation is performed using these aliases.

Outer Join

When you implement outer joins in Pig, records that do not have a match of the records in the other table are included with null values filled in for the missing fields. There are three types of outer joins:

- **Left outer join**—It returns all the rows from the left table, even if there are no matches in the right table.

  Let's consider a relation A and B, and have the same elements in it.

```
grunt> DUMP A;
(2, maggie)
(4, yepme)
(3, topreman)
(1, chings)
grunt> DUMP B;
(Nestle, 2)
(xyz,4)
(tops, 2)
(Kelogs, 0)
(itc, 3)
```

  These are the elements of both A and B. Now, on joining them on the basis of left outer join, it will be as follows:

```
grunt> C = JOIN A by $0 LEFT OUTER, B by $1
grunt> Dump C;
```

  The output for this is as follows:

```
(1, chings, ,)
(2, Maggie, nestle, 2)
(2, Maggie, top, 2)
(3, topreman, itc, 3)
(4, yepme, xyz, 4)
```

- **Right outer join**—It returns all the rows from the right table, even if there are no matches in the left table.

  For the above data relation, we get the result by applying the right outer join as follows:

```
grunt> C = JOIN A RIGHT OUTER JOIN, B ;
grunt> DUMP C;
```

  The output for this is as follows:

```
(Nestle, 2, maggie,2)
(XYZ, 4, yepme,4)
(top, 2, maggie,2)
(kelogs, 0, ,)
(ITC, 3, topreman, 3)
```

- **Full outer join**—It includes all the records from both sides even if they do not have any matches.

LIMIT

The `LIMIT` operator in Pig allows a user to limit the number of results. The syntax of the `LIMIT` operator is as follows:

```
alias = LIMIT alias n;
```

In the preceding syntax:

- **alias**—Refers to the name of a relation
- **n**—Refers to the number of tuples as output, which can be either a constant, such as 20, or a scalar used in an expression, such as h .add /10

Consider the following example that generates three tuples as output:

```
temp = load '/home/Your Dir/hadoop/pig/pig-0.12.0/students' AS
(first:int,second:int,third:int);
DUMP temp;
```

The output of the preceding syntax is as follows:

```
(2,2,3)
(3,2,4)
(7,3,5)
(3,2,3)
```

Now, consider the following statement, which only selects the first two results out of four:

```
Lmt_tmp= LIMIT temp 2;
DUMP lmt_tmp ;
```

The output of the preceding statement is as follows:

```
(2,2,3)
(3,2,4)
```

In the preceding output, you can see that only the first two results are displayed.

SAMPLE

The SAMPLE operator in Pig is used for selecting a random data sample by providing a sample size. It returns the percentage in rows in double values. For example, if the operator returns 0.2, it indicates 20%.

It is not always likely that the same number of rows will be returned for a particular sample size each time the SAMPLE operator is used. So, this operator is also termed a probabilistic operator.

The syntax for using the SAMPLE operator is as follows:

```
SAMPLE alias n;
```

In the preceding syntax:

- **alias**—Refers to the name of a relation
- **n**—Refers to sample size, which can be a constant that ranges from 0 to 1 or a scalar used in an expression

Consider the following example in which table Z will have 1% of the data present in table X:

```
X = LOAD 'data' AS (first:int,second:int,third:int);
Z = SAMPLE X 0.01;
```

SPLIT

The SPLIT operator partitions a given relation into two or more relations. The syntax for using the SPLIT operator is as follows:

```
SPLIT alias INTO alias IF expression, alias IF expression [, alias IF expression …]
[, alias OTHERWISE];
```

In the preceding syntax:

- **alias**—Refers to the name of a relation
- **INTO**—Refers to a keyword
- **IF**—Refers to a keyword
- **expression**—Refers to an expression
- **OTHERWISE**—Refers to an optional keyword that designates a default relation

A tuple may be assigned to more than one relation or may not be assigned to any relation, depending on the conditions given in the expression.

In the following example, the relation `table` is split into two relations, `tab1` and `tab2`:

```
table = LOAD 'data' AS (first:int,second:int,third:int);
DUMP table;
(1,3,5)
(2,4,6)
(5,7,8)
SPLIT table INTO tab1 IF first<5, tab2 IF second==7;
DUMP tab1;
(1,3,5)
(2,4,6)
DUMP tab2;
(5,7,8)
```

FLATTEN

The `FLATTEN` operator is used for un-nesting as well as collecting tuples (also known as bags). The `FLATTEN` operator seems syntactically similar to a user-defined function statement; however, it is actually an operator that allows the user to modify the structure of tuples and bags. In case of tuples, the `FLATTEN` operator replaces the fields of a tuple in place of the tuple. For instance, consider a relation that contains a tuple of the form `(x, (y, z))`. The expression `GENERATE $0, flatten($1)`, will change the form of this tuple to `(x, y, z)`.

In case of bags, the situation is a bit more complex. Whenever we un-nest a bag, we form new tuples. Consider a relation of the form `({(w,x),(y,z)})` and when you apply `GENERATE flatten($0)`, two tuples `(w,x)` and `(y,z)` are generated. Sometimes, you need to perform a cross product for removing a level of nesting from a bag. Consider a relation that contains a tuple in the form `(u, {(w,x), (y,z)})`. Now, when you apply the expression `GENERATE $0, flatten($1)` to this tuple, new tuples `(a, b, c)` and `(a, d, e)` are generated.

EXHIBIT 1: Process a Million Songs with Apache Pig

There is a dataset named Million Song Dataset (MSD), which contains detailed acoustic and contextual data about a million songs. For each song, you can find information like title, hotness, tempo, duration, danceability, and loudness as well as artist name, popularity, localization (latitude and longitude pair), and many other things. No music files are included here, but the links to MP3 song previews at 7digital.com can be easily constructed from the data.

The dataset consists of 339 tab-separated text files. Each file contains about 3000 songs, and each song is represented as a separate line of text. The dataset is publicly available, and you can find it at Infochimps or Amazon S3. Since the total size of this data sums up to around 218GB, processing it using one machine may take a very long time.

Definitely, a much more interesting and efficient approach is to use multiple machines and process the songs in parallel by taking advantage of open-source tools from the Apache Hadoop ecosystem (e.g., Apache Pig). If you have your own machines, you can simply use CDH (Cloudera's Distribution including Apache Hadoop), which includes the complete Apache Hadoop stack. CDH can be installed manually (by typing a couple of simple commands) or automatically by using Cloudera Manager Free Edition (which is Cloudera's recommended approach). Both CDH and Cloudera Manager are freely downloadable. Alternatively, you may rent some machines from Amazon with Hadoop already installed and process the data using Amazon's Elastic MapReduce.

Problem Definition

The idea is to process this dataset to find "exotic" (but still popular) songs. By exotic songs, we mean songs that are recorded by an artist who lives in some foreign country, far away from other artists. The general goal is to discover a couple of fancy folk songs that are associated with the culture of some country. A funny example could be the song "Koko Koko Euro Spoko" by Jarzębina, which was chosen by the Poles to be the official song of the Polish national football team during UEFA EURO 2012.

Apache Pig

Apache Pig is used to achieve this goal. It is a convenient tool created at Yahoo! to analyze large datasets easily and efficiently. It provides a high-level and easy-to-learn, understand-and-maintain data flow programming language called Pig Latin.

Pig Latin is quite similar to scripting languages. It supports many useful operations like filtering, sorting, aggregation, joining, and splitting, and provides several complex data types (tuples, bags, and maps). An exemplary Pig Latin script is 20 times shorter than its equivalent in Java MapReduce and takes a programmer 16 times less time to implement it, at the same time being only slightly slower than Java MapReduce. Thanks to these advantages, Apache Pig is often used by many well-recognized companies and organizations; e.g., Yahoo! (currently about 90% Hadoop jobs are written in Pig Latin), Twitter, Nokia Ovi Maps, AOL, Mendeley, LinkedIn, and ICM UW.

Source: *http://blog.cloudera.com/blog/2012/08/process-a-million-songs-with-apache-pig/*

Debugging Pig

Pig Latin has rich operators that can help to debug it. The main operators are as follows:

- **Dump**—It is used to run statements of Pig Latin and display results on screen. It is for interactive mode.
- **Describe**—It is used to view schema of relation.

- **Explain**—It is used to review logical, physical, and mapreduce execution plans, which are used for specified relationship.
- **Illustrate**—It allows to test your programs'on small datasets and shows step-by-step execution of sequence of statements.

Multi-Query Execution

Multi-query execution is the Pig process that processes the whole script or batches of statements in one go. That means we need not to execute the scripts one by one.

Turning the Multi-Query Execution On or Off

Multi-query execution remains turned on as by default it is set to "on." To turn off the multi-query execution and revert to Pig, use these statements "execute-on-dump/store" behavior or use the "-M" or "-no_multiquery" option. From this, the pre-default multi-query execution turns to offline mode.

To execute the script "script.pig" without optimization in it, execute Pig script file as follows:

```
$ pig -M script.pig
or
$ pig -no_multiquery script.pig
```

How It Works

Multi-query execution offers some changes with respect to Pig:

- On working with batch mode execution, the whole pig script is parsed to determine if transitional tasks can be combined to reduce the overall amount of work that needs to be done; parsing is done on priority and then execution starts only after parsing is completed (EXPLAIN operator, and the exec and run commands are used in this).
- There are two run scenarios, which are optimized and explained below: explicit and implicit splits and storing intermediate results.

Explicit and Implicit Splits

Sometimes, you need to process the same data differently on the separate parts of the same data stream. Let's consider some examples:

Example 1:

```
A = LOAD ...
...
SPLIT A' INTO B IF ..., C IF ...
...
STORE B' ...
STORE C' ...
```

Example 2:

```
A = LOAD ...
...
B = FILTER A' ...
C = FILTER A' ...
...
STORE B' ...
STORE C' ...
```

In the previous version of Pig, the above Example 1 will dump A′ to the local disk and then start the job for B′ and C′. Then, in Example 2, all the dependencies of B′ will get executed and stored. After this, it will execute all dependencies of C′ and store them as well. Both are equivalent, but they perform very differently.

Here are some steps, which a multi-query execution performs to increase the performance of Pig:

1. In Example 2, add an implicit split to transform the query to Example 1. This will eliminate the processing of A' multiple times in an enhanced manner.
2. The multiple query execution makes the split non-blocking and allows processing to continue. This helps to reduce the amount of data that has to be stored right at the split.
3. Multiple query execution allows multiple outputs from a job as one job can have one or more queries. This way some results can be stored as a side effect of the main job. This is also necessary to make the previous item work.
4. Multiple query execution allows multiple split branches to be carried on to the combiner/reducer. This will reduce the amount of IO, again in the case where multiple branches in the split can benefit from a combiner run.

Working with Functions in Pig

A function can be defined as a set of statements used for performing specific tasks. There are basically two types of functions in Pig: user-defined functions and built-in functions. As the name suggests, user-defined functions can be created by users as per their requirements. On the other hand, built-in functions are already defined in Pig. There are mainly five categories of built-in functions in Pig, which are as follows:

- **Eval or Evaluation functions**—These functions are used to evaluate a value by using an expression. Some commonly used eval functions are listed in Table 13.2:

Table 13.2: Eval Functions and Their Description

Function	Description	Syntax
Avg	Calculates the average of numeric values.	AVG(expression)
Concat	Joins two expressions of identical type.	CONCAT(expression expression)
Count	Calculates the number of elements in a bag.	COUNT(expression)
Count_Star	Calculates the number of elements in a bag. It also includes NULL values in the calculation.	COUNT_STAR(expression)
Diff	Compares two fields in a tuple.	DIFF(expression, expression)
IsEmpty	Verifies whether a bag or map is empty.	IsEmpty(expression)

Table 13.2: Eval Functions and Their Description

Function	Description	Syntax
Max	Calculates the maximum of numeric values or chararrays in a single-column bag.	MAX(expression)
Min	Calculates the minimum of numeric values or chararrays in a single-column bag.	MIN(expression)
Size	Calculates the number of elements on the basis of a Pig data type.	SIZE(expression)
Sum	Calculates the sum of the numeric values in a single-column bag.	SUM(expression)
Tokenize	Divides a string and returns a bag of words.	TOKENIZE(expression)

- **Math functions**—These functions are used to perform mathematical operations. Some commonly used mathematical functions are listed in Table 13.3:

Table 13.3: Math Functions and Their Description

Function	Description	Syntax
ABS	Computes the absolute value of an expression.	ABS(expression)
CBRT	Computes the cube root of an expression.	CBRT(expression)
CEIL	Provides the value of an expression after rounding it up to the nearest integer.	CEIL(expression)
EXP	Provides the exponential of an expression.	EXP(expression)
FLOOR	Computes the value of an expression after rounding it down to the nearest integer .	FLOOR(expression)
LOG	Computes the natural logarithm (base e) of an expression.	LOG(expression)
LOG10	Provides the base 10 logarithm of an expression.	LOG10(expression)
RANDOM	Provides a pseudo random number.	RANDOM( )

Table 13.3: Math Functions and Their Description		
Function	**Description**	**Syntax**
ROUND	Provides the value of an expression rounded to an integer.	ROUND(expression)
SQRT	Calculates the square root of an expression.	SQRT(expression)

- **String functions**—These functions are used to perform various operations on strings. Some commonly used string functions are listed in Table 13.4:

Table 13.4: String Functions and Their Description		
Function	**Description**	**Syntax**
INDEXOF	Provides the index of the first occurrence of a character in a string by searching in the forward direction from the starting index.	INDEXOF(string, 'character', startIndex)
LAST_INDEX_OF	Provides the index of the last occurrence of a character in a string by searching for it in the backward direction from the starting index.	LAST_INDEX_OF(expression)
LCFIRST	Changes the first character in a string to lower case.	LCFIRST(expression)
LOWER	Changes all characters in a string to lower case.	LOWER(expression)
REPLACE	Substitutes existing characters in a string with new characters.	REPLACE(string, 'oldChar', 'newChar');
STRSPLIT	Divides a string around matches of a given regular expression.	STRSPLIT(string, regex, limit)
SUBSTRING	Provides a substring from a given string.	SUBSTRING(string, startIndex, stopIndex)
TRIM	Provides a copy of a string after removing leading and trailing white spaces.	TRIM(expression)
UCFIRST	Provides a string after converting the first character into upper case.	UCFIRST(expression)
UPPER	Provides a string after converting it into upper case.	UPPER(expression)

- **Bag and Tuple functions**—These functions are used to perform operations on tuples and bags. Some commonly used bag and tuple functions are listed in Table 13.5:

Table 13.5: Bag and Tuple Functions

Function	Description	Syntax
TOBAG	Transforms one or more expressions to the type bag.	TOBAG(expression [, expression ...])
TOP	Returns the top-n tuples from a bag of tuples.	TOP(topN,column,relation)
TOTUPLE	Converts one or more expressions into the type tuple.	TOTUPLE(expression [, expression ...])

- **Load and Store functions**—These functions are used to load and extract data. Pig provides a set of built-in load and store functions, some of which are described in Table 13.6:

Table 13.6: Load and Store Functions

Function	Description	Syntax
BinStorage	Uses machine-readable format for loading and storing data	BinStorage()
PigDump	Uses UTF-8 format for storing data	PigDump()
PigStorage	Uses structured text files for loading and storing data	PigStorage(field_delimiter)
TextLoader	Uses UTF-8 format for loading unstructured data	TextLoader()

Error Handling in Pig

Multi-query execution in Pig processes an entire script or a batch of statements in a single step. By default, Pig always tries to run all the jobs that result from that; besides this, some of the jobs fail during execution. To check which jobs have succeeded or failed, we need to use one of the following options:

- Pig logs encapsulate all successful and failed store commands. These "Store commands" are identified by their output path. At the endpoint of execution, a summary line indicates the success, partial failure, or failure of all store commands.
- Pig returns different types of codes upon completion for these scenarios:
  - **Return code 0**—All jobs succeeded
  - **Return code 1**—Used for retrievable errors
  - **Return code 2**—All jobs have failed
  - **Return code 3**—Some jobs have failed

In some of the cases, it might be needed to withhold or sustain (i.e., fail) the whole script on detecting that the first code statement will fail failed in the script. To achieve this, we need to use the "-F" or "-stop_on_failure" command line flag. If these flags are used in the script, Pig will automatically stop execution when the first failed job is detected and discontinue the further processing. It also refers to the file commands that come after a failed "store" in the script and that will not be executed (this can be used to create "done" files).

This is how the flag is used:

```
$ pig -F myscript.pig
or
$ pig -stop_on_failure myscript.pig
```

Summary

This chapter discussed various aspects of data analysis using the Pig Latin language. After introducing Pig, the chapter explained Pig's architecture and the benefits of the language. After this, the chapter took you through the steps of installing Pig on your system. It also explained the properties of Pig and running the installed Pig. In addition, It described the structure of Pig. In the end, the chapter explained the operators and functions used in Pig.

Quick Revise

Multiple-Choice Questions

Q1. Pig was developed by:

a. Yahoo
b. Gmail
c. Twitter
d. Facebook

Ans. The correct option is a.

Q2. Which of the following operators is used for performing iteration?

a. FOREACH
b. ASSERT
c. FILTER
d. GROUP

Ans. The correct option is a.

Q3. UDF stands for:

a. Universal Defined Function
b. Unique Defined Function
c. Universal Disk Format
d. Unique Definition of Function

Ans. The correct option is c.

Q4. On starting Pig, you can specify Hadoop properties with which of the following options?

a. -A
b. -B
c. -P
d. -D

Ans. The correct option is d.

Q5. Which mode of Pig is also known as the Hadoop mode?

a. Local mode b. MapReduce mode

c. Global mode d. Universal mode

Ans. The correct option is b.

Subjective Questions

Q1. Discuss the two modes used for running the Pig scripts.

Ans. Pig scripts can be run in the following two modes:

- **Local mode**—In this mode, several scripts can run on a single machine without requiring Hadoop MapReduce and Hadoop Distributed File System (HDFS). This mode is useful for developing and testing Pig logic. Local mode is faster when you are using a small set of data to develop or test your code than the MapReduce infrastructure. This mode does not require Hadoop. The Pig program runs in the context of a local Java Virtual Machine (JVM). The data is accessed through the local file system of a single machine. This process is a separate one, outside of the Pig Latin compiler.
- **MapReduce mode**—It is also known as the Hadoop mode. In this case, the Pig script gets converted into a series of MapReduce jobs, which are then run on the Hadoop cluster.

Q2. What are the main reasons for developing Pig Latin?

Ans. The main reasons for developing Pig Latin are as follows:

- **Simple**—A streamlined method is provided in Pig Latin for interacting with MapReduce. This makes the creation of parallel programs simpler for analysis and processing on the Hadoop cluster. Complex tasks may need many interrelated transformations of data. These transformations can be easily encoded as data flow sequences in Pig Latin.
- **Smart**—The Pig Latin compiler transforms a Pig Latin program into a series of Java MapReduce jobs. The logic here is to ensure that the compiler can optimize the execution of these Java MapReduce jobs automatically. This allows the user to concentrate on semantics and not on how to optimize and access the data.
- **Extensible**—Pig Latin is extensible, which allows developers to add functions for addressing their business problems specifically.

Q3. What do you understand by Pig Latin application flow?

Ans. Pig Latin is regarded as a data flow language. This simply means that we can use Pig Latin to define a data stream and a sequence of transformations, which can be applied to the data as it moves throughout your application. In the case of a control flow language, on the other hand, we write a sequence of instructions. We also use concepts such as conditional logic and loops. In Pig Latin, we don't find loops and if statements.

The Pig syntax used for data processing flow is as follows:

```
X = LOAD 'file_name.txt';
...
Y = GROUP ...  ;
...
```

```
Z= FILTER ... ;
...
DUMP Y;
..
STORE Z into 'temp';
```

Q4. Discuss the use of the FOREACH operator.

Ans. The `FOREACH` operator performs iteration over every record to perform a transformation. When the given expressions are applied, the `FOREACH` operator generates a new collection of records. The syntax for using the `FOREACH` operator is as follows:

```
alias = FOREACH { block | nested_block };
```

In the preceding syntax,

- **alias—**Refers to the name of the relation, which is also known as a variable
- **block—**Refers to the outer block
- **nested_block—**Refers to the name of the inner block

Q5. What are the various statements used in flow of data processing in Pig Latin?

Ans. The statements used for data flow processing in Pig Latin are as follows:

- The `LOAD` statement is used for reading data from the file system. The data that requires to be manipulated is first loaded. It is typically stored in HDFS. For a Pig program to access the data, you first need to mention the file to use. For this, you use the `LOAD` statement. The specified file can be either an HDFS file or a directory. If a directory is specified, all files in that directory are loaded into the program.
- The `FILTER` statement is used for filtering the records.
- The `GROUP` statement is used for grouping the data.
- The `DUMP` statement is used for viewing the results on the screen. Typically, you use the 'DUMP' command to show the output on to the screen when the program needs to be debugged. When working in a production environment, you can use the `STORE` command to save the results in a file. These results can be used for further processing or analysis.
- The `STORE` statement is used for saving the results.

Q6. What is the use of the ASSERT operator in Pig Latin?

Ans. The `ASSERT` operator asserts a condition on the data. Assertions are used for ensuring that a condition is true on the data. The processing fails if any of the records violate the condition.

The syntax for using the `ASSERT` operator is as follows:

```
ASSERT alias BY expression [, message];
```

In the preceding syntax,

- **alias—**Refers to the name of the relation
- **BY—**Refers to a keyword

- **expression**—Refers to a boolean expression
- **message**—Refers to an error message when assertion fails

Q7. What is the use of the FILTER operator in Pig Latin?

Ans. The `FILTER` operator enables you to use a predicate for selecting the records that need to be retained in the pipeline. Only those records will be passed down the pipeline successfully for which the predicate defined in the `FILTER` statement remains true. The syntax for using the `FILTER` operator is as follows:

```
alias = FILTER alias BY expression;
```

In the preceding syntax:

- **alias**—Refers to the name of a table
- **BY**—Refers to a keyword
- **expression**—Refers to a boolean expression

Q8. Write a short note on the following operators:

- GROUP
- ORDER BY

Ans. Various operators are provided by Pig Latin for group and aggregate functions. The syntax of the `GROUP` operator in Pig Latin is similar to SQL, but it is different in functionality when compared to the `GROUP BY` clause in SQL. In Pig Latin, the `GROUP` operator is used for grouping data into single or multiple relations. The `GROUP BY` clause in SQL is used to create a group that can be input directly into single or multiple aggregate functions. You cannot include a star expression in a `GROUP BY` column in Pig Latin. The syntax for using the `GROUP` operator is as follows:

```
alias = GROUP alias { ALL | BY expression } [, alias ALL | BY expression…]
[ USING 'collected' | 'merge' ] [ PARTITION BY partitioner ] [ PARALLEL n ];
```

In the preceding syntax:

- **alias**—Refers to the name of a table
- **ALL**—Refers to the keyword used for inputting all the tuples into a group; for example, Z = GROUP A ALL;
- **BY**—Refers to a keyword used for grouping relations by field, tuple, or expression; for example, X = GROUP A BY f1;
- **PARTITION BY partitioner**—Describes the Hadoop partitioner

ORDER BY

The ORDER BY operator in Pig Latin is used for sorting a given relation depending on one or more fields. The syntax of the ORDER BY operator is as follows:

```
alias = ORDER alias BY {* [ASC|DESC] | field_alias [ASC | DESC] [, field_alias
[ASC|DESC]…] }
[PARALLEL n];
```

In the preceding syntax:

- **alias**—Refers to the name of a relation
- *—Signifies a tuple designator
- **field_alias**—Refers to a field in the relation
- **ASC**—Sorts data in ascending order
- **DESC**—Sorts data in descending order

Pig supports the ordering on fields with the simple types or by using the tuple designator (*). You cannot impose order fields with complex types or by expressions.

Q9. What is the use of DISTINCT operator in Pig Latin?

Ans. In Pig Latin, the `DISTINCT` operator works on the entire records and not on individual fields. This operator is used for removing duplicate fields from a given set of records. The syntax of the `DISTINCT` operator is as follows:

```
alias = DISTINCT alias [ PARTITION BY partitioner ] [ PARALLEL n ];
```

In the preceding syntax:

- **alias**—Refers to the name of the relation
- **PARTITION BY partitioner**—Refers to the Hadoop partitioner
- **PARALLEL n**—Enhances the parallelism of a task by mentioning the number of reduce tasks, n

Q10. What are joins? How many types of joins are there in Pig Latin?

Ans. The `JOIN` operator in Pig Latin is used for joining two or more relations. The joining of two rows is possible in case they have identical keys. If some records in the two rows do not match, these records can be deleted or dropped. The following two types of joins can be performed in Pig Latin:

- Inner join
- Outer join

The syntax of the `JOIN` operator is as follows:

```
alias = JOIN alias BY {expression|'('expression [, expression…]')'}
(, alias BY {expression|'('expression [, expression…]')'}…) [USING 'replicated' |
'skewed' | 'merge' | 'merge-sparse']
```

In the preceding syntax:

- **alias**—Refers to the name of a relation
- **BY**—Refers to a keyword
- **expression**—Refers to a field expression
- **USING**—Refers to a keyword

- **replicated**—Performs replicated joins
- **skewed**—Performs skewed joins
- **merge**—Performs merge joins
- **merge-sparse**—Performs merge-sparse joins

14

Using Oozie

A team of Yahoo! developers realized the scope of Hadoop-based data processing systems and developed Oozie. Oozie is a new workflow management and scheduling system. It was first released in 2010 as the GitHub project. Initially, it was developed for internal projects of Yahoo!, but as it is an open-source application, it has been adopted by other developers.

This chapter discusses various aspects of Oozie and its components in detail. It begins by introducing Oozie and then takes you through the steps of installing and configuring it. After this, the chapter discusses four important components of Oozie: the Oozie workflow, the Oozie coordinator, the Oozie bundle, and Oozie Parameterization with an Expression Language (EL). Toward the end, the chapter discusses the Oozie Job Execution Model, where you also learn about the various states of the model.

Introducing Oozie

Apache™ Oozie is a Java Web application that runs in a Java servlet container (i.e. Tomcat). Oozie is a server-based workflow engine and is used to schedule Apache Hadoop jobs.

Depending on the version, Oozie performs different functions as an engine. The three types of Oozie engines are as follows:

- A server-based workflow engine (Oozie v1)
- A server-based coordinator engine (Oozie v2)
- A server-based bundle engine (Oozie v3)

Oozie can store and run various Hadoop jobs like hive, pig, and so on. This essentially means it has a database to store workflow definitions and states as well as variables of any instances of a running workflow.

Oozie workflow is a set of actions specified by the control dependency DAG (Directed Acyclic Graph). This graph is specified in an XML Process Definition Language (xPDL).

Oozie performs the following jobs:

- **Oozie workflow jobs**—Workflow jobs are nodes in DAG. In other words, each node in DAG represents a job and the edges of the DAG represent jobs dependencies.
- **Oozie coordinator jobs**—These are recurrent Oozie workflow jobs that are triggered by availability of dependent data.

Oozie is distributed under the Apache license.

NOTE

DAG stands for Directed Acyclic Graph. It is a directed graph that does not have any directed cycle. It is commonly used in mathematics and computer science.

Figure 14.1 shows an example of DAG:

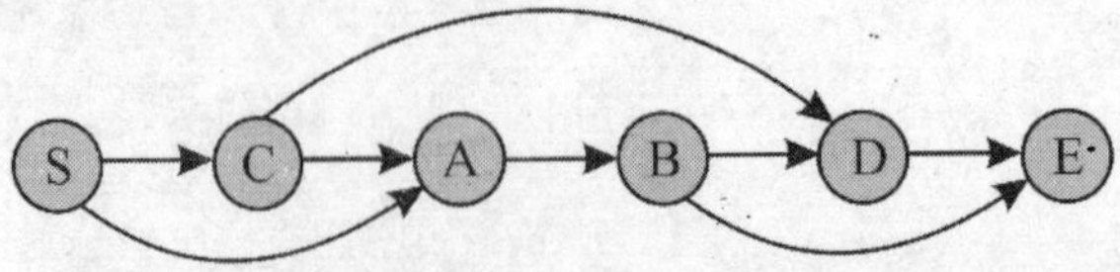

Figure 14.1: Example of DAG

In Figure 14.1, you can see that no directed cycle is formed from any node; thus, this graph is directed as well as a DAG.

Main Functional Components of Oozie

Oozie is a workflow scheduler and coordination system to manage Apache-Hadoop jobs. Oozie is only responsible for triggering (initiating) a task, while the execution of the task is done by Hadoop MapReduce. Oozie has four functional components:

- **Oozie workflow**—This component is used to specify the sequence of actions (or jobs) to be executed in the form of DAG.
- **Oozie coordinator**—This component automatically executes Oozie workflows on the basis of specified events and available system resources.
- **Oozie bundles**—This component defines and executes a bundle of applications with a coordinator application.
- **Oozie Service-Level Agreement (SLA)**—This component provides a way of tracking the whole execution process of workflows.

We will learn about these components of Oozie in detail in the further sections of the chapter. For now, let's look at their working with the help of a diagram.

Figure 14.2 shows the components of Oozie:

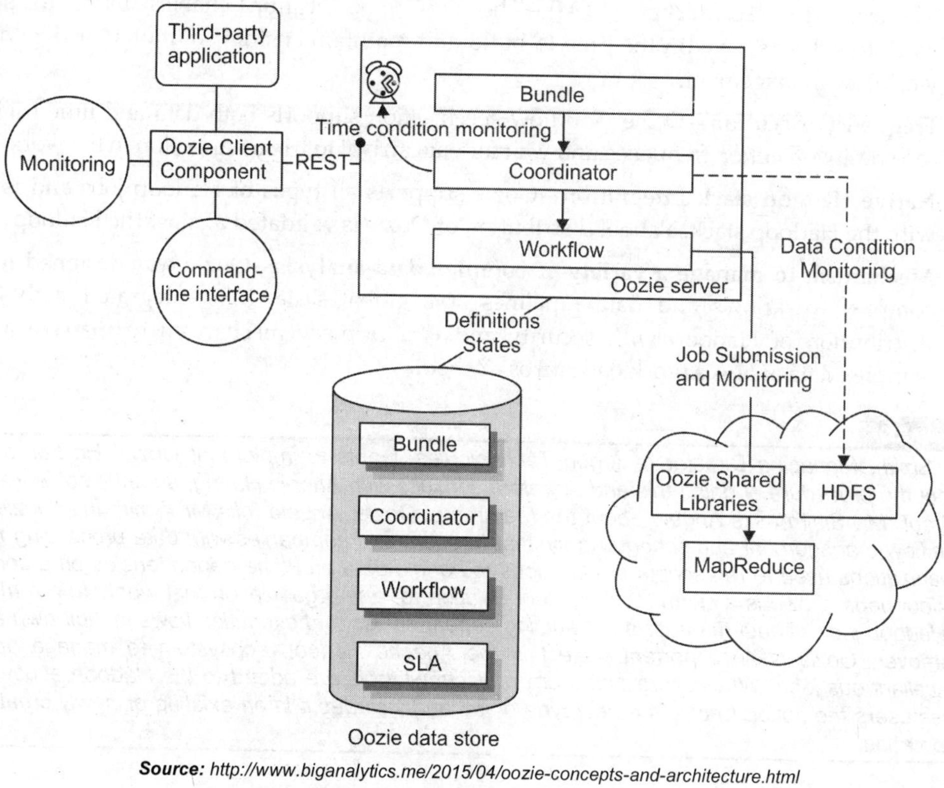

Source: *http://www.biganalytics.me/2015/04/oozie-concepts-and-architecture.html*

Figure 14.2: Components of Oozie

In Figure 14.2, you can see that one of the main components of Oozie is the Oozie server. This is a Web application and runs in a Java servlet container, i.e. Tomcat. It reads and executes workflows, coordinators, bundles, and SLA definitions.

The Oozie server implements a set of remote Web services Application Programming Interfaces (APIs) that can be invoked from Oozie's client components to third-party applications.

The Oozie server has a customizable database that can store corresponding states and process variables apart from workflows, coordinators, bundles, and SLA definitions. This database can be implemented by any of the following technologies: MySQL, Oracle, and Apache Derby.

Oozie provides a CLI (Command-Line Interface) interface on its client component, which is a thin Java wrapper (that is, a small Java container that provides access to Web service APIs through the command line) around Oozie Web service APIs. If they have sufficient permissions, these APIs can also be used by third-party applications.

Benefits of Oozie

The benefits of Oozie are as follows:

- **Complex workflow action dependencies**—The Oozie workflow contains actions and dependencies. Users create DAG to model their workflow. At runtime, Oozie manages dependencies and executes actions when the dependencies identified in the DAG are satisfied.
- **Reduces Time-To-Market (TTM)**—The DAG specification enables users to specify the workflow. Users save on the time to build and maintain custom solutions for dependency and workflow management.
- **Frequency execution**—Oozie workflow specification supports both data and time triggers. Users can specify execution frequency and wait for data arrival to trigger an action in the workflow.
- **Native Hadoop stack integration**—Oozie supports all types of Hadoop jobs and is integrated with the Hadoop stack. Yahoo! distribution of Oozie is validated against the Hadoop stack.
- **Mechanism to manage a variety of complex data analysis**—Oozie was designed for Yahoo!'s complex workflows and data pipelines at a global scale. It is integrated with the Yahoo! distribution of Hadoop with security and is a primary mechanism to manage a variety of complex data analysis workloads across Yahoo!

SCENARIO

Mr. Smith, Managing Director of Argon Technologies, wants to implement Oozie. He has some doubts about the procedure of doing this and therefore consults with Angelo Huang, a senior software engineer at Yahoo! Mr. Smith asks Angelo about the features of Oozie. Angelo tells Mr. Smith that Oozie provides a workflow management and scheduling system to users and companies with data processing needs. Most organizations used to run scripts or Cron jobs to handle data and time dependencies on a combination of Hadoop jobs. Oozie is a clean, cost-efficient solution for any organization that wants to run multiple types of Hadoop jobs without the hassle of handling dependencies and execution flows in their own applications. Moreover, Oozie is an important project in the Apache Hadoop ecosystem to manage and schedule miscellaneous jobs. When more and more projects or tools are added to the Hadoop ecosystem, Oozie gives users the option to plugin a new type of job and includes it in an existing or newly created workflow application.

Installing and Configuring Oozie

In this section, we are going to learn how to install and configure Oozie on a Linux platform. In order to process fairly large amounts of data, you would need to schedule the Hadoop jobs efficiently. Therefore, you would require a workflow scheduler. As mentioned earlier, Oozie workflow engine provides an effective solution for this. The installation and configuration of Oozie is done on a Linux operating system, Ubuntu.

You need to have the `Oozie TAR` setup file as well as the `Maven-3.0-4`, `openjdk-7-jdk`, and Hadoop packages installed on your Ubuntu operating system.

Now, perform the following steps to complete your installation:

1. Extract the Oozie package.
2. Create a new group named oozie by typing the following command:

```
$sudo addgroup oozie
```

After entering the preceding command, the terminal appears, as shown in Figure 14.3:

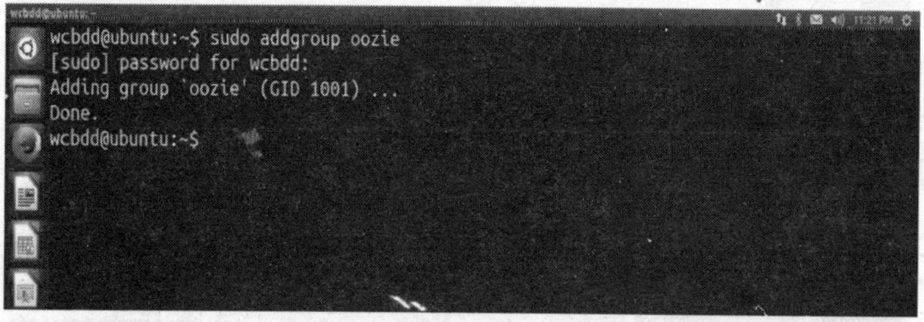

Figure 14.3: Creating a New Group for Installing Oozie

This group is created with a purpose of installing Oozie for particular users. As shown in Figure 14.3, you need to provide the password for the virtual lab environment to complete the process of creating the Oozie group.

3. Add a user named oozie to the oozie group by typing the following command:

```
$sudo adduser - -ingroup oozie oozie
```

The terminal, after entering the preceding command, appears as shown in Figure 14.4:

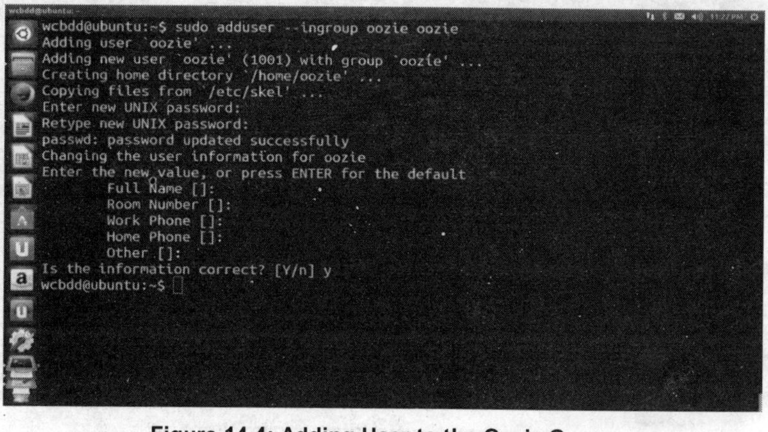

Figure 14.4: Adding User to the Oozie Group

4. Paste the following link in your Web browser to download the `Oozie TAR` setup file:

```
http://apache.mirros.pair.com/oozie/3.3.1/
```

The Apache Oozie Window opens, as shown in Figure 14.5:

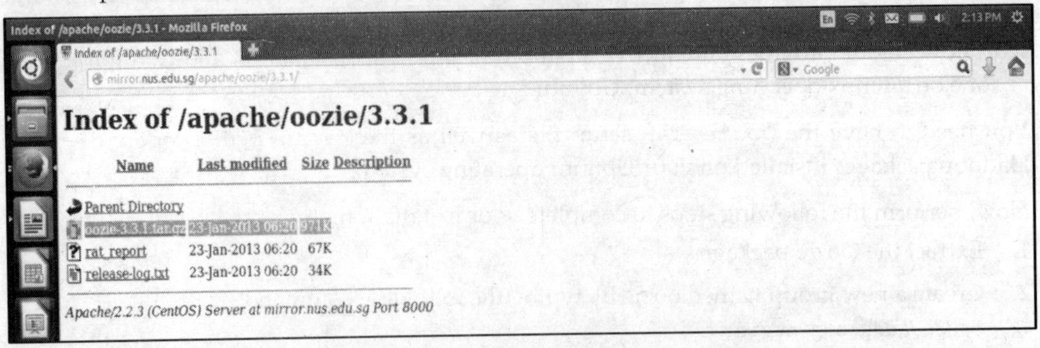

Figure 14.5: Downloading the Oozie Setup File

5. Extract the `Oozie TAR` package by typing the following command on the terminal:

```
$tar xfv oozie-3.3.1.tar.gz
```

6. Build Distro by typing the following commands on the terminal:

```
$ cd oozie-3.3.1
$ ./bin/mkdistro.sh -DskipTests
```

NOTE

After successful execution of the commands, all the requisite JARs will be downloaded. This step may take some additional time to execute.

The output, after the commands are successfully executed, is shown in Figure 14.6:

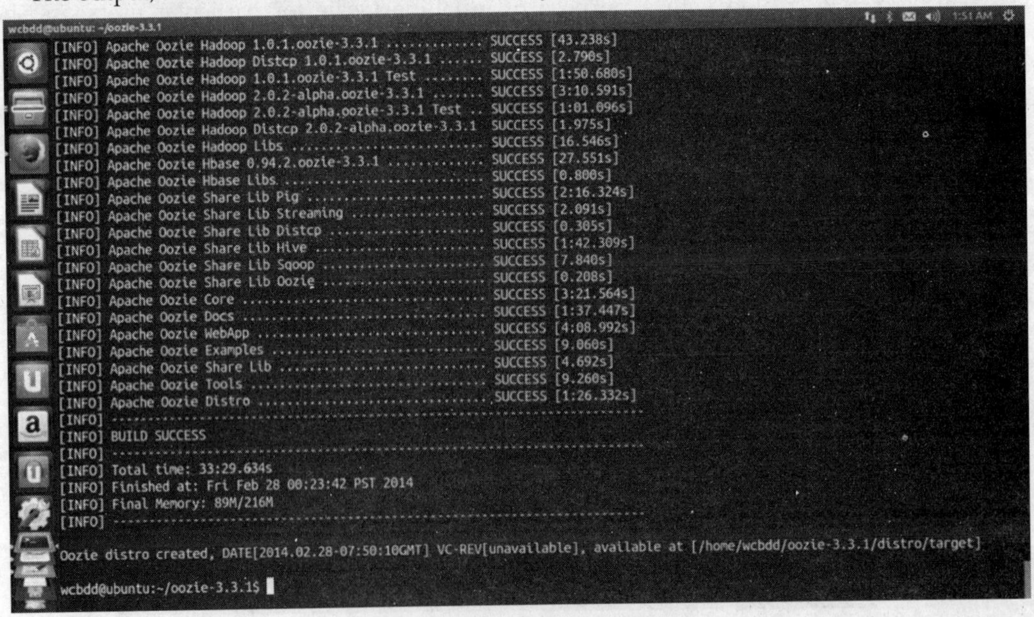

Figure 14.6: Building Oozie Distro

A new package file, `oozie-3.3.1-distro.tar.gz`, will be generated from the execution of the command.

7. Make the current user the owner of the `oozie-3.3.1` directory by typing the following command:

```
$sudo chown -R oozie:oozie /home/wcbdd/oozie-3.3.1
```

8. Set the value of the `OOZIE_HOME` and `HADOOP_HOME` variables by typing the following commands:

```
$ export OOZIE_HOME=/home/wcbdd/oozie-3.3.1
$ export HADOOP_HOME=/home/wcbdd/apache/hadoop-1.0.4
```

9. Move the Distro to the `OOZIE_HOME` location and extract it by typing the following commands:

```
$sudo -u oozie mv distro/target/oozie-3.3.1-distro.tar.gz 'dirname $OOZIE_HOME'
$cd dirname $OOZIE_HOME
$tar xvfz oozie-3.3.1-distro.tar.gz
```

The terminal, after entering the preceding commands, appears as shown in Figure 14.7:

Figure 14.7: Extracting Oozie Distro

10. Create a soft link for easily accessing Oozie by typing the following commands:

```
$ ln -s oozie-3.3.1 oozie
$ cd oozie
```

NOTE

A soft link (also known as a symbolic link or symlink) consists of a special type of file that serves as a reference to another file or directory. Unix/Linux-like operating systems often use soft links.

11. Download and extract the `ext-2.2.1.zip` file for the Oozie Web console interface, by typing the following command:

```
$sudo -u oozie wget http://dev.sencha.com/deploy/ext-2.2.1.zip && unzip ext-
2.2.1.zip -d ext-2.2.1
```

A snapshot of the directory in which the `ext-2.2.1.zip` file has been extracted is shown in Figure 14.8:

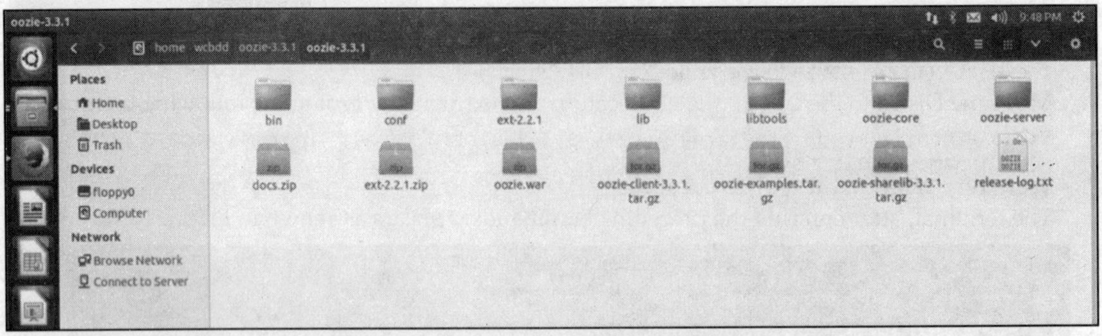

Figure 14.8: Storing the ext-2.2.1.zip File

12. Configure Oozie to use the required Java ARchives (JARs) by typing the following command:

```
$sudo -u oozie ./bin/oozie-setup.sh -hadoop 0.20.2 $HADOOP_HOME -extjs ext-2.2.1 -
jars "$HADOOP_HOME/lib/commons-configuration-1.6.jar $HADOOP_HOME/lib/jackson-core-
asl-1.8.8.jar:$HADOOP_HOME/ lib/jackson-mapper-asl-1.8.8.jar"
```

The terminal, after entering the preceding command, appears as shown in Figure 14.9:

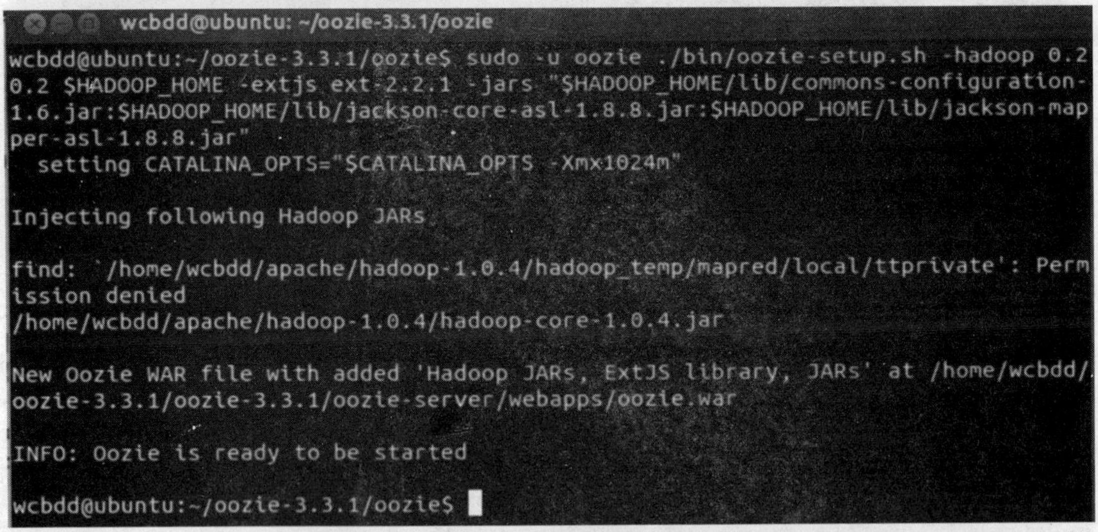

Figure 14.9: Adding the Required JARs to Oozie

13. Create a database, which is a requisite before starting Oozie, by typing the following command:

```
$sudo -u oozie ./bin/ooziedb.sh create -sqlfile oozie.sql -run
```

The terminal, after entering the preceding command, appears as shown in Figure 14.10:

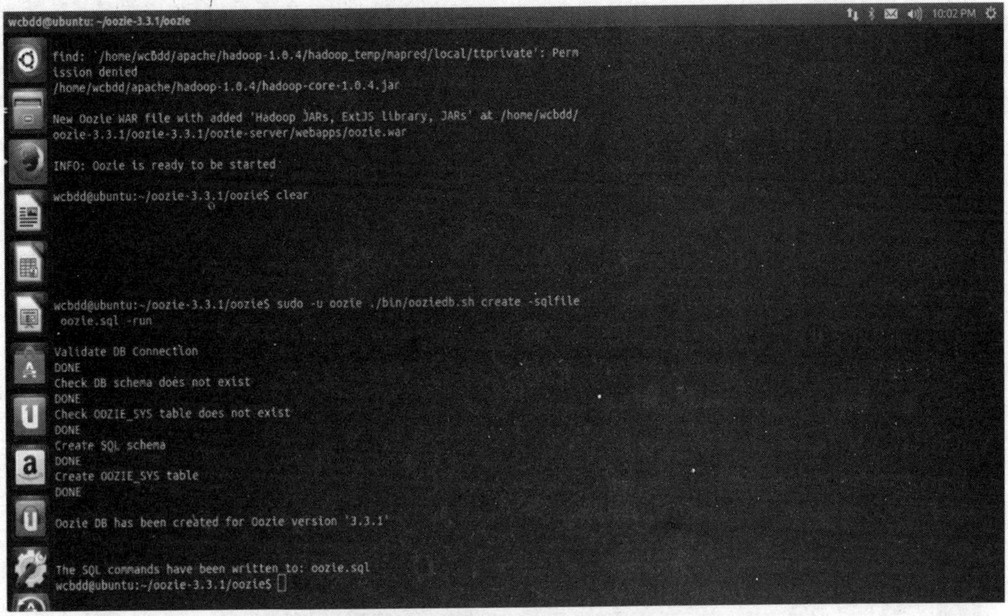

Figure 14.10: Creating a Database

14. Edit the `hdfs-site.xml` file by typing the following command:

```
$gedit /home/wcbdd/apache/hadoop-1.0.4/conf/hdfs-site.xml
```

15. Update the Hadoop `hdfs-site.xml` file to include the following property:

```
<property>
<name>dfs.permissions</name>
<value>false</value>
</property>
```

16. Start the Oozie server by typing the following command:

```
$sudo -u oozie ./bin/oozie-start.sh
```

The terminal, after entering the preceding command, appears as shown in Figure 14.11:

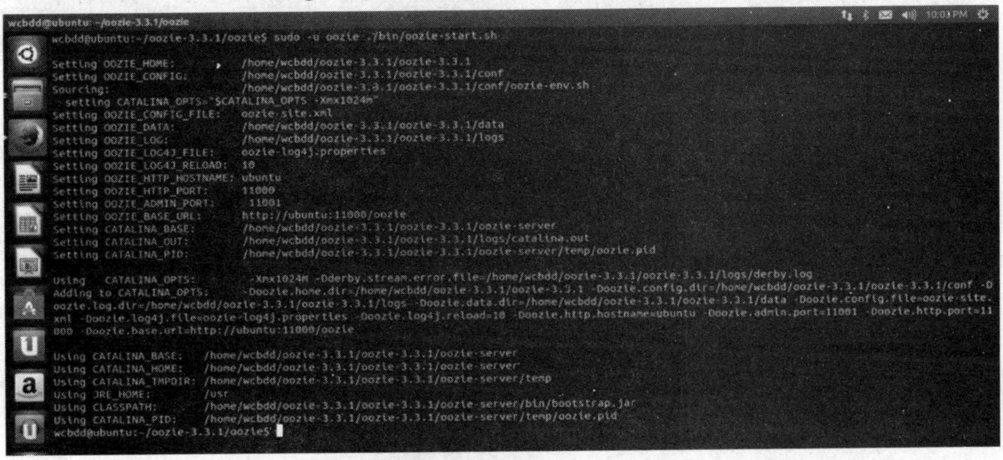

Figure 14.11: Starting the Oozie Server

17. Check the status of Oozie to verify the installation by typing the following commands:

```
$ export OOZIE_URL=http://localhost:11000/oozie
$ bin/oozie admin -status
```

After executing the commands, Oozie displays the System mode as Normal, as shown in Figure 14.12:

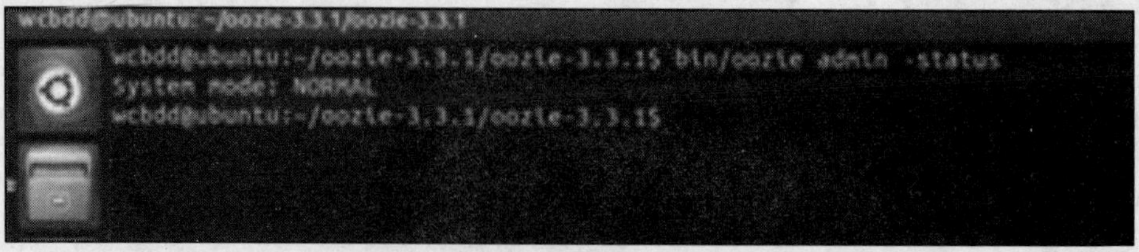

Figure 14.12: Verifying Installation

18. Check the Oozie Web console by pasting the following URL in the address bar of a Web browser like Chrome, Internet Explorer, etc.:

```
http://localhost:11000
```

The Web console appears as shown in Figure 14.13:

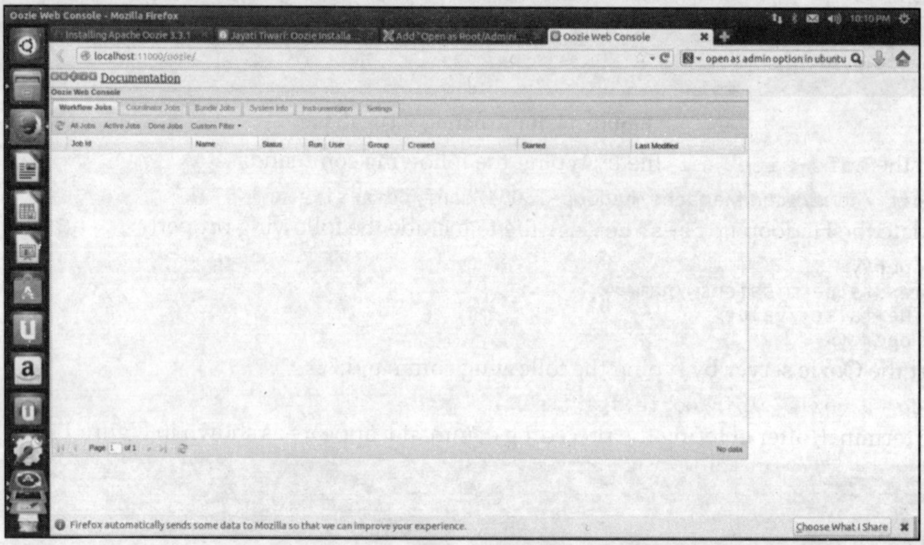

Figure 14.13: Viewing the Oozie Web Console

19. Update the Hadoop `core-site.xml` file located in the conf folder of Hadoop's directory files to include the following properties:

```
<property>
<name>hadoop.proxyuser.oozie.groups</name>
<value>oozie</value>
</property>
<property>
<name>hadoop.proxyuser.oozie.hosts</name>
<value>localhost</value>
</property>
```

20. Import the Oozie library to Hadoop Distributed File System (HDFS) by typing the following commands:

```
$ cd $OOZIE_HOME
$ sudo -u oozie tar xvfz oozie-sharelib-3.3.1.tar.gz
$ $HADOOP_HOME/bin/hadoop dfs -put share share
```

The terminal, after entering the preceding commands, appears as shown in Figure 14.14:

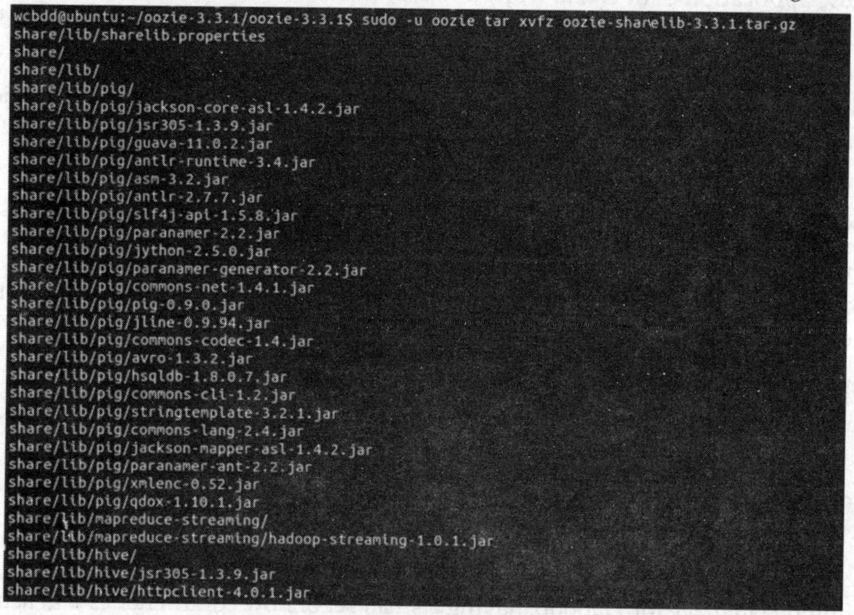

Figure 14.14: Importing the Oozie Library to HDFS

Oozie has now been installed and configured on your system.

CASELET

Suppose you are working on an issue as to solve the problem of the Oozie coordinator, which pools MyNode for data check. If most of the jobs are dependent, it will create an overhead on MyNode. Now, how can you validate your work on a large scale like 20000 jobs per day?

The answer is Mumak, a simulator that can simulate a Hadoop cluster. The latest release of Mumak is Mumak 0.21. JIRA and Ankus are other projects that can be used for the same purpose. Using Mumak or Ankus as a simulator for analysis will help you test your solution on various scales.

Understanding the Oozie Workflow

An Oozie workflow is a DAG (Directed Acyclic Graph) of Hadoop computation tasks (known as actions) and flow controls to coordinate tasks and handle dependencies among actions.

The Oozie workflow is based on the following terminologies:

- **Actions**—An action is a specification of an individual workflow task. It represents the execution of code, a Hive script, or a MapReduce job. The Oozie workflow action triggers jobs on remote nodes. As the execution of the current job is completed, the processes that executed the job call back to Oozie and notify it about the completion. After receiving the notification, Oozie starts the next job.

- **Transition**—After the completion of a given job or action, the action to be executed next is specified by a transaction. A transition also describes the dependency among the actions.
- **Workflow**—A collection of actions and transitions arranged in a dependency sequence graph is known as workflow.
- **Workflow application**—An Oozie workflow that is defined in the Oozie workflow language is known as a workflow application. The Oozie server can interpret and understand the Oozie workflow application. The Oozie server can store Oozie workflow applications in its database.
- **Workflow job**—The Oozie server runs the Oozie workflow definitions, and the Oozie workflow job controls the sequence of these workflow definitions.

Oozie also supports two more actions, which are as follows:

- **Synchronous**—A synchronous action executes on an execution thread of the Oozie server.
- **Asynchronous**—An asynchronous action executes on a Hadoop cluster in the form of a `MapReduce/Pig/Hive/Sqoop` job. The Oozie server initiates asynchronous action and waits till the completion of the action.

A transition is managed by the following two types of conditions:

- **Structural conditions**—These are conditions that are statically defined in a workflow DAG. A structural condition includes transition-changing states and fork-join constructs.
- **Runtime execution conditions**—These are the conditions on which an action can use the results of previously executed actions in the form of process variables.

Oozie describes workflows by using hPDL (Hadoop Process Definition Language). hPDL is a process-definition language for Hadoop, having a small set of flow control nodes and action nodes.

Flow control nodes define the flow of execution. They also define the beginning/end of a workflow and various control structures like decision, fork, and join nodes.

Table 14.1 describes the various flow control nodes in Oozie:

Table 14.1: Flow Control Nodes in Oozie

Flow Control Node	XML Element Type	Description
Start node	Start	This specifies a starting point for an Oozie workflow.
End node	End	This specifies an end point for an Oozie workflow.
Decision node	Decision	This expresses the switch-case logic.
Fork node	Fork	This splits the execution into multiple concurrent paths.
Join node	Join	This forces the workflow execution to wait until every concurrent execution path of a previous fork node arrives at the join node.
Sub-workflow node	Sub-workflow	This invokes a sub-workflow.
Kill node	Kill	This forces the Oozie server to kill the current workflow job.

An action node triggers the execution of a computation or processing task of the workflow. Oozie provides the following types of actions:

- Hadoop file system action
- Hadoop MapReduce action
- Java action
- Pig action
- Oozie sub-workflow action

Table 14.2 describes various action nodes in Oozie:

Table 14.2: Action Nodes in Oozie

Action Node	XML Element Type	Description	Type
Java action	Java	This invokes the main() method of the specified Java class.	Asynchronous
Pig action	Pig	This runs a Pig job.	Asynchronous
MapReduce action	MapReduce	This runs a Hadoop MapReduce job (This could be a Java MapReduce job, a streaming job, or a pipe job).	Asynchronous
Shell action	Fs	This enables you to define a sequence of delete, mkdir, move, and chmod commands executed on HDFS.	Synchronous

Additionally, Oozie supports the extensibility mechanism that allows users to create new customized actions.

Table 14.3 provides a brief description of the actions and their types performed by the XML element:

Table 14.3: Extension Actions in Oozie

Action Node	XML Element Type	Description	Type
Hive action	Hive	This runs a Hive job.	Asynchronous
Email action	Email	This sends an email.	Synchronous
SSH action	Ssh	This invokes an action in a specified shell script located on an Oozie server node (not HDFS).	Synchronous
Sqoop action	Sqoop	This runs a Sqoop job (as a MapReduce job).	Asynchronous
Distcp action	Distcp	This runs a distributed copy job (as a MapReduce job).	Asynchronous

You already know that Oozie supports synchronous and asynchronous actions. In Tables 14.2 and 14.3, you can see that Email, Ssh, Shell, and fs are synchronous actions, while all others are asynchronous actions. We will discuss the execution of asynchronous actions by Oozie next.

Figure 14.15 shows the Oozie workflow definition XML schema, also known as hPDL schema:

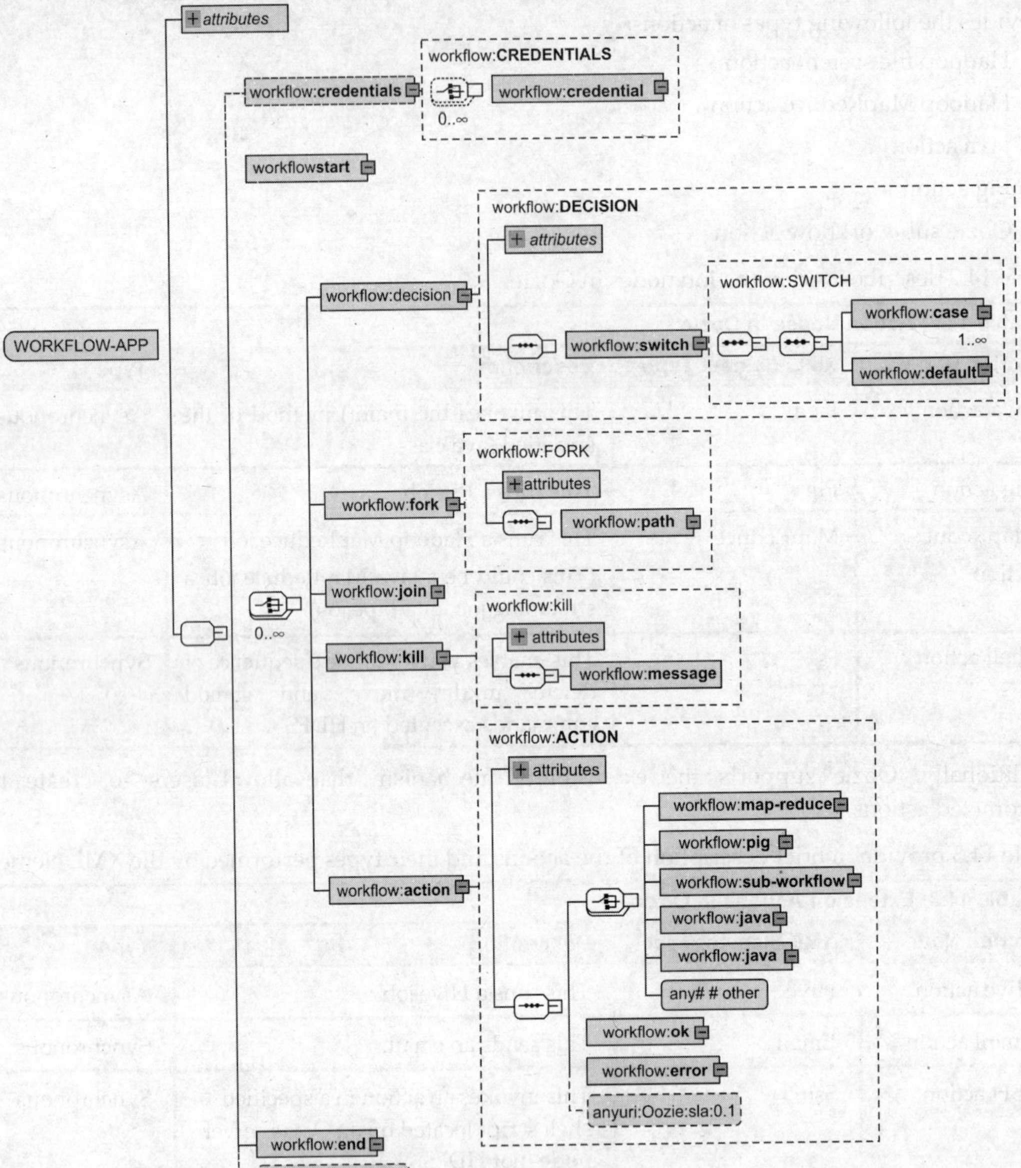

Figure 14.15: The hPDL Schema

Execution of Asynchronous Actions in Oozie

Any asynchronous action in the Hadoop cluster can be executed in the form of Hadoop MapReduce jobs. This makes Oozie scalable.

When you use Hadoop to perform processing/computation tasks triggered by a workflow action, workflow jobs must wait until the completion of these tasks before moving to the next node in the workflow. However, how does Oozie get to know the completion of the current processing/computation task? Oozie does this by the following two ways:

- **Through callback URL**—Before the starting of any processing/computation task, Oozie assigns a unique callback URL to the task. As the task finishes its execution, it gives a notification about it in the callback URL.
- **Through polling**—Sometimes, the current is unable to inform the callback URL about the task's completion for some reason, such as a transient network failure. In this case, Oozie uses the polling mechanism. In this mechanism, Oozie selects a task to execute and complete itself.

A single instance of an Oozie server can support thousands of jobs. The Action-Executor pattern mechanism is used to keep these jobs separate from one another. This mechanism also allows Oozie to conserve server resources.

Implementing the Oozie Workflow

Each Oozie asynchronous action uses an appropriate Action/Executor pair. The Oozie Executor framework is at the heart of the Oozie Server architecture.

NOTE

The Action/Executor pattern separates what must be done (the action) from how it is to be done (the execution). The classical example of this pattern is the Java concurrency API `(java.util.concurrent package).`

Listing 14.1 shows the implementation of the Oozie workflow to display 'Hello World':

Listing 14.1: Implementation of Oozie Workflow to Display 'Hello World'

```
<workflow-app name="HelloWorld-wf" xmlns="uri:oozie:workflow:0.3"
xmlns:sla="uri:oozie:sla:0.1">
<start to="cluster"/>
<action name="cluster">                Starts the execution of the program
1<java>
<prepare> [PREPARE SECTION] </prepare>
<main-class>HelloWorld</main-classarg>[PROGRAM ARGUMENT]</arg>


<!-Providing details about the main class and the arguments to the program - ->
<archive>[ARCHIVE SECTION]</archive>
<file>[FILE SECTION]</file>
</java>
<ok to="end "/>
<error to="kill "/>
</action>
2<kill name="fail"> ◄── Kill section begins
<message>
HelloWorld-wf failed to execute!
<!-Error message on failure - ->
</message>
</kill>
<end name="end"/>
</workflow-app>
```

The workflow shown in Listing 14.1 starts with the execution of the Java action. Here, the start node specifies the name of the first node to execute.

This Java action is implemented using the `HelloWorld` class with the specified program arguments. The `<main-class>` element specifies the Java class with the main method, which is used as a string point of executing the action code in the Hadoop job. With the `<prepare>`, `<archive>`, and `<file>` tags, you can specify additional information for class execution.

If the class execution completes successfully, that is, with an exit code of 0, the transition will progress to an end action otherwise the transition will progress to a kill action and produce a "HelloWorld-wf failed to execute!" message.

Because a kill action has no explicit transition specified, the next action, that is, end, will be invoked after the completion of the kill action. The end action stops the execution of the process.

Figure 14.16 shows the submission and execution of a MapReduce job in the Oozie Executor framework:

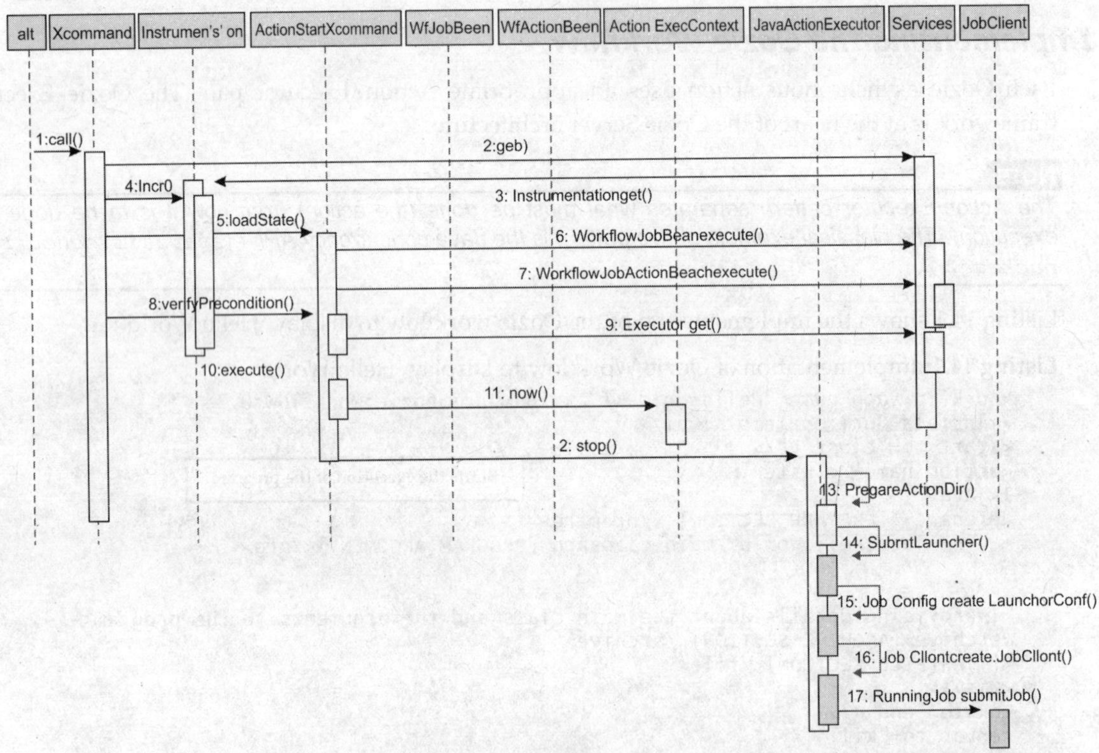

Figure 14.16: Submission of a Job for the Java Action in the Oozie Executor Framework

The submission and execution of the MapReduce job, as shown in Figure 14.16, can be explained as follows:

1. Processing of the Java command starts with the invocation of the `call()` method on the `XCommand` class. The `call()` method constructs a MapReduce job and submits it to the Java action.
2. The `call()` method obtains the instance of the `Instrumentation` class from the `Services` class and maintains a pool of `Instrumentation` instances. This instance is used to set up variables, locks, counters, and timers for the job.

3. Now, the operation uses the `loadState()` method of the `ActionStartXCommand` class and loads all required configurations of the job. Implementation of the `ActionStartXCommand` class is done by the Workflow object `wfJob` of the `WorkflowJobBean` class and the action object `wfAction`.
4. The `call()` method of the `XCommand` class uses the `verifyPrecondition()` method of the `ActionStartXCommand` class to check the job status and obtain the instance of `JavaActionExecutor` from the `Services` class, which maintains a pool of `ActionExecutor` instances.
5. The `call()`calls the `execute()` method of the `ActionStartXCommand` class to finish all remaining work.

The `execute()` method performs the following tasks:

- Prepares the Hadoop job configuration and defines all retry policies
- Creates the action execution context of the `ActionExecutorContext` class, which serves as the container of the job configuration elements
- Invokes a `start()` method on `JavaActionExecutor` to complete the invocation

The `start()` method of `JavaActionExecutor` leverages a set of launchers to implement different steps of the action invocation. These launchers are created during `ActionExecutor` initialization, as shown in Listing 14.2.

Listing 14.2: Launcher Classes in JavaActionExecutor

```
protected List<Class> getLauncherClasses() { List<Class> classes =
new ArrayList<Class>(); classes.add(LauncherMapper.class);
classes.add(LauncherSecurityManager.class);
classes.add(LauncherException.class);
classes.add(LauncherMainException.class);
classes.add(FileSystemActions.class);
classes.add(PrepareActionsDriver.class);
classes.add(ActionStats.class);
classes.add(ActionType.class);
return classes;
}
```

The `start()` method of `ActionStartCommand` performs the following tasks:

1. It calls the `prepareActionDir()` method, which moves the JAR file related to the launcher's job from the Oozie server node to the action directory on HDFS.
2. It invokes the `submitLauncher()` method, which does the following:
   - Parses the action XML configuration to set the configuration of Hadoop objects and the `JobConf` class by using the `HadoopAccessorService` class.
   - Configures the `LauncherMapper` object by setting the main class from the `<java-main>` Java action element and program arguments from the `<arg>` Java action elements.
   - Specifies the libraries (the `<archive>` section) and files (the `<file>` section), which will be moved to the Hadoop-distributed cache. The `submitLauncher()` method sets the credentials and names parameters, and creates an instance of the Hadoop `JobClient` class. The `JobClient` object is used by the `Java Executor` to submit the Hadoop job to the cluster and implement the retry logic.

- Retrieves the URL of the submitted job from the `JobConf` instance. The Oozie server uses this URL to track the job state in the Oozie console.

3. The `Java` class specified in the `Oozie java` action is actually invoked on the Hadoop cluster from the instance of the `LauncherMapper` class that implements the `org.apache.hadoop.mapred.Mapper` interface. In the `map()` method (called only once), it retrieves the class name specified in the Oozie action definition and invokes the `main` method of that class with the (simplified) code fragment, as shown in Listing 14.3:

Listing 14.3: Invocation of the Java Action Main Class on the Hadoop Cluster

```
// To obtain the job configuration assigned.............................................
String mainClass = getJobConf().get(CONF_OOZIE_ACTION_MAIN_CLASS);
String[] args = getMainArguments(getJobConf());
Class klass = getJobConf().getClass(CONF_OOZIE_ACTION_MAIN_CLASS, Object.class);
Method mainMethod = klass.getMethod("main", String[].class);
mainMethod.invoke(null, (Object) args);
.........................................................
```

`MapReduceActionExecutor` extends the `JavaActionExecutor` class by overriding several methods. The implementation of the `setupActionConf()` method supports the Streaming and Pipes parameters (if the map-reduce action specifies Pipes or Streaming APIs).

The implementation of the `getLauncherClasses()` method adds the main methods for different types of map-reduce invocations, including Pipes, Streaming, and so on, as shown in Listing 14.4:

Listing 14.4: Launchers for the mapReduce Action

```
protected List<Class> getLauncherClasses()

1{ List<Class> classes = super.getLauncherClasses();



2classes.add(LauncherMain.class);

classes.add(MapReduceMain.class);
classes.add(StreamingMain.class);
classes.add(PipesMain.class); return classes;
}
```

Classes is the object of the List class referring to the parent class

In the following lines, the object is added to the main-class of Launcher, MapReducer, streaming and Pipes.

When `jobClient.submitJob`(launcherJobConf) is invoked in the `submitLauncher()` method of the `JavaActionExecutor` (base) class, the MapReduceMain, StreamingMain, or PipesMain launcher is used. As an example, for the Java MapReduce action, this would effectively result in running `MapReduceMain.main`, which starts a new MapReduce job on the cluster.

Oozie Recovery Capabilities

Oozie can recover workflow jobs in two ways. First, when action starts successfully, Oozie applies the MapReduce retry mechanisms for recovery. On the other hand, if an action fails to start, Oozie uses some other recovery techniques according to the nature of the failure. For example, when any transient failure (remote system temporarily unavailable or any other types of network problems) occurs, Oozie first sets the Maximum Retries and Retry Interval values and then performs the retries.

Table 14.4 shows the parameter names of the OozieClient class with their default values:

Table 14.4: Parameter Names of OozieClient with their Default Values

Parameter Name	Default Value	Defined in Class
`oozie.wf.action.max.retries`	3	`org.apache.oozie.client.OozieClient`
`oozie.wf.action.retry.interval`	60 sec	`org.apache.oozie.client.OozieClient`

It is important to note that the Oozie workflow engine does not support the automatic start of workflow jobs, their repeated execution, and data dependencies among the workflow jobs. These activities are done by the Oozie coordinator, about which you will learn in a later section of the chapter.

Oozie Workflow Life Cycle

Once the workflow application is loaded to the workflow server, it is now known as a workflow job. The Oozie workflow lifecycle is shown in Figure 14.17:

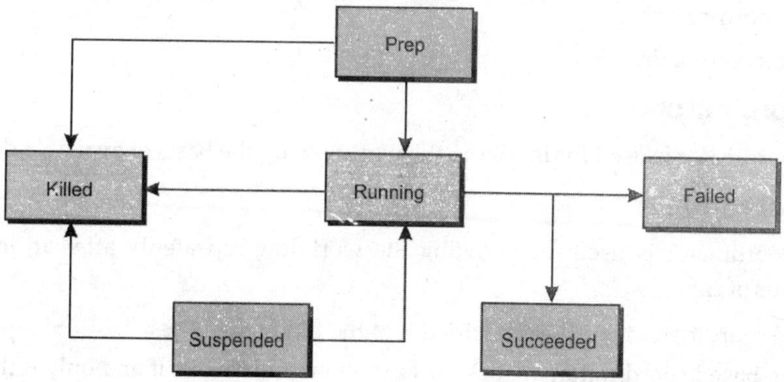

Figure 14.17: Lifecycle of Workflow Job

As you can see in Figure 14.17, the following possible states exist for any workflow job in Oozie:

- **PREP**—Oozie loads the workflow job in the PREP state.
- **RUNNING**—The job moves from the PREP state to the RUNNING state when it starts execution.
- **SUSPENDED**—When a running workflow is suspended by the user, it enters the SUSPENDED state.
- **SUCCEEDED**—When the running workflow reaches the desired goal, it enters the SUCCEEDED state.
- **KILLED**—The job moves from the PREP state to the KILLED state when it is deleted by the user.
- **FAILED**—When the workflow job fails to execute, it enters the FAILED state.

Oozie Coordinator

The Oozie coordinator is used to specify the conditions for a workflow in the form of predicates. It triggers the execution of the workflow at the specified time, on regular intervals, or on the basis of the available data.

A predicate is a conditional statement with some parameters like date, time, and occurrence of any external events. The workflow job/action starts if and only if the specified predicate is satisfied.

Oozie version 2.x and higher support coordinator jobs. A coordinator job can be defined in XPDL.

NOTE

XML Process Definition Language (XPDL) is a language to interchange the "business process definitions" among the various workflow products. The Workflow Management Coalition Working Group (WMCWG) introduced XPDL, now known as XPDL 1.0.

Types of Oozie Coordinator

According to the functionality, the Oozie coordinator can be classified into the following two types:

- File-based coordinator
- Time-based coordinator

File-based Coordinator

A file-based coordinator is used for invoking the workflow on the basis of available data and polling.

Time-based Coordinator

This type of coordinator is used for invoking the workflow repeatedly after an interval between specified periods of time.

The time-based coordinator is further classified into the following types:

- **Simple file-based coordinator**—An Oozie job/action will invoke if and only if the required data is available and the corresponding predicate is true.
- **Sliding window-based coordinator**—Oozie job/action can be invoked frequently and data are aggregated over multiple overlapping previous instances. For example, invoking it at a frequency of 30 seconds and running action on aggregated previous five instances of 30 second data.
- **Rollups-based coordinator**—It is invoked after a long period of time and data are aggregated over multiple previous instances from the last time of invocation. For example, it will run once a day, and trigger a workflow that aggregates 24 instances of hourly data.

The Oozie coordinator language is an XML dialect. Figure 14.18 shows the schema diagram of the Oozie coordinator language:

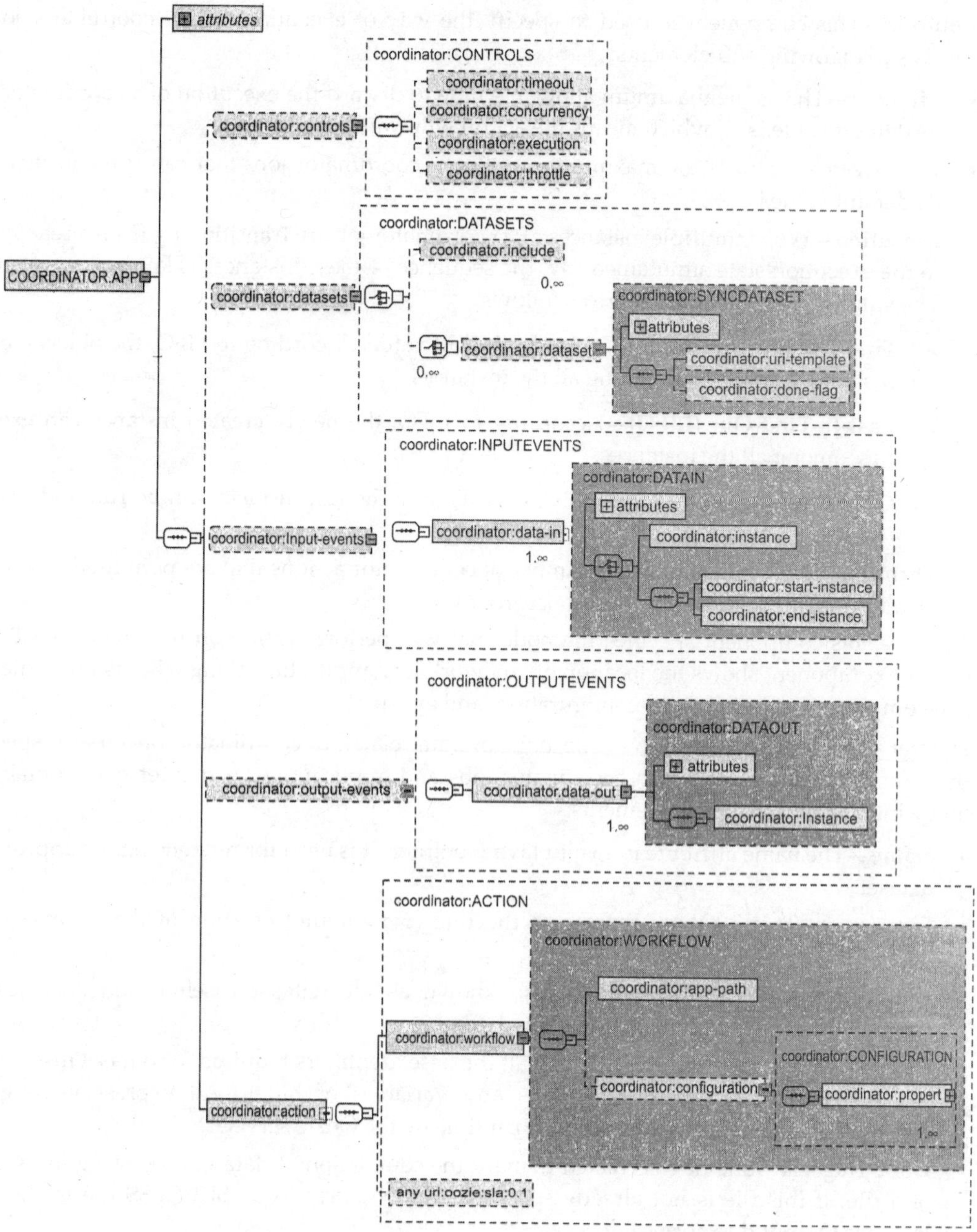

Figure 14.18: Coordinator Language Schema

The following is a description of the coordinator language schema:

- **Coordinator App**—This is a main component of the Oozie coordinator. It is a wrapper component that defines various attributes for a coordinator. It can include other components with the coordinator component. The attributes of the coordinator app are name, start/end, and frequency.

- **Controls**—This component is used to specify the way of execution of any coordinator job. It consists of following sub-elements:
  - **Timeout**—This is the maximum allowable time to discard the execution of a coordinator job. Its default value is -1, which means the action will wait forever.
  - **Concurrency**—This is the maximum number of coordinator jobs that can run concurrently. Its default value is 1.
  - **Execution**—When multiple instances of a coordinator job are transitioning from a ready state to the execution state simultaneously, the sequence of these instances is known as execution. The valid values of execution are as follows:
    - **First-In-First-Out (FIFO)**—This is a default value. According to FIFO, the oldest created instance executes first among all the instances.
    - **Last-In-First-Out (LIFO)**—According to LIFO, the newly created instance can execute first among all the instances.
    - **ONLYLAST**—According to ONLYLAST, only the last instance can be run and discard (forcefully) all older instances.
  - **Throttle**—This is the maximum number of coordinator actions that are permitted to wait for all additional conditions to fulfill concurrently.
- **Action**—This component specifies the node that will perform action on the given coordinator job. The component shows the location of any workflow application along with its properties. Its sub-components are workflow, configuration, and app-path.
- **Dataset**—This component shows collections of data related to coordinator jobs. It also specifies the data dependences between coordinator jobs and applications. A dataset may contain the following attributes and sub-elements:
  - **Name**—The name attribute is a valid Java identifier. It is used for referencing the appropriate dataset.
  - **Frequency**—This attribute represents the rate (per minute) creation of the instances of a dataset.
  - **Initial-instance**—This attribute is also known as the dataset baseline and specifies the creation time of the first instance of any dataset.
  - **URI-template**—This sub-element lists all the base identifiers required for dataset instances. It can be constructed by the constants and variables of hPDL. All expression language constants and variables are resolved at runtime by the Oozie server.
  - **Done-flag**—A Done-flag is created to mark the completion of dataset processing in the form of a file. If this file is not already specified, Hadoop creates a _SUCCESS file in the Data Instance Output directory.

Listing 14.5 shows a simple example of a dataset:

Listing 14.5: Example of a Dataset

```
<dataset name="MyDataSet" frequency="${coord:hours(5)}"
initial-instance="2015-01-01T09:00Z" timezone="${timezone}">
<uri-template>
${baseURI}/${YEAR}/${MONTH}/${DAY}/${HOUR}/${MINUTE}
```

```
</uri-template>
<done-flag>READY</done-flag>
</dataset>
```

The dataset defined in Listing 14.5 has a frequency of 5 hours (300 minutes). Let the variable `baseURI` be defined as `/user/Hdp/MySample`. The dataset defines the set of locations (or directories) for the dataset instances, as shown in Listing 14.6:

Listing 14.6: Dataset Instance Directories

```
/user/Hdp/MySample/2015/01/01/09/00
/user/Hdp/MySample/2015/01/01/14/00
/user/Hdp/MySample/2015/01/01/19/00
/user/Hdp/MySample/2015/01/01/00/00
/user/Hdp/MySample/2015/01/01/05/00
```

- **Input event**—This element specifies the input conditions for a coordinator application. It is specified with the `<input-events>` element, which can contain one or more `<data-in>` elements, each having the `name` attribute, `dataset` attribute, and the `<start-instance>` and `<end-instance>` elements.

  Alternatively, instead of the `<start-instance>` and `<end-instance>` elements, input-events can use a single `<instance>` sub-element. When both the `<start-instance>` and `<end-instance>` elements are used, they specify the range of dataset instances that should be available to start a coordinator job.

Oozie Coordinator Lifecycle Operations

The operations related to the Oozie coordinator's lifecycle are similar to Oozie workflow operations except for the start operation. The start operation is not present for Oozie coordinators. Figure 14.19 represents the lifecycle operations of the Oozie coordinator:

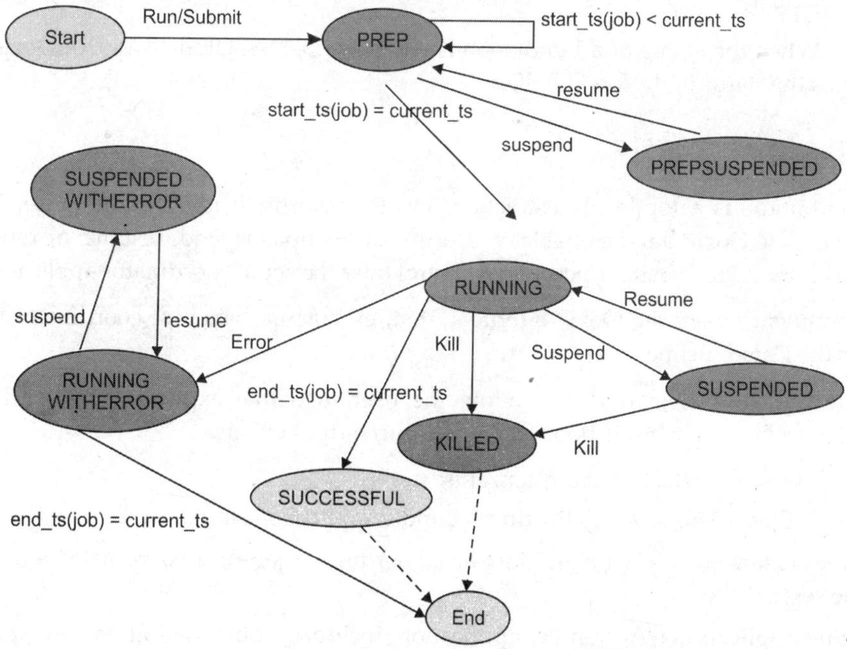

Figure 14.19: The Lifecycle Operations of Coordinator

The various stages or states of the Oozie coordinator's lifecycle, as shown in figure 14.19, can be explained as follows:

1. **Start**—This is the state where a user sends a request to start a bundle job.
2. **PREP**—When a bundle job is submitted, Oozie creates a record for the bundle and sets its status as PREP.
3. **RUNNING**—Also known as submit; in this state, the coordinator job is passed to the Oozie server for execution, but the submitted job lives in PREP state until the specified start time of the job.
4. **PREPSUSPENDED**—If a bundle job in the PREP state is suspended by the user's request, Oozie changes the status of the job to PREPSUSPENDED. When the user requests for a resumption of a PREPSUSPENDED status job, Oozie sets the job status as PREP.
5. **SUSPENDED**—A suspended operation is also known as pause. This operation temporarily suspends or pauses a coordinator job.
6. **DONEWITHERROR**—If all coordinator jobs could not finish, Oozie changes the status of the bundle job to DONEWITHERROR.
7. **RUNNINGWITHERROR**—If the job with the RUNNING status encounters any error, Oozie changes the status of the job to RUNNINGWITHERROR.
8. **SUSPENDEDWITHERROR**—If the job with the RUNNINGWITHERROR status is suspended by the user, Oozie changes the status of the job to SUSPENDEDWITHERROR.
9. **KILLED**—If the user requests to end any coordinator job forcefully, Oozie puts the job in the KILLED status and kills (terminates) all submitted coordinator jobs.
10. **SUCCESSFUL**—When a bundle job is executed successfully, Oozie changes its status to SUCCESSFUL.
11. **END**—When the status of a bundle job is either SUCCESSFUL or KILLED, Oozie immediately changes the status of the job to END.

Oozie Bundle

The Oozie bundle is a top-level abstraction. In other words, it is a bundle or set of coordinator applications. The Oozie bundle enables a user to start, stop, suspend, resume, or rerun a job at the bundle level. It provides better operational control over the set of coordinator applications.

The environment where the Oozie bundle system executes a bunch of coordinator applications is known as the Data pipeline.

The Oozie bundle system does not allow the user to define explicit dependencies among the coordinator applications; this is done through input/output events.

The Oozie bundle uses the following concepts:

- **Kick-off time**—This refers to the time a bundle application starts.
- **Bundle action**—It refers to the start of a coordinator job of a coordinator application by the Oozie server.
- **Bundle application**—A bundle application includes some definitions to specify a set of coordinator applications of the bundle through the Oozie bundle language.

- **Bundle job**—A bundle job describes all the applications in the Oozie bundle. The content of a bundle job helps the Oozie server to decide which bundle applications are required to be deployed.

A bundle language is an XML-based language.

Figure 14.20 shows a schema for the bundle language:

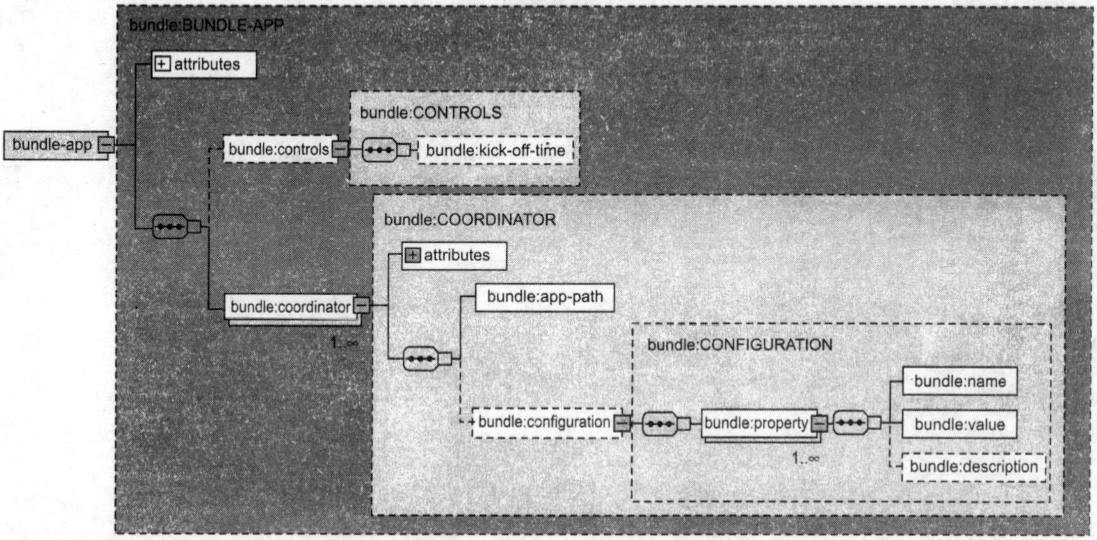

Figure 14.20: Bundle Language Schema

As you can see in Figure 14.20, the major elements of the bundle language are as follows:

- **Bundle-app**—This is the top-level element of the bundle application. Its attributes and sub-elements are name, coordinator, and controls. These can be briefly explained as follows:
  - **Name**—This is the name of the bundle and is used to refer to the bundle application in Hadoop CLI.
  - **Controls**—This element has a single attribute, kick-off time, which specifies the beginning (start time) of a bundle application.
  - **Coordinator**—This element describes coordinator applications of the bundle. A bundle application can have multiple coordinator elements.

  Every coordinator has the following attributes:

  - **name**—A name of the coordinator application is used to refer to the application through a bundle to control various actions like kill, return, or suspend.
  - **app-path**—This attribute is used to specify the location of definitions (such as.xml file) related to the coordinator.
  - **configuration**—This attribute provides a list of optional Hadoop configurations to pass parameters to corresponding coordinator applications.

Listing 14.7 shows an example of a bundle application that includes two coordinator applications:

Listing 14.7: Example of a Bundle Application

```
<bundle-app name='weather-forecast' xmlns:xsi='http://www.
w3.org/2001/XMLSchema-instance' xmlns='uri:oozie:bundle:0.1'>
<controls>
<kick-off-time>${kickOffTime}</kick-off-time>
</controls>
<coordinator name='monitor-weather-datastream' >
<app-path>${'monitor-weather-coord-path}</app-path>
<property>
<name>monitor-time</name>
<value>60</value>
</property>
<property>
<name>lang</name>
<value>${LANG}</value>
</property>
<configuration>
</coordinator>
<coordinator name='calc-publish-forecast' >
<app-path>${'calc-publish-coord-path}</app-path>
<configuration>
<property>
<name>monitor-time</name>
<value>600</value>
</property>
<property>
<name>client-list</name>
<value>${LIST}</value>
</property>
</configuration>
</configuration>
</coordinator>
</bundle-app>
```

The first application monitors and processes raw weather data and runs every 60 seconds, as specified in the <property> section.

The second application calculates and publishes the weather forecast every 10 minutes.

Oozie Parameterization with EL

Oozie applications (workflow, coordinator, and bundle) are parameterized with EL. EL provides a set of built-in functions that enable you to parameterize complex workflow action nodes and decision nodes. Here, you will learn about some important EL constants and functions of Oozie.

Basic EL functions provide support for operations with some parameters. Some examples of these are as follows:

- `concat(String s1, String s2)` —Refers to a function that concatenates two given strings.
- `trim(String s)` —Refers to a function that trims a given string.
- `urlEncode(String s)` —Refers to a function that converts a string into the MIME format.

Workflow Functions

Workflow EL functions provide access to workflow parameters. Some workflow functions are as follows:

- **`wf:id()`**—It returns the Oozie-ID of the current workflow job.
- **`wf:conf(String name)`**—It returns the detail about the configuration of the current workflow.
- **`wf:callback(String stateVar)`**—This function returns the callback URL for a given action.
- **`wf:transition(String node)`**—This function returns the name of the transition node from the specified node.
- **`wf:appPath()`**—It returns the application path of the current workflow.

Coordinator Functions

Coordinator EL functions provide access to coordinator parameters. The following are some coordinator functions:

- **`coord:nominalTime()`**—This function retrieves the time of the creation of a coordinator action, as specified in the coordinator application definition.
- **`coord:current(int n)`**—This function takes an integer value, say n, and returns the name of the nth dataset instance during input/output events.
- **`coord:dataIn(String name)`**—This function takes the name of the Oozie application and resolves all the URIs for the dataset instances specified in an input event dataset section.

Bundle Functions

No specific function exists for bundle. Bundle definition can use various basic EL functions. These functions are discussed in the next section.

EL Functions

Oozie provides functions, called EL functions, for writing expressions, which can be executed in the Oozie server. EL functions are used to provide access to the statistics of execution of any MapReduce job. For example, EL functions provide information like the name of the user who submitted the workflow, the external ID of a MapReduce job submitted by Oozie, concatenation of two strings, and much more. Some basic EL functions are as follows:

- **`String firstNotNull(String value1, String value2)`**—It returns NULL if both input values are null.
- **`String concat(String s1, String s2)`**—It returns the concatenation of strings passed into this function.
- **`String trim(String s)`**—It returns the trimmed value of a given string into the function.
- **`String urlEncode(String s)`**—It returns the URL UTF-8 encoded value of the given string. A string with the null value is considered an empty string.

Oozie Job Execution Model

Figure 14.21 shows a typical Oozie job execution model:

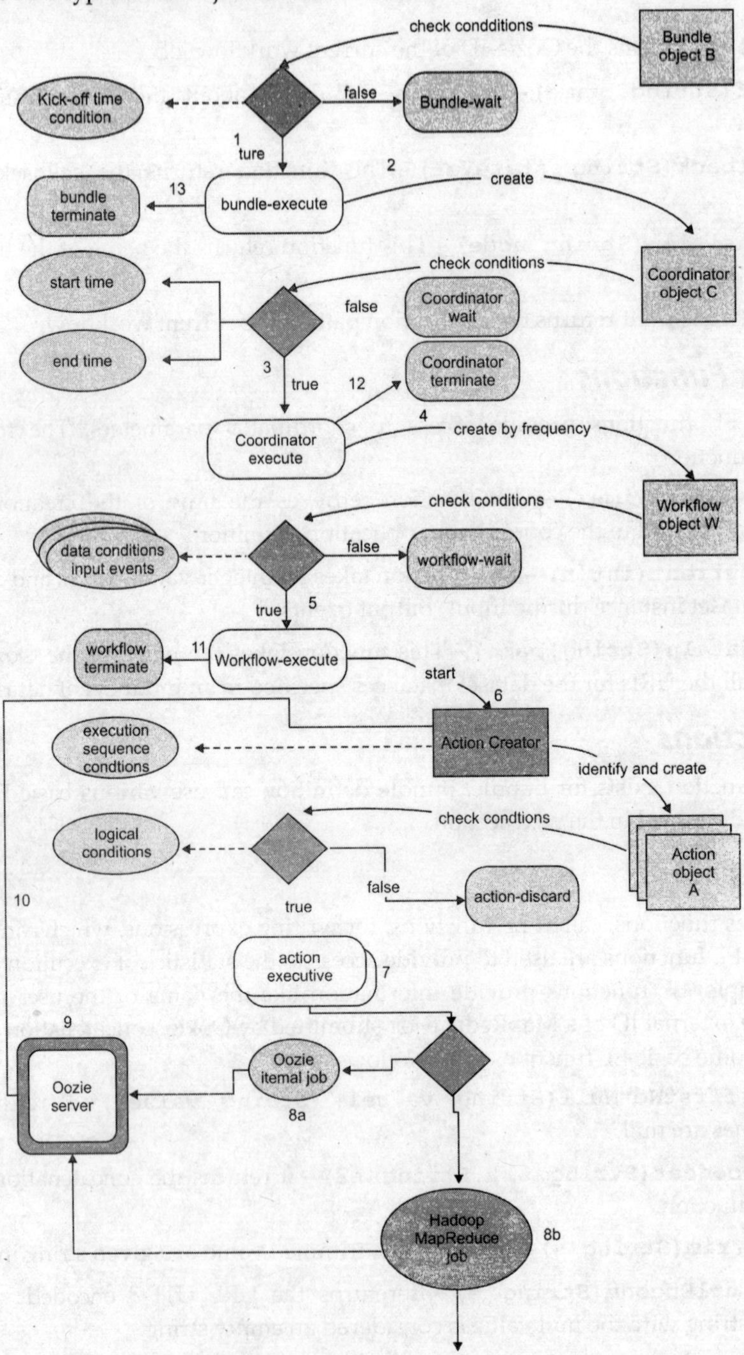

Figure 14.21: Oozie Job Execution Model

This is a simple model that covers the Oozie bundle, coordinator, workflow, workflow action, and jobs from Oozie to Hadoop cluster. This model does not show details like state transition for coordinator actions.

There are various types of objects that exist in an execution model, each representing a job (not an application). These objects can be explained as follows:

- **Workflow objects**—A workflow object contains a complete DAG of action nodes. Workflow objects are used to specify execution and control-flow nodes. The Oozie server only creates workflow objects by workflow applications or from bundle objects (defined below).
- **Coordinator objects**—Every coordinator object refers to one workflow object with some conditions. The Oozie server can create coordinator objects with the coordinator applications based on time conditions (these are Start, End, and Frequency). Coordinator objects wait for the data conditions and concurrency conditions to be satisfied before the creation of the appropriate workflow object. Coordinator objects are associated with data conditions, concurrency conditions, and time conditions.
- **Bundle objects**—A set of coordinator objects without any condition is known as a bundle object. The Oozie server creates a bundle object by bundle applications with some specified conditions (like kick-off time).
- **Action objects**—These objects represent an Oozie workflow action. They can be associated with a workflow object, execution sequence conditions, and logical conditions. The Oozie server creates these objects from workflow objects.
- **Hadoop jobs**—These simply refer to Hadoop jobs associated with specific workflow actions.

The following conditions are used for objects in an Oozie application:

- **Data conditions**—These conditions are related to coordinator objects and can be expressed through datasets and inputs.
- **Time conditions**—These conditions are also related to coordinator objects and can be expressed in terms of start time, end time, and frequency.
- **Logical conditions**—These conditions are related to action objects and can be expressed with data flow nodes.
- **Execution sequence conditions**—These conditions are also related to action objects and can be expressed through graphs in the workflow.
- **Concurrency conditions**—These are conditions under which coordinator objects are effectively executed in parallel.

All executable objects are associated with some conditions; these conditions can be either satisfied or not satisfied. The execution sequence condition for an action is said to be satisfied if and only if each earlier action in the DAG of the workflow has been executed.

An executable object has the following two states:

- **Wait state**—If an executable object is waiting for some conditions before it can be executed, that object is said to be in the waiting state.
- **Execution state**—If an executable object is executing, it is said to be in the execution state.

An object can transition from the wait state to the execution state if and only if all the preconditions associated with that object are fulfilled.

Some executable objects are associated with asynchronous actions, such as pig actions, map-reduce actions, Hive actions, Java actions, and sqoop actions. These objects are further associated with Hadoop jobs.

Other executable objects are associated with synchronous actions such as fs actions, ssh actions, and email actions. These objects can execute directly on the Oozie server.

The Oozie execution model has following attributes:

- Global scope attributes, such as time
- Coordinator scope attributes, such as start time and end time
- Workflow scope attributes used for defining and modifying workflows
- Action scope attributes used to define and modify actions

As shown in Figure 14.21, the execution model defines the way all these objects interact. This interaction can be explained through the following steps:

1. The bundle object is created and moved to the execution state based on the kick-off time.
2. As the bundle object B enters the execution state, the coordinator objects specified in bundle object B are created based on the time conditions (start time, end time, and frequency) specified for B.
3. Coordinator object C is moved to the execution state when all data and concurrency conditions associated with C are satisfied.
4. When the parent coordinator object is moved to the execution state, the workflow object W is created.
5. After the creation of the workflow object W, the coordinator waits until the execution of all preconditions of the workflow is complete.
6. The first action object A is created and moved to the execution state.
7. When the action object A is moved to the execution state, the job specified in the action is analyzed as follows:
   - If it is a synchronous action, it is directly executed on the Oozie server.
   - If it is an asynchronous action, the job is submitted to the Hadoop cluster.
8. If it is a synchronous action, it is executed directly on the Oozie server. If it is an asynchronous action, a corresponding job is submitted to the Hadoop cluster.
9. The Oozie server waits for the completion of the currently executing action (Under specific conditions, such as a join activity, a workflow waits for the completion of several activities before it can proceed).
10. After the action object execution is completed, the Oozie server analyzes the workflow and takes appropriate action. In the case of a fork-join, the Oozie server can wait until all action objects in the fork section complete execution according to the logical condition. The Oozie server then selects the next action to execute according to the sequence condition, creates action object A, and moves it into the executable state.

11. When a workflow reaches the end node, the workflow object W is terminated.
12. When the workflow object associated with coordinator C is terminated, coordinator C is terminated as well.
13. Bundle object B checks whether more coordinator objects are currently in the execution state. If so, nothing is done, otherwise bundle object B terminates.

Accessing Oozie

We can access the Oozie server programmatically in the following three ways:

- **Through Oozie Web Services APIs**—These APIs provide full capabilities of administration and job management. They are used by various Oozie tools like the Oozie execution console.
- **Through the Oozie CLI Interface**—This is an interface that is built on the top of Web Services APIs. Through this interface, you can perform all possible operations of the workflow job. An administrator can use this CLI interface to manage Oozie execution, while developers can write scripts for Oozie invocations using this interface.
- **Through Oozie-Java Client APIs**—These APIs are built on the top of Web Services APIs. Through these APIs, you can perform any workflow job operation. Moreover, Client APIs include a Local Oozie class that is useful for testing Oozie from within an IDE. Java APIs provide a base for Oozie to integrate with other applications.

Oozie SLA

Oozie SLA specifies the quality of an Oozie application in measurable terms. SLA can be determined after taking the business requirements and nature of software into consideration.

For example, for a project about a Web-based application, SLA may include:

- The average response time
- Maximum response time
- System availability

The SLA is always related to the following three terms:

- Maximum allowed time limit as to when the job should start
- Maximum allowed time limit as to when the job should end
- The time duration of the execution

Oozie workflows and coordinators jointly define these SLA parameters in the application definition XML. Oozie not only actively monitors the state of SLA-sensitive jobs, but also sends notifications for every condition met or missed in SLA.

In versions that are older than 4.x, the SLA feature was static, meaning that the user had to ask the Oozie client SLA API to fetch the status-related records of a job through a query. In addition, the user probably had to use his or her own custom calculation engine to compute the condition met or missed in SLA.

However, in the version 4.x, there is an SLA tab in the Oozie UI. Through this tab, the user can query for SLA information and have a summarized view of the status of jobs against SLAs.

Event Status

We know that there are three important criteria for any event or job: start time, end time, and time duration of execution. Corresponding to these criteria, your jobs can be either met or missed. The different states (or status types) of an event can be briefly explained as follows:

- **START_MET**—Refers to the status that is displayed when a job starts at the specified time
- **START_MISS**—Refers to the status that is displayed when a job does not start at the specified time
- **DURATION_MET**—Refers to the status when a job is completed within the specified duration
- **DURATION_MISS**—Refers to the status when a job is not completed within the specified duration
- **END_MET**—Refers to the status when a job completes successfully
- **END_MISS**—Refers to the status when a job does not end successfully; instead, goes to error state

SLA Status

The SLA status of a job can have any one of the following four states:

- **Not_Started**—Includes jobs that have not started yet
- **In_Process**—Includes jobs that are currently running
- **Met**—Includes jobs that have been successfully terminated
- **Miss**—Includes jobs that have been unsuccessfully terminated

Oozie Activity

An Oozie activity is any possible entity that can be tracked in Oozie functional subsystems (including coordinator, workflow jobs and actions) and Hadoop jobs (any job submitted by Oozie). The Oozie SLA defines, stores, and tracks the desired SLA information for any Oozie activity.

The Oozie SLA Subsystem

The Oozie SLA subsystem is a built-in support system for tracking SLAs in Oozie. This subsystem does not do monitoring. We can implement a process-monitoring system outside of the Oozie server.

SLA Language Schema

The SLA language can be specified by the XML schema, as shown in Figure 14.22:

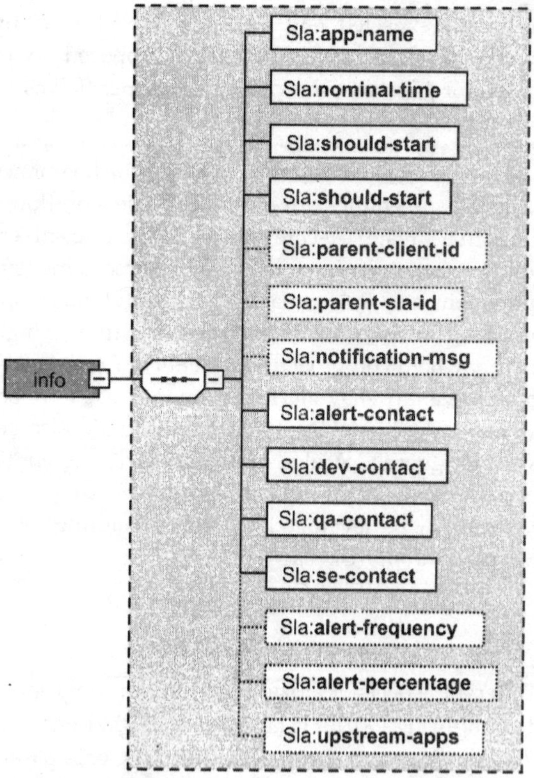

Figure 14.22: SLA Language Schema

Table 14.5 provides a description of the elements of the SLA Language Schema:

Table 14.5: Elements of the SLA Language Schema

Element Name	Description
`Info`	This is the root element of SLA definitions for the workflow or coordinator.
`app-name`	This element represents the names of the application with no namespace segregation done. It is up to the application developers to come up with a meaningful naming partition. For example, a package-naming structure similar to that used in Java could be used. The natural way to specify the value of an element in SLA is `${wf:name()}` or with the coordinator application name.
`nominal-time`	This is the time specified in coordinator.xml to start a coordinator action. In many cases, the value used for this element is `${coord:nominalTime()}`.
`should-start`	This is the expected start time for an activity. For example, if the actual action is expected to start five minutes after the coordinator job starts, the value can be specified as `<sla:shouldstart>${5 *MINUTES}</sla:should-start>`.

Table 14.5: Elements of the SLA Language Schema

Element Name	Description
should-end	This is the expected end time for this SLA relative to nominal time. For example, if an action is normally supposed to end two hours after the coordinator job starts, the value can be specified as <sla:shouldend>${2 * HOURS}</sla:should-end>.
parent-clientid, parent-sla-id	Processing entities (for example, Oozie coordinator actions) may create/execute processing sub-entities (for example, Oozie workflow jobs), and processing sub-entities may create/execute smaller processing sub-entities (for example, Oozie workflow actions). Knowing that a processing sub-entity missed an SLA requirement may help proactively identify bigger processing entities that may miss SLA requirements. SLAs traversing from a higher entity to a lower sub-entity may help you proactively identify SLA issues. An SLA violation for some processing entity may alert you to what else may be impacted because of the SLA miss. The hierarchical information could also be used by any monitoring system to ignore SLA alerts for processing sub-entities if an alert for a higher processing entity has been triggered already. Parent-child relationships of SLA activities can be leveraged by the monitoring system to provide a holistic navigation through SLA activities.

Summary

This chapter has covered different aspects of Oozie and its main components. It has taken you through the steps of installing and configuring Oozie. It has also discussed various other topics such as Oozie workflow, Oozie coordinator and its types, Oozie bundle, and Oozie parameterization with EL. Apart from this, it has explained the Oozie Job Execution Model, how to access Oozie, and Oozie SLA.

Quick Revise

Multiple-Choice Questions

Q1. The Oozie workflow component does the following:

a. Provides support for defining and executing a controlled sequence of MapReduce, Hive, and Pig jobs

b. Provides support for the automatic execution of workflows based on events and the presence of system resources

c. Provides a way to group a set of coordinator applications that can be managed together

d. Provides support for tracking the execution of workflow applications

Ans. The correct option is a.

Q2. The Oozie workflow is based on which of the following terminologies?

a. Transition
b. Transportation
c. Transaction
d. Transfusion

Ans. The correct option is a.

Q3. A transition is managed by which of the following conditions?

a. Overtime execution conditions
b. Runtime execution conditions
c. Limit time execution conditions
d. No time execution conditions

Ans. The correct option is b.

Q4. One of the action nodes provided by Oozie is:

a. COBRA action
b. Java 6 action
c. Pig action
d. Map action

Ans. The correct option is c.

Q5. Which of the following is an Oozie extension action?

a. Top action
b. JAVA action
c. Snoop action
d. Hive action

Ans. The correct option is d.

Q6. You are running an Oozie workflow application. Which mechanism will Oozie use to detect the completion of the application?

a. Backlog
b. Call up
c. Call back
d. Recall

Ans. The correct option is c.

Q7. If job execution on a Hadoop cluster fails, one of the pieces of information returned to the Oozie server is:

a. Thread-string parameter
b. Error message
c. Callback option
d. Boolean value

Ans. The correct option is d.

Q8. Which status is displayed when a job does not start at the specified time?

a. START_MET
b. START_MISS
c. DURATION_MET
d. DURATION_MISS

Ans. The correct option is b.

Q9. A MapReduce Oozie action effectively creates two MapReduce jobs. They are:

a. Oozie launcher and the actual job
b. Oozie launcher and a trial job
c. Oozie launcher and job execution
d. Oozie launcher and a debugging job

Ans. The correct option is a.

Q10. One of the elements of Oozie coordinator is:

a. Stipulated time
b. Executive action
c. Extra time
d. Actual time

Ans. The correct option is d.

Subjective Questions

Q1. List and explain the key concepts of the Oozie coordinator.

Ans. The Oozie coordinator is used to specify the conditions for a workflow in the form of predicates. It triggers the execution of the workflow at the specified time, on regular intervals, or on the basis of the available data.

A predicate is a conditional statement with some parameters like date, time, and occurrence of any external events. The workflow job/action starts if and only if the specified predicate is satisfied.

Oozie version 2.x and higher support coordinator jobs. A coordinator job can be defined in XPDL. According to the functionality, the Oozie coordinator can be classified into the following two types:

- File-based coordinator
- Time-based coordinator

A file-based coordinator is used for invoking the workflow on the basis of available data and polling. A time-based coordinator, on the other hand, is used for invoking the workflow repeatedly after an interval between specified periods of time.

The time-based coordinator is further classified into the following types:

- **Simple file-based coordinator**—An Oozie job/action will invoke if and only if the required data is available and the corresponding predicate is true.
- **Sliding window-based coordinator**—Oozie job/action can be invoked frequently and data are aggregated over multiple overlapping previous instances. For example, invoking it at a frequency of 30 seconds and running action on aggregated previous five instances of 30 second data.
- **Rollups-based coordinator**—It is invoked after a long period of time and data are aggregated over multiple previous instances from the last time of invocation. For example, it will run once a day and trigger a workflow that aggregates 24 instances of hourly data.

Q2. Discuss the three basic programmatic ways of accessing the Oozie server.

Ans. The three basic programmatic ways of accessing the Oozie server are as follows:

- **Through Oozie Web Services APIs**—These APIs provide full capabilities of administration and job management. They are used by various Oozie tools like the Oozie execution console.
- **Through the Oozie CLI Interface**—This is an interface that is built on top of Web Services APIs. Through this interface, you can perform all possible operations of the

workflow job. An administrator can use this CLI interface to manage Oozie execution, while developers can write scripts for Oozie invocations using this interface.

- **Through Oozie-Java Client APIs**—These APIs are built on the top of Web Services APIs. Through these APIs, you can perform any workflow job operation. Moreover, Client APIs include a Local Oozie class that is useful for testing Oozie from within an IDE. Java APIs provide a base for Oozie to integrate with other applications.

Q3. Discuss how Oozie as a Hadoop workflow engine is different from other workflow applications.

Ans. Oozie differs from other workflow applications with respect to the following points:

- Oozie is a workflow scheduler system used to manage Apache Hadoop jobs.
- Oozie workflow jobs are Directed Acyclic Graphs (DAGs) of actions.
- Oozie coordinator jobs are recurrent Oozie workflow jobs triggered by time (frequency) and data availability.
- Oozie is integrated with the rest of the Hadoop stack supporting several types of Hadoop jobs out of the box (such as Java map-reduce, Streaming map-reduce, Pig, Hive, Sqoop and Distcp) as well as system-specific jobs (such as Java programs and shell scripts).

Q4. Consider the following image of the Apache Oozie workflow engine:

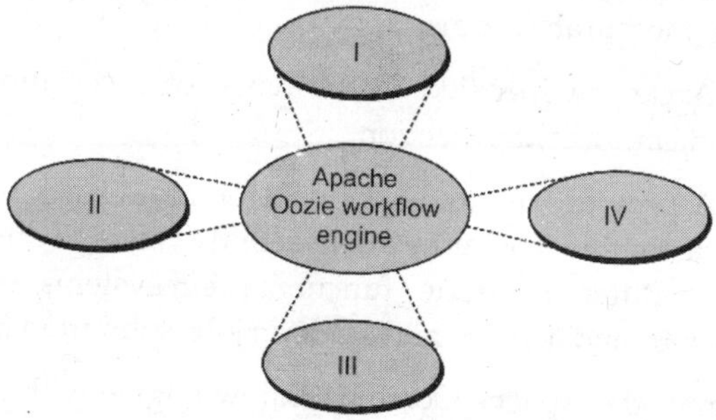

a. Mention the four main functional components of the Apache Oozie workflow engine.

b. Distinguish between Oozie workflow and Oozie bundle.

c. State the functions of SLAs.

d. Name any difficulty that can be removed by the Apache Oozie workflow engine.

Ans. a. The four main functional components of Oozie are:

- **Oozie workflow**—This component is used to specify the sequence of actions (or jobs) to be executed in the form of DAG.
- **Oozie coordinator**—This component automatically executes Oozie workflows on the basis of specified events and available system resources.
- **Oozie bundles**—This component defines and executes a bundle of applications with a coordinator application.

- **Oozie Service Level Agreement (SLA)** – This component provides a way of tracking the whole execution process of workflows.

b. Differences between Oozie workflow and Oozie bundle are shown in following table:

Oozie Workflow	Oozie Bundle
Oozie workflow supports the design and execution of the Directed Acyclic Graphs (DAGs) actions.	Oozie bundle is a top-level abstraction that enables the grouping of a set of coordinator applications into a bundle application.
Oozie workflow is based on the concepts of action, transition, workflow, and workflow application.	Oozie bundle is based on the concepts of bundle action, bundle application, and bundle job.
Oozie workflow is governed by two conditions: structural condition and runtime execution condition.	The execution of a bundle is specified by the controls element, which specifies a bundle start time.

c. The main functions of SLAs are as follows:

- An SLA is a standard part of a software contract that specifies the quality of the product in measurable terms.
- Oozie SLA can be specified in the scope of a coordinator application, workflow application, and workflow action.
- Oozie SLA provides a way to define, store, and track the desired SLA information for Oozie activities. The term Oozie activity refers to any possible entity that can be tracked in different Oozie functional subsystems, including coordinator and workflow jobs and actions, and Hadoop jobs submitted from Oozie.

d. The integration of the Apache Oozie workflow engine with other components simplifies the tasks of data engineers. The integration also enables better utilization of resources.

15

NoSQL Data Management

NoSQL is a non-relational database that varies from traditional relational database system. NoSQL database is provided for distributed data stores where there is a need for large scale of data storing. For example, Google and Facebook are collecting terabytes of data daily for their users. Such databases do not require fixed schema, avoid join operations, and scale data horizontally.

In a NoSQL database, tables are stored as ASCII files, with each tuple represented by a row and fields separated with tabs. The database is manipulated through shell scripts that can be combined to UNIX pipelines. As its name suggests, NoSQL doesn't use SQL as a query language.

NoSQL databases are still in the development stages and are going through a lot of changes. Software developers who work on databases have a mixed opinion about NoSQL. Some find it useful, while others point out flaws in it. Some are uncertain, and believe that it's just another hyped technology that will eventually vanish due to its immaturity.

This chapter discusses various aspects of NoSQL in detail. It begins by introducing NoSQL and then describes aggregate data models used in it. The chapter also discusses the key-value, column-oriented, document, and graph data models. Further, it explains the concept of relationships in NoSQL and schema-less databases. Apart from this, you learn about materialized views as well as distribution models. Toward the end, you also learn the concept of sharding.

Introduction to NoSQL

There are lots of data storage options available in the market. And yet, many more are still coming up as the nature of data, platforms, user requirements, architectures, and processes are constantly changing. We are living in the era of Big Data and are in search of ways of handling it. This has given impetus to, since 2009, the need for creating schema-free databases that can handle large amounts of data. These databases are scalable, enable availability of user, support replication, and are distributed and possibly open source. One such database is NoSQL.

Before you develop applications that can interact with NoSQL databases, you should first understand the need for maintaining a separation between data management and data storage in these databases. NoSQL mainly focuses on high-performance scalable data storage and provides low-level access to the data management layer. This allows data management tasks to be created easily in any programming language. Figure 15.1 shows the interaction of layers in a NoSQL database:

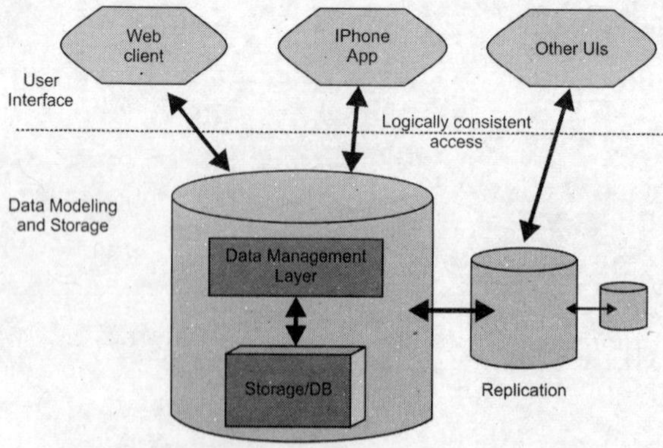

Source: *http://www.sitepen.com/blog/2010/05/11/nosql-architecture*

Figure 15.1: Interaction of Layers in NoSQL

Why NoSQL?

Modern NoSQL solutions can tackle applications that require a high degree of scalability, data distribution, and continuous availability. At the same time, we should also understand that relational databases have been used for transactional processing in organizations for a very long time. RDBMS is supported by several tools and a large trained workforce that implements and maintains them. Hence, the need to find an alternative to RDBMS is technical, functional, and perhaps financial.

SCENARIO

Consider the case of Argon Technologies that wants to scale up its systems or find viable alternatives to expensive proprietary software that can still address the company's business needs. Mr. Robinson, the data analyst in the company, does a comparison of NoSQL databases with relational databases, and lists the facts for and against NoSQL, as shown in Table 15.1:

Table 15.1: Benefits and Challenges of NoSQL

Benefits of NoSQL Databases	Challenges against NoSQL Databases
• Scale (horizontal) • Simple data model (fewer joins) • Streaming/volume • Reliability • Schema-less (no modelling or prototyping) • Rapid development • Flexible as it can handle semi-structured, unstructured, and structured data • Cheaper than the relational database • Creates a caching layer • Wide data type variety • Uses large binary objects for storing large data • Bulk upload • Graphs • Lower administration • Distributed storage • Real-time analysis	• ACID transactions • Cannot use SQL • Ecosystem/tools/add-ons • Cannot perform searches • Data loss • No referential integrity • Lack of availability of expertise

Characteristics of NoSQL

NoSQL databases do not use SQL; however, some of them have query languages. When the creators of NoSQL chose the name NoSQL, they meant to communicate the fact that here is a database query language that does not follow the principles of RDBMS. Another important characteristic of NoSQL databases is that they are generally open-source projects. The term NoSQL is frequently applied to an open-source phenomenon. Most NoSQL databases are driven by the need to run on clusters. This fact has an effect on their data model as well as their approach to consistency. For example, ACID transactions are used to maintain consistency across the whole database, which is also a characteristic of relational databases. NoSQL databases offer a range of options for consistency and distribution. You are allowed to freely add fields to database records without having to define any changes in the structure because NoSQL databases operate without a schema.

This comes particularly useful while dealing with non-uniform data and custom fields. We see relational databases as one option for data storage. This point of view is often referred to as polyglot persistence, and simply means using different data stores for different circumstances. We need to understand the nature of the data we are storing and how we want to manipulate it, instead of picking a relational database just because everyone is doing it. As a result, most organizations will have a mix of data storage technologies for different circumstances. However, Big Data has created an opportunity for people to think with a new perspective on their data storage needs. Some development teams see in NoSQL database the opportunity of improving their productivity by simplifying database access.

History of NoSQL

The NoSQL database was invented by an engineer named Carlo Strozzi in 1998. NoSQL (short for Not only SQL) provides a mechanism for the retrieval and storage of data. At that time, NoSQL did not provide SQL interface but was relational. Later, when Johan Oskarsson organized an event on open-source distributed databases, Eric Evans reintroduced the term NoSQL in 2009. Most of the NoSQL databases are non-relational, distributed, and do not follow ACID properties. The most popular NoSQL databases are MongoDB, Apache Cassandra, Redis, HBase, Splunk, and Neo4j.

Types of NoSQL Data Models

There are generally four types of NoSQL databases. Each of them has their own attributes and limitations. You cannot say a single solution is better among all of them because few databases are meant to solve specific problems.

Table 15.2 shows a comparison of various NoSQL data models:

Table 15.2: Comparison between Different NoSQL Data Models

Data Model	Performance	Scalability	Flexibility	Functionality
Key Value	High	High	High	Variable
Column-Oriented	High	High	Moderate	Minimal
Document	High	Variable (high)	High	Variable (low)
Graph	Variable	Variable	High	Graph Theory

Let's discuss these data models in detail.

Key Value Data Model

In the key value data model, the client can get the value for a key, put a value for a key, or delete a key from the data store. Here, the value is a Binary Large Object (BLOB) that is only concerned about data and not what is inside; it is the responsibility of the application to understand what exactly is stored. BLOB is also scalable because it uses primary key access for the different purposes.

A sample key/value database is shown in Figure 15.2:

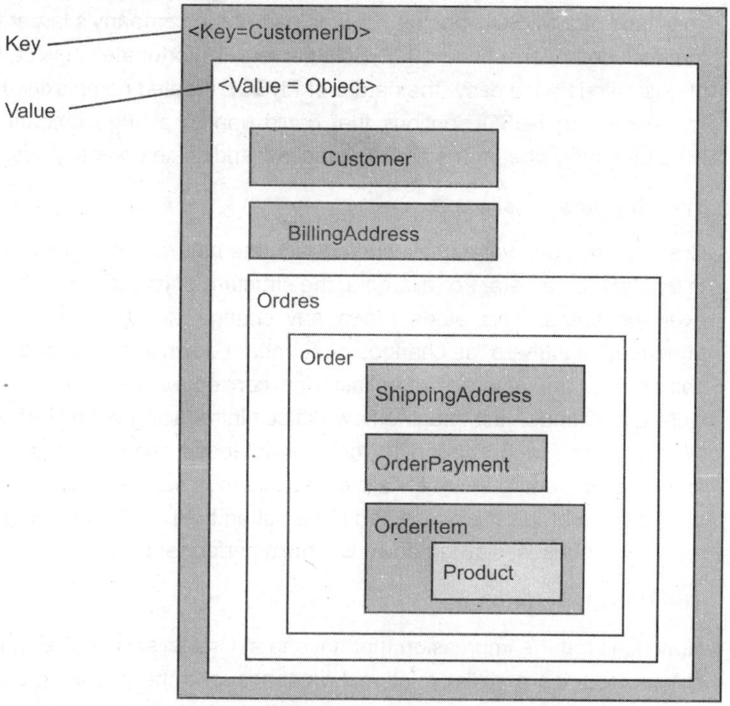

Source: *http://www.thoughtworks.com/insights/blog/nosql-databases-overview*

Figure 15.2: A Key Value Database

Some examples of popular key/value databases are Riak; Redis; Memcached and its versions; Berkeley DB; HamsterDB ; Amazon DynamoDB; Project Voldemort; and Couchbase. All key/value databases are not the same; there are major differences between these products; for example, Memcached data is not persistent, but Riak data is.

Therefore, we need to cache user preferences in Memcached data. If we implement user preferences in Memcached, they would need to be refreshed entirely in case any of the nodes are lost. On the other hand, we may not need to worry about losing data if it is stored in the Riak database. However, we need to consider how to update stale data. So, it is also important to choose the type of key/value databases as per our requirement.

EXHIBIT 1: The Craigslist Case Study for Big Data and NoSQL Solutions

Craigslist is a classified advertisements website with sections devoted to jobs, housing, personals, for sale, items wanted, services, community, gigs, résumés, and discussion forums. With more than 1.5 million new ads posting every day, Craigslist users have generated over a billion records, which can be considered as Big Data. What's more, legislation demands that these records can't simply be erased or overwritten at the whim of the company: after a 60-day retention period in the live portion of the site, records must be migrated over to an archival space for legislative compliance.

And how does Craigslist manage this large volume of data? Prior to 2011, an archive consisted of a MySQL cluster that was part of the company's larger database structure that included over a hundred MySQL servers. Unfortunately, instead of making the job of data persistence easy, the nature of MySQL created complexity, forcing Craigslist to start exploring NoSQL options that could handle a huge amount of incoming data, simultaneously stream the archive process, and scale up easily over time.

The 'Big Data' Challenge

Craigslist faced several challenges due to the nature and volume of data being stored in its MySQL servers. For example, the structure of its data had changed several times over the years. This alone made any change to the database schema a costly, prolonged nightmare, as changes often meant downtime, and of course, any alteration comes with the potential of unintended consequences. And if database alterations were a challenge, just imagine how difficult introducing entirely new features became. What's more, each change to the live database schema required a corresponding change to the entire archive – a process that took months every time. And during these updates, the archival process had to be put on hold, which meant stale data piled up in the live databases, slowing down the site's performance.

The NoSQL Solution

Now don't get the impression that anyone at Craigslist is criticizing MySQL. MySQL is still revered, it's a stellar relational database, and the people in charge didn't want to stop using it for data in active online postings. It was the dead postings that needed a better "graveyard". So what was the NoSQL solution? Craigslist passed that baton to MongoDB for archiving posts and the accompanying metadata. Craigslist archived these posts as documents instead of treating them as rows in a relational database table. And the process was a relatively speedy one. Including the time needed to sanitize and prepare the data, migrating 1.5 billion postings to the new archive database only took about three months.

Key Benefits of a NoSQL Solution like MongoDB for Big Data:

- Dynamic and flexible without being tied to a single schema
- Auto-sharding for horizontal scalability
- Built-in replication
- High availability
- Faster and less expensive than a relational database
- Document-based queries

Source: http://www.theserverside.com/feature/The-Craigslist-Dilemma-A-case-study-for-big-data-and-NoSQL-solutions

Column-Oriented Data Model

Column-oriented databases are based on columns and every column is considered individually. The values of a single column are stored contiguously. Some examples of column-oriented data models are Cassandra, BigTable, SimpleDB, and HBase. The data maintained by columns are in the form of column-specific files. In column-oriented data model, the performance on the aggregation queries such as COUNT, SUM, AVG, MIN, and MAX is high. The pictorial representation of the column-oriented data model is shown in Figure 15.3:

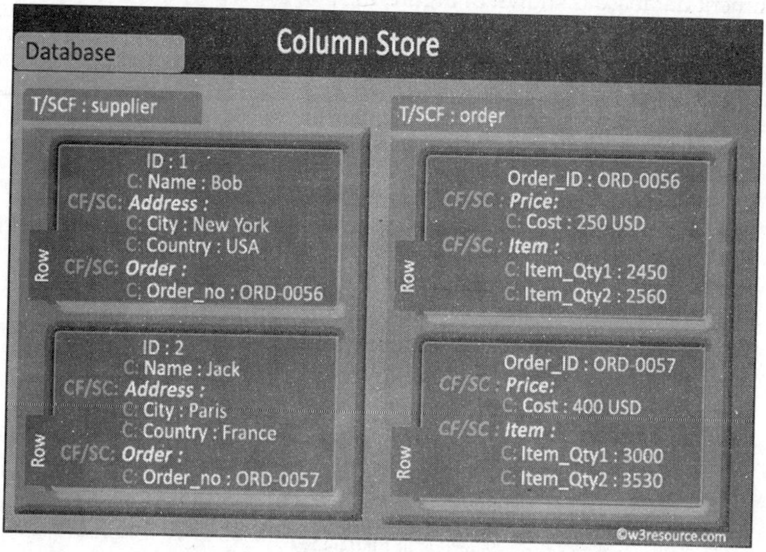

Source: *http://www.w3resource.com/mongodb/nosql.php*

Figure 15.3: Pictorial Representation of Column-Oriented Data Model

Document Data Model

There are many types of document databases, such as XML, JSON, BSON, etc. These document databases are self-describing, hierarchical tree data structures that can contain maps, collections, and scalar values. Document databases mainly store documents in the value part of the key/value store; think about document databases as key/value stores where the value is examinable. For easier transitions from relational databases, document databases provide indexing, and searching, etc. Figure 15.4 shows a comparison of the structure of the relational model and the document data model:

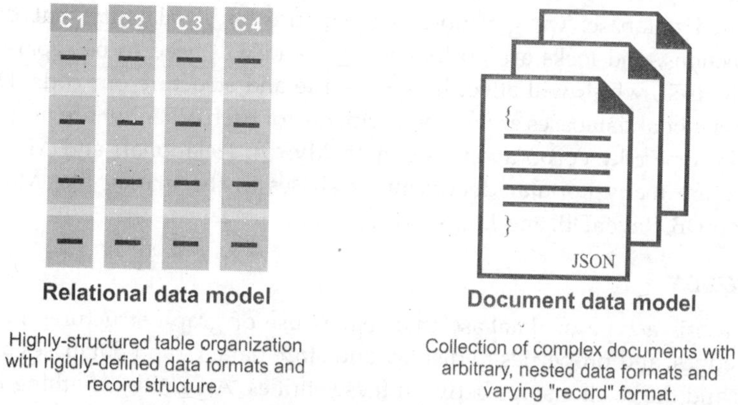

Source: *http://dataconomy.com/sql-vs-nosql-need-know/*

Figure 15.4: Comparing the Relational Data Model and the Document Data Model

Document databases have a different structure to store the information related to an entity unlike relational databases, which use tabular format.

A sample document database is shown in Figure 15.5:

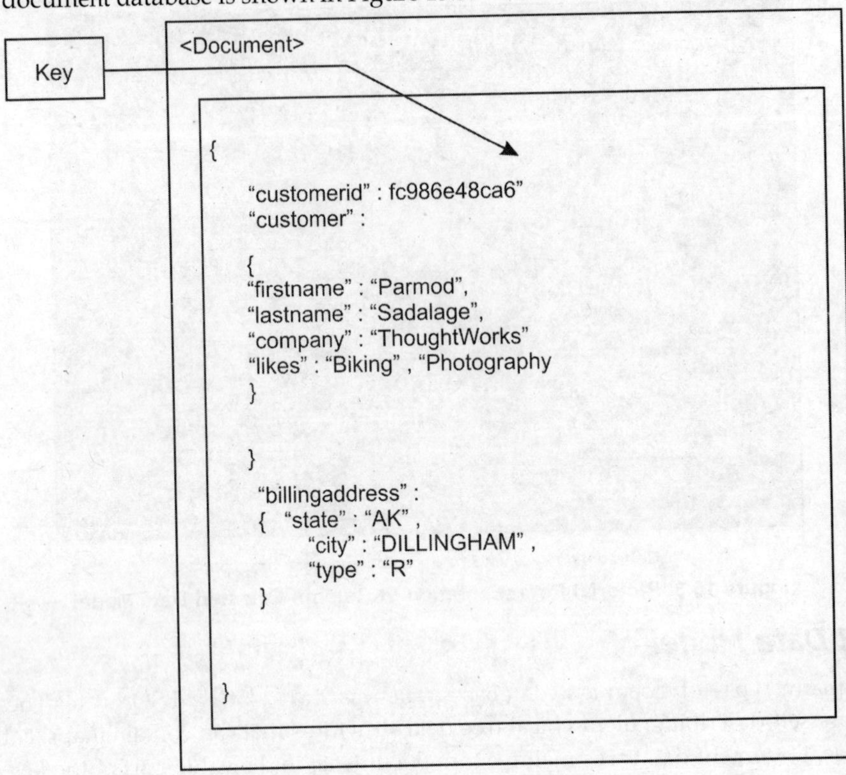

Source: *http://www.thoughtworks.com/insights/blog/nosql-databases-overview*

Figure 15.5: Document Database

Though the document-oriented model is rich in performance and scalability, it doesn't provide ACID and data integrity that a relational data model has by definition. So if we want to use a document-oriented database, we get more performance and scalability, but database-level data integrity, transactions, and locks are no longer there and will need to be separately embed in the application logic itself, which will affect how we write and structure our code. Document-oriented databases and relational databases are no replacements for each other but are useful in various ways. For example, the OpenSky corporation uses both MySQL (relational) and MongoDB (document-oriented). There are many popular document databases in the market like MongoDB, CouchDB, Terrastore, OrientDB, RavenDB, and Lotus Notes.

Graph Databases

A graph database is a type of database that makes use of graph structures for semantic queries having nodes, edges, and properties to display and store data. Graph databases are mainly used for storing entities and the relationships between these entities. An entity is nothing but a node with its own properties. A node can be perceived as an instance of an object in an application. Relations are also known as edges, and they can have properties as well. Edges are directions, and each direction has its own significance. The graph is organized, and the data in it are stored once but interpreted in different aspects based on the relationships. Figure 15.6 shows an example of a graph database:

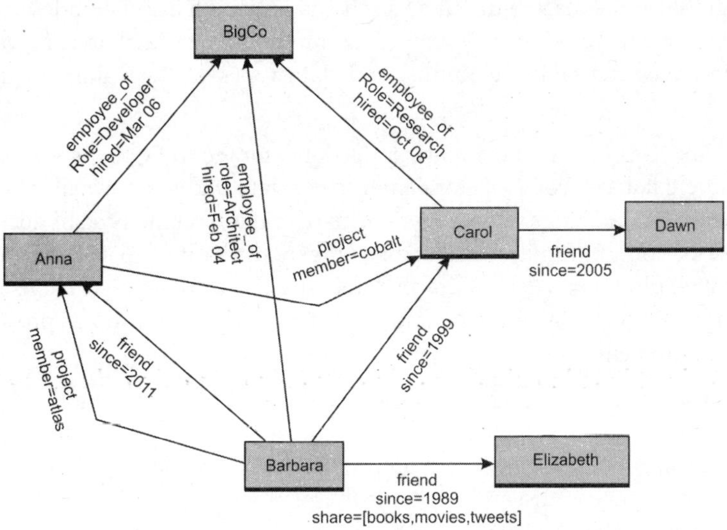

Source: *http://www.informit.com/articles/article.aspx?p=2266741*

Figure 15.6: A Graph Database

Whenever we store a graph-like structure in a relational database, it is stored for a single type of relationship. If we add another relationship to it, it means a lot of schema changes and data movement. However, this doesn't happen in the case of graph databases. Additionally, in relational databases, we model the graph based on the traversal. So, if the traversal changes, the data will have to change accordingly.

In graph databases, traversing the joins or relationships can be done very quickly. Moreover, the relationship between nodes is not calculated at the time of querying but is actually persisted as a relationship. The point is that we can have nodes with different types of relationships between them. This allows us to represent relationships between the major domain entities and secondary relationships for category, path, or linked lists for accessing sorted data. Moreover there is no limitation to the number and kind of relationships that can be formed, so relationships can be represented in the same graph database.

Relationships are of paramount importance in graph databases. They help in deriving most of the values in these databases. Relationships can have properties in addition to a start node and an end node. The most important concept of a database is relations among nodes.

Since relationships and their properties are integral to graph databases, you must invest a lot of time, thought, and design expertise to model the relationships in the domain you are trying to work with. Addition of new relationship types is easy. Changing existing nodes and their relationships is similar to migrating data, because the major changes must be done on each node and each relationship in your data. Some examples of popular graph databases are Neo4J, Infinite Graph, and FlockDB.

Schema-Less Databases

As the name suggests, a database without any schema is known as schema-less database. You need to define a schema or structure before storing data into relational databases. A well-defined schema of a database describes the tables, columns, and data types of the values in the columns of the database.

Storing data in NoSQL is easier in comparison to data storage in SQL. As discussed earlier, in the case of a key/value database, you can store any type of data under a particular key. This is also true in the case of document databases, where there is no restriction on the type of document you want to store. In the case of column-family databases, you can store any type of data under any column according to your requirement. Also, in graph databases, there are no restrictions in adding edges or properties to nodes. You can add edges and simultaneously define node properties as per your convenience or requirement.

In the case of a schema-defined database, you need to plan for the collection of data to be stored in the database. However, no such planning is required for schema-less databases, and the data type can be changed at run time, if required. If you find new data items while storing data, you can add them easily. Similarly, you can discard the items that you feel are not required, at run time, without worrying about existing related data like in case of schema or relational databases.

A schema-less database also makes it easier to arrange non-uniform information, where each record has an alternate set of fields. You also have various types of information in diverse columns similar to schema databases, which arrange all the rows of a table horizontally. You either end up with a set of invalid or null columns (a sparse table), or with unimportant, meaningless columns.

A schema-less database permits each record to contain exactly what it needs. This type of database also eliminates many conditions found in fixed-schema databases.

Materialized Views

The priority for developers and data administrators in data storage is often on how the data is stored, as opposed to how it is read. The chosen storage format is usually closely related to the format of the data, requirements for managing data size and data integrity, and the kind of store in use. For example, when using the document model, data is often represented as a series of aggregates, each of which contains all information about an entity.

However, this may have a negative effect on queries. When a query requires only a subset of the data from some entities, such as a summary of orders of several customers without all the order details, it needs to extract all of the data for the relevant entities in order to obtain the required information.

To support efficient querying, a common solution is to generate, in advance, a view that contains the data in a format most suited to generate the required dataset. This view is known as the materialized view. You can define the materialized view as a pattern that generates pre-populated views of data in environments where the source data is in a format that is not suitable for querying. In this case, generating a suitable query is also difficult, or its performance is poor due to the nature of the data or the data store. Figure 15.7 displays the materialized view:

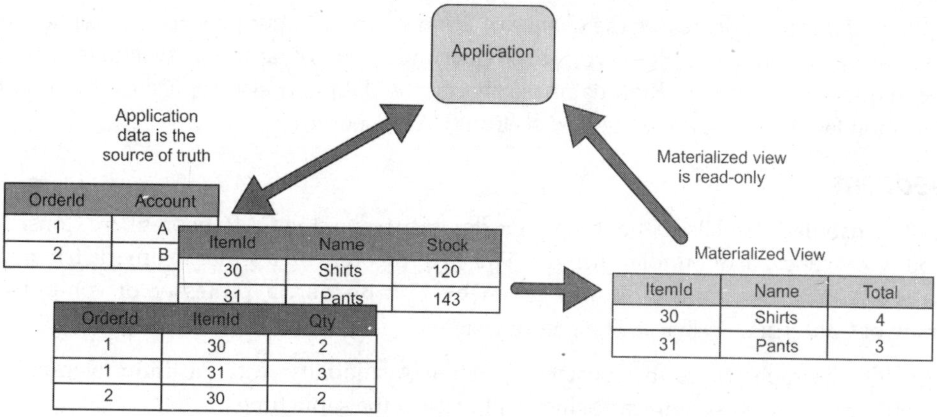

Source: *https://i-msdn.sec.s-msft.com/dynimg/IC709527.png*

Figure 15.7: Materialized View

These materialized views, which contain only data required by a query, allow applications to quickly obtain the information they need. In addition to joining tables or combining data entities, materialized views may include the current values of calculated columns or data items, the results of combining values or executing transformations on the data items, and values specified as part of the query. A materialized view may even be optimized for just a single query.

An important point to note here is that a materialized view and the data it contains are completely disposable because they can be entirely rebuilt from the source data stores. A materialized view is never updated directly by an application, and so it is effectively a specialized cache.

When there is a change in the source data while creating view, the view must be updated to include the new information. This may occur automatically on an appropriate schedule, or when the system detects a change in the original data. In other cases, it may be necessary to regenerate the view manually.

Distribution Models

Aggregate-oriented databases allow easy distribution of data. In such databases, the distribution mechanism is just concerned about the movement of aggregate data and not the related data, as all the related data is stored in the aggregate. Distribution of data can be done in two ways:

- **Through sharding**—Sharding is one of the major techniques of data distribution. It is used to distribute various types of data across multiple servers. Therefore, each server acts as a single source for a subset of data.
- **Through replication**—Replication is one of the major techniques for fault tolerance. The idea is to copy data across multiple servers so that each bit of data can be found in multiple places. Replication occurs in two forms:
  - Master-slave replication, which makes one node the authoritative copy that handles writes; while slaves, which are synchronized with the master, handle reads.
  - Peer-to-peer replication, which allows writes to any node without requiring authorization. Here, the nodes can coordinate with each other to synchronize their copies of the data.

Master-slave replication decreases the chance of update conflicts, but peer-to-peer replication avoids loading of all writes onto a single server, causing a single point of failure. A system may use either or both techniques. For example, Riak database shards the data and also replicates it that is based on the replication factor discussed in the next section (CAP Theorem).

CAP Theorem

In case of distributed databases, the three important aspects of the CAP theorem are Consistency (C), Availability (A), and Partition tolerance (P). The CAP theorem states that in any distributed system, we can select only two aspects. It was given by Eric Brewer, a professor of computer science, University of California, Berkeley. The theorem states:

"Though it's desirable to have Consistency, High-Availability and Partition-tolerance in every system, unfortunately no system can achieve all three at the same time".

Let us discuss the three aspects of the CAP theorem. The first one refers to the number of nodes that should respond to a read request before it is considered as a successful operation. The second is the number of nodes that should respond to a write request before it is considered a successful operation. The third is the number of nodes where the data is replicated or copied. Figure 15.8 provides an illustration of the CAP theorem:

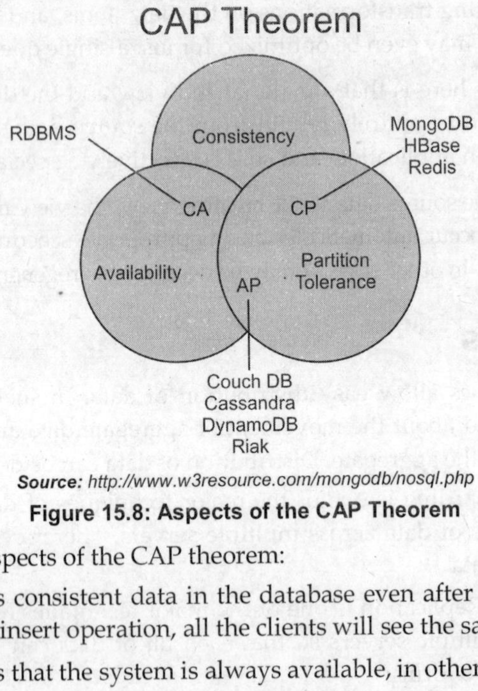

Source: *http://www.w3resource.com/mongodb/nosql.php*

Figure 15.8: Aspects of the CAP Theorem

Figure 15.8 shows three aspects of the CAP theorem:

- **Consistency**—Implies consistent data in the database even after the execution of an operation. For example, after an insert operation, all the clients will see the same data.
- **Availability**—Implies that the system is always available, in other words, there is no downtime.
- **Partition Tolerance**—Implies the system continues to work even though the communication among the servers is unreliable.

Generally, it is impossible to sustain all the three requirements. Therefore, according to CAP theorem, two out of the three requirements should be followed.

Let's discuss briefly the three combinations; CA, CP, and AP, shown in Figure 15.8:

- **CA**—Implies single site cluster in which all nodes communicate with each other.
- **CP**—Implies all the available data will be consistent or accurate, provided some data may not be available.
- **AP**—Implies some data returned may be inconsistent.

ACID Property

ACID (Atomicity, Consistency, Isolation, and Durability) transactions guarantee four properties:

- **Atomicity**—In this either all the operations in transaction will complete or not a single one. If any part of transaction fails, the entire transaction will fail.
- **Consistency**—A transaction must leave the database in an inconsistent state. This ensures that any transaction which is done will change the database to another valid state.
- **Isolation**—Transactions will not interfere with each other.
- **Durability**—The Successful completion of transaction will not be reversed.

Eric's CAP theorem says that if you want consistency, availability, and partition tolerance, then we can look out for two out of three. In a distributed system, partition tolerance means that system will continue to work unless there is a complete network failure.

An alternative to ACID is BASE:

- **Basic Availability**—System does not guarantee availability.
- **Soft-state**—System changes over time, even without input.
- **Eventual consistency**—The system will become consistent over time.

The NoSQL database provides options for database developers to fulfill their specific requirements. This, however, is both good and bad at the same time. This is good because it can design the system according to the requirements, and bad because there are several options available to it and it can make an incorrect choice in designing the system.

We all know that transactions are a major feature of relational databases. Our development methods are used in such a way to this feature that we cannot imagine databases without transactions. However, most NoSQL databases do not provide transaction support by default, which means the developers have to think of ways of implementing transactions.

Sharding

Database sharding can be defined as a partitioning scheme for large databases distributed across various servers, and is responsible for new levels of database performance and scalability. It divides a database into smaller parts called 'shards' and replicates those across a number of distributed servers. Figure 15.9 displays the technique of sharding:

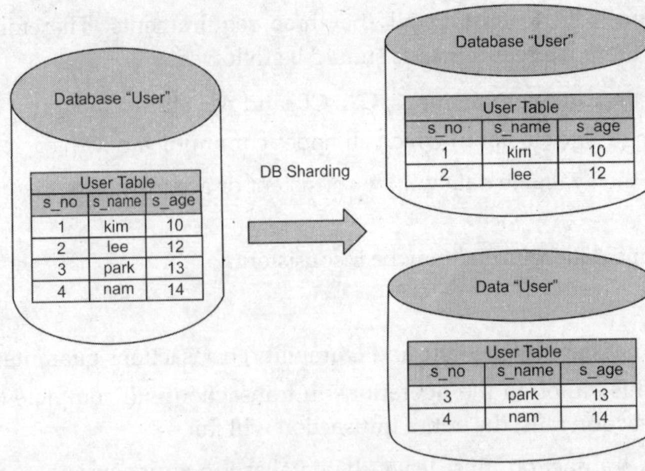

Source: *http://www.cubrid.org/manual/91/en/shard.html*

Figure 15.9: Database Sharding

The term 'sharding' was coined by Google engineers, and gained popularity through their publication of Big Table architecture. The concept of 'shared-nothing' database partitioning has been in use for more than a decade, and many implementations were provided for it over this period, specifically as high profile developed as in-house solutions by Internet leaders such as eBay, Amazon, Digg, YouTube, Facebook, Friendster, and Wikipedia. Database sharding has been gaining popularity due to the extensive growth in transactional volume and size of business application databases. It is popular among many successful e-service providers, Software as a Service (SaaS) companies, and social networking websites.

Database sharding employs a scalable approach for improving the throughput and overall performance of high-transaction, large database-centric business applications. Since the inception of RDBMS, application engineers and architects have been looking for ways to increase performance and capacity of the systems.

The fact is that business databases are continuously growing in terms of size, especially due to the commencement of the Internet economy, the Information Age, and the introduction of high-volume electronic commerce. As the size and transaction volume of databases increase in a linear pattern, the response time also grows logarithmically, as shown in Figure 15.10:

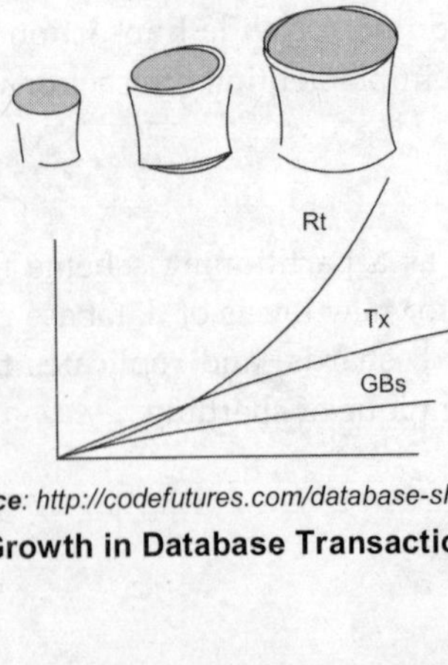

Source: *http://codefutures.com/database-sharding/*

Figure 15.10: Growth in Database Transactions and Volumes

The fundamental design of a database management system is based on two factors—performance and scalability. Databases are heavily dependent on the three components of a computer, i.e. CPU, memory, and disk space.

We know that each of these components on a single server can only scale up to a certain point, and then other measures have to be taken. While it is clear that disk I/O is a primary bottleneck as database management systems have improved, they also continue to take greater advantage of CPU and memory.

Therefore, as business applications gain sophistication and continue to grow in demand, architects, developers, and database administrators are faced with the constant challenge of maintaining database performance for critical systems. This is one of the major aspects that drive the need for database sharding.

Summary

This chapter has discussed various aspects of data management in NoSQL in detail. After introducing NoSQL, the chapter has explained types of data models. It has then described the key/value, column-oriented, and document data models. Apart from this, you have learned about graph and schema-less databases. You have also been made familiar with the concept of materialized views as well as distribution models. Moreover, you have learned about sharding.

Quick Revise

Multiple-Choice Questions

Q1. Which of the following is a disadvantage of relational databases?

a. Concurrency
b. Impedance mismatch
c. ACID transactions
d. Normalization

Ans. The correct option is b.

Q2. Which of the following is a disadvantage of NoSQL databases?

a. Scalability
b. Performance
c. High availability
d. Complex transaction support

Ans. The correct option is d.

Q3. Which of the following is not a NoSQL data model?

a. Object relational
b. Column-oriented store
c. Document-oriented store
d. Graph database

Ans. The correct option is a.

Q4. Which type of format cannot be stored or retrieved in the document data model?

a. JSON
b. XML
c. DOC
d. BSON

Ans. The correct option is c.

Q5. Which of the following data models can be used for social network mining?

a. Document data model
b. Schema-less data model
c. Key/value data model
d. Graph data model

Ans. The correct option is d.

Q6. Sharding is a type of ______ partitioning.

a. Vertical
b. Horizontal
c. Both vertical and horizontal
d. None of these

Ans. The correct option is b.

Subjective Questions

Q1. Compare relational databases with NoSQL databases.

Ans. A comparison of relational databases and NoSQL databases is shown in the following table:

	Relational Database	NoSQL Database
Dataset Size	Relational databases are designed to handle similar type of data and large datasets, for example, transactional data.	NoSQL databases are designed to handle different types of data as well as very large datasets, for example, Google or Facebook data.
Scalability	It provides less scalability.	It provides more scalability.
Data Consistency Model	Relational databases use ACID properties. As a result, a consistent and equivalent view of data for all users is guaranteed. So, the data which is committed will be available to the customer. For example, in case of online banking, consistency is a key criterion. Therefore, we have to use relational databases.	NoSQL follows Basic Availability, Soft State and Eventual Consistency (BASE). NoSQL is designed according to the client's requirements. For example, in case of a social media website, consistency is not an issue. Therefore, we can use NoSQL databases here.
CAP Theorem	RDBMS are also called CA systems, because they possess the features of consistency and availability.	NoSQL can be called CP or AP systems, which means that they have consistency and partitioning or availability and partitioning.
Data Model	RDBMS contains a data model in the form of rows and columns.	NoSQL does not have a fixed data model. No SQL can therefore be key/value, column-oriented, or document-oriented.
Data Integrity	Data integrity can be ensured in relational databases with the help of foreign keys and by defining fields like unique or not-null, etc.	The design of NoSQL is such that it does not provide data integrity; instead, it is the responsibility of an application to handle it.

	Relational Database	NoSQL Database
Querying	Relational databases use SQL for querying. One of the advantages of using these databases is that they support joins.	NoSQL does not use the concept of joins. For the purpose of querying, these databases require APIs, a proprietary language, or object graph navigation APIs or Map Reduce APIs, etc.
Schema Definition	RDBMS schema is fixed. We also need to defi the database schema before using it.	NoSQL has no schema-based restrictions.

Q2. What is a materialized view?

Ans. Materialized views are slightly different from normal views. These are disk-based and updated periodically as per the requirements of the query. This is an advantage because when we query a materialized view, we are basically querying a table, which can be indexed. Creating materialized views in the form of aggregate tables or copies of frequently executed queries can speed up the response time.

A disadvantage of a materialized view is that the data obtained from it is updated to the point or date it was last refreshed. Materialized views are mostly used in BI applications or Big Data, where query response time is a basic need.

Q3. What is the purpose of sharding? What is the difference between replication and sharding?

Ans. Sharding is a technique of providing horizontal scalability, which allows different sites to have different types of data. This scalability helps in reducing the work load of servers.

Replication is just a process of copying the same data across different sites while sharding is the process of distributing different datasets on different sites. In addition, sharding improves both read and write performance, while replication improves read performance but not write performance.

Q4. Explain the CAP theorem.

Ans. In case of distributed databases, the three important aspects of the CAP theorem are Consistency (C), Availability (A), and Partition tolerance (P). The CAP theorem states that in any distributed system, we can select only two aspects.

Let us discuss the three aspects of the CAP theorem. The first one refers to the number of nodes that should respond to a read request before it is considered as a successful operation. The second is the number of nodes that should respond to a write request before it is considered a successful operation. The third is the number of nodes where the data is replicated or copied.

Q5. Explain the ways in which data can be distributed.

Ans. Data distribution can be performed in the following two ways:

- **Through sharding**—Sharding is one of the major techniques of data distribution. It is used to distribute various types of data across multiple servers. Therefore, each server acts as a single source for a subset of data.

- **Through replication**—Replication is one of the major techniques for fault tolerance. The idea is to copy data across multiple servers so that each bit of data can be found in multiple places. Replication occurs in two forms:
  - Master-slave replication, which makes one node the authoritative copy that handles writes, while slaves, which are synchronized with the master, handle reads.
  - Peer-to-peer replication, which allows writes to any node without requiring authorization. Here, the nodes can coordinate with each other to synchronize their copies of the data.

16

Data Movement with Flume and Sqoop

A large amount of data is required for analytical processing, and data is loaded from different sources into Hadoop clusters. The process of loading huge data into Hadoop clusters from different sources faces problems like maintaining and ensuring data consistency and the best way of utilizing the resources. Both Sqoop and Flume pull the data from the heterogeneous source and push it to the Hadoop cluster. In this chapter, we will discuss the working of Flume and Sqoop in detail.

Flume is a framework developed by Apache developers keeping in mind that it should be capable of solving the recursively generating data, i.e., logs, crash reports, etc. Flume is used to collect data from different sources, such as logs, directories, etc. It scales data horizontally, and multiple flume agents can be put in action to collect large volumes of data from different sources and aggregate them. Thereafter, data logs are moved to a centralized data store, i.e., Hadoop Distributed File System (HDFS). Apache Flume is distributed, reliable and has a flexible architecture based on streaming data flows.

Sqoop is used to move data between Hadoop and other databases. It is designed to exchange information between Hadoop and relational database. It exchanges mass information between Apache Hadoop and organized data stores effectively. Sqoop is used to extract useful information from Hadoop and export them to the outside structured data stores. It works with relational databases; for example, Teradata, Netezza, Oracle, MySQL, Postgres, and HSQLDB.

This chapter discusses various aspects of Flume and its components in detail. It explains the flume architecture designed on the basis of concepts, such as Flume Event, Flume Agent, Flume Flow, and so on. It also discusses the concept of Sqoop that is designed to exchange information between Hadoop and relational database. Finally, this chapter describes importing data into hive and HDFS.

Flume Architecture

Flume architecture is designed in such a way that it is robust, fault-tolerant, and has tunable reliability mechanism for failover and recovery. The architecture of Apache Flume is based on the following core concepts:

- **Flume Event:** It is represented as the unit of data flowing, which has a byte payload and a set of strings with optional string headers.
- **Flume Agent**—It is a JVM process that hosts the components such as channels, sinks, and sources. It has the potential to receive, store, and forward the events from an external source to the next-hop destination.
- **Flume Flow**—It is the point of time the event is being generated, i.e., origin point to the final destination is considered to be simple flow or data flow.
- **Flume Client**—It refers to the interface where the client operates at the origin point of the event and delivers it to Flume agent.
- **Source**—A source that consumes events having a specific format and delivers it via specific mechanism. For example, when an Avro source receives events from the clients and the flume agents, it then stores these in one or more channels.
- **Channel**—It is a passive store where events are held by channel until the sink removes it for further transport.

- **Sink**—It removes the event from the channel and puts it on external repository like HDFS. The example of terminal sink is Flume HDFS sink. The example of regular sink is Flume Avro sink. In Flume Avro sink, a message is transmitted to other agents that are running Avro source.

Figure 16.1 shows the architecture of Apache Flume:

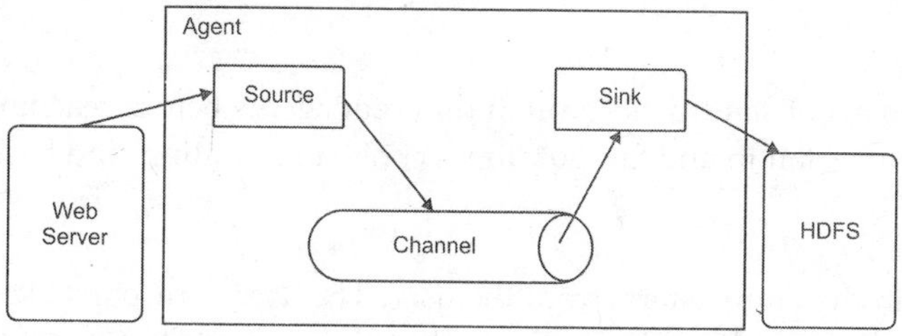

Figure 16.1: The Architecture of Apache Flume

The source of Flume uses an event, which is delivered to it by an external source. The target flume source receives the event in a readable format. It then stores it on one or more channels until flume sink removes the event for further processing. During this process, source and sink run asynchronously with the events directed in the channel.

Recoverability and Multihop Flows

To guarantee reliability of event delivery, flume uses transactional design. This design corresponds to event that is treated as transactions and events are staged in channels on each agent. In the flow, every event is delivered to next agents in the form of source bar. Events are only removed from the channel once it is confirmed that they have been further sent to the next agent or in terminal repository (like HDFS). This will help us to maintain the queue of current events till the storage confirmation is received.

This can only happen through sink and source as they encapsulate the storage or retrieval information in a transaction that is being provided by the channel. This will ensure that end-to-end reliability of the flow for single-hop message delivery semantics will happen in Flume.

Staging events in the channel help us to maintain recoverability. They manage recovery from failures. A durable file channel (a channel that provides a faultless data flow) is supported by Flume that is backed by the local file system. In other words, the durable file channel essentially maintains state to store on permanent storage. If any event is lost during system failure, it can be recovered when a durable file channel is used. A faster way to store the events in a memory queue is through memory channel. If agent process dies and events are still in memory channel, these events cannot be recovered. Figure 16.2 shows the multihop flow:

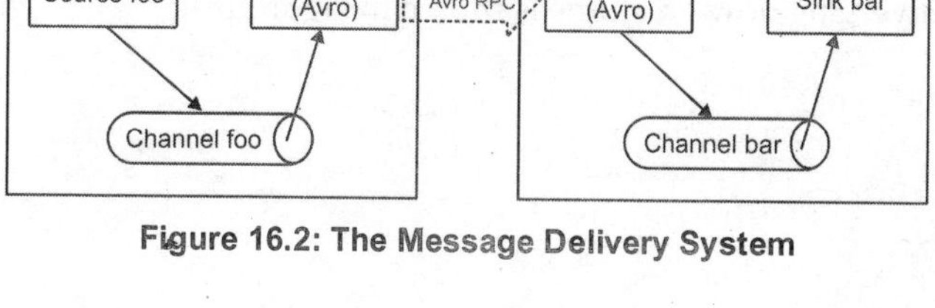

Figure 16.2: The Message Delivery System

Multihop flows are allowed in flume. A user is allowed to build an event where it can travel through multiple agents before reaching the final destination. In multihop flow, source from the next hop and sink from the previous hop have transactions process running. This is done to ensure data is safely stored in the channel for the next hop.

Complex Flow

In multihop flow, an event can travel through different agents before reaching the final destination. For failed hops, it allows fan-in and fan-out flows, contextual routing, and backup routes.

Flow Pipeline

A data signal flow in the Flume starts from the user. The user is responsible for the transmission of the event to the next intermediate destination, which is an agent. The event received by source will then send it to one or more channels. The event received by channels may be emptied by one or more sinks running within the same agents. Before sending the event further, we check that the sink is regular or terminal. In regular sink, an event is sent to the next destination that is another agent; whereas in terminal sink, event is sent to the final destination. The producer-consumer model is used by the channel for separating sources and sinks. This will help the sink and source to perform differently, and the attributes produced at runtime can use the physical resources that are available.

Figure 16.3 shows communication between various components:

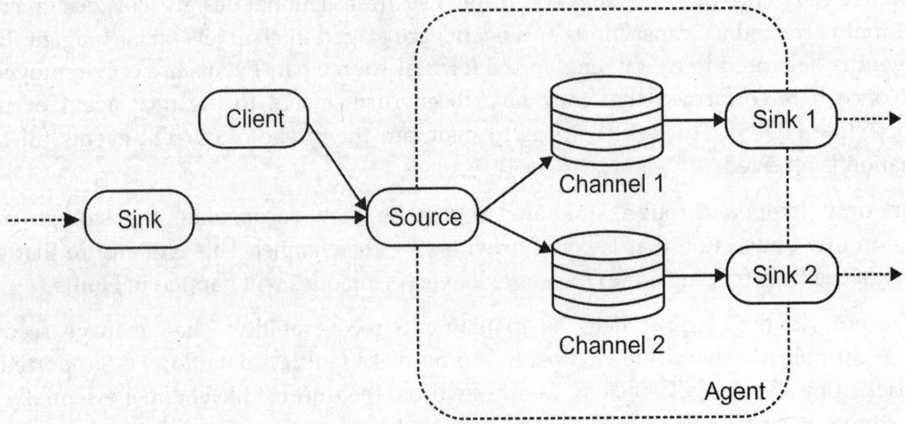

Figure 16.3: Communication between Various Components

By designing a source to convey the event to more than one channel, streams can fan out to more than one destination. This is shown in Figure 16.3, where the source inside the working agent composes the event out to two channels – Channels 1 and 2. On the other hand, streams can be focalized by numerous sources working inside the same operators while being in touch with the same channel. A simple converging flow on Flume is shown in Figure 16.4:

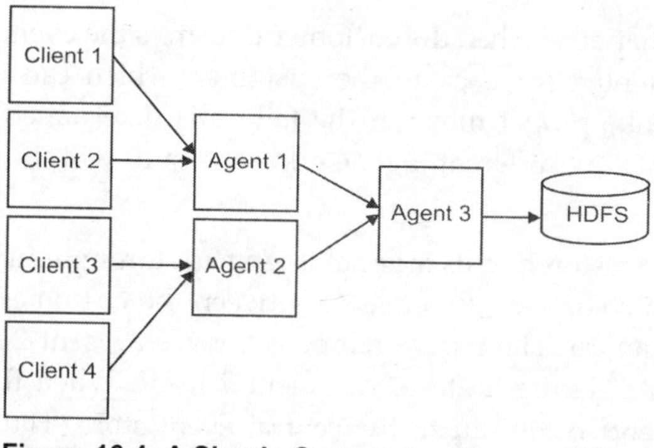

Figure 16.4: A Simple Converging Flow on Flume

Reliability and Failure Handling

The channel-based transaction is used by Flume for reliable message distribution. When a message starts moving from one agent to another, the following two transactions take place:

- First transaction at the agent's side who delivers the event
- Second transaction at the agent's side who receives the event

If the sender agent wants its transaction to be completed, it should receive a positive signal from the receiving agent. The receiving agents will send the positive signal if its transactions have been executed properly. This guarantees ensured message distribution between the hops that the stream makes. Figure 16.5 shows the transactional transfer of events between agents:

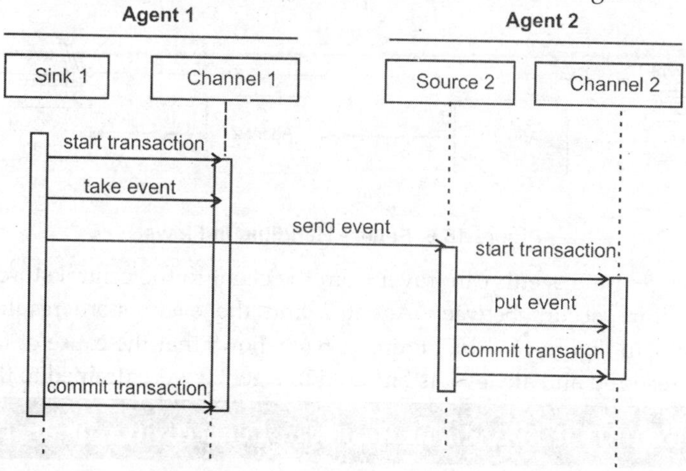

Figure 16.5: Transactional Transfer of Events between Agents

This mechanism frames the premise for failure handling in Flume. When a flow that passes through different agents experiences a communication failure on any leg of the flow, the affected events start getting buffered at the last unaffected agent in the flow. If a failure is not clarified on time, it will lead to the failure of the last agent that is unaffected. This will then drive the agent before it starts buffering the events.

Eventually, if the failure happens when the customer transmits the event to its first-jump destination, that failure will be accounted for back to the customer, which can then permit the application creating the events to make proper move. If the failure is determined before the first-jump agent fails, the buffered events in different agents downstream will begin depleting toward their destination.

Finally, the stream will be restored to its original trademark throughput levels. Figure 16.6 outlines a situation where a stream containing two agents between the customer and the central event store experiences a transient failure. The failure happens between Agent 2 and the central event store, bringing about the events getting buffered at Agent 2 itself. When the failing link is restored to normal, the buffered events drain out to the central event store. The flow is now restored to its original throughput characteristics.

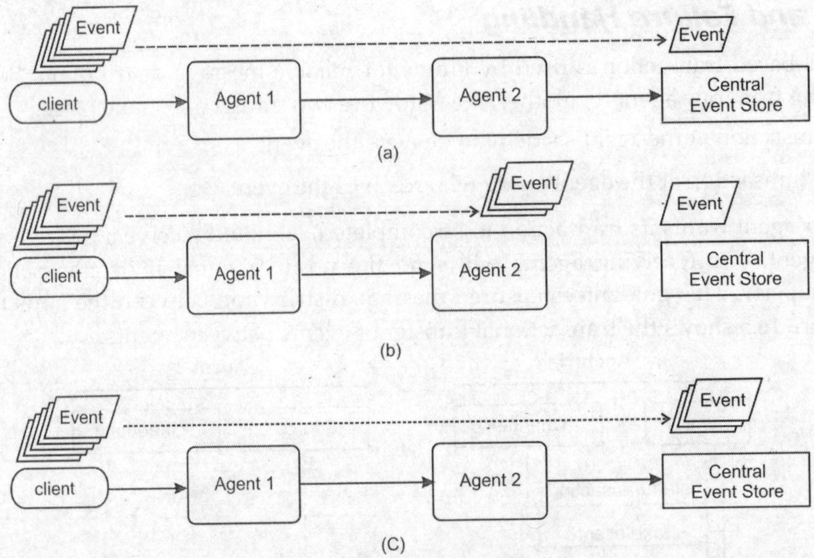

Figure 16.6: Failure Handling in Flows

The flow is normal and the events can travel from the client to the central store in Figure 16.6 (a). A communication failure occurs between Agent 2 and the event store resulting in events being buffered on Agent 2 in Figure 16.6 (b). Figure 16.6 (c) shows that the cause of failure was addressed and the flow was restored and any events buffered in Agent 2 were drained to the store.

EXHIBIT 1: Streamlining Healthcare Connectivity with Big Data

Company Overview

The connectivity and information technology subsidiary of a major pharmaceutical company was created to simplify how the business of healthcare is managed while making the delivery of care safer and more efficient. As more and more of the US healthcare system goes electronic, this organization meets challenges and opportunities through an open network that supports future growth via interoperability among organizations, systems, and solutions.

Business Challenges before Cloudera

With regulations such as the Health Insurance Portability and Accountability Act of 1996 (HIPAA), healthcare organizations are required to store healthcare data for extended periods of time. This health IT company instituted a policy of saving seven years' historical claims and remit data, but its in-house database systems had trouble meeting the data retention requirement while processing millions of claims every day.

A software engineer at the company explained, "All of our systems were maxed out. We were constantly having database issues. It was just too much data for what they were meant to handle. They were overworked and overloaded, and it started to cause problems with all of our real-time production processing."

Further, the organization sought a solution that would allow users to do more than just store data. The manager of software development at the company explained, "In today's data-driven world, data really is this huge asset. We wondered, 'What framework, what platform will allow us to optimize the data that we have?'"

The team set out to find a new solution. "We could have gone the SAN route, but it's expensive and cumbersome," said the software engineer. They did some searching online and came across Hadoop, MongoDB, and Cassandra. "We analyzed them and came up with a prototype for each one. In the end, we decided Hadoop was what we wanted."

Initially, the organization downloaded Hadoop from Apache and configured it to run on 10 Dell workstations that were already in-house. Once the small Hadoop cluster showed its functionality and demonstrated value, the team decided to make a commitment to the platform but would need support to do so. When evaluating various Hadoop distributions and management vendors, they recognized that Cloudera was different: its Hadoop distribution — CDH — is 100% Apache open source. This allows Cloudera customers to benefit from rapid innovations in the open source community while also taking advantage of enterprise-grade support and management tools offered with the Cloudera Enterprise subscription.

Use Case

When deciding to deploy CDH, the team set out to identify applications that were already seeing performance issues in production. "One of the big advantages of Hadoop has been to be able to segregate big data from transactional processing data and allow smoother processing of information. Basically, it allows us to offload a lot of stress from the database," said the company's manager of software development.

They quickly identified two areas that were a strong fit for Hadoop:

- Archiving seven years' claims and remit data, which requires complex processing to get into a normalized format
- Logging terabytes of data generated from transactional systems daily and storing them in CDH for analytical purposes

Today, the health IT organization uses Flume to move data from its source systems into the CDH cluster on a 24x7 basis. The company loads data from CDH to an Oracle

Online Transaction Processing (OLTP) database for billing purposes. This load runs once or twice each day via Sqoop.

Impact: Helping Providers Collect Payment Faster through Operational Efficiencies

"If you look at the margin that the average hospital has, it's between 2-3%," stated the manager of software development. "So their cash flow is very tight. Anything you can do to reduce the time to get paid is very valuable to a healthcare provider."

Since deploying Cloudera Enterprise, the organization has reduced the time it takes for healthcare providers to get paid by streamlining their transfer of messages to payers. The ability to expedite this process is especially valuable when regulatory changes come into play, such as the recent conversion from HIPAA 4010 to HIPAA 5010.

"We assist with the conversion and processing of these messages," said the company's manager of software development. "For example, 4010 messages came in and we'd convert them to 5010 to allow seamless processing. The providers didn't have to upgrade any of their systems when the regulations went into effect. We gave them a bit of a buffer to implement changes. And since we do a lot of electronic processing, we can do basic sanity checks on the messages as they come in and let providers know what adjustments need to be made in order to get paid faster."

Impact: Low Cost + Greater Analytic Flexibility

Since Hadoop uses industry standard hardware, the cost per terabyte of storage is, on average, 10x cheaper than a traditional relational data warehouse system. "One of my pet peeves is: you buy a machine, you buy SAN storage, and then you have to buy licensing for the storage in addition to the storage itself," explained the manager of software development. "You have to buy licensing for the blades, and it just becomes an untenable situation. With Hadoop you buy commodity hardware and you're good to go. In addition to the storage, you get a bigger bang for your buck because it gives you the ability to run analytics on the combined compute and storage. The solutions that we had in place previously really didn't allow for that. Even if the costs were equivalent, the benefit you get from storing data on a Hadoop type solution is far greater than what you'd get from storing it in a database."

Impact: Simple Deployment & Administration

After deciding on the Cloudera solution, "the deployment process into production with Hadoop was actually quite easy," said a software engineer at the company. "Cloudera Manager really helped us a lot. It's as easy as just clicking a few buttons, and you're up and running. It's really simple. And the support staff at Cloudera have been great. They really helped us out with a couple of issues we had along the way."

Several employees enrolled in Cloudera University training as well, which was "very beneficial" according to one software engineer. And with Cloudera Manager, the team spends very little time managing the cluster.

Further, this health IT organization appreciates the proactive customer support offered by Cloudera Enterprise. "We ask questions and we get them answered very quickly," commented their manager of software development. "Not only do the Cloudera Support folks answer the question, they come back and say, 'Do you have any other questions? Is there anything else we can help you with?' It's very different. The people that are on Cloudera's Support team — you can definitely tell they are Hadoop Committers. Not only will they find you the answer but they can tell you, 'This may not be the best practice, you may want to change the way you're doing your development to take advantage of other features.' The Cloudera Support organization is world class."

Source: *http://hadoopilluminated.com/hadoop_illuminated/cached_reports/Cloudera_Case_Study_Healthcare.pdf*

Sqoop

Sqoop is a tool designed to exchange information between Hadoop and relational database. As the compositional focus of Apache™ Hadoop, YARN coordinates information ingested from Apache Sqoop and different administrations that convey information into the Enterprise Hadoop group. Apache Sqoop effectively exchanges mass information between Apache Hadoop and organized data stores, for example, relational databases. Sqoop assists with offloading certain jobs, (for example, ETL handling) from the EDW (Enterprise Data Warehouse) to Hadoop for productive execution at a much lower expense. Sqoop is used to extract useful information from Hadoop and export it to outside structured data stores. It performs with relational databases such as Teradata, Netezza, Oracle, MySQL, Postgres, and HSQLDB. The following functions are used to merge the information between Hadoop and structured data stores:

- **Data import**—It moves certain data from EDW and external stores into Hadoop. This is done to optimize cost-effectiveness of the combined processing and data storage.
- **Parallel data transfer**—It is used when we want faster execution of information between Hadoop and data stores.
- **Fast data copies**—It copies data faster from external systems into Hadoop system.
- **Efficient data analysis**—It enhances efficiency of data analysis by combining unstructured data with structured data in a schema-on-read data lake.
- **Load balancing**—It reduces the excessive storage and processing loads by transferring them to other systems.

How Sqoop Works

Sqoop gives a pluggable component for ideal network and external systems. The Sqoop API gives a helpful structure for assembling new connectors. These connectors can be dropped into Sqoop installations to give network to different systems. Sqoop itself comes bundled with different types of connectors utilized for prevalent database and information warehousing systems. Figure 16.7 shows the architecture of Sqoop:

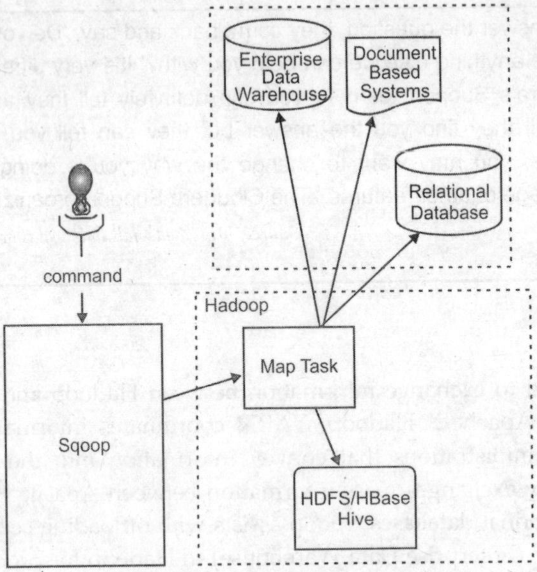

Figure 16.7: Architecture of Sqoop

Sqoop is a tool used for productive information transfers between relational databases and the Apache Hadoop biological system. One of the important advantages of Sqoop is that it is easy to handle and can work with a variety of frameworks within and outside the system. In this manner, with one tool, you can import or export information from all databases supporting the JDBC interface with the same charge line contentions uncovered by Sqoop. Moreover, Sqoop permits you to module specific additions to improve transfers for specific database systems.

Numerous clients utilize the words "connector" and "driver" conversely. However, these words mean totally distinctive things in the setting of Sqoop. In Sqoop, "driver" refers to a JDBC Driver. JDBC is a standard Java API. Java language recommends what classes and systems this interface contains, and JDK does not have any default usage. Along these lines, every database vendor is in charge of composing its own particular execution that will communicate with the corresponding database with its local convention. Thus, JDBC drivers regularly convey prohibitive licenses that restrict redistribution. Thus, every client needs to download the drivers independently and introduce them into Sqoop.

In spite of the presence of an SQL standard, each database vendor has its own criteria. The nuts and bolts more often than not work in the same way as over databases, although some edge conditions may be processed differently. Additionally, as SQL is a completely general query processing language, it may not generally be ideal for importing or exporting information out of the database server.

Connectors permit Sqoop to rise above SQL dialects while upgrading information transfer. A "connector" is a pluggable piece that gets metadata about transferred information (columns-related data sets) to move information in the most effective way. The most essential connector that ships with Sqoop is Generic JDBC Connector, and as the name suggests, it utilizes just the JDBC interface for getting to metadata and transferring information. Sqoop delivers specific connectors for MySQL, PostgreSQL, Oracle Database, Microsoft SQL Server, IBM DB2, and Netezza.

To show how drivers and connectors are utilized, let's understand how Sqoop joins with the database. Figure16.8 shows the connection of Sqoop with database:

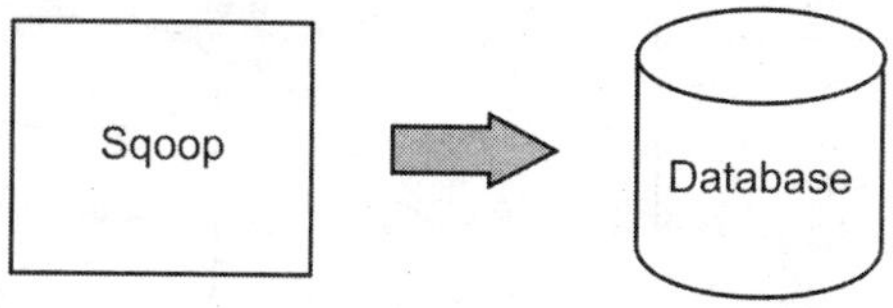

Figure 16.8: The Connection of Sqoop with Database

Depending on command line arguments and every single accessible connector, Sqoop attempts to stack the one offering the best execution. This procedure starts with Sqoop checking all additional physically downloaded connectors to confirm if one can be utilized. If there are no physically installed connectors or no installed connecters recognize themselves as candidates, Sqoop will check the JDBC URL (typically beginning with jdbc:) to check whether you are connecting with a database for which an inherent exceptional connector is accessible. For example, for the jdbc:mysql://URL that is utilized for MySQL, Sqoop will get the MySQL Connector. This is streamlined for MySQL. Finally, if no connector is yet confirmed for utilization, Sqoop will default to the Generic JDBC Connector.

We can use the argument connection manager with the class name of any self-assertive connector, if the selection procedure does not suit your ecosystem. In any case, remember that connectors are generally intended for one particular database vendor, and in this way, for instance, the MySQL Connector won't work with PostgreSQ. Figure 16.9 shows the introduction of the connector:

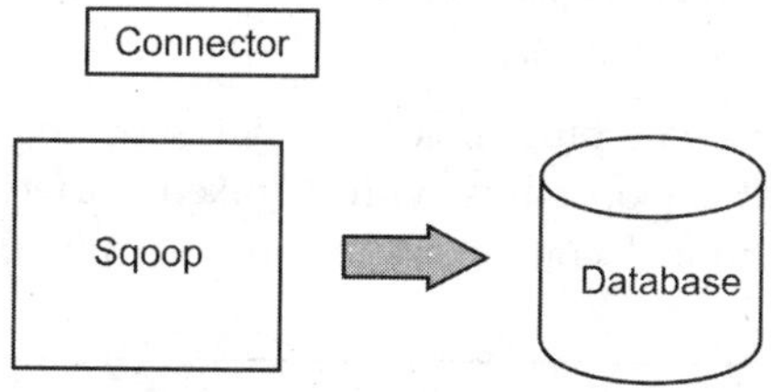

Figure 16.9: Introduction of Connector in Process Flow

Once the connector is selected, the next step is to select the JDBC driver. As most connectors and databases have only one JDBC driver accessible, the connector itself identifies which driver can be used for a given task. For example, MySQL JDBC Driver is repeatedly used by the MySQL connector. The special case is the Generic JDBC Connector, which is not attached to any database, and in this way, it cannot be figured out which JDBC Driver should be utilized. In fact, you need to supply the driver name in the driver parameter on the command line. However, it is important to be careful that using the driver parameter will always force Sqoop to use the Generic JDBC Connector even if a more specialized connector is available.

For instance, if the particular connector of MySQL would be utilized on the grounds that the URL begins with jdbc:mysql://, determining the driver alternative will constrain Sqoop to utilize the generic connector. In most of the cases, we need not use the driver options. Figure 16.10 shows the introduction of connector and driver:

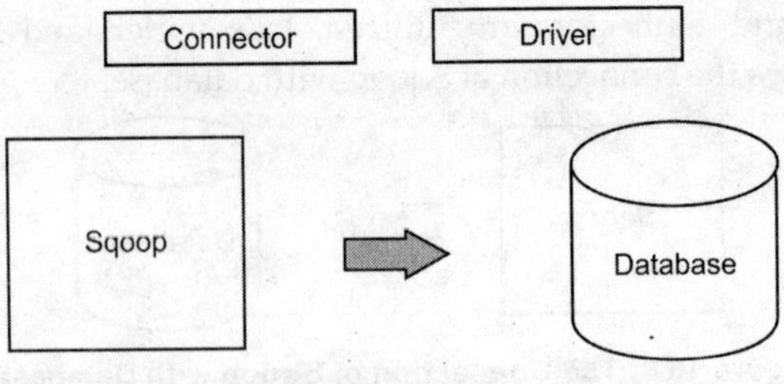

Figure 16.10: Introduction of Both Connection and Driver in Process Flow

After both connector and driver have been connected, the association between the Sqoop customer and the objective database can be built up, as shown in Figure 16.11:

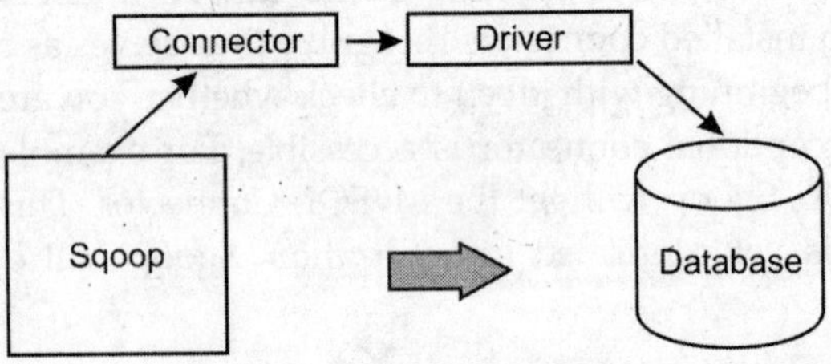

Figure 16.11: Flow of Connector and Driver in the Process Flow

Sqoop Architecture

As we have discussed all the pluggable pieces that Sqoop uses to connect with your database server, let's discuss about where every piece lives.

The connector is a Sqoop-particular plugin, so it is not shocking that it is a piece of the Sqoop establishment. The fact is that Sqoop ships with a mixed variety of connectors out of the box. Moreover, different extra-additional connectors can be downloaded and introduced into Sqoop effortlessly.

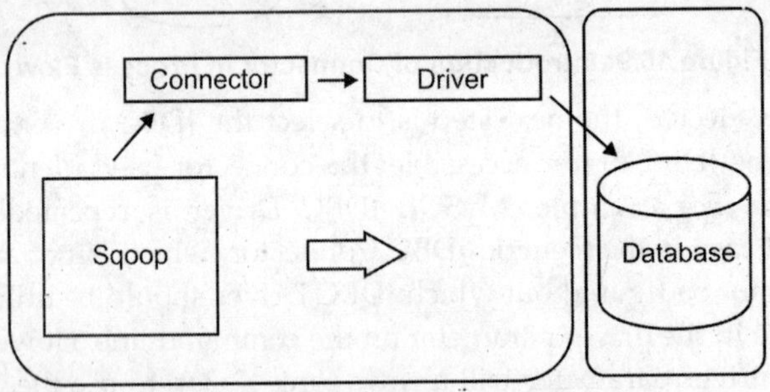

Figure 16.12: Architecture of Sqoop

Despite the fact that drivers are database-specific pieces, made and distributed by various database vendors, they are often not introduced alongside the database server. Rather, they should be introduced on the machine where Sqoop is executed because they are utilized by connectors to build up the connection with the database server. Suppose JDBC drivers are not delivered with Sqoop because of incompatible license issues. In this case, one must download and install the software manually. We can find the software drivers on the website of the database vendors.

Connectors and drivers should be introduced on the machine where Sqoop needs to be executed. You do not have to introduce them on all hubs in your Hadoop Cluster. Sqoop will spread them itself, whenever required.

Apache Sqoop is a device intended for productively exchanging mass information between Apache Hadoop and organized data stores; for example, relational databases, venture information distribution centers, and NoSQL frameworks systems. Sqoop can transform information into different file configurations, including CSV files, sequence files, or Avro information files. With the development of Parquet ubiquity, there are strong prerequisites of including Parquet support.

Importing Data

The import command of Sqoop is utilized to import a predefined table from a database to HDFS. Every row from a table is presented as a different record in HDFS. Records can be put away as content files (one record for every line) or in binary representation.

Sqoop imports information in two stages. At the first stage, Sqoop introspects the database to accumulate the vital metadata for the information being transported in databases. At the second stage Sqoop presents a MapReduce task. The job transfers the real information utilizing the metadata caught as a part of the past step to verify the data that is currently stored in database.

Importing Data into HDFS

The syntax is given as follows:

```
sqoop import \
--connect <JDBC connection string> \
--username <username> --password <password> \
--table <tablename> \
--target-dir <hdfs-dir>
```

The statement 'connect' indicates the JDBC connect string. The username and password indicate the verification information. The statement 'table' indicates the table to read. You may utilize query, which intends to import information from a discretionary SQL inquiry. The statement 'target-dir' indicates the destination in HDFS. Optionally, you can indicate the number map tasks by including m1.

You can import information to HDFS in Parquet group. You ought to determine it by utilizing the parquet file statement. With this statement, Sqoop will compose information records from a table in binary representation as Parquet files. To compose Parquet files, a construction is obliged to present to sorts in memory. Our process tends to choose Avro. Imported Parquet records can be used by other MapReduce tasks or tools having the tendency to access HDFS files.

If you import all data of table users from a MYSQL database to HDFS location *hdfs://jobtracker-host:jobtracker-port/import/mysql/users* with only one map task, the command will be as follows:

```
sqoop import \
--connect jdbc:mysql://the_mysql_server/the_mysql_database \
--username the_mysql_user --password the_mysql_password \
--table users \
--target-dir /import/mysql/users \
--as-parquetfile -m 1
```

When import is done effectively, Parquet files will be made at hdfs://jobtracker-host:jobtracker-port/import/mysql/users. To avoid potential name conflicts, we use UUID (Universally Unique IDentifier) as filenames. Before doing another import, Sqoop will check whether the target catalog exists or is unadulterated. Now, Sqoop will ensure that subcatalog.metadata exists or not as this catalog contains the data that is needed for export. If the data exists, then import will fail.

Importing Data into Hive

Suppose you have a Hive metastore connected with your HDFS cluster. Sqoop can likewise import the information into Hive by producing and executing a CREATE TABLE statement to characterize the information's format in Hive.

In Hive, Sqoop will convert data from the native data types within the external data store into the corresponding types. Importing data into Hive is as simple as adding the hive-import argument and hive-table argument to your Sqoop command line. It is important to note that the target-dir argument is not necessary for Hive import.

If we need to import all information of table clients from a MYSQL database to Hive table clients with map task, the command used would be:

```
sqoop import \
--connect jdbc:mysql://the_mysql_server/the_mysql_database \
--username the_mysql_user --password the_mysql_password \
--table users \
--hive-import -hive-table users \
--as-parquetfile -m 1
```

Like HDFS import, before doing another import, Sqoop will check whether the target Hive table exists or not. If it is present, this will fail for the import statement.

Sqoop2 vs Sqoop

Apache Sqoop utilizes a client model where the user needs to introduce Sqoop alongside connectors/drivers on the client. Sqoop2 uses a service-based model in which the connectors or drivers are introduced on the server. Additionally, all the installation should be done on the Sqoop2 server.

From the perspective of MapReduce, Sqoop presents a Map-only task, while Sqoop2 presents a MapReduce task where the Mappers would transport the information from the source, while the Reducers would change the information as indicated by the source determined. This gives a clear abstraction. In Sqoop, both the transportation and changes are given by Mappers only.

Another major difference in Sqoop2 is the security perspective. The administrator would set up the connections with the source and the targets, while the operator utilizes the established connections. The operator is not needed to know the details about the connections. Operators will be given access to a few connectors, if required.

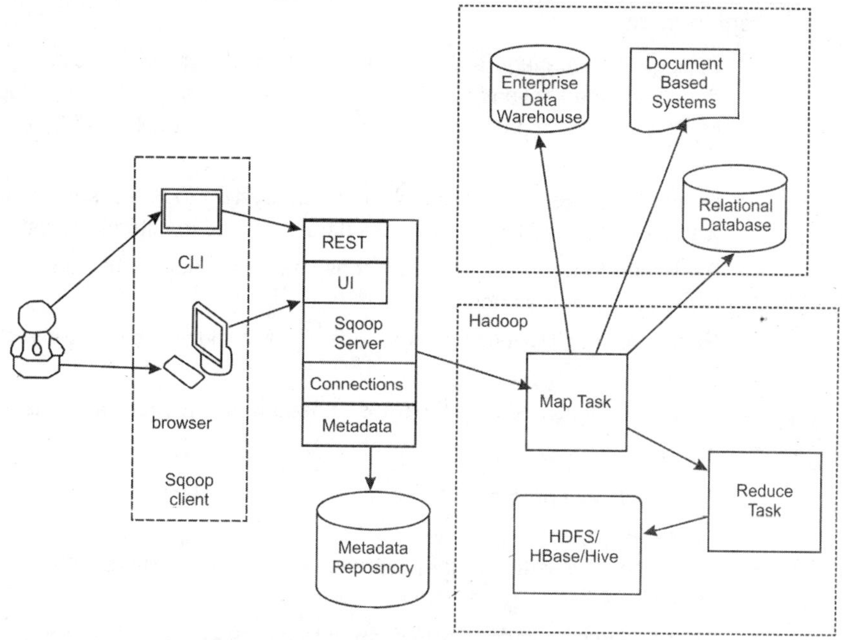

Figure 16.13: Architecture of Sqoop2

Alongside the continuation of the CLI (Command Line Interface), Web UI can likewise be utilized with Sqoop2. The CLI and the Web UI (User Interface) uses the REST (REpresentational State Transfer) services given by the Sqoop Server. One thing to note is that the Web UI is a segment of Hue-1214 and not a segment of the ASF (Apache Software Foundation). The Sqoop2 REST interface makes it simple to incorporate with different structures like Oozie to characterize a work process that includes Sqoop2.

EXHIBIT 2: Retail Chain

Introduction

The multiplication of retail channels and the increasing use of social media are empowering consumers. With a wealth of information readily available online, consumers are now better able to compare products, services, and prices—even as they shop in physical stores. When consumers interact with companies publically through social media, they have greater power to influence other customers or damage a brand.

In order for retailers to capitalize on these and other changes in the industry, they need ways to collect, manage, and analyze a tremendous volume, velocity, and variety of data. Hence, one of the retail chains wanted to generate valuable insights for personalizing marketing and improving the effectiveness of marketing campaigns, optimizing assortment and merchandising decisions, and removing inefficiencies in distribution and operations. This is where Corpus got in to address these challenges with Big Data Analytics.

Requirements

- Struggling to manage and extract value from the growing volume and variety of data and need to unify information across federated sources. Each disparate MySQL server records around 2 million updates, a total of 50-60 million updates daily.
- Unable to relate "raw" data collected from system logs, sensors, or click streams with customer and line-of-business data managed in enterprise systems
- Each end-to-end ELT process consumes 14 hours. This process should be completed within an hour.
- Real-time visibility into business operations including customer experience and behavior
- Most of the time spent on the transformations within data warehouse staging

Solutions

- Replaced Java program ELT with Hadoop for data transformation from MySQL to Data Warehouse using Apache Sqoop
- Replaced multi-staged data warehousing system with a common centralized warehouse
- Apache Pig was used to transform data that is in HDFS (Hadoop Distributed File System). Apache Pig is a platform for analyzing large data sets, which consists of a high-level language for expressing data analysis programs, coupled with infrastructure for evaluating these programs and with substantial parallelization.
- Integrated "Hive" with the existing data warehousing system for faster batch process, which facilitates easy data summarization, ad-hoc queries, and analysis of large datasets stored in Hadoop compatible file systems.
- Hive provides a mechanism to project structure onto this data and query the data using an SQL-like language called HiveQL. At the same time, this language also allows traditional map/reduce programmers to plug in their custom mappers and reducers when it is inconvenient or inefficient to express this logic in HiveQL.
- Achieved under 1 hour ELT process to meet the retail chain's data analytics needs
- Planned to implement MongoDB in the next phase to achieve near real-time analytics

Benefits

- Predict optimal pricing and maintain a price leadership position by analyzing price and demand elasticity
- Select the right merchandise for each channel and fine-tune local assortment planning by drawing on insights from social media, market reports, internal sales data, and customer buying patterns
- Optimize inventory across multiple channels by using leading indicators such as customer sentiment and promotional buzz to anticipate future demand
- Reduced costs and improved operational performance for the business

- Improved decision making and greater efficiencies in business processes
- Gained new insights by combining and analyzing data types in different ways
- Improved customer engagement

About Corpus

Corpus Software is one of the faster growing IT solution and services companies focused on Digital media entertainment, embedded technology and business analytics with offices and partners across Americas, Europe, APAC, Middle East, and Africa.

We work with clients in most emerging technologies, that's where we make their business strong and bring in real difference in the way the peer operates. A diverse workplace continuously focuses on developing unique ideas and contributions to make our clients business grow and to keep the momentum going.

Source: *http://www.corpus.com/pdfs/bigdata/Case_Study_Retail_Chain.pdf*

Summary

This chapter discussed various aspects of Flume and Sqoop. It explained the architecture of Flume and Sqoop. In addition, it described the importing of data into hive and HDFS. In the end, the chapter explained the comparison between Sqoop2 and Sqoop.

Quick Revise

Multiple-Choice Questions

Q1. Which of the following is represented as the unit of data flowing having a byte payload and set of strings with optional string headers?

a. Flume Event b. Flume Agent
c. Flume Flow d. Flume Client

Ans. The correct option is a.

Q2. Which of the following has the potential to receive, store, and forward the events from an external source to the next-hop destination?

a. Flume Event b. Flume Agent
c. Flume Flow d. Flume Client

Ans. The correct option is b.

Q3. _______ permits Sqoop to rise above SQL dialects while upgrading information transfer.

a. Connectors b. Drivers
c. Load balancing d. Efficient data analysis

Ans. The correct option is a.

Q4. Sqoop performs with which of the following relational databases?

a. Teradata, HSQLDB b. Netezza, Postgres
c. Oracle, MySQL d. All of the above

Ans. The correct option is d.

Q5. Which of the following removes the event from the channel and puts them on external repository like HDFS?

a. Flume Agent
b. Flume Client
c. Sink
d. Source

Ans. The correct option is c.

Subjective Questions

Q1. What is Flume? Discuss the architecture of Flume.

Ans. Flume is a framework developed by Apache developers keeping in mind that it should be capable of solving the recursively generating data, i.e., logs, crash reports, etc. Flume is used to collect data from different sources, such as logs, directories, etc. It scales data horizontally, and multiple flume agents can be put in action to collect large volumes of data from different sources and aggregate them. Thereafter, data logs are moved to a centralized data store, i.e., Hadoop Distributed File System (HDFS).

Flume Architecture

The Flume architecture is designed in such a way that it is robust, fault-tolerant, and has tunable reliability mechanism for failover and recovery. The architecture of Apache Flume is based on the following core concepts:

- **Flume Event**—It is represented as the unit of data flowing, which has a byte payload and a set of strings with optional string headers.
- **Flume Agent**—It is a JVM process that hosts the components such as channels, sinks, and sources. It has the potential to receive, store, and forward the events from an external source to the next-hop destination.
- **Flume Flow**—It is the point of time the event is being generated, i.e., origin point to the final destination is considered to be simple flow or data flow.
- **Flume Client**—It refers to the interface where the client operates at the origin point of the event and delivers it to Flume agent.
- **Source**—A source that consumes events having a specific format and delivers it via specific mechanism. For example, when an Avro source receives events from the clients and the flume agents, it then stores these in one or more channels.
- **Channel**—It is a passive store where events are held by channel until the sink removes it for further transport.
- **Sink**—It removes the event from the channel and puts it on external repository like HDFS. The example of terminal sink is Flume HDFS sink. The example of regular sink is Flume Avro sink. In Flume Avro sink, a message is transmitted to other agents that are running Avro source.

The following figure shows the architecture of Apache Flume:

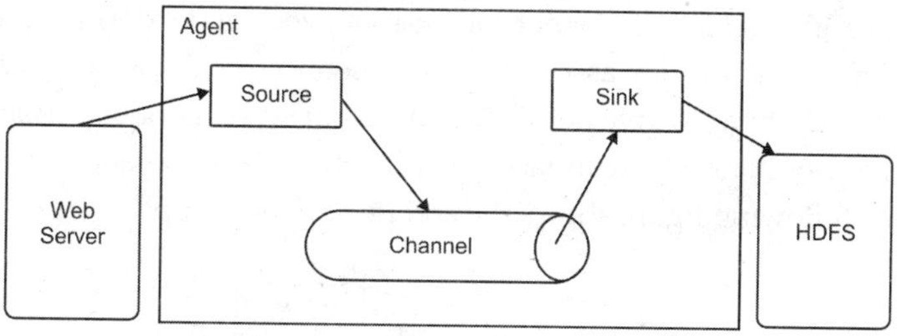

Figure: The Architecture of Apache Flume

The source of Flume uses an event, which is delivered to it by an external source. The target flume source receives the event in readable format. It then stores it on one or more channels until flume sink removes the event for further processing. During this process, source and sink run asynchronously with the events directed in the channel.

Q2. Give a brief introduction of Sqoop.

Ans. Sqoop is a tool designed to exchange information between Hadoop and relational database. As the compositional focus of Apache™ Hadoop, YARN coordinates information ingested from Apache Sqoop and different administrations that convey information into the Enterprise Hadoop group. Apache Sqoop effectively exchanges mass information between Apache Hadoop and organized data stores for example, relational databases. Sqoop assists with offloading certain jobs (for example, ETL handling) from the EDW (Enterprise Data Warehouse) to Hadoop for productive execution at a much lower expense.

Sqoop is used to extract useful information from Hadoop and export them to outside structured data stores. It performs with relational databases such as Teradata, Netezza, Oracle, MySQL, Postgres, and HSQLDB.

Q3. List the various functions of Sqoop and explain the working procedure of Sqoop.

Ans. The following functions are used to merge information between Hadoop and structured data stores:

- **Data import**—It moves certain data from EDW and external stores into Hadoop. This is done to optimize the cost-effectiveness of the combined processing and data storage.
- **Parallel data transfer**—It is used when we want faster execution of information between Hadoop and data stores.
- **Fast data copies**—It copies data faster from external systems into Hadoop system.
- **Efficient data analysis**—It enhances efficiency of data analysis by combining unstructured data with structured data in a schema-on-read data lake.
- **Load balancing**—It reduces the excessive storage and processing loads by transferring them to other systems.

Working Procedure of Sqoop

Sqoop gives a pluggable component for ideal network and external systems. The Sqoop API gives a helpful structure for assembling new connectors. These connectors can be dropped into Sqoop installations to give network to different systems. Sqoop itself comes bundled with different types of connectors utilized for prevalent database and information warehousing systems. The following figure shows the architecture of Sqoop:

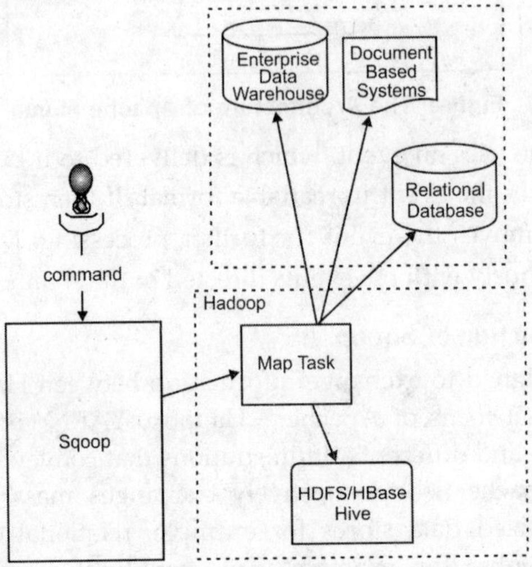

Figure: Architecture of Sqoop

Sqoop is a tool used for productive information transfers between relational databases and the Apache Hadoop biological system. One of the important advantages of Sqoop is that it is easy to handle and can work with a variety of frameworks within and outside the system. In this manner, with one tool, you can import or export information from all databases supporting the JDBC interface with the same charge line contentions uncovered by Sqoop. Moreover, Sqoop permits you to module specific additions to improve transfers for specific database systems.

Numerous clients utilize the words "connector" and "driver" conversely. However, these words mean totally distinctive things in the setting of Sqoop. In Sqoop, "driver" refers to a JDBC Driver. JDBC is a standard Java API. Java language recommends what classes and systems this interface contains, and JDK does not have any default usage. Along these lines, every database vendor is in charge of composing its own particular execution that will communicate with the corresponding database with its local convention. Thus, JDBC drivers regularly convey prohibitive licenses that restrict redistribution. Thus, every client needs to download the drivers independently and introduce them into Sqoop.

In spite of the presence of an SQL standard, each database vendor has its own criteria. The nuts and bolts more often than not work in the same way as over databases, although some edge conditions may be processed differently. Additionally, as SQL is a completely general query processing language, it may not generally be ideal for importing or exporting information out of the database server.

Connectors permit Sqoop to rise above SQL dialects while upgrading information transfer. A "connector" is a pluggable piece that gets metadata about transferred information (columns-related data sets) to move information in the most effective way. The most essential connector that ships with Sqoop is Generic JDBC Connector, and as the name suggests, it utilizes just the JDBC interface for getting to metadata and transferring information. Sqoop delivers specific connectors for MySQL, PostgreSQL, Oracle Database, Microsoft SQL Server, IBM DB2, and Netezza.

Q4. Discuss the procedure to import data into Hive.

Ans. Suppose you have a Hive metastore connected with your HDFS cluster. Sqoop can likewise import the information into Hive by producing and executing a CREATE TABLE statement to characterize the information's format in Hive.

In Hive, Sqoop will convert data from the native data types within the external data store into the corresponding types. Importing data into Hive is as simple as adding the hive-import argument and hive-table argument to your Sqoop command line. It is important to note that the target-dir argument is not necessary for Hive import.

If we need to import all information of table clients from a MYSQL database to Hive table clients with map task, the command used would be:

```
sqoop import \
--connect jdbc:mysql://the_mysql_server/the_mysql_database \
--username the_mysql_user --password the_mysql_password \
--table users \
--hive-import -hive-table users \
--as-parquetfile -m 1
```

Like HDFS import, before doing another import, Sqoop will check whether the target Hive table exists or not. If it is present, this will fail for the import statement.

Q5. Discuss the procedure to import data into HDFS.

Ans. The syntax is given as follows:

```
 sqoop import \
--connect <JDBC connection string> \
--username <username> --password <password> \
--table <tablename> \
--target-dir <hdfs-dir>
```

The statement 'connect' indicates the JDBC connect string. The username and password indicate the verification information. The statement 'table' indicates the table to read. You may utilize query, which intends to import information from a discretionary SQL inquiry. The statement 'target-dir' indicates the destination in HDFS. Optionally, you can indicate the number map tasks by including m1.

You can import information to HDFS in Parquet group. You ought to determine it by utilizing the parquet file statement. With this statement, Sqoop will compose information records from a table in binary representation as Parquet files. To compose Parquet files, a construction is obliged to present to sorts in memory.

Our process tends to choose Avro. Imported Parquet records can be used by other MapReduce tasks or tools having the tendency to access HDFS files.

If you import all data of table users from a MYSQL database to HDFS location *hdfs://jobtracker-host:jobtracker-port/import/mysql/users* with only one map task, the command will be as follows:

```
sqoop import \
--connect jdbc:mysql://the_mysql_server/the_mysql_database \
--username the_mysql_user --password the_mysql_password \
--table users \
--target-dir /import/mysql/users \
--as-parquetfile -m 1
```

When import is done effectively, Parquet files will be made at hdfs://jobtracker-host:jobtracker-port/import/mysql/users. To avoid potential name conflicts, we use UUID (Universally Unique IDentifier) as filenames. Before doing another import, Sqoop will check whether the target catalog exists or is unadulterated. Now, Sqoop will ensure that subcatalog.metadata exists or not, as this catalog contains the data that is needed for export. If the data exists, then import will fail.

17

Introduction to Mahout

We are living in an information age and have to deal with an abundance of data emanating from various sources like industries, networking websites, feedback forms, satellites, etc. In this competitive environment, the success of individuals as well as organizations depends on how quickly and efficiently they can transform huge amounts of data into processed information that could be put to some meaningful use.

In the previous chapters, we have learned about various analytical techniques used to mine and process Big Data. Technological advancements have caused a sharp increase in the sources of data generation, the amount of data generated and thus the need for tools and techniques that can sort, process, and analyze data more quickly and efficiently has never been felt greater. The machine learning environment has emerged as an answer to meet the demands of the current times.

In this chapter, you will learn about Apache Mahout, the open source library of scalable machine-learning algorithms. Next, the chapter discusses the machine learning technique and its two types: supervised and unsupervised learning. You next learn about the 3Cs of machine learning, which are collaborative filtering, clustering, and classification. The chapter also discusses some commonly used machine-learning algorithms, such as K-Means and Fuzzy K-Means. Towards the end, you will learn to install Mahout on the Linux operating system.

What is Mahout?

On hearing the word 'Mahout', the picture that most people get in their minds is that of a man riding an elephant. The Oxford Advanced Learner's Dictionary defines Mahout as "a person who works with, rides and cares for an elephant."

Apache Mahout is a library of scalable algorithms and since it runs on top of Hadoop, characterized by the mascot Elephant, it is given the name Mahout.

Mahout started as a subproject of Lucene, an API of Apache, which helps in searching and sorting out relevant data from heterogeneous data sources, such as XML files, MySQL database, Excel sheets, etc., at a very fast speed. With time, Mahout acquired functionalities of its own and emerged as an independent package of scalable and fast-executing machine-learning algorithms. Apache Mahout makes use of the MapReduce paradigm and Hadoop framework; however, it can also run algorithms in the standalone mode.

Some features of Apache Mahout are listed below:

- Mahout algorithms are written on the top of Hadoop and can easily run in Hadoop Distributed File System (HDFS) as well as on independent platforms.
- Mahout algorithms are highly scalable and compatible with the cloud network.
- Mahout provides a ready-to-use framework facilitating the developers to perform data mining on huge volumes of data.
- Mahout algorithms are very fast and efficient as compared to other Big Data analytic techniques.
- Algorithms of Mahout contain many MapReduce enabled clustering implementations such as K-Means, Fuzzy K-Means, Canopy, Dirichlet, and Mean-Shift.
- Mahout supports implementations of Distributed Naive Bayes and Complementary Naive Bayes.
- Mahout supports matrix and vector libraries.

EXHIBIT 1: More About Mahout

"Mahout" is a Hindi term for a person who rides an elephant. The elephant, in this case, is Hadoop -- and Mahout is one of the many projects that can sit on top of Hadoop, although you do not always need MapReduce to run it.

Mahout puts powerful mathematical tools in the hands of the mere mortal developers who write the Inter Webs. It's a package of implementations of the most popular and important machine-learning algorithms, with the majority of the implementations designed specifically to use Hadoop to enable scalable processing of huge data sets. Some algorithms are available only in a non-parallelizable "serial" form due to the nature of the algorithm, but all can take advantage of HDFS for convenient access to data in your Hadoop processing pipeline.

Machine learning is probably the most practical subset of Artificial Intelligence (AI), focusing on probabilistic and statistical learning techniques. For all you AI geeks, here are some of the machine-learning algorithms included with Mahout: K-Means clustering, Fuzzy K-Means clustering, K-Means, latent Dirichlet allocation, singular value decomposition, logistic regression, naive Bayes, and random forests. Mahout also features higher-level abstractions for generating "recommendations" (à la popular e-commerce sites or social networks).

Beyond recommendations

Mahout is far more than a fancy e-commerce API. In fact, other algorithms make predictions, classifications (such as the hidden Markov models that power most of the speech and language recognition on the Internet). It can even help you findclusters or, rather, group things, like cells ... of people or something so you can send them.... gift baskets to a single address.

Mahout is a great way to leverage a number of features from recommendation engines to pattern recognition to data mining.

Source: *http://www.infoworld.com/article/2608418/application-development/enjoy-machine-learning-with-mahout-on-hadoop.html*

Mahout works on the machine-learning framework that processes data on the basis of the following 3Cs:

- Collaborative filtering (also known as recommendation)
- Clustering
- Classification

However, before going into the details of the 3Cs of machine learning, let's learn about machine learning.

Machine Learning

Machine learning is a type of Artificial Intelligence (AI) that deals with the programming of computer systems. Algorithms based on the machine-learning techniques enable computer systems to learn and improve with experience. In other words, machine learning algorithms targets on the development of computer systems and programs, enabling them to analyze, grow, and adapt themselves to any changes in the volume and variety of data. The concept of machine learning is similar to that of data mining, as both search for and establish patterns of data.

Figure 17.1 shows the working of a machine learning algorithm:

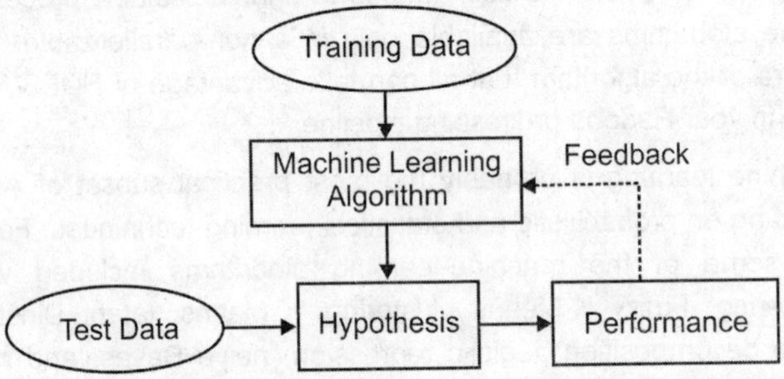

Figure 17.1: Machine Learning Algorithm

In Figure 17.1, a set of training data is sent to a machine learning algorithm for developing an Instance. After creating an instance, the algorithm values are sent to the Hypothesis ground to find whether this algorithm is good for the data or not. If the algorithm is good from the hypothesis point, then it is sent for performance. Performance is nothing but the actual state of the processing of the algorithm. Now if the performance is good, it sends a feedback signal to the machine learning algorithm that the algorithm, which is generated on the training data is performing fine or can be used with other input data and new data.

Machine-learning algorithms combine the principles of various fields such as logistics, statistics, probability theory, control theory, combinatorial optimization, search and reinforcement learning to deduce patterns from the given data and generate meaningful conclusions. Algorithms of machine learning are widely used in Big Data analytics and various filed applications. Some fields that use machine-learning algorithms in their applications are as follows:

- Vision processing
- Data mining
- Language processing
- Stock market forecasting
- Pattern recognition
- Robotics
- Games
- Advanced human artificial limbs

There are several ways to implement machine learning techniques, among which supervised learning and unsupervised learning are the most common.

Supervised Learning

A supervised learning algorithm analyzes the data gathered from various resources and generates a function that can be used for mapping new data on similar patterns. Neural networks, Support Vector Machines (SVMs), and Naive Bayes classifiers are some examples of supervised learning algorithms. The fields where supervised learning algorithms are used include:

1. Classification of tweets as private
2. Voice analysis
3. Labeling webpages based on their content

Figure 17.2 shows the mechanism of the supervised learning:

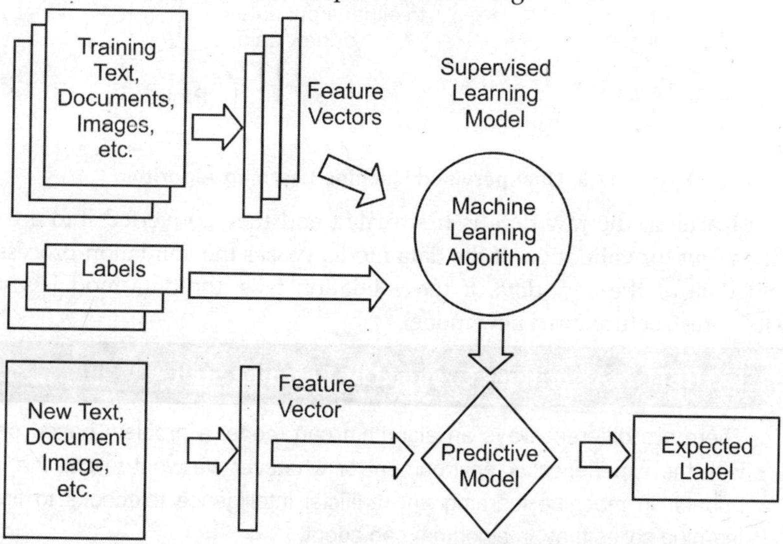

Figure 17.2: Supervised Machine Learning Algorithm

In Figure 17.2, the feature vectors are extracted from the training data or the "txt" files, and are provided to the machine learning algorithm for developing and processing the data file. Labels are generated and added to the machine learning algorithm so that they can be tracked from the huge stack of data. A predictive model is generated that already contains the result from the machine learning algorithm. Finally, the algorithm is processed in the predictive model to generate the label for the training data that was initially provided for the processing.

Unsupervised Learning

Unsupervised learning algorithm transforms the unlabeled data (data without any pre-defined datasets) into some meaningful form. This algorithm works by searching patterns and trends in raw data. It is basically used in clustering similar data into logical groups. Some examples where unsupervised learning techniques are used include K-Means hierarchical clustering algorithms.

Figure 17.3 shows the mechanism of the unsupervised learning:

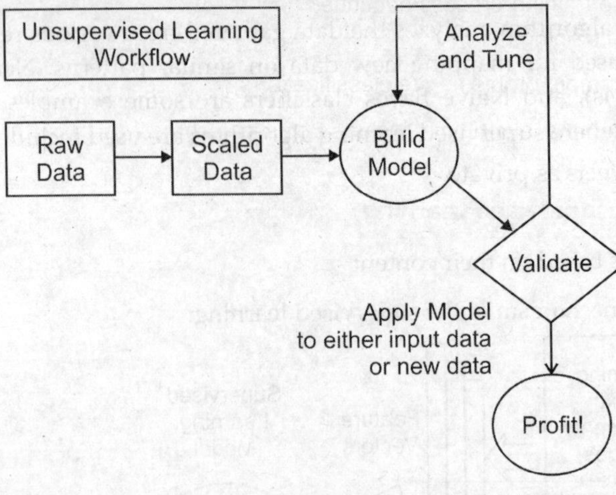

Figure 17.3: Unsupervised Machine Learning Algorithm

In unsupervised learning, the raw data is first scaled and then converted into a data model. This data model is then sent for validation. If the data model passes the validation process, it can be used for further input data or the new data. If the validation fails, the data model is sent back to the building stage to be restructured in a new model.

EXHIBIT 2: Algorithms Grouped by Learning Style

There are different ways an algorithm can model a problem based on its interaction with the experience or environment or whatever we want to call the input data. It is popular in machine learning and artificial intelligence textbooks to first consider the learning styles that an algorithm can adopt.

This taxonomy or way of organizing machine learning algorithms is useful because it forces you to think about the roles of the input data and the model preparation process and select one that is the most appropriate for your problem in order to get the best result.

Let's take a look at four different learning styles in machine learning algorithms:

Supervised Learning

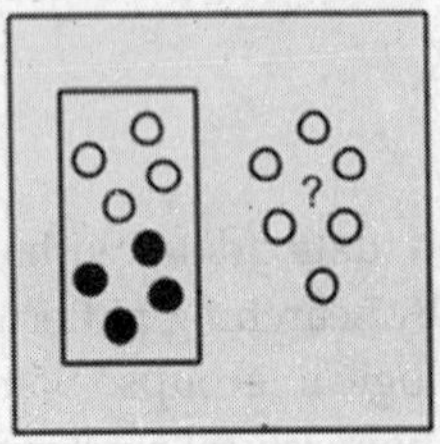

Supervised Learning Algorithms

Input data is called training data and has a known label or result such as spam/not-spam or a stock price at a time. A model is prepared through a training process where it is required to make predictions and is corrected when those predictions are wrong. The training process continues until the model achieves a desired level of accuracy on the training data.

Example problems are classification and regression.

Example algorithms include Logistic Regression and the Back Propagation Neural Network.

Unsupervised Learning

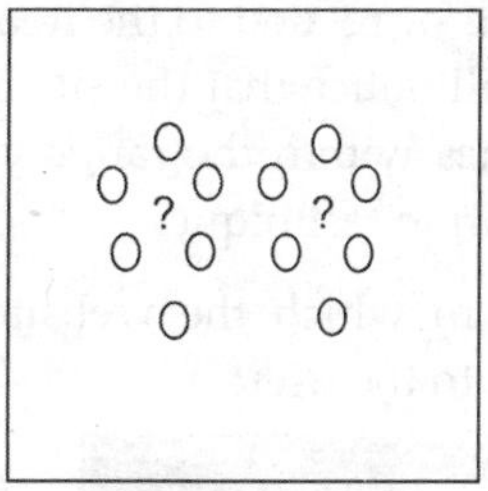

Unsupervised Learning Algorithms

Input data is not labeled and does not have a known result. A model is prepared by deducing structures present in the input data. This may be to extract general rules. It may, through a mathematical process, also be used to systematically reduce redundancy, or organize data by similarity.

Example problems are clustering, dimensionality reduction and association rule learning.

Example algorithms include the Apriori algorithm and K-Means.

Semi-Supervised Learning

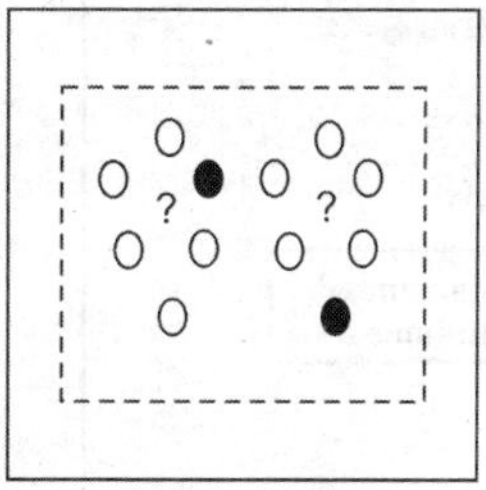

Semi-supervised Learning Algorithms

Input data is a mixture of labeled and unlabeled examples.

There is a desired prediction problem but the model must learn the structures to organize the data as well as make predictions.

Example problems are classification and regression.

Example algorithms are extensions to other flexible methods that make assumptions about how to model the unlabeled data.

Source: *http://machinelearningmastery.com/a-tour-of-machine-learning-algorithms/*

Now, let's discuss the 3Cs of machine learning in detail.

Collaborative Filtering (Recommendation)

You must have noticed that when you search for a particular item on the Internet, the side panel starts displaying other similar items suggesting that people who searched for this item also showed interest in these items. This is called collaborative filtering in which the user behavior is mined to derive certain patterns. This information is then used as a suggestion/recommendation for other users with similar likes and dislikes.

Let's take a scenario of a shopping site, say www.flipkart.com. Now, when you search for something on the website, it starts showing some items that are similar or related to the item you are searching for. For example, while surfing for mobiles phones, you will notice that the site itself starts showing you the recommended accessories or comparable cellphones within the range you selected. This is what is called the collaborative filtering or the recommendation technique.

Figure 17.4 shows an example of collaborative filtering in which the website is showing some recommendations of mobile phones and related accessories to the user:

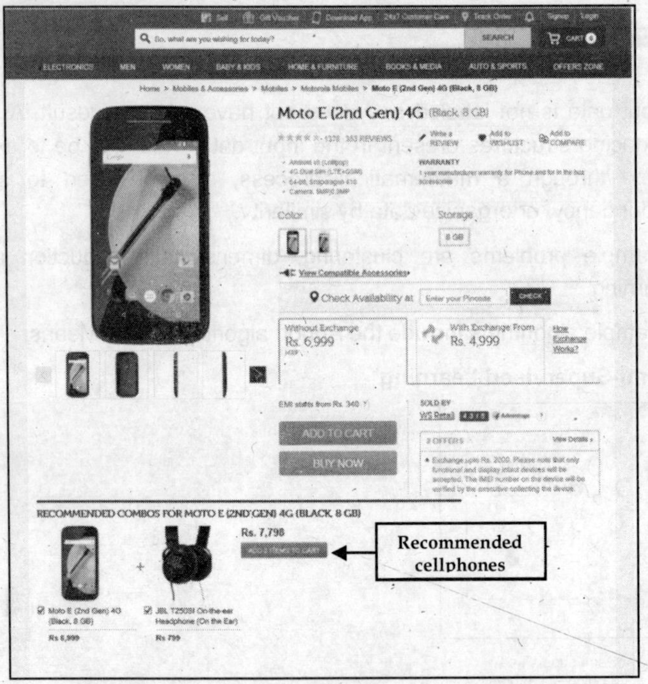

Figure 17.4: Showing Recommended Items

These recommendations are produced with the help of a recommendation engine. Some common recommendation engines supported by Mahout include:

- User-based recommendation
- Item-based recommendation

User-Based Recommendation

In a user-based recommendation, the inferences are drawn on the basis of the likes, dislikes and preferences of users. The data for this analysis is collected after studying the search patterns of a single or multiple users over a period of time. It is based on a simple concept in which to calculate the recommendations of a targeted user, the search data of all the other users having similar search patterns is analyzed. One of the most commonly used methods for doing this analysis is to calculate the correlation coefficient between the search patterns of different users.

Figure 17.5 shows an example of the working of the user-based recommendation engine:

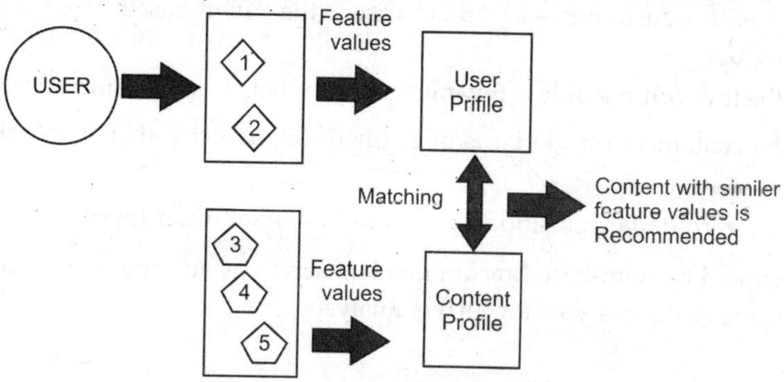

Figure 17.5: User-Based Recommendation

In a user-based recommendation, a user profile is created on the basis of the user's current search patterns. The algorithm also generates and displays the content profile of the item selected by the user. The user profile is now matched with the content profile of the selected item. If the profiles match, then the algorithm recommends all the items with the similar content profile.

In Mahout, we apply user-based recommendation on the given dataset by running the following command:

```
UserSimilarity similarity = new PearsonCorrelationSimilarity(model);
```

To decide the user that is most similar to the nearest recommender, we will use the similarity greater than 0.1, which is implemented through a ThresholdUserNeighborhood as:

```
UserNeighborhood neighborhood = new ThresholdUserNeighborhood(0.1, similarity,
model);
```

We can now create our recommender as we have all the portions of similarities. Run the following command to create a recommender:

```
UserBasedRecommender recommender = new GenericUserBasedRecommender(model,
neighborhood, similarity);
```

The recommender can now easily give recommendations for a single or multiple items.

For example, if we want to give three items for recommendations for the user withuserID 2, it will be generated in the following way:

```
List recommendations = recommender.recommend(2, 3);
for (RecommendedItem recommendation : recommendations)
{
  System.out.println(recommendation);
}
```

Item-Based Recommendation

Item-based recommendation is a flexible and easy-to-execute algorithm that can be applied in a variety of applications. The algorithm is based on the input of the customer about the items searched or purchased, generating an output that recommends similar items with a score reflecting whether a particular customer will "like" the recommended item or not. One of the advantages of item-based recommendation algorithms is that they are so flexible that they can adapt themselves to diverse working conditions and research interests.

For example, suppose we want to calculate the total number of orders received for a particular product from each customer. In this case, the item-based recommenders filter the recommendations by:

- Removing the low volume or low revenue gain products from consideration
- Clubbing the customers on the basis of segment or market rather than using customer's level data
- Removing the zero-dollar transitions, paybacks and other order types

The output generated by item-based recommenders serves as an input of downstream applications, such as ERP systems, websites, etc., for further analysis.

Clustering

Clustering algorithms act upon data and form groups of data units having similar characteristics. For example, customers are grouped together on the basis of their demographic information, gender, buying patterns, etc.

Clustering is a form of unsupervised learning that involves the following three steps:

1. **Similarity and Dissimilarity**—Whenever a new element is added in the group, the classification cluster verifies whether that element belongs to the present group or not. If the element doesn't belongs to some already existing group, then a new cluster is formed for it.
2. **Algorithm**—In this step, the element is inserted into the group to which it belongs by using the appropriate algorithm.
3. **Stopping Condition**—The stopping condition is imposed to define a point where no clustering or classification is further required. At this point, the clusters are dissolved.

The following are some common applications of clustering:

- Clustering is used in various applications that involve recognizing patterns, image processing, rendering, data analytics, etc.
- In the IT field, clustering is used to club several computer systems involved in the same project for easy sharing of documents, resources, etc.
- Clustering is used in search engines such as Google and Bing to group data with similar characteristics.
- Newsgroups also use clustering algorithms to group various articles based on related topics.

Mahout supports the following types of clustering algorithm:

- **K-Means clustering—**It is one of the simplest and most commonly used machine learning algorithm that is used for grouping objects. It is based on vector quantization in which the objects to be clustered are represented as a set of numerals. The user has to classify a given data set into a certain number of groups (referred to as k). A separate centroid, k, is defined for each cluster. In the next step, each point of the given data set is associated with its nearest centroid, that is the nearest k. The first level of clustering is completed when every point is joined to the centroid. The entire procedure is repeated again with new k points till the time a loop is generated and there is no more scope of movement for the k centroids.
- **Fuzzy K-Means (FKM)—**It is also known as Fuzzy-C-Means (FCM), and is basically an extension of the K-Means algorithm. However, unlike K-Means, FKM allows one set of data to belong to two or more clusters. In other words, in FKM, a data set can get associated with more than one centroid. Similar to K-Means, FKM does not cause any changes in the input directories and works on the objects that can be represented in n-dimensional vector space.

Classification

Classification is a machine learning technique that uses the knowledge of known data to determine new data, so that it can be arranged or classified into the existing categories of the data. In other words, classification involves identification of new datasets and categorization on the basis of certain predefined criteria.

The following are some widely-used applications of classification:

- If we download a new audio/video in our phone, then the installed audio/video player automatically classifies the new content and places it under the relevant category or creates a new playlist.
- Mail service providers also use classification algorithms to classify mails in different categories. These algorithms study user's pattern of marking and segregating mails and then decide in whether the mails should be delivered in the spam, junk or inbox folder.
- Classification algorithms are also widely used in financial and insurance organizations to analyze various risk factors related to monetary transactions or claims.

Mahout Algorithms

As already discussed, Mahout is a library of highly scalable machine-learning algorithms, some of which can run in the local mode and some in the distributed mode of Hadoop. There are some specific algorithms for every category of Mahout and each of these algorithms can be invoked through a specific command line. Table 17.1 lists some Mahout algorithms, which are compatible with HDFS, classified under three categories-collaborative filtering, clustering, and classification:

Table 17.1: HDFS Compatible Mahout Algorithms

Algorithm	Category	Description
Distributed Item-Based Collaborative Filtering	Collaborative Filtering	Estimates a user's preference for one item by looking at his/her preferences for similar items

Table 17.1: HDFS Compatible Mahout Algorithms

Algorithm	Category	Description
Collaborative Filtering Using a Parallel Matrix Factorization	Collaborative Filtering	Among a matrix of items that a user has not yet seen, predict which items the user might prefer
Canopy Clustering	Clustering	For preprocessing data before using a K-Means or Hierarchical clustering algorithm
Dirichlet Process Clustering	Clustering	Performs Bayesian mixture modeling
Fuzzy K-Means	Clustering	Discovers soft clusters where a particular point can belong to more than one cluster
Hierarchical Clustering	Clustering	Builds a hierarchy of clusters using either an *agglomerative*"bottom up" or *divisive* "top down" approach
K-Means Clustering	Clustering	Aims to partition *n* observations into *k* clusters in which each observation belongs to the cluster with the nearest mean
Latent Dirichlet Allocation	Clustering	Automatically and jointly clusters words into "topics" and documents into mixtures of topics
Mean Shift Clustering	Clustering	Finds modes or clusters in 2-dimensional space, where the number of clusters is unknown
Minhash Clustering	Clustering	Quickly estimates similarity between two data sets
Spectral Clustering	Clustering	Cluster points using eigenvectors of matrices derived from the data
Bayesian	Classification	Classifies objects into binary categories
Random Forests	Classification	Refers to an ensemble learning method for classification (and regression) that operates by constructing a multitude of decision trees

Source: *http://hortonworks.com/hadoop/mahout/*

NOTE

A complete list of Mahout algorithms can be found at http://mahout.apache.org/users/basics/ algorithms.html.

Environment for Mahout

Mahout works on top of Hadoop. It means that to run Mahout algorithms, you need to have Hadoop and Java installed on a Linux environment. In this section, you will learn to:

- Install Java on Linux
- Install Hadoop on Linux
- Install Mahout on Linux

Java Installation on Linux

Perform the following steps to install Java on a Linux-based machine:

1. Download the latest 32-bit or 64-bit compressed binary "tar.gz" file from [http://www.oracle.com/technetwork/indexes/downloads/index.html#java].
2. Uncompress the Java tar file by using the following command:

```
$ tar -xzvf jdk-8u3-linux-x64.tar.gz
```

3. Move the Java folder to the /usr/lib directory by using the following command:

```
$sudo mkdir -p /usr/lib/jvm
$sudo mv ./jdk1.8.0_03 /usr/lib/jvm/jdk1.8.0
```

4. Run the following update commands for Java:

```
$ sudo update-alternatives -install "/usr/bin/java" "java"
"/usr/lib/jvm/jdk1.8.0/bin/java" 1
$ sudo update-alternatives -install "/usr/bin/javac" "javac"
"/usr/lib/jvm/jdk1.8.0/bin/javac" 1
$ sudo update-alternatives -install "/usr/bin/javaws" "javaws"
"/usr/lib/jvm/jdk1.8.0/bin/javaws" 1
```

5. Set the ownership and permission for the executable file by using the following commands:

```
$sudo chmod a+x /usr/bin/java
$sudo chmod a+x /usr/bin/javac
$sudo chmod a+x /usr/bin/javaws
$sudo chown -R root:root /usr/lib/jvm/jdk1.8.0
```

6. Run the `$java -version` command to check the version of your new JDK 8 installation to get information about Java.
7. Now, update all the Java versions installed on your system by using the following commands:

```
$sudo update-alternatives -config java
$sudo update-alternatives -config javac
$sudo update-alternatives -config javaws
```

This is how Java is installed on a system. As you know, Java is the most important part of the Hadoop framework. In other words, without Java, Hadoop cannot work.

Hadoop Installation on Linux

For Mahout we are going to set up a Hadoop 2.x 2nd generation single node. There are a few pre-requisites for the installation of Hadoop and the services of Hadoop, which are as follows:

- Linux-based OS (can be fedora, Ubuntu, Red hat, CentOS,)
- Java installed on the system
- SSH server should be configured on the system.

The steps to install the Hadoop single node are as follows:

1. Create a folder named Hadoop in the '**opt**' directory of your Linux system. In our case, we have created /opt/hadoop-2.2.0-dist/.

   While creating the above folder, if the system shows an error like "don't have the permission for creating the folder", you can obtain the permission by executing the following command:

```
$sudo chmod -R xxx /opt/ (here xxx could be the Linux permission set like 777 for
the super user permission with {-r-w-e-re-we}).
```

2. Change the directory from/opt/ to $ cd/opt/hadoop-2.2.0-dist.
3. Download the latest 2.x version tar.gz file of Hadoop from the link, http://hadoop.apache.org/releases.html
4. Un-tar the latest Hadoop tar file to a folder named /opt/hadoop-2.2.0 by using the following command:

```
$tar -xzvf hadoop-name_of_file.tar.gz
```

5. Now, move the Hadoop setup folder to /opt/ by using the following command:

```
$mv hadoop-2.2.0/opt/
```

6. Run $cd/opt/hadoop-2.2.0 to enter in the directory where Hadoop is installed.

   Now before going further to install Hadoop on your system, you need to configure the environment variable, for which you need to open or create .bash_profile in the home folder of the user.

7. To open/create .bash_profile in the home folder of the user, run the following command:

```
$ sudo nano~/.bash_profile
```

8. Enter the following code in the .bash_profile of the home folder:

```
export HADOOP_PREFIX="/opt/hadoop-2.2.0/"
export PATH=$PATH:$HADOOP_PREFIX/sbin
export HADOOP_COMMON_HOME=${HADOOP_PREFIX}
export HADOOP_MAPRED_HOME=${HADOOP_PREFIX}
export HADOOP_HDFS_HOME=${HADOOP_PREFIX}
EXPORT YARN_HOME=${HADOOP_PREFIX}
export JAVA_HOME="/usr/lib/jvm/jdk1.8.0"
export PATH=$JAVA+HOME/bin
```

9. Save the code by pressing the Ctrl+X key combination. The system asks you whether you want to save your file. Press 'y' and then press the Enter key.
10. Run `$source ~/.bash_profile` to source .bash_profile so that the system can take the entire configuration that we entered in it.
11. To edit the configuration sites present in the Hadoop system, go to the directory /opt/hadoop-2.2.0/etc/hadoop/, and open the core-site.xml file and enter the following code:

```
<configuration>
    <property>
        <name>fs.defaultFS</name>
        <value>hdfs://localhost:8020</value>
        <final>true</final>
    </property>
    <property>
        <name>io.file.buffer.size</name>
        <value>131072</value>
    </property>
</configuration>
```

12. Now, go to the /opt/hadoop-2.2.0/etc/hadoop/ directory, open the hdfs-site.xml file, and enter the following code:

```
<configuration>
      <property>
 <name>dfs.namenode.name.dir</name>
<value>file:///opt/hadoop-2.2.0/hadoop_data/dfs/dfs.namenode.name.dir</value>
      </property>
     <property>
   <name>dfs.blocksize</name>
  <value>268435456</value>
    </property>
       <property>
   <name>dfs.namenode.handler.count</name>
   <value>100</value>
       </property>
         <property>
    <name>dfs.datanode.data.dir</name>
<value>file:///opt/hadoop-2.2.0/hadoop_data/dfs/dfs.datanode.data.dir</value>
         </property>
</configuration>
```

13. Go to the /opt/hadoop-2.2.0/etc/hadoop/ directory, open the mapred-site.xml file, and enter the following code:

```
<configuration>
     <property>
          <name>mapreduce.framework.name</name>
         <value>yarn</value>
    </property>
</configuration>
```

14. Switch to the /opt/hadoop-2.2.0/etc/hadoop/ directory, open the Yarn-site.xml file, and enter the following code:

```
<configuration>
        <property>
                <name>yarn.resourcemanager.address</name>
                <value>localhost:8032</value>
        </property>
        <property>
              <name>yarn.resourcemanager.scheduler.address</name>
              <value>localhost:8030</value>
       </property>
       <property>
     <name>yarn.resourcemanager.resource-tracker.address</name>
            <value>localhost:8031</value>
        </property>
       <property>
            <name>yarn.resourcemanager.admin.address</name>
            <value>localhost:8033</value>
       </property>
     <property>
              <name>yarn.resourcemanager.webapp.address</name>
             <value>localhost:8088</value>
    </property>
      <property>
          <name>yarn.resourcemanager.scheduler.class</name>
     <value>org.apache.hadoop.yarn.server.resourcemanager.scheduler.capacity.Capacit
yScheduler</value>
       </property>
</configuration>
```

15. Now, go to the /opt/hadoop-2.2.0/etc/hadoop directory to open or create the hadoop-env.sh file. Enter/change the java path, which is already given there to the Java path of our installation directory by using the following command:

```
export JAVA_HOME=/usr/lib/jvm/jdk1.8.0
```

16. Run `$echo $JAVA_HOME` to check your Java installation path.
17. Format the namenode by running the following command from the Hadoop folder:

```
$ hdfs namenode-format
```

Hadoop 2.2.0 is now successfully installed on your system. You can check it by running the following services:

Service	Command
Namenode	hadoop-daemon.sh start namenode
Datanode	hadoop-daemon.sh start datanode
Resourcemanager	yarn-daemon.sh start resourcemanager
Nodemanager	yarn-daemon.sh start nodemanager
Job History Server	mr-jobhistory-daemon.sh start historyserver

You can also see the Hadoop system logs by accessing the /opt/hadoop-2.2.0/logs folder.

Mahout Installation on Linux

Mahout is an open source Hadoop-based framework, which is also freely available on the Apache website. Mahout algorithms run on the maven platform; therefore, prior to installing Mahout, you need to install maven.

Perform the following steps to install maven and then Mahout on your system:

1. Install maven from the synaptic package manager or by running the following code:

```
$sudo apt-get install maven2
```

You can also install maven 3.0.04 manually by extracting the distribution archive of maven by using the following command:

$ tar –xzvf apache-maven-3.0.04 and uncompressing it in the /opt/ directory.

The maven-3.0.04 folder gets created in the /opt/ directory.

2. Set the home path for maven in .bash_profile by running the $sudo nano ~/.bash_profile command and enter the following code:

```
export M2_HOME=/opt/apache-maven-3.0.04
export M2=$M2_HOME/bin
export path=$M2:$PATH
export JAVA_HOME="/usr/lib/jvm/jdk1.8.0"
export PATH=$JAVA+HOME/bin
```

3. Run mvn –version to check whether you have correctly installed maven or not. Now, we are done with the maven installation and can proceed to Mahout.
4. Download the latest version of Mahout from http://apache.mirrors.lucidnetworks.net/mahout/.
5. Run $tar –xzvf mahout-distribution-0.9.tar.gz to decompress the Mahout installation file.

6. Run $mv mahout-distribution-0.9 /opt/ to move the Mahout files to the /opt/ directory to avoid any confusion during the home setting.
7. Check for the pom-site.xml file in your Mahout folder, i.e. /opt/mahout/. The presence of this file confirms that Mahout has been successfully installed.
8. Run the $mahout command to start working with Mahout.

Summary

This chapter introduced you to the basics of Mahout, the library of scalable machine-learning algorithms, and its features. Next, it explained the concept of machine learning and its two types: supervised and unsupervised learning. You also learned about the 3Cs of machine learning, which are collaborative filtering, clustering, and classification. The chapter also discussed some commonly used machine-learning algorithms, such as K-Means and Fuzzy K-Means. Finally, you learned to install Mahout on the Linux operating system.

Quick Revise

Multiple-Choice Questions

Q1. Mahout is a framework for________.

a. Data analysis
b. Data distribution
c. Data presentation
d. Data mining

Ans. The correct option is d.

Q2. Which of the following techniques suggests items on an e-commerce website?

a. Clustering
b. Recommendation
c. Classification
d. Machine learning

Ans. The correct option is b.

Q3. Which of the following is not a Mahout concept?

a. Data Mining
b. Recommendation
c. Bar-graph representation
d. Classification

Ans. The correct option is c.

Q4. Which of the following is a part of the supervised learning concept?

a. Classification of mails
b. Recommendation
c. Bar-graph representation
d. K-Means

Ans. The correct option is a.

Q5. Which of the following is a part of the unsupervised learning concept?

a. Data Mining
b. Recommendation
c. Bar-graph representation
d. K-Means

Ans. The correct option is d.

Subjective Questions

Q1. What is Mahout?

Ans. Apache Mahout is a library of scalable algorithms and since it runs on top of Hadoop, characterized by the mascot Elephant, it is given the name Mahout.

Mahout started as a subproject of Lucene, an API of Apache, which helps in searching and sorting out relevant data from heterogeneous data sources, such as XML files, MySQL database, Excel sheets, etc., at a very fast speed. With time, Mahout acquired functionalities of its own and emerged as an independent package of scalable and fast-executing machine-learning algorithms. Apache Mahout makes use of the MapReduce paradigm and Hadoop framework; however, it can also run algorithms in the standalone mode.

Q2. List some features of Apache Mahout.

Ans. Some features of Apache Mahout are listed below:

- Mahout algorithms are written on the top of Hadoop and can easily run in Hadoop Distributed File System (HDFS) as well as on independent platforms.
- Mahout algorithms are highly scalable and compatible with the cloud network.
- Mahout provides a ready-to-use framework facilitating the developers to perform data mining on huge volumes of data.
- Mahout algorithms are very fast and efficient as compared to other Big Data analytic techniques.
- Algorithms of Mahout contain many MapReduce enabled clustering implementations such as K-Means, Fuzzy K-Means, Canopy, Dirichlet, and Mean-Shift.
- Mahout supports implementations of Distributed Naive Bayes and Complementary Naive Bayes.
- Mahout supports matrix and vector libraries.

Q3. What do you understand by machine learning? Explain its types in brief.

Ans. Machine learning is a type of artificial intelligence (AI) which deals with the programming of computer systems. Algorithms based on the machine-learning techniques enable computer systems to learn and improve with experience. In other words, machine learning algorithms targets on the development of computer systems and programs, enabling them to analyze, grow, and adapt themselves to any changes in the volume and variety of data. The concept of machine learning is similar to that of data mining, as both search for and establish patterns of data.

Machine learning is of the following two types:

- **Supervised learning**—The supervised learning algorithm analyzes the data gathered from various resources and generates a function that can be used for mapping new data on similar patterns. Neural networks, Support Vector Machines (SVMs), and Naive Bayes classifiers are some examples of supervised learning algorithms.

- **Unsupervised learning**—The unsupervised learning algorithm transforms the unlabeled data (data without any pre-defined datasets) into some meaningful form. This algorithm works by searching patterns and trends in raw data. It is basically used in clustering similar data into logical groups. Some examples where unsupervised learning techniques are used include K-Means hierarchical clustering algorithms.

Q4. Explain the following terms:

a. User-based recommendation

b. Item-based recommendation

Ans.

a. In user-based recommendation, the inferences are drawn on the basis of the likes, dislikes and preferences of users. The data for this analysis is collected after studying the search patterns of a single or multiple users over a period of time. It is based on a simple concept in which to calculate the recommendations of a targeted user, the search data of all the other users having similar search patterns is analyzed. One of the most commonly used methods for doing this analysis is to calculate the correlation coefficient between the search patterns of different users.

b. Item-based recommendation is a flexible and easy-to-execute algorithm that can be applied in a variety of applications. The algorithm is based on the input of the customer about the items searched or purchased, generating an output which recommends similar items with a score reflecting whether a particular customer will "like" the recommended item or not. One of the advantages of item-based recommendation algorithms is that they are so flexible that they can adapt themselves to diverse working conditions and research interests.

Q5. Mention some applications of the clustering technique.

Ans. The following are some common applications of clustering:

- Clustering is used in various applications that involve recognizing patterns, image processing, rendering, data analytics, etc.
- In the IT field, clustering is used to club several computer systems involved in the same project for easy sharing of documents, resources, etc.
- Clustering is used in search engines such as Google and Bing to group data with similar characteristics.
- Newsgroups also use clustering algorithms to group various articles based on related topics.

Q6. What is classification? List its common applications.

Ans. Classification is a machine learning technique that uses the knowledge of known data to determine new data, so that it can be arranged or classified into the existing categories of the data. In other words, classification involves identification of new datasets and categorization on the basis of certain predefined criteria.

The following are some widely-used applications of classification:

- If we download a new audio/video in our phone, then the installed audio/video player automatically classifies the new content and places it under the relevant category or creates a new playlist.
- Mail service providers also use classification algorithms to classify mails in different categories. These algorithms study user's pattern of marking and segregating mails and then decide in whether the mails should be delivered in the spam, junk or the inbox folder.
- Classification algorithms are also widely used in financial and insurance organizations to analyze various risk factors related to the monetary transactions or claims.

Q7. Considering that Java and Hadoop are already installed on your Linux system, write the steps you need to perform to install Mahout on your system.

Ans. Mahout algorithms run on the maven platform; therefore prior to installing Mahout, you need to install maven. Perform the following steps to install maven and then Mahout on your system:

1. Install maven from the synaptic package manager or by running the following code:

```
$sudo apt-get install maven2
```

   You can also install maven 3.0.04 manually by extracting the distribution archive of maven by using the following command:

```
$ tar -xzvf apache-maven-3.0.04 and uncompressing it in the /opt/ directory.
```

   The maven-3.0.04 folder gets created in the /opt/ directory.

2. Set the home path for maven in .bash_profile by running the $sudo nano ~/.bash_profile command and enter the following code:

```
export M2_HOME=/opt/apache-maven-3.0.04
export M2=$M2_HOME/bin
export path=$M2:$PATH
export JAVA_HOME="/usr/lib/jvm/jdk1.8.0"
export PATH=$JAVA+HOME/bin
```

3. Run mvn –version to check whether you have correctly installed maven or not. Now we are done with the maven installation now we can proceed to Mahout.
4. Download the latest version of Mahout from http://apache.mirrors.lucidnetworks.net/mahout/.
5. Run $tar -xzvf mahout-distribution-0.9.tar.gz to decompress the Mahout installation file.
6. Run $mv mahout-distribution-0.9 /opt/ to move the Mahout files to the /opt/ directory to avoid any confusion during the home setting.
7. Check for the pom-site.xml file in your Mahout folder, i.e. /opt/mahout/. The presence of this file confirms that Mahout has been successfully installed.
8. Run the $mahout command to start working with Mahout.

18

Understanding Analytics and Big Data

Data without any analysis or interpretation is useless. At the same time, there is no "easy" button to generate a great analysis in one simple step. Analyzing statistics, writing a report, and using a modeling algorithm are each only one step of several required to obtain a great analysis. Not understanding the aim of the analysis and focusing only on these individual tasks without keeping the end goal or problem to be solved in mind can lead to wrong decisions and generate a lot of extra work. Therefore, instead of working on individual tasks, the data should be analyzed thoroughly by keeping the goal or objective in mind.

Big Data analytics refers to the process of collecting, organizing, and analyzing large sets of data to identify patterns and other important information. An analysis of Big Data helps organizations to take strategic decisions based on the information extracted from Big Data. For example, sales data can be analyzed to decide whether or not a product should be sold in a particular month based on the product's sales trend in that month. Generally, organizations require the information that comes after analyzing the data. As you know, data is available in structured and unstructured formats. So it becomes a challenge for organizations to perform data analysis. The data of different formats is collected, combined, and then analyzed. The focus of the chapter would be to help you understand what characterizes analysis and why it is required.

This chapter will also discuss a variety of concepts related to creating a great analysis. The principles discussed in this chapter are applied broadly and are not specific to Big Data analytics. Organizations will not be able to tame the Big Data tide simply by reports alone or by using existing analytics tools; for effective analysis, study and implementation of advanced analytics are also required.

In this chapter, we compare reporting and analysis, different types of analytics, and different points to be considered for analysis. We also learn to build an analytic team and understand the concept of text analytics. Toward the end of the chapter, we learn to design new analytical approaches to support Big Data.

Comparing Reporting and Analysis

A very common mistake organizations make is to relate reporting with analysis. An organization often requires both reporting and analysis to explore new business insights from Big Data. For this, it is essential to know the difference between a report and an analysis.

Reporting is a process in which data is organized and summarized in an easy-to-understand format. Reports enable organizations to monitor various performance parameters and improve customer satisfaction.

Analysis is a process in which data and reports are examined to get insights from them. These insights help an organization to perform important tasks in a timely manner, such as planning a new strategy, taking important business decisions, introducing a new product, and improving customer satisfaction.

In simple words, reporting can be considered as a process in which raw data is transformed into useful information and analysis as a process that transforms information into insights.

Reporting is used as a tool to monitor the day-to-day business operations of an organization. A good report enables an organization to ask the most relevant questions related to the business and customers. Analysis, on the other hand, enables organizations to answer these questions based on summarized data at a deeper level and thereby find ways to implement the insights. However, there exists one major difference between them. Reports enable an organization to understand what is happening but analysis helps an organization understand why it is happening and what action can be taken for it.

An analysis can result in reports, and reports can result in analysis. It is also possible to have an analysis that is completely based on reports. Reports are essential for the growth of a business and add value to it.

Let's understand reporting in detail.

Reporting

A reporting environment is also known as a Business Intelligence (BI) environment. Such an environment enables users to select and view reports, run them, and view the results. Reports might contain various visual elements to aid understandability, including graphs, charts, and tables. The key factors that define a report are as follows:

- They provide the data that the user has been asking for.
- They provide the data in a predefined format for easy understandability.
- They show the stakeholders what had happened in the past.
- They allow the data analyst to define several pieces of data with a few indices.

As a result, reports are quite inflexible. Different prompts and filters can be used to create complex report templates. The user usually fills information in the prompts and filters that are already in place.

Reports can be misused. When lots of reports are available, they can be mistakenly used for in-depth analysis. Usually, people in charge of the BI environment would often boast of having a world-class BI environment with 500 reports covering all the aspects of the business. However, the number of reports doesn't necessarily translate into in-depth analysis.

Let's illustrate this point. A stakeholder will not be satisfied by the reports used by an organization if they fail to provide the required business insights. This is quite possible because the information required may be scattered in many reports. When there are 500 reports to look into, it can get a little difficult to extract the required information. Further, every stakeholder might look at the reports in a different way and come up with a different analysis. In simple words, even 500 reports may prove to be inadequate in fulfilling all the business needs of a person. Even the perfect blend of all the reports may not provide the relevant analysis for the stakeholder.

In such a scenario, it is always better to generate a few reports that provide the required information for consumers rather than create 500 reports that fail to fulfill anyone's needs. It is worth repeating the fact that it is not the number of reports that matters, but their relevance.

A report need not be analyzed further if it provides the required information. For example, suppose an organization has a report of sales by product by week, and a manager needs to know whether the products have achieved the sales target last week. The manager gets the required information by running the report and no further analysis is required to get the answer. This example shows one way in which reports add value to business. They can be used to get answers of common questions quickly and easily. If the reports fail to provide all the answers, then it is time to do further analysis of the reports. Prior to performing an analysis, you must first ask yourself what problem you are trying to solve.

Let's now understand what analysis means.

Analysis

An analysis refers to a process that involves a person trying to solve a problem, finding the data required to obtain the required answer, analyzing the data, and interpreting the results to suggest a recommended course of action.

The following are the important points that define an analysis:

- It provides answers to the questions being raised.
- It provides the steps required to get answers to the questions.
- The analysis is specific to the questions being addressed.
- Analysis requires a person who guides the process.

Let's take an example to understand the process of analysis. Suppose the sales of product X of an organization called OFR Corporation has fallen drastically in the last quarter. The sales manager needs to know the reasons for the fall in sales figure of product X. For this, the manager must analyze the sales data for product X over the last quarter. Further, the manager must analyze the feedback of customers gathered from different social media platforms, such as the Internet, e-mails, and so on.

Before performing the analysis, the manager must ensure that the data he/she collects is structured in a predefined format. After analyzing the data on the basis of an existing model, the manager would come to know about the factors that have affected the sales of product X in the market. The result of the analysis would help the manager understand the areas that need attention.

On the basis of the results obtained by the manager, he/she can devise a plan to improve the sales of the product. Further, effective marketing plans can be created to improve the popularity of the product in the market.

Table 18.1 lists the main differences between reporting and analysis:

Table 18.1: Comparing Reporting with Analysis

Reporting	Analysis
Provides data	Provides answers to questions
Provides what is asked for satisfying stakeholders	Provides what is needed to take strategic decisions
Is typically standardized in format	Is typically customized in the form of text or reports
Does not involve a person as it is generated automatically	Involves a person leading the process
Is fairly inflexible as a rigid format is used	Is extremely flexible as it can be defined in any format

Interaction between reporting and analysis is common and each makes the other more effective. For instance, assume a sales manager has a sales summary report that displays monthly sales by region. He/she views this sales report every day to ensure that the business is on the right track. One day, he/she discovers that there is a drop in the sales figure of the western region between the 10th and 20th of every month. He/she notifies the analytics team about it and asks them to investigate the matter. The result was an analysis.

The data analyst investigates the problem and identifies some of the causes. For example, he/she identifies that most of the community activities in the western region occur between the 1st and 10th of the month when expenditure is high. After the community activities are over, the expenditure is checked again and is found to be low. As proof, the data analyst shows the reports of expenditures made before and after 10th to the sales manager for analysis. The manager finds the reports quite informative and useful. The analysis was conducted to identify the cause of a specific issue but the manager now wants the data to be analyzed on a daily basis to ensure that things are on track. The analysis done by the data analyst forms a new standard report.

In the case of Big Data, an organization can do a great analysis by simply piecing together existing information in different ways for a new purpose. This helps the organization to look at its business from a different perspective, one from which it has never done before. The job of the data analyst is to ensure that the data is ready for analysis.

It is also important to note that the value of analysis is in finding new ways of exploring and discovering hidden business insights rather than just analyzing data for the sake of it. Specially in the case of Big Data, a proper infrastructure should be in place to carry out the analysis and it should be meaningful and relevant. Suppose some anomalies in sales are recorded at a retail chain. One solution will be to build a complex predictive model to identify the drivers that have contributed in creating those anomalies. However, the correct way to deal with this sort of problem would be to determine whether there were any supply-chain issues. Possibly, there must have been a delay in shipment or inclement weather must have kept customers home. If the cause can be easily identified, then there is no requirement to create a model.

The process of analysis should not make a simple problem more difficult. Sometimes, all that it takes is a simple analysis that might solve the problem and provide all the answers. Looking at data differently can also help in deriving deep, new insights. There is no point investing time and effort into complex analytics when there is no requirement to do so.

In Big Data, analytics is viewed from two perspectives:

- **Decision-oriented analysis**—This approach is also called the traditional business intelligence approach. Here, analysts try to use the results of the analysis in the process of making business decisions.
- **Action-oriented analysis**—This approach is used when a rapid response or an action is expected to a critical situation. In this type of analysis, a particular pattern emerges or specific types of data are detected and an appropriate action is required to be taken. For example, if sales data is analyzed, you may find negative or missing values that need to be taken care of by taking the appropriate action.

Let's now understand the analytic process.

The Analytic Process

An analysis process contains all or some of the following phases:

1. **Business understanding**—The first phase involves identifying and understanding the business objectives. It deals with the problems to be solved and decisions to be made. The main goal is to enhance business profitability. Once the business objectives are determined, the analysts evaluate the situation, and identify the data mining goals. According to the defined goals, a project plan is created between the analytics team and the IT or development team.
2. **Data collection**—The process of collecting data is an important task in executing a project plan accurately. In this phase, data from different data sources is collected first and then described in terms of its application and need of the project. This process is also called data exploration. Exploration of data is required to ensure the quality of the collected data.
3. **Data preparation**—From the data thus collected, unnecessary or unwanted data is to be removed in this phase. In other words, the data must be prepared for the purpose of analysis.
4. **Data modeling**—In this phase, a model is created by using a data modeling technique. The data model is used to analyze the relationships between different selected objects in the data. Test cases are created to assess the applicability of model and data is structured according to the model.
5. **Data evaluation**—The results obtained from different test cases are evaluated and reviewed for errors. After validating the results, analysis reports are created for determining the next plan of action.
6. **Deployment**—In this phase, the plan is finalized for deployment. The deployed plan is constantly checked for errors and maintenance. This process is also termed as reviewing of the project.

The various phases of analysis are explained in Figure 18.1:

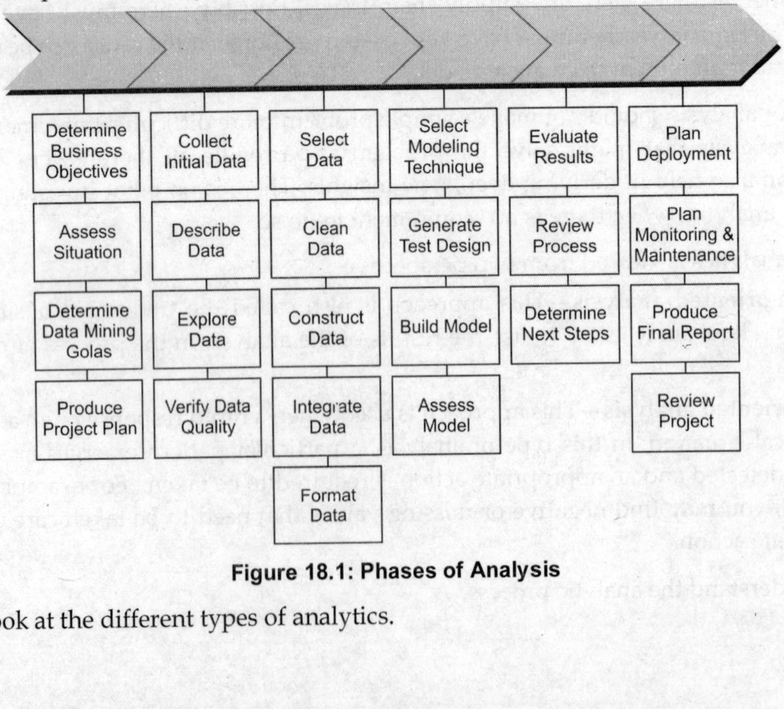

Figure 18.1: Phases of Analysis

Let's now look at the different types of analytics.

Types of Analytics

When you decide to dive into Big Data analysis, you must first identify the problem that you are trying to solve. To solve that problem, you might have a lot of data from which valuable insights can be derived. Further, important patterns may emerge out of that data.

You must know what you are interested in. For example, are you interested in analyzing customer behavior patterns? Or do you want to analyze your system log data to predict when problems are likely to occur? In order to solve these problems, four types of Big Data analytics are used. These are as follows:

- **Prescriptive**—It finds the best course of action for a given situation. According to Gartner, 13% of the organizations use predictive analysis, whereas only 3% of the organizations use prescriptive analytics. In order to understand the use of the prescriptive analytics, consider the example of health care industry where you can measure the count of patients who are obese. This type of analytics can be also done in other industries.
- **Predictive**—In this type of analytics, the future is predicted on the basis of past patterns. For sales' lead scoring, predictive analytics is used.
- **Diagnostic**—This analytics determines what has happened in the past and why. It can be used to assess the number of posts, likes and reviews in a social media marketing campaign.
- **Descriptive**—It helps in determining what is happening at the present time. It is useful to classify customers on the basis of their brand preference or sales cycle.

When analyzing data, you can also categorize Big Data analytics as follows:

- Basic analytics
- Advanced analytics
- Operational analytics
- Monetized analytics

SCENARIO

Horizon Wave Media Ltd. is a music company with an online store that sells music CDs and movies. Lately, the company has seen a sharp drop in the sales of music CDs. It tries many ways to boost sales through attractive discounts and advertising, but to no avail. The company finally decides to approach Argon Technology Ltd. with the problem. Argon Technology Ltd. appoints the data analyst Mark to analyze the problem.

Let's learn about the different types of analytics one by one, starting with basic analytics.

Basic Analytics

Basic analytics is used to explore the data whose value is not known. In other words, the data may or may not prove to be useful. Basic analytics usually involves visualizations of simple statistics. This type of analytics is used specially when a lot of disparate data needs to be analyzed. The process of basic analytics includes investigating what happened, when it happened, and its impact.

Let us consider an example to understand this better. Suppose a product manager in an organization needs to know about the sales promotion of certain products, which was performed last month. He/she also wants to know how many new customers have been associated with the organization due to the sales promotion. In this case, to know "what" happened, core analysis would help in understanding how many customers bought and used the products. To know the "impact" of this, core analysis would help in understanding how much money the new customers brought in, and this impacted when compared to the baseline.

NOTE

The data obtained from core analysis is provided by using standardized reports. The analysis involves the process of analyzing those reports, making conclusions, and suggesting a plan of action. Here, the analysis involves examining numerical data and ascertaining if the set objectives were fulfilled or not. Finally, the product manager can ascertain whether the promotion was a success or not.

Some examples of basic analysis are as follows:

- **Slicing and dicing**—It refers to the division of data into smaller groups that are easy to explore. For example, sales data can be divided or categorized on the basis of regions for better analysis.
- **Basic monitoring**—It is to the monitoring of huge volumes of data in real time. For instance, when your new ad campaign is launched, you might be interested in monitoring data related to every single minute.
- **Anomaly identification**—It refers to the identification of anomalies, for example, identification of an event that shows a difference between the actual observation and what you expected in your data. This may be due to some anomaly in the operations of an organization.

Advanced Analytics

Advanced analytics is not just confined to answering questions such as what happened, when it happened, and its impact. It goes one step beyond by finding the cause for what has happened and the measures that can be taken to avoid it from happening again in the future. Advanced analytics performs complex analysis of both structured and unstructured data by using algorithms. It also uses advanced data mining techniques such as neural networks, statistical models, machine learning, text analytics, and many more. Additionally, it uses several activities such as complex adhoc SQL, forecasting, optimization, predictive modeling, data mining, and so on. To determine different patterns in data, complex event processing, forecasting, and advanced analytics are used.

The following are some examples of advanced analytics:

- **Predictive modeling**—It refers to a data-mining solution that provides algorithms and techniques to use on structured and unstructured data to ascertain future outcomes. For instance, a telecommunications company can identify the customers who are about to drop its service by using a predictive model.
- **Text analytics**—It is to the process of examining unstructured text, extracting important information out of it, and transforming the information into structured information that can be leveraged in different ways.
- **Other statistical and data mining algorithms**—These algorithms use techniques such as advanced forecasting, optimization, cluster analysis for segmentation, and affinity analysis.

Consider a company that monitors the Web activities of its customers. It carries out an analysis to ascertain whether viewing a product online increases the probability of that product being purchased. It might be a daunting task to analyze the complete Web data and integrate it with other customer data. This is because Web data is constantly being generated and added to existing data.

As a starting point, correlation analysis can be performed. To analyze data for the first time, an expensive and elaborative model and process are not required. However, if a strong correlation exists between browsing data and sales data, then the company can market its products easily to users who browsed the website but did not make any purchases. May be later on, the analysts might think of quantifying the relationship more precisely and might make use of advanced analytic models.

Many statisticians and mathematicians have used techniques such as advanced analytics for several years but it was never a part of the analytics landscape. Let's take an example of companies that took the help of statisticians 20 years back to identify customers who might unsubscribe their services in the future. These statisticians predicted customer behavior on the basis of machine learning algorithms or advance survival analysis. Most employees in the company found it difficult to understand their meaning and how prediction can be used for benefit. Further, it was difficult to achieve the computational power and analyze changing data.

In today's world, advanced analytics has become more conventional. With the ever-increasing advancements in computational power, new developments in algorithms, enhanced data infrastructure, and the requirement for better insights from huge volumes of data, companies are now using advanced analytics as a part of their business-making process.

SCENARIO

Let's now go back to our scenario. Mark analyzes the data of Horizon Wave Media Ltd., and with the help of predictive modeling, finds that the offers and plans the company provides to the customer are too costly and that their competitors are providing CDs at much cheaper rates. Mark suggests the management to change the existing offers and plans.

Operationalized Analytics

Operational analytics means making analytics an important part of the business process. For instance, an insurance company can use a model to predict the probability of a claim being fraudulent. This model can be used by the company to form an important part of its claims-processing system to flag claims having a high probability of fraud. The fraudulent claims are then sent to a separate unit for investigation, which reviews the claims further. In some cases, the model will work for the end users from behind the scenes. For instance, in a company a model may be used to predict customers who can be good targets for selling products when they make calls. While an agent of the company is taking a call of a customer, he/she might receive a message about additional products to sell to the customer. In such cases, the agent might not be aware that a predictive model is working behind the scenes to make product recommendations.

Monetized Analytics

Monetized analytics helps businesses to take important and better decisions and earn revenues. However, Big Data analytics is also used to derive revenue beyond the insights it provides. You might be able to get a unique data set that is valuable for other companies. For example, credit card providers can use this data to offer value-added products. Similarly, telecommunications companies like financial institutions have started selling location-based insights to retailers.

Data of different types such as text-messaging data, location data, billing data and Web data are used to find inferences about customer behavior patterns. These patterns will help the retailers in finding useful information.

Characteristics of Big Data Analysis

There are few additional characteristics of Big Data analysis besides the three Vs—volume, velocity, and variety—that make it different from traditional analysis.

The following are the additional characteristics of Big Data analysis:

- **It can be programmatic**—Big Data analysts must use code to handle raw data. Analysts can use the code to manipulate or explore the data. This is specially useful when you have large volumes of data.
- **It can be data-driven**—A hypothesis-driven approach is used by several analysts to develop a premise and gather data to see if the premise is correct or not. However, Big Data uses a large volume of data to drive the analysis.
- **It can use a lot of attributes**—Analysts in the past used hundreds of attributes of the data set for analysis, and today Big Data uses thousands of attributes and millions of observations to conduct analysis.
- **It can be iterative**—Big Data analysts use iterations on models that provide more computational power. These models allow the analysts to do iterations to the required level of analysis. Because of this, new applications are designed and developed to analyze requirements and time frames to complete the analysis.

Points to Consider during Analysis

Every analysis performed should be taken seriously. One common trap to avoid is what is commonly called "cherry-picking". In this type of analysis, importance is given to only those findings that support your intuitions and ignoring the rest.

Most experienced business executives are good at making the right choices and decisions by using their experience, intuition, and common sense. They often request for an analysis to check whether the data is backed by an action being considered. When the analysis supports the action, only then is the decision said to be backed by the data.

The problem arises when the analysis shows that the executive's plan is not good enough to be considered. In such cases, if the organization and the executive believe in the analytics results, then the plan needs to be reconsidered.

The main objective should not be just to use analytics blindly when the results serve your purpose. If you plan to use analytics, then you should use it across the board consistently.

Frame the Problem Correctly

It is important to ask the right question to solve a problem, gather the right data, design the right analysis to solve the problem, and have a great analysis.

Framing the problem entails asking the right questions and laying critical assumptions. For instance, is the objective of a new initiative to drive more profit or more revenue? The choice will provide a big difference in the analysis and plan of action. Is the data required available or do we need to collect it? Do we have enough alternatives to design an analysis that would solve the problem? Without framing these questions, the rest of the work will be useless.

A great analysis begins with framing the right problem. This involves determining the data correctly, developing a solid plan for analysis, and taking into consideration the different technical and practical considerations in play.

Statistical Significance or Business Importance?

Analytic professionals concentrate more on the statistical significance of data. However, it just plays a part in delivering a great analysis. Statistical significance testing takes into consideration some assumptions and identifies the likelihood that the results that are ultimately generated would appear only if the assumptions are correct.

For instance, we would consider a coin to be fair in the sense that it will land heads and tails with equal probability, that is, the chances of each is 50 percent. Now, if the coin is fair, the chances of the odds of landing 10 tails in a row are quite small. If the coin throws up 10 tails in a row, then there are two explanations: First, that we have witnessed an occurrence that happens only once in 1,024 attempts. Second, that the coin is not fair. A significance test related to getting tails in a row would confirm that you can be 99.9 percent sure of the coin not being fair. This is because a fair coin will only yield a result 0.1 percent of the time. Such type of computation is referred to as statistical significance.

It becomes necessary to distinguish between statistical significance and business importance. The fact is that they are different. Let's know the difference in the following sections.

Statistical Significance

Statistical significance is usually used to calculate averages, percentages, and parameter estimates arising out of statistical models. Statistical significance testing is valuable to ensure that your data does not provide irrelevant information. By taking this mathematical perspective, you will come to know whether a difference is large enough to be considered significant. Sometimes a small difference can be very significant and sometimes a big difference does not seem to be significant enough.

A statistical test is performed to ensure that the right inferences are derived from the data. A different discipline has been developed for testing the data. In the business world, this discipline is called test and learn. In the test-and-learn environment, an experiment is performed to measure the effects of options and identify which options will work best.

On the other hand, businesses must ensure that they follow the correct and approved approach and do not just consider the obvious answer.

Let us take an example of two graduate school baseball players who played together for five seasons. Joe has a higher average score than Tom in each single of those five seasons. Now the question arises, who has the higher batting average across the five seasons?

Table 18.2 shows the performance of both the players in the five seasons:

Table 18.2: Baseball Batting Averages by Season

Season	Tom	Joe	Winner
1	.252	.255	Joe
2	.259	.266	Joe
3	.237	.241	Joe
4	.253	.255	Joe
5	.256	.257	Joe

As you can see in Table 18.2, there is no information about which player has the best overall batting average. There is not sufficient information in the table to understand who had the best batting average across all five seasons.

If Joe and Tom had the same number of attempts to bat in each season, then the answer would have been quite simple. Joe would have been the winner. However, what would happen if the number of attempts to bat is different? What if both Joe and Tom had played their best average in a season and suddenly Joe got hurt for the rest of the season, resulting in low averages? In such a case, Joe would have a lot more batting attempts.

This would mean that Tom would have a higher batting average than Joe even if Tom was beaten in each single season. This would not be a common case, but it is quite possible.

CASELET

When you know just a part of the story, you will always get a wrong result as the conclusion. You must not take an easy way out and assume that the results would be compelling. You must ensure that you have all the required data and that tests have been performed on the data before reaching any conclusion.

In the preceding example, without having the complete information, that is, without knowing in advance the total number of batting attempts, it is not possible to know which player did better overall. Take a look at Table 18.3 to see an example of how Tom could be the winner across the five-year period:

Table 18.3: Full Comparison of Batting Averages

Year	Tom: avg.	Tom: at bats	Tom: hits	Joe: avg.	Joe: at bats	Joe: hits	Winner
1	.252	123	31	.255	341	87	Joe
2	.259	355	92	.266	109	29	Joe
3	.237	139	33	.241	377	91	Joe
4	.253	304	77	.255	294	75	Joe
5	.256	363	93	.257	206	53	Joe
Total	.254	1,284	326	.252	1,327	335	

In Table 18.3, the difference between Tom's and Joe's batting averages is not statistically significant. Therefore, rather than Joe beating Tom, we conclude that Tom actually beat Joe. However, this case is also not so simple. Even if Tom has won the game, the margin of victory is not statistically significant. The conclusion is actually derived from a statistical perspective. The answer is more difficult to interpret than it appears.

Usually people will refer to Table 18.3 and go with the result shown in the table in which Joe had a better overall average. The case proves that you should never blindly go with the result. Ensure that you test and validate.

Another important aspect about statistical significance is that most people feel that the result is satisfactory if they are 95 percent or 99 percent sure that they have crossed a hurdle. The important point to understand here is that when you are 95 percent sure that you are right, there is still that 5 percent that can prove you wrong. It means that one out of every 20 times you perform an experiment, you can expect to get it wrong if you accept the result as it is.

Ensure that the level of certainty tests conducted matches with the level of risk that can be comfortably taken. For instance, if a company can go bankrupt by making an incorrect decision, then 95 percent certainty does not seem that great. In fact, 99.9 percent or higher should be the level of certainty one should aim for.

You must keep your significance bar very high to maintain the risk at a very low level. Clinical trials are performed for new drugs, and they usually use a very high bar as the result might lead to an inferior drug or even death. On the contrary, the decision taken by a company to place image A or image B at the top of a Web page involves a much lower risk.

Business Importance

Assume that statistical significance is found in analysis. You must answer some questions such as, is there a statistically significant result that is fantastic? Is it critical for the business to function? How is the result being used by the business, and how is the business going to take an action on that result? Is the result large enough to have a meaningful impact?

The results thus obtained must always be placed in a business context to take it as a final process of validation. Let's assume that an executive is 99 percent confident that the change in a process would result in the fetching of a 10 percent hike in the revenue. The decision works well for the business.

However, what if the hypothesis was based on a basic offer, whereas the change was tested on a bonus offer that costs twice as much? In such a case, even if you receive an extra 10 percent of response, it will not cover the extra costs. The fact that the response rate is higher will not matter. It is still not important from the business point of view.

You must see beyond significance tests and consider the bigger picture. What are the costs related to making the recommended changes? How much additional revenue is generated over a period of time? Is the new approach good enough to be implemented with the corporate strategy? Statistical significance is also very important, but it only matters to the extent it can be validated to do something important from the business point of view.

Making Inferences versus Computing Statistics

Consider that an analysis has unveiled significant statistics. The analytic professional also confirms that the findings are critical to the business. Now the analytic professional must know what should be done as a result. To find a great analysis, he/she must have an idea of the potential plan of action that must be taken into consideration to understand what can be done about the findings. Further, if there are actions that the analysis fails to support, then that should also be documented.

A great analysis makes decisions easy. The decision-maker must make the final call. An analysis summary offers suggestions. A good analysis must make initial inferences and not simply compute statistics. Just as a report is not an analysis, providing statistics or other technical information is also not an analysis. An analytic professional is one who offers analysis and recommendations and not reports or statistics. Analytic professionals analyze data and provide the result required to solve a problem. The big value is then added to those results that are interpreted, and a plan of action is obtained. This transforms reports into analysis and reporters into analytic professionals.

Let's understand this better with an illustration. It is not sufficient to just point out that option A has outperformed option B by 20 percent. The decision to be taken as a result is also required. A great analysis includes recommended steps. If option B outperformed option A by 20 percent, then you must conclude that option B should be implemented. This was a very simple case. However, there are many analyses that are more complicated. In such cases, guidance on what action the results imply is also very helpful. The decision-makers should not identify the options on their own. They should have the choice of either accepting or rejecting the options.

Let's now understand what makes a great analytics team.

Developing an Analytic Team

Organizations find it difficult to structure analytics teams. Analytic professionals do not have a fixed or permanent department in an organization like the human resources department or the finance department. Companies usually have different analytic professionals who work for different departments of the company. The problems they handle, the methods they use to solve the problems, and even the type of training they require are entirely different.

It is not so complicated in case of other departments. Usually, the job of the human resources department is fixed and consistent. The role of a recruiter is fairly consistent as per its job description but this is not true in case of data analysts or analytic professionals. The analytics required by the operations department is far different from that required by a merchandising department. Similarly, the focus of a risk management team is quite different from that of a marketing team. This conflict gives rise to the following important questions:

- How should an organization structure its analytics teams?
- Where do the teams fit in the organization?
- What will set the organization up for the most success?

Analytical teams must answer these questions if they want to tame Big Data.

In some industries, analytics is highly used in the decision-making process. Some examples include the banking, logistics, and financial industries. Organizations involved in these industries have various analytic professionals. For instance, risk management is driven by using analytics. Similarly, credit card solicitations received through mail are also driven using analytics. Before a card application reaches your mailbox, your data is examined thoroughly, and it is ascertained that you are a good risk for the offer in your hand.

There are companies that have explored analytics and there are others that have hardly used analytics. A very good example of this is the retail and manufacturing industries. Some manufacturers use analytics while some are hardly doing anything beyond spreadsheet-based analysis.

A great analysis helps a company change a number of important things about its business. The company is able to identify and correct the segments of customers that it had been targeting incorrectly and marketing with inappropriate messages. It can now fix that. The staff can work on a single view to promote performance instead of many views used in various parts of the company. A single view makes it easy to agree on where to invest and what will work. The organization can also implement a more user-specific view of its business with the introduction of customer measures to a different operational reports and analyses.

Skills Required for an Analyst

Although many fields lack talent, this is even truer in the case of the analytics field than in most others. That is, in part, because of the following two things:

- **Increasing demand for analytic professionals**—Books, articles, and blogs discussing the rapid increase in demand for analytical talent can be found everywhere. The fact is that there is an acute shortage of analytic professionals.
- **Short supply of analytic talent out of the educational system**—It is taking time for academic programs to adapt and scale in order to develop more talent.

Given that there are now software tools with user-friendly interfaces for performing advanced analytics, is it a good idea to let untrained people do their own analysis using these tools?

The issue underlying this question is that many people assume that if there is a tool that is easy to navigate via a nice point and click interface, then it implies that it is easy to use the tool correctly and appropriately. This is not true. Just because a tool is easy to use does not mean it is easy to use it correctly. In fact, the ease of use makes it incredibly easy to do exactly the wrong thing fast and unwittingly; for example, tools that generate SQL through a point and click interface will let users join data together in any way they please. This will put the syntax requested in place, but there is no guarantee that the syntax created will make any business sense at all.

Even if you know how to use a tool, you also need to have the right skills, experience, and perspective to use it properly. An analytics tool may save a user some programming, but he or she still needs to understand the analytics that is being generated. If you were confident that a novice was asking the right questions, that all of the data to answer the questions was ready and waiting in exactly the right format, and that the precise algorithm to apply was known, then virtually anybody could succeed. Under these terms, everything is laid out perfectly, and the user is truly just going through the motions of hitting the buttons. In the real world, this perfect setup is never actually the case.

A lot goes into building an appropriate analysis or model. The process goes beyond pointing and clicking a tool. Is the right behavior being predicted? Is the best set of independent variables to support that prediction available? Does the analytic professional have the experience to know when things do not look right? Does the analytic professional know how to address the problems that arise?

CASELET

Business people usually do not have any knowledge of analytics. Their main job is to sell the power of analytics upstream and transform the business processes to use analytics. The job of the analytic professional is to let business people drive analytics through the organization. If both the analytics team and the business team do what they do best, then it can be a win-win situation for everyone.

Convergence of IT and Analytics

While building an analytics team, a big issue faced by organizations is the struggle between analytic professionals and the IT or development team. This should no longer need to be so. To understand the issue better, let's have a look at the roles of both IT and analytic professionals in an organization.

An analytic professional is assigned the task of analyzing corporate data and extract new information out of it, which helps in taking important business decisions. An analytic professional must think out of the box and find new and innovative insights for the business.

IT people are hired by an organization to ensure that all the systems are functioning smoothly and that every employee is able to do his/her work properly. IT professionals must make sure that resources are allocated appropriately and everything is under control.

Often IT professionals and analytic professionals have differences of opinions because of the jobs that they have been assigned by their organization are inherently in conflict. The IT team is assigned with locking and controlling data and regulating the use of resources. The analytic team is assigned with the task of examining the data, using lots of resources, and finding new insights. Conflict between the two teams is bound to occur from time to time.

Table 18.4 depicts the roles of the analytics and IT professionals in an organization:

Table 18.4: Role of Analytics and IT Teams

Analytics Team	IT Team
Uses system resources heavily	Manages resource usage tightly
Creates tables and uses a lot of space	Limits table creation and reduces space usage
Runs complex ad hoc queries	Minimizes the use of complex ad hoc queries
Goes outside the box	Forces users to use traditional approaches for performing tasks
Experiments with new approaches	Follows approved approaches
Works with limited rules and restrictions	Enforces rules and restrictions

It is important for both the IT and analytics teams to come together and agree on how they plan to work together. It is possible for both teams to work in harmony with the available technology in hand and help each other coexist in the organization.

The good news is that most of the factors that lead to animosity no longer exist now. With these improvements, it is now possible to bridge the gap between the two teams. It is important that an organization must bridge the gap between both teams to create a great analytics team.

In case a team is provided with its own environment for analytics, it has the liberty to make some of the team members system administrators, production schedulers, and so forth. An analytic professional generally creates a new analytic process that runs on a weekly basis. The professional has to then monitor the process every week, identify how to account for changes to the data feeds, or any other changes in the system that might impact the process.

Analytic professionals usually do not like to do these things. Especially after the emergence of Big Data, analytics without the existence of a customized infrastructure and framework is impossible to implement for managing huge amounts of data. At the same time, analysts need applications and some custom scripts to perform analytics. Analytics teams can hand over the task of developing great tools, frameworks, backups, applications to IT people who are good at it. This will help the analytics team to concentrate on finding new and innovative ideas rather than just get processes to implement.

Understanding Text Analytics

Several methods exist for analyzing unstructured data. In the past, these methods came out of technical areas such as Natural Language Processing (NLP), data mining, information retrieval, knowledge discovery, and statistics.

Text analytics refers to the process of analyzing unstructured text, taking out relevant information from it, and transforming it into structured information that can be used in several ways. The process of analysis and extraction of data takes benefit from techniques that emerged in computational linguistics, and other computer science disciplines.

An example most often helps to explain a complicated topic. Consider that you work for the marketing department in a wireless phone company. You have launched two new calling plans, Plan A and Plan B, and you are not getting the update you wanted on Plan B. Therefore, information is available only on Plan A in the form of unstructured text received from call center notes. Figure 18.2 shows a part of the notes from the call center:

Customer XYZ called about Plan A promotion. Explained plan.
Customer thinks roll-over minutes should be included.

Customer ABC called about Plan A promotion. Customer thought
it was ridiculous that roll-over minutes were not in plan.

Potential called about Plan A promotion. Said that plan was expensive.

Potential called about Plan A promotion. Said that 4GB data not enough.

Customer XYT called about Plan A promotion, Said
that data plan was insufficient and stupid.

Figure 18.2: Call Center Notes

As shown in Figure 18.2, the underlined words will provide the information required to understand why Plan A was not adopted by the users. For example, Plan A appears in all the call center notes, indicating that the reports mention the plan. Terms such as 4GB data, roll-over minutes, expensive, and data plan indicate that there is a problem with the data plan, price, and roll-over minutes. Words such as ridiculous and stupid provide an insight into caller sentiment, which in this case is negative.

The text analytics process uses different algorithms, such as understanding the sentence structure, to analyze unstructured text and then extract and transform that information into structured data. The structured data extracted from unstructured text is shown in Table 18.5:

Table 18.5: Extracting Structured Data from Unstructured Text

Identifier	Entity	Problem	Sentiment
Cust XYZ	Plan A	Roll-over minutes	Neutral
Cust ABC	Plan A	Roll-over minutes	Negative
Cust ABC	Plan A	Expensive	Negative
Cust ABC	Plan A	Data plan	Neutral
Cust XYT	Plan A	Data plan	Negative

By looking at Table 18.5, we could have easily obtained the result by simply looking at the call center notes. However, these are just a small subset of information recorded from thousands of call center agents. Each agent might have a problem with a plan offered by the company. Agents will not have the time to share this information across all the call center agents who are getting similar calls about Plan A. However, after aggregating this information and processing the data by using text analytics algorithms, a trend might emerge from the unstructured data. That's what makes text analytics so powerful.

Summary

In the chapter, you have learned advanced analytical techniques that are used to organize and analyze Big Data. The chapter has compared reporting and analysis, explained different types of analytics, and familiarized you with the points that need to be considered for an analysis. You have learned that for an analysis to be effective, it must be guided, relevant, explainable, actionable, and timely. You have also learned basic analytics and how it answers the simple questions, viz., what happened? When did it happen? And what is the impact of what happened? Additionally, you have learned how to build an analytic team and understood the concept of text analytics.

Quick Revise

Multiple-Choice Questions

Q1. Which among the following is not a characteristic of reporting?

a. Provides data

b. Provides answers

c. Is fairly inflexible

d. Provides what is asked for

Ans. The correct option is b.

Q2. An organization requires its analytical team to increase the net profit of its retail stores. The analytical team starts the analysis but then realizes that the problem statement of the organization is not very clear in its approach. This is because the retail stores of the organization are divided into various regions. Which of the following characteristics is lacking from this analysis?

a. It is not guided
b. It is not relevant
c. It is not timely
d. It is not actionable

Ans. The correct option is a.

Q3. The senior management of an organization tells the analytics team to create an analysis to cater to the needs of the stores in region B. Because of certain problems, the analytical team is able to prepare the analysis only after the advent of the new fiscal year. Which of the following characteristics is lacking from this analysis?

a. It is not guided
b. It is not relevant
c. It is not timely
d. It is not actionable

Ans. The correct option is c.

Q4. Exploratory data analysis using graphs is nothing but:

a. Data cleaning
b. Basic reporting
c. Predictive modeling
d. Model implementation

Ans. The correct option is d.

Q5. Reporting does not involve:

a. Predictive models
b. Graphs
c. Charts
d. Tables

Ans. The correct option is a.

Q6. In a data analysis report, you will find:

a. Descriptive statistics
b. Optimization
c. Formatted text
d. White paper or journals

Ans. The correct option is b.

Q7. Data collection is one of the steps in statistical data analysis. This step is performed after which of the following steps?

a. Model building
b. Model implementation
c. Business objective
d. Evaluation

Ans. The correct option is c.

Q8. When we don't have access to a population, we tend to consider:

a. A simulated population
b. A survey
c. A random sample
d. Judgmental insights

Ans. The correct option is c.

Q9. Missing value treatment to the data is:

a. Necessary to get the correct results
b. Often leads to wrong results
c. Should never be practiced
d. Simply dropping all the missing records

Ans. The correct option is a.

Q10. Which of the following is not a task of an analytics team?

a. Heavily utilize resources
b. Work with limited rules and restrictions
c. Tightly manage resource usage
d. Run complex ad hoc queries

Ans. The correct option is c.

Subjective Questions

Q1. Discuss how advanced analytics can help the sales manager of T&E Corporation to analyze ways to increase the net profit of the retail stores of the organization.

Ans. Depending upon the behavior of the customers from past data, the sales manager can predict the future sales and increase the net profit of the retail stores.

Q2. Discuss how Big Data has helped advanced analytics in creating a great analysis for different organizations.

Ans. Advanced analytics is a multi-dimensional discipline. There is extensive use of mathematics and statistics, descriptive techniques, and predictive models to gain valuable knowledge from Big Data. The insights from data are used to recommend action or to guide decision making in organizations.

Q3. What are the roles of the IT and analytics teams in Big Data analytics projects?

Ans. The roles of the IT and analytics teams in Big Data analytics projects are:

a. Analytics teams are asked to:
   i. Heavily utilize system resources
   ii. Create tables and use a lot of space
   iii. Run complex ad-hoc queries
   iv. Go outside the box and forecast future patterns
   v. Experiment with new approaches and build strategies
   vi. Work with limited rules and restrictions
b. IT teams are asked to:
   i. Tightly manage resource usage
   ii. Limit table creation and space usage
   iii. Minimize use of complex ad-hoc queries
   iv. Allow users to use traditional approaches for performing tasks
   v. Stick to approved approaches
   vi. Enforce rules and restrictions

Q4. Explain reporting.

Ans. A reporting environment is also known as a Business Intelligence (BI) environment. Such an environment enables users to select and view reports, run them, and view the results. Reports might contain various visual elements to aid understandability, including graphs, charts, and tables. The key factors that define a report are as follows:

- They provide the data that the user has been asking for
- They provide the data in a predefined format for easy understandability
- They show the stakeholders what had happened in the past
- They allow the data analyst to define several pieces of data with a few indices

As a result, reports are quite inflexible. Different prompts and filters can be used to create complex report templates. The user usually fills information in the prompts and filters that are already in place. Reports can be misused. When lots of reports are available, they can be mistakenly used for in-depth analysis. Usually, people in charge of the BI environment would often boast of having a world-class BI environment with 500 reports covering all the aspects of the business. However, the number of reports doesn't necessarily translate into in-depth analysis.

A report need not be analyzed further if it provides the required information. For example, suppose an organization has a report of sales by product by week, and a manager needs to know whether the products have achieved the sales target last week. The manager gets the required information by running the report and no further analysis is required to get the answer. This example shows one way in which reports add value to business. They can be used to get answers of common questions quickly and easily. If the reports fail to provide all the answers, then it is time to do further analysis of the reports.

Q5. Explain the analytic process.

Ans. An analytic process contains all or some of the following phases:

1. **Business understanding**—The first phase involves identifying and understanding the business objectives. It deals with the problems to be solved and decisions to be made. The main goal is to enhance business profitability. Once the business objectives are determined, the analysts evaluate the situation, and identify the data mining goals. According to the defined goals, a project plan is created between the analytics team and the IT or development team.
2. **Data collection**—The process of collecting data is an important task in executing a project plan accurately. In this phase, data from different data sources is collected first and then described in terms of its application and need of the project. This process is also called data exploration. Exploration of data is required to ensure the quality of the collected data.
3. **Data preparation**—From the data thus collected, unnecessary or unwanted data is to be removed in this phase. In other words, the data must be prepared for the purpose of analysis.
4. **Data modeling**—In this phase, a model is created by using a data modeling technique. The data model is used to analyze the relationships between different selected objects in

the data. Test cases are created to assess the applicability of model and data is structured according to the model.

5. **Data evaluation**—The results obtained from different test cases are evaluated and reviewed for errors. After validating the results, analysis reports are created for determining the next plan of action.
6. **Deployment**—In this phase, the plan is finalized for deployment. The deployed plan is constantly checked for errors and maintenance. This process is also termed as reviewing of the project.

The various phases of analysis are explained in the following figure:

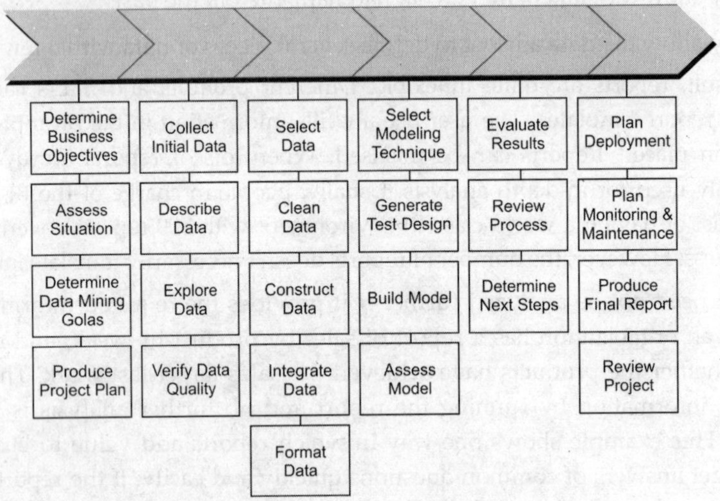

Q6. What do you mean by basic analytics?

Ans. Basic analytics is used to explore the data whose value is not known. In other words, the data may or may not prove to be useful. Basic analytics usually involves visualizations of simple statistics. This type of analytics is used specially when a lot of disparate data needs to be analyzed. The process of basic analytics includes investigating what happened, when it happened, and its impact.

Let us consider an example to understand this better. Suppose a product manager in an organization needs to know about the sales promotion of certain products, which was performed last month. He/she also wants to know how many new customers have been associated with the organization due to the sales promotion. In this case, to know "what" happened, core analysis would help in understanding how many customers bought and used the products. To know the "impact" of this, core analysis would help in understanding how much money the new customers brought in, and this impacted when compared to the baseline.

Some examples of basic analytics are as follows:

- **Slicing and dicing**—It refers to the division of data into smaller groups that are easy to explore. For example, sales data can be divided or categorized on the basis of regions for better analysis.

- **Basic monitoring**—It is the monitoring of huge volumes of data in real time. For instance, when your new ad campaign is launched, you might be interested in monitoring data related to every single minute.
- **Anomaly identification**—It refers to the identification of anomalies, for example, identification of an event that shows a difference between the actual observation and what you expected in your data. This may be due to some anomaly in the operations of an organization.

Q7. Describe advanced analytics.

Ans. Advanced analytics is not just confined to answering questions such as what happened, when it happened, and its impact. It goes one step beyond by finding the reason for what has happened and the measures that can be taken to avoid it from happening again in the future. Advanced analytics performs complex analysis of both structured and unstructured data by using algorithms. It also uses advanced data mining techniques such as neural networks, statistical models, machine learning, text analytics, and many more.

Additionally, it uses several activities such as complex ad hoc SQL, forecasting, optimization, predictive modeling, data mining, and so on. To determine different patterns in data, complex event processing, forecasting, and advanced analytics are used.

The following are some examples of advanced analytics:

- **Predictive modeling**—It refers to a data mining solution that provides algorithms and techniques to use on structured and unstructured data to ascertain future outcomes. For instance, a telecommunications company can identify the customers who are about to drop its service by using a predictive model.
- **Text analytics**—It is the process of examining unstructured text, extracting important information out of it, and transforming the information into structured information that can be leveraged in different ways.
- **Other statistical and data mining algorithms**—These algorithms use techniques such as advanced forecasting, optimization, cluster analysis for segmentation, and affinity analysis.

Q8. Explain operational analytics.

Ans. Operational analytics means making analytics an important part of the business process. For instance, an insurance company can use a model to predict the probability of a claim being fraudulent. This model can be used by the company to form an important part of its claims processing system to flag claims having a high probability of fraud. The fraudulent claims are then sent to a separate unit for investigation, which reviews the claims further. In some cases, the model will work for the end users from behind the scenes. For instance, in a company a model may be used to predict customers who can be good targets for selling products when they make calls.

While an agent of the company is taking a call from a customer, he/she might receive a message about additional products to sell to the customer. In such cases, the agent might not be aware that a predictive model is working behind the scenes to make product recommendations.

Q9. State the characteristics of Big Data analysis.

Ans. There are few additional characteristics of Big Data analysis that make it different from traditional ones besides the three Vs: volume, velocity, and variety. The following are the additional characteristics of Big Data analysis:

- **It can be programmatic**—Big Data analysts must use code to handle raw data. The analysts can use the code to manipulate or explore the data. This is especially useful when you have large volumes of data.
- **It can be data-driven**—A hypothesis-driven approach is used by several analysts to develop a premise and gather data to see if the premise is correct or not. However, Big Data uses a huge volume of data to drive the analysis.
- **It can use a lot of attributes**—Analysts in the past used hundreds of attributes of the data set for analysis, and today Big Data uses thousands of attributes and millions of observations to conduct analysis.
- **It can be iterative**—Big Data analysts use iterations on models that provide more computational power. These models allow the analysts to do iterations to the required level of analysis. Because of this, new applications are designed and developed to analyze requirements and time frames to complete the analysis.

Q10. Explain monetized analytics.

Ans. Monetized analytics helps businesses to take important and better decisions and helps earn revenues. However, Big Data analytics is also used to derive revenue beyond the insights it provides. You might be able to get a unique data set that is valuable for other companies. For example, credit card providers can use this data to offer value-added products. Similarly, telecommunications companies like financial institutions have started selling location-based insights to retailers. Data of different types such as text-messaging data, location data, billing data and Web data are used to find inferences about customer behavior patterns. These patterns will help the retailers in finding useful information.

Q11. What do you mean by statistical significance?

Ans. Statistical significance is usually used to calculate averages, percentages, and parameter estimates arising out of statistical models. Statistical significance testing is valuable to ensure that your data does not provide irrelevant information. By taking this mathematical perspective, you will come to know whether a difference is large enough to be considered significant. Sometimes a small difference can be very significant and sometimes a big difference does not seem to be significant enough.

A statistical test is performed to ensure that the right inferences are derived from the data. A different discipline has been developed for testing. In the business world, this discipline is called test and learn. In the test-and-learn environment, an experiment is performed to measure the effects of options and identify which options will work best.

19

Analytical Approaches and Tools to Analyze Data

Over the years, various tools have been used by analytic professionals to analyze data, execute algorithms, and determine results. With the passage of time, the functionality of these tools has increased and improved tremendously. Data analytic professionals use these tools and approaches to solve a problem—in this case, to sort and organize unstructured data into some meaningful patterns and derive meaningful insights. Modern tools, available today, have the ability to automate most of the common tasks, thereby enabling analytic professionals to pay more attention on the core data analysis process than to worry about implementation details.

In this chapter, you learn about the evolution of analytical tools and various types of analytical approaches—ensemble methods and text data analysis. The chapter also discusses the history of analytical tools and the development of various types of tools such as graphical user interfaces, point solutions, and data visualization. Next, you learn about some popular analytical tools such as R Project for Statistical Computing, IBM SPSS, and SAS. Towards the end, you learn to install R and RStudio on different types of operating systems.

SCENARIO

Mr. Smith, the data analyst at Argon Technology, is studying about various Big Data analytical approaches and tools to identify business trends and patterns. He decides to share this knowledge with his team.

Analytical Approaches

The ways adopted to sort, analyze, or solve problems are known as analytical approaches. Many analytical approaches have been in use over the years. However, as the size of the data to be analyzed grew, newer analytical approaches were adopted. Today, you can execute different types of algorithms on large datasets, which was not possible earlier.

The sections that follow discuss some of the commonly used analytical approaches, which are as follows:

- Ensemble methods
- Text data analysis

Ensemble Methods

Ensemble method refers to a process of generating multiple models and combining them to solve a specific problem. The process that we follow in an ensemble method is quite similar to what we follow in our day-to-day life. Similar to the ensemble method, where different models are merged to derive a final answer, in our daily lives, we take opinions from different experts before arriving at a final decision. For example, we take opinions from various doctors before going for a medical treatment or consider various user reviews before purchasing a particular mobile. Doing so helps in reducing the chances of selecting an incorrect medical treatment or a poor quality mobile.

The main aim of using an ensemble method is to minimize the probability of selecting a poor item and also improve the performance of a model. Ensemble models are based on the theory of the wisdom of crowds. According to **James Surowiecki**, *The Wisdom of Crowds explains the principle of group think, and the concept that the masses are better problem solvers, forecasters, and decision makers than any one individual.*

The following are some examples of different ensemble algorithms:

- **Bagging**—Bagging stands for bootstrap aggregating and refers to an ensemble algorithm wherein the following process is followed:
  1. Individual models on random samples of the same data size are developed.
  2. A classification or regression tree is applied to each sample.
  3. Finally, an average of the predictions obtained from different methods or votes on the classification of an observation is made to obtain the final predictions or classifications.

NOTE

Classification tree refers to a tree structure where the target variable can have finite or fixed values, such as male or female. Regression tree is a tree structure where the target variable can have continuous values or real numbers. Examples of real numbers include the price of a car, or the duration for which a patient stays in a hospital.

- **Boosting**—Boosting is another ensemble algorithm that generates multiple models and obtains weights to merge the predictions from these models into a single predicted classification.
- **Random forests**—Random forest is a data-mining algorithm wherein random samples of data are generated, multiple decision trees are constructed, and a random subset of inputs called predictors are evaluated for each tree.

NOTE

Decision tree refers to a structure similar to a flowchart wherein each node signifies a test performed on an attribute (for example, whether the candidate is male or female) and each branch indicates the result of the test (for example, male or female) and further, each leaf node indicates a class label (shows the decision taken after the computation of all the attributes).

Text Data Analysis

The processing and modeling of textual data to gain useful business insights is called text data analysis. Data analysis is done by using statistics, with or without the aid of computerized tools to analyze data. An essential part of text data analysis is text mining, which involves obtaining meaningful and high-quality information from textual data. This high-quality information is derived by finding relationships and useful business patterns and trends from a massive collection of text.

As the name suggests, text data analysis takes text as input. This text can be an e-mail, medical dictation, or even text that can be scanned from a hard copy and converted into electronic form.

Today, no organization can ignore customers' choices and opinions. Most of the information related to customer feedback can be extracted from e-mails, call center notes, customer satisfaction surveys, and other important documents interchanged between the organization and its customers. Text analytics helps in identifying and addressing causes of customer dissatisfaction in a timely manner, thereby improving the organization's brand image.

You already know that a huge amount of data is generated from various data sources, such as e-mails, social media platforms like Facebook and Twitter, online queries, and call center conversations. This data is mostly unstructured, and identifying meaningful patterns and trends out of it is not an easy task.

Table 19.1 shows some examples of data sources and different data structure types used in case of text data analysis:

Table 19.1: Data Sources and Data Structure Types for Text Data Analysis

Data Source	Data Format	Data Structure Type
Literature	TXT, DOC, HTML, or PDF	Unstructured
Web pages	HTML	Semi-structured
News articles	TXT, HTML, or scanned PDF	Unstructured
E-mail	TXT, MSG, or EML	Unstructured
Call center transcripts	TXT	Unstructured
Server logs	LOG or TXT	Semi-structured

Over the years, text analysis tools and methods have evolved tremendously. Modern text analysis tools can help you parse text into different words and phrases and even discover the meaning of those words and phrases. For instance, text analysis helps to find out answers of certain questions: how many of the e-mails received from customers had positive or negative tones? How frequently did a specific customer focus on a particular product line in his or her communication? This essentially creates some structured information from raw, unstructured data. Such a process of parsing and structuring text is called information extraction. Some popular commercial text analysis tools are offered by Attensity, IBM, SAS, and Clarabridge.

Advanced analytical tools also help in strengthening the safety mechanisms of various organizations and financial institutions and reduce the chances of fraudulent transactions. Studies indicate that by using simple text mining techniques, fraudulent transactions can be easily detected by financial institutions such as banks and insurance companies. These institutions capture a number of metrics containing information about user details that include names, contact numbers, and e-mail addresses. Although most of this information is fake, components such as e-mail addresses and telephone numbers can help in determining the area from which the accused is operating; thus, advanced analytics can be used to safeguard companies from falling into the trap of imposters and frauds.

Financial organizations usually take the following precautions to guard themselves against fraudulent practices:

- Record the information, such as contact number of customer, e-mail address, user name, password, and address found on an online purchase order form.
- Determine the IP addresses of customers from the mails sent or received by them.
- Perform research on the e-mail address and the attached domain, identify that it is a real e-mail address or a fake one, identify the domain name, and the country to which it belongs.
- Match the IP address, contact number, e-mail address, and address of the customer and determine whether all the information is from the same place or from different places.
- Search the given contact number and check whether it is reported for any kind of abuse or scam on the Internet.

History of Analytical Tools

In the late 1980s, analytics was considered to be a very daunting task due to the unavailability of the appropriate tools or computational systems. In those days, data analytics was performed by using a mainframe and by developing numerous program codes using the complicated Job Control Language (JCL). JCL is a complex language with different parameters, with each of these parameters having an effect that can take several pages to explain. Further, it also needs specific and correct placement of commas and blanks.

NOTE

JCL is a scripting language used to run batch jobs on mainframes.

Even graphs used to be very elementary and were generated by printing text characters on paper sheets. With time, graphical interfaces were introduced, allowing users to quickly create graphs by using point-and-click environments instead of coding.

NOTE

Point-and-click environment enables a user to move a mouse pointer on a specific location of a computer screen and perform a click operation. An example of such an environment can be a user clicking on a hyperlink to move from one Web page to another.

By the late 1990s, all the commercial analytical tools offered such interfaces. From then onwards, there were tremendous improvements in user interfaces to make more powerful graphics, visual workflow diagrams, and applications that are mainly focused on specific point solutions (solving a specific issue without considering any associated problems). One of the major improvements in this field is the introduction of workflow diagrams that opened the way for analytic professionals to look into individual steps of a process and forming a visual map where the tasks are all connected.

Till now, you have seen how analytical tools have evolved from graphical user interfaces to point solutions to data visualization tools. The sections that follow will discuss each of these tools in detail.

SCENARIO

You can use a free Web analytics tool to track the visitors on a website. This tool is offered by Google and used by Web Masters for tracking customers on the Web. This tool allows Web Masters to record details such as the location of the visitors, duration of the visitors' stay on the site, and all the links the visitors have viewed.

Graphical User Interfaces

Before the 1980s, the only way to perform statistical analysis on a given set of data was to write code. Today, we have various types of user interfaces and automatic analytical and graphical tools available for this task. The graphical user interfaces available today help in generating code that is already defined to perform a particular task. These tools help analytic professionals focus on analysis methods rather than on writing code. Further, software packages offer robust solutions that not only generate code quickly, but also help users through a predefined process that aimed at solving specific problems.

Moreover, the code generated automatically by a user interface is free of any errors and bugs, which mostly creep into the manual coding process. Although the code will be automatically generated by the interface, users should be able to understand the generated code and review and validate it for performing the intended tasks. Often, it happens that while working with a user interface, you click a few options and expect a certain result; however, on reviewing the code that the tool has generated, you realize that a different result has been intended by the developers.

Point Solutions

Analytic point solutions refer to software packages that solve a specific group of problems. Examples of point solutions are price optimization detection applications, fraud applications, and demand forecasting applications. Point solutions based on tool suites, such as SAS, will make use of some generic functionalities of the underlying toolset; however, the user interface will always be used for some specific set of problems. Implementing a one-point solution as a substitute for creating a custom solution for various problems can help organizations save money, effort, and time.

For example, a money-laundering detection application tool used in financial institutions provides some algorithms and business rules to detect suspicious patterns during the transfer of money. The interfaces of such an application are designed to identify suspicious activities and provide additional information, as and when required, to aid an investigation into the case. Such ready-made tools enable organizations to quickly use these tools instead of building a set of processes from scratch.

It requires a fair amount of knowledge and expertise to install and configure analytic point solutions and set up the parameters of the analytics to be run on them. Typical users of analytic point solutions are power users (users who use advanced features but their skill sets are not as advanced as those of analytic professionals) rather than average business people. After the solutions are set by experts, many tasks are automated so that power users can effectively keep an eye on the output of the tools and ensure everything is working and up-to-date.

One of the drawbacks of using point solutions is that they are quite expensive. It can cost around $10 million or more to get an enterprise license. An organization should opt for point solutions only if there is enough financial return to justify such a huge expense.

Data Visualization Tools

Simply analyzing data is not enough. The results must also be displayed in a user-friendly or visual manner so as to communicate the outcomes in an easy-to-understand format to the targeted audience. Many people prefer to see a visual depiction of a decision tree model than a long list of business rules. This is where data visualization tools help. In the world of analytics, visualization refers to the process of presenting data in the form of charts, graphs, and tables. Earlier, analytic software used keyboard characters to draw graphics, which used to be a cumbersome and time-consuming process.

For example, each bar in a bar chart was made of rows of semicolons (;), as displayed in Figure 19.1:

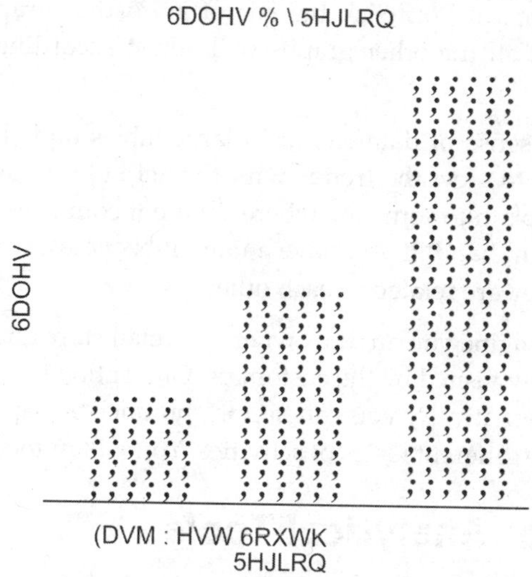

Figure 19.1: Early Rudimentary Bar Chart Style

Periods, commas, and dashes were used to make a pie chart. Similarly, a table was made up of dashes ("-") and pipe (" | ") characters.

Introduction of Office applications upgraded the graphics capabilities of analytical tools and they began to be used beyond text-based interfaces; however, most visualizations still used to be static. This means that a chart can be created using spreadsheet software; however, you need to manually update it, if required.

Nowadays, advanced visualization tools have made data interaction possible among almost all types of graphics and help to analyze and present data in new ways. Let us explore some common modern visualization tools.

Modern Visualization Tools

Visualization tools have evolved enormously. Tools such as Tableau, Quickview, JMP, Advizor, and Spotfire help analytic professionals and business users move beyond just graphics or data and help them to connect the dots between seemingly unrelated pieces of data, read between the lines, and interpret the processed information in various ways.

Visualizations can actually provide insights that cannot be easily detected by viewing the same data in a textual format. Analytic professionals extensively use visualization tools to analyze data, explore outcomes, and enhance graphics. Visualization tools are much faster and robust as compared to traditional charting tools. They can handle almost all types of questions asked during a presentation by providing quick answers. This means that the old approach of noting down the query, promising an answer, generating a new chart, and sending it to the person who raised the query is already outdated.

Visualization tools also allow users to link multiple tabs of graphs and charts to each other and to the underlying data. For instance, if you click the bar of a weather graph for extracting information about the Northeast region, all the other graphs will adjust accordingly and will display only the Northeast data.

It is very difficult to make sense of data stored in large tables and sheets and identify trends and patterns, but it is very easy to view the trends with the help of an appropriate visual. Just imagine how hard it would be to explain to someone where different countries are located on a geographical map without having a map in hand. If you have a map, it becomes easier to understand the location of the countries and how they are related to each other.

To take another example, imagine you are the owner of a retail store and want to know which parts of your store are most frequently visited by the customers. One option is to create spreadsheets and try to figure out the patterns. Alternatively, you can simply produce a map of the store floor plan where different colors represent the different levels of activities. You will immediately get the answer.

Introducing Popular Analytical Tools

Various types of analytical tools are available in the market, but no company can buy and implement all of them. Some of the open-source analytical tools are as follows:

- GridGain
- HPCC
- Storm
- Terrastore
- Neo4j

The decision to invest in an analytical tool is a crucial one and needs careful consideration on the part of a company on various parameters, such as size and type of the company, the kind of products or services it offers, the locations and ways to interact with customers, the stakeholders involved in the business, the manner in which the company receives feedback from customers, the amount of data generated by all these various sources and activities, future goals and perspectives, etc. A careful consideration of all these factors helps companies select the tool that is best suited to its individual requirements.

The following are some popular analytical tools:

- The R Project for Statistical Computing
- IBM SPSS
- SAS

NOTE

SPSS stands for Statistical Package for the Social Sciences and SAS refers to Statistical Analysis System.

The R Project for Statistical Computing

The R Project for Statistical Computing is also popularly known as R. It is a free, open source analytics package. R is an implementation of the S programming language, which was earlier being used for statistical analysis. R derived its name from its creators, Robert Gentleman and Ross Ihaka. R is widely used by several analytic professionals and is usually used in the academic, research and development environments.

Features of R

R has the following remarkable features:

- As compared to other analytical tools, R is more object-oriented.
- As R is can be easily linked with programming languages such as C++ and Java, it is possible to embed it in different applications.
- R can now be implemented from commercial analytical tools.
- R is an extensible language. Developers can create their own software and distribute it as add-on packages.

One of the major advantages of using R is its compatibility with most new modeling and analysis approaches. R can be used for different types of non-statistical tasks, such as data processing, graphic visualization, and analysis of all types of data. It is usually used in domains such as finance, biology, and market research.

Limitations of R

One of the major disadvantages of R is its lack of scalability. Some improvements have been made recently, but R is still not able to scale to the level of other commercial tools and databases. The R software runs in memory as compared to running against files. This implies that it can only manage datasets of the size of the memory available on a machine. The memory available in even a high configuration machine is quite less than what is required for managing enterprise-level datasets, and if you consider Big Data, the memory is definitely not enough. Therefore, if a big organization aims to analyze Big Data, then R can be a better solution, but it will not be the only solution. Programming in R is a fairly difficult process. Although R offers some graphical interfaces, still many developers prefer writing code.

IBM SPSS

The SPSS analytical tool was introduced in 1968. In 2009, its name was changed to IBM SPSS Statistics, after the IBM Group acquired the SPSS business. The functionality of IBM SPSS can be accessed with the help of a proprietary 4GL (fourth generation programming language), known as the syntax language, and using a graphical interface offering menus. The menus produce a syntax which the user cannot see, unless he or she requests to paste the syntax into the command window.

NOTE

4GLs are much closer to natural languages then third generation high-level programming languages, such as C or Java. The languages that are used to access databases are categorized as 4GLs.

Even a less experienced user can easily use the graphical interface as it is very user-friendly and quite simple to use. Further, the syntax language is also helpful in combining lengthy and complicated operations together and repeats common tasks by recording the syntax.

All the functionalities of R cannot be found in SPSS. However, the syntax and database format offered by SPSS are compatible with R. SPSS, like R, can also manage huge volumes of data.

Note that certain functionalities of R cannot be accessed by using graphical interfaces. For that, you will have to use R commands, which can be launched in the interactive mode or in the batch mode with the help of the production facility module. You can also use a macro language for automating the task of repeating commands on the basis of the given parameters. R also offers a script language to create dialog boxes.

NOTE

In an interactive mode, commands are provided to the command line shell one by one and the results are shown for each statement instantly. In the batch mode, a set of programs is executed without any manual intervention.

The main window of IBM SPSS Statistics, known as the data editor, looks similar to a spreadsheet wherein you can input data directly. Figure 19.2 shows an IBM SPSS sheet:

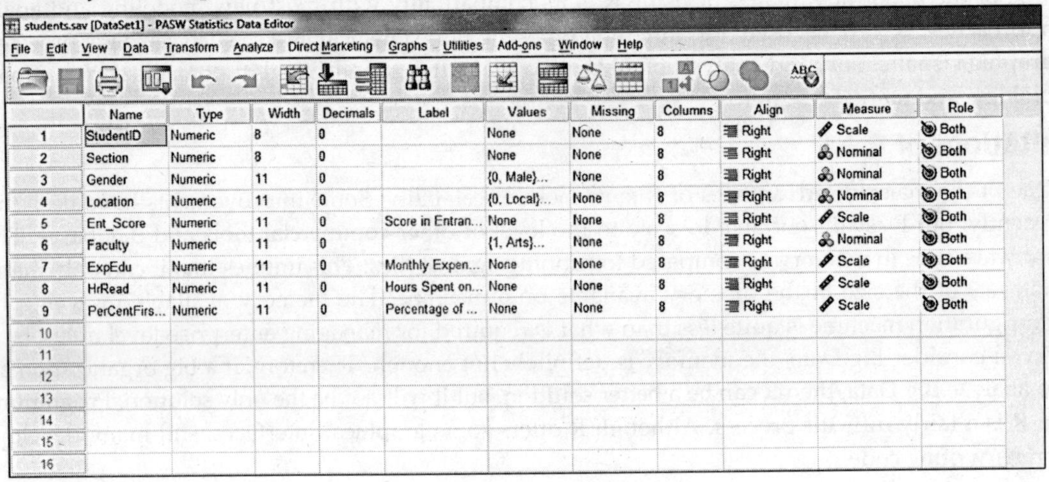

Figure 19.2: IBM SPSS Statistics

Features of IBM SPSS

IBM SPSS provides the following features:

- SPSS commands are executed one line at a time to update tables and add results to the output editor window. You can also store the executed syntaxes with their times of execution in this window.
- IBM SPSS Statistics can read data from and write to ASCII files, databases, and tables of other statistical software. This tool also helps in providing basic data management functions, such as sorting, aggregation, and table merge.

- IBM SPSS Statistics can send the output directly to a file, instead of the Output Editor window. The file can be in the .txt, .html, or .xml format. The Output Management System (OMS) helps in storing the outputs obtained from a large number of iterated calculations in a single file by creating a loop using a macro.
- IBM SPSS Statistics can be installed on different platforms such as Windows, Mac OS X, and Unix.

CASELET

A telecommunication service provider wants to get feedback from its customers to increase the customer retention rate. Using SPSS database management, the service provider conducts surveys over the Internet, mobile phones, and through face-to-face interactions. The feedback obtained from the customers helps the company to improve the level of its services, ultimately resulting in a high customer retention rate.

SAS

Statistical Analysis System (SAS) refers to an information delivery system, which is an integrated and hardware-independent computing package. SAS was introduced in 1976 in the IBM mainframe world to handle large volumes of data. Its capacity to handle data increased with the implementation of a parallel architecture in 1996.

NOTE

A parallel architecture refers to a set of procedural elements that work together to solve large problems faster.

As SAS is an information delivery system, it provides a broad and independent environment for organizational databases; therefore, data analysts can easily transform datasets into useful information that helps them in taking important decisions.

Similar to IBM SPSS Statistics, SAS is based on a 4GL programming language. A SAS program consists of data steps, procedure steps, and macros, if required. Several procedures provide a comprehensive range of functions, such as statistics, graphics, and utilities. In the data step, the user is allowed to open files or import databases, read each record, write to another file or export to a database, merge a number of files, and close the files.

SAS provides well-organized and timely information delivery, by:

- Delivering universal data access
- Providing a good user interface
- Increasing the functionalities of applications in software
- Taking the advantages of computer hardware platforms

SAS analysis allows users to navigate through data with the help of various analysis procedures. These procedures facilitate users to read and analyze data in a concise form.

SAS products, commonly known as modules, are mostly used by social and behavioral scientists. These modules allow users to perform various types of functions, such as spreadsheet analysis, data access, statistical analysis, application construction, and management. SAS products can be sold separately or in sets.

Features of SAS

Some key features of SAS are listed as follows:

- **Statistics**—SAS statistics offers a variety of statistical software. The information collected by using statistical analytics tools allows organizations to improve procedures, enterprise development, and profits. SAS statistical analysis helps organizations to retain their customers.
- **Data and text mining**—Business organizations collect large amounts of data from various sources. Organizations use this collected data for data mining and text mining in order to develop new strategies and take better decisions.
- **Data visualization**—SAS data visualization provides a user-friendly interface and permits users to work with graphs and charts to explain the results of the analysis.
- **Forecasting**—SAS uniquely supports all types of forecasting tools that help to analyze and forecast various types of processes. Forecasting helps organizations identify new business strategies and expect variations to more effectively plan for future prospects. SAS also provides several tools to understand previous business strategies and forecast plans to take the business process further.
- **Optimization**—SAS tools provide optimization, project scheduling, and simulation techniques to achieve maximum results while operating within restrictions and limited resources. These enable organizations to:
    - Improve contact strategy
    - Consider contingencies
    - Determine the best allocation of resources
- **Model management and deployment**—SAS model manager simplifies the tedious process of creating, managing, and deploying analytical models. The manager regularly verifies the accuracy and usefulness of the models.
- **Quality improvement**—SAS provides some Quality Control (QC) tools to enhance the quality of products, improve processes, and increase customer satisfaction. It encourages organizations to go beyond traditional and basic processes and includes some advanced statistical analyses to improve the product development process.

NOTE

Some important points about data and text mining are listed as follows:

- *Data mining is the process of exploring and analyzing datasets in order to find unknown or hidden rules, associations, or tendencies.*
- *Text mining also uses both predictive and descriptive analysis techniques for text-based documents.*

SAS works well with different types of operating systems and computers such as mainframes, personal computers, and Macintoshes.

Comparing Various Analytical Tools

The following presents a brief comparison of different analytical tools such as R, IBM SPSS, and SAS:

- **User interface**—Before the introduction of SAS Enterprise Guide, SPSS was significantly ahead with regard to user-friendliness, as it has an interface similar to Microsoft standards. SPSS is also very successful in sectors, such as marketing and the social sciences. IBM SPSS Statistics has a graphical interface containing menus. R does not have a universal graphical interface, and all of its functions are not integrated into various graphical interfaces distributed in its packages. However, to learn and practice hands-on analytics, R is an excellent tool. It enables analysts to master different steps and commands.
- **Decision making**—IBM SPSS Statistics is considered better than SAS because of its lower price and the possibility of obtaining the Answer tree for the generated decision trees without the need to purchase the data mining suite. In case you need to construct decision trees with SAS, you will have to buy Enterprise Miner. IBM SPSS offers more tree algorithms than R, and thus it is a better choice in cases where you need to take a lot of decisions.
- **File management and stability**—SAS is more complete and flexible with regard to file management. It has an enhanced procedure called TRANSPOSE to manage both relational and SAS tables efficiently. Suppose there is no index applied on the join keys. Then, it is better to merge two tables quickly with the help of an SQL join instead of a SAS merge as SAS merge needs a preliminary sorting of the tables before merging. When it comes to large volumes of data, SAS is best for processing. In terms of performance, SAS is considered the most stable of the three systems.
- **Data management**—In data management, SAS has an edge over IBM SPSS and is somewhat better than R. A major drawback of R is that most of its functions have to load all the data into memory prior to execution. This brings a limit on the volumes to be handled; however, some packages have started to break free of this limitation. An example of data management is the `biglm` package designed for linear models.
- **Documentation**—The technical documentation designed for SAS is very comprehensive. For instance, almost 8,000 pages cover the procedures of just the SAS/STAT module, which is just a part of the process.

In comparison to IBM SPSS Statistics, SAS provides many predefined functions, such as mathematical and financial functions. These include depreciation, compound interest, cash flow, hyperbolic functions, factorials, combinations and arrangements, and others. Further, the predictive and descriptive algorithms available in R and SAS are more in number as compared to IBM SPSS Statistics. The statistical indicators in SAS are more detailed and there are more possibilities of parameter setting. Finally, as compared to SPSS, the SAS macro language is more flexible and complete.

Figure 19.3 shows comparison between SAS, R, and SPSS:

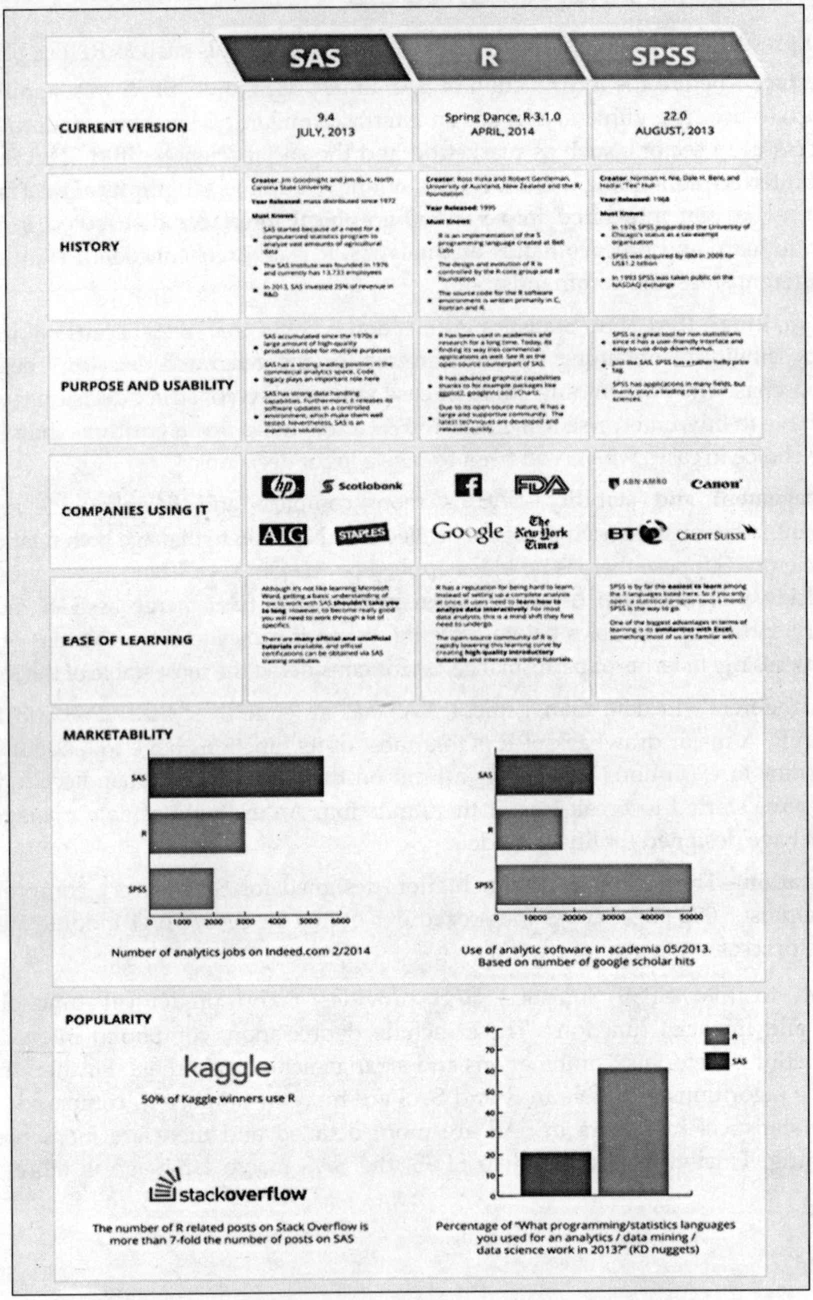

***Source**: http://datacamp.wpengine.com/wp-content/uploads/2014/05/infograph.png*

Figure 19.3: Comparing SAS, R, and SPSS

As R is an open-source programming language and provides a software environment for statistical computation and graphics, we will look into its installation next.

Installing R

Analyzing large customer data enables businesses to maximize their profitability, customer satisfaction, and productivity. If large volumes of data are analyzed manually, it becomes a daunting and time-consuming process. However, the time and effort to analyze data can be reduced tremendously by using R statistical data analytics. You may have seen that files working on one operating system may or may not work on another operating system. This is because different operating systems have different specifications and require different configuration of files. In this section, we will learn to install R on different operating systems, such as Windows, Macintosh, and Linux.

SCENARIO

Smith of Argon Technology decides to give demonstrations of installing R on various platforms such as Windows, Macintosh, and Linux. This is because in future projects, the company might have to work with the R tool.

Installing R on a Windows Computer

Microsoft's Windows operating system is one of the most popular and widely used operating systems across the globe. In this section, you learn to install the R tool on the Windows operating system.

To install R on the Windows operating system, perform the following steps:

1. Download R from its official website using the following location:

   http://ftp.heanet.ie/mirrors/cran.r-project.org

   The Comprehensive R Archive Network (CRAN) window appears, as shown in Figure 19.4:

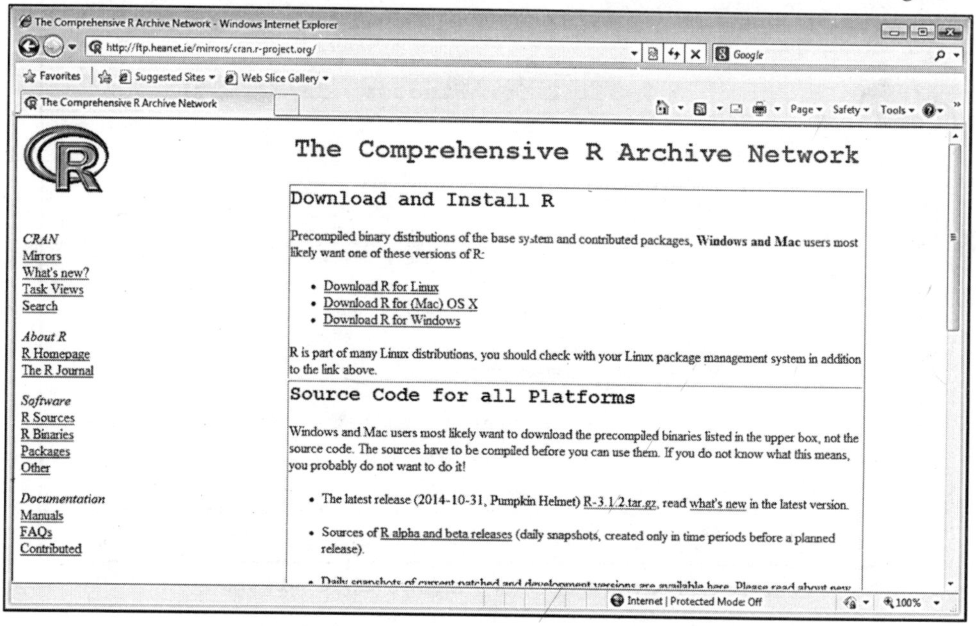

Figure 19.4: Download R from the CRAN Window

2. Click the `Download R for Windows` link to download the R tool for the Windows operating system (Figure 19.4). The R for Windows page appears, as shown in Figure 19.5:

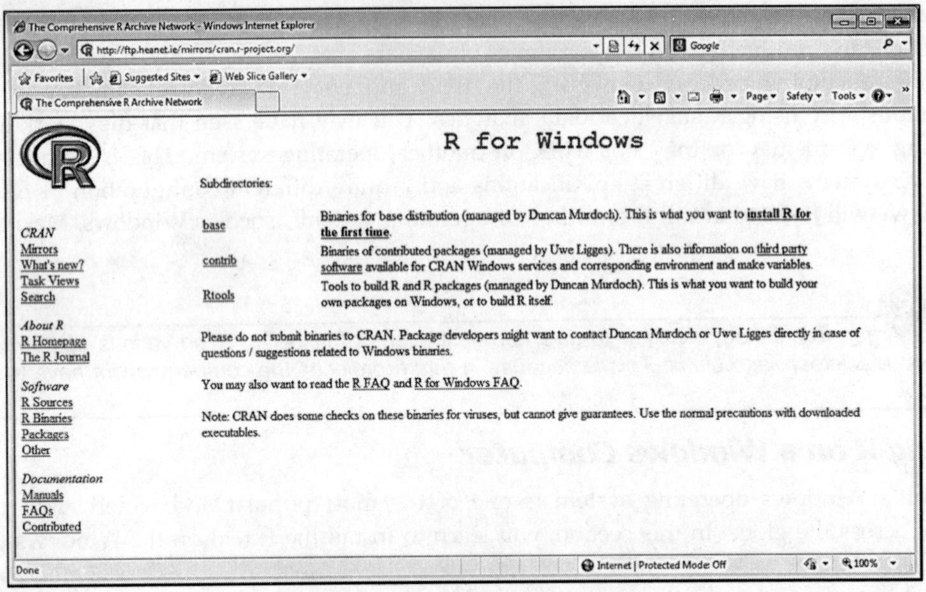

Figure 19.5: The R for Windows Page

3. Click the `install R for the first time` link (Figure 19.5). The R-3.1.2 for Windows (32/64 bit) page appears, as shown in Figure 19.6:

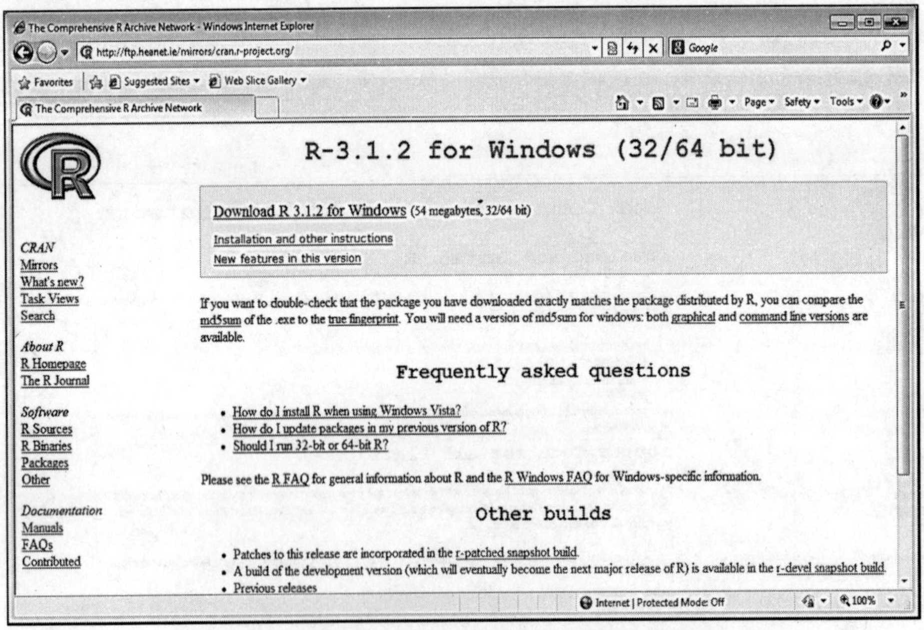

Figure 19.6: The R-3.1.2 for Windows (32/64 bit) Page

4. Click the `Download R 3.1.2 for Windows` link (Figure 19.6).
5. Save and run the setup file of R on your system. A dialog box appears, asking you to select a language, as shown in Figure 19.7:

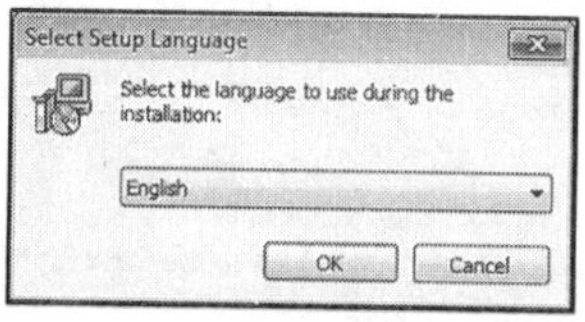

Figure 19.7: Select Setup Language Dialog Box

6. Select English as the language and click the OK button (Figure 19.7). The R Setup wizard appears, as shown in Figure 19.8:

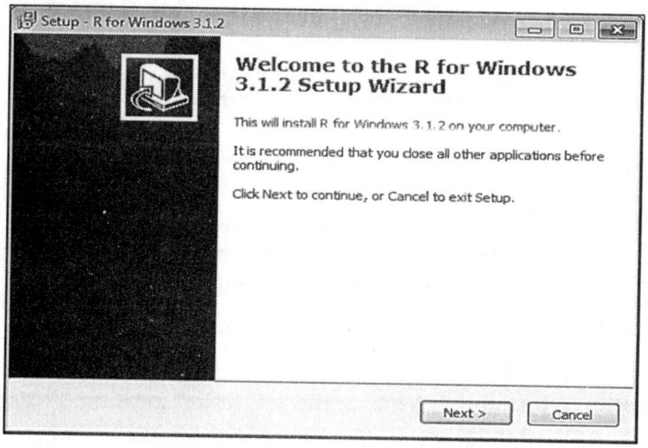

Figure 19.8: The R Setup Wizard

7. Click the Next button on the R Setup wizard. The next page of the R Setup wizard appears, as shown in Figure 19.9:

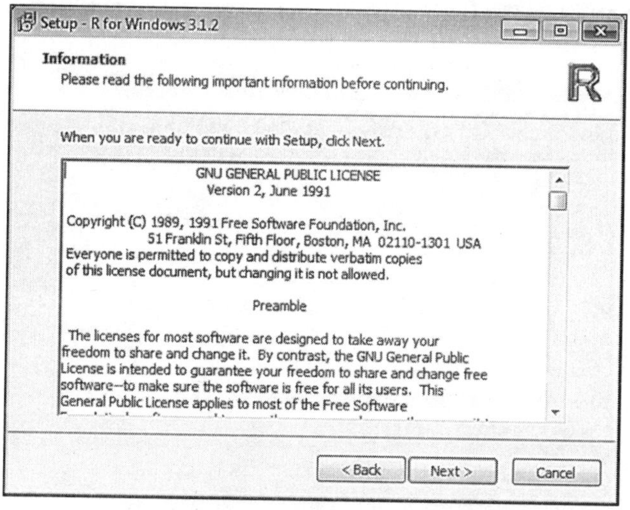

Figure 19.9: The Information Page

8. Click the Next button (Figure 19.9) to go to the Select Destination Location page of the wizard, as shown in Figure 19.10:

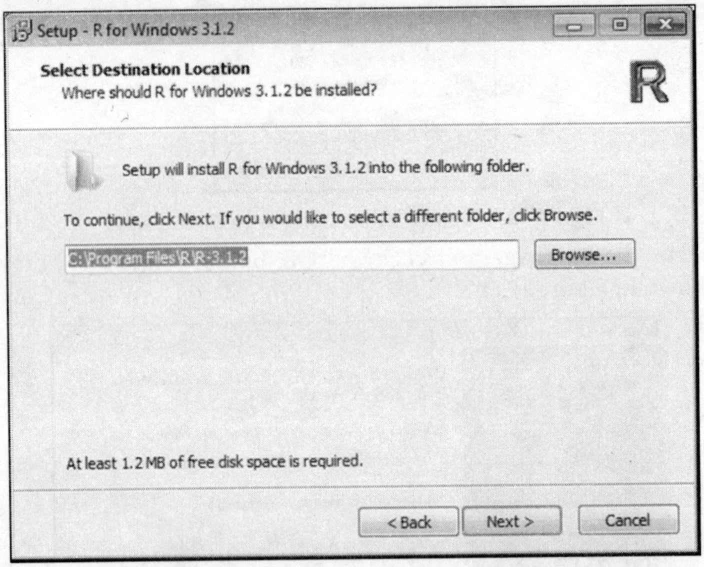

Figure 19.10: The Select Destination Location Page

The Select Destination Location page shows the default location as `C:\Program Files` for installing R on your computer.

9. Click the Next button to install the R tool at the suggested location. Please note that you can also change the location to store the R setup at a different location on your computer.

   The Select Components page appears, as shown in Figure 19.11:

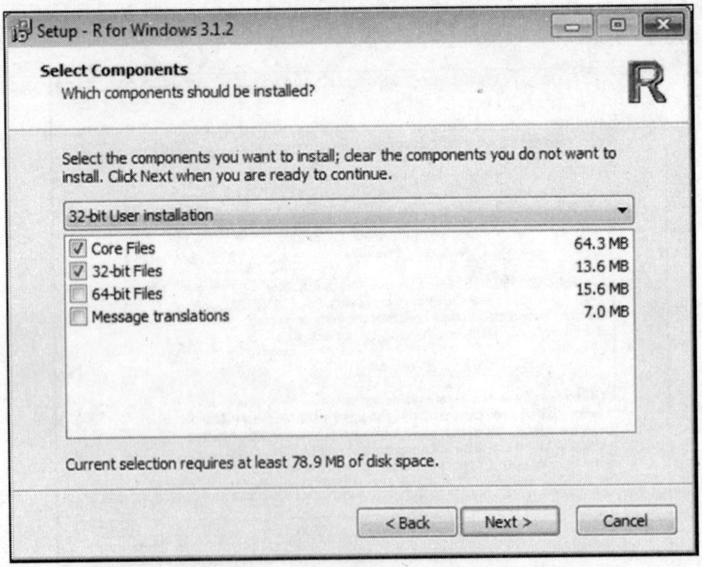

Figure 19.11: The Select Components Page

10. Click the Next button (Figure 19.11). The Startup options page appears, asking whether you want to customize the startup options, as shown in Figure 19.12:

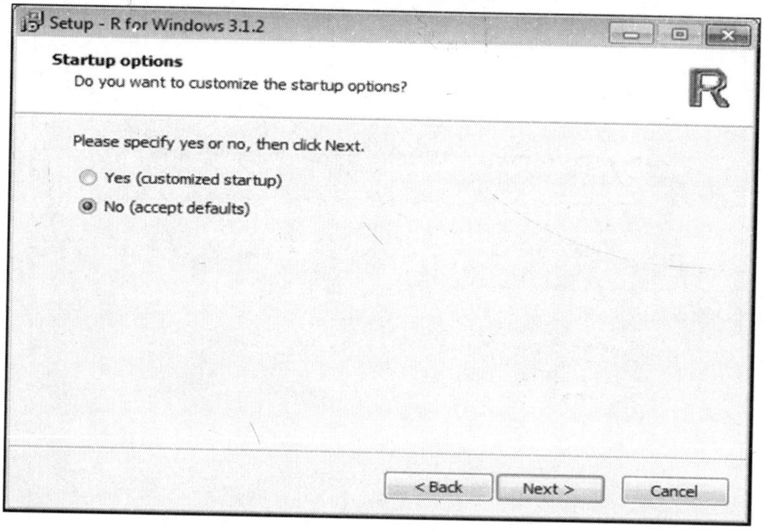

Figure 19.12: The Startup options Page

11. Click the Next button, as in this case, we are going with the default settings (Figure 19.12). The Select Start Menu Folder page of the R Setup wizard appears, as shown in Figure 19.13:

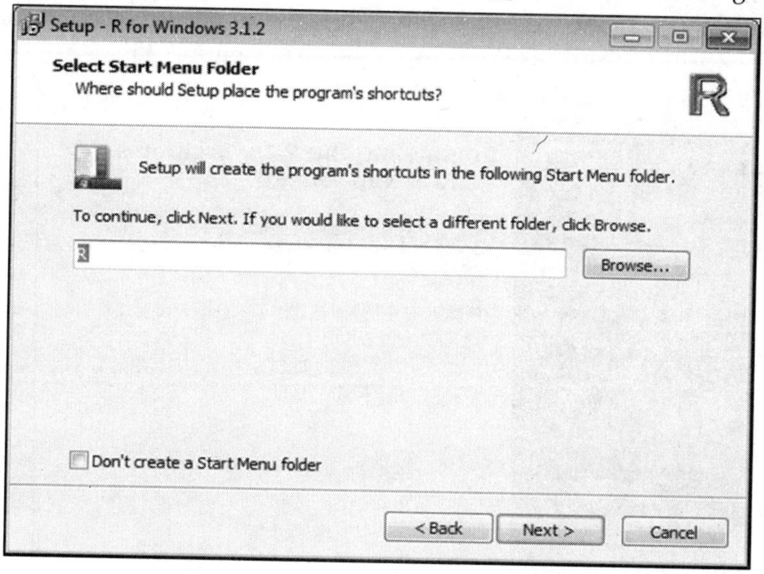

Figure 19.13: The Select Start Menu Folder Page

12. Click the Next button (Figure 19.13) to move to the Select Additional Tasks page of the wizard, as shown in Figure 19.14:

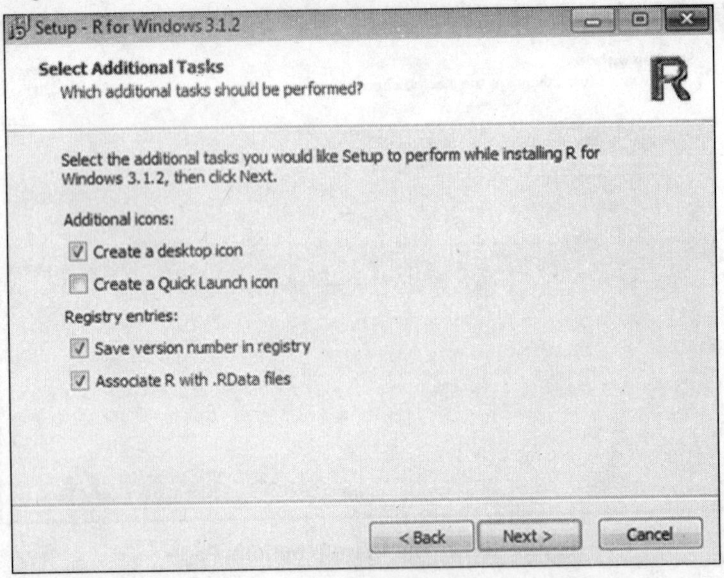

Figure 19.14: The Select Additional Tasks Page

13. Click the Next button on the Select Additional Tasks page. The installation of R starts. It will take a few minutes. When the installation process is completed, the Completing the R for Windows 3.1.2 Setup Wizard page appears, as shown in Figure 19.15:

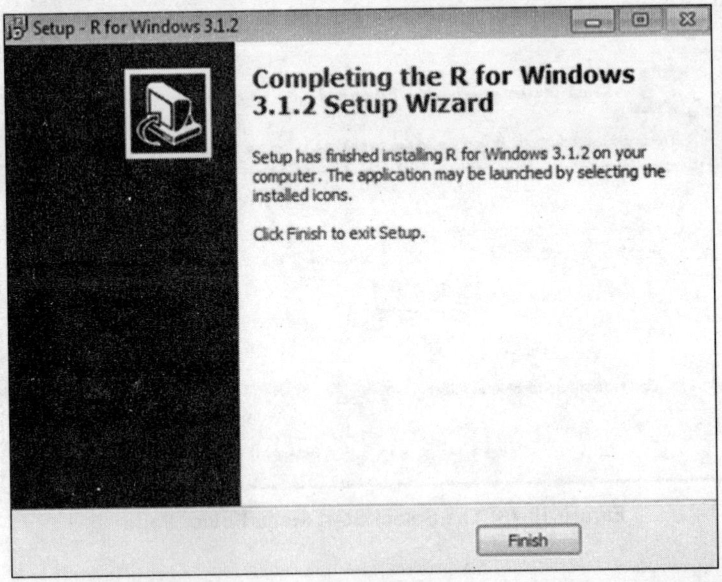

Figure 19.15: The Completing the R for Windows 3.1.2 Setup Wizard Page

14. Click the Finish button to exit the R Setup wizard. This completes the installation of R on the Windows operating system.

Installing R on a Macintosh Computer

The Macintosh operating system does not support the Windows file extension, .exe. This means that to work with R in a Macintosh, we need to download and install the Macintosh-supported R file on the system. In this section, you will learn the steps to download and install R on a Macintosh system.

To install R on the Macintosh operating system, perform the following steps:

1. Download the R file that can be installed on a Macintosh operating system from the following official website of R:

   http://ftp.iitm.ac.in/cran/

2. Click the `Download R for (Mac) OS X` link.
3. Click the link for the latest version of R (`R x.x.x.pkg`). You will be directed to a Web page, namely R for Mac OS X.
4. Click the setup file to install the R tool on your system, as shown in Figure 19.16:

Figure 19.16: Start Setup Dialog Box

The Introduction dialog box appears on the screen, as shown in Figure 19.17:

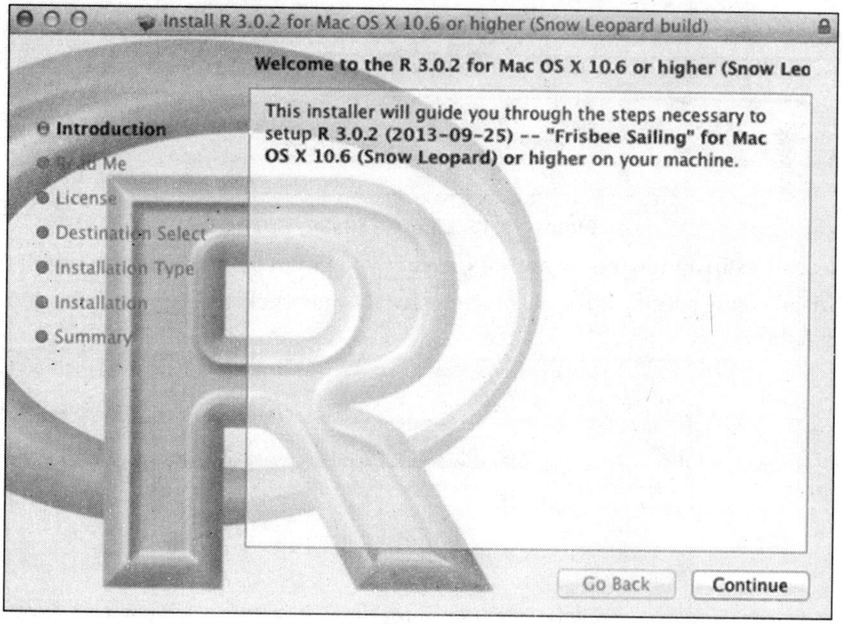

Figure 19.17: Introduction Dialog Box

5. Click the Continue button (Figure 19.17). The Read Me dialog box appears on the screen, as shown in Figure 19.18:

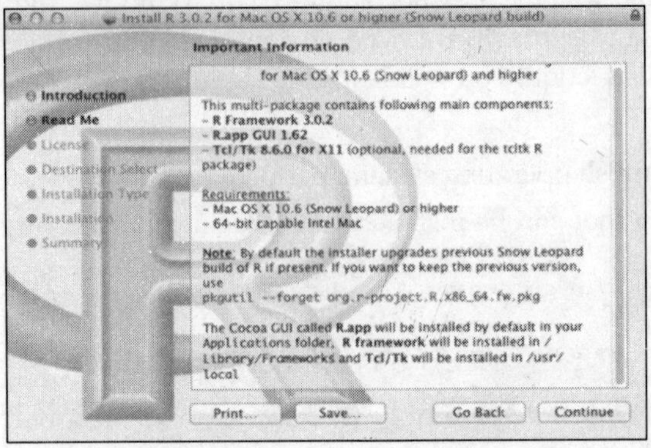

Figure 19.18: Read Me Dialog Box

6. Click the Continue button two more times, and a pop-up box containing the license agreement terms appears, asking you to accept the license agreements, as shown in Figure 19.19:
7. Click the Agree button, as shown in Figure 19.19:

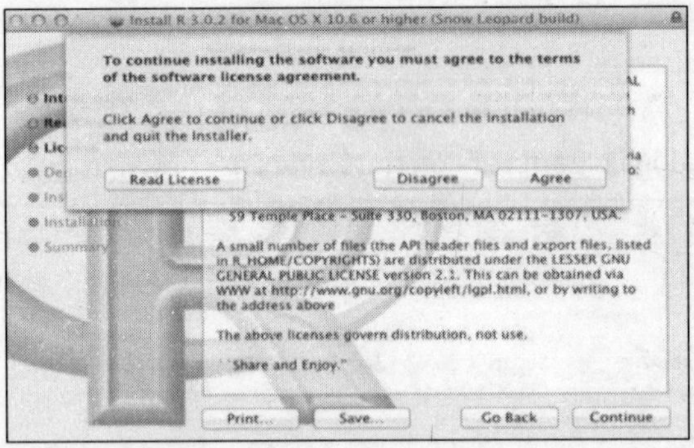

Figure 19.19: License Dialog Box

The Select a Destination window appears, asking you how you would like to install this software.

8. Select Install on a specific disk → Macintosh HD and click the Continue button, as shown in Figure 19.20:

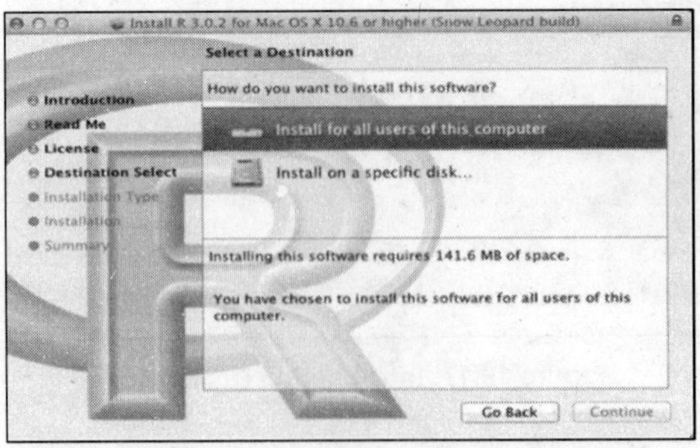

Figure 19.20: The Select a Destination Window

The Standard Install on "Macintosh HD" window appears, as shown in Figure 19.21:

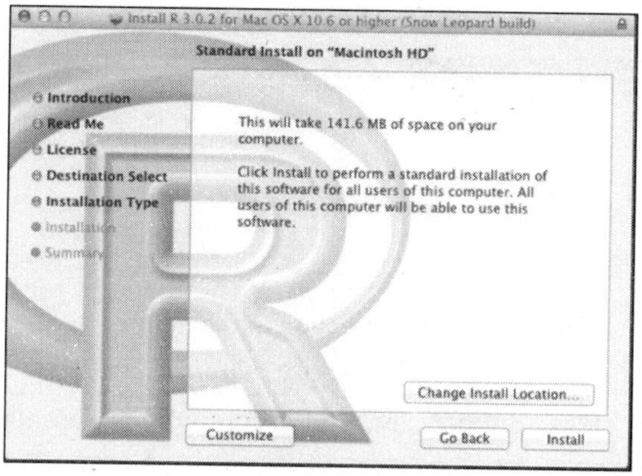

Figure 19.21: Standard Install on "Macintosh HD" Window

9. Click the Install button on the Standard Install on "Macintosh HD" window (Figure 19.21). The installation process takes a few minutes to complete, and the installation was completed successfully window appears, showing the summary of installation.
10. Click the Close button to exit the R setup, as shown in Figure 19.22:

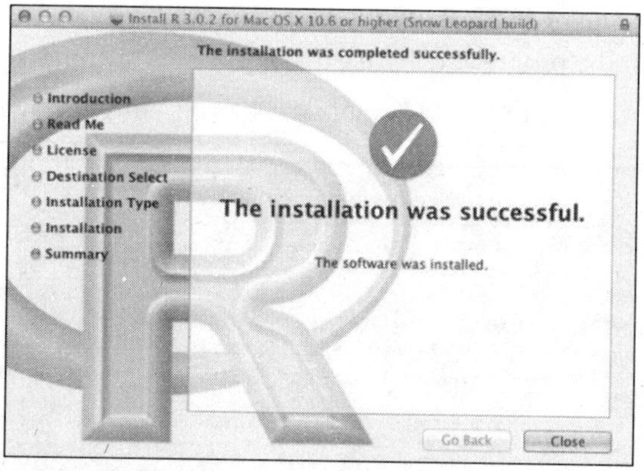

Figure 19.22: The installation was completed successfully Window

Installing R on a Linux Computer

The Linux operating system is considered one of the most secure operating systems in the world. As Linux operates on a different file system, you need to download the R file that can be installed on Linux computers.

In this section, you will learn to download and install the R file on the Linux operating system.

Downloading the Linux-supported R file for installation is a prerequisite for installing R on a Linux system. The download steps are given as follows:

1. Open the official website of R: *http://ftp.iitm.ac.in/cran/*.
2. Download R by clicking the link `R-x.x.x.tar.gz` (`x.x.x` refers to the version of R) and save the `.tar.gz` file on your computer.

3. Type `tar -xzf R-x.x.x.tar.gz` at the command prompt. Then, enter `cd R-x.x.x`, as shown in Figure 19.23:

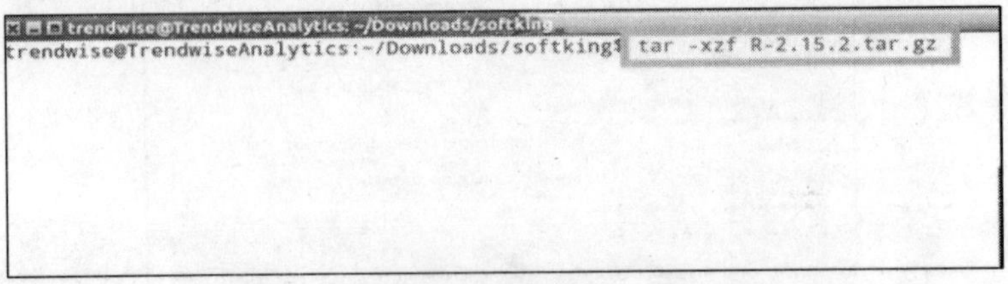

Figure 19.23: Extraction of the .tar.gz File

The program will be extracted to a subdirectory named `R-x.x.x`.

4. Type `./configure` at the command prompt to configure the program to run on your operating system, as shown in Figure 19.24:

Figure 19.24: Configuration of R into the System

The configuration of the program will take a few minutes to complete.

5. Type `make` at the command prompt to compile the program, as shown in Figure 19.25:

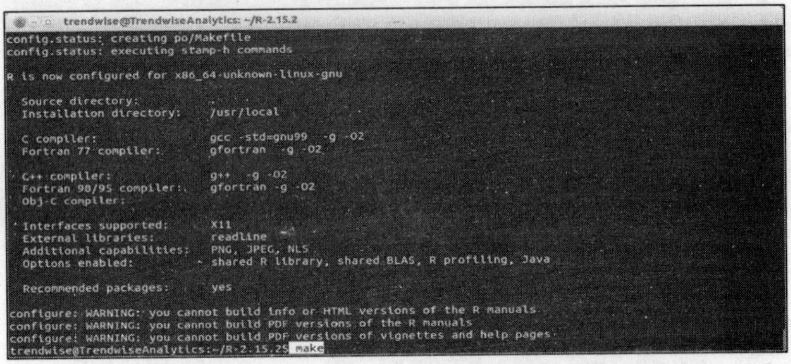

Figure 19.25: R Setup Compilation Window

6. Type `make install` at the command prompt to install the program on your computer, as shown in Figure 19.26:

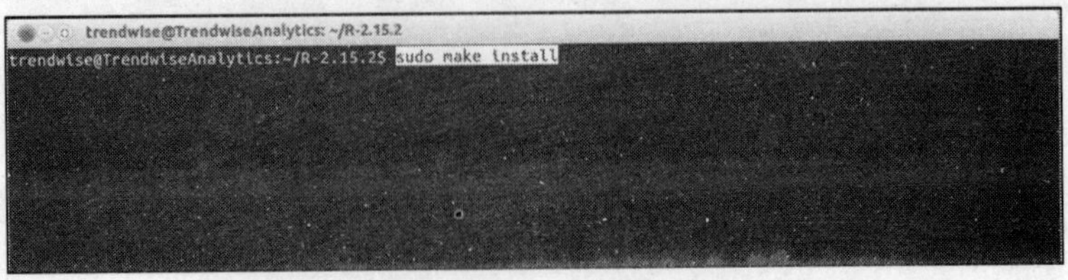

Figure 19.26: R Setup Installation Window

The program will be installed and stored at the `/bin` or `/usr/bin` location.

After the completion of the installation process, the terminal window appears, as shown in Figure 19.27:

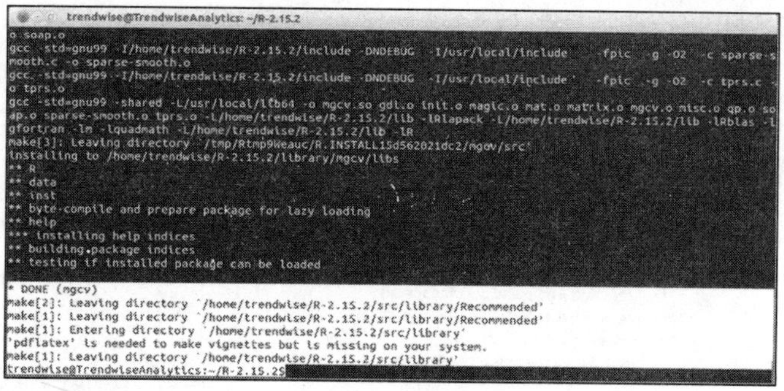

Figure 19.27: Terminal Window after the Completion of the Installation

Installing RStudio

In this section, you will learn to install RStudio, a complete package for working with R, on a Windows system. The RStudio IDE offers an efficient and versatile user interface for R. It is available as free and open source software, and can be used with Windows and Linux.

SCENARIO

After installing R on different platforms, Smith gives a presentation on installing RStudio on the Windows and Linux operating systems.

Installing RStudio on Windows

Before starting the lab, you need to download RStudio from the official website of R.

Perform the following steps to install RStudio on the Windows operating system:

1. Download RStudio for the Windows system from the following official website:

   http://www.rstudio.com/products/rstudio/

   The RStudio IDE window appears, as shown in Figure 19.28:

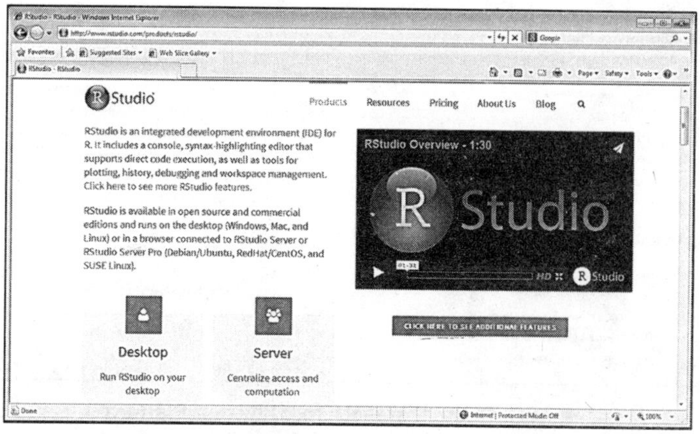

Figure 19.28: Showing the RStudio IDE Window

2. Click the Desktop button (Figure 19.28). A Web page appears that provides an overview of the RStudio Desktop IDE, as shown in Figure 19.29:

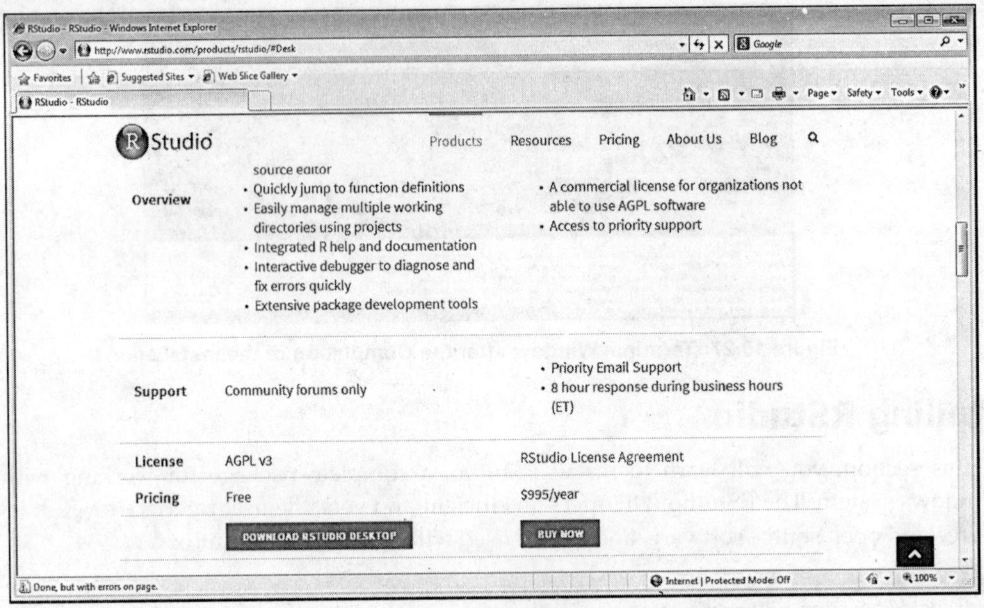

Figure 19.29: Overview of the RStudio Desktop IDE

3. Click the DOWNLOAD RSTUDIO DESKTOP (Figure 19.29) button. The Web page appears with the installer files for different platforms, as shown in Figure 19.30:

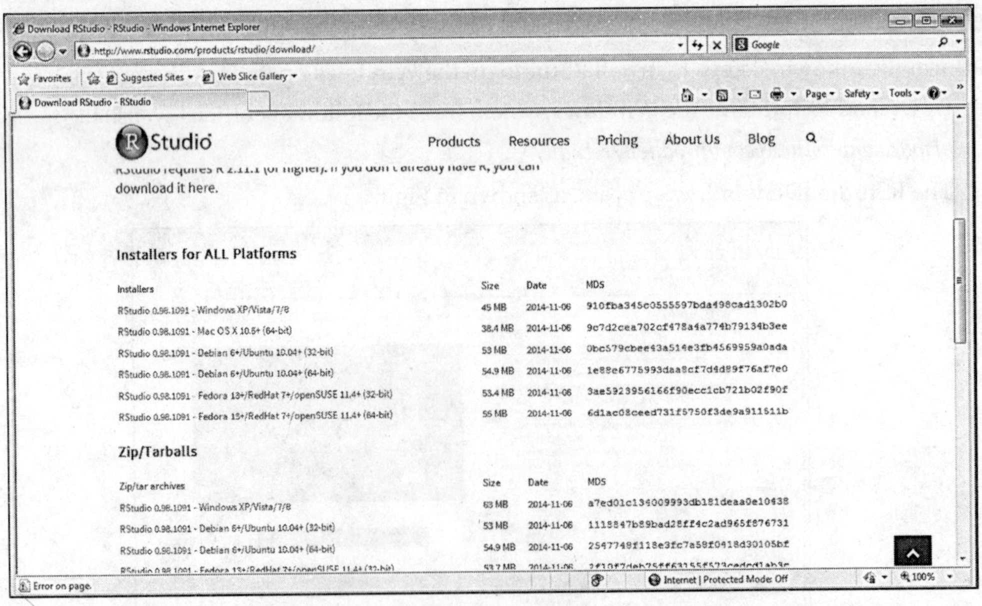

Figure 19.30: Installers for Different Platforms

4. Click the `RStudio 0.98.1091 - Windows XP/Vista/7/8` link and save the `RStudio-0.98.1091.exe` file for RStudio setup on your Windows computer.
5. Run the `RStudio-0.98.1091.exe` file. The RStudio Setup wizard appears, as shown in Figure 19.31:

Figure 19.31: RStudio Setup Wizard

6. Click the Next button (Figure 19.31). The Choose Install Location page of the wizard appears, as shown in Figure 19.32:

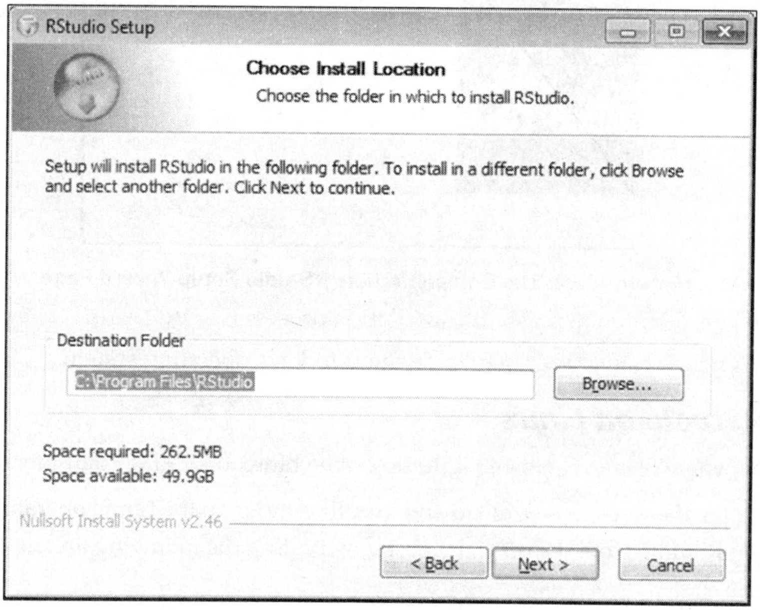

Figure 19.32: The Choose Install Location Page

7. Click the Next button without changing the default installation location (Figure 19.32). The Choose Start Menu Folder page appears, as shown in Figure 19.33:

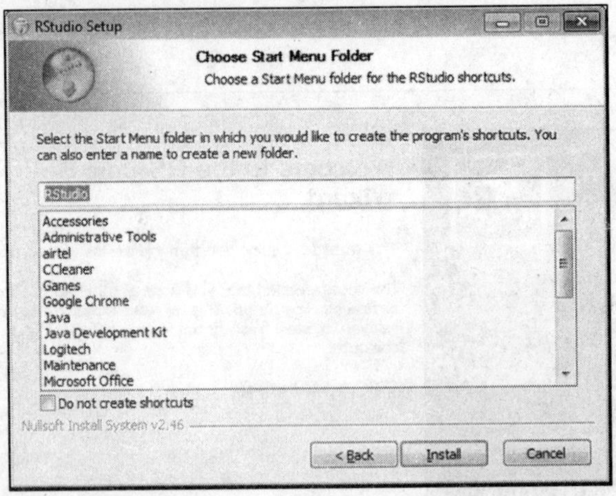

Figure 19.33: The Choose Start Menu Folder Page

8. Click the Install button to install RStudio (Figure 19.33). The installation process begins. After the installation, the Completing the RStudio Setup Wizard page appears, as shown in Figure 19.34:

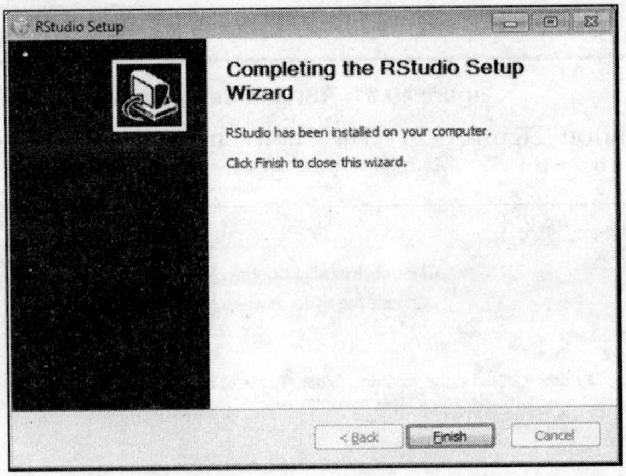

Figure 19.34: The Completing the RStudio Setup Wizard Page

9. Click the Finish button to finish the installation process (Figure 19.34).

   RStudio is now installed successfully on the Windows operating system.

Installing RStudio on Linux

In this section, you will learn to install RStudio on the Linux operating computer.

The following are the steps to download and install RStudio on the Linux operating system:

1. Download RStudio from the official website by pasting the following link in your Web browser:

   http://www.rstudio.com/products/rstudio/

   The RStudio IDE window appears (Figure 19.28).

2. Click the Desktop button (Figure 19.28). A Web page appears that provides an overview of the RStudio Desktop IDE (Figure 19.29).
3. Click the DOWNLOAD RSTUDIO DESKTOP (Figure 19.29) button. The Web page appears with the installer files for different platforms (Figure 19.30).
4. Click the `RStudio 0.98.1091 - Debian 6+/Ubuntu 10.04+ (32-bit)` link and save the `rstudio-0.98.1091-i386.deb` file for RStudio setup on your Ubuntu computer.
5. Right-click the `.deb` file and select the Open with Ubuntu Software center option to install RStudio, as shown in Figure 19.35:

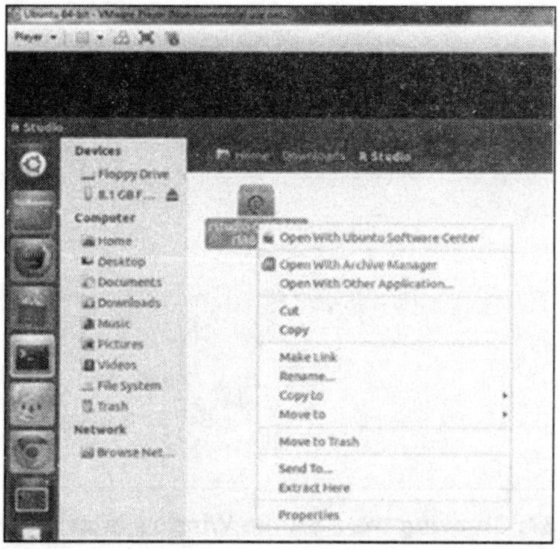

Figure 19.35: Starting the Installation of RStudio

The Ubuntu Software Center window appears, as shown in Figure 19.36:

Figure 19.36: Initiating the Installation of RStudio

After the installation is complete, the RStudio window appears, as shown in Figure 19.37:

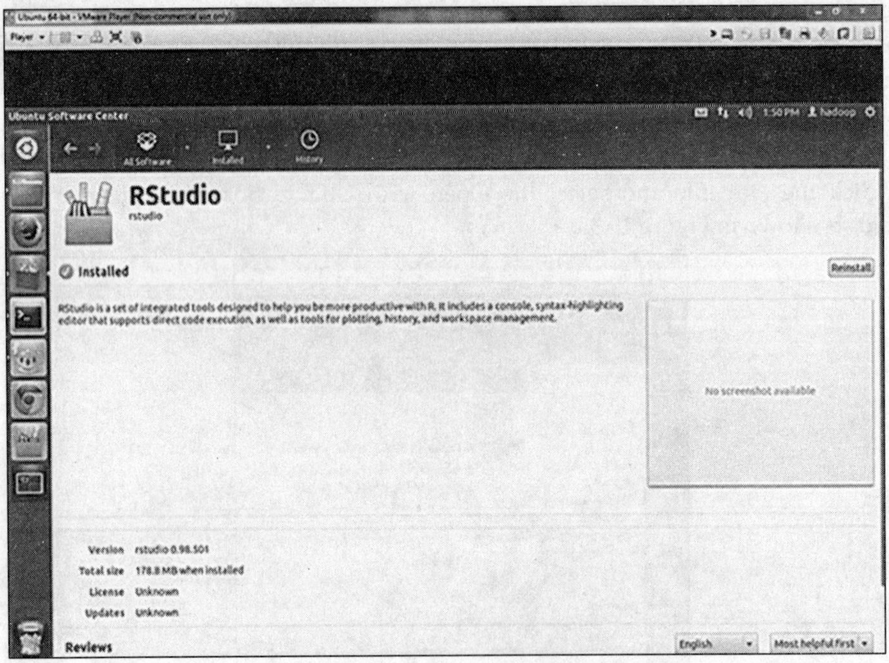

Figure 19.37: Showing the RStudio Window after Installation

RStudio is now successfully installed on the Linux OS.

Summary

In this chapter, you learned about analytical approaches and the evolution of analytical tools. You learned about ensemble methods that combine the results of multiple models to get the best results. You also learned about text data analysis, which has become an essential part of Big Data analytics. Next, you learned about the evolution of various analytical tools, such as graphical user interface, point solutions, and data visualization tools. Tools like IBM SPSS and SAS were also discussed in detail. The chapter also compared different analytical tools. Towards the end, you learned to install R and RStudio on different types of operating systems.

Quick Revise

Multiple-Choice Questions

Q1. Which of the following statements is correct for R?

a. R cannot connect with other languages.

b. R does not support extensions.

c. R is more object-oriented than many other analytical tool sets.

d. R is not compatible with multiple formats.

Ans. The correct option is c.

Q2. Which of the following is a commercial text analysis tool?

a. Tableau
b. Clarabridge
c. JMP
d. Spotfire

Ans. The correct option is b.

Q3. Which of the following analytical tools is mostly used in social sciences, marketing, and healthcare?

a. R
b. SPSS
c. JMP
d. Spotfire

Ans. The correct option is b.

Q4. Which of the following is a data visualization tool?

a. Attensity
b. Advizor
c. Clarabridge
d. SAS

Ans. The correct option is b.

Q5. Which of the following is a limitation of a graphical user interface?

a. Code created through a user interface generates unintended code quickly.
b. Code created through a user interface increases the complexity of the code.
c. Code created through a user interface is difficult to understand.
d. Code created through a user interface is mostly incorrect.

Ans. The correct option is a.

Q6. Kent, a data analyst with Mara Mia Consultancy, has been asked to analyze clients' requirements and propose an appropriate solution. One of the clients is a telecommunication company that wants to increase customer satisfaction. Which feature of SAS would be best suited for this client?

a. The company can use the SAS optimization feature.
b. The company can use the SAS quality improvement feature.
c. The company can use the SAS data visualization feature.
d. The company can use the SAS forecasting feature.

Ans. The correct option is b.

Q7. Scott is a data analyst at Apex Widgets—a leading manufacturer of widgets. He wants to compare the sales in two regions to prepare a report suggesting ways to increase sales. For this, Scott runs the core Business Intelligence (BI) report to check the sales and average income of each region for the previous quarter. To perform the analysis, he uses the SAS tool and finds that the profit margin of one region is better than that of the other. Now, two scenarios can appear:

- **In the first scenario, one region beats the other.**
- **In the second scenario, sales and profit difference can be coincidental in some quarters.**

Which of the following features of the SAS tool can help Scott make the final analysis?

a. Graphical Outputs
b. SAS DI
c. Statistics
d. Quality improvement

Ans. The correct option is c.

Q8. Angle Medicare Solutions is a service provider for various industries, and it collects thousands of reviews every day. The company also observes that it gets several fake reviews from many review sites. Which of the following tools should Angle Medicare Solutions use to manage this huge amount of unstructured data?

a. SAS b. SPSS
c. R d. Clarabridge

Ans. The correct option is d.

Q9. Jacob, a financial manager, wants to collect data from several associates in different formats. He wants to collate the data and prepare reports in various formats, including PDF and Excel files. Which of the following tools should Jacob use?

a. SPSS b. SAS
c. Tableau d. Any of the above

Ans. The correct option is d.

Q10. Imagine you have the sales data of the past six months of a product. Which of the following analytical tools would you use to predict the sales of the product in the next year?

a. Tableau b. SPSS
c. JMP d. Spotfire

Ans. The correct option is b.

Q11. A sports goods manufacturing company wants to analyze the reorder and inventory levels of its manufactured goods. Which of the following features of SPSS can help the organization to perform this analysis?

a. Statistical b. Data Manipulation
c. Data Visualization d. Forecasting

Ans. The correct option is a.

Q12. Kent, a data analyst with Mara Mia consultancy, has been asked to analyze clients' requirements and propose an appropriate solution. One of the clients is a mobile manufacturing company that wants to allocate its resources more appropriately. Which feature of SAS would be best suited for this client?

a. SAS optimization feature b. SAS quality improvement feature
c. SAS data visualization feature d. SAS forecasting feature

Ans. The correct option is a.

Subjective Questions

Q1. Give some examples of ensemble algorithms.

Ans. The following are some examples of different ensemble algorithms:

- **Bagging**—Bagging stands for bootstrap aggregating and refers to an ensemble algorithm wherein the following process is followed:
  - Individual models on random samples of the same data size are developed.

- A classification or regression tree is applied to each sample.
- Finally, an average of the predictions obtained from different methods or votes on the classification of an observation is made to obtain the final predictions or classifications.

- **Boosting**—Boosting is another ensemble algorithm that generates multiple models and obtains weights to merge the predictions from these models into a single predicted classification.
- **Random forests**—Random forest is a data mining algorithm wherein random samples of data are generated, multiple decision trees are constructed, and a random subset of inputs called predictors are evaluated for each tree.

Q2. Define text data analysis.

Ans. The processing and modeling of textual data to gain useful business insights is called text data analysis. An essential part of text data analysis is text mining, which involves obtaining meaningful and high-quality information from textual data.

This high-quality information is derived by finding relationships and useful business patterns and trends from a massive collection of text.

As the name suggests, text data analysis takes text as input. This text can be an e-mail, medical dictation, or even text that can be scanned from a hard copy and converted into electronic form.

Q3. List some precautions that financial organizations should take to guard themselves against fraudulent practices.

Ans. Financial organizations usually take the following precautions to guard themselves against fraudulent practices:

- Record the information, such as contact number of customer, e-mail address, user name, password, and address found on an online purchase order form.
- Determine the IP addresses of customers from the mails sent or received by them.
- Perform research on the e-mail address and the attached domain, identify that it is a real e-mail address or a fake one, identify the domain name and the country to which it belongs.
- Match the IP address, contact number, e-mail address, and address of the customer and determine whether all the information are from the same place or from different places.
- Search the given contact number and check whether it is reported for any kind of abuse or scam on the Internet.

Q4. What are analytic point solutions?

Ans. Analytic point solutions refer to software packages that solve a specific group of problems. Examples of point solutions are price optimization applications, fraud detection applications, and demand forecasting applications. Point solutions based on tool suites, such as SAS, will make use of some generic functionalities of the underlying toolset; however, the user interface will always be used for some specific set of problems.

Implementing a one point solution as a substitute for creating a custom solution for various problems can help organizations save money, effort, and time.

For example, a money-laundering detection application tool used in financial institutions provides some algorithms and business rules to detect suspicious patterns during the transfer of money. The interfaces of such an application are designed to identify suspicious activities and provide additional information, as and when required, to aid an investigation into the case. Such ready-made tools enable organizations to quickly use the tools instead of building a set of processes from scratch.

Q5. List some important features of IBM SPSS.

Ans. IBM SPSS provides the following features:

- SPSS commands are executed one line at a time to update tables and add results to the output editor window. You can also store the executed syntaxes with their times of execution in this window.
- IBM SPSS Statistics can read data from and write to ASCII files, databases, and tables of other statistical software. This tool also helps in providing basic data management functions, such as sorting, aggregation, and table merge.
- IBM SPSS Statistics can send the output directly to a file, instead of the Output Editor window. The file can be in the .txt, .html, or .xml format. Output Management System (OMS) helps in storing the outputs obtained from a large number of iterated calculations in a single file by creating a loop using a macro.
- IBM SPSS Statistics can be installed in different platforms such as Windows, Mac OS X, and Unix.

20

Exploring R

R is a cross-platform programming language as well as a software environment for statistical computing and graphics. Generally, it is used by statisticians and data miners for developing statistical software and doing data analysis. It is also believed that R is an implementation of the S programming language combined with lexical scoping semantics. The S language was created by John Chambers at Bell Labs, while R was created by Ross Ihaka and Robert Gentleman at the University of Auckland, New Zealand. Therefore, the name of R language is derived from the initial letters of the names of its authors. Currently, R language is developed by the R Development Core Team. R is a GNU project, which is freely available under the GNU General Public License and its pre-compiled binary versions are provided for various operating systems. R programs can be compiled and run on a wide variety of UNIX platforms, Windows and MacOS.

In this chapter, you learn about the basic features of R. Next, you will learn how to open and work in RGUI and RStudio. You also learn to perform basic arithmetic functions in R, interact with users, and handle data in R Workspace. Toward the end, you learn to execute scripts, create plots, and use the help and documentation facilities in R.

SCENARIO

Gabriel has joined Argon Technology as a data analyst. He is given the task of analyzing the data of IBIBI bank. He is provided with a dataset containing information about bank account holders and their transactions history. He wants to analyze the data and present the outcome in a pictographic form so that the bank staff can easily interpret the results and use the knowledge gained to provide better facilities to their customers. To perform this task, Gabriel decides to use R as it provides the following features:

- *It is of high quality*
- *It helps you think critically*
- *It is an open source software*
- *It allows automation*
- *It can handle and generate maps*

Exploring Basic Features of R

R is a data analysis and data visualization tool that allows you to represent complex data in the form of charts, plots, and graphs. It provides a variety of statistical and graphical techniques, such as linear and nonlinear modeling, statistical tests, time series analysis, classification, clustering, etc. The functionalities provided by R can be extended by using functions and user-defined packages. There are several GUI editors of R language, out of which RGUI and RStudio are commonly used. To handle R projects, developers use a command line interface as well as several graphical front-ends for it. Some common characteristics of the R language are as follows:

- Effective and powerful data handling and storage facilities
- Arrays and matrices for handling data
- Graphical representation of the analysis

You can install R in your computer system by downloading its software from the official website of R, i.e. *www.r-project.org*.

Figure 20.1 shows the screenshot of this website:

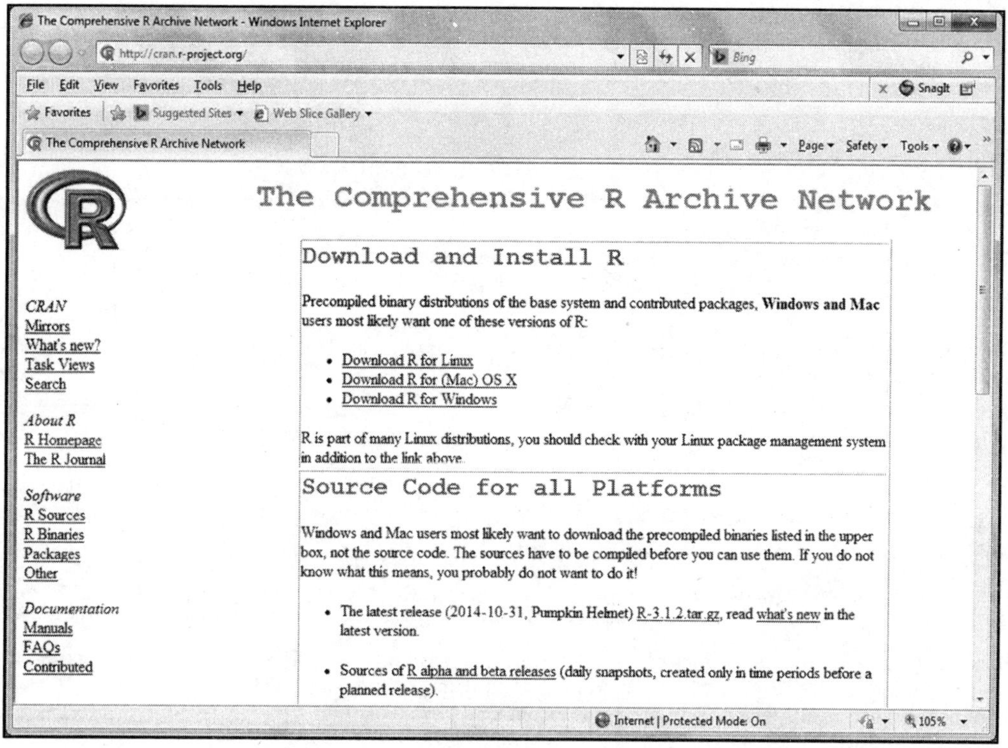

Figure 20.1: Displaying Official Website of R

This website also has general documentation and libraries of routines related to R. You can also get the installation files for many versions of Linux on the R website.

Statistical Features

R provides various statistical and graphical techniques, such as linear and nonlinear modeling, classical statistical tests, time-series analysis, classification, clustering, etc. R can be extended through various predefined and user-defined functions and packages. R language also inherited various features from its parent language, S; therefore, it is a stronger object-oriented programming language than other statistical computing languages.

Any ordinary version of R can generate static graphs and mathematical symbols. However, to generate dynamic and interactive graphics, you have to install additional packages.

Programming Features

R is an interpreted language, so it uses a command line interpreter for execution of commands. Figure 20.2 shows the programming features of the R language:

- R supports matrix arithmetic.
- R includes data structures like scalars, vectors, matrices, data frames, and lists.
- R provides an extensible object system, which includes the objects for regression models, time series, and geo-spatial coordinates.
- R provides support for procedural programming with functions, and supports object-oriented programming with generic functions.
- R language can also be used with several other scripting languages such as Python, Perl, Ruby, F#, and Julia.
- Some popular text editors and integrated development environments (IDEs) that support R programming development are: ConTEXT, Eclipse (StatET), Emacs (Emacs Speaks Statistics), Vim, jEdit, Kate, RStudio, WinEdt (R Package RWinEdt), Tinn-R, and Notepad++.

Figure 20.2: Programming Features of the R Language

NOTE

The operation of a generic function depends on the type of arguments passed in it. An example of a generic function in R is print() function. This function can print any type of object in R with the use of "print(objectname)" syntax.

Packages

A package is a collection of functions and datasets. To access the contents of a package, you have to load it first. The R language provides two types of packages, standard (or called base packages) and contributed packages (user-defined packages). Standard packages are considered as an in-built part of the R source code. These packages consist of basic functions that allow R to work, and the datasets and standard statistical and graphical functions. On the other hand, contributed packages are written by different users as they are user-defined. These packages are developed primarily in R, and sometimes in Java, C, C++, or FORTRAN. They consist of specialized statistical methods that can access data as well as hardware for processing. Some of the recommended packages are automatically available with every binary distribution of R, while others can be downloaded from the CRAN website (*http://CRAN.R-project.org/*) and its mirrors. The "Task Views" page on the CRAN website provides a list of fields for which contributed packages are available. Some examples of these fields are: Finance, Genetics, High Performance Computing, Machine Learning, Medical Imaging, Social Sciences, and Spatial Statistics.

Graphical User Interfaces

There are several GUI editors in the R language. Some of them are as follows:

- **RGUI**—Specifies a tool with the pre-compiled version of R for Microsoft Windows.
- **RStudio**—Specifies a cross-platform and open source IDE for R programming development.
- **Deducer**—Specifies a GUI tool for menu-driven data analysis.
- **RKWard**—Specifies an extensible GUI and IDE for R.
- **RWeka**—Specifies a tool for using data mining capabilities in Weka and statistical analysis in R.
- **Eclipse StatET**—Specifies a powerful IDE containing R add-in, called StatET. It is generally preferred for large-scale software development projects.
- **Emacs Speaks Statistics**—Specifies a combination of text and code editor, which is widely used on the Linux and Windows platforms. This tool has a statistics add-in, called Emacs Speaks Statistics (ESS), which is popular for providing keyboard shortcuts for almost every command.

From the above-mentioned editors, RGUI and RStudio are the most popular and commonly used ones. Let's explore these editors in detail.

Exploring RGUI

RGUI stands for R Graphical User Interface. You can download and install it from the official website of R, *www.r-project.org*. After installation, you see the and icons on your system's desktop and in the Programs menu. Open the editor window of RGUI by navigating the following path:

Start→All Programs→R→ R i386 3.1.2 or R x64 3.1.2

Figure 20.3 shows how to open RGUI on Windows:

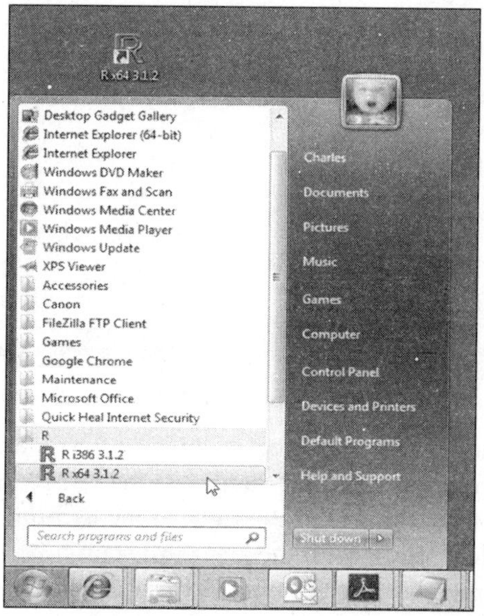

Figure 20.3: Opening RGUI

NOTE

You can select either R i386 3.1.2 or R x64 3.1.2 option according to your computer system type.

The main window of the RGUI editor is R console.

R Console

When you open the R Console window, it displays some basic information about R, such as the version of R, its release date, its licensing conditions, etc. Figure 20.4 shows a newly opened R Console window:

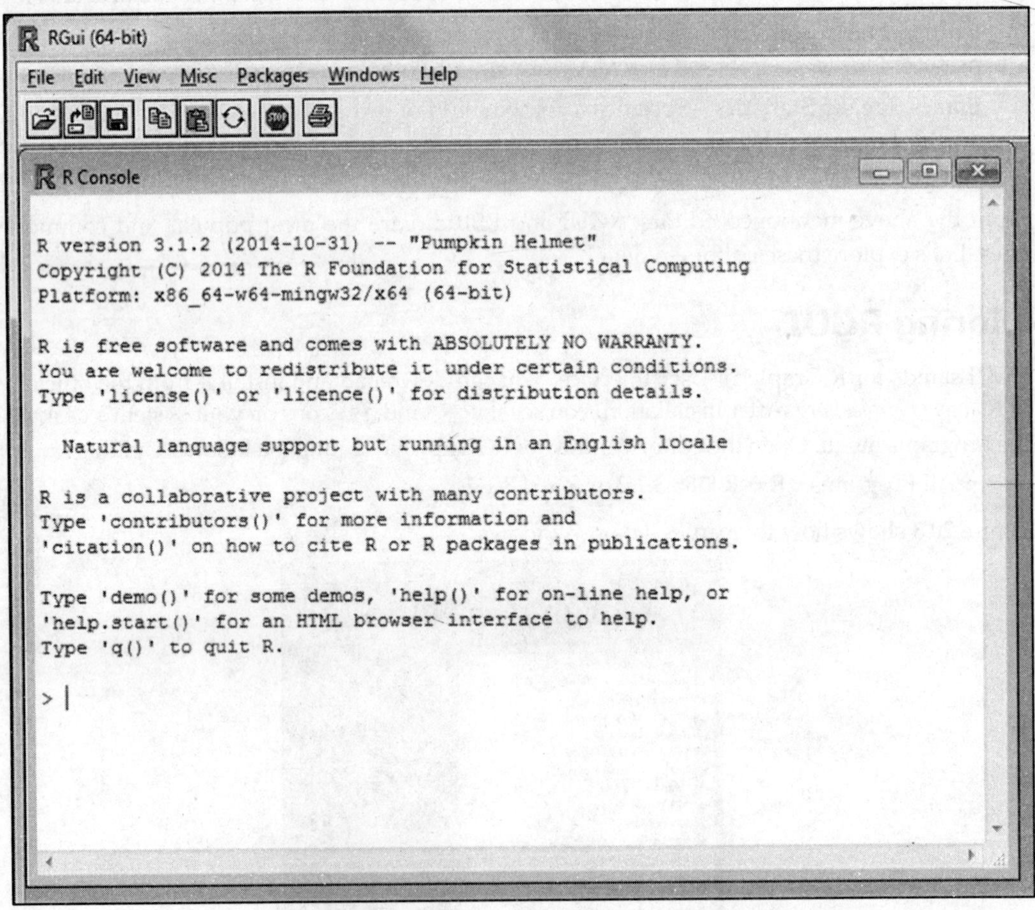

Figure 20.4: Displaying R Console Window

In Figure 20.4, you can notice a `'>'` symbol below the information. This is called the R prompt, which allows users to write commands and then press the `ENTER` key to execute the command. Also, note that a blinking cursor is available to the right of the R prompt for writing the command. You can also handle the console window with the keyboard shortcuts. To view the information related to the handling of console through keyboard, type Help→Console. The output is shown in Figure 20.5:

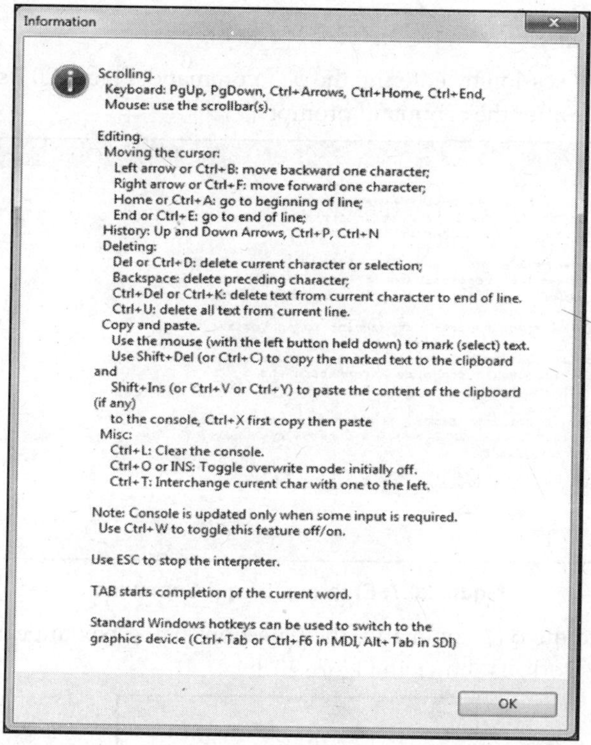

Figure 20.5: Console Handling through Keyboard Information

Developing a Program

Let's now learn to write a simple program in R. In this program, we are using the `print()` function to display "Hello world" in the R Console window, as shown in Figure 20.6:

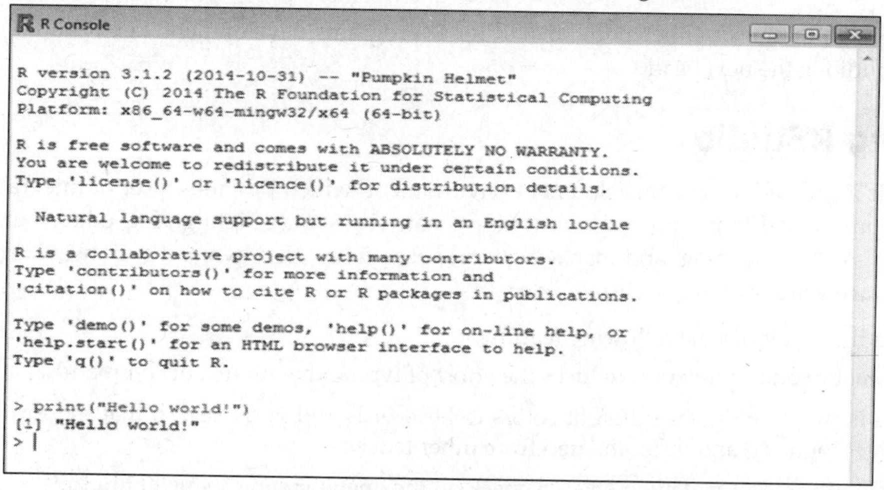

Figure 20.6: Using Print Command to Display Hello World Message

In Figure 20.6, you can see that the code begins with the > symbol, and the output line begins with `[1]`.

Quitting R

You can quit an active R session by entering the `q()` command. Figure 20.7 shows the use of the `q()` command in the console after the command prompt `(>)`:

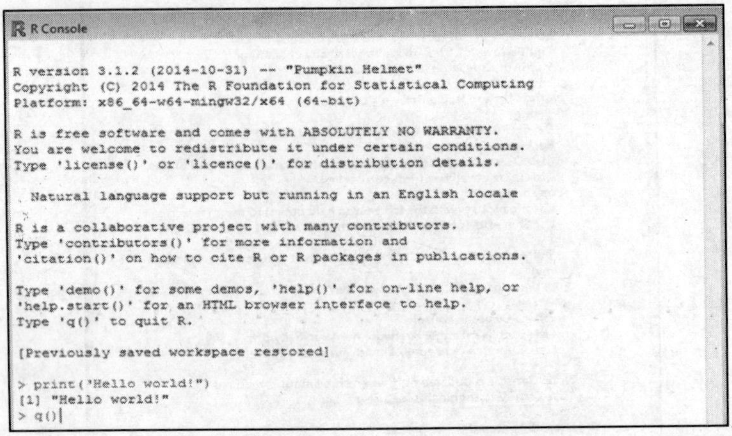

Figure 20.7: Entering the q () Command

Whenever you execute the `q()` command, the Question dialog box appears asking whether or not you wish to save your work, as shown in Figure 20.8:

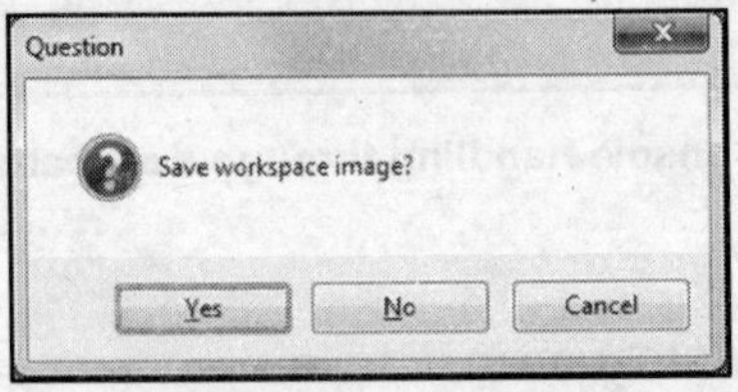

Figure 20.8: Displaying the Question Dialog Box

Besides RGUI, there is another popular IDE for R programs development, i.e., RStudio. Let's learn about RStudio in the next head.

Exploring RStudio

RStudio is a code editor and development environment, which provides a set of integrated tools to develop productive R programs. It provides a console, syntax-highlighting editor, and tools for plotting history, debugging, and managing workspace. You can download and install RStudio from its official website, i.e., *http://www.rstudio.org/*.

RStudio editor provides the following features:

- Automatic code completion reduces the effort of typing the full text of commands.
- Code highlighting gives different colors to keywords and variables, so that these words can be easily recognized and differentiated from other text.
- Automatic bracket matching keeps a check on the opening and closing of brackets.
- Easy access to R Help allows you to understand the role of various functions and other concepts of R.

- Easy exploration of variables, values, functions, packages, etc.

After installation, you can see the RStudio symbol on your desktop and in the Programs menu of Windows. Open the editor window of RStudio by navigating the following path:
Start→All Programs→RStudio→RStudio
Figure 20.9 shows how to open RStudio on Windows:

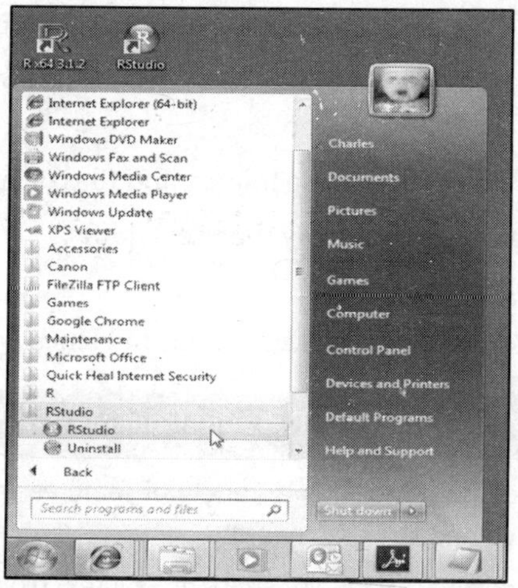

Figure 20.9: Opening RStudio on Windows

The RStudio window opens (Figure 20.10). Select File→New File→ R Script. This action opens four panes in the RStudio window, as shown in Figure 20.10:

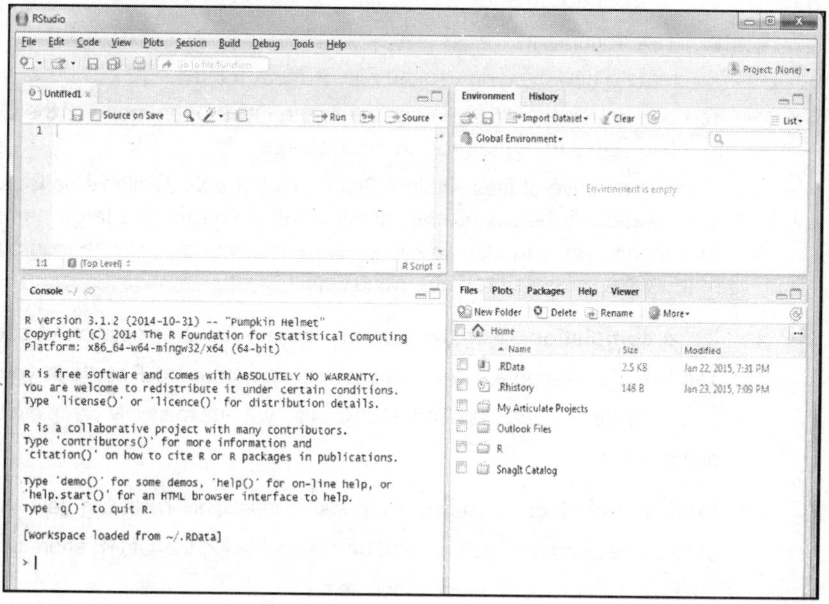

Figure 20.10: Opening RStudio with Different Panes

In Figure 20.10, you see the following panes in the RStudio window:

- **Script pane**—Refers to an editor pane at the top left corner of the RStudio window. This pane is used to edit and save a collection of commands or scripts.
- **Console pane**—Refers to a command pane at the bottom left corner of the RStudio window. In this pane, you can enter commands after the > prompt.
- **Workspace / History pane**—Refers to a pane at the top right corner of the RStudio window. The workspace pane allows you to see the data and values that R has in its memory. You can edit these data or values. The History pane shows what has been typed before.
- **Files, Plots, Package, and Help pane**—Refers to a pane at the bottom right corner of the RStudio window. It gives access to the following tools:
  - **Files**—This tool allows a user to browse folders and files on a computer.
  - **Plots**—This tool allows a user to display the user's plots.
  - **Packages**—This tool allows a user to have a view of all the installed packages.
  - **Help**—This tool allows a user to browse the built-in Help system of R.

EXHIBIT 1: Working in the RStudio Console

The RStudio console includes a variety of features intended to make working with R more productive and straightforward:

- **Managing files**—RStudio supports syntax highlighting and other specialized code-editing features for the following types of files:
  - R scripts
  - Sweave documents
  - TeX documents

  To create a new file, you use the File → New menu.

  To open an existing file, you use either the File→Open menu or the Open Recent menu to select from the recently opened files.

  If you open several files within RStudio, they are all available as tabs to facilitate quick switching between open documents. If you have a large number of open documents, you can also navigate between them using the >> icon on the tab bar or the View → Switch to Tab) menu item.

- **Code completion**—RStudio supports the automatic completion of code using the Tab key. For example, if you have an object named pollResults in your workspace you can type poll and then Tab and RStudio will automatically complete the full name of the object.

- **Find and replace**—RStudio supports finding and replacing text within source documents. Find and replace can be opened using the Ctrl+F shortcut key, or from the Edit → Find and Replace menu item.

- **Extract function**—RStudio can analyze a selection of code from within the source editor and automatically convert it into a re-usable function. Any "free" variables within the selection (objects that are referenced but not created within the selection) are converted into function arguments.
- **Comment/uncomment**—You can comment and uncomment entire selections of code using the Edit → Comment/Uncomment Lines menu item (you can also do this using the Ctrl+/ keyboard shortcut).
- **Indentation**—As you write R code in RStudio, it is automatically indented according to the current indentation options. R code is also re-indented:

  1. Whenever new code is pasted into a source document.
  2. When the Reindent Lines command is invoked.

  Note that RStudio automatic indentation is R syntax-aware and is therefore only used on source files containing R code.
- **Executing code**—RStudio supports the direct execution of code from the source editor.

  To execute the line of source code where the cursor currently resides you press the Ctrl+Enter key (or use the Run toolbar button):

  After executing the line of code, RStudio automatically advances the cursor to the next line. This enables you to single-step through a sequence of lines.
- **Executing multiple lines**—There are three ways to execute multiple lines within the editor:

  - Select the lines and press the Ctrl+Enter key (or use the Run toolbar button).
  - After executing a selection of code, use the Re-Run Previous Region command (or its associated toolbar button) to run the same selection again. Note that changes to the selection including additional, removal, and modification of lines will be reflected in this subsequent run of the selection.
  - To run the entire document, press the Ctrl+Shift+Enter key (or use the Source toolbar button).
- **Source on save**—When editing re-usable functions (as opposed to freestanding lines of R), you may wish to set the Source on Save option for the document (available on the toolbar next to the Save icon). Enabling this option will cause the file to automatically be sourced into the global environment every time it is saved.

  Setting Source on Save ensures that the copy of a function within the global environment is always in sync with its source, and also provides a good way to arrange for frequent syntax checking as you develop a function.
- **Keyboard shortcuts**—Beyond the keyboard shortcuts described above, there is a wide variety of other shortcuts available.

  Some of the more useful ones include:

  - Ctrl+Shift+N — New document
  - Ctrl+O — Open document

- Ctrl+S — Save active document
- Ctrl+1 — Move focus to the Source Editor
- Ctrl+2 — Move focus to the Console

Source: https://support.rstudio.com/hc/en-us/articles/200484448-Editing-and-Executing-Code

Handling Basic Expressions in R

Let's start working in R. Anything that you type on the R Console gets evaluated immediately on pressing the Enter key. Type "Getting Started with R" on the R Console, as shown in Figure 20.11:

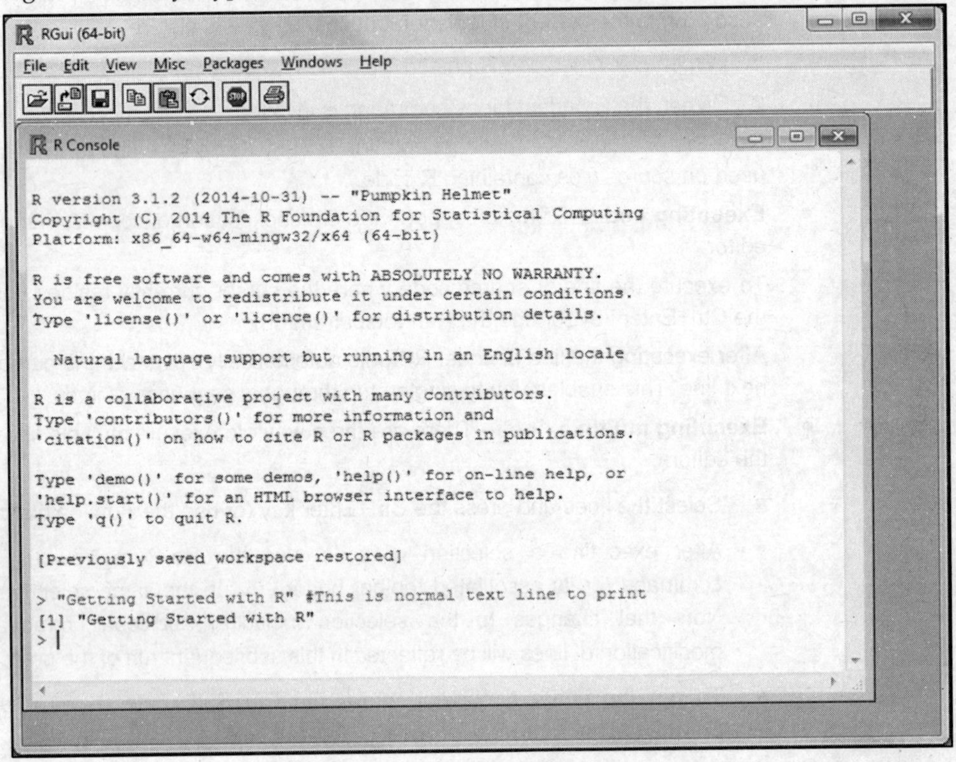

Figure 20.11: Entering a Text in R Console

In Figure 20.11, you can see that all characters after # are treated as comments.

Basic Arithmetic in R

You can use R like a calculator to perform complex mathematical and statistical calculations. For example, you can perform simple arithmetic operations in R by typing the following command:

```
12 + 45 + 9 - 7
```

Enters values for simple mathematical operation

Figure 20.12 shows the result of executing the preceding command in R:

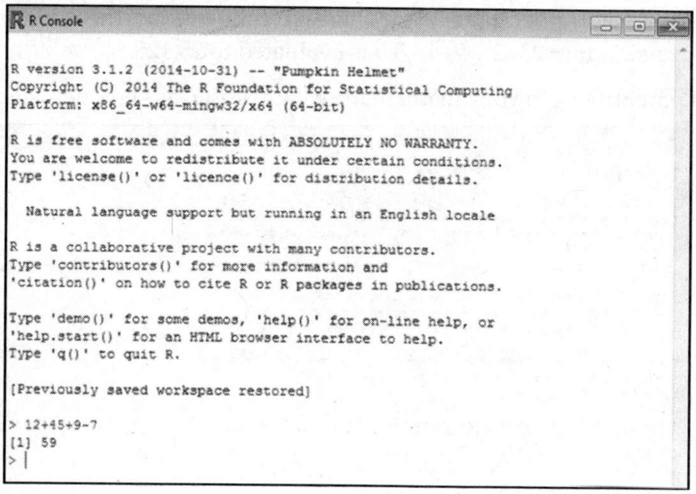

Figure 20.12: Displaying the Result of Simple Mathematical Operators

NOTE

In this chapter, we have used RGUI for R programming.

R executes the 12 + 45 + 9 – 7 expression in the following order:

1. 12 + 45 + 9 = 66
2. 66 – 7 = 59

Now, let's perform some complex calculations in R. Type the following command on R Console:

```
18 + 23/2 -5/4 * 3.5
```

Enters values for complex mathematical operation

Figure 20.13 shows the output of executing the preceding command in R:

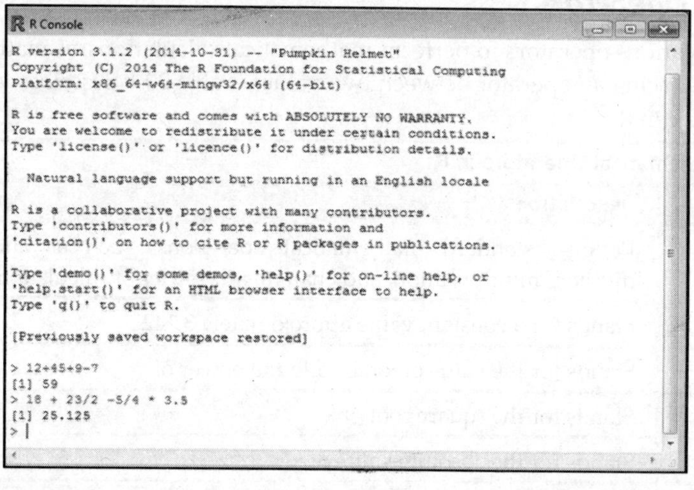

Figure 20.13: Performing Complex Calculation Using Mathematical Operators

To calculate this expression, R follows the standard rules of BODMAS according to which the multiplication and division operations are done first, followed by the additions and subtractions. Therefore, the expression 18 + 23/2 – 5/4 * 3.5 is evaluated to 25.125.

You can also add parentheses to your mathematical expression, as shown in Figure 20.14:

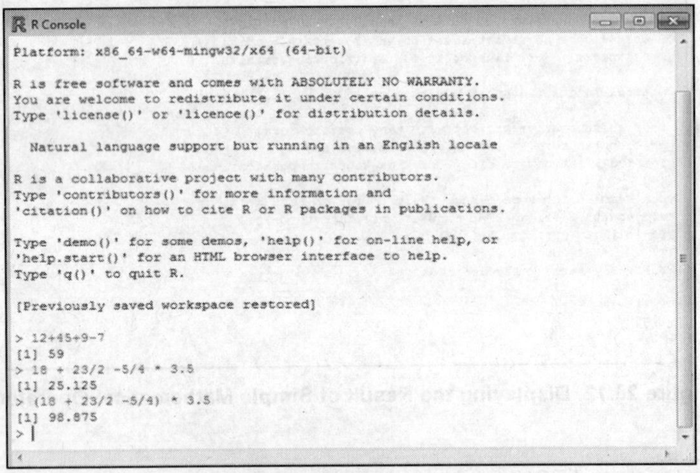

Figure 20.14: Using Parentheses in R

In Figure 20.14, you can see that the output of (18 + 23/2 -5/4) * 3.5 is evaluated to 98.875. This is because, as per the rule of BODMAS, R evaluates the expression inside the parentheses first, and then the result is multiplied by 3.5 to give the final result.

NOTE

R ignores spaces. Hence, there is no need to include spaces while entering mathematical expressions in R. However, in practice, the use of spaces makes it easy to understand a command and reduces the chances of errors.

Mathematical Operators

R also provides various operators to perform mathematical calculations. A mathematical calculation is performed by placing an operator between two values. Table 20.1 describes various mathematical operators available in R:

Table 20.1: Mathematical Operators in R

Operators	Description
+ - / * ( )	Perform standard mathematical operations, such as addition, subtraction, division, multiplication, and changing the order of calculation
pi	Stands for a constant value approximately 3.142
x^y	Stands for the value of x raised to the power of y
sqrt(x)	Stands for the square root of x
abs(x)	Stands for the absolute value of x
factorial(x)	Stands for the factorial of x

Table 20.1: Mathematical Operators in R	
Operators	**Description**
log(x, base = n)	Stands for the logarithm of x using base = n (natural log if none specified)
log10(x) log2(x)	Stand for logarithms of x to the base of 10 or 2
exp(x)	Stands for the exponent of x
cos(x) sin(x) tan(x) acos(x) asin(x) atan(x)	Stand for trigonometric functions for cosine, sine, tangent, arccosine, arcsine, and arctangent, respectively, in radians

Variables in R

Variables are symbols that are used to contain and store values. There are two ways to assign a value to a variable in R:

- Using the "=" symbol:
  - Num=10
- Using the "<-" symbol:
  - Num<-10

Figure 20.15 shows the assignment operations in R:

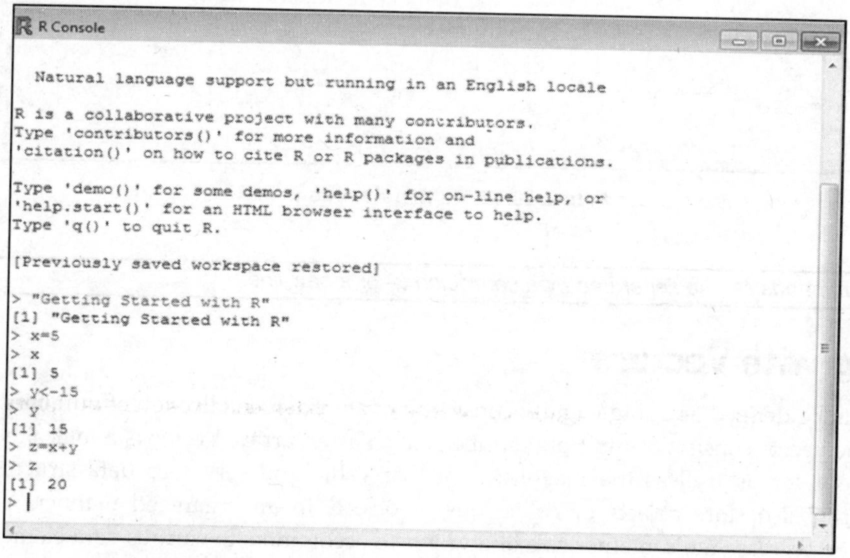

Figure 20.15: Assigning and Displaying the Values of Variables

In Figure 20.15, you can see that `x` is assigned with a number, `5`, and `y` is assigned with a number, `15`. The `z` variable is assigned with the addition of `x+y`, i.e., `20`. For displaying the content of a variable, you just need to type the name of the variable and press the ENTER key. It should be noted that you can also reassign values to the existing variables.

NOTE

R organizes numbers in three formats:

- ***Scalar***—*Represents a single number (0-dimensional)*
- ***Vector***—*Signifies a row of numbers, also called arrays (1-dimensional)*
- ***Matrix***—*Signifies a table like structure (2-dimensional)*

Calling Functions in R

To invoke predefined functions in R, you need to type their names on the R Console, followed by comma-separated parameters as arguments within parentheses.

Figure 20.16 shows calling of various predefined functions in R:

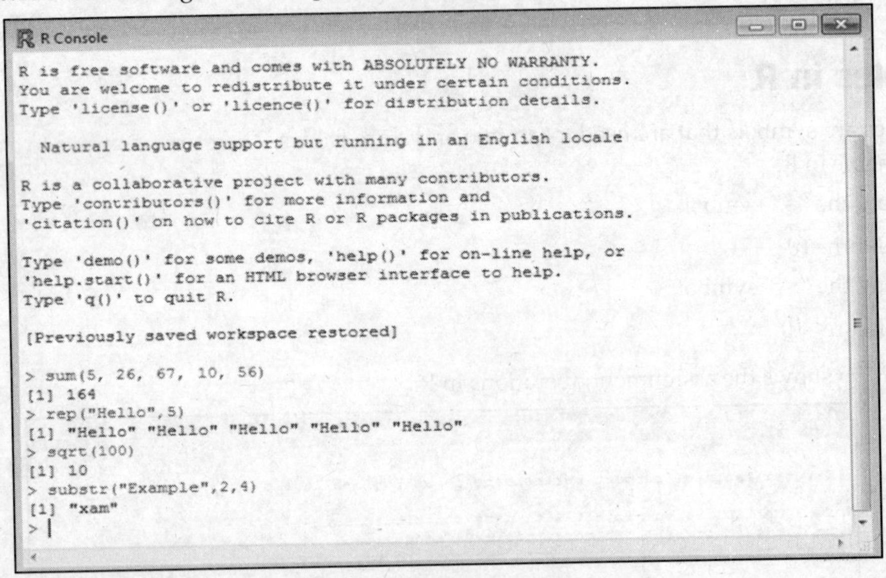

Figure 20.16: Calling Functions in R

NOTE

Two R commands can be separated by a semicolon (;) or a new line.

Working with Vectors

Vector can be defined as a single entity consisting of an ordered collection of numbers. For example, a numeric vector consists of multiple numbers, such as an array. Vector is a logical element, which holds the value as well as the magnitude of that value and serves as data structure containers. Vectors can also store objects or collections of objects in an organized manner. You can easily increase or decrease the container size of a vector to accommodate various data elements. However, this type of change cannot be done in arrays. Listing 20.1 shows how to construct a vector in R:

Listing 20.1: Constructing a Vector in R

```
c(10,20,30,40,50)
```

Shows the implementation of the c() function to create a vector

Figure 20.17 shows the output of executing the `c()` function:

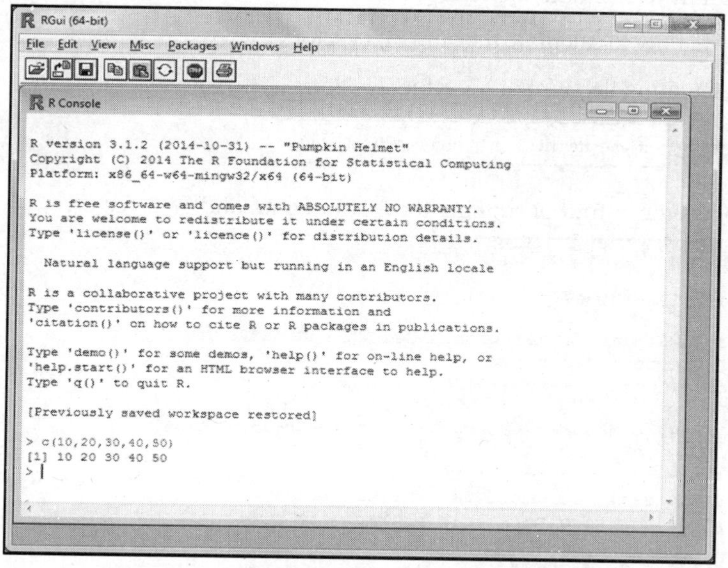

Figure 20.17: Showing the Output of the `c()` Function

In Listing 20.1, the `c()` function is used to construct a vector with five integers. It should be noted that the values or numbers written inside the parentheses are referred to as arguments.

A vector can also be created by using the `':'` operator between the range of numbers. Listing 20.2 shows how to create a vector in R by using the sequence `(:)` operator:

Listing 20.2: Creating a Vector Using `(:)` Operator

```
1:15
```

← **Generates numbers from 1 to 15**

The output of Listing 20.2 is shown in Figure 20.18:

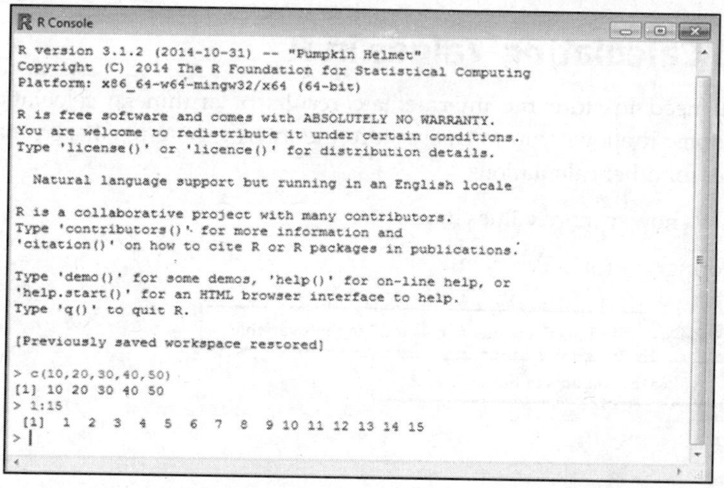

Figure 20.18: Showing the Output of the Sequence Operator

Let's now learn how to calculate the sum of the vector created in Figure 20.18.

Listing 20.3 shows how to calculate the sum of a vector:

Listing 20.3: Calculating the Sum of a Vector

```
sum(1:15)
```

← Generates the sum of numbers from 1 to 15

Figure 20.19 shows the output of running the `sum()` command on a vector:

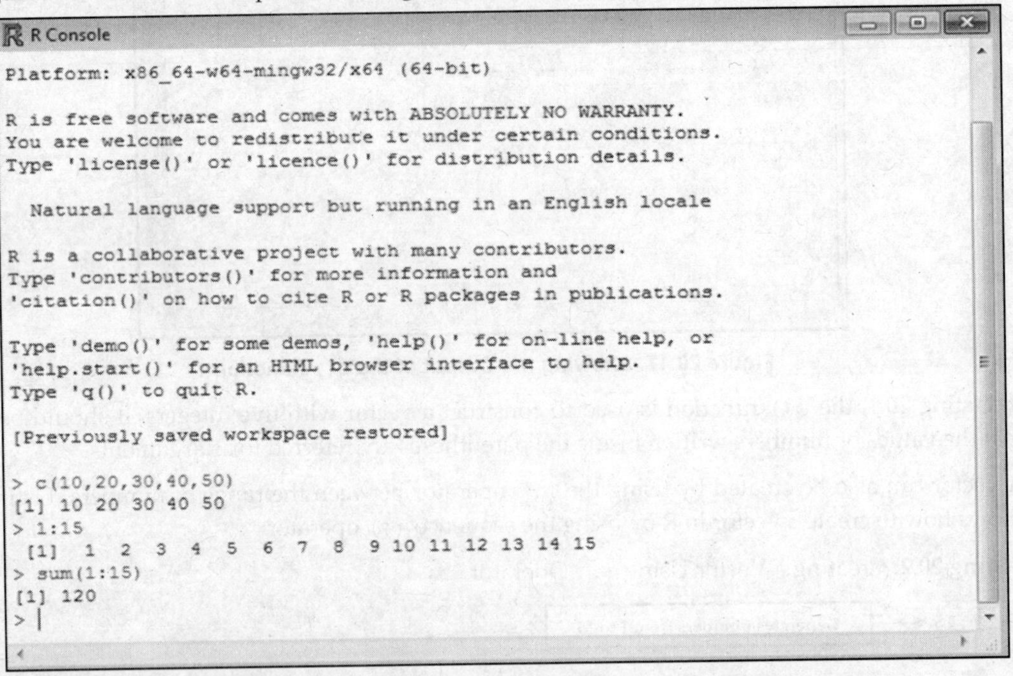

Figure 20.19: Showing the Output of the sum() Command

Storing and Calculating Values in R

Sometimes you need to store the intermediate results of arithmetic calculations for performing further calculations. R allows you to easily store the intermediate results, so that the stored values can be used later for other calculations.

Listing 20.4 shows how to store values in R:

Listing 20.4: Storing Values in R

```
>x <- 1:15
>x
```

← Assigns the values from 1 to 15 in the x variable

← Invokes the contents of the x variable

Figure 20.20 shows the output of Listing 20.4:

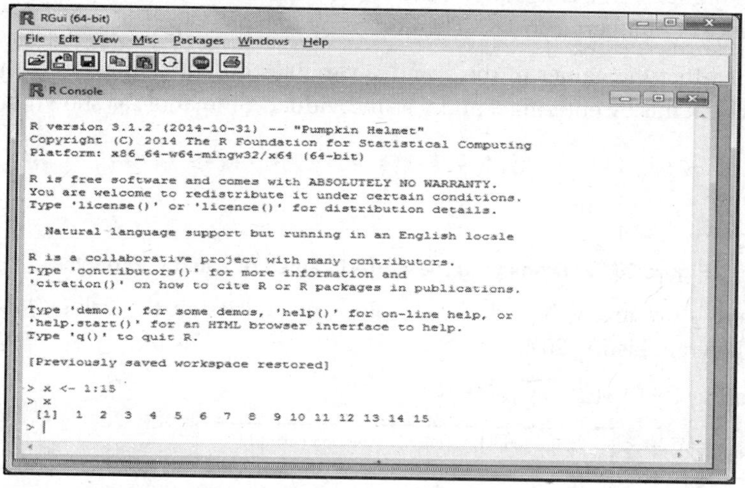

Figure 20.20: Displaying the Contents of Variable x in R

In Listing 20.4, the sequence 1:15 is assigned to a variable, `x`. The <- symbol is the assignment operator in R. To print the value of `x`, type `x` in the console and press the ENTER key.

Now, let's create a second variable, `y`, assign it the value `30`, and add the values of `x` and `y`.

Listing 20.5 shows the addition of two variables, `x` and `y`:

Listing 20.5: Adding Variables in R

```
>y <- 30
>x + y
```

- `>y <- 30` — Assigns a number, 30, to a variable y
- `>x + y` — Adds the values of x and y variables

Figure 20.21 shows the output of Listing 20.5:

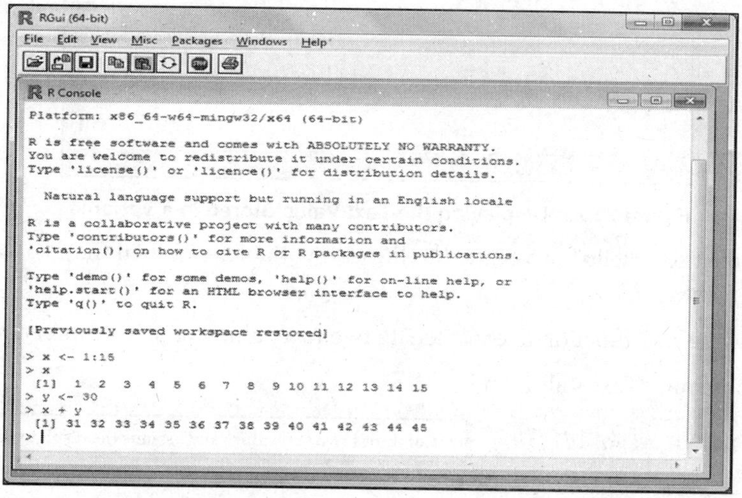

Figure 20.21: Displaying the Addition of x and y Variables

In Listing 20.5, a number, `30`, is assigned to variable, `y`. Then, the `x+y` expression adds the number `30` in the sequence of numbers `1` to `15`. Therefore, you see the output as: `31, 32, 33.......45.`

It should be noted that the values of the `x` and `y` variables do not change unless you assign a new value. You can check this by entering `x` and `y` as individual commands, as shown in Figure 20.22:

```
> x
  [1] 1 2 3 4 5 6 7 8 9 10 11 12 13 14 15
> y
[1] 30
> |
```

Figure 20.22: Displaying the Stored Values of x and y Variables

Variables can also store text values. For example, you can assign the value "Hello" to a variable called `msg`, as shown in Listing 20.6:

Listing 20.6: Storing Text Values in a Variable

```
>msg <- "Hello"   ← Assigns a text, "Hello", to the msg variable

>msg   ← Invokes the content of the msg variable
```

Figure 20.23 shows the output of Listing 20.6:

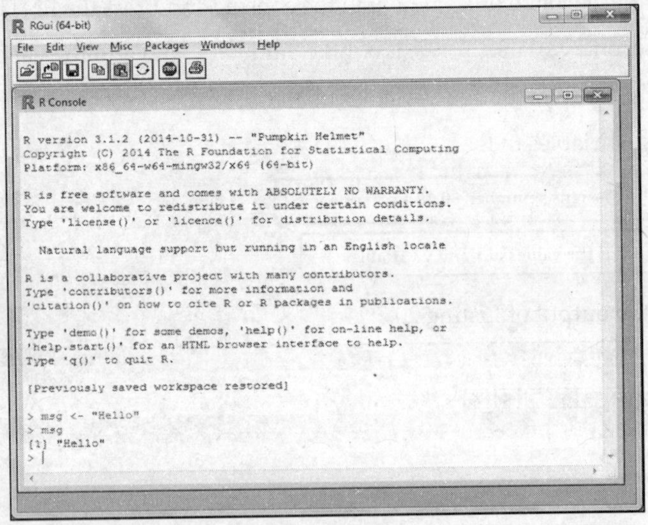

Figure 20.23: Displaying the Text Value Stored in a Variable

In Listing 20.6, the text "Hello" is assigned to the `msg` variable, and then the `msg` variable is invoked to display its content.

You can also use the `c()` function to concatenate two text values, as shown in Listing 20.7:

Listing 20.7: Combining Text Values in R

```
>hw <- c("Hello", "World!")   ← Combines two text values and assigns the result to the hw variable

>hw   ← Invokes the value of the hw variable
```

Figure 20.24 shows the output of Listing 20.7:

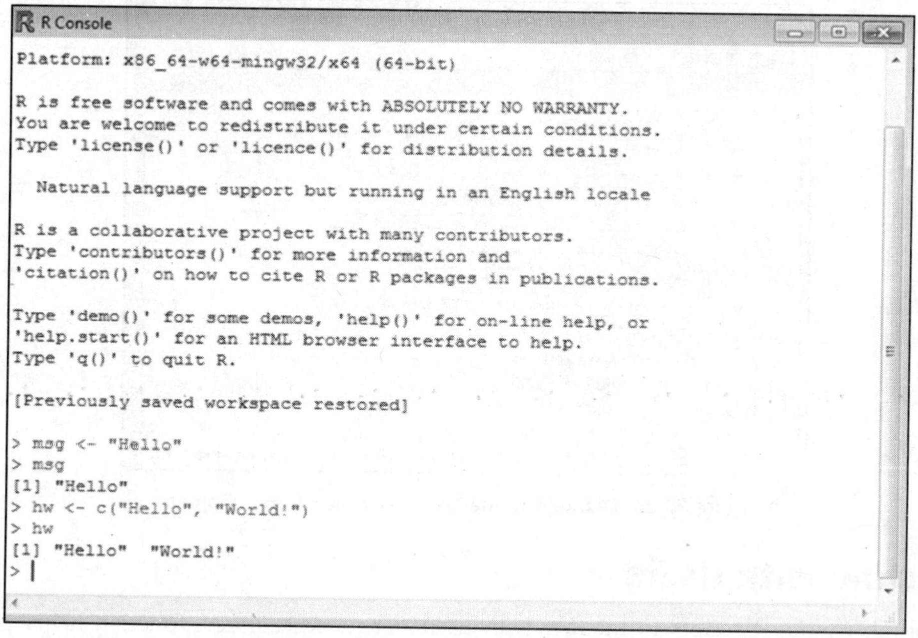

Figure 20.24: Combining Two Text Values

In Listing 20.7, the `c()` function is used to combine two text values "Hello" and "World!" and assign it to a variable, `hw`. Then, the `hw` variable is invoked to display the result.

TIP

You can also use the paste() function to concatenate multiple text elements. The paste() function, by default, adds a space between different elements, as shown in the following figure:

```
> paste ("Displaying", "the", "use", "of", "paste", "function")
[1] "Displaying the use of paste function"
>|
```

Creating and Using Objects

R uses objects to store the result of a computation. For example, you can store the result of 16+7+27 in an object. To store the result in an object, type the following command:

```
object.name = mathematical.expression
```

Listing 20.8 shows how to create an object in R:

Listing 20.8: Creating and Invoking an Object

```
>myObj = 25 + 12/2 - 16 + (7 * pi/2)
>myObj
```

Assigns a mathematical expression to an object, `myObj`

Invokes the `myObj` object

Figure 20.25 shows the output of Listing 20.8:

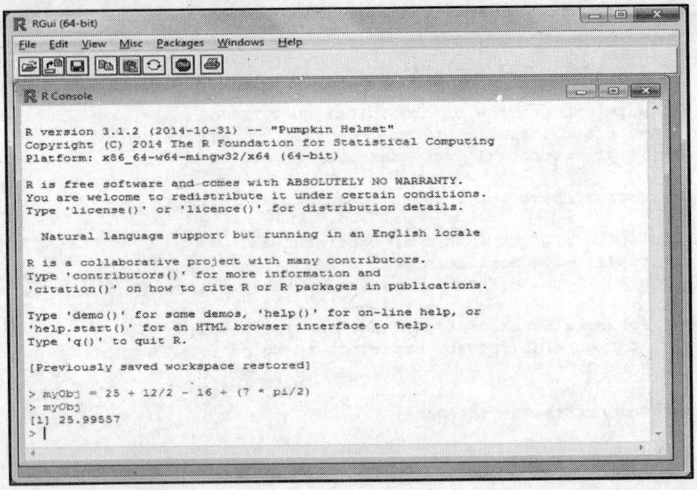

Figure 20.25: Displaying the Output of the `myObj` Object

Interacting with Users

You can also write R scripts to interact with users. The `readline()` function helps you to ask questions from users.

Listing 20.9 shows the use of the `readline()` function:

Listing 20.9: Using the `readline()` Function in R

```
>msg <- "Hello"

>yourname <- readline("What is your name?")

What is your name?
>paste(msg, yourname)
```

Displays a question, "What is your name?"

Figure 20.26 shows the output of Listing 20.9:

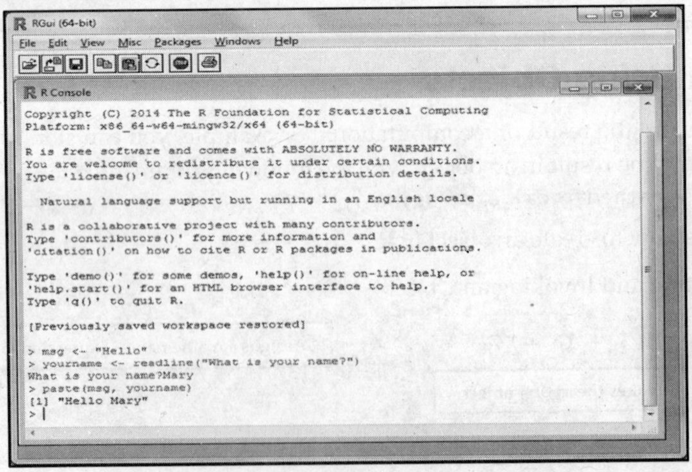

Figure 20.26: Using the readline() Function

In Listing 20.9, the text "Hello" is assigned to the `msg` variable. Then, the `readline()` function is used to assign a question to the `yourname` variable. The execution of this line demands a name from the user's side. In our case, we have provided the name, Mary. Then, the `paste()` function is used to display the concatenation of the text values stored in the `msg` and `yourname` variables.

Handling Data in R Workspace

The current R working environment includes variables, functions, vectors, matrices, data frames, and lists (collectively called user-defined objects). When an active session of R ends, the user can save the image of the current workspace that will be automatically reloaded the next time R is started.

Let's now learn about the following functions that allow users to handle data in R Workspace:

- The `ls()` function
- The `rm()` function
- The `getwd()` function
- The `save()` function
- The `load()` function

The ls() Function

The `ls()` function is used to view all the created variables in a current active workspace.

Figure 20.27 shows the use of the `ls()` function:

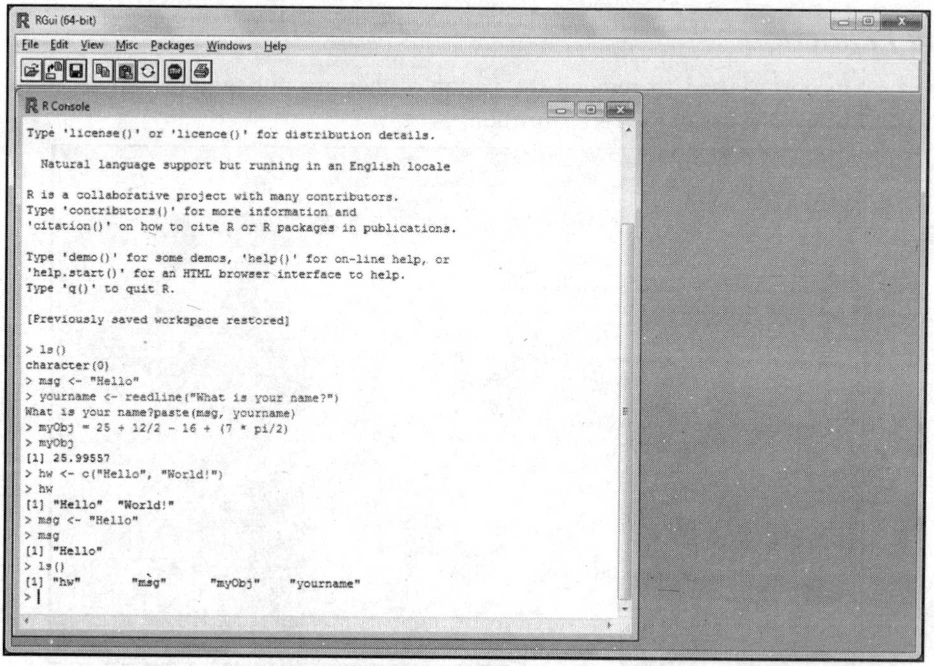

Figure 20.27: Using the ls() Function

Figure 20.27 shows the names of all the variables created in the active session.

If you use RStudio, you can see the values of all the variables in the top right window even without typing any R commands. By default, the top right window of RStudio has two tabs: Environment and History. The Environment tab displays the values of all the variables created in the current active workspace and the History tab keeps a record of all the previously used commands. Figure 20.28 shows the contents of the Environment tab:

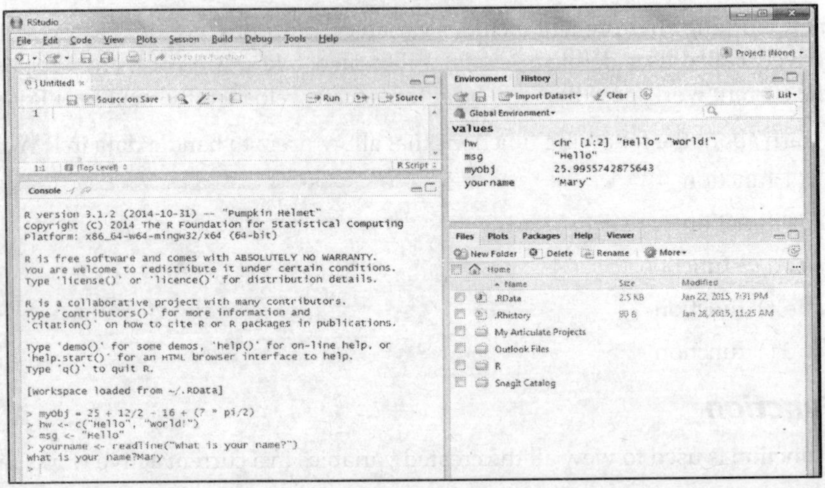

Figure 20.28: Displaying a List of Variables and their Stored Values in the Environment Tab

The rm() Function

The `rm()` function is used to remove the variables that are not required anymore in a session. Figure 20.29 shows the use of the `rm()` function:

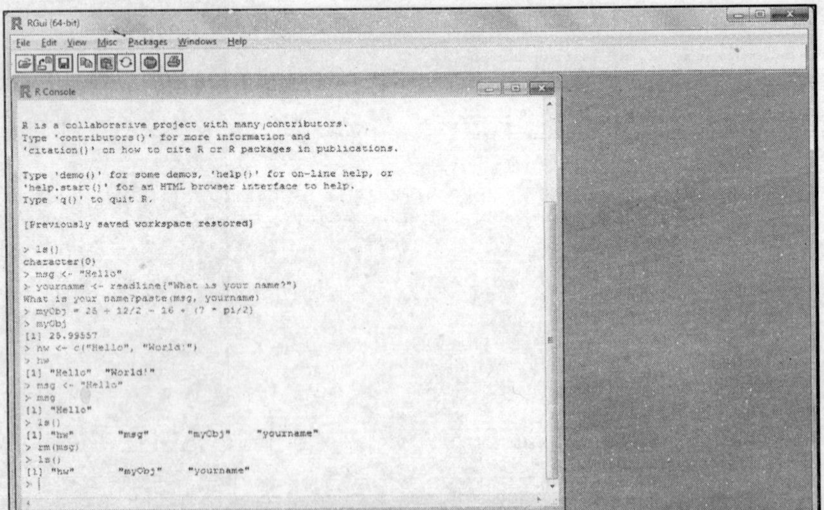

Figure 20.29: Using the rm() Function

In Figure 20.29, you can see that the `rm()` function has removed the `msg` variable and the execution of the `ls()` function does not list the `msg` variable in the current active session.

The getwd() Function

The `getwd()` function is used to display the current working directory of the user. Figure 20.30 shows the use of the `getwd()` function:

```
> getwd()
[1]"D:/MyFiles"
```

Figure 20.30: Using the getwd() Function

NOTE

In RGUI, you can set your working directory by navigating the File→Change dir…. Option.

The save() Function

The `save()` function is used to save the variables created in an active session. Suppose you want to save the value of a variable, `yourname`. Figure 20.31 shows the use of the `save()` function to save the `yourname` variable:

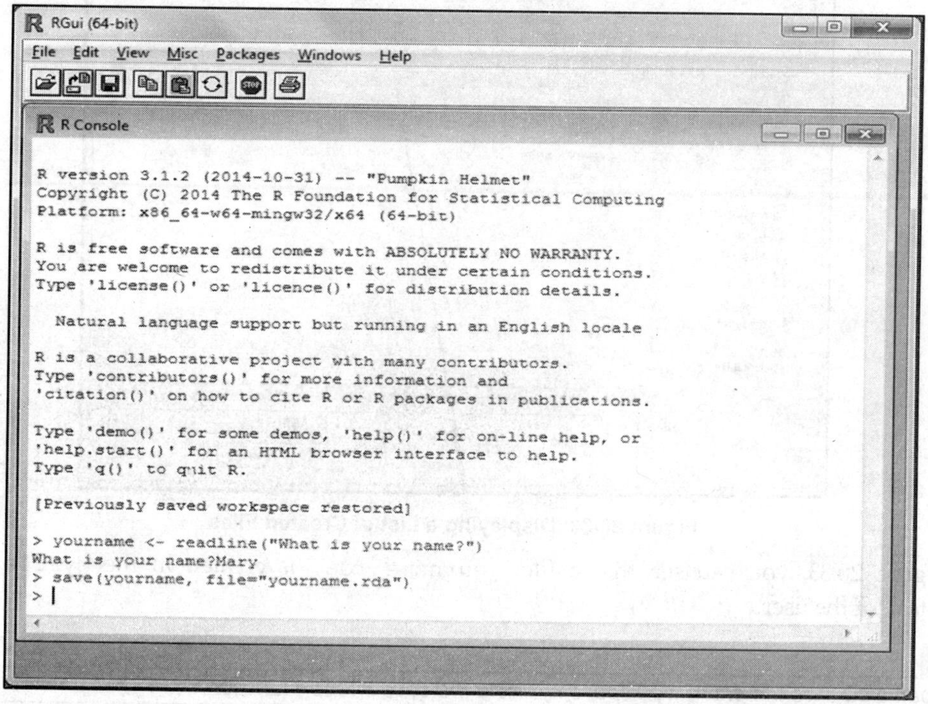

Figure 20.31: Using the save() Function

It should be noted that R silently saves the file in the working directory, which means that no confirmation message is displayed in the console. However, you can check whether the file has been stored or not by selecting the File→Display file(s) option, as shown in Figure 20.32:

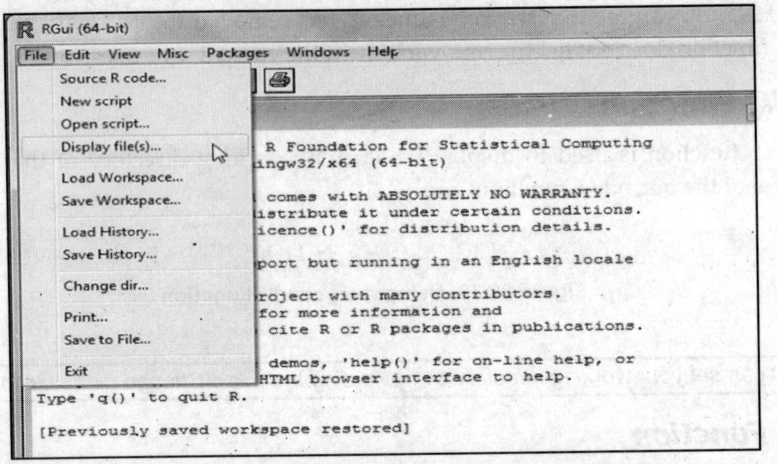

Figure 20.32: Selecting the File→Display file(s) Option

This action displays the list of files created in your working directory, as shown in Figure 20.33:

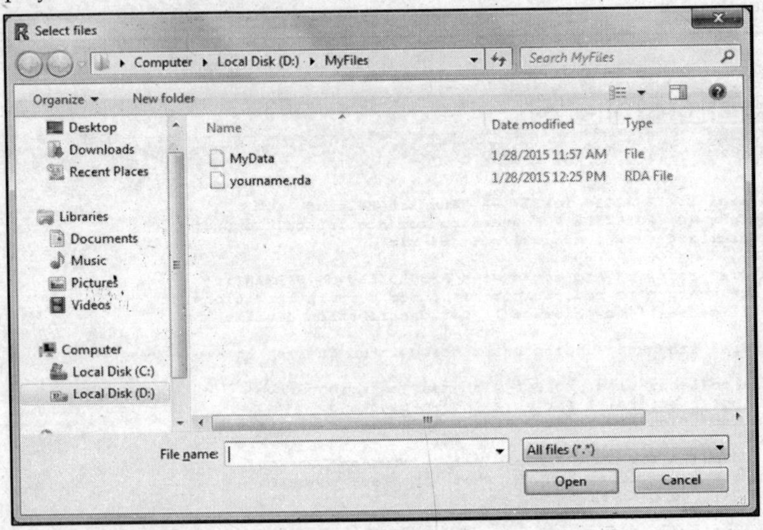

Figure 20.33: Displaying a List of Created Files

In Figure 20.33, you can see that a file, `yourname.rda`, is created in the `MyFiles` working directory of the user.

TIP

You can also save the entire workspace by using the save.image() function.

The load () Function

The `load()` function is used to retrieve the saved data. For example, you remove the `yourname` variable from your current session by using the `rm()` function. Now, the `load()` function can be used to retrieve the `yourname` variable back from the `yourname.rda` file, as shown in Figure 20.34:

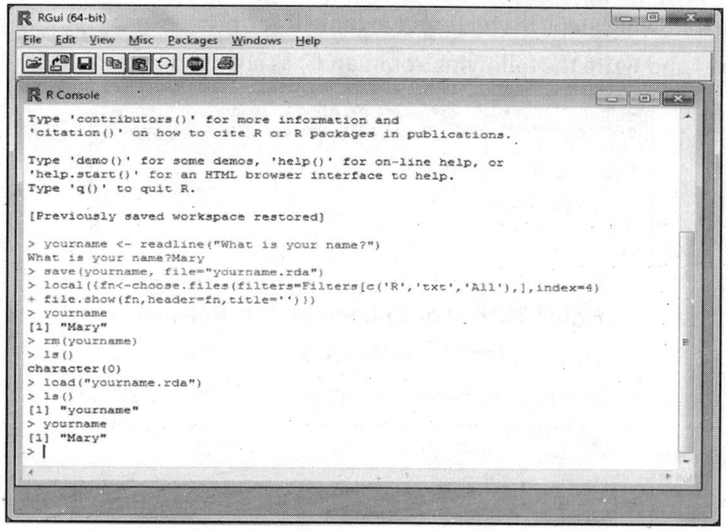

Figure 20.34: Using the load() Function

In Figure 20.34, you can see that the `rm()` function removes the `yourname` variable, and the `load()` function reloads this variable in the active session.

Executing Scripts

Till now, you have worked directly in the R Console by issuing individual commands in an interactive style of coding. In this section, you will learn to create scripts and execute them. To prepare a script to be sourced, first the entire script is written in an editor window. In RGUI, you can open R Editor by selecting the File →New Script option, as shown in Figure 20.35:

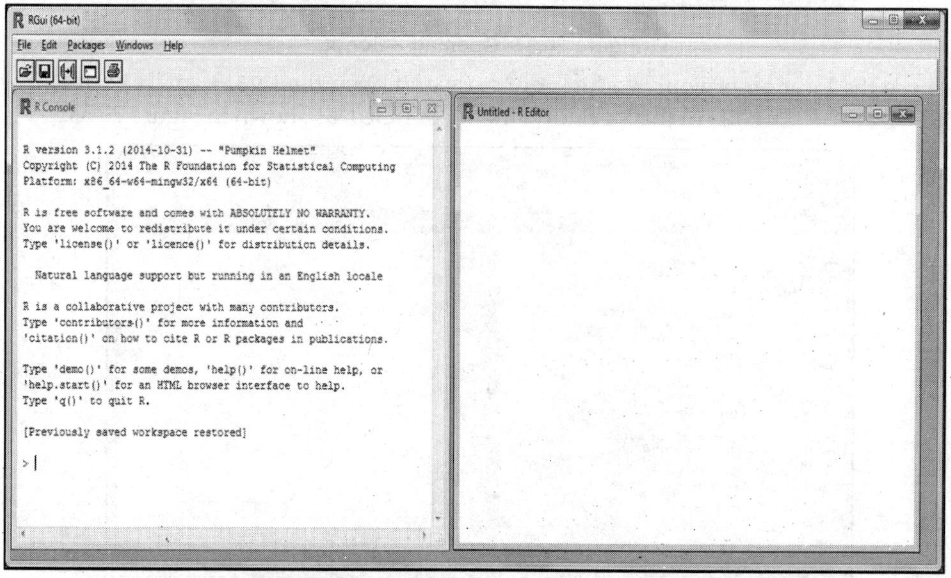

Figure 20.35: Displaying R Editor in RGUI

Let's perform the following steps to create and execute R scripts:

1. Open Notepad and write the following commands, as shown in Figure 20.36:

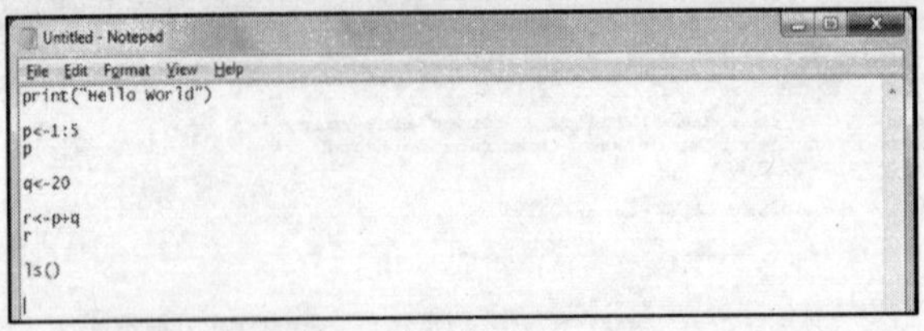

Figure 20.36: Writing Commands in Notepad

2. Save the file as `MyScript.txt` in the current working directory.
3. Open RGUI tool and select File→Open script, as shown in Figure 20.37:

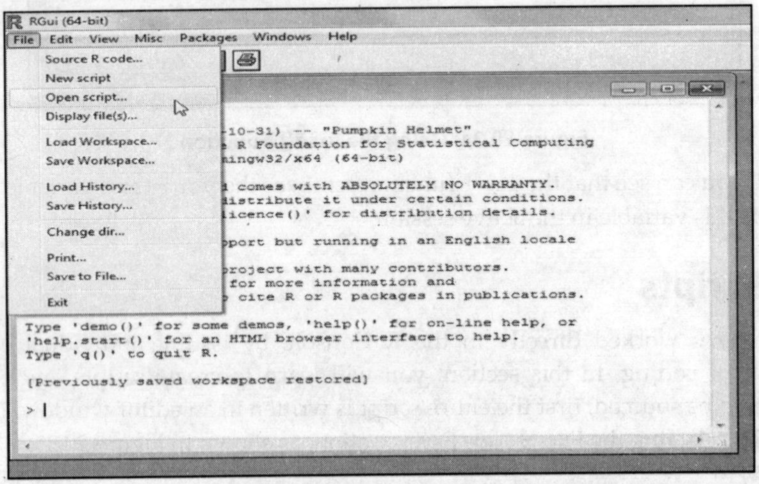

Figure 20.37: Opening a Script

4. Browse the location of your working directory and open the `MyScript.txt` file. It will open the `MyScript.txt` file in the R Editor window of RGUI, as shown in Figure 20.38:

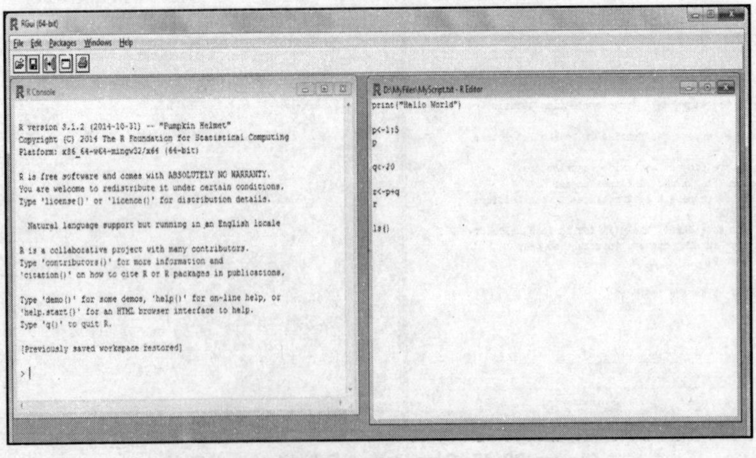

Figure 20.38: Displaying a Script in R Editor

5. Select Edit→Run all to execute all the commands listed in the `MyScript.txt` file, as shown in Figure 20.39:

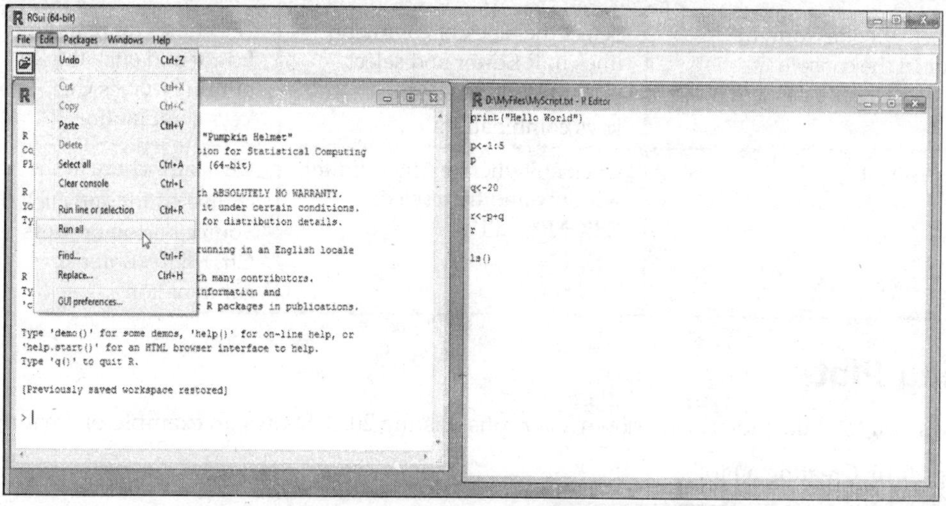

Figure 20.39: Executing All Commands of a Script File

Figure 20.40 displays the result of executing commands listed in the `MyScript.txt` file:

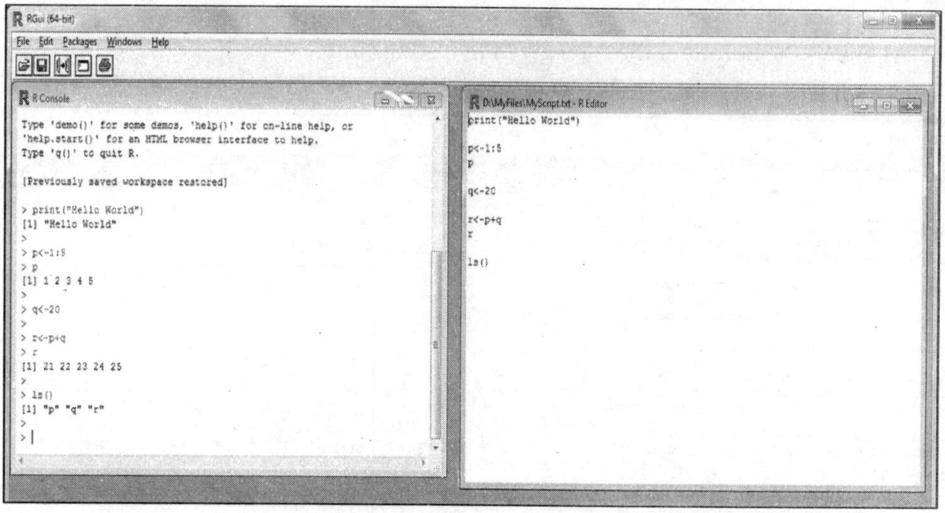

Figure 20.40: Displaying the Result of Commands of a Script File

Table 20.2 lists the ways in which a script file can be executed in RGUI or RStudio:

Table 20.2: Different Ways of Script Execution in RGUI and RStudio

Execution	RGUI	RStudio
Individual line of code from the editor to the console	Select the command line in R Editor and select Edit→Run line or press Ctrl+R keys combination	Select the command line in the Editor and click the Run button or press the Ctrl+Enter keys combination

Table 20.2: Different Ways of Script Execution in RGUI and RStudio

Execution	RGUI	RStudio
A block of code from the editor to the console	Select the block of command lines in R Editor and select Edit→Run line or press Ctrl+R keys combination	Select the command line in the Editor and click the Run button or press Ctrl+Enter keys combination
Entire script	Click anywhere in the R Editor window and then select Edit→Run all	Click anywhere in the source editor and click the Source button or press Ctrl+Shift+Enter keys combination

Creating Plots

R allows you to make plots, also known as graphs. Listing 20.10 shows an example of creating a plot:

Listing 20.10: Creating a Plot

```
x = rnorm(200)
plot(x)
```

Creates a graph

Figure 20.41 shows the output of the code given in Listing 20.10:

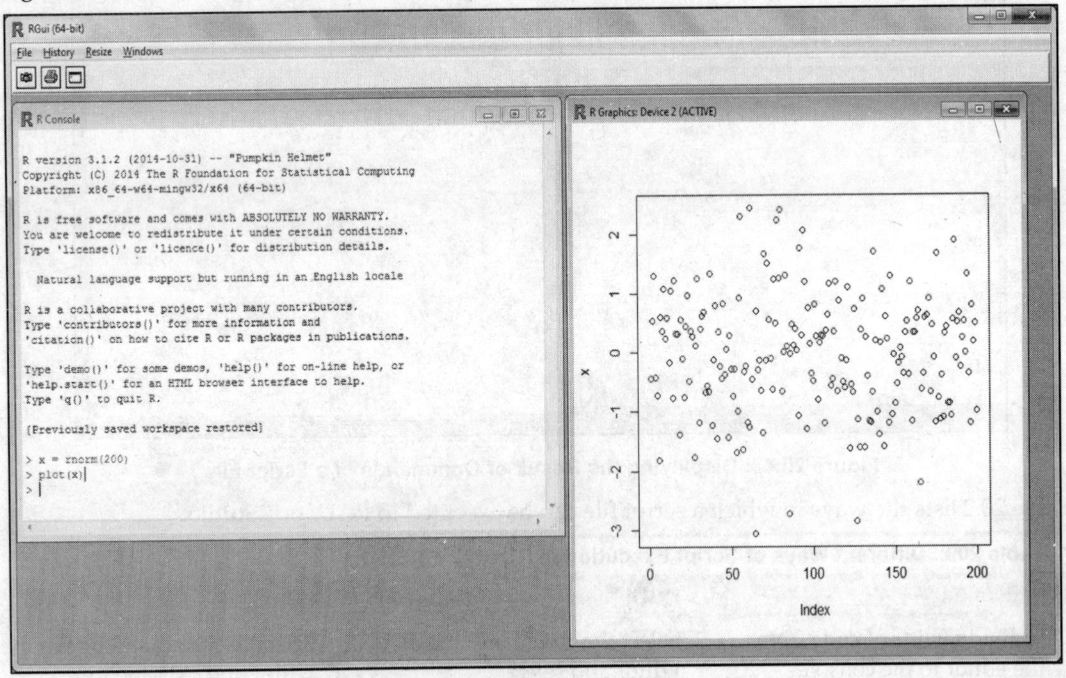

Figure 20.41: Displaying a Plot Example

In Figure 20.41, 200 random numbers are assigned to the variable x, which becomes a vector by this operation. Then, all these values are plotted in the plot window.

Accessing Help and Documentation in R

R provides a large amount of free documentation and help files. Listing 20.11 shows the use of the `help()` and `example()` commands:

Listing 20.11: The `help()` and `example()` Commands

```
help(rnorm)       <- Uses the help() command
example(rnorm)    <- Uses the example() command
```

Figure 20.42 shows the output of the commands given in Listing 20.11:

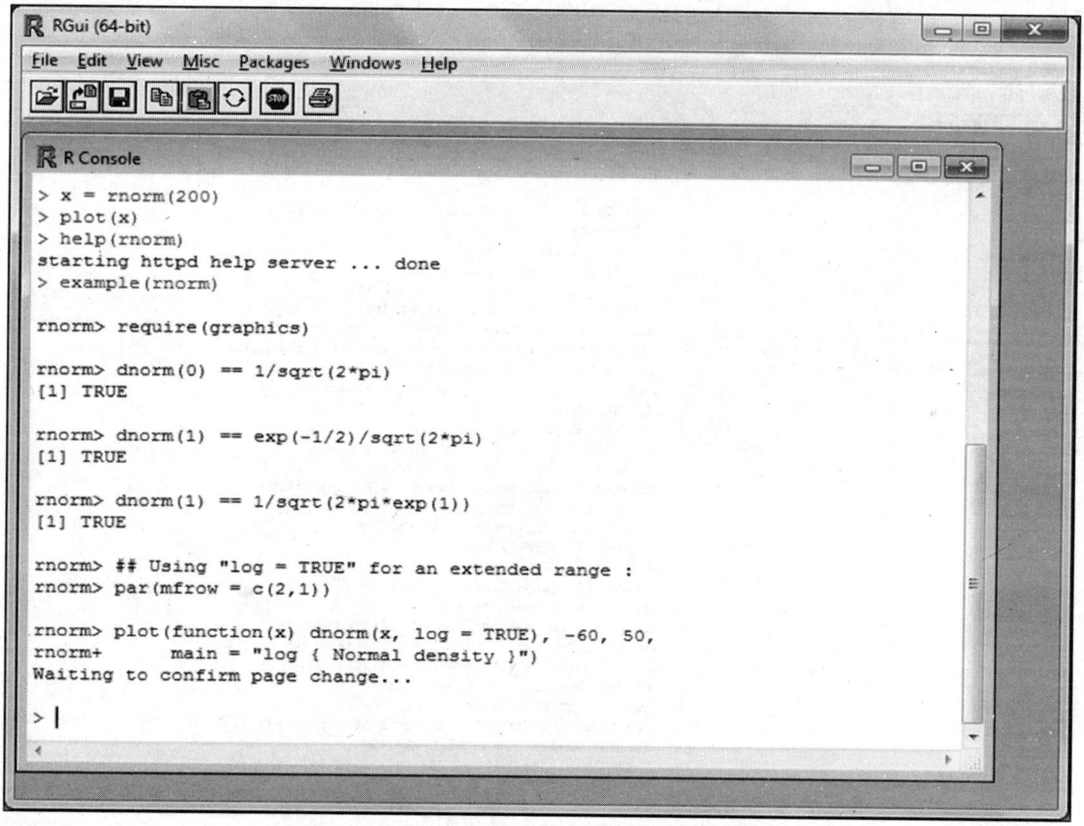

Figure 20.42: Using the help() and example() Commands

In Figure 20.42, you can see that the `help()` command opens the free documentation on `httpd help server`, while the `example()` command gives some examples of how a particular function can be used.

Using Built-in Datasets in R

SCENARIO

The head of the data analyst team asked Gabriel to provide the list of all the built-in datasets in R. Gabriel decides to retrieve the list by using the data() command.

Type the following command on the R console to see the list of all built-in datasets:

```
data()   <-- Generates the list of built-in datasets
```

The output will appear as shown in Figure 20.43:

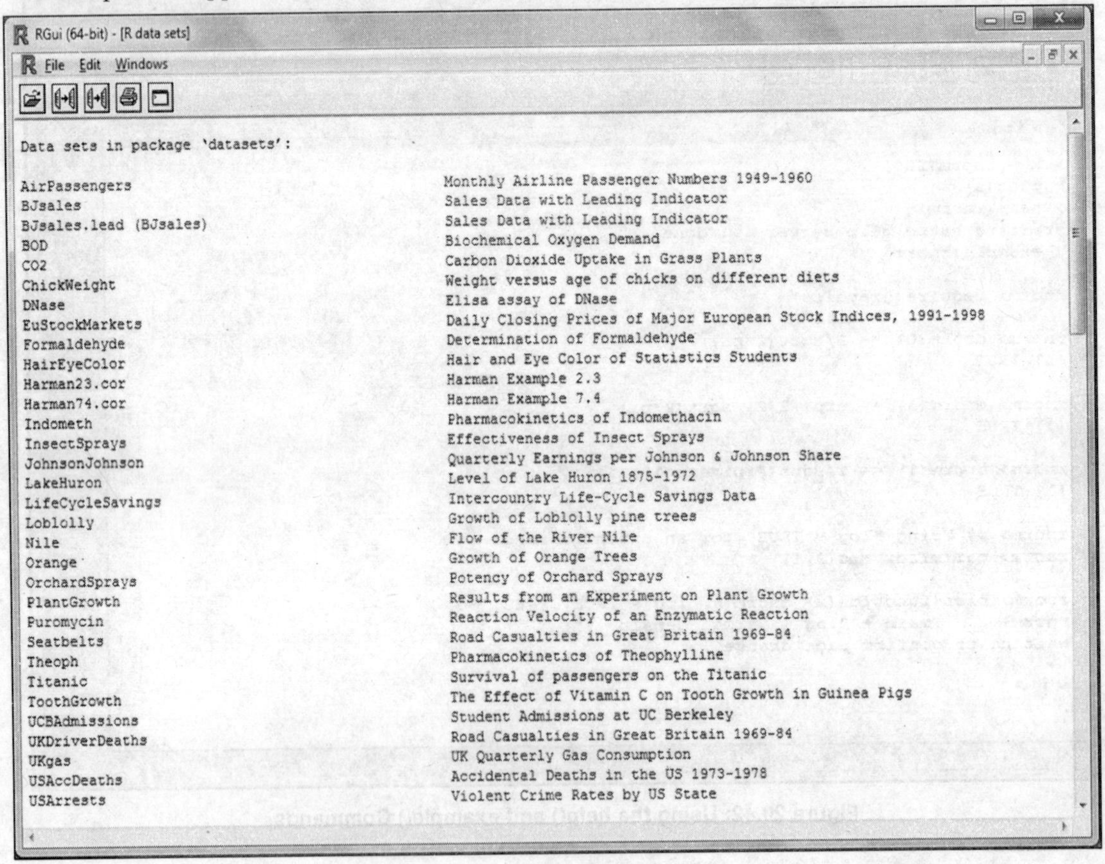

Figure 20.43: List of Built-in Datasets in R

The following command lists the built-in datasets in all the currently installed packages:

```
data(package = .packages(all.available = TRUE))
```

Displays the datasets in all currently installed packages

To access a particular dataset, you need to specify some conditions on the basis of which R should search that dataset. Listing 20.12 shows commands to search the IRIS dataset:

Listing 20.12: Searching the IRIS Dataset

```
data(iris)
iris
```

The output of executing the preceding commands is displayed in Figure 20.44:

```
> data(iris)
> iris
   Sepal.Length Sepal.Width Petal.Length Petal.Width  Species
1           5.1         3.5          1.4         0.2   setosa
2           4.9         3.0          1.4         0.2   setosa
3           4.7         3.2          1.3         0.2   setosa
4           4.6         3.1          1.5         0.2   setosa
5           5.0         3.6          1.4         0.2   setosa
6           5.4         3.9          1.7         0.4   setosa
7           4.6         3.4          1.4         0.3   setosa
8           5.0         3.4          1.5         0.2   setosa
9           4.4         2.9          1.4         0.2   setosa
10          4.9         3.1          1.5         0.1   setosa
11          5.4         3.7          1.5         0.2   setosa
12          4.8         3.4          1.6         0.2   setosa
13          4.8         3.0          1.4         0.1   setosa
14          4.3         3.0          1.1         0.1   setosa
15          5.8         4.0          1.2         0.2   setosa
16          5.7         4.4          1.5         0.4   setosa
17          5.4         3.9          1.3         0.4   setosa
18          5.1         3.5          1.4         0.3   setosa
19          5.7         3.8          1.7         0.3   setosa
20          5.1         3.8          1.5         0.3   setosa
21          5.4         3.4          1.7         0.2   setosa
22          5.1         3.7          1.5         0.4   setosa
23          4.6         3.6          1.0         0.2   setosa
24          5.1         3.3          1.7         0.5   setosa
25          4.8         3.4          1.9         0.2   setosa
26          5.0         3.0          1.6         0.2   setosa
27          5.0         3.4          1.6         0.4   setosa
28          5.2         3.5          1.5         0.2   setosa
29          5.2         3.4          1.4         0.2   setosa
30          4.7         3.2          1.6         0.2   setosa
31          4.8         3.1          1.6         0.2   setosa
32          5.4         3.4          1.5         0.4   setosa
33          5.2         4.1          1.5         0.1   setosa
34          5.5         4.2          1.4         0.2   setosa
```

Figure 20.44: Retrieving Built-in Datasets on the Basis of Specified Conditions

You can also access datasets from particular packages, as shown in Listing 20.13:

Listing 20.13: Accessing Datasets from a Particular Package

```
data(Cars93, package="MASS")
Cars93
```

The output of executing the preceding commands is displayed in Figure 20.45:

```
> data(Cars93, package="MASS")
> Cars93
   Manufacturer       Model    Type Min.Price Price Max.Price MPG.city MPG.highway            AirBags DriveTrain Cylinders EngineSize Horsepower  RPM Rev.per.mile
1         Acura     Integra   Small      12.9  15.9      18.8       25          31               None      Front         4        1.8        140 6300         2890
2         Acura      Legend Midsize      29.2  33.9      38.7       18          25 Driver & Passenger      Front         6        3.2        200 5500         2335
3          Audi          90 Compact      25.9  29.1      32.3       20          26        Driver only      Front         6        2.8        172 5500         2280
4          Audi         100 Midsize      30.8  37.7      44.6       19          26 Driver & Passenger      Front         6        2.8        172 5500         2535
5           BMW        535i Midsize      23.7  30.0      36.2       22          30        Driver only       Rear         4        3.5        208 5700         2545
6         Buick     Century Midsize      14.2  15.7      17.3       22          31        Driver only      Front         4        2.2        110 5200         2565
7         Buick     LeSabre   Large      19.9  20.8      21.7       19          28        Driver only      Front         6        3.8        170 4800         1570
8         Buick  Roadmaster   Large      22.6  23.7      24.9       16          25        Driver only       Rear         6        5.7        180 4000         1320
9         Buick     Riviera Midsize      26.3  26.3      26.3       19          27        Driver only      Front         6        3.8        170 4800         1690
10     Cadillac     DeVille   Large      33.0  34.7      36.3       16          25        Driver only      Front         8        4.9        200 4100         1510
11     Cadillac     Seville Midsize      37.5  40.1      42.7       16          25 Driver & Passenger      Front         8        4.6        295 6000         1985
12    Chevrolet    Cavalier Compact       8.5  13.4      18.3       25          36               None      Front         4        2.2        110 5200         2380
13    Chevrolet     Corsica Compact      11.4  11.4      11.4       25          34        Driver only      Front         4        2.2        110 5200         2665
14    Chevrolet      Camaro  Sporty      13.4  15.1      16.8       19          28 Driver & Passenger       Rear         6        3.4        160 4600         1805
15    Chevrolet      Lumina Midsize      13.4  15.9      18.4       21          29               None      Front         4        2.2        110 5200         2595
16    Chevrolet  Lumina_APV     Van      14.7  16.3      18.0       18          23               None      Front         6        3.8        170 4800         1690
17    Chevrolet       Astro     Van      14.7  16.6      18.6       15          20               None        4WD         6        4.3        165 4000         1790
18    Chevrolet     Caprice   Large      18.0  18.8      19.6       17          26        Driver only       Rear         8        5.0        170 4200         1350
19    Chevrolet    Corvette  Sporty      34.6  38.0      41.5       17          25        Driver only       Rear         8        5.7        300 5000         1450
20      Chrylser    Concorde   Large      18.4  18.4      18.4       20          28 Driver & Passenger      Front         6        3.3        153 5300         1990
21     Chrysler     LeBaron Compact      14.5  15.8      17.1       23          28 Driver & Passenger      Front         4        3.0        141 5000         2090
22     Chrysler    Imperial   Large      29.5  29.5      29.5       20          26        Driver only      Front         6        3.3        147 4800         1785
23        Dodge        Colt   Small       7.9   9.2      10.6       29          33               None      Front         4        1.5         92 6000         3285
24        Dodge      Shadow   Small       8.4  11.3      14.2       23          29        Driver only      Front         4        2.2         93 4800         2595
25        Dodge      Spirit Compact      11.9  13.3      14.7       22          27        Driver only      Front         4        2.5        100 4800         2535
26        Dodge     Caravan     Van      13.6  19.0      24.4       17          21        Driver only        4WD         6        3.0        142 5000         1970
27        Dodge     Dynasty Midsize      14.8  15.6      16.4       21          27        Driver only      Front         4        2.5        100 4800         2465
28        Dodge     Stealth  Sporty      18.5  25.8      33.1       18          24        Driver only        4WD         6        3.0        300 6000         2120
29        Eagle      Summit   Small       7.9  12.2      16.5       29          33               None      Front         4        1.5         92 6000         2505
30        Eagle      Vision   Large      17.5  19.3      21.2       20          28 Driver & Passenger      Front         6        3.5        214 5800         1980
31         Ford     Festiva   Small       6.9   7.4       7.9       31          33               None      Front         4        1.3         63 5000         3150
32         Ford      Escort   Small       8.4  10.1      11.9       23          30               None      Front         4        1.8        127 6500         2410
33         Ford       Tempo Compact      10.4  11.3      12.2       22          27               None      Front         4        2.3         96 4200         2805
34         Ford     Mustang  Sporty      10.8  15.9      21.0       22          29        Driver only       Rear         4        2.3        105 4600         2285
35         Ford       Probe  Sporty      12.8  14.0      15.2       24          30        Driver only      Front         4        2.0        115 5500         2340
```

Figure 20.45: Accessing Built-in Datasets from a Package

To summarize a dataset, enter the commands, shown in Listing 20.14:

Listing 20.14: Summarizing a Dataset

```
data(ToothGrowth)
summary(ToothGrowth)
```

← **Summarizes the ToothGrowth dataset**

The output of executing the preceding commands is displayed in Figure 20.46:

```
> data(ToothGrowth)
> summary(ToothGrowth)
      len        supp         dose      
 Min.   : 4.20   OJ:30   Min.   :0.500  
 1st Qu.:13.07   VC:30   1st Qu.:0.500  
 Median :19.25           Median :1.000  
 Mean   :18.81           Mean   :1.167  
 3rd Qu.:25.27           3rd Qu.:2.000  
 Max.   :33.90           Max.   :2.000  
```

Figure 20.46: Summarizing a Dataset

The following command plots the graph of the `ToothGrowth` dataset:

```
plot(ToothGrowth)
```

The output of executing the preceding command is displayed in Figure 20.47:

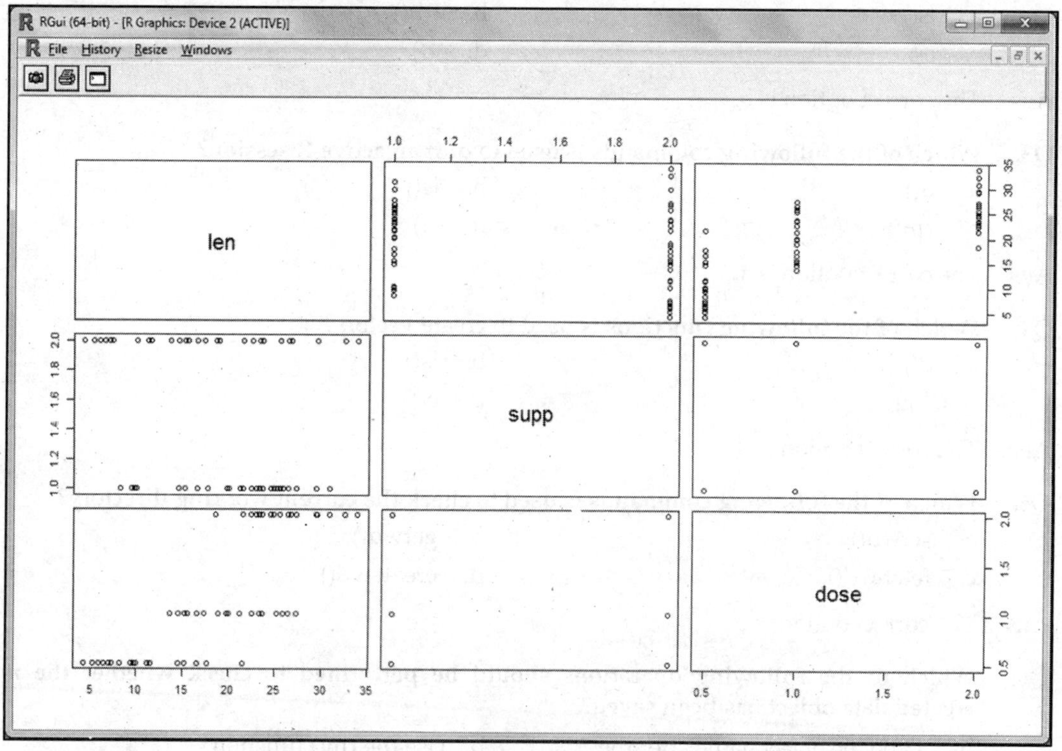

Figure 20.47: Plotting Graph of the `ToothGrowth` Dataset

Summary

This chapter familiarized you with R language. R is a cross-platform programming language as well as a software environment for statistical computing and graphics. The chapter first discussed the basic features of R, such as its statistical and programming features. Next, you learned how to start RGUI and how to write, save, and execute programs in R. You further learned about RStudio and how to perform various tasks in R, such as storing and calculating values. The chapter also discussed to handle data in R Workspace. Toward the end, you learned to execute scripts, create plots, and access help and documentation in R.

Quick Revise

Multiple-Choice Questions

Q1. Which of the following functions is used in R to generate a list of already existing data objects?

a. ls()
b. rm()
c. c()
d. q()

Ans. The correct option is a.

Q2. Which of the following functions is used in R to remove the existing data objects?

a. ls()
b. rm()
c. c()
d. q()

Ans. The correct option is b.

Q3. Which of the following commands is used to quit an active R session?

a. q()
b. ls()
c. rm()
d. c()

Ans. The correct option is a.

Q4. Which of the following functions is used to create vectors?

a. q()
b. ls()
c. rm()
d. c()

Ans. The correct option is d.

Q5. Which of the following commands is used to check the current working directory?

a. setwd()
b. getwd()
c. fetchwd()
d. createwd()

Ans. The correct option is b.

Q6. Which of the following operations should be performed to check whether the newly created data object has been saved?

a. Type the object name after the prompt in the console or use the ls() function
b. Use the rm() function
c. Quit the active R session and start a new session
d. Use help in R

Ans. The correct option is a.

Q7. RStudio provides four windows for user interaction. Which of the following windows is not a part of RStudio?

a. Source window
b. Console window
c. Workspace and history window
d. Print preview window

Ans. The correct option is d.

Q8. Typing each command in the R Console and executing the entire program step by step is one approach of using R for statistical computations. The various editors available for R make scripting and executing code easy. The process of developing scripts in editors and executing the entire code in the console at one go is known as:

a. Sourcing a script
b. Printing a script
c. Developing a script
d. Editing a script

Ans. The correct option is a.

Q9. Sourcing a script in R is an efficient way to reduce the efforts of programmers. Which of the following is not a way to implement sourcing of script in R?

a. Send an individual line of code from the editor to the console

b. Send a block of highlighted code to the console

c. Execute the script step by step in the console

d. Send the entire script to the console

Ans. The correct option is c.

Q10. Vectors are the basic data types in R. R can perform operations simultaneously on all the elements of a vector. One way for creating vectors in R is by using the c() function. Which among the following is the other method used to create vectors?

a. Use of the sequence operator

b. Use of the rm() function

c. Use of the ls() function

d. Use of the load() command

Ans. The correct option is a.

Subjective Questions

Q1. List some common characteristics of the R language.

Ans. Some common characteristics of the R language are as follows:

- Effective and powerful data handling and storage facilities
- Arrays and matrices for handling data
- Graphical representation of the analysis

Q2. Write a script to generate the following list of numerical values with spaces:

6 7 8 9 10 11

Ans. The script is as follows:

```
Data= c(6 ,7, 8, 9 ,10 ,11)
Data
```

Q3. Write a script to concatenate text and numerical values in R in the following manner:

a. Text 1: Sam scored

b. Text 2: 10

c. Text 3: marks

Ans. The script is as follows:

```
cat("sam scored",10, "marks")
```

Q4. The following table shows the number of units of different products sold on different days:

Product	Monday	Tuesday	Wednesday	Thursday	Friday
Cola cans	10	1	37	5	12
Milk cans	8	3	19	6	4
Bread packets	18	9	1	2	4
Detergent packets	12	13	16	9	10
Chocolate bars	8	27	6	32	23

Create five simple numeric vectors from this data.

Ans. Numeric vectors created from the given data are as follows:

```
Product = c(Monday ,Tuesday, Wednesday ,Thursday, Friday)
Colacans = c(10, 1, 37, 5, 12)
Milkcans = c( 8, 3, 19, 6, 4)
Breadpackets = c( 18 ,9 ,1, 2 ,4)
Detergentpackets c(12, 13, 16, 9, 10)
Chocolatebars = c(8, 27, 6 ,32, 23)
data =
data.frame(Colacans,Milkcans,Breadpackets,Detergentpackets,Chocolatebars,Product)
```

21

Reading Datasets and Exporting Data from R

Analytics refers to the process of studying large amounts of data (Big Data) to find new patterns and information trends, which help an organisation to take better decisions, analyze the effects of certain events and previously taken decisions, evaluate the performance of a given tool or application. Analysis cannot be performed without data, so getting data into R is an important task. Big Data analytics includes creating complex samples, examining lengthy sets of data, and putting data into R for computational purposes. Reading and writing data plays an important role in R as you may need to import data from other sources to R. You also need to move the processed data out of R, i.e., export data from R to other sources.

This chapter discusses various types of R commands to import data into and export data from R. Here, you will first learn about the `c()` command that is used to combine or concatenate data. Next, the chapter discusses the `scan()` command, which is used to read large datasets and retrieve data from Comma Separated Values (CSV) files. Next, you learn to use `read.csv()`, `read.table()`, `write.csv()`, and `write.table()` commands. Finally, you learn how to import data in RStudio and export data from R to a disk or text file.

Using the c() Command

The `c()` command is used to combine or concatenate two or more values. The syntax for using the `c()` command is:

```
>c(sampleitem1, sampleitem2, sampleitem3, sampleitem4)
```

In the preceding syntax, the values given within the parentheses are combined. If you want to assign the combined values to a variable, use the syntax given below:

```
>sampleitems = c(sampleitem1, sampleitem2, sampleitem3, sampleitem4)
```

In the given syntax, the combined values are stored in the `sampleitems` variable. To read the data values of a small dataset, the `c()` command is used. As you know, the data can be in numeric as well as in the text format, so let's understand how the `c()` command is used to read and combine both types of data in R.

Reading and Combining Numerical Data

Numeric values are passed within the parentheses of the `c()` command with the comma separation. Suppose you want to enter the following dataset or values in R:

580 467 679 368 890 382 456 299 789 283 388 623 947

To enter the given data and store it in a variable, run the commands given in Listing 21.1:

Listing 21.1: Running the `c()` Command to Enter Numeric Values

Enters the numeric values using the c() command in a variable

```
>sampledata = c(580,467,679,368,890,382,456,299,789,283,388,623,947)
>sampledata
```

Displays the values

In Listing 21.1, the `sampledata` variable stores the concatenated numeric values. Figure 21.1 shows the execution of the commands given in Listing 21.1:

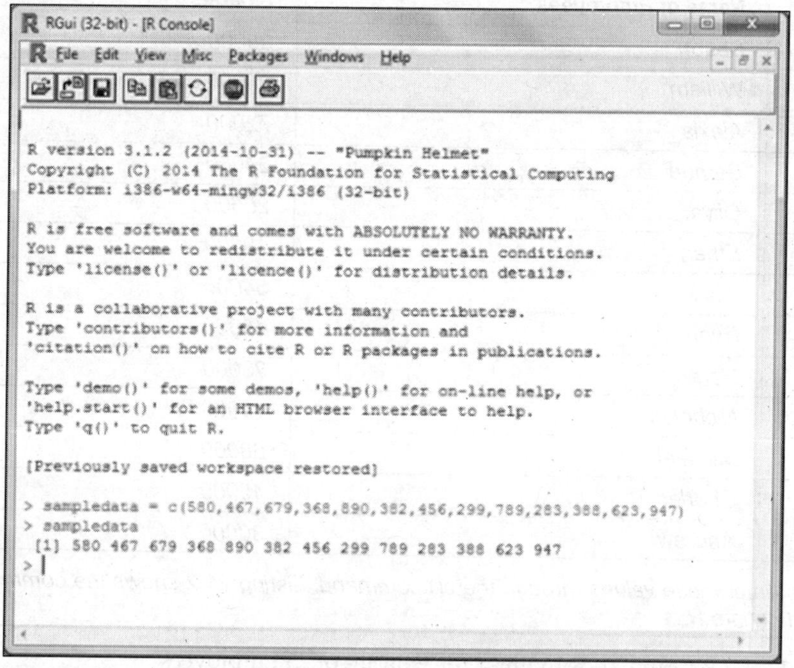

Figure 21.1: Concatenated Numeric Values

SCENARIO

The data analyst of Argon Technology, Mr. Smith, needs to enter the salaries of 25 employees in R. The salaries of the employees are given in Table 21.1:

Table 21.1: Salaries of Employees

S. No.	*Name of Employees*	*Salaries*
1.	Smith	21000
2.	Kate	55000
3.	Jonathan	67000
4.	Chris	54000
5.	Reddy	50000
6.	James	70000
7.	John	56000
8.	Zara	55000
9.	Farah	40000
10.	Ricky	30000
11.	David	20000
12.	Peter	10000

Table 21.1: Salaries of Employees		
S. No.	***Name of Employees***	***Salaries***
13.	*Shaun*	*25000*
14.	*William*	*38000*
15.	*Alexis*	*72000*
16.	*Samuel*	*24000*
17.	*Oliver*	*20000*
18.	*Ethan*	*18000*
19.	*Jack*	*54000*
20.	*Ryan*	*45000*
21.	*Harry*	*23000*
22.	*Nicholas*	*19000*
23.	*Michael*	*68000*
24.	*Charles*	*45000*
25.	*Andrew*	*30000*

He decides to enter these values through the c() command. Listing 21.2 shows the commands Smith used to enter this data into R:

Listing 21.2: Using R Commands to Enter the Salaries of 25 Employees

```
>salaries = c(21000, 55000, 67000, 54000, 50000, 70000, 56000, 55000, 40000, 30000,
20000, 10000, 25000, 38000, 72000, 24000, 20000, 18000, 54000, 45000, 23000, 19000,
68000, 45000, 30000)
>salaries
```

Figure 21.2 shows the execution of the commands given in Listing 21.2:

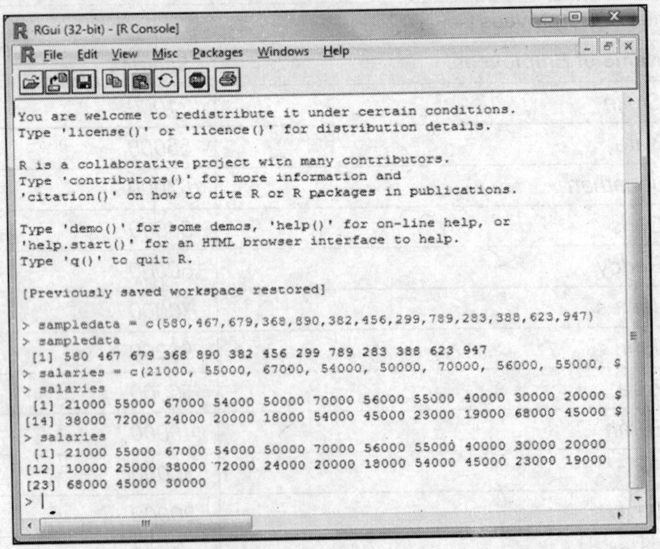

Figure 21.2: Output of the Salaries of Employees

In Figure 21.2, you can see that different rows of values are starting from [1], [12], and [23]. This indicates that the first row contains the 11 values and the second row starts with the 12th value. The last row begins with [23], depicting that the salaries of 25 employees are entered in the `salaries` variable.

SCENARIO

Now, Mr. Smith wants to add the salaries of 5 new employees in the existing data. For this, he uses the salaries variable along with the salaries of the new employees.

Listing 21.3 shows the commands to join datasets with new values in R:

Listing 21.3: Incorporating Existing Data Objects with New Values

Defines new values | Uses existing data object

```
>salaries
>newsalaries = c(salaries, 55000, 30000, 20000, 12000, 67000)
>newsalaries
```

In Listing 21.3, first the data object `salaries` is taken and some extra values are added to it to create a new data object, `newsalaries`. Figure 21.3 shows the output of the commands given in Listing 21.3:

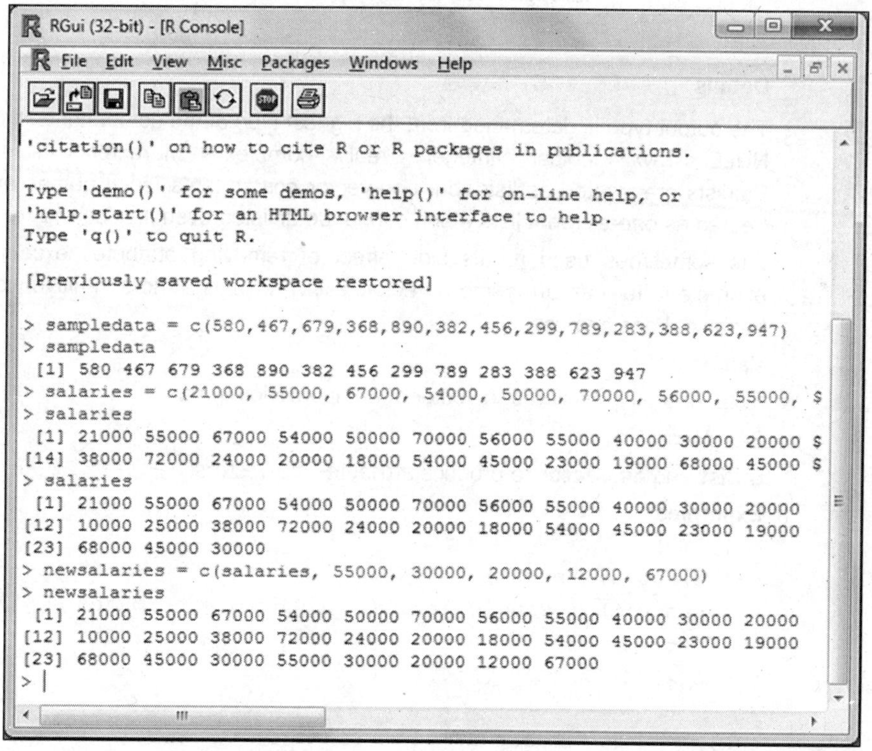

Figure 21.3: Output of Existing Data Object with New Values

The output, shown in Figure 21.3, combines the existing data with the new values in R. Now, let's learn to read the text items in R using the `c()` command.

EXHIBIT 1: The c() Command

Combine Values into a Vector or List

Description

This is a generic function which combines its arguments.

The default method combines its arguments to form a vector. All arguments are coerced to a common type which is the type of the returned value, and all attributes except names are removed.

Usage

```
c(..., recursive=FALSE)
```

Arguments

`...`	objects to be concatenated.
`recursive`	logical. If `recursive = TRUE`, the function recursively descends through lists (and pairlists) combining all their elements into a vector.

Details

The output type is determined from the highest type of the components in the hierarchy NULL < raw < logical < integer < real < complex < character < list < expression. Pairlists are treated as lists, but non-vector components (such names and calls) are treated as one-element lists which cannot be unlisted even if `recursive = TRUE`.

`c` is sometimes used for its side effect of removing attributes except names, for example to turn an array into a vector. `as.vector` is a more intuitive way to do this, but also drops names.

Value

`NULL` or an expression or a vector of an appropriate mode.

See Also

unlist and **as.vector** to produce attribute-free vectors.

Examples

```
c(1,7:9)
c(1:5, 10.5, "next")
## uses with a single argument to drop attributes
x <- 1:4
names(x) <- letters[1:4]
x
c(x)           # has names
as.vector(x)  # no names
dim(x) <- c(2,2)
x
c(x)
as.vector(x)
```

```
## append to a list:
ll <- list(A = 1, c="C")
## do *not* use
c(ll, d = 1:3) # which is == c(ll, as.list(c(d=1:3))
## but rather
c(ll, d = list(1:3))# c() combining two lists
c(list(A=c(B=1)), recursive=TRUE)
c(options(), recursive=TRUE)
c(list(A=c(B=1,C=2), B=c(E=7)), recursive=TRUE)
```

Source: *http://astrostatistics.psu.edu/su07/R/html/base/html/c.html*

Reading and Combining Text Data

The text data is entered using quotes. There is no difference between using single or double quotes as R converts all the quotes to double quotes. The syntaxes to read the text data using the `c()` command are:

```
>c('sampleitem1', 'sampleitem2', 'sampleitem3', 'sampleitem4')
>c("sampleitem1","sampleitem2","sampleitem3","sampleitem4")
>c("sampleitem1",'sampleitem2',"sampleitem3",'sampleitem4')
```

SCENARIO

Reconsider the scenario of Argon Technology, where Smith, the data analyst, wants to enter the name of the employees in R using the c() command.

For this, he runs the commands shown in Listing 21.4:

Listing 21.4: Combining and Reading the Text Data

```
>empnames = c("Smith", "Kate", "Jonathan", "Chris", "Reddy", "James", "John",
"Zara", "Farah", "Ricky", "David", "Peter", "Shaun", "William", "Alexis", "Samuel",
"Oliver", "Ethan", "Jack", "Ryan", "Harry", "Nicholas", "Michael", "Charles", "Andrew")
>empnames
```

As shown in the commands of Listing 21.4, the names of employees are provided in the double quotes. Figure 21.4 shows the output of the commands used in Listing 21.4:

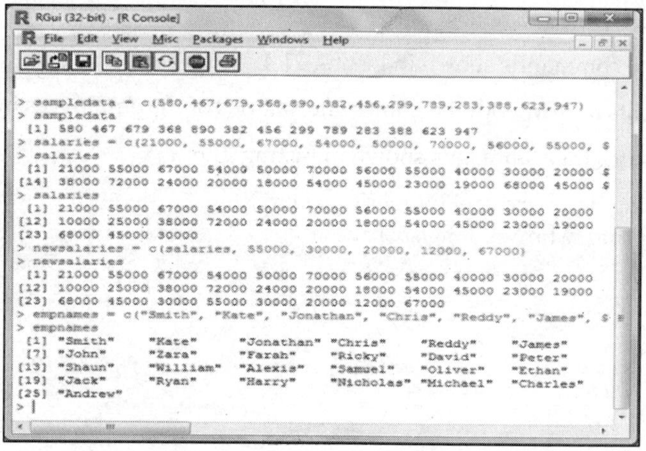

Figure 21.4: Output of Reading the Text Data

Similar to the numeric data, let's look to add new data to the existing data object, `empnames`. Listing 21.5 shows the commands to combine the data object with new values:

Listing 21.5: Adding New Text Values to the Existing Data Object

```
>newempnames = c(empnames, "Mark", "Ruby", "Emily", "Lily", "Sophia")
>newempnames
```

Figure 21.5 shows the output of the commands given in Listing 21.5:

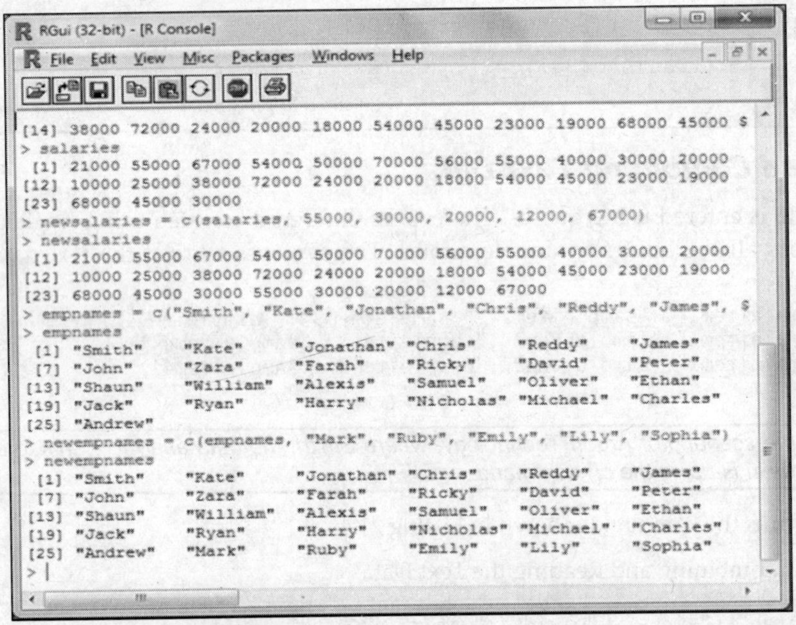

Figure 21.5: Output of Reading Text Data Object with New Values

Reading Both Numeric and Text Values in R

When text and numbers are combined, the entire data object becomes a text variable and the numbers are also converted to text.

For this, he runs the commands shown in Listing 21.4.

Mr. Smith now wants to read both the names and salaries of the employees in the dataset.

To do this, he executes the commands shown in Listing 21.6:

Listing 21.6: Reading Both Text and Numeric Data in R

```
> combine = c(newsalaries, newempnames)
> combine
```

Figure 21.6 shows the output of the commands:

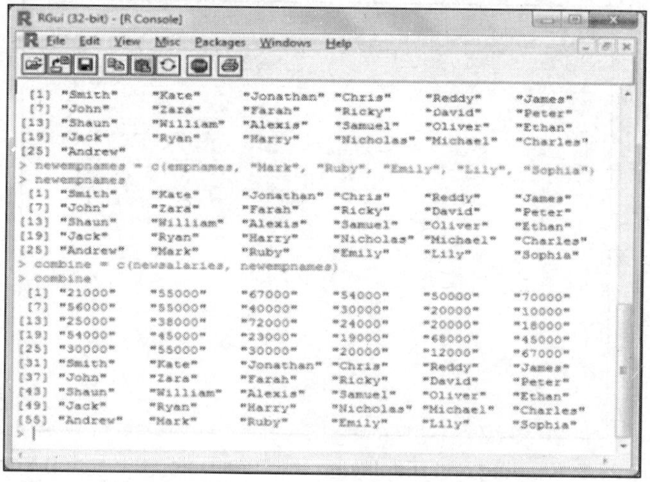

Figure 21.6: Combined Numeric and Text Data

You should note that in Figure 21.6, the numeric data is also available in double quotes like the text data. The `c()` command used in the previous examples is a quick way of getting a series of values stored in a data object. This command is useful when the samples are small but can be tedious when a lot of typing is involved. You have learned that the `c()` command is used to read and combine any type of data. Let's now explore some more ways of putting data in R.

Using the scan() Command

When using the `c()` command, you may find typing all the commas to separate values a little tedious. You can do the same job without using the commas through the `scan()` command. Apart from using the `scan()` command to enter text or numeric data into datasets, you can use this command with the clipboard to get the data from files. Unlike the `c()` command, the `scan()` command uses empty parentheses. After executing the command and pressing the Enter key, you are prompted to enter the desired data, as shown in Figure 21.7:

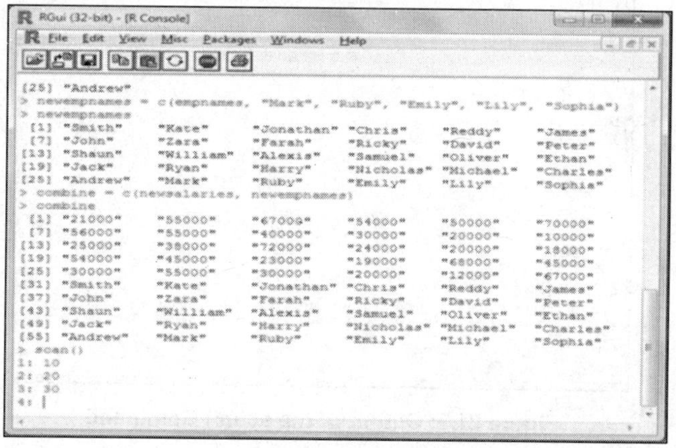

Figure 21.7: Output of the scan() Command

The output of the `scan()` command after reading the data is shown in Figure 21.8:

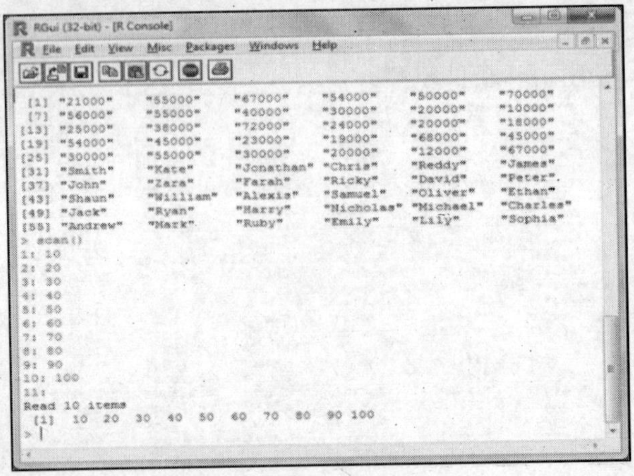

Figure 21.8: Reading and Displaying the Data Using the scan() Command

As shown in Figure 21.8, when you press the Enter key without providing the data, the prompt stops to accept more data and display the read values. You can also store these values in a variable.

SCENARIO

Reconsider the scenario of reading the salaries of employees.

Now, we will read the values using the `scan()` command, as shown in Listing 21.7:

Listing 21.7: Reading the Numeric Values Using the `scan()` Command

```
>empsalaries = scan()
```

After executing this command, you are prompted to enter the salaries of employees. After reading the values of the dataset, run the `empsalaries` command to display the entered values. The output is displayed in Figure 21.9:

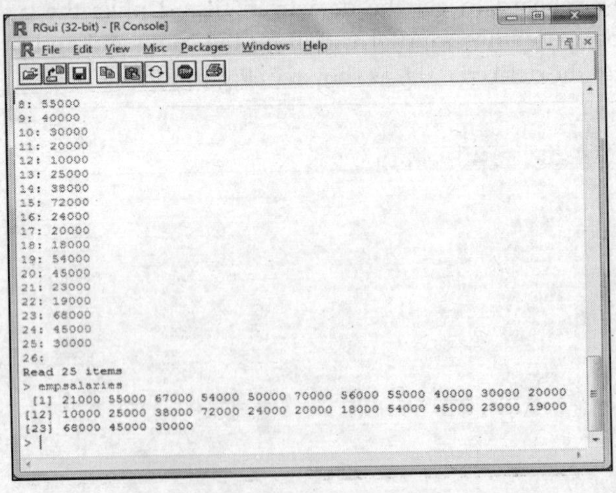

Figure 21.9: Output of the scan() Command

Now, let's learn to read the text data by using the `scan()` command.

Reading the Text Data Using the scan() Command

You can also use the `scan()` command to enter text into datasets. Simply entering the items in quotes will generate an error message, as shown in Figure 21.10:

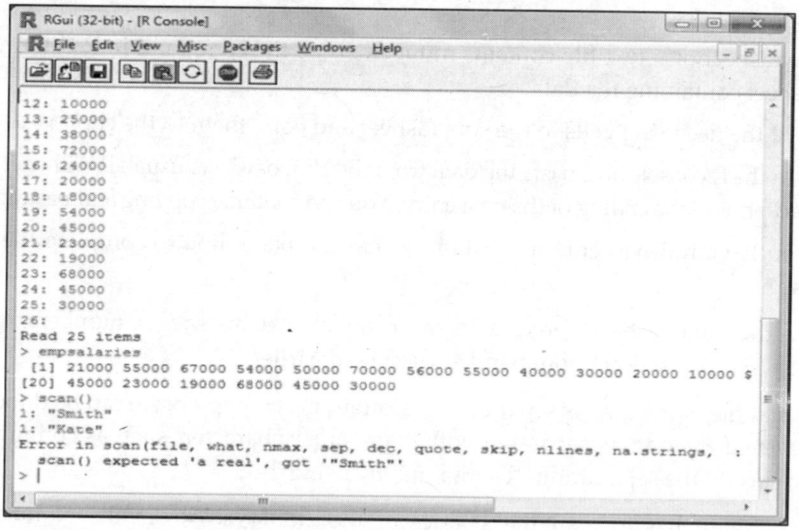

Figure 21.10: Displaying the Error Message while Entering Text Values as Double Quotes

The syntax for entering the text data in the `scan()` command is:

```
>scan(what = 'character')
```

The preceding syntax depicts that the user is specifying that the items entered will be characters and not numbers. After executing the given syntax, you are prompted to enter the text data. Now, you do not need to enter the text data using double quotes, as shown in Figure 21.11:

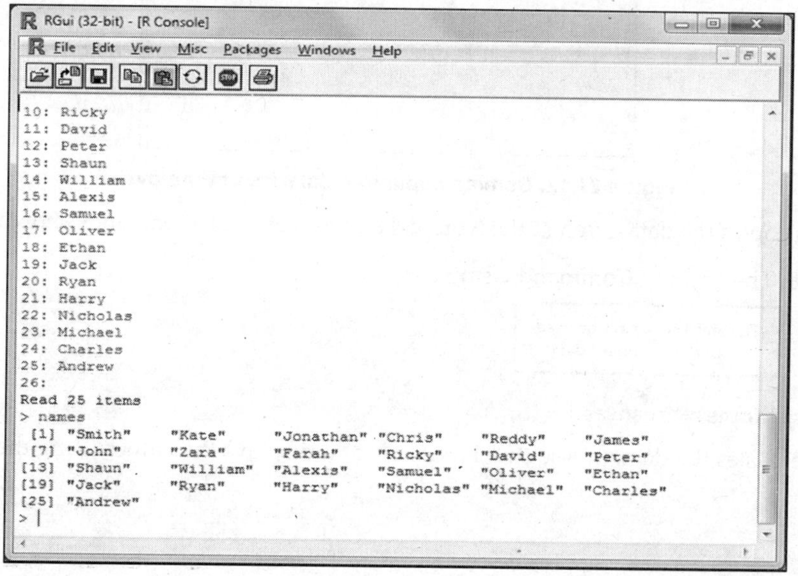

Figure 21.11: Accepting the Names of Employees in the scan() Command

Using Clipboard to Create the Data

You can enter data from other programs such as a text file or a spreadsheet by using the scan() command with the clipboard. Perform the following steps to copy the data from a spreadsheet and read it in R:

1. If a spreadsheet or a text file contains numbers, type the command in R before switching to the spreadsheet containing the data.
2. Highlight the necessary cells in the spreadsheet and copy them to the clipboard.
3. Return to the R console and paste the data from the clipboard. As usual, R will wait until a blank link is entered prior to the ending of the data entry. You can continue copying and pasting data in R.
4. Once you have finished entering data in R, enter a blank line to complete the data acceptance process.

However, if the data to be entered is in the form of text instead of numbers, add the `what = 'character'` to the `scan()` command as discussed earlier.

In case of a text file, if the data is separated by simple spaces, copy paste can be done to read the data in R. However, if the data is separated with some other character, such as comma (,) or period (.), you need to specify the separator in R command by using `sep = ','` or `sep ='.'`.

Suppose Mr. Smith has to read the salaries of the employees from the Notepad file shown in Figure 21.12:

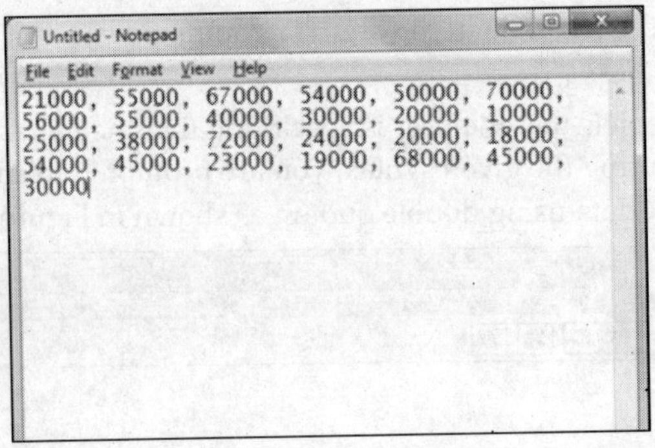

Figure 21.12: Comma Separated Salaries of Employees

For this, he copies the data given in the Notepad and executes the commands shown in Listing 21.8:

Listing 21.8: The `scan()` Command Using `sep`

Defines the separator used in the clipboard data

```
>csv_salaries = scan(sep = ',')
```

Further, he pastes the data, presses the Enter key, and displays the values using the `csv_salaries` variable.

The output is shown in Figure 21.13:

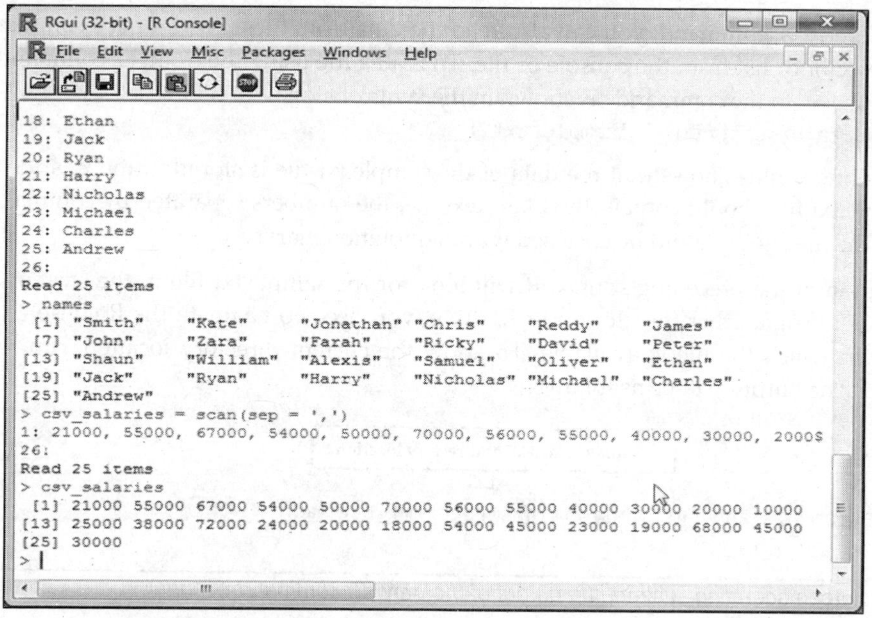

Figure 21.13: Output Using the sep in the scan() Command

As shown in Listing 21.8, the separator should be enclosed in quotes. You need to press the Enter key to finish the data-entry process. In case any value has decimal points, R appends decimals to all the data so that all of it has the same level of precision, as shown in Figure 21.14:

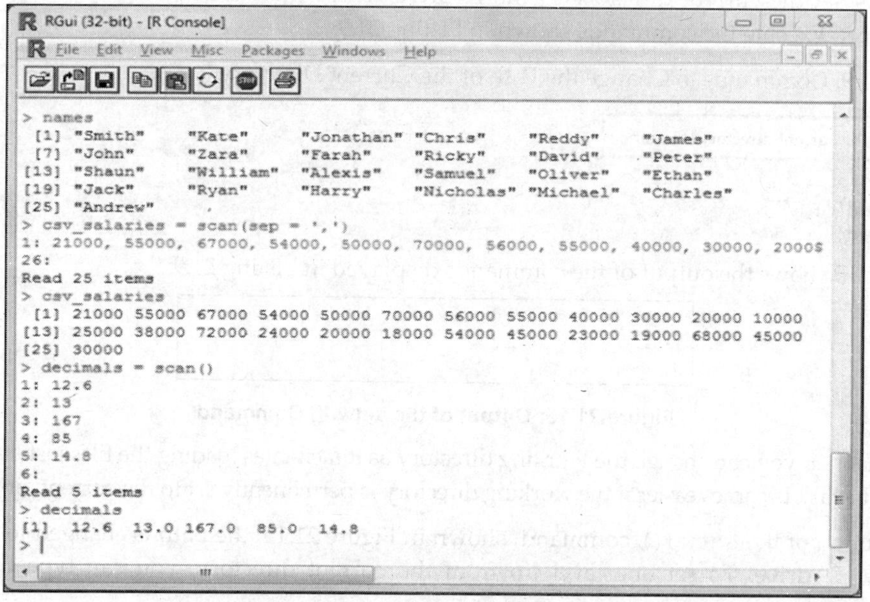

Figure 21.14: Reading and Displaying the Decimal Point Values

If the data is separated by a tab, use `\t` as the separator to inform R about it.

Reading the Data of a File from Disk

Using the `scan()` command, you can also read the data from files. The `scan()` command can read data in a vector or list from the console or file. To read a file using the `scan()` command, add `file = 'filename'` to the command, as shown in the syntax below:

```
>readdata = scan(file = 'sample.txt')
```

The preceding syntax shows that the data of the sample.txt file is stored in the `readdata` variable. The sample.txt file should contain the plain text, i.e. the numbers separated by comma. You should note that the file name should be enclosed within quotation marks.

On execution of the preceding syntax, R will look for the sample.txt file in the current directory. If your file is in some other directory, say E: drive, you need to navigate the R console to locate the directory in which the file is available. To know the current directory location, run the `getwd()` command. The output will be as follows:

Displays curr0065nt directory location

```
"C:/Documents and Settings/Administrator/My Documents"
```

NOTE

In the Macintosh operating system, the output of the getwd() command will be:
"/Users/Administrator"
In the Linux operating system, the output of the getwd() command will be:
"/home/Administrator"
Note that in the above output, the forward slash is used instead of the backslash character.

Now, let's set the current directory to the E: drive where the names of countries are stored in a spreadsheet. Execute the commands shown in Listing 21.9:

Listing 21.9: Commands to Change the Path of the Current Directory

Changes the current directory location

```
>setwd('E:/')
>getwd()
```

Figure 21.15 shows the output of the commands displayed in Listing 21.9:

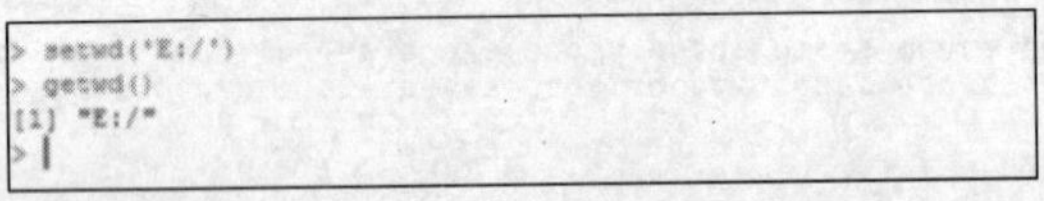

Figure 21.15: Output of the setwd() Command

In this manner, you can change the working directory as it facilitates loading the files just by typing their names. The task becomes easier if the working directory is permanently set to the current directory.

On execution of the `setwd()` command, shown in Figure 21.15, the path is changed to the working directory, E: drive. To set one level up from the current directory, you can type the following command:

```
>setwd('..')
```

To display the list of the files/folders available in the current directory, use the `dir()` or `list.files()` commands. The output of these commands is shown in Figure 21.16:

```
> setwd('E:/')
> getwd()
[1] "E:/"
> dir()
 [1] "$RECYCLE.BIN"               "26_11_2014"
 [3] "AlbumArtSmall.jpg"          "Dell Vostro 2520 Drivers"
 [5] "DT_BACKUP"                  "Folder.jpg"
 [7] "jars"                       "Outlook"
 [9] "Referring Data"             "suchita_kogent"
[11] "System Volume Information" "XML"
> list.files()
 [1] "$RECYCLE.BIN"               "26_11_2014"
 [3] "AlbumArtSmall.jpg"          "Dell Vostro 2520 Drivers"
 [5] "DT_BACKUP"                  "Folder.jpg"
 [7] "jars"                       "Outlook"
 [9] "Referring Data"             "suchita_kogent"
[11] "System Volume Information" "XML"
> |
```

Figure 21.16: Output of the dir() and list.files() Commands

By default, the files and folders of the current working directory are displayed; however, if you provide the path for any other directory, the files and folders of that directory will be displayed. For example, the files and folders available in the `DT_BACKUP` directory are displayed in Figure 21.17:

```
> setwd('E:/')
> getwd()
[1] "E:/"
> dir()
 [1] "$RECYCLE.BIN"               "26_11_2014"
 [3] "AlbumArtSmall.jpg"          "Dell Vostro 2520 Drivers"
 [5] "DT_BACKUP"                  "Folder.jpg"
 [7] "jars"                       "Outlook"
 [9] "Referring Data"             "suchita_kogent"
[11] "System Volume Information" "XML"
> list.files()
 [1] "$RECYCLE.BIN"               "26_11_2014"
 [3] "AlbumArtSmall.jpg"          "Dell Vostro 2520 Drivers"
 [5] "DT_BACKUP"                  "Folder.jpg"
 [7] "jars"                       "Outlook"
 [9] "Referring Data"             "suchita_kogent"
[11] "System Volume Information" "XML"
> dir('E:/DT_BACKUP')
[1] "Running Projects"
> |
```

Figure 21.17: Displaying Directories of a Specific Folder

Note that the listing of files and folders is in the alphabetical order, and the files are shown along with their extensions, whereas folders are displayed by their names. If the files are not displayed with extensions, it will be difficult to differentiate between them and folders. By default, invisible files are not displayed but can be seen by running the following command:

```
>dir(all.files = TRUE)
```

In Windows and Macintosh operating systems, instead of specifying the names of the files, you can select the file of your choice from the given list.

For this, add `file.choose()` in the `scan()` command, as shown in Figure 21.18:

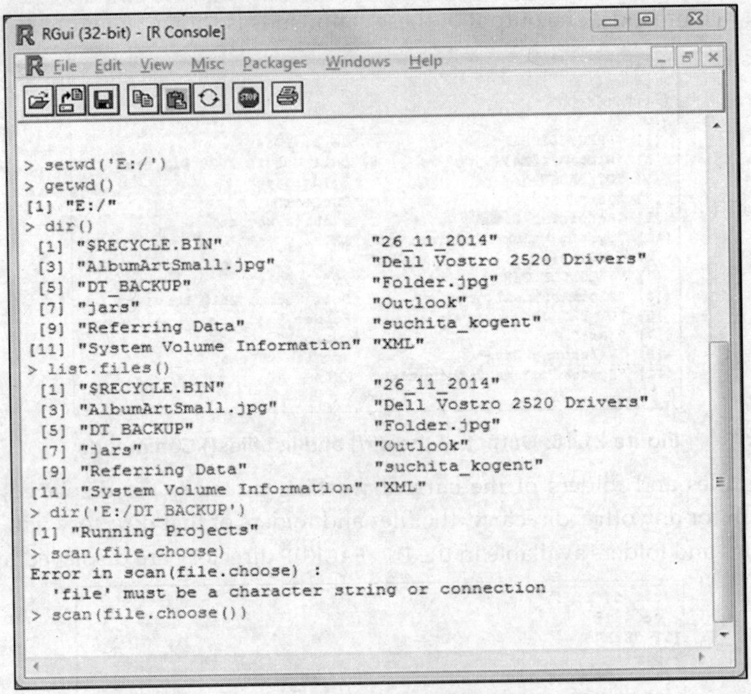

Figure 21.18: Running the file.choose() Command

On execution of the command, the Select file dialog box opens, as shown in Figure 21.19:

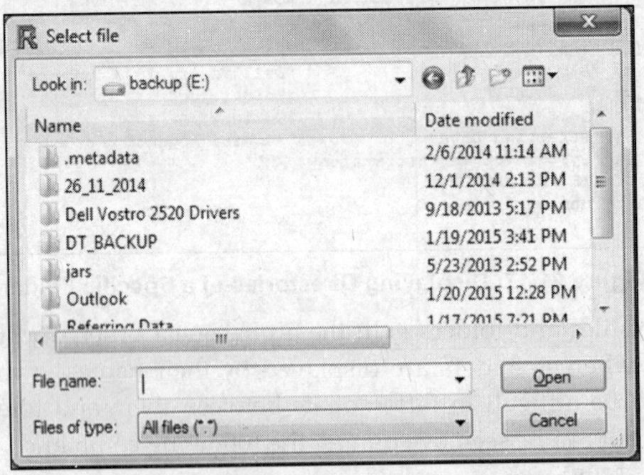

Figure 21.19: The Select file Dialog Box

When you select a file, the data contained in it is displayed on the R console. The plain text file containing the numeric values should be selected. However, to select the file containing characters, separated by commas, run the command shown in Listing 21.10:

Listing 21.10: The Command to Read a CSV File

```
>choosefile = scan(file.choose(), what = 'character', sep = ',')
>choosefile
```

Suppose we choose a file containing the names of the employees with comma separation. The output is displayed in Figure 21.20:

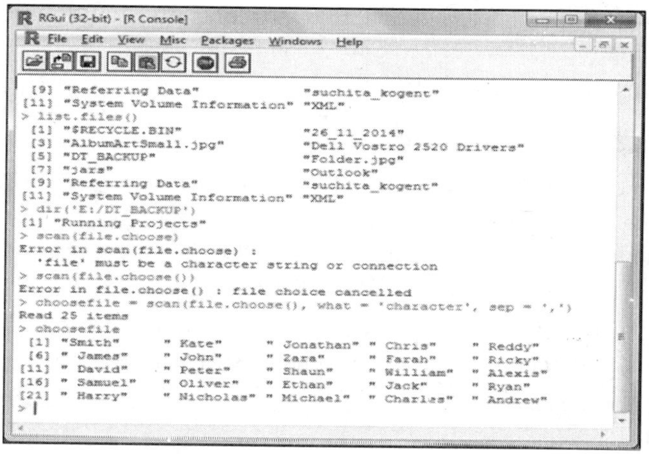

Figure 21.20: Output of Reading a Comma Separated Text Data File Using the file.choose() Command

NOTE

The `file.choose()` command does not work on the Linux operating system.

The `file.choose()` command helps to select a file from any location without altering the working directory or typing the complete name of the file with its path.

Reading Multiple Data Values from Large Files

Till now, the data items created or read were simple as they contained a single value. Let's now learn to read multiple data values in R.

SCENARIO

Suppose Mr. Smith wants to read the complete data shown in Table 21.1. The data of employees is maintained in a CSV file containing data in various fields, such as S.No. Names, Country, and Salaries, as shown in Figure 21.21:

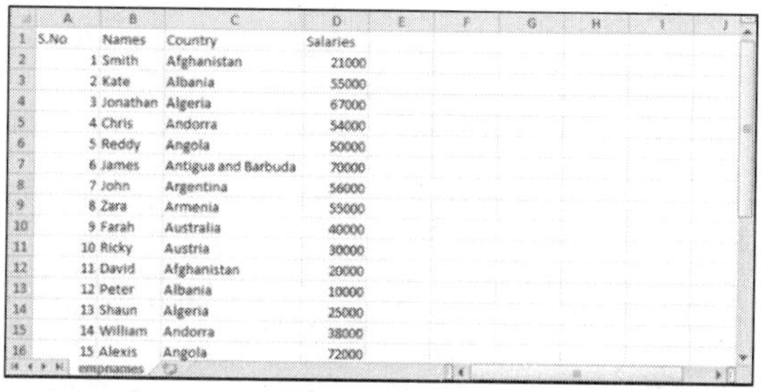

S.No	Names	Country	Salaries
1	Smith	Afghanistan	21000
2	Kate	Albania	55000
3	Jonathan	Algeria	67000
4	Chris	Andorra	54000
5	Reddy	Angola	50000
6	James	Antigua and Barbuda	70000
7	John	Argentina	56000
8	Zara	Armenia	55000
9	Farah	Australia	40000
10	Ricky	Austria	30000
11	David	Afghanistan	20000
12	Peter	Albania	10000
13	Shaun	Algeria	25000
14	William	Andorra	38000
15	Alexis	Angola	72000

Figure 21.21: Displaying the Data of Employees

The list of data items, shown in Figure 21.21, is known as a vector. A vector can have a single value or multiple values. While displaying the list, R provides an index to see how many items are available. Generally, R deals with large datasets than single vectors of values. The `scan()` command is used to read simple vectors.

To read a large amount of data from complicated files containing multiple items or spreadsheets, like the one shown in Figure 21.21, the `read.csv()` command is used.

Let's work with the `read.csv()` command.

Using the read.csv() Command

Generally, large amounts of data would be taken from spreadsheets and using the clipboard for this purpose would be a complex task. Therefore, for reading these data from spreadsheets, the `read.csv()` command is used. The syntax for using this command is:

```
>read.csv()
```

The given syntax will read the entire CSV file and display the data on the console. You can add various instructions with the `read.csv()` command, such as:

- **file** to specify the file name
- **sep** to provide the separator
- **header** to specify whether or not the first row of the CSV file should be set as column names. By default, the value is set to TRUE
- **rows.names** to specify row names for the data. Generally, this will be a column in the dataset. You can set the row names by setting the `row.names = n`, where n is the column number

To read the data from the spreadsheet shown in Figure 21.21, Mr. Smith runs the commands shown in Listing 21.11:

Listing 21.11: Command to Read the Data from a Spreadsheet

```
>read.csv(file.choose(), header = TRUE, row.names = 1)
```

Before executing the command shown in Listing 21.11, ensure that the file to be read is saved in an appropriate format (for example, XLS). Assign a name to the file and open it from the Select file dialog box. The output will be displayed, as shown in Figure 21.22:

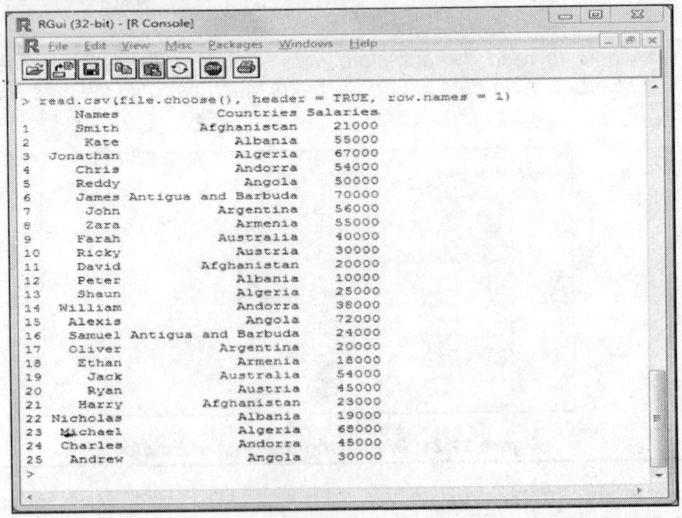

Figure 21.22: Output of Executing the read.csv() Command

In Figure 21.22, each row is labelled with a simple index number. Here, the data is less so it may not seem of great relevance; however, this command is of great help when you need to work with large amounts of data. Reading data from a CSV file using the `read.csv()` command implies that you have to type less for data entries.

NOTE

Most computer programs produce CSV format files, including spreadsheets.

Using the read.table() Command

Apart from the CSV format, the data can be available in other formats, including spaces or tabs as separators. The `read.table()` command is generally used to read plain, text data, which is generally in the form of tables.

To read the data separated with spaces, run the command shown in Listing 21.12:

Listing 21.12: Using the `read.table()` Command

```
>readfile = read.table(file.choose(), header = TRUE)
>readfile
```

Execution of the preceding command prompts you to select the file. After selecting the file in which the names of the employees are stored as a single column, the output is displayed as shown in Figure 21.23:

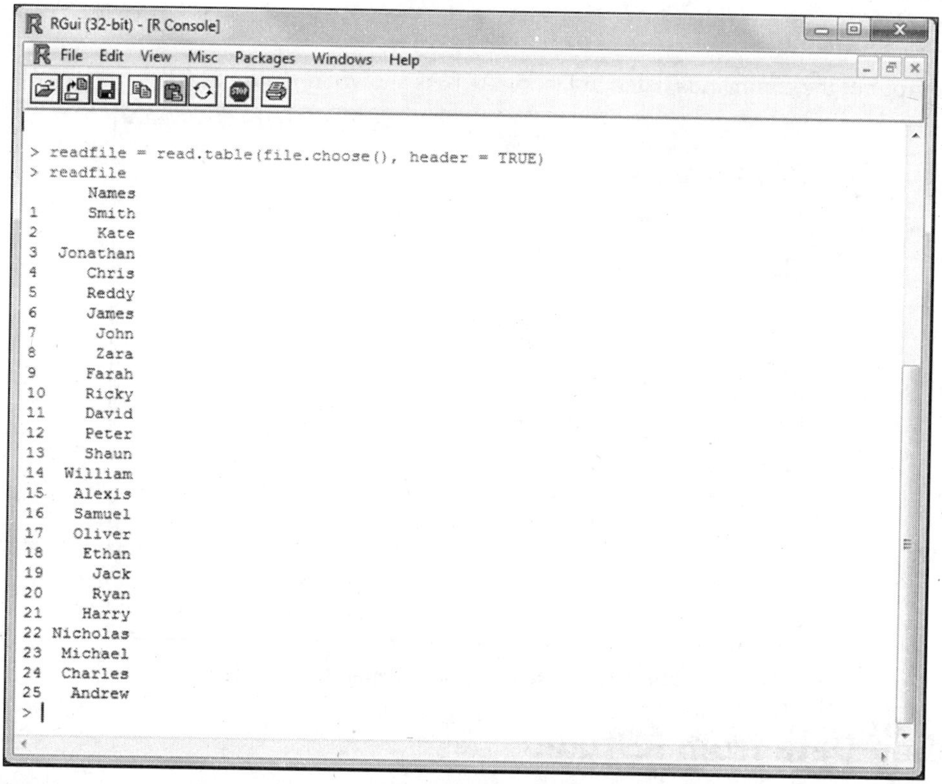

Figure 21.23: Output of the read.table() Command Reading the File Separated by Spaces

Now, suppose the values saved in the `employees.txt` file are separated by tabs, as shown in Figure 21.24:

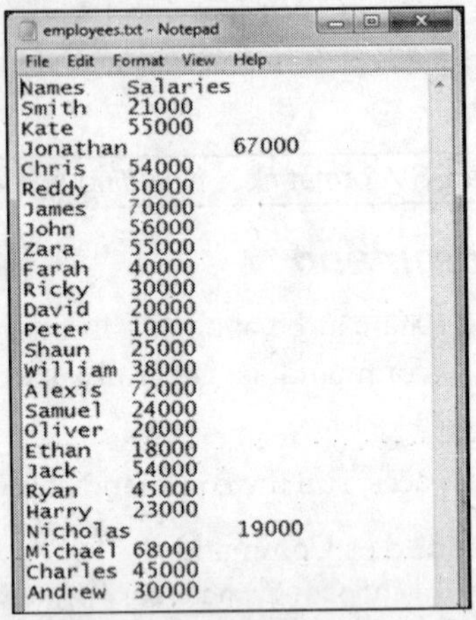

Figure 21.24: Data Separated by Tabs

To read the data from this file, you need to run the commands shown in Listing 21.13:

Listing 21.13: Read Tab Separated Data

```
>readfile_tab = read.table(file.choose(), header = TRUE, sep = '\t')
> readfile_tab
```

The output of the commands listed in Listing 21.13 is shown in Figure 21.25:

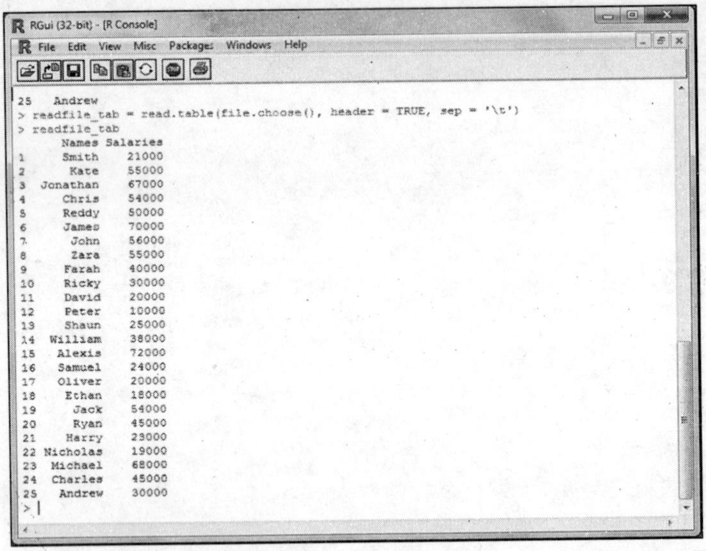

Figure 21.25: Reading Data Separated by Tabs

Reading Data from RStudio

Apart from reading the data using various commands on the R console, you can directly read the data using the RStudio GUI. RStudio allows you to import datasets into the R environment without executing a series of commands. Perform the following steps to read a CSV/txt file using the RStudio GUI:

1. Select Start→All Programs→RStudio→RStudio. The RStudio workspace opens.
2. In the RStudio workspace, click the Import Dataset option (Figure 21.26).
3. Select the From Text File option, as shown in Figure 21.26:

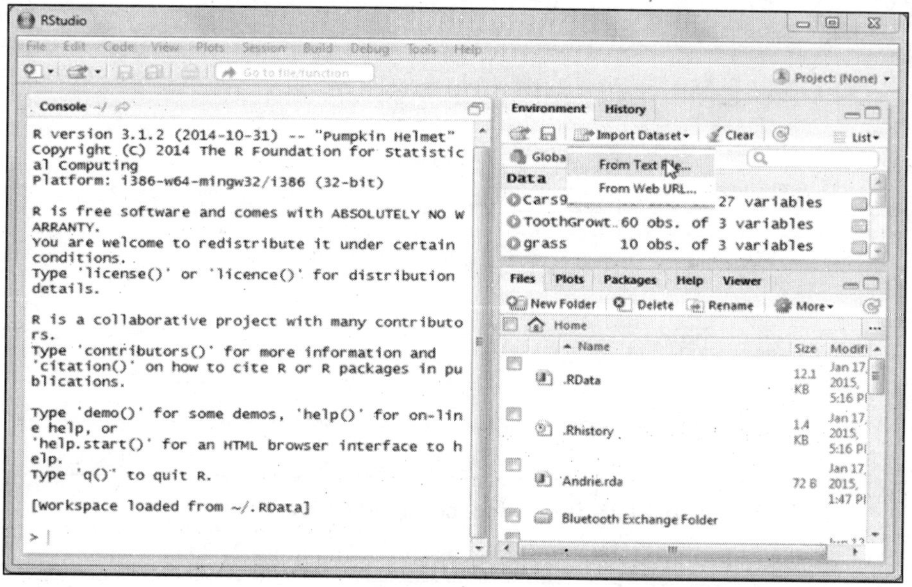

Figure 21.26: Selecting the Option to Import Dataset in RStudio

The Select File to Import dialog box opens (Figure 21.27).

4. Navigate to the appropriate location, select the file to be imported, and click the Open button. In our case, we have selected the `empnames.csv` file, as shown in Figure 21.27:

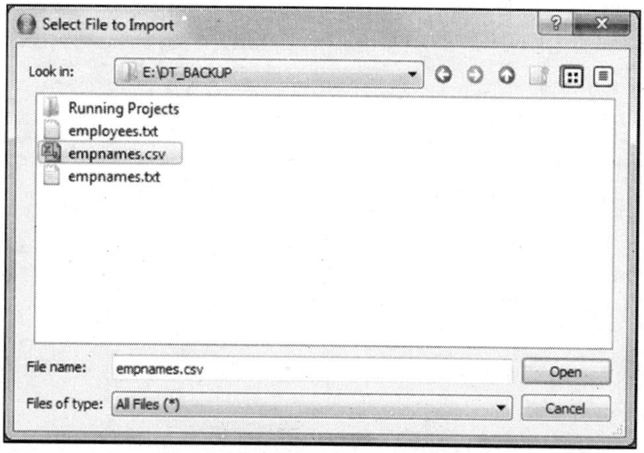

Figure 21.27: The Select File to Import Dialog Box

The Import Dataset pane opens, displaying the data of the input file and data frame. Figure 21.28 displays the data of the `empnames.csv` file.

5. Click the Import button, as shown in Figure 21.28:

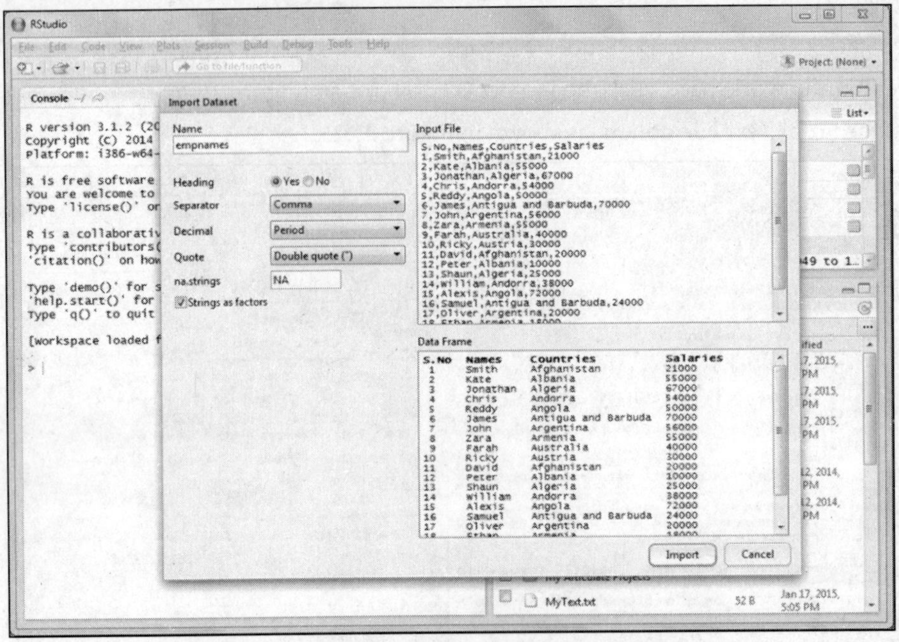

Figure 21.28: Displaying the Import Dataset Pane

The output of the file is displayed in the RStudio, as shown in Figure 21.29:

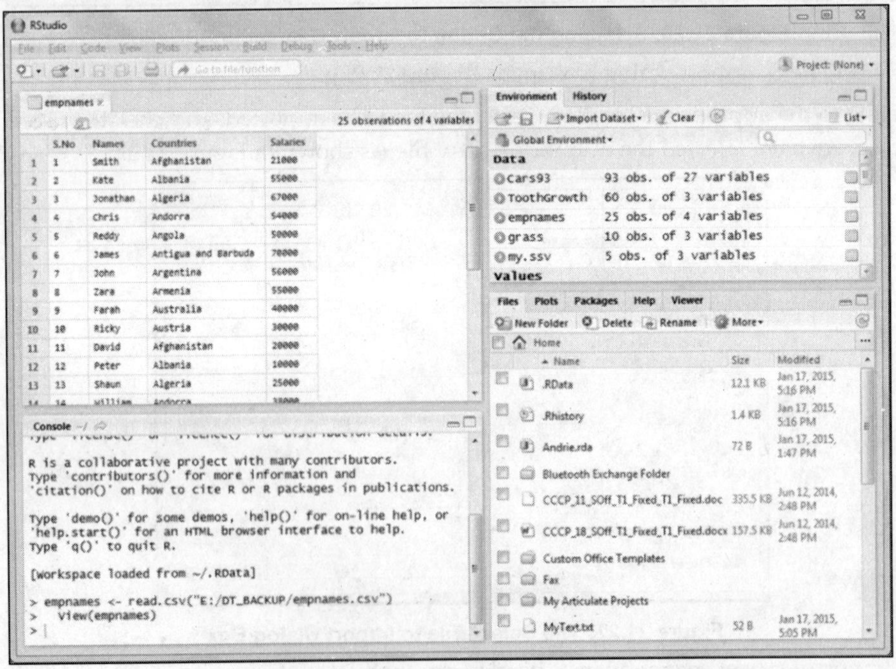

Figure 21.29: Data from the CSV File Imported to RStudio

Exporting Data from R

After undergoing computations in R, the data now needs to be used in reports or various other sources. Therefore, we need to extract data from R. Exporting data from R to other applications in the CSV format is as simple as reading data from other source files into R. To create a CSV file, the `write.csv()` function is used. Similar to the `read.csv()` and `read.table()` commands, the `write.csv()` and `write.table()` commands are used to extract data from R.

Using the write.table() Command

The `write.table()` command is used to write the data stored in a vector to a file. The data is saved using the delimiters such as spaces or tabs. Here, let's use the `readfile_tab` data to write to the `mydata.txt` file. The data in this file will be saved using tabs. Run the following command to write the data in a text file:

```
>write.table(readfile_tab, "E:/mydata.txt", sep = "\t")
```

The command execution is shown in Figure 21.30:

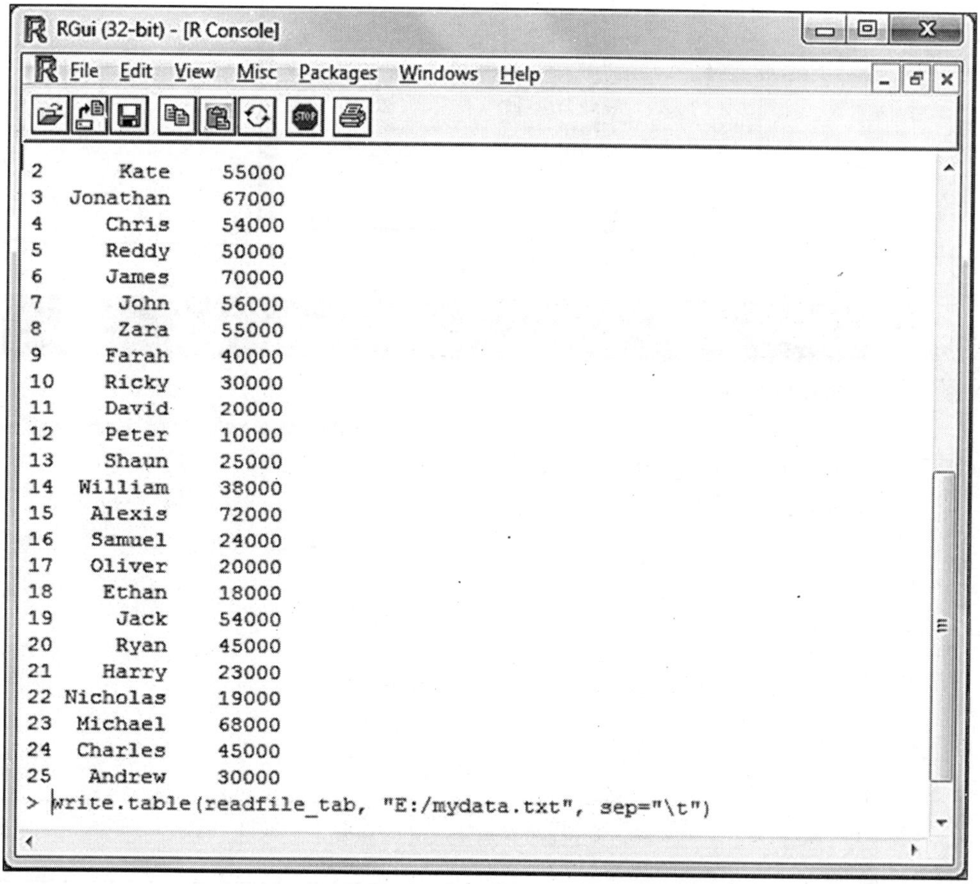

Figure 21.30: Executing the write.table() Command

The output will be saved in the `mydata.txt` file, as shown in Figure 21.31:

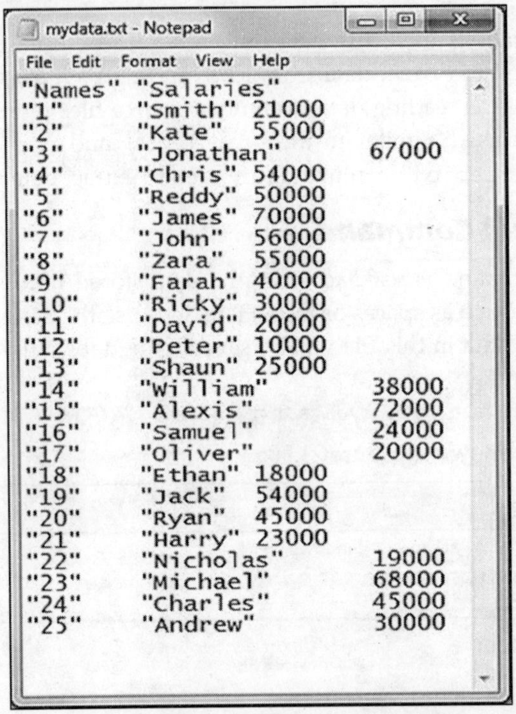

```
"Names" "Salaries"
"1"     "Smith" 21000
"2"     "Kate"  55000
"3"     "Jonathan"      67000
"4"     "Chris" 54000
"5"     "Reddy" 50000
"6"     "James" 70000
"7"     "John"  56000
"8"     "Zara"  55000
"9"     "Farah" 40000
"10"    "Ricky" 30000
"11"    "David" 20000
"12"    "Peter" 10000
"13"    "Shaun" 25000
"14"    "William"       38000
"15"    "Alexis"        72000
"16"    "Samuel"        24000
"17"    "Oliver"        20000
"18"    "Ethan" 18000
"19"    "Jack"  54000
"20"    "Ryan"  45000
"21"    "Harry" 23000
"22"    "Nicholas"      19000
"23"    "Michael"       68000
"24"    "Charles"       45000
"25"    "Andrew"        30000
```

Figure 21.31: Tab Data Stored in a Text File

EXHIBIT 2: The write.table () Command

Description

`write.table` prints its required argument `x` (after converting it to a data frame if it is not one nor a matrix) to a file or connection.

Usage

```
write.table(x, file = "", append = FALSE, quote = TRUE,
  sep = " ",
eol = "\n", na = "NA", dec = ".", row.names = TRUE,
col.names = TRUE, qmethod = c("escape", "double"),
fileEncoding = "")
write.csv(...)
write.csv2(...)
```

`x`	the object to be written, preferably a matrix or data frame. If not, it is attempted to coerce `x` to a data frame.
`file`	either a character string naming a file or a connection open for writing. "" indicates output to the console.

`append`	logical. Only relevant if `file` is a character string. If `TRUE`, the output is appended to the file. If `FALSE`, any existing file of the name is destroyed.
`quote`	a logical value (`TRUE` or `FALSE`) or a numeric vector. If `TRUE`, any character or factor columns will be surrounded by double quotes. If a numeric vector, its elements are taken as the indices of columns to quote. In both cases, row and column names are quoted if they are written. If `FALSE`, nothing is quoted.
`sep`	the field separator string. Values within each row of `x` are separated by this string.
`eol`	the character(s) to print at the end of each line (row). For example, `eol = "\r\n"` will produce Windows' line endings on a Unix-alike OS, and `eol = "\r"` will produce files as expected by Excel:mac 2004.
`na`	the string to use for missing values in the data.
`dec`	the string to use for decimal points in numeric or complex columns: must be a single character.
`row.names`	either a logical value indicating whether the row names of x are to be written along with x, or a character vector of row names to be written.
`col.names`	either a logical value indicating whether the column names of x are to be written along with x, or a character vector of column names to be written. See the section on 'CSV files' for the meaning of `col.names = NA`.
`qmethod`	a character string specifying how to deal with embedded double quote characters when quoting strings. Must be one of "`escape`" (default for `write.table`), in which case the quote character is escaped in C style by a backslash, or"`double`" (default for `write.csv` and `write.csv2`), in which case it is doubled. You can specify just the initial letter.
`fileEncoding`	character string: if non-empty declares the encoding to be used on a file (not a connection) so the character data can be re-encoded as they are written. See `file`.
`...`	arguments to `write.table: append, col.names, sep, dec` and `qmethod` cannot be altered.

Details

If the table has no columns the rownames will be written only if `row.names = TRUE`, and vice versa.

Real and complex numbers are written to the maximal possible precision.

If a data frame has matrix-like columns these will be converted to multiple columns in the result (via as.matrix) and so a character `col.names` or a numeric `quote` should refer to the columns in the result, not the input. Such matrix-like columns are unquoted by default.

Any columns in a data frame which are lists or have a class (e.g., dates) will be converted by the appropriate `as.character` method: such columns are unquoted by default. On the other hand, any class information for a matrix is discarded and non-atomic (e.g., list) matrices are coerced to character.

Only columns which have been converted to character will be quoted if specified by `quote`.

The `dec` argument only applies to columns that are not subject to conversion to character because they have a class or are part of a matrix-like column (or matrix), in particular to columns protected by I (). Use options("`OutDec`") to control such conversions.

In almost all cases, the conversion of numeric quantities is governed by the option "`scipen`" (see options), but with the internal equivalent of `digits = 15`. For finer control, use format to make a character matrix/data frame, and call `write.table` on that.

These functions check for a user interrupt every 1000 lines of output.

If `file` is a non-open connection, an attempt is made to open it and then close it after use.

To write a Unix-style file on Windows, use a binary connection, e.g. `file = file("filename", "wb")`.

CSV files

By default, there is no column name for a column of row names. If `col.names = NA` and `row.names = TRUE` a blank column name is added, which is the convention used for CSV files to be read by spreadsheets. Note that such CSV files can be read in R by

```
read.csv(file = "<filename>", row.names = 1)
```

`write.csv` and `write.csv2` provide convenience wrappers for writing CSV files. They set `sep` and `dec` (see below), `qmethod = "double"`, and `col.names` to `NA` if `row.names = TRUE` (the default) and to `TRUE` otherwise.

`write.csv` uses "`.`" for the decimal point and a comma for the separator.

`write.csv2` uses a comma for the decimal point and a semicolon for the separator, the Excel convention for CSV files in some Western European locales.

These wrappers are deliberately inflexible: they are designed to ensure that the correct conventions are used to write a valid file. Attempts to change `append`, `col.names`, `sep`, `dec` or `qmethod` are ignored, with a warning.

CSV files do not record an encoding, and this causes problems if they are not ASCII for many other applications. Windows Excel 2007/10 will open files (e.g., by the file association mechanism) correctly if they are ASCII or UTF-16 (use `fileEncoding = "UTF-16LE"`) or perhaps in the current Windows codepage (e.g., `"CP1252"`), but the 'Text Import Wizard' (from the 'Data' tab) allows far more choice of encodings. Excel:mac 2004/8 can *import* only 'Macintosh' (which seems to mean Mac Roman), 'Windows' (perhaps Latin-1) and 'PC-8' files. OpenOffice 3.x asks for the character set when opening the file.

There is an IETF RFC4180 (https://tools.ietf.org/html/rfc4180) for CSV files, which mandates comma as the separator and CRLF line endings. `write.csv` writes compliant files on Windows: use `eol = "\r\n"` on other platforms.

Note

`write.table` can be slow for data frames with large numbers (hundreds or more) of columns: this is inevitable as each column could be of a different class and so must be handled separately. If they are all of the same class, consider using a matrix instead.

Source: https://stat.ethz.ch/R-manual/R-devel/library/utils/html/write.table.html

Using the write.csv() Command

Apart from the delimiters, such as period or tab, the comma separated values can also be stored in files. Write the data in the CSV file using the `write.csv()` command. The following command is executed to store the data using the comma delimiter:

```
>write.csv(readfile_tab, "E:/sampledata.txt")
```

The execution of the preceding command on the R console is shown in Figure 21.32:

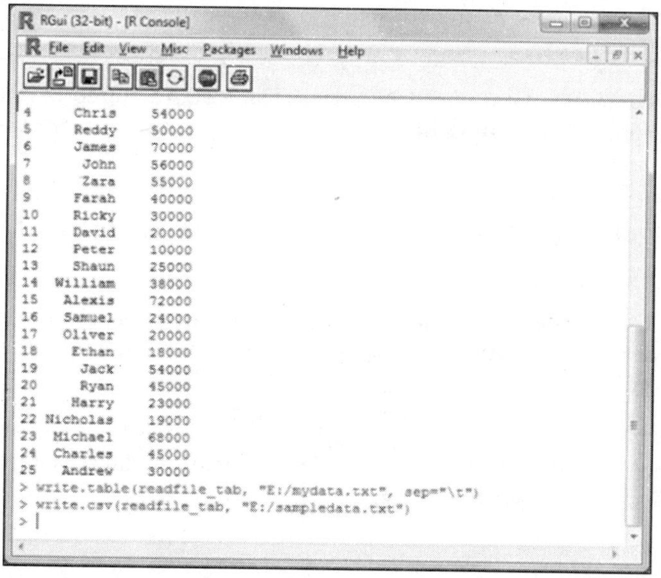

Figure 21.32: Execution of the write.csv() Command

The data will be stored as a CSV file, as shown in Figure 21.33:

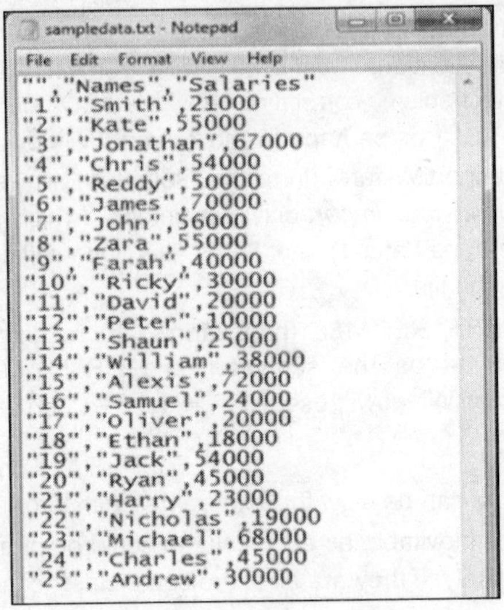

```
sampledata.txt - Notepad
File Edit Format View Help
"","Names","Salaries"
"1","Smith",21000
"2","Kate",55000
"3","Jonathan",67000
"4","Chris",54000
"5","Reddy",50000
"6","James",70000
"7","John",56000
"8","Zara",55000
"9","Farah",40000
"10","Ricky",30000
"11","David",20000
"12","Peter",10000
"13","Shaun",25000
"14","William",38000
"15","Alexis",72000
"16","Samuel",24000
"17","Oliver",20000
"18","Ethan",18000
"19","Jack",54000
"20","Ryan",45000
"21","Harry",23000
"22","Nicholas",19000
"23","Michael",68000
"24","Charles",45000
"25","Andrew",30000
```

Figure 21.33: Data Stored as the Comma Separated Values

Summary

In this chapter, you learned about the R commands, such as `c()`, `scan()`, `read.csv()`, `read.table()`, `write.csv()`, and `write.table()`, used to read and export data from datasets. You also learned to import and export data using RStudio.

Quick Revise

Multiple-Choice Questions

Q1. There are two datasets, data1 and data2. data1 has 1 2 3 4 5 stored in it and data2 has 6 7 8 9 stored in it. Which of the following is the correct command to place the data of data2 after the data of data1?

a. > data3 =c(data1, data2)
b. > data3 =c(data2, data1)
c. > data3 =c(data1,data2)
d. > data3 =c(data2,data1)

Ans. The correct option is a.

Q2. Considering the datasets used in the previous question, select the correct command to combine the data of data1 and data2 in a manner that the resultant dataset has entries in the following form:

6 7 1 2 3 4 5 8 9

a. > data3 =c(6, 7, data1, 8, 9)
b. > data3 =c(data1, data2)
c. > data3 =c(data2, data1)
d. > data3 =c(6, 7, 8, 9, data1)

Ans. The correct option is a.

Q3. Which of the following is the correct format for entering text as data by using the scan() command?

a. > scan(character)
b. > scan(what = 'character')

c. > scan(what = character)

d. > Scan(what ="character")

Ans. The correct option is b.

Q4. A programmer wishes to use the scan() command for entering the following text in a dataset in R:

2, 3, 4, 5, 6.7, 7, 8.1, 9

Which of the following is the correct syntax to create a dataset, data4, containing the above data?

a. > data4 = scan (2, 3, 4, 5, 6.7, 7, 8.1, 9)

b. > data4 = scan(sep = ,) 2, 3, 4, 5, 6.7, 7, 8.1, 9

c. > data4 = scan(sep = ',') 2, 3, 4, 5, 6.7, 7, 8.1, 9

d. > data4 = scan(sep = 2,3,4,5,6.7,7,8.1,9)

Ans. The correct option is c.

Q5. Which among the following is the correct output of the dataset created in the previous question?

a. [1] 2 3 4 5 6.7 7 8.1 9

b. [1] 2, 3, 4, 5, 6.7, 7, 8.1, 9

c. [1] 2.0 3.0 4.0 5.0 6.7 7.0 8.1 9.0

d. [1] 2 3 4 5 6 7 8 9

Ans. The correct option is c.

Q6. Which command among the following is used to change the working directory in R?

a. getwd()

b. setwd()

c. c()

d. ls()

Ans. The correct option is b.

Q7. While using the scan() function, which command is used to input files that have data separated by characters other than a comma?

a. file.open()

b. file.choose()

c. file.select()

d. file()

Ans. The correct option is b.

Q8. At the time of exiting an active R session, a programmer wishes to save the entire progress of the session. Which of the following commands should the programmer use?

a. save(list = ls(all=TRUE), file = 'filename')

b. save.image(file = 'filename')

c. write(x, file = "data", ncolumns = if(is.character(x)) 1 else 5, sep = " ")

d. save(list, file = 'filename')

Ans. The correct option is b.

Q9. The write.table() command is used for writing matrix and data frame objects to disk. In the following write.table() command syntax, what does 'myselect' signify?

```
write.table(myselect, file = 'filename', row.names = TRUE, sep = ' ', col.names =
TRUE)
```

a. Data item that the user wishes to write to the disk

b. Name of the file where the data will be stored

c. A random R variable

d. Source directory for the file

Ans. The correct option is a.

Q10. In the syntax shown in the previous question, what does 'filename' signify?

a. Data item that the user wishes to write to the disk

b. Name of the file where the data will be stored

c. A random R variable

d. Source directory for the file

Ans. The correct option is b.

Subjective Questions

Q1. Explain the working of the c() command in R.

Ans. The c() command in R is used to combine or concatenate two or more values. The syntax for using the c() command is:

```
>c(sampleitem1, sampleitem2, sampleitem3, sampleitem4)
```

In the preceding syntax, the values given within the parentheses are combined. If you want to assign the combined values to a variable, use the syntax given below:

```
>sampleitems = c(sampleitem1, sampleitem2, sampleitem3, sampleitem4)
```

In the given syntax, the combined values are stored in the sampleitems variable. To read the data values of a small dataset, the `c()` command is used.

Q2. Explain the working of the scan() command in R.

Ans. When using the `c()` command, you may find typing all the commas to separate values a little tedious. You can do the same job without using the commas through the `scan()` command. Apart from using the `scan()` command to enter text or numeric data into datasets, you can use this command with the clipboard to get the data from files.

Unlike the `c()` command, the `scan()` command uses empty parentheses. After executing the command and pressing the Enter key, you are prompted to enter the desired data.

Q3. Compare the write.table() and write.csv() commands.

Ans. The `write.table()` command is used to write the data stored in a vector to a file. The data is saved using the delimiters, such as spaces or tabs. Apart from the delimiters, such as period or tab, the comma separated values can also be stored in files. The `write.csv()` command is used to write the data in the CSV file.

22

Manipulating and Processing Data in R

A data structure is a specialized format for organizing and storing data values. R provides various types of data structures, such as vectors and data frames. It also provides various types of functions to manipulate and process the data stored in different data structures. Some examples of such functions are `subset()`, `merge()`, and `order()`. The `subset()` function helps in extracting particular datasets from data structures. The `merge()` function helps in joining the data of data structures. The `order()` function helps in sorting data in ascending order or descending order. In addition, R provides techniques for reshaping and formatting data, for example, changing the shape of data from a wide format to a long format.

In this chapter, you will learn how to manipulate and process data in R. First, you learn how to select an appropriate data structure to store your data. Next, you learn how to create data subsets from different types of data structures, how to combine or merge datasets in R, and how to sort the datasets in ascending or descending order. Towards the end, you learn how to reshape data in different formats, like in long or wide formats.

Selecting the Most Appropriate Data Structure

SCENARIO

Jon Martin has joined as a new member in the data analytics team of Argon Technology. He has to analyze various types of data. Before analyzing the data, he needs to place data in R, and for this, he needs to select appropriate data structures.

In computer terminology, a data structure refers to a particular way of arranging data in the memory of a computer. Different applications use different types of data structures as per their computing and storage requirements. R provides the following types of data structures:

- **Vector**—It is a structure that can contain one or more values of a single type, such as character, number, or integer. It can be compared to a single column or row in a spreadsheet or a database table. Vectors are used to represent only one-dimensional data, such as a set of digits.
- **Matrix**—It is a two-dimensional vector. You can create a matrix by using the `matrix()` function. This function takes the parameters of numbers to be displayed in either the column or row format. The ncol argument is used to specify the number of columns, and the nrow argument is used to specify the number of rows.
- **Data frame**—It is a list of named vectors of the same length. It resembles a spreadsheet or a table in a database with columns and a heading for each column. In other words, a data frame can be defined as a matrix in which data is stored in columns having names. Data frames are generally used to represent time series.
- **List**—It is a collection of objects that fall under a similar category. A list is not fixed in length and can contain other lists.

We have already discussed that depending upon their requirements, different applications may use different types of data structures. The following are some guidelines to select an appropriate data structure:

- To store one-dimensional data, such as a set of digits, use vectors.
- To store data that has more than one dimension, such as a set of digits and alphabets, use matrices, lists, or data frames.

- To store data belonging to a single class, use matrices or higher dimensional arrays.
- To store data belonging to multiple classes, use lists or data frames.
- To store a collection of objects that cannot be represented as an array or a data frame, you can use lists, as they can contain all kinds of objects, including other lists or data frames.

Creating Data Subsets

You already know that R deals with large amounts of data, not all of which is useful. Therefore, the first step in the analysis process is to sort out the data containing any relevant or useful information. The extracted datasets are then divided into small subsets of data for further processing. You can use the `subset()` function to create data subsets in R. The following operators help you to form subsets of data in R:

- $—The dollar operator is used to select a single element of data. When this operator is used with a data frame, the result is always a vector.
- [[—The double square brackets operator is used to return a single element. It provides the flexibility of referring to the elements by their position rather than by name. Generally, it is used to represent the data stored in data frames and lists.
- [ ]—The single square brackets operator is used to extract multiple elements of data.

Let's now see how the `subset()` function and these operators are used to create subsets of data.

Creating Subsets in Vectors

To create the subsets of data stored in a vector, you can use the `subset()` function or the `[]` brackets.

Listing 22.1 shows the use of the `subset()` function and the `[]` brackets to create subsets of a vector:

Listing 22.1: Using the `subset()` Function and the `[]` Brackets

```
# A sample vector
v <- c(1,5,6,3,2,4,2)

subset(v, v<4) #Using subset function

v[v<4] #Using square brackets

# Another vector

t <- c("one","one","two","three","four","two")

# Remove "one" entries
subset(t, t!="one")

t[t!="one"]
```

Creates a vector, v, with a list of numbers

Creates a subset of numbers greater than 4 by using the subset() function

Creates a subset of numbers greater than 4 by using [ ] brackets

Creates a vector, t, with a list of texts

Creates a subset of texts after removing the word, "one", using the subset() function

Creates a subset of texts after removing the word, "one", using [ ] brackets

Figure 22.1 shows the output of executing the code given in Listing 22.1:

```
R Console
> # A sample vector
> v <- c(1,5,6,3,2,4,2)
>
> subset(v, v<4) #Using subset function
[1] 1 3 2 2
>
> v[v<4] #Using square brackets
[1] 1 3 2 2
>
> # Another vector
> t <- c("one", "one", "two", "three", "four", "two")
>
> # Remove "one" entries
> subset(t, t!="one")
[1] "two"   "three" "four"  "two"
>
> t[t!="one"]
[1] "two"   "three" "four"  "two"
> |
```

Figure 22.1: Creating Subsets in Vectors

In Listing 22.1, two sample vectors, v and t, are created. The v vector is initialized with a list of numbers, and the `t` vector is initialized with a series of texts. First, the `subset()` function and `[]` brackets are used to create a subset of numbers greater than 4. Then, the `subset()` function and `[]` brackets are used to create a subset of texts after removing the text, "one".

An important difference between the `subset()` function and square brackets is that by using square brackets, you can assign values to elements; however, you cannot do that by using the `subset()` function, as shown in Listing 22.2:

Listing 22.2: Assigning Values Using `[]` Brackets

```
v[v<3] <- 7
subset(v, v<3) <- 7   <-- Gives an error
v
```

Figure 22.2 shows the output of Listing 22.2:

```
> v[v<3] <- 7
>
>
> subset(v, v<3) <- 7
Error in subset(v, v < 3) <- 7 : could not find function "subset<-"
>
> v
[1] 7 5 6 3 7 4 7
> |
```

Figure 22.2: Assigning Values by Using the Square Brackets

In Listing 22.2, the `[]` brackets are used with the assignment operator to replace the numbers less than 3 with a new number 7. However, if you try to do the same task by using the `subset()` function and assignment operator, you get an error.

Creating Subsets in Data Frames

In this section, you learn to create subsets of data frames by using the `subset()` function and the `[]` brackets. Listing 22.3 shows a sample of a data frame and how to create a subset of the data frame by using the `subset()` function and `[]` brackets:

Listing 22.3: Creating Simple Subsets of Data Frames

```
# A sample data frame
data <- read.table(header=T, text='
 subject class marks
       1    1    99
       2    2    84
       3    1    89
       4    2    79
 ')

subset(data, subject < 3)

data[data$subject < 3, ]
```

Creates a subset of subject less than 3 by using the subset() function

Creates a subset of subject less than 3 by using the [ ] brackets

Figure 22.3 shows the output of executing the code shown in Listing 22.3:

```
> # A sample data frame
> data <- read.table(header=T, text='
+  subject class marks
+        1     1    99
+        2     2    84
+        3     1    89
+        4     2    79
+  ')
> subset(data, subject < 3)
  subject class marks
1       1     1    99
2       2     2    84
> data[data$subject < 3, ]
  subject class marks
1       1     1    99
2       2     2    84
```

Figure 22.3: Creating Subsets in Data Frames

In Listing 22.3, a sample of a data frame, named data, is created with a table. Then, the `subset()` function and `[]` brackets are used to create subsets of data, where subject is less than 3.

Listing 22.4 shows how to create subsets of particular rows and columns:

Listing 22.4: Creating Subsets of Particular Rows and Columns

```
# Subset of particular rows and columns

subset(data, subject < 3, select = -subject)
```

Creates a subset where the subject column is not included and the subject is less than 3 by using the subset() function

```
subset(data, subject < 3, select = c(class,marks))
subset(data, subject < 3, select = class:marks)

data[data$subject < 3, c("class","marks")]
```

Creates a subset where the subject column is not included and the subject is less than 3 by using the [ ] brackets

Figure 22.4 shows the output of executing the code given in Listing 22.4:

```
> # Subset of particular rows and columns
> subset(data, subject < 3, select = -subject)
  class marks
1     1    99
2     2    84
> subset(data, subject < 3, select = c(class,marks))
  class marks
1     1    99
2     2    84
> subset(data, subject < 3, select = class:marks)
  class marks
1     1    99
2     2    84
> data[data$subject < 3, c("class","marks")]
  class marks
1     1    99
2     2    84
>
```

Figure 22.4: Creating Subsets on Particular Rows and Columns of a Data Frame

Listing 22.4 shows how to display records without including the subject column first by using the `subset()` function and then by using the `[]` brackets.

Listing 22.5 shows how to create subsets of different logical conditions:

Listing 22.5: Creating Subsets of Different Logical Conditions

```
# Logical AND of two conditions

subset(data, subject < 3  &  class==2)
data[data$subject < 3  &  data$class==2, ]

# Logical OR of two conditions

subset(data, subject < 3  |  class==2)

data[data$subject < 3  |  data$class==2, ]
```

Creates a subset where the subject column subject is less than 3 or the class equals to 2 by using the [ ] brackets

Creates a subset where the subject column subject is less than 3 and the class equals to 2 by using the subset() function

Creates a subset where the subject column subject is less than 3 or the class equals to 2 by using the subset() function

Creates a subset where the subject column is less than 3 and the class equals to 2 by using the [ ] brackets

Figure 22.5 shows the output of executing the code given in Listing 22.5:

```
> # Logical AND of two conditions
> subset(data, subject < 3  &  class==2)
  subject class marks
2       2     2    84
> data[data$subject < 3  &  data$class==2, ]
  subject class marks
2       2     2    84
>
>
> # Logical OR of two conditions
> subset(data, subject < 3  |  class==2)
  subject class marks
1       1     1    99
2       2     2    84
4       4     2    79
> data[data$subject < 3  |  data$class==2, ]
  subject class marks
1       1     1    99
2       2     2    84
4       4     2    79
>
```

Figure 22.5: Creating Subsets of Logical AND and OR of Two Conditions

In Listing 22.5, the `subset()` function and `[]` brackets are used to display the records of data where the subject is less than 3 and the class equals to 2. Next, the `subset()` function and `[]` brackets are used to display the records of data, where either the subject is less than 3 or the class equals to 2.

Merging Datasets in R

Sometimes, similar datasets obtained from different sources need to be merged together for further processing. R provides the following functions to combine different sets of data:

- **The `merge()` function**—It is used to merge the data contained in different data frames on the basis of columns and rows.
- **The `cbind()` function**—It is used to add the columns of datasets having an equal set and identical order of rows.
- **The `rbind()` function**—It is used to add rows in datasets having an equal number of columns.

Figure 22.6 shows some ways of merging different datasets in R:

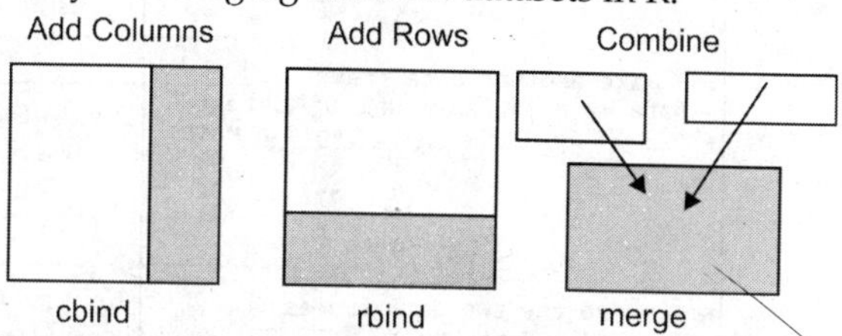

Figure 22.6: Ways of Merging Different Datasets in R

Using the merge() Function

The `merge()` function combines the data of two data frames on the basis of the existence of a common column between the two. The `merge()` function takes the following arguments:

- **x**—Specifies a data frame
- **y**—Specifies a data frame
- **by, by.x, by.y**—Specify the names of the columns common in both x and y.
- **all, all.x, all.y**—Specify logical values for the type of merge. The default value is `all = FALSE`.

Listing 22.6 shows how to create two data frames and combine them by using the `merge()` function:

Listing 22.6: Creating and Merging Two Data Frames

```
# Make first data frame
df1 <- read.table(header=T, text='
   ID  Name
    1  Anne
    2  John
    3  Berkeley
')
# Make another data frame
data <- read.table(header=T, text='
  ID English Maths
   1   67      98
   2   89      98
   3   70      87
')

# Merge the two data frames

merge(df1, data, "ID")
```

Combines the data of df1 and df2 on the basis of "ID" column

Figure 22.7 shows the output of executing the code given in Listing 22.6:

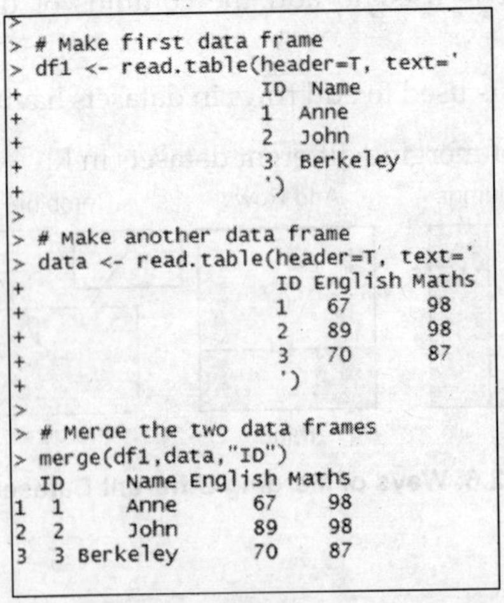

```
>
> # Make first data frame
> df1 <- read.table(header=T, text='
+                   ID  Name
+                   1  Anne
+                   2  John
+                   3  Berkeley
+                   ')
>
> # Make another data frame
> data <- read.table(header=T, text='
+                   ID English Maths
+                   1   67      98
+                   2   89      98
+                   3   70      87
+                   ')
>
> # Merge the two data frames
> merge(df1,data,"ID")
  ID     Name English Maths
1  1     Anne      67    98
2  2     John      89    98
3  3 Berkeley      70    87
```

Figure 22.7: Merging Two Data Frames Using Same Column Name

In Listing 22.6, a dataframe, `df1`, is created with two columns, `ID` and `Name`. The second data frame, `data`, consists of three columns, `ID`, `English`, and `Maths`. The `merge()` function combines the data of `df1` and `data` on the basis of a single common column, `ID`.

If the two data frames have different column names, you can explicitly specify the column name on the basis of which you have to combine data, as shown in Listing 22.7:

Listing 22.7: Combining Two Data Frames Using Different Column Names

```
# In this case, the column is named 'StudentID' instead of ID
df3 <- read.table(header=T, text='
  StudentID  Name
       1     Anne
       2     John
       3     Berkeley
')
# Merge on df3$StudentID and df2$ID

merge(x=df3, y=data, by.x="StudentID", by.y="ID")
```

Combines the data of df3 and df2 on the basis of "StudentID" and "ID" columns, respectively

Figure 22.8 shows the output of executing the code given in Listing 22.7:

```
> # In this case, the column is named 'StudentID' inst
ead of ID
> df3 <- read.table(header=T, text='
+                    StudentID  Name
+                    1          Anne
+                    2          John
+                    3          Berkeley
+                    ')
>
> # Merge on df3$StudentID and df2$ID

> merge(x=df3, y=data, by.x="StudentID", by.y="ID")
  StudentID     Name English Maths
1         1     Anne      67    98
2         2     John      89    98
3         3 Berkeley      70    87
> |
```

Figure 22.8: Merging Data by Specifying Column Names Explicitly

In Listing 22.7, a data frame, `df3`, is created with two columns, `StudentID` and `Name`. The `merge()` function combines the data of `df3` and `df2` on the basis of the `StudentID` column of `df3` and the `ID` column of `df2`. You can also combine different data frames by using multiple column names, as shown in Listing 22.8:

Listing 22.8: Combining Data Using Multiple Columns of Data Frames

```
# Make up more data
Details <- read.table(header=T, text='
   ID  Name     Class
   1   Anne     4
   2   John     3
   5   Martin   4
   6   Thomas   3
')

Marks <- read.table(header=T, text='
```

```
  ID Name     English Maths
   1 Anne     67      98
   2 John     89      98
   3 Berkeley 70      87
   4 Mary     69      79
')

merge(Details, Marks, c("ID","Name"))
```

Combines the data of Details and Marks on the basis of two columns "ID" and "Name"

Figure 22.9 shows the output of executing the code given in Listing 22.8:

```
> # Make up more data
> Details <- read.table(header=T, text='
+    ID  Name     Class
+    1   Anne     4
+    2   John     3
+    5   Martin   4
+    6   Thomas   3
+ ')
>
> Marks <- read.table(header=T, text='
+   ID Name     English Maths
+    1 Anne     67      98
+    2 John     89      98
+    3 Berkeley 70      87
+    4 Mary     69      79
+ ')
>
> merge(Details, Marks, c("ID","Name"))
  ID Name Class English Maths
1  1 Anne     4      67    98
2  2 John     3      89    98
> |
```

Figure 22.9: Merging Data Using Two Column Names

In Listing 22.8, a data frame, `Details`, is created with three columns, `ID`, `Name`, and `Class`. The second data frame, `Marks`, consists of four columns, `ID`, `Name`, `English`, and `Maths`. The `merge()` function combines the data of `Details` and `Marks` on the basis of two columns, `ID` and `Name`.

Table 22.1 shows four ways to combine data by using the `merge()` function:

Table 22.1: Different Ways of Combining Data by Using the `merge()` Function

Join Type	Description	Argument	Example
Natural join	To keep only rows that match with the data frames	all=FALSE	merge(x = Details, y = Marks, by = "ID", all = FALSE)
Full outer join	To keep all rows from both data frames	all=TRUE	merge(x = Details, y = Marks, by = "ID", all = TRUE)
Left outer join	To include all the rows of your data frame x and only those from y that match	all.x=TRUE	merge(x = Details, y = Marks, by = "ID", all.x=TRUE)

Table 22.1: Different Ways of Combining Data by Using the `merge()` Function

Join Type	Description	Argument	Example
Right outer join	To include all the rows of your data frame y and only those from x that match	all.y=TRUE	merge(x = Details, y = Marks, by = "ID", all.y=TRUE)
Cross join	To display all records in all possible combinations		merge(x = Details, y = Marks, by = NULL)

Using the cbind() Function

The `cbind()` function is used to bind the column names of two datasets. It helps in restricting the number of columns to be included in the new dataset. Listing 22.9 shows the use of the `cbind()` function:

Listing 22.9: Using the `cbind()` Function

```
Details
Marks
cbind(Details[,c(1,2,3)],Marks[,c(3,4)])
```

Combines 1, 2, and 3 columns of Details and 3 and 4 columns of Marks

Figure 22.10 shows the output of executing the code given in Listing 22.9:

```
> Details
  ID   Name Class
1  1   Anne     4
2  2   John     3
3  5 Martin     4
4  6 Thomas     3
> Marks
  ID     Name English Maths
1  1     Anne      67    98
2  2     John      89    98
3  3 Berkeley      70    87
4  4     Mary      69    79
> cbind(Details[,c(1,2,3)],Marks[,c(3,4)])
  ID   Name Class English Maths
1  1   Anne     4      67    98
2  2   John     3      89    98
3  5 Martin     4      70    87
4  6 Thomas     3      69    79
> |
```

Figure 22.10: Using the cbind() Function

In Figure 22.9, first the data of the `Details` and `Marks` data frames is displayed. Then, the `cbind()` function is used to combine the first, second, and third columns of the `Details` data frame and the third and fourth columns of the `Marks` data frame.

Using the rbind() Function

The `rbind()` function is used to bind the rows of two datasets. It helps in restricting the number of columns to be included in the new data frame. Listing 22.10 shows the use of the `rbind()` function:

Listing 22.10: Using the `rbind()` Function

```
Data1 <- read.table(header=T, text='
   ID  Name
```

```
   1  Anne
   2  John
   3  Berkeley
')
Data2 <- read.table(header=T, text='
  ID  Name
   4  Addi
   5  David
   6  James
   7  Thomson
')
rbind(Data1, Data2)
```

Combines the rows of Data1 and Data2

Figure 22.11 shows the output of executing the code given in Listing 22.10:

```
> Data1 <- read.table(header=T, text='
+     ID  Name
+      1  Anne
+      2  John
+      3  Berkeley
+ ')
> Data2 <- read.table(header=T, text='
+     ID  Name
+      4  Addi
+      5  David
+      6  James
+      7  Thomson
+ ')
> rbind(Data1, Data2)
  ID     Name
1  1     Anne
2  2     John
3  3 Berkeley
4  4     Addi
5  5    David
6  6    James
7  7  Thomson
> |
```

Figure 22.11: Using the rbind() Function

In Listing 22.10, two data frames, `Data1` and `Data2`, are created. Then, the `rbind()` function is used to combine the rows of `Data1` and `Data2`.

Sorting Data

SCENARIO

The head of the data analytics team asked Martin to sort out the data stored in different data structures, such as vector, matrix, or data frame. Martin decides to perform this task by using the sort() and order() functions.

R provides various functions that allow you to define the order of your data in a data structure. The `sort()` and `order()` functions are the most commonly used functions to perform this task. Let's learn about these functions in the following sections.

Sorting Data

The `sort()` function is used to sort the values contained in a vector. Listing 22.11 shows an example of sorting a vector in ascending and descending orders:

Listing 22.11: Sorting and Reverse Sorting of a Vector

```
vec1<-c(23,45,10,34,89,20,67,99)
# Sorting of a vector

sort(vec1)

# Reverse sorting
sort(vec1, decreasing=TRUE)
```

Sorts a vector in ascending order

Sorts a vector in descending order

Figure 22.12 shows the output of executing the code given in Listing 22.11:

```
> vec1<-c(23,45,10,34,89,20,67,99)
> # Sorting of a vector
> sort(vec1)
[1] 10 20 23 34 45 67 89 99
> # Reverse sorting
> sort(vec1, decreasing=TRUE)
[1] 99 89 67 45 34 23 20 10
>
```

Figure 22.12: Displaying Sorting and Reverse Sorting on a Vector

In Listing 22.11, a vector, named `vec1`, is created of a list of numbers. The sort function is used to sort `vec1` in ascending and descending orders. It should be noted that when we pass the `decreasing=TRUE` argument within the `sort()` function, the function displays the numbers in the descending order.

Ordering Data

The `order()` function is used to organize/arrange values or columns in a dataset. Listing 22.12 shows the commands to create a data frame and use the `order()` function in different ways to sort one or more columns of the data frame:

Listing 22.12: Creating and Sorting a Data Frame

```
# Make a data frame
SampleDataFrame <- data.frame (id=1:5,
         weight=c(25,37,14,62,55),
size=c("small", "large", "medium", "large", "medium"))

SampleDataFrame[ order(SampleDataFrame$weight), ]

# Sort by size, then by weight
SampleDataFrame[ order(SampleDataFrame$size, SampleDataFrame$weight), ]

# Sort by all columns in the data frame, from left to right
```

Creates SampleDataFrame

Sorts SampleDataFrame by the weight column

Sorts SampleDataFrame first by the size column and then by the weight column

```
SampleDataFrame[ do.call(order, as.list(SampleDataFrame)), ]   <- Sorts SampleDataFrame by all columns

# In this particular example, the order will be unchanged
```

Figure 22.13 shows the output of executing the code given in Listing 22.12:

```
> # Make a data frame
> SampleDataFrame <- data.frame (id=1:5,
+               weight=c(25,37,14,62,55),
+               size=c("small", "large", "medium", "large", "medium"))
> SampleDataFrame[ order(SampleDataFrame$weight), ]
  id weight   size
3  3     14 medium
1  1     25  small
2  2     37  large
5  5     55 medium
4  4     62  large
>
> # Sort by size, then by weight
> SampleDataFrame[ order(SampleDataFrame$size, SampleDataFrame$weight), ]
  id weight   size
2  2     37  large
4  4     62  large
3  3     14 medium
5  5     55 medium
1  1     25  small
>
> # Sort by all columns in the data frame, from left to right
> SampleDataFrame[ do.call(order, as.list(SampleDataFrame)), ]
  id weight   size
1  1     25  small
2  2     37  large
3  3     14 medium
4  4     62  large
5  5     55 medium
> # In this particular example, the order will be unchanged
> |
```

Figure 22.13: Displaying Different Ways to Sort a Data Frame

In Listing 22.12, a data frame, `SampleDataFrame`, is created with some data. Then, the `order()` function sorts the values contained in `SampleDataFrame` on the basis of a single column, `weight`. Next, the `order()` function sorts `SampleDataFrame` on the basis of multiple columns, by size and then by weight. Finally, the `do.call()` and `as.list()` functions are used to sort all the columns of `SampleDataFrame`.

Reverse Sort

You can reverse the order of the data contained in the column of a data frame in two ways: by using the argument, `decreasing=TRUE`, in the `order()` function or by using the minus(-) before the column name. Listing 22.13 shows examples of sorting data of a data frame in the decreasing order:

Listing 22.13: Sorting of Data Frame in Decreasing Order

```
SampleDataFrame[ order(SampleDataFrame$weight, decreasing=TRUE), ]
SampleDataFrame[ order(SampleDataFrame$size, -SampleDataFrame$id), ]
```

Sorts SampleDataFrame in decreasing order of the weight column

Sorts SampleDataFrame in increasing order of size and then by decreasing order of the id column

Figure 22.14 shows the output of executing the code given in Listing 22.13:

```
> SampleDataFrame[ order(SampleDataFrame$weight, decreasing=TRUE), ]
  id weight   size
4  4     62  large
5  5     55 medium
2  2     37  large
1  1     25  small
3  3     14 medium
> SampleDataFrame[ order(SampleDataFrame$size, -SampleDataFrame$id), ]
  id weight   size
4  4     62  large
2  2     37  large
5  5     55 medium
3  3     14 medium
1  1     25  small
> |
```

Figure 22.14: Sorting Data Frames in Descending Order

In Listing 22.13, first, the `order()` function sorts `SampleDataFrame` in the decreasing order of the `weight` column with the help of the argument, `decreasing=TRUE`. Then, the `order()` function sorts `SampleDataFrame` in the increasing order of the `size` column and then in the decreasing order of the `weight` column. In this case, the decreasing order is specified by using the minus(-) symbol.

It should be noted that if you wish to sort a column of factors in the decreasing order by using the minus symbol, you need to use the `xtfrm()` function. Listing 22.14 shows an example of using the `xtfrm()` function:

Listing 22.14: Using the `xtfrm()` Function

Works on factors

```
SampleDataFrame[ order(-xtfrm(SampleDataFrame$size), SampleDataFrame$weight), ]
SampleDataFrame[ order(-SampleDataFrame$size, SampleDataFrame$weight), ]
```

Displays a warning

Figure 22.15 shows the output of executing the code given in Listing 22.14:

```
> SampleDataFrame[ order(-xtfrm(SampleDataFrame$size), SampleDataFrame$weight), ]
  id weight   size
1  1     25  small
3  3     14 medium
5  5     55 medium
2  2     37  large
4  4     62  large
> SampleDataFrame[ order(-SampleDataFrame$size, SampleDataFrame$weight), ]
  id weight   size
3  3     14 medium
1  1     25  small
2  2     37  large
5  5     55 medium
4  4     62  large
Warning message:
In Ops.factor(SampleDataFrame$size) : '-' not meaningful for factors
> |
```

Figure 22.15: Using the xtfrm() Function

In Listing 22.14, the `order()` function sorts `SampleDataFrame` in the decreasing order of the `size` column and then in the increasing order of the `weight` column. It should be noted that the `size` column stores factors, so you need to use the `xtfrm()` function; otherwise, a warning will be displayed (Figure 22.15).

Putting Your Data into Shape

R provides a variety of methods for reshaping data prior to its analysis. Some of these methods are as follows:

- Transposing data
- Converting data between the wide and long formats

Let's learn about these methods in the following sections.

Transposing Data

You can use the `t()` function to transpose a matrix or a data frame. This function transposes rows into columns and columns into rows.

Listing 22.15 shows the use of the `t()` function:

Listing 22.15: Using the `t()` Function

```
SampleDataFrame
t(SampleDataFrame)  ← Transposes SampleDataFrame
```

Figure 22.16 shows the output of executing the code of Listing 22.15:

```
> SampleDataFrame
  id weight   size
1  1     25  small
2  2     37  large
3  3     14 medium
4  4     62  large
5  5     55 medium
> t(SampleDataFrame)
       [,1]    [,2]    [,3]     [,4]    [,5]
id     "1"     "2"     "3"      "4"     "5"
weight "25"    "37"    "14"     "62"    "55"
size   "small" "large" "medium" "large" "medium"
> |
```

Figure 22.16: Using the t() Function for Transposing Data

Converting Data to Wide or Long Formats

Wide data contains more columns and fewer rows as compared to long data. R provides the following functions of the reshape package to convert data into wide or long formats:

- Use the `melt()` function to convert wide data into the long format
- Use the `dcast()` function to convert long data into the wide format

NOTE

Use the acast() function to convert the format of data in arrays.

When converting data between the long and wide formats, it is important to understand the concept of identifier variables and measured variables. Identifier (ID) variables identify the observations. These act like the keys that identify your observations. However, the measured variables represent the observed measurements.

Let's now learn how to melt data to long format.

Melting Data to Long Format

You need to use the `melt()` function for converting the data from the wide format into the long format. The `melt()` function is contained in the `reshape2` package. Therefore, to execute the `melt()` function, you must install the `reshape2` package in R. Listing 22.16 shows the use of the `melt()` function:

Listing 22.16: Using the `melt()` Function

```
data <- read.table(header=T, text='
 subject sex control cond1 cond2
     1    M     8.9    11.3    10.6
     2    F     6.2    10.7    12.1
     3    F     9.4    12.1    13.6
     4    M    10.5    13.5    13.9
 ')

library(reshape2)

newdata.long<-melt(data)
newdata.long
```

Loads reshape2

Melts a wide format data into long format

Figure 22.17 shows the output of executing the code given in Listing 22.16:

```
> data <- read.table(header=T, text='
+  subject sex control cond1 cond2
+        1   M     8.9  11.3  10.6
+        2   F     6.2  10.7  12.1
+        3   F     9.4  12.1  13.6
+        4   M    10.5  13.5  13.9
+  ')
> data
  subject sex control cond1 cond2
1       1   M     8.9  11.3  10.6
2       2   F     6.2  10.7  12.1
3       3   F     9.4  12.1  13.6
4       4   M    10.5  13.5  13.9
>
```

Figure 22.17: Melting a Data Frame from Wide Format to Long Format

In Listing 22.16, a data frame, named `data`, is created. Then, the command library is used to load the `reshape2` package in R. After that, the `melt()` function of the `reshape2` package is used to convert the wide format data into a long format in the `newdata.long` data frame.

NOTE

To download and install the reshape2 package, use install.packages()as follows: install.packages("reshape2")

The `melt()` function, by default, considers all categorical variables as identifier variables. You can also specify the `melt()` function with other options, as shown in Listing 22.17:

Listing 22.17: Specifying Other Options with the `melt()` Function

```
newdata.long <- melt(data,
    id.vars=c("subject","sex"),
    measure.vars=c("control", "cond1", "cond2" ),
    variable.name="condition",
    value.name="measurement"
    )

newdata.long
```

Specifies ID variables, source columns, destination columns, and measurement column

Figure 22.18 shows the output of executing the code given in Listing 22.17:

```
> newdata.long <- melt(data,
+     id.vars=c("subject","sex"),
+     measure.vars=c("control", "cond1", "cond2" ),
+     variable.name="condition",
+     value.name="measurement"
+     )
>
> newdata.long
   subject sex condition measurement
1        1   M   control         8.9
2        2   F   control         6.2
3        3   F   control         9.4
4        4   M   control        10.5
5        1   M     cond1        11.3
6        2   F     cond1        10.7
7        3   F     cond1        12.1
8        4   M     cond1        13.5
9        1   M     cond2        10.6
10       2   F     cond2        12.1
11       3   F     cond2        13.6
12       4   M     cond2        13.9
> |
```

Figure 22.18: Specifying the melt() Function with Other Options

In Listing 22.17, the `melt()` function explicitly specifies ID variables, source columns, the destination column, and the measurement column. It should be noted that if you leave out the `measure.vars` variable, the `melt()` function automatically uses all the other variables as `id.vars`. In addition, if you do not specify `variable.name`, the `melt()` function will name that column as "variable", and if you do not specify `value.name`, it will name that column as "measurement".

Casting Data to Wide Format

The `dcast()` function is used to reshape data again in its original format. Listing 22.18 shows the use of the `dcast()` function to reshape data from the long format to the wide format:

Listing 22.18: Casting Data from Long Format to Wide Format

```
#Casting long format into wide format
newdata.wide <- dcast(newdata.long, subject
+ sex ~ condition, value.var="measurement")

#Displaying newdata.wide with original data
newdata.wide
data

#Modifying the columns names in wide format
names(newdata.wide)[names(newdata.wide)=="cond1"] <- "first"
names(newdata.wide)[names(newdata.wide)=="cond2"] <- "second"
newdata.wide
```

Converts long format into wide format

Figure 22.19 shows the output of executing the code given in Listing 22.18:

```
> #Casting long format into wide format
> newdata.wide <- dcast(newdata.long, subject + sex ~ condition, value.var="measurement")
>
> #Displaying newdata.wide with original data
> newdata.wide
  subject sex control cond1 cond2
1       1   M     8.9  11.3  10.6
2       2   F     6.2  10.7  12.1
3       3   F     9.4  12.1  13.6
4       4   M    10.5  13.5  13.9
> data
  subject sex control cond1 cond2
1       1   M     8.9  11.3  10.6
2       2   F     6.2  10.7  12.1
3       3   F     9.4  12.1  13.6
4       4   M    10.5  13.5  13.9
>
> #Modifying the columns names in wide format
> names(newdata.wide)[names(newdata.wide)=="cond1"] <- "first"
> names(newdata.wide)[names(newdata.wide)=="cond2"] <- "second"
> newdata.wide
  subject sex control first second
1       1   M     8.9  11.3   10.6
2       2   F     6.2  10.7   12.1
3       3   F     9.4  12.1   13.6
4       4   M    10.5  13.5   13.9
> |
```

Figure 22.19: Converting Long Format Data into Wide Format

In Listing 22.18, the `dcast()` function is used to cast the data from long format to wide format. The `names()` function is used to rename the column names.

Managing Data in R Using Matrices

Before creating, manipulating, and accessing matrix data, you should know how data is entered in the tabular format and how that data is stored in a matrix. In this head, you will learn how to create a matrix, reshape a vector into a matrix, access a matrix, and create subsets of the data stored in a matrix.

Let's create a matrix consisting of five columns and three rows, as shown in Listing 22.19:

Listing 22.19: Creating Matrices

```
matrix(1, 3, 5)   ← Creates a matrix of 3 rows and 5 columns
a <-1:15
matrix(a,3,5)
matrix(5, 5, 5)   ← Creates a matrix of 5 rows and 5 columns
```

Figure 22.20 shows the output of executing the code given in Listing 22.19:

```
> matrix(1, 3, 5)
     [,1] [,2] [,3] [,4] [,5]
[1,]    1    1    1    1    1
[2,]    1    1    1    1    1
[3,]    1    1    1    1    1
>
> a <-1:15
> matrix(a,3,5)
     [,1] [,2] [,3] [,4] [,5]
[1,]    1    4    7   10   13
[2,]    2    5    8   11   14
[3,]    3    6    9   12   15
>
> matrix(5, 5, 5)
     [,1] [,2] [,3] [,4] [,5]
[1,]    5    5    5    5    5
[2,]    5    5    5    5    5
[3,]    5    5    5    5    5
[4,]    5    5    5    5    5
[5,]    5    5    5    5    5
> |
```

Figure 22.20: Creating Matrices

In Listing 22.19, first of all, the `matrix()` function creates a matrix of 3 rows and 5 columns, and all the fields in the matrix are set at 1. Next, a series of numbers from 1 to 15 is assigned to a variable, `a`. Then, the `matrix()` function creates a matrix of 3 rows and 5 columns with the numbers stored in the `a` variable. Further, calling of the `matrix()` function creates a matrix of 5 rows, 5 columns, and all the fields in the matrix are set at 5 (Figure 22.20). This type of matrix is also called a square matrix.

Reshaping a Vector into a Matrix

To reshape a vector into a matrix, first of all, set the dimensions of the matrix by using the `dim()` function. Listing 22.20 shows a set of commands to create a vector and convert it into a matrix:

Listing 22.20: Creating a Vector and Converting it into a Matrix

```
matVector <- 1:20   ← Creates a vector

dim(matVector)<-c(4,5) # 4 rows and 5 columns   ← Converts a vector into a matrix

matVector
```

Figure 22.21 shows the output of executing the code given in Listing 22.20:

```
> matVector <- 1:20
> dim(matVector)<-c(4,5) # 4 rows and 5 columns
> matVector
     [,1] [,2] [,3] [,4] [,5]
[1,]    1    5    9   13   17
[2,]    2    6   10   14   18
[3,]    3    7   11   15   19
[4,]    4    8   12   16   20
>
```

Figure 22.21: Converting a Vector into a Matrix

In Listing 22.20, a vector, named `matVector` is created and assigned with a sequence of numbers 1 to 20. Then, the `dim()` and `c()` functions are used to create a matrix of 4 rows and 5 columns and assign this structure to the values of `matVector`. In this way, `matVector` is actually converted into a matrix, and its content is displayed.

NOTE

In R, the class() function is used to determine the class of an object, i.e., whether the object is a matrix, a number, or a data frame. You can determine the class of an object, matVector, by using the following commands:

class(matVector)

print(matVector) # printing dataframe ← Prints the content of matVector

The following figure shows the output of executing the preceding commands:

```
> class(matVector)
[1] "matrix"
> print(matVector) # printing dataframe
     [,1] [,2] [,3] [,4] [,5]
[1,]    1    5    9   13   17
[2,]    2    6   10   14   18
[3,]    3    7   11   15   19
[4,]    4    8   12   16   20
>
```

Here, the class() function is used to determine the class of matVector, and the print() function is used to print the content of matVector.

Accessing Matrix and Subsetting the Data

You can access an element of a matrix by mentioning the position of the element in two dimensions, separated from each other by a comma, within square brackets. Listing 22.21 shows the command to access an element of a matrix:

Listing 22.21: Accessing Elements of a Matrix

```
matVector[2,4]   ← Displays the second row in the fourth column of matVector

matVector[2, ]   ← Displays the second row of matVector

matVector[ ,3]   ← Displays the third column of matVector
```

```
matVector[,1:3]       ← Displays first, second, and third rows of matVector

matVector[1,3] <-55   ← Replaces the value of field of first row and third column

print(matVector)
```

Figure 22.22 shows the output of executing the code given in Listing 22.21:

```
> matVector[2,4]
[1] 14
> matVector[2, ]
[1]  2  6 10 14 18
> matVector[ ,3]
[1]  9 10 11 12
> matVector[,1:3]
     [,1] [,2] [,3]
[1,]    1    5    9
[2,]    2    6   10
[3,]    3    7   11
[4,]    4    8   12
> matVector[1,3] <-55
> print(matVector)
     [,1] [,2] [,3] [,4] [,5]
[1,]    1    5   55   13   17
[2,]    2    6   10   14   18
[3,]    3    7   11   15   19
[4,]    4    8   12   16   20
> |
```

Figure 22.22: Accessing Elements of a Matrix

In Listing 22.21, the `matVector` command first displays the value at the second row and fourth column and then at the second row and third column. Next, the command displays the records of the first three rows. Then, `[]` brackets are used to replace the value of the first row and the third column with the number 55. Finally, the `print()` function displays the content of `matVector`.

Managing Data in R Using Data Frames

A data frame is a list of vectors that are equal in length. In this head, you learn the steps of creating data frames, storing values in them, accessing the data stored in data frames, and using data to perform various operations. So let's start with creating data frames.

Creating Data Frames

Listing 22.22 shows how to create and display vectors and data frames:

Listing 22.22: Creating and Displaying Vectors and Data Frames

```
# Creating and displaying vectors
personNames <- c('Gremish','Symons','Simond','Guntoo','Simond','Darek','Churan')
salary <- c(9000, 5000, 12000, 7500, 18000, 10000, 15000);
bonus <- c(800,490,1200,300,1830,1000,1280);
personNames
salary
bonus

#Creating and displaying data frame

company<-data.frame(personNames,salary,bonus)  ← Creates company data frame by using personNames, salary, and bonus vectors
print(company)
```

Figure 22.23 shows the output of executing the code of Listing 22.22:

```
> # Creating and displaying vectors
> personNames <- c('Gremish','Symons','Simond','Guntoo','Simond','Darek','Churan')
> salary <- c(9000, 5000, 12000, 7500, 18000, 10000, 15000);
> bonus <- c(800,490,1200,300,1830,1000,1280);
> personNames
[1] "Gremish" "Symons"  "Simond"  "Guntoo"  "Simond"  "Darek"   "Churan"
> salary
[1]  9000  5000 12000  7500 18000 10000 15000
> bonus
[1]  800  490 1200  300 1830 1000 1280
>
> #Creating and displaying data frame
>
> company<-data.frame(personNames,salary,bonus)
> print(company)
  personNames salary bonus
1     Gremish   9000   800
2      Symons   5000   490
3      Simond  12000  1200
4      Guntoo   7500   300
5      Simond  18000  1830
6       Darek  10000  1000
7      Churan  15000  1280
> |
```

Figure 22.23: Creating and Displaying Vectors and Data Frames

In Listing 22.22, three vectors `personNames`, `salary`, and `bonus` are created and displayed. All these vectors are of equal length. Then, a data frame, `company`, is created by using these three vectors and printed by using the `print()` function.

Accessing Data Frames

Data frames can be accessed as individual columns by providing their index numbers within double square brackets preceded by the name of the data frame. Listing 22.23 shows different ways of accessing data from data frames

Listing 22.23: Accessing Data Frames in Different Ways

```
company[[2]]  <- Displays second column of company data frame

company[["salary"]]

company$salary
company[['personNames']] #printing by column names  <- Displays the personNames column of company data frame

company[1,]  <- Displays first row of company data frame

head(company, n=5) # print first rows of data  <- Displays first 5 rows of company data frame

tail(company,n=3) # print last 3 rows of data  <- Displays last 3 rows of company data frame
```

Figure 22.24 shows the output of executing the code of Listing 22.23:

```
> company[[2]]
[1]  9000  5000 12000  7500 18000 10000 15000
> company[["salary"]]
[1]  9000  5000 12000  7500 18000 10000 15000
> company$salary
[1]  9000  5000 12000  7500 18000 10000 15000
> company[['personNames']] #printing by column names
[1] Gremish Symons  Simond  Guntoo  Simond  Darek   Churan
Levels: Churan Darek Gremish Guntoo Simond Symons
> company[1,]
  personNames salary bonus
1     Gremish   9000   800
> head(company, n=5) # print first rows of data
  personNames salary bonus
1     Gremish   9000   800
2      Symons   5000   490
3      Simond  12000  1200
4      Guntoo   7500   300
5      Simond  18000  1830
> tail(company,n=3) # print last 3 rows of data
  personNames salary bonus
5      Simond  18000  1830
6       Darek  10000  1000
7      Churan  15000  1280
```

Figure 22.24: Accessing Data Frames in Different Ways

In Listing 22.23, the first three commands display different ways to access the salary column by using double square brackets and the dollar ($) symbol. Next, two commands display the data of the `personNames` column and the first row. Then, the `head()` and `tail()` functions are used to display the top 5 rows and the bottom 3 rows, respectively.

Merging Data Frames

The `merge()` function takes two tables as arguments, with the left table being the `x` frame and the right table being the `y` frame. The `merge()` function joins two tables by default on the basis of columns with the same name. Let's create some sample data frames, as shown in Listing 22.24:

Listing 22.24: Creating Two Sample Data Frames

```
area <- read.table(header=T, text='
Area      AreaCode
Essen     90
Dutchess  7
Sussex    56
Pike      45
Orange    34
ManMouth  23
Rockland  43
Hunterdon 59
Nassau    78
Putnam    28
')
area
popuVehicle <- read.table(header=T, text='
Area      Population No_of_vehicles
Essen     232343     987
Dutchess  454400     560
Sussex    454325     543
Pike      425243     766
Orange    452344     890
ManMouth  555435     789
```

```
Rockland  343903      100
Hunterdon 387734      324
Nassau    342343      800
Putnam    983783      322
')
popuVehicle
```

Figure 22.25 shows the output of executing the code of Listing 22.24:

```
> area <- read.table(header=T, text='
+ Area       AreaCode
+ Essen      90
+ Dutchess   7
+ Sussex     56
+ Pike       45
+ Orange     34
+ ManMouth   23
+ Rockland   43
+ Hunterdon  59
+ Nassau     78
+ Putnam     28
+ ')
> area
        Area AreaCode
1      Essen       90
2   Dutchess        7
3     Sussex       56
4       Pike       45
5     Orange       34
6   ManMouth       23
7   Rockland       43
8  Hunterdon       59
9     Nassau       78
10    Putnam       28
>
> popuVehicle <- read.table(header=T, text='
+ Area       Population No_of_vehicles
+ Essen      232343     987
+ Dutchess   454400     560
+ Sussex     454325     543
+ Pike       425243     766
+ Orange     452344     890
+ ManMouth   555435     789
+ Rockland   343903     100
+ Hunterdon  387734     324
+ Nassau     342343     800
+ Putnam     983783     322
+ ')
> popuVehicle
        Area Population No_of_vehicles
1      Essen     232343            987
2   Dutchess     454400            560
3     Sussex     454325            543
4       Pike     425243            766
5     Orange     452344            890
6   ManMouth     555435            789
7   Rockland     343903            100
8  Hunterdon     387734            324
9     Nassau     342343            800
10    Putnam     983783            322
>
```

Figure 22.25: Displaying Two Sample Data Frames

In Listing 22.24, two data frames, `area` and `popuVehicle`, are created.

Let's try to merge these two data frames, as shown in Listing 22.25:

Listing 22.25: Merging Data Frames

```
mergeData = merge(x = area, y = popuVehicle)
mergeData
dim(mergeData)
```

```
colnames(mergeData)
rownames(mergeData)
names(mergeData)  ← Displays column names

cbind(area[,c(1,2)],popuVehicle[,2])  ← Restricts column numbers
```

Figure 22.26 shows the output of executing the code given in Listing 22.25:

```
> mergeData = merge(x = area, y = popuVehicle)
> mergeData
        Area AreaCode Population No_of_vehicles
1   Dutchess        7     454400            560
2      Essen       90     232343            987
3  Hunterdon       59     387734            324
4   ManMouth       23     555435            789
5     Nassau       78     342343            800
6     Orange       34     452344            890
7       Pike       45     425243            766
8     Putnam       28     983783            322
9   Rockland       43     343903            100
10    Sussex       56     454325            543
> dim(mergeData)
[1] 10  4
> colnames(mergeData)
[1] "Area"           "AreaCode"        "Population"      "No_of_vehicles"
> rownames(mergeData)
 [1] "1"  "2"  "3"  "4"  "5"  "6"  "7"  "8"  "9"  "10"
> names(mergeData)
[1] "Area"           "AreaCode"        "Population"      "No_of_vehicles"
> cbind(area[,c(1,2)],popuVehicle[,2])
        Area AreaCode popuVehicle[, 2]
1      Essen       90           232343
2   Dutchess        7           454400
3     Sussex       56           454325
4       Pike       45           425243
5     Orange       34           452344
6   ManMouth       23           555435
7   Rockland       43           343903
8  Hunterdon       59           387734
9     Nassau       78           342343
10    Putnam       28           983783
```

Figure 22.26: Merging Two Data Frames

In Listing 22.25, the `merge()` function is used to merge the data of the `area` and `popuVehicle` data frames. The merged data is stored in a new data frame, `mergeData`. The `dim()` function displays the number of columns and rows of `mergeData`. The `colnames()` and `rownames()` functions display the column names and rows names of `mergeData`, respectively.

The `names()` function also displays the column names of `mergeData`. Finally, the `cbind()` function is used to restrict the number of columns of the `area` and `popuVehicle` data frames. It displays the first and second columns of `area` and the second column of `popuVehicle`.

Performing Operations on Data Frames

Now, let's learn to perform some basic operations on data frames, like sorting and transposing. Listing 22.26 shows how to perform operations on data frames:

Listing 22.26: Performing Operations on Data Frames

```
mergeData
mergeData[order(mergeData$AreaCode, decreasing=T), ]
t(mergeData)
as.data.frame(t(mergeData))   ← Returns a data frame
```

Figure 22.27 shows the output of Listing 22.26:

```
> mergeData
        Area AreaCode Population No_of_vehicles
1   Dutchess        7     454400            560
2      Essen       90     232343            987
3  Hunterdon       59     387734            324
4   ManMouth       23     555435            789
5     Nassau       78     342343            800
6     Orange       34     452344            890
7       Pike       45     425243            766
8     Putnam       28     983783            322
9   Rockland       43     343903            100
10    Sussex       56     454325            543
> mergeData[order(mergeData$AreaCode, decreasing=T), ]
        Area AreaCode Population No_of_vehicles
2      Essen       90     232343            987
5     Nassau       78     342343            800
3  Hunterdon       59     387734            324
10    Sussex       56     454325            543
7       Pike       45     425243            766
9   Rockland       43     343903            100
6     Orange       34     452344            890
8     Putnam       28     983783            322
4   ManMouth       23     555435            789
1   Dutchess        7     454400            560
> t(mergeData)
               [,1]       [,2]     [,3]        [,4]       [,5]     [,6]     [,7]     [,8]     [,9]       [,10]
Area           "Dutchess" "Essen"  "Hunterdon" "ManMouth" "Nassau" "Orange" "Pike"   "Putnam" "Rockland" "Sussex"
AreaCode       " 7"       "90"     "59"        "23"       "78"     "34"     "45"     "28"     "43"       "56"
Population     "454400"   "232343" "387734"    "555435"   "342343" "452344" "425243" "983783" "343903"   "454325"
No_of_vehicles "560"      "987"    "324"       "789"      "800"    "890"    "766"    "322"    "100"      "543"
> as.data.frame(t(mergeData))
                     V1     V2        V3       V4     V5     V6     V7     V8       V9    V10
Area           Dutchess  Essen Hunterdon ManMouth Nassau Orange   Pike Putnam Rockland Sussex
AreaCode              7     90        59       23     78     34     45     28       43     56
Population       454400 232343    387734   555435 342343 452344 425243 983783   343903 454325
No_of_vehicles      560    987       324      789    800    890    766    322      100    543
>
```

Figure 22.27: Performing Operations on Data Frames

In Listing 22.26, the `order()` function is used to sort the `mergeData` data frame in descending order. The `t()` function is used to swap the columns of `mergeData` into rows and vice versa. After swapping rows and columns, `mergeData` no longer remains a data frame. You can convert it into a data frame by using the `as.data.frame()` function.

Summary

In this chapter, you learned about various types of data structures available in R. Next, you learned how to create data subsets from different types of data structures by using the `subset()` function and different operators, like `[]`. Then, you learned how to combine or merge datasets in R by using the `merge()`, `cbind()`, and `rbind()` functions. After that, you learned how to sort datasets in ascending or descending order by using the `sort()` and `order()` functions. Finally, you learned to reshape the data in different formats.

Quick Revise

Multiple-Choice Questions

Q1. Which of the following is the correct syntax to sort the elements of dataset X in the decreasing order?

a. > order(X$E1, decreasing=TRUE)
b. > order(X, decreasing)
c. > order(X)
d. > order(X, decreasing=FALSE)

Ans. The correct option is a.

Q2. You have a dataset ACE in wide format and want to convert it into long format. Which of the following statements will you use to perform this task?

a. > mACE <- melt(ACE)
b. > ACE <- melt(ACE)
c. > X <- ACE
d. > ACE <- merge(ACE)

Ans. The correct option is a.

Q3. Which of the following data objects should be used in R if the data consists of one or more values of a single type?

a. Vector
b. Matrix
c. List
d. Data frame

Ans. The correct option is a.

Q4. Which of the following data objects should be used in R if the data consists of one or more values of any type?

a. Vector
b. Matrix
c. List
d. Data Frame

Ans. The correct option is c.

Q5. Which of the following subset operators should be used to get an output with multiple elements of your data?

a. $
b. [[
c. [
d. c()

Ans. The correct option is c.

Q6. Which of the following is not a type of merge operation performed in R?

a. Full outer join
b. Left outer join
c. Common join
d. Natural join

Ans. The correct option is c.

Q7. ____________ are used to represent only one-dimensional data, like a set of digits.

a. Vectors
b. Matrices
c. Data frames
d. Lists

Ans. The correct option is a.

Q8. The ____________ function is used to sort a data frame.

a. sort()
b. order()
c. melt()
d. dcast()

Ans. The correct option is b.

Subjective Questions

Q1. List some types of data structures available in R.

Ans. R provides the following types of data structures:

- **Vector**—It is a structure that can contain one or more values of a single type, such as character, number, or integer. It can be compared to a single column or row in a spreadsheet or a database table. Vectors are used to represent only one-dimensional data, such as a set of digits.
- **Matrix**—It is a two-dimensional vector. You can create a matrix by using the `matrix()` function. This function takes the parameters of numbers to be displayed in either the column or row format. The ncol argument is used to specify the number of columns, and the nrow argument is used to specify the number of rows.
- **Data frame**—It is a list of named vectors of the same length. It resembles a spreadsheet or a table in a database with columns and a heading for each column. In other words, a data frame can be defined as a matrix in which data is stored in columns having names. Data frames are generally used to represent time series.
- **List**—It is a collection of objects that fall under a similar category. A list is not fixed in length and can contain other lists.

Q2. Name some operators used to form data subsets in R.

Ans. The following operators help you to form subsets of data in R:

- **$**—The dollar operator is used to select a single element of data. When this operator is used with a data frame, the result is always a vector.
- **[[**—The double square brackets operator is used to return a single element. It provides the flexibility of referring to the elements by their position rather than by name. Generally, it is used to represent the data stored in data frames and lists.
- **[ ]**—The single square brackets operator is used to extract multiple elements of data.

Q3. List the functions provided by R to combine different sets of data.

Ans. R provides the following functions to combine different sets of data:

- **The `merge()` function**—It is used to merge the data contained in different data frames on the basis of columns as well as rows.
- **The `cbind()` function**—It is used to add the columns of datasets having an equal set and identical order of rows.
- **The `rbind()` function**—It is used to add rows in datasets having an equal number of columns.

Q4. Suppose you have two datasets, A and B. Dataset A has the following data: 1 2 3 4. Dataset B has the following data: 5 6 7 8. Using the `merge()` function, combine the data from both datasets into dataset C.

Ans. Dataset A and dataset B can be combined by using the merge() function, as shown below:

```
> A<-c(1,2,3,4)
> B<-c(5,6,7,8)
> c<-merge(A,B)
> c
   x y
1  1 5
2  2 5
3  3 5
4  4 5
5  1 6
6  2 6
7  3 6
8  4 6
9  1 7
10 2 7
11 3 7
12 4 7
13 1 8
14 2 8
15 3 8
16 4 8
> |
```

23

Working with Functions and Packages in R

You know already how to write a script in R to perform a specific task. A script in R is just a simple text file containing executable commands. These commands can be entered using the R command line. R scripts are not very flexible to run with variable input values. Moreover, due to complexity of the task at hand, the program developed for the task execution may become lengthy and tedious. Such a program is difficult to understand, and debug programs are also difficult to maintain. These programs are also prone to errors and take long time to execute. To overcome these problems, functions are used in programs.

Functions refer to smaller groups/blocks of statements which a large program is divided. Like every programming language, R also supports the concept of functions. R offers a range of predefined functions, such as `round()` and `sqrt()`. R also allows users to define functions according to their requirements. Such functions are termed as user-defined functions.

The predefined functions are categorized as per their functionalities and grouped into containers known as **packages**. For example, all the functions used for performing mathematical calculations are grouped under the `Maths` package. You can access any of these functions by just including this package in your R program. In this way, you can call any function, whenever required.

This chapter familiarizes you to the concept of functions and how to define, declare, and access them in R. You also learn to declare arguments in functions. The chapter next lists various types of functions along with their descriptions. You also learn about packages and how to work with them in R.

Using Functions Instead of Scripts

A function refers to a named block of statements in a program, which is executed when called from some other part of the program. A large program can be broken down into smaller parts using functions, which help in making the program more readable. A function needs to be declared or defined in a program before using it in that program. You can create as many functions as you want and call them from any part of a program. Each defined function in a program has a name, and when this name is called from any part of a program, the statements written inside the function get executed. When all the statements written inside a function get executed, the control of the program returns back to the calling statement. The statements in a function are arranged in such a way that each performs a particular task.

NOTE

Different programming languages use different terms to refer to functions, such as methods, procedures, or subroutines.

Using functions in R provides the following two main advantages:

- They can work with variable inputs, i.e., with different values.
- They return the result as an object. This result can further be used as an input for another function or program.

Transforming the R Script into a Function

To transform the R script into a function, you first need to create the R script, then the R function, and then transform the script into the function. You already know that you can create the R script by using any text editor, such as Notepad, Microsoft Word, etc. and then saving the file with the .R extension in your working directory. Basically, the `source()` function is used for reading files in R.

Creating a Script

Suppose you create a file named `Myfile.R` in Notepad. To read this file in R, type the following command in the R console:

```
>source ("Myfile.R")
```

The contents of the file will be read by R.

Now, let's write an R script to create and display the first ten multiples of 2, as shown in Listing 23.1:

Listing 23.1: Displaying the First Ten Multiples of 2 in R

```
z <- c(1,2,3, 4,5,6,7,8,9,10)   ← Sets the z object for containing ten numbers

table <- round(z* 2)   ← Multiplies each value of z with 2

res <- paste(table, sep = "")
print("Table of 2:")

print (res)   ← Displays the output
```

Now, save the script file with appropriate name. In our case, we have saved the file with the name `DisplayTable.R`. Next, call the file by using the `source()` function, as shown in Figure 23.1.

The output of Listing 23.1 is shown in Figure 23.1:

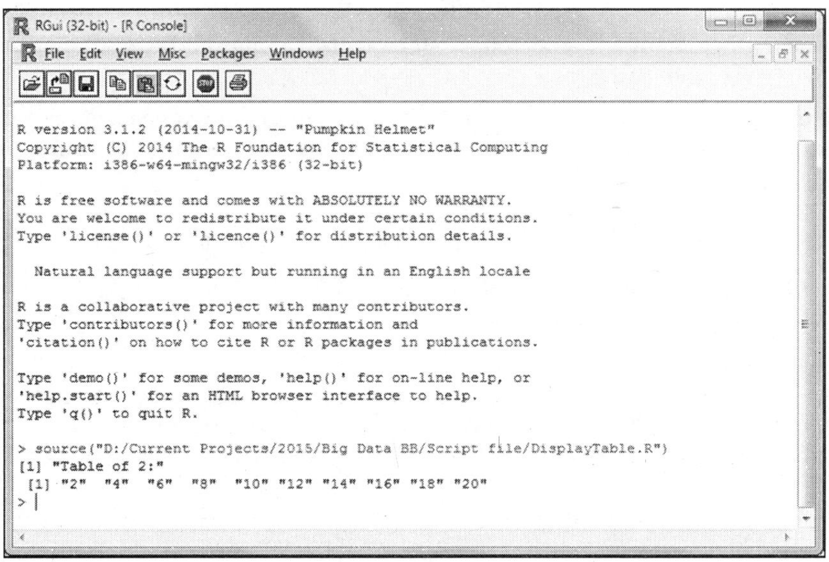

Figure 23.1: Displaying the Multiples of 2 in R

NOTE

In most editors, you can source a script (send a complete script file to the R console) with one simple click. In RStudio, this is done by clicking the Source button or by pressing Ctrl+Shift+Enter.

Creating a Function

You can also convert a script created on any platform (Notepad, MS-Word, MS-Excel) into an R function. Let's first learn to create a function in R by performing the following steps:

1. Define a function with an appropriate name.
2. Declare the function keyword using parentheses.
3. Provide arguments to the function.
4. Declare the return statement, if required.

The syntax for defining a function in R is as follows:

```
<functionname> <-function(arg1,arg2,…)
{
    Statement 1
    Statement 2
    . ….
return(output)
}
```

In the preceding syntax:

- **<functionname>**—Refers to the name of the function.
- **function**—Refers to the keyword used for defining a function.
- **(arg1, arg2,..)**—Refers to the set of arguments given to a function. A function can have one or more arguments; however, it is not necessary to specify arguments in a function. The arguments of a function are separated by commas and are enclosed within parentheses. Dots given in braces are known as "dot arguments", which means we can add the third argument that will be other than arg1 and arg2 during the runtime.
- **Statement 1, Statement 2 ...and return statement**—Define the body of the function and are always written within curly braces.
- **Return(output)**—Calls the output so that it can return to the main screen. For example, in the code fragment (given below), `print()` is the function used to return the output variable or the value held by the variable "b".

```
>print ("Area of circle after removing r=")
>print(b)   // this will give output which is held by "b"
```

Now, let's create a simple function in R that prints "`hello`" as output. Listing 23.2 shows the code to print "`hello`" in R:

Listing 23.2: Creating a Simple Function in R

```
MyFirstFunc<-function(){
print("hello")
}
```

Creates a simple function with the name '`MyFirstFunc`'

You can invoke or call a function in R by specifying the source of the script file and writing the name of the function in RGui. However, before calling a function, you must check whether it is available in the R workspace or not. You can check the availability of the function by using the `ls()` function. A function, when invoked without any argument, returns the list of all the functions the user has defined in the program.

The syntax for calling a function is as follows:

```
Functionname(list of arguments)
```

In the preceding syntax, the arguments of the function are optional.

The output of Listing 23.2 is shown in Figure 23.2:

```
> source("D:/Current Projects/2015/Big Data BB/Script file/simpleFunction.R")
> MyFirstFunc()
[1] "hello"
> |
```

Figure 23.2: Printing "hello" in R

Let's now transform the script given in Listing 23.1 into a user-defined function, which when invoked will print the first ten multiples of 2. Listing 23.3 shows how to create a user-defined function:

Listing 23.3: Creating a User-Defined Function

```
showTable<-function(){

z <- c(1,2,3, 4,5,6,7,8,9,10)
table <- round(z* 2)
res <- paste(table, sep = "")
print("Table of 2:")
return (res)
}
```

Defines a function with the name 'showTable'

Returns the result of the showTable() function

In Listing 23.3, we have created the `showTable()` function, which will perform the same task as the code given in Listing 23.1.

The output of Listing 23.3 is shown in Figure 23.3:

```
> source("D:/Current Projects/2015/Big Data BB/Script file/DisplayTable.R")
> ls()
[1] "showTable"
> showTable()
[1] "Table of 2:"
 [1] "2"  "4"  "6"  "8"  "10" "12" "14" "16" "18" "20"
> |
```

Figure 23.3: Calling the showTable() Function

NOTE

A function is no longer required, it can be removed from the R workspace by using the rm() function.

Returning Results in R

The `return` statement is optional in case of functions, because by default, R will always return the value of the last line of code written in the function body.

You know that the `return` statement is used for returning results of a function. What happens if the `return` statement is not used in the function? Let's rewrite the `showTable()` function without using the `return` statement.

Listing 23.4 shows the code to define the `showTable()` function without using the `return` statement:

Listing 23.4: Writing Code Without Using the `Return` Statement

```
showTable<-function(){
z <- c(1,2,3, 4,5,6,7,8,9,10)
table <- round(z* 2)
res <- paste(table, sep = "")
print("Table of 2:")
print(res)
}
```

In Listing 23.4, you can see that no `return` statement is specified. However, the output of the function remains the same, as shown in Figure 23.4:

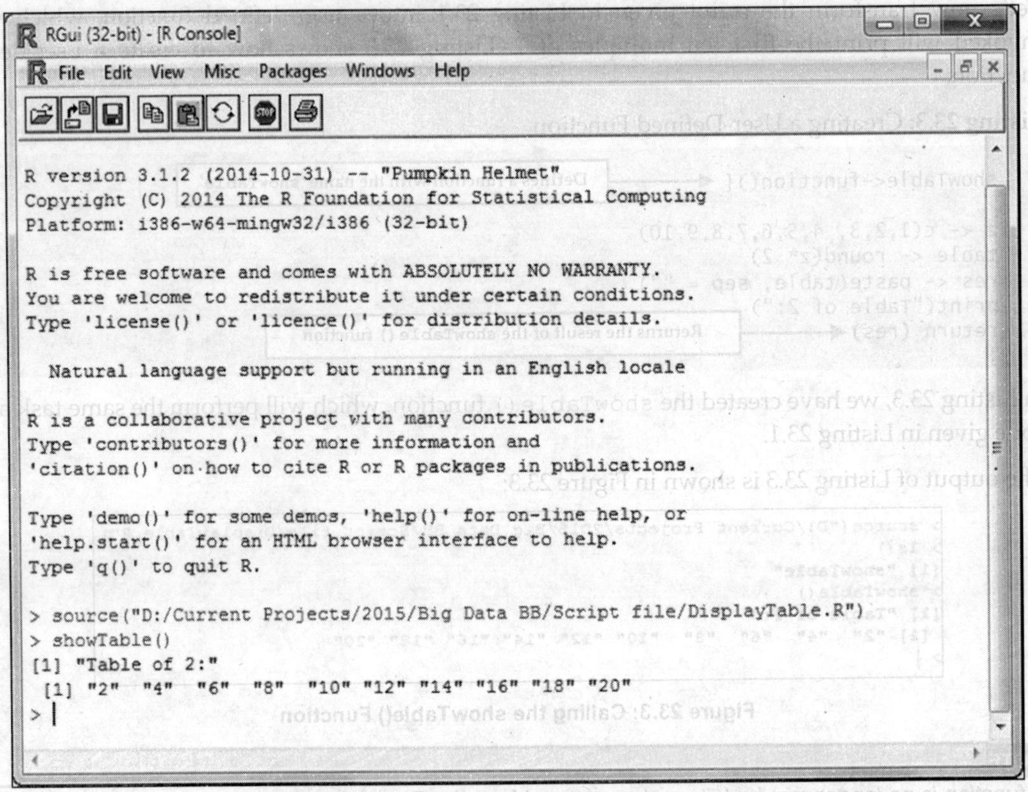

Figure 23.4: Displaying the Output Without Using the Return Statement

It may seem as if the `return` statement is not of any use in a function. However, this is not so. You require the `return` statement to exit from a function without waiting for the whole code written in the function body to be executed.

Suppose you want to check whether the value passed for printing a table is numeric or not. You can check this by adding the following statement:

```
If(!is.numeric(x)) return (NULL )
```

The preceding statement will return NULL if the data type of the value passed in the function is not a numeric. Listing 23.5 shows the code for checking the data type of the value:

Listing 23.5: Checking the Data Type of a Value

```
showTable<-function(x){
z <- c(1,2,3,4,5,6,7,8,9,10)
if(!is.numeric(x)) return (NULL)
table <- round(z* x)
paste(table, sep = "")
}
```

Checks whether x is numeric or not

The output of Listing 23.5 is shown in Figure 23.5:

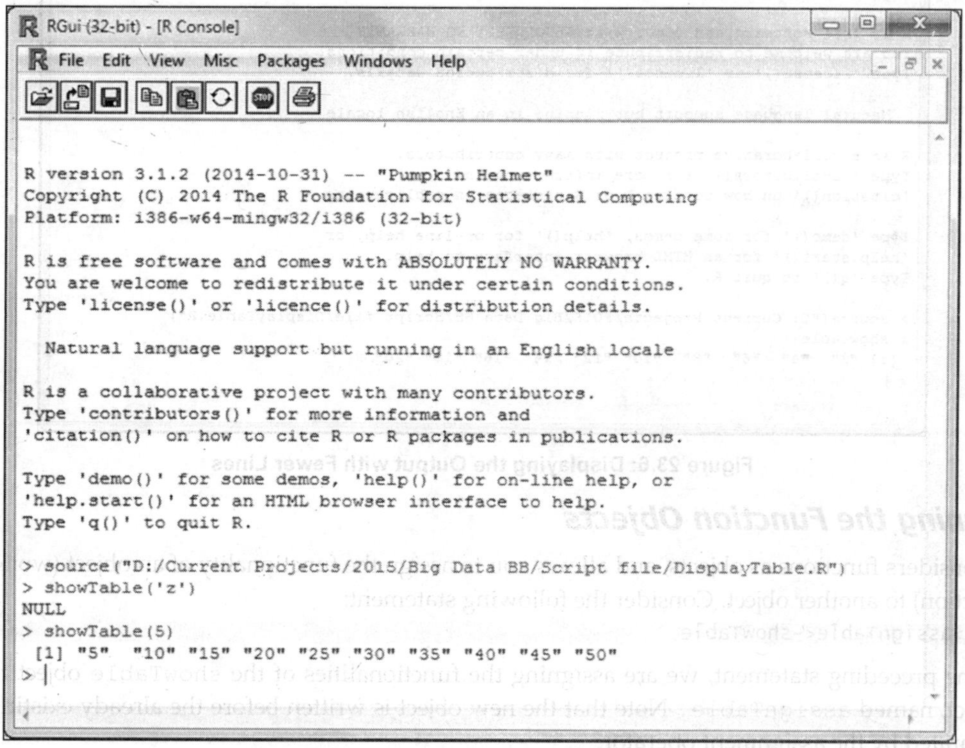

Figure 23.5: Checking Whether the Data Type of the Value is Numeric

In Figure 23.5, you can see that the function returns NULL when the character value is passed in it. However, when the numeric value is passed, the first ten multiples of that number are displayed.

Reducing the Number of Lines in an R Function

You can also reduce the number of lines in R code without affecting the output of the program. Listing 23.6 shows how to write the `showTable()` function with fewer lines of code:

Listing 23.6: Writing the Function with fewer Lines of Code

```
showTable<-function(){
z <- c(1,2,3, 4,5,6,7,8,9,10)
table <- round(z* 2)
paste(table, sep = "")}
```

You can see that in Listing 23.6, we have replaced two print commands given in Listing 23.4 with a single paste statement.

The program in Listing 23.6 provides the output shown in Figure 23.6:

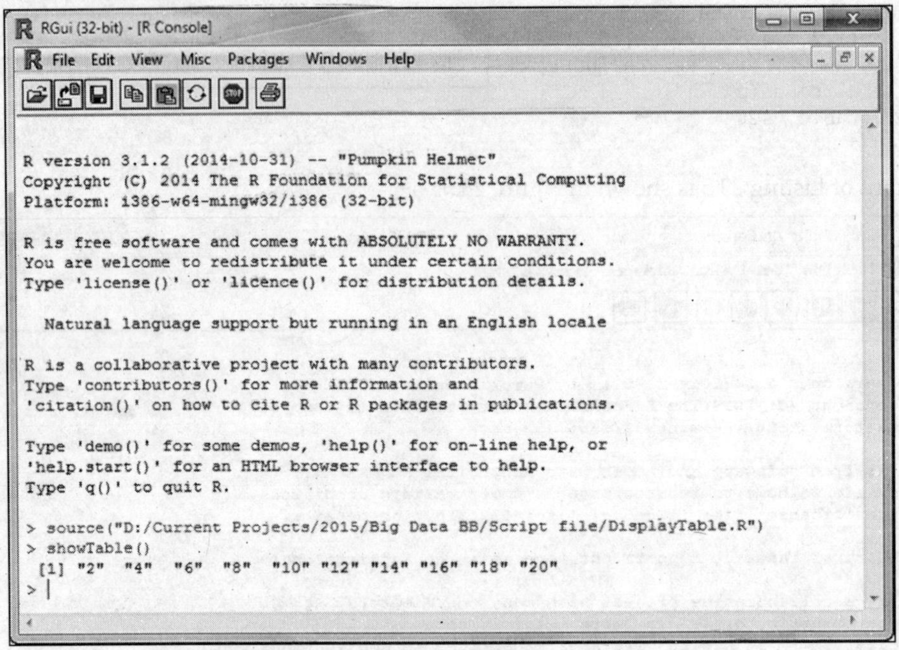

Figure 23.6: Displaying the Output with Fewer Lines

Assigning the Function Objects

R considers functions as objects, and allows you to assign the functionality of an object (working as a function) to another object. Consider the following statement:

```
>assignTable<-showTable
```

In the preceding statement, we are assigning the functionalities of the `showTable` object to a new object, named `assignTable`. Note that the new object is written before the already existing object, separated by the assignment operator.

Figure 23.7 displays the output of calling the `assignTable` object:

```
>  source("D:/Current Projects/2015/Big Data BB/Script file/DisplayTable.R")
> assignTable<-showTable
> assignTable
function(){
z <- c(1,2,3, 4,5,6,7,8,9,10)
table <- round(z* 2)
res <- paste(table, sep = "")
print("Table of 2:")
return (res)
}
> assignTable()
[1] "Table of 2:"
 [1] "2"  "4"  "6"  "8"  "10" "12" "14" "16" "18" "20"
>
```

Figure 23.7: Displaying the Output of Calling the `assignTable` Object

In Figure 23.7, notice that calling the `assignTable` object without parenthesis displays the body of the function; while calling the `assignTable` object with parenthesis makes it act like a function and displays the first ten multiples of the number 2.

You must be careful while naming objects. If you declare a new object with the name of an existing object, you might lose data.

Writing Function Without Braces

If a function contains only a single line of code, then you can define the function without using parentheses. You only need to write the code after specifying the arguments. R will consider the body of the function after specifying the arguments. Listing 23.7 shows a program to calculate the square of a number:

Listing 23.7: Calculating the Square of a Number

```
calSquare<-function(y) y*y
```

Creates the `calSquare()` function without using braces

In Listing 23.7, you can see that no braces or return statements have been specified, but the program works perfectly. The output of Listing 23.7 is shown in Figure 23.8:

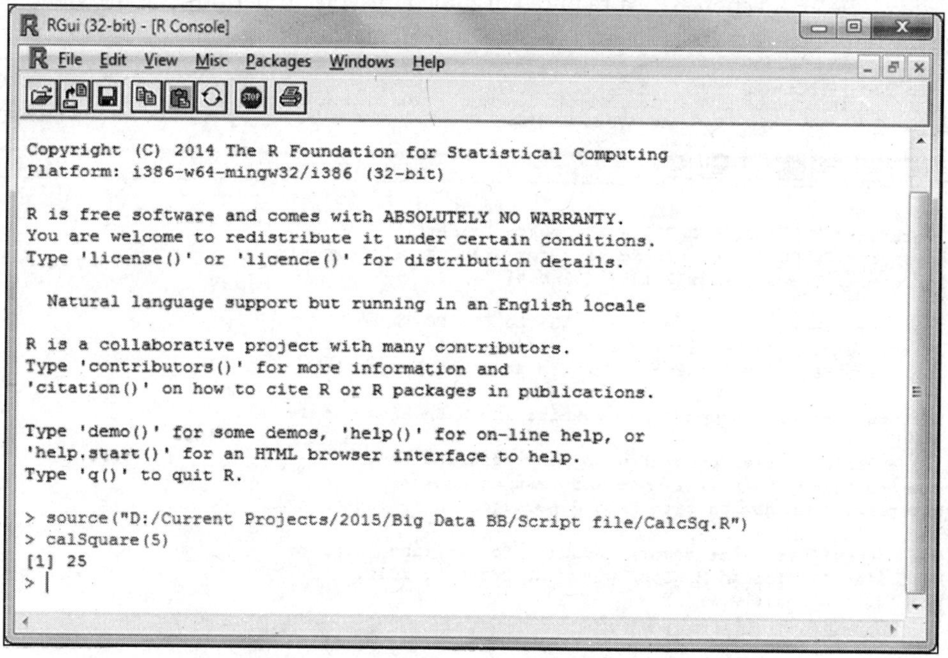

Figure 23.8: Displaying the Square of a Number

Skipping braces reduces the lines of the code and less code saves space, but saving space is not of any use if the program is not readable. You must write a function in such a manner that it can be easily understood when read by another person.

Using Arguments in Functions

Arguments can be defined as variables, constants, or expressions that contain values which can be used in a function. As discussed earlier, a function may or may not have arguments. The arguments of a function receive the value from the user at runtime. These values can be used in a function for computational purposes.

NOTE

In a programming language, arguments are also known as parameters. The functions containing parameters are known as parameterized functions, while the functions defined without using parameters are known as non-parameterized functions.

There are two types of arguments in R: optional and required. The arguments that already contain a default value are known as optional arguments because it is optional for a user to define their values. The required arguments, on the other hand, are those arguments whose value needs to be specified while calling a function. Consider the following function:

```
calCube<-function(x, y=3) x^y
```

Calculates the cube of a number

In the `calCube()` function, `x` is a required argument. If you do not provide the value of `x` while calling the function, it provides an error, as shown in Figure 23.9:

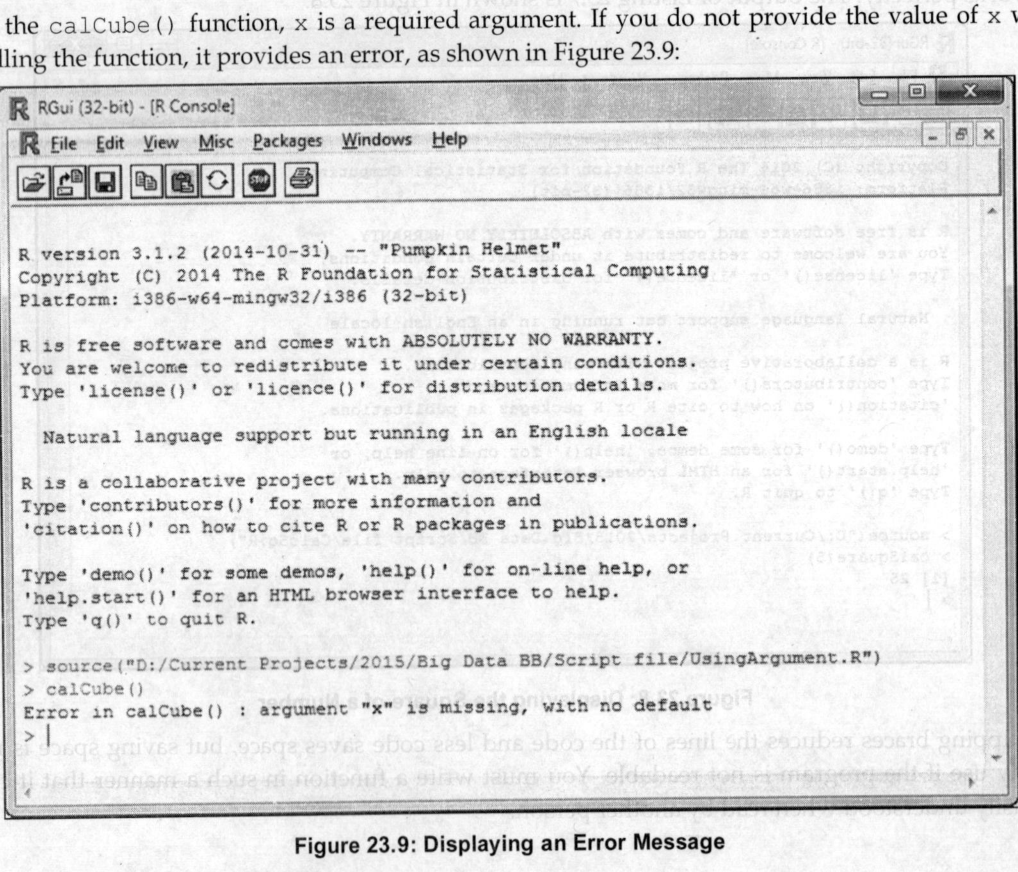

Figure 23.9: Displaying an Error Message

The y argument is optional in the `calCube()` function because it contains a default value of 3. This means that even if you do not provide the value of y, the function will use the value 3 and not throw an error, as shown in Figure 23.10:

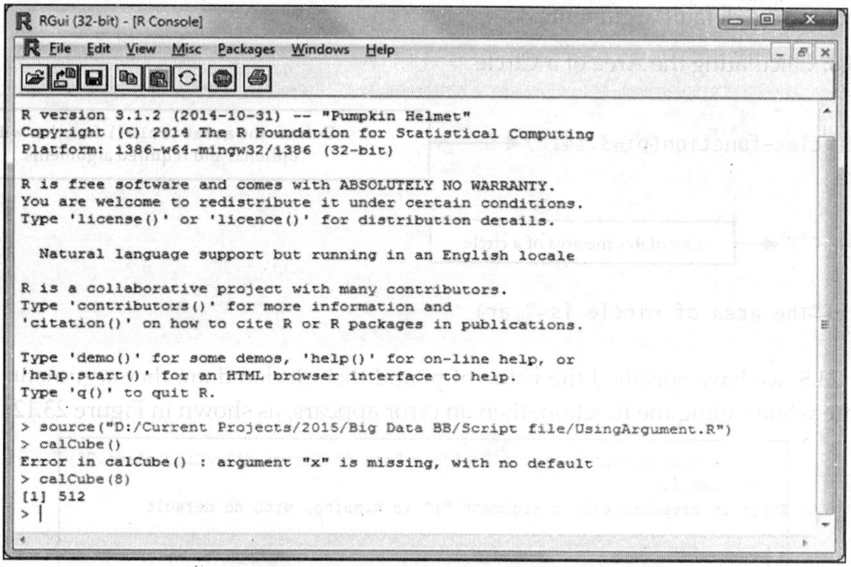

Figure 23.10: Displaying the Output of a Function

The main advantage of providing a default value to an argument is that you do not need to provide a value to the argument every time you call a function. Moreover, you can also provide a value to an optional argument while calling the function, as shown in Figure 23.11:

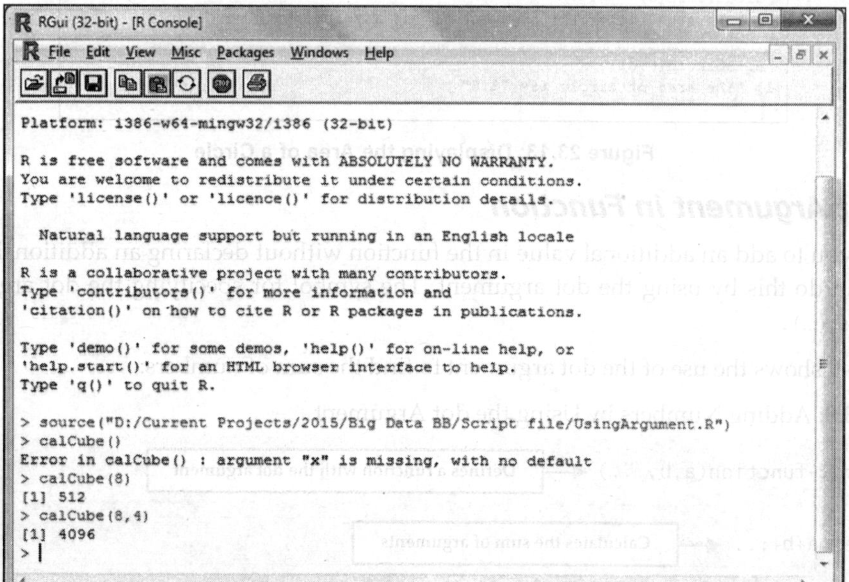

Figure 23.11: Providing Value to the Optional Argument

In Figure 23.11, you can see that we have provided a value of 4 to the optional argument. Now, the output will be calculated as 4 to the power of 8, which is 4096. Basically, the default value is provided to those arguments whose values do not change frequently. Listing 23.8 calculates the area of a circle using the default argument `pi`:

Listing 23.8: Calculating the Area of a Circle

```
areaCircle<-function(pi=3.14,r)
{
 ar=pi*r*r
 paste("The area of circle is=",ar)
}
```

Defines the `areaCircle()` function with optional and required arguments

Calculates the area of a circle

In Listing 23.8, we have specified the value of pi and then declared another argument `r`. If you only pass a value while calling the function, then an error appears, as shown in Figure 23.12:

```
> source("D:/Current Projects/2015/Big Data BB/Script file/CircleArea.R")
> areaCircle(5)
Error in areaCircle(5) : argument "r" is missing, with no default
>
> |
```

Figure 23.12: Displaying the Error

This error can be removed by passing the argument with a name and a value, as shown in Figure 23.13:

```
> source("D:/Current Projects/2015/Big Data BB/Script file/CircleArea.R")
> areaCircle(5)
Error in areaCircle(5) : argument "r" is missing, with no default
>
> areaCircle(r=5)
[1] "The area of circle is= 78.5"
> |
```

Figure 23.13: Displaying the Area of a Circle

Using Dot Argument in Function

R allows you to add an additional value in the function without declaring an additional argument in it. You can do this by using the dot argument. The symbol for specifying the dot argument in the function is (...).

Listing 23.9 shows the use of the dot argument to find the sum of numbers:

Listing 23.9: Adding Numbers by Using the dot Argument

```
dotArg<-function(a,b,...)
{
   res=a+b+...
  paste("The sum of numbers is=",res)
}
```

Defines a function with the dot argument

Calculates the sum of arguments

In Listing 23.9, the `dotArg()` function is called with two arguments, and calculates the sum of two numbers. The output on executing the code of Listing 23.9 is shown in Figure 23.14:

```
> source("D:/Current Projects/2015/Big Data BB/Script file/DotArguments.R")
> dotArg(3,4)
[1] "The sum of numbers is= 7"
> |
```

Figure 23.14: Calculating the Sum of Two Numbers

When the `dotArg()` function is called with three arguments, it will display the sum of three numbers, as shown in Figure 23.15:

```
> source("D:/Current Projects/2015/Big Data BB/Script file/DotArguments.R")
> dotArg(3,4)
[1] "The sum of numbers is= 7"
> dotArg(3,4,6)
[1] "The sum of numbers is= 13"
> |
```

Figure 23.15: Calculating the Sum of Three Numbers

NOTE

The dot argument can also be used to pass a value from one function to another.

Passing Functions as Arguments

R allows you to pass functions as arguments. Consider Listing 23.10 in which the `round()` function is passed as an argument for rounding the area of a circle:

Listing 23.10: Using the Function as an Argument

```
funArg<-function(r,pi=3.14,FUN=round,...){
result<-FUN(pi*r*r)
paste(result)
}
```

Defines the **funArg()** function containing the **round()** function as an argument

In Listing 23.10, the `round()` function is passed as an argument, which will round off the result obtained after calculating the area of the circle. The output of Listing 23.10 is shown in Figure 23.16:

```
> source("D:/Current Projects/2015/Big Data BB/Script file/FunctionArg.R")
> funArg(5)
[1] "78"
> |
```

Figure 23.16: Passing a Function as an Argument

NOTE

In order to avoid errors, you must assign the function to the argument without using parentheses.

Anonymous Functions

Functions created without any names are known as anonymous functions. These functions are used for writing one-line codes. An anonymous function can be written like an argument in a function. The entire body of an anonymous function is written as an argument in its body; therefore, you do not need to provide any name to the function. The syntax of defining an anonymous function in R is as follows:

```
function(argument list)expression
```

In Listing 23.11, an anonymous function is used to find the area of a circle:

Listing 23.11: Using an Anonymous Function to calculate the Area of a Circle

```
(function(pi=3.14,r)pi*r*r)(r=5)
```

Creates an Anonymous Function

The output of Listing 23.11 is shown in Figure 23.17:

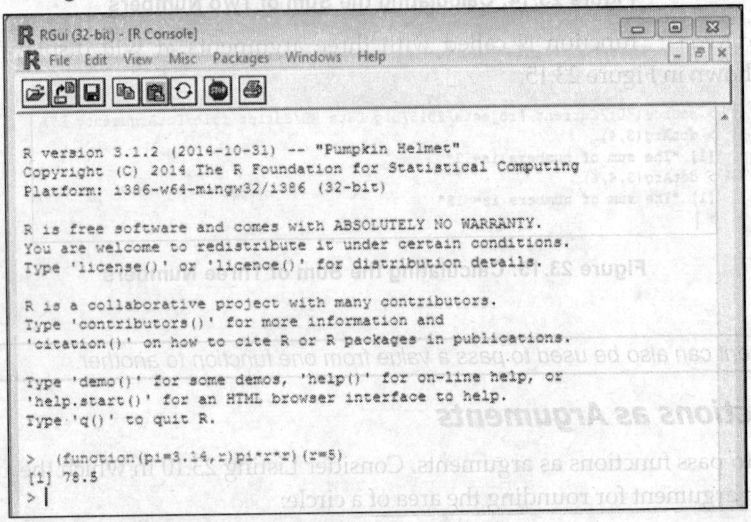

Figure 23.17: Displaying an Anonymous Function

Local and Global Environment of Functions

The workspace of R is known as the global environment in which the function operates; whereas, the environment used in a function is known as the local environment of that function. The local environment is the subset of the global environment. In other words, you can say that the local environment is nested within the global environment. The environment outside the function is known as its global environment, while the environment inside the function is known as its local environment.

NOTE

The global environment is also known as the parent environment.

The object residing in the global environment can be accessed inside the local environment. On the other hand, the object residing in the local environment cannot be accessed outside it. After the execution of the function, the object in the local environment is destroyed.

Let's understand the concept of global and local environment of functions with the help of Listing 23.12:

Listing 23.12: Displaying the Accessibility of an External Object

```
r=5
calarea<-function(pi=3.14,r=10)
{
  a=pi*r*r
  rm(r)
```

Defines the calarea () function

Removes the variable r

```
  b=pi*r*r
  print("Area of circle before removing r")
 print(a)
 print ("Area of circle after removing r=")
 print(b)
 }
```

Computes the area of a circle with the global r variable

In Listing 23.12, first the area of a circle is calculated by using the local variable `r`. When the local variable gets removed from the function by using the `rm()` function, then the area gets calculated by using the global variable `r` present in the workspace. The removal of the local variable from the function will not give any error as the variable of the same name is present in the global workspace.

TIP

The `rm()` function helps you to delete those objects of a function from the memory that are no more required by the program. This way, you can save a lot of space.

The output of Listing 23.12 is shown in Figure 23.18:

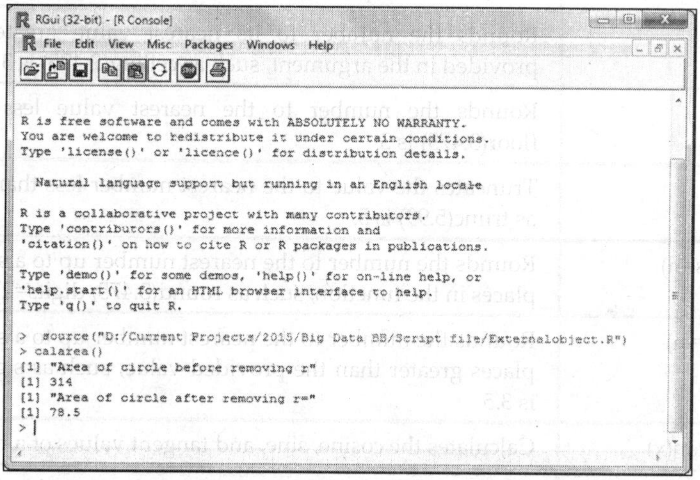

Figure 23.18: Using the External Objects

Built-in Functions in R

Functions that are already defined in the R library are known as built-in or predefined functions. The advantage of using these functions is that you do not need to define the body of the function. Instead, you can use these functions by just writing their names in the script.

SCENARIO

Mr. Samuel Roberts, the senior developer of Argon Technology was checking the code developed by one of his new team members, Michelle, and noticed that it was too lengthy and difficult to understand. He found that Michelle has defined complex user-defined functions at most of the places in the program. Mr. Roberts tells Michelle that most of these functions are already available in the R library and she only needs to include the name of the packages containing the functions in her program. This would not only save her time, but also make the code much concise and clear.

Some common categories of predefined functions in R are as follows:

- Numeric functions
- Character functions
- Statistical Probability functions
- Miscellaneous functions

Numeric Functions

Numeric functions are used to perform mathematical operations. Table 23.1 lists the most commonly used numeric functions along with their descriptions:

Table 23.1: Numeric Functions

Function	Description
abs(x)	Calculates the absolute value of a number such as abs(-6) is 6
sqrt(x)	Calculates the square root of a number such as sqrt(25) is 5
ceiling(x)	Rounds the number to its nearest value greater than the value provided in the argument, such as ceiling(2.475) is 3
floor(x)	Rounds the number to the nearest value less than x, such as floor(3.475) is 3
trunc(x)	Truncates the value to the nearest number less than the number, such as trunc(5.99) is 5.
round(x, digits=n)	Rounds the number to the nearest number up to a specified number of places in the function, such as round(3.475, digits=2) is 3.48
signif(x, digits=n)	Rounds the number to the nearest number up to a specified number of places greater than the provided value, such as signif(3.475, digits=2) is 3.5
cos(x), sin(x), tan(x)	Calculates the cosine, sine, and tangent values of a number
log(x)	Calculates the natural logarithm of a number, such as log(2) is 0.6931472
log10(x)	Calculates the common logarithm of a number, such as log10(100)=2
exp(x)	Calculates the exponential of a number, such as exp(0.6931472) is 2

Character Functions

Character functions are used to perform character operations on an array of characters or strings. Table 23.2 lists the most commonly used character functions along with their descriptions:

Table 23.2: Character Functions

Function	Description
substr(x, start=n1, stop=n2)	Extracts or replaces substrings in a string. z <- "abcdef"

Table 23.2: Character Functions	
Function	**Description**
	substr(z, 2, 4) is "bcd" substr(z, 2, 4) <- "11111" is "a111ef"
grep(pattern, x , ignore.case=FALSE, fixed=FALSE)	Searches for a pattern in x. If the value of the fixed argument is set as FALSE, then the pattern is considered as a regular expression. On the other hand, if the value of the argument is set as TRUE, then the pattern is considered as a text string. This function returns matching indices. grep("X", y("z","X","a"), fixed=TRUE) returns 2
sub(pattern, replacement, x, ignore.case =FALSE, fixed=FALSE)	Finds pattern in x and replaces it with the replacement text provided in the function. If the value of the fixed argument is set as FALSE then the pattern is considered as a regular expression. On the other hand, if the value of the fixed argument is set as TRUE, then the pattern is considered as a text string. sub("\\s",".","Hi There") returns "Hi.There"
strsplit(x, split)	Splits the elements of character vector x at split. strsplit("xyz", "") returns 3 element vector "x","y","z"
paste(..., sep="")	Joins strings after using the sep string to separate them. paste("z",1:3,sep="") returns c("z1","z2" "z3") paste("z",1:3,sep="Y") returns c("zY1","zY2" "zY3") paste("The current date is", date())
toupper(x)	Changes the letter of the string to uppercase
tolower(x)	Changes the letter of the string to lowercase

Statistical Probability Functions

Statistical probability functions are used in calculations of the probability distributions. Table 23.3 lists the most commonly used statistical probability functions along with their descriptions:

Table 23.3: Statistical Probability Functions	
Function	**Description**
dnorm(x)	Calculates the normal density in statistical calculations
pnorm(x)	Calculates the cumulative normal probability for the number provided
qnorm(p)	Calculates the p percentile of normal distribution
rnorm(n, m=0,sd=1)	Calculates the n random normal deviates with mean m and standard deviation sd
dbinom(x, size, prob) pbinom(q, size, prob) qbinom(p, size, prob) rbinom(n, size, prob)	Calculates binomial distribution where size is the sample size and prob is the probability of heads (pi)

Table 23.3: Statistical Probability Functions

Function	Description
dpois(x, lambda) ppois(q, lambda) qpois(p, lambda) rpois(n, lambda)	Calculates the poisson distribution with m=std=lamda
dunif(x, min=0, max=1) punif(q, min=0, max=1) qunif(p, min=0, max=1) runif(n, min=0, max=1)	Calculates the uniform distribution by following the same pattern as in the case of normal distribution
mean(x, trim=0, na.rm=FALSE)	Calculates the mean of object x
sd(x)	Calculates the standard deviation of object x
median(x)	Calculates the median of object x
quantile(x, probs)	Calculates the quantiles where x is the numeric vector whose quantiles are desired and probs is a numeric vector with probabilities in [0,1]
range(x)	Provides the range of object x
sum(x)	Calculates the sum of object x
diff(x, lag=1)	Calculates the lagged differences, with lag indicating which lag to use
min(x)	Calculates the minimum value of object x
max(x)	Calculates the maximum value of object x

Miscellaneous Functions

Besides the preceding built-in functions, there are some miscellaneous functions. Table 23.4 lists some miscellaneous functions in R along with their descriptions:

Table 23.4: Displaying Some Miscellaneous Functions and their Description

Function	Description
seq(from , to, by)	Generates a sequence such as indices <- seq(2,10,2) #indices is c(2,4, 6, 8,10)
rep(x, ntimes)	Repeats the value of x upto n times such as rep(1:5, 3) 1, 2, 3,4,5 1, 2, 3,4,5,1,2,3,4,5
cut(x, n)	Divides the continuous variable in factor with n levels cut(x, 3)

Introducing Packages

As already discussed, packages act as containers for functions. The main advantage of using packages is that they help to prevent any ambiguity that may arise in case two or more functions, belonging to different categories, have the same name.

Besides functions, packages in R also include help files, example datasets and command scripts for providing knowledge about the usage of functions.

Whenever you start the R interface, several packages get automatically installed. You can use the `search()` function to know about the packages installed by default while loading the R environment. Figure 23.19 shows the output of executing the `search()` function:

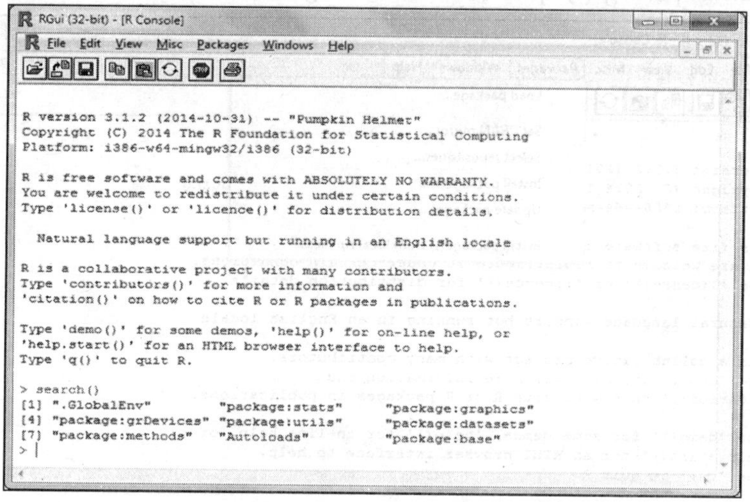

Figure 23.19: Displaying the Default Packages

Working with Packages

To view the complete list of packages available in the R library, type the following command:

```
installed.packages()
```

The output of running the preceding command is shown in Figure 23.20:

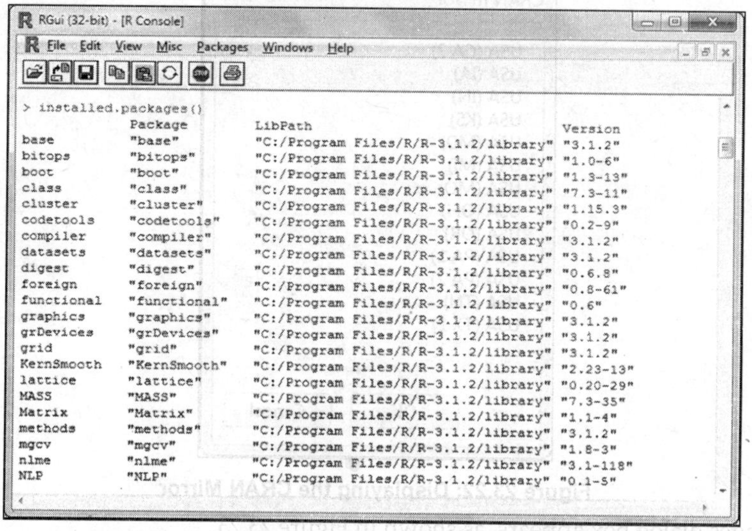

Figure 23.20: Displaying the Complete List of Packages

You can select the packages that you need to install from the list of packages shown in Figure 23.20.

Perform the following steps to install packages in R:

1. Open the RGui and select the Packages tab (Figure 23.21).
2. Select the Install package(s) option, as shown in Figure 23.21:

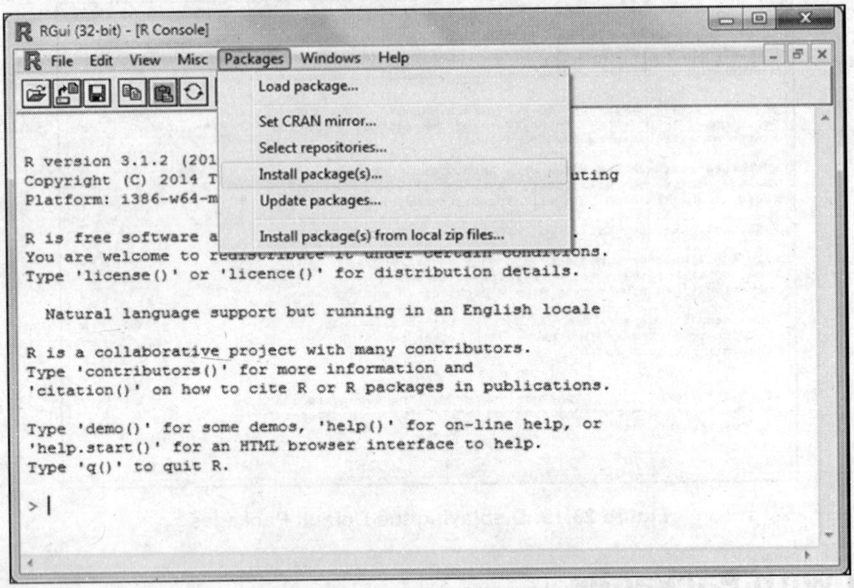

Figure 23.21: Using the Install Package(s) Option

The CRAN mirror dialog box appears.

3. Select the country of your choice and click the OK button, as shown in Figure 23.22:

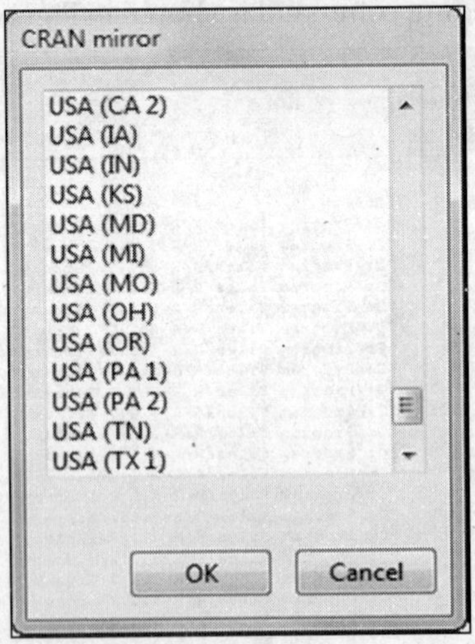

Figure 23.22: Displaying the CRAN Mirror

The Packages dialog box appears, as shown in Figure 23.23.

4. Select the packages that you want to include in your R library. In our case, we have selected the `bigdata` package, as shown in Figure 23.23:

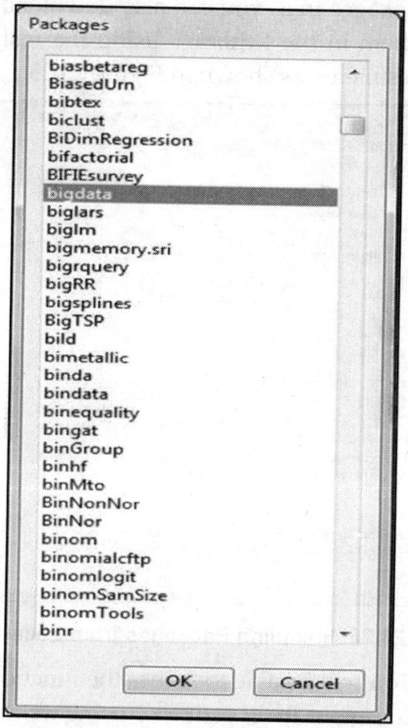

Figure 23.23: Selecting the `bigdata` Package

The `bigdata` package gets installed in the R console, as shown in Figure 23.24:

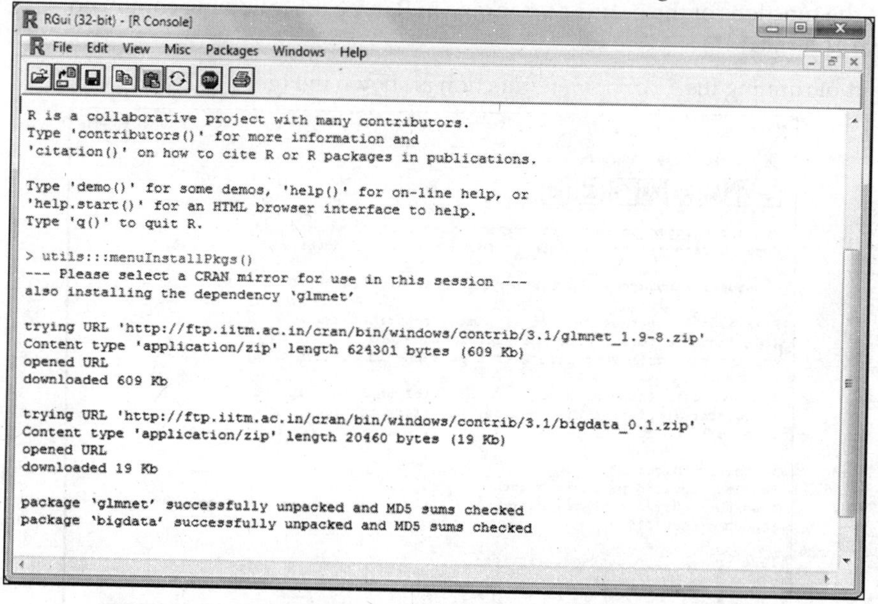

Figure 23.24: Displaying the Successful Installation of Package

In addition to the available packages in R, you can also download the packages from Internet in the form of zip files and install them in the R library using the Install package(s) from local zip files option available in the Packages menu, as shown in Figure 23.25:

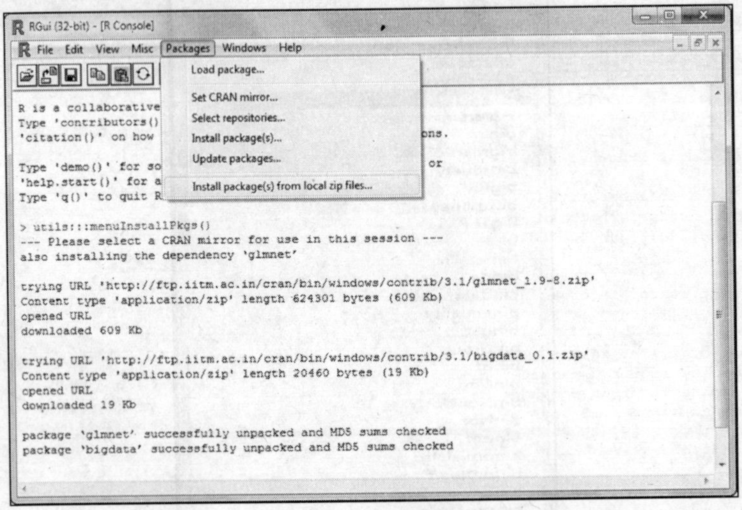

Figure 23.25: Installing Packages from Local Zip Files

After installing the package, you will be able to access the functions and commands available in that package. You can load the package in the R script by using the `library()` function. The syntax of using the `library()` function is as follows:

```
library("package-name")
```

To access the functions of the `bigdata` package in R, type the following command:

```
library("bigdata")
```

The output of running the `library()` function is shown in Figure 23.26:

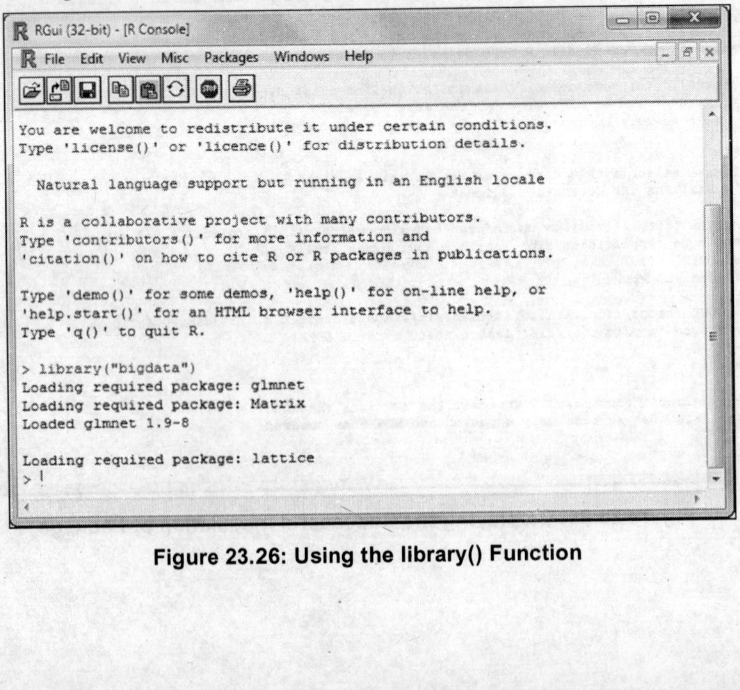

Figure 23.26: Using the library() Function

You can also load and update packages by using the `Load` package or `Update` packages options, respectively, from the Packages menu, as shown in Figure 23.27:

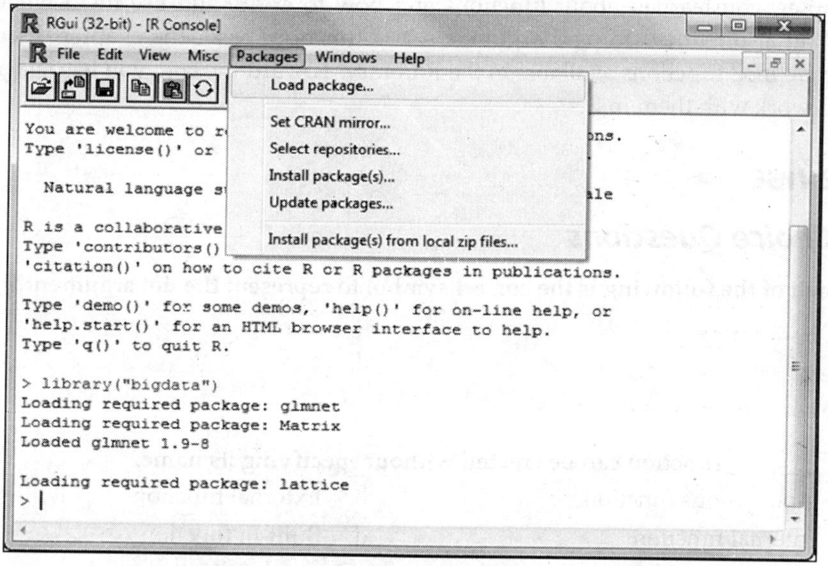

Figure 23.27: Using the Load Package Option

You can unload or remove a package from the R library by using the `detach()` function. The syntax of writing the `detach()` function is as follows:

```
detach(package:<name of package>)
```

In the preceding syntax, the `package` is a keyword; while `<name of the package>` specifies the name of the package.

To view the working of the `detach()` function, first load a package using the `library()` function. In this case, we have loaded the `bigdata` package. Then, write the `search()` function to view the list of loaded packages. Now, remove the `bigdata` package by using the `detach()` function, as shown in Figure 23.28:

```
> library("bigdata")
Loading required package: glmnet
Loading required package: Matrix
Loaded glmnet 1.9-8

Loading required package: lattice
> search()
 [1] ".GlobalEnv"             "package:bigdata"    "package:lattice"
 [4] "package:glmnet"         "package:Matrix"     "package:stats"
 [7] "package:graphics"       "package:grDevices"  "package:utils"
[10] "package:datasets"       "package:methods"    "Autoloads"
[13] "package:base"
> detach(package:bigdata)
> search()
 [1] ".GlobalEnv"             "package:lattice"    "package:glmnet"
 [4] "package:Matrix"         "package:stats"      "package:graphics"
 [7] "package:grDevices"      "package:utils"      "package:datasets"
[10] "package:methods"        "Autoloads"          "package:base"
> |
```

Figure 23.28: Detaching the bigdata Package

Summary

In this chapter, you learned about functions and how to create and use them while writing an R program. You also learned to pass arguments in a function. Next, the chapter discussed different types of predefined functions available in the R library. Toward the end, you learned about packages and how to work with them in R.

Quick Revise

Multiple-Choice Questions

Q1. Which of the following is the correct symbol to represent the dot argument?

a. … … … … b. … … …

c. … … d. …

Ans. The correct option is d.

Q2. ___________ function can be created without specifying its name.

a. Anonymous function b. External function

c. Internal function d. Built-in function

Ans. The correct option is a.

Q3. The environment inside a function is known as the ___________ environment.

a. global b. nested

c. local d. child

Ans. The correct option is c.

Q4. Which character function is used for extracting characters from a string?

a. grep() b. substr()

c. sub() d. paste()

Ans. The correct option is b.

Q5. Consider the following command:

X<-rep(1:3,2)

The output of running the preceding command is:

a. (1,2,3,2) b. (1:3,1:3)

c. (1,2,1,2) d. (1,2,3,1,2,3)

Ans. The correct option is d.

Subjective Questions

Q1. What are functions?

Ans. A function refers to a named block of code that performs a specific task in a program, which is executed when it is called from some other part of the program.

A large program can be broken down into smaller parts using functions, which help in making that program more readable. A function needs to be declared or defined in a program before using it in that program. You can create as many functions as you want in a program and call them from any part of that program.

Q2. What are the two main advantages of using functions over scripts?

Ans. Using functions in R provides the following two main advantages:

- Functions have the capability of working with variable inputs, i.e., with different values.
- Functions return the result as an object. This result can be further used as an input for another function or program.

Q3. Discuss the syntax of defining a function in R.

Ans. The syntax of defining a function in R is as follows:

```
<functionname><-function(arg1,arg2,…)
{
 Statement 1
 Statement 2
 . ….
return(output)
}
```

In the preceding syntax:

- **<functionname>**—Refers to the name of the function.
- **function**—Refers to the keyword used for defining a function.
- **(arg1, arg2,..)**—Refers to the set of arguments given to a function. A function can have one or more arguments; however it is not necessary to specify arguments in a function. The arguments of a function are separated by commas and are enclosed within parentheses. Dots given in braces are known as "dot arguments", which means we can add the third argument that will be other than arg1 and arg2 during the runtime.
- **Statement 1, Statement 2 ...and return statement**—Define the body of the function and are always written within curly braces.
- **Return(output)**—Calls the output so that it can return to the main screen. For example, in the code fragment (given below), `print()` is the function used to return the output variable or the value held by the variable "b".

```
>print ("Area of circle after removing r=")
>print(b)   // this will give output which is held by "b"
```

Q4. What are arguments? Why are they used in functions?

Ans. Arguments can be defined as variables, constants, or expressions that contain values which can be used in functions. As discussed earlier, a function may or may not have arguments. The arguments of a function receive the value from the user at runtime. These values can be used in a function for computational purposes.

Q5. What is the difference between optional and required arguments?

Ans. The arguments that already contain a default value are known as optional arguments because it is optional for a user to define its values. The required arguments, on the other hand, are those arguments whose value needs to be specified while calling a function.

Q6. What do you understand by the local and global environment of a function?

Ans. The workspace of R is known as the global environment in which the function operates; whereas, the environment used in a function is known as the local environment of that function. The local environment is the subset of the global environment. In other words, you can say that local environment is nested within the global environment. The environment outside the function is known as its global environment, while the environment inside the function is known as its local environment.

24

Performing Graphical Analysis in R

Statistics is a field of study concerned with the analyses of historical data and prediction of common trends on the basis of those analyses. The R programming tool helps analysts to analyze large historical datasets and predict the patterns of market trends through graphs, histograms, and charts.

As you know, statistical analysis is solely based on numerical techniques, such as confidence intervals, hypothesis testing, regression analysis, and so on. However, most of these statistical techniques are based on suppositions about the present usage of data. You can find if data follows to these suppositions by analyzing its graph, because a graph can provide deeper details into the properties of the plotted dataset. One of the main reasons for doing statistical computing is that it produces high-quality graphics. The main advantage of using graphs is that they are particularly useful for analyzing non-numerical data, such as colors, flavors, brand names, and more, where performing computations is difficult or impossible. This chapter explains how to organize data graphically in a convenient form so you can easily analyze it.

SCENARIO

Almost all organizations use statistical data analysis to draw inferences about their production and sales processes. The data analysts at Argon technology, a provider of Big Data analytical solutions, collect some general data about customers from a local market and store it in the `dailySpend.csv` dataset. The company intends to use this data to get important insights regarding the behavior and buying tendencies of customers.

In this chapter, you first learn about the concept of plots. Further, this chapter discusses different types of plotting mechanisms such as plotting for a single variable, two variables, multiple variables and designing special plots. Next, you learn to plot for a single variable by using histograms, index plots, time series plots, pie charts, and strip charts; for two variables using the scatter plot graph; and for a third variable by using the `pairs()` function and `coplot()` function. This chapter also discusses about design and bubble plots. In the end, this chapter discusses about saving graphs in external files.

Using Plots

R provides excellent graphics and plotting capabilities. It can efficiently display information graphically with the help of its "`plot()`" commands and functions. The data displayed onto different graphs can be read from files or can be entered directly. Symbols and colors are used in graphs to differentiate between different datasets. Some useful functions used in plotting graphs or interacting with graphs are lines, points, abline, curve, text, rug, legend segments, arrows, polygon locator, identify, etc. Some of the common plots in R are:

- Strip charts
- Histograms
- Time series plots
- Scatter plots
- Index plots
- Bubble plots

All the preceding graphs can be drawn by using the following techniques:

- Using plots for a single variable
- Using plots for two variables

- Using plots for multiple variables
- Designing special plots

Let's learn about each of these techniques in detail.

Using Plots for a Single Variable

R allows you to plot a graph even for a single variable; however, the choice of plots remains limited in this case. Plotting the daily sales of a product is an example of a single variable graph. R provides the following functions to plot single variable graphs:

- **hist(y)** — Used for plotting histograms to display a frequency distribution
- **plot(y)** — Used for plotting indices to display the values of y in sequence
- **plot.ts(y)** — Used for plotting values in a time series graph
- **pie(x)** — Used for plotting compositional graphs such as pie diagrams

Now, let's learn how to plot for a single variable by using histograms, index plots, time series plots, pie charts, and `stripchart()` function.

Histograms

A histogram comprises parallel vertical bars displaying the frequency distribution of a quantitative variable in a graphical format. The area occupied by each bar is equal to the frequency of items searched.

A histogram is the best displaying mode to represent structured data. The values of response variables are distributed across the x axis and each occupied area is known as a bin. It is a little tricky to plot a histogram, as its plotting requires subjective judgments for deciding where exactly to put the bin margins. Let's create a histogram by using the `rnorm()` and `hist()` functions as follows:

```
NormDist<-rnorm(n=500,m=24.2,sd=2.2)
hist(NormDist)
```

The `rnorm()` function in the preceding command contains three arguments:

- **n**—Specifies the random numbers
- **m**—Specifies the mean value
- **sd**—Specifies the standard deviation

Figure 24.1 shows the histogram generated by executing the preceding set of commands:

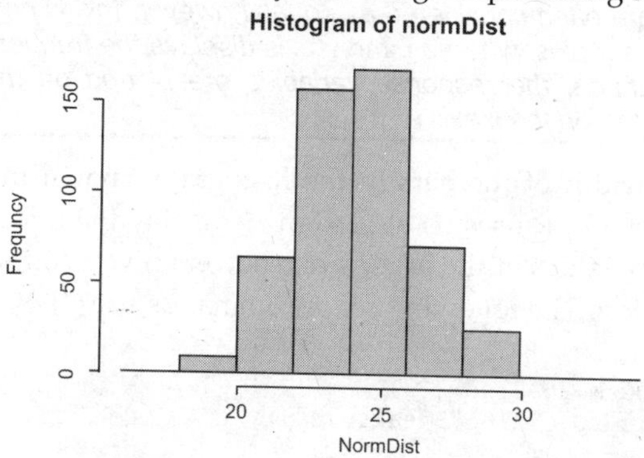

Figure 24.1: Displaying the Histogram of Normal Distribution

Apart from creating histograms, the `hist()` function can also be used to perform a number of tasks. The information about these tasks can be viewed by using the following commands:

```
>histinfo<-hist(NormDist)
>histinfo
```

The output of executing the preceding commands is shown in Figure 24.2:

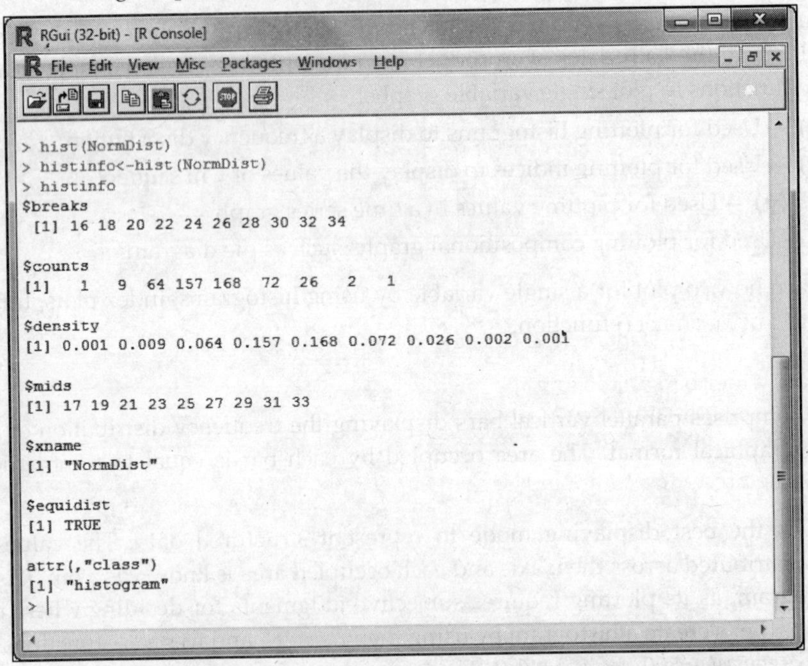

Figure 24.2: Displaying Information about a Histogram

Figure 24.2 displays the information about the histogram created in Figure 24.1. This information includes the number of breaks, also called the bins cutoff points, counts, density and midpoints for each bin. It also displays the names of the variable and object's class, and whether the bins are equidistant or not.

NOTE

Histograms and bar charts are often considered as equal; however, this is not the case. Histograms have the response variables on the x axis; whereas, the y axis displays the frequency of different values of the response. In case of bar charts, the response variables are plotted on the y axis and a categorical explanatory variable is depicted on the x axis.

You can also change the width of the bars in the histogram, shown in Figure 24.1, by using the `breaks()` function. By default, R uses its algorithm to display the information into finer or wider bars according to the given values of the arguments; however, you can set the width of the bars by using the `breaks()` function. The following set of commands uses the `break()` function to define the width of the bars:

```
NormDist<-rnorm(n=500,m=24.2,sd=2.2)
hist(NormDist, breaks=20, main="Breaks=20")
```

The output of executing the preceding command is shown in Figure 24.3:

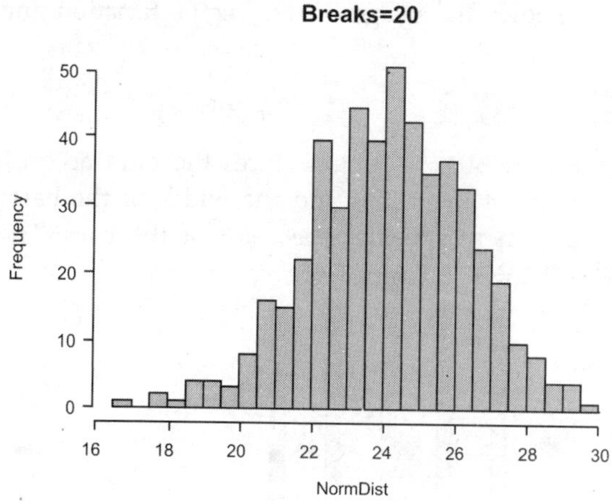

Figure 24.3: Displaying Finer Histogram Bars

Let's now draw wider bars in the graph by using the following set of commands:

```
NormDist<-rnorm(n=500,m=24.2,sd=2.2)
hist(NormDist, breaks=5, main="Breaks=5")
```

The output of the preceding commands is shown in Figure 24.4:

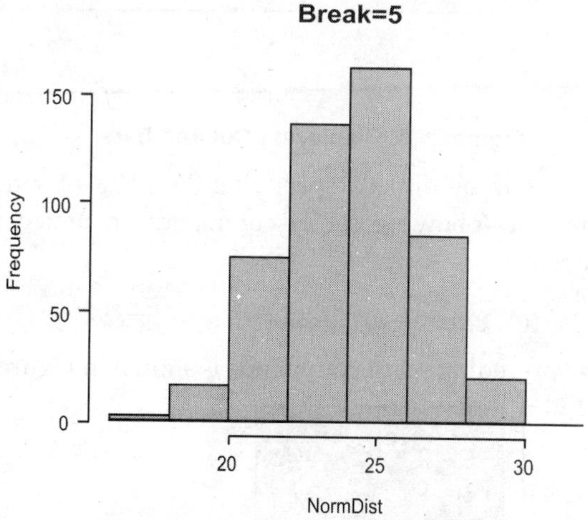

Figure 24.4: Displaying the Wider Bars

In the `hist()` function, you can also vary the size of the bars by specifying the bin boundaries using the `seq()` function. The conventions adopted in R for displaying the bin boundaries are as follows:

- [x,y) means 'greater than or equal to x but less than y
- (x,y] means 'greater than x but less than or equal to y

From the preceding standards, it is clear that a bin gets a given number when that number falls exactly on a boundary between two bins. If the number falls on the minimum or maximum value, it gets easier to determine which bin gets a given number. You must ensure that the bins are accommodated on the basis of both the minimum and maximum values.

You can also fill colors in the bars by using the `col` argument in the `hist()` function. The following set of commands shows the usage of the `seq()` function and the col argument in the `hist()` function:

```
numobj<-c(1,2,3,4,5)
hist(numobj, seq (0,10,0.25) ,col ="grey", main="")
```

In the preceding commands, the `numobj` object stores the data according to which bars will be drawn on the x-axis. The range of the x-axis and the width of the bars are defined by using the `seq()` function. The `col` argument specifies the color of the bars. The output of executing the preceding set of commands is shown in Figure 24.5:

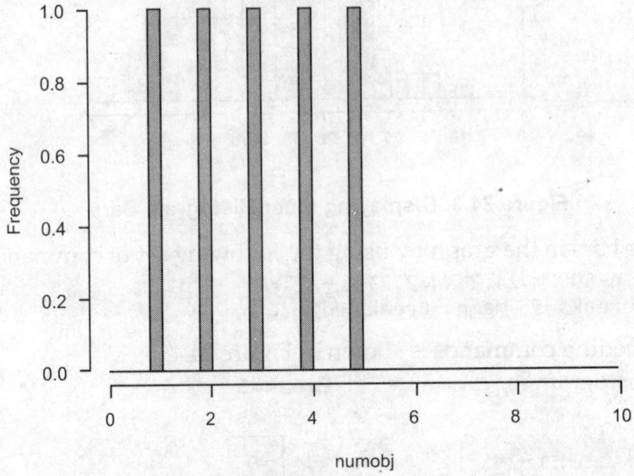

Figure 24.5: Displaying Colored Bars

You can also draw the histogram by directly specifying the values for the width of the bins in the `hist()` function. Consider the following set of commands in which the values (0,2,4,8,10) are provided in the `hist()` function:

```
numobj<-c(1,2,3,4,5)
hist(numobj,c(0,2,4,8,10),col="grey",main="")
```

The output of executing the preceding set of commands is shown in Figure 24.6:

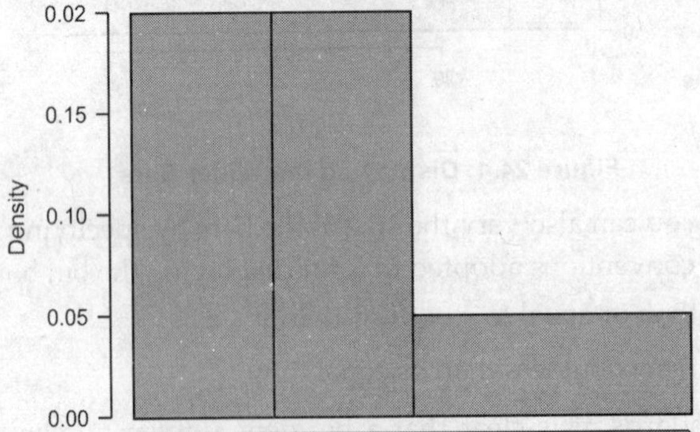

Figure 24.6: Displaying Bars of Varying Width

Now, let's learn to derive results from histograms. Enter the following set of commands to load a dataset in the R environment. In our case, we have used the dataset, `healthClaim.csv`.

```
healthClaim=read.csv("Datasets/healthClaim.csv",header=T).
>head(healthClaim)
```

The output of executing the preceding set of commands is shown in Figure 24.7:

```
> healthClaim=read. csv ("datasets/healthClaim.csv", header=T
>   head (healthClaim)
  Patient_id age Distance_from_clinic Days_admitted
1          6  74                 3500             8
2         14  40                13700             4
3         16  64                11362             8
4         45  26                    1             8
5         75  49                10257             6
6         83  53                12414             6
  Num_medical_bills Claim_amount Year Month
1                 1          746 2013    12
2                 1        13216 2013    12
3                 1         6232 2013    12
4                 1            0 2013    12
5                 2         1365 2013    12
6                 1          214 2013    12
> |
```

Figure 24.7: Loading the healthClaim Dataset

Now, let's create a histogram for the values given in the age variable. To do this, enter the following command:

```
>hist(healthClaim$age)
```

Figure 24.8 shows the output of executing the preceding command:

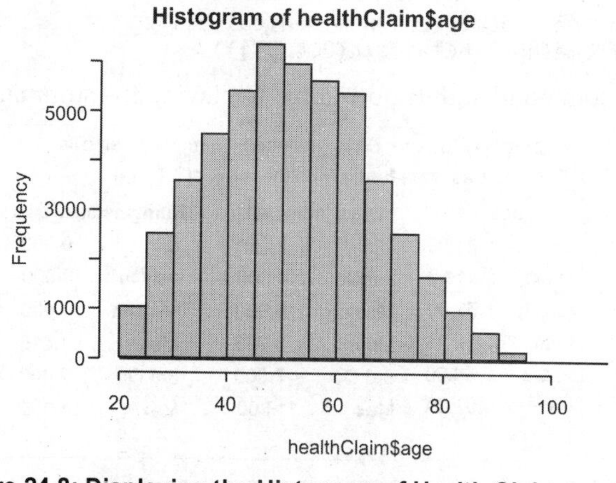

Figure 24.8: Displaying the Histogram of Health Claims and Age

From the histogram shown in Figure 24.8, we can conclude that people in the age group of 40–50 years face most health issues and are more likely to claim health insurance. We can determine the distribution to be bell-shaped or skewed toward left or right by drawing the skewness curve, as shown in the following set of commands:

```
#Drawingskewness curve over histogram
# installing SuppDists package
```

```
install.packages("SuppDists")
library(SuppDists)
hist(healthClaim$age,freq=F) # without frequency
# Fita Johnson distribution to the data
parms<-JohnsonFit(healthClaim$age, moment="find")
# Print out the parameters
sJohnson(parms)
# add the Johnson function to the histogram
plot(function(x)dJohnson(x,parms), -100, 100, add=TRUE, col="red")
```

Figure 24.9 shows the output of executing the preceding commands:

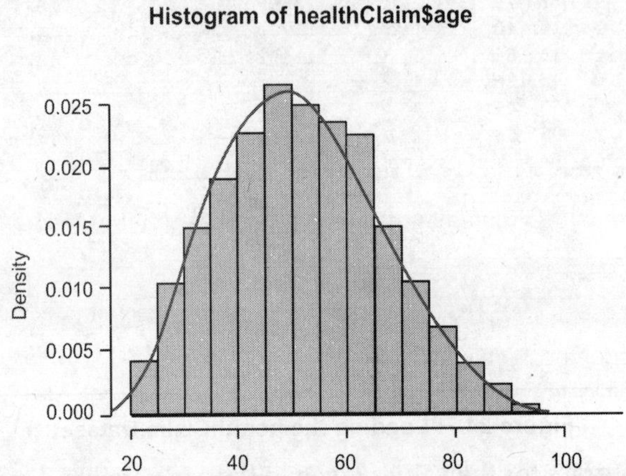

Figure 24.9: Displaying the Skewness Curve on a Histogram

Enter the following set of commands to get some particular columns of the data in the summarized form by using the `summary()` function:

```
# Summary for age, Days_admitted, Num_medical_bills
summary(as.data.frame(healthClaim[,c(2,4,5)]))
```

Figure 24.10 shows the command and its output by displaying the summary of data:

```
> # Summary for age, Days_admitted, Num_medical_bills
> Simmary( as. data.frame (healthClaim[, c(2,4,5)]))
      age            Days_admitted       Num_medical_bills
Min     : 21.00    Min     : 2.000    Min     : 0.000
1st Qu  : 41.00    1st Qu  : 4.000    1st Qu  : 0.000
Median  : 52.00    Median  : 6.000    Median  : 1.000
Mean    : 52.21    Mean    : 5.723    Mean    : 1.015
3rd Qu  : 63.00    3rd Qu  : 7.000    3rd Qu  : 2.000
Max     :107.00    Max     :11.000    Max     :14.000
>|
```

Figure 24.10: Displaying the Summary of Data

For the summary created with the heading `Num_medical_bills`, we can plot the histogram by using the following set of commands:

```
> #histograme for Num_medical_bills
>table(healthClaim$Num_medical_bills)
>hist(healthClaim$Num_medical_bills,freq=T)
```

Figure 24.11 shows the output of executing the preceding set of commands:

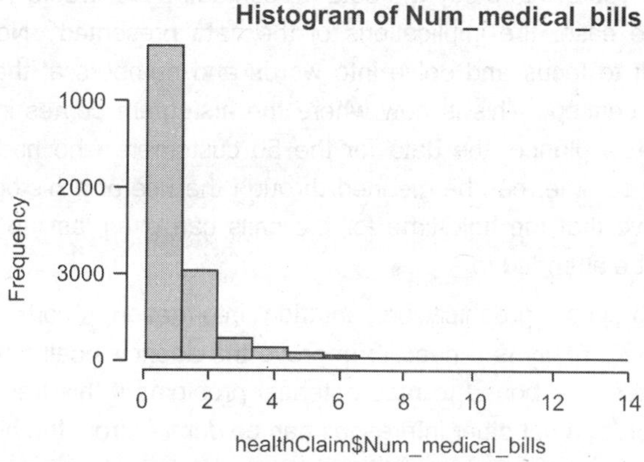

Figure 24.11: Displaying a Histogram of Number of Medical Bills

EXHIBIT 1: Graphical Analysis of Call Center's Failure for Rapid Response

A call center agency wants to improve its system as an inbound call center and service agency. Although there's no specific industry standard to which handling of calls should adhere, the agency's goal is to sustain its ability to respond rapidly to customers' calls. Currently, the hold-time it takes for their agents to respond has been falling short of the previous track record of less than a minute.

In line with this, a study was conducted in order to determine if the agency needed more staff to attend to the customers. Fifty (50) inbound calls for technical support took more than a minute before a help-desk technician could attend to the customers' requests for assistance. In fact, it was observed that half of the fifty calls took more than five minutes, which can be gleaned from the following data gathered during the course of the observations.

Number of Minutes the Customers Were On Hold

- 0-1 minute = This is the rapid-response time by which phone calls should be answered.
- 1-2 minutes = Two (2) customers had hung up their phones.
- 2-3 minutes = Five (5) more customers had hung up.
- 3-4 minutes = Eight (8) customers also gave up on holding.
- 4-5 minutes = Ten (10) customers stayed on the line and were attended to.
- 5-6 minutes = Another set of (10) customers who waited while on hold, had been given assistance.
- 6-7 minutes = Seven (7) more customers had been provided with technical assistance.
- 7-8 minutes = Another set of four (4) customers waited for their turn to be served.
- 8-9 minutes = Three (3) of the customers simply gave up and decided to hang-up.
- 9-10 minutes = One (1) customer's patience paid-off and he was finally served.

Now if you are to study the data presented above, would you be able to perceive with relative ease, the implications of the data presented? Not quite, because it's a bit difficult to focus and delve into words and numbers at the same time to visualize a larger concept. This is now where the histogram comes in as a useful and practical tool. At a glance, the data for the 50 customers who had waited beyond the rapid-response time, can be gleaned through the use of a histogram. Planners can readily perceive that the hold-time for the calls can even last up to 10 minutes before they could be attended to.

By this simple graphical presentation, information is communicated to a project team that there really is a need to improve the agency's call-handling systems. Otherwise, the agency is bound to face potential problems if this trend is allowed to continue or get worse. What other inferences can be derived from the histogram?

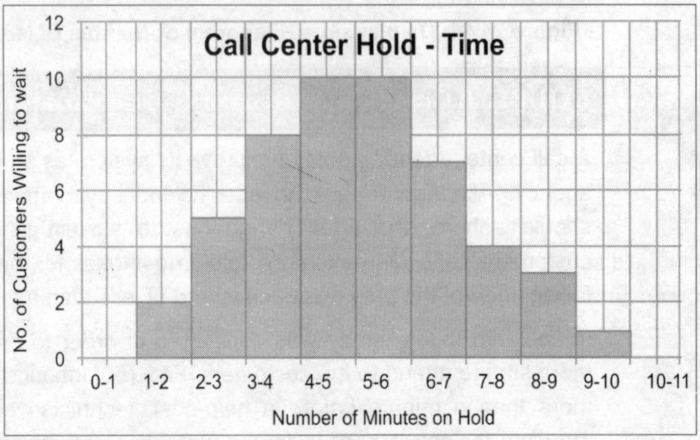

- Understanding histograms entails not just comprehending the bars and their frequencies. It can be taken further by adding a trend line over the bars' heights to determine the distribution shape.
- The graph can be taken further by connecting the end points of each bar for purposes of plotting the distribution shape, as shown in the following figure:

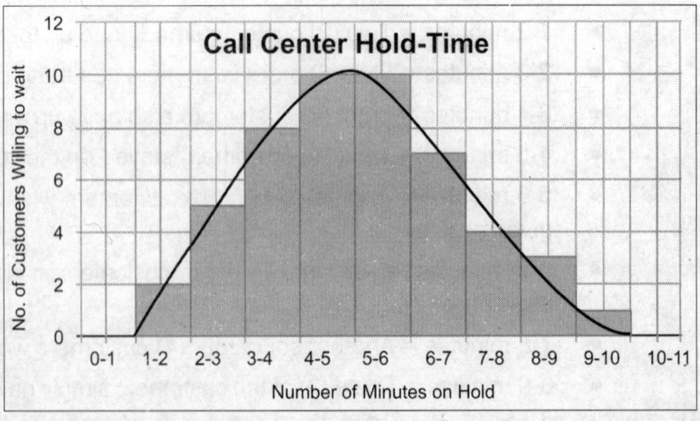

From here the following information can be readily extracted:

- Half of the customers were observed to have waited for 6 minutes or more. This can be easily arrived at by adding the number of customers who waited between 5-6 minutes through 9-10 minutes: 10 + 7 + 4 + 3 + 1 = 25 customers, which is also equivalent to half of the 50 customers observed.
- Two sets of data had 10 counts each and both groups waited between 4-5 and 5-6 minutes. This could be taken as the mode or an indication that these customers regarded it as the norm at this call center agency. Perhaps they have been through this as a routine and somehow expected the availability of the service any minute.
- These are only inferences but the project team would also have to consider analyzing the technical problems being encountered by the technicians. There is the possibility that an alternative solution for improving the system is to add a special line for those who need quick-fix solutions in order to decongest phone call traffic.

Source:*http://www.brighthubpm.com/six-sigma/13445-understanding-histograms-and-their-uses/#imgn_2*

Index Plots

Index plots take a single argument, which is a continuous variable, and plots the values on the *y* axis, with the *x* coordinate identified by the position of the number in the vector. The commands used to create an index plot are as follows:

```
numobj<-c(1,2,3,4,5)
plot(numobj)
```

The output of executing the preceding commands is shown in Figure 24.12:

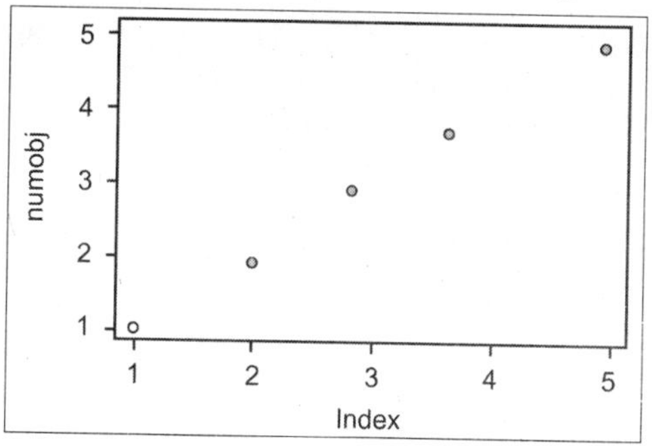

Figure 24.12: Displaying the Index plot

You can use the `which()` function for determining the index, as shown in the following command:

```
which(numobj>3)
```

The output of executing the preceding command will be 4 and 5.

Time Series Plots

R provides the facility of analyzing time related data. In a time series graph, data is plotted against the time by plotting dots, which are further joined to produce the graph. The time series graph provides more accurate results when no data is missing over a period of time. The limitation with the time series graph is that it does not provide any information about the missing values. For example, the value sale for a particular month of a year may be missed or the sales values of many months may be missed during the last ten years but all this may be not reflected in the time series graph. The `ts()` and `plot()` functions are used for plotting the time series graph. The `ts()` function converts a numeric vector into an object of R time series. The syntax for using the `ts()` function is as follows:

```
<name of object><-ts(vector, start=, end=, frequency=)
```

In the preceding syntax, start and end refer to the times of the first and last observations. The frequency refers to the number of observations per unit time. In case of frequency, 1 denotes annual, 4 denotes quarterly, and 12 denotes monthly.

SCENARIO

Consider the case of Argon Technology that provides Big Data solutions. The company wants to assess the attrition rate of employees from the year 2010 to 2014. The company collects data about the employees who left in the last five years. The data of attrition rate of the employees is as follows:

Year	2010	2011	2012	2013	2014
Number of employees who left company	10	5	6	2	1

Now, let's plot the time series graph in R using the preceding data. Enter the following commands:

```
myvector<-c(10,5,6,2,1)
myts<-ts(myvector, start=c(2010), end=c(2014), frequency=1)
plot(myts)
```

In the preceding commands, the `myvector` object is a numeric vector that contains the data of the employees who left the company in the past five years. The `ts()` and `plot()` functions are used for plotting the graph. Figure 24.13 shows the time series graph:

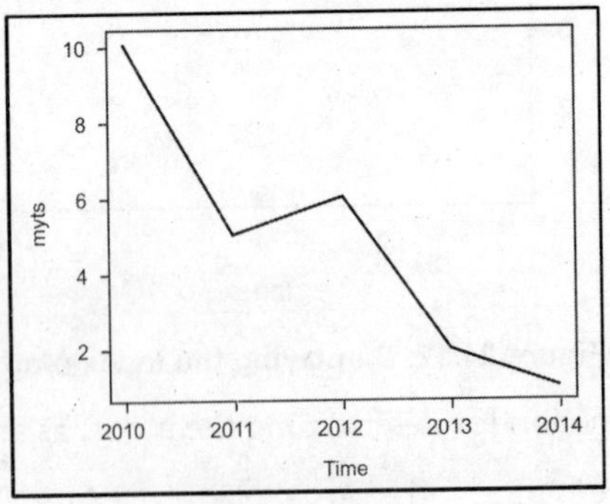

Figure 24.13: Displaying the Time Series Graph

From the preceding graph, it can be easily seen that the attrition rate of the company has gone down from 2010 to 2014. You can also change the color of the line by using the plot function. Use the following command to change the color of the line:

```
plot(myts,color='blue')
```

The time series graph will appear as a blue line.

You can also change the captions of `x` and `y` axes using the following command:

```
Plot(myts, color='blue',ylab="Number of employees",xlab="Year")
```

The output of executing the preceding command is shown in Figure 24.14:

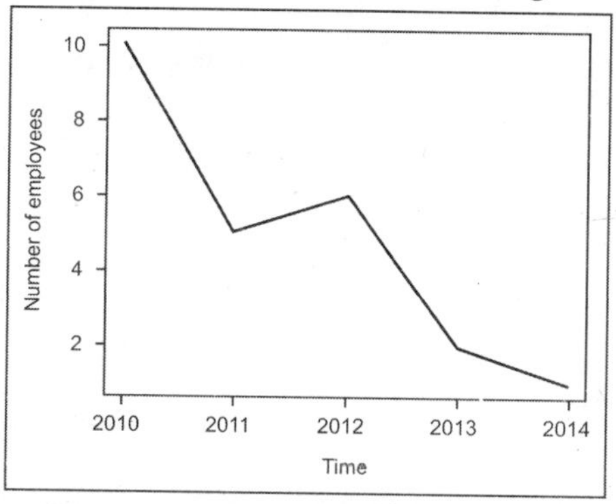

Figure 24.14: Displaying the Changed Captions of Axes

You can also display the line in different formats such as dashed, dash dot, and continuous. You only need to set the `lty` argument to dashed in the `plot()` function. You can do this by using the following commands:

```
Plot(myts, color='blue',ylab="Number of employees",xlab="Year",lty='dashed')
```

The execution of the preceding command generates a dashed line.

You can also draw multiple lines in a time series graph for comparing data. Consider the following data showing the percentage of adults who are using social networking sites since 2005:

Year	All_Internet_ Users	Ages(18-29)	Ages(30-49)	Ages(50-64)	Ages(65+)
2005	8	9	7	6	
2006	16	49	8	4	1
2008	29	67	25	11	7
2009	46	76	48	24	13
2010	61	86	61	47	26
2011	64	87	68	49	29
2012	66	86	72	50	34
2012	69	92	73	57	38
2012	67	83	77	52	32
2013	72	89	78	60	43
2013	73	90	78	65	46
2014	74	89	82	65	49

Source: *http://www.pewinternet.org/data-trend/social-media/social-media-use-by-age-group/*

Save this data in a CSV file, say `SNS_Users.csv`. You must add the `ggplot2` package in R before plotting the time series graph. Enter the following command for adding the `ggplot2` package:

```
library("ggplot2")
```

The `ggplot2` package allows you to use the `ggplot()` function. Now, read the `SNS_Users.csv` file by using the following command:

```
MyData <- read.csv(file="C:/Users/Puneet/Documents/SNS_Users.csv", header=TRUE,
sep=",")
```

After reading the file, enter the following command for displaying the graph:

```
ggplot() +
geom_line(data = MyData, aes(x = Year, y =
All_Internet_Users),color="red",linetype="solid") +
geom_line(data = MyData, aes(x = Year, y = Ages_18_29) ,color="blue",
linetype="dotted") +
geom_line(data = MyData, aes(x = Year, y = Ages_30_49) ,color="green",
linetype="longdash") +
geom_line(data = MyData, aes(x = Year, y = Ages_50_64) ,color="yellow",
linetype="twodash") +
geom_line(data = MyData, aes(x = Year, y = Ages_65_More) ,color="black",
linetype="dotdash") + ylab("Percentage of Internet Users") + xlab("Year")
```

In the preceding command, the `ggplot()` function is used to plot a graph and the `geom_line()` function is used to draw a line and set its type and color. The output of the preceding command is shown in Figure 24.15:

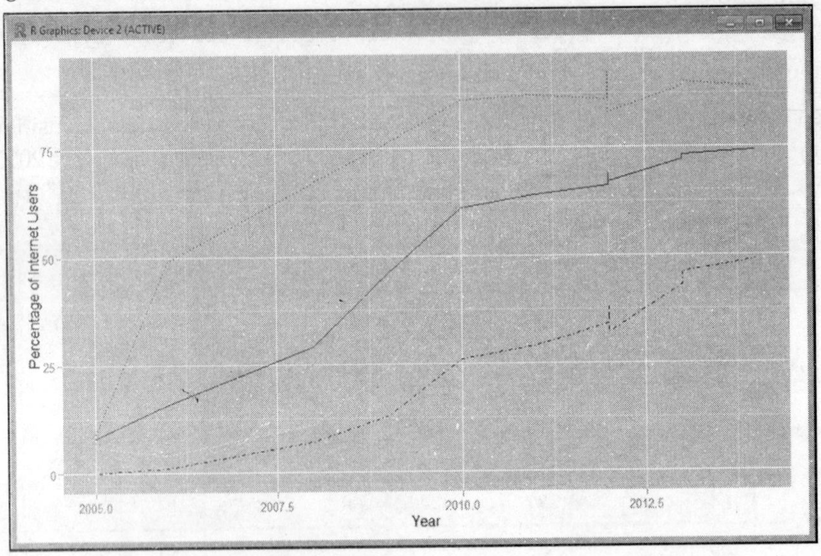

Figure 24.15: Displaying Multiple Lines in a Time Series Graph

The description of the lines, shown in Figure 24.15 is as follows:

- **Solid red color line**—Depicts the percentage of the All_Internet_Users column
- **Blue dotted line**—Depicts the percentage of users whose age is between 18 to 29 years
- **Green longdash line**—Depicts the percentage of users whose age is between 30 to 49 years
- **Yellow twodash line**—Depicts the percentage of users whose age is between 50 to 64 years
- **Black dotdash line**—Depicts the percentage of users whose age is more than 65 years

EXHIBIT 2: The Untapped Potential of Time Series Data Mining

By Wayne Thompson, UdoSglavo and Sascha Schubert

Financial planning and budgeting, supply chain management, retail replenishment and planning – these are just a few of the critical business functions that benefit greatly from data mining, forecasting and time series analysis, three established disciplines of analytics. These three disciplines are used in many industries for many different functions, but now leading organizations are recognizing the impact of combining them to create a more powerful brand of predictive analytics. Before describing the wide array of business advantages that can be gained by integrating data mining, time series analysis and forecasting, let's look at some definitions.

Data mining is a collection of analytical techniques that enable automated search for patterns and relations within a large portfolio of characteristics to find relationships that can be used for improved decision-making. For example, based on the characteristics of a customer – such as age, demographics, product portfolio, contact history and others – data mining can be used to identify a set of customers most likely to respond to a specific marketing offer.

Time series analysis and forecasting are used to detect temporal patterns from historical time-dependent data and project the detected patterns (such as trend or seasonality) into the future. For example, time series analysis plays a crucial role in forecasting electricity demand for the utilities industry. Electricity demand follows long-term trends, such as population growth and industrial activity, as well as shorter seasonal cycles for time of year (summer versus winter), day of the week (business days versus weekends) and time of day (peak demand to drive air conditioning on hot summer afternoons, and low demand in the middle of the night). Good software detects and reconciles the various temporal patterns and provides both the long-range and near-term forecasts that utility companies require.

Time series data mining combines data mining with time series analysis to:

- Extract features of time series data (such as seasonal patterns, etc.) for building better predictive models.
- Reduce time series data into fewer dimensions by using data mining methods, such as variable selection and clustering.
- Conduct similarity analysis of time series data (pattern detection) for segmenting data, or validating forecasts of new products.

Some practical applications of time series data mining include:

- **Marketing**—To predict the response of a customer to a specific marketing offer, the recency of contact plays an important role. Customers who have reacted positively to a recent offer are more likely to react positively again. Marketing departments across all industries have been using this insight for more targeted customer relationship management. Advanced predictive models often use proxy variables to capture the temporal aspect of the relationship between historical customer behavior and desired future outcome. For example, analysts often manually summarize transactional data about product usage into a set of time series, such as total monthly air minutes, maximum total air use, and change from previous month for mobile phone use. The time series data is then used as input to the predictive models.But because the integration of this temporal effect was managed manually, it further complicates the already tedious data preparation. Time series data mining (TSDM) tools automate the data preparation phase to include temporal relationships in predictive modeling. This will help speed up the data preparation, as well as improve the accuracy of predictive models.

- **Inventory management**—Often, time series information is collected on a very granular level in organizations. For example, retailers measure sales of items in a store on the SKU level and in daily time intervals. For stores with thousands of items, this results in a large amount of time series with many records because historical data is sometimes collected over many years. This large amount of data often makes it difficult to extract information relevant for decision-making. TSDM tools help analysts quickly reduce the dimensionality of the problem under investigation and extract signals from the noise. SKUs with similar sales trends can be combined into segments without losing critical information. Time series analysis techniques, such as smoothing, can help compress detailed information into a picture that makes general patterns easier to spot.
- **Fraud detection**—The similarity analysis provided with TSDM tools work on the most detailed level in order to spot exceptions to average behavior. Credit card providers can use time series data mining to automate the detection of fraudulent behavior in financial transactions. They do this by comparing many detailed transactional time series against a known pattern of abusive behavior. It is often only in looking across the temporal representation of behavior that undesired behavior becomes apparent.

  The similarity analysis tool can quickly detect behavior over time with known signatures of fraud and create flags for further investigation if similar patterns are detected.
- **New product forecasting**—A never-ending challenge for consumer goods manufacturers and retailers, new product forecasting situations include: predicting entirely new types of products, new markets for existing products (such as expanding a regional brand nationally or globally) and refinements of existing products (such as "new and improved" versions or packaging changes). All of them require a forecast of future sales without historic data for the new product. However, by using techniques such as similarity analysis, an analyst can examine the demand patterns of past new products having similar attributes and identify the range of demand curves that can be used to model demand for the new product. By integrating data mining with time series analysis and forecasting, organizations can take the next step in extracting more value from their data to improve decision making.

Source: *http://www.analytics-magazine.org/special-articles/392-the-untapped-potential-of-time-series-data-mining*

Pie Charts

A pie chart is commonly used for data visualization. These charts are circular charts that are divided into sectors. Each sector displays a size according to a specific value, as shown in Figure 24.16:

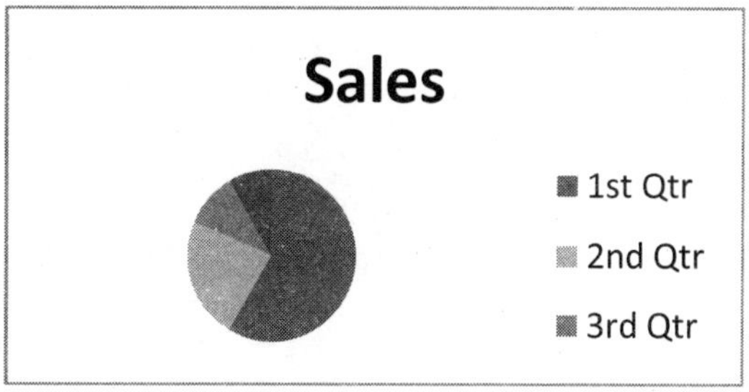

Figure 24.16: Displaying a Pie Chart of Sales

In R, the `pie()` function is used to display a pie chart and define the labels for its sectors. Let's create a pie chart for the number of employees who left the organization in the last five years. Consider the following data:

Year	2010	2011	2012	2013	2014
Percentage of employees left company	20	15	26	22	17

Let's draw a pie chart of the preceding data by using the `pie()` function. The command for drawing the pie chart is as follows:

```
datayear<-c(2010,2011,2012,2013,2014)
dataperc<-c(20,15,26,22,17)
pie(dataperc,labels=as.character(datayear))
```

The output of the preceding command is shown in Figure 24.17:

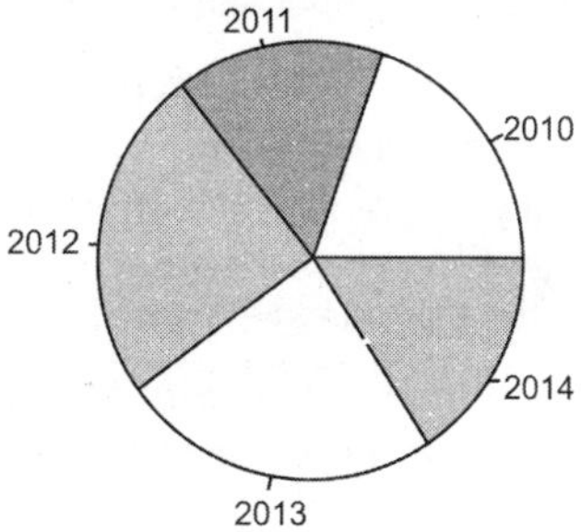

Figure 24.17: Displaying a Pie Chart

In Figure 24.17, the pie chart gets created with the default colors. You can also provide the colors to the pie chart by setting the `col` argument in the `pie()` function. Consider the following commands for providing colors to the pie chart:

```
datayear<-c(2010,2011,2012,2013,2014)
dataperc<-c(20,15,26,22,17)
colors = c("red", "yellow", "green", "violet","pink")
pie(dataperc, labels=as.character(datayear),col=colors)
```

The output of the preceding command is shown in Figure 24.18:

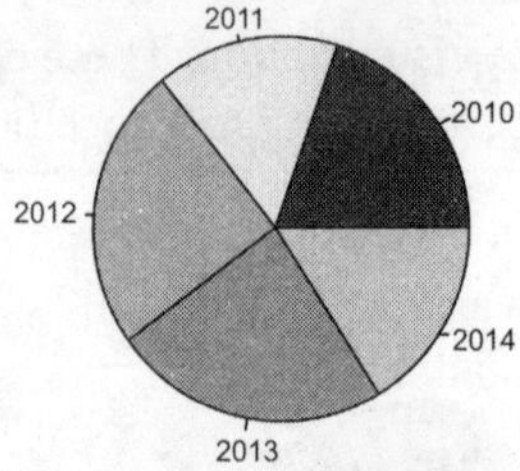

Figure 24.18: Displaying a Colorful Pie Chart

Strip Chart

A strip chart plots data in sequence along a line and each data point is specified as a box. It is mainly used when the sample size is too small, for example, when the observations are less than 30. The main aim of using a strip chart is to carefully view the location of each value present in the small sample, and for comparing values across cases. The `stripchart()` function is used for plotting a strip chart. Let's create a simple strip chart with some values using the following command:

```
values<-c(20,15,26,22,17)
stripchart(values)
```

The output of the preceding command is shown in Figure 24.19:

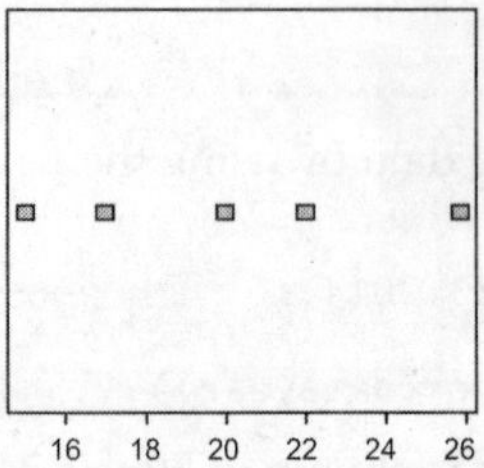

Figure 24.19: Displaying a Strip Chart

In Figure 24.19, you can see that a simple strip chart is created without captions on the x and y axes. You can set the `xlab` and `ylab` arguments in the **s**`tripchart()` function for providing captions to x and y axes, respectively. You can also create a vertical strip chart by using the following command:

```
values<-c(20,15,26,22,17)
stripchart(dataperc,ylab="values",method="stack",vertical="true")
```

In the preceding command, the `stack` method is used to create the stack of repeated values. The vertical argument is set as true for creating a vertical strip chart. The output of the preceding command is shown in Figure 24.20:

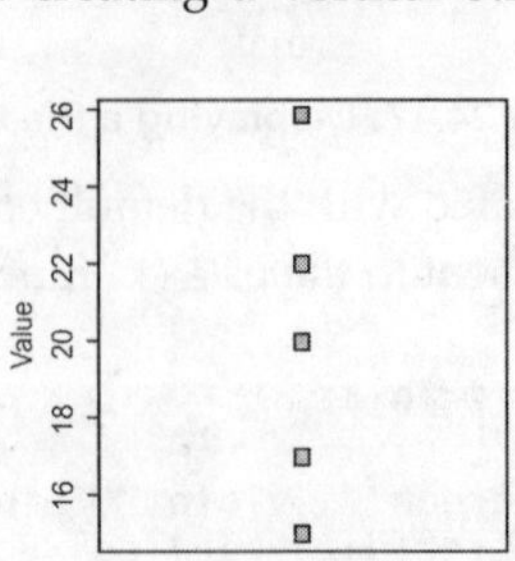

Figure 24.20: Displaying a Vertical Strip Chart

Using Plots for Two Variables

Response variable and explanatory variable are the two types of variables used in graphical analysis. The response variable is specified on the y axis, and the explanatory variable is specified on the x axis.

The type of the plot that you generate depends upon the explanatory variable. For example, if the explanatory variable is a continuous variable, like length, weight, or altitude, then the scatter plot is the most appropriate plot to use. A scatter plot displays the relationship between two number sets by using the graphical representation.

On the other hand, if the explanatory variable is categorical, like color or gender, then a box-and-whisker plot or a bar plot must be used. A box-and-whisker plot is a graphical means of displaying sets of numeric data by using the quartiles and is based on the minimum and maximum values, and upper and lower quartiles, as shown in Figure 24.21:

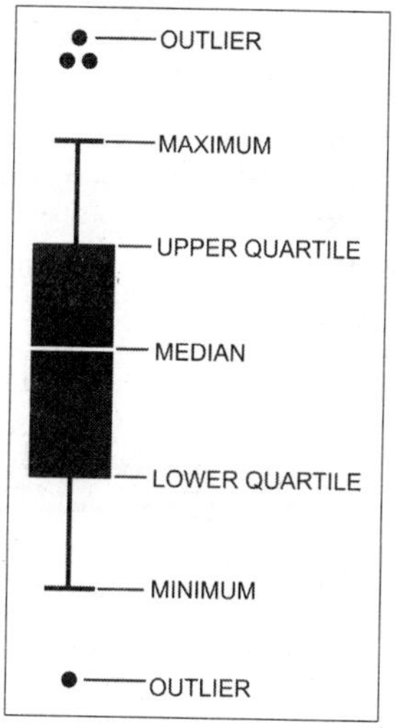

Figure 24.21: Displaying a Box-and-Whisker Plot

The bar plot represents the data graphically using bar charts. Figure 24.22 displays a bar plot:

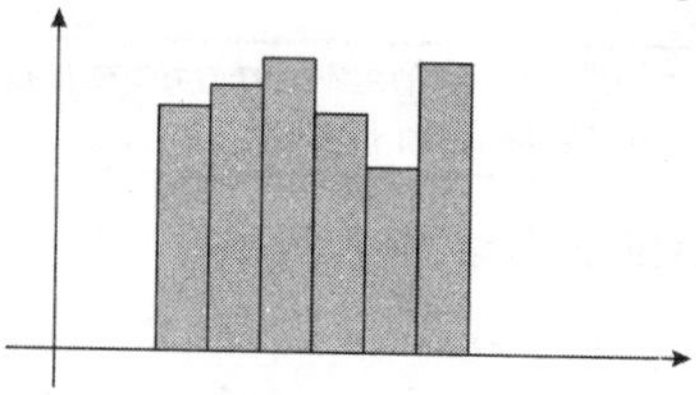

Figure 24.22: Displaying a Bar plot

The following functions are used for plotting graphs of two variables in R:

- `plot (x, y)` —Creates a scatter plot using x and y
- `plot (factor, y)`—Creates the box-and-whisker plot of y at each factor level
- `barplot (y)`—Creates bar plot using a vector of y values

Plotting a Two-Variable Scatter Plot Graph

As you know, scatter plots are graphs drawn with two continuous explanatory variables. The following commands load the CSV file, `scatterRaw1.csv`, into the R environment as `object rawData1` and plot variable `aa` against `bb`:

```
> # Plotting with two continuous explanatory variables: scatterplots
> rawData1<-read.csv("Datasets/scatterRaw1.csv",header=T)
>names(rawData1)
[1] "aa" "bb"
>plot(rawData1$aa,rawData1$bb,col="blue",xlab="Explanatory variable"
,ylab="Responsive variable")
```

You can also add regression lines to the plot by using the `abline()` function by entering the following commands:

```
> # adding regression lines to graph
>abline(lm(rawData1$bb~rawData1$aa))
> rawData2<-read.table("Datasets/scatterRaw2.txt",header=T)
>names(rawData2)
[1] "aa2" "bb2"
>points(rawData2$aa2,rawData2$bb2,col="red")
> # adding second regression lines to graph
>abline(lm(rawData2$bb2~rawData2$aa2))
```

Figure 24.23 shows the scatter plot graph along with regression lines:

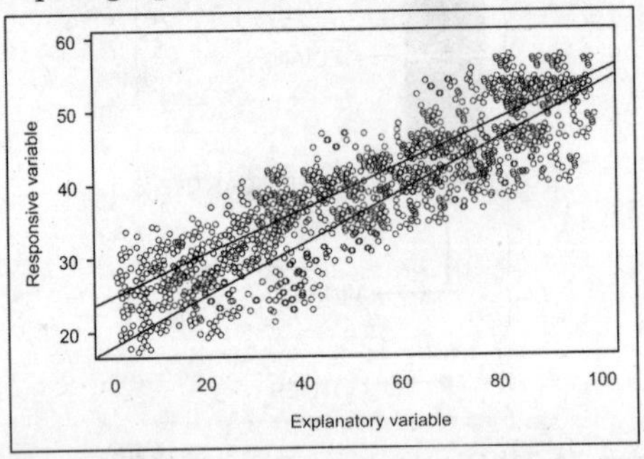

Figure 24.23: Displaying the Scatter Plot Graph with Regression Lines

NOTE

A legend is added for explaining the difference between different colors of points in the scatter plot. The `legend()` *function is used for adding the legend in the scatter plot graph.*

Using a Third Variable to Label a Scatter Plot

You can notice that in the scatter plot, shown in Figure 24.23, the points are not labeled with their values. You can label these points by using a third variable, as shown in the following set of commands:

```
# Using a third variable to label a scatterplot
pragmaticAcid<-read.table("Datasets/pragmaticAcid.txt",header=T)
attach(pragmaticAcid)
```

The `names()` function is used to find the names of the columns in the text file as follows:

```
names(pragmaticAcid)
[1] "feacalRate" "index" "pH"
```

Now, enter the following commands for displaying the labeled points in the output:

```
plot(pragmaticAcid$index,pragmaticAcid$pH)
text(pragmaticAcid$index, pragmaticAcid$pH, labels=round(pragmaticAcid$feacalRate,
   2), pos=1, offset=0.5,cex=0.7)
```

The output with the labeled points is shown in Figure 24.24:

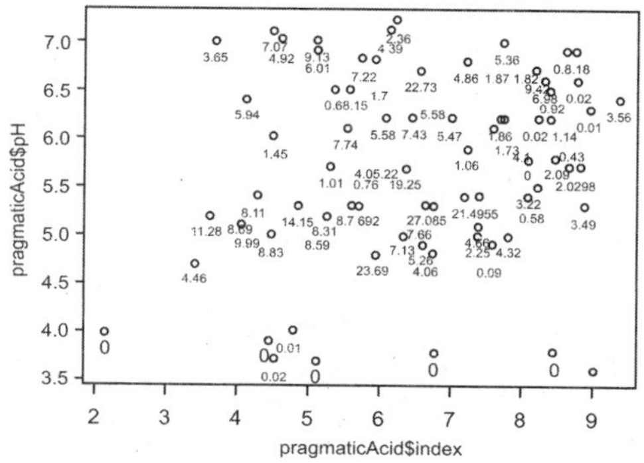

Figure 24.24: Displaying the Scatter Plot with Third Variable

NOTE

To join the points on a scatter plot by lines, it is essential to ensure that the points on the x *axis are ordered. If they are not ordered, the result will be a mess as shown in the following figure:*

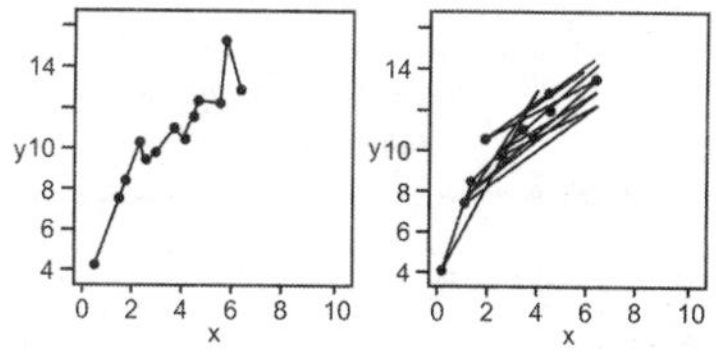

Plotting a Categorical Explanatory Variable

Enter the following commands to plot a categorical explanatory variable:

```
>cExpData<-read.table("Datasets/compExp.txt",header=T)
>plot(cExpData$exp,cExpData$output,xlab="Exp.",ylab="output")
```

In the preceding commands, firstly, the `compExp.txt` file is read using the `read.table()` function. After that, the `plot()` function is used for plotting the graph. Figure 24.25 shows the graph created as an outcome of these commands:

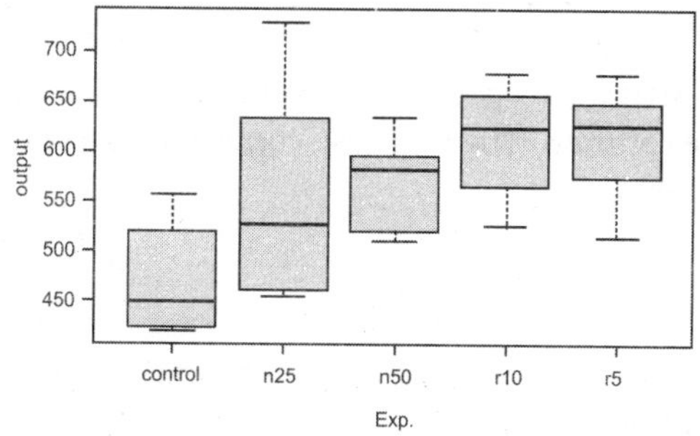

Figure 24.25: Displaying a Graph Using a Categorical Explanatory Variable

Using Plots for Multiple Variables

The main plotting functions that are used for representing multiple variables are:

- The `pairs()` function
- The `coplot()` function

Now, let's learn how to plot graphs using the preceding functions:

The pairs() Function

The `pairs()` function is used for plotting every variable in the data frame on the `y` axis with respect to every other variable on the `x` axis. Having two or more continuous explanatory variables, it is valuable to verify the intricate dependencies between the explanatory variables. The following commands show how to use the `pairs()` function:

```
ozonedata<- read, table ("c : \\temp\\ozone.data.txt", header=T)
attach (ozonedata)
names (ozonedata)
[1] "rad" "temp" "wind" "ozone"
```

The `pairs()` function needs only the name of the whole data frame as its first argument. Now, enter the following command used for generating the graph:

```
pairs(ozonedata,panel=panel.smooth)
```

The output of the preceding command is shown in Figure 24.26:

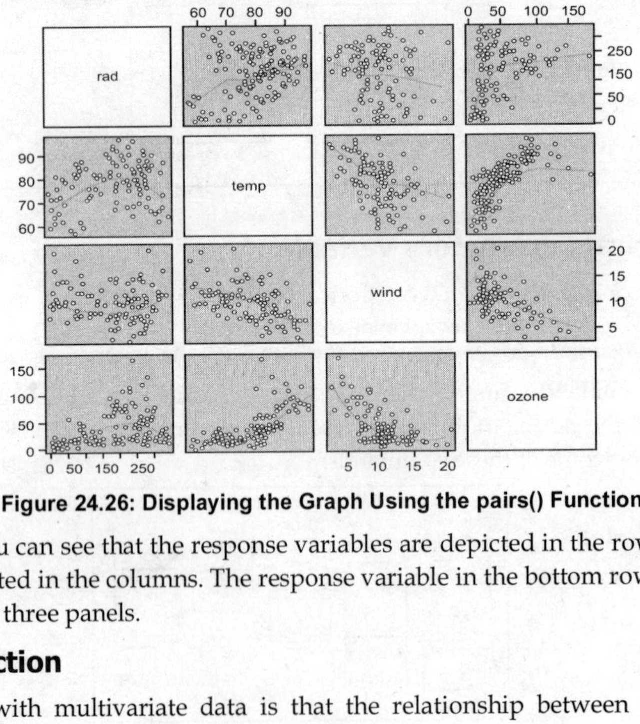

Figure 24.26: Displaying the Graph Using the pairs() Function

In Figure 24.26, you can see that the response variables are depicted in the rows and the explanatory variables are depicted in the columns. The response variable in the bottom row, which is ozone, is on the `y` axis of all the three panels.

The coplot() Function

A real difficulty with multivariate data is that the relationship between two variables may be obscured. In the simplest case, we have one response variable (ozone) and just two explanatory variables (wind speed and air temperature).

Enter the following command to draw a multivariable graph by using the `coplot()` function:

```
>coplot(ozonedata$ozone~ozonedata$wind|ozonedata$temp,panel = panel.smooth)
```

Figure 24.27 shows the graph plotted by using the `coplot()` function:

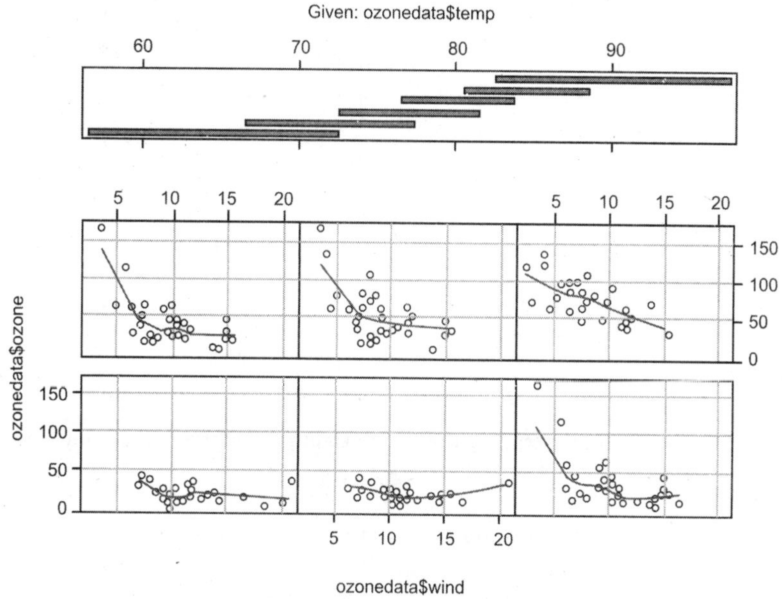

Figure 24.27: Displaying the Graph Using coplot() Function

You can see that the response variable is on the left of the tilde and the explanatory variable on the *x* axis is on the right, with the conditioning variable and the conditioning operator (|). In Figure 24.27, you can see that the coplot panels are ordered from the lower left to the upper right corner. Therefore, the lower left plot is for the lowest temperature and the upper right plot is for the highest temperature.

Designing Special Plots

R has the capability of producing scatter plots from the data present in different kinds of formats. In R, you can generate high level and low level plots according to requirements. The low level plots are referred to as the basic graphs that you can build in a step-by-step procedure. On the other hand, the high levels plots in R have in-built types and styles for the graphical representation of data.

R also provides some special types of plots, which are as follows:

- Design plots
- Bubble plots

Design Plots

An efficient method of visualizing the effective sizes in experiments is done by the `plot.design()` function. This function is used just like a model formula. Enter the following command to create a design plot by using the `plot.design()` function:

```
>plot.design(growthRate~water*detergent*daphnia,fun="sd")
```

The preceding command plots the graph on the basis of the growth rate and factors. The `sd` value of the `fun` argument refers to the standard deviation. The output of the preceding command is shown in Figure 24.28:

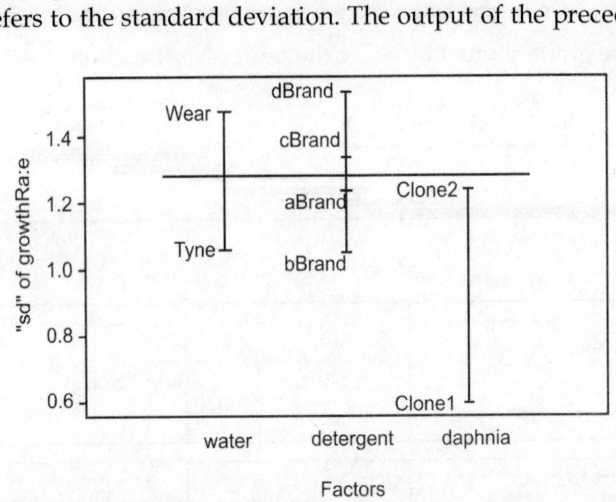

Figure 24.28: Displaying the Graph Using the plot.design() Function

Bubble Plots

The bubble plot is used for displaying the information using bubbles. The bubble plot is useful for explaining variations in a third variable by using its size across different locations in the `x-y` plane. Enter the following commands for creating bubble plots on a dataset:

```
>plotcreateBubble<-function(firstValue,secondValue,rv,bs=0.1){
+ r<-rv/max(rv)
+ yscale<-max(secondValue)-min(secondValue)
+ xscale<-max(firstValue)-min(firstValue)
+ plot(firstValue,secondValue,type="n", xlab=deparse(substitute(firstValue)),
+ ylab=deparse(substitute(secondValue)))
+ for (i in 1:length(firstValue)) createBubble(firstValue[i],secondVal
ue[i],r[i],bs,xscale,yscale) }
>createBubble<-function (x,y,r,createBubble.size,xscale,yscale) {
+ theta<-seq(0,2*pi,pi/200)
+ secondValue<-r*sin(theta)*createBubble.size*yscale
+ firstValue<-r*cos(theta)* createBubble.size*xscale
+ lines(x+firstValue,y+secondValue) }
>pragmaticAcid<-read.table("Datasets/pragmaticAcid.txt",header=T)
>attach(pragmaticAcid)
```

The following object is masked from `pragmaticAcid` (position 3):

```
feacalRate, index, pH
```

The following object is masked from `ddd`:

```
pH
>names(pragmaticAcid)
[1] "feacalRate" "index" "pH"
>plotcreateBubble(index,pH,feacalRate)
```

The output of the preceding commands is shown in Figure 24.29:

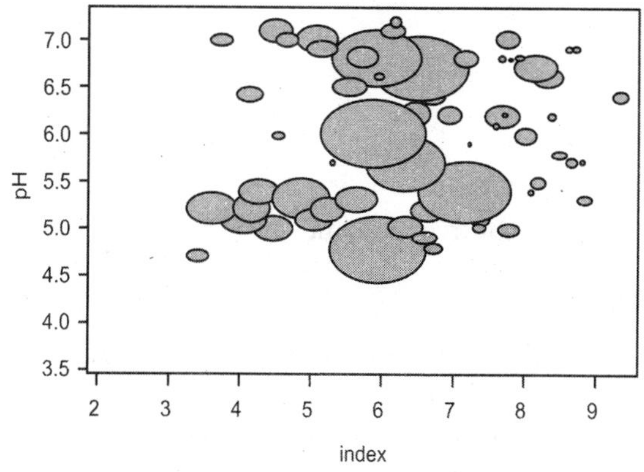

Figure 24.29: Displaying Bubble Plots

In Figure 24.29, the values of two variables, i.e. `index` and `pH`, are shown on the `x-y` plane; whereas, the effect of the third variable, `feacalRate`, is displayed by using the size of the bubble.

Saving Graphs to External Files

You can save graphs or plots that you have created as PDF or PostScript files. To save graphs in R, you need to switch off the device on which you are working. The default device is your monitor, and you can get a ready copy of the graph which can then be pasted into a document outside R with the help of the following command:

```
data<- read, table ("D :\\Script\\voters.txt", header=T)
attach(data)
```

You can save the graphics to a PDF file by using the following command:

```
pdf ("D : \\Script\\Voting.pdf", width=7, height=4)
par(mfrow=c(1,2))
plot (Region,Voting)
plot(Temp,Voting)
dev.off()
```

In the preceding set of commands, the `dev.off()` command is used to switch off the device.

You can also save the graphics to a `PostScript` file, using the following command:

```
postscript ("D : \\Script\\Voting.ps " , width=7, height=4)
par(mfrow=c(1,2))
plot (Region,Voting)
plot(Temp,Voting)
dev.off()
```

Various options are used in the pdf and postscript functions for getting the desired output, but width and height options are the ones modified most of the time.

Advanced Features of R

Some of the advanced features of R help data analysts to complete their work efficiently.

These features are as follows:

- Swapping X and Y axes
- Plotting discrete datasets
- Plotting continuous datasets
- Reversing the direction of an axis

Let's discuss the aforementioned features in detail.

Swapping X and Y Axes

The "ggplot2" package, created by Hadley Wickham, offers a powerful graphics language for creating elegant, concise and complex plots. Let us consider an example of a simple boxplot. This is the basic boxplot that we will work with, using the built-in `PlantGrowth` dataset. Now, enter the following commands:

```
>library (ggplot2) //# here we include the library package of ggplot2 for more
   visualization of data//
>bp <- ggplot(PlantGrowth, aes(x=group, y=weight)) + geom_boxplot()
>bp
```

The output of executing the preceding commands is shown in Figure 24.30:

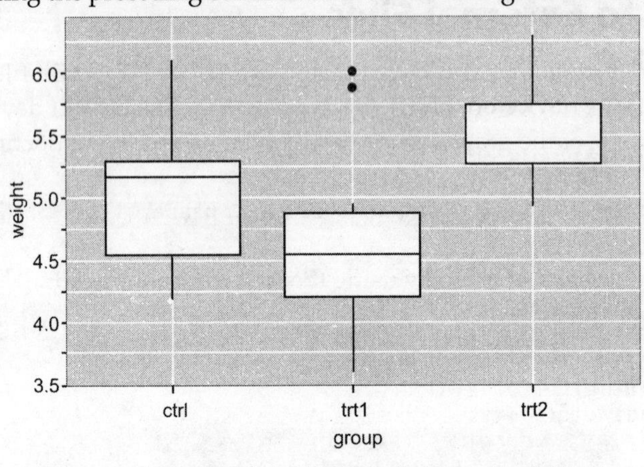

Figure 24.30: Boxplot Showing the Growth of Plant

The preceding commands are explained as follows:

1. **`Library (ggplot2)`:** This function is used to include the package in the script. The name of the package is written in the braces as an argument of the function.
2. **`bp <- ggplot(PlantGrowth, aes(x=group, y=weight))`:** The variable "bp" holds the command to plot group on x-axis and weight on y-axis. Basically, `ggplot(objectname, aes(x=field, y=field))` is the syntax of plotting the graph.
3. **`geom_boxplot()`:** It is a function in the package of ggplot2, which plots the "box graph" as per the provided data.
4. **bp:** When `bp` command is given on the script window, it will show the graph on the plot window of the R studio.

In Figure 24.30, the graph represents weight field on y-axis and group field on x-axis. Swapping axis means changing the weight field to x-axis and the group field to y-axis. In this case, `coord_flip()` function is used to flip or swap the axis. Enter the following command to swap x and y axes:

```
bp + coord_flip()
```

Figure 24.31 shows the output of execution of the preceding command:

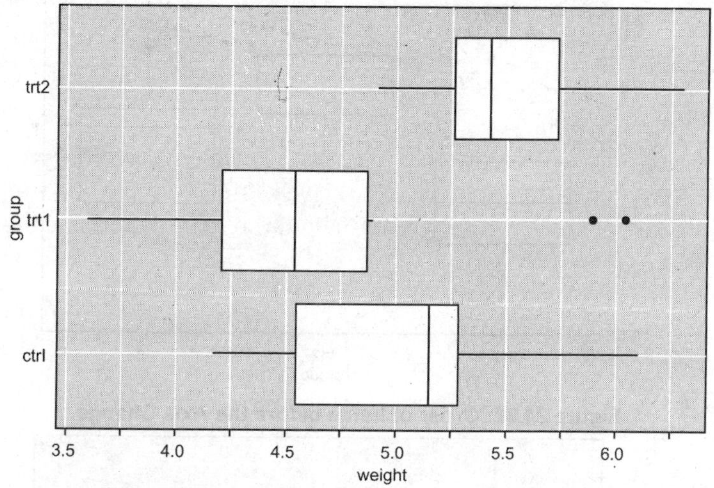

Figure 24.31: The Swapping of Axes

Plotting Discrete Datasets

Discrete axis is used to plot datasets that are discrete in nature. There are a few modes to represent these datasets. Some of these are as follows:

Changing the Order of Items

Enter the following commands to change the order of items:

```
# Manually set the order of a discrete-valued axis
>bp + scale_x_discrete(limits=c("trt1","trt2","ctrl"))
# here we scale x axis and gives the divisions like trt1,trt2,ctrl so that we can
identify easily the exact value on X-axis or in this case the plant growth respect to x-
axis.
# Reverse the order of a discrete-valued axis

# Get the levels of the factor

>flevels <- levels(PlantGrowth$group)

>flevels

[1] "ctrl" "trt1" "trt2"

# Reverse the order

>flevels <- rev(flevels)

>flevels

[1] "trt2" "trt1" "ctrl"
```

```
>bp + scale_x_discrete(limits=flevels)

# Or it can be done in one line:
>bp + scale_x_discrete(limits = rev(levels(PlantGrowth$group)))
```

The output of executing the preceding commands is shown in Figures 24.32 and 24.33:

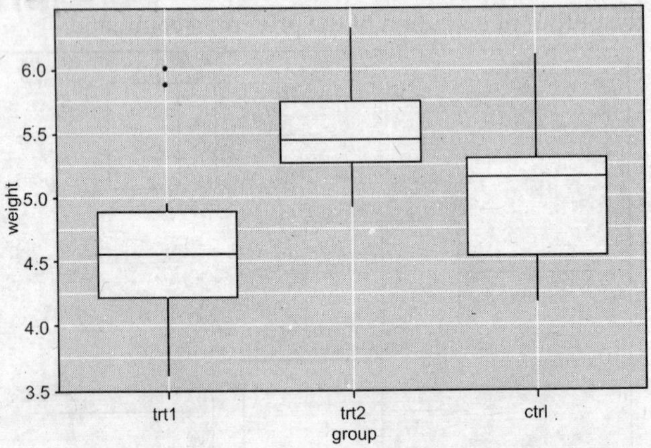

Figure 24.32: Order of Items before the Axis Change

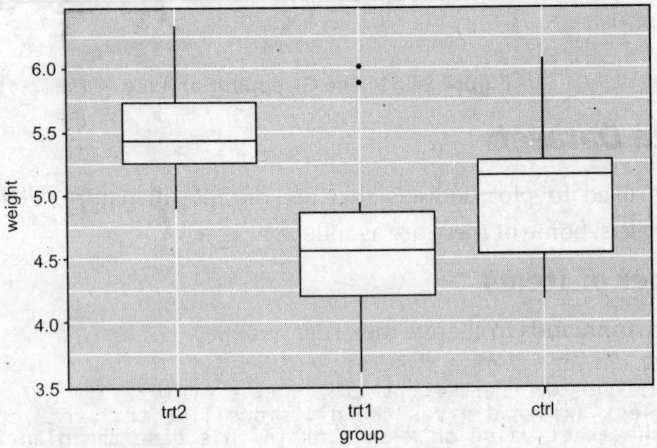

Figure 24.33: Order of Items after the Axis Change

Putting Tick Mark Labels on Fields

For the representation of discrete variables on the axis, tick mark labels are taken directly from levels of factors. Levels of factor are given in short or abbreviated forms that are unsuitable for professional presentations. So, we mark labels on fields that depict their meanings or names. Now, enter the following commands:

```
    # here we break the old names like ctrl, trt1, trt2 with the new labels Like for
ctrl we give it control, for trt1 we give it as Treat 1 and similarly for trt2=treat2

       >bp + scale_x_discrete(breaks=c("ctrl", "trt1", "trt2"),labels=c("Control",
"Treat 1",   "Treat 2"))
```

The output of the preceding command is shown in Figure 24.34:

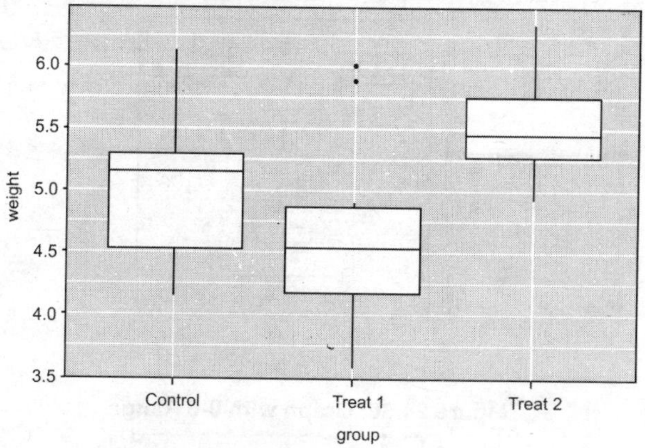

Figure 24.34: Labels on the Axis

In order to hide the labels on any axis, enter the following commands:

```
# Hide x tick marks, labels, and grid lines

>bp + scale_x_discrete(breaks=NULL)

# Hide all tick marks and labels (on X axis), but keep the gridlines

>bp + theme(axis.ticks = element_blank(), axis.text.x = element_blank())
```

Figure 24.35 shows the output of the execution of the preceding commands:

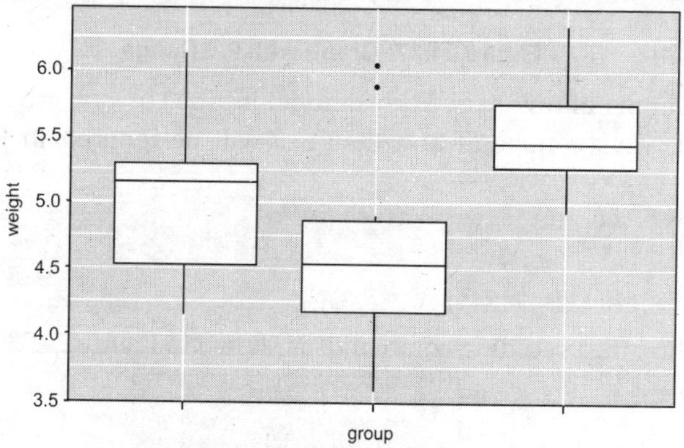

Figure 24.35: Hidden Labels of Axis

Plotting Continuous Datasets

The continuous axis plots the successive dataset values. We use `expand_limits()` function to expand the range of an axis. Let's enter the following commands:

```
# Make sure to include 0 in the y axis
>bp + expand_limits(y=0)
# Make sure to include 0 and 8 in the y axis
>bp + expand_limits(y=c(0,8))
```

Figures 24.36 and 24.37 represent the output of the execution of the preceding commands:

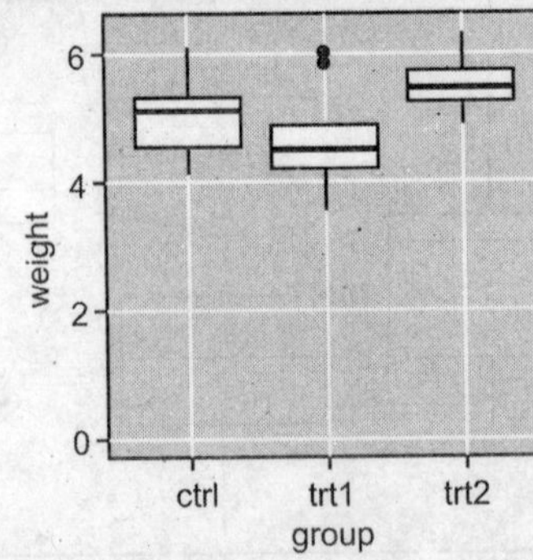

Figure 24.36: Graph with 0-6 Range

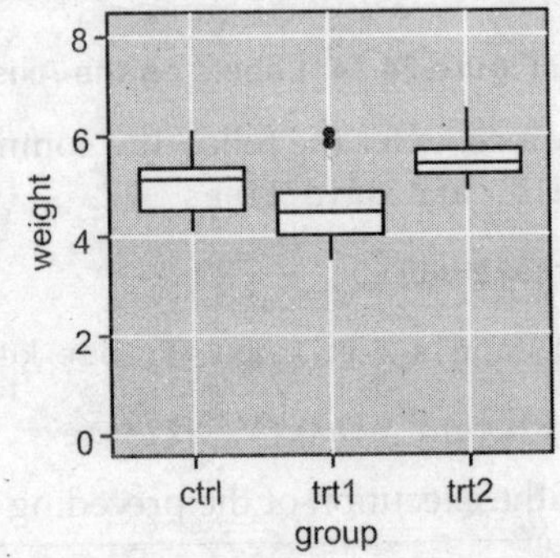

Figure 24.37: Graph with 0-8 Range

We can also set the limits of any axis. For example, if `scale_y_continuous` command is used, then it will override `ylim` command and the `ylim` will be ignored in the code. Now, enter the following commands:

```
# Set the range of a continuous-valued axis
# These are equivalent
>bp + ylim(0, 8)
>bp + scale_y_continuous(limits=c(0, 8))
```

The output of executing the preceding commands is shown in Figure 24.38:

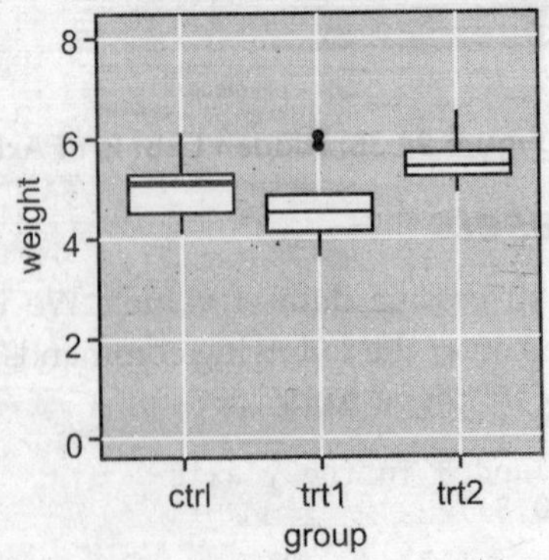

Figure 24.38: Overriding of the ylim

If the range of y-axis is reduced by using the preceding command, then data outside the range are ignored. This can be good for a scatter plot; however, it can be problematic for boxplots. If the range of the graph does not include 0 in bar graphs, then bars in the graph will not be visible. To avoid such type of problem, we use `coord_cartesian` function. It will set the viewing area of data instead of setting their limits. The following commands show the use of `coord_cartesian` function:

```
# These two do the same thing; all data points outside the graphing range are
# dropped, resulting in a misleading box plot
>bp + ylim(5, 7.5)
# Warning: Removed 13 rows containing non-finite values (stat_boxplot).
>bp + scale_y_continuous(limits=c(5, 7.5))
# Using coord_cartesian "zooms" into the area
>bp + coord_cartesian(ylim=c(5, 7.5))
# Specify tick marks directly
>bp + coord_cartesian(ylim=c(5, 7.5)) + scale_y_continuous(breaks=seq(0, 10, 0.25))
# Ticks from 0-10, every .25
```

Figures 24.39 and 24.40 show the output of the execution of the preceding commands:

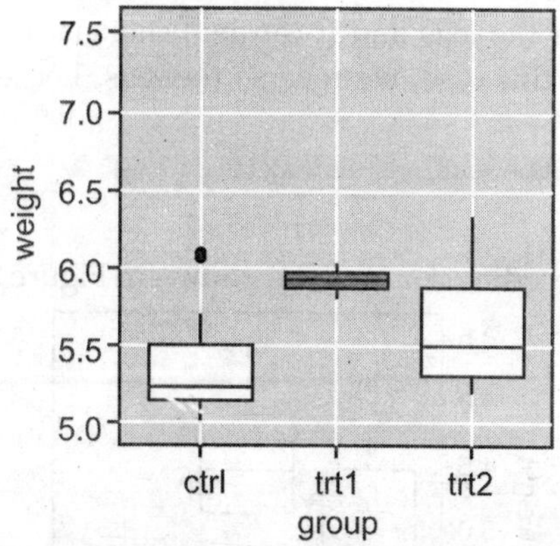

Figure 24.39: Normal View of the Plotted Graph with Defined Limits

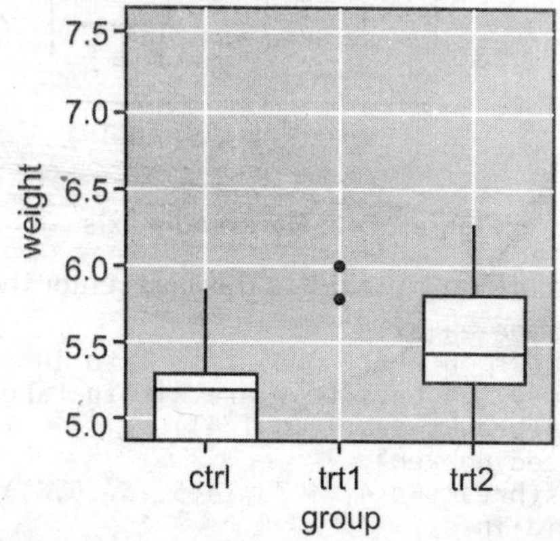

Figure 24.40: View of the Plotted Graph without Limits

In Figure 24.41, we have added 0.25 in every division (from 5-7.5) to expand the view of the graph.

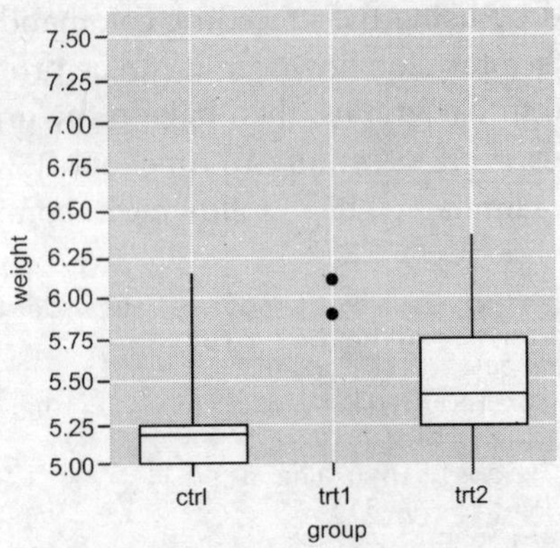

Figure 24.41: Extended View of the Graph

Reversing the Direction of an Axis

This is a method of converting the axis and it can be beneficial in making reports such as annual report, financial report, etc. In this case, we reverse the axis. Let' enter the following command to understand it better:

```
# Reverse order of a continuous-valued axis
>bp + scale_y_reverse()
```

The output of executing the preceding command is shown in Figure 24.42:

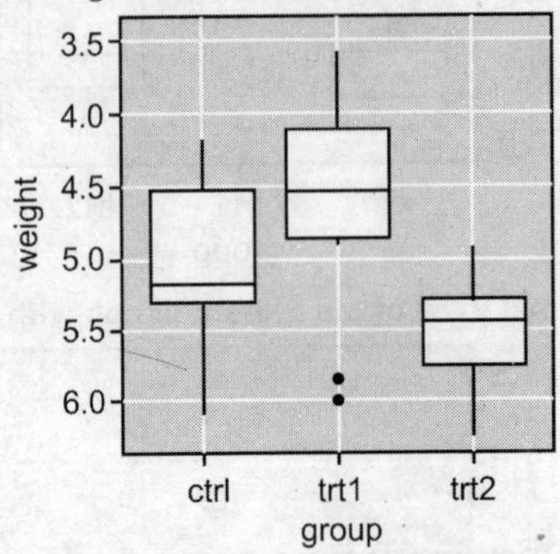

Figure 24.42: Reversed y-axis

In ggplot2, we can set the tick mark on any axis. In this case, enter the following commands:

```
# setting the tick marks on an axis
# This will show tick marks on every 0.25 from 1 to 10
# The scale will show only the ones that are within range (3.50-6.25 in this case)
>bp + scale_y_continuous(breaks=seq(1,10,1/4))
# The breaks can be spaced unevenly
>bp + scale_y_continuous(breaks=c(4, 4.25, 4.5, 5, 6,8))
# suppress ticks and gridlines
>bp + scale_y_continuous(breaks=NULL)
# Hide tick marks and labels (on Y axis), but keep the gridlines
>bp + theme(axis.ticks = element_blank(), axis.text.y = element_blank())
```

The following figures show the output of the execution of preceding commands:

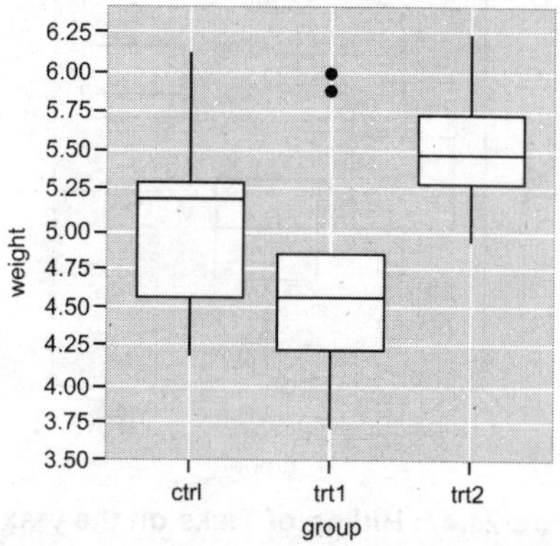

Figure 24.43: Setting Ticks on Every .25 Range

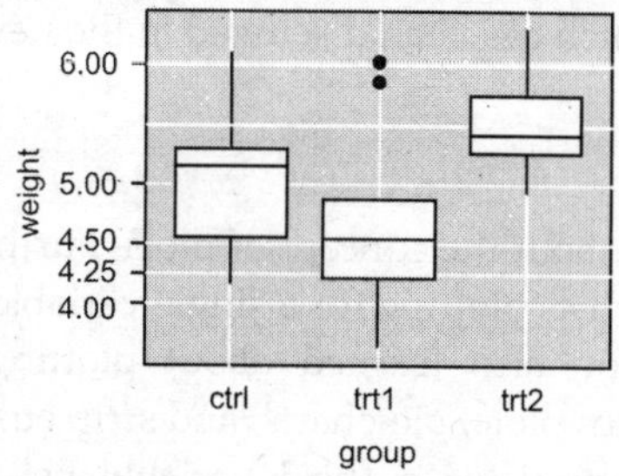

Figure 24.44: Creating the Break in between Ticks

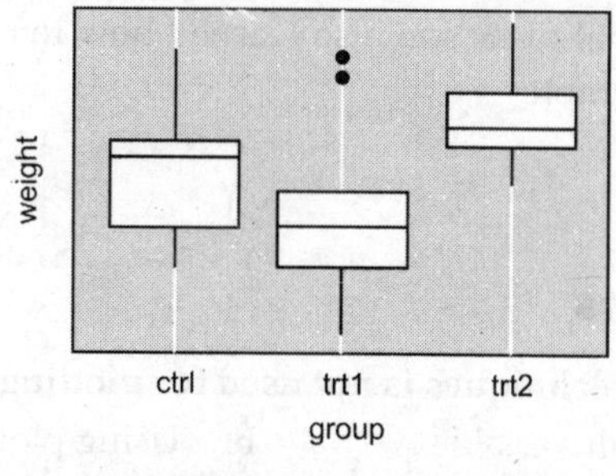

Figure 24.45: Hiding the Horizontal Ticks

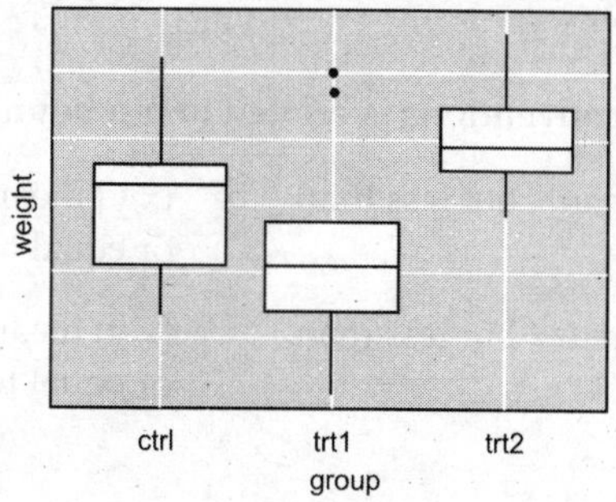

Figure 24.46: Removal of Ticks on the y-axis

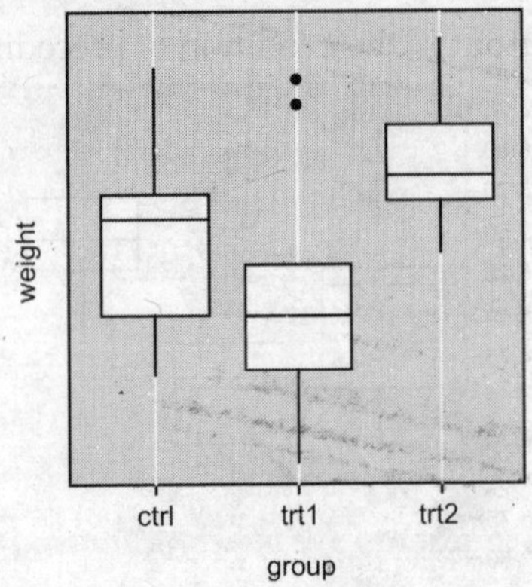

Figure 24.47: Hiding of Ticks on the y-axis

In this way, we use R for plotting and making different types of graphs on different datasets. We can also integrate R with Hadoop, which has been discussed in the next chapter.

Summary

In this chapter, you first learned about the concept of plots. Further, this chapter discussed different types of plotting mechanisms such as plotting for a single variable, two variables, multiple variables, and designing special plots. You also learned about plotting for a single variable by using histograms, index plots, time series plots, pie-charts, and strip chart; plotting for two variables using the scatter plot graph; and plotting for a third variable by using the `pairs()` function and `coplot()` function. This chapter next discussed design and bubble plots. Towards the end, you learned to save graphs in external files. You also learned how to change the axis of the graph, how to insert ticks and labels in the graph.

Quick Revise

Multiple-Choice Questions

Q1. Which of the following techniques is not used for plotting mechanism?

a. Using plots for default variable
b. Using plots for single variable
c. Using plots for two variables
d. Using plots for multiple variables

Ans. The correct option is a.

Q2. Which of the following conventions is related to bin boundaries?

a. [x,y] means greater than x but less than or equal to y
b. (x,y] means greater than x but less than or equal to y
c. (x,y) means greater than x but less than or equal to y
d. [x,y) means greater than x but less than or equal to y

Ans. The correct option is b.

Q3. Which of the following arguments is used in the `hist()` function for setting the color of a histogram?

a. color
b. clr
c. col
d. crl

Ans. The correct option is c.

Q4. Which of the following plots is circular?

a. Index
b. Histogram
c. Bar
d. Pie

Ans. The correct option is d.

Q5. Which of the following arguments are commonly used to provide captions to x and y axes in a graph?

a. xlab and ylab
b. xaxis and yaxis
c. labx and laby
d. x and y

Ans. The correct option is a.

Subjective Questions

Q1. What do you understand by plotting in R?

Ans. R provides excellent graphics and plotting capabilities. It can efficiently display information graphically with the help of its plotting commands and functions. The data displayed onto different graphs can be read from files or can be entered directly. The symbols and colors are used in graphs to differentiate between different datasets. Some useful functions used in plotting graphs or interacting with graphs are lines, points, abline, curve, text, rug, legend segments, arrows, polygon locator, identify, etc.

Some of the common plots in R are:

- Strip charts
- Histograms
- Time series plots
- Scatter plots
- Index plots
- Bubble plots

Q2. List the techniques used to draw graphs in R.

Ans. Graphs in R can be drawn by using the following techniques:

- Using plots for a single variable
- Using plots for two variables
- Using plots for multiple variables
- Designing special plots

Q3. What is a histogram?

Ans. A histogram comprises parallel vertical bars displaying the frequency distribution of a quantitative variable in a graphical format. The area occupied by each bar is equal to the frequency of items searched. A histogram is the best displaying mode to represent structured data. The values of response variables are distributed across the x axis and each occupied area is known as a bin. It is little tricky to plot a histogram, as its plotting requires subjective judgments for deciding where exactly to put the bin margins.

Q4. Write a short note on time series plots.

Ans. R provides the facility of analyzing the time related data. In the time series graph, the data is plotted against the time by plotting dots which are further joined to produce the graph. The time series graph provides more accurate results when no data is missing over a period of time. The limitation with time series graph is that it does not provide any information about the missed values. For example, the value sale for a particular month of a year may be missed or the sales values of many months may be missed during the last ten years but all this may not be reflected in the time series graph. The `ts()` and `plot()` functions are used for plotting the time series graph. The `ts()` function converts a numeric vector into an object of R time series. The syntax of using the `ts()` function is as follows:

```
<name of object><-ts(vector, start=, end=, frequency=)
```

In the preceding syntax, `start` and `end` refer to the times of the first and last observations. The `frequency` refers to the number of observations per unit time. In case of frequency, 1 denotes annual, 4 denotes quarterly, and 12 denotes monthly.

Q5. What is a strip chart?

Ans. A strip chart plots the data in sequence along a line and each data point is specified as a box. It is mainly used when the sample size is too small, for example, when the observations are less than 30. The main aim of using a strip chart is to carefully view the location of each individual value present in the small sample, and to compare values across cases. The `stripchart()` function is used for plotting a strip chart.

25

Integrating R and Hadoop and Understanding Hive

You have already learned to perform advanced analytics in R. Like R, Hadoop is used for performing statistical computing and provides efficient algorithms for processing and storing distributed data. However, both applications have their own environments; thus, to integrate R with Hadoop, it is important to bridge the gap between these two applications.

Hadoop has two major components: Hadoop Distributed File System (HDFS) for storing distributed data and MapReduce for processing the data stored in a distributed environment. Integration between R and Hadoop should be such that R functions can directly access the data stored in the HDFS component. Moreover, all R functions should follow the MapReduce model to process the distributed data, thereby, allowing programmers to handle distributed data and make use of parallel processing.

One way of integrating R with Hadoop is by using the `rmr` package. This package allows programmers to directly write code for the Hadoop's MapReduce model and copy data to and from HDFS. Another advantage of using the `rmr` package is that programmers can also write their own algorithms, and this may help them in dealing with many Big Data problems.

This chapter talks about the need and importance of integrating the technologies of R and Hadoop. Here, you first learn about the integration of R with Hadoop. Further, you learn about the installation of RHadoop and use of RHadoop in data analytics. Next, the chapter discusses the use of text mining in processing data on the RHadoop platform. Toward the end, you learn about data mining in Hive and the MapReduce technique.

RHadoop—An Integration of R and Hadoop

R is one of the most well-known statistical software to analyze Big Data. R packages are very powerful, support parallel processing, and are widely used for data analysis by organizations. However, even the computational processes of R prove to be insufficient, when it comes to complex Big Data analytics. Similarly, Hadoop alone is also not able to fulfill all the requirements of data analytics. To take advantage of the capabilities of both Hadoop and R, you need to integrate the two. RHadoop is an open-source project that allows programmers to define their own map and reduce functions and directly use the functionality of MapReduce in R.

NOTE

RHadoop project has been developed by Revolution Analytics, a software company that develops open-source statistical software. The company was established in 2007 as REvolution Computing for providing support and services in R. In 2010, the company changed its name to Revolution Analytics and started developing open-source versions of R for both academic and commercial uses.

The integration of R with Hadoop allows programmers to write their own programs in MapReduce using R. In other words, RHadoop allows programmers to make full use of the features and existing environment of R and the Hadoop platform.

RHadoop includes the following three packages:

- **`rhdfs`**—Provides the basic connectivity for HDFS. With the help of this package, programmers can access, read, create, and modify the files stored in HDFS.

This package includes the following important functions:

- **File manipulation functions**—These include the `hdfs().copy()`, `hdfs.rename()`, `hdfs.move()`, `hdfs.delete()`, `hdfs.rm()`, `hdfs.del()`, `hdfs.chown()`, `hdfs.put()`, and `hdfs().get()` functions.
- **File read/write functions**—These include the `hdfs.write()`, `hdfs.close()`, `hdfs.flush()`, and `hdfs.read()` functions.
- **Directory functions**—These include the `hdfs.dircreate()` and `hdfs.mkdir()` functions.
- **Utility functions**—These include the `hdfs.list.files()` and `hdfs.file.info()` functions.
- **Initialization functions**—These include the `hdfs.init()` and `hdfs.defaults functions()`.

❑ **`rhbase`**—This package provides the functionality to manipulate tables. With the help of this package, programmers can access, read, create, and modify tables stored in the Hadoop platform.

This package includes the following important functions:

- **Table manipulation functions**—These include the `hb.new.table()`, `hb.delete.table()`, and `hb.set.table.mode()` functions.
- **Table read/write functions**—These include the `hb.insert()`, `hb.insert.data.frame()`, `hb.get.data.frame()`, and `hb.scan()` functions.
- **Utility function**—This induces the `hb.list.tables()` function.
- **Initialization functions**—These include the `hb.defaults()` and `hb.init()` functions.

❑ **`rmr`**—This package allows programmers to directly write code that is executed by Hadoop's MapReduce component. With the help of this package, analysts can write MapReduce algorithms in the R language. To install this package, the analyst needs to install each node on the Hadoop cluster. In addition, all packages are installed on a default location that can be accessed by all users. Nowadays, a new and updated version of **`rmr`** known as **rmr 3.3.1** or **rmr2** is available.

The RHadoop platform also provides the following two types of graph engines for generating graphs of the given data:

❑ **Database Graph Engine**—This engine supports the development of real-time, traversal-based algorithms over a linked list graph on a single server. Some vendors who provide these types of graphs are Neo4j, InfiniteGraph, and DEX.

❑ **Batch-Processing Graph Engine**—This engine is used to represent batch-processing algorithms over a group of computers. These graph engines are included in the Hama, Golden Orb, and Pregel graph-processing applications.

Installing RHadoop

To install RHadoop, you first need to install the following R packages:

❑ RJSONIO

- rmr or rmr2
- rJava
- Rcpp
- bitops
- digest
- functional
- stringr
- plyr
- reshape2

You can install the preceding packages by using the following command for the respecting package:

```
install.packages("RJSONIO")
install.packages("rJava")
install.packages("Rcpp")
install.packages("bitops")
install.packages("digest")
install.packages("functional")
install.packages("stringr")
install.packages("plyr")
install.packages("reshape2")
```

Besides the preceding commands, you can also install these packages by using the graphical user interface (GUI) of R. Perform the following steps to install R packages in Hadoop:

1. Open the R GUI (Figure 25.1).
2. Open the Packages Menu (Figure 25.1).
3. Click the Install package(s) option, as shown in Figure 25.1:

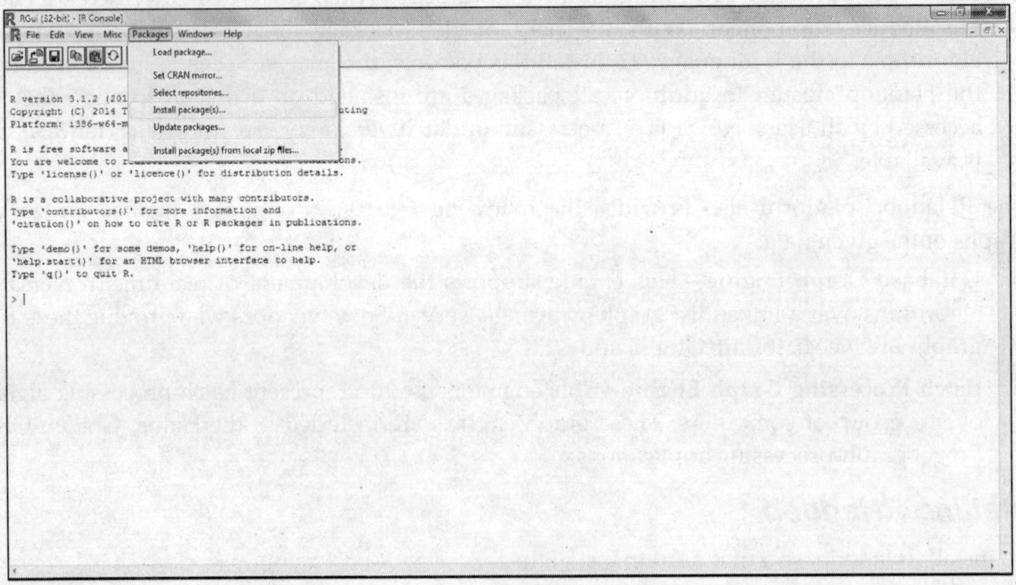

Figure 25.1: Using the Packages Menu

The CRAN mirror dialog box appears (Figure 25.2).

4. Select the appropriate country for downloading the packages. In our case, we have chosen India. (Figure 25.2).
5. Click the OK button, as shown in Figure 25.2:

Figure 25.2: Selecting the Country

The Packages dialog box appears (Figure 25.3).

6. Select the `RJSONIO` package, as shown in Figure 25.3:

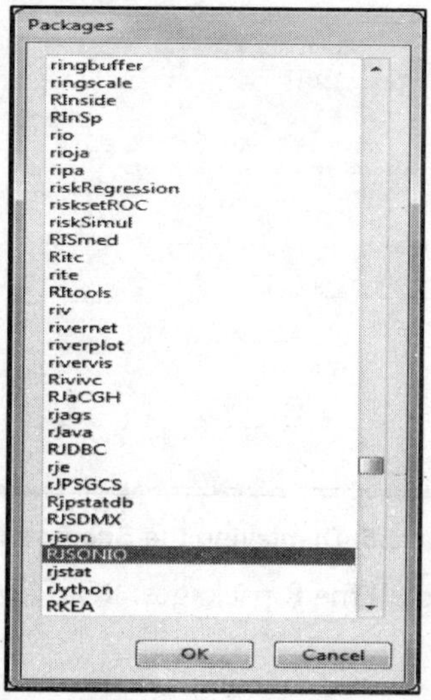

Figure 25.3: Selecting a Package

The installation process of the `RJSONIO` package starts. The installation box appears, displaying the downloading of the package in the progress bar, as shown in Figure 25.4:

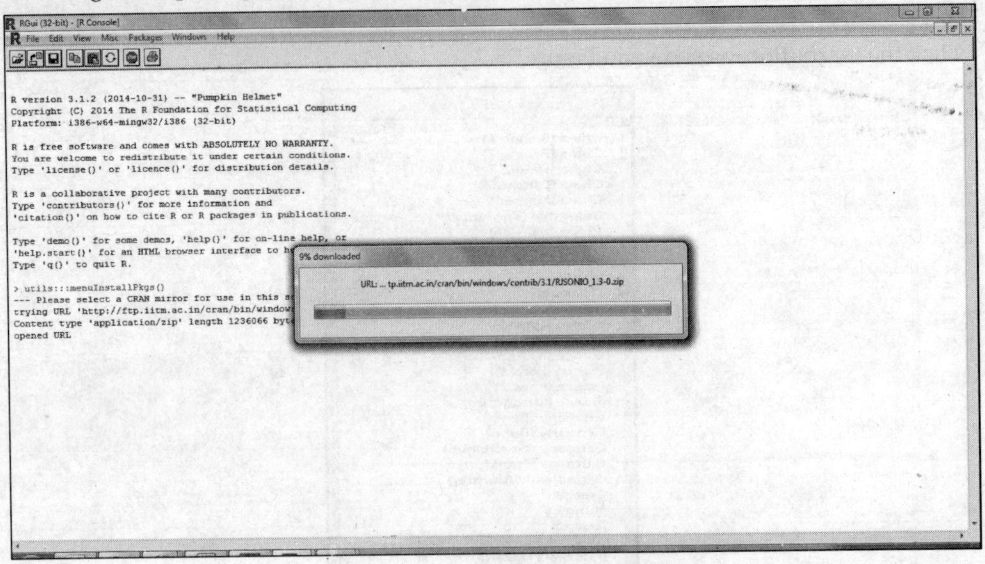

Figure 25.4: Installing the Package

Figure 25.5 shows the message that appears after the successful installation of the package:

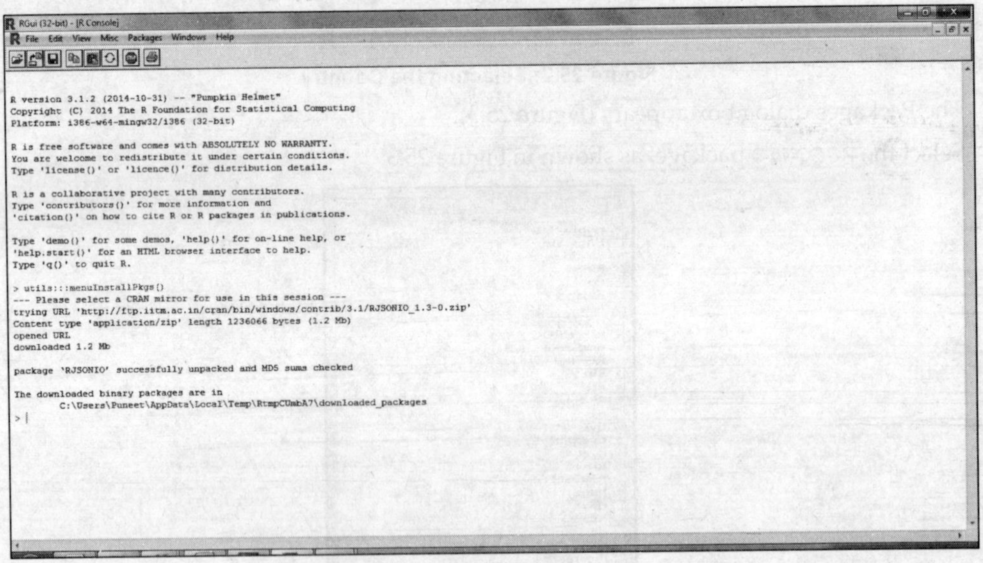

Figure 25.5: Displaying the Success Message

Once you have finished installing all the R packages, RGui opens, displaying the installed packages, as shown in Figure 25.6:

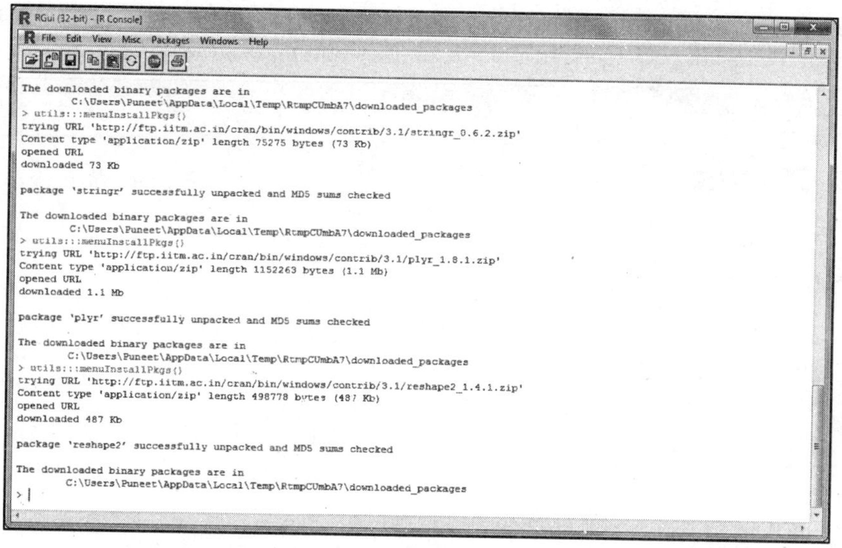

Figure 25.6: Displaying RGui after the Installation of Packages

With this, the installation of R packages is complete.

After installing R packages, you need to install RHadoop packages, such as `rhdfs`, `rhbase`, and `rmr2` to integrate R with Hadoop. For this, you need to download the files of these packages.

Perform the following steps to install RHadoop packages:

1. Open the following URL to download the files of RHadoop packages:

   https://github.com/RevolutionAnalytics/RHadoop/wiki/Downloads

   The Downloads window opens, as shown in Figure 25.7:

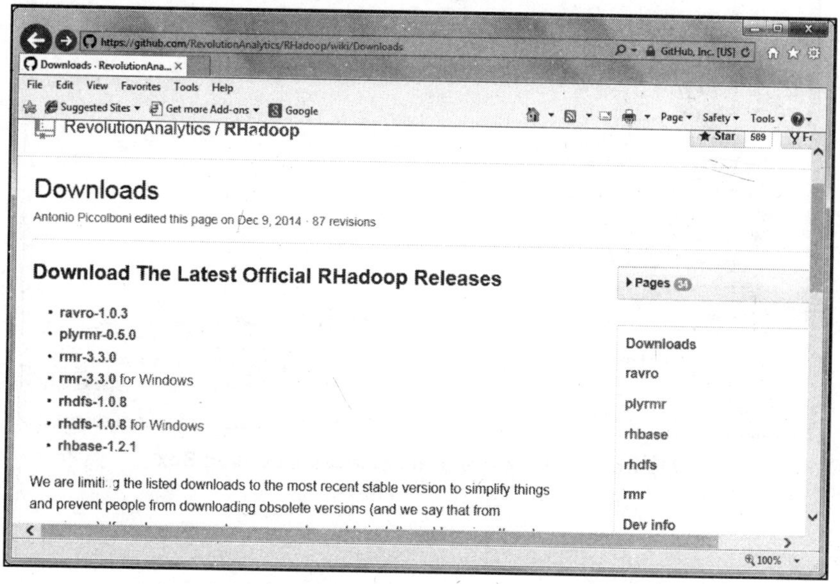

Figure 25.7: Displaying the Packages to be Downloaded

2. Save the packages to the appropriate location in your computer. Now, open the Packages menu and select the Install package(s) from local zip files option, as shown in Figure 25.8:

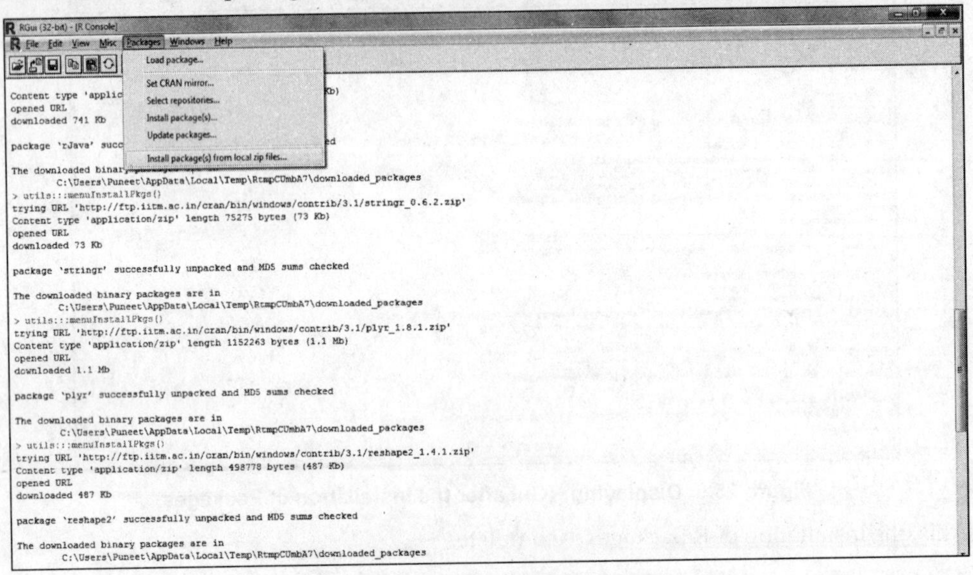

Figure 25.8: Installing Packages from the zip File

The Select files dialog box appears, as shown in Figure 25.9:

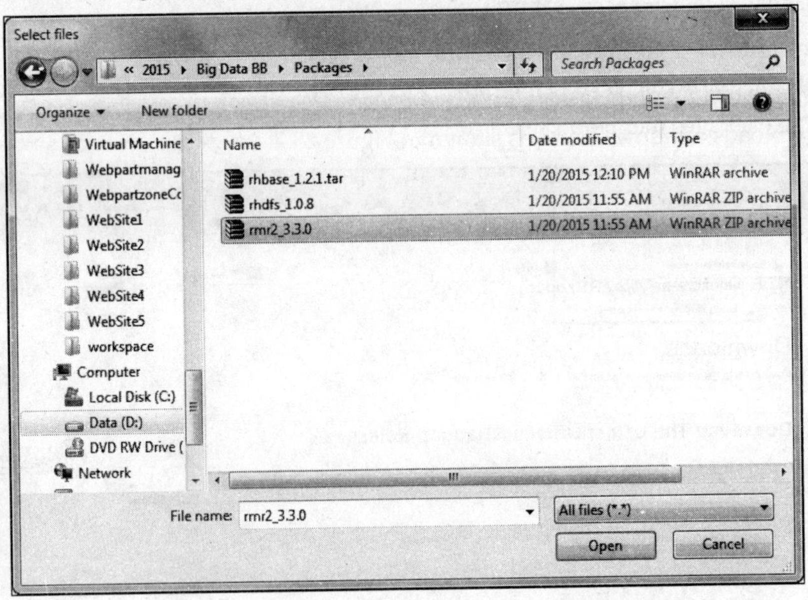

Figure 25.9: Displaying the Select files Dialog Box

Figure 25.10 shows the message that appears after the successful installation of RHadoop packages:

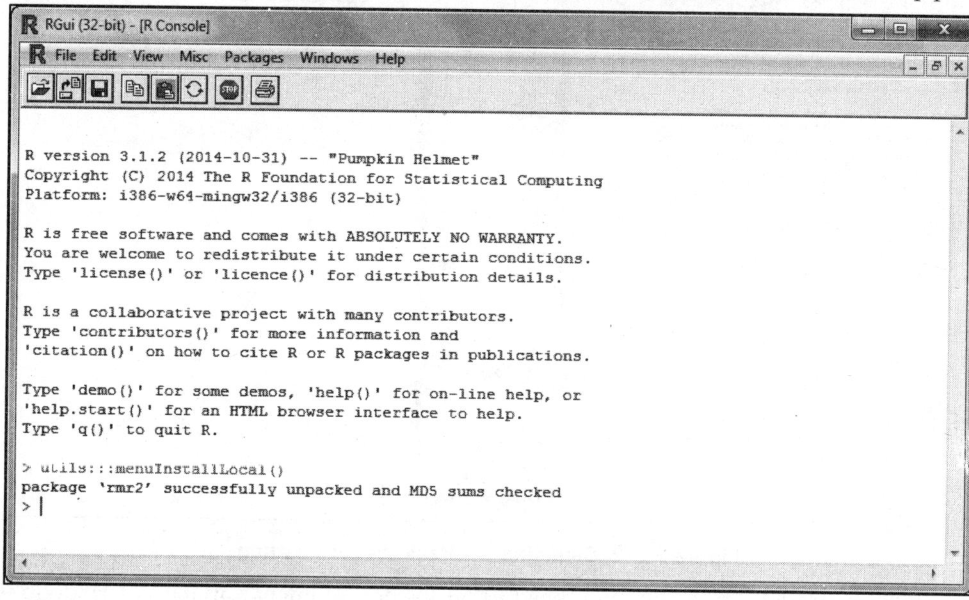

Figure 25.10: Displaying the Success Message

Alternatively, you can also install the RHadoop packages by using the following commands:

```
install.packages("<path>/rhdfs_1.0.8.tar.gz", repos = NULL, type="source")
install.packages("<path>/rhbase_1.2.1.tar.gz", repos = NULL, type="source")
install.packages("<path>/rmr2_3.3.0.tar.gz", repos = NULL, type="source")
```

Perform the following steps to load RHadoop packages:

1. Open the Packages menu and select the Load package option, as shown in Figure 25.11:

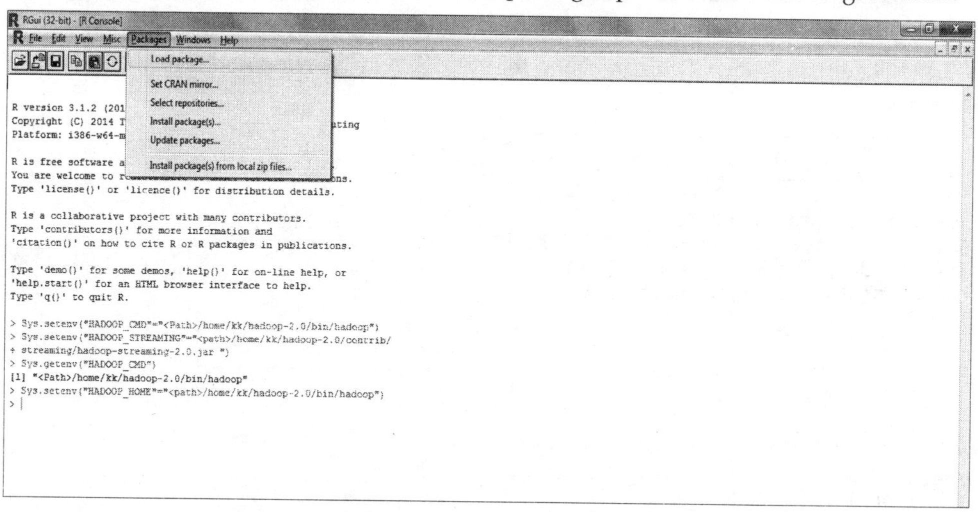

Figure 25.11: Loading the Package

2. Select the package that you want to load and click the OK button. In our case, we have selected the `rmr2` package, as shown in Figure 25.12:

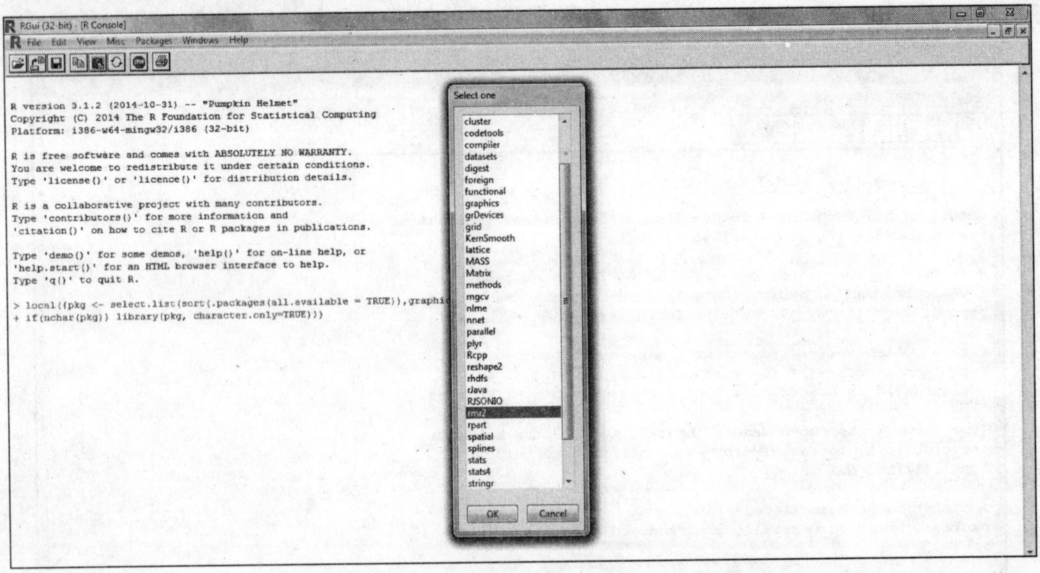

Figure 25.12: Selecting the Package for Loading

After installing RHadoop packages, you need to set the environment variables of Hadoop within R functions. You can use the following commands to set environment variables:

```
Sys.setenv("HADOOP_CMD"="<Path>/hadoop-2.6.0/bin/hadoop")
Sys.setenv("HADOOP_STREAMING"="<path>/hadoop-2.6.0/contrib/
streaming/hadoop-streaming-2.6.0.jar ")
Sys.getenv("HADOOP_CMD")
```

RHadoop is now installed on your system.

To test whether RHadoop packages have been successfully installed, type the following command:

```
Sys.setenv("HADOOP_HOME"="<path>/hadoop-2.6.0/bin/hadoop")
```

Load the package `rmr2` and `rhdfs` by using the `library()` function and type the following code in the R console:

Declaring the range of numbers

```
small.ints = to.dfs(1:500)
out = mapreduce( input = small.ints, map = function(k, v) keyval(v, v^2))
df = as.data.frame( from.dfs( out) )
colnames(df) = c(/n/, /n2/)
str(df)
```

Assigning value of out variable to df variable

Using the mapreduce() function

The output of the preceding code is as follows:

```
/data.frame/: 500 obs. of 2 variables:
$ n :int 1 2 3 4 5 6 7 8 9 10 ...
$ n2: num 1 4 9 16 25 36 4 9 64 81 100 ...
```

Using RHadoop

Now that you have installed RHadoop, let's look at an example that makes use of the combined capabilities of R and Hadoop.

Suppose you want to calculate the Cumulative Moving Average (CMA) of stocks. The data for this file is stored in the **stock.cvs** file and contains the following variables for each stock:

```
Symbol, Date, Open, High, Low, Close, Volume, Adj Close
```

A subset of the data stored in the **stock.cvs** file is shown below:

```
$ head -6 test-data/stock.txt
AAPL, 2009-01-02, 85.88, 91.04, 85.16, 90.75, 2664300, 90.75
AAPL, 2008-01-02, 199.27, 200.26, 192.55, 194.84, 38542100, 194.84
APPL, 2007-01-03, 86.29, 86.58, 81.90, 83.80, 44225700, 83.80
```

You already know that in RHadoop, programmers can define map and reduce functions invoked by MapReduce. Listing 25.1 provides the code for calculating CMA for the given stocks in RHadoop:

Listing 25.1: Calculating CMA in RHadoop

```
1  #! /usr/bin/envRscript

install.packages("rmr")

library(rmr)

2 map <- function(k,v){ fields <-unlist(strsplit(v,","))
keyval(fields[1], mean(as.double(c(fields[3], fields [6]))))
}
3 reduce <- function(k,v){keyval(k,mean(as.numeric(unlist(vv)))
}
4 Kvtextoutputformat=function(k,v){ paste(c(k,v,"\n"), collapse ="\t")
5 mapreduce(
input = stocks_input.txt
output="stock_output",
textinputformat=rawinputtextformat,
textoutputformat=kvtextoutputformat,
map = map,
reduce = reduce)
```

Installing rmr package

Using rmr library

Defining the map () function

Defining the reduce () function

Executing the MapReduce() function

The code given in Listing 25.1 is explained as follows:

1. Installs and loads the `rmr` library.
2. Defines the `map()` function. This function generates key value pairs from input splits. The `map()` function is called for each input split and gives key/value output tuple.
3. Defines the `reduce()` function. This function is called once for each uniquely mapped key. K is the key and v is the value.
4. Defines the reduce output key value separator.
5. Runs MapReduce.

To execute the code in Listing 25.1, you have to run the following commands:

```
$ HADOOP_HOME=<Hadoop installation directory>
$ HADOOP_HOME/bin/hadoopfs -put test-data/stocks.txt stocks_input.txt
$ src/Home/R/Rcode/caclulate_stock.R
$ hadoopfs -cat stock_output/part*
```

```
CSCO 30.8985
MSFT 44.6725
AAPL 68.997
GOOG 419.943
YHOO 70.971
```

Figure 25.13 shows how the code given in Listing 25.1 is executed by MapReduce:

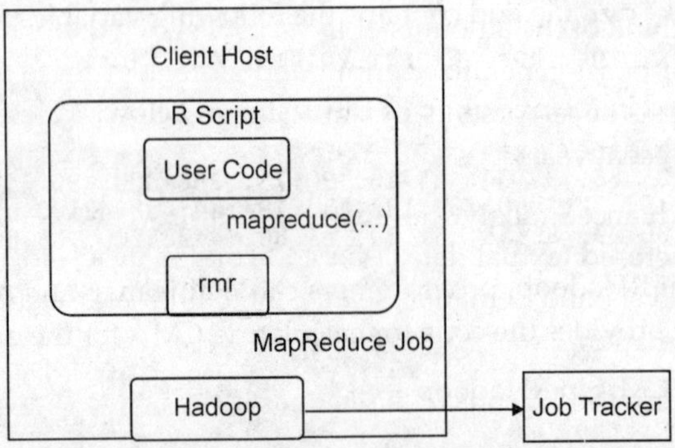

Figure 25.13: Displaying the Execution of Code

The `rmr` package creates a client-side environment for `MapReduce` to execute the `map()` and `reduce()` functions. This allows these functions to access variables outside their scope. The `rmr` package also allows programmers to seamlessly work with the inputs and outputs of MapReduce. Programmers can also write R variables to HDFS, use these variables as input for MapReduce, and load them back to R's data structure after completing the job.

The simple example given here is just to show you how to calculate the CMA for stocks by using the RHadoop. However, RHadoop or the integration of Hadoop with RStudio is generally used in text mining for processing large amounts of textual data to derive useful information. Let's now learn about text mining and how it is used to derive useful information from raw text data.

RHadoop is a collection of five R packages, which allow users to manage and analyze data with Hadoop. The five packages are as follows:

- **ravro**—It reads and write files in avro format.
- **plyrmr**—It is higher level plyr-like data processing for structured data, powered by rmr.
- **rmr**—This package offers Hadoop MapReduce functionalities in R.
- **rhdfs**—It is an interface between R and HDFS. It can be used to read/write data and modify files stored in HDFS.
- **rhbase**—This package allows R developers to use Hadoop HBase. R programmers can use rhbase to read/write data and modify tables stored in HBase.

Text Mining in RHadoop

Text mining is a set of techniques and methods used for the automatic processing of text data available in large quantities. This text is usually in the form of computer files. The aim of text mining is to extract the unstructured text and structure the text for quick (non-literary) analysis in order to discover hidden data for automatic decision making. Text mining is different from stylometry, which is the study of the style of texts to identify the author or date of the work, but it has much in common with lexicometry or lexical statistics (also known as linguistic statistics or quantitative linguistics). Text mining is an extension of lexical statistics and uses advanced methods of multidimensional statistics. You can show this schematically as:

- Text mining = Lexicometry + Data mining

The concept of text mining originated partly in response to the huge volume of text data created and diffused in our society (think of the amounts of laws, orders, regulations, contracts, for example) and partly for the purpose of quasi-generalized input and storage of these data in computer systems. It also owes its acceptance to developments in statistical and data processing tools whose power has increased greatly in the recent years.

Text analytics is an advanced analytical method that reveals new, unfamiliar, and practical information from unstructured textual data. Text analytics analyzes unstructured text, categorizes it, performs sentiment analysis and semantic search matching, and examines customer feedback to extract meaningful information.

Text mining devises patterns and trends in large amounts of text to derive some useful information.

A typical text mining process includes:

- Categorizing text
- Clustering
- Extracting concept/entity relationship
- Generating taxonomies
- Performing sentiment analysis
- Summarizing document
- Modeling entity relationship

In simple words, the text mining process includes the following steps:

- Text gathering (collection of unstructured text data)
- Text pre-processing (structuring text data)
- Data analysis
- Visualisation
- Evaluation

This is just a very basic introduction of text mining. Let's now understand the implementation of text mining on the RHadoop platform.

Text mining is one of the most commonly used applications of RHadoop. R's `tm` package is used for text mining. This package contains about 50 news articles with additional metadata information in the form of 21578 XML datasets. This package is developed to work with plain text, articles, papers, surveys, and Web documents in the form of Hypertext Markup Language (HTML), Extensible Markup Language (XML), and Standard Generalized Markup Language (SGML). Perform the following steps to mine the text:

1. Load the `tm` package by using the following command:

```
Library ("tm")
```

When you run this command, the following message is displayed:

```
Loading required package: slam
```

2. Load the input from the `reuters_xml` file, which is available in the `tm` package, by using the following command:

```
>input<-"~ /Data/Reuters/reuters_xml"
```

3. Store the input in the `co` object by using the following command:

```
>co<-Corpus(DirSource(input), [...])
```

4. Use the following command to view the details of the `co` object:

```
>co
```

When you run the preceding command, the following message will be displayed on the screen:

```
A corpus with 21578 text documents
```

5. Display the size of the `co` object in Mb (megabytes) by using the following command:

```
>print(object.size(co), units ="M b")
```

When you run the preceding command, the size of the `co` object will be displayed in Mbs, as follows:

```
65.5 Mb
```

You have now loaded a single corpus and retrieved its size. This is a simple text mining example. You can also load files from multiple locations, a process called **distributed text mining**. Let's look at an example of distributed text mining.

Suppose you want to load two files and retrieve their size. You can do this by performing the following steps:

1. Define a source file, `corpus.R`, by using the following command:

```
>source("corpus.R")
```

2. Define another source file, `reader.R`, by using the following command:

```
>source ( "reader.R")
```

3. Take both files as input by using the following command:

```
>dc<-DistributedCorpus(DirSource(input), [...])
```

4. Access the information about the `dc` object by using the following command:

```
>dc
```

When you run the preceding command, the following message will be displayed on your screen:

```
A corpus with 21578 text documents
```

5. Access the first line of the content of the `dc` object by using the following command:

```
>dc[[1]]
```

When you run the preceding command, the following line of text will be displayed on the screen:

```
Showers continued throughout the week in
```

6. Print the size of the `dc` object in Mbs by using the following command:

```
>print(object.size(dc), units ="Mb")
```

When you run the preceding command, the size of the `dc` object will be displayed in Mbs, as follows:

```
1.9 Mb
```

The preceding steps can be used in RHadoop to perform distributed text mining.

To store text files in HDFS, you must first have access to the files via R; however, this is a difficult job because Hadoop provides random output after calling the mapper function. The output, in the form of chunks, is automatically renamed to `part-xxxxx`. A solution to this problem is to update metadata information for each chunk, such as name and position in the chunk, and then update the distributed corpus after calling the mapper function.

Data Analysis Using the MapReduce Technique in RHadoop

SCENARIO

Consider the scenario of Argon Technology, the organization that specializes in providing Big Data analytical solutions to its customers. Mr. Smith, the data analyst of Argon Technology, receives a request from one of their clients, a reputed restaurant, to process its customer feedback that is available largely in an unstructured format. The top management of the restaurant wants to analyze the positive and negative feedback from customers about the maintenance, waiter service, food quality, neatness, hygiene, and other operations of the restaurant. The aim of this exercise is to further improve the quality of the services for better customer satisfaction.

The restaurant has a large volume of unstructured data (in the range of gigabytes) collected from various social media sites, feedback log books, and other sources.

Mr. Smith decides to use the MapReduce technique in RHadoop for analyzing the customer feedback data.

Before starting the data analysis, we need to know the way the MapReduce model is applied in the text analysis operation. This model is used to analyze text data by counting the frequency of repeated words. The application of the MapReduce WordCount program can be explained as follows:

- WordCount reads the text files and counts the number of times each word appears in the text (frequency of words). Both the input and the output are text files. Each line of the output file contains a word that is separated by a tab from the number of times the word appears in the input file.
- To find out the word frequency, we implement a simple MapReduce algorithm, which includes the following steps:
  - Each mapper first takes a string as an input and then splits it into input splits. Then, the key/value of each word is emitted, along with 1.
  - Each reducer sums the counts for each word and emits a single key/value with the word and sum.

The combiner is also used as a reducer on the map output. This reduces the amount of data sent across the network by combining each word into a single record. In the end, the outcomes of the analysis are viewed and exported to the local system.

Let's start by writing R scripts for mapper and reducer programs. The `mapper.R` code to integrate R with Hadoop includes the following set of commands:

```
trimWhiteSpace<- function(line) gsub("(^ +)|( +$)", "", line)
# Removes blank spaces splitIntoWords<- function(line)
unlist(strsplit(line, "[[:space:]]+"))
#splits words separated by blank spaces
```

The file read operation is performed by using the following command:

```
>con<- file("stdin", open = "r")
while (length(line <- readLines(con, n = 1, warn = FALSE)) > 0) {
line<- trimWhiteSpace(line)
words<- splitIntoWords(line)
## The following two lines of the code can be written as
cat(paste(words, "\t1\n", sep=""), sep="") also.
for (w in words)
cat(w, "\t1\n", sep="")
}
>close(con) #closes the connection
```

The `reducer.R` code to integrate R with Hadoop includes the following commands:

```
>trimWhiteSpace<- function(line) gsub("(^ +)|( +$)", "", line)
>splitLine<- function(line) {
val<- unlist(strsplit(line, "\t"))
list(word = val[1], count = as.integer(val[2]))
}
>env<- new.env(hash = TRUE)
>con<- file("stdin", open = "r")
while (length(line <- readLines(con, n = 1, warn = FALSE)) > 0) {
line<- trimWhiteSpace(line)
split<- splitLine(line)
word<- split$word
count<- split$count
if (exists(word, envir = env, inherits = FALSE)) {
oldcount<- get(word, envir = env)
assign(word, oldcount + count, envir = env)
} else assign(word, count, envir = env)
}
>close(con)
for (w in ls(env, all = TRUE))
cat(w, "\t", get(w, envir = env), "\n", sep = "")
```

After creating the map and reduce programs, you must ensure that Hadoop is running.

For this, type `jps` on the terminal. The running processes should be visible as follows:

- NameNode
- DataNode
- JobTracker
- TaskTracker
- SecondaryNameNode
- JPS

Next, you need to copy the input files to HDFS. To do this, type the following commands on the terminal:

```
bin/hadoopdfs -copyFromLocal '/ atasets/input.txt' /readme
bin/hadoopdfs -ls /
```

The command `-copyFromLocal` is used to copy a file from the local file system and then paste it in the distributed file system. `-ls` shows all the directories and files present in HDFS.

Next, run the MapReduce model to perform the analysis operation. To do this, type the following commands on the terminal:

```
bin/hadoop jar '/hadoop-2.6.0/contrib/streaming/hadoop-streaming-2.6.0.jar' -file
```

```
'/Chapter 25/mapper.R -mapper'
'/Chapter 25/mapper.R -file'
'/Chapter 25/reducer.R -reducer'
'/Chapter 25/reducer.R' -input /readme -output /RCount2
```

After this, the results of the analysis are viewed and exported. To do this, type the following command on the terminal:

```
bin/hadoopfs -cat /RCount2/part-00000
```

`-cat` command is used to view the file and its output in the Linux-based system.

In the end, the results must be copied to the local system. To do this, type the following command on the terminal:

```
bin/hadoopdfs -get /RCount2/part-00000 '/Chapter 25/wcOutput'
```

`-get` command is used to copy the file from HDFS and then paste it in the local file system.

For an efficient and smooth operation of RHadoop, you should remove the folder RCount, which stores all the data in HDFS. To do this, type the following command on the terminal:

```
bin/hadoopdfs -rmr /RCount2
```

`-rmr` command removes the present directory from the Linux-based system. It is used for both HDFS and local file system.

Data Mining in Hive

Hive is a batch-oriented and data-warehousing layer created on the basic elements of Hadoop, such as HDFS and MapReduce. This layer plays an important role in the mining of Big Data. Hive offers a simple SQLite implementation called HiveQL to SQL users without losing access through mappers and reducers. Hive provides you an SQL-like retrieval of the structured data and critical Big Data analysis by using MapReduce.

Hive does not provide fast responses to queries as compared to most data warehouses. Sometimes, queries may take several minutes or even hours, depending on the intricacy of the queries. Therefore, Hive can be best used for data mining and deeper analytics that do not need to be executed in real time. Hive depends upon the foundation of Hadoop and is a very robust, extensible, and scalable platform.

Hive uses the following three mechanisms to organize data:

- **Tables**—Hive tables are very much similar to RDBMS tables, which consist of rows and columns. Hive tables can be mapped to directories present in the file system because Hive is layered on the Hadoop HDFS. Moreover, Hive provides support to tables present in other native file systems.
- **Partitions**—One or more partitions can be supported by a Hive table. These partitions are already mapped with subdirectories present in the file system and display the distribution of data throughout the table. Consider an example in which a table, *cars,* has a key value of *3456* and a maker value *Hundai.* The path to the partition of this table would be `/hivewh/cars/kv=3456/Hundai`.
- **Buckets**—Data can be divided into buckets that are saved as files in the partition directory of the present file system. The basis of buckets is hash of a column in the table. In the earlier example, you might have a bucket called *i10,* having all the attributes of a Hundai i10car.

Metastores are used to store Hive metadata externally. It is a relational database that contains thorough descriptions of the Hive schema, which includes column types, owners, key and value data, table statistics, etc. A metastore has the ability to synchronize catalog data with other metadata services in the Hadoop ecosystem.

Hive also supports HiveQL, which is an SQL-like language. HiveQL provides support to most SQL primitives, such as select, join, aggregate, union, etc. It also provides support to multitable queries and shares the input data in a single HiveQL statement. HiveQL also plays a major role in user-defined aggregation, column transformation, and embedded MapReduce scripts.

Summary

In this chapter, you first learned about the importance of integrating R with Hadoop in Big Data analytics. Next, you learned to install and use RHadoop packages in R. The chapter further discussed the concept of text mining and how it is used to process data in RHadoop. Finally, you learned to implement data mining in Hive and use the MapReduce technique for data analysis.

Quick Revise

Multiple-Choice Questions

Q1. HDFS stands for:

a. Hadoop Distributed File System
b. Hadoop Dependent File System
c. Hadoop Distributed Files System
d. Hadoop Discrete File System

Ans. The correct option is a.

Q2. Which component of Hadoop is used for processing the data stored in a distributed environment?

a. HDFS
b. MapReduce
c. rmr
d. RJSONIO

Ans. The correct option is b.

Q3. Name the package that allows programmers to directly write code for the Hadoop's MapReduce model.

a. hdfc
b. Mapreduce
c. rmr
d. RJSONIO

Ans. The correct option is c.

Q4. Which of the following packages provides the functionality to manipulate tables?

a. rhdfs
b. rmr
c. rhbase
d. hdfs

Ans. The correct option is c.

Q5. Name the engine that supports the development of real-time, traversal-based algorithms over a linked list graph on a single server.

a. Database Graph engine

b. Batch-Processing Graph engine

c. Search engine

d. Golden Orb

Ans. The correct option is a.

Subjective Questions

Q1. What do you understand by RHadoop?

Ans. RHadoop is an approach for integrating R and Hadoop. It is an open-source project that allows programmers to define their own map and reduce functions and directly use the functionality of MapReduce in R code. The integration of R with Hadoop allows programmers to write their own programs in MapReduce using R. In other words, RHadoop allows programmers to make full use of the environment of R and the Hadoop platform.

Q2. List the different functions of the `rhbase` package.

Ans. The `rhbase` package provides the functionality to manipulate tables. With the help of this package, programmers can access, read, create, and modify tables stored in the Hadoop platform.

This package includes the following important functions:

- **Table manipulation functions**—These include the `hb.new.table()`, `hb.delete().Table()`, and `hb.set.table.mode()` functions.
- **Table read/write functions**—These include the `hb.insert()`, `hb.insert.data.frame()`, `hb.get.data.frame()`, and `hb.scan()` functions.
- **Utility function**—This includes the `hb.list.tables()` function.
- **Initialization functions**—These include the `hb.defaults()` and `hb.init()` functions.

Q3. Discuss the functionality of the `rmr` package.

Ans. The `rmr` package allows programmers to directly write code that is executed by Hadoop's MapReduce component. With the help of this package, analysts can write MapReduce algorithms in the R language. To install this package, the analyst needs to install each node on the Hadoop cluster. In addition, all packages are installed on a default location that can be accessed by all users.

Q4. What do you understand by text mining?

Ans. Text mining is a set of techniques and methods used for the automatic processing of text data available in large quantities. This text is usually in the form of computer files. The aim of text mining is to extract and structure the text for quick (non-literary) analysis in order to discover hidden data for automatic decision making.

Text mining is different from stylometry, which is the study of the style of texts to identify the author or date the work, but it has much in common with lexicometry or lexical statistics (also known as linguistic statistics or quantitative linguistics).

Text mining is an extension of lexical statistics and uses advanced methods of multidimensional statistics. You can show this schematically as:

- Text mining = Lexicometry + Data mining

The concept of text mining originated partly in response to the huge volume of text data created and diffused in our society (think of the amounts of laws, orders, regulations, contracts, for example) and partly for the purpose of quasi-generalized input and storage of these data in computer systems. It also owes its acceptance to developments in statistical and data processing tools whose power has increased greatly in the recent years.

Q5. List the different processes included in text mining.

Ans. A typical text mining process includes:

- Categorizing text
- Clustering
- Extracting concept/entity relationship
- Generating taxonomies
- Performing sentiment analysis
- Summarizing document
- Modeling entity relationship

Q6. What are the different steps used in a text mining process?

Ans. The text mining process includes following steps:

- Structuring input text
- Adding language rules
- Removing useless terms
- Inserting structured data into the database
- Identifying patterns in stored data
- Analyzing patterns
- Generating useful information

Q7. Name the two types of graph engines provided by RHadoop for generating graphs of the given data.

Ans. The RHadoop platform provides the following two types of engines for generating graphs of the given data:

- **Database Graph Engine**—This engine supports the development of real-time, traversal-based algorithms over a linked list graph on a single server. Some vendors who provide these types of graphs are Neo4j, InfiniteGraph, and DEX.
- **Batch-Processing Graph Engine**—This engine is used to represent batch-processing algorithms over a group of computers. These graph engines are included in the Hama, Golden Orb, and Pregel graph-processing applications.

26

Data Visualization-I

Visualization is a pictorial or visual representation technique. Anything which is represented in pictorial or graphical form, with the help of diagrams, charts, pictures, flowcharts, etc. is known as visualization. Data presented in the form of graphics can be analyzed better than the data presented in words.

Data visualization is a pictorial or visual representation of data with the help of visual aids such as graphs, bar, histograms, tables, pie charts, mind maps, etc. Depending upon the complexity of data and the aspects from which it is analyzed, visuals can vary in terms of their dimensions (one-/two-/multi-dimensional) or types, such as temporal, hierarchical, network, etc. All these visuals are used for presenting different types of datasets. Different types of tools are available in the market for visualizing data. One of the most commonly used data visualization tools is Tableau, which is available for free as Tableau Public. We can use Tableau products for both individual as well as corporate purposes, creating several types of 1D, 2D, and 3D visualizations. But what is the use of data visualization in Big Data? Is it necessary to use it? Let's first track down the real meaning of visualization in the context of Big Data analytics.

This chapter familiarizes you with the concept of data visualization and the need to visualize data in Big Data analytics. You also learn about different types of data visualizations. Next, you learn about various types of tools using which data or information can be presented in a visual format. The chapter also discusses the basics and the installation process of the Tableau Public tool.

Ways of Representing Visual Data

The data is first analyzed and then the result of that analysis is visualized in different ways as discussed above. There are two ways to visualize a data—infographics and data visualization.

Infographics are the visual representation of information or data rapidly and accurately. The use of colorful graphics in drawing charts and graphs helps in improving the interpretation of a given data. Figure 26.1 shows an example of infographics:

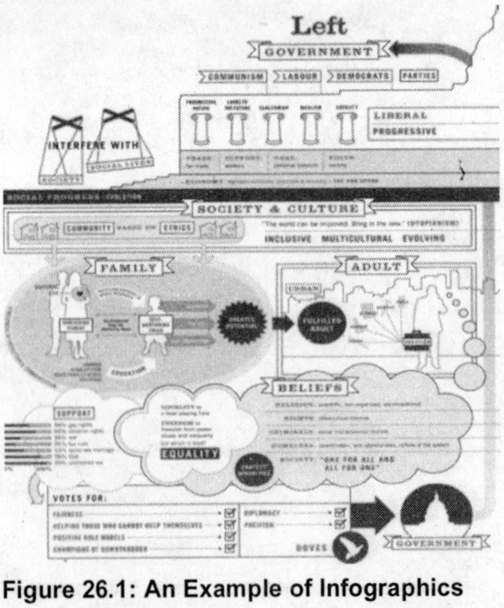

Figure 26.1: An Example of Infographics

Source: *http://www.jackhagley.com/What-s-the-difference-between-an-Infographic-and-a-Data-Visualisation*

Data Visualization

SCENARIO

Mr. Robert Smith, the technical head of Argon Technology, thought of finding better ways to present the data that is stored in their databases as Comma Separated Value (CSV) files. Mr. Smith learned about the availability of various data visualization tools that can be used to visually present the stored data. He tells his team members about data visualization, its techniques, and various data visualization tools available in the market.

Data visualization is a different approach from the Infographics. It is the study of representing data or information in a visual form. With the advancement of digital technologies, the scope of multimedia has increased manifold. Visuals in the form of graphs, images, diagrams, or animations have completely proliferated the media industry and the Internet. It is an established fact that the human mind can comprehend information more easily if it is presented in the form of visuals. Instructional designers focus on abstract and model-based scientific visualizations to make the learning content more interesting and easy to understand. Nowadays, scientific data is also presented through digitally constructed images. These images are generally created with the help of computer software.

NOTE

Visual analytics combines the power of algorithm intelligence and computational power of modern computers.

Visualization is an excellent medium to analyze, comprehend, and share information. Let's see why:

- Visual images help to transmit a huge amount of information to the human brain at a glance.
- Visual images help in establishing relationships and distinction between different patterns or processes easily.
- Visual interpretations help in exploring data from different angles, which help gain insights.
- Visualization helps in identifying problems and understanding trends and outliers.
- Visualizations point out key or interesting breakthroughs in a large dataset.

Data can be classified on the basis of the following three criteria irrespective of whether it is presented as data visualization or infographics:

- **Method of creation**—It refers to the type of content used while creating any graphical representation.
- **Quantity of data displayed**—It refers to the amount of data which is represented. For example, geographical map, companies financial data, etc.
- **Degree of creativity applied**—It refers to the extent to which the data is created graphically or designed in a colorful way or it is just showing some important data in black and white diagrams.

On the basis of above evaluation, we can understand which is the correct form of representation for a given data type. Let's discuss the various content types:

- **Graph**—A representation in which X and Y axes are used to depict the meaning of the information
- **Diagram**—A two-dimensional representation of information to show how something works

- **Timeline**—A representation of important events in a sequence with the help of self-explanatory visual material
- **Template**—A layout is a design for presenting information
- **Checklist**—A list of items for comparison and verification
- **Flowchart**—A representation of instructions which shows how something works or a step-by-step procedure to perform a task
- **Mind Map**—A type of diagram which is used to visually organize information

Techniques Used for Visual Data Representation

Data can be presented in various visual forms, which include simple line diagrams, bar graphs, tables, matrices, etc. Some techniques used for a visual presentation of data are as follows:

- **Isoline**—It is a 2D data representation of a curved line that moves constantly on the surface of a graph. The plotting of an isoline is based on data arrangement rather than data visualization. Figure 26.2 shows a set of isolines:

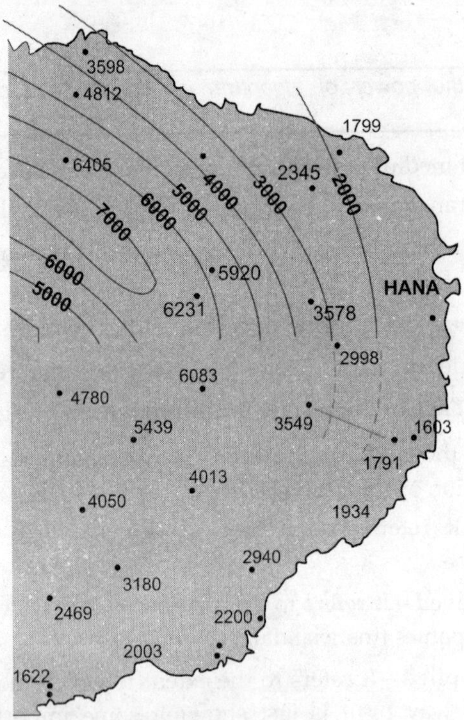

Figure 26.2: Isolines

- **Isosurface**—It is a 3D representation of an isoline. Isosurfaces are designed to represent points that are bound by a constant value in a volume of space, i.e., in a domain that covers 3D space.

Figure 26.3 shows how isosurfaces look like:

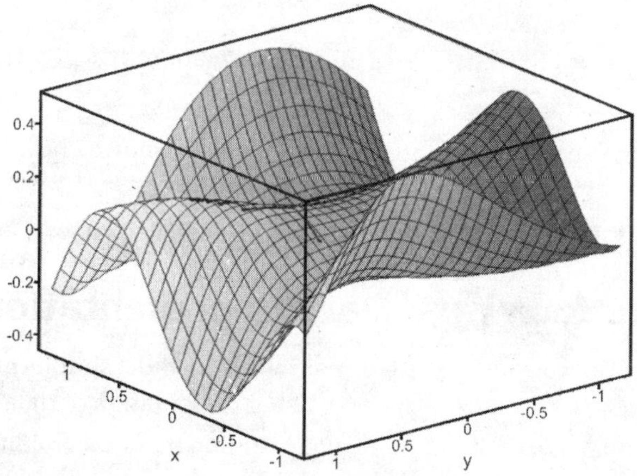

Figure 26.3: Isosurfaces

- **Direct Volume Rendering (DVR)**—It is a method used for obtaining a 2D projection for a 3D dataset. A 3D record is projected in a 2D form through DVR for a clearer and more transparent visualization.

  Figure 26.4 shows a 2D DVR of a 3D image:

Figure 26.4: 2D Image DVR

- **Streamline**—It is a field line that results from the velocity vector field description of the data flow.

  Figure 26.5 shows a set of streamlines:

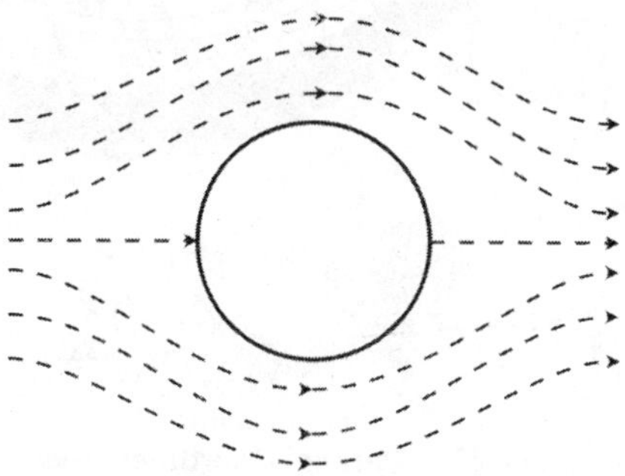

Figure 26.5: Streamlines

- **Map**—It is a visual representation of locations within a specific area. It is depicted on a planar surface.

Figure 26.6 shows an instance of Google Map:

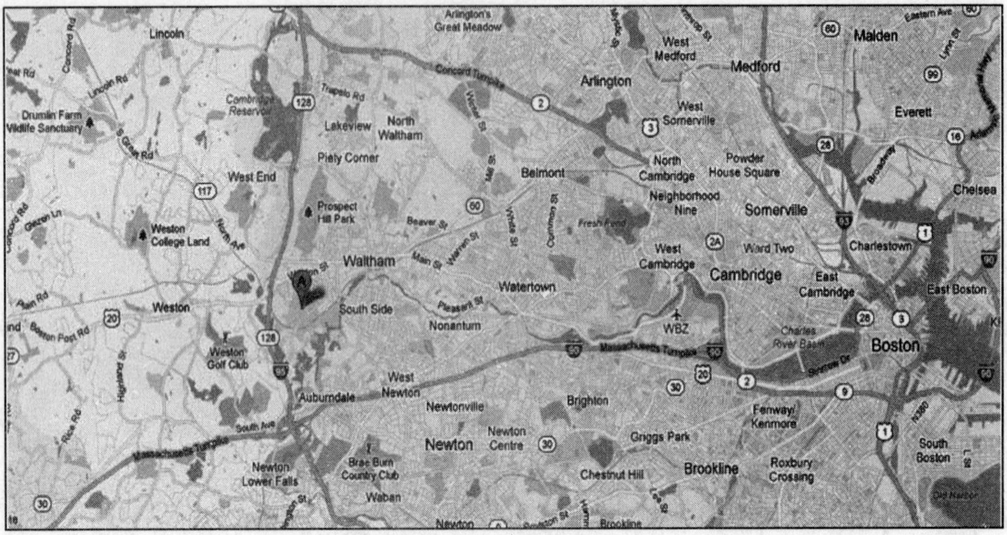

Figure 26.6: Google Map

- **Parallel Coordinate Plot**—It is a visualization technique of representing multidimensional data.

  Figure 26.7 shows a parallel coordinate plot:

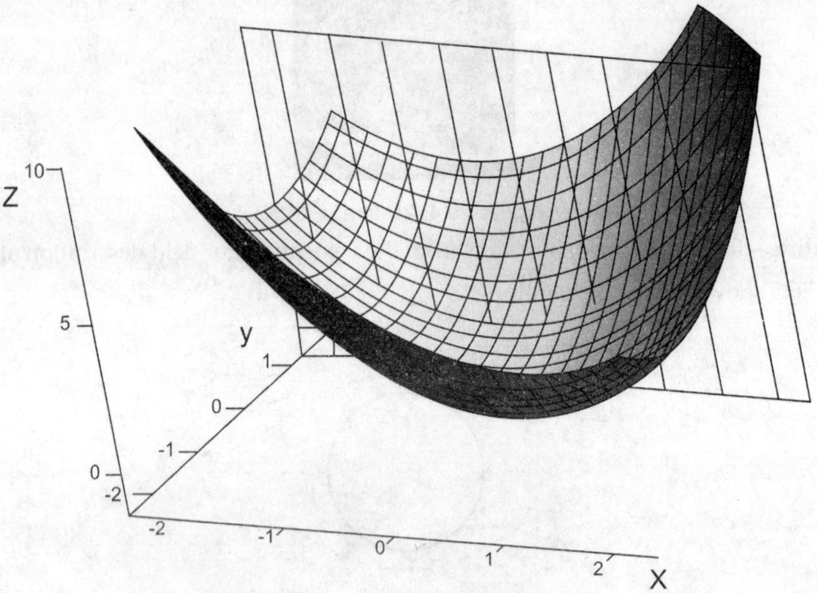

Figure 26.7: Parallel Coordinate Plot

- **Venn Diagram**—It is used to represent logical relations between finite collections of sets.

Figure 26.8 shows a Venn diagram for a set of relations:

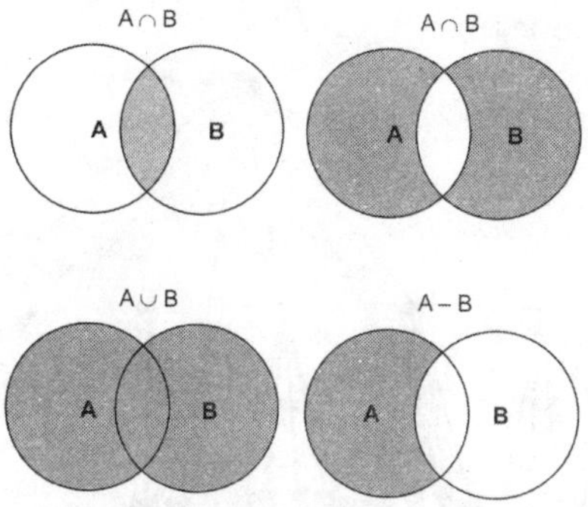

Figure 26.8: Venn Diagrams

- **Timeline**—It is used to represent a chronological display of events.

  Figure 26.9 shows an example of a timeline for some critical event sets:

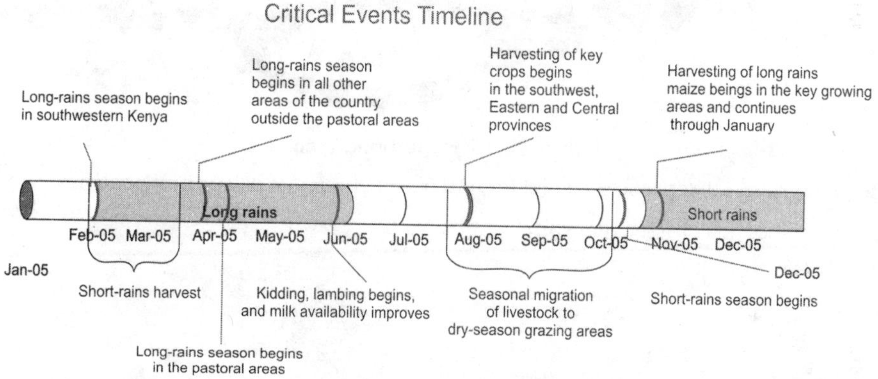

Figure 26.9: Timeline for Some Critical Events

- **Euler Diagram**—It is a representation of the relationships between sets.

  Figure 26.10 shows an example of an Euler diagram:

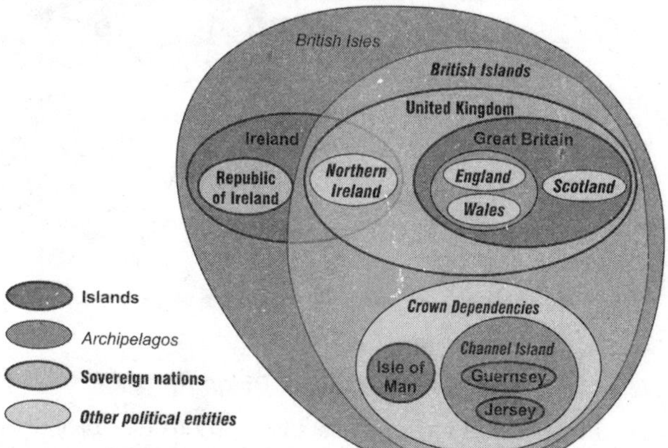

Figure 26.10: Euler Diagram

- **Hyperbolic Trees** – They represent graphs that are drawn using the hyperbolic geometry. Figure 26.11 shows a hyperbolic tree:

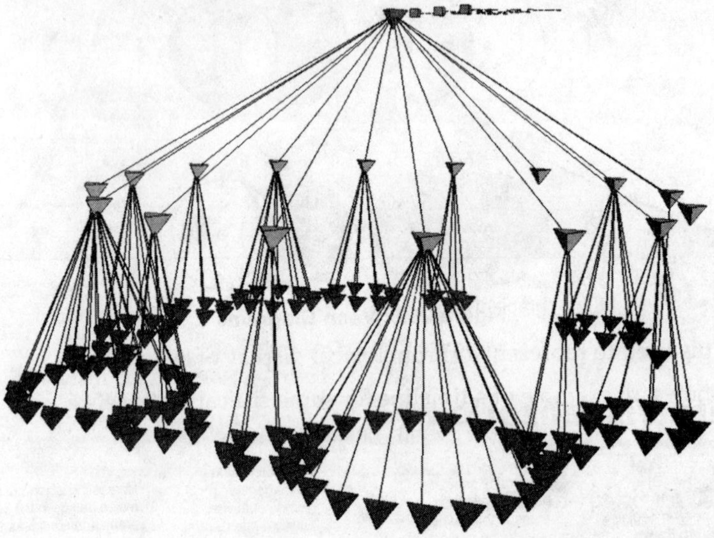

Figure 26.11: Hyperbolic Tree

- **Cluster Diagram** – It represents a cluster, such as a cluster of astronomic entities. Figure 26.12 shows a cluster diagram:

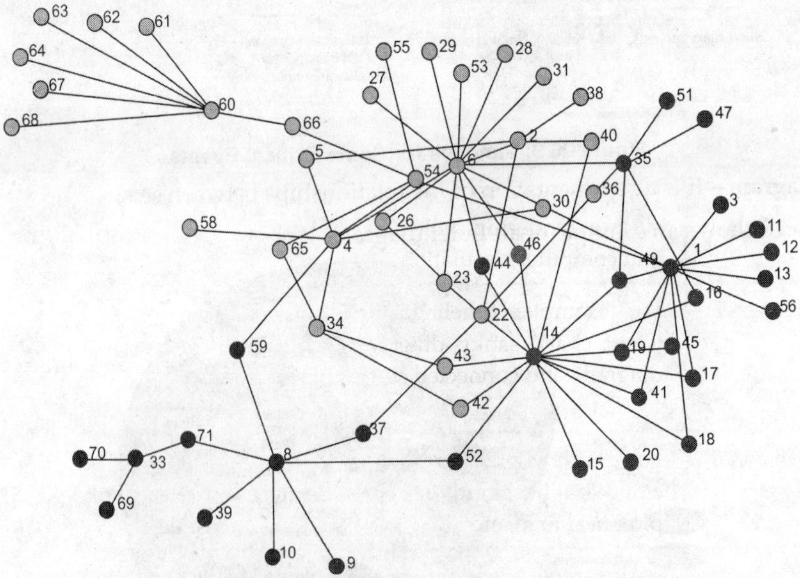

Figure 26.12: Cluster Diagram

- **Ordinogram** – It is used to analyze various sets of multivariate objects.

Figure 26.13 shows an ordinogram:

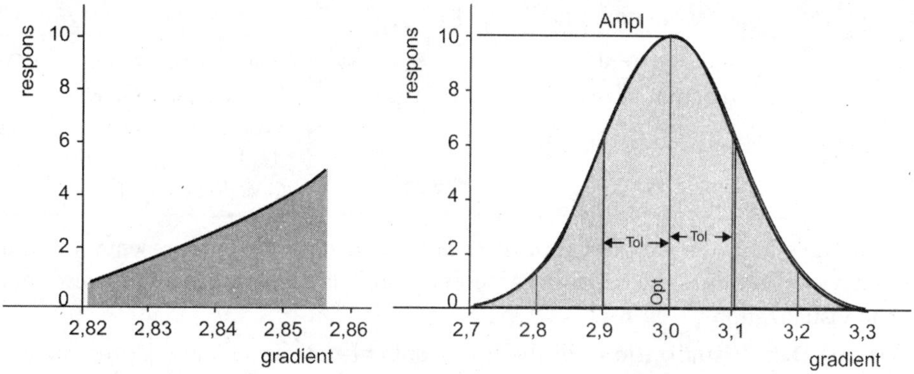

Figure 26.13: Ordinogram

Types of Data Visualization

You already know that data can be visualized in many ways, such as in the forms of 1D, 2D, or 3D structures. Table 26.1 briefly describes the different types of data visualization:

Table 26.1: Data Visualization Types

Name	Description	Tool
1D/Linear	For example, a list of items organized in a predefined manner	Generally, no tool is used for 1D visualization
2D/Planar	For example, choropleth, cartogram, dot distribution map, and proportional symbol map	GeoCommons, Google Fusion Tables, Google Maps API, Polymaps, Many Eyes, Google Charts, and Tableau Public
3D/Volumetric	For example, 3D computer models, surface rendering, volume rendering, and computer simulations	AC3D, AutoQ3D, TrueSpace
Temporal	For example, timeline, time series, Gantt chart, sanky diagram, alluvial diagram, and connected scatter plot	TimeFlow, Timeline JS, Excel, Timeplot, TimeSearcher, Google Charts, Tableau Public, and Google Fusion Tables
Multidimensional	For example, pie chart, histogram, tag cloud, bubble cloud, bar chart, scatter plot, heat map, etc.	Many Eyes, Google Charts, Tableau Public, and Google Fusion Tables
Tree/Hierarchical	For example, dendogram, radial tree, hyperbolic tree, and wedge stack graph	d3, Google Charts, and Network Workbench/Sci2

Table 26.1: Data Visualization Types

Name	Description	Tool
Network	For example, matrix, node link diagram, hive plot, and tube map	Pajek, Gephi, NodeXL, VOSviewer, UCINET, GUESS, Network Workbench/Sci2, sigma.js, d3/Protovis, Many Eyes, and Google Fusion Tables

As shown in Table 26.1, the simplest type of data visualization is 1D representation and the most complex data visualization is the network representation. The following is a brief description of each of these data visualizations:

- **1D (Linear) Data Visualization**—In the linear data visualization, data is presented in the form of lists. Hence, we cannot term it as visualization. It is rather a data organization technique. Therefore, no tool is required to visualize data in a linear manner.
- **2D (Planar) Data Visualization**—This technique presents data in the form of images, diagrams, or charts on a plane surface. Cartogram and dot distribution map are examples of 2D data visualization. Some tools used to create 2D data visualization patterns are GeoCommons, Google Fusion Tables, Google Maps API, Polymaps, Tableau Public, etc.
- **3D (Volumetric) Data Visualization**—In this method, data presentation involves exactly three dimensions to show simulations, surface and volume rendering, etc. Generally, it is used in scientific studies. Today, many organizations use 3D computer modeling and volume rendering in advertisements to provide users a better feel of their products. To create 3D visualizations, we use some visualization tools that involve AC3D, AutoQ3D, TrueSpace, etc.
- **Temporal Data Visualization**—Sometimes, visualizations are time dependent. To visualize the dependence of analyses on time, the temporal data visualization is used, which includes Gantt chart, time series, sanky diagram, etc. TimeFlow, Timeline JS, Excel, Timeplot, TimeSearcher, Google Charts, Tableau Public, Google Fusion Tables, etc. are some tools used to create temporal data visualization.
- **Multidimensional Data Visualization**—In this type of data visualization, numerous dimensions are used to present data. We have pie charts, histograms, bar charts, etc. to exemplify multidimensional data visualization. Many Eyes, Google Charts, Tableau Public, etc. are some tools used to create multidimensional data visualization.
- **Tree/Hierarchical Data Visualization**—Sometimes, data relationships need to be shown in the form of hierarchies. To represent such kind of relationships, we use tree or hierarchical data visualizations. Examples of tree/hierarchical data visualization include hyperbolic tree, wedge-stack graph, etc. Some tools to create hierarchical data visualization are d3, Google Charts, and Network Workbench/Sci2.
- **Network Data Visualization**—It is used to represent data relations that are too complex to be represented in the form of hierarchies. Some examples of network data visualization tools include matrix, node link diagram, hive plot, Pajek, Gephi, NodeXL, VOSviewer, UCINET, GUESS, Network Workbench/Sci2, sigma.js, d3/Protovis, Many Eyes, Google Fusion Tables, etc.

Applications of Data Visualization

Data visualization tools and techniques are used in various applications. Some of the areas in which we apply data visualization are as follows:

- **Education**—Visualization is applied to teach a topic that requires simulation or modeling of any object or process. Have you ever wondered how difficult it would be to explain any organ or organ system without any visuals? Organ system or structure of an atom is best described with the help of diagrams or animations.
- **Information**—Visualization is applied to transform abstract data into visual forms for easy interpretation and further exploration.
- **Production**—Various applications are used to create 3D models of products for better viewing and manipulation. Real estate, communication, and automobile industry extensively use 3D advertisements to provide a better look and feel to their products.
- **Science**—Every field of science including fluid dynamics, astrophysics, and medicine use visual representation of information. Isosurfaces and direct volume rendering are typically used to explain scientific concepts.
- **Systems visualization**—Systems visualization is a relatively new concept that integrates visual techniques to better describe complex systems.
- **Visual communication**—Multimedia and entertainment industry use visuals to communicate their ideas and information.
- **Visual analytics**—It refers to the science of analytical reasoning supported by the interactive visual interface. The data generated by social media interaction is interpreted using visual analytics techniques.

Visualizing Big Data

Visual analysis of data is not a new thing. For years, statisticians and analysts have been using visualization tools and techniques to interpret and present the outcomes of their analyses.

Almost every organization today is struggling to tackle the huge amount of data pouring in every day. Data visualization is a great way to reduce the turn-around time consumed in interpreting Big Data. Traditional visualization techniques are not efficient enough to capture or interpret the information that Big Data possesses. For example, such techniques are not able to interpret videos, audios, and complex sentences. Apart from the type of data, the volume and speed with which it is generating pose a great challenge. Most of the traditional analytics techniques are unable to cater to any of these problems.

Big Data comprises both structured as well as unstructured forms of data collected from various sources. Heterogeneity of data sources, data streaming, and real-time data are also difficult to handle by using traditional tools. Traditional tools are developed by using relational models that work best on static interaction. Big Data is highly dynamic in function and therefore, most traditional tools are not able to generate quality results. The response time of traditional tools is quite high, making it unfit for quality interaction.

Deriving Business Solutions

The most common notation used for Big Data is 3Vs—volume, velocity, and variety. But, the most exciting feature is the way in which value is filtered from the haystack of data. Big Data generated through social media sites is a valuable source of information to understand consumer sentiments and demographics. Almost every company nowadays is working with Big Data and facing the following challenges:

- Most data is in unstructured form
- Data is not analyzed in real time
- The amount of data generated is huge
- There is a lack of efficient tools and techniques

Considering all these factors, IT companies are focusing more on research and development of robust algorithms, software, and tools to analyze the data that is scattered in the Internet space. Tools such as Hadoop are providing the state-of-the-art technology to store and process Big Data. Analytical tools are now able to produce interpretations on smartphones and tablets. It is possible because of the advanced visual analytics that is enabling business owners and researchers to explore data for finding out trends and patterns.

Turning Data into Information

The most exciting part of any analytical study is to find useful information from a plethora of data. Visualization facilitates identification of patterns in the form of graphs or charts, which in turn helps to derive useful information. Data reduction and abstraction are generally followed during data mining to get valuable information.

Visual data mining also works on the same principle as simple data mining; however, it involves the integration of information visualization and human–computer interaction. Visualization of data produces cluttered images that are filtered with the help of clutter-reduction techniques. Uniform sampling and dimension reduction are two commonly used clutter-reduction techniques.

Visual data reduction process involves automated data analysis to measure density, outliers, and their differences. These measures are then used as quality metrics to evaluate data-reduction activity. Visual quality metrics can be categorized as:

- Size metrics (e.g. number of data points)
- Visual effectiveness metrics (e.g. data density, collisions)
- Feature preservation metrics (e.g. discovering and preserving data density differences)

In general, we can conclude that a visual analytics tool should be:

- Simple enough so that even non-technical users can operate it
- Interactive to connect with different sources of data
- Competent to create appropriate visuals for interpretations
- Able to interpret Big Data and share information

Apart from representing data, a visualization tool must be able to establish links between different data values, restore the missing data, and polish data for further analysis.

Tools Used in Data Visualization

Some useful visualization tools are listed as follows:

- **Excel**—It is a new tool that is used for data analysis. It helps you to track and visualize data for deriving better insights. This tool provides various ways to share data and analytical conclusions within and across organizations.

  Figure 26.14 shows an example of Excel sheet:

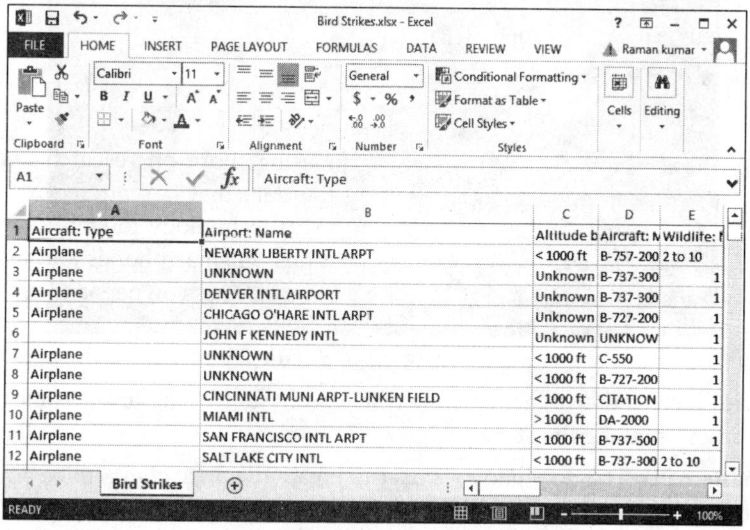

Figure 26.14: Excel Sheet

- **Last.Forward**—It is open-source software provided by last.fm for analyzing and visualizing social music network.

  Figure 26.15 shows an example of a Last.Forward visual:

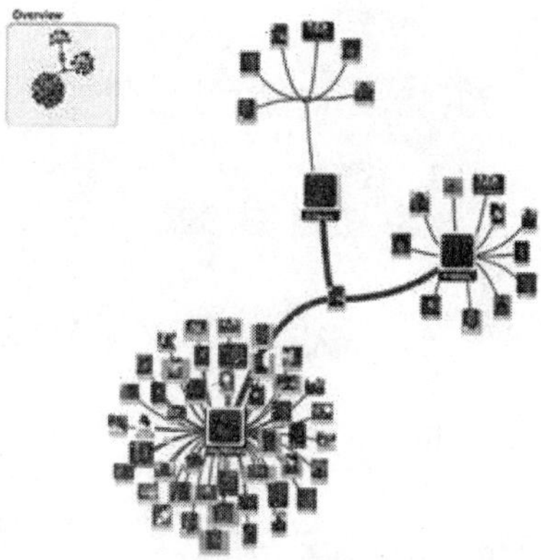

Figure 26.15: Last.Forward Visual

- **Digg.com**—Digg.com provides some of the best Web-based visualization tools.
- **Pics**—This tool is used to track the activity of images on the website.

- **Arc**—It is used to display the topics and stories in a spherical form. Here, a sphere is used to display stories and topic, and bunches of stories are aligned at the outer circumference of sphere. Figure 26.16 shows Digg Arc:

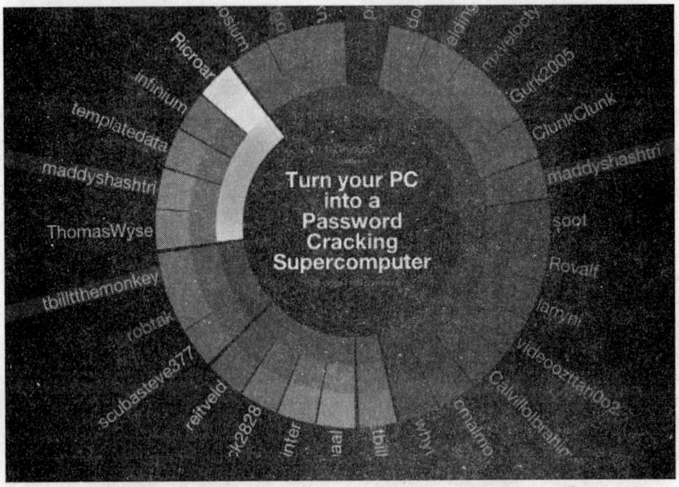

Figure 26.16: Digg Arc Visual

Larger stories have more diggs, as shown in Figure 26.16. The arc becomes thicker with the number of times users dig the story.

- **Google Charts API**—This tool allows a user to create dynamic charts to be embedded in a Web page. A chart obtained from the data and formatting parameters supplied in a HyperText Transfer Protocol (HTTP) request is converted into a Portable Network Graphics (PNG) image by Google to simplify the embedding process.

  Figure 26.17 shows some charts created by using Google Charts API:

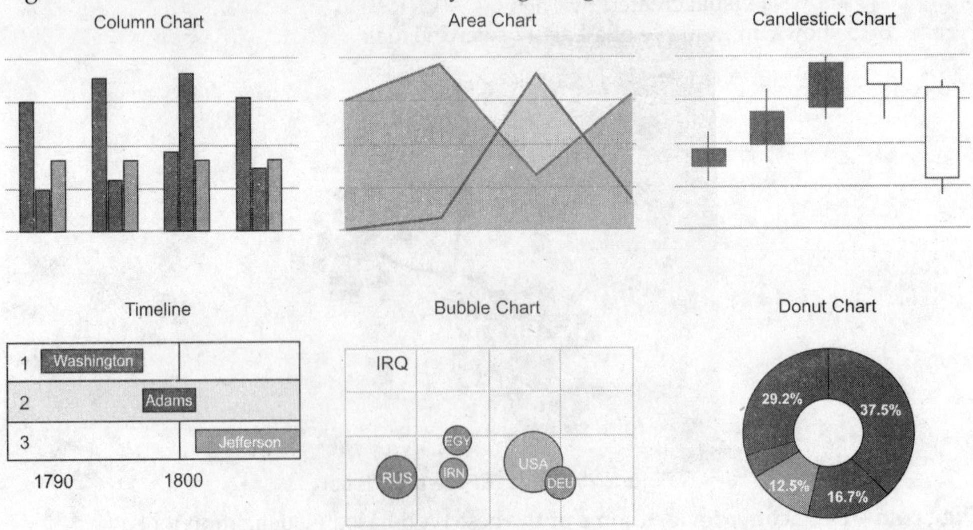

Figure 26.17: Charts Obtained from Google Charts API

- **TwittEarth**—This tool is capable of showing live tweets from all over the world on a 3D globe. It is an effort to improve social media visualization and provide a global image mapping in tweets.

  Figure 26.18 shows an example of a TwittEarth visual:

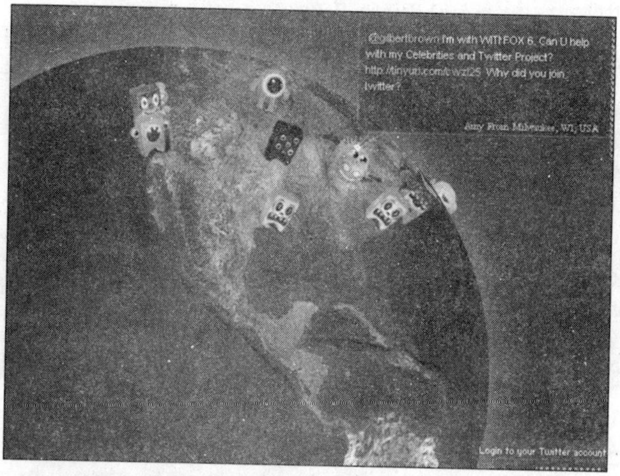

Figure 26.18: TwittEarth Visual

Source: *http://cybergyaan.com/2010/01/10-supercool-ways-to-visualize-internet.html*

- **Tag Galaxy**—Tag Galaxy provides a stunning way of finding a collection of Flickr images. It is an unusual site which provides search tool which makes the online combing process a memorable visual experience. If you want to search a picture, you have to enter a tag of your choice and it will find the picture. The central (core) star contains all the images directly relating to the initial tag and the revolving planets consist of similar or corresponding tags. Click on a planet and additional sub-categories will appear. Click on the central star and Flickr images gather and land on a gigantic 3D sphere.

  Figure 26.19 shows a visual created by Tag Galaxy:

Figure 26.19: Tag Galaxy Visual

Source: *Taggalaxy.de*

- **D3**—D3 allows you to bind arbitrary data to a Document Object Model (DOM) and then applies data-driven transformations to the document. For example, you can use D3 to generate an HTML table from an array of numbers. Or, use the same data to create an interactive SVG bar chart with smooth transitions and interactions.

  Figure 26.20 shows some complex visuals created through D3:

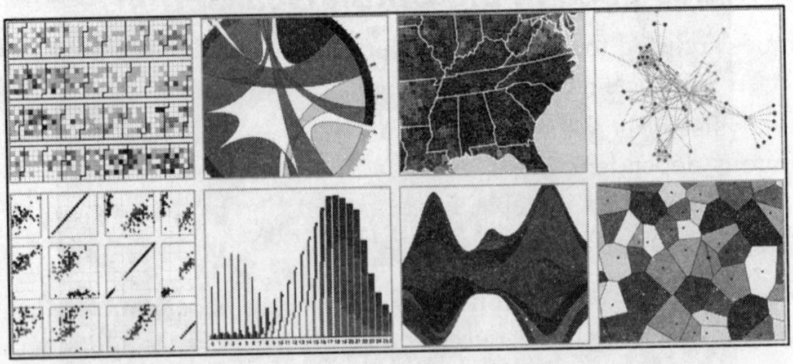

Figure 26.20: Some Visuals Obtained from D3

Source: http://d3js.org/

- **Rootzmap Mapping the Internet**—It is a tool to generate a series of maps on the basis of the datasets provided by the National Aeronautics and Space Administration (NASA). Figure 26.21 shows an example of the Internet mapping through Rootzmap:

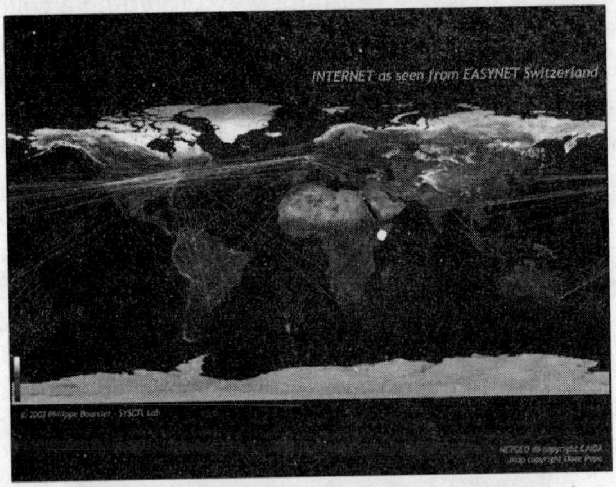

Figure 26.21: Internet Mapping Visual

Source: *http://www.sysctl.org/rootzmap/e-map.jpg*

Open-Source Data Visualization Tools

We already know that Big Data analytics requires the implementation of advanced tools and technologies. Due to economic and infrastructural limitations, every organization cannot purchase all the applications required for analyzing data. Therefore, to fulfill their requirement of advanced tools and technologies, organizations often turn to open-source libraries. These libraries can be defined as pools of freely available applications and analytical tools. Some examples of open-source tools available for data visualization are VTK, Cave5D, ELKI, Tulip, Gephi, IBM OpenDX, Tableau Public, and Vis5D.

Open-source tools are easy to use, consistent, and reusable. They deliver high-quality performance and are compliant with the Web as wel! as mobile Web security. In addition, they provide multichannel analytics for modeling as well as customized business solutions that can be altered with changing business demands.

Analytical Techniques Used in Big Data Visualization

Analytical techniques are used to analyze complex relationships among variables. The following are some commonly used analytical techniques for Big Data solutions:

- **Regression analysis**—It is a statistical tool used for prediction. Regression analysis is used to predict continuous dependent variables from independent variables. In this, we try to find the effect of one variable on other variable. For example, sales increase when prices decrease.

  Types of regression analysis are as follows:

  - **Ordinary least squares regression**—It is used when dependent variable is continuous and there exists some relationship between the dependent variable and independent variable.
  - **Logistic regression**—It is used when dependent variable has only two potential results.
  - **Hierarchical linear modeling**—It is used when data is in nested form.
  - **Duration models**—It is used to measure length of process.
- **Grouping methods**—The technique of categorizing observation into significant or purposeful blocks is called grouping. The recognition of features to create a distinction between groups is called discriminant analysis.
- **Multiple equation models**—It is used to analyze causal pathways from independent variables to dependent variables. Types of multiple equation models are as follows:
  - Path analysis
  - Structural equation modeling

Tableau Products

Till now, you have learned about some general tools and techniques used in Big Data visualization. Let's now learn about Tableau products that are most widely used for Big Data visualization. Some common Tableau products used for Big Data visualization are listed as follows along with their use:

- Tableau Desktop
  - Access ad hoc analytics, dashboards, reports, graphs
  - Explore, visualize, and analyze data
  - Create dashboards to consolidate multiple views
  - Deliver interactive data experiences
- Tableau Server
  - Provide a business intelligence solution that scales to organizations of all sizes
  - Share visual analytics with anyone using a Web browser
  - Publish interactive analytics or dashboards
  - Secure information and manage metadata

- Collaborate with others

❑ Tableau Reader

- Share visualizations and dashboards on the desktop
- Filter, sort, and page through views
- Use "Acrobat for Data"
- Can be downloaded free

❑ Tableau Public

- Create and publish interactive visualizations and dashboards
- Embed in websites and blogs
- Get free download and free hosting service

Installation of Tableau Public

Tableau Public is an open-source tool that is used for data visualization. You can download the product to install it on your computer system. We have downloaded Tableau Public version 8.3 on our Windows 8.1 operating system. Perform the following steps to download and install Tableau Public on a Windows desktop:

1. Open the following link in your Web browser:

   http://www.tableau.com/public/

   The home page of Tableau Public will appear, as shown in Figure 26.22:

Figure 26.22: Home Page of Tableau Public

2. Click the DOWNLOAD Tableau Public link (Figure 26.22). The Download Tableau Public window appears, as shown in Figure 26.23:

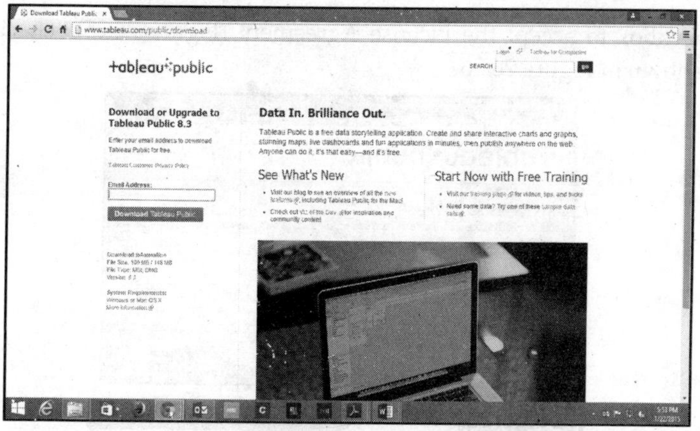

Figure 26.23: The Download Tableau Public Window

3. Enter your e-mail ID in the Email Address text box and click the Download Tableau Public button (Figure 26.23).

   The Thanks for choosing Tableau Public window appears, as shown in Figure 26.24:

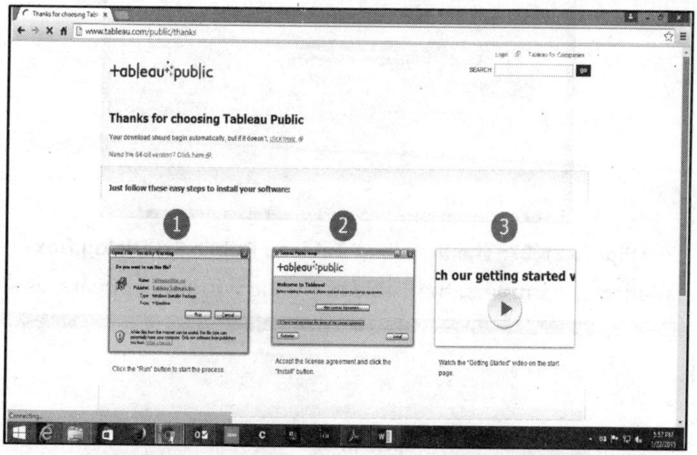

Figure 26.24: The Thanks for choosing Tableau Public Window

4. Go to the location in your system where you have saved the Tableau Public setup and double click the executable file. The Welcome to Tableau! dialog box appears, as shown in Figure 26.25:

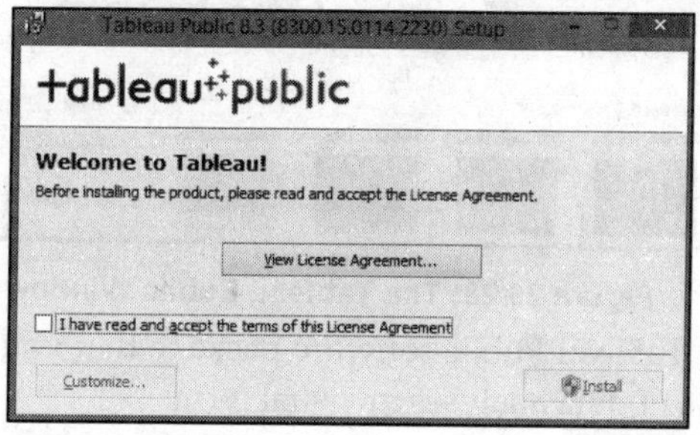

Figure 26.25: The Welcome to Tableau! Dialog Box

5. Click the checkbox to accept the License Agreement (Figure 26.25). The Install button will be enabled, as shown in Figure 26.26:

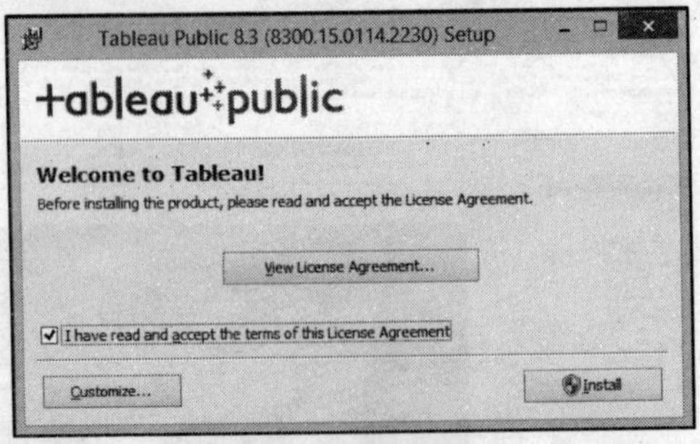

Figure 26.26: Enabling the Install Button

6. Click the Install button. The Installing Tableau Public <version number> dialog box appears, depicting the progress of the setup installation, as shown in Figure 26.27:

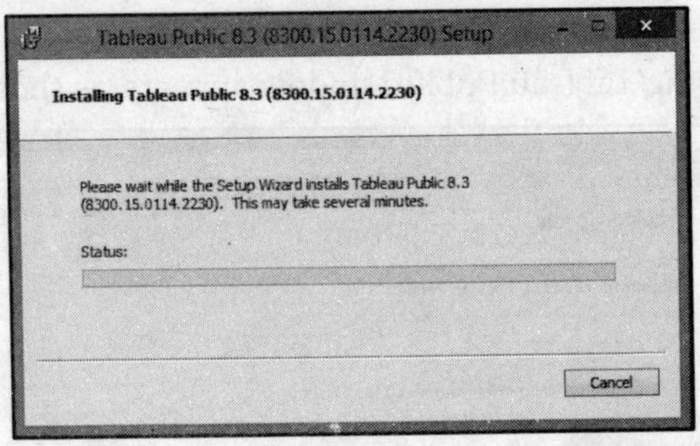

Figure 26.27: The Installing Tableau Public 8.3 Dialog Box

After the installation is complete, the Tableau Public window appears, as shown in Figure 26.28:

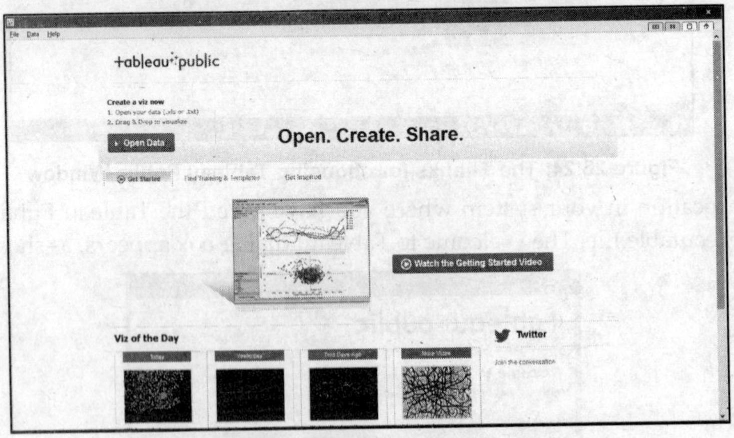

Figure 26.28: The Tableau Public Window

Now, you can use the Tableau Public software package that you have downloaded and installed to represent the results of data analyses in visual form.

7. Click the Open Data button (Figure 26.28) to start loading data in Tableau Public. The connectivity window appears, as shown in Figure 26.29:

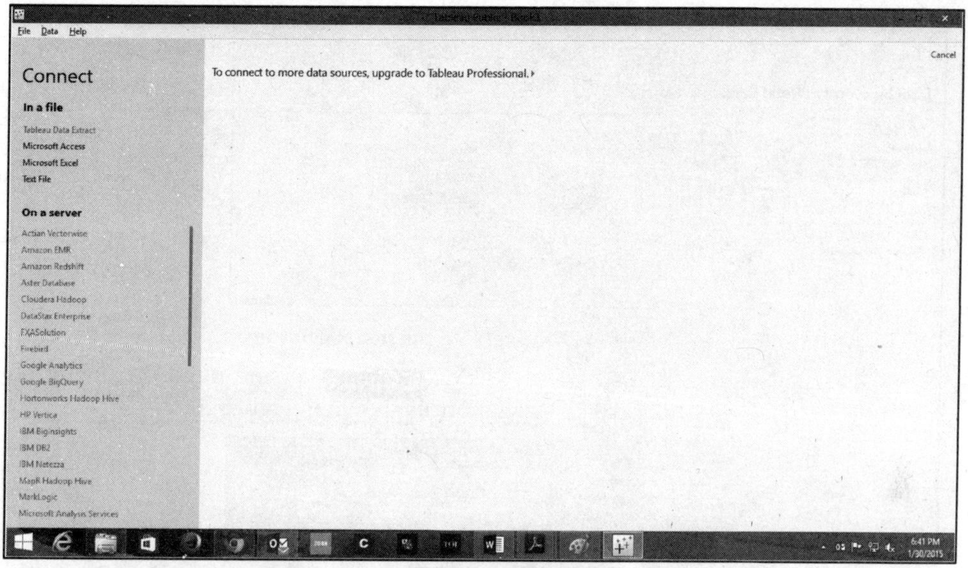

Figure 26.29: The Data Connectivity Window

You can load data stored either in a file (Microsoft Excel, Microsoft Access, or Text file) or on a server. In this case, we are loading a sample set of data, stored in an Excel file, by clicking the Microsoft Excel link (Figure 26.29). You will be prompted to select the file.

Once the data is loaded, the next window appears, as shown in Figure 26.30:

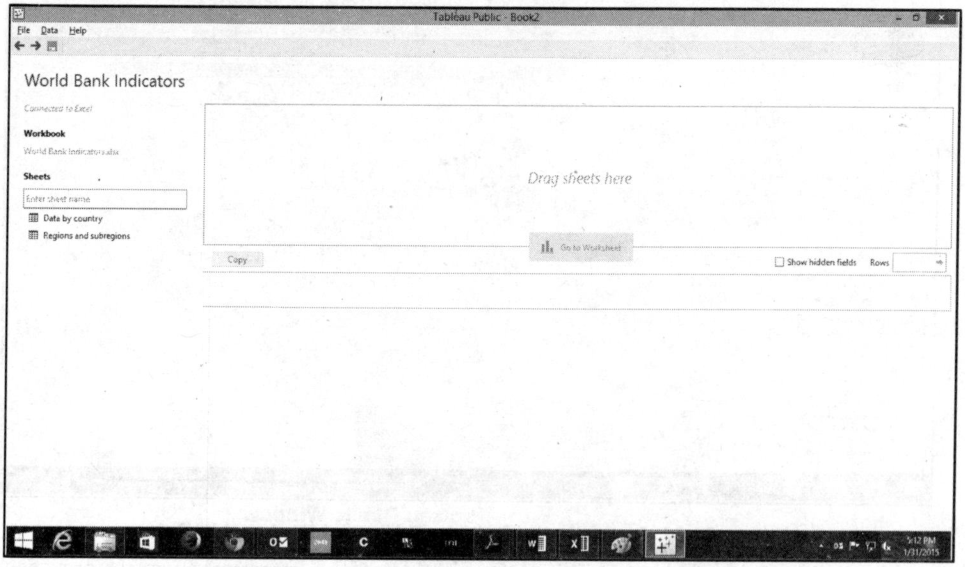

Figure 26.30: The Window after Connecting to the Data

8. Drag and drop your data sheets from the left frame to the right frame or double click a data sheet to see the next window, as shown in Figure 26.31:

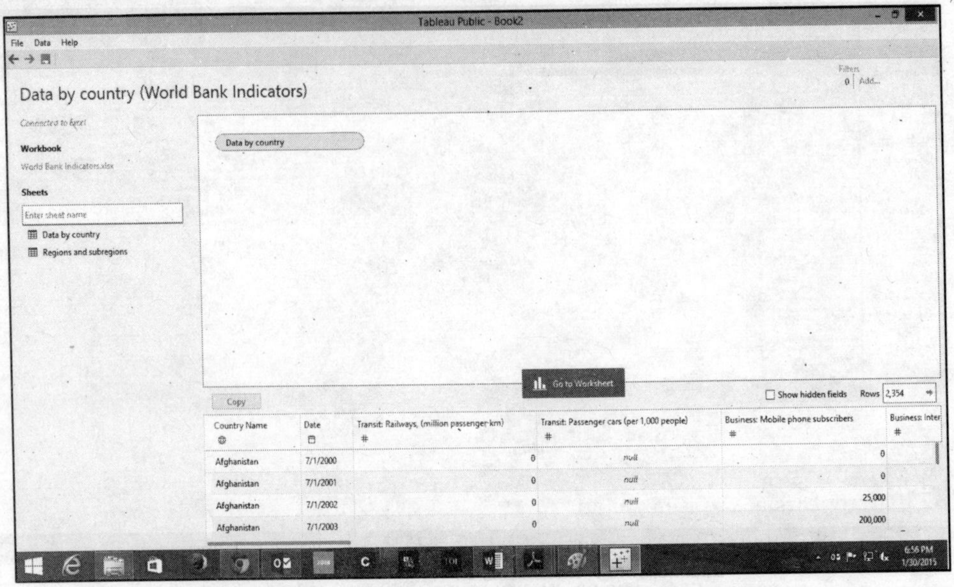

Figure 26.31: Showing the Loaded Data Sheet

9. Click the Go to Worksheet button (Figure 26.31).

   The window showing the datasheet view of the loaded data appears, as shown in Figure 26.32:

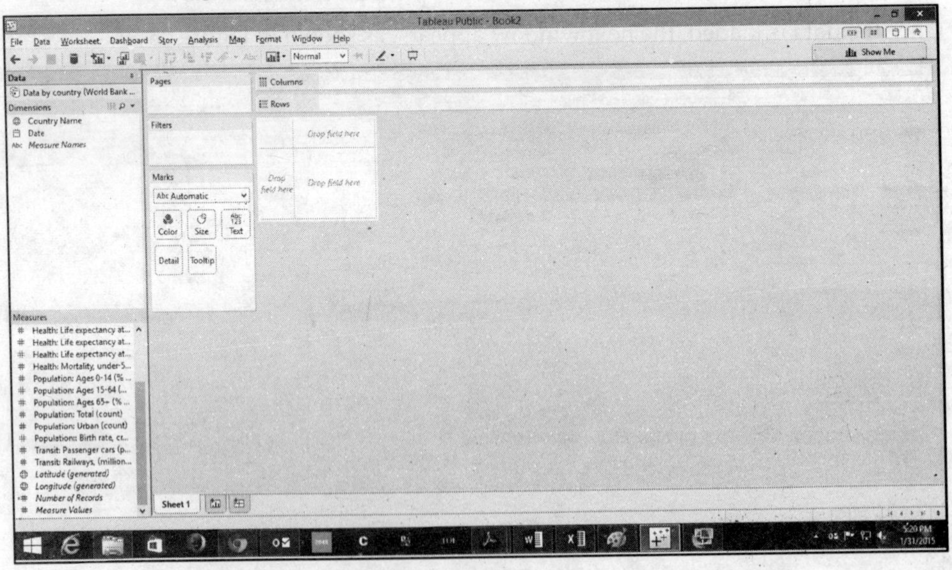

Figure 26.32: Showing the Datasheet View of the Loaded Data

10. Double click individual sheets to view the plotting in the graphical form. In our case, we have clicked the Country Name sheet.

A scatter plot is created between longitude and latitude, as shown in Figure 26.33:

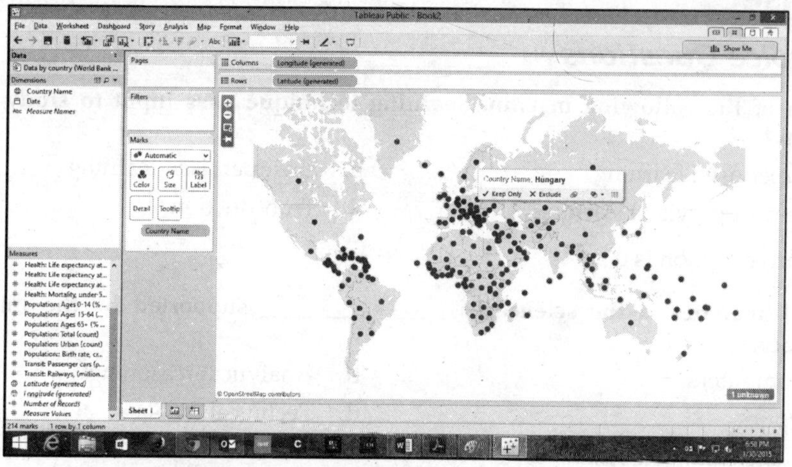

Figure 26.33: Showing Scatter Plot for Country Name

11. You can also select any other type of graphical view for the sheet from the Show Me selection box that appears at the right-hand corner of the screen. In our case, we have selected the map view, as shown in Figure 26.34:

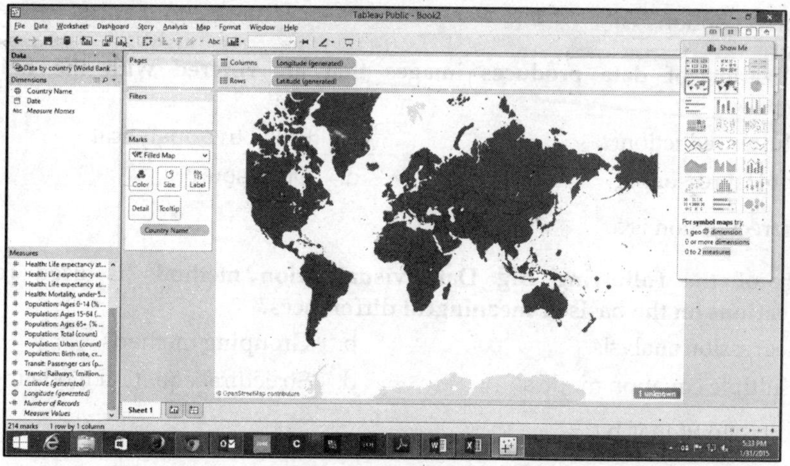

Figure 26.34: Showing Map View for Country Name

Thus, you can easily create various types of visuals for your data in Tableau Public.

Summary

In this chapter, you learned about the basics of data visualization, types of data visualization, and the various techniques used for visualizing data. Next, you learned about the application of data visualization techniques in various industries. Towards the end, you learned to install the Tableau Public tool.

Quick Revise

Multiple-Choice Questions

Q1. Which of the following machine learning technique uses input to study the effects on outputs?

a. Supervised learning
b. Unsupervised learning
c. Semi-supervised learning
d. Transduction

Ans. The correct option is d.

Q2. Visual analytics is the science of ____________ supported by the interactive visual interface.

a. Computers
b. Analytical reasoning
c. Optics
d. Technical tools

Ans. The correct option is b.

Q3. Which of the following tools provides state-of-the-art technology to store and process Big Data?

a. Yahoo
b. Google Analytics
c. Twitter Map
d. Hadoop

Ans. The correct option is d.

Q4. Visualization of data produces images that are filtered with the help of ________ techniques.

a. Clutter reduction
b. Predictive analytical
c. Logical reasoning
d. Open source

Ans. The correct option is a.

Q5. Which of the following Big Data visualization methods is used for categorizing observations on the basis of meaningful differences?

a. Regression analysis
b. Grouping methods
c. Multiple equation models
d. Structural equation modeling

Ans. The correct option is b.

Subjective Questions

Q1. 'Visualization is an excellent medium to analyze, comprehend, and share information.' Justify this statement.

Ans. Visualization is a very effective technique for representing the result of data analysis as:

- Visual images help to transmit a huge amount of information into the human brain at a glance.
- Visual images help in establishing relationships and distinction between different patterns or processes easily.

- Visual interpretations help in exploring data from different angles, which help gain insights.
- Visualization helps in identifying problems and understanding trends and outliers.
- Visualization points out key or interesting breakthroughs in a large dataset.

Q2. Which technique is used to analyze multivariate sets?

Ans. Ordinogram is used in the analysis of multivariate sets.

Q3. Name a few data visualization tools.

Ans. Some commonly used data visualization tools are:

- Excel
- Last.Forward
- Arc
- Google Charts API
- TwittEarth
- Tag Galaxy
- D3
- Rootzmap

Q4. Discuss some applications of data visualization.

Ans. Data visualization tools and techniques are used in various applications. Some of the areas in which we apply data visualization are as follows:

- **Education**—Visualization is applied to teach a topic that requires simulation or modeling of any object or process. Have you ever wondered how difficult it would be to explain any organ or organ system without any visuals? Organ system or structure of an atom is best described with the help of diagrams or animations.
- **Information**—Visualization is applied to transform abstract data into visual forms for easy interpretation and further exploration.
- **Production**—Various applications are used to create 3D models of products for better viewing and manipulation. Real estate, communication, and automobile industry extensively use 3D advertisements to provide a better look and feel to their products.
- **Science**—Every field of science, including fluid dynamics, astrophysics, and medicine use visual representation of information. Isosurfaces and direct volume rendering are typically used to explain scientific concepts.
- **Systems visualization**—Systems visualization is a relatively new concept that integrates visual techniques to better describe complex systems.
- **Visual communication**—Multimedia and entertainment industry use visuals to communicate their ideas and information.

- **Visual analytics**—It refers to the science of analytical reasoning supported by the interactive visual interface. The data generated by social media interaction is interpreted using visual analytics techniques.

Q5. List and discuss various types of data visualizations.

Ans. The different types of data visualizations are as follows:

- **1D (Linear) Data Visualization**—In the linear data visualization, data is presented in the form of lists. Hence, we cannot term it as visualization. It is rather a data organization technique. Therefore, no tool is required to visualize data in a linear manner.
- **2D (Planar) Data Visualization**—This technique presents data in the form of images, diagrams, or charts on a plane surface. Cartogram and dot distribution map are examples of 2D data visualization. Some tools used to create 2D data visualization patterns are GeoCommons, Google Fusion Tables, Google Maps API, Polymaps, Tableau Public, etc.
- **3D (Volumetric) Data Visualization**—In this method, data presentation involves exactly three dimensions to show simulations, surface and volume rendering, etc. Generally, it is used in scientific studies. Today, many organizations use 3D computer modeling and volume rendering in advertisements to provide users a better feel of their products. To create 3D visualizations, we use some visualization tools that involve AC3D, AutoQ3D, TrueSpace, etc.
- **Temporal Data Visualization**—Sometimes, visualizations are time dependent. To visualize the dependence of analyses on time, the temporal data visualization is used, which includes Gantt chart, time series, sanky diagram, etc. TimeFlow, Timeline JS, Excel, Timeplot, TimeSearcher, Google Charts, Tableau Public, Google Fusion Tables, etc. are some tools used to create temporal data visualization.
- **Multidimensional Data Visualization**—In this type of data visualization, numerous dimensions are used to present data. We have pie charts, histograms, bar charts, etc. to exemplify multidimensional data visualization. Many Eyes, Google Charts, Tableau Public, etc. are some tools used to create multidimensional data visualization.
- **Tree/Hierarchical Data Visualization**—Sometimes, data relationships need to be shown in the form of hierarchies. To represent such kind of relationships, we use tree or hierarchical data visualizations. Examples of tree/hierarchical data visualization include hyperbolic tree, wedge-stack graph, etc. Some tools to create hierarchical data visualization are d3, Google Charts, and Network Workbench/Sci2.
- **Network Data Visualization**—It is used to represent data relations that are too complex to be represented in the form of hierarchies. Some examples of network data visualization tools include matrix, node link diagram, hive plot, Pajek, Gephi, NodeXL, VOSviewer, UCINET, GUESS, Network Workbench/Sci2, sigma.js, d3/Protovis, Many Eyes, Google Fusion Tables, etc.

27

Data Visualization with Tableau (Data Visualization-II)

In the previous chapter, you learned about data visualization and its importance in Big Data analytics. You also learned about the various types of tools and techniques used to visualize data. Among the various tools and techniques used for analyzing data, Tableau is the most commonly used software tool that can generate various kinds of visuals for data representation. Various types of Tableau products are available in the market, which include Tableau Desktop, Tableau Server, Tableau Reader, Tableau Public, etc. We have already discussed the basics and the installation process of the Tableau Public tool in the previous chapter. Tableau tools are easy to use and can create complex visualizations from given datasets. Along with this, they involve sharing and filtering features as well. Additionally, you can access multiple file formats and types for presenting different visual patterns, such as graphs, maps, charts, plots, etc.

In this chapter, you learn about the Tableau software, especially the installation and usage of Tableau Desktop and Tableau Public software tools. The chapter also outlines some technical specifications of Tableau and its use in various departments and data environments. You also learn about the Tableau workspace and how to present data visually in Tableau.

SCENARIO

Ms. Rachel Keith, a data analytics professional employed with Argon Technology, has been asked by the organization's marketing head, Mr. Richard Taylor, to provide some samples of data analytics visuals. Mr. Taylor intends to show these samples to a prestigious client of the organization in order to get some quotations. Ms. Keith creates these visuals by using Tableau, which she downloaded from its official website, www.tableau.com. All the knowledge she gathered and all the tasks she performed during the creation of visuals are provided in this chapter.

Introduction to Tableau Software

Tableau products are the most widely used software tools for data visualization. There are various types of Tableau products available in the market. Some of the commonly known products include Tableau Desktop, Tableau Server, Tableau Online, Tableau Reader, and Tableau Public.

One of the most popular applications of Tableau software tools is Tableau Desktop, which provides various facilities to create visualizations. The breakthrough approach used to build the Tableau Desktop tool takes pictures of data and converts them into optimized database queries, which help users in spotting patterns, identifying trends, and deriving logical conclusions and insights.

While working with the Tableau Desktop, the data analyst need not write any code; all the insights can, instead, be discovered by just connecting to the data and following the thoughts that strike the mind naturally. You can easily connect to your data, which is either in the memory or on the server. Tableau Desktop allows you to directly retrieve data from the server or load it in the Tableau data engine from a disk. The speed of Tableau Desktop is as fast as the thoughts of human beings, and everything can be done with drag-and-drop technology.

Tableau Desktop provides options for data sharing in the form of dashboards, which can be used to reflect relationships by highlighting and filtering data. Dashboards can also help you create story line in a guided manner for explaining the insights obtained from data. Moreover, you can use Tableau variants, such as the Tableau Online and Tableau Server tools, for sharing content.

The important features of Tableau software include the following:

- Single-click data analytics in visual form

- In-depth statistical analysis
- Management of metadata
- In-built, top-class data analytic practices
- In-built data engine
- Big Data analytics
- Quick and accurate data discovery
- Business dashboards creation
- Various types of data visualization
- Social media analytics, including Facebook and Twitter
- Easy and quick integration of R
- Business intelligence through mobile
- Analysis of time series data
- Analysis of data from surveys

While using Tableau, you can get all-round support from the Tableau team that offers product support, online training, consulting facilities, certification, etc. The customer service provided by Tableau is measured in terms of customer satisfaction. Tableau software can be used in various industries and data environments. The main industries where Big Data analysis is carried out by using Tableau Desktop include banking, gaming, education, government analytics, healthcare, insurance, manufacturing, telecommunication analytics, etc.

Tableau has primarily been used within the following data environments:

- All data sources
- Amazon redshift
- Excel charts and graphs
- Google analytics
- Google BigQuery
- Hadoop
- HP Vertica
- SAP
- Splunk

Tableau is a useful software tool for data analysis and its graphical representation. It helps to track and keep a record of the Web traffic. An example of analyzing the Web traffic is shown in Figure 27.1:

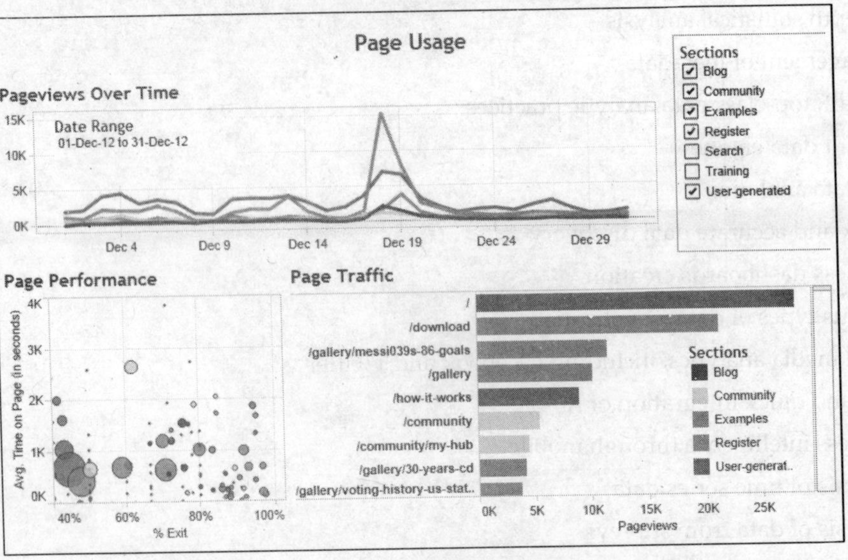

Source: www.tableau.com

Figure 27.1: Analyzing Web Traffic in Tableau

Tableau can help to detect fire hot spots in forests. Figure 27.2 shows an example of it:

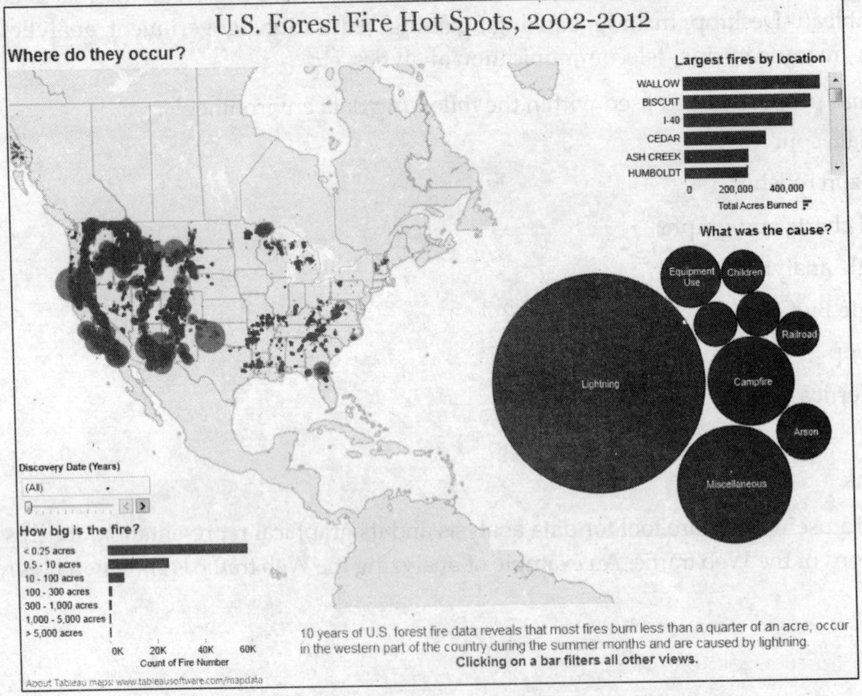

Figure 27.2: Detecting Forest Fire Hot Spots with Tableau

Tableau can display the structure and organization of a sports team. Figure 27.3 shows the organization of a college football team:

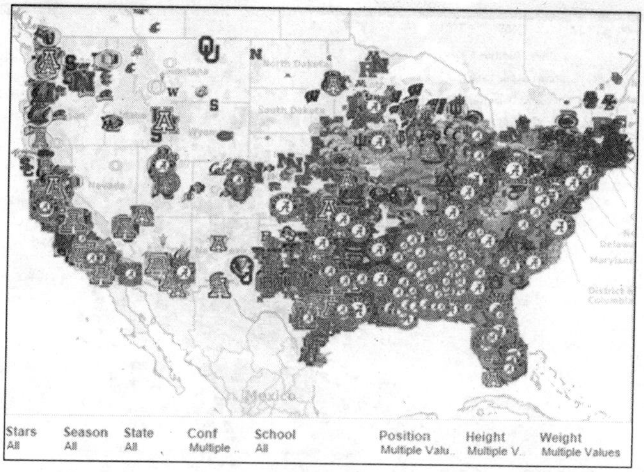

Figure 27.3: Displaying Organization of a College Football Team

Tableau can be used to compare the performance of various business enterprises in the market. Figure 27.4 compares the growth of top 100 entrepreneurs:

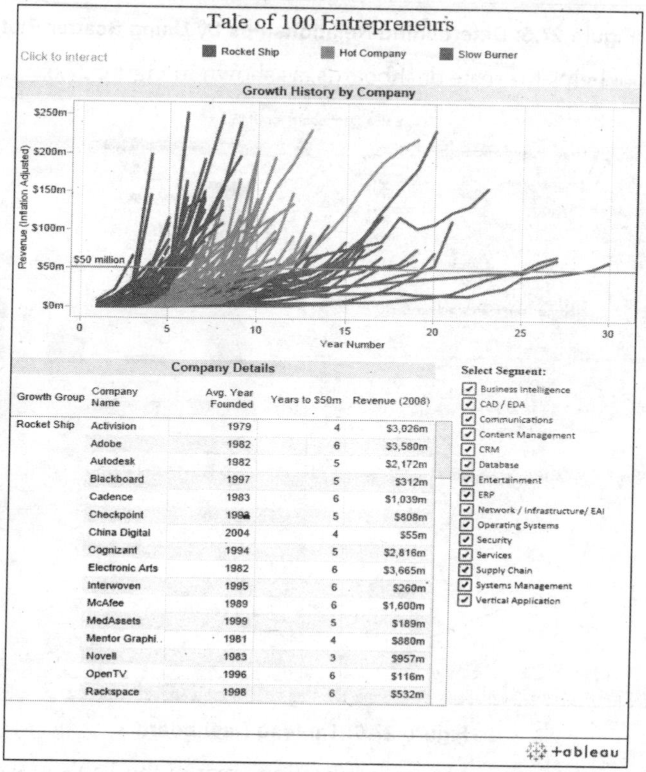

Figure 27.4: Comparing Performance Growth of Top 100 Entrepreneurs

Scatter plots in Tableau help to determine relationships between different elements. An example is shown in Figure 27.5:

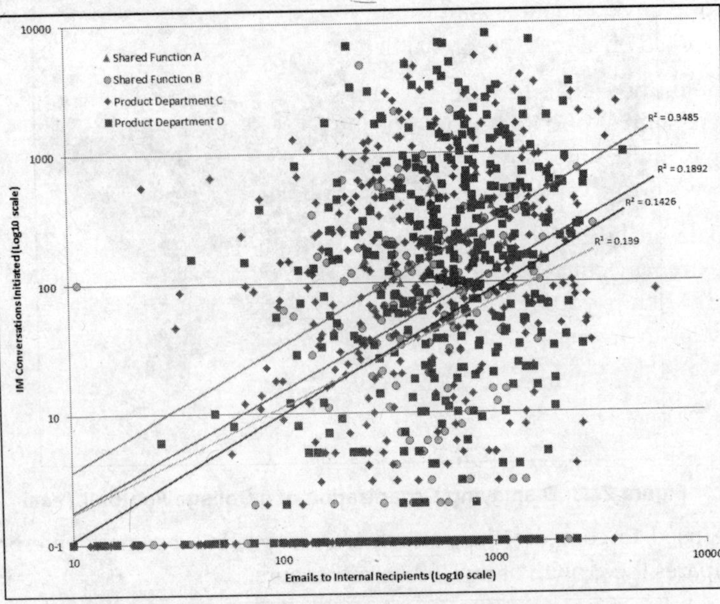

Figure 27.5: Determining Relationships by Using Scatter Plot

Tableau software tool helps to create dashboards, as shown in Figure 27.6:

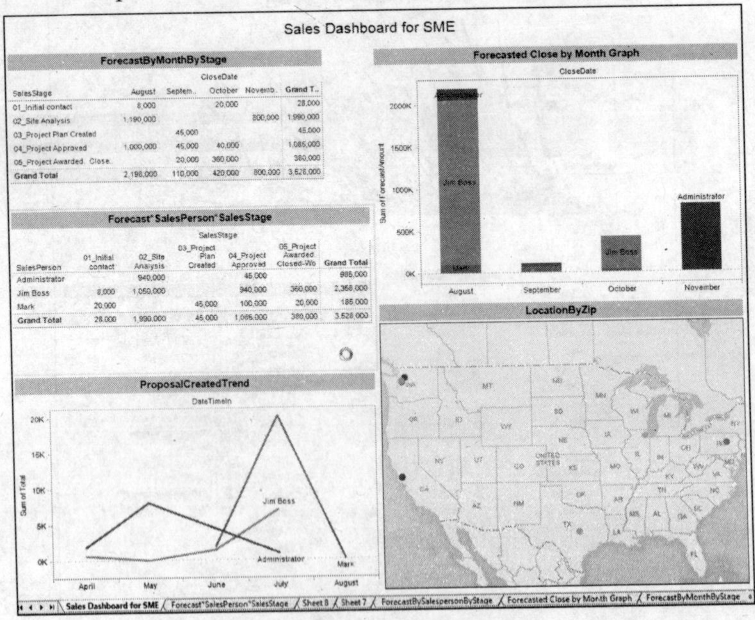

Figure 27.6: Tableau Dashboard

After learning about a few of the various application areas of the Tableau software tool, let's proceed to discuss Tableau Desktop Workspace and its connectivity with data sources.

Tableau Desktop Workspace

Tableau's desktop environment is simple and easy to learn almost for anyone. However, those who have already worked on spreadsheets or other analytical tools would find it even simpler.

It should be noted here that Tableau's website provides a connector that can be downloaded to connect different sources of data listed in the On a Server section of the Tableau Desktop tool's data connection page. It is quite simple to download a connector, and you can install several data connection drivers. Some vendors may ask for a validation license to download their connectors.

The Tableau data analytics tool analyzes data with almost the speed of thought. In other words, Tableau is an extremely efficient tool, which can answer your questions about data analytics quickly. To use Tableau Desktop, you first need to download and install the tool on your computer. Perform the following steps to download and install the Tableau software:

1. Open the following link in a Web browser:

   http://www.tableau.com/products/desktop

   The home page of Tableau desktop will appear, as shown in Figure 27.7:

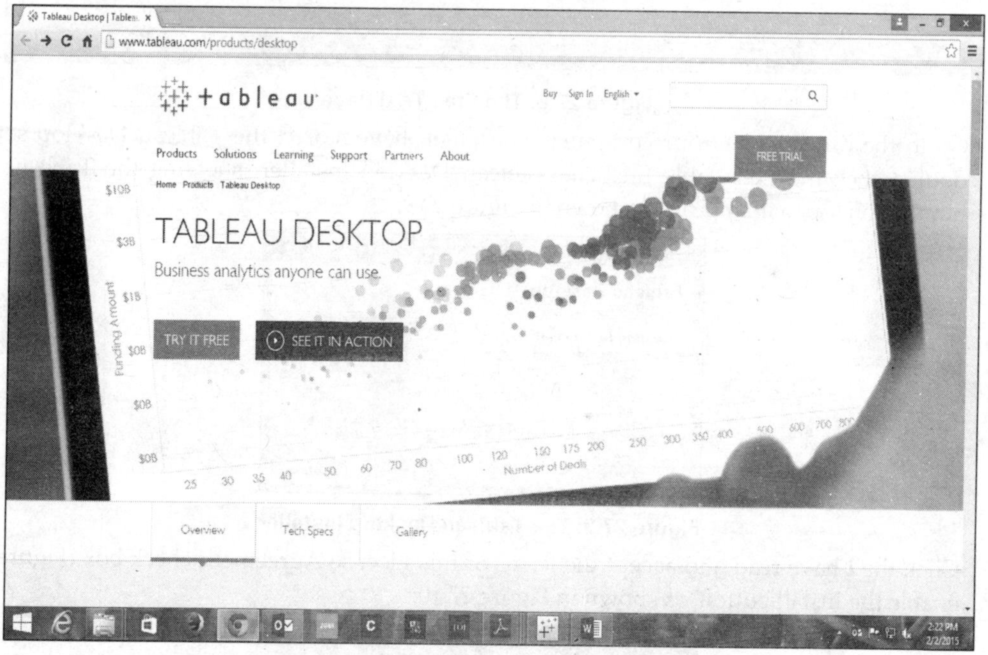

Figure 27.7: The Tableau Desktop Home Page

2. Download the trial version of the Tableau Desktop by clicking the TRY IT FREE button (Figure 27.7). The downloading process will start and the Thanks for choosing a free trial of Tableau Desktop screen appears, as shown in Figure 27.8:

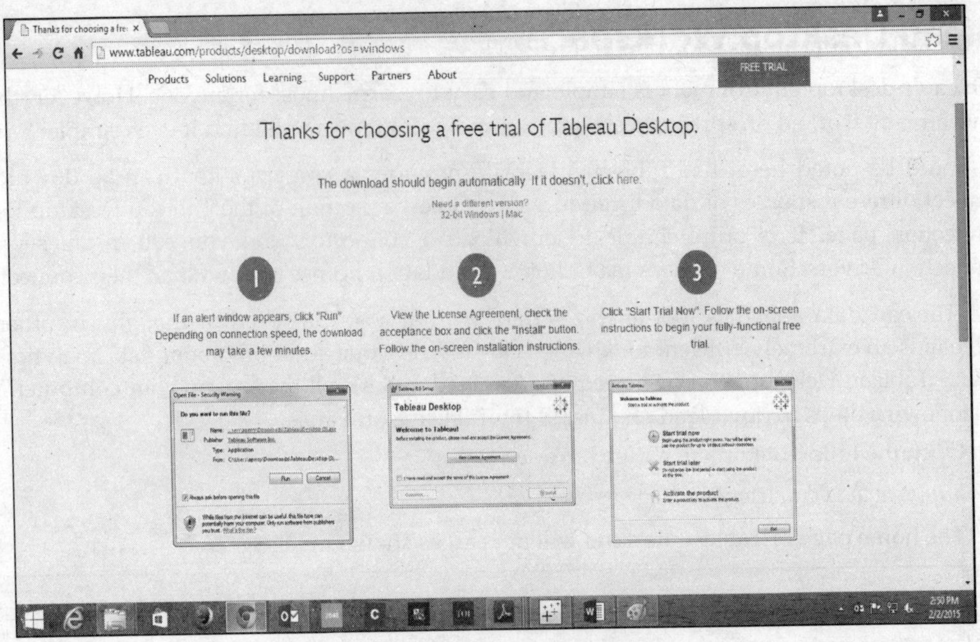

Figure 27.8: The Free Trial Page

3. Go to the directory of your computer where you have stored the Tableau Desktop setup and double click the executable file. The Tableau Desktop installer, showing the Tableau version number on top, will appear, as shown in Figure 27.9:

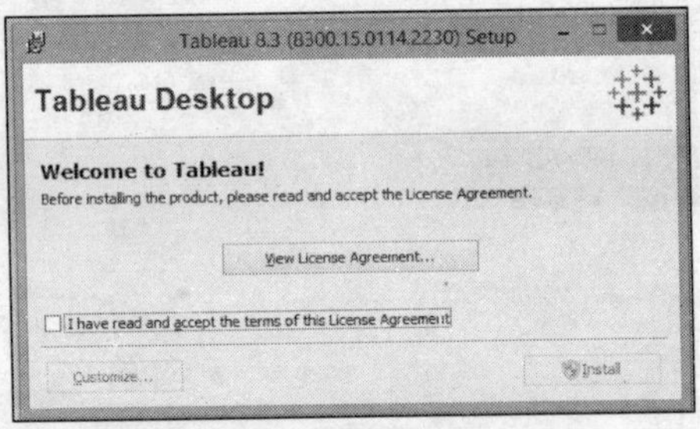

Figure 27.9: The Tableau Desktop Installer

4. Click the I have read and accept the terms of this License Agreement check box (Figure 27.9) to enable the Install button, as shown in Figure 27.10:

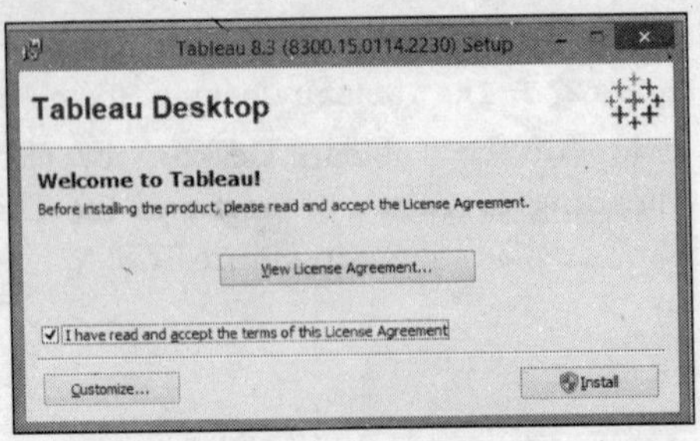

Figure 27.10: Enabling the Install Button

5. Click the Install button to start the installation of the Tableau Desktop. The progress of installation appears, as shown in Figure 27.11:

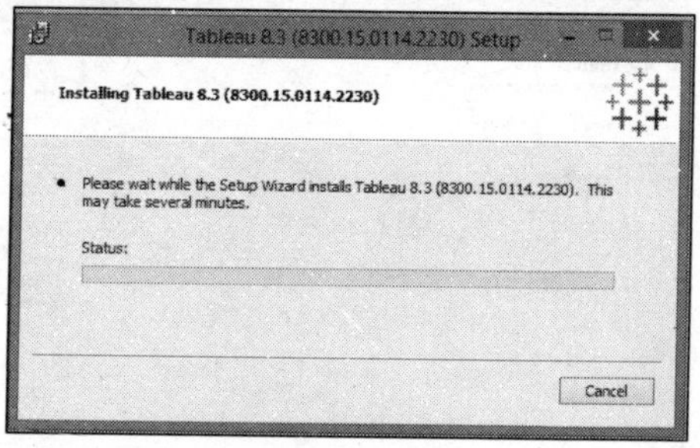

Figure 27.11: Showing the Progress of Tableau Installation

The installation of Tableau gets completed. The Activate Tableau dialog box appears, as shown in Figure 27.12:

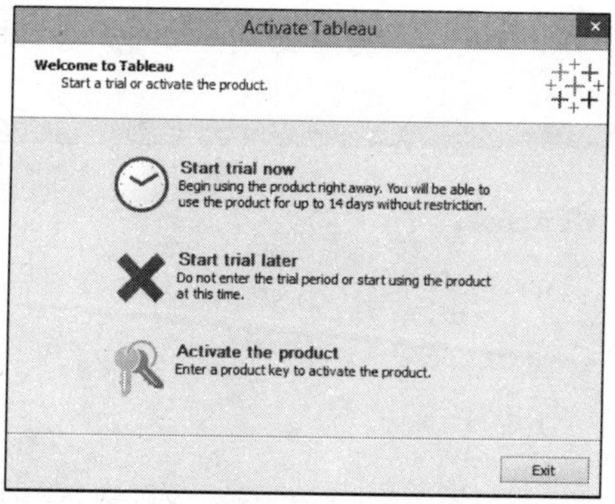

Figure 27.12: The Activate Tableau Dialog Box

The Activate Tableau dialog box contains three options: Start trial now, Start trial later, and activate the product. To activate the product, you require a product key, which needs to be purchased from the Tableau website. However, you are eligible to continue the trial by clicking the Start trial now option.

6. Click the Start trial now option (Figure 27.12). This will ask for registration, as shown in Figure 27.13:

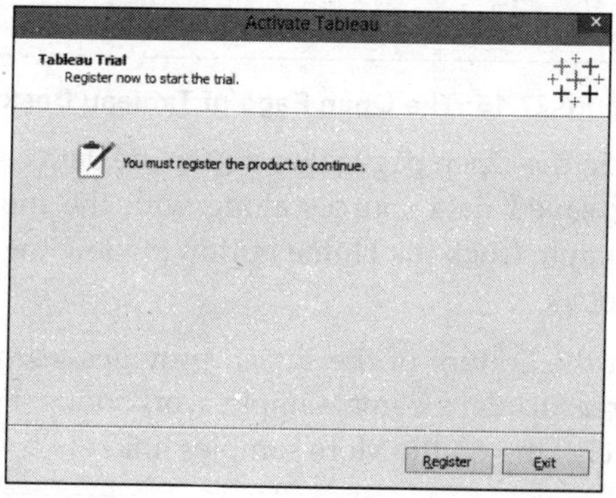

Figure 27.13: The Tableau Trial Dialog Box for Registration

7. Click the Register button to open the registration form and provide all the required details. Figure 27.14 shows the completion of the registration process:

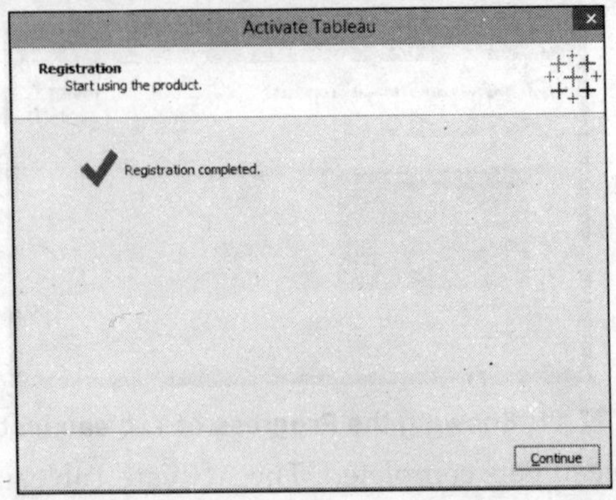

Figure 27.14: The Dialog Box after Completing Registration

Click the Continue button (Figure 27.14). The open page of Tableau tool appears, as shown in Figure 27.15:

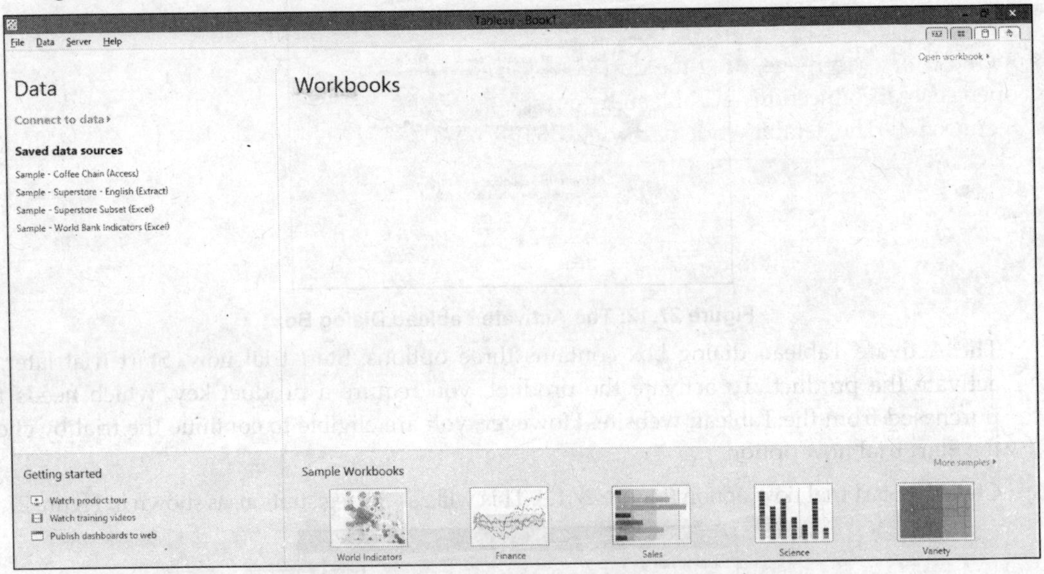

Figure 27.15: The Open Page of Tableau Desktop

The Connect to data button in the Open page takes you to the data connection workspace, where you can see the list of all your saved data sources along with the four sample data sources that are provided by Tableau, by default. Click the Home button to view the Workbooks area. Tableau saves the last opened nine workbooks.

The Getting Started area at the bottom of the screen provides learning and promotional materials. The Sample Workbooks area displays some sample workbooks. For more samples, you can visit Tableau's visual gallery by clicking on the More samples link.

The Tableau's visual gallery is shown in Figure 27.16:

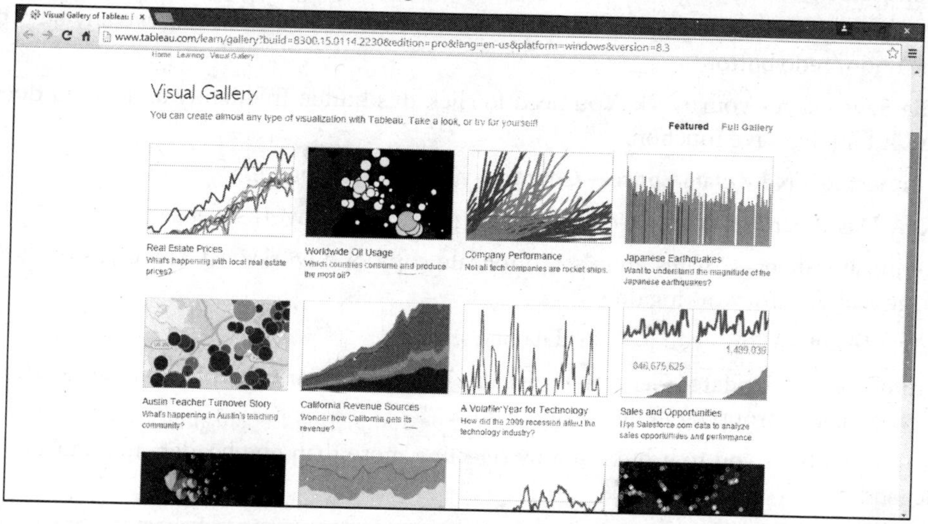

Figure 27.16: Tableau's Visual Gallery

To open a workspace page, drag the desired data source icon and drop it on the Tableau icon. You can open several connections in Tableau by going to the start or data connection page and selecting a new connection. The default workspace view of Tableau is shown in Figure 27.17:

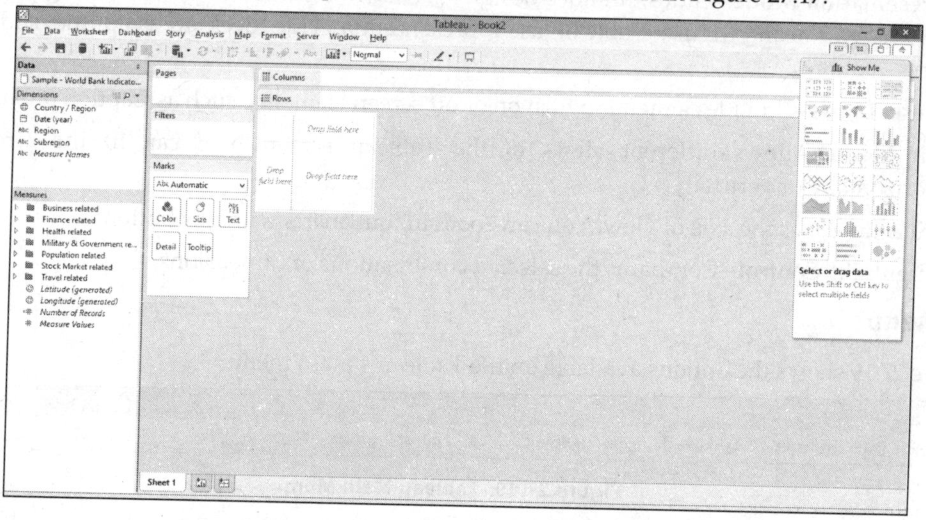

Figure 27.17: Default Workspace View

Toolbar Icons

Tableau is a GUI-oriented drag and drop tool. Figure 27.18 shows the icons present on the Tableau toolbar:

Figure 27.18: Showing Tableau Toolbar

The icons, shown in Figure 27.18, are discussed as follows:

- **Undo/Redo**—Scrolls backward or forward on the screen. You can retrieve any step by clicking the undo/redo button.
- **File Save**—Saves your work. You need to click this button frequently as Tableau does not have the automated save function.
- **Connect to a New Data Source**—Connects you to a data source.
- **New Dashboard or Worksheet**—Adds new pages to your worksheet.
- **Duplicate Sheet**—Creates an exact/duplicate copy of a worksheet as well as of the dashboard page that you are working on.
- **Clear Sheet**—Allows you to clear data of a sheet.
- **Auto/Manual Update**—Generates visuals. It is particularly helpful for large datasets where dragging and dropping items consume time.
- **Group**—Allows you to group data by selecting more than one headers in a table or values in a legend.
- **Pivot Worksheet**—Allows you to create a pivot table on a new worksheet.
- **Ascending/Descending Sort**—Sorts selected items in an ascending or descending order.
- **Label Marks**—Turns on or off screen elements.
- **Presentation Mode**—Hides/unhides design shelves. It is particularly used during presentations where you want to use Tableau as a presentation slide deck to keep the slides of the presentation.
- **Reset Cards**—Provides a menu to turn on or off screen elements, such as Caption or Summary.
- **Fit Menu**—Allows different views of the Tableau screen. You can fit the screen either horizontally or vertically.
- **Fit Axis**—Fixes the axis of view. You can zoom in/out charts with this button.
- **Highlight Control**—Compares the selected combinations of dimensions.

Main Menu

Figure 27.19 shows the options available on the Tableau's main menu:

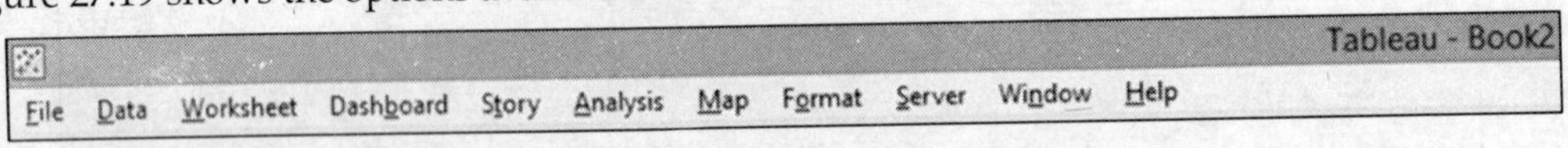

Figure 27.19: Tableau Main Menu

The main menu options, shown in Figure 27.19, are discussed as follows:

- **File**—Contains general functions, such as Open, Save, and Save As. Other functions are Print to pdf and Repository Location Function to review and change the default location of the saved file.
- **Data**—Helps to analyze the tabular data on the Tableau website. The Edit Relationships option is used to blend data when the field names in two data sources are not identical.
- **Worksheet**—Provides options such as Export option, Excel crosstab, and Duplicate as crosstab.

- **Dashboard—**Provides the Actions menu, which is the most important option on the Dashboard menu because all the actions related to Tableau worksheets and dashboards are defined within the Actions menu. The Actions menu is present under the Worksheet menu as well.
- **Story—**Provides the New Story option that is used for explaining the relationship among facts, providing context to certain events, showing the dependency between decisions and outcomes, etc. A story is created to link various events, occurring one after another.
- **Analysis—**Provides the Aggregate Measures and Stack Mark options. To create new measures or dimensions, use Create Calculated Field or Edit Calculated Field.
- **Map—**Provides options to change the color scheme and replace the default maps. You can also import geocoding for custom locations by using the Geocoding menu.
- **Format—**Contains options like Cell Size and Workbook Theme. It is one of the least used menus as you can access most of its features by simply right clicking at the point where you want to make any changes.
- **Server—**Provides options to publish your work on the Tableau server. This menu is available for those who are not using Tableau professionally.
- **Window—**Provides the Bookmark menu, which is used to create .tbm files that can be shared with different users.
- **Help—**Provides options to access Tableau's online manual, training videos, and sample workbooks.

Tableau Server

Tableau Server is a great tool for those who need to upload their files regularly and share their work with others. It can automatically refresh data extracts published in it by the users.

Tableau Server can be accessed either by having a named user license or a core license. A named user license is ideal for smaller deployments (> 150 users), whereas a core license is good for those who need dynamic access. Core license is a cost-effective solution because it drastically reduces administrative tasks.

Tableau Server is compliant with security laws and permits its customers to access tailored reports (as defined by the server administrator). Its user interface is intuitive and provides functions to find and organize reports.

Data Window

Data source in Tableau appears as a data window. You can open different data connections in a single data window. Figure 27.20 shows two different data connections in a single data window:

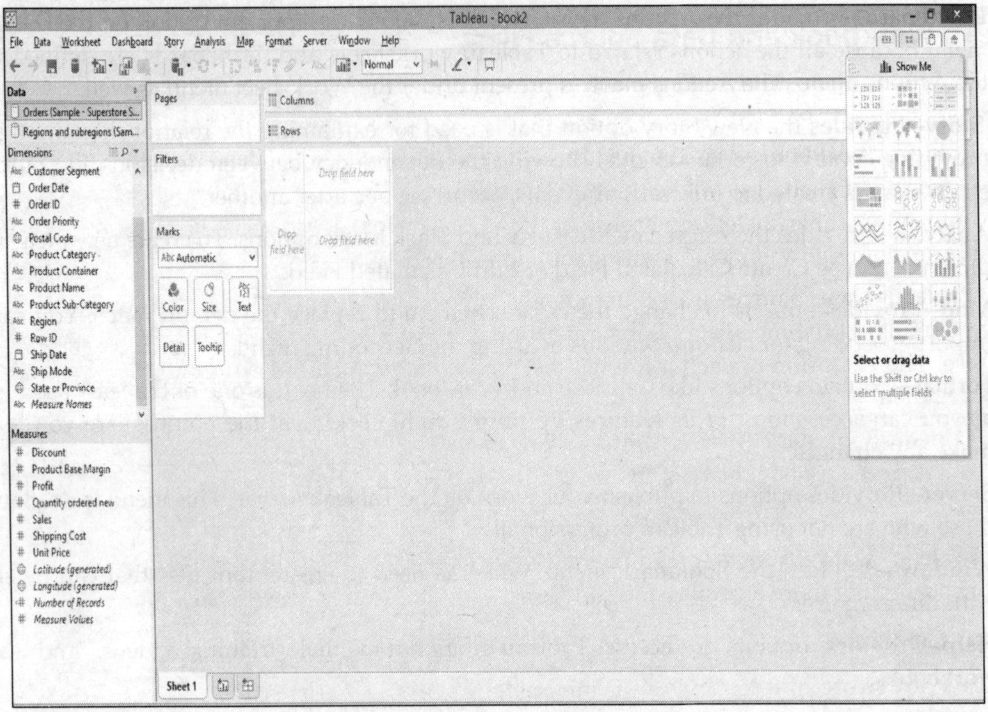

Figure 27.20: Tableau Data Window

In Tableau, visuals are created by automatically assigning and placing data in Rows or Columns shelves. Measuring shelves helps to determine whether a field belongs to the Rows field or the Columns field. If you do not find the automatically placed field correct, you can manually drag it to the right position. Although Tableau places fields at the correct position, sometimes errors may occur when numbers are used to represent dimensions.

Data Types

Tableau stores data sources in data types. If data types are not specified by the user, Tableau assigns them itself. The following are some common data types supported by Tableau:

- Text values
- Date values
- Date and time values
- Numerical values
- Geographical values
- Boolean values

Tableau Workbook and Data Source Files

Depending on their utility and the amount of information they contain, Tableau saves and shares files as:

- **Tableau Workbook—**It is the default save type when you save your work on the desktop. The extension of such files will be `.twb`. The files with extension `.twbx` can be shared with people not having Tableau Desktop license or those who cannot access the data source. The `.twb` files are small in size and include information to visualize data.
- **Tableau Data Source—**If you frequently connect to a specific data source or if you have manipulated the metadata of any data source, saving the file as Tableau data source is of great use. The extension of such a file will be `.tds`, and it includes server address, password, and metadata.
- **Tableau Bookmark—**If you want to share any specific file with others, use Tableau bookmark. You can create a bookmark by following the path—

  `File menu/Window/Bookmark/Create bookmark`. The extension will be `.tbm`.
- **Tableau Data Extract—**It compresses your extracted data and improves performance by incorporating more formulas and functions. The extension of a Tableau Data Extract file is .tde.

Tableau Charts

Tableau can create different types of univariate, bivariate, and multivariate charts, depending on your requirements. The following are some of the common chart types that Tableau can create:

- **Tables—**Tables are an excellent choice of presenting data as they preserve all the information, which in turn minimize the chances of misinterpretation.
- **Scatter Plots—**Scatter plots are used to describe the relationship between two variables. These plots cannot explain a causal relationship.
- **Trend Lines—**Trend lines are used to analyze the relationship between variables as well as predict the future outcome.
- **Bullet Graph—**Bullet graph is just like a bar graph and is generally used in qualitative analysis. It helps in measuring the same variable in different categories.
- **Box Plot—**Box plot represents distribution of data and is used in the comparison of multiple sets of data. It can effectively compute:
  - Minimum and maximum value
  - Median
  - 25% and 75% quartile
- **Treemap—**Treemap is one of the best compact techniques to visualize the part-to-whole relationships as well as hierarchical models.
- **Bubble Charts—**Bubble charts help in categorizing and comparing different values and factors in the data with the help of bubbles.

An example of a bubble chart is shown in Figure 27.21:

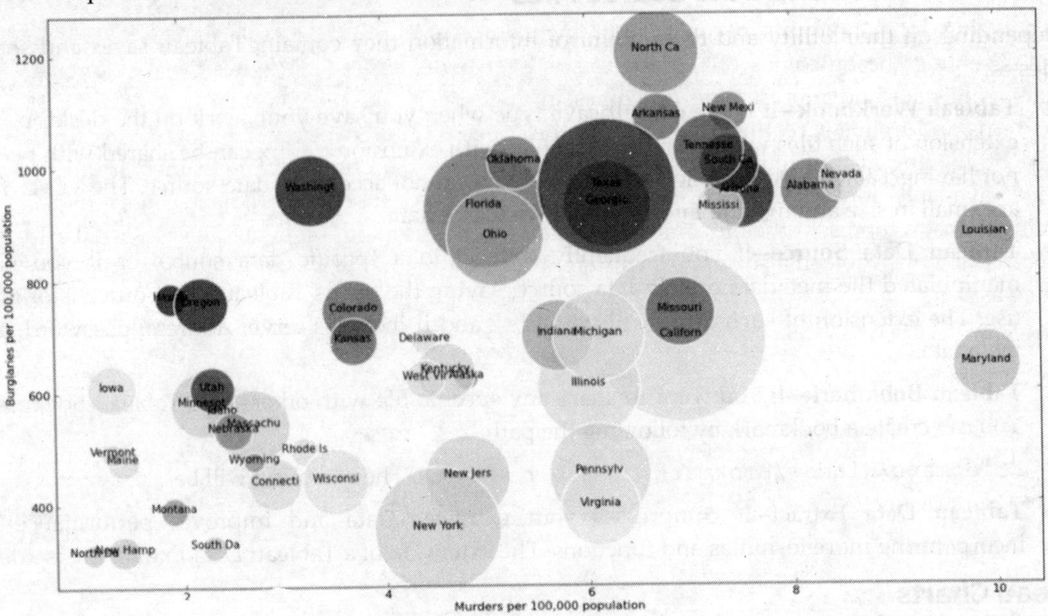

Figure 27.21: Bubble Chart

- **Word Cloud**—Word cloud is an interesting type of visualization that Tableau has incorporated in its 8.0 version. Similar to bubble charts, the words in a word cloud are sized according to the frequency at which they appear in the content.

An example of a word cloud is shown in Figure 27.22:

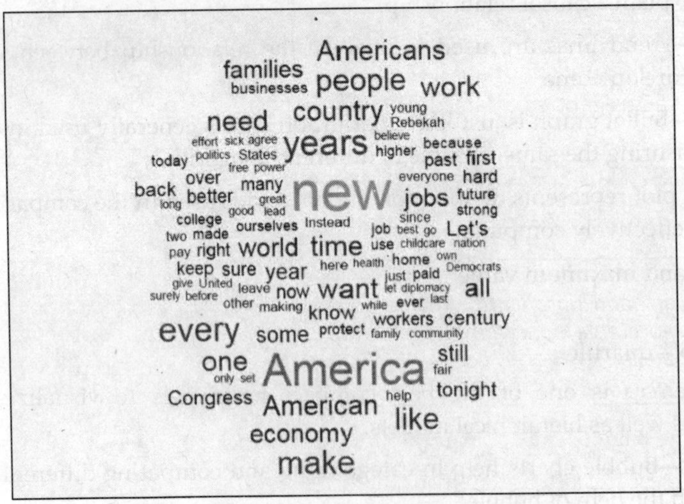

Figure 27.22: Word Cloud

Operations on Data

Analyzing large amounts of data involving complex and intricate patterns is a tedious task. Representing the outcomes of the analysis is even more difficult. We need some techniques for analyzing data and representing outcomes in a systematic manner so that it is easy to interpret patterns and trends. Creating visualizations on a given dataset makes it easy to interpret patterns just by looking at the figures and charts prepared from the dataset. Among the various software tools available for the creation of visualizations and dashboards, Tableau Public is used by statisticians to represent the outcomes of data analysis carried out on large datasets. Similar to other analytical tools, Tableau also supports different types of mathematical and statistical data operations such as:

- Sum
- Average
- Median
- Count
- Count distinct
- Minimum
- Maximum
- Standard deviation
- Standard deviation of a population
- Variance
- Variance of a population
- Attribute
- Dimension

In Tableau, you can also use conditional statement such as if else. Additionally, Tableau permits you to alter the default aggregation of data and change its level.

Data Analytics in Tableau Public

SCENARIO

According to the requirements outlined by Mr. Richard Taylor, Ms. Rachel Keith takes a sample dataset provided with the Tableau Public setup. The dataset is an Excel sheet file named OlympicAthletes_0.xlsx. She uses the data to create some graphs and dashboards on Tableau Public software that she earlier downloaded and installed on her Windows 8.1 operating system. The steps performed by Ms. Keith in creating visuals are discussed as follows.

1. Open the Home page of the Tableau Public tool.
2. Select the Connect to Data option from the Data menu to connect to the given dataset, as shown in Figure 27.23:

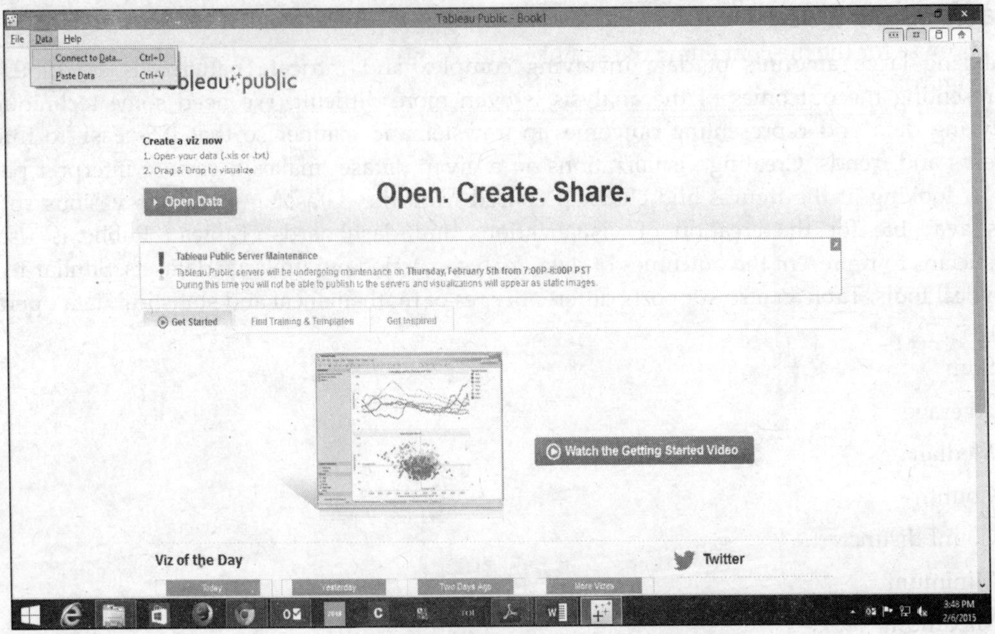

Figure 27.23: Connecting to Data in Tableau Public

A window appears with the Connect frame on its left-hand side (Figure 27.24). You can also establish the connection to the data by using the Open Data button (Figure 27.23).

3. Select the file type in which the data is stored from the Connect frame. In our case, we have selected Microsoft Excel, as shown in Figure 27.24:

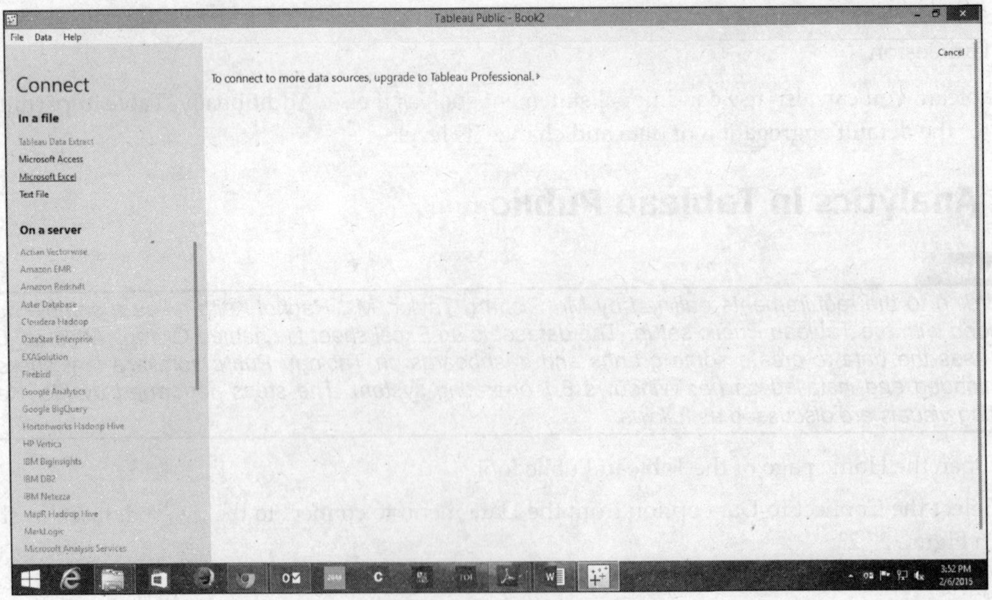

Figure 27.24: Selecting the File Type

The Open dialog box appears (Figure 27.25).

4. Browse for the file containing the sample data used by Ms. Keith and double click it, as shown in Figure 27.25:

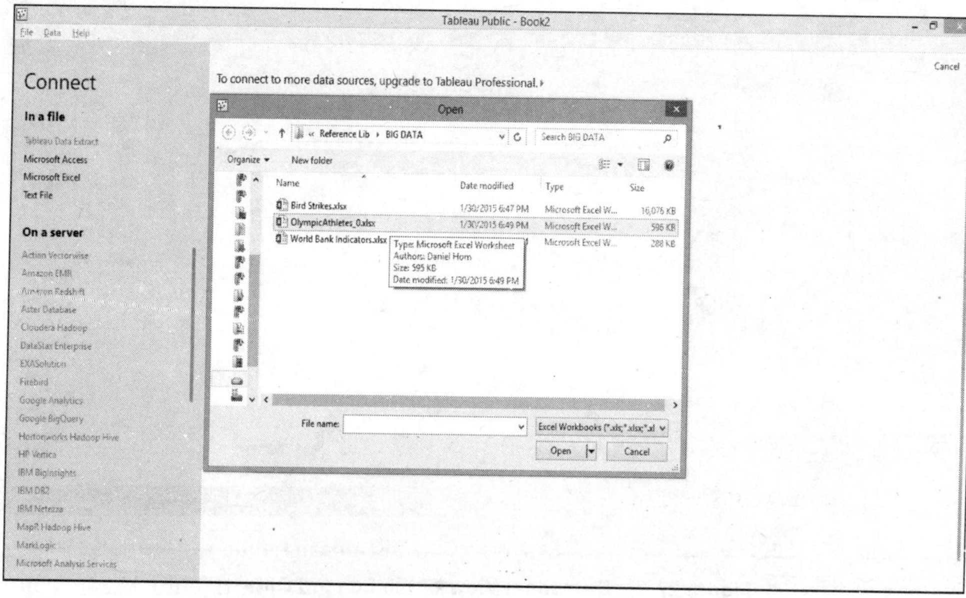

Figure 27.25: Selecting a Particular File for Analysis in Tableau

The data connection establishment process completes after the file has been selected. The Tableau Public screen appears, as shown in Figure 27.26:

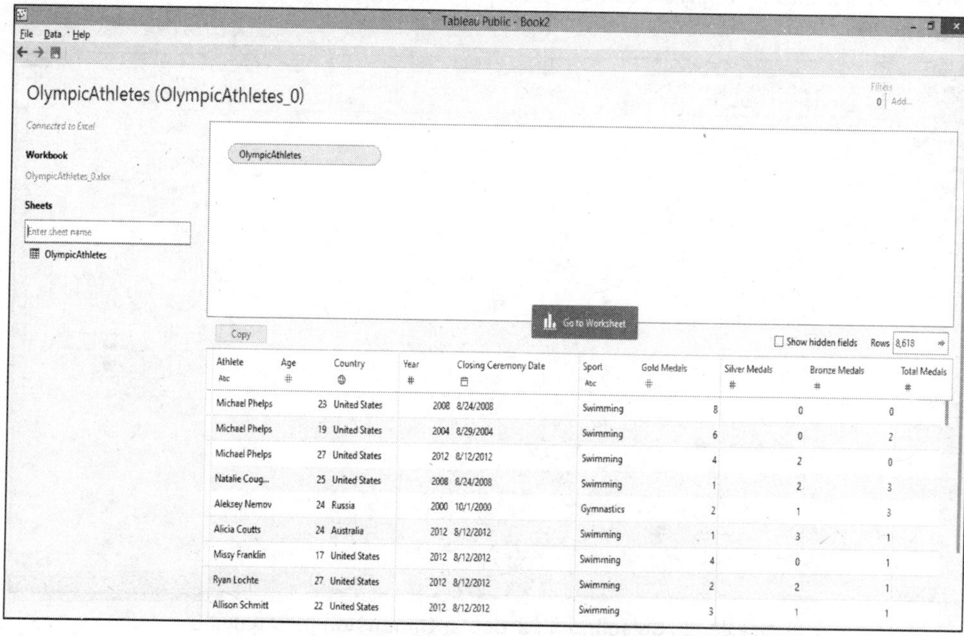

Figure 27.26: Tableau Public Screen after Data Connection

5. Click the Go to Worksheet button (Figure 27.26) to get the data in the Worksheet form, as shown in Figure 27.27:

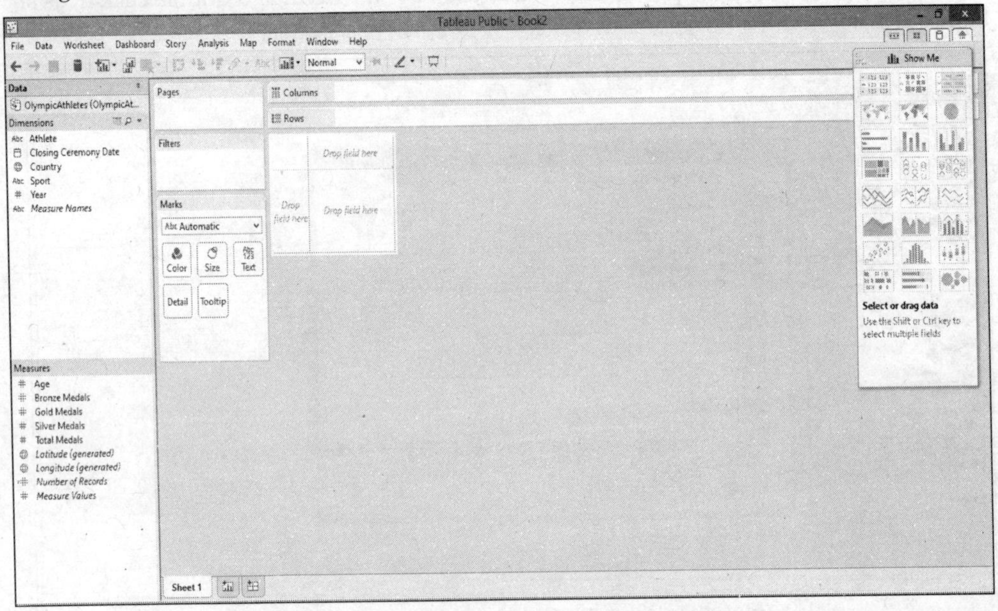

Figure 27.27: Datasheet View of the Loaded Data

Now, we can use the datasheet view of the data in Tableau to develop various kinds of visuals.

6. Drag a dimension from the left-hand sidebar and drop it in the Rows or Columns field for analysis. In our case, we have dropped the Sport dimension in the Columns field, as shown in Figure 27.28:

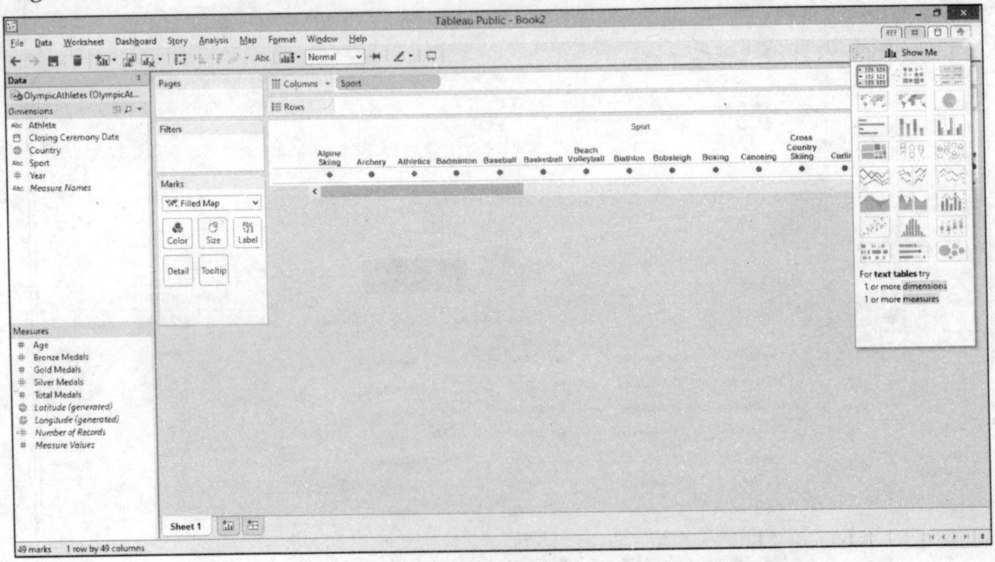

Figure 27.28: Selecting a Particular Dimension for Analysis

You can add more dimensions to the Columns field. In our case, we have added the Year dimension, as shown in Figure 27.29:

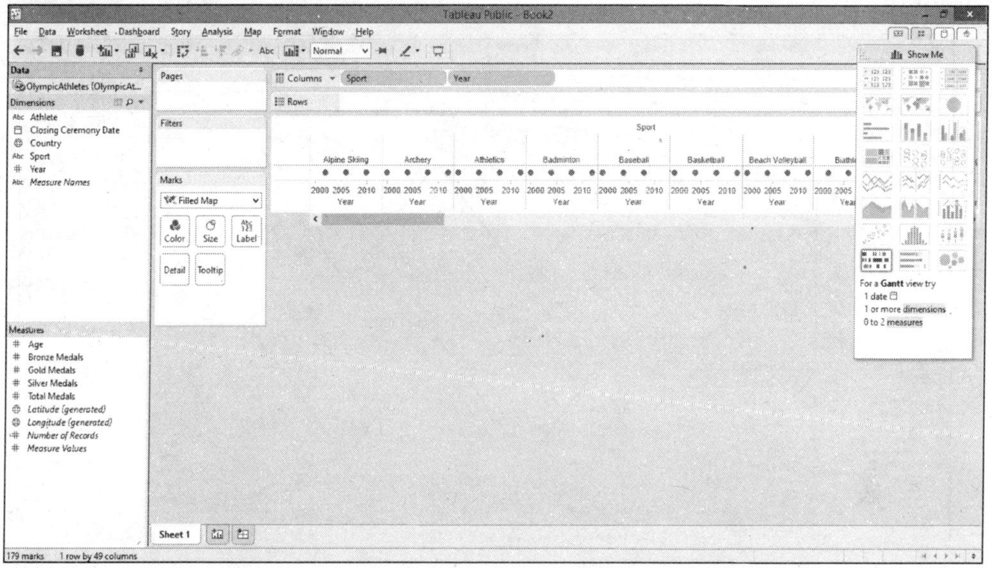

Figure 27.29: Adding More Dimensions for Analysis

7. Specify particular analytical measures by dragging individual dimensions from the Measures section and dropping them in the Rows field. In our case, we have selected Total Medals dimension, as shown in Figure 27.30:

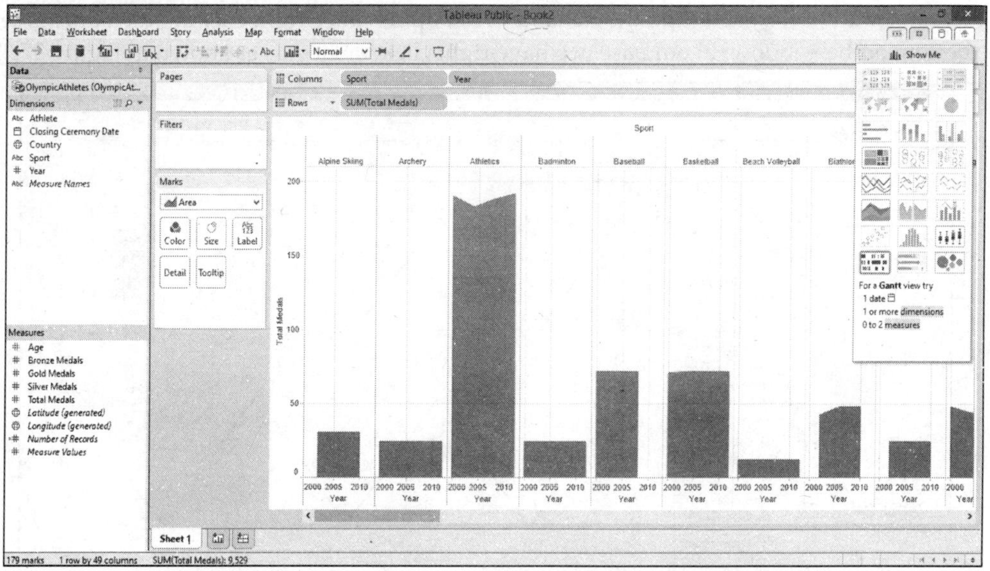

Figure 27.30: Showing a Graph for Selected Dimensions

8. Select a different kind of chart from the Show Me selection box, appearing on the upper right corner, to view a different pattern. In our case, we have selected the lines chart, as shown in Figure 27.31:

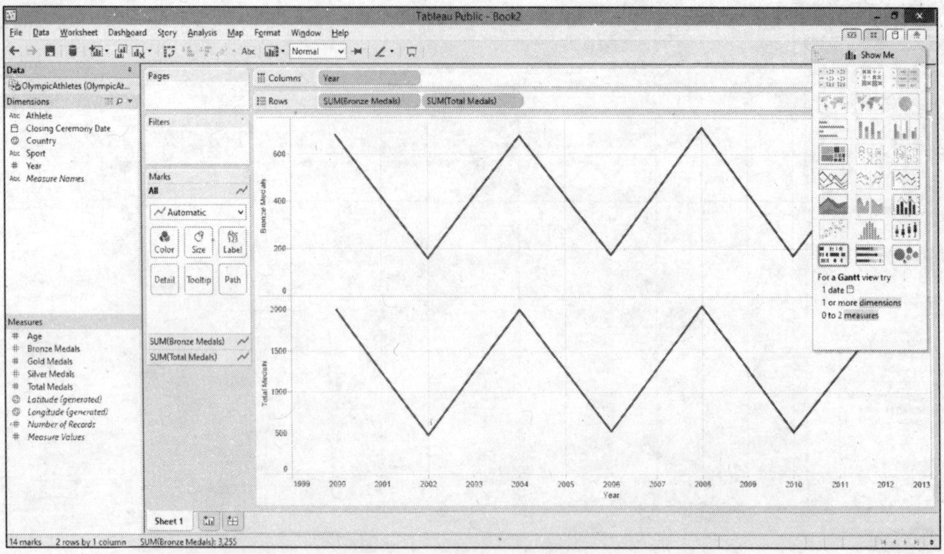

Figure 27.31: Line Chart for Selected Dimensions

NOTE

A line chart cannot be drawn for dimensions involving more than one column.

9. Rename the sheet by selecting the Rename Sheet option after right clicking the panel given at the bottom of the window. In our case, we have right clicked Sheet 1, as shown in Figure 27.32:

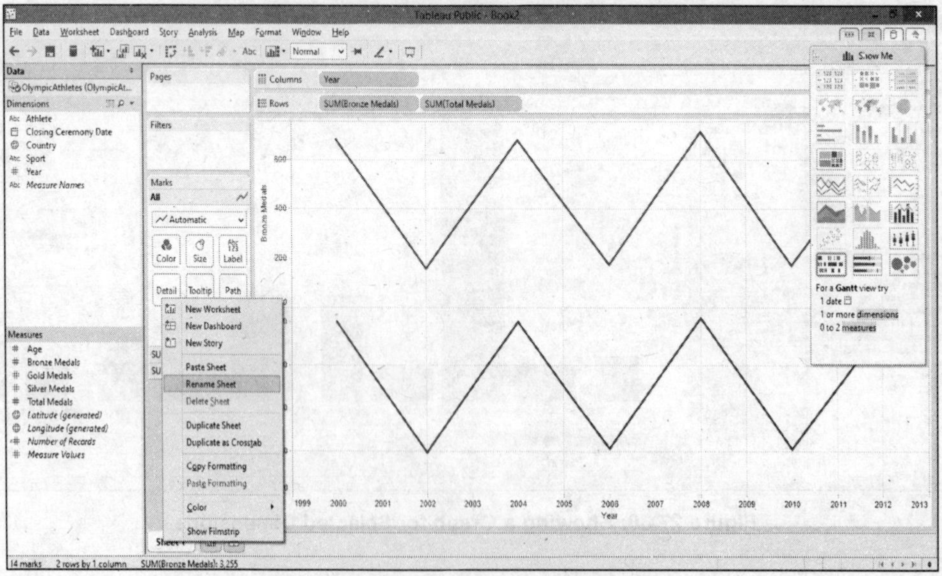

Figure 27.32: Renaming the Sheet

You can create more visuals, including bar chart, discrete line chart, bubble chart, etc., by clicking different options from the Show Me selection box.

10. Create a bar chart for the bronze medals won by different countries over the years by clicking the bar chart option, as shown in Figure 27.33:

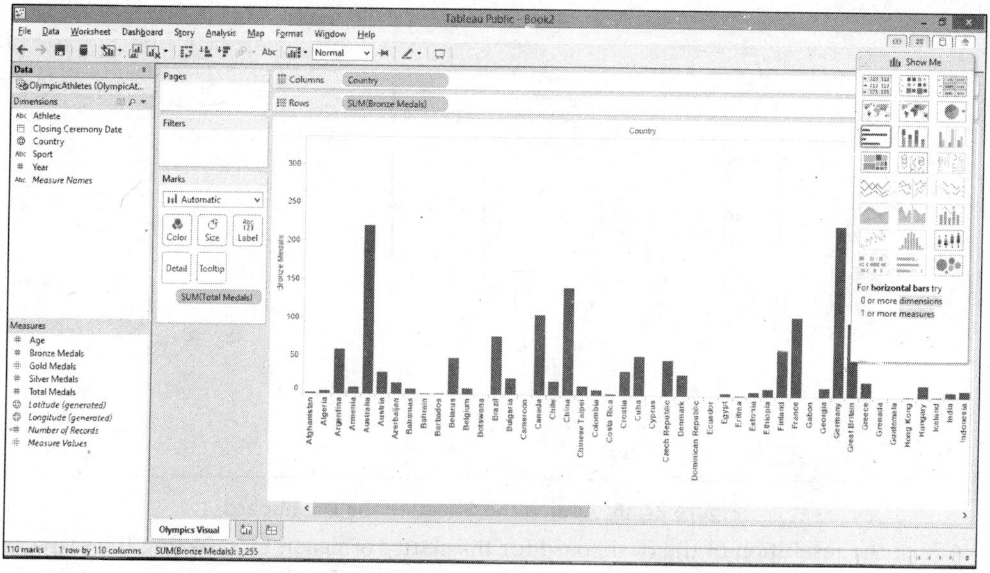

Figure 27.33: Creating a Bar Chart for Selected Dimensions

11. In Tableau, it is possible to create dashboards. To create a dashboard for your analysis, you need to click the New Dashboard icon, the right-most icon given on the status bar of the Tableau Public window. A new dashboard appears, showing the sheets of the dataset being used, as shown in Figure 27.34:

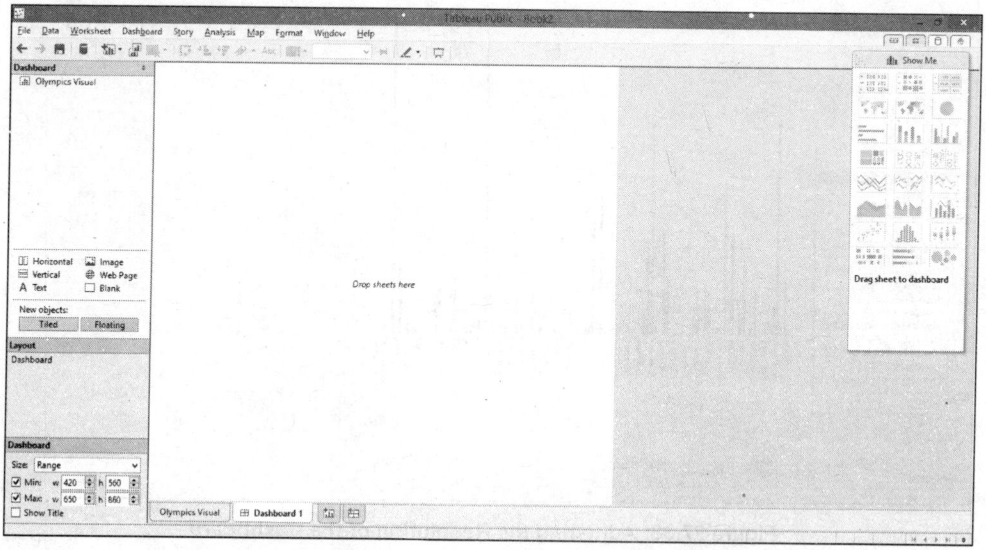

Figure 27.34: Showing the Dashboard with the Selected Data

12. Drag the sheet from the left-hand sidebar and drop it on the dashboard, as shown in Figure 27.35:

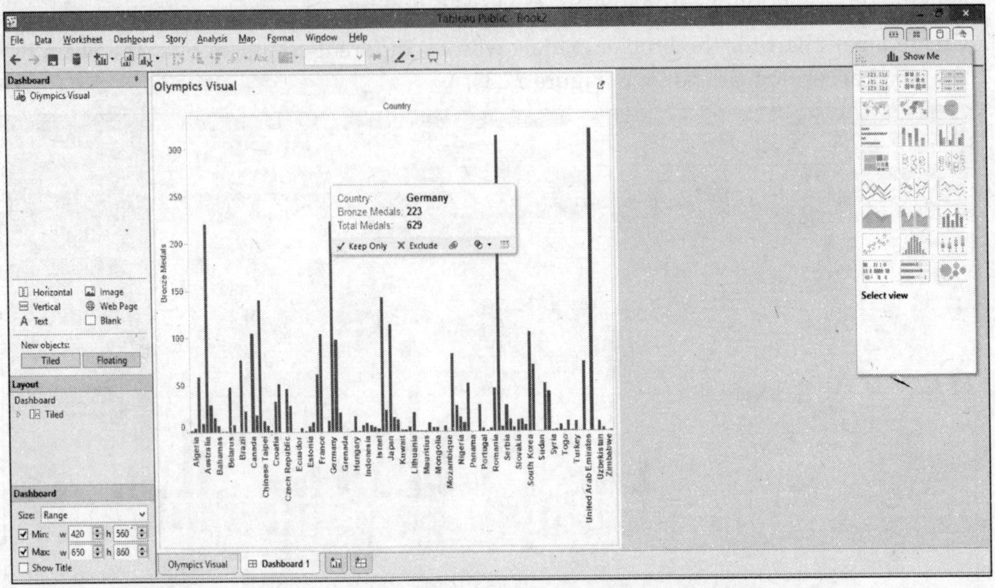

Figure 27.35: Adding the Sheet on the Dashboard

13. Adjust the resolution of the dashboard for the clarity of vision by selecting the respective range of the resolution from the Dashboard section on the lower left corner, as shown in Figure 27.36:

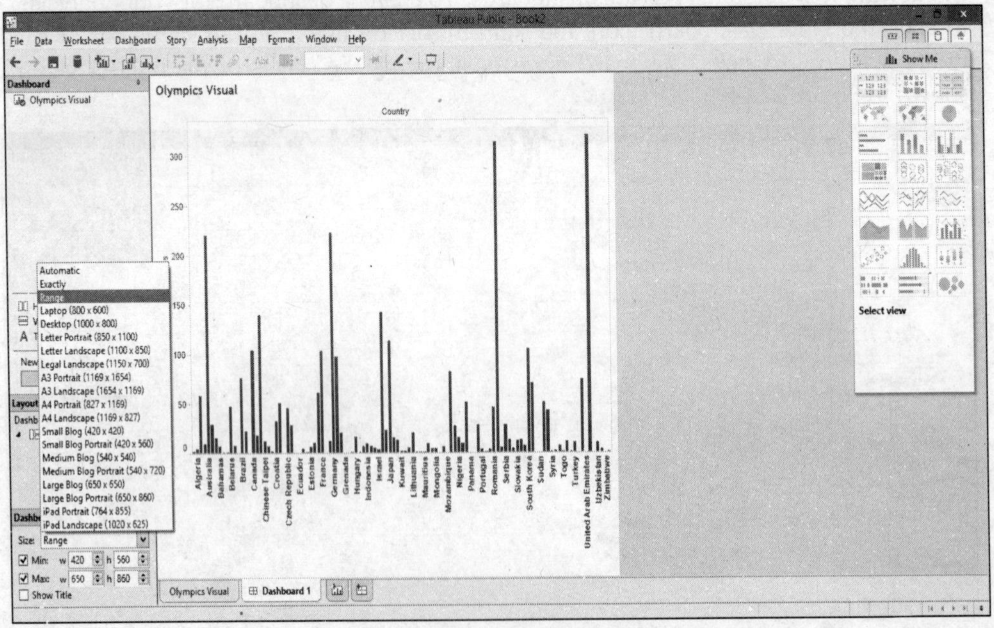

Figure 27.36: Adjusting the Resolution of the Dashboard

EXHIBIT 1: MainPower – From Spreadsheets to Speed and Agility with Tableau

While MainPower brought power to the people, its data analysis needed an extra spark. Data was siloed and team members spent time determining the true numbers rather than making decisions. Identifying that its previous data analysis system was time-consuming, slow, and cumbersome, MainPower turned to Tableau for a centralised solution to increase business efficiency and clarity of information.

Today with Tableau MainPower has:

- Improved efficiencies with better insight into maintenance scheduling
- Cut hours from data analysis timelines
- Provided self-service, intuitive data analysis that employees have embraced

For nearly 100 years, MainPower has been distributing electricity to homes and businesses across the North Canterbury region in New Zealand. It distributes electricity to over 37,000 customers via 4,873 kilometers of overhead lines and underground cables across an area of almost 12,000 square kilometers. The company continually strives to provide a safe, secure and reliable service, recognised by its community as a leading regional electricity distribution company. One of 29 electricity distribution companies in New Zealand, MainPower is a community-owned company that owns and manages a regional and urban electricity distribution network. The company is also responsible for overseeing, on behalf of electricity retailers, the supply of electricity for customers. MainPower ensures the safety, reliability and security of these networks.

Sustainability-savvy, MainPower constantly seeks opportunities to take advantage of renewable resources. The organisation focuses on expanding and upgrading its distribution network to keep up with the demand for electricity supply while preserving the existing network. "We're relatively small but like to think we're powerful," says Sean Fahey, MainPower Database Administrator (DBA). "We've got around 180 employees including the field staff out on the road servicing the poles and wires."

Difficulty deciphering data

To maintain its standards for excellence in customer service, MainPower analyses a wide scope of data from varying sources. Most information is sourced through a GIS system to map all assets with coordinates. The organisation also employs Tech One, an ERP system. The electricity provider began to see limitations in the way it collected, viewed and understood data, as monitoring extensive data sets manually can be cumbersome and time-consuming. "We were using numerous huge spreadsheets on seemingly endless sheets of paper in tiny font. You can imagine exactly why that was an issue," says Fahey with a laugh. "Exporting and analysing spreadsheets was slow and tedious with the methodology offering little flexibility." Fahey reports each unique data set could include up to 40 attributes.

The type of information collected is crucial to operations. MainPower collected data spanning from maintenance history and reports to power ratings, outages and voltages, and customer records. Even New Zealand's flora and fauna have their place in MainPower's knowledge banks—trees are often responsible for power outages, falling on lines during storms or strong winds. "We were experiencing an influx of data from each source. Our analysis method simply couldn't keep up," says Fahey.

MainPower's data was often siloed—it didn't have the chance to 'speak' to other sets.

"The information we were gathering tended to be quite scattered," says Stuart Wilson, MainPower's Network Manager of Development. "We wanted to reduce conflicts within the organisation because at that stage we had everyone looking at data sets from different perspectives; there was no unity of information, methodology or centralised depository." "We also feared that important connections between sets were being overlooked. We simply had no way of compiling and easily viewing data sets collected across different departments and maintenance history." Double-handling specific sets of data also hindered business efficiency and diluted employees' capacity to concentrate on other tasks, with several sets of eyes viewing the same spreadsheets but interpreting them to suit individual needs.

From spreadsheets to speed and agility

While spreadsheets certainly capture a wealth of information, MainPower soon learned they are less than optimal for presenting and understanding trends and patterns. The system was leaving information static and siloed while data analysis was slow and impacted business efficiency. MainPower started to build a data warehouse to make the data held in multiple systems centralised, useful and accessible. "We attended a series of seminars held by independent consultancy Montage to look into business intelligence solutions," explains Fahey. "At one of these events Montage presented six BI solutions and the standout was certainly Tableau." We entered into discussions with Montage that very night, keen to learn whether Tableau could improve our operations."

In further meetings, the Montage team explained that Tableau was renowned for its visualisations and analytics offerings, mentioning the software would allow MainPower employees to compile and share data visualisations and dashboards in an easy-to-understand environment. "Tableau seemed to tick all the boxes and we were optimistic it could assist with some of the challenges we had been facing. We were excited to give it a go," says Fahey. Progressing with Tableau Desktop, Montage worked with MainPower to create a pilot program in order to ensure the solution was able to meet the company's needs. This was then complemented by a further targeted statement of work, using best-of-breed solutions (which could be built on later), to present to MainPower's executives. "The use of MainPower's real-time data in that initial presentation opened our eyes to the true power of the software," says Fahey.

After successful trials, Tableau indeed proved to be the optimum solution for MainPower. Over the next few weeks, Montage worked closely with internal teams to integrate the software into the organisation's pre-existing environment. The setup and installation process was streamlined and easy, with a representative from Montage available every step of the journey.

"Chip Felton from Montage has been great. The deployment was easy and he comes in a few days a month to answer our questions and ensure everything is running smoothly. He's available for support when we're trying to get our head around new aspects of the software," says Wilson. "Although we haven't had to call upon it yet, it's also nice to know we can contact Tableau's internal support team at any time."

Once the initial process of connecting existing data collection points to flow through Tableau was complete, staff showed enthusiasm for sinking their teeth into the program. "We found that no matter what the department, our employees are able to pick up Tableau quickly and effectively, with a little assistance from Montage. We now have four or five staff regularly using the software."

A powerful perception: saving time and money

After the first 12 months of MainPower's journey with Tableau, the company can see the value of a cohesive solution. Improved speed-to-insight is one significant benefit. "We've been able to cut down on the hours spent analysing data; our employees are no longer doubling up to look at the same information because it's centralised."

Compiling exhaustive quantities of data has also become more efficient. "The input doesn't seem so much like an avalanche anymore. It's certainly a refreshing change that several sets of eyes can easily explore data sets that relate to them," Wilson says. "Previously, I might have been the only one looking at a data set, because I put it together and was probably better equipped to understand it. Now we have four or five other team members who can get more involved and view and understand information that relates to them," Wilson says. Also, now that data sets from different teams can be blended in a single view, employees have developed a new perspective on their data. "We've uncovered some unexpected insights through the new software, simply because now we're able to join data from different sources, linking it together to ask questions we weren't previously able to," says Fahey. These new connections especially highlight where data collection is lacking or of poor quality. Another key observation has been mapping maintenance issues. Information can now be displayed on a geographical map, allowing MainPower to reorganise and optimise its maintenance schedules for improved physical infrastructure.

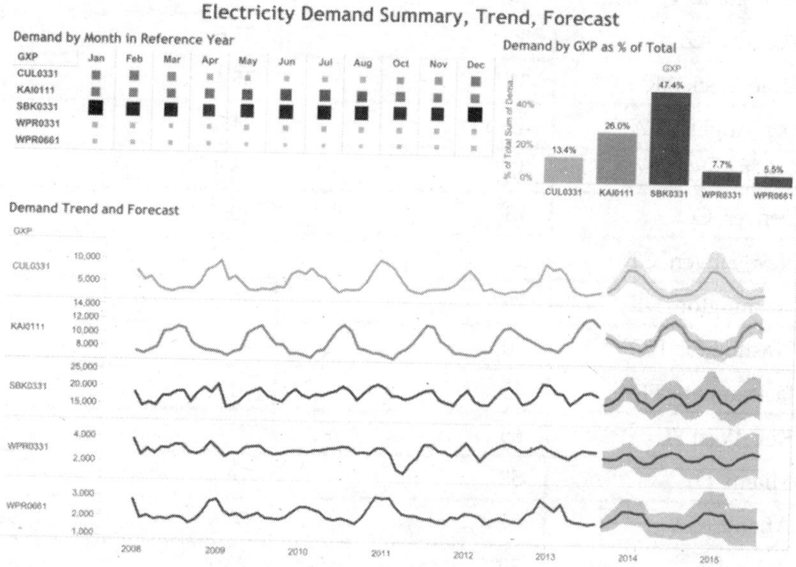

"Through this, we were able to see problem areas on a map and prioritise which jobs need to be attended first," says Wilson. "It also meant we could group work in one particular area to make sure it all happens in the same work package in the same year. This saw us save time and money as well being much more efficient."

Finally, Fahey applauds the user experience and ease of implementation Tableau has provided. "One thing that stands out for me is Tableau's not an engineering tool, it's not a financial tool and it's not even an IT tool." It's something that is easily understood, everyone can implement it in their work. Rather than buying separate tools we're able to use software that works for all employees within the company. Tableau has been more helpful than we could have imagined.

Source: https://www.tableau.com/learn/stories/mainpower-spreadsheets-speed-and-agility-tableau

Using Visual Controls in Tableau Public

Tableau Public software provides a number of controls for creating visualizations for a given dataset For example, we are taking a sample dataset for the temperature of some cities. The sample dataset is stored in an excel sheet, named `city_temp data.xls`, which contains certain information that includes the city name in the `City` column, average temperature of the city in the month of January in the `JanTemp` column, and latitude and longitude values in the `Lat` and `Long` columns. You can connect to this data in Tableau in the same way as you did earlier to load the excel sheet data. The dataset, in our case, appears as shown in Table 27.1:

Table 27.1: Sample Dataset Containing Average City Temperature

City	JanTemp	Lat	Long
Mobile AL	44	31.2	88.5
Montgomery AL	38	32.9	86.8
Phoenix AZ	35	33.6	112.5
Little_Rock AR	31	35.4	92.8
Los_Angeles CA	47	34.3	118.7
San_Francisco CA	42	38.4	123
Denver CO	15	40.7	105.3
New_Haven CT	22	41.7	73.4
Wilmington DE	26	40.5	76.3
Washington DC	30	39.7	77.5
Jacksonville FL	45	31	82.3
Key_West FL	65	25	82
Miami FL	58	26.3	80.7
Atlanta GA	37	33.9	85
Boise ID	22	43.7	117.1

Table 27.1: Sample Dataset Containing Average City Temperature

City	JanTemp	Lat	Long
Chicago IL	19	42.3	88
Indianapolis IN	21	39.8	86.9
Des_Moines IA	11	41.8	93.6
Wichita KS	22	38.1	97.6
Louisville KY	27	39	86.5
New_Orleans LA	45	30.8	90.2
Portland ME	12	44.2	70.5
Baltimore MD	25	39.7	77.3
Boston MA	23	42.7	71.4
Detroit MI	21	43.1	83.9
Minneapolis MN	2	45.9	93.9
St_Louis MO	24	39.3	90.5
Helena MT	8	47.1	112.4
Omaha NE	13	41.9	96.1
Concord NH	11	43.5	71.9
Atlantic_City NJ	27	39.8	75.3
Albuquerque NM	24	35.1	106.7
Albany NY	14	42.6	73.7
New_York NY	27	40.8	74.6
Charlotte NC	34	35.9	81.5
Raleigh NC	31	36.4	78.9
Bismarck ND	0	47.1	101
Cincinnati OH	26	39.2	85
Cleveland OH	21	42.3	82.5
Oklahoma_City OK	28	35.9	97.5
Portland OR	33	45.6	123.2
Harrisburg PA	24	40.9	77.8
Philadelphia PA	24	40.9	75.5
Charleston SC	38	33.3	80.8
Nashville TN	31	36.7	87.6
Amarillo TX	24	35.6	101.9

Table 27.1: Sample Dataset Containing Average City Temperature			
City	**JanTemp**	**Lat**	**Long**
Galveston TX	49	29.4	95.5
Houston TX	44	30.1	95.9
Salt_Lake_City UT	18	41.1	112.3
Burlington VT	7	45	73.9
Norfolk VA	32	37	76.6
Seattle WA	33	48.1	122.5
Spokane WA	19	48.1	117.9
Madison WI	9	43.4	90.2
Milwaukee WI	13	43.3	88.1
Cheyenne WY	14	41.2	104.9

We are using the Tableau Public UI to show how visual controls are applied on the given dataset to create visualizations. When you are using visual controls in Tableau Public, the window with the connected data appears, as shown in Figure 27.37:

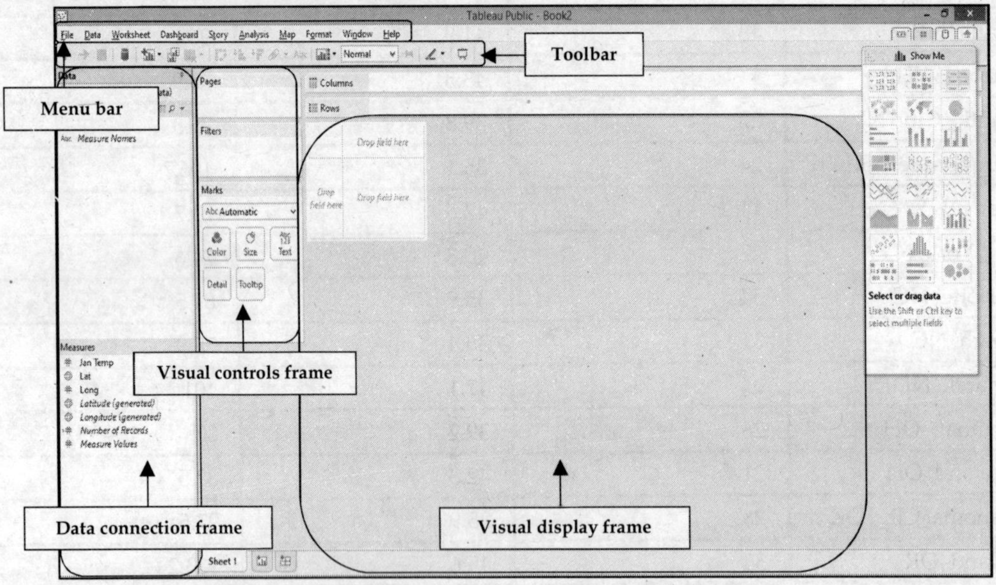

Figure 27.37: Window after Connecting to Data

The window contains different sections that include menu bar, toolbar, data connection frame (showing dimensions and measures), visual controls frame (showing pages, filters, and marks), and visual display frame. In addition, we have four control options that are used to direct the flow and visual representation of data. We have already studied about menu bar, toolbar, and the data connection frame. Now, let's take a look at how we can use the elements of the visual controls frame.

We need to first create visualization by using some fields. Usually, when you double click a dimension, the Tableau software tries to place the values in the appropriate fields deciding by itself whether a value belongs to the Columns field or the Rows field. You can also manually drag and drop values in the desired fields. Now, double click the City tab from the data connection frame. A map (plotted with the help of longitude and latitude values) appears, as shown in Figure 27.38:

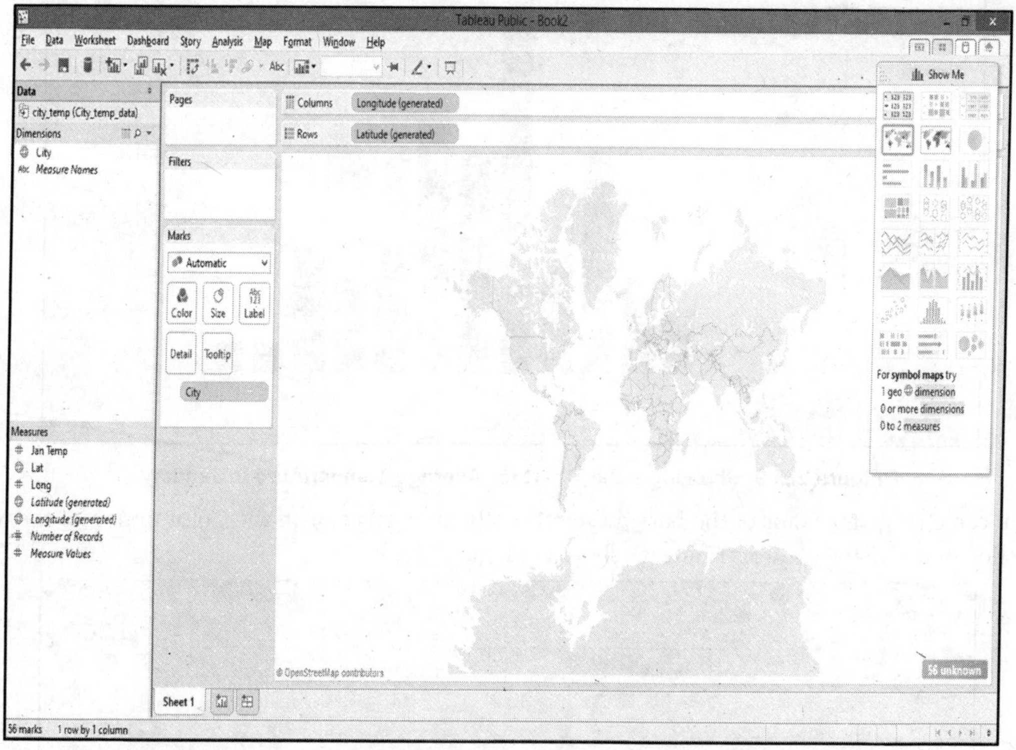

Figure 27.38: Showing a Map Plotted with Longitude and Latitude Values

You can use more dimensions to create various kinds of visuals shown in the Show Me selection box and apply different marks on the created visualizations. You can fill different colors in different sections, find out details about a dimension or measure, or define the size (or range) of your dimensions or measures. All of these can be done by using the Marks section of the visual controls frame. You can define filtering levels by dragging individual dimensions or measures and dropping them in the Filters section of your visual controls frame. In the same manner, you can perform other operations by using different controls in your visualization. As an instance, we have created a bar chart for the average January temperature by using the JanTemp field and its total count for cities, as shown in Figure 27.39:

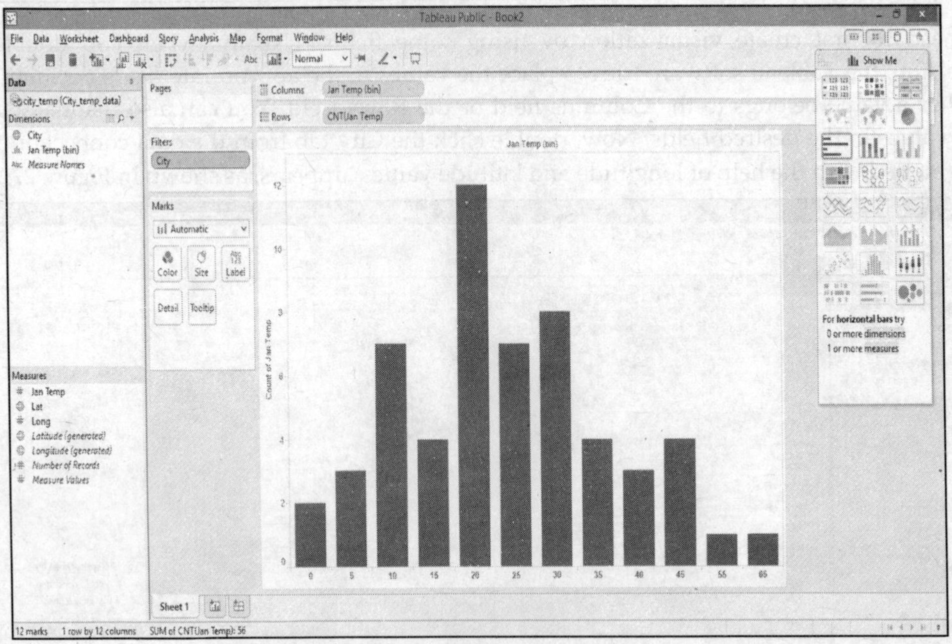

Figure 27.39: Showing a Bar Chart for Average Temperature in January

You can change the color of the bars by selecting the desired color in the Color option of the Marks section of the visual controls frame, as shown in Figure 27.40:

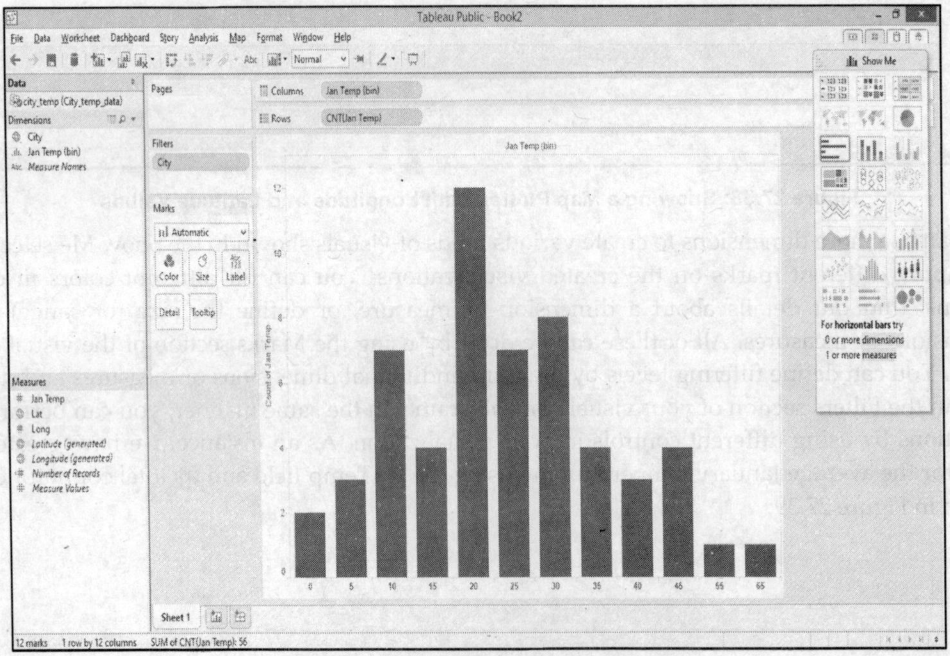

Figure 27.40: Changing the Bar Color

Click the Detail option of the Marks section and then select a bar from the bar chart to see the details about the selected bar, as shown in Figure 27.41:

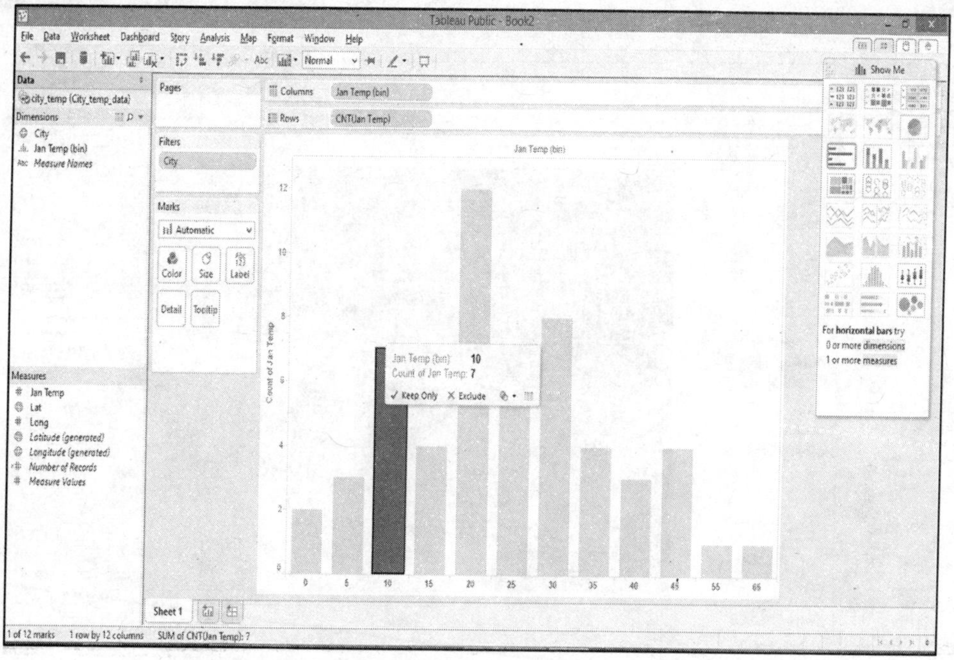

Figure 27.41: Getting Details

You can also present the visuals in other format. For example, Figure 27.42 shows a bubble chart created for the same dimensions as above:

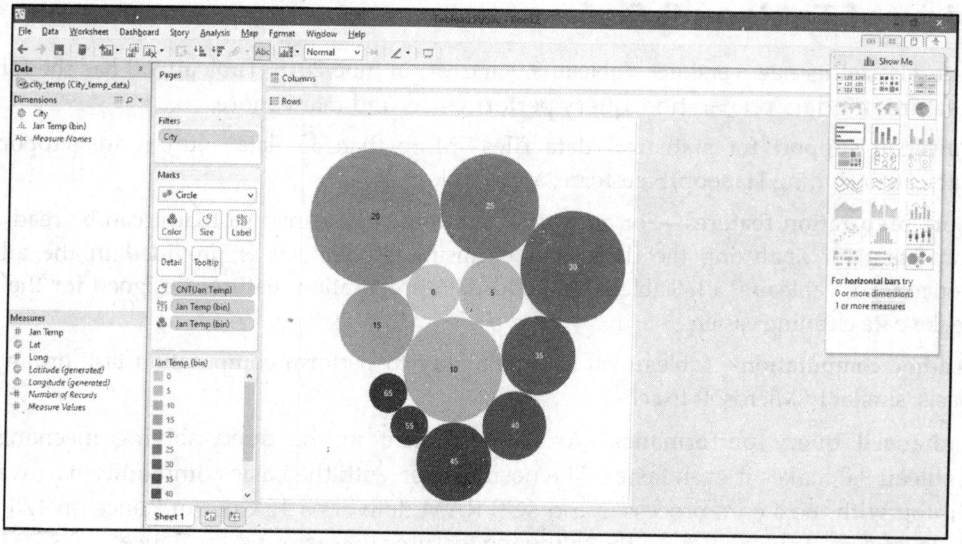

Figure 27.42: Showing a Bubble Chart

Figure 27.43 shows a Treemap for the same dimensions:

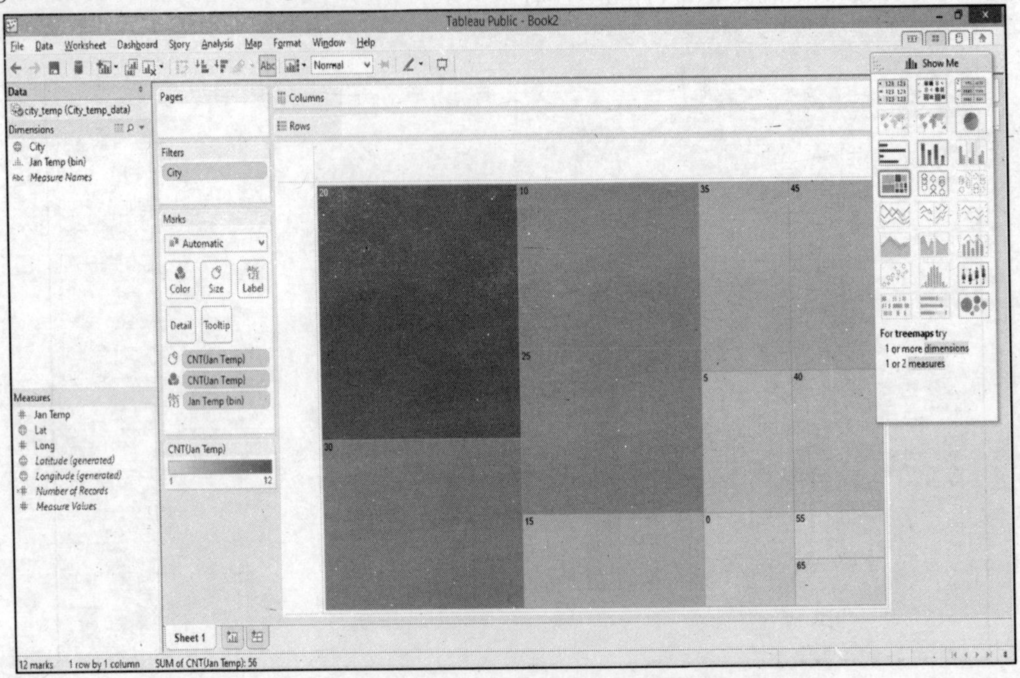

Figure 27.43: Showing a Treemap

In the same way, you can use other types of datasets to see various kinds of visuals in Tableau Public.

Overview of Tableau 9.0

Tableau released its new versions, Tableau 9.0 and 9+, in June 2015. Tableau 9.0 has the following new features for data preparation, query performance, and many more:

1. **Powerful support for statistical data files**—More than 45 data sources are supported by Tableau, including Hadoop, Salesforce, and Excel.
2. **Data preparation features**—For analytics, data must be cleaned so that it can be read. This is important for analyzing the data. This cleansing mechanism is provided in the advanced version, i.e. Tableau 9.3.1. Tableau will add data preparation features designed for the user to make data cleaning easier.
3. **Ad-hoc computation**—Tableau 9.0 has the ability to perform computation task on an ad-hoc basis, similar to Microsoft Excel.
4. **Enhanced query performance**—An improvement in the query-solving mechanisms in Tableau 9.0 makes it even faster. The normal user with the basic commodity hardware, say laptop with the 4 core processor and 4GB RAM delivers a 10X performance on 173 million rows of data. Tableau 9.0 has the following features for faster performance:
   - Multi-core query execution
   - Vector operations

- Parallel queries
- Pan and zoom
- Persisted query cache for resuming the previous task on next window opening

Tableau 9.0 grabs the better part of source databases to execute more powerful queries at a given time for faster and efficient dashboard performance on desktop and server. It introduces a new technology for database connections called Query Fusion that takes all the queries and simplifies them, and converts them in few queries that increases throughput with less work.

5. **Smart maps**—Tableau 9.0 introduces new selection controls that include geocoding data and geographic search capabilities, which make it easier for end users to answer questions that circulate around the notion of "where?" For example, new radial and lasso selection controls.
6. **Admin views**—In Tableau 9.0, a powerful admin view is introduced in which an admin can track on activities of the user like providing resources, identifying bugs, and at the same time admin can debug it and report a log for the same issue.

Let's have the first look of Tableau 9.0.

1. Start Tableau 9.0 on Windows 7.

   Figure 27.44 shows the start-up of the Tableau 9 public edition on Windows 7:

Figure 27.44: The Start-up of Tableau (Version 9.0)

2. After opening Tableau 9.0, the first window which we get is shown in Figure 27.45:

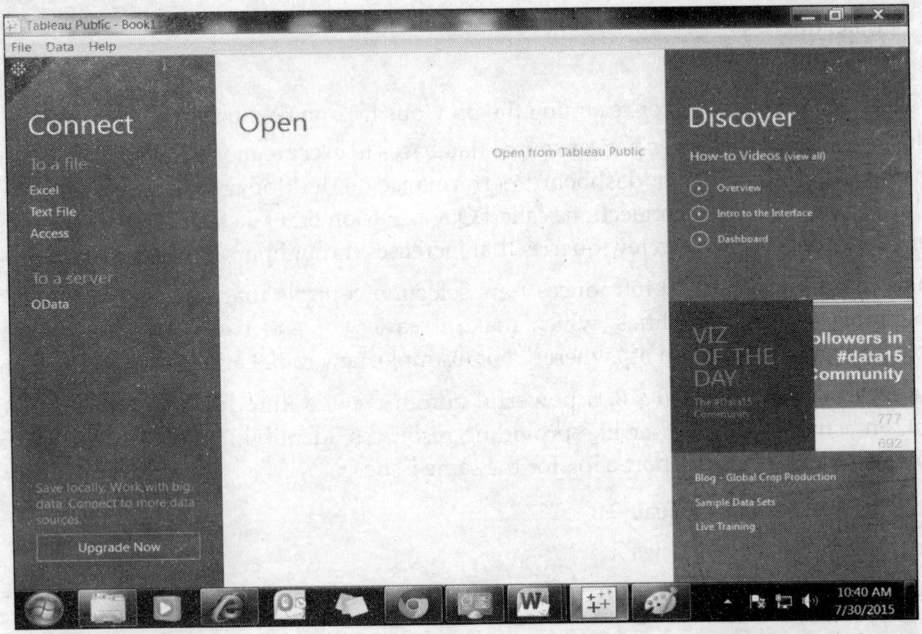

Figure 27.45: Opening of Tableau 9.0

3. Figure 27.46 shows how the data is uploaded on Tableau 9.0 for the data analysis:

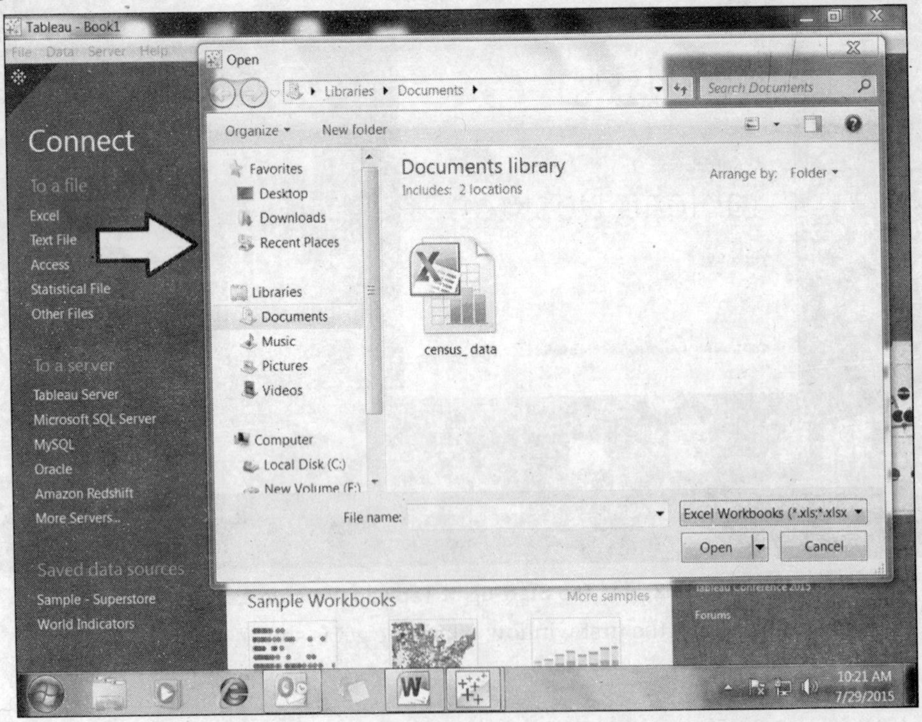

Figure 27.46: Uploading of Data in Tableau 9.0

4. The screen appears after loading the data in Tableau 9.0, as shown in Figure 27.47:

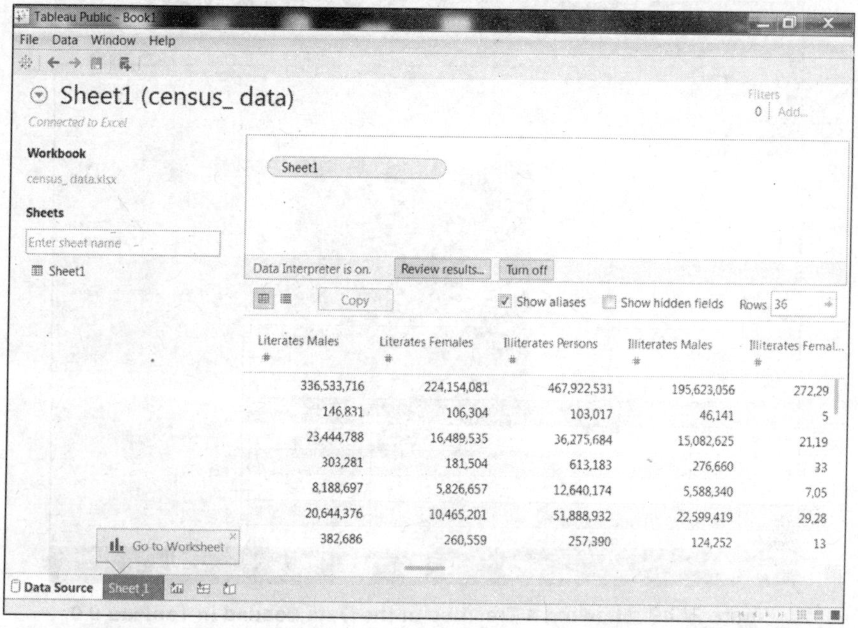

Figure 27.47: Showing how Data is represented in Tableau 9.0 after Loading

5. Now, the data is represented in the bar graph, which is shown in Figure 27.48:

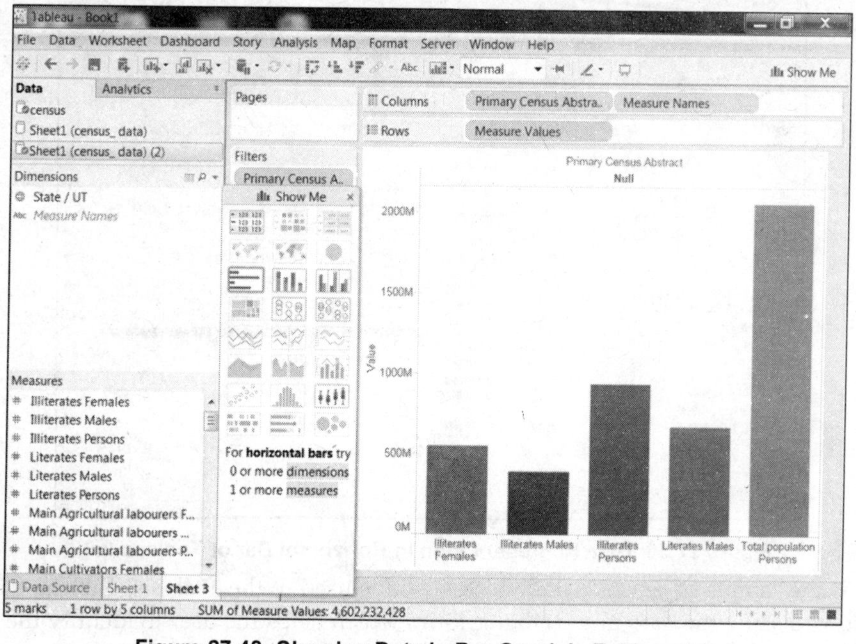

Figure 27.48: Showing Data in Bar Graph in Tableau 9.0

Figure 27.49 shows the Treemap of census data, which is given state-wise in Tableau 9.0:

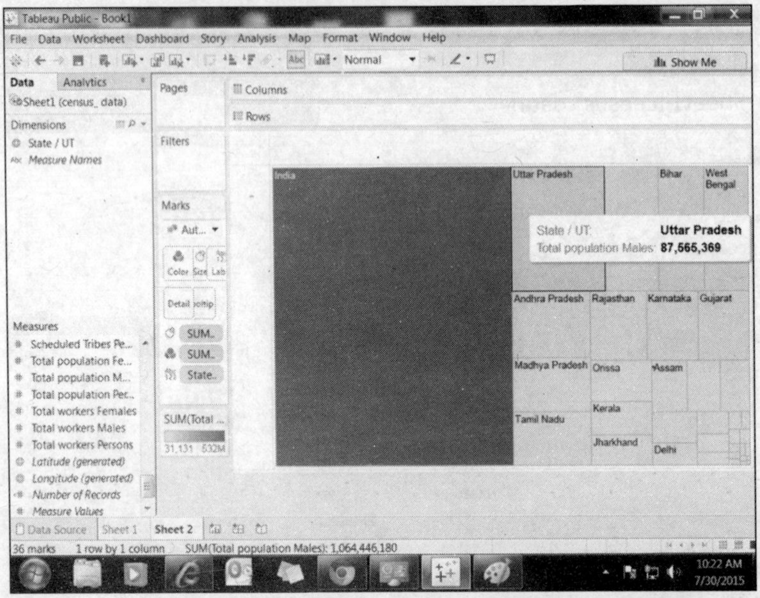

Figure 27.49: Showing a Treemap of the Data Loaded in Tableau 9.0

Figure 27.50 shows the state-wise population in Tableau 9.0 public edition:

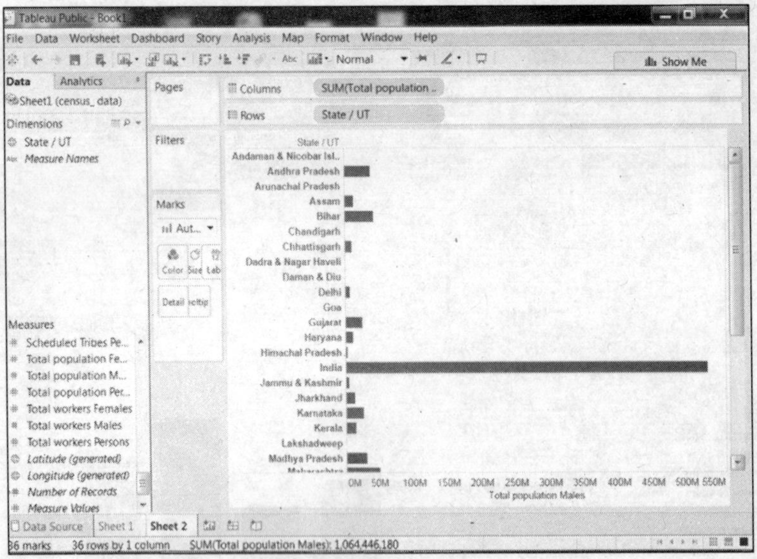

Figure 27.50: Data Representation in Horizontal Bar of Tableau 9.0

6. Here is the sample of census data, which we have used in the analysis. Tableau 9.0 has its own window to show the data in the tabular form, which helps the user to identify the null value in that data.

Figure 27.51 gives the field information of the data:

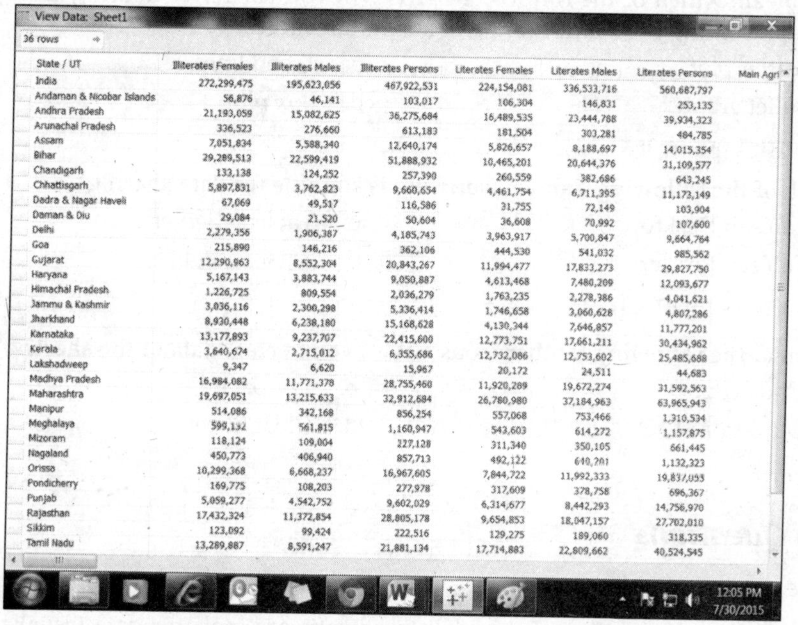

View Data: Sheet1

36 rows

State / UT	Illiterates Females	Illiterates Males	Illiterates Persons	Literates Females	Literates Males	Literates Persons	Main Agri
India	272,299,475	195,623,056	467,922,531	224,154,081	336,533,716	560,687,797	
Andaman & Nicobar Islands	56,876	46,141	103,017	106,304	146,831	253,135	
Andhra Pradesh	21,193,059	15,082,625	36,275,684	16,489,535	23,444,788	39,934,323	
Arunachal Pradesh	336,523	276,660	613,183	181,504	303,281	484,785	
Assam	7,051,834	5,588,340	12,640,174	5,826,657	8,188,697	14,015,354	
Bihar	29,289,513	22,599,419	51,888,932	10,465,201	20,644,376	31,109,577	
Chandigarh	133,138	124,252	257,390	260,559	382,686	643,245	
Chhattisgarh	5,897,831	3,762,823	9,660,654	4,461,754	6,711,395	11,173,149	
Dadra & Nagar Haveli	67,069	49,517	116,586	31,755	72,149	103,904	
Daman & Diu	29,084	21,520	50,604	36,608	70,992	107,600	
Delhi	2,279,356	1,906,387	4,185,743	3,963,917	5,700,847	9,664,764	
Goa	215,890	146,216	362,106	444,530	541,032	985,562	
Gujarat	12,290,963	8,552,304	20,843,267	11,994,477	17,833,273	29,827,750	
Haryana	5,167,143	3,883,744	9,050,887	4,613,468	7,480,209	12,093,677	
Himachal Pradesh	1,226,725	809,554	2,036,279	1,763,235	2,278,386	4,041,621	
Jammu & Kashmir	3,036,116	2,300,298	5,336,414	1,746,658	3,060,628	4,807,286	
Jharkhand	8,930,448	6,238,180	15,168,628	4,130,344	7,646,857	11,777,201	
Karnataka	13,177,893	9,237,707	22,415,600	12,773,751	17,661,211	30,434,962	
Kerala	3,640,674	2,715,012	6,355,686	12,732,086	12,753,602	25,485,688	
Lakshadweep	9,347	6,620	15,967	20,172	24,511	44,683	
Madhya Pradesh	16,984,082	11,771,378	28,755,460	11,920,289	19,672,274	31,592,563	
Maharashtra	19,697,051	13,215,633	32,912,684	26,780,980	37,184,963	63,965,943	
Manipur	514,086	342,168	856,254	557,068	753,466	1,310,534	
Meghalaya	599,132	561,815	1,160,947	543,603	614,272	1,157,875	
Mizoram	118,124	109,004	227,128	311,340	350,105	661,445	
Nagaland	450,773	406,940	857,713	492,122	640,201	1,132,323	
Orissa	10,299,368	6,668,237	16,967,605	7,844,722	11,992,333	19,837,055	
Pondicherry	169,775	108,203	277,978	317,609	378,758	696,367	
Punjab	5,059,277	4,542,752	9,602,029	6,314,677	8,442,293	14,756,970	
Rajasthan	17,432,324	11,372,854	28,805,178	9,654,853	18,047,157	27,702,010	
Sikkim	123,092	99,424	222,516	129,275	189,060	318,335	
Tamil Nadu	13,289,887	8,591,247	21,881,134	17,714,883	22,809,662	40,524,545	

Figure 27.51: Dataset used for the Tableau Analysis

Summary

This chapter introduced you to the basics of Tableau software, especially the installation and usage of Tableau Desktop and Tableau Public software tools. It started with an overview of the Tableau software tool. Next, it outlined some technical specifications of the Tableau software tool and its use in different data environments. You also learned about the Tableau workspace and how the results of data analytics are presented in a visual format.

Quick Revise

Multiple-Choice Questions

Q1. Which of the following main menu options will you use to publish your work on the server of Tableau?

a. Map
b. Format
c. Server
d. Window

Ans. The correct option is a.

Q2. ____________ provides a menu to turn on or off screen elements.

a. Reset cards
b. Label marks
c. Duplicate sheets
d. Fit axis

Ans. The correct option is b.

Q3. In Tableau, which of the following charts will you use for comparing multiple sets of data and representing their minimum and maximum values?

a. Scatter plot
b. Trend lines
c. Bullet graph
d. Box plot

Ans. The correct option is c.

Q4. Which of the following Tableau software is suitable for data sharing?

a. Tableau Desktop
b. Tableau Server
c. Tableau Reader
d. Tableau Public

Ans. The correct option is b.

Q5. Which of the following toolbar icons allows you to clear data of the sheet?

a. Undo/Redo
b. File Save
c. Duplicate Sheet
d. Clear Sheet

Ans. The correct option is d.

Subjective Questions

Q1. Write a note on Tableau products.

Ans. Tableau products are the most widely used software tools for data visualization. There are various types of Tableau products available in the market. Some of the commonly known products include Tableau Desktop, Tableau Server, Tableau Online, Tableau Reader, and Tableau Public.

One of the most popular applications of Tableau software tools is Tableau Desktop, which provides various facilities to create visualizations. The breakthrough approach used to build the Tableau Desktop tool takes pictures of data and converts them into optimized database queries, which help users in spotting patterns, identifying trends, and deriving logical conclusions and insights. While working with the Tableau Desktop, the data analyst need not write any code; all the insights can, instead, be discovered by just connecting to the data and following the thoughts that strike the mind naturally. You can easily connect to your data, which is either in the memory or on the server. Tableau Desktop allows you to directly retrieve data from the server or load it in the Tableau data engine from a disk. The speed of Tableau Desktop is as fast as the thoughts of human beings, and everything can be done with drag-and-drop technology.

Tableau Desktop provides options for data sharing in the form of dashboards, which can be used to reflect relationships by highlighting and filtering data. Dashboards can also help you create story line in a guided manner for explaining the insights obtained from data. Moreover, you can use Tableau variants, such as the Tableau Online and Tableau Server tools, for sharing content.

Q2. List some important features of Tableau software.

Ans. The important features of Tableau software include the following:

- Single-click data analytics in visual form
- In-depth statistical analysis
- Management of metadata
- In-built, top-class data analytic practices
- In-built data engine
- Big Data analytics
- Quick and accurate data discovery
- Business dashboards creation
- Various types of data visualization
- Social media analytics, including Facebook and Twitter
- Easy and quick integration of R
- Business intelligence through mobile
- Analysis of time series data
- Analysis of data from surveys

Q3. How would you open a new workspace page in Tableau?

Ans. To open a workspace page, drag the desired data source icon and drop it on the Tableau icon. You can open several connections in Tableau by going to the start or data connection page and selecting a new connection.

Q4. List and discuss the icons present on the Tableau toolbar.

Ans. The following icons are present on the Tableau toolbar:

- **Undo/Redo**—Scrolls backward or forward on the screen. You can retrieve any step by clicking the undo/redo button.
- **File Save**—Saves your work. You need to click this button frequently as Tableau does not have the automated save function.
- **Connect to a New Data Source**—Connects you to a data source.
- **New Dashboard or Worksheet**—Adds new pages to your worksheet.
- **Duplicate Sheet**—Creates an exact/duplicate copy of a worksheet as well as of the dashboard page that you are working on.
- **Clear Sheet**—Allows you to clear data of a sheet.
- **Auto/Manual Update**—Generates visuals. It is particularly helpful for large datasets where dragging and dropping items consume time.

- **Group**—Allows you to group data by selecting more than one headers in a table or values in a legend.
- **Pivot Worksheet**—Allows you to create a pivot table on a new worksheet.
- **Ascending/Descending Sort**—Sorts selected items in an ascending or descending order.
- **Label Marks**—Turns on or off screen elements.
- **Presentation Mode**—Hides/unhides design shelves. It is particularly used during presentations where you want to use Tableau as a presentation slide deck to keep the slides of the presentation.
- **Reset Cards**—Provides a menu to turn on or the screen elements, such as Caption or Summary.
- **Fit Menu**—Allows different views of the Tableau screen. You can fit the screen either horizontally or vertically.
- **Fit Axis**—Fixes the axis of view. You can zoom in/out charts with this button.
- **Highlight Control**—Compares the selected combinations of dimensions.

Q5. What is a Tableau Server?

Ans. Tableau Server is a great tool for those who need to upload their files regularly and share their work with others. It can automatically refresh data extracts published in it by the users.

Tableau Server can be accessed either by having a named user license or a core license. A named user license is ideal for smaller deployments (> 150 users), whereas a core license is good for those who need dynamic access. Core license is a cost-effective solution because it drastically reduces administrative tasks.

Tableau Server is compliant with security laws and permits its customers to access tailored reports (as defined by the server administrator). Its user interface is intuitive and provides functions to find and organize reports.

28

Social Media Analytics and Text Mining

In a world where information is readily available via Internet on the click of a button, organizations need to remain abreast with the ongoing events and latest happenings in order to gain a competitive edge over business markets. Apart from that, organizations also need to interact with their consumers more effectively in order to gain an insight about the ongoing business trends and the market position of particular products. Social media provides an opportunity to business organizations and individuals to connect and interact with each other worldwide. With the evolution of social media as a tool to connect with the existing and potential customers, business organizations have begun to recognize the requirement of employing social media analytics for gaining crucial business insights and taking timely decisions.

Social media analytics is the practice of gathering data from blogs and social media websites and analyze the data to take crucial business decisions. Generally, the data obtained from the social media is mined to identify customer sentiments and opinions regarding particular products and services. Such an analysis helps organizations to enhance their products and services, improve marketing strategies, provide better customer services, reduce costs, and gain a competitive edge in the market.

This chapter discusses the role of social media and the importance of conducting social media analytics by business organizations. These analyses help organizations to evaluate feedback from consumers and gauge their current and future position in the market. Further you will learn about text mining and sentiment analysis. The chapter ends with a presentation on how to perform social media analytics and opinion mining on tweets.

Introducing Social Media

Simply put, social media refers to a computer-mediated, interactive, and Internet-based platform that allows people to create, distribute, and share a wide range of content and information, such as text and images. Social media technologies unleash and leverage the power of social networks to enable interaction and information exchange.

Jesse Farmer, cofounder, Dev Bootcamp, quotes social network as a collection of people bound together via a specific set of social relations. Social media, in turn, denotes a group of Internet-based applications build over the foundations of Web 2.0 that supports the creation and exchange of user-generated content. In other words, social media relies on Web-based technologies to generate interactive platforms where people and organizations can create, co-create, recreate, share, discuss, and modify user-generated content.

Prior to the advent of social media as an open-system approach to exchange content effectively, business organizations and public relation practitioners rarely focused on business dynamics to manage brand images. With the changing business environments due to the evolution of social media, business organizations also adopted the open-system approach based on reciprocal feedback. This, in turn, has completely transformed the way information was communicated or the manner by which public relations were developed. The new approach encourages active participation in development and distribution of information by merging innovative technologies and sociology.

Social media provides a collaborative environment which can be employed for:

- Building relationships
- Distributing content
- Rating products and services
- Engaging target audience

Social media provides an equally open platform for novices as well as experts to express and share their viewpoints and feedback on various events and issues. This information can, in turn, be employed by business organizations to gain insights about customers' perspective on their products and services. In this manner, social media enables business organizations to receive a feedback and promote a dialog between customers, potential customers, and the organization. In other words, social media allows business organizations to promote participation, conversation, sharing, and publishing of content.

Social media, however, can take different forms, which can be categorized as follows:

- **Social networking websites**—These provide a Web-based platform to users where they can create a personalized profile, summarizing and showcasing their interests, define other members as connections or contacts, and communicate and share content with their contacts. Examples of social networking websites include Facebook, LinkedIn, MySpace, Hi5, and Bebo.
- **Blogs**—Short for 'Web logs', blogs represent online journals to showcase the content organized in the reverse chronological order. Examples of blogging sites include Blogger, WordPress, and Tumblr.
- **Microblogs**—These allow people to share and showcase small posts and are suitable for quick sharing of content in a few lines of text or an individual photo or video. Twitter is a well-known microblogging website.
- **Content communities and media sharing sites**—These allow users to organize and share different types of media content such as videos and images. The members can also comment on the shared content. Examples include YouTube, Pinterest, Flikr, and Instagram.
- **Wiki**—It represents a collective website in which the members can create and modify content in a community-based database. In other words, the users can modify the content of any hosted page and can also create new pages in the website based on the wiki technology. One of the most popular examples of Wiki websites is Wikipedia, which is an online encyclopedia.
- **Social bookmarking websites**—These websites allow users to organize and manage tags and links to other websites. Well-known examples include Reddit, StumbleUpon, and Digg.

Apart from the listed ones, social media may include websites that showcase reviews and ratings, such as Yelp, forums, and discussion boards, such as Yahoo!, and websites that showcase virtual social worlds that create a virtual environment where people can interact, such as SecondLife.

Figure 28.1 depicts the forms of conversations possible via social media:

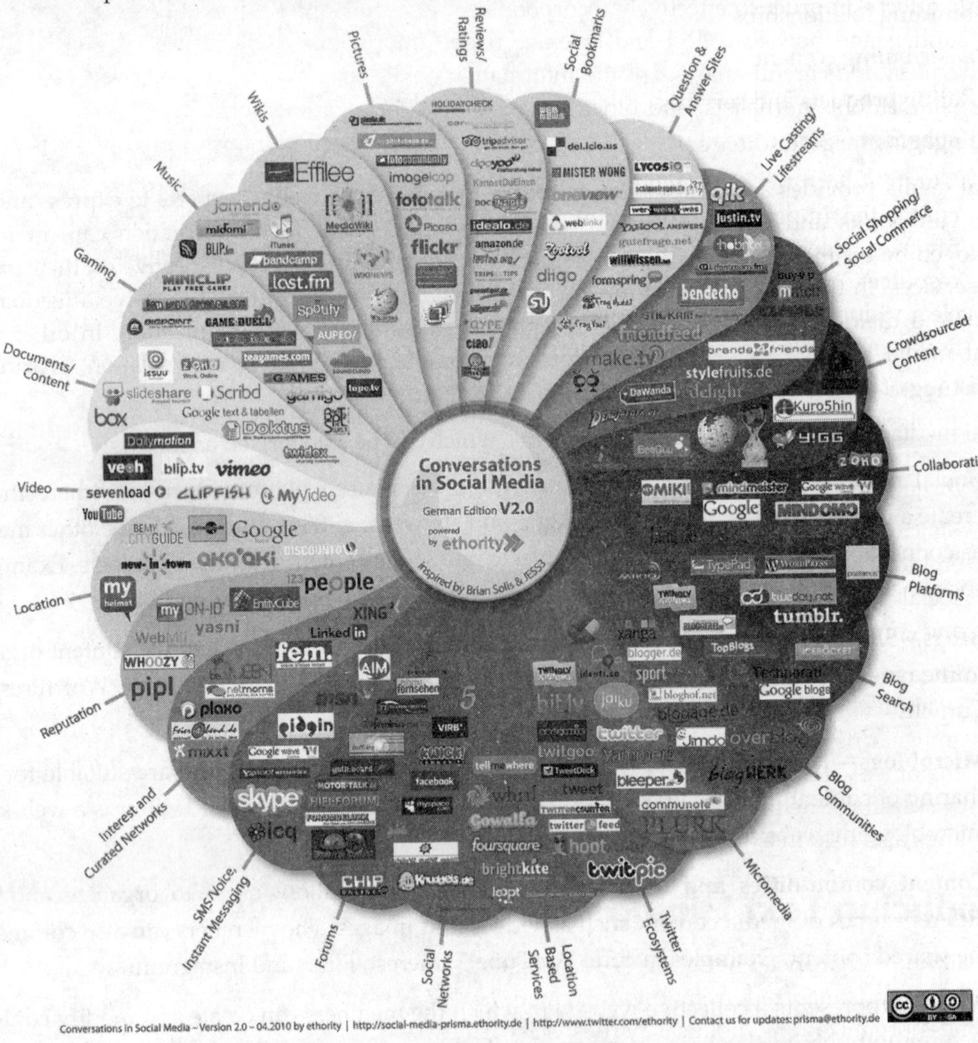

Figure 28.1: Possible Forms of Conversation via Social Media

SCENARIO

The marketing executives at Argon Technology are planning to incorporate social media in their marketing strategy to reach more and more customers and improve their services based on customer feedback.

Introducing Key Elements of Social Media

Incorporating social media into everyday sales and marketing routines of an organization is not easy and requires gaining a command over certain set of tactics and tools related to the efficient management and utilization of social media. In order to effectively leverage the possibilities provided by social media for the growth of business, the organizations need to focus on certain key elements of social media along with the corresponding techniques.

Social media participation involves a focus on the following key elements:

- **Collect**—In order to effectively incorporate social media, the business organizations first need to understand how to collect and leverage useful information and market artifacts. This involves critical and careful analysis of the information coming from various sources such as customers, competitors, journalists, and other market influencers. Various tools, such as feed readers, blog subscriptions, and email newsletters, can be employed to collect information from various sources.
- **Curate**—Once the information is collected from various sources, the next step is to effectively curate the important information to be sent to the clients and internal stakeholders. This involves intelligent filtering and aggregation of the information collected from various resources. This not only provides an effective insight to the customers but also helps in having a clear vision about the current industry standards and market trends. Various curation tools such as Newsle, LinkedIn, and RSS readers can be employed for this task.
- **Create**—After collection and curation of the collected information, the organizations need to create valuable content objects that can provide a focus and industry buzz to them. This is an effective marketing strategy to create a leader position in the industry. This can be accomplished by employing various publishing programs and sharing routines.
- **Share**—A key element for implementing effective social media is sharing of information. This employs sharing your content, information, and ideas with others. This helps in expanding the social media network. Various tools, such as Feedly and Hootsuite, help in sharing information and content over the social media.
- **Engage**—The basic idea behind social media is to engage the existing and prospective customers. The tools and routines of social media and the regular practice of listening, curation, and sharing help executives and sales personnel of an organization in engaging more and more customers, stakeholders, prospective customers, journalists, and industry influencers. Tools such as Salesforce help to connect people from different categories. Apart from that, various mobile apps also help in expanding the realm of reaching more and more people.

Introducing Text Mining

We all know that social networks are a rich source of information. A lot of valuable content can be extracted and analyzed from this information to serve the knowledge requirements of various business organizations, political parties, scientific research departments, social science fraternities, and other interested domains. Social networks generally support the exchange of information and data in various formats, such as text, videos, and photos. However, the most common form of information and content exchange on social networking sites is text.

Online marketers and business analysts examine and interpret the online content using social media analytics. This analysis helps them to amend and mold their business objectives as per the customer behavior. For example, the reviews posted by customers on websites or social marketing media in the form of text or rating score enable organizations to understand and analyze customer's perspectives and expectations.

The insight obtained from such reviews can help organizations to identify their key areas of improvement and enhance their performance. However, certain tools and methodologies are required to read, interpret, and analyze the large number of reviews received on a daily basis. This is accomplished by text mining.

It is pretty difficult for any database administrator, marketing professional, or a researcher to explore and extract the desired information from the huge amount of data and information generated and exchanged online on a daily basis. The problem is multiplied manifold by the text-based social networking communications and documents exchanged during business operations. Although keyword searching provides some scope to search the desired information; however, they cannot every time relate to the exact terms in the document.

Text mining or text analytics comes as a handy tool to quantitatively examine the text generated by social media and filtered in the form of different clusters, patterns, and trends. In other words, text mining represents the set of tools, techniques, and methods applied for automatically processing natural language textual data provided in huge amounts in the form of computer files. The extracted and structured content and themes are used for rapid analysis, identification of hidden data and information, and automatic decision making. Text mining tools are often based on the principles of information retrieval and natural learning processes.

Complex linkage structure makes text mining in social networks a challenging job, requiring the help of automated tools and sorting techniques. A number of text mining tools and algorithms have been developed to enable easy extraction of information from different textual resources. The recent developments in statistical and data processing tools have added to the evolution in the domain of text mining.

Text mining employs the concepts obtained from various fields, ranging from linguistics and statistics to Information and Communication Technologies (ICT). Statistical pattern learning is applied to create patterns from the extracted text, which are further examined to obtain valuable information. The overall process of text mining comprises retrieval of information, lexical analysis, creation and recognition of patterns, tagging, extraction of information, application of data mining techniques, and predictive analytics. This can be summarized as follows:

Text mining = Lexicometry + Data mining

TIP

Lexicometry or lexical statistics refers to the study of identifying the frequency of occurrence of words in textual data.

The process is initiated with the retrieval of information, which involves collection and identification of information from a set of textual material. The information can come from various sources, such as websites, database, documents, or content management system. The textual information is processed by parsers and other linguistic analysis tools to examine and recognize textual features, such as people, organizations, names of places, stock ticker symbols, and abbreviations.

Figure 28.2 depicts the text mining process:

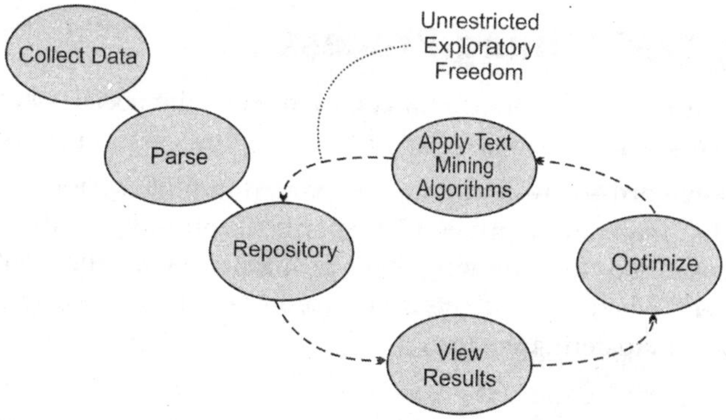

Figure 28.2: Text Mining Process

TIP

The process of analyzing a string of symbols, either in natural or computer language on the basis of formal grammar rules is termed as parsing or syntactic analysis.

On the basis of certain identified patterns, other quantities such as entities, emails, and telephone numbers are identified. Further, sentiment analysis is applied to identify the underlying attitude. Finally, the psychological profiling is determined by conducting quantitative text analysis.

The overall purpose of text mining analytics is to transform unstructured text into valuable structured data, which can be further analyzed and applied for various domains, such as research, investigation, exploratory data analysis, biomedical applications, and business intelligence.

Statistical analysis tools, such as R and word count, aid in the assessment of the overall review. Further, positive and negative relationships can be explored using various plotting techniques, such as scatter plot. Apart from the listed application areas, text mining techniques can be further applied for analysis of demographics, financial status, and buying tendencies of customers.

To sum up, text mining can be applied in the following areas:

- **Competitive intelligence**—In order to succeed, business organizations need to know about not only the key players in the industry but also the strengths and weaknesses of their competitors. Text mining provides factual data to organizations that can be applied for strategic decision making.
- **Community leveraging**—Text mining facilitates the identification and extraction of the information embedded in community interaction. This information can be applied for amending marketing strategies.
- **Law enforcement**—Text mining can be applied in the domain of government intelligence for countering anti-terrorist activities.
- **Life sciences**—Text mining can also be effectively applied in the area of research and development of drugs. Bioinformatics companies, such as PubGen, are applying biomedical text mining combined with network visualization as an Internet service.

Understanding Text Mining Process

The enormous amount of unstructured data collected from the social media makes text mining a very challenging process. The key steps for any text mining process can be summed up as follows:

1. **Extracting the keyword**—Any text analysis process begins by identification of relevant and precise keyword(s) that can be applied for specific queries. Next, the content and the linkage patterns are considered for applying keyword searches as the content related to similar keywords is often linked. The selected keywords act as social network nodes and play an important role while clustering the text.
2. **Classifying and clustering the text**—Various algorithms are applied for classifying text from the source content. For this process, the nodes are associated with labels prior to classification. After that, the classified text is clustered on the basis of similarity. The classification and clustering of the text are greatly influenced by the linkage structure of data. Accurate results can be obtained by applying node labeling and content-based classification techniques.
3. **Identifying patterns**—Trend analysis applies the principle that even for the same content, the clusters collected at different nodes can have different concept distributions. For this reason, the concepts at various nodes are compared and classified accordingly in the same or different subcollections.

Obtaining desired results for a specific query involves careful processing of the relevant document. For effective text mining, several stages of processing need to be applied on a document, such as:

- **Text preprocessing**—This involves the identification of all the unique words in a document. Non-informative words, such as the, and, or, and when, are filtered out from the document text before applying word stemming. Word stemming refers to the process of reducing the inflected or derived words to their stem base. For example, words such as cat, cats, catlike, and catty will all be mapped to the same stem base 'cat'. Terms such as stemmers or stemming algorithms are also used interchangeably in stemming programs. Affix stemmers trim down both suffix and prefix, such as ed, ly, and ing, from a given word. Popular stemmers include Brute Force algorithm and Suffix Tripping algorithm.
- **Document representation**—A document is basically represented in words and terms.
- **Document retrieval**—This involves the retrieval of a document based on some query. Accurate results are ensured using text indexing and accuracy measures. Text indexing and searching capabilities can be incorporated in an application using Lucene, which is a Java library.
- **Document clustering**—This involves the grouping of conceptually related documents to ensure fast retrieval. A term for a given query can be searched faster from the well-clustered documents.

  Document clustering can be implemented using the following techniques:

  - Hierarchical clustering
  - One-pass clustering
  - Buckshot clustering

Once clustered, the documents are then organized into user-defined categories or taxonomies. Figure 28.3 depicts the stages of document processing:

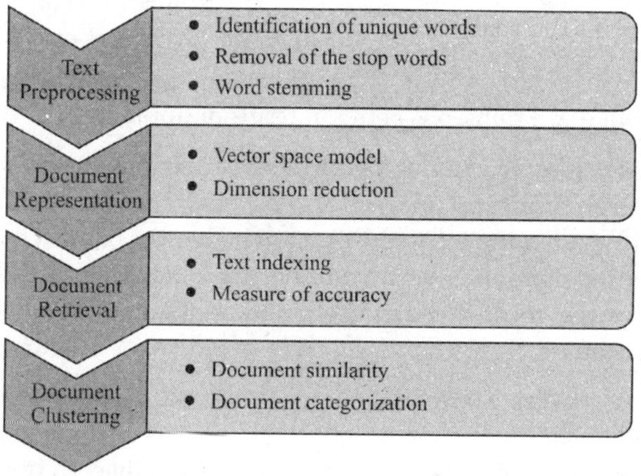

Figure 28.3: Stages of Document Processing in Text Mining

Both structured and unstructured data are involved in text mining. Unstructured data comes from reviews and summaries while the structured data is obtained from organized spreadsheets. Text mining tools identify themes, patterns, and insights hidden in the structured as well as unstructured data. Various text mining software are employed by organizations for different data mining applications. The following are some commonly used text mining software:

- **R**—Used for statistical data analysis, text processing, and sentiment analysis
- **ActivePoint**—Applied for natural language processing and online catalog-based contextual search
- **Attensity**—Used for extraction of facts, including who, what, where, and why and then identifying people, places, and events and how they are related
- **Crossminder**—Applied for cross-lingual text analytics
- **Compare Suite**—Used for comparing texts by keywords and highlighting common and unique keywords
- **IBM SPSS Predictive Analytics Suite**—Applied for data and text mining
- **Monarch**—Applied for analysis and transformation of reports into live data
- **SAS Text Miner**—Provides a rich suite of text processing and analysis tools
- **Textalyzer**—Used for online text analysis

Apart from these, some other text mining tools include AeroText, Angoss, Autonomy, Clarabridge, IBM LanguageWare, IBM SPSS, WordStat, and Lexalytics

Now, let's explore an important component of text mining, i.e., sentiment analysis.

Sentiment Analysis

Sentiment analysis is one of the most important components of text mining. Also termed as opinion mining, it involves careful analysis of people's opinions, sentiments, attitudes, appraisals, and evaluations. This is accomplished by examining large amounts of unstructured data obtained from the Internet on the basis of positive, negative, or neutral view of the end user.

Sentiment analysis involves the analysis of following sentences:

- **Facts**—Product A is better than product B.
- **Opinions**—I don't like A. I think B is better in terms of durability.

Similar to Web analysis, specific queries are applied in sentiment analysis to retrieve and rank relevant content. However, sentiment analysis also differs from Web analysis in certain factors. It is possible to determine from a sentiment analysis that whether the content expresses an opinion on the topic and also whether the opinion is positive or negative. Ranking in Web analysis is done on the basis of the frequency of keywords. On the other hand, ranking in sentiment analysis is done on the basis of polarity of the attitude.

With the widespread use of Web 2.0 technologies, a huge volume of opinionated data is available on the social media. People using social media put their reviews and comments about products used and also share their feedback, opinions and experiences with others in their network. These reviews and feedback are utilized by organizations to improve and upgrade their products and services and enhance their brand equity. Sentiment analysis applies other domains such as linguistics, digital technologies, text analysis tools, artificial intelligence, and Natural Language Processing (NLP) for identification and extraction of useful information. This greatly influences various domains, ranging from politics and science to social science.

TIP

Artificial intelligence is a technology and a branch of science that deals with the study and development of intelligent machines and software. Natural language processing is a domain of computer science, artificial intelligence, and linguistics that deals with the interactions between computers and human (natural) languages.

CASELET

The most common application of sentiment analysis is in the field of consumer products and services. This also provides valuable information to competing organizations and candidates. Sentiment analysis can effectively track voters' expectations, perspectives, and feedback. Apart from that, sentiment analysis can be applied in automated scoring systems and rating applications to provide scores and ratings to public companies. An example of rating applications is Stock Sonar that generates automatic rating by analyzing articles, blogs, and tweets.

The process of sentiment analysis begins by tagging words using Parts of Speech (POS), such as subject, verb phrase, verb, noun phrase, determiner, and prepositions. Defined patterns are filtered to identify their sentiment orientation. For example, 'beautiful room' has an adjective followed by noun. The adjective 'beautiful' indicates a positive perspective about the noun 'room'. At this stage, the emotional factor in the phrase is also examined and analyzed. After that, an average sentiment orientation of all the phrases is computed and analyzed to conclude if a product is recommended by a user.

Following parameters may be applied to classify the given text in the process of sentiment analysis:

- Polarity, which can be positive, negative, or neutral
- Emotional states, which can be sad, angry, or happy
- Scaling system or numeric values

- Subjectivity or objectivity
- Features based on key entities such as durability of furniture, screen size of cell phone, and lens quality of camera

Automated sentiment analysis is still evolving as it is difficult to interpret the conditional phrases used by people to express their sentiments on social media. For example, 'if you don't like A, try B'. In this sentence, the user clearly shows his/her positivity toward B but doesn't indicate clear views about A. After removing 'if', the first clause clearly indicates negativity toward A.

However, sentiment analysis employs various online tools to effectively interpret consumer sentiments. Some of the online tools are listed as follows:

- **Topsy**—It is used to measure success of a Website on Twitter. It tracks the occurrence of given and related keywords, website name, and website URL in tweets.
- **BackTweets**—This toll is applied to improve search engine ranking of a website. It tracks tweets that link back to a website.
- **Twitterfall**—It locates tweets that are important for a website. It can be used to stay in touch with the customers and consumers and respond to their queries and suggestions in real time.
- **TweetBeep**—This is used to send timely updates or alerts for the topics of interest.
- **Reachli**—Designed especially for Pinterest, it is a content-sharing website. This tool helps in tracking data and scheduling and organizing pins (denote the updates in Pinterest) in advance.

Apart from these, some other sentiment analysis tools include Social Mention, AlertRank Sentiment Analysis, and Twitter Sentiment Analysis. The business organizations can apply specific tools as per their requirements and sentiment analysis needs.

Performing Social Media Analytics and Opinion Mining on Tweets

In today's IT-driven world, social media has emerged as the most popular means of communicating and sharing views and information across the world. Some examples of social media are social networking websites, such as Facebook and Twitter. These websites act as global platforms that allow people to share their likes, dislikes, and opinions on various topics.

In this section, you will practice deriving useful information from the data obtained from social networking sites.

Every day, millions of people use social platforms to express their opinions about almost everything under the sun. This is why most organizations prefer to collect data from these websites to know the public opinion about their products and services. This information helps organizations to take timely and crucial business decisions. R is a statistical programming tool that implements modern statistical algorithms to perform various types of analytical activities. This section takes you through the step-by-step process of gathering, segregating, and analyzing text data using the R tool. A mobile phone manufacturing company hires a data analyst to review the opinion given by people on its products. This information will help the company to know about the current market trends and further enhance the quality of its products based on the insights. The data analyst decides to collect data from the tweets of people, and then examine it under three categories: positive, negative, and neutral.

Here, you are going to help him download tweets and analyze them to derive valuable information. Before performing the social media analytics, you need to load some library utilities into the current R environment and verify the Twitter authentication information to work with the tweets.

Enter the following commands to load required packages to work with online tweets:

```
install.packages("twitteR")
install.packages("bitops")
install.packages("digest")
install.packages("RCurl")
# If there is any error while installing RCurl, follow the below
command using terminal
#sudo apt-get install libcurl4-openssl-dev
install.packages("ROAuth")
install.packages("tm")
install.packages("stringr")
install.packages("plyr")
library(twitteR)
library(ROAuth)
library(RCurl)
library(plyr)
library(stringr)
library(tm)
```

If you are working on Windows Operating System, you may face Secured Socket Layer (SSL) certificate issues.

You can avoid that by providing certificate authentication information in the `options()` function through the following command:

```
options(RCurlOptions = list(cainfo =
system.file("CurlSSL","cacert.pem",package="RCurl")))
```

After loading the required R utilities and providing the SSL certificate authentication information, load the Twitter authentication information. This information will be used to download tweets later.

Enter the following commands to load Twitter authentication information using your own Twitter credentials:

```
load("/Datasets/twitter_cred.RData")
registerTwitterOAuth(cred)
```

Figure 28.4 shows the use of Twitter credentials for Twitter authentication in R:

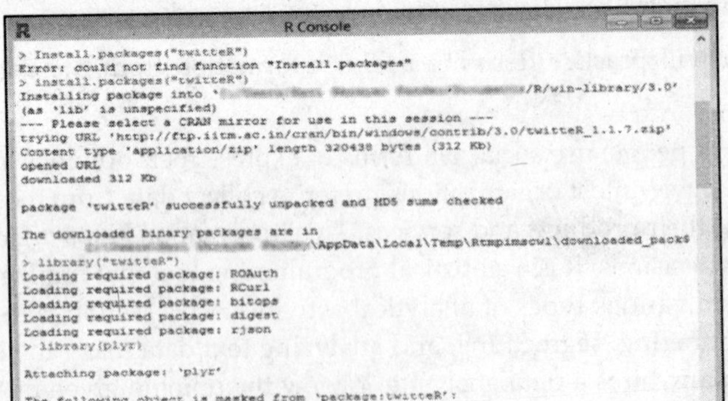

Figure 28.4: Using Twitter Credentials for Twitter Authentication in R

To analyze tweets, you first need to segregate and download them on the basis of some specific keywords.

NOTE

R provides automatic downloading of tweets by using the searchTwitter() function, which takes as its arguments the language in which the tweets need to be searched, the keyword (term to be searched on the Internet), and the number of tweets that need to be extracted containing the keyword.

Now, enter the following command to download 1000 English language (specified as `lang="en"` argument to the `searchTwitter()` function) tweets, containing the word `"nokia"`:

```
input_tweets=searchTwitter("nokia", n=1000,lang="en")
```

We can take a list of tweets at a time to analyze different opinions, as shown by the following command:

```
input_tweets[1:3]
```

Figure 28.5 shows the commands along with their outputs:

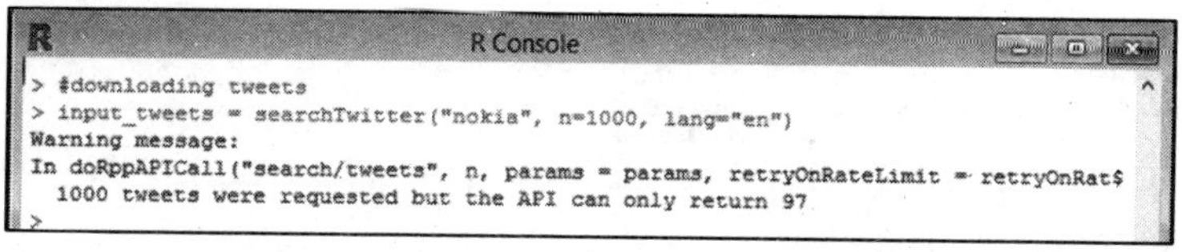

Figure 28.5: Searching a Keyword in a Specified Number of Tweets

Some tweets, containing the search word, may be insignificant for our analysis. Therefore, we need to extract tweets only with the relevant texts. Enter the following command to extract a specific set of words as a text string:

```
tweet=sapply(input_tweets,function(x) x$getText())
```

The strings can be viewed as vectors by entering the following command:

```
input_tweets[1:4]
```

The next task is to segregate tweets on the nature of the feedback they provide. The feedback would be positive, negative, or neutral. In our case, we are using only positive and negative words.

The function for sentiment analysis is given as follows:

```
score.sentiment = function(sentences, pos.words,neg.words,.progress='none')
{ scores = laply(sentences, function(sentence, pos.words, neg.words)
{ sentence = gsub("[[:punct:]]", "", sentence)
sentence = gsub("[[:cntrl:]]", "", sentence)
sentence = gsub('\\d+', '', sentence)
tryTolower = function(x)
{
y = NA
try_error = tryCatch(tolower(x), error=function(e) e)
if (!inherits(try_error, "error"))
y = tolower(x)
return(y)}
sentence = sapply(sentence, tryTolower)
word.list = str_split(sentence, "\\s+")
words = unlist(word.list)
pos.matches = match(words, pos.words)
neg.matches = match(words, neg.words)
pos.matches = !is.na(pos.matches)
neg.matches = !is.na(neg.matches)
```

```
score = sum(pos.matches) - sum(neg.matches)
return(score)
}, pos.words, neg.words, .progress=.progress )
scores.df = data.frame(text=sentences, score=scores)
return(scores.df)}
```

After writing the preceding function, the files containing positive and negative words are loaded to run the sentiment function. Enter the following commands to load the data file containing positive and negative words, respectively:

```
pos=readLines("/Datasets/positive-words.txt") # find file positive_words.txt
neg=readLines("/Datasets/negative-words.txt") # find file negative_words.txt
```

Categorize each tweet as positive, negative, or neutral by using the following code:

```
scores = score.sentiment(tweet, pos, neg, .progress='text')
scores$very.pos = as.numeric(scores$score > 0)
scores$very.neg = as.numeric(scores$score < 0)
scores$very.neu = as.numeric(scores$score == 0)
```

Figure 28.6 shows the commands along with their outputs:

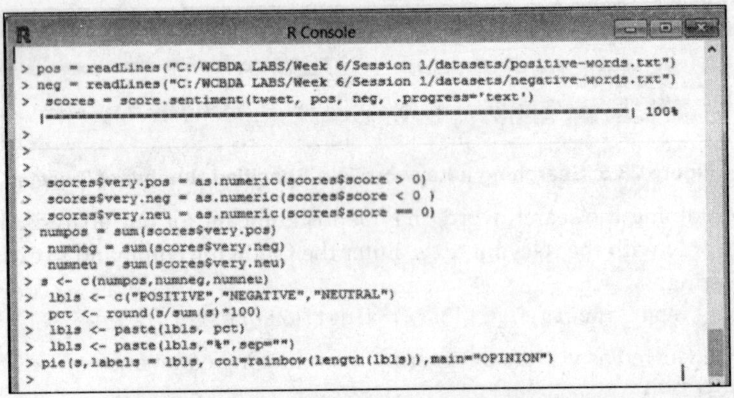

Figure 28.6: Assigning Sentiment Scores to Tweets

Enter the following commands to find out the number of positive, negative, and neutral tweets:

```
# Number of positive, neutral, and negative tweets
numpos = sum(scores$very.pos)
numneg = sum(scores$very.neg)
numneu = sum(scores$very.neu)
```

Now, aggregate the final results by using the following commands:

```
#Final results aggregation
<- c(numpos,numneg,numneu)lbls <-c("POSITIVE","NEGATIVE","NEUTRAL")pct <-
round(s/sum(s)*100)lbls <- paste(lbls, pct)lbls
<-paste(lbls,"%",sep="")
```

After the sentiments are categorized and the number of positive, negative, and neutral tweets is found out, plot the results by using the following command:

```
#Plot the results
pie(s,labels = lbls, col = rainbow(length(lbls)),main="OPINION")
```

The Pie chart for the analyzed sentiment score is shown in Figure 28.7:

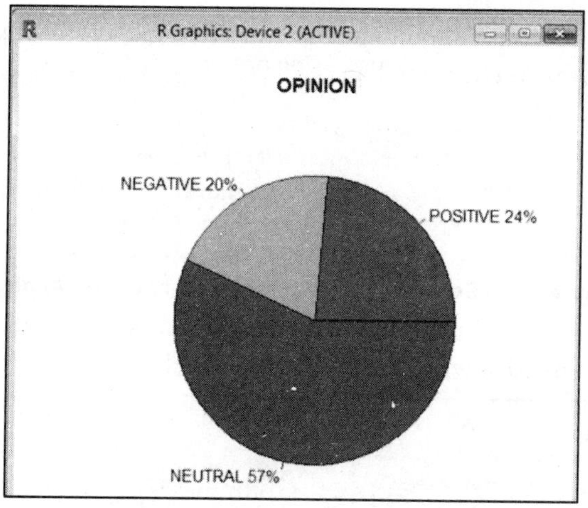

Figure 28.7: Pie Chart for the Sentiment Score

Online Social Media Analysis

We can use online tools for the analysis of text generating from social media. One of the major online social media analysis tools is Social Mention. The process of analyzing the text through Social Mention is given as follows.

The analysis of the text to find out positive, negative, and neutral views can also be performed online by performing the following steps (you will need an Internet connection to perform this):

1. Open the following link in your browser:

   http://socialmention.com/

   The Social Mention website will appear, as shown in Figure 28.8:

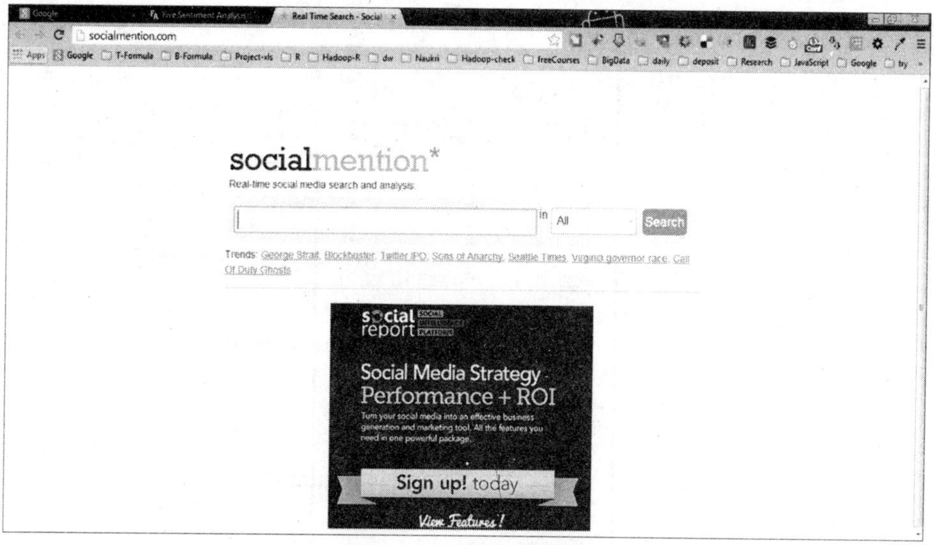

Figure 28.8: Showing the Social Mention Website

2. Type the name of the product about which you need to gather information in the Search box and press the Search button, as shown in Figure 28.9:

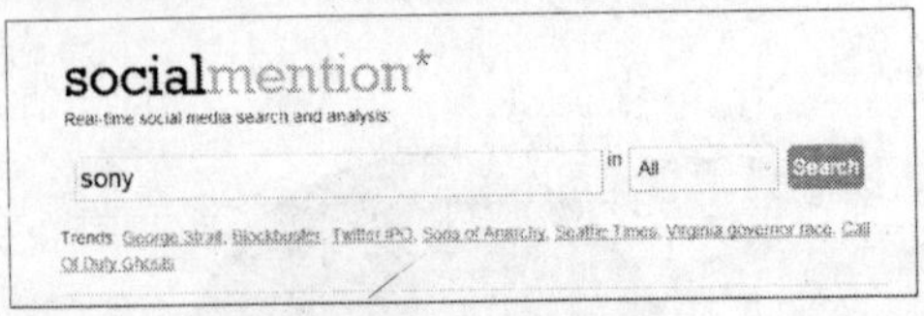

Figure 28.9: Searching a Product for Online Text Analysis

A Web page appears with the sentiment score for the product (Sony, in our case) being displayed on the left-hand side, as shown in Figure 28.10:

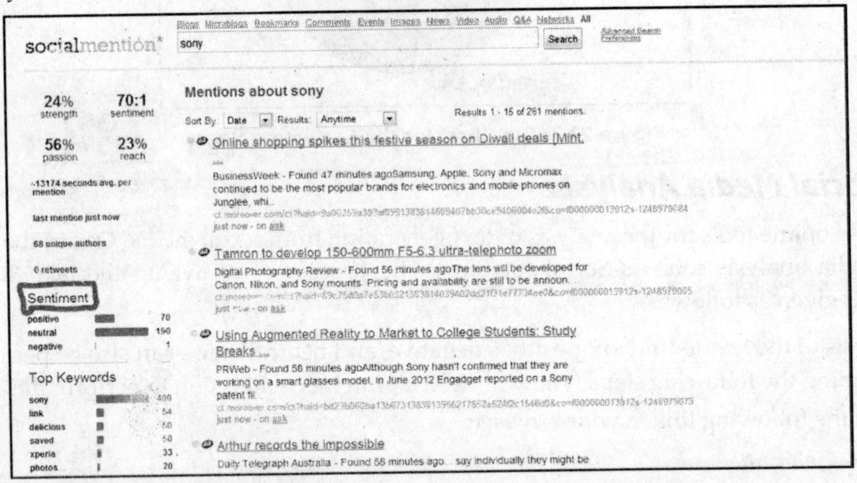

Figure 28.10: Showing the Web Page with Sentiment Score for the Product

The extended view of the Sentiment score, marked in Figure 28.10 is shown in Figure 28.11:

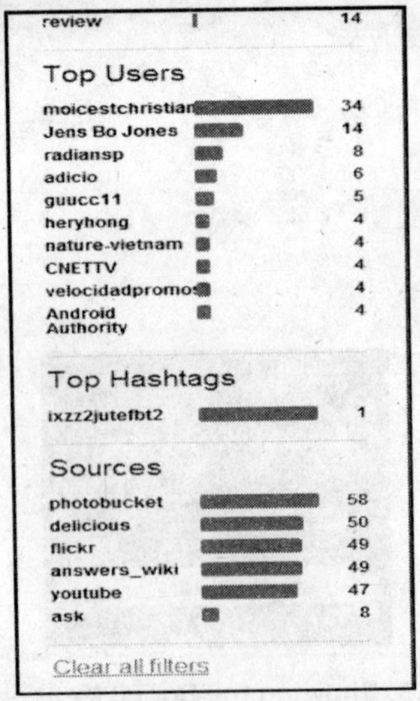

Figure 28.11: Showing the Sentiment Score for the Product and Related Information

You can get more information on the feedback of the product by clicking any link on the Web page shown in Figure 28.10.

Apart from R, you can also use the Sentiment140 tool to analyze data on the basis of the feedback given by users. Sentiment140 uses Twitter's data for the analysis purpose.

Figure 28.12 shows the Web page of the Sentiment140 text analysis tool:

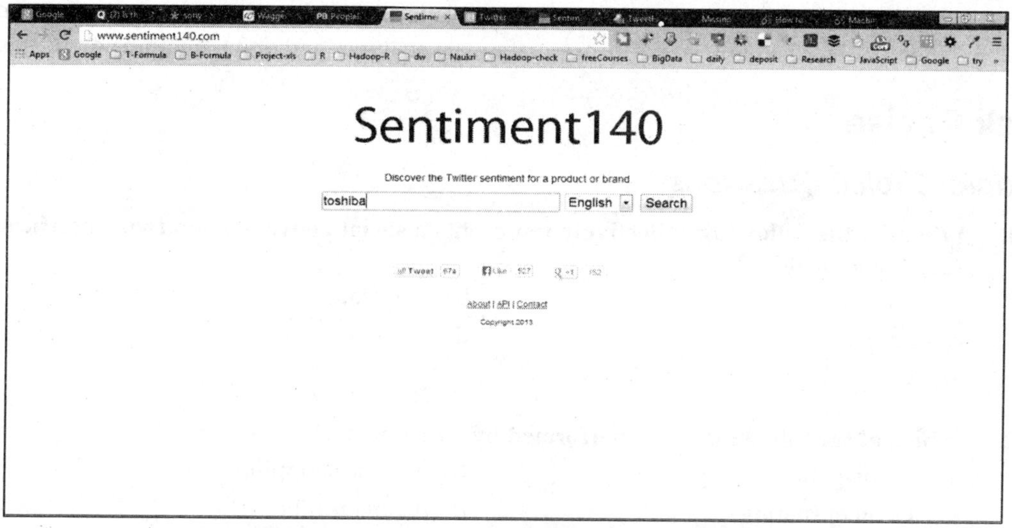

Figure 28.12: Showing the Web Page of Sentiment140

Figure 28.13 shows the online analysis of views for Toshiba products:

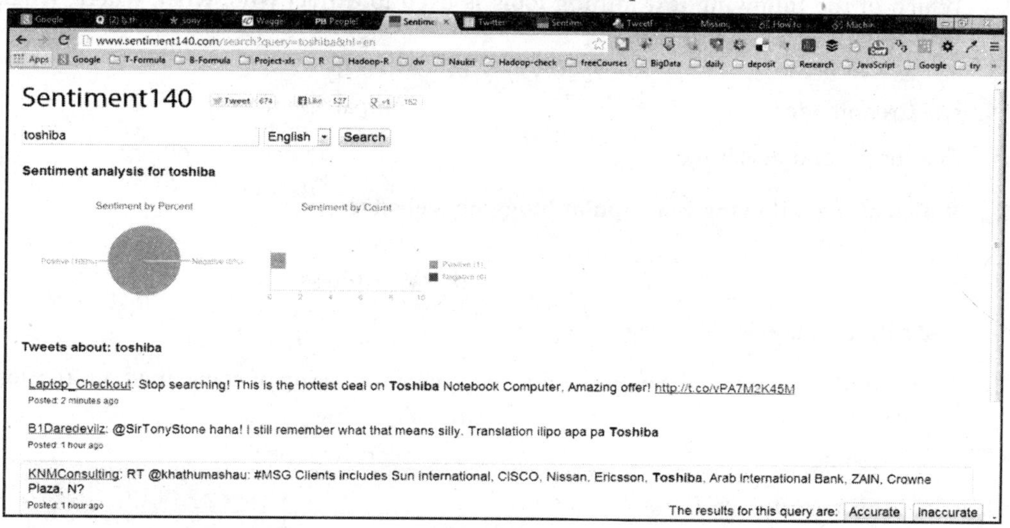

Figure 28.13: Showing the Online Analysis for Toshiba Products Using the Sentiment140 Tool

Summary

In this chapter, you learned about the growing involvement of social media in almost every arena of our life and the need to analyze the huge amount of data collected from social media platforms. The chapter highlighted the key elements of social media and their importance in analyzing business data. The chapter further introduced you to the concept and process of text mining. You also learned about sentiment analysis, its importance, and the tools to perform sentiment analysis. Towards the end, the chapter described how to perform social media analytics and opinion mining on tweets.

Quick Revise

Multiple-Choice Questions

Q1. Which of the following collectively represents a social network bound via specific sets of social relationships?

a. Websites
b. Big Data
c. People
d. Analytics tools

Ans. The correct option is c.

Q2. Which of the following is not performed by social media?

a. Participation
b. Online shopping
c. Content sharing
d. Conversation

Ans. The correct option is b.

Q3. Which of the following text mining tools is used to extract who, what, where, when, and why facts?

a. Active-Point
b. Attensity
c. Crossminder
d. Compare Suite

Ans. The correct option is b.

Q4. Which of the following is a popular blogging website?

a. Facebook
b. LinkedIn
c. Twitter
d. WordPress

Ans. The correct option is d.

Q5. Which of the following terms represents passive observation of social media activities?

a. Participation
b. Engaging
c. Listening
d. Interpretation

Ans. The correct options are a and d.

Subjective Questions

Q1. List some key elements of social media.

Ans. Social media involves the following key elements:

- **Collect**—In order to effectively incorporate social media, the business organizations first need to understand how to collect and leverage useful information and market artifacts. This involves critical and careful analysis of the information coming from various sources such as customers, competitors, journalists, and other market influencers. Various tools, such as feed readers, blog subscriptions, and email newsletters, can be employed to collect information from various sources.
- **Curate**—Once the information is collected from various sources, the next step is to effectively curate the important information to be sent to the clients and internal stakeholders. This involves intelligent filtering and aggregation of the information collected from various resources. This not only provides an effective insight to the customers but also helps in having a clear vision about the current industry standards and market trends. Various curation tools such as Newsle, LinkedIn, and RSS readers can be employed for this task.
- **Create**—After collection and curation of the collected information, the organizations need to create valuable content objects that can provide a focus and industry buzz to them. This is an effective marketing strategy to create a leader position in the industry. This can be accomplished by employing various publishing programs and sharing routines.
- **Share**—A key element for implementing effective social media is sharing of information. This employs sharing your content, information, and ideas with others. This helps in expanding the social media network. Various tools, such as Feedly and Hootsuite, help in sharing information and content over the social media.
- **Engage**—The basic idea behind social media is to engage the existing and prospective customers. The tools and routines of social media and the regular practice of listening, curation, and sharing help executives and sales personnel of an organization in engaging more and more customers, stakeholders, prospective customers, journalists, and industry influencers. Tools such as Salesforce help to connect people from different categories. Apart from that, various mobile apps also help in expanding the realm of reaching more and more people.

Q2. What is text mining?

Ans. Text mining represents the set of tools, techniques, and methods applied for automatically processing natural language textual data provided in huge amounts in the form of computer files. The extracted and structured content and themes are used for rapid analysis, identification of hidden data and information, and automatic decision making. Text mining tools are often based on the principles of information retrieval and natural learning processes.

Complex linkage structure makes text mining in social networks a challenging job, requiring the help of automated tools and sorting techniques. A number of text mining tools and algorithms have been developed to enable easy extraction of information from different textual resources. The recent developments in statistical and data processing tools have added to the evolution in the domain of text mining.

Text mining employs the concepts obtained from various fields, ranging from linguistics and statistics to Information and Communication Technologies (ICT). Statistical pattern learning is applied to create patterns from the extracted text, which are further examined to obtain valuable information. The overall process of text mining comprises retrieval of information, lexical analysis, creation and recognition of patterns, tagging, extraction of information, application of data mining techniques, and predictive analytics. This can be summarized as follows:

Text mining = Lexicometry + Data mining

The process is initiated with the retrieval of information, which involves collection and identification of information from a set of textual material. The information can come from various sources, such as websites, database, documents, or content management system. The textual information is processed by parsers and other linguistic analysis tools to examine and recognize textual features, such as people, organizations, names of places, stock ticker symbols, and abbreviations.

Q3. Describe the steps to perform text mining.

Ans. The key steps to perform text mining are given as follows:

1. **Extracting the keyword**—Any text analysis process begins by identification of relevant and precise keyword(s) that can be applied for specific queries. Next, the content and the linkage patterns are considered for applying keyword searches as the content related to similar keywords is often linked. The selected keywords act as social network nodes and play an important role while clustering the text.

2. **Classifying and clustering the text**—Various algorithms are applied for classifying text from the source content. For this process, the nodes are associated with labels prior to classification. After that, the classified text are clustered on the basis of similarity. The classification and clustering of the text are greatly influenced by the linkage structure of data. Accurate results can be obtained by applying node labeling and content-based classification techniques.

3. **Identifying patterns**—Trend analysis applies the principle that even for the same content, the clusters collected at different nodes can have different concept distributions. For this reason, the concepts at various nodes are compared and classified accordingly in the same or different subcollections.

Q4. Name some commonly used text mining software.

Ans. The following are some commonly used text mining software:

- **ActivePoint**—Applied for natural language processing and online catalog-based contextual search
- **Attensity**—Used for extraction of facts, including who, what, where, and why and then identifying people, places, and events and how they are related
- **Crossminder**—Applied for cross-lingual text analytics
- **Compare Suite**—Used for comparing texts by keywords and highlighting common and unique keywords
- **IBM SPSS Predictive Analytics Suite**—Applied for data and text mining
- **Monarch**—Applied for analysis and transformation of reports into live data
- **SAS Text Miner**—Provides a rich suite of text processing and analysis tools
- **Textalyzer**—Used for online text analysis

Q5. What do you understand by sentiment analysis?

Ans. Sentiment analysis is one of the most important components of text mining. Also termed as opinion mining, it involves careful analysis of people's opinions, sentiments, attitudes, appraisals, and evaluations. This is accomplished by examining large amounts of unstructured data obtained from the Internet on the basis of positive, negative, or neutral view of the end user.

Sentiment analysis involves the analysis of following sentences:

- **Facts**—Product A is better than product B.
- **Opinions**—I don't like A. I think B is better in terms of durability.

Similar to Web analysis, specific queries are applied in sentiment analysis to retrieve and rank relevant content. However, sentiment analysis also differs from Web analysis in certain factors. It is possible to determine from a sentiment analysis that whether the content expresses an opinion on the topic and also whether the opinion is positive or negative. Ranking in Web analysis is done on the basis of the frequency of keywords. On the other hand, ranking in sentiment analysis is done on the basis of polarity of the attitude.

Q6. List some common online tools used to perform sentiment analysis.

Ans. Some online tools to perform sentiment analysis are listed as follows:

- **Topsy**—It is used to measure success of a Website on Twitter. It tracks the occurrence of given and related keywords, website name, and website URL in tweets.
- **BackTweets**—This tool is applied to improve search engine ranking of a website. It tracks tweets that link back to a website.

- **Twitterfall**– This tool locates tweets that are important for a website. It can be used to stay in touch with the customers and consumers and respond to their queries and suggestions in real time.
- **TweetBeep**–This is used to send timely updates or alerts for the topics of interest.
- **Reachli**–Designed especially for Pinterest, it is a content-sharing website. This tool helps in tracking data and scheduling and organizing pins (denote the updates in Pinterest) in advance.

29

Mobile Analytics

If you need information on:	*See page:*

The first mobile phone was launched in 1973 by Motorola. Technologically, it was a big step because it allowed you to make calls wirelessly irrespective of the distance between the caller and the receiver. Since then, the mobile phone has changed a lot from just being a calling device. Nowadays, you can use your phone to make voice/video calls, do sale/purchase, socialize with friends, enjoy online/offline gaming, and share text/music/videos files. The rapid growth of data that is being used on mobile devices has prompted organizations to study how users use their phones. The information gathered from such an exercise, the organizations hope, would help them to develop products and services that are more suited to the user's requirements and needs.

As we know, Web analytics is the study of the behavior of visitors on a website. In a similar way, we need to have a tool that can study the behavior of users with its mobile devices. This study can help service providers or organizations make improvement in existing services/products and give organizations innovative ideas to develop new applications. This would make the users or customers happy and help the organization to maximize its profit.

Mobile analytics is a service that performs the collection and analysis of data related to any application (or app) of a business organization. Here, an app is a software application running on a mobile device. In this chapter, the terms application and app have been used interchangeably.

Mobile analytics provides a technical view (like a graph or chart) of data collected from a mobile device. Different types of mobile analytics collect and represent different data in various ways; for example, mobile analytics tools related to online gaming collect information related to the time spent by the user with any game; e-commerce-related mobile analytics tools track and collect information related to the purchase habits of users; and online-trading-related mobile analytics tools track day-to-day sales.

The data collected through mobile analytics is converted into information that the organization can use. This information relates to the behavior of a user or customer with respect to any application in the mobile device. By analyzing this behavior, organizations can know the buying pattern and likes and dislikes of users and offer services or products to them accordingly. In this way, mobile analytics helps organizations to gain customer loyalty and maximize organizational profit.

Mobile analytics is useful in a wide range of industries related to finance, Business Process Outsourcing (BPO), healthcare, and online traders.

In this chapter, you will learn about the definition, types, and challenges of mobile analytics. You will also learn how to perform analysis using mobile analytics.

Introducing Mobile Analytics

We are now using fourth-generation (4G) wireless mobile technologies. When you look at the past, you will see that wireless mobile technologies have shown a steady growth, evolving from 1G to 4G. With every major shift in the technology, there has been a corresponding improvement in both the speed and efficiency of mobile devices.

First generation (1G) mobile devices provided only a "mobile voice", but in second-generation (2G) devices, larger coverage and improved digital quality were provided. Third-generation (3G) technology focused on multimedia applications like videoconferencing through mobile phones. 3G opened the gates for the mobile broadband, which was seen in fourth-generation (4G) devices. 4G provides wide range access, multiservice capacity, integration of all older mobile technologies, and low bit cost to the user.

Figure 29.1 shows the evolution of different generations of mobile technologies:

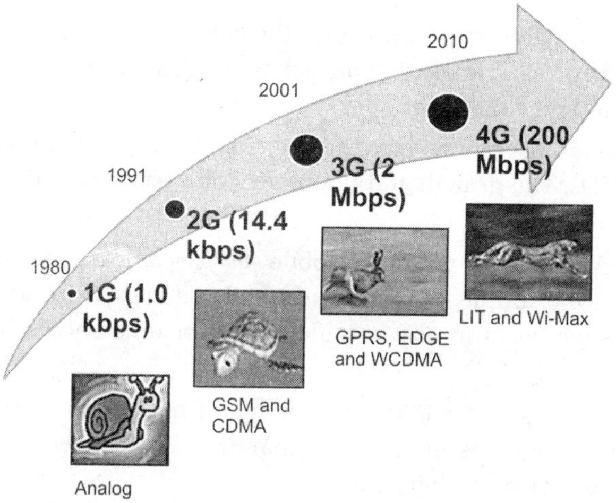

Source: *3GPP Alliance, UMTS forums, Informa telecoms, Motorola, ZTI.*

Figure 29.1: Evolution of Mobile Technologies

NOTE

The full forms of the terms used in Figure 29.1 are as follows:

- ***GSM**—Global System for Mobile Communications*
- ***CDMA**—Code Division Multiple Access*
- ***GPRS**—General Packet Radio Service*
- ***EDGE**—Enhanced Data rates for GSM Evolution*
- ***WCDMA**—Wideband Code Division Multiple Access*
- ***LIT**—Long Term Evolution*

"Forget what we have taken for granted on how consumers use the Internet," said Karsten Weide, research vice president, Media and Entertainment. "Soon, more users will access the Web using mobile devices than using PCs, and it's going to make the Internet a very different place."

According to International Telecommunication Union (ITU), an agency of the United Nations (UN) responsible for information and communication technologies-related issues, the number of mobile users in 2008 was 548 million. This number increased to 6835 million in 2012.

According to Informa, a research firm in the US, there were over 3.3 billion active cell phone subscriptions in 2007 all over the world. This effectively means that around half of the total population of the earth is using mobile devices.

Given the above statistics, it is imperative for organizations to find ways of analyzing data related to mobile devices and use the data to market and sell their products and services through these devices. Mobile analytics is one tool that organizations have to do this.

Define Mobile Analytics

Marketers want to know what their customers want to see and do on their mobile device so that they can target the customer.

Similar to the process of analytics used to study the behavior of users on the Web or social media, mobile analytics is the process of analyzing the behavior of mobile users. The primary goal of mobile analytics is to understand the following:

- **New users**—These are users who have just started using a mobile service. Users are identified by unique device IDs. The growth and popularity of a service greatly depend on the number of new users it is able to attract.
- **Active users**—These are users who use mobile services at least once in a specified period. If the period is one day, for example, the active user will use the service several times during the day. The number of active users in any specific period of time shows the popularity of a service during that period.
- **Percentage of new users**—This is the percentage of new users over the total active users of a mobile service. This figure is always less than 100%, but a very low value means that the particular service or app is not doing very well.
- **Sessions**—When a user opens an app, it is counted as one session. In other words, the session starts with the launching of the app and finishes with the app's termination. Note that a session is not related to how long the app has been used by the user.
- **Average usage duration**—This is the average duration that a mobile user uses the service.
- **Accumulated users**—This refers to the total number of users (old as well as new) who have used an app before a specific time.
- **Bounce rate**—The bounce rate is calculated in percentage (%). It can be calculated as follows:
    - Bounce rate = Number of terminated sessions on any specific page of an app/Total number of sessions of the app*100.
    - The bounce rate can be used by service providers to help them monitor and improve their service so that customers remain satisfied and do not leave the service.
- **User retention**—After a certain period of time, the total number of new users still using any app is known as the user retention of that app.

Commercially, mobile analytics can be defined as the study of data that is collected to achieve the following purposes:

- **Track sales**—Mobile analytics can track the sale of products.
- **Analyze screen flow**—Mobile analytics can track how and where a user touches the screen. This information can be used to make interactive GUIs and also decide the place for mobile ads.
- **Keep customers engaged**—Mobile analytics studies the behavior of the users or customers, and display ads and other screens to keep them engaged.
- **Analyze the preferences of visitors**—On the basis of the user's touch, tap and other behavior on the screen, mobile analytics can analyze their preferences.

- **Convert potential buyers into buyers**—According to the users' likes and dislikes, mobile analytics offers different products and services to them. The purpose of this exercise is to convert a visitor to a buyer.
- **Analyze m-commerce activities of visitors**—Mobile analytics can analyze the m-commerce activities of the visitors and find out a lot of useful information like a user's frequency of making a purchase and the amount he is willing to spend.
- **Track Web links that users visit on their mobile phones**—Mobile analytics can be used to analyze the visited Web links of users and know their preferences.

NOTE

Mobile commerce (or m-commerce) refers to the delivery of electronic commerce capabilities directly into the consumer's hand anywhere, via wireless technology.

Mobile Analytics and Web Analytics

Mobile analytics has several similarities with Web and social analytics, such as both can analyze the behavior of the user with regard to an application and send this information to the service provider. However, there are also several important differences between Web analytics and mobile analytics.

Some of the main differences between Web analytics and mobile analytics are as follows:

- **Analytics segmentation**—Mobile analytics works on the basis of location of the mobile devices. For example, suppose a company is offering cab service in a city like New York. In this case, the company can use mobile analytics to identify the target people travelling in New York. Mobile analytics works for location-based segments, while Web analytics works globally.
- **Complexity of code**—Mobile analytics requires more complex code and programming languages to implement than Web analytics, which is easier to code.
- **Network service providers**—Mobile analytics is totally dependent on Network Service Providers (NSPs), while Web analytics is independent of this factor.
- **Measure**—Sometimes, it is difficult to measure information from the mobile analytics apps because they can run offline. Web analytics always runs online. So, we can easily measure vital information with it.
- **Tools**—To do the ultimate analysis on data, we require some other tools of Web analytics with mobile analytics tools. Web analytics, on the other hand, does not require any other tool for analysis.

Types of Results from Mobile Analytics

The study of consumer behavior helps business firms or other organizations to improve their marketing strategies. Nowadays, every organization is making extra effort to understand and know the behavior of its consumers.

Mobile analytics provides an effective way of measuring large amounts of mobile data for organizations. It also shows how useful marketing tools, such as ads, are converting potential buyers to actual purchasers. It also offers deep insight into what makes people buy a product or service and what makes them quit a service.

The technologies behind mobile analytics, like Global Positioning System (GPS), are more sophisticated than those used in Web analytics; hence, compared to Web analytics, users can be tracked and targeted more accurately with mobile analytics.

Mobile analytics can easily and effectively collect data from various data sources and manipulate it into useful information. Mobile analytics keeps track of the following information:

- **Total time spent**—This information shows the total time spent by the user with an application.
- **Visitors' location**—This information shows the location of the user using any particular application.
- **Number of total visitors**—This is the total number of users using any particular application, useful in knowing the application's popularity.
- **Click paths of the visitors**—Mobile analytics tracks of the activities of a user visiting the pages of any application.
- **Pages viewed by the visitor**—Mobile analytics tracks the pages of any application visited by the user, which again reflects the popular sections of the application.
- **Downloading choice of users**—Mobile analytics keeps track of files downloaded by the user. This helps app owners to understand the type of data users like to download.
- **Type of mobile device and network used**—Mobile analytics tracks the type of mobile device and network used by the user. This information helps mobile service providers and mobile phone sellers understand the popularity of mobile devices and networks and make further improvements as required.
- **Screen resolution of the mobile phone used**—Any information or content that appears on mobile devices is according to the screen size of these devices. This important aspect of ensuring that the content fits a particular device screen is done through mobile analytics.
- **Performance of advertising campaigns**—Mobile analytics is used to keep track of the performance of advertising campaigns and other activities by analyzing the number of visitors and time spent by them as well as other methods.

Types of Applications for Mobile Analytics

There are two types of applications made for mobile analytics. They are:

- Mobile Web analytics
- Mobile application analytics

Let's learn about these types of applications in detail in the following sections.

Mobile Web Analytics

Mobile Web refers to the use of mobile phones or other devices like tablets to view online content via a light-weight browser. The name of any mobile-specific site can be the form of m.example.com. Mobile Web sometimes depends on the size of the screen of the devices. For example, if you design an application for a small screen, its images would appear blurred on a big screen; similarly, if you make your site for the big screen, it can be heavy for a small screen device. Some organizations are starting to build sites specifically for tablets because they have found that neither their mobile-specific site nor their main website ideally serves the tablet segment. To solve this problem, mobile

Web should have a responsive design. In other words, it should have the property to adapt the content to the screen size of the user's device.

Figure 29.2 shows the difference between a website, a mobile site, and a responsive-design site:

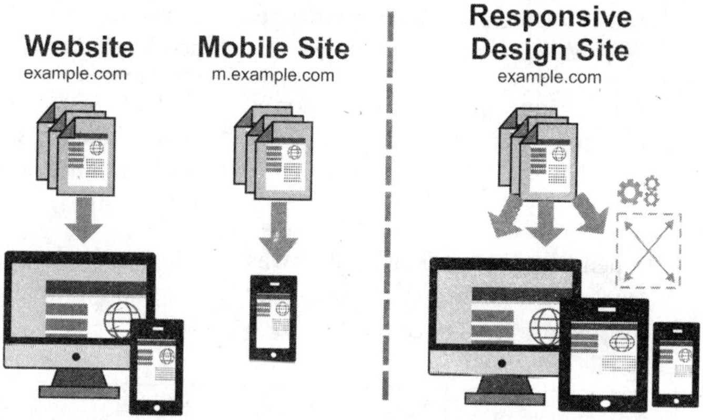

Figure 29.2: Difference among a Website, Mobile Site, and Responsive-design Site

In Figure 29.2, you can see that a website can be opened on both computers and mobile phones, while a mobile site can be opened only on mobile phones; responsive-design sites, on the other hand, can be opened on any device like a computer, tablet, or mobile phone.

Mobile Application Analytics

The term mobile app is short for the term mobile application software. It is an application program designed to run on smartphones and other mobile devices.

Mobile apps are usually available through application distribution platforms like Apple App Store and Google Play. Application distribution platforms are typically operated by the owner of the mobile operating system. Examples of mobile operating systems include the Apple App Store, Google Play, Windows Phone Store, and BlackBerry App World. Some mobile apps are freely available, while others must be bought.

Depending on the objective of analytics, an organization should decide whether it needs a mobile application or a mobile website. If the organization wants to create an interactive engagement with users on mobile devices, mobile app is a good option; however, for business purposes, mobile websites are more suitable than mobile apps.

Table 29.1 lists the main differences between mobile app analytics and mobile Web analytics:

Table 29.1: Differences between Mobile App Analytics and Mobile Web Analytics

Factors	Mobile App Analytics	Mobile Web Analytics
Screen and Page	Mobile app analytics does not have pages. The user can interact with various screens.	Mobile Web analytics has pages like normal websites, and users do interact with various pages.

Table 29.1: Differences between Mobile App Analytics and Mobile Web Analytics

Factors	Mobile App Analytics	Mobile Web Analytics
Use of built-in features of mobile devices	Mobile app analytics can access built-in features, such as gyroscope, GPS, accelerometer, and storage.	Mobile Web analytics does not use built-in features, like gyroscope, GPS, accelerometer, etc.
Session time	Mobile app analytics has shorter session timeouts (around 30 seconds).	Mobile Web analytics has longer session timeouts. In general, a session will end after 30 minutes of inactivity for websites.
Online/Offline	Depending on how it was developed, mobile app analytics may not require to be connected to a mobile network.	Mobile Web analytics requires an Internet connection and can run online only.
Updates	App owners provide frequent updates and new versions of the apps.	Updates are not frequent.

CASELET

According to Google, the percentage of search queries on mobile phones has increased manifold in the last few years. Some of the most searched industries on mobiles are as follows: restaurants (29.6%), auto (16.8%), electronics (15.5%), and insurance (15.4%).

Introducing Mobile Analytics Tools

Advances in analytic technologies and business intelligence are allowing CIOs to go big, go fast, go deep, go cheap and go mobile with business data. —*www.CIO.com*

The fundamental task of the mobile analytics tool is similar to other digital analytical tools like Web analytics. They capture data, collect it, and help to generate reports that can be used meaningfully after processing.

The selection of analytics tools is not an easy process because these tools are new and undergo rapid enhancements as compared to traditional Web analytics tools. Companies frequently upgrade their existing analytical tools as well as launch new tools with new features.

Mobile analytics tools have some technical limitations; all mobile analytics tools do not perform all the services, so must find out which tool can be beneficial for you. Following are some points to be considered while selecting mobile analytics tools:

- **What is your analytical goal?**—No single mobile analytics tool can fulfill all your needs; therefore, it is essential to set your analytical goal so that you can select the right tools. You can take the help of experts to make your goal in terms of the capabilities of the tools.
- **Analysis techniques**—Various analysis techniques exist to analyze the information of mobile users' behavior. For example, through 'packet sniffing' an intruder can obtain important personal information of users from data packets; 'image-based tagging' uses a query string to guess the activities of the user; and 'data collection scripts' analyze users' requests.

- **Way of presentation**—Information flows between a mobile device and the server according to the client-server architecture. Mobile analytics captures data as it passes through the mobile network. The data capture is done on a server that is different from the actual server. This server is placed between mobile devices and its actual server. This type of tracking generates a large amount of data in the form of log files. The reading of these log files is again a daunting task.

Now, the question is, 'how is the information presented to you?' You must choose an analytical tool that best suits your requirements.

There are two classes of mobile analytics tools:

- **Internal mobile analytics tools**—These refer to software that is provided by the SaaS (Software as a Service) vendors. It can be software installed and maintained by the IT department of any data center. Some examples of internal mobile analytics tools are Localytics and WebTrends.
- **External mobile analytics tools**—These are services provided by third-party data vendors, which are responsible for collecting, manipulating, analyzing, and generating reports for the customers from their proprietary systems. Some examples of external mobile analytics tools are comScore and Groundtruth.

According to Aconitum Mobile (a software development company in the US), the top four mobile analytics tools (or packages) are as follows:

1. **Localytics**—This is a big marketing and analytics platform for mobile and Web apps. Its developer is Localytics, in Boston. It supports cross-platform and Web-based applications. For more details, you can check out their website at www.localytics.com.

   Localytics supports push messaging, business analytics, and acquisition campaigns management. Localytics has a list of big customers like Microsoft, New York Times, ESPN, Soundcloud, and eBay.

2. **Appsee**—Appsee was founded by Zahi Boussiba and Yoni Douek, in 2012 based in Tel Aviv, Israel. It provides analytical services with features like conversion funnel analysis, heatmaps, and much more. For more details, you can check out their website at http://www.appsee.com.

3. **Google Analytics**—Google Analytics is a great free service provided by Google. It is a cross-platform, Web-based application. It offers analytics services to mobile app and mobile developers. You can check out the tool at www.google.com/analytics.

4. **Mixpanel**—Mixpanel is a 'business analytics service.' It is also a cross-platform and Web-based application. It can continually follow the user and mobile Web interactions and provide attractive tool offers to the user. For more information, you can visit the website at www.mixpanel.com.

Mobile analytics tools can be categorized as follows:

- Location-based tracking tools
- Real-time analytics tools
- User behavior tracking tools

We will learn about these tools in the following sections.

SCENARIO

Mr. Smith, the brand manager of Argon, is due to launch an online campaign for the organization's new breakfast cereal. The campaign will consist of a product launch video, and he hopes that it will become viral, and the content is in the form of user-generated images, and a fan forum is monitored by brand advocates. A previous campaign he was responsible for had failed due to high video abandonment rates and negative comments left in the forum relating to poor user experience. This time, Mr. Smith is using customer personas based on device preference and visitor context to develop a more targeted customer experience-messaging that reflects visitor context and a mobile Web experience adapted to the device capabilities.

Location-based Tracking Tools

A location-based tracking tool stores information about the location of mobile devices (or the location of user). These tools are software applications for mobile devices, and they continuously monitor the location of the devices and manipulate information thus obtained in various ways. For example, it can display the location of friends (persons in the contact list of your mobile phone), ATMs, cafés, hotels, and nearby police stations. The following are some location-based tracking tools:

- **Geoloqi**—This tool is a platform for location-based services, and it was launched in 2010 by the founder, Amber Case in the United States. It supports the creation of location-based notes and time-limited private location sharing.
- **Placed**—Placed provides a 'ratings service' by measuring various types of information such as place visited and duration of visit. This is an efficient tool to explain offline consumer behavior.

SCENARIO

Mr. Jeff, the marketing director of Argon, is preparing a campaign to sell holiday packages. He wants to target different mobile device users with different promotional offers. He struggles to segment his audience as he doesn't know what portion of his site's California-based visitors have GPS enabled phones, how many of those generally have GPS switched on, what portion browses the site while in or near a store, and whether they abandon the buying process when low on battery or bandwidth.

He finds an equal number of users of tablets and smartphones. He decides to build separate presentation views for these devices with adaptive content based on users. The created presentation includes devices that have 3G and GPS enabled. He decides to offer a rebate for users that are within a certain distance from the outlets of the company during opening hours. Smith can now not only devise the right strategy for each campaign, but also monitor conversions post-launch, almost instantly being able to pinpoint the causes of success and failure to adjust the strategy in real time.

Real-time Analytics Tools

"The 6.8 billion subscribers are approaching the 7.1 billion world population" (ITU). This is illustrated in Figure 29.3.

Figure 29.3 shows the growth of mobile phone users (in billions) with respect to years:

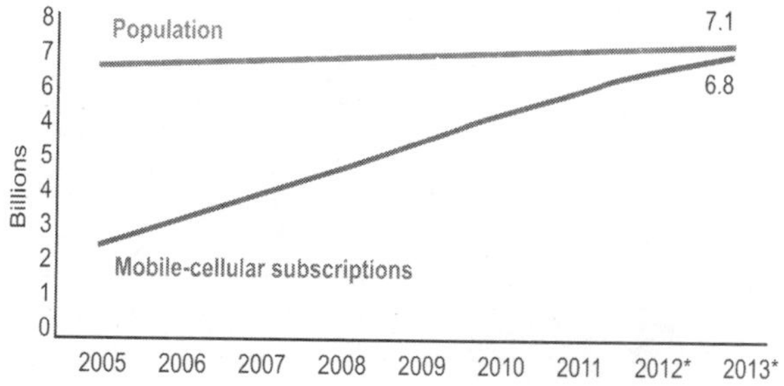

Figure 29.3: Growth of Mobile Subscribers

With the increase in the popularity of mobile phones and mobile Web, business organizations want to know more about the behavior of the user. Real-time analytics tools refer to software tools that analyze and report data in real time.

The following are some real-time analytics tools:

- **Geckoboard**—Geckoboard is a real-time dashboard that can collect, display, report, and share data that is important for you and your business in real time. According to Damian Kimmelman, the founder and CEO at Duedil, "Geckoboard simplifies the decision-making process. It is hard to dispute something that's right in front of you."

  Figure 29.4 shows the Geckoboard application:

Figure 29.4: Geckoboard Application

- **Mixpanel**—Mixpanel is a Web-based, cross-platform service. It is a business analytics service that tracks user interactions with mobile Web applications. It offers services to users on the basis of user behavior. Mixpanel does all its activities in real time. Suhail Doshi and Tim Trefren founded Mixpanel in 2009 in San Francisco, California.

Figure 29.5 shows the Mixpanel applications:

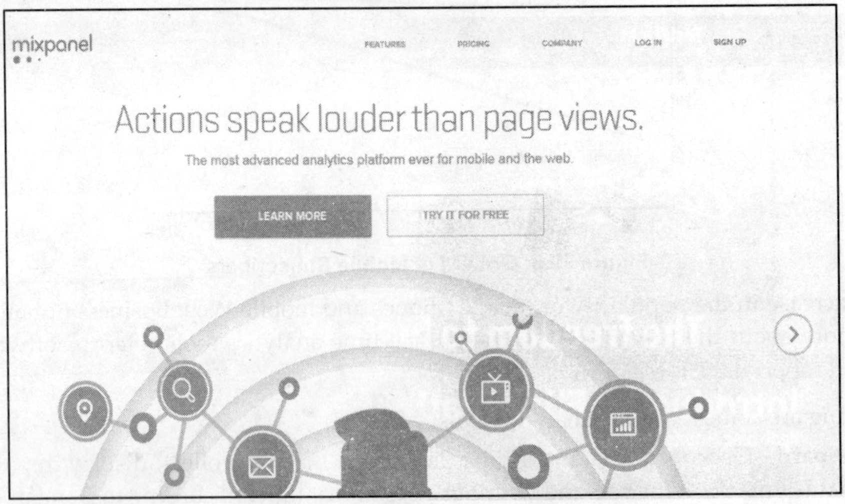

Figure 29.5: Mixpanel Application

User Behavior Tracking Tools

User behavior tracking tool is a software tool that tracks user behavior with any particular mobile application.

These behavior reports can help organizations to improve their applications and services. You can get a lot of information about your users, such as:

- Screens viewed in a session
- Number of screens viewed in a session
- Technical errors faced by the user
- The frequency of the user using any particular app
- Sessions life
- Time taken in the loading of any app elements
- Any specific action performed with the content, such as clicking of ads

These reports provide an excellent way for an organization to know how users use specific applications on their mobile phones. By customizing the tracking settings, an organization can observe the behavior of the user on any particular page (such as the product listing page) and use the information to fulfill their business objectives. The following are some popular behavior-tracking tools:

- **TestFlight**—Let's suppose a company has many testers, spread over different countries (or locations). The company has a new app that it wants to test. How is it going to test the app? The solution is TestFlight. TestFlight is a free software platform. Using TestFlight, a team of developers can use beta and internal iOS applications to manage the testing and feedback using the dashboard of TestFlight. The TestFlight SDK has a wide range of useful APIs to test application from various dimensions.

Figure 29.6 shows the TestFlight application:

Figure 29.6: TestFlight Application

- **Mobile App Tracking**—This tool tracks and analyzes mobile app installations. It can report user engagement and Lifetime Value (LTV) beyond the installations. It is efficient in scaling mobile advertising campaigns. It can collect customer's behavior related to an ad just through tapping.

NOTE

Lifetime Value (LTV) is related to the net profit gained by the entire future relationship with the customer.

Figure 29.7 shows the Mobile App Tracking application:

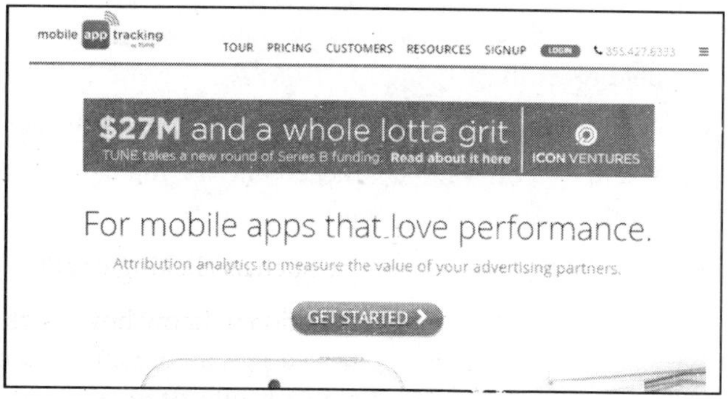

Figure 29.7: Mobile App Tracking Application

Performing Mobile Analytics

In this section, you will first understand the basic steps to integrate mobile analytics within your business processes. Then, you will do a practical where you will analyze datasets on mobile phones by using mobile applications.

To integrate mobile analytics with business processes, you must perform the following basic steps:

- Select the appropriate mobile device like a smartphone or tablet.

- List the objectives of mobile analytics for your business process.
- Identify the target audience and create a dataset for it.
- Modify the dataset by adding missing values and removing unnecessary data.
- Use the dimension-reduction technique and transform data (if possible).
- Perform some required data mining techniques, like text mining.
- Select data mining algorithms and do some analysis for mobile mining.
- Apply data mining algorithm and verify the relationships among the variables.
- Evaluate the result/interpretation.

As we have discussed in the earlier section, the whole process of mobile communication is done through the client-server method. So, the mobile analytics process can be done either on a mobile device or on the server providing services to the mobile device. According to the location of data collection, mobile analytics is categorized as follows:

- Data collection through mobile device
- Data collection on server

Data Collection through Mobile Device

Data for analysis is collected on the mobile devices and sent back to the server for further manipulation. This collection process may be done online as well as offline. This simply means that some data collection processes require an Internet connection to send collected data to the server but, on the other hand, several applications collect data into spreadsheets, and they do not require an Internet connection. Collected data can be stored in various formats.

Data collection through mobile devices has the following benefits:

- Allows data collection in real time
- Proves beneficial for field executives
- Allows data collection to be stored in various formats like text, graphs, images, etc.
- Allows the location of field executives to be tracked and the management to assign tasks to them according to their location
- Reduces unnecessary paperwork
- Prevents data redundancy because the data is collected and shared with the entire team within seconds

The following are some commonly used data collection applications:

- Numbers is a very simple-to-use tool. It can be used to organize data, perform calculations, and manage lists for you with a few taps. It provides various templates for making graphs and charts. Moreover, you can create your own templates too. It has around 250 functions that can perform simple-to-complex calculations for you. You can create your own formulas through built-in functions and the help feature.

Figure 29.8 shows the GUI of numbers:

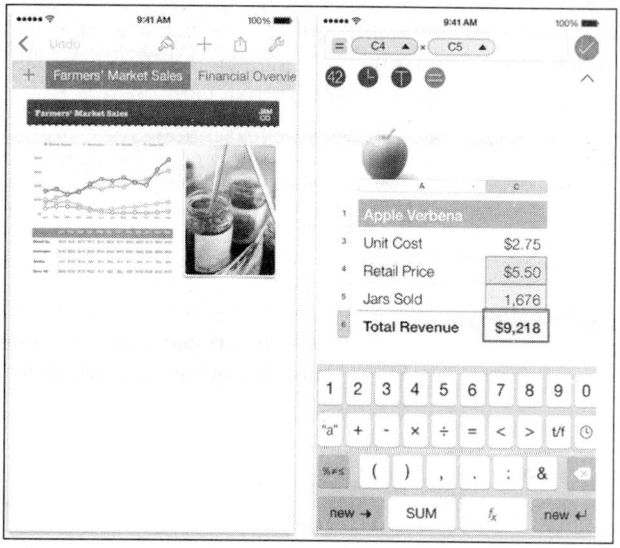

Figure 29.8: GUI of Numbers

- HanDBase is a relational database management system. It was initially designed to run on Palm PDAs, but can run on almost any handheld platform. HanDBase is not as full-featured as Oracle, Sybase, and DB2, but it still has various other features that make it important for computing. It is simple enough, supports multiple handheld platforms, and provides high security. The company offers a few apps to download free from its website.

HanDBase®

Figure 29.9 shows the GUI of HanDBase:

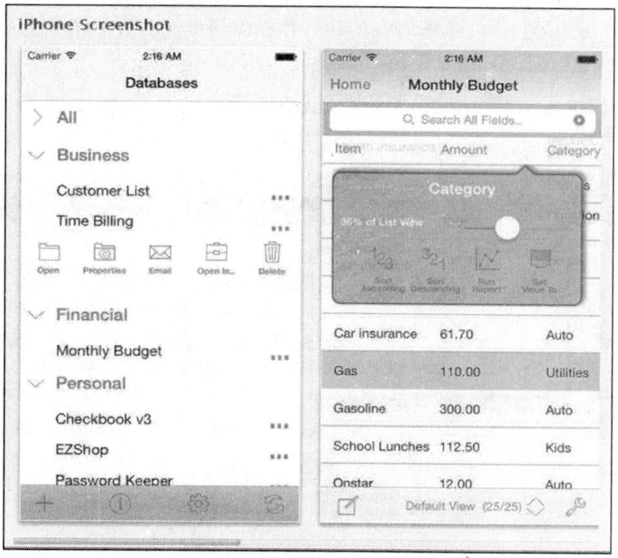

Figure 29.9: GUI of HanDBase

- Statistics Visualizer is a tool for iPads and is nicknamed as StatViz. It is a perfect statistical data tool for students and researchers. It performs statistical calculations and provides results with detailed explanations. The main feature of this tool is the dynamic graph, which helps you to quickly understand difficult statistical concepts.

  Figure 29.10 shows the GUI of StatViz:

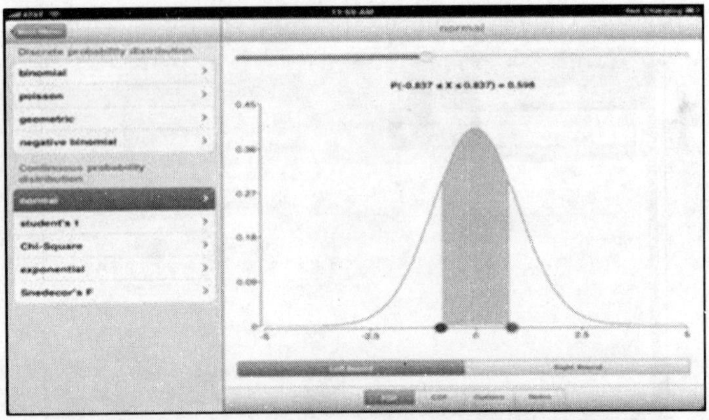

Figure 29.10: GUI of StatViz

Data Collection on Server

As we have studied in the previous section, data collected by a mobile device is ultimately transferred to its server for analysis. A server stores the received data, performs analysis over it, and creates reports.

The following are some popular applications that collect data into the server:

- DataWinners is the data collection service design for experts. This application converts paper forms into digital questionnaires. Team members can submit their data through any service like SMS, Web, etc. DataWinners provides an efficient data collection facility that can reduce users' decision-making time.

  The home page of the DataWinners application is shown in Figure 29.11:

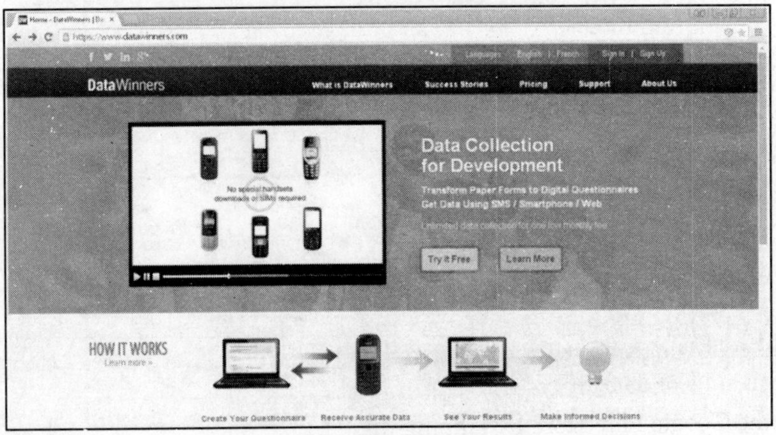

Figure 29.11: Home Page of DataWinners

- COMMANDmobile is an application that can perform mobile data collection and workforce management services. COMMANDmobile is more accurate and efficient than traditional paper and pencil approaches. The application uploads the data as soon as it is collected. Its response time is very small; thus, it can perform well in emergencies. It gives very good ROI (Return on Investment).

  The home page of COMMANDmobile application is shown in Figure 29.12:

Figure 29.12: Home Page of COMMANDmobile

Till now, you have studied various fundamental concepts related to mobile analytics. Now, let us do a practical activity with mobile analytics.

Get ready to analyze datasets on mobile phones using a mobile application. We have already discussed the key points for analyzing data by using mobile phones and tablets. Now, through this hands-on practice, you will analyze data stored in a given dataset available on a mobile device. You must have an android mobile phone and an Internet connection to do this practical work.

The objective of the activity is as follows: The marketing manager of a company performed an analysis on the listed price of items that his/her company needs to purchase from the company's peers. He/she wants to present the results of the analysis to the top management of his/her company during a meeting. He/she wants to use graphical techniques for presenting the analysis results on a tablet that runs on the android Operating System (OS). The marketing manager will use a mobile application, which he/she needs to download and install on his/her tablet for demonstrating the analysis results. You are going to help him/her download and install the application and create graphs using the application.

Perform the following steps to download and install the Graph Trial app, and then create a graph to present the results of data analysis:

1. Open the Google Play Store by tapping the Play Store icon on the screen of any android phone or tablet. A window appears, showing the contents of the play store (Figure 29.13).

2. Type Graph Trial in the search box, and tap the button to start the search operation, as shown in Figure 29.13:

Figure 29.13: Showing the Google Play Store Window

A window appears, containing the list of available apps for the particular search item (Figure 29.14).

3. Select the first app, named Graph trial, from the window by tapping it, as shown in Figure 29.14:

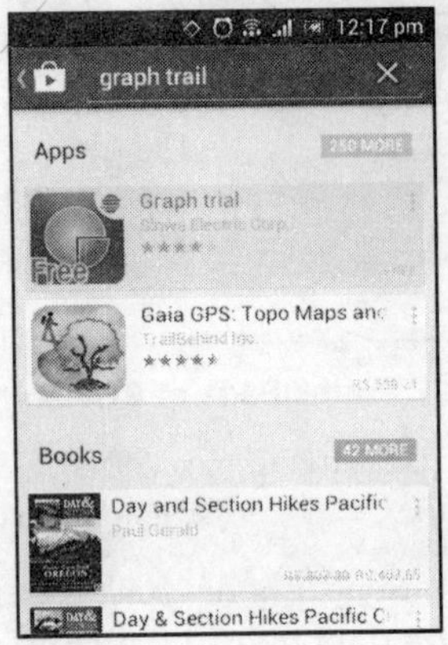

Figure 29.14: Selecting the Graph Trial App from the List

The next window appears, asking for permission to install the app (Figure 29.15).

4. Tap the ACCEPT button to install the app on your device, as shown in Figure 29.15:

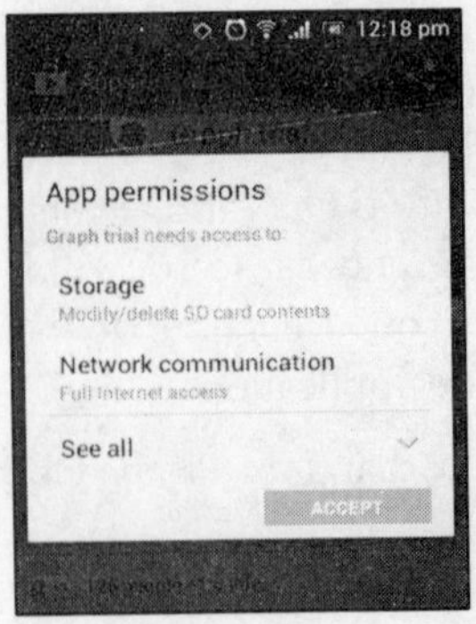

Figure 29.15: Showing the Installation Permission Window

A new window appears with the INSTALL button (Figure 29.16).

5. Tap the INSTALL button to install the app, as shown in Figure 29.16:

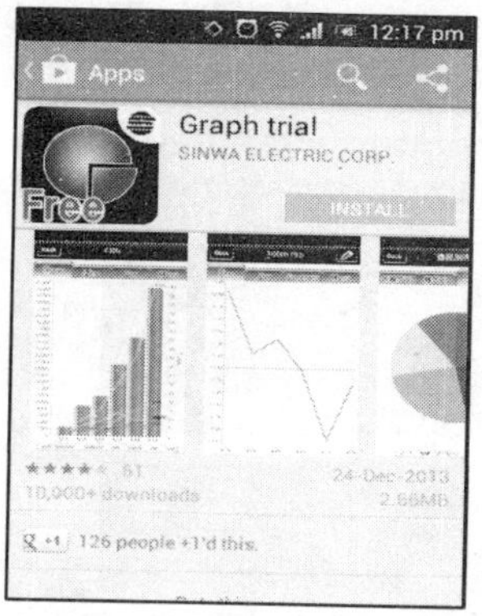

Figure 29.16: Showing the Install App Window

The downloading and installation process of the Graph trial app begins, as shown in Figure 29.17:

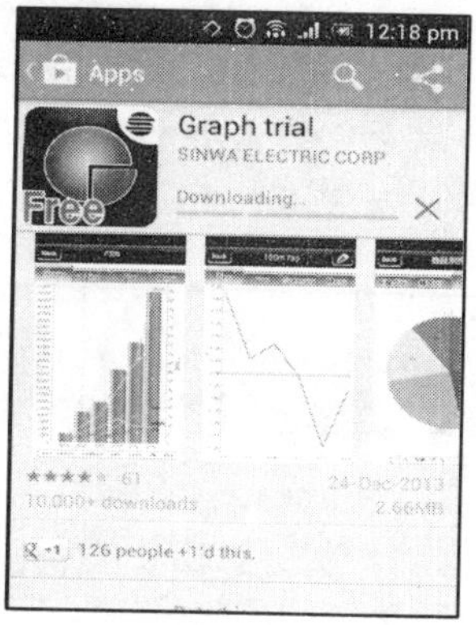

Figure 29.17: Showing the Downloading Window

After the installation is completed, the Graph trial icon appears on the tablet's screen, as shown in Figure 29.18:

Figure 29.18: Showing the Tablet Screen Containing the Installed App Icon

6. Tap the Graph trial icon (Figure 29.18) to get to the home screen, as shown in Figure 29.19:

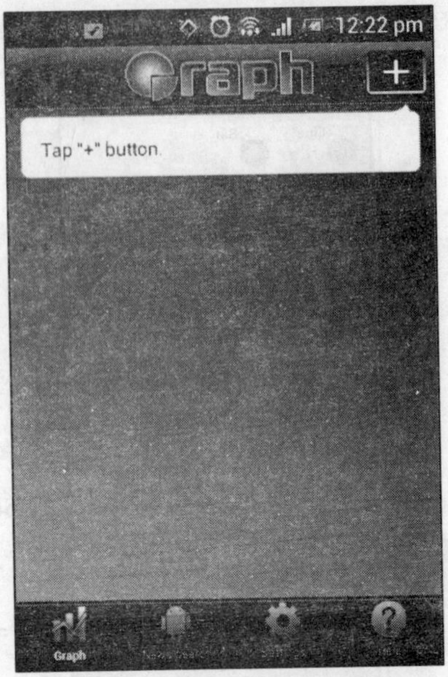

Figure 29.19: Showing the App Home Screen

7. Tap the [+] button (Figure 29.19) to get the graph type selection window, as shown in Figure 29.20:

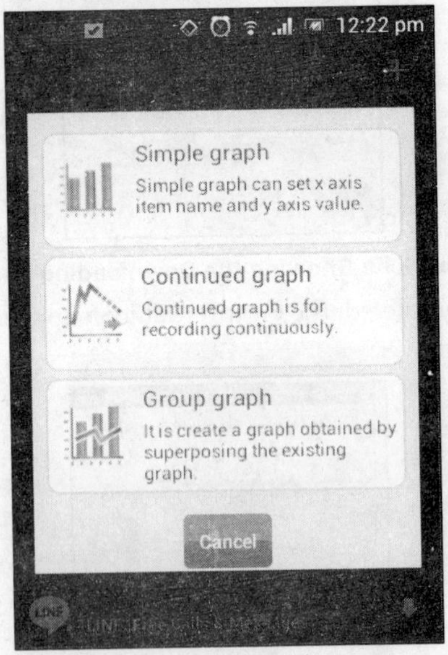

Figure 29.20: Showing the Graph Type Selection Window

8. Select the type of graph (Figure 29.20) you want to create by tapping on its icon. In our case, we have selected simple graph. The Create simple graph window appears (Figure 29.21).

9. Select the simple type of graph from the Graph type tab. In our case, we have selected the Bar graph, as shown in Figure 29.21:

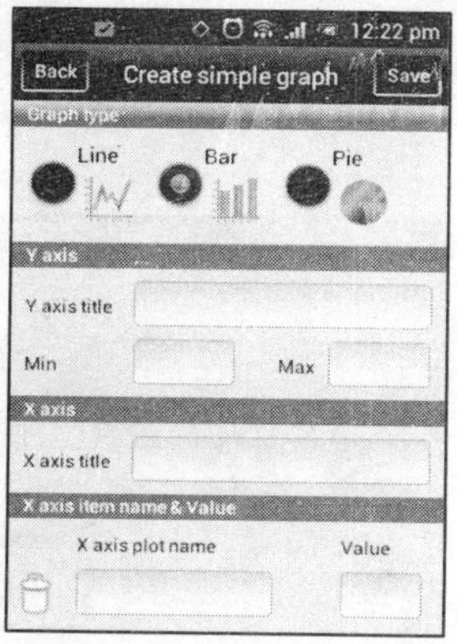

Figure 29.21: Showing the Create Simple Graph Window

10. Input the details in the Y axis title, Min, and Max fields, as shown in Figure 29.22:

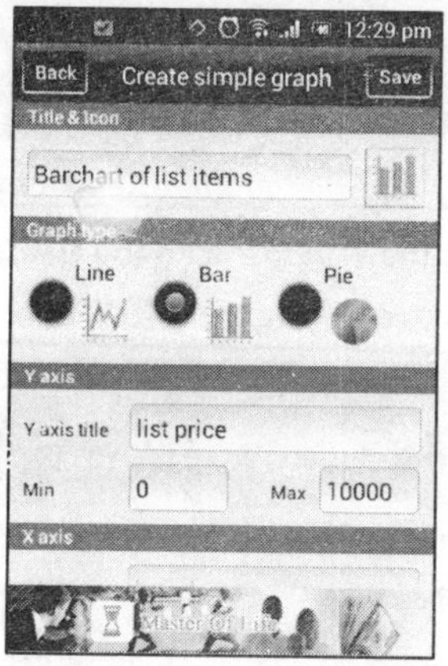

Figure 29.22: Showing the Bar Graph Window

11. Scroll down the window to input details in other fields, as shown in Figure 29.23:

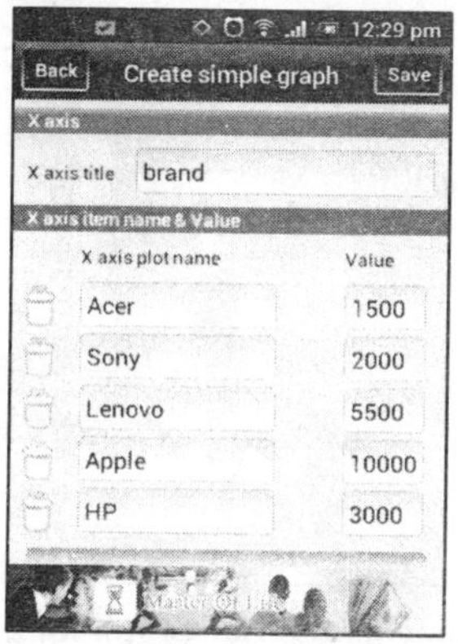

Figure 29.23: Showing the Data Input Window

12. Tap the Save button (Figure 29.23) to get the Barchart of list items icon, as shown in Figure 29.24:

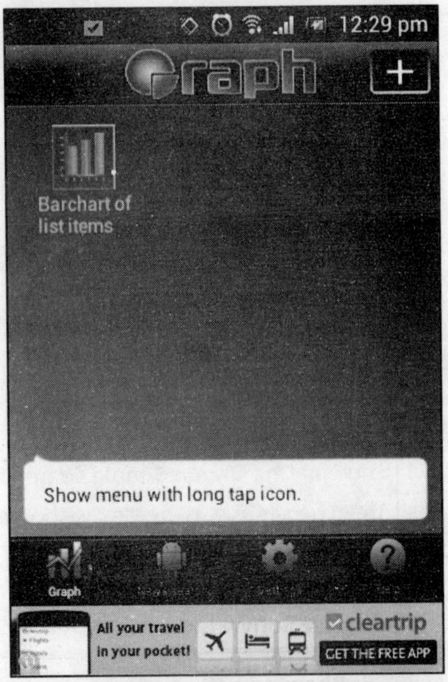

Figure 29.24: Showing the Window with the Barchart of list items Icon

13. Long tap the Barchart of list items icon (Figure 29.24) to see the graph, as shown in Figure 29.25:

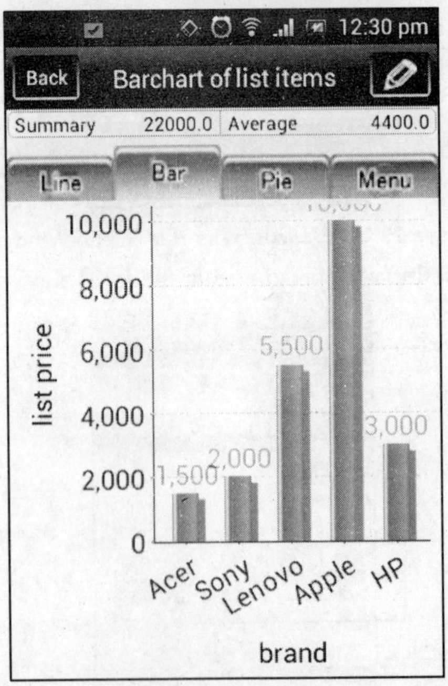

Figure 29.25: Showing the Bar Graph for a Given Dataset

14. Select the Pie tab (Figure 29.25) by tapping it to get a pie chart, as shown in Figure 29.26:

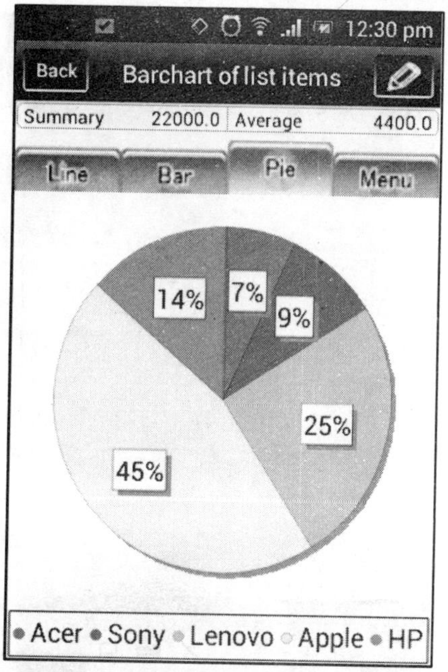

Figure 29.26: Showing a Pie Chart for the Given Dataset

15. Select the Line tab (Figure 29.26) by tapping it to get a line chart, as shown in Figure 29.27:

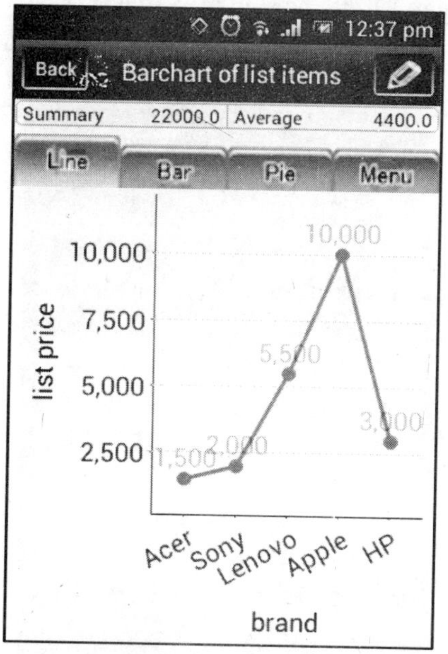

Figure 29.27: Showing a Line Chart for the Given Dataset

Till now, we have created different types of simple graphs for a sample dataset provided in our virtual lab.

Let's now create a bar graph by loading a dataset stored as a Comma Separated Value (CSV) file in the tablet's memory.

16. Tap the Settings button to open a Settings window, as shown in Figure 29.28:

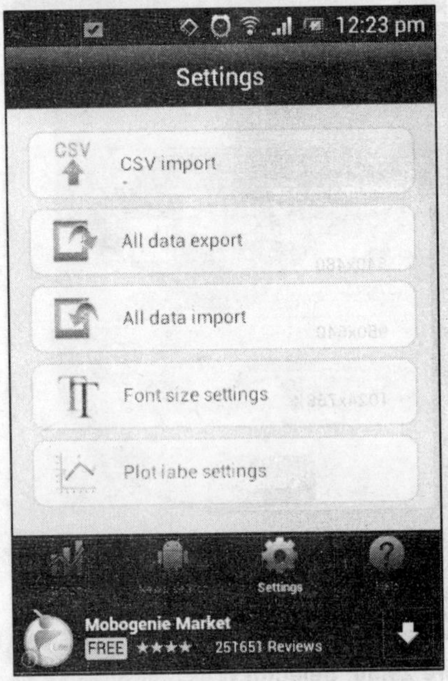

Figure 29.28: Showing the Settings Window

17. Tap the CSV import option (Figure 29.28) to open the window listing the CSV files in the selected location, as shown in Figure 29.29:

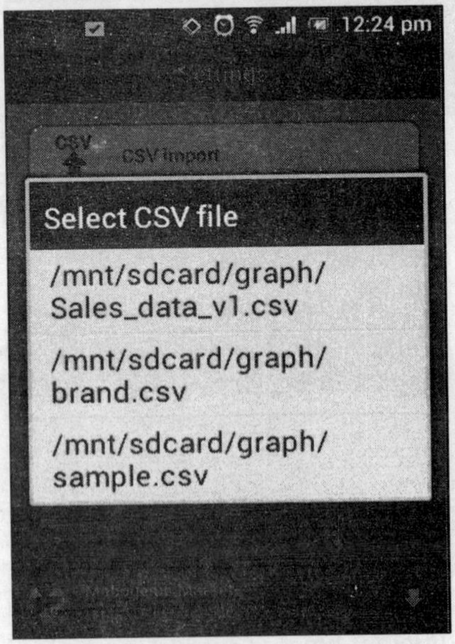

Figure 29.29: Showing the List of CSV File in a Memory Location

18. Select the particular file name (Figure 29.29) to get a graph for the dataset.
19. Select the size of the graph by tapping an option from the Select image size window, as shown in Figure 29.30:

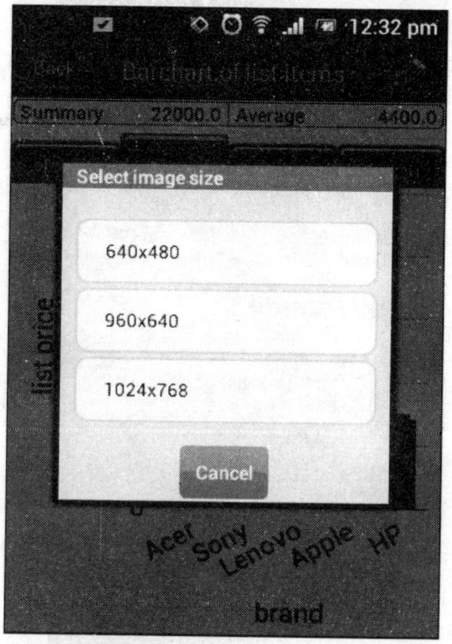

Figure 29.30: Selecting the Graph Size

20. Tap the OK button to save the graph in the form of an image, as shown in Figure 29.31:

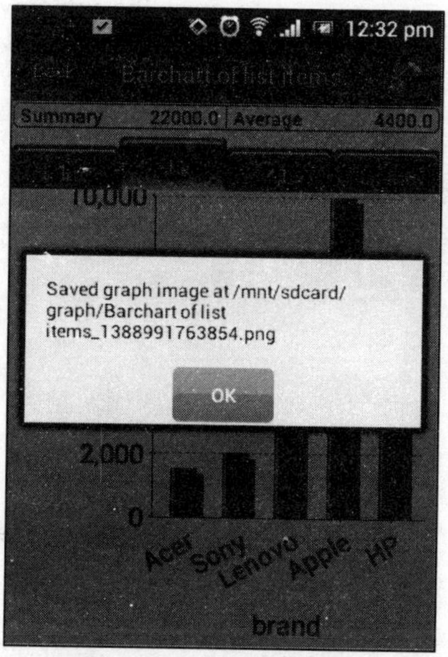

Figure 29.31: Saving a Graph as an Image

After saving the graph as an image, you can share it via e-mail. To do this, proceed to the next step.

21. Tap the Share option to open the Share graph image window, as shown in Figure 29.32:

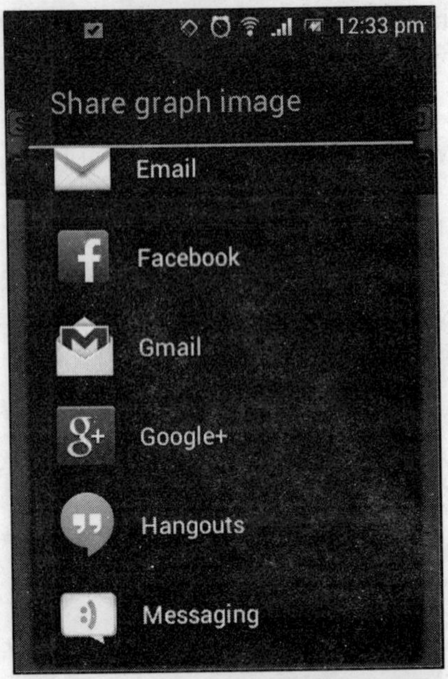

Figure 29.32: Showing the Share graph image Window

22. Tap the option through which you want to share the image. In our case, we have selected Gmail, as shown in Figure 29.33:

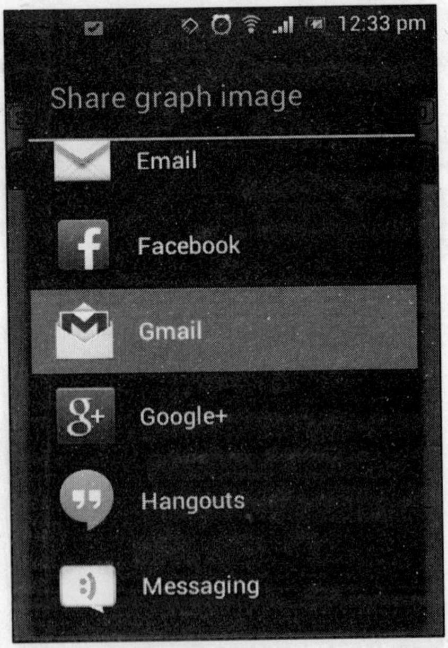

Figure 29.33: Selecting the Particular Option for Sharing the Graph Image

23. Enter the details in the required fields, as shown in Figure 29.34:

Figure 29.34: Entering Details

24. Tap the Share button and exit the application by pressing the OK button on the pop-up box that appears, as shown in Figure 29.35:

Figure 29.35: Sharing the Graph Image

We can quickly create some dashboards by using the above procedure to create a presentation of the analysis on a mobile phone or a tablet. The charts included in the presentation can also be shared quickly through e-mails.

EXHIBIT 1: Premier Inn Generates £1m in Revenues through Mobile Analytics

Premier Inn is a chain of hotels in UK. It is the largest hotel brand of UK, having around 650 hotels. Premier Inn launched a mobile app in January 2011 to make bookings online. Through this mobile app, Premier Inn was able to generate revenues of over £1m in just three months of launching the app. Since then, the app has achieved more than two million downloads. Around 77% of the total bookings are made through the mobile app.

How was the hotel able to achieve such big revenues? Actually, the magic behind the success of the Premier Inn mobile app was mobile data analytics provided by Grapple, a mobile-innovation agency. Grapple collected data from its 300 branded applications of clients. Branded applications are those which either offer a utility or make the life of the customer easier when he or she is on the move. Grapple analyzed this data from 325 smartphone and tablet devices to enable companies, such as Premier Inn, to better understand customer behavior and help the company to improve sales, customer retention, and loyalty. Premier Inn used Grapple's analysis to improve the features and functionality of its mobile application and increase sales conversion rates from 3% to 5.9% and generated revenues of £1m in a short period of three months.

Challenges of Mobile Analytics

Mobile analytics has its own challenges. Some of the main ones can be listed as follows:

- **Unavailability of uniform technology**—Different mobile phones support different technologies. For example, some mobile phones support images, JavaScript, HTML, and cookies while others do not.
- **Random change in subscriber identity**—TMSI (Temporary Mobile Subscriber Identity) is the identity of mobile devices and can be known by the mobile network being used. This identity is randomly assigned by the VLR (Visitor Location Register) to every mobile in the area as it is switched on. This random change in the subscriber ID makes it difficult to gather important information such as the location of user, etc.
- **Redirect**—Some mobile devices do not support redirects. The term 'redirect' is used to describe the process in which the system automatically opens another page.
- **Special characters in the URL**—In some mobile devices, some special characters in the URL are not supported.
- **Interrupted connections**—The mobile connection with the tower is not always dedicated. It can be interrupted when the user is moving from one tower to another tower. This interruption in the connection breaks the requests sent by the devices.

Together with generalized issues mentioned above, mobile analysts are also facing the following critical issues, which discourage mobile analytics marketing:

- **Limited understanding of the network operators**—Network operators are unable to understand the business processes happening outside the carrier's firewall.
- **True real-time analysis**—True real-time data analysis is not always possible with mobile analytics due to various reasons such as signal interruption, variation in technology used in mobiles, random change in subscriber ID, etc.
- **Security issues**—Mobile technology has various important features but some of these features, such as GPS, cookies, Wi-Fi, and beacons can disclose important information of the user. Information like details of credit cards, bank accounts, medical history, or other personal content can be easily misused. Some techniques like Deep Packet Inspection (DPI), Deep Packet Capture (DPC), and application logs can increase security threats.

To cope with such security threats, business organizations must intelligently monitor all communications in real time and make sure that personal data is not accessible to everyone.

Summary

The chapter covered different aspects of mobile analytics. It began by defining mobile analytics. It then explained the difference between mobile analytics and Web analytics. In addition, it discussed the types and applications of mobile analytics. Various mobile analytics tools, such as location-based tracking tools, real-time analytics tools, and user behavior tracking tools, are also discussed in detail. Apart from this, you learned the two techniques used for performing mobile analytics: through the mobile device and through the server. Toward the end, the chapter elaborated on the challenges associated with mobile analytics.

Quick Revise

Multiple-Choice Questions

Q1. Which of the following technologies supports LIT and Wi-Max techniques?

a. 1G
b. 2G
c. 3G
d. 4G

Ans. The correct option is d.

Q2. Which of the following mobile analytics tools will you use to work on all mobile platforms for the measurement of user acquisition, engagement, and outcomes in native mobile apps?

a. AdMob
b. Bango
c. Google Analytics
d. Localytics

Ans. The correct option is c.

Q3. Which of the following location-based mobile analytics tracking tools will you use to incorporate advanced geolocation functionality to mobile devices running on iOS, Windows, as well as Android?

a. Geoloqi
b. Placed

c. Geckoboard
d. Mixpanel

Ans. The correct option is a.

Q4. Which of the following mobile analytics tools is used to test an app?

a. TestFlight
b. Mobile App Tracking
c. Apsalar
d. Mixpanel

Ans. The correct option is a.

Q5. Which of the following mobile analytics data collection tools provides data collection services and reduces decision-making time by interpreting data efficiently?

a. Open Data Kit
b. DataWinners
c. COMMANDmobile®
d. Enterprise Server

Ans. The correct option is b.

Q6. Which of the following types of mobile app analytics reports will you use to understand the demographics of the people using a particular mobile application?

a. Audience
b. Acquisition
c. Behavior
d. Conversion

Ans. The correct option is a.

Q7. Which of the following statements is true about DPI?

a. It is the process of diverting Web traffic of a network.
b. It is the process of filtering data packets over a network.
c. It is the process of authenticating users over a mobile network.
d. It is the process of managing data for mobile apps.

Ans. The correct option is c.

Q8. Which of the following reports will you use to display the details about the actual sign-ups and sale of mobile applications?

a. Acquisition
b. Audience
c. Behavior
d. Conversion

Ans. The correct option is d.

Q9. Which of the following is an example of a mobile application?

a. Android
b. HTML
c. Blackberry
d. JavaScript

Ans. The correct option is d.

Q10. Localytics is an example of a:

a. Mobile device
b. Mobile application
c. Mobile platform
d. Mobile analytics tool

Ans. The correct option is d.

Subjective Questions

Q1. Discuss some application areas of mobile analytics.

Ans. Mobile analytics is used in various fields, such as the following:

- Location-based services
- Traffic solutions
- Mobile e-commerce

Q2. Briefly explain some popular mobile analytics tools available in the market.

Ans. Mobile analytics tools are classified as internal tools and external tools. Some of the popular mobile analytics tools include:

- **AdMob**—It lets you analyze information related to visitors' behavior.
- **Bango**—It is one of the most well-known mobile analytics programs that can track mobiles as well as websites.
- **Google Analytics**—It works on all mobile platforms and enables the measurement of user acquisition, engagement, and outcomes in native mobile apps.
- **Localytics**—It is the leading marketing and analytics platform for mobile applications. It provides a complete solution for mobile analytics, including real-time analysis and behavior tracking. It provides insights for Android, iPhones, and Blackberry.

Q3. Discuss some fields where mobile analytics can be used.

Ans. Mobile analytics can be used to:

- Determine the size, demographics, and psychometrics of the audience
- Identify the content that interests the audience of an organization using the data interpreted by mobile analytics to present products or services effectively on mobile sites
- Improve the performance of other marketing areas using the results from mobile analytics
- Improve the overall performance of a business by incorporating results from mobile analytics with the results of other analytics
- Determine the utility of mobile channels as a marketing mix
- Determine the lifetime of a customer on a mobile network

Q4. What is the importance of location-based tracking tools?

Ans. Knowing the geographic location of visitors helps an organization to optimize the Website or application accordingly. It is not easy to locate the visitors because it is not always based on the GPS signal but rather on the IP address of the gateway. For these purposes, and for many other reasons, location-based tracking tools are very important.

Q5. Discuss the necessity of keeping data secure while conducting analytics.

Ans. Cookies, beacons, GPS, and Wi-Fi can reveal important information about users. This information may include bank account details, medical history, or private content that can be mishandled. Deep Packet Inspection (DPI) and Deep Packet Capture (DPC) can examine and extract data at the desired level of specificity.

Data captured from devices or application logs certainly increases security threats. To meet such security threats, business organizations should be able to secure data in a way that can be intelligently monitored for real-time alerts. Data should not be made accessible to everyone.

30

Finding a Job in the Big Data Market

The field of Big Data has grown and expanded rapidly over the years and is expected to maintain this trend in the future as well. When we talk about Big Data, we are referring to the storage, processing, analysis, and visualization of large sets of data stored in databases. Such vast amounts of data cannot be handled by traditional database systems. In the earlier chapters, we learned how Big Data has changed the way business is done. Big Data has tremendous potential for driving business forward. However, as the field is new and the opportunities in it are immense, lack of experienced workforce in Big Data technologies has emerged as a major challenge for organizations. There is an acute shortage of experienced professionals who can be directly taken to manage different Big Data roles. These involve executive-level posts as well as posts at the operational level. Therefore, there is a need for educating and training more and more professionals to handle Big Data so that the shortage of workforce can be overcome as soon as possible.

What seems to be challenging for a Big Data professional is the varying nature of jobs in this field. These jobs require different levels of knowledge, experience as well as skill sets. A postgraduate degree in mathematics, statistics, and/or computer science would be ideal for an operational-level professional while a masters in business administration and/or a doctorate in mathematics, statistics, or computers may be required for executive-level professionals. Thus, acquiring the required educational qualifications is important. After this, the job search can begin.

You need to create your own brand before seeking a job in the Big Data market. Create a winning resume, follow the preferred and potential employers, and apply for various job openings in order to get your dream job. Also, you must use your personal and/or online network to land a job. Make ample use of social media to help you in your quest.

In this chapter, you will learn different ways of preparing and then looking for an ideal job in the field of Big Data. The chapter starts with a discussion about the importance and scope of Big Data jobs. Next, you learn about the various opportunities that the Big Data field provides prospective job seekers. Moreover, you learn how to assess your skills and know your suitability for a Big Data job. The chapter also discusses the roles and responsibilities of a Big Data professional. In addition, you are made familiar with the basic educational qualifications and technological knowledge requirements for gaining a foothold in the Big Data field. The different kinds of jobs for Big Data professionals, such as consultants and in-house specialists, are also discussed. The chapter also provides the guidelines for preparing for a Big Data interview. Toward the end, the chapter explains how you can take the help of social media in your hunt for the Big Data job.

Scenario

Argon Technology is an organization that deals with Big Data analysis and data visualization. Mrs. Linda Arnold, its Chief Executive Officer (CEO), contacted a well-known US university, asking it to train 25 students of the university in the field of Big Data so that they can become competent Big Data professionals and serve the organization at different levels. The faculty members of the university introduced the students to different aspects of Big Data and provided hands-on experience to them on different business situations they might have to deal with as Big Data professionals. Let's learn the different aspects the students were trained in by the faculty members of the university through this chapter.

Importance and Scope of Big Data Jobs

Big Data is a term that is today commonly used in the world of advanced Information Technology (IT) to describe a large collection of different types of data, taken from various sources. The concept of Big Data involves four Vs, i.e., Volume, Velocity, Variety, and Veracity. Each of these Vs plays an important role in providing the fifth V, i.e., Value, to Big Data.

The value of Big Data is that it consists of different types of data—structured, semi-structured, and unstructured. This data is received and processed at a high velocity. The accuracy of input data as well as output information may vary according to the needs and availability of resources. Hence, the volume, velocity, variety, and veracity of data are the key players in determining the value of information.

Big Data is usually handled in different stages where the data is collected, stored, organized, analyzed, etc., with a view to discover new insights and improve business decisions. The different phases involved in handling Big Data can be briefly explained as follows:

1. **Data Collection**—In this phase, data is collected from various types of data sources, including databases, data marts, and data warehouses.
2. **Storage**—In this phase, the data gathered from various sources is stored at one logical location or space. The physical location of the data may be different, and this is usually the case because the distributed database system used for handling Big Data comprises many physical machines with their own memory and processors; so, the physical location of data normally varies.
3. **Data Organization**—This phase involves the arrangement of the data to facilitate easy and quick analysis. You need to organize the structured, unstructured, and semi-structured data you have in data warehouses, relational databases, and access stores, such as NoSQL and Hadoop Distributed File System (HDFS).
4. **Data Analysis**—Now that the data is stored and arranged properly, you can carry out statistical and business analytics activities by using various tools and techniques. These analytical activities reveal interesting facts and outcomes that can assist in decision making in organizations and chart the future course of action of businesses.
5. **Data Visualization**—The revelations obtained from the data analysis phase need to be presented in a manner that can be comprehended by managers and decision makers in an organization. One of the most effective ways to present Big Data analysis results is through visuals. Data visualization techniques are used to represent the obtained insights in the form of figures, graphs, dashboards, etc.
6. **Action or Result Utilization**—The last phase in building a Big Data handling platform is result utilization or taking action based on the visual representation of the outcomes. The visualized results are used in business decision making and determination of the future course of action.

Figure 30.1 shows the phases involved in building a Big Data platform:

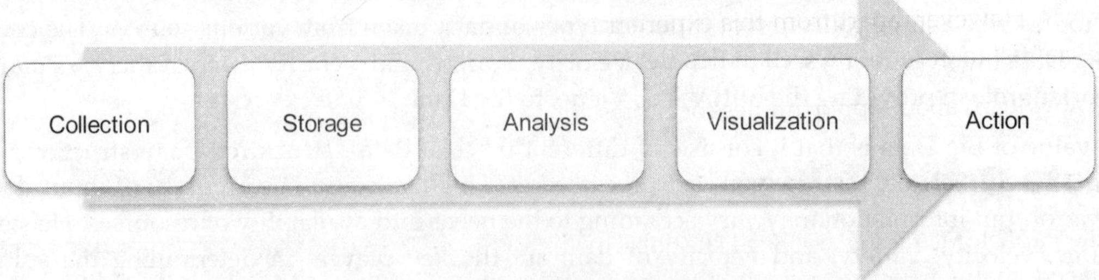

Figure 30.1: Sequence of Phases in Building a Big Data Platform

One of the major positive impacts of Big Data analysis has been that organizations have become more customer-centric. Marketing strategies, where data analysis plays a crucial role, play a big role in driving businesses forward. Today, nearly every industry deals with analyzed data and uses the results in improving their business decisions and future actions. The main areas where Big Data is used include risk management, compliance, financial services, healthcare organizations, government undertakings, retail industry, etc. Figure 30.2 shows some of the top industries where Big Data is used:

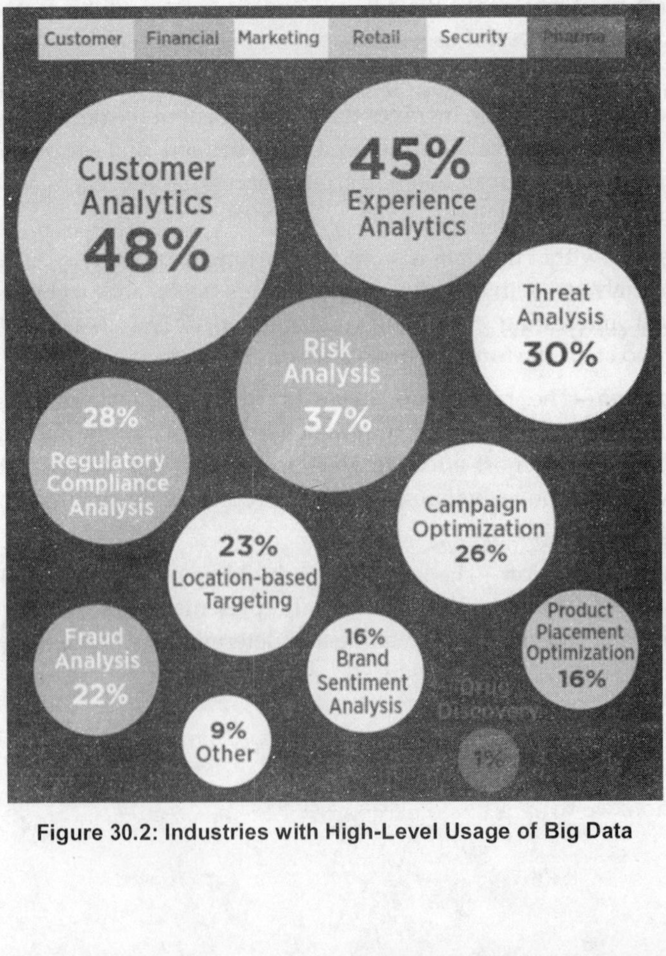

Figure 30.2: Industries with High-Level Usage of Big Data

As you can see in Figure 30.2, Big Data is a big player in different industries. Big Data provides a lot of opportunities for people who want to make a career in the field. There is a lot of scope for young professionals, especially those who have good hands-on experience in the fields of technology and analytics. However, apart from this experience, you also need to have the skills and knowledge of a data scientist in order to do well in this field.

Let's now learn about opportunities for professionals in the field of Big Data.

Big Data Opportunities

People capable of taking up Big Data jobs include specialized programmers, statistical modelers, advanced mathematicians, etc. In the Big Data industry, these people are referred to as data scientists, and they help organizations by handling data analytics. The professionals working in the field of Big Data need to have experience in the following fields:

- Marketing and analysis
- Statistics
- Applied mathematics
- Data visualization and movement
- Cloud computing
- NoSQL
- Relational databases
- Product placement and management
- MapReduce programming

The opportunities for professionals having experience in these areas can be found in diverse domains. These professionals can therefore find jobs in different fields. Some of the fields with prominent requirements for Big Data scientists are as follows:

- Public sector undertakings
- Academics
- Big Data organizations
- Commercial organizations
- Corporate information technology companies
- Marketing departments and businesses
- Risk management organizations

Big Data provides a wide range of opportunities, which are expected to increase in the future with more and more organizations making use of Big Data analysis to help them in their business. But, before entering this field, whether as a novice or an experienced professional, one must honestly assess one's abilities, knowledge, and interest in the field. The person must assess his skills and aptitude to make sure he has what it takes to do well in the chosen field.

In the following section, we will discuss the importance of skill assessment for Big Data jobs.

Skill Assessment for Big Data Jobs

The challenges in the field of Big Data are as difficult and wide as the field itself. However, careful study and planning would provide you an edge to excel in Big Data jobs. The roles and responsibilities of a Big Data scientist would determine what skills and educational qualifications a person wanting to enter the field must have. The prospective job seekers need to properly assess their interests, education, and skill sets so that it becomes easier for them to decide whether they are capable of taking the responsibilities of a Big Data job. They need to do a thorough study of the future of Big Data, assess themselves as well as their skill sets according to the challenges of Big Data, and determine the direction they want to take in the field.

The study of the future prospects of Big Data involves the following activities:

- Checking the growth of Big Data jobs
- Forecasting the future of Big Data in the coming years

Professionals who want to take a Big Data job or those who are already employed in this field will be happy to know that according to current trends, the number of jobs available in the Big Data industry is expected to continue to grow. Moreover, various surveys and reports point to the fact that Big Data technology, which is still in its early phase, is maturing. This is borne out by the studies done by Gartner and McKinsey. According to a 2012 report of Gartner, the number of Big Data jobs is expected to be around 5 million by the end of 2015. However, Gartner also predicted that the number of jobs that will be filled will be below 2 million, which is less than 40% of the jobs available in the field. McKinsey's prediction, on the other hand, elaborates that the unfilled jobs in Big Data would range between 1 million and 1.2 million in the US alone till 2018. Hence, both the studies reveal that the possibilities are endless in this field.

Big Data professionals and organizations hiring them indicate that the jobs will continue to grow in this field due to several factors. The three main factors that contribute to a continuous growth in Big Data jobs are as follows:

- Lack of adoption of Big Data at large scale in organizations
- Continuously increasing amount of data that is generated by customers, employees, and third parties
- Consistently increasing amount of venture capital investment in Big Data

In a Gartner survey, almost three-fourth of the total respondents have a plan to increase investment in Big Data but more than 60% of those lack the required skills and infrastructure base. This effectively means that your knowledge of Big Data will help you a lot in your career. Data is being generated at a fast pace, but existing database technologies lack the speed and scalability to fulfill the increasing demands for volume and velocity. Hence, a wide gap exists between the expected level of predictive analysis for Big Data and the actual level of the results obtained. Therefore, people with Big Data skills have a lot of opportunities for growth in the field.

An important aspect of the future of Big Data is that organizations are ready to invest more capital in this field because of the prospects it offers. The increasing amount of investment means that the number of jobs will continue to surge.

It is very easy to predict the future of something on the basis of surveys and reports, but the accuracy of the predictions or whether they would actually come out to be true cannot be guaranteed. This is more so in the case of Big Data. We may have predicted a bright future for Big Data, but how much will individuals and organizations actually be able to benefit from it is still a matter of conjecture.

In the last few years, there have been two very significant advancements in the field of technology: cloud computing and Big Data. However, in the recent years, Big Data has got more attention across the IT industry than cloud computing. The search trends on Google are testimony to this fact, as Figure 30.3 shows:

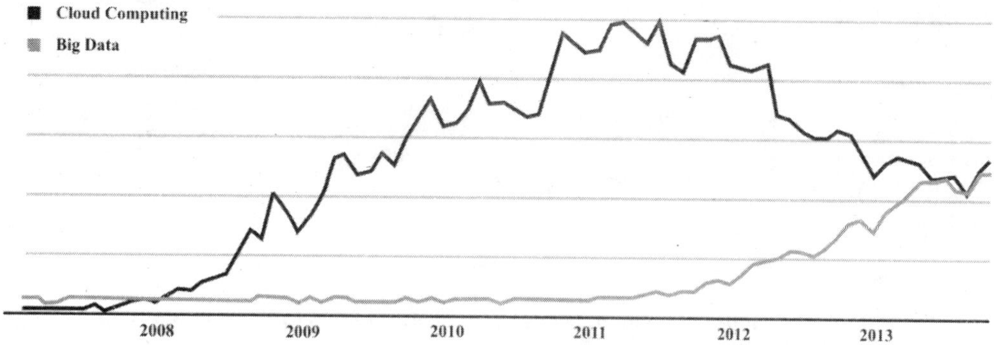

Figure 30.3: Search Trends for Big Data and Cloud Computing

As you can see in Figure 30.3, in 2012, there has been an increase in the number of searches for Big Data and a reduction in the searches for cloud computing. And in 2013, Big Data searches took a huge leap and went ahead of cloud computing.

According to various reports and surveys, the Big Data industry is expected to acquire a large workforce in the next five years. The jobs will require individuals to possess specific skills in software development, business analysis, and scientific study of data. All of these skills must be matched with a strong mathematical aptitude. A software developer with a high level of programming skills in one or more languages will be an ideal choice for Big Data solution development. Similarly, as Big Data should ultimately help organizations in their business, the Big Data professional must possess a strong business sense and proficiency. The professionals can analyze data only if they possess good analytical reasoning and strong mathematical aptitude for statistical analysis.

As discussed earlier, you need to do a self-assessment of your Big Data skills in order to know if you have the skills and aptitude to do a Big Data job competently. Skill assessment can be performed in four different areas, which are as follows:

- Aptitude evaluation
- Skill set assessment
- Gap filling
- Execution plan

In each of the areas listed above, you need to assess the roles and responsibilities according to your capabilities and interests. For example, the roles and responsibilities that may be suited to you according to your interests and aptitude would belong to the first category, the skills required to excel in the Big Data field can be segregated in the second category, filling the gaps by identifying weaknesses and ways of overcoming them can be put into the third category and, finally, goals and success metrics can be set in the last category. Figure 30.4 illustrates the process taken in the self-assessment of skills in the field of Big Data:

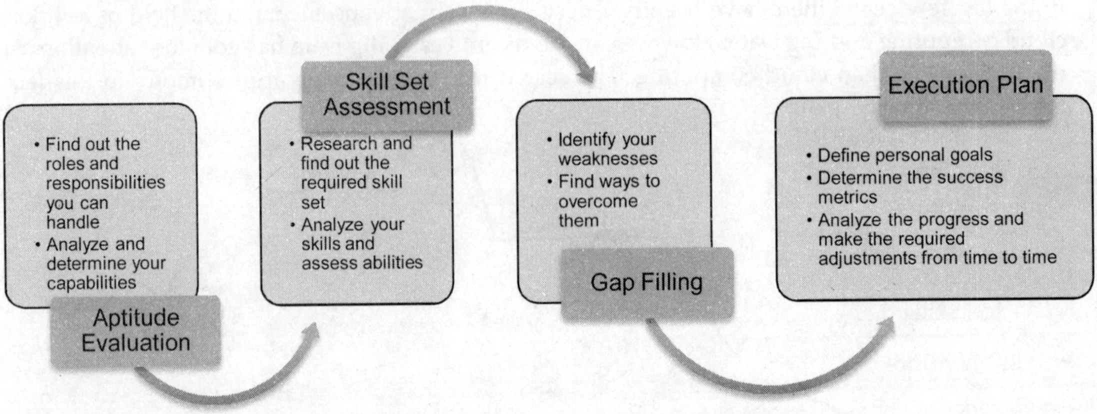

Figure 30.4: Self-Assessment Process for Professionals to Excel in Big Data

A self-assessment plan must be properly charted after conducting research and additional study if you do not have complete information about the required set of skills and educational qualifications. For help, you can use Table 30.1 as an assessment worksheet for your skills:

Table 30.1: Self-Assessment Worksheet for Big Data

Big Data Skills	Skill Rating (1-10)	Notes
Programming		
Relational Database Design		
Relational Database Programming		
Java		
C++		
Python		
Hadoop		
Hive		
Pig/Pig Latin		
Spark		
MapReduce		
Visualization Tools		

Table 30.1: Self-Assessment Worksheet for Big Data

Big Data Skills	Skill Rating (1-10)	Notes
Business Analysis		
SQL/Database Programming		
Financial Analysis		
Predictive Analytics Models		
What-if Analysis		
Business Writing		
Presentation Skills		
Mad Excel Skills		
Visualization Tools		
Data Science		
Statistics		
Math Theory		
Graph Theory		
Machine Learning		
Artificial Intelligence (AI)		
Signals Processing		
Natural Language Processing		
Visualization Tools		
Advanced Degree (Masters and Higher)		

The list shown in Table 30.1 includes a number of criteria that would determine your level of knowledge. You can use these criteria to get a fair assessment of your skills and aptitude for handling Big Data jobs. You can rate yourself on a scale of 1 to 10, where a rating of 1 indicates that you have a basic awareness of a particular skill and a rating of 10 means that you have full awareness or expertise in the skill.

In assigning a value to a particular skill, you need to understand the relationship between the value you assign and the experience you have in that particular field. For example, a 5-year experience in the field of NoSQL database could be given a rating of 7, and the value for relational database may be marked anywhere between 4 and 6. Here, you need to assess yourself properly so as to assign the correct values for your skills and knowledge level.

Once you have figured out the roles and responsibilities suited to you and analyzed the required knowledge and skills, you can try to find out the gaps in your educational qualifications, technical expertise, and business understanding. You can start filling the gaps by analyzing your current position in the professional career and finding out the areas where you can improve yourself. You can mark these areas of improvement with a value of 4, for example, in your assessment worksheet.

In order to fill the gaps, you need to properly analyze the specific things that you need to do. For example, you might need to continue your education till you obtain a master's or doctorate degree in mathematics or statistics. However, getting formal education is not always a viable option because it may take years—valuable time that you might not be in a position to sacrifice. Therefore, you must clearly assess your present situation and decide whether less money at present is important or the prospect of getting more income in 2–3 years down the line is a better option. Hence, whether you want to invest some time in getting a formal education or want to do a job must be a step that you must take after considering all aspects carefully. Sometimes, your situation (financial or otherwise) may force you to do a job, and formal education may not be a possibility for the time being. In such a situation, you can continue your learning through the Internet or other methods while doing the job simultaneously. This way, you can be more valuable in your Big Data job with education as well as experience. The combination may help to give you an edge in the market over others.

When you are ready with knowledge, skills, and experience, you can carefully plan your journey in the Big Data field by defining the milestones you want to achieve and the timelines to achieve them in. For this, you can prepare a worksheet similar to the one shown in Table 30.2:

Table 30.2: Preparing a Milestone and Timeline Worksheet

Milestone and Timeline Worksheet			
Item	**Task**	**Duration (In Days)**	**Notes**
1.	Learn PHP	15	Target a rating point of 4–6
2.	Gain practical experience in MapReduce	8	Target a rating point of 3 or 4
3.	Take on Hadoop pilot at work	20	Target a rating point of 4–6
4.	Learn the data science visualization tool	7	Target a rating point of 3 or 4
5.	Apply the learning at work	20	Target a rating point of 4–6
6.	Learn Graph Theory	17	Target a rating point of 5
Reassess		3	Assessment of skills and goals after improvement
Total Duration		90	

Table 30.2 shows the tasks that would help you in your job in the field of Big Data as well as the time you would need to be proficient in these tasks. Remember, fix a particular time frame to finish your tasks and stick to it. In other words, you can vary the time allotted for each task, but the total time taken to finish all the tasks should not change.

The goal, in the end, is to gain enough knowledge so that your target can be achieved. Therefore, plan your learning accordingly and move ahead.

Once you have achieved your targets, you can measure your expertise through the results obtained. In this process of reassessment, you need to check all that you have learned and the methods you have used. You will also come to know how effective the learning methods have been. However, as you have spent most of your time on learning new things, you will not have much time to assess or evaluate your skills and knowledge you have gained. It is also possible that you may need to skip the evaluation phase altogether. The reasons for skipping the evaluation phase include the following:

- No time to look back
- Time spent on evaluation would be unproductive for the organization you are working for, which is only concerned with meeting deadlines
- Fear of not being able to match the level or standard you set for yourself

Despite the reasons, it is still better to perform an evaluation in order to know where you stand.

Now, let's learn about the roles and responsibilities in Big Data jobs.

Roles and Responsibilities in Big Data Jobs

Every role requires a set of skills and experience. Big Data primarily involves business decision making by analyzing business situations and requirements. Therefore, the roles and responsibilities in Big Data jobs are divided into the following categories:

- Business analysis
- Data science
- Software development

All these job roles are suitable for people who have keen interest in mathematics, analytics, business analysis, analytical programming, and problem solving. Let's examine these roles and requirements one by one in the following sections.

Business Analyst for Big Data

The origin of Big Data projects is strongly connected to some business cases wherein the objective of the project is driven with a concept to improve business decision making in the given circumstances. Most of the practices in businesses are technology-oriented, but no technology is useful without a definite objective in place for the use of that technology. The use of visualization tools and data analysis outcomes has also been helpful in boosting businesses. However, they also have little value for a business without clearly defined objectives. This is where the role of the business analyst comes in. Business analysts play a crucial part in improving business processes by determining the goals and objectives of technological implementation. Through the analysis of Big Data, organizations can further improve the decision-making processes, where business analysts play a crucial role.

A business analyst plays an important role in different industries, spanning corporate IT companies, software firms specializing in Big Data, or consulting companies. Organizations are increasingly luring business analysts with attractive payments, ranging between $75000 and $109000 annually on an average.

Business analysts are crucial for the overall functioning of an organization. They may be given other job titles, such as marketing analyst, data analyst, system analyst, etc. However, before deciding to choose the role of a business analyst as a career option, you need to properly assess whether you have the requisite skills for the job. You can succeed as a good business analyst if you possess the following skills:

- Natural inquisitiveness that requires closely observing and analyzing business situations so that the best option can be taken
- Vision to enhance the current circumstances for benefitting the business scenario by focusing on the right areas
- Ability to quickly switch between creativity and analytics
- Knowledge of the target audience and understanding their demands and preferences

The responsibilities of business analysts may not be clearly specified in most job postings, because a clear specification of a job role for such a post is difficult. However, the main responsibilities include focus on business problem solving with effective business communication skills and an analytical bent of mind that can create a balance between analytics and technology.

Apart from business analyst, another important role in the field of Big Data is that of a data scientist. Let's discuss this role in the next section.

Big Data Scientist

A data scientist in Big Data has the responsibility of communicating with business analysts so that inputs for business decisions can be taken and the tasks based on the inputs can be performed. Some of the most important tasks performed by data scientists on the recommendations of a business analyst are as follows:

- Preparation of technical cases
- Creation of mathematical models
- Discovery of patterns, trends, and correlations in data

A data scientist also needs to assess his/her area of interest in the same way as business analysts before deciding on the Big Data profession as a career. The following questions would help the data scientist to make the decision:

- Do you possess a natural inquisitive instinct to conduct deep analysis of important issues? Also, do you have a passion for technology?
- Do you have the determination to fulfill the educational requirements of a data scientist?
- Are you self-motivated and can work without external guidance?
- Can you manage multiple disciplines and work on several areas such as statistics, mathematics, computer science, etc.?
- Are you able to convert an idea into reality?

If a person answers most of these questions in the affirmative, he/she should probably think about choosing data scientist as a career option. The field provides a lot of opportunities for growth. The job postings for the role of a data scientist may appear in the form of data consultants or research scientists in the field of physiological data modeling. A fresh college pass-out student would be preferred as a data consultant, whereas individuals with some experience in this role would usually be given the title of a research scientist.

Next, let's learn the role played by a software developer in the Big Data industry.

Software Developer for Big Data

The Big Data industry always welcomes professionals who possess programming knowledge and experience. It is particularly looking for individuals who have worked in more than one programming language, and those who have worked on analytical tools get preference over fresh graduates with little knowledge of either field. Today, no business can succeed without the help of technology. Therefore, software developers have a distinct place in the Big Data industry, which drives businesses through technological implementations. A software developer needs to assess his/her skills before choosing the role of software developer in the Big Data industry. The main characteristics required for a Big Data software developer are as follows:

- Ability to work with teams
- Knowledge of multiple programming languages
- Willingness to learn and adopt

Usually, Big Data jobs require Big Data developers with certain basic qualifications as well as additional skills and abilities. Basic qualifications may include a few years of experience in particular programming languages, ability to learn quickly, and a bachelor's degree. Additional skills can be experienced in particular technologies, specific development methods, or certain designing techniques and approaches.

After learning about the roles and responsibilities of different professionals in the field of Big Data, let's now study how one can gain a foothold in the Big Data market.

Gaining a Foothold in the Big Data Market

Starting from the very beginning in any field is not difficult. However, gaining a foothold in the field is a different matter altogether. This is more so in the case of relatively newer industries such as Big Data than in traditional fields. However, a little research and analysis may be helpful for professionals possessing Big Data experience of some kind. For example, Big Data education must be pursued with a definite goal in mind that you want to achieve. If you are working as a business intelligence professional, for example, your next goal should be to become a visual analytics professional. Similarly, a Java professional can take the Hadoop MapReduce paradigm to the next level so that he/she can get better job opportunities in the future. To understand your abilities and skills and to plan your journey in the field of Big Data in a better way, you need to analyze your shortcomings and fill gaps by acquiring more knowledge and skills. The best way to do this is to acquire knowledge at your own speed and prepare Big Data test cases on your own. No single path can guarantee you success, but you can plan your career in a way that is most likely to bring you the success you want.

The fruit of patience is always sweet; therefore, you need to be patient and have faith in your education and knowledge of Big Data. You may not end up with the perfect job in your first attempt, but if you have the required amount of knowledge and skills to sustain the demands of Big Data, you will be definitely rewarded in the end.

Take Your Time

The first thing you need to do to acquire more knowledge and skills in Big Data is to decide your learning goals. In other words, decide the level you want to reach. When you have decided on the level, you must try to find ways of reaching it. There are two ways to reach the desired level of skill or knowledge. These are formal and informal. These will eventually help you to establish a foothold in the Big Data industry. There are different ways of educating yourself about Big Data in order to establish a foothold in the field. These include the following:

- **Reading books**—To begin with, you need to read books that could help you learn theoretical concepts through practical examples. The advantage of reading books is that you get a desktop reference through them after acquiring the knowledge of a tool. To become a business analyst, for example, you should start by learning the basic concepts related to Big Data. Similarly, you can learn about modeling tools, programming techniques, scripting engines, etc. in order to strengthen your knowledge as a software developer, or you can explore some new modeling techniques for managing unstructured data in databases in order to enhance your role as a database administrator.
- **Accessing online tutorials**—Online tutorials are another means by which a person can improve his or her knowledge and skills. Some people do not like to read books. Such people can use the Internet to access information according to their interests and requirements. They may find online tutorials very effective in boosting their knowledge. Online tutorials are available either as step-by-step guides or as instructional videos. You can access both to enhance your knowledge of Big Data.
- **Joining online communities**—Online communities enable global audiences to unite easily for improving knowledge and skills as well as for information sharing. Programmers and data analysts find online communities an ideal platform to discuss various aspects of programming and analytics. An online community may exist in the following forms:
    - Boards and forums
    - Internet Relay Chat (IRC)
    - Open-source development communities
    - Software foundations
- **On-the-job training**—On-the-job training is another effective way to learn and grow in your chosen profession. However, you need to be proactive and find projects of your liking and requirements through which you can learn at the workplace. The working environment of an organization is an ideal place to learn and enhance your skills. Sometimes, this may require you to move from your comfort zone in order to learn something new. But, it is always worth the effort and pays handsomely in the long run as a professional.

Preparing the Big Data Skill Learning and Testing Mechanism

Once you have acquired the knowledge required to do well in the field of Big Data, you need to build your own mechanism to test your knowledge. One drawback of self-learning or training is that you have no guide or teacher to push or test you or correct your mistakes. Therefore, you need to devise your own ways to do this. You can use the following steps to prepare your testing mechanism:

1. Define your goals
2. Define the required skill sets
3. Assess the knowledge gaps
4. Acquire the knowledge to fill the gaps

After completing the learning process, you need to assess your skills and abilities. For this, you need to assess the time taken in learning to use certain tools with some amount of effort involved. When you are reassessing your skills, you can use three process levers, which are as follows:

- **Tools**—Refer to the tools used in Big Data learning
- **Time**—Refers to the time taken in learning the use of the tools
- **Effort**—Refers to the effort made (such as using the Internet, books, videos, personal guidance, etc.) in learning the tools

The preceding three levers will lead to a set of outcome levers, which are as follows:

- **Knowledge**—Refers to the level of knowledge obtained after learning
- **Learning objectives**—Refer to the objectives fulfilled during the learning process
- **Value**—Refers to the value that the learning provides to your Big Data career

From the discussion so far, we have come to know different ways of learning about Big Data and improving our knowledge in order to gain a foothold in this field.

Next, let's learn the basic educational requirements to become a competent Big Data professional.

Basic Educational Requirements for Big Data Jobs

Some years back, career choices were usually made at very early ages, when children had barely entered their teen years. However, today, the scenario is very different. The world has witnessed a lot of changes in all spheres in recent times, and these changes are reflected in the educational system as well. As a result, people today have a wide range of careers to choose from. This is in part due to the different specializations that have come up in subjects that were once single subjects. For example, some years ago, the fields of computer science and information technology had very few specializations, but today, these fields have become complex and cover several specializations. Consequently, decisions regarding careers are also being taken at a later stage in life.

The field of education has to keep pace with these changes. For example, a career in Big Data requires one to have knowledge about different fields such as statistics, mathematics, analytics, IT, etc. Therefore, one needs to study these fields in order to do well as a Big Data professional.

Big Data education would preferably, at present, require one to get specialized education (degree) in one or more subjects given in the following list:

- Statistics and Mathematics
- Computer Science and Engineering
- Business Administration

Earlier, we discussed the important role played by a business analyst in the field of Big Data. For a person to become a Big Data business analyst, he/she should ideally have a degree in Statistics and/or Mathematics. This is because the analyst traditionally performs statistical analysis of data. Big Data specific degrees are not available in universities and colleges, but several programs, courses, and degrees are specifically designed to suit the requirements of the Big Data industry. These programs, courses, and degrees focus particularly on teaching students concepts related to computational theory, statistics, and probability.

Big Data is a blend of different disciplines. You need to be able to apply your analytical skills, which come by having knowledge of mathematics, computer science, and business administration. Computer science, along with its various subfields, plays a vital role in the use of Big Data at the organizational level. Some of the fields integrated with Big Data handling include the following:

- Artificial Intelligence (AI)
- Machine learning
- Data theory

Knowledge of these fields is important for using and managing Big Data. However, you can also choose one of these disciplines for specialization so that you can perform certain tasks related to Big Data where mathematical theories are applied practically on business problems.

When it comes to businesses, Big Data has been very influential in improving the decision-making process and marketing strategies. Almost every business is benefiting from Big Data in one way or another. However, as a Big Data professional, you need to have good knowledge of various business situations so that you can help the organization deal with any issues. This requires experience as well as study. Neither the study nor the experience alone can help you deal with real-world business situations. Apart from having experience in various business situations, you also need to have a degree in marketing, business intelligence, predictive analysis, etc.

You should have at least a degree in mathematics, statistics, computer science and engineering, or business administration before taking up a role in Big Data. However, if you are already working in the field of technology after having abandoned your studies earlier, you can join a continual program to obtain specific knowledge related to Big Data.

A few years back, it was not possible to predict the emergence or growth of Big Data. Therefore, some of us might not have felt the need to go for higher education. Such people can now continue with their education and take up jobs as data analysts, programmers, or business analysts. In the continual study system, you can go for a specialized short-duration program in statistics or analytics, but for this, you need to already possess some knowledge of statistics, calculus, accounting basics, marketing concepts, and so on. Each of these fields may have its implications on your career in your Big Data job. In an analytics program, you may choose to go for a course in business intelligence, statistical analysis, management course, or stochastic simulation. Moreover, you could have elective subject options that include data mining, applied multivariable methods, forecasting methods, quality management and six-sigma, and a number of other subjects.

Next, let's learn the basic technological requirements for Big Data jobs.

Basic Technological Requirements for Big Data Jobs

Big Data infrastructure is based on various technologies. Therefore, a person looking for a Big Data job should have some basic understanding of various technologies in order to do well as a Big Data professional. Some of the technologies you should be familiar with include Hadoop, NoSQL, Relational Database Management Systems (RDBMSs), data visualization tools, etc. The Big Data ecosystem is witnessing a very fast expansion in the use of tools for handling Big Data. Discussing the types, categories, and vendors of all the tools used in the Big Data ecosystem is beyond the scope of this chapter. In the initial stages of your career, it is sufficient to have basic knowledge of the core technologies on the basis of which you can acquire more knowledge in the field of Big Data as the field continues to evolve.

Big Data uses large datasets that are difficult to handle, and the traditional data-handling techniques are failing to meet the exacting demands of adaptability and scalability. Today, we are facing a kind of data explosion mainly because the data is generated through machines and social media. Not only has the volume of data increased, but also the speed at which data is being generated and the variety of data sources in which data is collected have made it difficult to handle Big Data. Therefore, people with specific skills and technological understanding are required in this field. The true potential of Big Data can be realized from the unique types of tools and techniques employed to manage it. The different types of tools that are commonly used to handle Big Data are as follows:

- **Database tools**—Databases are important in Big Data handling because of the large amounts of data that need to be stored and processed. Big Data is basically generation of large volumes of different types of data at a fast pace. This means that we need to have special data-handling tools that can store and process large data volumes efficiently. However, traditional databases, such as RDBMSs, have failed to satisfy the exacting demands of the Big Data world. We needed a different type of technology to handle Big Data. That technology is NoSQL or Not Only SQL. NoSQL includes many features of RDBMSs apart from a number of new implementations that help to handle large amounts of data. There are two types of database tools, which are discussed as follows:

  - **Relational databases**—RDBMSs, which were originally used in online analytical processing systems, are the base of Big Data projects. RDBMSs contain data in the form of tables arranged in rows and columns. Relationships between these tables exist in the form of associations and links. The data and the relationships between various data elements are accessed by using a set of commands that are defined in a common data access language called Structured Query Language (SQL). However, with the increased variety, velocity, and volume of data, it became infeasible to use these traditional databases for performing the required tasks. The evolution of database technologies led to the development of NoSQL databases.
  - **NoSQL databases**—NoSQL databases are newly developed techniques for handling Big Data. Traditional database technologies fail to keep pace with the amount and speed of data generation. Therefore, development of NoSQL databases became inevitable. NoSQL databases include most of the important features of SQL databases. Additionally, these

databases are flexible, scalable, easier to manage, and can keep pace with the speed of data generation. There are various types of NoSQL databases, which can be listed as follows:

- Key-value pair data stores
- Document databases
- Graph-based databases
- Column-oriented databases

- **Framework technologies to handle Big Data**—Big Data is not only about data storage but also involves access, organization, analysis, and manipulation of data as part of Big Data handling. Some important Big Data framework technologies are as follows:
  - Hadoop framework
  - Pig
  - Hive
  - Spark
- **Analytical tools to handle Big Data**—Big Data analytics is mostly, if not entirely, dependent on its analytical tools that are used to process large amounts of data stored in various databases and analyze the data for insights. Some commonly used tools for handling Big Data analytics activities are as follows:
  - Business analytics tools
  - Visualization tools
  - Sentiment analysis tools
  - Machine learning tools

Apart from obtaining knowledge and some hands-on practice with regard to the common tools and technologies, you need to stay updated with the current market developments in Big Data.

Now, let's discuss the tools used to manage Big Data.

Tools Supporting Big Data

Big Data is supported by various tools and techniques. The main techniques include analytical and visualization techniques. Additionally, there are various types of tools for handling Big Data. Many of these tools are available for free in the form of Web-based applications on the Internet. You can download and install these tools on your computer, become familiar with their interfaces, and use them for your benefit. For example:

- You can create data visualizations by using R packages such as, RCharts and RMaps.
- You can scrap your data by using Import.io.
- You can collect images by using ImageQuilts.
- You can use DataWrangler for wrangling the data.
- You can use Tableau Public for exploring data.
- You can use Gephi for fast data processing and analysis.
- You can perform machine-learning operations through the WEKA suite.
- You can use Weave to get a Web-based platform for the visualization of data.
- You can also use the platform known as Knoema to visualize your data.

These tools are used by professionals to manage Big Data in an efficient way for the benefit of the organization they are working for.

The different kinds of work profiles for Big Data professionals may include the job of a consultant or an in-house specialist in an organization. Let's learn about these specific job positions in the next section.

Consultants and In-House Specialists in Big Data

The Big Data industry offers jobs for consultants and in-house specialists. The term consultant means different things to different people. However, it is commonly defined as someone who offers some advice/solution/perspective on an issue or topic as and when it is required by using their experience. The main characteristic of a consultant is that he/she is a problem solver. Consultants have to clearly analyze issues or problems and devise strategies to deal with them. The role of an in-house specialist in an organization is similar to that of a consultant. The difference between the two is that industry exposure and earning potential for in-house specialists would be lesser and their work schedule would be more relaxed.

Big Data Consultants

Big Data consultants occupy an important position in an organization. They are expected to develop strategies for solving business problems and taking the organization forward. There are different roles of a consultant in Big Data organizations. However, there are two categories of consultants performing different roles:

- **Management consultants**—The primary responsibilities of management consultants are planning and strategizing. These people are usually deputed at the executive level and are responsible for solving business-related issues that could have serious implications on the balance sheet. Most management consultants are directly recruited from top-grade institutions that provide a degree in business administration. Some of the questions management consultants have to deal within organizations are as follows:
  - What is the meaning of Big Data for an organization and how will the organization react to this new field?
  - Marketing executives in organizations claim to use social media data in determining the price of products. How is this method of price determination justified and in what ways does it affect the privacy of the organization?
  - How can an organization plan to employ its resources if it needs to use Big Data in the business decision-making process?
  - In case a new business unit of an organization is being launched, what steps would you take in the initial planning and strategizing of the unit? How can the historical data of the organization be taken into operation and what can be its possible impact on the balance sheet?
- **System integrators**—A person occupying the post of system integrator mainly takes the responsibility of actual system implementation or product delivery. Some of the common questions posed for system integrators to answer are as follows:
  - How can a system integrator help in building a new Big Data team?

- How can the best data management practices be established to support the marketing team of a company through Big Data?
- How can a system integrator help a company's IT department, if no one in the department has experience in working with Hadoop?

There are various organizations in the market that are working as Big Data consultants. The largest players in the Big Data market as far as management consulting is concerned are two groups of companies. These are known as Big Three and Big Four in the field of Big Data consulting.

The Big Three include:

- McKinsey and Company
- The Boston Consulting Group
- Bain and Company

The Big Four are:

- PricewaterhouseCoopers
- Deloitte
- Ernst and Young
- KPMG

Big Data system integration tasks are different, and therefore, a different set of companies has been dominating this field. Some of the dominant market players in Big Data system integration are as follows:

- Accenture
- Capgemini
- Cognizant
- CSC
- TCS
- Infosys
- Wipro

Consultants in Big Data have great scope of growth. However, different organizations offer different career paths. Consultants may start off as associates and become partners of organizations. The general pattern of a consultant's career path is shown in Figure 30.5:

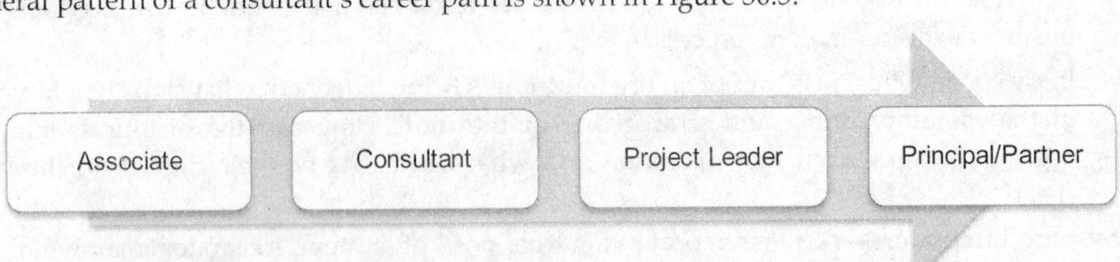

Figure 30.5: Career Path of a Business Consultant

Every role in a business has both its positives and negatives. The positive aspects of a business consultant are diverse, which may include:

- Exposure to different companies and industries
- Opportunity to work at the strategic level
- Opportunity for extensive travel
- Potential for high earnings

On the other hand, some of the negative aspects of a business consultant's job are as follows:

- Excessive travelling
- Demanding work hours
- Difficult schedules, priorities of work, deliverables, etc.
- Difficulty in dealing with clients
- Competition in the work environment

In-House Big Data Experts

Some Big Data professionals may not like working as consultants because of the demanding work schedules and various other issues. However, they could be hired by organizations to serve as in-house specialists or experts. You might not have been hired as a Big Data professional but knowing a technology can help you to be an expert in your own company. Today, corporate IT is a familiar term for technology professionals. It is a term associated with providing IT support to corporate houses and businesses. All kinds of IT support is provided to organizations by corporate IT companies that hire people who are specialists in a certain technology.

These specialists work in the following categories:

- **Centralized IT companies**—Centralized IT companies are generally looking for specialists who can handle corporate infrastructure tasks, analytics programmers, and systems administrators and architects. You need to explore the vacancies and job postings for corporate IT roles in order to understand the responsibilities and the required experiences for them.
- **Business units**—A business unit may be willing to hire specialized individuals instead of corporate IT support so that new revenue opportunities, insights, and innovations can be driven within the business unit itself. This is beneficial for the individuals as well as the business units. These individuals have full authority and responsibility of the entire business; therefore, they can work freely in their position.

The positives associated with the role of a person working as a specialist are as follows:

- Possesses unique skills
- Has the opportunity to thoroughly understand the working of a business
- Has the opportunity to be more impactful and visible within the organization

The negatives associated with the job of an in-house specialist are as follows:

- Limited guidance and few opportunities for gaining knowledge and developing career
- Chances of getting stuck in the same role or position
- Limited potential for earning

From the discussion so far, it is clear that you need to carefully examine the different roles, responsibilities, and requirements in the field of Big Data and plan your journey accordingly.

Let's now learn about the tactics that can help you find the best Big Data job.

Tactics for Searching Big Data Jobs

The Big Data industry is not only driven by knowledge and skills. Personal networking and contacts also play a significant role in this field. You can get your dream job in Big Data by building a network and brand of yourself through real-world connections as well as online social networks. Moreover, creating a winning resume is also required to catch the eye of potential recruiters. Today's job market is clearly defined by brand building, which may include the use of online social media or networking by personal connections in the real word. The evolution of Internet technologies and Web services has made it necessary to focus on online brand-building tactics. However, your day-to-day contacts, whom you meet in person on a regular basis, can also prove beneficial for you. You need to concentrate on building your brand, and jobs will follow.

Network Building Tactics

All of us have friends who keep in touch with other people or seem to know people everywhere they go. These friends are naturally interactive and can build networks easily. Being interactive and contact building is an art that does not come easily to some people, but it can be developed.

You develop contacts or connections with others with or without expecting anything in return. However, remember that the connections you establish form the foundation on the basis of which you will get jobs in the market. Therefore, you need to be aware of the requirements of the industry and the type of people who can be helpful in your job search. The best places to search for such people are as follows:

- **Industry interest groups**—These groups involve people of similar mindsets who like to discuss and share their ideas and promote innovative approaches by making connections. You can find such groups by exploring the Internet for the industry you want to join. Industry interest groups can be found at the following places:
  - Conferences
  - Trade shows
  - Vendor summits
  - Meetings
- **Alumni networks**—In addition to interest groups, you can find out and connect with alumni networks. The following are some examples of alumni networks:
  - Alumni databases
  - Career services
  - Alumni associations
  - University lifelong learning groups

Establishing connections with people is a difficult task, especially if you are not naturally interactive. However, you need to make an effort in this direction as it may lead you to your dream job. Some of the points to keep in mind while establishing connections and networks are as follows:

- Have a story and be ready to tell it
- Be honest about your abilities while describing yourself to people
- Be straightforward while discussing yourself and your goals with others
- Take the initiative to ask people for regular meetings

Before you build your brand and create connections, you need to carefully plan how you would like to go about doing it. The following steps would help you in this regard:

- Define your goals clearly
- Prepare the current network list
- Identify groups for engagement
- Enhance your online profile
- Evaluate your prospects

This way, you would be better prepared to land the perfect job in the field of Big Data.

Resume Building Tactics

Having a perfect resume is one of the basic requirements for a job search in any field. You should understand that your resume is the first step towards your goal of getting the job. Any kind of hiring process begins with the resume. Therefore, you need to be very careful about what you include in your resume. Make sure that the information included in your resume is relevant and true and projects a positive image of you to the potential employer.

The strategy you adopt to write your resume and the content you decide to highlight in it depend on common market trends, job descriptions, and positions for which the vacancy is open. You need to go through the Careers page of different organizations to understand the requirements of the Big Data industry. That would help you to create a winning resume on the basis of the requirements. A hiring process normally involves a number of steps starting with job postings spread on social media or in forums offering job consulting services for both employers and job seekers. The applications for these posts are filled and sent along with the resumes of the applicants to the employer. After this, the Human Resource (HR) team shortlists the resumes so that interviews can be conducted.

Remember that resumes are shortlisted on the basis of certain keywords related to the job posting. Resumes that do not contain these keywords would therefore be most likely be ignored. Hence, you must make sure that your resume contains these keywords if you want it to get noticed and shortlisted.

There can be some do's and don'ts that you need to follow while creating a resume. The following are some basic do's while creating a resume:

- Make the resume simple, concise, and one that grabs the attention of the potential employer easily.

- Mention the information in relevant sections for clarity. These sections can be as follows:
  - Career Objective
  - Technical Skills
  - Educational Qualification
  - Professional Experience
  - Training and Certificates
- Highlight your achievement with sentences that start with action verbs such as 'Developed a multimedia program by applying a specific innovative approach.'
- Avoid spelling mistakes or grammatical errors
- Use consistent fonts and format throughout

The following are some don'ts that need to be observed while creating a resume:

- Don't make your resume too long. Two pages is the ideal length.
- Don't include unconvincing work experience.
- Avoid inexplicable conflicts between dates, employers, etc.
- Avoid spelling mistakes and errors in punctuation and grammar.

After creating your resume, make sure to check it thoroughly to spot and correct errors. Also, ensure that you haven't forgotten to include any important detail while keeping the document concise. Finally, make sure to include relevant information in different sections such as career objective, technical skills, work experience, etc. Mention the details properly, carefully, and clearly in your resume in order to get shortlisted for the job you applied for.

Once you get shortlisted, the hiring organization would most probably call you for an interview. Let's discuss this important stage in the next section.

Preparing for Interviews

A job interview can be stressful if you are not prepared for it. Interviews require a combination of skills, including public speaking, ability to accept different views, and willingness to be judged by others. While the importance of the interview cannot be denied, it should be borne in mind that it is not the determinant of your entire future and career. There is more to a career than clearing just one interview. Therefore, more important than preparing for the interview is taking its outcome, be it positive or negative, in the right spirit and learn from the experience. Also remember that preparing for something does not guarantee success, however, not preparing for it ensures failure. Therefore, be prepared, and the rest of the things will take their own course.

Interviews can be of different types, such as technical interviews, non-technical interviews, panel interviews, individual interviews, phone interviews, in-person meetings, etc. You need to specifically find out the type of interview you are going to appear for, and then prepare accordingly.

The following points should be taken into consideration while preparing for an interview:

- You should analyze and gather information about the nature and requirements of the position, history and nature of the company, the ways in which you can relate your experiences with the current position, etc.

- You need to be ready with the questions you want to ask. For example, you could ask the type of work you would be expected to do in a typical date if you were given the job or the challenges you could expect to face.
- You should decide what sort of personal information you would like to reveal during the interview. Mostly, you should describe your professional journey and relate your experience with the position being offered, explaining why you think you are fit for the job.

An important aspect of interviews is trying to understand the type of answers the interviewer expects to hear from you and replying accordingly. Your resume says a lot of things about your personal and professional life, but there may be certain questions that the interviewer would like to ask you in order to make sure what you have written in the resume is true or justified. Moreover, the interviewer might be interested in assessing how you behave under certain situations as well as your communication skills, etc. You should be careful while answering questions about personal issues or that seek confidential information, information about previous or current employers, etc.

When it comes to facing interviews in the field of Big Data, you may be provided a business-related problem and asked to solve it. Solving such a problem would help the interviewer assess your analytical skills and showcase your understanding of business-related issues, industry knowledge, presentation skills, etc. through case interviews. You can use this opportunity to force your claim on the position so that the potential employer hires you. The assessment of your technical and business understanding is usually done during a technical interview, which is conducted by a panel of experts or board members of the company.

After the technical interview, you will have another interview to assess your non-technical skills. These interviews are often a way of assessing a person's knowledge, attitude, behavior, personality traits, and adaptability to the work culture of the organization. When you are preparing for a Big Data interview, you should ensure that you are updated about the requirements in the industry for the position you want to apply for. You should check out the Careers page on the website of the organization, read the information given on the About Us page, and search for the information about the company on some social sites on which former and current employees post their experiences, before you appear for an interview with the organization.

There is no certain way for cracking an interview. There are also no specific set of questions that one can prepare for in order to ensure success. However, there are some questions that are commonly asked during various job interviews. These questions can be listed as follows:

- Can you tell me about yourself?
- What are your goals?
- Have you ever disagreed with your boss? If so, how did you handle it?
- Why do you want to work here?
- Why should we hire you?
- Why do you want to leave your current job?
- How do others view you?
- Can you tell me about a time when you made a mistake? What lesson did you learn from it?
- Can you tell me about some of your accomplishments?

These days, social media provides a great way of interacting with people and telling them about your interests or views on various issues. It is also one of the ways of getting your dream job in the field of Big Data. Let us learn about the great utility of social media and how you can use it to get a job in Big Data.

Obtaining Big Data Jobs through Social Media

The development of social networking sites such as Twitter, Facebook, and LinkedIn has been one of the most advantageous developments for companies and individuals. The information you put online is your brand. Social media platforms have been widely used for advertising and gaining popularity. A well-managed brand on social media attracts a lot of viewers, including potential recruiters who could contact you after seeing your profile on social media. There are various ways through which you can maintain your profile in social media. Some of these ways are as follows:

- **Searching yourself on Google**—A search for your own profile in Google will provide a clear idea about the kind of information is visible to the employers about you. Your public image tells others the kind of person you are. You need to ensure that your photos, videos, etc., posted by you in social networking sites come up on a Google search and give a positive impression of you to others.
- **Removing unflattering pictures**—A Google search for your profile may reveal some annoying or awkward photos that you may not like your potential employer to see. It is better to remove these photos so that your image on social media remains clean and positive.
- **Scrutinizing and editing for oneself**—Blogs, photos, videos, or any other work related to writing, image editing, or video making are usually posted on the Internet and available for everyone to see. You need to identify the best ways to scrutinize your own work to ensure that potential employers do not see what you don't want them to see.
- **Using the Google+ platform**—The Google+ platform is a part of the Google brand, so your updated profile on Google+ would be prioritized on Google searches. Hence, you will be easily visible to employers.
- **Maintaining LinkedIn network profile in a professional manner**—Your use of LinkedIn matters a lot today in your job hunt. The LinkedIn platform is the largest social network for professionals to share their experience. Therefore, you need to create a professional, well-managed profile on LinkedIn that would impress a potential employer. The full benefits of the LinkedIn network can be exploited in the following ways:
  - Your LinkedIn profile can be used as a resume.
  - You can use the profile to highlight your personal and professional achievements.
  - Make sure that the profile includes a suitable Display Picture (DP).
  - Follow companies and industry influencers.
  - Your LinkedIn profile should be short and impressive.
  - Set a customized visibility setting for the profile.

- **Using Blogger and other blogging sites**—The Internet has made it possible for everyone to express themselves in one way or another. Blogging is one of the primary ways of doing this. Before writing about a certain topic or issue in a blog, make sure that you have adequate information about it by doing a little research. There are numerous blogging sites, such as Blogger, WordPress, Tumblr, etc., on which you can create a blog and post regularly. Also, make sure that the blogs you create are updated regularly. An employer would not like a blog with no updates in a long time.
- **Become an expert of your craft**—Some of the websites nowadays provide a platform for experts to voice their opinion about certain topics or themes or answer questions. Some examples of such sites are Stack Overflow and Quora. You should attach the links of your answers to your public profile available online.
- **Focus on Facebook**—You can use Facebook in multiple ways. Facebook not only provides you a way to stay connected with your friends, families, and other individuals but also enables you to get a new job through the Facebook network. However, to land a job through Facebook may require you to write your profile in a way that it focuses more on your professional history or achievements than on personal information. You can also connect with companies for job openings. However, you should be careful about your posts and the information you share on Facebook.
- **Share on Twitter**—Twitter has become an extremely powerful tool in managing brands online. You can follow the Twitter handles of your potential employers and the dream companies where you want to work someday in the future. This way, you can stay updated about these companies/employers. Moreover, you can use Twitter to find information about employers and hiring companies.

As is clear from the preceding discussion, social media can be a great way of getting jobs, especially in the new and expanding field of Big Data. The opportunities in this field are immense and still growing. There is an acute requirement for both novices and experienced individuals, and social media provides the perfect tool for such people to showcase their talent to prospective employers.

Summary

This chapter discussed the potential of Big Data, which is a new and growing field requiring a large number of talented professionals. In the beginning, the chapter described the basics of Big Data, which involves the generation of large volumes of data at a high velocity in different forms. It also explained the importance of Big Data for businesses and scope of Big Data as a paradigm. Moreover, you were made familiar with the opportunities provided in field of Big Data. The chapter also explained how to assess your skills in order to determine how suitable you would be as a Big Data professional. The roles and responsibilities of Big Data professionals were discussed next. After this, the different kinds of jobs for Big Data professionals such as consultants and in-house specialists were described in detail. Toward the end of the chapter, you learned how to prepare for a Big Data interview and how to use social media as a tool to help you get your dream job in the Big Data industry.

Quick Revise

Multiple-Choice Questions

Q1. In which of the following areas do you need to assess your Big Data skills?

a. Aptitude evaluation
b. Skillset assessment
c. Execution plan
d. All of the above

Ans. The correct option is b.

Q2. Which of the following is not a category for Big Data jobs?

a. Business analysis
b. Business process outsourcing
c. Data science
d. Software development

Ans. The correct option is b.

Q3. Which of the following is the primary skill set of a data scientist?

a. Team playing skills
b. Knowledge of multiple programming languages
c. Preparation of technical cases and creation of mathematical models
d. Willingness to learn and adopt

Ans. The correct option is c.

Q4. What does IRC stand for?

a. Internet Relay Chat
b. Indian Railway Check
c. International Relay Check
d. None of the above

Ans. The correct option is a.

Q5. Which of the following is not an NoSQL database system?

a. Document databases
b. Graph-based databases
c. Column-oriented databases
d. Relational tables

Ans. The correct option is d.

Subjective Questions

Q1. What is the importance and scope of jobs in Big Data?

Ans. Big Data is a term that is today commonly used in the world of advanced Information Technology (IT) to describe a large collection of different types of data, taken from various sources. The concept of Big Data involves four Vs, i.e., Volume, Velocity, Variety, and Veracity. Each of these Vs plays an important role in providing the fifth V, i.e., Value, to Big Data.

The value of Big Data is that it consists of different types of data—structured, semi-structured, and unstructured. This data is received and processed at a high velocity. The accuracy of input data as well as output information may vary according to the needs and availability of resources. Hence, the volume, velocity, variety, and veracity of data are the key players in determining the value of information.

Big Data is usually handled in different stages where the data is collected, stored, organized, analyzed, etc., with a view to discover new insights and improve business decisions.

One of the major positive impacts of Big Data analysis has been that organizations have become more customer-centric. Marketing strategies, where data analysis plays a crucial role, play a big role in driving businesses forward. Today, nearly every industry deals with analyzed data and uses the results in improving their business decisions and future actions. The main areas where Big Data is used include risk management, compliance, financial services, healthcare organizations, government undertakings, retail industry, etc.

Big Data is a big player in different industries. It provides a lot of opportunities for people who want to make a career in the field. There is a lot of scope for young professionals, especially those who have good hands-on experience in the fields of technology and analytics. However, apart from this experience, you also need to have the skills and knowledge of a data scientist in order to do well in this field.

Q2. Discuss the importance of skill assessment when looking for jobs in the field of Big Data.

Ans. You need to do a self-assessment of your Big Data skills in order to know if you have the skills and aptitude to do a Big Data job competently. Skill assessment can be performed in four different areas, which are as follows:

- Aptitude evaluation
- Skill set assessment
- Gap filling
- Execution plan

In each of the areas listed above, you need to assess the roles and responsibilities according to your capability and interests. For example, the roles and responsibilities that may be suited to you according to your interests and aptitude would belong to the first category, the skills required to excel in the Big Data field can be segregated in the second category, filling the gaps by identifying weaknesses and ways of overcoming them can be put into the third category and, finally, goals and success metrics can be set in the last category. The following figure illustrates the process taken in the self-assessment of skills in the field of Big Data:

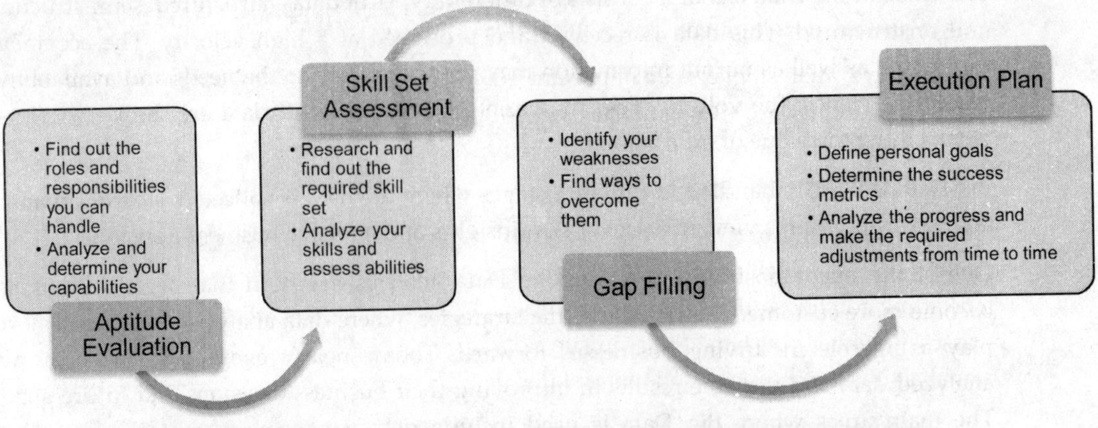

Figure: Self-Assessment Process for Professionals to Excel in Big Data

Once you have figured out the roles and responsibilities suited to you and analyzed the required knowledge and skills, you can try to find out the gaps in your educational qualifications, technical expertise, and business understanding. You can start filling the gaps by analyzing your current position in the professional career and finding out the areas where you can improve yourself.

In order to fill the gaps, you need to properly analyze the specific things that you need to do. For example, you might need to continue your education till you obtain a master's or doctorate degree in mathematics or statistics. However, getting formal education is not always a viable option because it may take years—valuable time that you might not be in a position to sacrifice. Therefore, you must clearly assess your present situation and decide whether less money at present is important or the prospect of getting more income in 2–3 years down the line is a better option. Hence, whether you want to invest some time in getting a formal education or want to do a job must be a step that you must take after considering all aspects carefully. Sometimes, your situation (financial or otherwise) may force you to do a job, and formal education may not be a possibility for the time being. In such a situation, you can continue your learning through the Internet or other methods while doing the job simultaneously. This way, you can be more valuable in your Big Data job with education as well as experience. The combination may help to give you an edge in the market over others.

When you are ready with knowledge, skills, and experience, you can carefully plan your journey in the Big Data field by defining the milestones you want to achieve and the timelines to achieve them in.

Q3. What are the different roles and responsibilities in Big Data jobs?

Ans. Every role requires a set of skills and experience. Big Data primarily involves business decision making by analyzing business situations and requirements. Therefore, the roles and responsibilities in Big Data jobs are divided into the following categories:

- Business analysis

- Data science
- Software development

A business analyst plays an important role in different industries, spanning corporate IT companies, software firms specializing in Big Data, or consulting companies. Organizations are increasingly luring business analysts with attractive payments, ranging between $75000 and $109000 annually on an average.

Business analysts are crucial for the overall functioning of an organization. They may be given other job titles, such as marketing analyst, data analyst, system analyst, etc. However, before deciding to choose the role of a business analyst as a career option, you need to properly assess whether you have the requisite skills for the job. You can succeed as a good business analyst if you possess the following skills:

- Natural inquisitiveness that requires closely observing and analyzing business situations so that the best option can be taken
- Vision to enhance the current circumstances for benefitting the business scenario by focusing on the right areas
- Ability to quickly switch between creativity and analytics
- Knowledge of the target audience and understanding their demands and preferences

A data scientist in Big Data use cases has the responsibility of communicating with business analysts so that inputs for business decisions can be taken and the tasks based on the inputs can be performed. Some of the most important tasks performed by data scientists on the recommendations of a business analyst are as follows:

- Preparation of technical cases
- Creation of mathematical models
- Discovery of patterns, trends, and correlations in data

A data scientist also needs to assess his/her area of interest in the same way as business analysts before deciding on the Big Data profession as a career. The following questions would help the data scientist to make the decision:

- Do you possess a natural inquisitive instinct to conduct deep analysis of important issues? Also, do you have a passion for technology?
- Do you have the determination to fulfill the educational requirements of a data scientist?
- Are you self-motivated and can work without external guidance?
- Can you manage multiple disciplines and work on several areas such as statistics, mathematics, computer science, etc.?
- Are you able to convert an idea into reality?

If a person answers most of these questions in the affirmative, he/she should probably think about choosing data scientist as a career option.

Today, no business can succeed without the help of technology. Therefore, software developers have a distinct place in the Big Data industry, which drives businesses through technological implementations. A software developer needs to assess his/her skills before choosing the role of software developer in the Big Data industry. The main characteristics required for a Big Data software developer are as follows:

- Ability to work with teams
- Knowledge of multiple programming languages
- Willingness to learn and adopt

Usually, Big Data jobs require Big Data developers with certain basic qualifications as well as additional skills and abilities. Basic qualifications may include a few years of experience in particular programming languages, ability to learn quickly, and a bachelor's degree. Additional skills can be experience in particular technologies, specific development methods, or certain designing techniques and approaches.

Q4. What is the basic educational qualification required for a Big Data job?

Ans. Some years back, career choices were usually made at very early ages, when children had barely entered their teen years. However, today, the scenario is very different. The world has witnessed a lot of changes in all spheres in recent times, and these changes are reflected in the educational system as well. As a result, people today have a wide range of careers to choose from. This is in part due to the different specializations that have come up in subjects that were once single subjects. For example, some years ago, the fields of computer science and information technology had very few specializations, but today, these fields have become complex and cover several specializations. Consequently, decisions regarding careers are also being taken at a later stage in life.

The field of education has to keep pace with these changes. For example, a career in Big Data requires one to have knowledge about different fields such as statistics, mathematics, analytics, IT, etc. Therefore, one needs to study these fields in order to do well as a Big Data professional.

Big Data education would preferably, at present, require one to get specialized education (degree) in one or more subjects given in the following list:

- Statistics and Mathematics
- Computer Science and Engineering
- Business Administration

Earlier, we discussed the important role played by a business analyst in the field of Big Data. For a person to become a Big Data business analyst, he/she should ideally have a degree in Statistics and/or Mathematics. This is because the analyst traditionally performs statistical analysis of data. Big Data specific degrees are not available in universities and colleges, but several programs, courses, and degrees are specifically designed to suit the requirements of the Big Data industry. These programs, courses, and degrees focus particularly on teaching students concepts related to computational theory, statistics, and probability.

Big Data is a blend of different disciplines. You need to be able to apply your analytical skills, which come by having knowledge of mathematics, computer science, and business administration. Computer science, along with its various subfields, plays a vital role in the use of Big Data at the organizational level. Some of the fields integrated with Big Data handling include the following:

- Artificial Intelligence (AI)
- Machine learning
- Data theory

Knowledge of these fields is important for using and managing Big Data. However, you can also choose one of these disciplines for specialization so that you can perform certain tasks related to Big Data where mathematical theories are applied practically on business problems.

When it comes to businesses, Big Data has been very influential in improving the decision-making process and marketing strategies. Almost every business is benefiting from Big Data in one way or another. However, as a Big Data professional, you need to have good knowledge of various business situations so that you can help the organization deal with any issues. This requires experience as well as study. Neither the study nor the experience alone can help you deal with real-world business situations. Apart from having experience in various business situations, you also need to have a degree in marketing, business intelligence, predictive analysis, etc.

You should have at least a degree in mathematics, statistics, computer science and engineering, or business administration before taking up a role in Big Data. However, if you are already working in the field of technology after having abandoned your studies earlier, you can join a continual program to obtain specific knowledge related to Big Data.

A few years back, it was not possible to predict the emergence or growth of Big Data. Therefore, some of us might not have felt the need to go for higher education. Such people can now continue with their education and take up jobs as data analysts, programmers, or business analysts. In the continual study system, you can go for a specialized short-duration program in statistics or analytics, but for this, you need to already possess some knowledge of statistics, calculus, accounting basics, marketing concepts, and so on. Each of these fields may have its implications on your career in your Big Data job. In an analytics program, you may choose to go for a course in business intelligence, statistical analysis, management course, or stochastic simulation. Moreover, you could have elective subject options that include data mining, applied multivariable methods, forecasting methods, quality management and six-sigma, and a number of other subjects.

Q5. Describe the main tools used to handle Big Data.

Ans. Big Data is supported by various tools and techniques. The main techniques include analytical and visualization techniques. Additionally, there are various types of tools for handling Big Data. Many of these tools are available for free in the form of Web-based applications on the Internet. You can download and install these tools on your computer, become familiar with their interfaces, and use them for your benefit. For example:

- You can create data visualizations by using R packages such as, Rcharts and Rmaps.
- You can scrap your data by using Import.io.
- You can collect images by using ImageQuilts.
- You can use DataWrangler for wrangling the data.
- You can use Tableau Public for exploring data.
- You can use Gephi for fast data processing and analysis.
- You can perform machine-learning operations through the WEKA suite.
- You can use Weave to get a Web-based platform for the visualization of data.
- You can also use the platform known as Knoema to visualize your data.

These tools are used by professionals to manage Big Data in an efficient way for the benefit of the organization they are working for.

Q6. Discuss the importance of networking as a tool to search for a Big Data job.

Ans. All of us have friends who keep in touch with other people or seem to know people everywhere they go. These friends are naturally interactive and can build networks easily. Being interactive and contact building is an art that does not come easily to some people, but it can be developed.

You develop contacts or connections with others with or without expecting anything in return. However, remember that the connections you establish form the foundation on the basis of which you will get jobs in the market. Therefore, you need to be aware of the requirements of the industry and the type of people who can be helpful in your job search. The best places to search for such people are as follows:

- **Industry interest groups**—These groups involve people of similar mindsets who like to discuss and share their ideas and promote innovative approaches by making connections. You can find such groups by exploring the Internet for the industry you want to join. Industry interest groups can be found at the following places:
  - Conferences
  - Trade shows
  - Vendor summits
  - Meetings

- **Alumni networks**—In addition to interest groups, you can find out and connect with alumni networks. The following are some examples of alumni networks:
  - Alumni databases
  - Career services
  - Alumni associations
  - University lifelong learning groups

Establishing connections with people is a difficult task, especially if you are not naturally interactive. However, you need to make an effort in this direction as it may lead you to your dream job. Some of the points to keep in mind while establishing connections and networks are as follows:

- Have a story and be ready to tell it
- Be honest about your abilities while describing yourself to people
- Be straightforward while discussing yourself and your goals with others
- Take the initiative to ask people for regular meetings

Before you build your brand and create connections, you need to carefully plan how you would like to go about doing it. The following steps would help you in this regard:

- Define your goals clearly
- Prepare the current network list
- Identify groups for engagement
- Enhance your online profile
- Evaluate your prospects

This way, you would be better prepared to land the perfect job in the field of Big Data.

Q7. What points should you consider while creating a resume for a job in the field of Big Data?

Ans. Having a perfect resume is one of the basic requirements for a job search in any field. You should understand that your resume is the first step towards your goal of getting the job. Any kind of hiring process begins with the resume. Therefore, you need to be very careful about what you include in your resume. Make sure that the information included in your resume is relevant and true and projects a positive image of you to the potential employer.

The strategy you adopt to write your resume and the content you decide to highlight in it depend on common market trends, job descriptions, and positions for which the vacancy is open. You need to go through the Careers page of different organizations to understand the requirements of the Big Data industry. That would help you to create a winning resume on the basis of the requirements. A hiring process normally involves a number of steps starting with job postings spread on social media or in forums offering job consulting services for both employers and job seekers. The applications for these posts are filled and sent along with the resumes of the applicants to the employer. After this, the Human Resource (HR) team shortlists the resumes so that interviews can be conducted.

Remember that resumes are shortlisted on the basis of certain keywords related to the job posting. Resumes that do not contain these keywords would therefore be most likely be ignored. Hence, you must make sure that your resume contains these keywords if you want it to get noticed and shortlisted.

There can be some do's and don'ts that you need to follow while creating a resume. The following are some basic do's while creating a resume:

- Make the resume simple, concise, and one that grabs the attention of the potential employer easily.
- Mention the information in relevant sections for clarity. These sections can be as follows:
  - Career Objective
  - Technical Skills
  - Educational Qualification
  - Professional Experience
  - Training and Certificates
- Highlight your achievement with sentences that start with action verbs such as 'Developed a multimedia program by applying a specific innovative approach.'
- Avoid spelling mistakes or grammatical errors
- Use consistent fonts and format throughout

The following are some don'ts that need to be observed while creating a resume:

- Don't make your resume too long. Two pages is the ideal length.
- Don't include unconvincing work experience.
- Avoid inexplicable conflicts between dates, employers, etc.
- Avoid spelling mistakes and errors in punctuation and grammar.

After creating your resume, make sure to check it thoroughly to spot and correct errors. Also, ensure that you haven't forgotten to include any important detail while keeping the document concise. Finally, make sure to include relevant information in different sections such as career objective, technical skills, work experience, etc. Mention the details properly, carefully, and clearly in your resume in order to get shortlisted for the job you applied for.

Q8. How can you use social media to help you get a job in Big Data?

Ans. The development of social networking sites such as Twitter, Facebook, and LinkedIn has been one of the most advantageous developments for companies and individuals. The information you put online is your brand. Social media platforms have been widely used for advertising and gaining popularity. A well-managed brand on social media attracts a lot of viewers, including potential recruiters who could contact you after seeing your profile on social media.

There are various ways through which you can maintain your profile in social media. Some of these ways are as follows:

- **Searching yourself on Google**—A search for your own profile in Google will provide a clear idea about the kind of information is visible to the employers about you. Your public image tells others the kind of person you are. You need to ensure that your photos, videos, etc., posted by you in social networking sites come up on a Google search and give a positive impression of you to others.
- **Removing unflattering pictures**—A Google search for your profile may reveal some annoying or awkward photos that you may not like your potential employer to see. It is better to remove these photos so that your image on social media remains clean and positive.
- **Scrutinizing and editing for oneself**—Blogs, photos, videos, or any other work related to writing, image editing, or video making are usually posted on the Internet and available for everyone to see. You need to identify the best ways to scrutinize your own work to ensure that potential employers do not see what you don't want them to see.
- **Using the Google+ platform**—The Google+ platform is a part of the Google brand, so your updated profile on Google+ would be prioritized on Google searches. Hence, you will be easily visible to employers.
- **Maintaining LinkedIn network profile in a professional manner**—Your use of LinkedIn matters a lot today in your job hunt. The LinkedIn platform is the largest social network for professionals to share their experience. Therefore, you need to create a professional, well-managed profile on LinkedIn that would impress a potential employer. The full benefits of the LinkedIn network can be exploited in the following ways:
  - Your LinkedIn profile can be used as a resume.
  - You can use the profile to highlight your personal and professional achievements.
  - Make sure that the profile includes a suitable Display Picture (DP).
  - Follow companies and industry influencers.
  - Your LinkedIn profile should be short and impressive.
  - Set a customized visibility setting for the profile.
- **Using Blogger and other blogging sites**—The Internet has made it possible for everyone to express themselves in one way or another. Blogging is one of the primary ways of doing this. Before writing about a certain topic or issue in a blog, make sure that you have adequate information about it by doing a little research. There are numerous blogging sites, such as Blogger, WordPress, Tumblr, etc., on which you can create a blog and post regularly. Also, make sure that the blogs you create are updated regularly. An employer would not like a blog with no updates in a long time.
- **Become an expert of your craft**—Some of the websites nowadays provide a platform for experts to voice their opinion about certain topics or themes or answer questions. Some examples of such sites are Stack Overflow and Quora. You should attach the links of your answers to your public profile available online.

- **Focus on Facebook**—You can use Facebook in multiple ways. Facebook not only provides you a way to stay connected with your friends, families, and other individuals but also enables you to get a new job through the Facebook network. However, to land a job through Facebook may require you to write your profile in a way that it focuses more on your professional history or achievements than on personal information. You can also connect with companies for job openings. However, you should be careful about your posts and the information you share on Facebook.
- **Share on Twitter**—Twitter has become an extremely powerful tool in managing brands online. You can follow the Twitter handles of your potential employers and the dream companies where you want to work someday in the future. This way, you can stay updated about these companies/employers. Moreover, you can use Twitter to find information about employers and hiring companies.

Big Data Practical

The Hadoop ecosystem is a Big Data management environment that combines a number of data storage, processing, access, visualization, and distribution technologies. In this ecosystem, the core processing tasks are handled by the MapReduce programming paradigm in which a large task is divided into smaller subtasks that are processed in a parallel distributed environment. This ecosystem can be implemented on various frameworks. One of these frameworks is Cloudera, a part of Apache Software Foundation's open source projects, which enables massive data storage and faster processing. Additionally, the Hadoop ecosystem includes a number of technologies, such as HBase, Hive, Pig, etc. These technologies have their own importance in Big Data management.

The objective of **Big Data Practical** is to introduce you to some basic functions of various technologies that are used to handle Big Data. The Practical includes some labs on the MapReduce programming paradigm. It implements the basics of Pig. It also explains some basic commands in Hive and HBase. Finally, it discusses the updated labs on R and Tableau 9.0 public.

Labs on MapReduce

Lab 1—To Create a Job and Submit it to Cluster

Solution—The syntax to create a job and submit it to a cluster is as follows:

```
hadoop jar /Jar_File_Path Package_Name /Source_Path /Destination_Path
```

The following command is used to create a job and submit it to a cluster:

```
hadoop jar /home/cloudera/Desktop/EnergyProjDemo.jar Energy_Package.Energy_Driver
  /tmp/IBM/Energy_ProjDemo/input/sincal.txt /tmp/IBM/Energy_ProjDemo/outputTest
```

After entering the preceding command, a new job will be created and submitted to the cluster. The output after the job is created and it is shown in Figure 1:

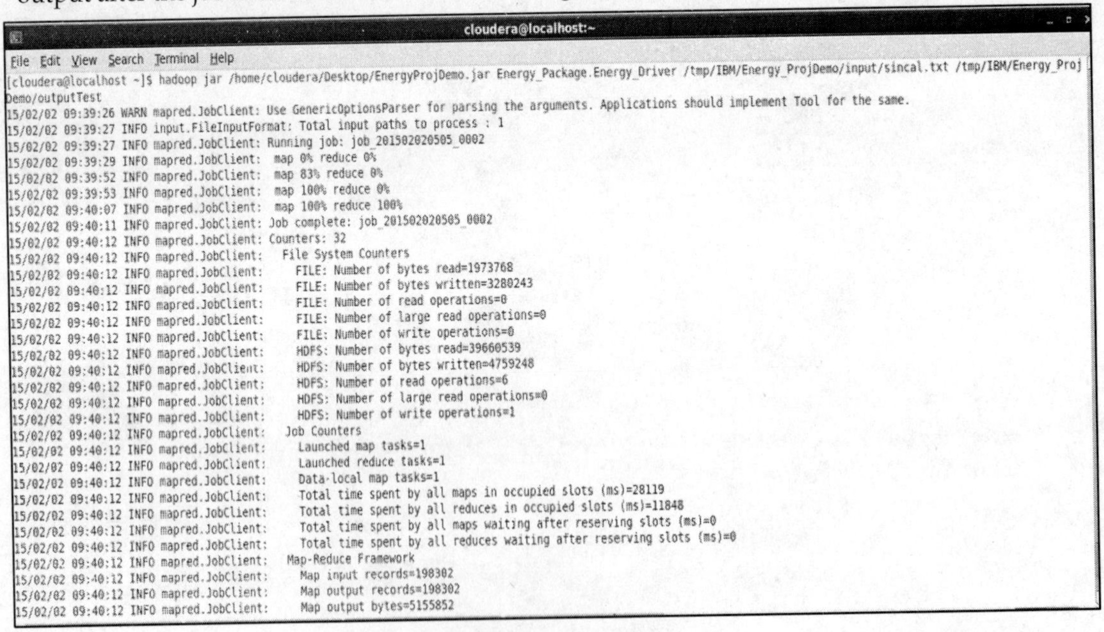

Figure 1: Creating a Job

The output screen, after the submission of the newly created job to the cluster, appears as shown in Figure 2:

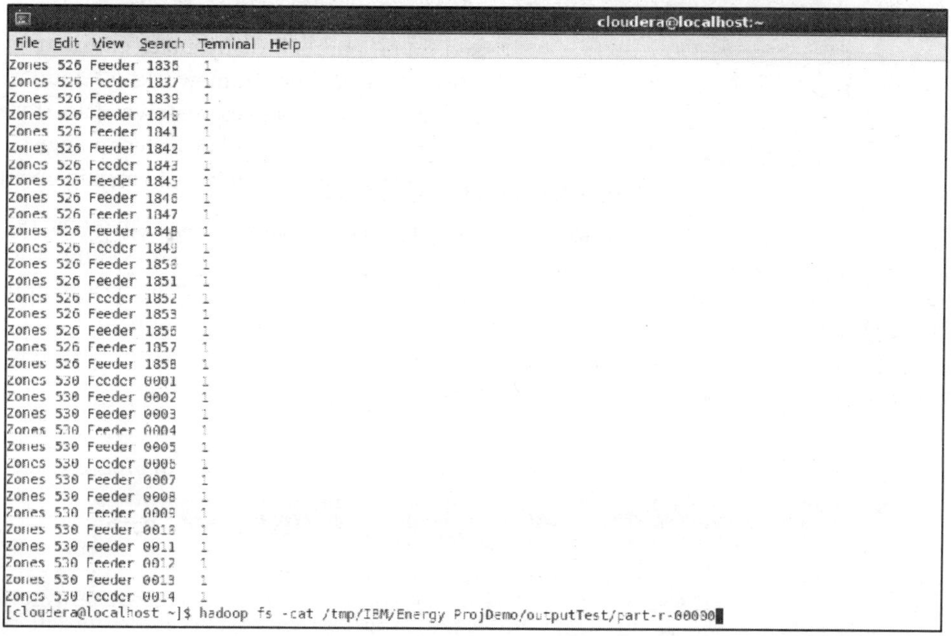

Figure 2: Submitting a Job to a Cluster

Lab 2—To Track Job Information

Solution—The Hadoop cluster contains some important daemons running on a cluster. These daemons are as follows:

- NameNode
- DataNode
- JobTracker
- TaskTracker

Among these daemons, the JobTracker daemon distributes tasks to specific nodes in the cluster. The JobTracker daemon is responsible for performing the following tasks:

- It communicates with NameNode to determine the location of data.
- It locates TaskTracker nodes with available slots at or near the data.
- It submits the tasks to TaskTracker on the selected nodes. These nodes are monitored. If they do not submit heartbeat signals often, they are assumed to have failed, and the work is scheduled on a different TaskTracker.
- It updates its status after the completion of the job.
- It can be polled by the client for information.

In Hadoop, the command to get tracking information about a job is as follows:

```
hadoop job -list
```

After entering the preceding command, you will see the job details listed as shown in Figure 3:

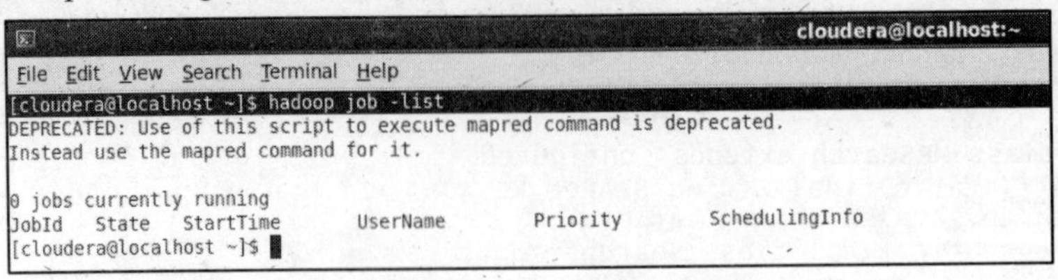

Figure 3: Listing the Jobs Details

Since no job is running at present, there will be no job details available. Instead, the screen shows a message that reads **0 jobs currently running**.

Lab 3—To Terminate a Job

Solution—The command to terminate or kill a job is as follows:

```
hadoop job -kill
```

As shown in Figure 4, there are no jobs running. Therefore, no jobs are killed as a result of the execution of the preceding command. The output screen appears, as shown in Figure 4:

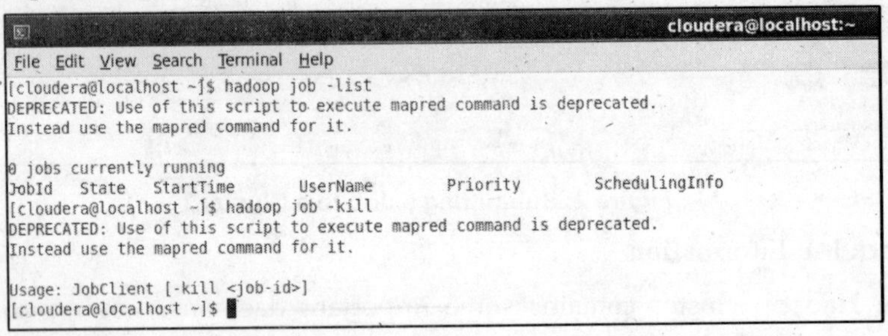

Figure 4: Running the kill Command

Lab 4—To Search a Key in MapReduce Jobs

Solution—To search a key in MapReduce jobs, we need to create the following two classes:

- The `Mapper` class
- The `Driver` class

The `Mapper` class contains the business logic for searching a key. The `Driver` class is the main class through which an instance of the `Mapper` class is created and run.

Listing 1 shows the code to create the `Mapper` class:

Listing 1: The `Mapper` Class

```
package com.MRSearch;
import java.io.IOException;
import org.apache.hadoop.conf.Configured;
import org.apache.hadoop.fs.Path;
import org.apache.hadoop.io.LongWritable;
import org.apache.hadoop.io.NullWritable;
import org.apache.hadoop.io.Text;
import org.apache.hadoop.mapreduce.Job;
import org.apache.hadoop.mapreduce.Mapper;
import org.apache.hadoop.mapreduce.Mapper.Context;
import org.apache.hadoop.mapreduce.lib.input.FileInputFormat;
```

```
import org.apache.hadoop.mapreduce.lib.input.FileSplit;
import org.apache.hadoop.mapreduce.lib.input.TextInputFormat;
import org.apache.hadoop.mapreduce.lib.output.FileOutputFormat;
import org.apache.hadoop.util.Tool;
import org.apache.hadoop.util.ToolRunner;

public class MRSearch extends Configured implements Tool {
  private static final String SEARCH_KEYWORD_KEY =
  "MRSearch.samples.search.keyword";
  public static final class SearcherMapper extends
              Mapper<LongWritable, Text, Text, Text> {
        private Text valueFileName = null;
        private Text keywordKey = null;
        private String keyword = "";
        @Override
        protected void setup(Context context) throws IOException,
                    InterruptedException {
              super.setup(context);
              FileSplit split = (FileSplit) context.getInputSplit();
              fileNameValue = new Text(split.getPath().getName());
              keyword = context.getConfiguration().get(SEARCH_KEYWORD_KEY);
              keywordKey = new Text(keyword);
        }
        @Override
        protected void map(LongWritable key, Text value, Context context)
                    throws IOException, InterruptedException {
              String line = value.toString();
              if (line.contains(keyword)) {
                    context.write(keywordKey, fileNameValue);
              }
        }
  }
  @Override
  public int run(String[] args) throws Exception {
        Job job = new Job();
        job.setJarByClass(getClass());
        job.setJobName("Map Reduce Searcher");
        job.setMapperClass(SearcherMapper.class);
        job.setMapOutputKeyClass(Text.class);
        job.setMapOutputValueClass(NullWritable.class);
        job.setOutputKeyClass(Text.class);
        job.setOutputValueClass(Text.class);
        job.setNumReduceTasks(0);
        job.setInputFormatClass(TextInputFormat.class);
        FileInputFormat.setInputPaths(job, new Path(args[0]));
        FileOutputFormat.setOutputPath(job, new Path(args[1]));
        job.getConfiguration().set(SEARCH_KEYWORD_KEY, args[2]);
        job.waitForCompletion(true);
        return 0;       }
```

In Listing 1, the `MRSearch` class extends the `Configured` class and implements the `Tool` interface. The class overrides the `setup()`, `map()`, and `run()` methods.

Listing 2 shows the code of the `Driver` class:

Listing 2: The `Driver` Class

```
public static void main(String[] args) throws Exception {
        ToolRunner.run(new MRSearch(), args);
  }
}
```

In Listing 2, the `Driver` class implements the `main()` method in which the `run()` method is invoked by passing the `MRSearch` class as an argument.

Figure 5 shows the input to the `MRSearch` class:

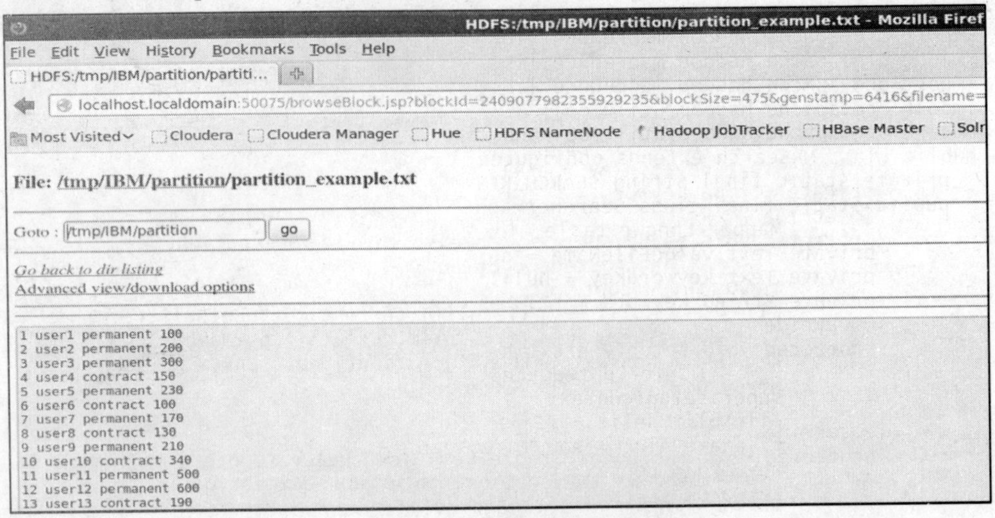

Figure 5: Input to the MRSearch Class

Figure 6 shows the output based on the input provided to the `MRSearch` class:

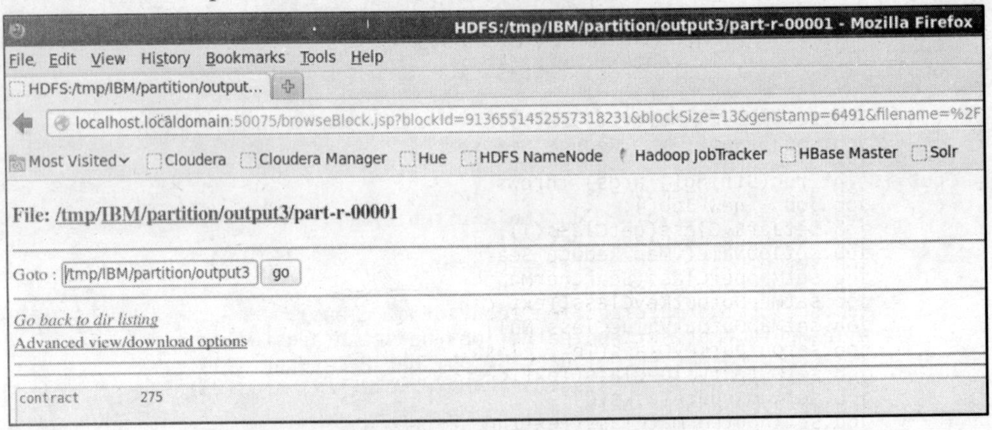

Figure 6: Output of the MRSearch Class

Lab 5—To Run Map-Only Jobs and Provide a Generic Map Example

Solution—Here also, you will create two classes, i.e., `MRSearch` and `Driver`. Listing 3 shows the code of the `MRSearch` class:

Listing 3: The `MRSearch` Class

```
package com.MapOnlyJob;
import java.io.IOException;
import org.apache.hadoop.conf.Configured;
import org.apache.hadoop.fs.Path;
import org.apache.hadoop.io.LongWritable;
```

```
import org.apache.hadoop.io.NullWritable;
import org.apache.hadoop.io.Text;
import org.apache.hadoop.mapreduce.Job;
import org.apache.hadoop.mapreduce.Mapper;
import org.apache.hadoop.mapreduce.Mapper.Context;
import org.apache.hadoop.mapreduce.lib.input.FileInputFormat;
import org.apache.hadoop.mapreduce.lib.input.FileSplit;
import org.apache.hadoop.mapreduce.lib.input.TextInputFormat;
import org.apache.hadoop.mapreduce.lib.output.FileOutputFormat;
import org.apache.hadoop.util.Tool;
import org.apache.hadoop.util.ToolRunner;
public class MRSearch extends Configured implements Tool {
  private static final String SEARCH_KEYWORD_KEY = "MapOnlyJobs ";
  public static final class SearcherMapper extends
              Mapper<LongWritable, Text, Text, Text> {
        private Text valueFileName = null;
        private Text keywordKey = null;
        private String keyword = "";
        @Override
        protected void setup(Context context) throws IOException,
                     InterruptedException {
              super.setup(context);
              FileSplit split = (FileSplit) context.getInputSplit();
              fileNameValue = new Text(split.getPath().getName());
              keyword = context.getConfiguration().get(SEARCH_KEYWORD_KEY);
              keywordKey = new Text(keyword);
        }
        @Override
        protected void map(LongWritable key, Text value, Context context)
                     throws IOException, InterruptedException {
              String line = value.toString();
              if (line.contains(keyword)) {
                     context.write(keywordKey, fileNameValue);
              }
        }
  }
  @Override
  public int run(String[] args) throws Exception {
        Job job = new Job();
        job.setJarByClass(getClass());
        job.setJobName("Map Reduce Searcher");
        job.setMapperClass(SearcherMapper.class);
        job.setMapOutputKeyClass(Text.class);
        job.setMapOutputValueClass(NullWritable.class);
        job.setOutputKeyClass(Text.class);
        job.setOutputValueClass(Text.class);
        job.setNumReduceTasks(0);
        job.setInputFormatClass(TextInputFormat.class);
        FileInputFormat.setInputPaths(job, new Path(args[0]));
        FileOutputFormat.setOutputPath(job, new Path(args[1]));
        job.getConfiguration().set(SEARCH_KEYWORD_KEY, args[2]);
        job.waitForCompletion(true);
        return 0;
  }
```

In the code given in Listing 3, the only change as compared to the code given in Listing 1 is the value of the string SEARCH_KEYWORD_KEY. Listing 4 shows the code of the `Driver` class:

Listing 4: The `Driver` Class

```
    public static void main(String[] args) throws Exception {
            ToolRunner.run(new MRSearch(), args);
        }
    }
```

In Listing 4, an instance of the `MRSearch` class is passed to the `run()` method as an argument.

In map-only jobs, we have the output of the `Mapper` class only, and the same is saved in the specified destination folder. The output is saved in HDFS on the basis of the number of mappers that ran on a file or on different blocks.

Based on the input, we can say that two mappers ran on two blocks of data, as highlighted in Figure 7:

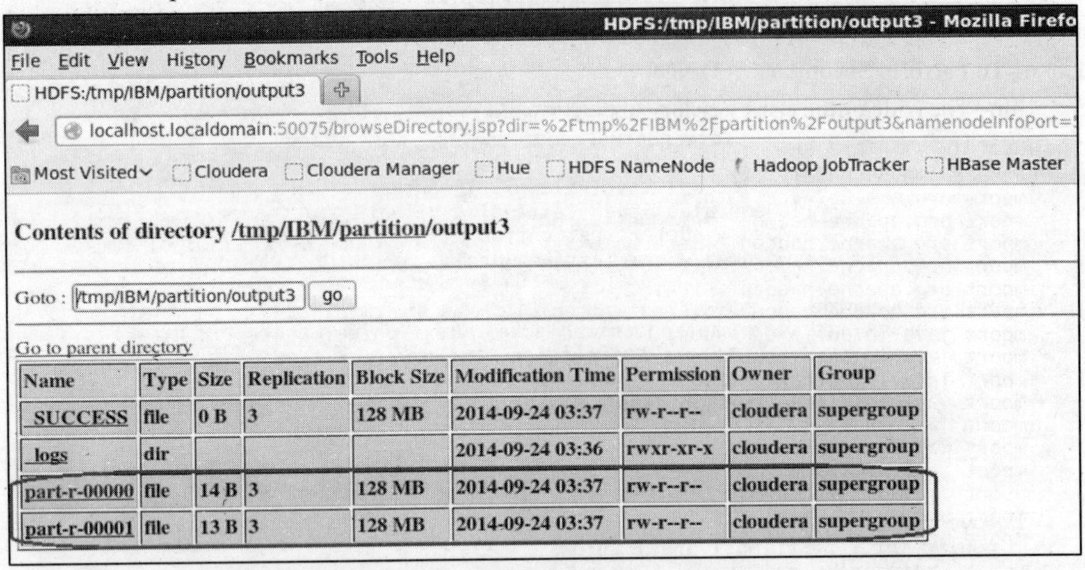

Figure 7: Map-Only Jobs Running on Different Data Blocks

The first output will appear as shown in Figure 8:

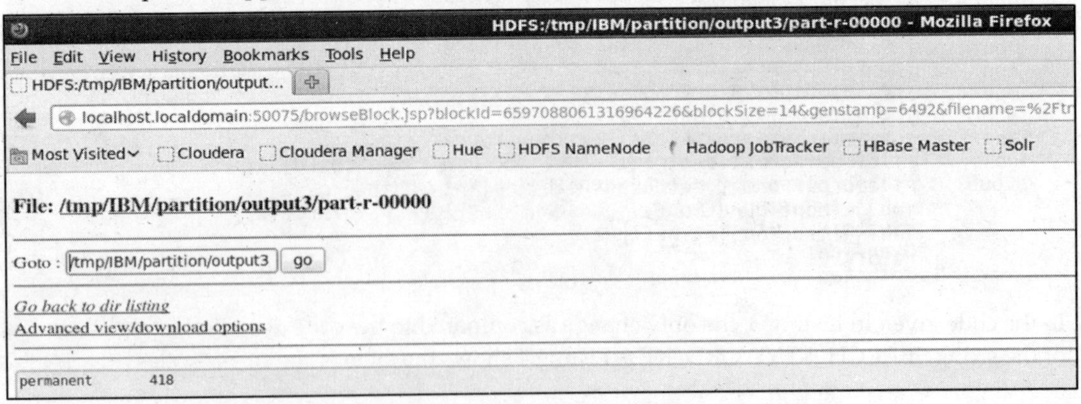

Figure 8: First Output of the Running MapReduce Jobs

The second output will appear as shown in Figure 9:

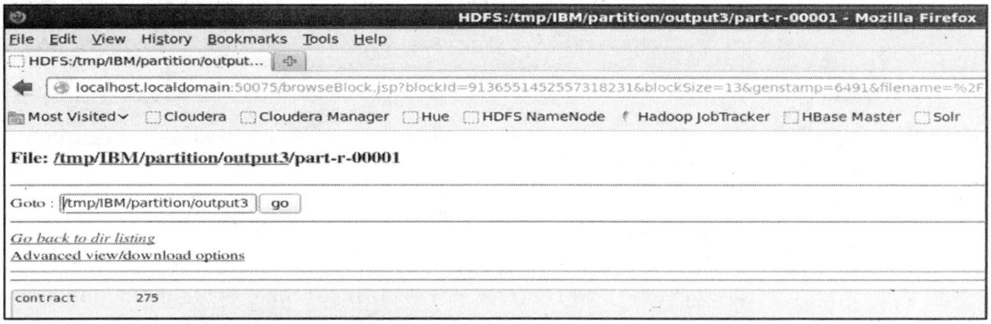

Figure 9: Second Output of the Running MapReduce Jobs

Lab 6—To Perform Secondary Sorting

Solution—The code of the `Mapper` class to perform secondary sorting is shown in Listing 5:

Listing 5: The `Mapper` Class

```
package com.SecondarySort;
import org.apache.hadoop.conf.Configuration;
import org.apache.hadoop.conf.Configured;
import org.apache.hadoop.filecache.DistributedCache;
import org.apache.hadoop.fs.FileSystem;
import org.apache.hadoop.fs.Path;
import org.apache.hadoop.io.FloatWritable;
import java.io.BufferedReader;
import java.io.DataInput;
import java.io.DataOutput;
import java.io.FileReader;
import java.io.IOException;
import java.util.HashMap;
import java.util.Map;
import org.apache.hadoop.mapreduce.lib.input.FileInputFormat;
import org.apache.hadoop.mapreduce.lib.input.TextInputFormat;
import org.apache.hadoop.mapreduce.lib.output.FileOutputFormat;
import org.apache.hadoop.mapreduce.lib.output.TextOutputFormat;
import org.apache.hadoop.mapreduce.Job;
import org.apache.hadoop.mapreduce.Mapper;
import org.apache.hadoop.mapreduce.Partitioner;
import org.apache.hadoop.io.LongWritable;
import org.apache.hadoop.io.Text;
import org.apache.hadoop.io.WritableComparable;
import org.apache.hadoop.io.WritableComparator;
import org.apache.hadoop.mapreduce.Reducer;
import org.apache.hadoop.util.Tool;
import org.apache.hadoop.util.ToolRunner;
public class SecondarySort extends Configured implements Tool {
  public static class MJMapper extends
            Mapper<LongWritable, Text, sceneRatings, FloatWritable> {
      private Map<String, String> scenes = null;
      @Override
      protected void setup(Context context) throws IOException,
                  InterruptedException {
            scenes = new HashMap<String, String>();
            Path[] files = DistributedCache.getLocalCacheFiles(context
                        .getConfiguration());
            BufferedReader reader = new BufferedReader(new FileReader(
                        files[0].toString()));
            String line;
            String[] fields;
```

```
            while ((line = reader.readLine()) != null) {
                    fields = line.split("::");
                    scenes.put(fields[0], fields[1]);
            }
        }
        @Override
        protected void map(LongWritable key, Text value, Context context)
                    throws IOException, InterruptedException {
            String record = value.toString();
            String[] fields = record.split("::");
            String sceneId = fields[1];
            if (scenes.containsKey(sceneId)) {
                    FloatWritable ratingValue = new FloatWritable(
                                    Float.parseFloat(fields[2]));
                    context.write(new sceneRatings(new Text(scenes.get(sceneId)),
                                    ratingValue), ratingValue);
            }
    }
    }
```

In Listing 5, the `SecondarySort` class extends the `Configured` class and implements the `Tool` interface. Now, let us look at the code of the `Reducer` class shown in Listing 6:

Listing 6: The `Reducer` Class

```
public static class MJReducer extends
            Reducer<sceneRatings, FloatWritable, Text, FloatWritable> {
        protected void reduce(sceneRatings key, Iterable<FloatWritable> values,
                    Context context) throws IOException, InterruptedException {
            for (FloatWritable value : values) {
                    context.write(key.getsceneName(), value);
            }
    }
    }
```

The `Reducer` class, named `MJReducer`, extends the `Reducer` class and provides the body to the `reduce()` method. Now, we need to create a custom data type class for which the code is shown in Listing 7:

Listing 7: Custom Data Type Class

```
public static class sceneRatings implements
            WritableComparable<sceneRatings> {
        public sceneRatings() {
            sceneName = new Text();
            rating = new FloatWritable();
        }

        public sceneRatings(Text sceneName, FloatWritable rating) {
            setsceneName(sceneName);
            setRating(rating);
        }
        private Text sceneName;;
        private FloatWritable rating;

        public Text getsceneName() {
            return sceneName;
        }
        public void setsceneName(Text sceneName) {
            this.sceneName = sceneName;
        }
        public FloatWritable getRating() {
            return rating;
        }
```

```
	public void setRating(FloatWritable rating) {
		this.rating = rating;
	}
	@Override
	public void write(DataOutput out) throws IOException {
		sceneName.write(out);
		rating.write(out);
	}
	@Override
	public void readFields(DataInput in) throws IOException {
		sceneName.readFields(in);
		rating.readFields(in);
	}

	@Override
	public int hashCode() {
		final int prime = 31;
		int result = 1;
		result = prime * result
				+ ((sceneName == null) ? 0 : sceneName.hashCode());
		result = prime * result
				+ ((rating == null) ? 0 : rating.hashCode());
		return result;
	}
	@Override
	public String toString() {
		return sceneName + "\t" + rating;
	}
	@Override
	public boolean equals(Object obj) {
		if (this == obj)
			return true;
		if (obj == null)
			return false;
		if (getClass() != obj.getClass())
			return false;
		sceneRatings other = (sceneRatings) obj;
		if (sceneName == null) {
			if (other.sceneName != null)
				return false;
		} else if (!sceneName.equals(other.sceneName))
			return false;
		if (rating == null) {
			if (other.rating != null)
				return false;
		} else if (!rating.equals(other.rating))
			return false;
		return true;
	}
	@Override
	public int compareTo(sceneRatings o) {
		int compareValue = sceneName.compareTo(o.getsceneName());
		/*
		 * if (compareValue == 0) { compareValue = ((sceneRatings)
		 * o).getRating().compareTo(getRating()); }
		 */
		return compareValue;
	}
}
```

Further, you need to create the `partitioner` class, the code of which is shown in Listing 8:

Listing 8: The `Partitioner` Class

```
public static class sceneNamePartitioner extends
            Partitioner<sceneRatings, FloatWritable> {
      @Override
      public int getPartition(sceneRatings key, FloatWritable value,
                  int numPartitions) {
            return (key.getsceneName().hashCode() & Integer.MAX_VALUE)
                        % numPartitions;
      }     }
```

In Listing 8, the `getPartition()` method is overridden and the class named `sceneNamePartitioner` extends the `Partitioner` class.

Now, you need to create the `Comparator` class for which the code is shown in Listing 9:

Listing 9: The `Comparator` Class

```
public static class sceneRatingsComparator extends WritableComparator {
      protected sceneRatingsComparator() {
            super(sceneRatings.class, true);
// Very critical to set true for create instances
      }
      @SuppressWarnings("rawtypes")
      @Override
      public int compare(WritableComparable a, WritableComparable b) {
            int compareValue = ((sceneRatings) a).getsceneName().compareTo(
                        ((sceneRatings) b).getsceneName());
            if (compareValue == 0) {
                  compareValue = ((sceneRatings) b).getRating().compareTo(
                              ((sceneRatings) a).getRating());
            }
            return compareValue;
      }     }
   public static class sceneNameGroupComparator extends WritableComparator {
      protected sceneNameGroupComparator() {
            super(sceneRatings.class, true);
// Very critical to set true for create instances
      }
      @SuppressWarnings("rawtypes")
      @Override
      public int compare(WritableComparable a, WritableComparable b) {
            return ((sceneRatings) a).getsceneName().compareTo(
                        ((sceneRatings) b).getsceneName());
      }     }
```

In Listing 9, the `sceneRatingsComparator` class extends the `WritableComparator` class and overrides the `compare()` method. Finally, you need to create the `Driver` class, which is the main class for executing the program. The code for the `Driver` class is shown in Listing 10:

Listing 10: The `Driver` Class

```
public int run(String[] args) throws Exception {
      if (args.length < 2) {
      System.out.println("Usage: com.vp.samples.SecondarySort input output");
      return -2;
      }
      Configuration localConf = new Configuration();
      // localConf.set("mapred.job.tracker", "local");
      // localConf.set("fs.default.name", "file:///");
      Job secondarySortJob = new Job(localConf);
```

```
        secondarySortJob.setJarByClass(SecondarySort.class);
        secondarySortJob.setJobName("Sort Movies with Ratings");
        secondarySortJob.setMapperClass(MJMapper.class);
        secondarySortJob.setReducerClass(MJReducer.class);
        secondarySortJob.setInputFormatClass(TextInputFormat.class);
        secondarySortJob.setOutputFormatClass(TextOutputFormat.class);
        secondarySortJob.setMapOutputKeyClass(MovieRatings.class);
        secondarySortJob.setMapOutputValueClass(FloatWritable.class);
        secondarySortJob.setOutputKeyClass(Text.class);
        secondarySortJob.setOutputValueClass(FloatWritable.class);
        secondarySortJob.setPartitionerClass(MovieNamePartioner.class);
        secondarySortJob.setSortComparatorClass(MovieRatingsComparator.class);
        secondarySortJob.setGroupingComparatorClass(MovieNameGroupComparator.class);
        FileInputFormat.setInputPaths(secondarySortJob, new Path(args[0]));
        FileOutputFormat.setOutputPath(secondarySortJob, new Path(args[1]));
        DistributedCache.addFileToClassPath(new Path("ml-1m/movies.dat"),
                        secondarySortJob.getConfiguration(),
                        FileSystem.get(secondarySortJob.getConfiguration()));
        if (secondarySortJob.waitForCompletion(true)) {
                return 0;
        } else {
                return -1;
        }       }
    public static void main(String[] args) throws Exception {
        if (ToolRunner.run(new SecondarySort(), args) == 0) {
                System.out.println("Job Success");
        } else {
                System.out.println("Job Failed");
        }       }       }
```

The primary task in this example is counting the occurrences of each word. At the same time, we are arranging or sorting the words in an alphabetical order. As the sorting or arranging task is not on priority; therefore, it is called secondary sorting.

The output of secondary sorting is shown in Figure 10:

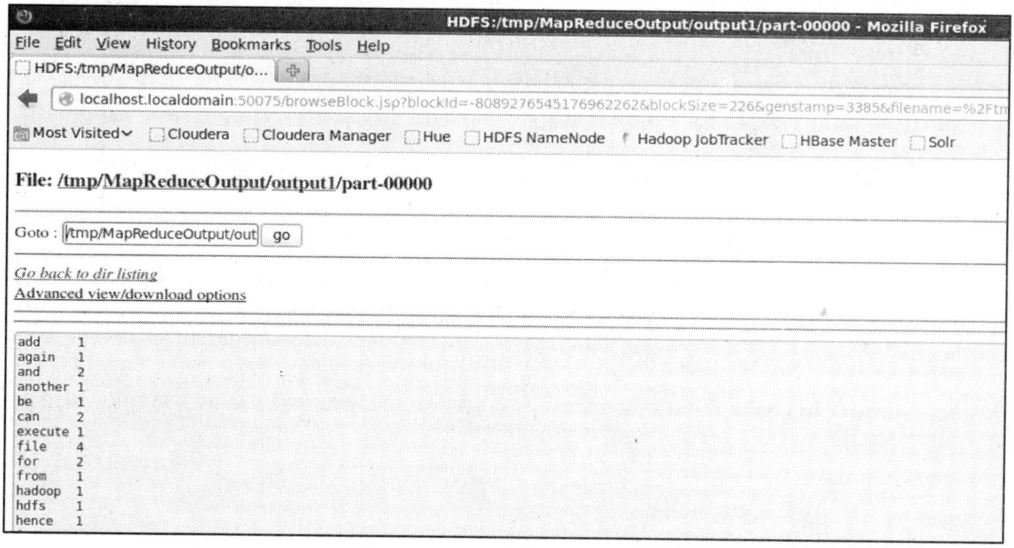

Figure 10: Secondary Sorting

Lab 7—To Arrange Jobs in a Chain

Solution—There are two methods of creating a job chain in a MapReduce program:

- In the first method, you need to create the `JobConf` object "job1" for the first job and set all the parameters with "input" as the input directory and "temp" as the output directory. Then, you need to execute the first job by using the command `JobClient.run(job1)`. This is followed by creation of the `JobConf` object "job2" for the second job, and setting of all the parameters with "temp" as the input directory and "output" as the output directory. Finally, you need to execute the second job by using the command `JobClient.run(job2)`.
- In the second method, we create two `JobConf` objects and set all the parameters as done in the first method, except the execution of the `JobClient.run()` method. We then create the two Job objects with `jobconfs` as parameters, as shown in the following code snippet:

```
Job job1=new Job(jobconf1);
Job job2=new Job(jobconf2);
```

Using the `jobControl` object, we specify the job dependencies and then run the jobs, as shown in the following code snippet:

```
jbcntrl=new JobControl("jbcntrl");
jbcntrl.addJob(job1);
jbcntrl.addJob(job2);
 job2.addDependingJob(job1);
jbcntrl.run();
```

The output of the job chaining process is shown in Figure 11:

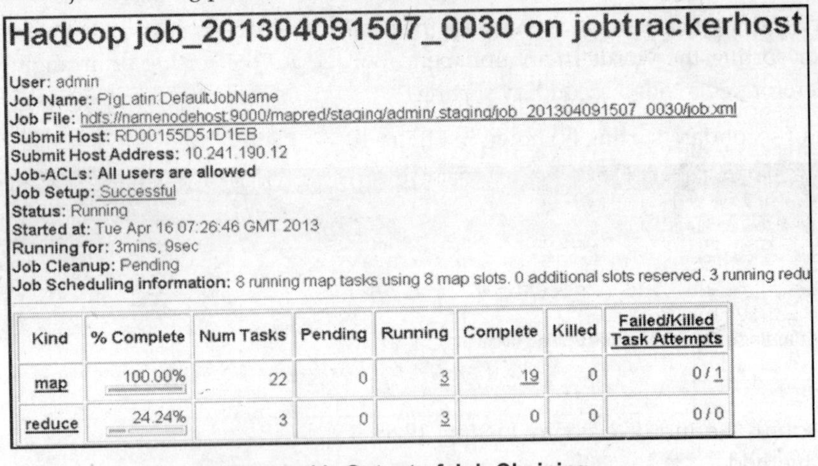

Figure 11: Output of Job Chaining

Lab 8—To Count the Occurrences of Words in an Input File

Solution—In order to count the occurrences of words in an input text file in a MapReduce program, you need to create the following classes:

1. The Mapper class
2. The Reducer class
3. The Driver class

Listing 11 shows the code of the `Mapper` class for a counting application, which in our case is `WordCount`:

Listing 11: The `Mapper` Class

```
package wordCount_Package;
import java.io.IOException;
import org.apache.hadoop.io.IntWritable;
import org.apache.hadoop.io.LongWritable;
import org.apache.hadoop.io.Text;
import org.apache.hadoop.mapreduce.Mapper;
public class WordCount_Mapper extends
  Mapper<LongWritable, Text, Text, IntWritable> {
  Text outkey = new Text();
  IntWritable outvalue = new IntWritable();
  public void map(LongWritable key, Text value, Context Context) throws IOException,
  InterruptedException {
        String[] words = value.toString().split(",");
        for (String word : words) {
               outkey.set(word);
               outvalue.set(1);
               Context.write(outkey, outvalue);
        }      }      }
```

In Listing 11, the `WordCount_Mapper` class extends the `Mapper` class and implements the `map()` method. Now, let's create the `Reducer` class for which the code is shown in Listing 12:

Listing 12: The `Reducer` Class

```
package wordCount_Package;
import java.io.IOException;
import org.apache.hadoop.io.IntWritable;
import org.apache.hadoop.io.Text;
import org.apache.hadoop.mapreduce.Reducer;
public class WordCount_Reducer extends
        Reducer<Text, IntWritable, Text, IntWritable> {
  IntWritable outvalue = new IntWritable();
  public void reduce(Text key, Iterable<IntWritable> values, Context Context) throws
  IOException, InterruptedException {
        int sum = 0;
        for (IntWritable value : values) {
               sum = sum + value.get();
        }
        outvalue.set(sum);
        Context.write(key, outvalue);
  }
  }
```

The `WordCount_Reducer` class in Listing 12 extends the `Reducer` class and implements the `reduce()` method.

Now, we need to define the `Driver` class. The code of this class is shown in Listing 13:

Listing 13: The `Driver` Class

```
package wordCount_Package;
import java.io.IOException;
import org.apache.hadoop.conf.Configuration;
import org.apache.hadoop.fs.Path;
import org.apache.hadoop.io.IntWritable;
import org.apache.hadoop.io.Text;
import org.apache.hadoop.mapreduce.Job;
import org.apache.hadoop.mapreduce.lib.input.FileInputFormat;
```

```
import org.apache.hadoop.mapreduce.lib.output.FileOutputFormat;
public class WordCount_Driver {
  public static void main(String[] args) throws IOException, InterruptedException,
  ClassNotFoundException {
  Configuration conf = new Configuration();
  Job job = new Job(conf, "My First MR program");
  job.setJarByClass(WordCount_Driver.class);
  job.setMapperClass(WordCount_Mapper.class);
  job.setReducerClass(WordCount_Reducer.class);
  job.setMapOutputKeyClass(Text.class);
  job.setMapOutputValueClass(IntWritable.class);
  job.setOutputKeyClass(Text.class);
  job.setOutputValueClass(IntWritable.class);
  FileInputFormat.addInputPath(job, new Path(args[0]));
  FileOutputFormat.setOutputPath(job, new Path(args[1]));
  System.exit(job.waitForCompletion(true) ? 0 : 1);
  }     }
```

The following command is used to execute the `WordCount` example:

```
hadoop jar /home/cloudera/wordcount.jar wcount.wcnt /tmp/IBM/fruits /tmp/nothing1
```

The `WordCount` example takes the fruits file as input, as Figure 12 shows:

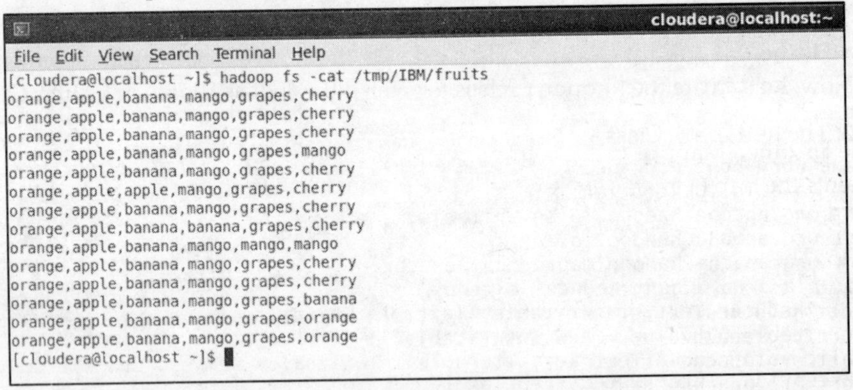

Figure 12: Input to the WordCount Example

The output screen displays the number of occurrences of each word, as shown in Figure 13:

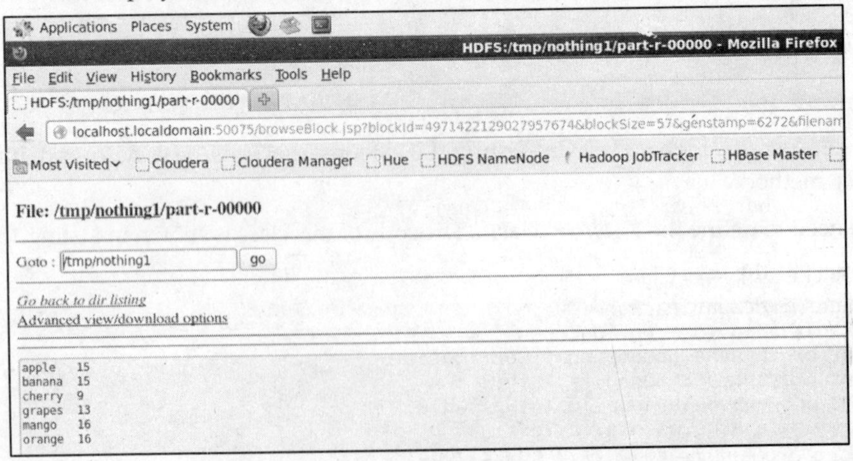

Figure 13: Output of the WordCount Example

Lab 9—To Identify the Transactions Performed for Sports Accessories on the Basis of a Customer's Transaction from Different Parts of the US

Solution—Listing 14 shows the code for the `Mapper` class to handle data of a customer's transactions done from different parts of the US:

Listing 14: The `Mapper` Class

```
package cityTransaction;
import java.io.IOException;
import org.apache.hadoop.io.IntWritable;
import org.apache.hadoop.io.LongWritable;
import org.apache.hadoop.io.Text;
import org.apache.hadoop.mapreduce.Mapper;
public class cityTrans_Mapper extends
        Mapper<LongWritable, Text, Text, IntWritable> {
    Text outKey = new Text();
    IntWritable outValue = new IntWritable();
    public void map(LongWritable key, Text value, Context context) throws IOException,
    InterruptedException {
        String word[] = value.toString().split(",");
        // outValue.set((int) Float.parseFloat(word[3]));
        outValue.set(Integer.parseInt(word[3]));
        outKey.set(word[4] + word[5]);
        // outKey.set(word[4] + word[6]);
        context.write(outKey, outValue);
    }    }
```

As done in other Mapper classes, the `cityTrans_Mapper` class extends the `Mapper` class and implements the `map()` method. Now, let's create the `Reducer` class, the code of which is shown in Listing 15:

Listing 15: The `Reducer` Class

```
package cityTransaction;
import java.io.IOException;
import org.apache.hadoop.io.IntWritable;
import org.apache.hadoop.io.Text;
import org.apache.hadoop.mapreduce.Reducer;
public class cityTrans_Reducer extends
        Reducer<Text, IntWritable, Text, IntWritable> {
        public void reduce(Text key, Iterable<IntWritable> values,
                Context context) throws IOException, InterruptedException {
        IntWritable outValue = new IntWritable();
        int max = 0;
        for (IntWritable value : values) {
                if (max < value.get()) {
                        max = value.get();
                }       }
        outValue.set(max);
        context.write(key, outValue);
    }   }
```

In Listing 15, the `cityTrans_Reducer` class is created, which extends the `Reducer` class and implements the `reduce()` method. Finally, we need to create the `Driver` class, for which the code is shown in Listing 16:

Listing 16: The `Driver` Class

```
package cityTransaction;
import java.io.IOException;
import org.apache.hadoop.conf.Configuration;
import org.apache.hadoop.fs.Path;
```

```
import org.apache.hadoop.io.IntWritable;
import org.apache.hadoop.io.Text;
import org.apache.hadoop.mapreduce.Job;
import org.apache.hadoop.mapreduce.lib.input.FileInputFormat;
import org.apache.hadoop.mapreduce.lib.output.FileOutputFormat;
public class cityTrans_Driver {
  public static void main(String[] args) throws IOException, InterruptedException,
ClassNotFoundException {
        Configuration conf = new Configuration();
        Job job = new Job(conf, "My First MR program");
        job.setJarByClass(cityTrans_Driver.class);
        job.setMapperClass(cityTrans_Mapper.class);
        job.setReducerClass(cityTrans_Reducer.class);
        job.setMapOutputKeyClass(Text.class);
        job.setMapOutputValueClass(IntWritable.class);
        job.setOutputKeyClass(Text.class);
        job.setOutputValueClass(IntWritable.class);
        FileInputFormat.addInputPath(job, new Path(args[0]));
        FileOutputFormat.setOutputPath(job, new Path(args[1]));
        System.exit(job.waitForCompletion(true) ? 0 : 1);
  }     }
```

In Listing 16, the `Mapper` and `Reducer` classes are configured.

The following command is used to run the MapReduce program:

```
   hadoop jar /home/cloudera/Desktop/custom.jar transCustomDT.customDriver
/tmp/IBM/transactions /tmp/transoutIBM1
```

The file being taken as input by the MapReduce program is shown in Figure 14:

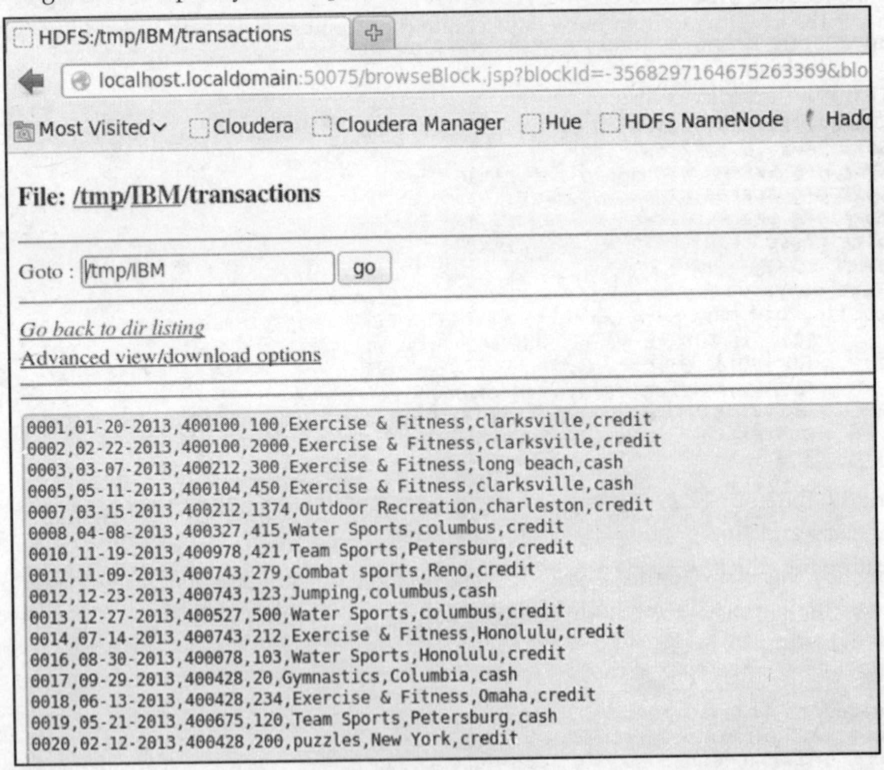

Figure 14: Input of the MapReduce Program to Handle Customer's Transactions

The output screen displays the number of occurrences of each sport accessory, as shown in Figure 15:

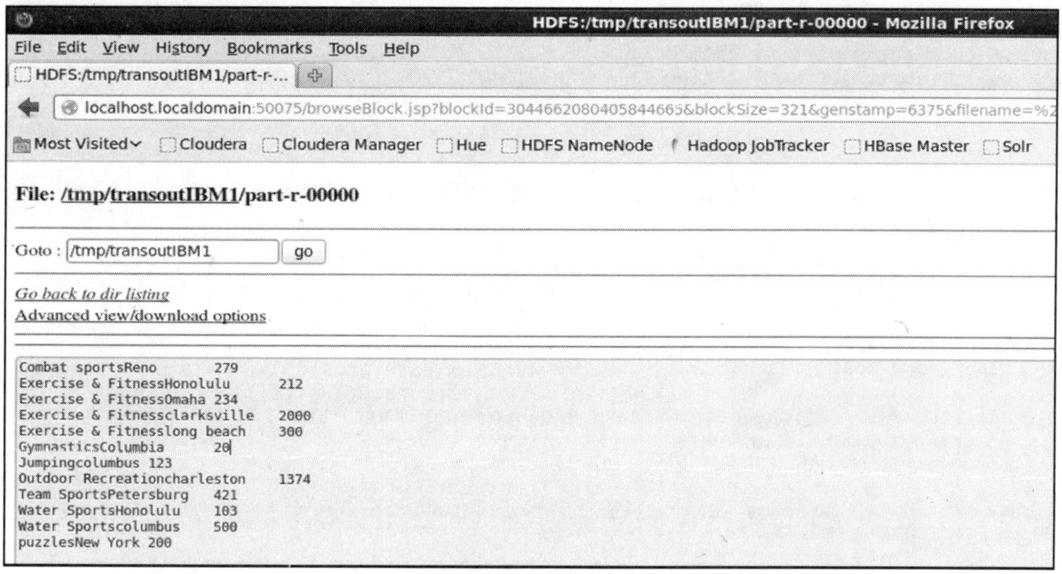

Figure 15: Output of the Sports Example

Lab 10—To Reduce Side Joins to Analyze Movies and Rating Files from HDFS

Solution—Listing 17 shows the code of the `Reduce Side Join Mapper Class` for movies:

Listing 17: Code of the `Reduce Side Join Mapper Class` for Movies

```
package com.hadoop.reduceJoin;
import java.io.IOException;
import org.apache.hadoop.io.LongWritable;
import org.apache.hadoop.io.Text;
import org.apache.hadoop.mapreduce.Mapper;
public class rsJoinMovieMapper extends Mapper<LongWritable, Text, Text, Text> {
  Text outKey = new Text();
  Text outValue = new Text();
  public void map(LongWritable key, Text value, Context context)
               throws IOException, InterruptedException {
        String[] lines = value.toString().split("::");
        outKey.set(lines[0]);
        outValue.set("genre\t"+ lines[2]);
        context.write(outKey, outValue);
  }     }
```

In Listing 17, the `rsJoinMovieMapper` class is defined as the mapper class; therefore, it extends the `Mapper` class and implements the `map()` method. Now, we need to create the Mapper class for movie rating for which the code is given in Listing 18:

Listing 18: Code of the `Rating Mapper` Class

```
package com.hadoop.reduceJoin;
import java.io.IOException;
import org.apache.hadoop.io.LongWritable;
import org.apache.hadoop.io.Text;
import org.apache.hadoop.mapreduce.Mapper;
public class rsJoinRatingMapper extends Mapper<LongWritable, Text, Text, Text> {
  Text outKey = new Text();
```

```
    Text outValue = new Text();
      public void map(LongWritable key, Text value, Context context) throws IOException,
      InterruptedException {
            String[] lines = value.toString().split("::");
            outKey.set(lines[1]);
            outValue.set("rating\t" + lines[2]);
            context.write(outKey, outValue);
            }
      }
```

Let's now define the `Reducer` class for movies and their ratings. The code is given in Listing 19:

Listing 19: The `Reducer` Class

```
package com.hadoop.reduceJoin;
import java.io.IOException;
import org.apache.hadoop.io.Text;
import org.apache.hadoop.mapreduce.Reducer;

public class rsJoinReducer extends Reducer<Text, Text, Text, Text> {
  Text outvalue = new Text();
  public void reduce(Text key, Iterable<Text> values, Context context)

                throws IOException, InterruptedException {
        int sum = 0;
        int count = 0;
        int avg = 0;
        String gen = null;
        for (Text value : values) {
                String[] line = value.toString().split("\t");
                if (line[0].equals("genre")) {
                        gen = line[1];
                }
                if (line[0].equals("rating")) {
                        sum = sum + Integer.parseInt(line[1]);
                        count++;
                }
        }
        if (count != 0) {
                avg = sum / count;
        }
        outvalue.set("Movie Avg Rating  = " + avg + "  Movie Genre is:" + gen);
        context.write(key, outvalue);
}
}
```

We now need to create the `Driver` class. The code for this class is shown in Listing 20:

Listing 20: The `Driver` Class

```
package com.hadoop.reduceJoin;
import java.io.IOException;
import org.apache.hadoop.conf.Configuration;
import org.apache.hadoop.fs.Path;

import org.apache.hadoop.io.Text;
import org.apache.hadoop.mapreduce.Job;
import org.apache.hadoop.mapreduce.lib.input.MultipleInputs;
import org.apache.hadoop.mapreduce.lib.input.TextInputFormat;

import org.apache.hadoop.mapreduce.lib.output.FileOutputFormat;
public class rsJoinDriver {
```

```
    public static void main(String[] args) throws IOException,
                    InterruptedException, ClassNotFoundException {
            Configuration conf = new Configuration();
            Job job = new Job(conf, "Custom Data Type Example");
            job.setJarByClass(rsJoinDriver.class);
            job.setReducerClass(rsJoinReducer.class);

            job.setOutputKeyClass(Text.class);
            job.setOutputValueClass(Text.class);
            MultipleInputs.addInputPath(job, new Path(args[0]),
                           TextInputFormat.class, rsJoinMovieMapper.class);
            MultipleInputs.addInputPath(job, new Path(args[1]),

                           TextInputFormat.class, rsJoinRatingMapper.class);
            Path outputPath = new Path(args[2]);
            FileOutputFormat.setOutputPath(job, outputPath);
            System.exit(job.waitForCompletion(true) ? 0 : 1);
        }
    }
```

The following command is used to run the reduce side join movie rating MapReduce program:

```
    hadoop jar /home/cloudera/Desktop/rsjoin.jar com.hadoop.reduceJoin.rsJoinDriver
/tmp/IBM/rsjoin/input/movies.dat /tmp/IBM/rsjoin/input/ratings.dat
/tmp/IBM/rsjoin/output
```

Figure 16 shows the input file for the Movies example:

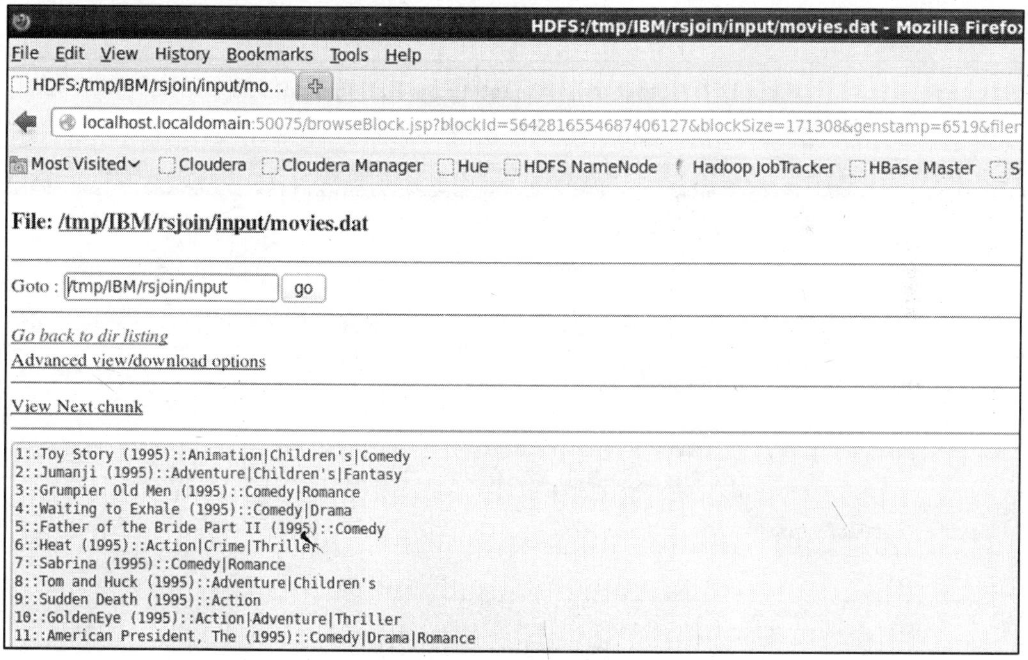

Figure 16: Accepting the Input File

Figure 17 shows the output of the program after accepting the rating input file:

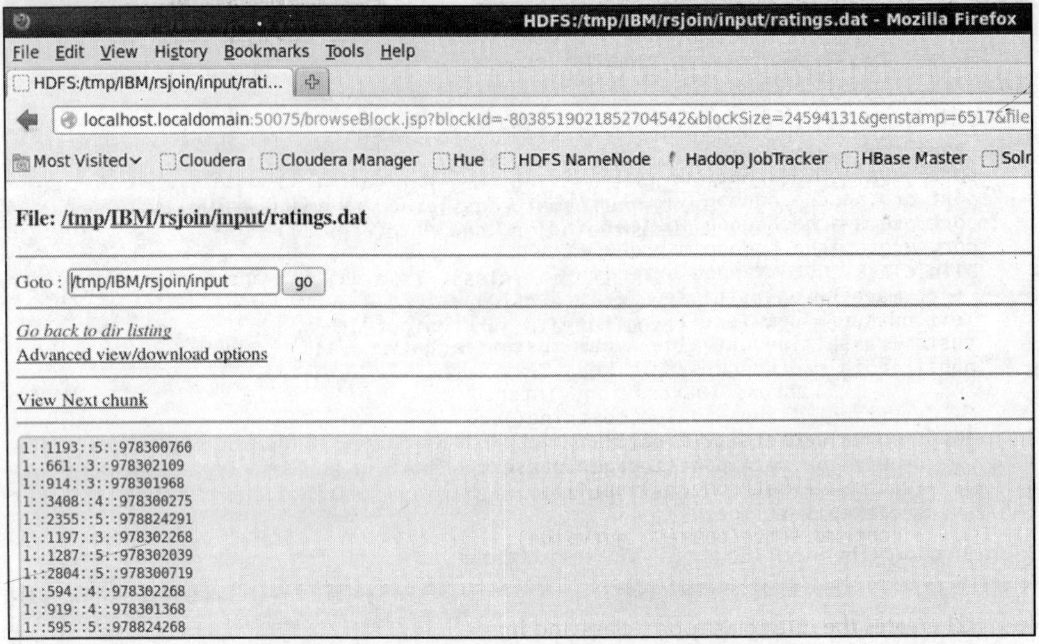

Figure 17: Output after Accepting the Rating Input File

The output of the MapReduce program is shown in Figure 18:

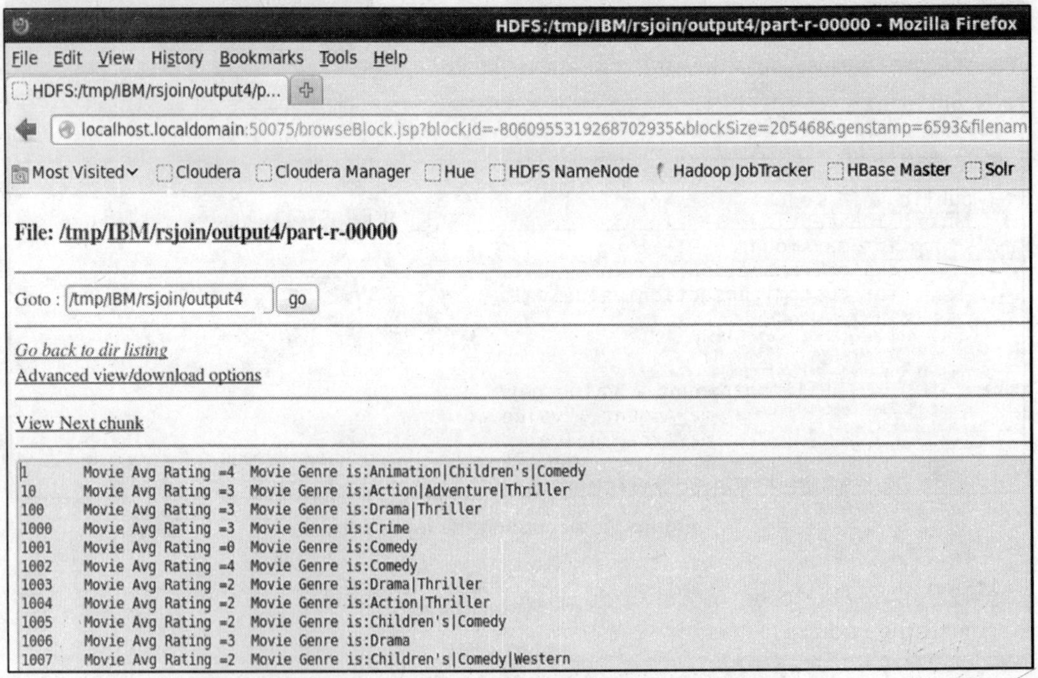

Figure 18: Output of the Movie Rating MapReduce Program

Lab 11—To Define a Custom Data Type

Solution—MapReduce provides the functionality to create custom data types while writing results to the output file. Here, for the custom data type example, we will create the Mapper, Reducer, Custom Data Type, and Driver classes. Listing 21 shows the code of the `Mapper` class:

Listing 21: The `Mapper` Class for the Custom Data Type Program

```
package transCustomDT;
import java.io.IOException;
import org.apache.hadoop.io.LongWritable;
import org.apache.hadoop.io.Text;
import org.apache.hadoop.mapreduce.Mapper;
public class customMapper extends
        Mapper<LongWritable, Text, Text, customTransaction> {
   Text outKey = new Text();
   customTransaction outValue = new customTransaction();
   public void map(LongWritable key, Text value, Context context)
              throws IOException, InterruptedException {
        String[] line = value.toString().split(",");
        outValue.setCity(line[5]);
        outValue.setAmount(Integer.parseInt(line[3]));
        outValue.setProduct(line[4]);
        outKey.set(line[0]);
        context.write(outKey, outValue);
   }
}
```

Listing 21 creates the `customMapper` class and implements the `map()` method. Now, let's create the `Reducer` class, named `customReducer`, for which the code is shown in Listing 22:

Listing 22: The `Reducer` Class for the Custom Data Type Program

```
package transCustomDT;
import java.io.IOException;
import org.apache.hadoop.io.Text;

import org.apache.hadoop.mapreduce.Reducer;
public class customReducer extends Reducer<Text, customTransaction, Text, Text>{
Text outValue = new Text();

   public void reduce(Text key, Iterable<customTransaction> values, Context context)
   throws IOException, InterruptedException {
         int maxAmount = 0;
         customTransaction maxTxn = null;
         for(customTransaction value:values)

         {

                if(maxAmount < value.getAmount()){
                       maxAmount = value.getAmount();
                       maxTxn = value;
                }      }
         outValue.set("Product = " + maxTxn.getProduct()+ " "+ "City" +
   maxTxn.getCity() +" "+ "Amount" + maxTxn.getAmount() );
   context.write(key, outValue);
   }     }
```

Listing 22 shows the code of the `customReducer` class that extends the `Reducer` class and implements the `reduce()` method. Let's now write the custom data type class code, which is given in Listing 23:

Listing 23: The Custom Data Type Class

```
package transCustomDT;
import java.io.DataInput;
import java.io.DataOutput;
import java.io.IOException;

import org.apache.hadoop.io.Writable;
public class customTransaction implements Writable {
  private String product;
  private String city;
  private int amount;

  public String getProduct() {
        return product;
  }
  public void setProduct(String product) {
        this.product = product;
  }
  public String getCity() {
        return city;
  }
  public void setCity(String city) {
        this.city = city;
  }
  public int getAmount() {
        return amount;
  }
  public void setAmount(int amount) {
        this.amount = amount;
  }
  public void readFields(DataInput In) throws IOException {
        this.amount = In.readInt();
        this.city = In.readUTF();
        this.product = In.readUTF();
  }
  public void write(DataOutput Out) throws IOException {
        Out.writeInt(this.amount);
        Out.writeUTF(this.city);
        Out.writeUTF(this.product);
  }
}
```

In Listing 23, the custom data type class, named `customTransaction`, is defined with the accessor and mutator methods.

Now, let's create the `Driver` class. Listing 24 shows the code of the `Driver` class:

Listing 24: The `Driver` Class

```
package transCustomDT;
import java.io.IOException;
import org.apache.hadoop.conf.Configuration;
import org.apache.hadoop.fs.Path;
import org.apache.hadoop.io.IntWritable;

import org.apache.hadoop.io.Text;
import org.apache.hadoop.mapreduce.Job;
import org.apache.hadoop.mapreduce.lib.input.FileInputFormat;
import org.apache.hadoop.mapreduce.lib.output.FileOutputFormat;

public class customDriver {
```

```
    public static void main(String[] args) throws IOException, InterruptedException,
        ClassNotFoundException {
            Configuration conf = new Configuration();
            Job job = new Job(conf, "Custom Data Type Program");
            job.setJarByClass(customDriver.class);
            job.setMapperClass(customMapper.class);

            job.setReducerClass(customReducer.class);
            job.setCombinerClass(customReducer.class);
            job.setMapOutputKeyClass(Text.class);
            job.setMapOutputValueClass(customTransaction.class);
            job.setOutputKeyClass(Text.class);

            job.setOutputValueClass(IntWritable.class);
            FileInputFormat.addInputPath(job, new Path(args[0]));
            FileOutputFormat.setOutputPath(job, new Path(args[1]));
            System.exit(job.waitForCompletion(true) ? 0 : 1);
        }
    }
```

The following command is used to run the custom data type program:

```
    hadoop jar /home/cloudera/custom.jar transCustomDT /tmp/IBM/transactions
/tmp/transoutIBM1
```

Figure 19 shows the input for the custom data type example:

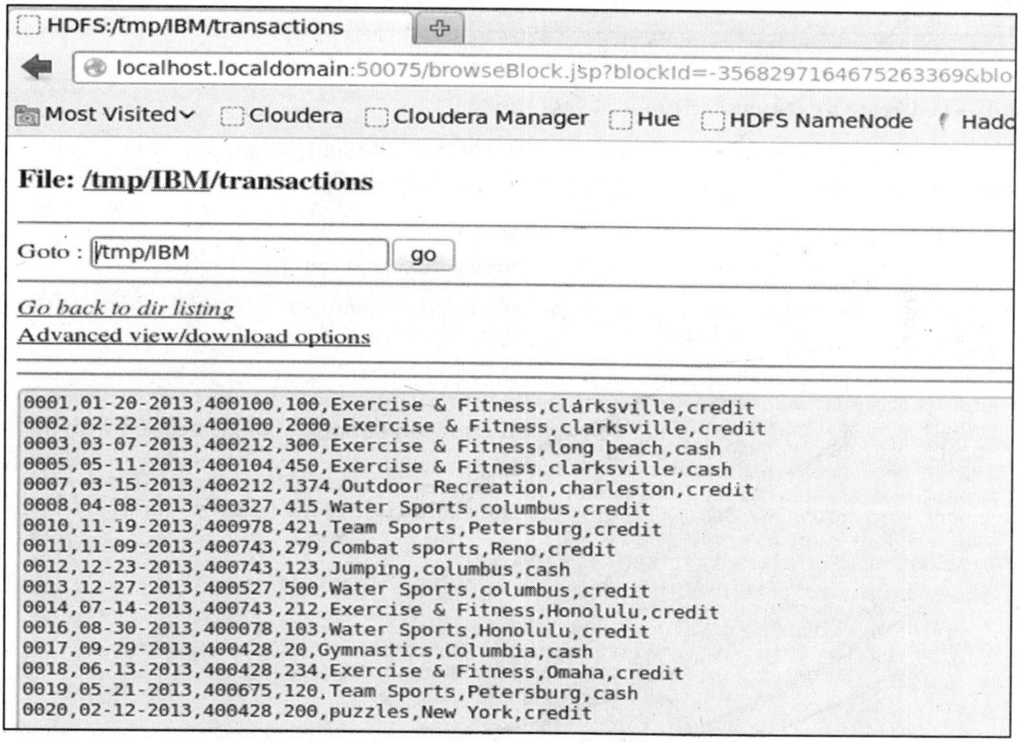

Figure 19: Input for Custom Data Type Program

The output of the program is displayed in Figure 20:

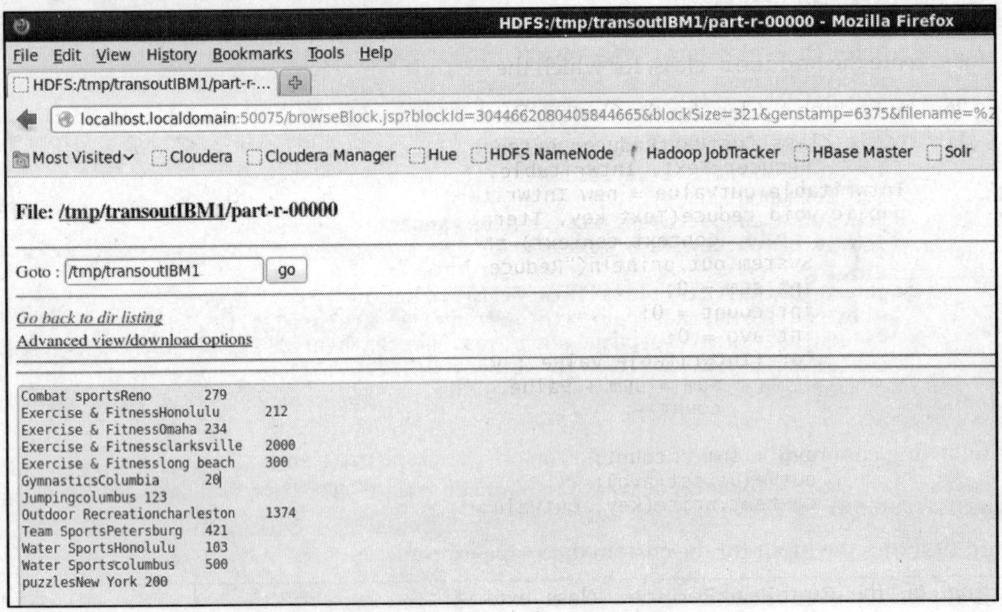

Figure 20: Output of the Custom Data Type Program

Lab 12—To Create a Custom Partitioner Class

Solution—Here, we will create the `Mapper`, `Reducer`, `Driver`, and `custom partitioner` classes. The code to create the `Mapper` class is shown in Listing 25:

Listing 25: The `Mapper` Class for the Custom Partitioner Program

```
package com.hadoop.mr;
import java.io.IOException;
import org.apache.hadoop.conf.Configuration;
import org.apache.hadoop.fs.Path;
import org.apache.hadoop.io.IntWritable;
import org.apache.hadoop.io.LongWritable;
import org.apache.hadoop.io.Text;
import org.apache.hadoop.mapreduce.Job;
import org.apache.hadoop.mapreduce.Mapper;
import org.apache.hadoop.mapreduce.Reducer;
import org.apache.hadoop.mapreduce.lib.input.FileInputFormat;
import org.apache.hadoop.mapreduce.lib.output.FileOutputFormat;
public class CustomPartitioner {
   public static class CustPartMapper extends
            Mapper<LongWritable, Text, Text, IntWritable> {
        Text outKey = new Text();
        IntWritable outValue = new IntWritable();
        public void map(LongWritable key, Text value, Context context)
                throws IOException, InterruptedException {
            System.out.println("Mapper code");
            String line = value.toString();
            String[] columns = line.split(" ");
            outKey.set(columns[2]);
            outValue.set(Integer.parseInt(columns[3]));
            context.write(outKey, outValue);
        }
}
```

In Listing 25, the `CustPartMapper` class extends the `Mapper` class and implements the `map()` method.

Now, let's create the `Reducer` class, for which the code is shown in Listing 26:

Listing 26: The `Reducer` Class for the Custom Partitioner Program

```
public static class CustPartReducer extends
            Reducer<Text, IntWritable, Text, IntWritable> {
        IntWritable outValue = new IntWritable();
        public void reduce(Text key, Iterable<IntWritable> values,
                    Context context) throws IOException, InterruptedException {
            System.out.println("Reducer code");
            int sum = 0;
            int count = 0;
            int avg = 0;
            for (IntWritable value : values) {
                    sum = sum + value.get();
                    count++;
            }
            avg = sum / count;
            outValue.set(avg);
            context.write(key, outValue);
        }
}
```

In Listing 26, the `CustPartReducer` class extends the `Reducer` class and implements the `reduce()` method. Next, the code of the `Driver` class is shown in Listing 27:

Listing 27: The `Driver` Class for the Custom Partitioner Program

```
public static void main(String[] args) throws IOException, InterruptedException,
  ClassNotFoundException {
        Configuration conf = new Configuration();
        Job job = new Job(conf, "Partition Example");
        job.setJarByClass(CustomPartitioner.class);
        job.setMapperClass(CustPartMapper.class);
        job.setReducerClass(CustPartReducer.class);
        job.setMapOutputKeyClass(Text.class);
        job.setMapOutputValueClass(IntWritable.class);
        job.setPartitionerClass(EmpTypePartitioner.class);
        job.setNumReduceTasks(2);
        job.setOutputKeyClass(Text.class);
        job.setOutputValueClass(IntWritable.class);
        FileInputFormat.addInputPath(job, new Path(args[0]));
        FileOutputFormat.setOutputPath(job, new Path(args[1]));
        System.exit(job.waitForCompletion(true) ? 0 : 1);
  }
}
```

The `Driver` class sets the Mapper and Reducer classes and provides the implementation for the `main()` method. Finally, the code of the `Partitioner` class is shown in Listing 28:

Listing 28: `Custom Partitioner` Class

```
package com.hadoop.mr;
import org.apache.hadoop.io.IntWritable;
import org.apache.hadoop.io.Text;
import org.apache.hadoop.mapreduce.Partitioner;
public class EmpTypePartitioner extends Partitioner<Text, IntWritable>{
   @Override
     public int getPartition(Text key, IntWritable value, int numPartitions) {
            System.out.println("Partitioner code");
```

```
            int reduceNumbers = (key.toString().charAt(0)) % numPartitions;
            //int number = p%2
            //int number = c%2
            return reduceNumbers;
        }
    }
```

The following command is used to run the custom partitioner program:

```
    hadoop jar /home/cloudera/Desktop/partition1.jar com.hadoop.empPartiotion_Driver
/tmp/IBM/partition/partition_example.txt /tmp/IBM/partition/output3
```

Figure 21 shows the input provided to the custom partitioner program:

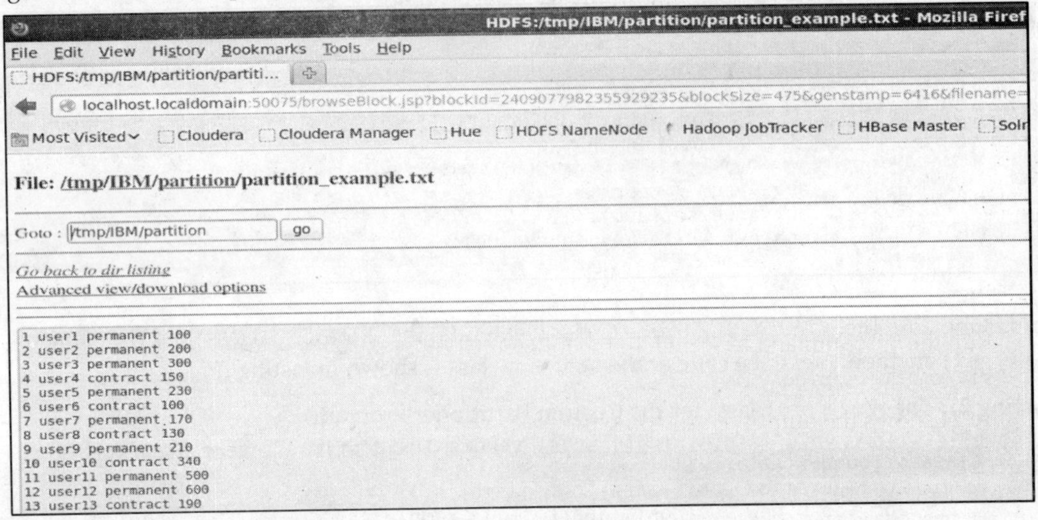

Figure 21: Input for Custom Partitioner Program

Figure 22 shows the output of the custom partitioner program:

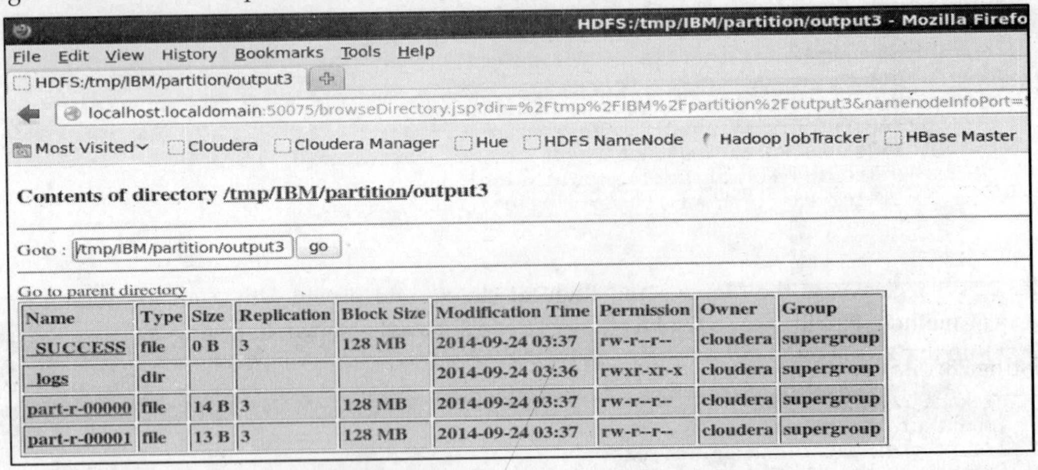

Figure 22: Output of the Custom Partitioner Program

Labs on Pig

Lab 1—To Identify the Most Popular Website with the Maximum Number of Users

Solution—Perform the following steps to find the most popular website with the maximum number of users:

1. Run the following command:

```
pig
```

The output of the command is shown in Figure 23:

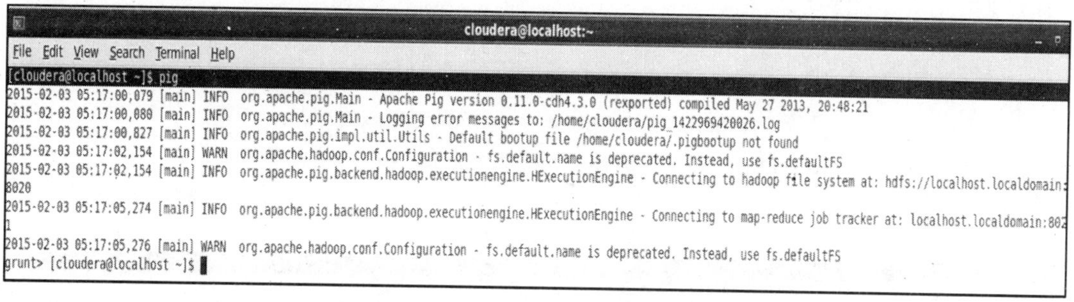

Figure 23: Output of the pig Command

2. Run the `vi` command as shown in the following code snippet:

```
vi /tmp/Test/pigdata3
```

Figure 24 shows the output of executing the preceding command:

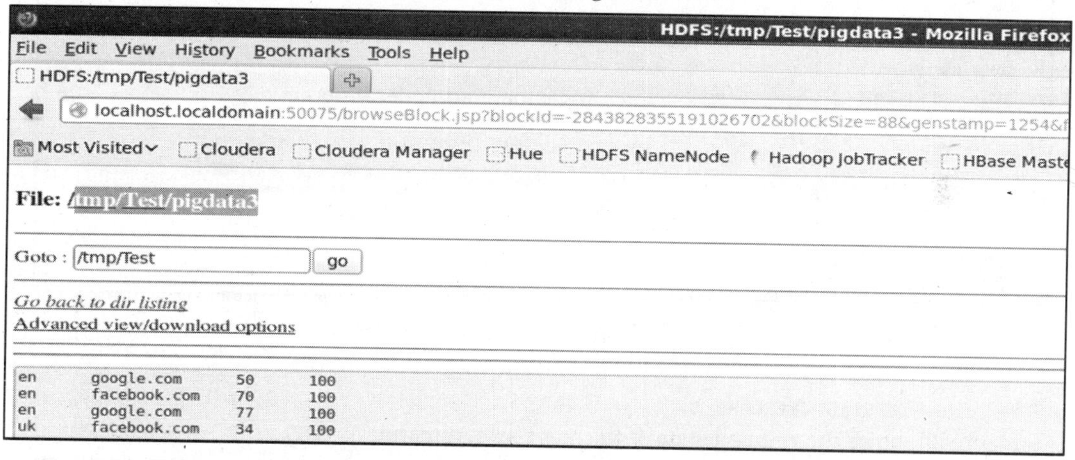

Figure 24: Output of the vi Command

3. Run the `load` command, as shown in the following code snippet:

```
dataLoad = LOAD '/tmp/Test/pigdata3' as (c1:chararray, c2:chararray, c3:int,
c4:int);
```

Figure 25 shows the output of executing the preceding command:

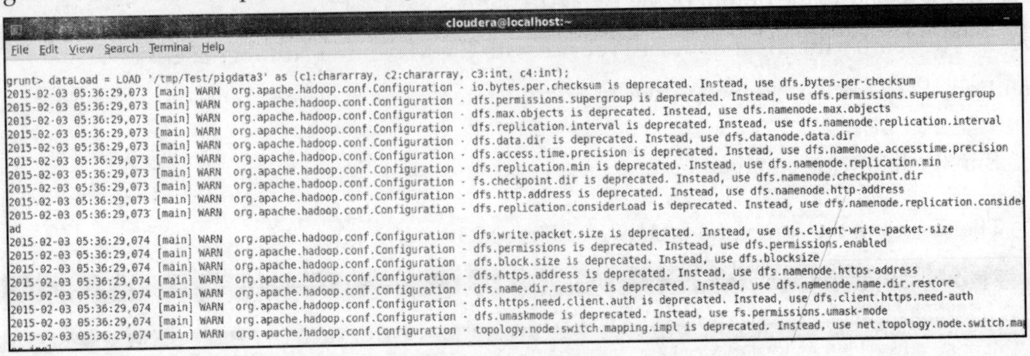

```
cloudera@localhost:~
File Edit View Search Terminal Help
grunt> dataLoad = LOAD '/tmp/Test/pigdata3' as (c1:chararray, c2:chararray, c3:int, c4:int);
2015-02-03 05:36:29,073 [main] WARN  org.apache.hadoop.conf.Configuration - io.bytes.per.checksum is deprecated. Instead, use dfs.bytes-per-checksum
2015-02-03 05:36:29,073 [main] WARN  org.apache.hadoop.conf.Configuration - dfs.permissions.supergroup is deprecated. Instead, use dfs.permissions.superusergroup
2015-02-03 05:36:29,073 [main] WARN  org.apache.hadoop.conf.Configuration - dfs.max.objects is deprecated. Instead, use dfs.namenode.max.objects
2015-02-03 05:36:29,073 [main] WARN  org.apache.hadoop.conf.Configuration - dfs.replication.interval is deprecated. Instead, use dfs.namenode.replication.interval
2015-02-03 05:36:29,073 [main] WARN  org.apache.hadoop.conf.Configuration - dfs.data.dir is deprecated. Instead, use dfs.datanode.data.dir
2015-02-03 05:36:29,073 [main] WARN  org.apache.hadoop.conf.Configuration - dfs.access.time.precision is deprecated. Instead, use dfs.namenode.accesstime.precision
2015-02-03 05:36:29,073 [main] WARN  org.apache.hadoop.conf.Configuration - dfs.replication.min is deprecated. Instead, use dfs.namenode.replication.min
2015-02-03 05:36:29,073 [main] WARN  org.apache.hadoop.conf.Configuration - fs.checkpoint.dir is deprecated. Instead, use dfs.namenode.checkpoint.dir
2015-02-03 05:36:29,073 [main] WARN  org.apache.hadoop.conf.Configuration - dfs.http.address is deprecated. Instead, use dfs.namenode.http-address
2015-02-03 05:36:29,073 [main] WARN  org.apache.hadoop.conf.Configuration - dfs.replication.considerLoad is deprecated. Instead, use dfs.namenode.replication.conside
ad
2015-02-03 05:36:29,074 [main] WARN  org.apache.hadoop.conf.Configuration - dfs.write.packet.size is deprecated. Instead, use dfs.client-write-packet-size
2015-02-03 05:36:29,074 [main] WARN  org.apache.hadoop.conf.Configuration - dfs.permissions is deprecated. Instead, use dfs.permissions.enabled
2015-02-03 05:36:29,074 [main] WARN  org.apache.hadoop.conf.Configuration - dfs.block.size is deprecated. Instead, use dfs.blocksize
2015-02-03 05:36:29,074 [main] WARN  org.apache.hadoop.conf.Configuration - dfs.https.address is deprecated. Instead, use dfs.namenode.https-address
2015-02-03 05:36:29,074 [main] WARN  org.apache.hadoop.conf.Configuration - dfs.name.dir.restore is deprecated. Instead, use dfs.namenode.name.dir.restore
2015-02-03 05:36:29,074 [main] WARN  org.apache.hadoop.conf.Configuration - dfs.https.need.client.auth is deprecated. Instead, use dfs.client.https.need-auth
2015-02-03 05:36:29,074 [main] WARN  org.apache.hadoop.conf.Configuration - dfs.umaskmode is deprecated. Instead, use fs.permissions.umask-mode
2015-02-03 05:36:29,074 [main] WARN  org.apache.hadoop.conf.Configuration - topology.node.switch.mapping.impl is deprecated. Instead, use net.topology.node.switch.ma
```

Figure 25: Output of the load Command

4. Run the dump command, as shown in the following code snippet:

```
DUMP dataLoad;
```

Figure 26 shows the output of the preceding command:

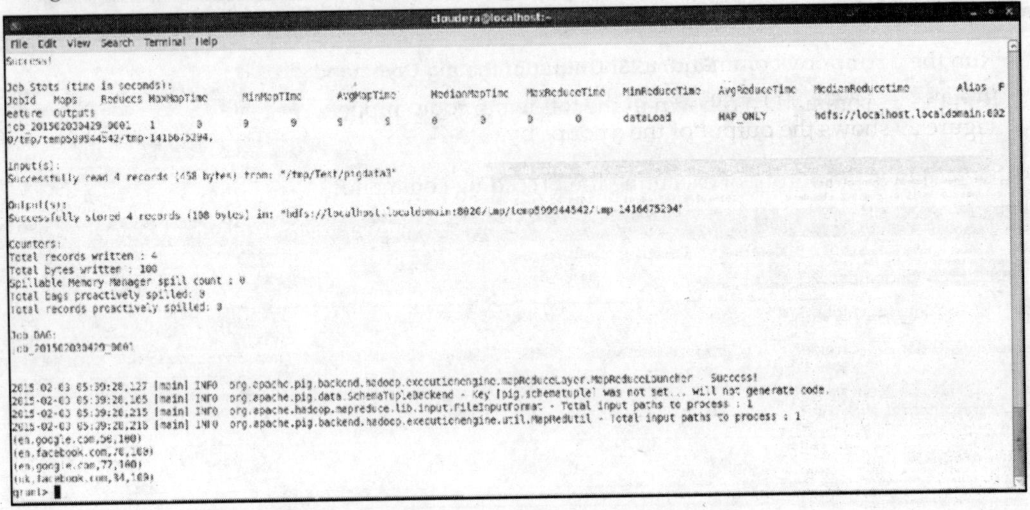

```
cloudera@localhost:~
File Edit View Search Terminal Help
Success!

Job Stats (time in seconds):
JobId  Maps  Reduces MaxMapTime  MinMapTime  AvgMapTime  MedianMapTime  MaxReduceTime  MinReduceTime  AvgReduceTime  MedianReducetime  Alias  F
eature  Outputs
job_201502030429_0001  1  0  9  9  9  9  0  0  0  0  dataLoad  MAP_ONLY  hdfs://localhost.localdomain:802
0/tmp/temp599644542/tmp-1416675294,

Input(s):
Successfully read 4 records (458 bytes) from: "/tmp/Test/pigdata3"

Output(s):
Successfully stored 4 records (108 bytes) in: "hdfs://localhost.localdomain:8020/tmp/temp599644542/tmp-1416675294"

Counters:
Total records written : 4
Total bytes written : 100
Spillable Memory Manager spill count : 0
Total bags proactively spilled: 0
Total records proactively spilled: 0

Job DAG:
job_201502030429_0001


2015-02-03 05:39:28,127 [main] INFO  org.apache.pig.backend.hadoop.executionengine.mapReduceLayer.MapReduceLauncher - Success!
2015-02-03 05:39:28,165 [main] INFO  org.apache.pig.data.SchemaTupleBackend - Key [pig.schematuple] was not set... will not generate code.
2015-02-03 05:39:28,215 [main] INFO  org.apache.hadoop.mapreduce.lib.input.FileInputFormat - Total input paths to process : 1
2015-02-03 05:39:28,216 [main] INFO  org.apache.pig.backend.hadoop.executionengine.util.MapRedUtil - Total input paths to process : 1
(en,google.com,50,100)
(en,facebook.com,70,100)
(en,google.com,77,100)
(uk,facebook.com,34,100)
grunt>
```

Figure 26: Output of the dump Command

5. Run the `filter` command, as shown in the following code snippet:

```
fil_rec = FILTER dataLoad by c1 == 'en';
```

Figure 27 shows the running state of the `filter` command:

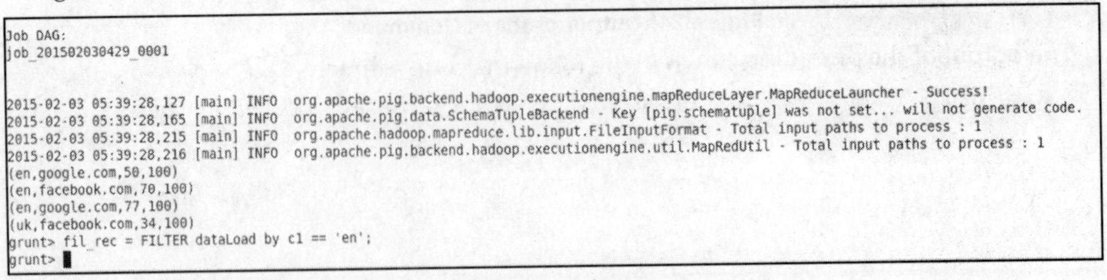

```
Job DAG:
job_201502030429_0001


2015-02-03 05:39:28,127 [main] INFO  org.apache.pig.backend.hadoop.executionengine.mapReduceLayer.MapReduceLauncher - Success!
2015-02-03 05:39:28,165 [main] INFO  org.apache.pig.data.SchemaTupleBackend - Key [pig.schematuple] was not set... will not generate code.
2015-02-03 05:39:28,215 [main] INFO  org.apache.hadoop.mapreduce.lib.input.FileInputFormat - Total input paths to process : 1
2015-02-03 05:39:28,216 [main] INFO  org.apache.pig.backend.hadoop.executionengine.util.MapRedUtil - Total input paths to process : 1
(en,google.com,50,100)
(en,facebook.com,70,100)
(en,google.com,77,100)
(uk,facebook.com,34,100)
grunt> fil_rec = FILTER dataLoad by c1 == 'en';
grunt>
```

Figure 27: Running the filter Command

Figure 28 shows the output of the `filter` command:

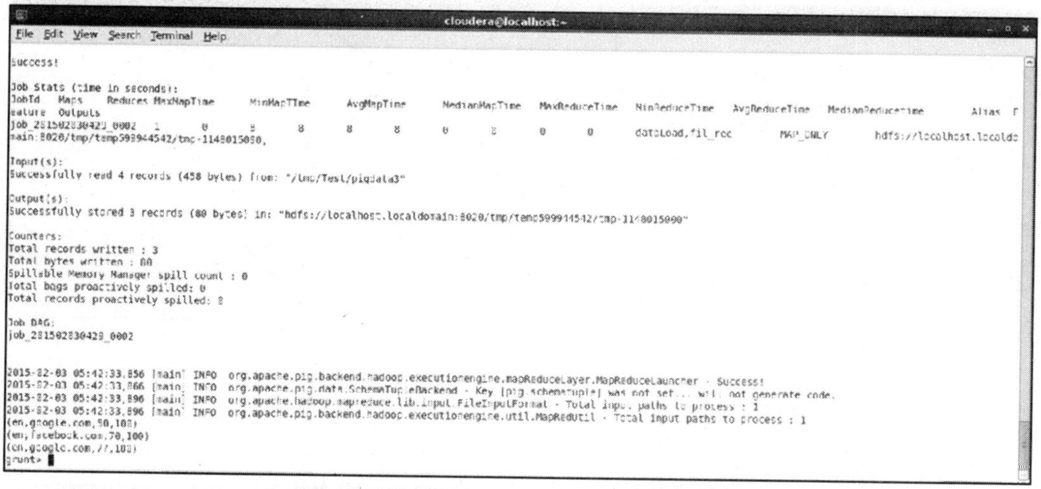

Figure 28: Output of the filter Command

6. Run the `group by` command, as shown in the following code snippet:

```
grp_rec = GROUP fil_rec by c2;
```

Figure 29 shows the output of the `group by` command:

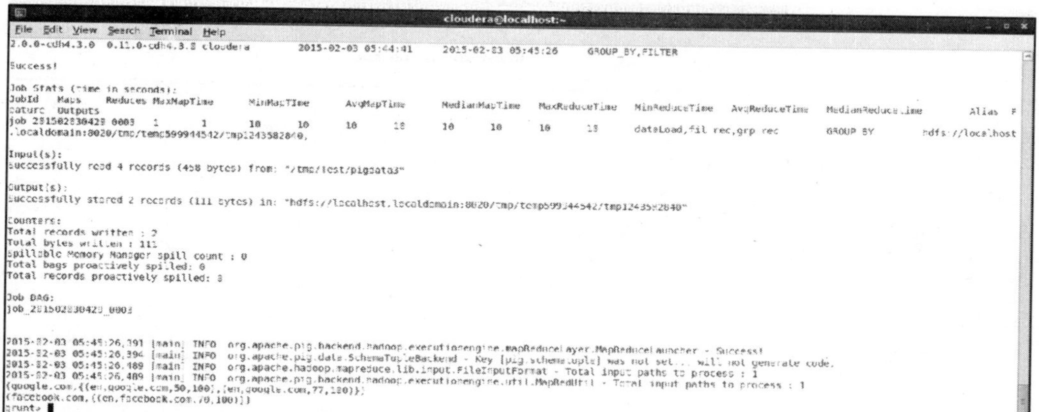

Figure 29: Output of the group by Command

7. Run the `foreach` command, as shown in the following code snippet:

```
results = FOREACH grp_rec generate group, SUM(fil_rec.c3);
```

The output of the preceding command is shown in Figure 30:

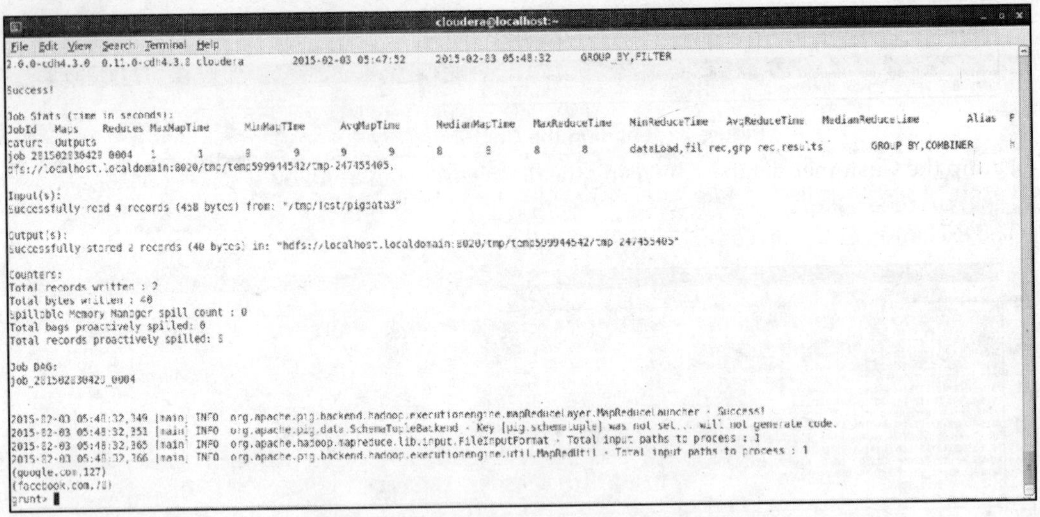

Figure 30: Output of the foreach Command

8. Run the `order by` command in the following manner to arrange records in the descending order:

```
sort = ORDER results by $1 desc;
```

The output of the `order by` command is shown in Figure 31:

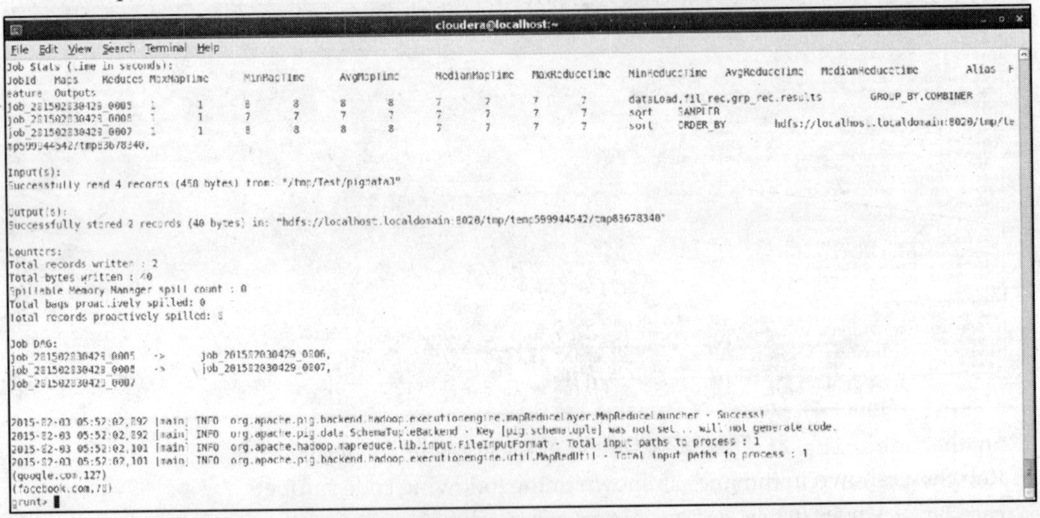

Figure 31: Output of the order by Command

Lab 2—To Load a Customer File to HDFS to be Processed Using the Pig Ecosystem and Find out the Maximum Purchase of Products and their Costs

Solution—Perform the following steps to find out the maximum purchase and cost of products:

1. Load the Customer file by using the following command:

```
customer_DB = LOAD '/tmp/Cust_Test/cust' using PigStorage(',') as (custID:chararray,
custFName:chararray, custLName:chararray, custAge:int, custProf:chararray);
```

The execution of the preceding command is shown in Figure 32:

Figure 32: Loading the Customer Data to Pig

2. Dump the Customer database by using the `dump` command as follows:

```
DUMP customer_DB;
```

The execution of the preceding command is shown in Figure 33:

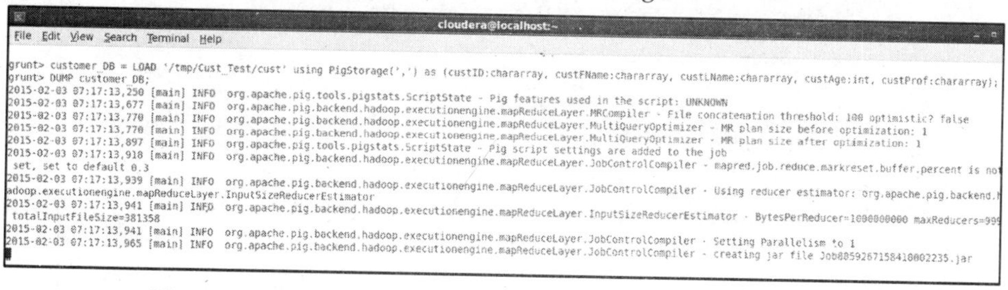

Figure 33: Execution of the dump Command on Customer Data

The output of the `dump` command is shown in Figure 34:

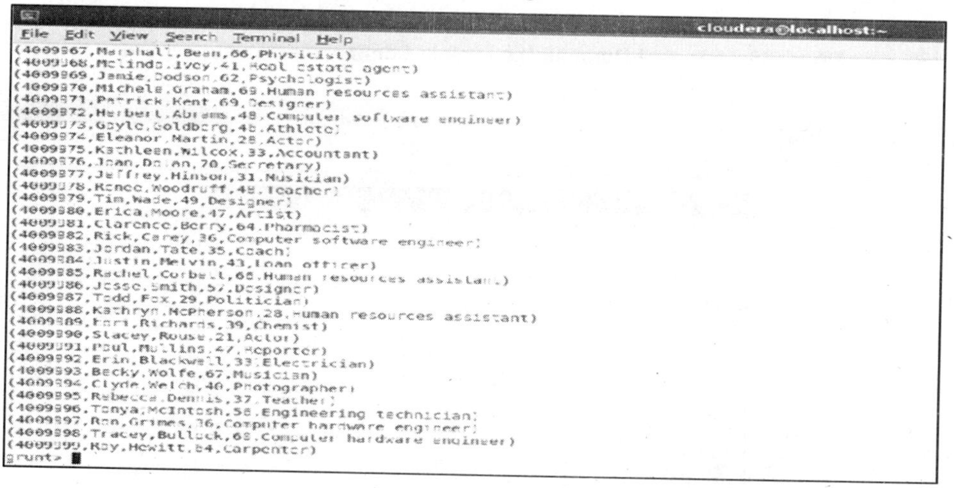

Figure 34: Output of Running the dump Command on Customer Data

3. Run the `describe` command to get the details of the rows and columns of the customer database, as shown in the following code snippet:

```
DESCRIBE customer_DB;
```

The output of executing the preceding command is shown in Figure 35:

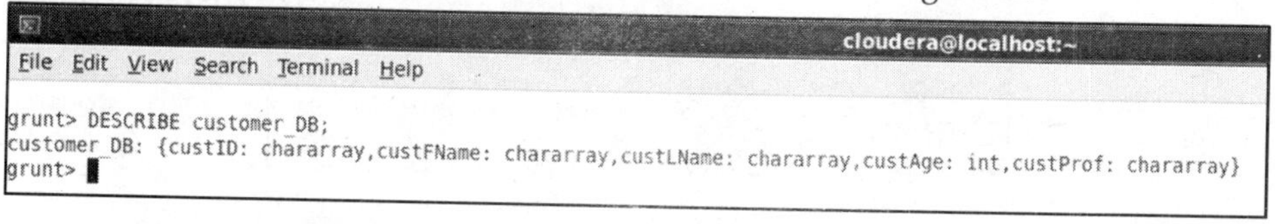

Figure 35: Output of Running the describe Command on Customer Data

4. Run the `explain` command in the following manner to get the description of the customer database:

```
EXPLAIN customer_DB;
```

Figure 36 shows the output of executing the `explain` command on customer data:

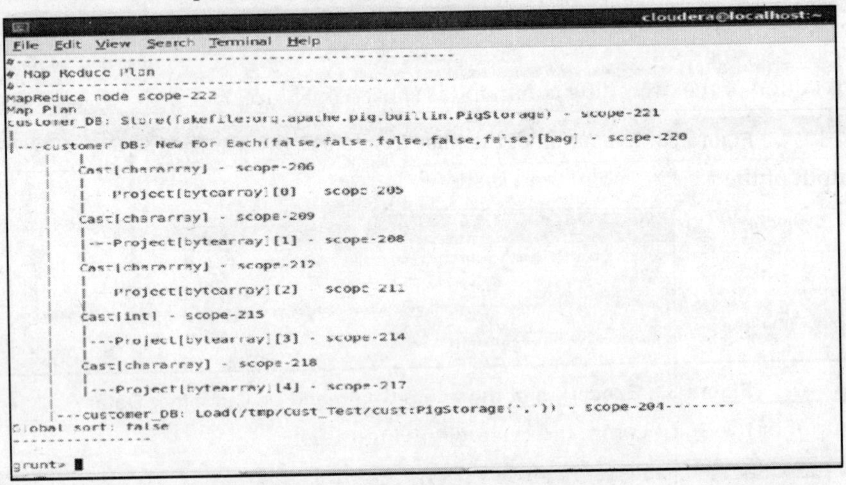

Figure 36: Output of Running the explain Command on Customer Data

5. Run the `illustrates` command as follows:

```
ILLUSTRATES customer_DB;
```

Figure 37 shows the output of executing the preceding command:

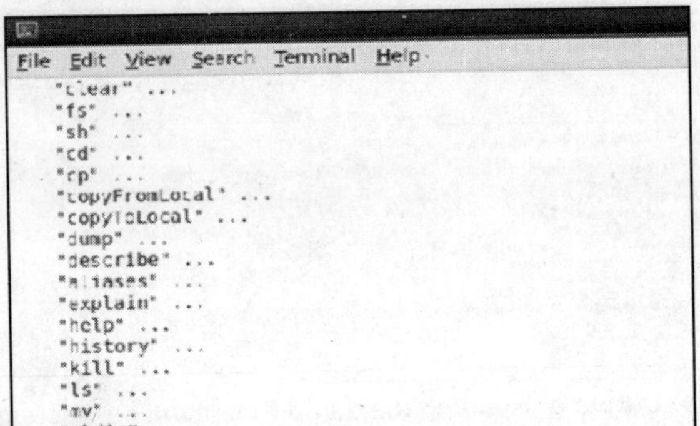

Figure 37: Output of Running the illustrates Command on Customer Data

6. Run the `filter` command to filter the customer data based on the profession as Pilot. For this, run the following command:

```
cust_filter = FILTER customer_DB by custProf = 'Pilot';
```

Figure 38 shows the execution of the preceding command:

Figure 38: Execution of the filter Command on Customer Data

The output of the `filter` command is shown in Figure 39:

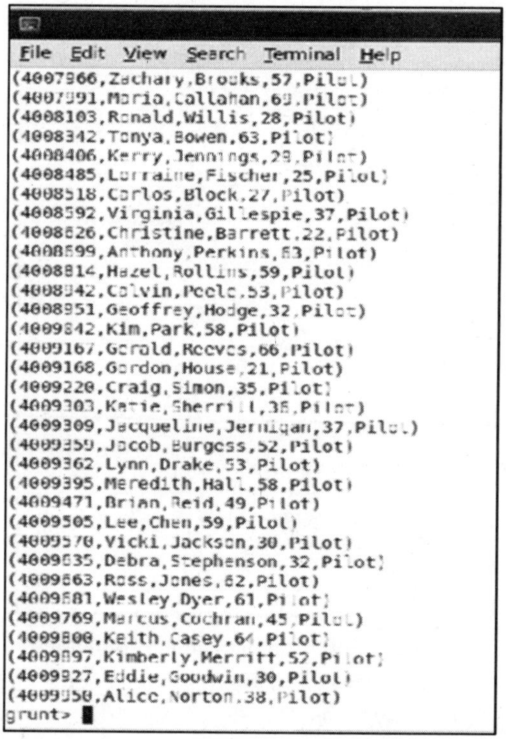

Figure 39: Output of the filter Command Execution on Customer Data

7. Run the `distinct` command to display the unique records. The command is given as follows:

```
cust_unique = DISTINCT cust_filter;
```

Figure 40 shows the execution of the `distinct` command:

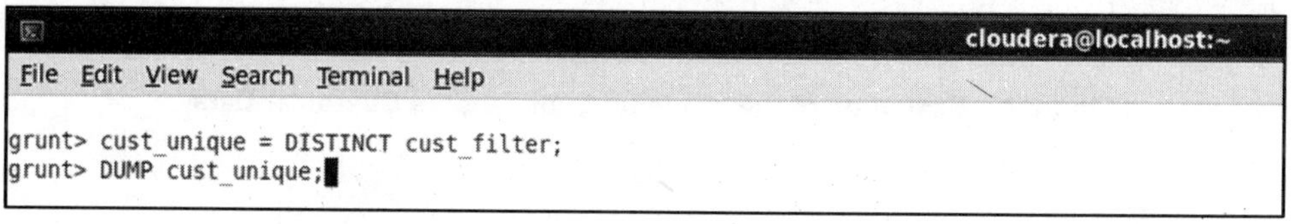

Figure 40: Execution of the distinct Command

Figure 41 shows the distinct records of the customers:

```
File Edit View Search Terminal Help
(4007966,Zachary,Brooks,57,Pilot)
(4007991,Maria,Callahan,69,Pilot)
(4008103,Ronald,Willis,28,Pilot)
(4008342,Tonya,Bowen,63,Pilot)
(4008406,Kerry,Jennings,29,Pilot)
(4008485,Lorraine,Fischer,25,Pilot)
(4008518,Carlos,Block,27,Pilot)
(4008592,Virginia,Gillespie,37,Pilot)
(4008626,Christine,Barrett,22,Pilot)
(4008699,Anthony,Perkins,63,Pilot)
(4008814,Hazel,Rollins,59,Pilot)
(4008842,Calvin,Poole,53,Pilot)
(4008951,Geoffrey,Hodge,32,Pilot)
(4009842,Kim,Park,58,Pilot)
(4009167,Gerald,Reeves,66,Pilot)
(4009168,Gordon,House,21,Pilot)
(4009220,Craig,Simon,35,Pilot)
(4009303,Katie,Sherrill,36,Pilot)
(4009309,Jacqueline,Jernigan,37,Pilot)
(4009359,Jacob,Burgess,52,Pilot)
(4009362,Lynn,Drake,53,Pilot)
(4009395,Meredith,Hall,58,Pilot)
(4009471,Brian,Reid,49,Pilot)
(4009505,Lee,Chen,59,Pilot)
(4009570,Vicki,Jackson,30,Pilot)
(4009635,Debra,Stephenson,32,Pilot)
(4009663,Ross,Jones,62,Pilot)
(4009681,Wesley,Dyer,61,Pilot)
(4009769,Marcus,Cochran,45,Pilot)
(4009800,Keith,Casey,64,Pilot)
(4009897,Kimberly,Merritt,52,Pilot)
(4009927,Eddie,Goodwin,30,Pilot)
(4009950,Alice,Norton,38,Pilot)
grunt>
```

Figure 41: Output of the distinct Command

8. Run the `group by` command, as shown in the following code snippet:

```
grpbyprof = GROUP customer_DB by custProf;
```

Figure 42 shows the execution of the `group by` command on customer data:

```
cloudera@localhost:~
File Edit View Search Terminal Help

grunt> grpbyprof = GROUP customer_DB by custProf;
grunt> DUMP grpbyprof
```

Figure 42: Execution of the group by Command on Customer Data

Figure 43 shows the output of the execution of the `group by` command on customer data:

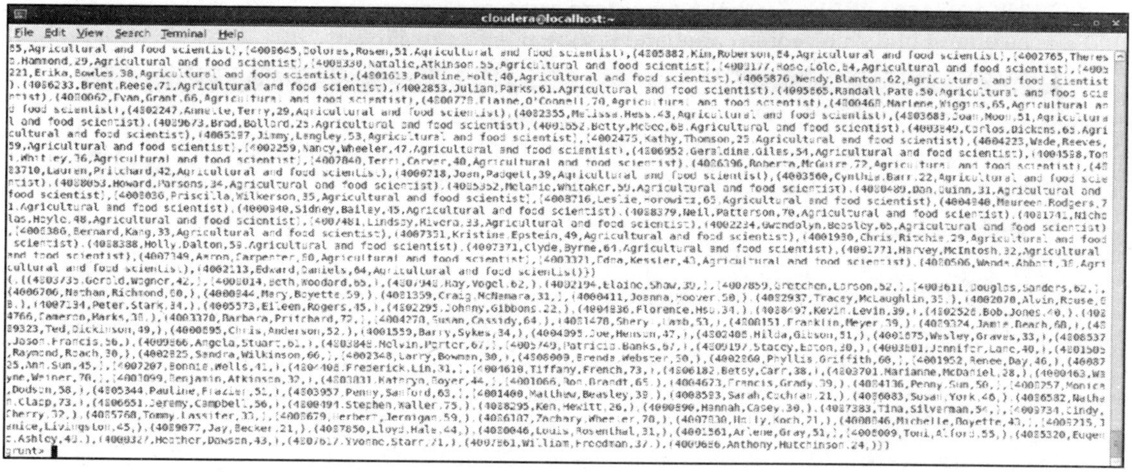

Figure 43: Output of the group by Command Execution on Customer Data

Lab 3—To Find the Maximum Temperature of a Particular Year in an Input File

Solution—Perform the following steps to find the maximum temperature of a year:

1. Load the climate data by using the following command:

```
Climate = LOAD '/ tmp/Test/maxTemp/input/maxTemp' using PigStorage ',' as
(year:int, temp:int);
```

The output of the preceding command is shown in Figure 44:

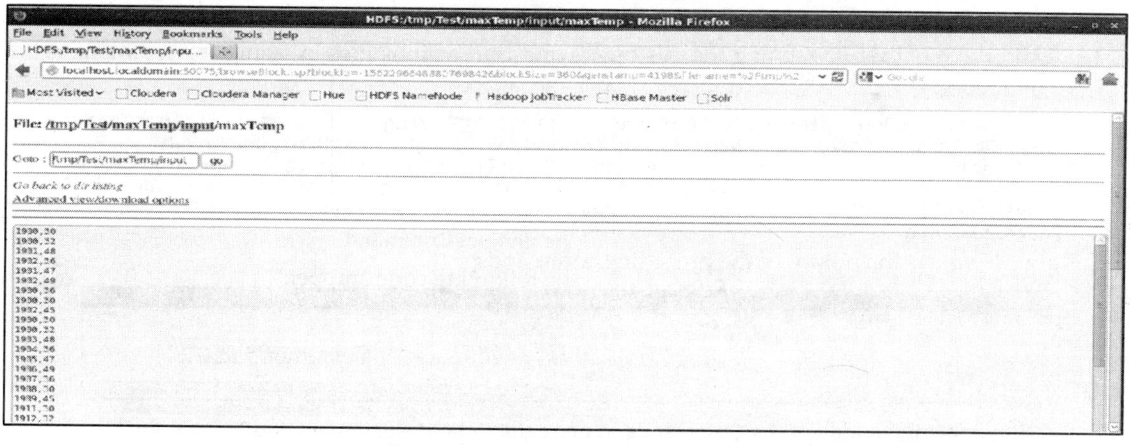

Figure 44: Loading the Climate Data

2. Run the following commands to extract data on the basis of various criteria:

```
Grunt> filter_env = FILTER env by temp> 30;
Grunt> group_env = GROUP env by year;
Grunt> max_temp = FOREACH group_env GENERATE GROUP, MAX (env.temp);
```

In the preceding commands, we are trying to find the maximum temperature of a particular year. We are using the group commands schema on the basis of which we will get the maximum temperature.

The following command is used to display the maximum temperature:

```
STORE max_temp INTO '/ tmp/Test/maxTemp/output;
```

The output of the preceding command is shown in Figure 45:

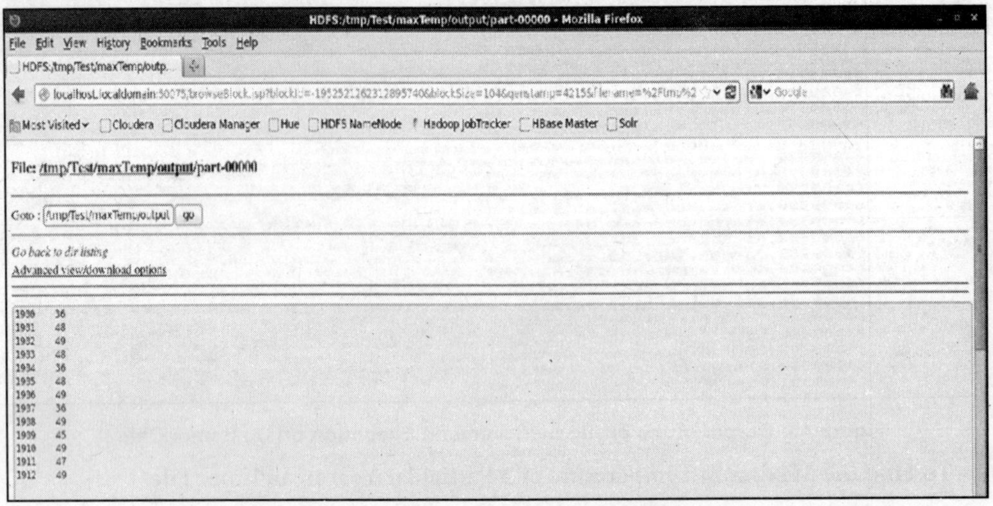

Figure 45: Displaying the Maximum Temperature

Lab 4—To Group Customers and Transactions Files to Limit the Records and Perform the Union Operation and Split the Files on the Basis of Multiple Conditions

Solution—Perform the following steps to group two files to restrict the count of the displayed records:

1. Load the database containing the customers and transactions files by using the following set of commands:

```
customers = LOAD '/tmp/Cust_Test/cust' using PigStorage (',') as (custID:chararray,
custFName:chararray, custLName:chararray, custAge:int, custProf:chararray);
transactions = LOAD '/tmp/Cust_Test/txns ' using PigStorage (',') as
(transId:chararray, transDate:chararray, transCustId:chararray, transAmt:double,
transCat:chararray, transProd:chararray, transCity:chararray, transState:chararray,
transType:chararray);
```

Figure 46 shows the output of the preceding commands:

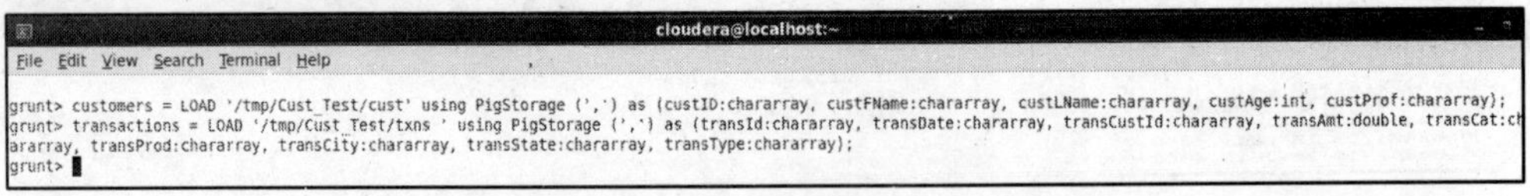

Figure 46: Execution of the Commands to Load the Data of Customers and Transactions

Figure 47 shows the customer data:

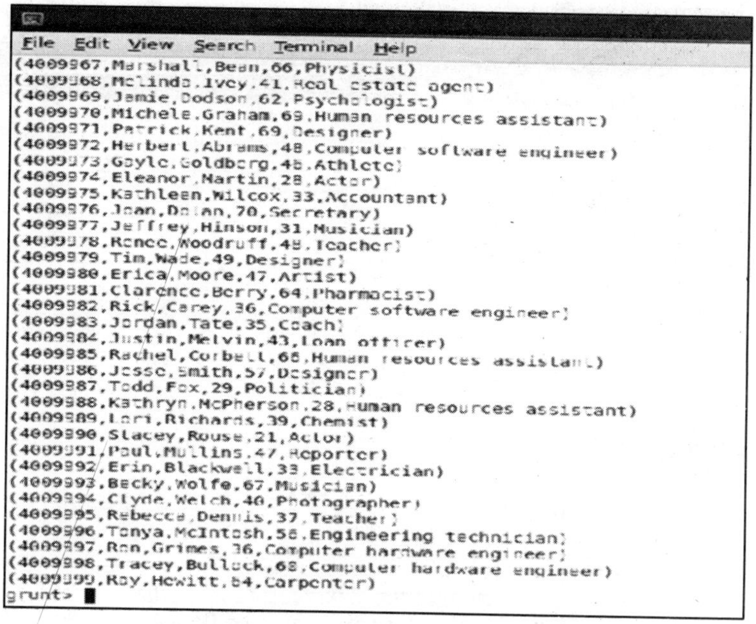

Figure 47: The Customer Data

Figure 48 shows the transactions data:

Figure 48: The Transactions Data

2. Combine the data of the customers and transactions by running the following command:

```
customerWithTransaction = JOIN customers BY custID, transactions BY transCustId;
```

Figure 49 shows the output of executing the preceding command:

Figure 49: Execution of the Commands to Combine Data of Customers and Transactions

The progress of combining the data of customers and transactions is shown in Figure 50:

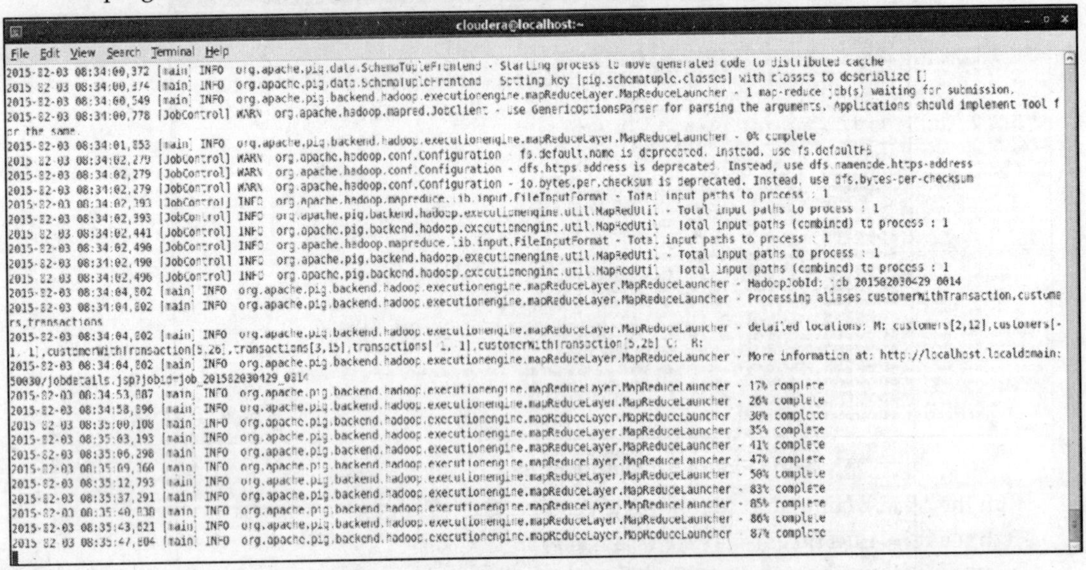

Figure 50: Progress of Combining Data

The output, after combining the data of both files, is shown in Figure 51:

Figure 51: Output after Joining Data

3. Run the `cross` command, as shown in the following code snippet:

```
crossProd = CROSS customers, transactions;
```

Figure 52 shows the output of the `cross` command:

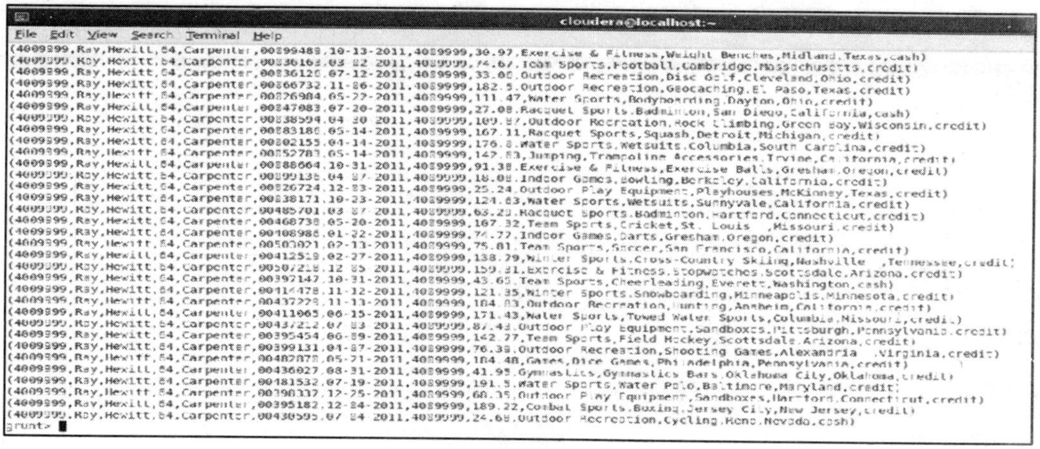

Figure 52: Output of the cross Command

4. Run the `limit` command as follows to restrict the customer transactions to 20:

```
limitCust = LIMIT customerwithTransaction 20;
```

Figure 53 shows the output of executing the `limit` command on the combined data:

Figure 53: Execution of the limit Command on the Combined Data

The output of the `limit` command is shown in Figure 54:

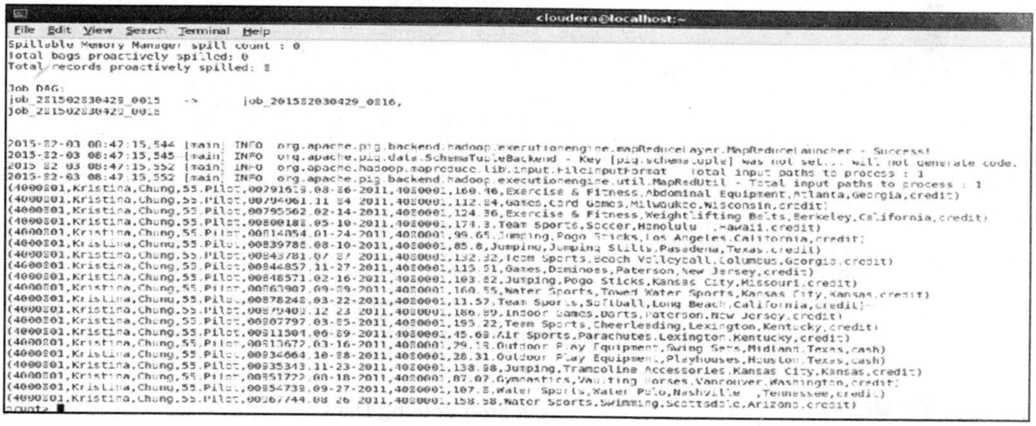

Figure 54: Output of the limit Command

5. Run the `union` command as follows to join the output of the customers and transactions files:

```
unionCustTrans = UNION customers, transactions;
```

Figure 55 shows the output of the `union` command:

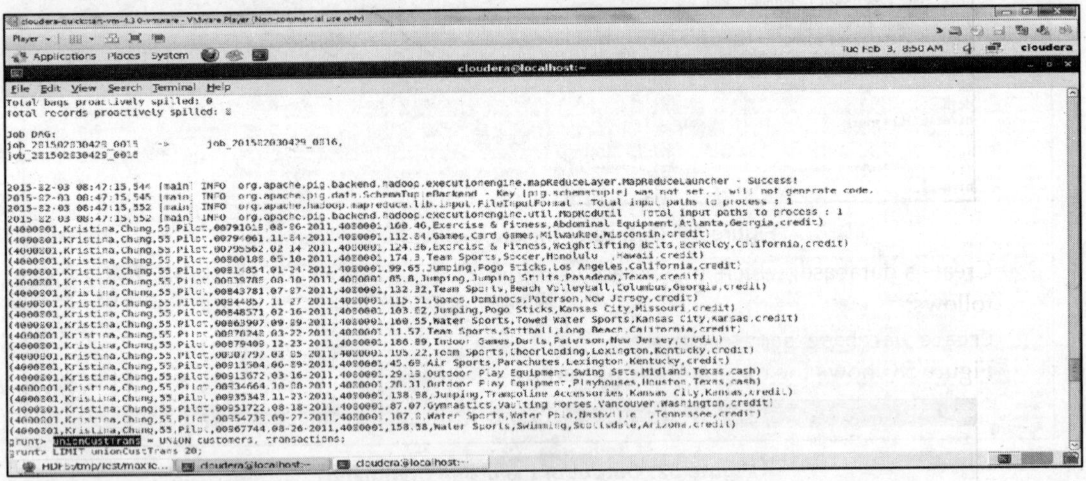

Figure 55: Output of the union Command

6. Run the `split` command as follows:

```
SPLIT unionCustTrans INTO X IF custAge<15, Y IF (custAge<30 OR custAge>40), Z IF
custAge>60;
DUMP X;
DUMP Y;
DUMP Z;
```

Figure 56 shows the output of the preceding command:

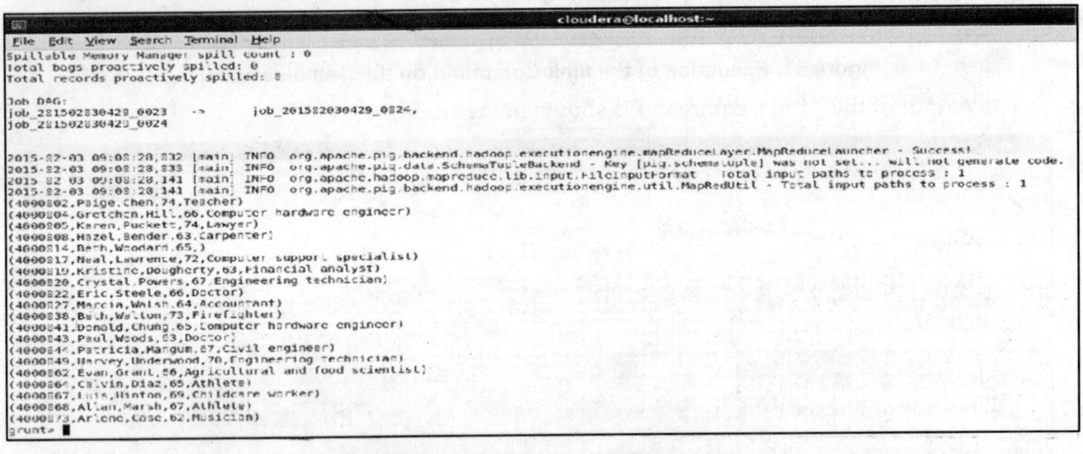

Figure 56: Output of the split Command

Labs on Hive

Lab 1—To Create an Internal Table and Work with Employees' Details

Solution—Perform the following steps to create a table containing employees' details and work with the data of the table:

1. Run the `show databases` command, as shown in Figure 57, to view the available databases:

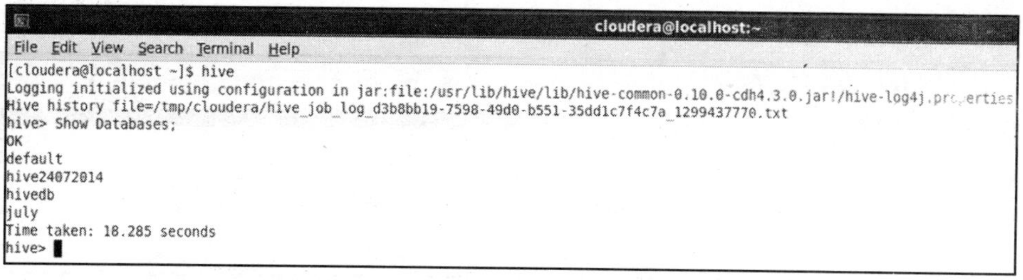

```
cloudera@localhost:~
File Edit View Search Terminal Help
[cloudera@localhost ~]$ hive
Logging initialized using configuration in jar:file:/usr/lib/hive/lib/hive-common-0.10.0-cdh4.3.0.jar!/hive-log4j.properties
Hive history file=/tmp/cloudera/hive_job_log_d3b8bb19-7598-49d0-b551-35dd1c7f4c7a_1299437770.txt
hive> Show Databases;
OK
default
hive24072014
hivedb
july
Time taken: 18.285 seconds
hive>
```

Figure 57: Output of the show databases Command

2. Create a database (which, in our case, is sampleemp) using the `create database` command as follows:

```
Create Database sampleemp;
```

Figure 58 shows the output of the preceding command:

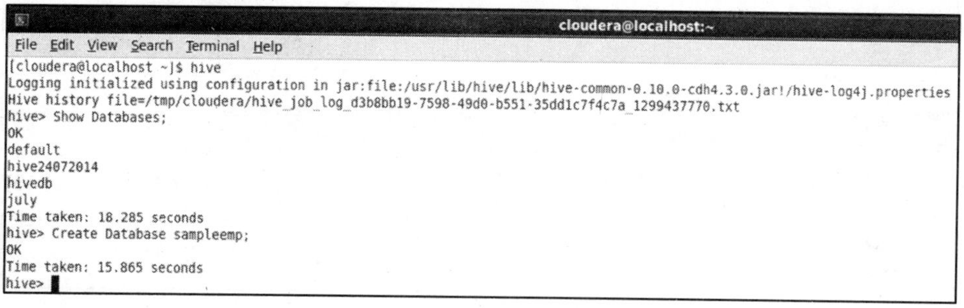

```
cloudera@localhost:~
File Edit View Search Terminal Help
[cloudera@localhost ~]$ hive
Logging initialized using configuration in jar:file:/usr/lib/hive/lib/hive-common-0.10.0-cdh4.3.0.jar!/hive-log4j.properties
Hive history file=/tmp/cloudera/hive_job_log_d3b8bb19-7598-49d0-b551-35dd1c7f4c7a_1299437770.txt
hive> Show Databases;
OK
default
hive24072014
hivedb
july
Time taken: 18.285 seconds
hive> Create Database sampleemp;
OK
Time taken: 15.865 seconds
hive>
```

Figure 58: Creating a Database

3. Use the database by executing the `use` command as follows:

```
use sampleemp;
```

Figure 59 shows the output of the preceding command:

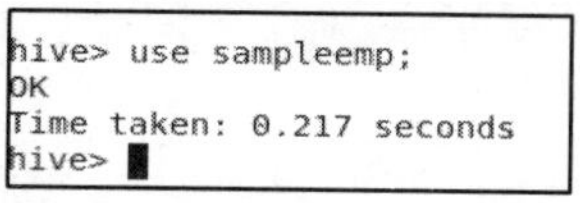

```
hive> use sampleemp;
OK
Time taken: 0.217 seconds
hive>
```

Figure 59: Using a Database

4. Create a table (which, in our case, is named employee) by using the `create table` command as follows:

```
create table employee(firstname string, salary int, project string) row format
delimited fields terminated by ',';
```

The output of executing the preceding command is shown in Figure 60:

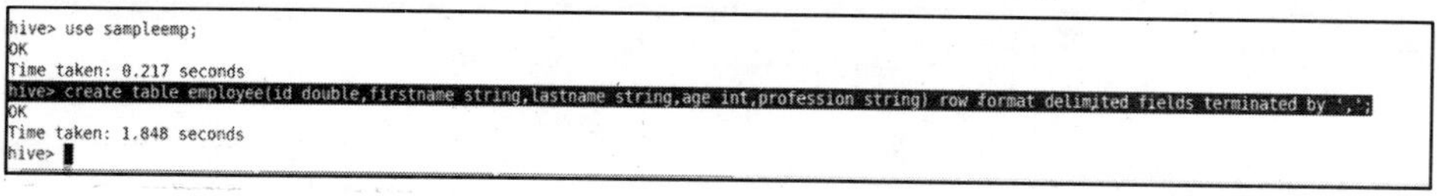

```
hive> use sampleemp;
OK
Time taken: 0.217 seconds
hive> create table employee(id double,firstname string,lastname string,age int,profession string) row format delimited fields terminated by ',';
OK
Time taken: 1.848 seconds
hive>
```

Figure 60: Creating a Table in a Database

5. Load the data in the table by using the `load data` command as follows:

```
load data local inpath '/home/cloudera/employeeHive' into table employee;
```

Figure 61 shows the output of the preceding command:

```
Time taken: 0.148 seconds
hive> create table employee(firstname string, salary int, project string) row format delimited fields terminated by ',';
OK
Time taken: 0.416 seconds
hive> load data local inpath '/home/cloudera/employeeHive' into table employee;
Copying data from file:/home/cloudera/employeeHive
Copying file: file:/home/cloudera/employeeHive
Loading data to table july.employee
Table july.employee stats: [num_partitions: 0, num_files: 1, num_rows: 0, total_size: 77, raw_data_size: 0]
OK
Time taken: 2.866 seconds
hive> █
```

Figure 61: Loading Data into a Database Table

6. Display the data of the table by using the following command:

```
select *from employee where salary between 8000 and 20000;
```

Figure 62 shows the record of employees whose salaries lie between 8000 and 20000:

```
hive> select *from employee where salary between 8000 and 20000;
Total MapReduce jobs = 1
Launching Job 1 out of 1
Number of reduce tasks is set to 0 since there's no reduce operator
Starting Job = job_201502030429_0025, Tracking URL = http://localhost.localdomain:50030/jobdetails.jsp?jobid=job_201502030429_0025
Kill Command = /usr/lib/hadoop/bin/hadoop job  -kill job_201502030429_0025
Hadoop job information for Stage-1: number of mappers: 1; number of reducers: 0
2015-02-03 09:57:54,987 Stage-1 map = 0%,  reduce = 0%
2015-02-03 09:58:01,539 Stage-1 map = 100%,  reduce = 0%, Cumulative CPU 0.89 sec
2015-02-03 09:58:02,568 Stage-1 map = 100%,  reduce = 0%, Cumulative CPU 0.89 sec
2015-02-03 09:58:03,584 Stage-1 map = 100%,  reduce = 0%, Cumulative CPU 0.89 sec
2015-02-03 09:58:04,601 Stage-1 map = 100%,  reduce = 0%, Cumulative CPU 0.89 sec
2015-02-03 09:58:05,665 Stage-1 map = 100%,  reduce = 0%, Cumulative CPU 0.89 sec
2015-02-03 09:58:06,686 Stage-1 map = 100%,  reduce = 100%, Cumulative CPU 0.89 sec
MapReduce Total cumulative CPU time: 890 msec
Ended Job = job_201502030429_0025
MapReduce Jobs Launched:
Job 0: Map: 1   Cumulative CPU: 0.89 sec   HDFS Read: 281 HDFS Write: 18 SUCCESS
Total MapReduce CPU Time Spent: 890 msec
OK
Deepti  20000   BHPB
Time taken: 29.511 seconds
hive> █
```

Figure 62: Displaying Employees' Salary Records lying between 8000 and 2000

7. Display the number of rows available in the employees table by using the following command:

```
select count(*) from employee;
```

Figure 63 shows the output of the preceding command:

```
cloudera@localhost:~
File Edit View Search Terminal Help
hive> select count(*) from employee;
Total MapReduce jobs = 1
Launching Job 1 out of 1
Number of reduce tasks determined at compile time: 1
In order to change the average load for a reducer (in bytes):
  set hive.exec.reducers.bytes.per.reducer=<number>
In order to limit the maximum number of reducers:
  set hive.exec.reducers.max=<number>
In order to set a constant number of reducers:
  set mapred.reduce.tasks=<number>
Starting Job = job_201502030429_0026, Tracking URL = http://localhost.localdomain:50030/jobdetails.jsp?jobid=job_201502030429_0026
Kill Command = /usr/lib/hadoop/bin/hadoop job  -kill job_201502030429_0026
Hadoop job information for Stage-1: number of mappers: 1; number of reducers: 1
2015-02-03 10:00:41,853 Stage-1 map = 0%,  reduce = 0%
2015-02-03 10:00:57,156 Stage-1 map = 100%,  reduce = 0%, Cumulative CPU 0.61 sec
2015-02-03 10:00:58,185 Stage-1 map = 100%,  reduce = 0%, Cumulative CPU 0.61 sec
2015-02-03 10:00:59,201 Stage-1 map = 100%,  reduce = 0%, Cumulative CPU 0.61 sec
2015-02-03 10:01:00,231 Stage-1 map = 100%,  reduce = 0%, Cumulative CPU 0.61 sec
2015-02-03 10:01:01,261 Stage-1 map = 100%,  reduce = 0%, Cumulative CPU 0.61 sec
2015-02-03 10:01:02,278 Stage-1 map = 100%,  reduce = 0%, Cumulative CPU 0.61 sec
2015-02-03 10:01:03,297 Stage-1 map = 100%,  reduce = 0%, Cumulative CPU 0.61 sec
2015-02-03 10:01:04,316 Stage-1 map = 100%,  reduce = 0%, Cumulative CPU 0.61 sec
2015-02-03 10:01:05,423 Stage-1 map = 100%,  reduce = 100%, Cumulative CPU 1.19 sec
2015-02-03 10:01:06,438 Stage-1 map = 100%,  reduce = 100%, Cumulative CPU 1.19 sec
2015-02-03 10:01:07,457 Stage-1 map = 100%,  reduce = 100%, Cumulative CPU 1.19 sec
2015-02-03 10:01:08,474 Stage-1 map = 100%,  reduce = 100%, Cumulative CPU 1.19 sec
2015-02-03 10:01:09,496 Stage-1 map = 100%,  reduce = 100%, Cumulative CPU 1.19 sec
MapReduce Total cumulative CPU time: 1 seconds 190 msec
Ended Job = job_201502030429_0026
MapReduce Jobs Launched:
Job 0: Map: 1  Reduce: 1   Cumulative CPU: 1.19 sec   HDFS Read: 281 HDFS Write: 2 SUCCESS
Total MapReduce CPU Time Spent: 1 seconds 190 msec
OK
4
```

Figure 63: Counting the Number of Rows in a Table

8. Type the following command to alter the employees table by adding a column named profession of the string type:

```
Alter table employee ADD COLUMNS(profession string);
```

The output of the preceding command is shown in Figure 64:

```
hive> Alter table employee ADD COLUMNS(profession string);
OK
Time taken: 0.671 seconds
hive>
```

Figure 64: Adding a New Column to a Table

9. Display the records where the salary is not null by using the following command:

```
select *from employee where salary is not null;
```

Figure 65 shows the output of executing the `is not null` command:

```
hive> select *from employee where salary is not null;
Total MapReduce jobs = 1
Launching Job 1 out of 1
Number of reduce tasks is set to 0 since there's no reduce operator
Starting Job = job_201502030429_0027, Tracking URL = http://localhost.localdomain:50030/jobdetails.jsp?jobid=job_201502030429_0027
Kill Command = /usr/lib/hadoop/bin/hadoop job  -kill job_201502030429_0027
Hadoop job information for Stage-1: number of mappers: 1; number of reducers: 0
2015-02-03 10:06:45,136 Stage-1 map = 0%,  reduce = 0%
2015-02-03 10:06:53,192 Stage-1 map = 100%,  reduce = 0%, Cumulative CPU 0.9 sec
2015-02-03 10:06:54,207 Stage-1 map = 100%,  reduce = 0%, Cumulative CPU 0.9 sec
2015-02-03 10:06:55,303 Stage-1 map = 100%,  reduce = 0%, Cumulative CPU 0.9 sec
2015-02-03 10:06:56,323 Stage-1 map = 100%,  reduce = 0%, Cumulative CPU 0.9 sec
2015-02-03 10:06.57,339 Stage-1 map = 100%,  reduce = 0%, Cumulative CPU 0.9 sec
2015-02-03 10:06:58,355 Stage-1 map = 100%,  reduce = 0%, Cumulative CPU 0.9 sec
2015-02-03 10:06:59,377 Stage-1 map = 100%,  reduce = 100%, Cumulative CPU 0.9 sec
MapReduce Total cumulative CPU time: 900 msec
Ended Job = job_201502030429_0027
MapReduce Jobs Launched:
Job 0: Map: 1   Cumulative CPU: 0.9 sec   HDFS Read: 281 HDFS Write: 89 SUCCESS
Total MapReduce CPU Time Spent: 900 msec
OK
Ravi    100000  DuPont  NULL
Deepti  20000   BHPB    NULL
Mayur   5000    bhpb    NULL
Amar    33333   BHP Billiton    NULL
Time taken: 24.592 seconds
hive>
```

Figure 65: Extracting the Records Containing the not Null Salary Values

10. Run the `group by` command as follows to group the records on the basis of projects undertaken by employees:

```
select project, SUM(salary) from employee group by project;
```

Figure 66 shows the output of the `group by` command:

```
cloudera@localhost:~
File  Edit  View  Search  Terminal  Help
In order to limit the maximum number of reducers:
  set hive.exec.reducers.max=<number>
In order to set a constant number of reducers:
  set mapred.reduce.tasks=<number>
Starting Job = job_201502030429_0028, Tracking URL = http://localhost.localdomain:50030/jobdetails.jsp?jobid=job_201502030429_0028
Kill Command = /usr/lib/hadoop/bin/hadoop job  -kill job_201502030429_0028
Hadoop job information for Stage-1: number of mappers: 1; number of reducers: 1
2015-02-03 10:09:52,721 Stage-1 map = 0%,  reduce = 0%
2015-02-03 10:10:01,776 Stage-1 map = 100%,  reduce = 0%, Cumulative CPU 1.25 sec
2015-02-03 10:10:02,797 Stage-1 map = 100%,  reduce = 0%, Cumulative CPU 1.25 sec
2015-02-03 10:10:03,810 Stage-1 map = 100%,  reduce = 0%, Cumulative CPU 1.25 sec
2015-02-03 10:10:04,829 Stage-1 map = 100%,  reduce = 0%, Cumulative CPU 1.25 sec
2015-02-03 10:10:05,851 Stage-1 map = 100%,  reduce = 0%, Cumulative CPU 1.25 sec
2015-02-03 10:10:06,873 Stage-1 map = 100%,  reduce = 0%, Cumulative CPU 1.25 sec
2015-02-03 10:10:07,892 Stage-1 map = 100%,  reduce = 0%, Cumulative CPU 1.25 sec
2015-02-03 10:10:08,906 Stage-1 map = 100%,  reduce = 0%, Cumulative CPU 1.25 sec
2015-02-03 10:10:09,936 Stage-1 map = 100%,  reduce = 100%, Cumulative CPU 3.54 sec
2015-02-03 10:10:10,950 Stage-1 map = 100%,  reduce = 100%, Cumulative CPU 3.54 sec
2015-02-03 10:10:11,969 Stage-1 map = 100%,  reduce = 100%, Cumulative CPU 3.54 sec
2015-02-03 10:10:13,055 Stage-1 map = 100%,  reduce = 100%, Cumulative CPU 3.54 sec
2015-02-03 10:10:14,068 Stage-1 map = 100%,  reduce = 100%, Cumulative CPU 3.54 sec
2015-02-03 10:10:15,090 Stage-1 map = 100%,  reduce = 100%, Cumulative CPU 3.54 sec
MapReduce Total cumulative CPU time: 3 seconds 540 msec
Ended Job = job_201502030429_0028
MapReduce Jobs Launched:
Job 0: Map: 1  Reduce: 1   Cumulative CPU: 3.54 sec   HDFS Read: 281 HDFS Write: 54 SUCCESS
Total MapReduce CPU Time Spent: 3 seconds 540 msec
OK
BHP Billiton    33333
BHPB    20000
DuPont  100000
bhpb    5000
Time taken: 33.272 seconds
hive>
```

Figure 66: Combining Employee Records by Project

Lab 2—To Create an External Table and Perform the Basic Operations in it

Solution—Perform the following steps to create an external table and perform basic operations in it:

1. Execute the following command to create an external table:

```
Create External Table customerext (custID int, firstName string, lastName string,
age int, profession string) ROW FORMAT DELIMITED FIELDS TERMINATED BY ',';
```

The output of the preceding command is shown in Figure 67:

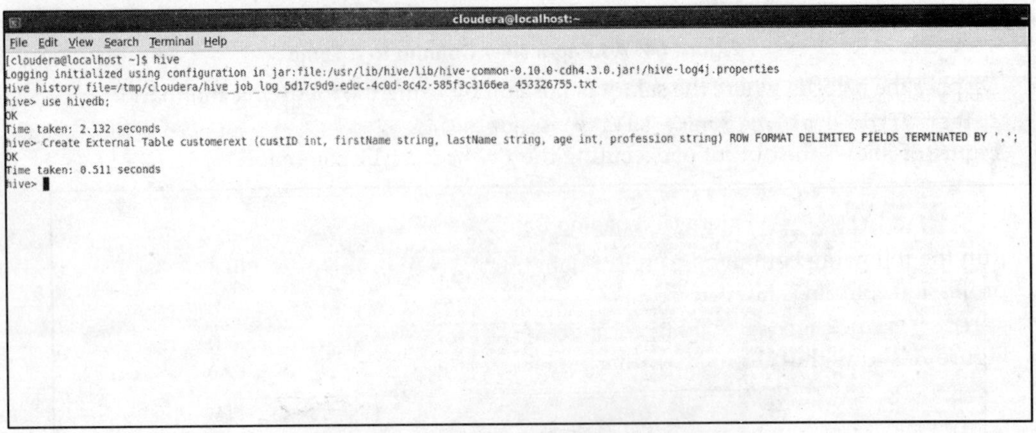

Figure 67: Creating an External Table

2. Load the data in the table by using the following command:

```
load data inpath '/tmp/Cust_Test/cust' into table customerext;
```

Figure 68 shows the input data for loading into the table:

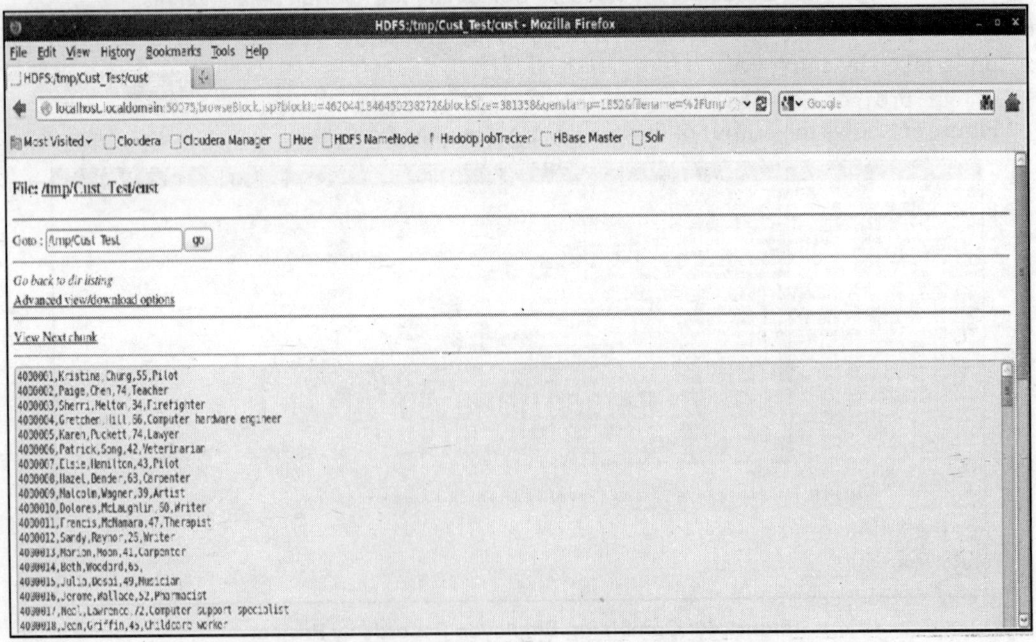

Figure 68: Accepting the Input Data for Loading Data in a Table

Figure 69 shows the output of the `load data` command:

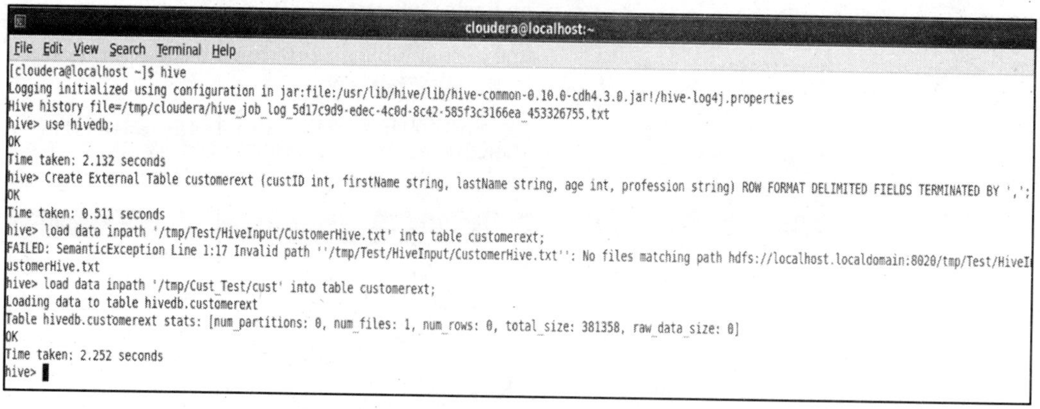

Figure 69: Loading Data in an External Table

3. Run the following command to select data from the `customerext` table where the value of the profession column is lawyer:

```
select * from customerext where profession = 'Lawyer';
```

Figure 70 shows the output after filtering records on the basis of the given condition:

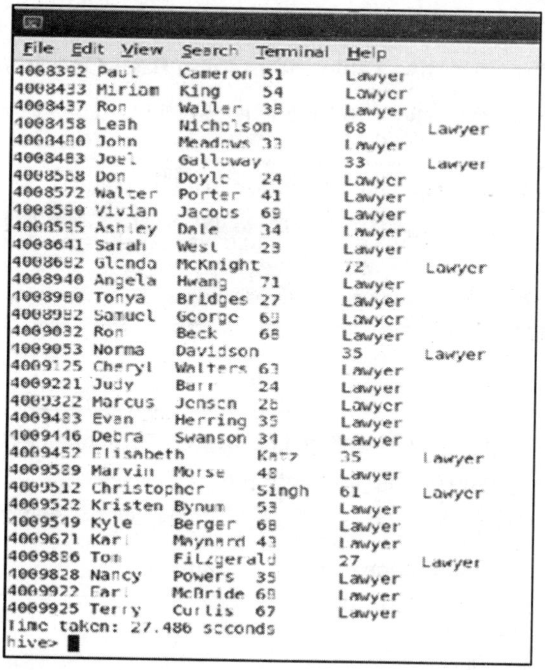

Figure 70: Records of the Employees Whose Profession is Lawyer

4. Enter the following command to display the employee records where profession is Pilot or age is greater than 40:

```
select * from customerext where profession = 'Pilot', age > 40;
```

Figure 71 shows the output of executing the preceding command:

```
File  Edit  View  Search  Terminal  Help
4009947 Betsy   Casey   78      Athlete
4009948 Cameron Ferrell 61      Recreation and fitness worker
4009951 Dana    Wolfe   54      Athlete
4009953 Marianne        McIntosh        56      Librarian
4009954 Sharon  Tate    44      Environmental scientist
4009955 Natalie Barbee  52      Economist
4009957 Thelma  Cooper  69      Secretary
4009958 Dorothy Shah    41      Computer software engineer
4009961 Betty   Grady   73      Athlete
4009962 Pam     Berger  47      Recreation and fitness worker
4009964 Jan     Wells   58      Real estate agent
4009965 Bob     McKinney        74      Librarian
4009967 Marshall        Bean    66      Physicist
4009968 Melinda Ivey    41      Real estate agent
4009969 Jamie   Dodson  62      Psychologist
4009970 Michele Graham  69      Human resources assistant
4009971 Patrick Kent    69      Designer
4009972 Herbert Abrams  48      Computer software engineer
4009973 Gayle   Goldberg        46      Athlete
4009976 Joan    Dolan   78      Secretary
4009978 Renee   Woodruff        48      Teacher
4009979 Tim     Wade    49      Designer
4009980 Erica   Moore   47      Artist
4009981 Clarence        Berry   64      Pharmacist
4009984 Justin  Melvin  43      Loan officer
4009985 Rachel  Corbett 66      Human resources assistant
4009986 Jesse   Smith   57      Designer
4009991 Paul    Mullins 47      Reporter
4009993 Becky   Wolfe   67      Musician
4009996 Tonya   McIntosh        56      Engineering technician
4009998 Tracey  Bullock 68      Computer hardware engineer
4009999 Ray     Hewitt  64      Carpenter
Time taken: 24.382 seconds
hive> ▮
```

Figure 71: Set of records in which Profession is Pilot and the Age is greater than 40

Lab 3—To Create a Partition in a Hive Table and Perform Basic Operations in the Partition

Solution—Perform the following steps to create a partition in a Hive table and perform basic operations:

1. Run the following command to create a partition in a Hive table:

```
Create Table IF NOT EXISTS  customerpart (custID int, firstName string, lastName string, age int, profession string) PARTITIONED BY (exchange STRING, symbol STRING) ROW FORMAT DELIMITED FIELDS TERMINATED BY ',' ;
```

Figure 72 shows the output of executing the preceding command:

```
hive> Create Table IF NOT EXISTS  customerpart (custID int, firstName string, lastName string, age int, profession string) PARTITIONED BY (exchange STRING, symbol STRIN
G) ROW FORMAT DELIMITED FIELDS TERMINATED BY ',' ;
OK
Time taken: 5.609 seconds
hive> ▮
```

Figure 72: Output of the Command to Create a Partition in a Hive Table

2. Run the following command to load data into the partitioner:

```
LOAD DATA INPATH '/tmp/cust_test/cust' INTO TABLE customerpart [PARTITION (exchange = 'US', symbol = 'CA')];
```

Figure 73 shows the execution of the preceding command:

```
hive> LOAD DATA LOCAL INPATH '/home/cloudera/CustomerHive' INTO TABLE customerpart PARTITION (exchange = 'US', symbol = 'CA');
Copying data from file:/home/cloudera/CustomerHive
Copying file: file:/home/cloudera/CustomerHive
Loading data to table hivedb.customerpart partition (exchange=US, symbol=CA)
Partition hivedb.customerpart{exchange=US, symbol=CA} stats: [num_files: 1, num_rows: 0, total_size: 2036, raw_data_size: 0]
Table hivedb.customerpart stats: [num_partitions: 1, num_files: 1, num_rows: 0, total_size: 2036, raw_data_size: 0]
OK
Time taken: 7.206 seconds
hive> ▮
```

Figure 73: Loading Data into a Table

Figure 74 shows the output of creating a partition:

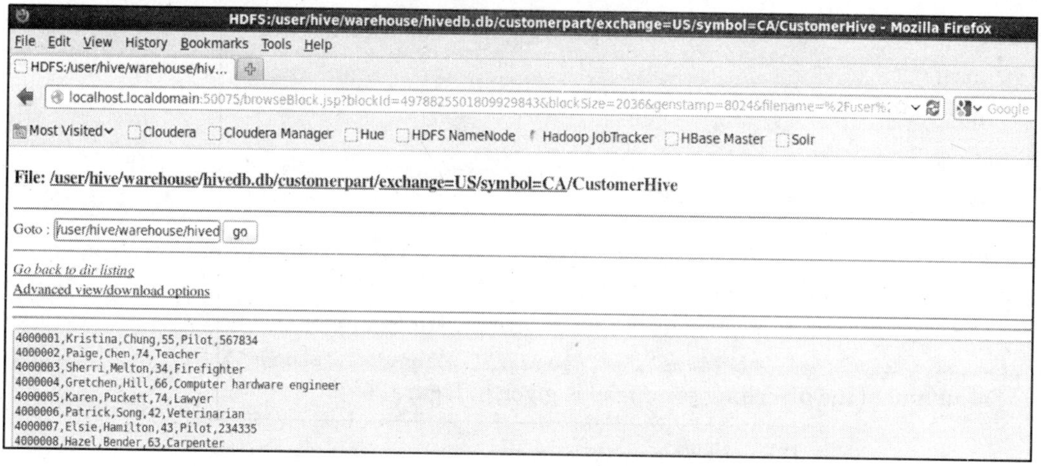

Figure 74: Partitioning the customerpart Table

You can see that in Figure 74, we have a table named 'customerpart' with two partitions named 'exchange' and 'symbol'.

NOTE

The columns that we have created as partition columns are actually folders in the Hive Data warehouse.

Lab 4—To Change the Name of a Table in Hive

Solution—Run the following command to rename a table:

```
ALTER TABLE customerpart RENAME TO customerrename;
```

Figure 75 shows the output of the preceding command:

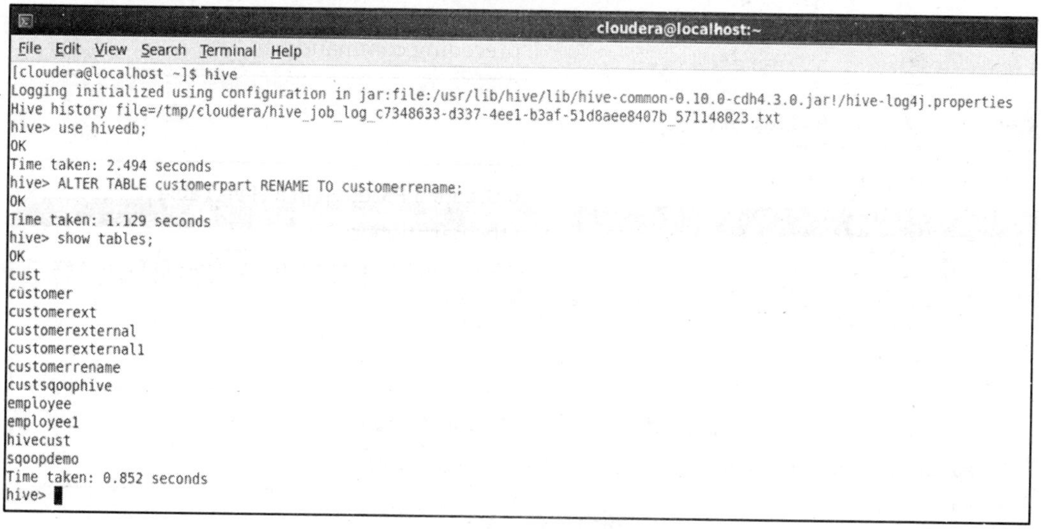

Figure 75: Renaming a Table

Lab 5—To Understand the Role of Different Methods Used in Hive

Solution—Here, you will learn about the following methods used in Hive:

- Concat
- Trim
- Reverse
- Lower
- Upper

Let us discuss each of these methods one by one.

1. **`Concat()` method**—Concatenates the given strings. For example:

```
CONCAT ('Hive','-','performs','-','good','-','in','-','Hadoop');
```

The output of the preceding command is given in Figure 76:

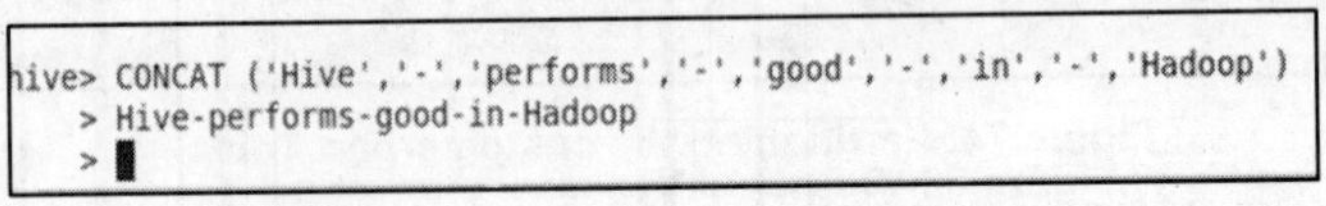

Figure 76: Output of the concat Command

Another form of the `concat` command is as follows:

```
CONCAT_WS ('-','Hive','performs','good','in','Hadoop');
```

Figure 77 shows the output of the preceding command:

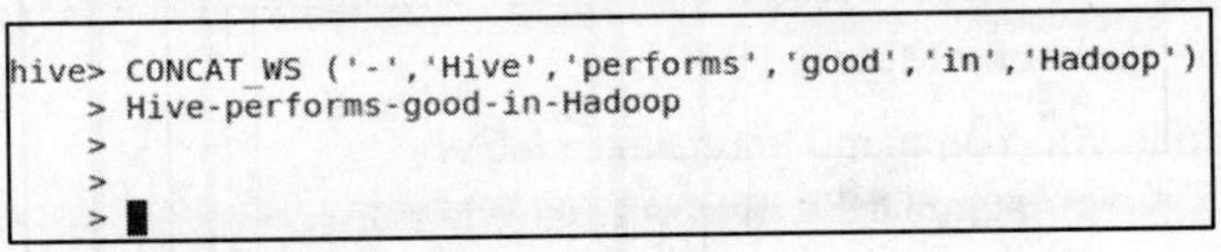

Figure 77: Output of the concat_ws Command

2. **`Trim()` method**—Removes spaces from a string. For example, the following code snippet executes the `trim` command:

```
Hive> TRIM('  Hadoop  ');
Hive> LTRIM('  Hadoop');
Hive> RTRIM('Hadoop  ');
```

Figure 78 shows the output of the `trim` command:

Figure 78: Output of the trim Command

3. **`Reverse()` method**—Reverses the given string. For example:

```
Reverse('Hadoop')
```

Figure 79 shows the output of the `reverse()` method:

```
hive> REVERSE('Hadoop')
    > poodaH
```

Figure 79: Output of the reverse() Method

4. **`Lower()` method**—Changes the given string to lowercase. For example:

```
LOWER('HADOOP');
LCASE('HADOOP');
```

Figure 80 shows the output of the preceding command:

```
hive> LOWER('HADOOP')
    > hadoop
    >
    >
    >
```

Figure 80: Output of the lower Command

5. **`Upper()` method**—Changes the given string to uppercase. For example:

```
UPPER('Hadoop');
UCASE('Hadoop');
```

Figure 81 shows the output of the preceding command:

```
hive> UPPER('Hadoop')
    > HADOOP
    >
```

Figure 81: Output of the upper Command

Labs on HBase

Lab 1—To Access the HBase Shell

Solution—Type the following command to access the HBase shell:

```
Hbase shell
```

Figure 82 shows the output of the preceding command:

```
cloudera@localhost:~
File Edit View Search Terminal Help
[cloudera@localhost ~]$ hbase shell
15/02/05 08:07:38 WARN conf.Configuration: hadoop.native.lib is deprecated. Instead, use io.native.lib.available
HBase Shell; enter 'help<RETURN>' for list of supported commands.
Type "exit<RETURN>" to leave the HBase Shell
Version 0.94.6-cdh4.3.0, rUnknown, Mon May 27 20:22:05 PDT 2013

hbase(main):001:0>
```

Figure 82: Accessing the HBase Shell

Lab 2—To List all the Tables Present in HBase

Solution—Type the following command to list all the tables in HBase:

```
list
```

Figure 83 shows the output of the preceding command:

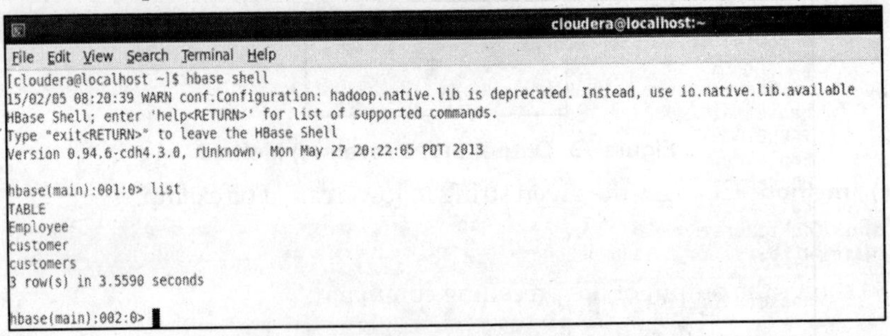

Figure 83: Displaying HBase Tables

Lab 3—To Check whether the HRegionServer and HMaster Services are Running in the System/Cluster

Solution—The following command is used to check whether the services are running or not:

```
sudo jps
```

Figure 84 shows the output of the preceding command:

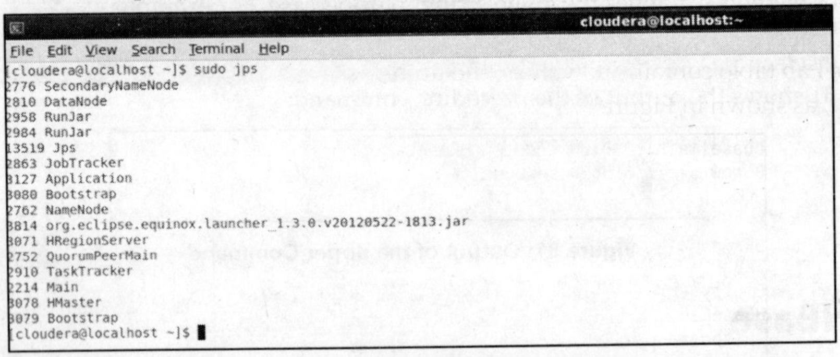

Figure 84: Displaying the Running Services

Lab 4—To Create a Table in the HBase Data Warehouse

Solution—The command to create a table in HBase is as follows:

```
create 'HBaseLab','Personal'
```

Figure 85 shows the output of executing the preceding command:

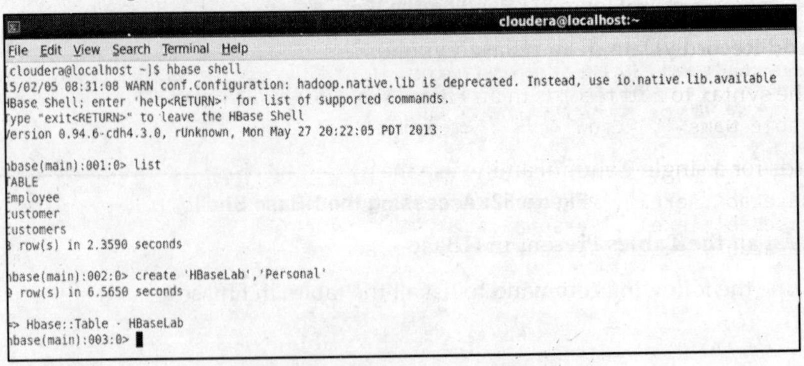

Figure 85: Creating a Table in HBase

You can verify whether the table is created or not by using the `list` command, as shown in Figure 86:

```
hbase(main):002:0> create 'HBaseLab','Personal'
0 row(s) in 6.5650 seconds

=> Hbase::Table - HBaseLab
hbase(main):003:0> list
TABLE
Employee
HBaseLab
customer
customers
4 row(s) in 0.1460 seconds

hbase(main):004:0> ▌
```

Figure 86: Displaying the HBaseLab Table in the List of Tables

Lab 5—To Get Values from a Table

Solution—The syntax to retrieve values from a table is as follows:

```
Scan <table name>
```

The preceding command is run as follows to display the values of the HBaseLab table:

```
scan HBaseLab
```

As the HBaseLab table contains no values, the uninitialized constant HBaseLab message is displayed in the output, as shown in Figure 87:

```
hbase(main):002:0> create 'HBaseLab','Personal'
0 row(s) in 6.5650 seconds

=> Hbase::Table - HBaseLab
hbase(main):003:0> list
TABLE
Employee
HBaseLab
customer
customers
4 row(s) in 0.1460 seconds

hbase(main):004:0> scan HBaseLab
NameError: uninitialized constant HBaseLab

hbase(main):005:0> ▌
```

Figure 87: Reading the Values from a Table

Lab 6—To Add Records/Data in an HBase Table for a Single ColumnFamily

Solution—The syntax to add records in an HBase table is as follows:

```
put '<Table Name>','<Crow Key>','<Columns Family_1 : Column Name_1>', '<Value>'
```

To add records for a single ColumnFamily, use the preceding command in the following manner:

```
put 'HBaseLab','exe1','Personal:Name','Angelina'
put 'HBaseLab','exe1','Personal:Age','40'
put 'HBaseLab','exe1','Personal:Password',' BradPit'
```

Figure 88 shows the output of the preceding set of commands:

```
cloudera@localhost:~
File  Edit  View  Search  Terminal  Help
[cloudera@localhost ~]$ hbase shell
15/02/05 09:21:37 WARN conf.Configuration: hadoop.native.lib is deprecated. Instead, use io.native.lib.available
HBase Shell; enter 'help<RETURN>' for list of supported commands.
Type "exit<RETURN>" to leave the HBase Shell
Version 0.94.6-cdh4.3.0, rUnknown, Mon May 27 20:22:05 PDT 2013

hbase(main):001:0> list
TABLE
Employee
HBaseLab
customer
customers
4 row(s) in 3.7540 seconds

hbase(main):002:0> put 'HBaseLab','exe1','Personal:Name','Angelina'
0 row(s) in 0.9150 seconds

hbase(main):003:0> put 'HBaseLab','exe1','Personal:Age','40'
0 row(s) in 0.1170 seconds

hbase(main):004:0> put 'HBaseLab','exe1','Personal:Password',' BradPit'
0 row(s) in 0.0130 seconds

hbase(main):005:0>
```

Figure 88: Adding Records for a ColumnFamily of an HBase Table

Lab 7—To Fetch Records from the HBaseLab Table

Solution—The `get` command is used as follows to retrieve records from a table:

```
get '<Table_Name>','<Roy_Key>'
```

The command to retrieve records of the HBaseLab table is as follows:

```
get 'HBaseLab','exe1'
```

Figure 89 shows the output of the preceding command:

```
hbase(main):006:0> get 'HBaseLab','exe1'
COLUMN                    CELL
 Personal:Age             timestamp=1423157106026, value=40
 Personal:Name            timestamp=1423157048158, value=Angelina
 Personal:Password        timestamp=1423157142012, value= BradPit
3 row(s) in 0.1230 seconds

hbase(main):007:0>
```

Figure 89: Extracting Records from an HBase Table

Lab 8—To Update the Data in a Table

Solution—The syntax of the command used for updating the data in a table is as follows:

```
put '<Table Name>','<Crow Key>','<Columns Family_1 : Column Name_1>', '<Value_1>'
```

Enter the following commands to update the data in the HBaseLab table:

```
put 'HBaseLab','exe1','Personal:Name','Katrina'
put 'HBaseLab','exe1','Personal:Age','27'
put 'HBaseLab','exe1','Personal:Password','Cool'
```

The output of the preceding commands is shown in Figure 90:

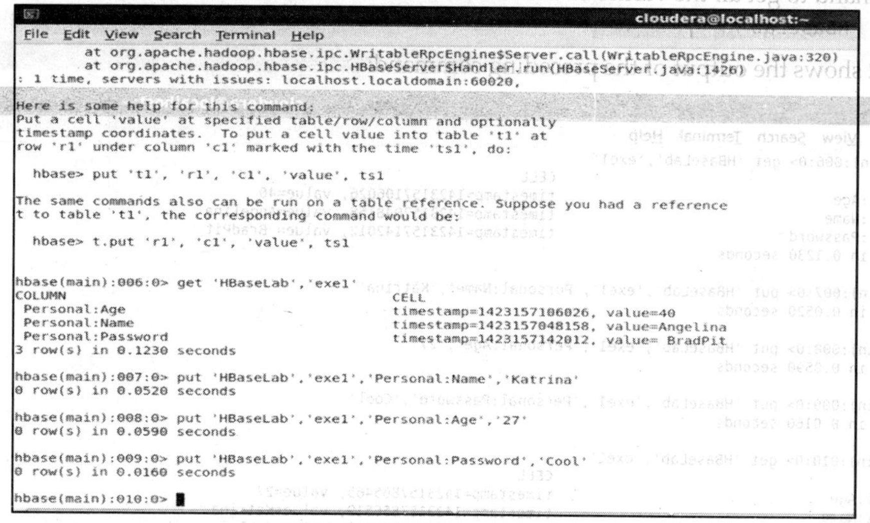

Figure 90: Updating Records in an HBase Table

The highlighted portions in Figure 91 reflect the changes in the values of the HBaseLab table against the 'exe1' row key:

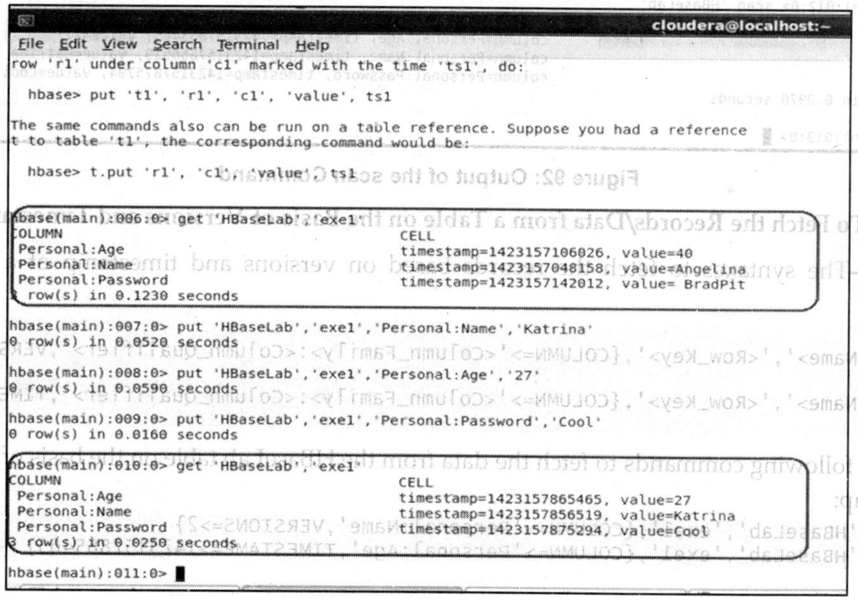

Figure 91: Changing Specific Values in an HBase Table

Lab 9—To get all the Values from a Table

Solution—The `scan` command is used as follows to get all the values of an HBase table:

```
scan <Table Name>
```

The command to get all the values of the HBaseLab table is as follows:

```
scan 'HBaseLab'
```

Figure 92 shows the output of the preceding command:

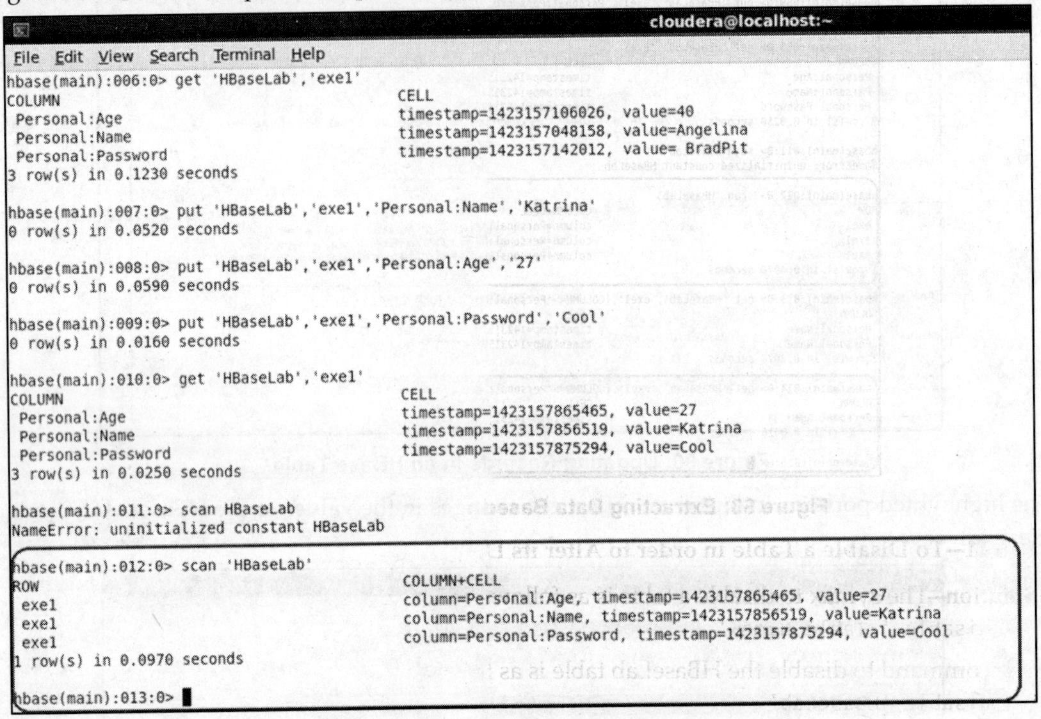

Figure 92: Output of the scan Command

Lab 10—To Fetch the Records/Data from a Table on the Basis of Versions and Timestamp

Solution—The syntaxes to fetch the records based on versions and timestamp of a table are as follows:

```
get
'<Table_Name>','<Row_Key>',{COLUMN=>'<Column_Family>:<Column_Qualifier>',VERSIONS=>2}
get
'<Table_Name>','<Row_Key>',{COLUMN=>'<Column_Family>:<Column_Qualifier>',TIMESTAMP=>2123
}
```

Type the following commands to fetch the data from the HBaseLab table on the basis of versions and timestamp:

```
get 'HBaseLab','exe1',{COLUMN=>'Personal:Name',VERSIONS=>2}
get 'HBaseLab','exe1',{COLUMN=>'Personal:Age',TIMESTAMP=>1423157865465}
```

Figure 93 shows the output of the preceding commands:

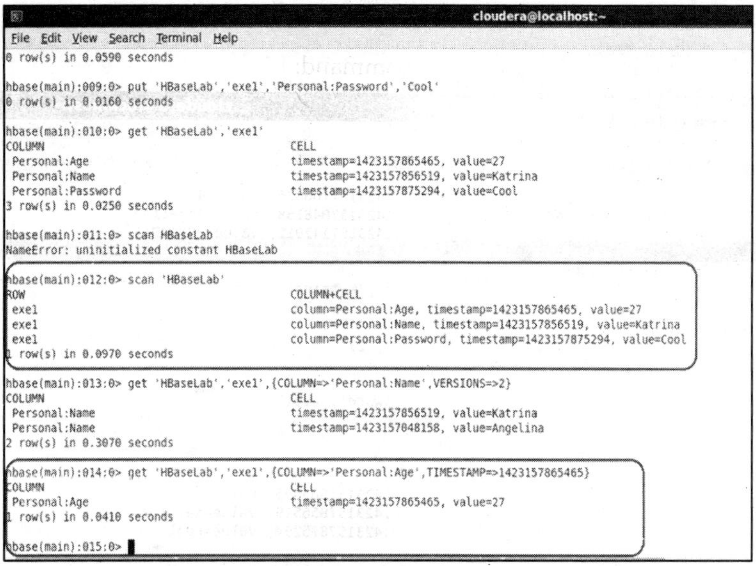

Figure 93: Extracting Data Based on Timestamp and Versions

Lab 11—To Disable a Table in order to Alter its Data

Solution—The syntax to disable a table is as follows:

```
disable '<Table_Name>'
```

The command to disable the HBaseLab table is as follows:

```
disable 'HBaseLab'
```

Figure 94 shows the output of the `disable` command:

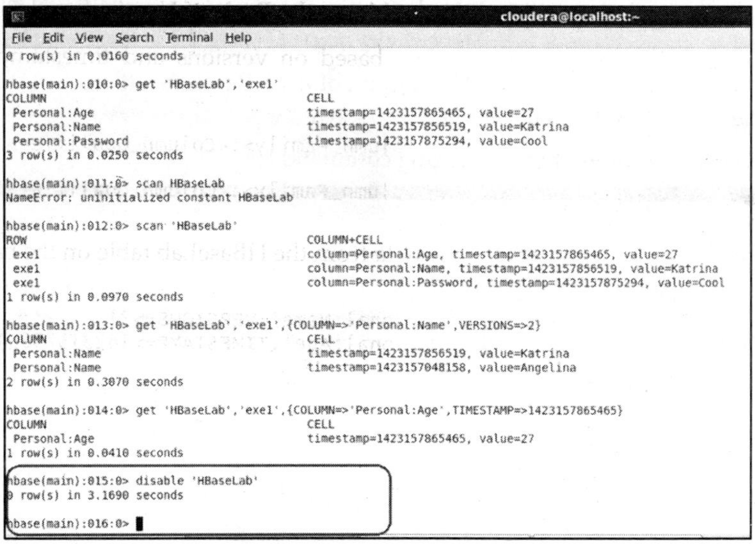

Figure 94: Disabling an HBase Table

The `is_enabled` command is used to check whether the HBase table is really disabled. The syntax of this command is as follows:

```
is_enabled '<Table_Name>'
```

The following command is to verify whether or not the HBaseLab table is enabled:

```
is_enabled 'HBaseLab'
```

Once the HBaseLab table is disabled, we can start the HBase table alteration process.

Figure 95 shows the output of the `is_enabled` command:

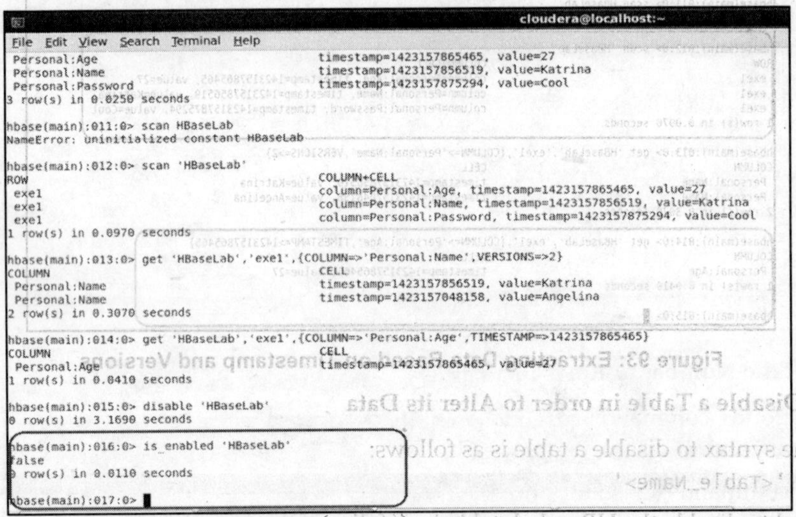

Figure 95: Output of the is_enabled Command

Lab 12—To Alter HBase Table by Adding a Column Qualifier

Solution—The syntax to alter an HBase table by adding a new column qualifier is as follows:

```
alter '<Table_Name>',{NAME=>'<New_Column_Qualifier>'}
```

The following command is used to alter the column of the HBaseLab table:

```
alter 'HBaseLab',{NAME=>'Address'}
```

Figure 96 shows the execution of the preceding command:

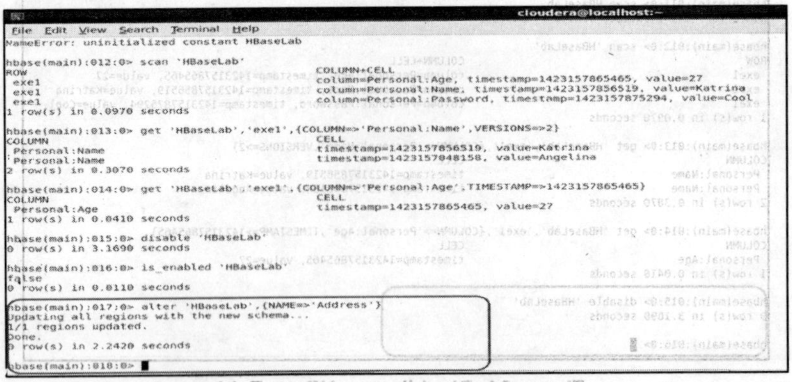

Figure 96: Execution of the alter Command

Once table alteration is done, you need to enable the HBase table again so as to execute the queries, as shown in Figure 97:

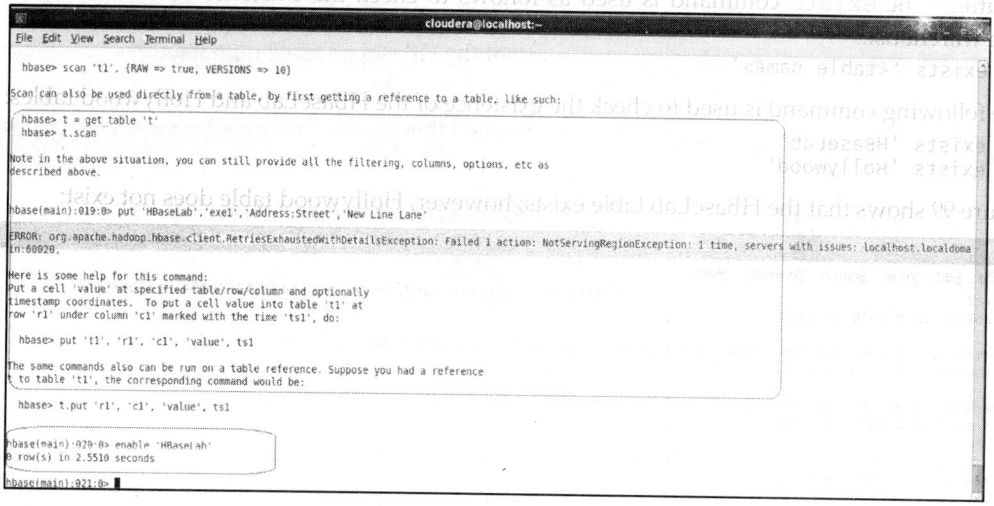

Figure 97: Re-enabling an HBase Table

Lab 13—Count the Number of Rows in a Table

Solution—The `count` command is used to count the number of rows in an HBase table, as follows:

```
count '<table name>'
```

The following command is used to count the rows of the HBaseLab table:

```
count 'HBaseLab'
```

Figure 98 shows the output of the preceding command:

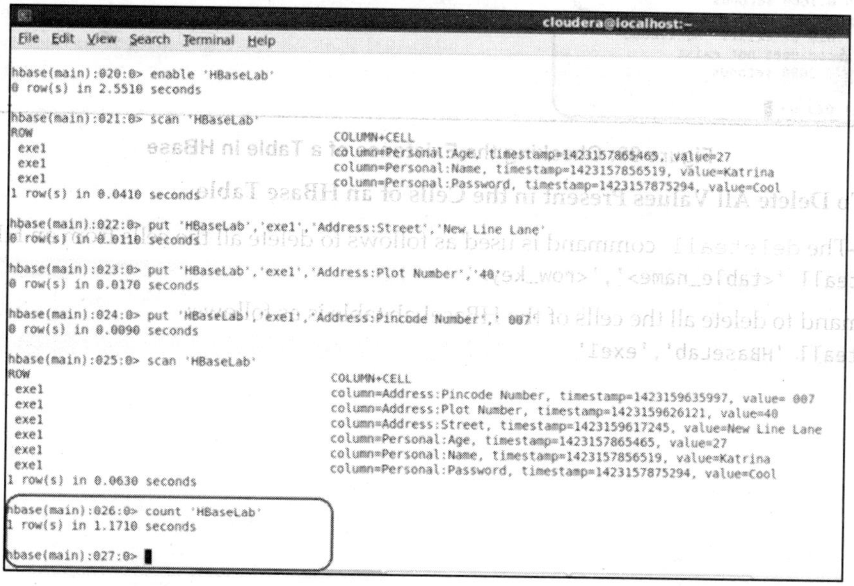

Figure 98: Counting Number of Rows in an HBase Table

Lab 14—To Check the Existence of the HBase Table in HBase Data Warehouse

Solution—The `exists` command is used as follows to check the existence of a table in the HBase data warehouse:

```
exists '<table name>'
```

The following command is used to check the existence of the HBaseLab and Hollywood tables:

```
exists 'HBaseLab'
exists 'Hollywood'
```

Figure 99 shows that the HBaseLab table exists; however, Hollywood table does not exist:

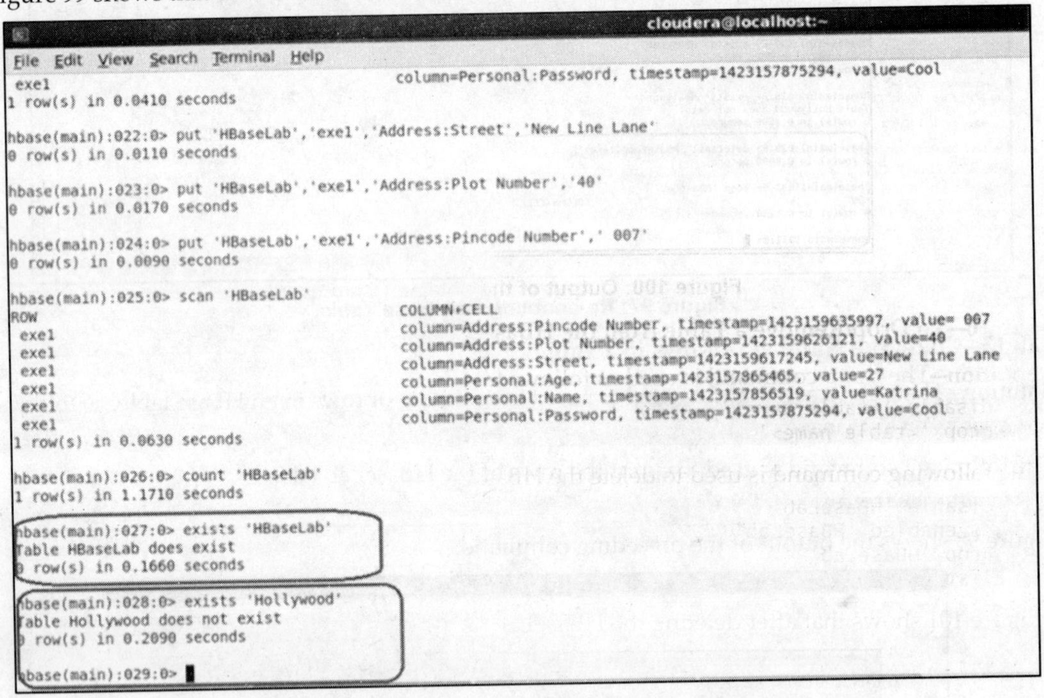

Figure 99: Checking the Existence of a Table in HBase

Lab 15—To Delete All Values Present in the Cells of an HBase Table

Solution—The `deleteall` command is used as follows to delete all the cells from an HBase table:

```
deleteall '<table_name>','<row_key>'
```

The command to delete all the cells of the HBaseLab table is as follows:

```
deleteall 'HBaseLab','exel'
```

Figure 100 shows the output of the `deleteall` command:

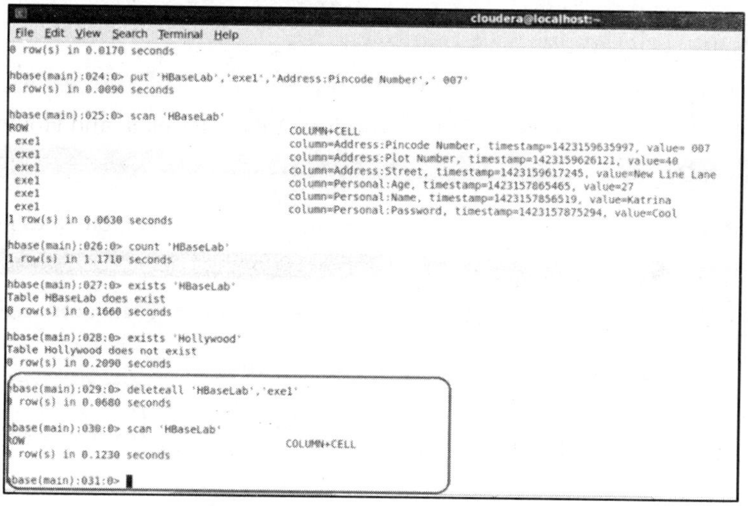

Figure 100: Output of the deleteall Command

Lab 16—To Drop/Remove a Table from the HBase Data Warehouse

Solution—The `drop` command is used as follows to remove an HBase table:

```
disable '<table name>'
drop '<table name>'
```

The following command is used to delete the HBaseLab table:

```
disable 'HBaseLab'
is_enabled 'HBaseLab'
drop 'HBaseLab'
list
```

Figure 101 shows that after deleting the HBaseLab table, it does not appear in the data warehouse:

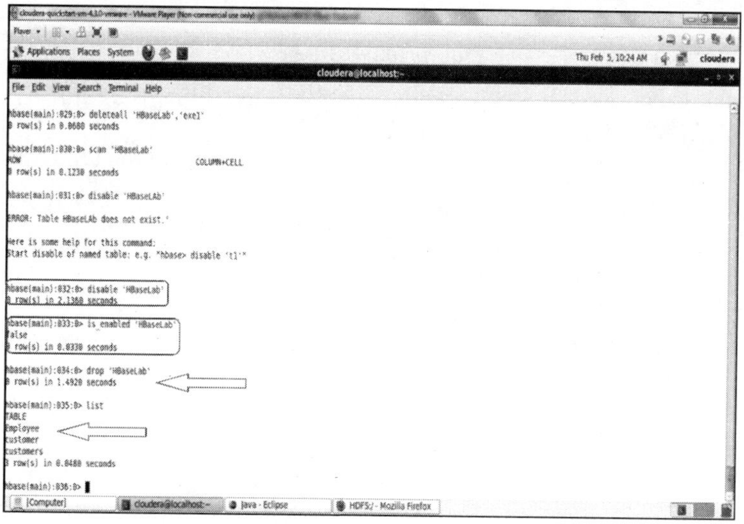

Figure 101: Deleting a Specific HBase Table

Labs on R

Lab 1—To Print the "hello world" with Your Name

Solution—Perform the following steps to print the "hello world" with your name:

1. Run the RStudio and open its workspace. Figure 102 shows you the outlook of the RStudio:

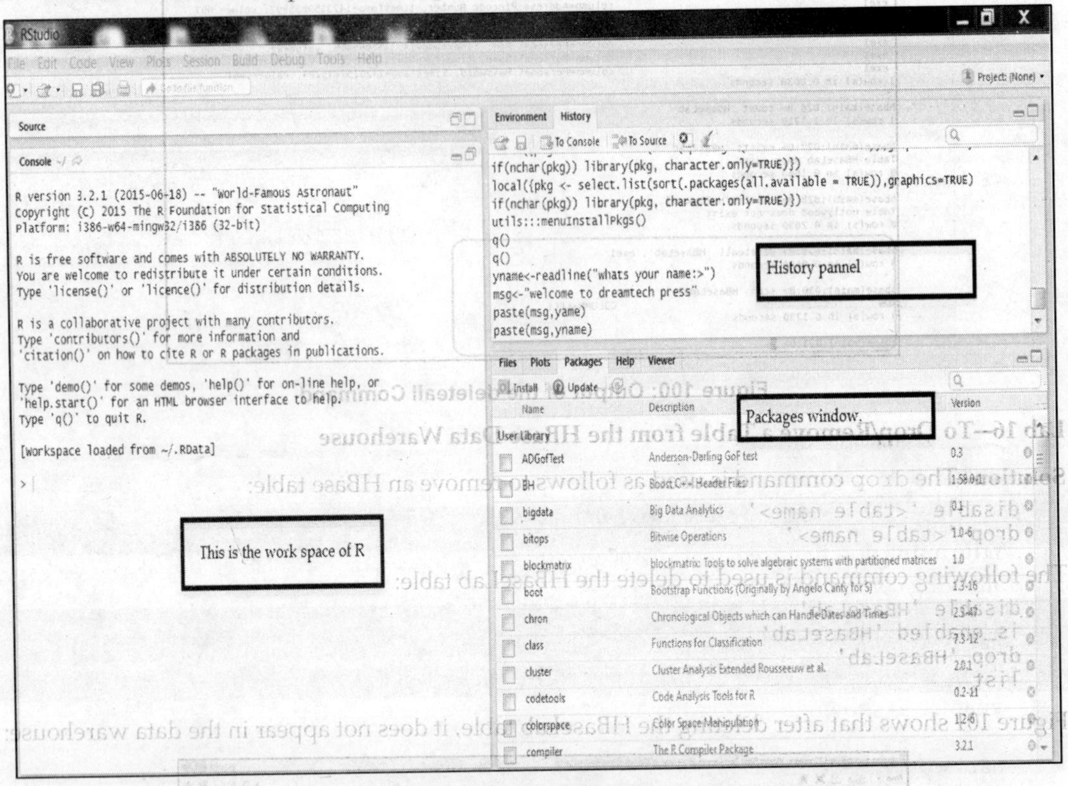

Figure 102: RStudio

2. Create a variable to hold the statement, as shown in the following code snippet:

```
Msg<-"Hello World welcome to RStudio"
>msg
[1] Hello World welcome to RStudio
```

Figure 103 shows the output of the preceding code on RStudio:

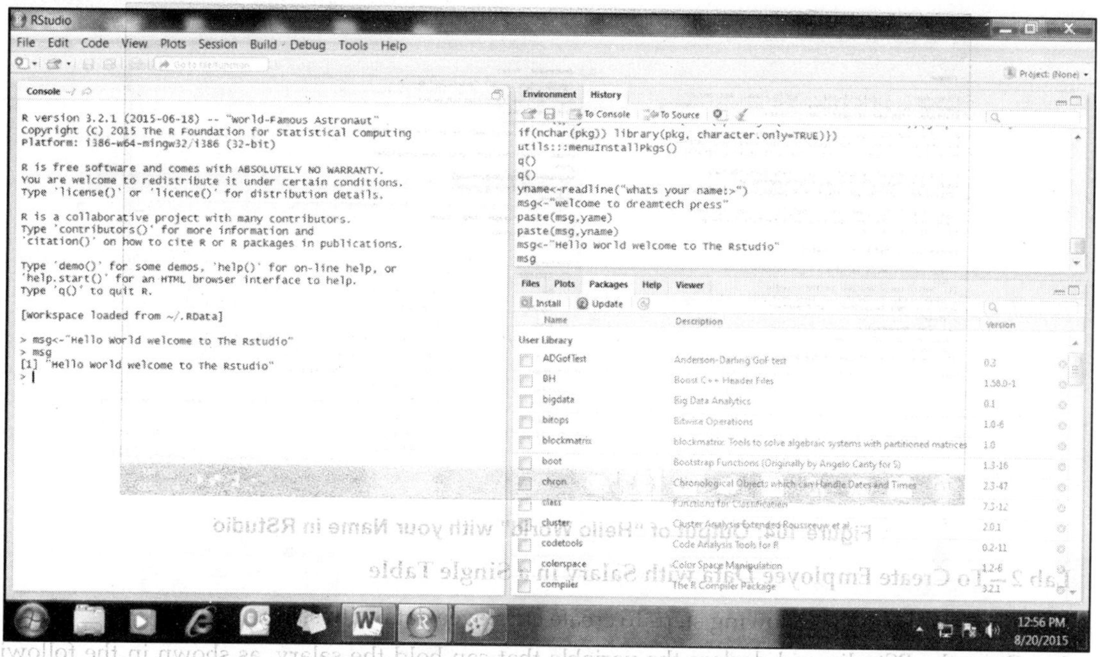

Figure 103: Output of the Created Variable

3. Write a function that asks your name on run time and again it stores it in a variable by using the following command:

```
> yname<-readline("what's your name Developer: ")
What's your name Developer: Iam Dreamtech
```

4. Check whether the preceding command is executed properly or not. For this, you need to call "yname" as shown in the following command:

```
> yname<-readline("what's your name Developer: ")
What's your name Developer: Iam Dreamtech
> yname
[1] "Iam Dreamtech"
>
```

5. Merge your "msg" message with the "yname" so that it prints the message with your name, as shown below:

```
msgname<-paste(msg,yname)
```

6. Call the "msgname" to get the msg with your name, as given in the following code snippet:

```
msg<-"Hello World welcome to The Rstudio"
> msg
[1] "Hello World welcome to The Rstudio"
> yname<-readline("what's your name Developer: ")
What's your name Developer: Iam Dreamtech
> yname
[1] "Iam Dreamtech"
> msgname<-paste(msg,yname)
> msgname
[1] "Hello World welcome to The Rstudio Iam Dreamtech"

>
```

Figure 104 shows the onscreen output of the preceding code:

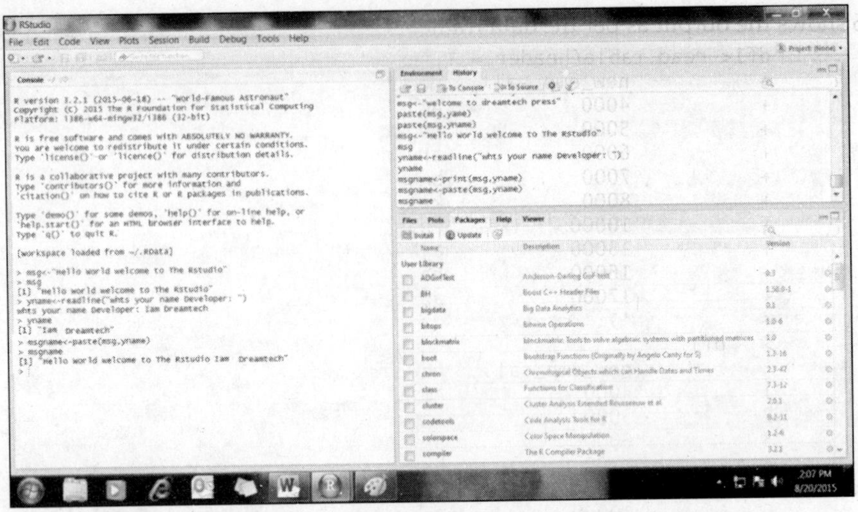

Figure 104: Output of "Hello World" with your Name in RStudio

Lab 2—To Create Employee Data with Salary in a Single Table

Solution—Perform the following steps to create employee data with salary:

1. Open the RStudio and declare the variable that can hold the salary, as shown in the following code snippet:

```
emp_sal=c("4000," "5000," "6000," "7000," "8000")
```

2. Similarly, create another variable for the name, as given below:

```
emp_name=c("Amit","ragav","arvind","baby","Kalu")
```

3. Enter a few other emp names, as given in the following code snippet:

```
new_emp_name=c(emp_name,"rajeev","ajay","hafin","aphimchi")
```

4. Next, salary of the new employee should be included, as mentioned below:

```
new_emp_sal=c(emp_sal,10000,15000,16000,17000)
```

5. Check the output of new_emp_sal and new_emp_name, as shown below:

```
new_emp_name
[1] "Amit"     "ragav"    "arvind"    "baby"     "Kalu"     "rajeev"
[7] "ajay"     "hafin"    "aphimchi"
> new_emp_sal
[1] "4000"  "5000"  "6000"  "7000"  "8000"  "10000" "15000" "16000"
[9] "17000"
```

6. Now, sum up the salary with the employees name.

   There are two methods to sum up the records: Combine method and Data frame method.

   Figure 105 shows the output as per the combine method:

```
combine=c(new_emp_sal,new_emp_name)
> combine
 [1] "4000"    "5000"    "6000"    "7000"    "8000"    "100
 00"
 [7] "15000"   "16000"   "17000"   "Amit"    "ragav"   "arv
 ind"
[13] "baby"    "Kalu"    "rajeev"  "ajay"    "hafin"   "aph
 imchi"
```

Figure 105: The Output of the Combine Method

Figure 106 shows the output as per the data frame method:

```
df1<-read.table(header = T,text='
+            new_emp_sal     new_emp_name
+            4000            Amit
+            5000            ragav
+            6000            arvind
+            7000            baby
+            8000            kalu
+            10000           rajeev
+            15000           ajay
+            16000           hafin
+            17000           aphichi
+            ')
>   df1
             new_emp_sal     new_emp_name
1            4000            Amit
2            5000            ragav
3            6000            arvind
4            7000            baby
5            8000            kalu
6            10000           rajeev
7            15000           ajay
8            16000           hafin
9            17000           aphichi
>
```

Figure 106: The Output of the Data Frame Method

Figure 107 shows the final output on the RStudio:

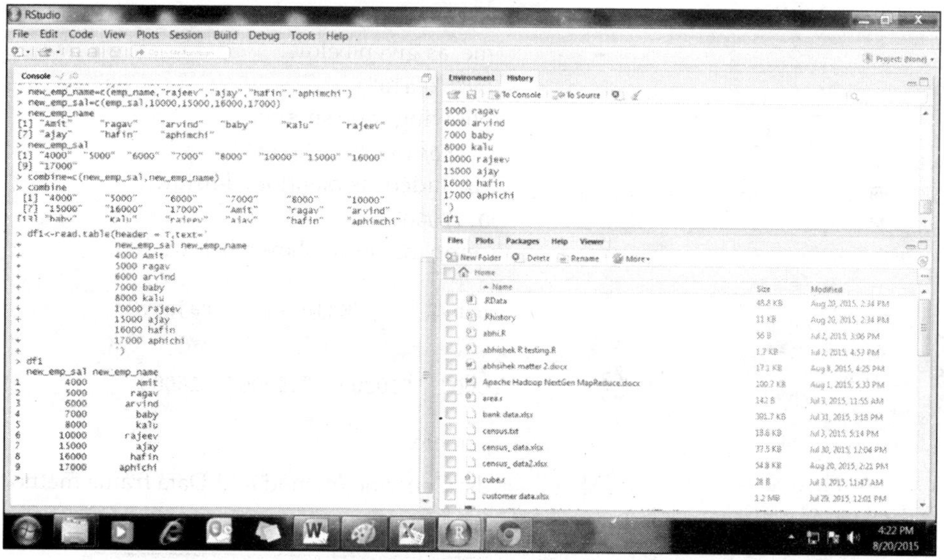

Figure 107: Output of Employee Data with Salary in a Single Table

Lab 3—To Merge Two Data Frames

Solution—Perform the following steps to merge two data frames:

1. Make a data frame and enter the details of students by using the following command:

```
df1<-read.table(header=T, text = '
+ roll name clas
```

```
+ 1 aryan 5
+ 2 aastha 5
+ 3 anita 5
+ 4 raj 5
+ 5 golu 5
+ 6 john 5
+ 7 tinu 5
+ ')
>data1<-df1
>
```

2. Create another data frame with subjects, roll no. and marks, as shown in the following command:

```
data2<-read.table(header = T,text='
+ roll subject marks_subject
+ 1 english 98
+ 2 maths 87
+ 3 hindi 76
+ 4 science 97
+ 5 science 78
+ 6 maths 90
+ 7 english 80
+ ')
```

3. Check the data frame 1 whether it gets the data in the correct form or not, by using the following code snippet:

```
>data1
  roll   name clas
1    1  aryan    5
2    2 aastha    5
3    3  anita    5
4    4    raj    5
5    5   golu    5
6    6   john    5
7    7   tinu    5
>
```

4. Check the data frame 2 by using the following code:

```
>data2
  roll subject marks_subject
1    1 english            98
2    2   maths            87
3    3   hindi            76
4    4 science            97
5    5 science            78
6    6   maths            90
7    7 english            80
```

5. Merge these two data frames in accordance with the "roll", as shown below:

```
>merge(data1,data2,"roll")
  roll   name clas subject marks_subject
1    1  aryan    5 english            98
2    2 aastha    5   maths            87
3    3  anita    5   hindi            76
4    4    raj    5 science            97
5    5   golu    5 science            78
6    6   john    5   maths            90
7    7   tinu    5 english            80
>
```

Figure 108 shows the output of the preceding commands:

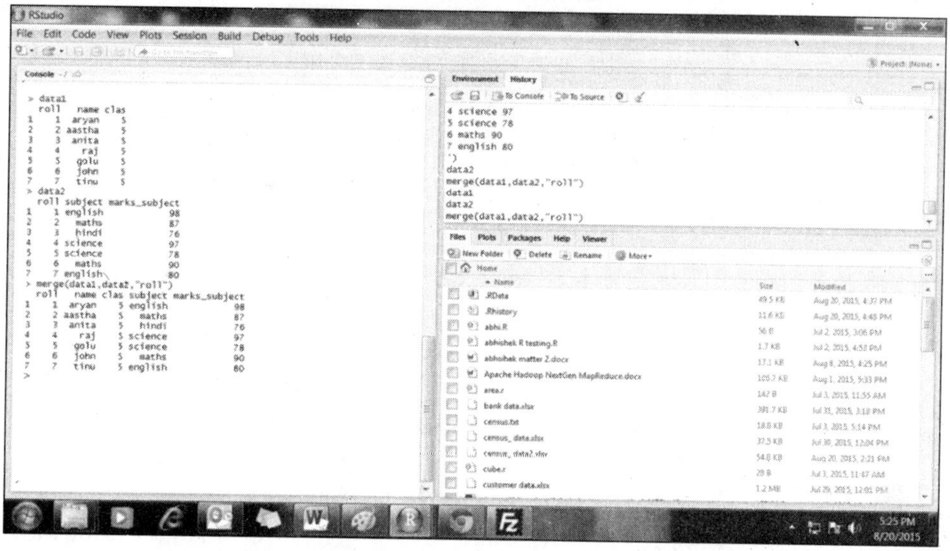

Figure 108: The Merging of Two Data Frames

Lab 4—To Define a Function in a Script, Source it to the RStudio and Print the Multiples of a Number

Solution—Perform the following steps to print the table (multiples) of the number:

1. Open the RStudio and on the top-left in Window, you get a script area where you enter the function declaration by using the following command:

```
mytable<-function(x){
}
```

2. Write the code in between the parenthesis, as shown below:

```
a<- c(1, 2, 3, 4, 5, 6, 7, 8, 9, 10, 11, 12, 13, 14, 15, 16, 18, 19, 20)
```

3. Insert the following logic so that the code will be effective on use:

```
a<- c(1, 2, 3, 4, 5, 6, 7, 8, 9, 10, 11, 12, 13,14, 15, 16, 18, 19, 20)
num_table<-round(a* x)
result<-paste(num_table,sep = "")
print("table of number:")
print(result)
```

4. Now, save the script and source it in the console panel so that we call and print the table in the console area. Use the following commands for reference:

```
> source('~/tablefun_.R')
> mytable(15)
[1] "table of number:"
 [1] "15"  "30"  "45"  "60"  "75"  "90"  "105" "120" "135" "150" "165"
[12] "180" "195" "210" "225" "240" "270" "285" "300"
```

In between the argument braces, we enter the number; for example "15". On pressing Enter key, it will give the table of 15. Figure 109 shows you the output of the preceding commands:

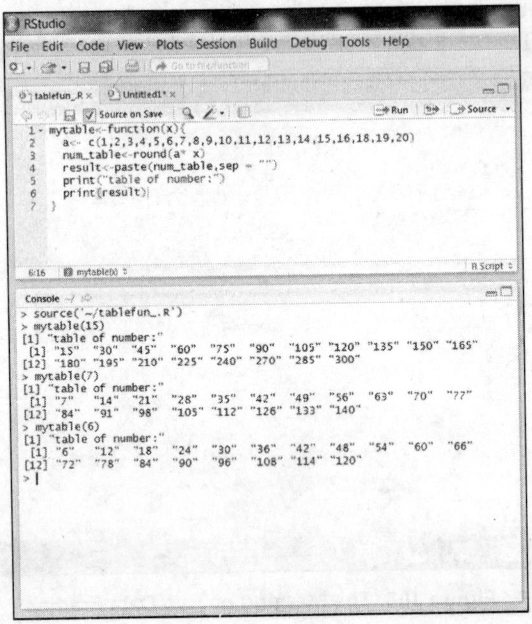

Figure 109: Output of External Script in RStudio

Labs on Tableau

Lab 1—To Load and Display the Dataset on Tableau

Solution— Perform the following steps to load and display the dataset on Tableau:

1. Load the data in Tableau by selecting the file format. Open the Tableau and click the file formats such as xls, csv, txt, etc. Figure 110 shows the dataset in Tableau:

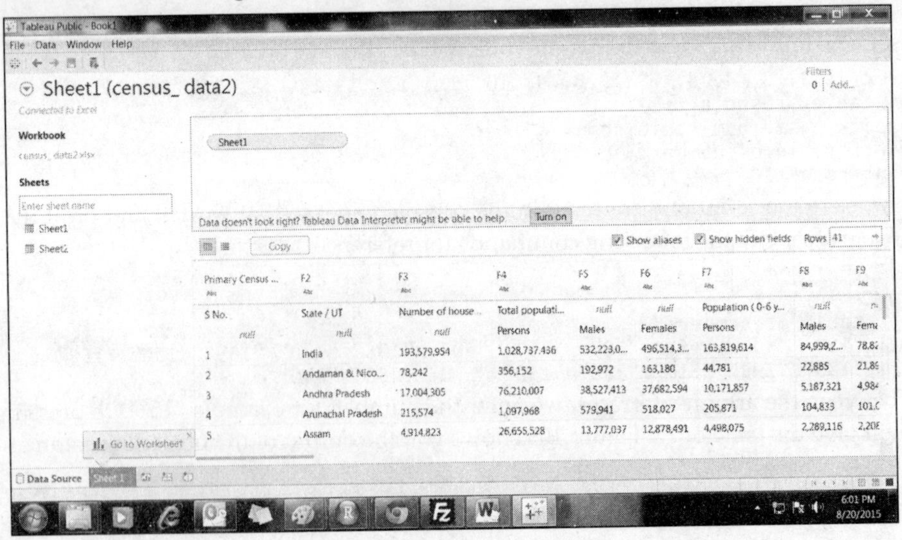

Figure 110: Dataset in Tableau

2. Analyze the data that you have loaded in Tableau. For analyzing the data, you need to go to the worksheet of the Tableau. Figure111 shows the worksheet of Tableau:

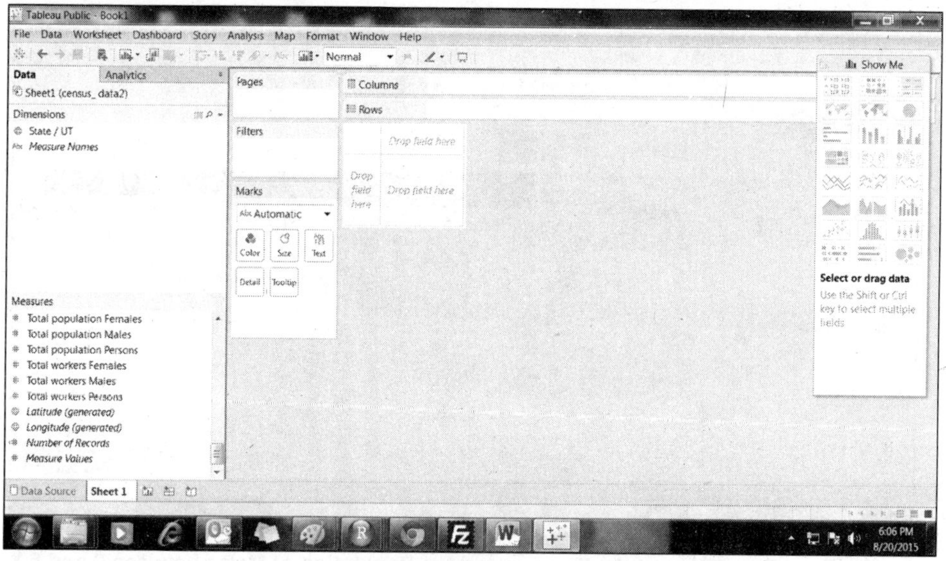

Figure 111: Worksheet of Tableau

3. In the left side of Figure 111, there are two divisions – measures and dimensions – used for data analytics. Now, take any measure in row as well as dimension in column to analyze. Figure 112 shows the measures and the dimensions in the worksheet of Tableau:

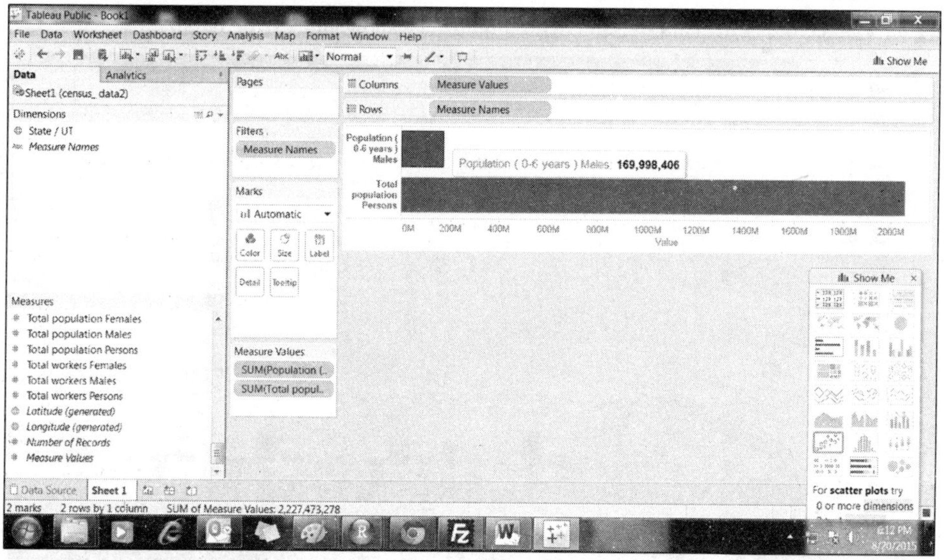

Figure 112: Measures and Dimensions in the Worksheet of Tableau

Figure 113 shows the total population of the persons and the population of males between 0 and 6 years:

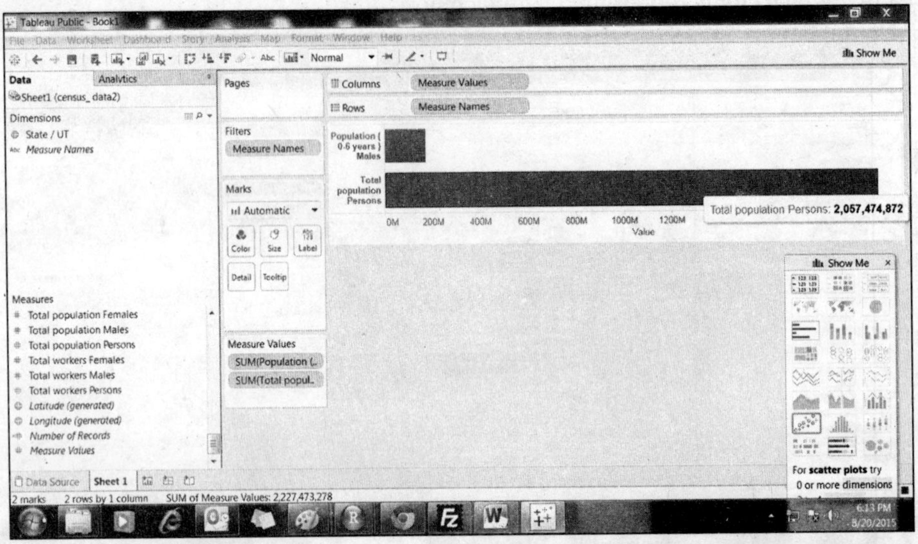

Figure 113: Total Population of the Persons and the Population of Males between 0 and 6 Years

Lab 2— To Plot a Graph to show the Data in Histogram

Solution—For this, we need to perform the following steps:

1. Load the data and get the measures.
2. We have taken the crime data of San Diego. Figure 114 shows the crime data:

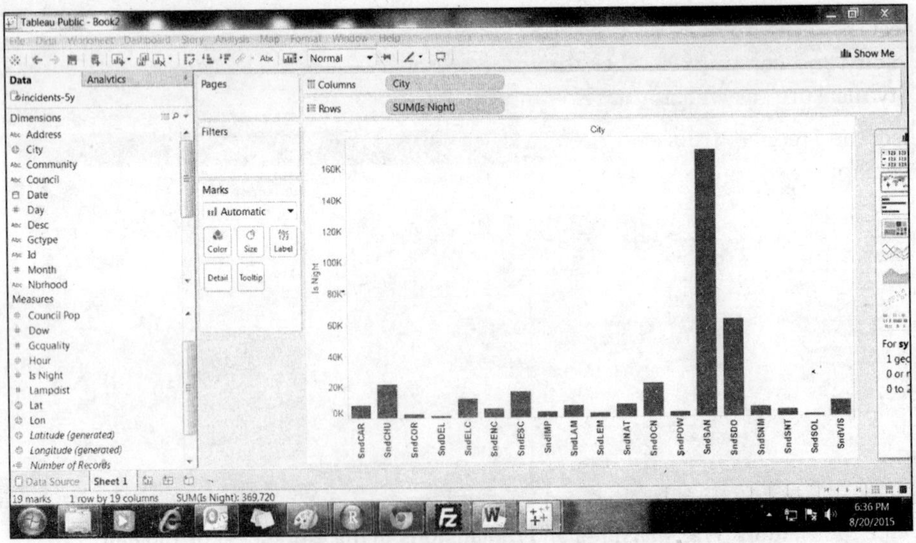

Figure 114: Crime Data of San Diego

In Figure 114, the horizontal axis shows the cities and the vertical axis shows the count of the crime.

3. Now, click to the mark plane and click on "show marks".
4. Analyze the data on horizontal bars and labels in the vertical axis. This analysis gives you an idea that which city is represented by which horizontal bar. Figure 115 shows the labels with the horizontal bars:

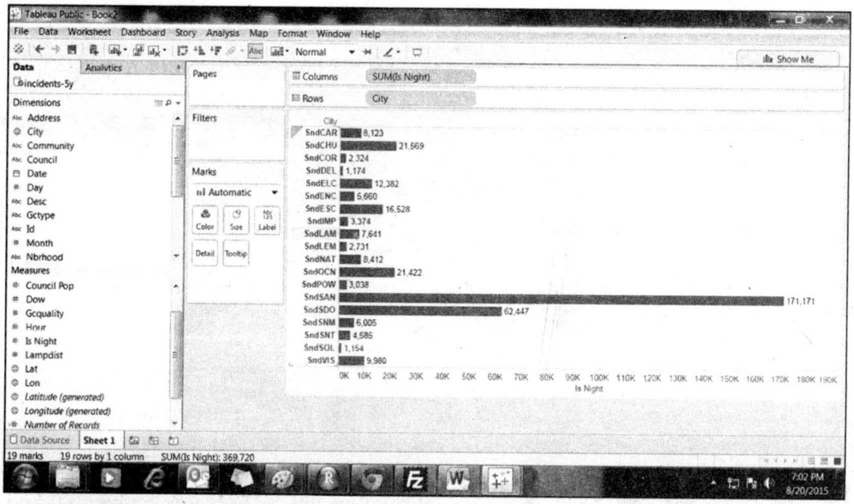

Figure 115: Labels and Associated Horizontal Bars of Histogram

Lab 3—To Show Data in Treemap

Solution—Treemap is the graphical representation of a dataset in rectangular boxes. These boxes are somehow associated with each other. Now, perform the following steps to show data in Treemap:

1. Load the data in Tableau.
2. Select the measure that has to be analyzed. In this, we have selected the "sum of crimes in night" in a city and community. Then, drag the measure "sum of crimes in night" in the column and "City measure" as well as the "Community measure" in the row bar.
3. Select the Treemap from the "Show Me" panel. Figure 116 shows the "Show Me", indicating the Treemap:

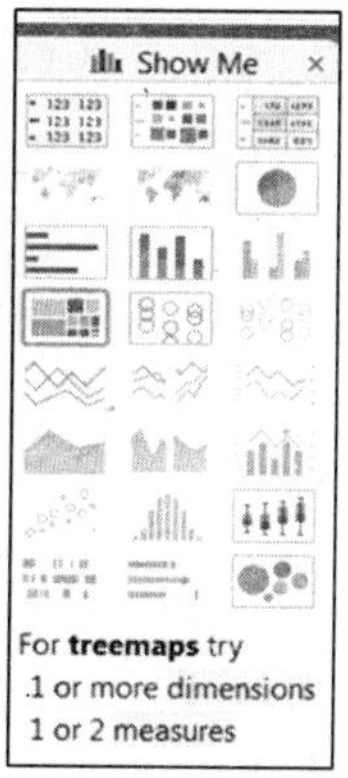

Figure 116: Show Me Panel

4. Once you select the Treemap, it automatically shows the Treemap structure in the worksheet. Figure 117 shows the Treemap regarding the crime in the city and community:

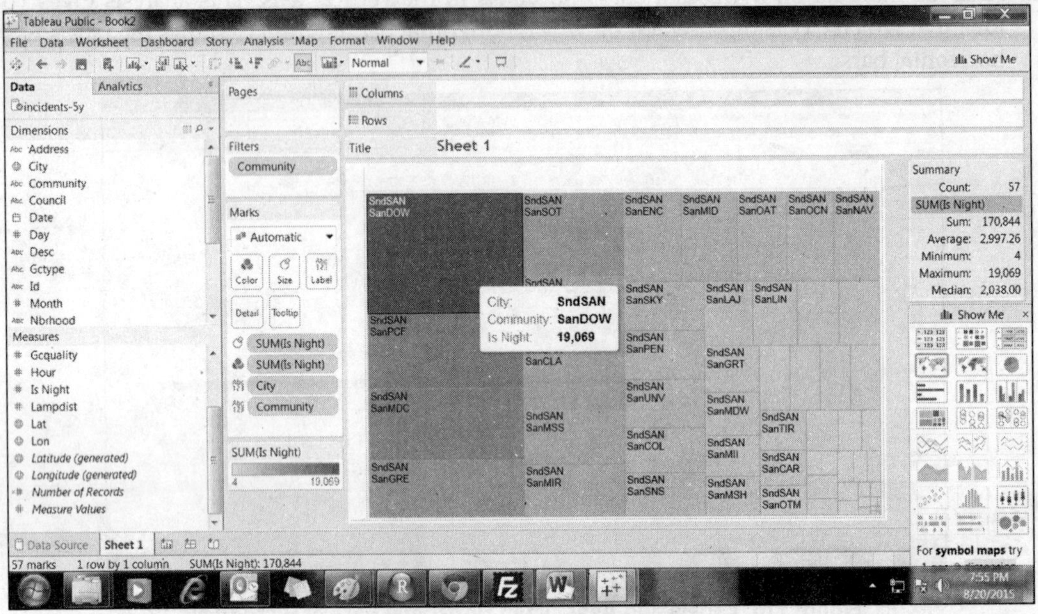

Figure 117: Treemap in Tableau

A

Cassandra

All of us are aware how Facebook changed the meaning of social media networking, but most of us don't know that it has brought a huge revolution in the Information Technology (IT) industry as well.

Have you ever thought of how Facebook handles the huge amount of data that millions and trillions of people share on it continuously round the clock? Probably, you did not. Well, the answer lies in the power of Apache Cassandra, which is an open source distributed database system based on the NoSQL database technology. It was first developed by Facebook to handle large amounts of data and to increase the throughput and response time of the website. It became a part of the incubator project for Apache in 2008. Over time, Cassandra gained popularity and acceptance due to its reliability, performance, and efficiency. Now, it has become a hugely popular and in-demand technology that is being used in almost every known platform.

Key Features of Apache Cassandra

Some key features of the Cassandra database system are as follows:

- **Peer-to-peer communication**—Contains no single point of failure (as there is no traditional master/slave architecture), and therefore allows continuous availability of business-critical applications that cannot afford to go down.
- **Ease of scalability**—Improves the response time with linear scalability. This means that the throughput of the system increases with the inclusion of additional nodes. For example, adding one more node to the system improves its throughput as much as the strength of the added node. You can easily add new machines to the database system without any system downtime or interruption to applications.
- **Flexible data storage**—Accommodates the full range of data formats including structured, semi-structured, and unstructured data.
- **Simple data distribution**—Maintains consistency in read/write operations and automatically synchronizes the data across clusters. You can perform data replication operations across multiple environments that may also involve mixed cloud environment or on-premise cloud systems.

- **Ease of operation**—Allows operational ease as all nodes in a cluster are identical, and there is no complex configuration to manage. Decreasing/increasing node count happens seamlessly throughout the cluster.
- **Column oriented**—Stores data in sparse, multidimensional hash tables. Cassandra does not maintain any relationships between data elements as in RDMS.
- **Contextual Query Language (CQL)**—Follows CQL, which uses an SQL-like syntax, wherein data modelling is simplified.

Structure of Cassandra Database System

Cassandra provides the distributed database structure, which means that the entire data is spread across multiple database servers at the same time. An important feature of Cassandra database system is that it does not have a single point of failure. If we take a look at the traditional client-server approach that follows the master-slave structure, the failure of master causes a collapse and shutdown of the entire system, causing all the slaves to stop responding. However, this basic architecture in Cassandra has been improved by encouraging peer-to-peer communication.

Cassandra handles database operations through a number of nodes. A node in Cassandra refers to an instance of the Cassandra database. Each node in a Cassandra database system contains some data. Now if one node in the database system fails, the entire system will not go down because all the tasks assigned to the non-responding node would be shifted to some other node, which has the same structure as the non-responding node.

In Cassandra, nodes are put together to form a cluster. Nodes within a cluster communicate with each other, thus they provide peer-to-peer communication. One important thing to note here is that not every node contains the same set of data. For example, in a University database, details of students and teachers may reside separately at different nodes. Cassandra database system also provides the facility to copy the same set of data on multiple nodes.

NOTE

Copying the same dataset on different nodes is known as data replication.

Before going further, let's discuss about some basic terms used in Cassandra.

Basic Terms in Cassandra

Cassandra uses a number of basic terms that are described as follows:

- **Replication factor**—It is the number of data copies you need to create across different nodes. This means if the replication factor is 1, then a single copy of the data will be maintained throughout the database system. A replication factor of 2 means that 2 copies of the data will be maintained on two different nodes in Cassandra. The following two types of replication strategies are available:
    - **Simple strategy**—It places the first replica on a node determined by the partitioner. All other replicas are placed on the next nodes clockwise in the ring. This is used for a single data center only.
    - **Network topology strategy**—It places replicas in the same data center ring clockwise until reaching the first node in another rack. Network topology strategy is used for multiple data centers.

- **CAP Theorem**—Replication of data may create inconsistency in the database system. A database system is characterized by its consistency, availability, and partition tolerance. The three characteristics of a database system are referred to as CAP and follow the principle of the CAP theorem, which is applicable to any distributed system that shares data across nodes. CAP states that you can achieve only two of the three characteristics at one time. One of the characteristics has to be sacrificed in order to achieve the other two.

  These terms can be defined in read/write operations in the following manner:

  - **Consistency**—A read is guaranteed to return the most recent write for a given client.
  - **Availability**—A non-failing node will return a reasonable response within a reasonable amount of time. There would be no error and timeout.
  - **Partition tolerance**—The system will continue to function during the partitioning of the network.

- **Partitioners**—Partitioners are used for the distribution of data across various nodes in Cassandra. Once you have decided to divide the data in certain partitions, you cannot overturn the data distribution without flushing the entire data off the database system. Hence, extra care needs to be taken to decide on the type of partitioner you want to use.

  Partitioner, together with replication strategy, is responsible for what data is placed on which node in a cluster. Partitioner uses a partition key to identify a unique row.

- **Keyspace**—It is identical to relational database systems and is used to store the application data. Every cluster has one keyspace assigned to it. You can consider a keyspace in NoSQL database systems to be the same as a database schema in relational databases.

- **Column family**—It is a tuple consisting of a key-value pair. When we write data to a column family in Cassandra, we specify values for one or more columns. This collection of values together with a unique identifier is called a row. The row has a unique key, called the row key, which is used as the primary key for that row. A NoSQL column family is comparable to a table in relational database.

Consider a default Keyspace named Employee, which is defined as follows:

```
Employee {
key: 641109{ name: Stephen, phone: 480-444-8888,
address: 400 N. Hayden Rd., city: Scottsdale, state: AZ, zip: 85255}
key: 641079 { name: Scott  , phone: 480-333-3333,
address: 3000 N. Scottsdale Rd, city: Scottsdale, state: AZ, zip: 85255}
key: CAS_021 { name: Washington,  phone: 415-222-2222,
address: 181 3rd Street, city: San Francisco, state: CA, zip: 94103}
key: NYN_042 { name: vanisha , phone: 212-555-5555,
address: 301 Park Ave, city: New York, state: NY, zip: 10019}
}
```

In this example, the row **key** is a unique primary key for the Employee and the columns are name, phone, address, city, state, and zip.

- **MemTable**—It is an in-memory cache with content stored as key/column. In MemTable, data is sorted by the keys.

After being familiar with the basic terminology, let's understand how read and write operations are performed in Cassandra.

Performing read/write Operations in Cassandra

The write Operation

Whenever the write request is received by a client, Cassandra writes the modified data first into the commit log. The write operation is not considered successful until the modified data is appended to the commitlog.

Cassandra also writes the data to an in memory structure, **MemTable,** where the data is stored in a key-value pair from. Each ColumnFamily has a separate MemTable and the column data is retrieved by the ColumnFamily on the basis of the key.

Once MemTable is full, the sorted data is written out sequentially to the disk in the form of SSTables. This process is known as flushing.

Let's suppose we have to maintain the copy of data in more than one node. So, when should be the acknowledgement of a successful write operation sent to the client—at the time when the very first copy is updated or after each subsequent copy is updated? To clarify this, we need to understand the concept of write consistency.

Write Consistency

When a client sends a write operation request, the determination of the number of copies or nodes that we need to write before sending the success message back to the client is known as write consistency. This means, a client may consider a write operation as complete when some replicas have not yet committed the data.

Write consistency has different levels, which are explained as follows:

Level	Write
ONE	Returns the control when one replica commits data
QUORUM	Returns the control when majority of replicas commit data
ALL	Returns the control when all replicas commit data

Let's consider a case where on performing a write operation, the replica node gets down or fails. When the node comes back to life, it has an updated ColumnFamily. This creates an inconsistency in the database system. To resolve this inconsistency, the hinted hand off concept comes into picture.

Hinted Hand Off

Let's suppose that the consistency level defined by the client is set to ALL. This implies that the acknowledgement would be sent to the client only when all replicas are updated. Now, if any of the replica nodes is down, the write operation consistency cannot be achieved until the node is up.

Cassandra provides a hint to a live replica node. This replica node will communicate the down node of changes once it is up and running. This way it reduces the latency when a replica is temporarily down.

Figure A.1 shows the concept of hinted handoff in performing the write operation in Cassandra:

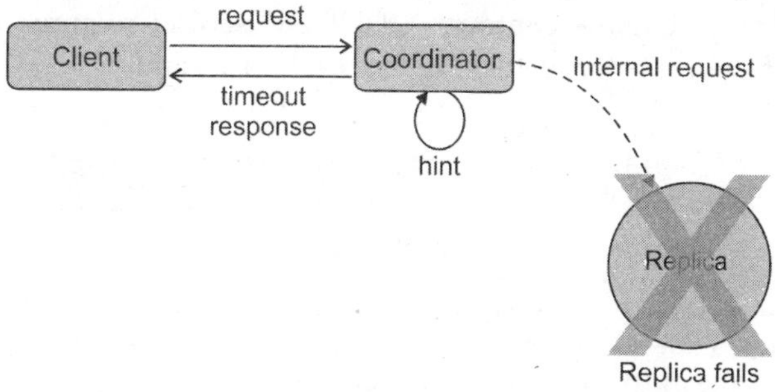

Figure A.1: Hinted Handoff in a write Operation in Cassandra

Figure A.2 shows how the flow of data works during a Cassandra write operation:

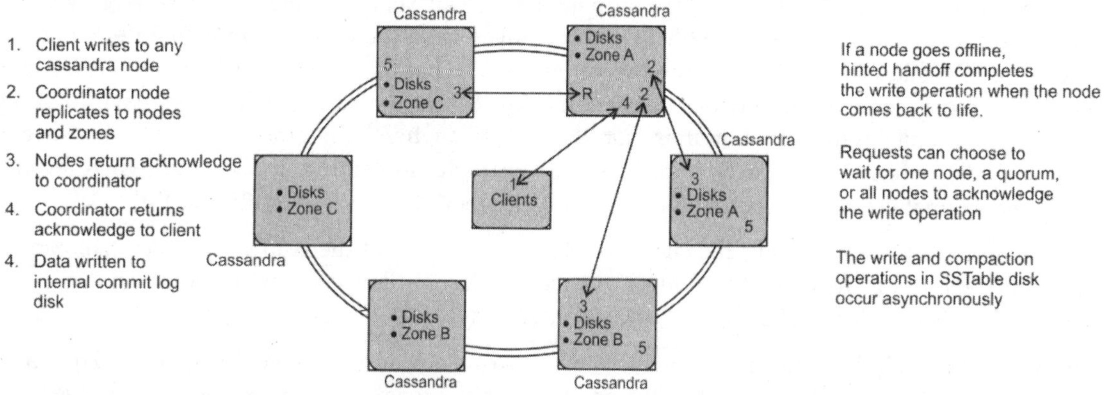

Figure A.2: Flow of Data in a Cassandra write Operation

The read Operation

As of now, we are aware what MemTable is and how data is stored in a MemTable. Let's now discuss how read operations are performed in Cassandra.

Whenever a read request comes from a client, Cassandra first checks whether the data is available in the in-memory database, i.e. MemTable. If it is found there, then a response is sent back to the client. If, however, the data is unavailable in MemTable, Cassandra reaches to SSTable and will read all the SSTables for that ColumnFamily.

We studied about the concept of write consistency and became aware that some nodes may contain outdated data. To avoid the storage of outdated data, we need to learn the concept of read consistency.

Read Consistency

In Cassandra, we maintain a copy of data in different nodes. So, when a client asks for a data, it may happen that some of the nodes have outdated data. Read consistency tells us about the number of nodes we need to read before responding back to the client.

Setting the consistency level to ONE, Cassandra will return the result to the requester after receiving response from one replica. On the contrary, QUORUM setting requires receiving a majority of replicas (2 replicas) to respond before returning the result to a client.

The following are the levels of consistency:

Level	Write
ONE	Returns data from the nearest replica
QUORUM	Returns the most recent data from majority of replicas
ALL	Returns the most recent data from all replicas

Let's understand the read operation with respect to the write operation through an example.

Suppose, in a cluster, we have a key as company name (say Microsoft) and value as its turnover in billion (say 10.3). Now if we update Microsoft's turnover to 10, the write is sent to N different nodes, each of which takes some time to write the value. Now, what happens when a read request comes for Microsoft, as some of those nodes might still have 10.3 for the value while others have 10? They will all eventually return 10 but it is not guaranteed "**when**" (in practice, usually just a few milliseconds), which is extremely important. For example, in trading applications where even a microsecond matters, a millisecond time would be thousand times more significant.

As discussed, Cassandra allows the client to select the strength of the read consistency (All, Single, Quorum). Based on the consistency level you have selected, the data will be returned. So, if the selected consistency level is Single read, the proxy returns the first response it gets.

In the background, the read repair operation also takes place on inconsistent responses. The proxy will send a write request to any node returning older values to ensure that the nodes return the latest value in future.

Figure A.3 clearly describes the read operation in Cassandra:

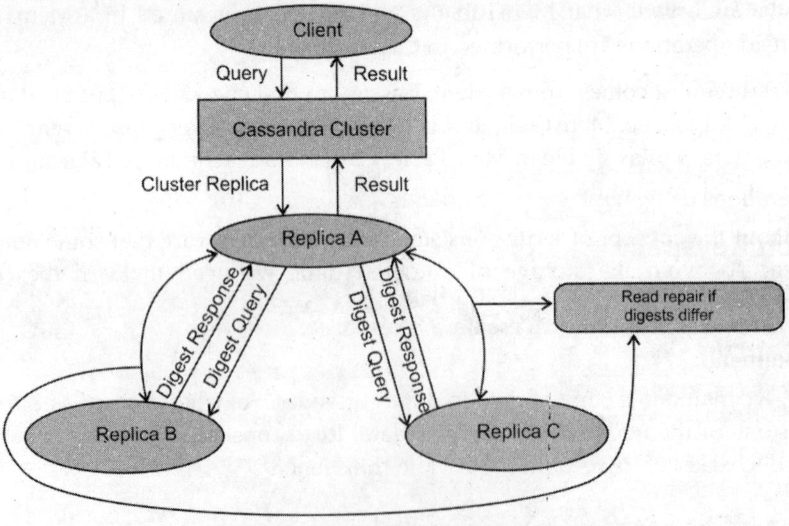

Figure A.3: Describing read Operation in Cassandra

Delete Operation

As SSTables are not mutable, we cannot simply delete data from them. Another problem that lies with the delete operation in Cassandra is if one of the replicas is down during the delete operation, then we cannot delete data from the other replica as this will create inconsistency. To resolve these issues, Cassandra has Tombstone Column. When a client requests a row to be deleted, Cassandra updates the column value with a special value called Tombstone. A read query will consider a tombstoned column as deleted.

Cassandra will keep the column for at least gc_grace_seconds (whose default value is 10 days). If a replica is down for more than 10 days, we need to do a manual data sync before bringing it back online.

Data access operations in every database system are performed through a query language. Cassandra also being a database system provides data access through a query language known as CQL. Let's learn about it in the following section.

Contextual Query Language (CQL)

CQL is the query language used by Cassandra. CQL is similar to Structured Query Language (SQL). It has borrowed many SQL features such as creation of table, use of orderby clause, etc. CQL is the recommended way to interact with Cassandra database system.

To launch a CQL shell, you need to perform the following steps:

1. If you have Cassandra installed and running on your system, open a command prompt terminal.
2. Go to the CASSANDRA_HOME directory of the system through the command prompt.

   For example, if you have Cassandra setup in the **/home/user/Cassandra/** directory on your computer, then you need to enter the following command on the terminal:

```
cd /home/user/Cassandra
```

3. To launch a CQL shell, type the following command:

```
$ bin/cqlsh
```

This will open the CQL shell.

CQL shell is used to communicate with the databases created in Cassandra database system. This communication is established through some CQL commands. Let's now learn to perform some database operations using basic CQL commands.

Operations on Keyspace

When you create a keyspace, you have to specify the replication strategy you are using and the replication factor. For example, to create a keyspace by the name Users, you need to enter the following command:

```
cqlsh> CREATE KEYSPACE Users
WITH REPLICATION = { 'class' :  'SimpleStrategy', 'replication_factor' : 1 };
```

Next, to use the keyspace we have just created, enter the following command:

```
cqlsh> USE Users;
```

To describe all the existing keyspaces, enter the following command:

```
cqlsh> DESC KEYSPACES;
```

Operations on ColumnFamily

As discussed earlier, a ColumnFamily in Cassandra is similar to a database table created in RDMBS. We can perform a number of operations on a ColumnFamily created in Cassandra. These operations include creating a ColumnFamily, inserting data in a ColumnFamily, extracting data from a ColumnFamily, updating a ColumnFamily, deleting a ColumnFamily, etc. Let's discuss about these operations.

The Create Operation

Let's now create a table, named employees, in the Keyspace Users so that we can insert some data in our database. First, use the Keysapce Users by entering the following command:

```
cqlsh> USE Users;
```

Now, let's create the table by using the following command:

```
cqlsh> CREATE TABLE employees (
 firstname text,
lastname text,
employeeId int,
age int,
email text,
salary double,
PRIMARY KEY (employeeId));
```

To see the various attributes of the employees table, type the following command:

```
cqlsh:users> DESC SCHEMA;
```

The Insert Operation

Let's now insert some data in our newly created table by entering the following commands:

```
cqlsh> INSERT INTO employees (firstname, lastname, employeeId, age, email, salary)
VALUES ('Mesel', 'Hoffman', 46, 24, 'mhoffman@gmail.com', 60000);
cqlsh> INSERT INTO employees (firstname, lastname, employeeId, age, email, salary)
VALUES ('Katia', 'Stuart', 46, 24, 'kStuart@gmail.com', 50000);
cqlsh> INSERT INTO employees (firstname, lastname, employeeId, age, email, salary)
VALUES ('Joe', 'Byrne', 46, 24, 'jbyrne@gmail.com', 90000);
```

The Select Operation

Now, perform the SELECT query on the employees table:

```
cqlsh:users> SELECT * FROM employees;
```

All the records of the employees table will be displayed as the output.

The Update Operation

Use the UPDATE command to update any change in the data stored in a table. You need to specify the primary key to identify the record that needs to be updated. Here, we are changing the user's city from Beverly Hills to San Jose by using the following command:

```
cqlsh:users> UPDATE employees SET city= 'San Jose' WHERE lastname= 'Byrne';
```

The Delete Operation

Use the DELETE command to delete a row of data as:

```
cqlsh:demo> DELETE from users WHERE lastname = “Byrne”;
```

B

ZooKeeper

Assume you are assembling a large-scale distributed system. Different administrations of Hadoop ecosystem should be brought online and correlate with each other. It is not necessary that every service of Hadoop ecosystem will have a permanent address of master IP. Let us consider an example in which we have started a same service on 100 nodes. The first 100 nodes that boot will choose the master IP. The problem is that the communication between these nodes must communicate with each other. In addition, how every node will find out the master IP address of the different services and how nodes will decide who is the master among them.

ZooKeeper is a service intended to handle these issues. It permits you to store data in a centralized location. It gives facilitated access to this data. In particular, it gives high accessibility. ZooKeeper service is expected to run on different machines as it will help us to avoid the loss of individual node. However, these nodes communicate data in a cautious manner, guaranteeing that all nodes in the ZooKeeper cluster give the same reliable response to a request, regardless of which ZooKeeper server you contact.

Overview of ZooKeeper

ZooKeeper permits distribution procedures to coordinate with one another. This can be done through a shared hierarchal namespace. The namespace comprises data registers. These data registers are known as znodes. The data of ZooKeeper is kept in-memory. This means that ZooKeeper can attain high throughput and low latency numbers. The best example of ZooKeeper is a large distributed system.

The namespace given by ZooKeeper is much like a standard document framework. A "name" is an arrangement of path components separated by a slash (/). Each znode in ZooKeeper's namespace is recognized by a path. Furthermore, every znode has a parent whose path is a prefix of the znode with one less component; the exemption to this rule is root (/) which has no parent. Additionally, like standard document frameworks, a znode cannot be erased in the event if it has any children.

The primary differences between ZooKeeper and a standard file system are that each znode can have information connected with it (each record can likewise be a directory and vice versa) and znodes are restricted to the measure of information that they can have. ZooKeeper is designed to store information such as status data, configuration, location data, and so on. This type of metadata is normally measured in kilobytes. ZooKeeper has a built-in facility of sanity check of 1MB data, which does not allow it to be used by huge data store. It is basically used for storing small bits of information. Figure B.1 shows the client-server model of ZooKeeper:

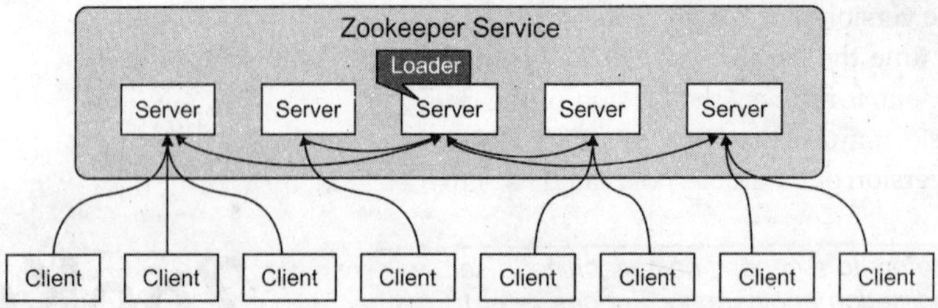

Figure B.1: Client-Server Model of ZooKeeper

In the client-server model of ZooKeeper (Refer to Figure B.1), clients are nodes, i.e. machines. These nodes make use of the service. In addition, servers are nodes that provide the service. There is a collection of servers of ZooKeeper. The servers that constitute the ZooKeeper service must be familiar with each other. This collection of servers forms a ZooKeeper group. At any given time, one client is connected to one server of ZooKeeper. Each server can handle various client connections simultaneously. Each client maintains a TCP (Transmission Control Protocol) connection by which it sends requests and heartbeats, and gets responses and watch events. If the client does not receive an acknowledgment from the server within the specified time or the TCP connection to the server breaks, it connects to a different server.

Let's discuss data model of ZooKeeper.

Data Model

ZooKeeper has a hierarchal namespace similar to a distributed file system. The main difference is that every node in the namespace can have information connected with it and children. It is similar to a file system that permits a file to also be a directory. Path to nodes are treated as canonical, slash-separated paths. Any unicode character can be utilized as a path subject to the limitations. These limitations are as follows:

- The invalid character (\u0000) cannot be a part of a path name (These cause problems with the C binding).
- These characters cannot be utilized because they don't show well, or render in perplexing ways: \u0001 - \u0019 and \u007F - \u009F.
- These characters are not permitted: \ud800 - uF8FFF, \uFFF0-uFFFF, \uXFFFE - \uXFFFF (where X is a digit 1 - E), \uF0000 - \uFFFFF.
- The "." character can be utilized as a feature of another name, however "." and ".." can't the only one to be utilized to show a node along a path, because ZooKeeper does not utilize relative path. "/a/b/./c" or "/a/b/../c" is invalid.
- The token "ZooKeeper" is reserved.

Let's learn about znodes in detail.

Znodes

Every node in a ZooKeeper tree is known as a znode. Znodes maintain a stat structure. The stat structure includes version numbers for data changes and ACL (Access Control List) changes. It also has timestamps. The version number and timestamp permit ZooKeeper to accept the cache and to organize updates. Every time the data of znode changes, the version number increases. For example, when a client retrieves data, it receives the version of the data as well. In addition, when a client performs an update or a delete, it must supply the version of the data of the znode it is changing. On the other hand, if the supplied version of data does not match its actual version, then the update fails.

NOTE

The word node refers to a generic host machine, a server, a member of an ensemble, and a client process in distributed application engineering. Znodes refer to data nodes in ZooKeeper documentation. Servers refer to machines that make up the ZooKeeper service; quorum peers refer to the servers that make up a gathering; client refers to any host or procedure which utilizes a ZooKeeper administration.

Znode is the primary entity that a developer accesses. It has many qualities, which are as follows:

- **Watches**—Customers can set watches on znodes. The changes to the znode trigger the watch and then clear that watch. When a watch triggers, at the same time, ZooKeeper sends the customer a notice.
- **Data Access**—The data stored at each znode in a namespace is read and composed automatically. Reads get all the data bytes connected with a znode and a write replaces all the data. Every node has an access control list that confines who can do what.
- **Ephemeral Nodes**—In ZooKeeper, ephemeral nodes are used for transient data. These nodes exist till the time session that made the znode active. As soon as the session terminates, the znode is erased and hence ephemeral znodes are not allowed to have children.
- **Sequence Nodes-Unique Naming**—When we create a znode, you can request ZooKeeper to affix a monotonically expanding counter to the end of the path. This counter is interesting to the parent znode. The counter has a configuration of %010d, i.e. 10 digits with 0 (zero) padding (the counter is organized along these lines to streamline sorting), i.e. "<path>0000000001.

It is important to note that the counter stores the next sequence number. This number is managed by the parent node. The sequence number is signed int, which holds 4 bytes. When the value of counter is beyond 2147483647, the counter overflows. This overflow results in a name "<path>-2147483647".

Let's discuss time in ZooKeeper.

Time in ZooKeeper

ZooKeeper tracks time in numerous ways:

- **Zxid**—Whenever there is a change in ZooKeeper state, it receives a stamp. This stamp is in the form of zxid (ZooKeeper Transaction Id). This zxid helps us in calculating the total changes executed in the ordered sequence to the ZooKeeper. Every change has a unique zxid. For example, if zxid1 is smaller than zxid2, then zxid1 is executed before zxid2.
- **Version numbers**—Each change to a node will bring an increase to one of the version numbers of that node. The three version numbers are version (number of changes to the data of a znode), cversion (number of changes made to the children of a znode), and aversion (number of changes to the ACL of a znode).

- **Ticks**—When utilizing multi-server ZooKeeper, servers use ticks to characterize timing of events; for example, status uploads, session timeouts, connection timeouts between companions, and so on. The tick time is indirectly uncovered through the minimum session timeout (2 times the tick time); if a client demands a session timeout less than minimum session timeout, the server will tell the client that the session timeout is really the minimum session timeout.
- **Real time**—ZooKeeper does not utilize real time or clock time at all but to place timestamps into the stat structure on znode creation and znode modification.

ZooKeeper Sessions

When we design a client session, the application code must be in the form of a string. This string in the code must be a separated list of host:port pairs. This list will refer to the ZooKeeper server, for example "127.0.0.1:4545" or "127.0.0.1:4000, 127.0.0.1:4001, 127.0.0.1:4002". The ZooKeeper client library will randomly try to connect to the server. If this attempt fails due to any reason, the client will try to connect to the different server. Until the client connects to a server , it will keep trying automatically.

When a customer gets a handle to the ZooKeeper service, ZooKeeper makes a ZooKeeper session, and it is represented as a 64-bit number allotted to the client. In other sense, if the client establishes other connection to an alternate ZooKeeper server, it sends the session id for new connection handshake. As a security measure, the server defines a password for the session id that any ZooKeeper server can validate. The password is sent back to the client with the session id when the client establishes the session. The client sends this password with the session id every time when it establishes the session with a new server.

One of the parameters that the ZooKeeper client library calls to make a ZooKeeper session is the session timeout in milliseconds. The client sends requested timeout, and the server reacts with the timeout that it can provide the client. The other parameter is default watcher. Watchers are informed when any state change happens in the client. Let's consider an example if the client loses connection to the server, the client will get an alert, or if the client's session lapses, and so on. This watcher should consider the initial state to be disconnected (i.e. prior to any state changes events are sent to the watcher by the client lib). In the case of the new connection, the first event sent to the watcher is commonly the session connection event.

The session is kept alive by the request sent by the client. If the session is idle for a period of time which would timeout the session, the customer will send a PING request to keep that session alive. This PING request permits the ZooKeeper server to realize that the client is still alive. It also permits the client to check that its connection with the ZooKeeper server is still active. The timing of the PING is sufficiently moderate to guarantee sensible time to recognize a dead connection and reconnect to the other server.

When a connection with the server is effectively established, there are two situations where the client lib creates connection loss (the result code in C binding, exception in Java) when either a synchronous or asynchronous operation is performed and one of the following holds:

- The application calls an operation on a session that is not alive or valid.
- The ZooKeeper client separates from a server when there are pending operations to that server, i.e., there is a pending asynchronous call.

ZooKeeper Watches

All the read operations - getData(), getChildren(), and exists() of ZooKeeper have choice of setting a watch as a side effect. The following points are considered for the meaning of a watch:

- **One-time trigger—**When the data is changed, one watch event will be sent to the client. For example, if a client executes a getData("/znode1", true) and later the data for/znode1 is changed or removed, the client will receive a watch event for/znode1. If that /znode1 changes again, no watch event will be sent unless the client has done another read that sets another watch.
- **Sent to the client—**This suggests that an event is on way to the client, yet may not reach the client before the effective return code to the change operation reaches the client that started the change. Watches are sent asynchronously to watchers. ZooKeeper gives a requesting guarantee: a client will never see a change for which it has set a watch until it first sees the watch event. System delays or other factors may bring about other clients to see watches and return codes from updates at distinct times. The key point is that everything seen by the distinct clients will have a consistent order.
- **The information for which the watch was set—**This refers to the distinct ways a node can change. It helps ZooKeeper in maintaining two lists of watches: data watches and child watches. getData() and exists() set data watches. getChildren() sets child watches. Alternately, it may help to consider watches being set by sort of data returned. getData() and exists() return information about the data of the node(terminal), while getChildren() gives back a list of children. Consequently, setData() will trigger data watches for the znode being set (assuming the set is successful). A successful create() will trigger a data watch for the znode being made and a child watch for the parent znode. An effective delete() will trigger both data watch and a child watch (since there can be no more children) for a znode being deleted and in addition a child watch for the parent znode.

Watches are preserved locally at the ZooKeeper server to which the clients are attached. This permits watches to be light weight to set, maintain, and dispatch. When a client unites with another server, the watch will be triggered for any session events. Watches won't be received while disconnected from a server. When a client reconnects, any enrolled watches will be re-registered and triggered if necessary. This happens transparently. There is one situation where a watch may be missed: a watch for the existence of a znode not yet made will be remembered if the znode is made and deleted while disconnected.

What ZooKeeper Guarantees about Watches

With respect to watches, ZooKeeper maintains the following guarantees:

- Watches are requested as for other events, watches, and asynchronous replies. The ZooKeeper client libraries guarantee that everything dispatched is in order.
- A client will see a watch event for a znode it is watching before seeing the new data that relates to that znode.
- The form of watch events from ZooKeeper relates to the form of the updates as seen by the ZooKeeper service.

Things to Remember about Watches

The following things to be remembered about watches:

- Watches are one-time triggers. If you get a watch event and you want to get notified, you must set another watch.
- Because watches are one-time triggers and there is latency between getting the event and sending another request to get a watch you can't see each change that happens to a node in ZooKeeper. You must be prepared to handle the situation where the znode changes various times between getting the event and setting the watch again.
- A watch object or function pair may be triggered once for a given notification. If the same watch object is registered for an exists and a getData call for the same file, then that file is deleted. The watch object would be invoked once with the cancellation warning for the file.
- When you detach from a server (when the server fails), you won't get any watches until the re-connection. For this reason, session events are sent to all remarkable watch handlers. Use session events to go into a protected mode as you won't be getting events while detached, so your process should act conservatively.

Let's discuss data storage in ZooKeeper.

Data Storage in Zookeeper

Many ZooKeeper daemons can begin on distinct terminals. Clients can connect to any daemons and they will see the same view of ZooKeeper without depending on which daemon they are connected to in the cluster. Data are stored in objects, and follow a hierarchical addressing system. This system is similar to the conventional file system. It uses a root object named /, and additional nodes are in a tree-like fashion. Every node inside tree can hold data (act as a file) and have child nodes (act like a directory). Data stored in thé object are of very small size, i.e. not more than 1MB. It is small because data is stored in the RAM of ZooKeeper machines.

This permits requests to be dispatched with high throughput. Changes are made in disk to give permanency. However, read operations are taken care by cached memory. For example, ZooKeeper may know about the filename in another traditional file system, which contains the configuration for distributed system. The distributed system first contacts ZooKeeper and gets filename, and then obtains that file for the configuration.

Index

$

-

.

4

A

B

C

D

O

P

Q

R

S

T

U

V